S0-AEM-383

LEO BAECK INSTITUTE

YEAR BOOK

1987

Probably the first photograph of a Jewish family in Germany
Family Hahn, Hamburg 1843
Daguerrotype by Hermann Biow

By courtesy of the Museum für Kunst und Gewerbe, Hamburg and Collection Dr. Nachum T. Gidal, Jerusalem

LEO BAECK INSTITUTE

YEAR BOOK XXXII

1987

SECKER & WARBURG · LONDON
PUBLISHED FOR THE INSTITUTE
LONDON · JERUSALEM · NEW YORK

THE LEO BAECK INSTITUTE
was founded in 1955 by the
COUNCIL OF JEWS FROM GERMANY
for the purpose of collecting material on and sponsoring research into the history of the Jewish Community in Germany and in other German-speaking countries from the Emancipation to its decline and new dispersion. The Institute is named in honour of the man who was the last representative figure of German Jewry in Germany during the Nazi period.

The Council of Jews from Germany was established after the war by the principal organisations of Jews from Germany in Israel, U.S.A. and U.K. for the protection of their rights and interests.

OFFICES OF THE
LEO BAECK INSTITUTE

JERUSALEM (ISRAEL): 33 Bustanai Street
LONDON: 4 Devonshire Street, W.1
NEW YORK: 129 East 73rd Street

THIS PUBLICATION WAS SUPPORTED
BY GRANTS FROM
THE BRITISH ACADEMY
AND THE
MEMORIAL FOUNDATION FOR JEWISH CULTURE

Published by Martin Secker & Warburg Limited
54 Poland Street, London W1V 3DF
SBN 436 25546 4
Photoset by Wilmaset, Birkenhead, Wirral
Printed in Great Britain by Richard Clay (The Chaucer Press), Limited, Bungay, Suffolk

Contents

IV. FAR WEST/FAR EAST

V. JEWS AND THE CAMERA

Illustrations

Preface

The spread of antisemitism in the late nineteenth century and the outlawing of Germany's Jewish population in the Third *Reich* are the two central topics of Year Book XXXII and it seems doubly important to stress yet once again that it has always been the task of this publication to present both the positive and the negative of the German-Jewish encounter. A maxim of editorial policy expounded by Robert Weltsch and upheld by the present Editor is the firm maintaining of a balanced view. The propagation of fatalism has ever been alien to us. As highlighted again and again in the writings of George Mosse and so eloquently expressed by Peter Gay in his initial address to the recent Leo Baeck Institute Conference on 'The Jews in Nazi Germany' in Berlin in October 1985, there were always two Germanies and Germany's Jews rightly held fast to the better, the Liberal, the nobler one. The Editor is therefore most grateful to George Mosse for undertaking to introduce this volume to the reader with a paper he delivered in May 1986 in Königswinter at a joint Conference of the London Leo Baeck Institute and the Friedrich-Naumann-Stiftung on 'The German Jews and Liberalism', which deals precisely with this Jewish Liberal commitment. We know only too well that the ties with Liberalism were never without problems for the Jewish community and that with the *Machtübernahme* some strayed momentarily from the Liberal path. And yet the Liberal heritage of German Jewry – "liberal" transcending here the party-political meaning – strongly reasserts itself to this very day.

The spirit of Liberalism and humanism also pervades the lecture which Gordon Craig delivered in December 1985 at a meeting of the American Historical Association in New York under the auspices of the New York Leo Baeck Institute. If it has a "message" it but complements and reaffirms what George Mosse has to say in his Introduction to the Year Book. The Liberal commitment was vital; Jewish emancipation was irrevocably linked with it. On the other hand, many of the components of the emancipation ideology are bound to be re-evaluated. Much of David Sorkin's essay is devoted to such a critical survey; and in November 1987, shortly after the publication of this volume, a Conference of the London Leo Baeck Institute held in association with the Max-Planck-Institut in Göttingen at Schloss Ringberg, will not only attempt a summing-up of forty years of post-war German-Jewish historiography but will also scrutinise accepted formulae and probe the validity of concepts which have come to be generally accepted by the historians of Jewish emancipation and assimilation for the past one-hundred-and-fifty years.

In the first of the two major sections of this Year Book Norbert Kampe now completes his meticulous investigation of student antisemitism in Imperial Berlin (begun in Year Book XXX). The proliferation of antisemitic fraternities, their internecine squabbling as to who sported the more valid antisemitic "credentials", the protracted and petty university intrigues, are certainly not without their tragi-comical note. The spouting of half-digested racialist notions and the confused thinking of pseudo philosophers must have turned the heads of many gifted individuals who – one would have thought – could have bestowed their spare time to better advantage elsewhere. Still, even steering away from worrying theories of predestination, the elements of continuity in the behaviour and thinking of a large part of Germany's intellectual elite provide a disturbing pointer to a grim future. Three essays on regional and rural antisemitism by James Harris, Michael Riff and David Peal complete this part of the Year Book. They serve once more to accentuate the value of local studies as opposed to mere generalising. "Antisemitism" and "prejudice" existed and persist in endless permutations. To understand what eventually befell German Jewry we will increasingly have to examine local factors and special conditions.

What better way to start the central section on Jewry under the Nazi heel than with Chaim Schatzker's comprehensive study (to be completed in Year Book XXXIII) on the Jewish youth movement? The rebellion and realignment of Jewish youth in Germany had already commenced prior to Nazi rule – but now our own lives and consciousness were most deeply affected; most of us quickly accepted that we no longer had any future in the country of our birth. Yet just because Zionism assumed such a major influence on the Jewish youth movement from 1933 on, our previous observation on the profundity of the impact of *Deutschtum* on the German Zionists, made in Year Book XXXI, must be restated here. Despite the process of alienation and the changing state of self-awareness, on which the author rightly focuses, a good measure of *Deutsches Wesen* continued to prevail in virtually all the strands of the Jewish youth movement – as we, its surviving members, can readily testify. It is conveyed by the linguistics and thought structure of the movement, so sharply recaptured by Schatzker's contribution. And how could it have been otherwise? We were so deeply rooted in the German world.

From this broad and ambitious sweep we come once more to one of the smaller units of the youth movement, when Jehuda Reinharz completes his story of *Hashomer Hazair* in Germany which he commenced in Year Book XXXI. We need both: the generous, boldly painted picture, as well as the detailed, finished study of the smaller group. We have commented on *Hashomer Hazair* before and therefore let us pinpoint only the fact that here was a segment of the Jewish youth movement which received both a Marxist and a Zionist indoctrination under the very nose of the Nazis (not the only Jewish youth group subjected to this two-pronged form of education). Again, for the other side of the Jewish spectrum, Francis Nicosia now provides us with the conclusion of his survey of Revisionism in Germany (started in Year Book XXXI). Revisionism's own youth organisation, the *Betar*, receives but short shrift here, but the essay as such must again be seen in juxtaposition to Reinharz's study. The inescapable conclusion is that right-wing Zionism was not a success story in Germany even under the stifling influence of the Nazi state. The soil was not suitable – German Jewry's political traditions were too well established – and most Jewish historians will take comfort from this fact.

One of the major Nazi obsessions was with the imaginary perils of Freemasonry. And thus even the Order *B'nai B'rith*, benevolent, charitable – no nest of conspirators here – had the dubious privilege of being amongst the first Jewish organisations to be dissolved by Nazi decree. Karin Voelker has carefully reconstructed from the German archives the closing down of its lodges and the confiscation of its assets. Elements of continuity – again – in anti-Jewish bias are found in Donald McKale's investigation into German Foreign Office records. In all fairness it must be said that there were exceptions, honourable German diplomats who at all times sought to protect Jewish interests and individuals, but the author here makes out a case for general "aloofness" or, often, wholehearted support for Nazi measures. That the Conservative elite, which manned the German Foreign Office, should have acted very differently was perhaps not really to be expected. We know after all that even the Nationalist-Conservative July 1944 "resisters" were not exactly enamoured with the idea of the restoration of Jewish civil rights.

Even those who are not unqualified admirers of psycho-history will be impressed by Peter Loewenberg's exposition of the measures planned against the captive Jewish community during the *"Kristallnacht"* or the November pogrom in 1938. (Incidentally, the use of the term *"Kristallnacht"* is now repeatedly under attack, as the original reference, to broken shop windows, conveys a cheerful belittling by unconcerned German spectators as to the extent of what actually took place. However, as every student of semantics knows, terms change their meaning, assume quite different properties, and today the word *"Kristallnacht"* carries for all of us the stark horror of what really transpired then in the centre of so-called civilised Europe; to do away with the term after fifty years of usage does not seem particularly helpful.) The discerning observer will not only note the vicious measures contemplated by the Nazi potentates but also the puerile glee with which the humiliations were determined on. German National Socialism, easily the greatest manifestation of evil in the history of mankind had also – and it makes it no less macabre – its clownish aspect. But perhaps it needed Charlie Chaplin's 'Great Dictator' to show us that.

David Bankier tells of the policies and tactics doled out by the illegal Communist Party in Nazi Germany on the "Jewish Question" and the persecution of the Jews. The record is mixed, as the KPD approach had to go along with the "accepted tenets" and so naturally suffered from ill-conceived and outworn stereotyping. Quite apart from that, the underground cadres had much to swallow from the vagaries and convolutions of the party line, subject as it was to the exigencies of Soviet foreign policy, all the way up to the Hitler-Stalin pact and beyond. Granted all this, yet we must not forget that German Communists – amongst them many young Jews – were in the forefront of a self-sacrificing struggle. It was a Conservative German statesman, none less than the President of the German Federal Republic, Richard von Weizsäcker, who on the 8th of May 1985, in a speech to the *Bundestag* on the 40th anniversary of the liberation of Europe, when commemorating all the German opponents of Hitler also paid his respects to this heroic Communist resistance to the Nazi regime.

If one man embodied the Liberal heritage of German Jewry of which we spoke above, it was Otto Hirsch who, as its supreme "civil servant", led the community in the period of its greatest trial. A profile in the Year Book of this distinguished man has been asked for for years. Much of the strength of Paul Sauer's concise biography lies in outlining Hirsch's antecedents and earlier career; author and editor are aware that a great deal of further work is now being done, particularly in Israel, on the activity of Otto Hirsch in the *Reichsvertretung/Reichsvereinigung*. Yet we did not wish to delay this long overdue appreciation. What deserves to be added though is that documentation recently become available sheds further light on the efforts of Otto Hirsch and his associates in the *Reichsvereinigung* to frustrate Nazi measures. Their brave attempts can surely be categorised as Jewish resistance.

Yet open resistance was shunned by the official representation of German Jewry and we know that those of the Jewish leadership who remained – with the remnant of the Jewish community held hostage – tried to the last to dissuade Jewish youth from direct acts of resistance. Herbert Baum and his group – on whom Eric Brothers has painstakingly assembled many new facts – thought otherwise. It could be argued that anti-war/anti-Nazi propaganda was always the right course of action while the act of sabotage in the Lustgarten (opposed within the Baum group itself) was perhaps mistaken. In 1942 the knowledge that all Jews were inevitably doomed was not universal and who are we with the wisdom of hindsight to sit in judgment here? Faced with deportation and likely death individual Jews saw their tasks differently. For myself I would say that both Otto Hirsch, the middle-class Liberal, and Herbert Baum, the Communist activist, died in the fight against German fascism; they both died for the Jewish people.

We have spoken of those left behind; as to the majority fortunate enough to have escaped in time, more than one speaker at the Berlin Conference emphasised the participation of German Jews in the world-wide battle against Nazism. We hope to deal, in a future essay in this Year Book, with the part played by a whole German-Jewish generation, as soldiers and partisans, as scientists and factory workers, in the military defeat of Nazi Germany.

In a further section Kennee Switzer-Rakos and Suzanne Rutland write on Jewish emigration from Europe and flight from Tsarist and Nazi oppression. In the late nineteenth century Western Jews gave substantial assistance to Eastern Jews in their plight. Half a century later, in 1939, almost 20,000 "visaless" German and Austrian Jewish refugees could be dumped in Shanghai because of the city's semi-colonial status and the international concessions granted to Japan and the European powers. In 1945, after having been freed from the Japanese occupation, these same refugees faced years of procrastination by the democratic countries of the West before they could finally be settled. In the end it was for the newly founded State of Israel to offer them a home.

This volume ends with an essay on the innovatory role of Jewish photographers from Central Europe in the development of the art of photography. It has been written for us by Nachum Tim Gidal, who is himself one of this notable band of photographers and photo-journalists.

Before the usual acknowledgements a word should for once be said about the increasing number of German historians who in recent years have contributed the results of their research to the Year Book. It does constitute an almost symbolic break with a bitter German past. True, there have been certain lapses of late, yet notwithstanding some ugly symptoms of a revisionist historiography in the recent "historians' debate" the Editor would like to associate himself with the tribute the British historian A. J. Nicholls paid in *The Times Literary Supplement* of 7th November 1986 to the "admirably brave and scrupulous historical profession" of Western Germany.

In addition to all those who by now guarantee the smooth and punctual appearance of the Year Book special thanks are due this year to Werner Angress, New York, Werner Becker, Bonn, Ursula Büttner, Hamburg, Helga Eberhard, Hamburg, Evyatar Friesel, Jerusalem, Nachum Tim Gidal, Jerusalem, Fred Grubel, New York, Hans George and Helen Hirsch, Maryland, Werner Jochmann, Hamburg, James Joll, London, Konrad Kwiet, Sydney, Walter Laqueur, Washington D.C., Anneliese Löffler, Cologne, Cécile Lowenthal-Hensel, Berlin, Ernst Lowenthal, Berlin, Wolfgang Madai, Dohna/Sachsen, Shlomo Mayer, Jerusalem, Arie Navon, Tel-Aviv, Pauline Paucker, London, Eva Reichmann, London, Ismar Schorsch, New York, Renate Steinchen, New York and Johannes Wachten, Frankfurt a. Main. The Editor would also like to express his gratitude for the unflinching support he has received from his friends and colleagues on the London Executive of the Leo Baeck Institute, Julius Carlebach, Hans Feld, John Grenville, Werner Mosse and Peter Pulzer.

London *Arnold Paucker*

German Jews and Liberalism in Retrospect

Introduction to Year Book XXXII

BY GEORGE L. MOSSE

To analyse the relationship between German Jews and Liberalism from hindsight runs the danger of foreshortening history, of ignoring the restraints of time.* Nevertheless, it is worthwhile to undertake this task in order to draw some conclusions from this long-standing identification which might enable us better to understand problems inherent in Liberalism itself, and those which haunted German Jews in their period of assimilation. Though I intend to approach this analysis from the point of view of German Jews, it is impossible to separate the problems of Liberalism from those faced by the Jews in modern times; their identification was too close for that. This essay is merely a preliminary stocktaking of a relationship which went beyond the usual alliance between a political or ideological movement and a group of the population, but instead determined the self-identification of many, and perhaps even most, German Jews.[1]

The overwhelming majority of Jews in Germany felt that they had no alternative but to accept the process of emancipation, however incomplete, and to enter into the process of assimilation – no Jew wanted to return to the ghetto, to a time of unfreedom, and every Jew wanted to become a citizen. Jews wanted to become Germans, but what sort of German? – for there were many different definitions of what it meant to be a part of the German people. The Liberal *Bildungsbürger* as defined by Wilhelm von Humboldt provided the model for German citizenship for newly emancipated Jews: through fostering the growth of reason and aesthetic taste, each man would cultivate his own personality until he became an autonomous, harmonious individual. This was a process of education and character building in which everyone could join regardless of religion or background; only the individual mattered. Liberalism during the age of Jewish emancipation was founded on an attitude of mind which, it was hoped, could be translated into Liberal politics.

Yet this emancipation was not the result of political necessities – though considerations of usefulness to the state played an important part – but due in

*This is a revised and expanded version of a paper first delivered by Professor George Mosse at a seminar in Königswinter organised jointly by the Leo Baeck Institute, London and the Friedrich-Naumann-Stiftung on 20th to 23rd May 1986. A German translation will be published in Friedrich-Naumann-Stiftung (Hrsg.), *Das deutsche Judentum und der Liberalismus*, St. Augustin 1987 – (Ed.).

[1]See George L. Mosse, *German Jews Beyond Judaism*, Bloomington, Illinois 1985.

large measure to the acceptance of Enlightenment thought with its belief in the potential of human reason, in the kind of self-education and *Bildung* which Wilhelm von Humboldt tried to make into an integral part of the Prussian educational system. The emancipation of the Jews in Germany was a cultural emancipation and its political consequences were only apparent much later. This historical development explains to a large extent the depth to which the concept of *Bildung* based upon the Enlightenment penetrated Jewish secular and religious thought: by acquiring the proper culture Jews would enter German citizenship. Liberal thought, destined to remain valid for German Jews because it had legitimised their emancipation, was conceived as a continuation of the Enlightenment. German citizenship meant developing one's own intellectual potential, a continuous process which depended upon self-cultivation. German Liberalism in its origins was not as in England primarily a philosophy of prosperity,[2] though as it became attuned to the Railway Age, it came to concentrate upon political and economic reality as well, but at the expense of its original impetus – that system of Liberal thought which found its roots in the Industrial Revolution, rather than in a philosophical system, was shared by Germany only towards the end of the nineteenth century. This difference is important for the distinction between Liberal thought and Liberal politics which, as we shall see, was to haunt the relationship between Jews and Liberalism.

The hopes for a more complete Jewish emancipation were symbolised by the conviction of nineteenth-century Liberals that intellectual development and national progress were identical.[3] Jews could freely enter into the process of *Bildung* through school and university, through the cultivation of their own personalities. The belief that those who entered into this process of *Bildung* would also make the best citizens seemed full of promise for Jews who desired to obtain equal rights with their Christian neighbours.

The difference between Liberal thought and Liberal politics provides one of the principal themes for any analysis of the symbiosis between Jews and Liberalism. Many Jews, during the first half of the nineteenth century, inclined towards political Conservatism or thought unquestioning obedience towards the State part of their newly acquired citizenship, while others – perhaps the majority – were politically passive.[4] However, despite such diverse political attitudes, most German Jews accepted Liberal thought as given, an article of faith upon which their hope for full emancipation depended.

Thus the expectation that the hopes placed in emancipation would be fulfilled was closely identified with belief in Liberal ideals, and these, in turn, were an integral part of the German-Jewish identity. Lessing's *Nathan der Weise* became a *Magna Charta* of German Judaism, but the Liberal heritage was also absorbed by a major trend of German-Jewish religious thought – it became an integral part of the essence of Judaism. This was a trend in Jewish theology

[2]Werner E. Mosse, *Liberal Europe*, London 1974, Chapter 5.

[3]Theodor Schieder, *Das Deutsche Kaiserreich als Nationalstaat*, Köln-Opladen 1961, p. 61.

[4]Jacob Toury, *Die politischen Orientierungen der Juden in Deutschland. Von Jena bis Weimar*, Tübingen 1966 (Schriftenreihe wissenschaftlicher Abhandlungen des Leo Baeck Instituts 15), pp. 17, 19.

which can be discerned from the very beginning of the process of emancipation,[5] and which was crowned by a work which many German Jews regarded as their second *Magna Charta*: Leo Baeck's *The Essence of Judaism* (*Das Wesen des Judentums*, 1906) (a book, by the way, which was presented by the Jewish community of Berlin during the Weimar Republic to every Jewish student who had passed his *Abitur*). *The Essence of Judaism* emphasised the autonomy of each individual; respect for his freedom as over against the State is designated as a religious duty. For Baeck the State was based upon bourgeois property rights, and though it is part of the blessings which such property confers to help the poor and the helpless, the principal task must be to prevent the existence of a property-less class. Finally, as in Humboldt's definition of *Bildung*, neither the State nor the human personality are fully formed products of history or circumstance, but in constant development. This development reaches out for the universal, to humanity, through the unremitting self-cultivation of the individual personality.[6] The much invoked "Mission of Judaism" was based upon such an ideal long before Leo Baeck wrote his famous book.

Even those Jews who fought against Liberalism with all their might were influenced by Liberal thought. Many of the most important Jewish Socialists attempted to soften Marxist orthodoxy, using Liberal thought in order to move the individual increasingly into the centre of Socialist theory. As I have shown elsewhere,[7] for such men the final victory of the working class and the abolition of existing property relationships would issue in the triumph of humanity, but this victory would be meaningless unless it was based upon *Bildung* and the Enlightenment. Such a revision of Marxism can be found to a greater or lesser extent in the thoughts of men like Kurt Eisner, the young Georg Lukács or the Frankfurt School, as well as amongst the so-called left-wing intellectuals during the Weimar Republic. These were men who used Liberal ideals in order to transcend their outsiderdom in society and in the labour movement, even as they rejected Liberalism as the ideology of Capitalism. Ernst Bloch stated, typically enough, that the humanism of the Enlightenment had been absorbed by Marxism, but it was the Italian Jewish Socialist Carlo Roselli who formulated the connection between Liberalism and Socialism, dear to such men, with greatest clarity: the spiritual substance of Liberalism can only be preserved in a Socialist society.[8]

Even German Zionism, publicly the sworn enemy of Liberalism, in reality absorbed much of its thought. Leaders such as Martin Buber, Robert Weltsch or Georg Landauer saw in Jewish nationalism a necessary ingredient of the never-ending cultivation of their own personalities: such nationalism was not a purpose in and of itself, but instead a necessary step towards the union with all mankind.[9] The Liberal ideals which derived from the period of emancipation

[5]George L. Mosse, *Masses and Man*, New York 1980, Chapter 13.

[6]Leo Baeck, *Das Wesen des Judentums*, Frankfurt a. Main [4]1926, pp. 90, 228, 232–233.

[7]George L. Mosse, *German Jews Beyond Judaism*, pp. 56ff.

[8]Ernst Bloch, *Auswahl aus seinen Schriften*, Frankfurt a. Main 1967, p. 158; Emilio Lussu, *Sul Partito d'Azione e gli altri*, Milan 1968, p. 40.

[9]See Georg Landauer, *Der Zionismus im Wandel dreier Jahrzehnte*, Tel-Aviv 1957.

were given equal weight with nationalism, a unique phenomenon in our own century, the only attempt I know of not to abolish but to humanise nationalism in an ever more nationalistic age. The use of the Liberal heritage of the age of emancipation in order to humanise Socialism and nationalism needs further investigation. The disproportionate part Jews played in this enterprise cannot be ignored, though non-Jews were, of course, also involved. Beyond the evidence which this phenomenon provides as to the penetration of Liberal thought even among those Jews who would reject it, such use of Liberalism raises two questions the answers to which are of importance for the relationship of Jews and Liberalism in retrospect: firstly, how intertwined were Liberal theory and practice, and, secondly, to what extent did theory dominate or even displace practice in the alliance of Liberalism and the Jews?

For most Jewish citizens the difference between Liberal theory and practice must have been irrelevant, at least until the last years of the Weimar Republic. They supported Liberal parties and organisations, and sought to transform Liberal thought into practice through their support of political Liberalism. Strong Liberal parties during most of the Empire encouraged such unity (it has been estimated that two-thirds of the Jews in the Empire voted for the Progressive Party).[10] This unity of theory and practice varied with the strength or weakness of Liberal political parties. Thus, Liberal thought existed without much of a political base in the age of Jewish emancipation, with a rapidly diminishing political infrastructure during the Weimar Republic and with none at all during the Third *Reich*. Such a changing relationship between Liberal thought and its political structure must necessarily influence any analysis of the relationship of Jews to Liberalism, and it raises the question of how one might evaluate the Liberalism of German Jews which during most of its history had little chance of realisation: did the belief of most emancipated Jews that such a chance existed blind them to political realities, giving an almost fatal irreality to their political aspirations? This, of course, seen merely in retrospect.

That so many Jews clung to Liberal parties in Wilhelminian and Weimar Germany, even when these supported antisemitic candidates, shows to what extent the urge to establish a unity between theory and practice blocked the consideration of political alternatives to those of the Liberal parties. When the Social Democrats defended Jewish rights at the turn of the century, the leaders of the major Jewish organisations saw in such action a danger to their own respectability.[11] Theodor Barth, the leader of the Progressive Liberals, discovered by the turn of the century a Liberal potential among the right wing of the Social Democrats and suggested an electoral alliance with that party. When such an alliance came about in 1912, it became easier for many Jews of the Establishment to sympathise with the SPD.[12] But the "red danger" was not

[10]Ernest Hamburger, *Juden im öffentlichen Leben Deutschlands. Regierungsmitglieder, Beamte und Parlamentarier in der monarchischen Zeit 1848–1918*, Tübingen 1968 (Schriftenreihe wissenschaftlicher Abhandlungen des Leo Baeck Instituts 19), p. 163.

[11]Marjorie Lamberti, *Jewish Activism in Imperial Germany*, New Haven 1978, pp. 25, 37.

[12]James J. Sheehan, *German Liberalism in the Nineteenth Century*, Chicago 1978, p. 266; Lamberti, *op. cit.*, p. 118.

exorcised so easily, and until 1930, at least, the vast majority of German Jews remained loyal to the Liberal parties which were becoming an ever more insignificant political force. As historians we can see in retrospect that during the Weimar Republic the Social Democrats increasingly co-opted the Liberal space in German politics, but we cannot expect that the leaders of German Jewry and most of their followers, who had grown up before the First World War, would be aware of this fact. This the more so as their allegiance to Liberalism, despite the search for ideological and political unity, was based in the final resort upon their faith in Liberal ideals, and not upon the primacy of political Liberalism.

It was easier in the end phase of the Weimar Republic for Thomas Mann to confess his allegiance to Social Democracy than for the German Jews who knew full well how much they owed to Liberal thought, and who wanted to attain full membership in the bourgeoisie. This though Thomas Mann, himself a convinced bourgeois, used the same argument which Carlo Roselli and many Jewish Socialists had voiced as well, namely that his new political engagement would preserve Liberalism within Germany.[13] If after 1930 many Jews drew close to or even joined the Social Democratic Party, now almost their only defender, many nevertheless remained with the *Staatspartei*, the insignificant remnant of political Liberalism in Germany.[14]

Analysing the alliance between German Jews and Liberalism in retrospect means comprehending the problems inherent in this close relationship: above all, the depth of allegiance to that theory which had legitimised the process of Jewish emancipation, and the tenuous chance of its political realisation determined by the fate of Liberal political parties. The Third *Reich* put the relationship between Jews and Liberalism to its crucial test, just as all German-Jewish problems were now up for reconsideration, seen, so to speak, through a magnifying glass. The relationship of Liberal theory to Liberal practice became part of the internal Jewish debate, not as an urge to modernise Liberalism – which one can find among the Socialists we have mentioned – but as a life-belt instead.

Because the Third *Reich* forced Jews to reconsider a Liberalism which they had taken for granted, it tested the depth of that allegiance, and the extent to which ideals which had stood Jews in good stead during the process of emancipation and assimilation could be maintained or had to be discarded. Though Liberal allegiance was tested throughout the German-Jewish community, I want to single out as an example a group who formed the most committed citadel of Liberalism. Here one can follow the testing of a Jewish Liberal identity at its most extreme, characterised through its unbending allegiance to

[13]Kurt Sontheimer, *Thomas Mann und die Deutschen*, Frankfurt a. Main 1961, p. 77.

[14]Arnold Paucker, *Der jüdische Abwehrkampf gegen Antisemitismus und Nationalsozialismus in den letzten Jahren der Weimarer Republik*, 2nd edn. Hamburg 1969 (Hamburger Beiträge zur Zeitgeschichte Band IV), pp. 91ff.; Ernest Hamburger and Peter Pulzer, 'Jews as Voters in the Weimar Republic', in *LBI Year Book XXX* (1985), pp. 52ff.; Arnold Paucker, 'Jewish Self-Defence', in *Die Juden im Nationalsozialistischen Deutschland/The Jews in Nazi Germany 1933–1943*, herausgegeben von Arnold Paucker mit Sylvia Gilchrist und Barbara Suchy, Tübingen 1986 (Schriftenreihe wissenschaftlicher Abhandlungen des Leo Baeck Instituts 45), pp. 58–60.

the tenets of Enlightenment Liberal thought. It does not matter for our purposes that the membership of the *Jüdische Reformgemeinde* was as small as it was distinguished and influential; concentrating upon the reaction of the congregation to the new situation of Jews in Nazi Germany brings into sharper focus Liberal dilemmas which were faced by more moderate Liberal congregations as well.

The *Jüdische Reformgemeinde* was the most radical wing of Liberal Judaism. It was founded in 1845 in order to eliminate from Jewish religious practice customs which seemed to conflict with German citizenship. All signs of particularism, like the Hebrew language and reference to Jerusalem, were thought to be out of place for Jews as German citizens. Between 1845 and 1932 no less than eleven revisions of the Prayer Book were undertaken, adjusting it to the changing times, until a book of only 64 small pages remained.[15] The goal of these reforms was to strengthen German identity, but the Germany with which this congregation identified was a Liberal Germany.

To be sure, especially after the First World War, not all members of this Congregation were committed Liberals. Then the leaders of the *Verband nationaldeutscher Juden* and some of their followers were members of the *Reformgemeinde*. They were, no doubt, attracted by the emphasis upon German citizenship, the rejection of any religious practices which might set Jews apart from Germans. The fact that this Congregation attracted virtually no East European Jewish immigrants – regarded with open enmity by the *Verband* – must have given them satisfaction as well. But their Conservative nationalist definition of what constituted a German differed from that of most of the congregation. The leaders of this Jewish Reform rejected what they saw as the radicalism of the *Verband nationaldeutscher Juden*,[16] even though a member of that *Verband* was for a time the president of the Congregation. Moreover, many members were also part of the *Reichsbund jüdischer Frontsoldaten* whose leader sat on the board of the *Jüdische Reformgemeinde*. Such membership might have pushed the Congregation to abandon its Liberal stance, to recognise the realities of the new Germany which both the *Nationaldeutsche Juden* and the leadership of the Jewish veterans organisation saw as the triumph of the ideal of a *völkisch* community, the latter perhaps more for tactical than patriotic reasons.[17] But, as we shall see, the Congregation itself refused to follow here: the contrast between the unanimous stand taken, for example, by the rabbis of the Congregation under the tyranny of National Socialism and the members of these organisations could not have been greater.

[15]Wolfgang Hamburger, 'The Reactions of Reform Jews to Nazi Rule', in Herbert A. Strauss and Kurt R. Grossmann (eds.), *Gegenwart im Rückblick. Festgabe für die Jüdische Gemeinde zu Berlin 25 Jahre nach dem Neubeginn*, Heidelberg 1970, pp. 150–152 treats their commitment to Germany in excellent fashion, but does not address the problem of Liberalism; Klaus J. Herrmann, 'Weltanschauliche Aspekte der *Jüdischen Reformgemeinde* in Berlin', *Emuna*, IX, Nr. 2 (März-April 1974), pp. 83–92, is the best and most thorough discussion of the post-First World War *Gemeinde* to date.

[16]Herrmann, *loc. cit.*, p. 91.

[17]On the *Reichsbund* as a forum for right-wing Jewish *Bünde* after 1933, see George L. Mosse, *Germans and Jews. The Right, the Left, and the Search for a "Third Force" in Pre-Nazi Germany*, New York 1970, p. 105. There is need for an examination of the liberal potential which might exist here in contrast to German veterans' organisations.

Königswinter Conference on German Jews and Liberalism, May 1986
Friedrich-Naumann-Stiftung – Leo Baeck Institute, London
From left to right: Reinhard Rürup, Werner Mosse, Gerhart Raichle, Peter Pulzer, George Mosse

The fact that the *Reformgemeinde* even under the Nazis took their German identity for granted has obscured the discussion which took place at the time about the kind of German tradition they regarded as their own. Theirs was not the Germany of a Conservative nationalism, for in the sermons of the rabbis and the pages of the Congregation's journal, the *Mitteilungen der Jüdischen Reformgemeinde*, the basic principles of Liberalism remained intact before and after the Nazi seizure of power. For example, the *Bar-Mitzvah* candidates of 1931 were told that the triumph of the critical spirit over blind faith constituted the essence of Judaism.[18] Individualism was always in the forefront: thus we hear from the pulpit, in 1932, that individuals created religions and political parties, and this sermon on the theme of 'Religion and Politics' ended with the exclamation "the human being first and foremost, and the human within all things" ("der Mensch über alles und der Mensch in allem").[19] The identical thoughts were repeated from the pulpit in 1935 – that is two years after the seizure of power – only out of the individual himself can a community be regenerated, and though the concept of the community must be given its due, Jews must remain nonconformists who confront the present with the eternal worth of the individual in mind.[20] Surely for such men German *Patriotismus* could not be exclusive – Jews who know only the German people and care only about the future of Germany – as the leader of the *Verband nationaldeutscher Juden* put it.[21] Their commitment to Germany pointed back to a time when patriotism had been paired with a concern for all humanity and where nationalism was seen as a step in the free development of the individual. Here Liberal thought attempted to humanise nationalism, a function which it also filled for the Zionists mentioned above. Certainly, a comparison of both such nationalisms, the Jewish-German and the German Zionist, might lead to interesting results. If, for example, men like Robert Weltsch saw in nationalism a phase of personal development which would, in the end, benefit all mankind, so the Chief Rabbi of the Jewish Reform Congregation preached at a patriotic ceremony before the First World War that he who serves the fatherland serves all mankind because this service will help develop his individual personality, and thus enable him to benefit all communities.[22]

This Liberal patriotism was bound to be tested in the radically changed environment after 1933; what seemed at risk, above all, was that individualism upon which their outlook upon the world was founded. It was the youth group of the *Reformgemeinde* which called for more coherence among Jews, for the creation of a true community. This challenge to Liberalism was not inspired by a wish to imitate the *Volksgemeinschaft* which the Nazis proclaimed, but by the

[18]Julius Jelsky, 'Konfirmationspredigt', *Mitteilungen der Jüdischen Reformgemeinde* (from now on, *Mitteilungen*), 1st May 1931, p. 9.

[19]Benno Gottschalk, 'Religion und Politik', *Mitteilungen*, 1st July 1932, p. 11.

[20]Karl Rosenthal, 'Ernst Machen!', *Mitteilungen*, 15th February 1935, p. 23.

[21]Kurt Loewenstein, 'Die innerjüdische Reaktion auf die Krise der deutschen Demokratie', in *Entscheidungsjahr 1932. Zur Judenfrage in der Endphase der Weimarer Republik*. Ein Sammelband herausgegeben von Werner E. Mosse unter Mitwirkung von Arnold Paucker, Tübingen 1966 (Schriftenreihe wissenschaftlicher Abhandlungen des Leo Baeck Instituts 13), p. 371.

[22]*Zum Gedächtnis an Dr. Moritz Levin*, 13th December 1914, p. 9.

new situation of Jews thrown back upon their own resources, the creation of a ghetto even if its walls were completed only over a period of time. Surely the Congregation had always regarded itself as a community, but as a religious community only, one dedicated to study and learning free from myths and symbols – an intellectual community lacking that appeal to the emotions which the German Right, but also the German youth movement, had made their own. Because of the resistance by the leadership of the Congregation to the acceptance of an emotion-laden concept of community, the debate initiated by the Congregation's youth became a test of Liberalism. The Congregation's intellectualised concept of community was based once again upon individualism: nonconformity was a quality which would protect Jews against assimilation.[23] But after 1933 such a definition could no longer satisfy youth – particularly hard hit by Nazi discrimination – and it is possible to follow in the *Mitteilungsblätter der Jüdischen Reformgemeinde* how the youth group tried to infuse the Liberalism of the Congregation with the ideal of a true community based upon shared emotions. For example, they suggested ridding the *Heim-Abende* of more or less abstruse intellectual discussions in order to concentrate upon individual encounters instead.[24] But a retreat into the apparent comfort of close personal relationships was not a tactic designed to strengthen communal bonds. Thus, in 1934 the youth group of the Congregation obtained a uniform, as well as a flag, and a special dress uniform to be worn on festive occasions. The first flag was consecrated on the 23rd of August, 1934, and at the same time roving through the countryside became an important activity of the group.[25] The symbols and the spirit of the German youth movement were copied by the youth group at this late date in order to create the feeling of community.

However, inspite of this apparent acceptance of the German ideal of *Gemeinschaft*, traditional Liberal values were not abandoned by the Congregation, but reaffirmed instead. The *Reformgemeinde* saw itself even now as a Liberal community asserting the need for pluralism in all walks of life. Not "Jewish-*völkisch*" personalities were needed, Karl Rosenthal, one of the Congregation's youthful and vigorous rabbis, tells us in a sermon entitled 'Within the New *Reich*' (September, 1933), but individual personalities, and yet, so he continues, the religious community through performing its spiritual tasks must become a truer community.[26] The conflict between Liberalism and the search for a true community had been fought out in Germany itself long ago, and the community had been the victor. But the symbiosis between Judaism and Liberalism was too deep-seated and could not be destroyed at the first onslaught.

The Liberal Jewish paper, *Der Morgen*, closer to the mainstream of German Jewry than the publications of the *Reformgemeinde*, published in June 1931 an article by the non-Jewish writer Wilhelm Michel in which he analysed what he

[23]Rosenthal, 'Ernst Machen!', *loc. cit.*, p. 23.
[24]*Mitteilungen*, 15th January 1935, p. 12.
[25]*Ibid.*, 15th January 1934, p. 10; *Ibid.*, 15th September 1934, p. 11; on the importance of the Jewish youth movement for the hard-pressed Jewish youth in the Third *Reich*, see Werner T. Angress, *Generation zwischen Furcht und Hoffnung. Jüdische Jugend im Dritten Reich*, Hamburg 1985, *passim*.
[26]Karl Rosenthal, 'Im neuen Reich', *Mitteilungen*, 1st September 1933, p. 3.

called the end of Liberalism. It was time, he wrote, to join in the hopes and feelings which moved all Germans, to fight against the exaggerated concept of freedom which Liberalism had advocated.[27] Liberal Jews themselves wrote frequently after 1933 about a "converted Liberalism", one which did not ignore the need of order in its concern with freedom. Already during the crisis of 1920–1921 with its upsurge of nationalism and antisemitism, the *Mitteilungen der Jüdischen Reformgemeinde* had called for putting some restraint upon the worship of reason in order to give enthusiasm and the emotions of the heart their rightful place.[28] At the same time Leo Baeck, who in the original edition of his *The Essence of Judaism* had condemned all mysticism, now in a revised edition of his work defined mysticism as something within us which encourages men to unfold their personality freely, joining men to God.[29] Such ideas reflected the hunger for myth during the Weimar Republic, but they never got the upper hand over the tradition of the Enlightenment; they were constantly negated through an emphasis upon reason and the individual personality. But now, under National Socialism, among Jews of all Liberal persuasions there was a strenuous effort to "convert" their Liberalism to a greater emphasis upon the principle of order.

Nevertheless, the ". . . Jewish love for Humanity and the age of Humanism"[30] – to quote a 1936 article in the *Mitteilungen* – lived on. It did so as part of a retreat from an unpalatable reality into that preoccupation with culture as humanistic *Bildung* which had been prepared by the primacy of Liberal thought over Liberal practice, a theme which has accompanied us throughout this analysis. The primacy of *Bildung* provided refuge during the Third *Reich* for Jews and many Gentiles alike, but for the Jews the attainment of *Bildung* as an extension of the Enlightenment had been one of the chief signs of their emancipation. Within the increasingly narrow bounds of their German ghetto culture was severed from political, social or economic reality, became a refuge and at the same time the guarantee of their German-Jewish identity. Thus in 1934 it was proudly stated that the *Kulturbund deutscher Juden* (the newly-created Jewish organisation which sponsored all cultural activity) considered culture as a good in itself, not related to any extraneous goals or activities. And in 1937 the *Jüdische Reformgemeinde* mourned the decline, caused by economic pressures, of *Bildung* among its hard-pressed youth. *Bildung* as art, philosophy and history would never become unfashionable and there could be no excuse for abandoning one's self-cultivation.[31]

The conflict between Liberalism and ideas of community was not abolished but disguised through emphasis upon the cultural inheritance which, as these

[27]Wilhelm Michel, 'Was heisst: Ende des Liberalismus?', *Der Morgen*, vol. 8, No. 2 (June 1932), p. 83.

[28]Joseph Lehmann, 'Judentum und Deutschtum', *Mitteilungen*, 1st July 1920, *passim*.

[29]Baeck, *op. cit.*, p. 165; Leonard Baker, *Days of Sorrow and Pain. Leo Baeck and the Berlin Jews*, New York 1978, p. 131.

[30]Lutz Weltmann, 'Zur Antigone-Aufführung des Kulturbundes', *Mitteilungen*, 14th April 1936, p. 36.

[31]Hans Margolius, 'Der Kulturbund Deutscher Juden', *Mitteilungen*, 15th August 1934, pp. 6–7; Paul Rothkugel, 'Zur geistigen Situation der Jüdischen Jugend', *Mitteilungen*, 10th May 1937, p. 56.

German Jews viewed it, was a Liberal bequest. There were many established leaders of the Jewish community who explicitly demanded the separation of Liberalism from its political infrastructure, a demand that, as we saw, young Jewish Socialists like Carlo Roselli had made much earlier. Manfred Swarsensky, a young rabbi at an important Berlin Liberal synagogue, wrote in 1933, representative for many others, that Jewish Liberalism was a child of European Liberalism, and could not be traced to specifically Jewish roots like the Talmud and Torah. Thus the crisis of general Liberalism had affected Jewish Liberalism as well. Nevertheless, it must not be discarded, for without Liberalism Jews would have found no inner relationship to their faith.[32] Thus while Liberalism did not grow out of Judaism, it served to renew its spirit. His criticism was directed at the balance between rationalism and irrationalism which had not been kept and which must be restored. But this could only happen if the fateful mistake of joining religious to political Liberalism were to be corrected.[33] Attempting to salvage religious Liberalism meant in this context saving the tradition of Liberal thought which was interwoven with Jewish religiosity: indeed, as we saw Liberal religion had absorbed and protected the humanistic Liberal tradition.

The *Jüdische Reformgemeinde* joined this argument. The reaction of that Congregation in 1936 to the closing of the *Jüdische Allgemeine Zeitung*, representing a more moderate Liberalism, was typical. We have attempted, so the *Mitteilungen* wrote, during the last twenty years to separate religious from political Liberalism, ". . . and what we were not able to do the passage of time has accomplished".[34] This is surely an astonishing statement given the involvement of so many members and leaders of the Congregation with Liberal political parties. Perhaps this was wishful thinking projected onto the past, or an acknowledgement that theory had always had precedence over practice. Such a reaction on the part of the most dogmatically Liberal of all German-Jewish congregations demonstrates that even here reality had to be faced, leading to a repudiation of Liberal politics and a retreat into culture as the bastion of besieged Liberal values.

The Jewish *Kulturbund* fulfilled a central function in the preservation and transmission of these values. To be sure, many cultural events sponsored by that organisation reflected the light entertainment found in many German theatre and concert programmes as well; but it seems – in the absence of a detailed stocktaking – that the major part of its programme was devoted to that theatre and music which had traditionally provided the sign of a humanistic *Bildung*. I have attempted to outline elsewhere how the *Kulturbund* functioned in transmitting the Liberal heritage.[35] Of course, here also this heritage was under

[32]Manfred Swarsensky, 'Liberale Bestimmung', *Die Gemeinschaft*, ed. by Liberale Synagoge Norden in Berlin, No. 21–22, (24th November 1934), pp. 3–4.
[33]*Ibid.* pp. 4–5.
[34]Heinrich Stern, 'Abschied vom Neu-Aufbau', *Mitteilungen*, 10th September 1936, p. 96.
[35]George L. Mosse, *German Jews Beyond Judaism*, pp. 78ff. See now Herbert Freeden, 'Kultur "nur für Juden": "Kulturkampf" in der jüdischen Presse in Nazideutschland', in *Juden im Nationalsozialistischen Deutschland*, *op. cit.*, pp. 259–271, and elsewhere in this symposium volume.

pressure, not just from Nazi censorship but also from the perceived necessity of defining its "Jewish" content. This quest was never successful, once plays with a specific, generally East-European Jewish note had proved unpopular, and it seemed easier to introduce a specifically Jewish content (such as the compositions of Ernest Bloch) into the musical programme. For example, in order to make *Nathan der Weise* more "Jewish," he was made in one performance to hum a *hasidic* tune in the first act (one wonders how many in the audience might have recognised it), and a *menorah* as well as a prayer stool graced with the Star of David were placed in his house. Subsequently it seemed sufficient that the actor himself would portray Jewish dignity through his comportment, whatever the play.[36] The Liberal heritage dominated the specifically Jewish in most of the *Kulturbund*'s performances, and the *Kulturbund* played an important role in preserving the alliance between Jews and Liberal thought in dark times.

The amputation of Liberal culture from Liberalism as a political, social or economic movement did lead to a certain vagueness in the definition of ideas like freedom and humanity. But while in Germany itself Liberal ideals threatened to degenerate into the transmission of Liberal slogans through popular journals like the *Gartenlaube* and in politics, Jews remained deadly serious in their commitment to Liberal thought. It stood for the positive in the German-Jewish experience, the hopes aroused by the process of emancipation. Nevertheless, these noble ideals tended to become a utopia unless they were tied to a concept of politics which accorded to some extent with the political realities of the times. But after the First World War this was less and less the case, as I have pointed out, and under the Nazis, while contemplating this Liberal tradition, one is projected into a world of dreams. Yet these Liberal ideas were models for a better and healthier world, and their preservation in Nazi times was a historic deed. Whether non-Jews were also attracted to that German tradition within which so many plays of the *Kulturbund* had their place (or just by the quality of the performances), whether they also bought the books it recommended – many openly praising ideals of tolerance and the Enlightenment – is still unknown. And yet, such possible interaction during the Third *Reich* between Germans and German Jews largely on the basis of a shared Liberalism would be an important part of the history of Liberalism in Germany.

There is scattered evidence that this interaction may have been attempted. The often-repeated warnings and threats against so-called Aryans attending *Kulturbund* performances might lead to such a conclusion. A correspondent of *The Manchester Guardian* wrote in 1937 that not even foreigners could attend the *Kulturbund* unless they could prove that they were Jews. These restrictions, he continued, may have been a necessary precaution by the authorities, for if the Jewish theatre were open to the general public it might prove too attractive.[37] German Jews were now, as in the past, one of the chief conveyors of the Enlightenment Liberal tradition; they had, as we saw briefly above, attempted

[36]George L. Mosse, *German Jews Beyond Judaism*, pp. 16, 80.

[37]'Jüdischer Kulturbund. Intellectual Life of German Jewry', *The Manchester Guardian*, 15th October 1937, p. 316; (Wiener Library, London, clipping collection).

to infuse it into non-Liberal movements such as Marxism or Nationalism with indifferent success, and at the end of their history in Germany they stood as its sole guardians. Surely there were many non-Jewish Germans who shared these ideals and Liberal Jews had always found Liberal partners in Gentile Society. But here, under the Nazis, only the Jews were permitted to advocate this Liberalism through their cultural activities. Just as surely not all Jews were wedded to this heritage; some were religiously Orthodox and others orthodox Marxists and a very few even political Conservatives. But to a greater or lesser extent most of them were influenced by that system of ideas which had stood at the beginning of their history as Germans. We still lack research on the diffusion of Liberalism through all branches of German Jewry, but it seems safe to say that the majority were, or aspired to be, *Bildungsbürger* in the classical sense of this term.

Liberal thought made a decisive contribution to Jewish emancipation and its influence upon German Jews is easily understood, but this Liberalism may also have contributed to clouding their understanding of modern politics. That mass politics which began its triumphal march in post-war Germany was largely based upon a militant nationalism and a concept of the *Volk* which embraced all Germans except the Jews. German-Jewish *Bildungsbürger*, like some of their Christian counterparts, could find no relationship to such a nationalism or to these kind of politics; they were perplexed or attempted to trivialise a phenomenon so foreign to their cast of mind. Joseph Lehmann, the best known rabbi of the *Reformgemeinde*, did not have this post-war nationalism in mind when he wrote in 1933 that the feeling of belonging to Germany was the source of Jewish religiosity.[38] He had made clear what he meant by such national feeling earlier, in response to the first wave of antisemitism and racism which swept post-war Germany. His conclusions were not much different from those of his arch-enemies, the German Zionists. The opponents of emancipation, he wrote, had discovered their national soul, as if all the world was rooted in unchanging national sentiment. But the Jews were destined to stir up cultural ferment for all mankind.[39] These sentiments were reminiscent of a phrase from Leo Baeck's *The Essence of Judaism*, that the Jews were the leavening of history.[40]

Just as, on the one hand, the symbiosis between Liberalism and the Jews made it possible for Jews in the Third *Reich* to preserve this Liberal heritage, so, on the other, it blocked off political alternatives and the comprehension of political realities. Ideals such as Baeck's, or those of the other rabbis we have cited, did not encourage the joining of mass movements. Indeed, in the last years of the Weimar Republic, the Democratic Party, a remnant of the once influential Liberal parties, attempted to regenerate itself and acquire a mass base by joining with the *Jungdeutscher Orden*, a former German youth movement, which though *völkisch* in attitude, had quarrelled with the German political Right. The new party was to be a synthesis of national and Liberal traditions.[41] The

[38]Joseph Lehmann, 'Unsere Stellung', *Mitteilungen*, 1st May 1933, p. 2.
[39]Joseph Lehmann, 'Judentum und Deutschtum', *Mitteilungen*, 1st July 1920, p. 11.
[40]Baeck, *op. cit.*, p. 281.
[41]Klaus Hornung, *Der Jungdeutsche Orden*, Düsseldorf 1958, p. 99 and *passim*.

very name of the new party, *Staatspartei*, shows how much Liberal substance had vanished in what turned out to be an unsuccessful attempt to compete with existing mass political parties. Liberal thought with its roots in the Enlightenment found it difficult, if not impossible, to accommodate itself to the political right. But, as we have seen, until shortly before Hitler's accession to power, Social Democracy was also under suspicion; its class rhetoric disguised the reality of its Liberal stance.

These observations are a critique of a Liberalism which after 1918 increasingly by-passed political realities which it did not or could not understand. Yet a better grasp of political reality by such Liberals would not, I believe, have stopped the German catastrophe either. Jewish emancipation and assimilation with all their consequences seemed time-bound after 1918, an emancipation and assimilation against the times which called for the formation of a true community as the centre of a civic religion. Conformity, and not a pluralistic and tolerant state, was in demand in a society which felt itself increasingly threatened.

But despite all the criticism which might be directed in retrospect against the alliance between Jews and Liberalism, it seems to me to have been most fruitful precisely where it was most vulnerable: in its intellectualism and in its unrealistic timelessness. It did more than its share to preserve the values of the Enlightenment, the emphasis upon the individual and the unity of all mankind. While in Germany the alliance between Liberalism and the Enlightenment was constantly weakened, here it held firm. The extent to which the German-Jewish Liberal bourgeoisie contributed to the survival of the Liberal heritage into post-war Germany still needs investigation. But that they attempted to transmit it is certain. It was nothing less than the tearing apart of theory and practice, so alarming before 1933, which made the survival of this heritage possible. Seen from this perspective the alliance of Jews and Liberalism defied its critics and justified itself.

Emancipation

Frederick the Great and Moses Mendelssohn: Thoughts on Jewish Emancipation

BY GORDON A. CRAIG

Historians are fond of calling attention to anniversaries, and it is a double anniversary that supplies the occasion for these remarks, for next year* will be the 200th anniversary of the deaths of both Moses Mendelssohn, who died on 4th January 1786, and of Frederick II of Prussia, who died on 17th August of that year.

One may object, of course, that this coincidence is a poor excuse for lumping together such disparate personalities, but, in truth, Moses Mendelssohn and Frederick were not so different as all that. To be sure, one was a King and the other was not; but, despite that salient discrepancy, there were striking similarities between them. In both cases, for example, their adolescence and early manhood were troubled and painful, with much deprivation, much drudgery over unrewarding tasks, and a considerable amount of physical and psychological torment. Frederick, of course, never had to worry about where his next meal was coming from, as Mendelssohn sometimes did; but then Mendelssohn never had to suffer the anguish of having to watch his closest friend being beheaded and of having subsequently to sit for weeks in confinement, waiting to learn whether he would suffer the same fate.[1]

Both men overcame the difficulties of their early lives by means of strict discipline and prodigious intellectual labours; both became voracious readers of systematic works on philosophy, theology, politics and – in Frederick's case – military science, as well as dramatic works and epic verse; and both, using models that they found in their reading, trained themselves to write about serious subjects with clarity, grace and authority. Writing seems, indeed, to have become for them a psychological necessity, in which they sought perspective and perhaps reassurance in times of doubt and danger; Mendelssohn's pen was always his friend and comforter, while Frederick, after his defeat at Kolin in 1757, not only wrote floods of letters and analyses of recent operations and reflections on how his conduct of battle might be improved, but told his correspondents that misfortune had re-awakened his desire to write poetry.[2] So too, after the murderous fight at Hochkirch in 1758, the King noted, "You will often find me engrossed in reading and writing. I need this diversion at a time when I am preoccupied with gloomy thoughts."[3] Wilhelm Dilthey was

*This paper was delivered by the author in New York on 28th December 1985 at a function of the Leo Baeck Institute on the occasion of the 100th meeting of the American Historical Association.

[1]On this, see Theodor Fontane, *Wanderungen durch die Mark Brandenburg*, II, Munich 1960, pp. 284ff.

[2]Christopher Duffy, *The Military Life of Frederick the Great*, New York 1986, p. 132.

[3]*Ibid.*, p. 181.

perhaps guilty of exaggeration when he described Frederick as one of the four great writers of his age, the others being Voltaire, Diderot and Lessing[4], but the King's histories of his own time are still accorded respect for their substance as well as their style. As for Mendelssohn, who wrote in a language that he had had to acquire painfully in his first years in Berlin, his works were praised by such discerning critics as Nicolai, Kant and Hamann.

Even the accomplishments of their mature years are, while different in nature, comparable in grandeur.

By the sheer force of his personality, Frederick – against forbidding odds and the armed opposition of all of his neighbours – transformed a relatively poor and heterogeneous collection of territories into a great European power and made it at the same time not only the newest but also the most modern state in Europe, a land of unlimited opportunities that served as a magnet for talented young men in all parts of Germany. Mendelssohn's achievement was no less a victory of personality. In a society that regarded Jews with contempt and suspicion, he showed by his own example how mistaken stereotypical German views of the Jews really were. To his own people, he demonstrated – as Hans I. Bach has written – that "the transition from the secluded life of medieval Jewry to participation in Western civilization could be achieved without loss of faith . . . Without his example, the emancipation of the Jews, the freedom to take their place as valued citizens of the Western world, could never have been contemplated."[5]

Finally, both Mendelssohn and Frederick were leading representatives of the Enlightenment, that proud and self-confident movement of the eighteenth century which based itself on the faith that human reason was capable not only of determining the universal laws of nature but also of re-fashioning the world and freeing it from the burden of superstition, prejudice, outmoded institutions and injustice, and which expressed this in an ambitious programme of secularism, humanity, cosmopolitanism, and freedom in all of its forms.

About the legitimacy of Mendelssohn's credentials as an *Aufklärer*, there is no question. His biographer Alexander Altmann has described his almost herculean labours during his first Berlin years to acquire the languages necessary to study the work of the great *philosophes*, of his laborious reading of Locke's *Essay Concerning Human Understanding*, which he had to translate word by word from an edition in Latin, and of the formative influence upon his thinking of Leibniz, Shaftesbury and Wolff.[6] Accustomed by his training in Jewish doctrine to believe in the efficacy of reason, its compatibility with the Law, and the merits of tolerance, he had no difficulty in making the ideals of the *Aufklärung* his own, and all of his subsequent activities and works, from his correspondence with Lessing and Nicolai and Kant to his collaboration with Christian Wilhelm von Dohm, the author of the treatise *On the Civic Improvement*

[4]Wilhelm Dilthey, *Gesammelte Schriften*, III, ed. by Paul Ritter, Leipzig 1927, p. 100ff.

[5]Hans I. Bach, *The German Jew. A Synthesis of Judaism and Western Civilization, 1730–1930*. New York 1984, p. 44.

[6]Alexander Altmann, *Moses Mendelssohn. A Biographical Study*, University of Alabama 1973, pp. 15–25.

of the Jews, testify to his abiding faith in reason, his love of humanity, his belief in the intrinsic goodness and unity of human nature, and his willingness to be modern at the expense of the traditional and the Orthodox.

More problematical is Frederick's right to be considered as a true *Aufklärer*. The friend of Voltaire, the ruler who sometimes styled himself the *philosophe de Sans Souci*, was in the end repudiated by his fellow philosophers as a recreant and traitor to the cause, and Rousseau was speaking for the majority of them when he wrote in 1758 that he was an "admirer of the talents of the King of Prussia, but in no way his partisan", adding, "I can neither esteem nor love a man without principles, who tramples on all international law, who does not love virtue but considers it as a bait with which to amuse fools, and who began his Machiavellianism by refuting Machiavelli".[7] In our own time, Peter Gay has written that Frederick, like Catherine of Russia, "forced [himself] on a movement to whose ideals [his] policy owed little".[8]

It is possible that these judgements are too severe. What most people know about Frederick's treatise against Machiavelli, which was written in 1739, is that it was followed almost immediately by his unprovoked assault upon the territories of Empress Maria Theresia, the so-called rape of Silesia. But no one who reads the *Anti-Machiavel*, or the work that preceded it, the *Considérations sur l'état présent du corps politique de l'Europe* of 1737–1738, can remain entirely unimpressed by the strong strain of idealism that runs through them. When Frederick declares in the former work that politics should be regarded not as a storehouse of cunning artifices and tricks, but as the totality of the wisdom of princes; when he writes that their task should be to ban falsehood and intrigue from international affairs and to promote the welfare of their subjects, when, in place of Machiavelli's hero Cesare di Borgia, he sets up Fénélon's Télémaque as a model for rulers and as the embodiment of goodness, justice and restraint, there is no reason to believe, simply because his later actions did not conform to his professions, that he was being deliberately insincere. Even as he wrote, he was painfully aware that, once he assumed the throne, he would be confronted with the dilemma that is posed for every responsible political leader by the contrast between the world as it is and the world as it should be. Even in his fulminations against Machiavelli, he did not ignore the Florentine's warning that a prince's freedom of action was circumscribed by necessity – that of maintaining his realm against jealous and unscrupulous foes –, and that his best-designed plans were at the mercy of fortune's whims, and that in such circumstances his greatest resource was *virtú*. But Frederick's definition of *virtú* was "*Qui dit la vertu, dit la raison*".[9]

This definition should be remembered in any evaluation of Frederick's work as a ruler. There is no doubt that the deeper one penetrates the details of his internal policy the clearer it becomes that its chief aim was the enhancement of

[7]Peter Gay, *The Enlightenment: An Interpretation*, vol. II, *The Science of Freedom*, New York 1969, p. 458.
[8]*Ibid.*, vol. I, *The Rise of Modern Paganism*, New York 1966, p. 11.
[9]Theodor Schieder, *Friedrich der Grosse. Ein Königtum der Widersprüche*, Frankfurt a. Main 1983, p. 105; *Die Werke Friedrichs des Grossen*, ed. by Gustav Berthold Volz, vol. VII, Berlin 1913, especially pp. 106–107.

the power of the State. Yet the reforms that he made to accomplish that purpose – the decree of tolerance, the abolition of torture, the reform of the legal system, the economic and colonisation projects, the measures to improve the efficiency of the State administration – were part of a rational process, an application of *Staatsvernunft* or Reason of State, which was, of course, a salient feature of the politics of the Enlightenment. What could be more characteristic of the spirit of the Enlightenment than Frederick's insistence in his *Political Testament* of 1752 that "a well-conducted government ought to have a system as coherent as a system of philosophy?"[10]

Moreover, Reason of State was not entirely incompatible with the idealism that had found expression in the *Anti-Machiavel*. In the latest biography of Frederick, Theodor Schieder has written that the King never got over his youthful belief that *Staatsvernunft* must serve not purely utilitarian ends, but "the higher goals of justice, humanity, and happiness".[11] It is not difficult to find passages in both the *Testament* of 1752 and that of 1768 that support this view, as do some of the major reforms, notably the encouragement of the formulation of rules of war as a means of introducing a measure of restraint to the century's intermittent blood-letting. This impulse doubtless weakened with time and was overborne by political considerations and by Frederick's deepening cynicism. Even so, he never became a heedless *Realpolitiker*. He was always the philosopher who reflected upon his actions and for whom, as Schieder says, "the power with which he worked was always an intellectual problem".[12]

Having said all this, one must nevertheless admit that most of Frederick's statements about "the higher goals of justice, humanity, and happiness" suffered from their abstract quality. Otto Hintze's view that the *Political Testaments* in part reflect French and American theories of the rights of the individual is not persuasive. Frederick was not accustomed to thinking of individuals and their specific needs, and his comments about his subjects as human beings were not infrequently atrabilious. As ruler and reformer, he tended rather to think in terms of functional groupings with specific roles in society, and this necessarily diminished the humanitarian content of his reforms, while negating his professed desire to promote justice. No better example of this can be found than his attitude towards his Jewish subjects.

In eighteenth-century Prussia, the Jews were a small – there were only 333 Jewish families resident in Berlin in 1743, with a total Jewish population of less than 2,000 – under-privileged, over-taxed minority that was tolerated for its economic usefulness but was often an object of abuse and mistreatment. Their rights of residence and movement were, except in the case of a small elite of *Generalprivilegierten*, restricted, and they were subject to expulsion from their places of domicile at the caprice of local authorities. They were excluded from the public service; they could not belong to guilds; they were forbidden to engage in certain trades, to open barber's shops, for example, to sell spirits, baked goods, fish, meat and milk products; and they were taxed mercilessly

[10] *Politische Testamente der Hohenzollern*, ed. by Richard Dietrich, Munich 1981, p. 174.
[11] Schieder, *Friedrich der Grosse, op. cit.*, p. 307.
[12] *Ibid.*

and, as Henri Brunschwig has written, on every possible occasion, when travelling, when marrying, when buying a house, taxed for the right to remain in the city, taxed whenever they left it, taxed for the privilege of being excluded from the armed forces, and so forth. The story is an old one and does not bear repeating. The civic disabilities of the Jews seemed to most of the *philosophes* to cry for correction, although it should be noted that there was a certain ambivalence in their attitude, since the Jewish religion seemed to them to be even more benighted and obscurantist than that of the various Christian sects. Hence Voltaire's mixed feelings about the Jews.[13]

There was, however, no ambivalence about the feelings of the philosopher king. His ordinance of 1750 divided Jews into four categories, defined their rights, and placed all matters concerning them under the control of the General Directory, but it in no way improved their condition. Frederick recognised them as an economic resource that could be tapped when needed (when the *Königliche Porzellanmanufaktur* needed shoring up, for example, he decreed that Jews must buy large amounts of its products on set occasions), but otherwise regarded them with a distaste bordering on contempt. In the *Political Testament* of 1752, in the section on religious denominations, he wrote:

> "The Jews are the most dangerous of all these sects because they do damage to the trade of Christians and because they are unusable as far as the State is concerned. We need this people in order to maintain a certain amount of trade with Poland, but one must prevent their numbers from growing and must limit them not only to a fixed number of families but also to a fixed number of individuals. One must also restrict their business activities, preventing them from engaging in wholesale trade, for they should only be retailers."[14]

Sixteen years later, in the *Testament* of 1768, he showed that his views had not changed. In the section on "future plans", he wrote:

> "We have too many Jews in the cities. On the borders of Poland they are necessary, because in that land only the Jews are traders. As soon as a town is distant from Poland, the Jews become harmful because of the usury they practise, the smuggling that goes through their hands, and the thousand rascalities that work to the disadvantage of *Bürger* and of Christian merchants. I have never persecuted the members of this sect, or anyone else. However, I think it wise to watch that their number does not increase too greatly."[15]

On 16th April 1786, four months before his death, Frederick granted an interview to Count Gabriel Honoré de Mirabeau.[16] The French reformer was interested in two subjects: Frederick's views of Christian Wilhelm von Dohm's treatise *On the Civic Improvement of the Jews*, and his reasons for failing to encourage or even recognise native German literature, which was already, in the works of Klopstock, Lessing and the young Goethe, showing a vitality equal to that of the French literature that Frederick preferred. We do not know what Frederick said on the first point, but it is unlikely that he confessed to being moved by Dohm's arguments, and it is possible that he gave an answer similar to the one he gave to Mirabeau's second question: "What could I have done for

[13]See Theodore Bestermann, *Voltaire*, Chicago 1969, pp. 92, 572.

[14]Dietrich (ed.), *Politische Testamente, op. cit.*, p. 167. This passage has been omitted from the *Testamente* as printed in Volz (ed.), *Die Werke Friedrichs des Grossen*, vol. VII, *op. cit.*, p. 148.

[15]Dietrich (ed.), *Politische Testamente, op. cit.*, p. 281.

[16]Schieder, *Friedrich der Grosse, op. cit.*, pp. 465–472.

German writers that equalled the advantage I granted them by *not* bothering about them and *not* reading their books?"

Frederick's aversion to the Jews was unalloyed by any appreciation of the achievements of the most brilliant members of the Jewish community. Long after Moses Mendelssohn had become one of the best known inhabitants of Berlin, with a reputation as a philosopher that extended well beyond the borders of Frederick's kingdom – indeed, long after he had become a friend of the King's confidant the Marquis d'Argens and a consultant on appointments to the minister of education, Karl von Zedlitz – the King acted as if he did not exist. It was only with difficulty that Mendelssohn, in 1763, received the royal *Schutzprivilegium* that entitled him to maintain a residence of his own, and in 1779, when he tried to have it extended to his children, Frederick refused.[17]

In February 1771, the Royal Academy in Berlin voted to propose to the King that Mendelssohn be appointed to fill a vacancy in its philosophical section, and Friedrich Nicolai wrote jubilantly to Lessing: "Our friend Moses was elected a regular member of the Academy ... last Thursday. True, the King's confirmation has not yet been received from Potsdam, but no one doubts it."[18] Nicolai, who admired Frederick as extravagantly as he did Mendelssohn, can be forgiven for believing that the philosopher of Sans Souci would recognise a kindred spirit in the author of the *Phaedon*. But the King left the Academy's proposals unanswered, and after an uncomfortable pause the academicians lost heart and submitted another list of candidates, which did not include Mendelssohn's name.

Mendelssohn did receive an invitation to Sans Souci in September 1771, when a cabinet minister from Saxony, Baron Thomas von Fritsche, who was visiting Frederick, expressed a desire to meet the Jewish philosopher, and the King undertook to make this possible. Mendelssohn was summoned to appear in Potsdam on 30th September, which coincided with the festival of Shemini Atseret, during which travel is not permitted. A council of experts on the Law, meeting with the Chief Rabbi of Berlin, decided that, because of the special circumstances, a dispensation was in order, and Mendelssohn went off to Potsdam.[19] The visit aroused enough public attention to persuade the Berlin artist Daniel Chodowiecki to commemorate it in a fine print that shows the diminutive philosopher handing his papers over to a lieutenant of the *Garde du Corps* while a grenadier with shouldered musket and bayonet towers above him.[20] Conspicuous by its absence from Chodowiecki's print is the figure of the King, but then he was absent from the interview too. In fact, the two men never met, and it may be just as well, for it is difficult to see what they could have talked about.

The slights that he suffered at the King's hand, Mendelssohn bore with equanimity. He was not immune to the force of Frederick's personality or

[17]*Moses Mendelssohn zur 200jährigen Wiederkehr seines Geburtstages*, herausgegeben von der Encyclopaedia Judaica, Berlin 1929, p. 19.

[18]Altmann, *Moses Mendelssohn, op. cit.*, pp. 264–265.

[19]*Ibid.*, pp. 275ff.

[20]*Mendelssohn zur 200jährigen Wiederkehr, op. cit.*, p. 81.

insensitive to his great talents. In 1757, after the battle of Leuthen, he composed a sermon praising the King that was read in the Berlin synagogue, and in 1760, in a review of Frederick's *Poésies diverses* for Nicolai's *Literaturbriefe*, he wrote that it would be difficult to find another poet who combined so much philosophy, sublimity of sentiment, psychological insight, felicity of imagery, tenderness of feeling and naturalness of language, adding mildly that it was a pity that he wrote in French rather than in German and that he borrowed so heavily from a philosopher as shallow as Epicurus.[21] Frederick's failure to ratify his election to the Academy disappointed him, but he comforted himself with the reflection that he had at least been recognised as worthy of election by his peers. Mendelssohn was not given to recrimination, nor did he ever associate himself with Lessing's not infrequent sneers about the lack of real freedom in Prussia. He was too conscious of what he himself had been able to accomplish, despite the humblest of beginnings and the most discouraging of odds, to be cast down by minor setbacks. And he was too much a man of the Enlightenment to doubt that reason would in the end triumph over prejudice and injustice and inequality. His own experience and his faith in the *Aufklärung* formed the basis of his belief in the emancipation of his people, and his example and his optimism encouraged generations of German Jews to believe as he did that complete integration in German society was possible by means of moral growth and self-improvement, or – if you will – by *Bildung*.

It would be easy to argue that Frederick's deepening cynicism and his growing conviction that power and human folly between them did more to determine the course of history than reason was more realistic than Mendelssohn's faith in the future. The influence of the Enlightenment in Germany was never as great as Mendelssohn believed. It was confined to the large urban centres, and particularly to Berlin, and even there it affected only the middle class and part of the nobility. The masses knew nothing of the writings of the *philosophes* or Lessing's faith in the education of the human race,[22] or Dohm's *Civic Improvement of the Jews*. Their minds were still moved by old prejudices; they lived in a world governed by passion rather than rationality, by myth and symbol rather than the printed word. Through the very process of their emancipation, the Jews were alienated from the common people, and their faith in *Bildung* was not sufficient to integrate them even with those classes that shared it with them. When Frederick and Mendelssohn died in 1786, the intellectual atmosphere was already changing in Germany; with the coming of the French Revolution and the advent of Napoleon, the Enlightenment shrivelled before the triumphant onslaught of romantic nationalism and Teutomania, which proved to be long-lived and, for Jewish emancipation, ominous. As George L. Mosse has pointed out in his Efroysom Lectures, as a result of all this the more the Jews came to resemble the Germans the more they were rejected by them.[23]

To leave it at that, however, would be to do an injustice to Mendelssohn. Surely the world of reason that he envisioned was a nobler goal than the world of

[21]Altmann, *Moses Mendelssohn, op. cit.*, pp. 30, 67–68, 71–72.
[22]For Lessing's appreciation of this point, see his play *Die Juden.*
[23]George L. Mosse, *German Jews Beyond Judaism*, Bloomington, Illinois 1985, chapter 1.

power that Frederick and his successors accepted. And – leaving that aside – who would argue that Mendelssohn's faith in the ability of his people to integrate themselves into German society was misplaced? Can it not be said that, despite the ultimate rejection and the horrors of the Holocaust, the rich contribution that German Jews made to their country's culture – to German art and literature and music and science – is powerful testimony to the contrary. In any case, the record is not complete; history did not end in 1945. Mendelssohn's faith in reason and humanity, his confidence in the inevitability of the full emancipation of his people, have not lost their power to inspire and, indeed, as Hans Bach has written, "still form the basis of the continued existence of the Jews, in the Jewish State of Israel as well as in the Dispersion".[24]

[24]Bach, *The German Jew*, *op. cit.*, p. 44.

The Genesis of the Ideology of Emancipation: 1806–1840

BY DAVID SORKIN

In German-Jewish history the period from 1781 to 1871 was known as the age of emancipation. The achievement of political and civic rights appeared to contemporaries as the pre-eminent issue during that ninety-year period. Emancipation not only served as the cardinal indicator of the Jews' changing position in Germany's multiple states, but also had a formative influence on the way in which they adjusted to modern German social and political life. The Jews' response to the protracted process of emancipation was therefore central to their experience in nineteenth-century Germany. Yet that response, especially in the first half of the nineteenth century, has not received the attention it deserves. Scholarship has subordinated it to other issues: either the internal issue of the redefinition of Judaism and the reform of Jewish ritual and practice, or the external issue of the role of the states and various political groupings in the unfolding of the emancipation process.[1]

In the following article I will therefore examine how a group of Jewish intellectuals (whom I shall call the ideologues of emancipation) responded to the challenge of emancipation by developing a distinct ideology. That ideology was an articulated set of ideas – encompassing politics, history, culture, society and, only lastly, religion – through which the ideologues defined the Jews' understanding of emancipation and offered a programme of action. The ideologues elaborated this during the Napoleonic era when emancipation appeared to be imminent. The development of the ideology can be dated so closely because at that point the ideologues created the institutions that were the prerequisite for it, a German-language public sphere. In this new sphere the ideologues radicalised the ideas of the preceding period, the *Haskalah*, transforming them into a coherent programme for the age of emancipation.

[1]For the subordination of the Jews' response to the issue of religious change see Max Wiener, *Jüdische Religion im Zeitalter der Emanzipation*, Berlin 1933; Jacob Katz, *Out of the Ghetto*, New York 1978; Michael A. Meyer, *The Origins of the Modern Jew. Jewish Identity and European Culture in Germany, 1749–1824*, Detroit 1967, pp. 115–143; Heinz Moshe Graupe, *The Rise of Modern Judaism. An Intellectual History of German Jewry, 1650–1942*, trs. John Robinson, Huntington, New York 1978; and Hans I. Bach, *The German Jew. A Synthesis of Judaism and Western Civilization*, New York 1984. One of the best treatments of the Jews' response to emancipation is Ismar Schorsch's *Jewish Responses to German Anti-Semitism, 1870–1914*, New York 1972, pp. 1–13. Yet Schorsch also understands the response primarily in terms of religion. H. D. Schmidt in his, 'The Terms of Emancipation 1781–1812', in *LBI Year Book I* (1956), pp. 28–47, devoted the bulk of his penetrating analysis to the German and not the Jewish side of the emancipation process. For important recent treatments of the emancipation process from the German side see the works of Reinhard Rürup, *Emanzipation und Antisemitismus. Studien zur "Judenfrage" der bürgerlichen Gesellschaft*, Göttingen 1975, as well as his articles in the *LBI Year Book*.

Emancipation, the achievement of civic and political equality,[2] belonged to the transformation of Germany from states and estate societies to a nation-state and a civil society. One distinguishing characteristic of that transformation was that the elites of the estate order – autocrat, aristocracy – presided over it, maintaining their political preponderance. They regarded that transformation with manifest ambivalence and barely concealed disdain. They therefore allowed the process to proceed only when internal developments or external pressure forced them to do so. The fact that Jewish emancipation remained incomplete for so long derived from the fitful progress of Germany's overall transformation. For the old political elites it was one among a number of undesirable consequences of Germany's transformation.[3]

The continuing preponderance of the old political elites gave rise to another conspicuous characteristic of the emancipation process: its state-centredness. When compelled, autocrat and aristocracy initiated social change through the mechanism of the bureaucracy. The bureaucracy, in turn, created the terms in which emancipation proceeded. The bourgeoisie of education or *Gebildeten* who staffed the bureaucracy conceived of emancipation as a *quid pro quo* of regeneration for rights. They did so because they thought the Jews were degenerate: either because they held Judaism to be an immoral religion, or because they viewed the Jews' occupations and social practices as fundamentally immoral.[4] While among the liberal *Gebildeten* who advocated emancipation there was a consensus about the exchange of rights for regeneration, there was a spectrum of opinion about the timing of that exchange. Some, like Christian Wilhelm Dohm, whose *On the Civic Amelioration of the Jews* (1781) inaugurated the discussion of emancipation in Germany,[5] thought rights should be given unconditionally, since only the ennobling condition of freedom would allow the Jews to be regenerated. Others thought

[2]For the origins of the term see Jacob Katz, 'The Term Jewish Emancipation. Its Origin and Historical Impact', in Alexander Altmann (ed.), *Studies in Nineteenth-Century Jewish Intellectual History*, Cambridge 1964, pp. 1–25; and Reinhard Rürup, 'Emanzipation. Anmerkungen zur Begriffsgeschichte', in *Emanzipation und Antisemitismus*, *op. cit.*, pp. 126–132.

[3]For this view of German history see Leonard Krieger, *The German Idea of Freedom*, Chicago 1957; Werner Conze (ed.), *Staat und Gesellschaft im deutschen Vormärz 1815–1848*, Stuttgart 1962; Hans Rosenberg, *Bureaucracy, Aristocracy and Autocracy*, Boston 1966; and Reinhart Koselleck, *Preussen zwischen Reform und Revolution*, Stuttgart 1967.

[4]For the prevalent image of the Jews see S. Ettinger, 'The Beginnings of the Change in the Attitude of European Society Towards the Jews', in *Scripta Hierosolymitana*, 7 (1961) pp. 193–219; Hans Liebeschütz, *Das Judentum im deutschen Geschichtsbild von Hegel bis Max Weber*, Tübingen 1967 (Schriftenreihe wissenschaftlicher Abhandlungen des Leo Baeck Instituts 17), pp. 1–24; Arthur Hertzberg, *The French Enlightenment and the Jews*, New York 1970; Felix Priebatsch, 'Die Judenpolitik des fürstlichen Absolutismus im 17. und 18. Jahrhundert', in *Festschrift Dietrich Schäfer*, Jena 1915 pp. 601–639; Jacob Katz, *From Prejudice to Destruction. Anti-Semitism 1700–1933*, Cambridge, Mass. 1980, pp. 51–106, 147–222.

[5]For Dohm's impact see Franz Reuss, *Christian Wilhelm Dohms Schrift, "Über die bürgerliche Verbesserung der Juden", und deren Einwirkung auf die gebildeten Stände Deutschlands*, Kaiserslautern 1891; and, more recently, Horst Möller, 'Aufklärung, Judentum und Staat: Ursprung und Wirkung von Dohms Schrift über die bürgerliche Verbesserung der Juden', in Walter Grab (ed.), *Deutsche Aufklärung und Judenemanzipation*, Beiheft 3 of *Jahrbuch des Instituts für deutsche Geschichte*, Tel-Aviv 1980, pp. 119–149.

that rights should be made conditional upon regeneration.[6] This formula of an exchange was the one that prevailed in the actions of the states. Emancipation became an incremental process under the supervision of the tutelary states. Rights were granted on a piecemeal basis, or granted during the revolutionary era and then slowly rescinded in the *Vormärz*, with the states monitoring the Jews' regeneration throughout.

One response by Jewish intellectuals to the transformation of German society, the German Enlightenment and the dim prospect of emancipation was the Jewish Enlightenment or *Haskalah* (*circa* 1760–1795). It represented a visionary programme for the reform of the Jews and Jewish society based on the renewal of an aesthetic sense through the study of Hebrew, German and the Bible; the acquisition of secular knowledge, especially the sciences and languages; and the restructuring of the Jews' economic life through a shift towards the productive occupations of artisanry and farming.[7] Yet in advocating this programme the *Maskilim*, no matter how radical, did not accept the equation of rights for prior regeneration. Moses Mendelssohn, a representative of the conservative *Haskalah*, argued on the basis of natural rights doctrine that the Jews should be emancipated unconditionally.[8] David Friedländer, a radical *Maskil*, accepted the premise that the Jews required regeneration, but held fast to the notion that rights had to precede it.[9] In these arguments the *Maskilim* retained elements of the political dualism characteristic of the medieval and early modern Jewish community, that is, they recognised the authority of the state but attempted to safeguard a sphere of autonomy. In the Napoleonic era the ideologues were to repudiate this legacy of the autonomous community.

THE IMPACT OF NAPOLEON

Emancipation first came to Germany's Jews in the baggage trains of Napoleon's armies. After Napoleon defeated the continental partners to the Third

[6]See Pastor Schwager's response to Dohm's tract in *Über die bürgerliche Verbesserung der Juden*, Stettin 1782, 2, pp. 89–111.

[7]On the *Haskalah* see Isaac Eisenstein-Barzilay, 'The Ideology of the Berlin Haskalah', in *Proceedings of the American Academy of Jewish Research*, 25 (1956), pp. 1–38; Jacob Katz, *Tradition and Crisis*, New York 1971, pp. 245–274. For the economic and social background see [Bernard] Dov Weinryb, 'Economic and Social Causes of the Haskala in Germany', (Hebrew) in *Knesset*, 3 (1938) pp. 416–436. For occupational restructuring see Mordechai Levin's *Arkhei Hevra ve-Kalkalah be-Ideologiya shel Tekufat ha-Haskala*, Jerusalem 1975. For the precursors of the *Haskalah* see Azriel Shohat, *Im Hilufei Tekufot*, Jerusalem 1960; Joseph Eschelbacher, 'Die Anfänge allgemeiner Bildung unter den deutschen Juden vor Mendelssohn', in *Festschrift Martin Philippsons*, Leipzig 1916, pp. 168–177; Isaac Eisenstein-Barzilay, 'The Background of the Berlin Haskalah', in Joseph L. Blau (ed.), *Essays on Jewish Life and Thought Presented in Honor of Salo Wittmayer Baron*, New York 1959, pp. 183–198, and Steven and Henry Schwarzschild, 'Two Lives in the Jewish Frühaufklärung. Raphael Levi Hannover and Moses Abraham Wolff', in *LBI Year Book XXIX* (1984), pp. 229–276.

[8]*Moses Mendelssohn's Gesammelte Schriften, Jubiläumsausgabe*, ed. by Fritz Bamberger *et al.* 19 vols., Stuttgart 1971, 8, pp. 99–204. (Henceforth *JubA*). See also Alexander Altmann, *Die trostvolle Aufklärung. Studien zur Metaphysik und politischen Theorie Moses Mendelssohn*, Stuttgart 1982, pp. 164–243.

[9]*Akten-Stücke, die Reform der Jüdischen Kolonieen in den Preussischen Staaten betreffend*, Berlin 1793, p. 28.

Coalition, Austria and Russia, at Austerlitz (December 1805), he dissolved the Holy Roman Empire, the political framework of Central Europe for over eight centuries, and reorganised the German states.[10] Napoleon's reorganisation of Germany coincided with his reconsideration of the status of the Jews in France. These concomitant events raised prospects that emancipation would now be imported into Germany. Napoleon thought that the equal rights revolutionary France had granted the Jews in 1790 and 1791 had been an act of "unwise generosity",[11] which required rectification. On 30th May 1806 he issued a decree convening an Assembly of Jewish Notables in Paris which was to answer a list of questions designed to ascertain whether the Jews deserved to be citizens of France.[12] Although Napoleon intended the Assembly to be a vehicle for introducing discriminatory legislation that would correct allegedly abusive Jewish practices, particularly usury, the Jews of Europe greeted the Assembly and its successor, the Sanhedrin, as the acts of a magnanimous liberator.[13]

Napoleon's commissioners posed twelve questions which forced the delegates to the Assembly to attempt a theoretical reconciliation of *Halakhah* with an authoritarian and centralised yet, as an inheritance of the Revolution, for the time radically secular French state. Not surprisingly, Mendelssohn's *Jerusalem* served the intellectual leaders of the Assembly, especially David Sintzheim (1745–1812), the Assembly's self-appointed arbiter on *Halakhah*, as a guide. In formulating answers to questions about Judaism's view of marriage (bigamy; divorce; intermarriage), relations to non-Jews (do Jews consider Frenchmen their brethren), the office of Rabbi (who appoints him, what are his powers), and economic practices (can Jews practise all professions; is usury permitted equally among Jews and non-Jews), the Assembly accepted Mendelssohn's fundamental premise that Judaism does not clash with the secular State as well as the distinctions he had drawn between political and ceremonial laws.[14] Sintzheim and the Assembly utilised this distinction in order to acknowledge the unquestioned validity of the State's civil law. They asserted that Judaism made no claims to civil or political authority, requiring instead only the right to free religious observance.

The Assembly thus renounced all claims to corporate status and power. It

[10]He elevated Bavaria and Württemberg to the status of kingdoms, turned Baden and Hesse-Darmstadt into grand duchies, and gathered the states along the east bank of the Rhine into a new client "Confederation of the Rhine". This reorganisation took place between the signing of the Peace of Pressburg in December 1805 and the actual signing and ratification of the Treaty of the Confederation by the South German states in late July of 1806. Throughout those seven months news of the impending changes circulated. See Herbert A. L. Fisher, *Studies in Napoleonic Statesmanship, Germany*, Oxford 1903, pp. 94–121.

[11]This was the formulation of one of his aides, Beugnot. See Simon Schwarzfuchs, *Napoleon, the Jews and the Sanhedrin*, London 1979, p. 47. For the relations between French and German Jewry see Jonathan I. Helfand, 'The Symbiotic Relationship between French and German Jewry in the Age of Emancipation', in *LBI Year Book XXIX* (1984), pp. 331–350.

[12]The decree is reprinted in F. D. Kirwan (trans.), *Transactions of the Paris Sanhedrin*, London 1807, pp. 105–107.

[13]See the documents collected in Barukh Mevorakh, *Napoleon u-Tekufato*, Jerusalem 1968, pp. 133–169.

[14]See the references to Mendelssohn in *Transactions of the Paris Sanhedrin*, pp. 149, 159.

did this by redefining the application of the rabbinic dictum, "the law of the land is the law". That dictum had served as the political theory of the autonomous Jewish community of medieval and early modern Europe.[15] Whereas in the autonomous community the dictum had been applied only to profane matters of public law e.g. the kind and rate of taxes the Emperor could legitimately impose, but never to matters of religious life, the Assembly applied the dictum to matters of religious ritual. In answer to a question about Jewish marriage practices, for example, the Assembly asserted: "In the eyes of every Israelite, without exception, submission to the prince is the first of duties. It is a principle generally acknowledged among them, that, in everything relating to civil or political interests, the law of the State is the supreme law."[16] In so defining the dictum the Assembly also abjured the element of resistance that had previously been integral to it. In the autonomous community the dictum served as "the basic legal norm for the recognition of what is just in laws that are not derived from Hebrew jurisprudence".[17] Were a law deemed unjust according to *halakhic* standards, the Jews could refuse to comply with it. The Assembly thus transformed a doctrine of both recognition and resistance into a doctrine of recognition alone. Utilising Mendelssohn's thought, then, the predominantly French Assembly created a precedent which was to encourage German-Jewish ideologues in their own efforts to discard all remnants of the political dualism that had been characteristic of the autonomous community.[18]

THE PUBLIC SPHERE

The establishment of the Confederation of the Rhine and the convocation of the Assembly of Notables convinced the heirs of the *Haskalah* that equal rights would now reach Germany's Jews under Napoleonic auspices. The extension of French hegemony eastward created a mood of anticipation among the Jewish ideologues. They sensed that emancipation was imminent. In this frame of mind they undertook an entirely new venture. They established the German-

[15]On the dictum see Shmuel Shilo, *Dina de-Malkhuta Dina*, Jerusalem 1975; Gil Graff, *Separation of Church and State in Thought and Practice. Application and Extension of 'Dina de-Malkhuta Dina' in Jewish Law, 1750–1848*, unpublished Ph.d. Thesis, University of California, Los Angeles 1982; and Max Wiener, *Jüdische Religion im Zeitalter der Emanzipation*, Berlin 1933, pp. 30–32. For its function as a political theory see Haim Hillel Ben-Sasson, *Toldot Yisrael bi-Mei ha-Beinayim*, vol. 2 of *Toldot Am Yisrael*, ed. by *idem*. Tel-Aviv 1969, pp. 111f.

[16]*Transactions of the Paris Sanhedrin*, p. 152. For Sintzheim and the Assembly see Charles Touati, 'Le Grand Sanhedrin de 1807 et le droit rabbinique', in Bernhard Blumenkranz and Albert Soboul (eds.), *Le Grand Sanhédrin de Napoléon*, Toulouse 1979, pp. 27–49, esp. pp. 33–39; for the expansive redefinition of the dictum "the law of the land is the law" see Graff, *Separation of Church and State*, *op. cit.*, pp. 98–128.

[17]Shilo, *Dina de-Malkhuta Dina, op. cit.*, p. 433. For a detailed study of the case of Regensburg, for example, where the Jews invoked the dictum in an effort to defend themselves against subjection to municipal taxes in the thirteenth century see Berthold Altmann, 'Studies in Medieval German Jewish History', in *Proceedings of the American Academy of Jewish Research*, 10 (1940) pp. 5–98, esp. pp. 11–12.

[18]The *Sulamith* did not report on the Assembly and the Sanhedrin until they had adjourned. The report was understandably enthusiastic. See *Sulamith*, I, 2 (1807) pp. 1–27.

language media of the journal (*Sulamith*, July 1806), and the sermon. Dessau was the home of both the *Sulamith* and the first sermons, and their creators proved prescient. Anhalt-Dessau joined the Confederation of the Rhine on 18th April 1807.[19] It was in these organs that the ideology of emancipation was to be coherently formulated and extensively disseminated. The journal and the sermon together represented the beginnings of a new German-language public sphere. The emergence of the ideology not only entailed a shift from Hebrew to German, but also new institutional forms of expression. As a result, the new public sphere differed radically from the autonomous community's forms of expression.

The cultural corollary of the autonomous community's dualist political structure was that in the early modern period a clear distinction existed between literature intended for fellow Jews and apologetic literature addressed to Christians. The autonomous community had conducted its civil and religious life in various Hebrew and Yiddish genres that had been accessible, with few exceptions, exclusively to Jews. German or Latin had served as the medium of apologetic literature and contact with Gentile political authority. This exclusivity of the autonomous community's internal literary forms was slow to disappear.

The *Haskalah* not only accepted this exclusivity, but in fact reinforced it by attempting to transform Hebrew into a serviceable literary medium. Hence Mendelssohn, for example, maintained the distinction between different kinds of literature in the structure of his works. He used German for his general philosophical works and for those works on Judaism which had a decidedly apologetic purpose.[20] He wrote in Hebrew when he intended to educate his fellow Jews. *Hame'asef*, the *Haskalah*'s journal, while using the form of an *Aufklärung* journal, was also accessible only to Hebrew readers. A few radical authors did write books on Judaism in German which were intended for Jews in the last decades of the eighteenth century, but these were isolated individuals.[21] It was only with the appearance of the *Sulamith* and the German-language sermon that there were distinct organs in which the distinction between internal and apologetic no longer obtained. The journal and the sermon were structurally beyond the autonomous community's dualism in that they were as accessible to non-Jews as to Jews: not only was their language German, but their forms were borrowed from the *Aufklärung*.

The *Sulamith* was a direct heir to *Hame'asef*. It took over its format and also proposed a similar list of suitable topics: moral and religious subjects; translations from the Bible and other Jewish sources; reports on customs and lives of various nations and the diverse Jewish sects; essays on technical

[19]Huber, *Deutsche Verfassungsgeschichte*, 1, p. 76.

[20]For example, his *Ritualgesetze der Juden*, Berlin 1778, designed to familiarise German courts with Jewish law, and his *Jerusalem*. In the 1830s Samson Raphael Hirsch was to regret the fact that Mendelssohn undertook his full-scale elaboration of Judaism, *Jerusalem*, as an apologetic rather than an internal work. See his, *Igrot Tsafon. Neunzehn Briefe über Judenthum*, Altona 1836, p. 93.

[21]See for example Lazarus ben David (1762–1832), *Etwas zur Charakteristik der Juden*, Leipzig 1793; and Saul Ascher (1767–1822), *Leviathan, oder über Religion in Rücksicht des Judenthums*, Berlin 1792.

subjects, especially commerce.[22] Both directly imitated the journals of the *Aufklärung*. Yet the *Sulamith* had a very different notion of its intended audience. The editors believed that the benevolence and goodwill of Christians was as integral to emancipation as the Jews' own actions.[23] The *Sulamith* consequently aimed to create a new public, consisting of both Jews and non-Jews, to support the emancipation process. David Fränkel (1779–1865), one of the journal's founders and co-editors, made this intention clear in his introductory article. Fränkel thought *Hame'asef* had failed precisely because of the exclusivity of its language. In the 1780s and 1790s the "clear-sighted savants" among the Jews could read German; the religious traditionalists who knew the language refused to read the journal; and the majority of Jews did not know sufficient Hebrew. The *Sulamith* aimed to capture the eager Jewish readers who, fluent in the "German mother tongue", desired "systematic education" (*Bildung*).[24] At the same time Fränkel, unlike the *Hame'asef*, hoped to enlist the public of "educated men (*gebildete Menschen*)" for the cause of emancipation and regeneration.[25] He proclaimed the *Sulamith* to be a forum "for every friend of mankind, be he of whatever religion he may",[26] and in fact the journal had a number of Christian contributors, *Gebildete*, mainly pastors and teachers, with whom Fränkel was acquainted. The *Sulamith* radicalised *Hame'asef*'s form, then, by shifting to German and breaking down the distinction between apology for non-Jews and internal works for Jews.

The German-language sermon also broke down that distinction, though in a far more extreme fashion than in the journal, since the form of the sermon itself represented a radical departure. The sermon replaced the Hebrew *derasha*. The *derasha* was based on a difficult legal problem or an opaque biblical passage which the rabbi or itinerant preacher illuminated by analysing a diverse and often bewildering array of sources. It was meant to impress and delight through the range of its topics and the ingenuity used to solve the stated problem which, serving as a point of departure, often disappeared in the course of the *derasha* only to make a startling reappearance at the end. The *derasha* presupposed an audience that knew the Hebrew and Aramaic sources and was familiar with the exegetical method, often casuistic, used to expound them. In its very form, then, the *derasha* belonged to the tradition of Hebrew *musar* literature, assuming the socio-cultural situation of civil and religious autonomy: an exclusivist community of common knowledge and practice which gathered to have its values reconfirmed either by the rabbi's display of an awesome mastery of the tradition, or the preacher's exhortations and exegesis.[27]

[22]For *Hame'asef*'s suggested topics see *Nahal Besor*, Königsberg 1784, pp. 1–3; the *Sulamith* listed topics on the inside front and back covers. For the relationship between the two journals see Siegfried Stein, 'Die Zeitschrift "Sulamith" ', in *Zeitschrift für die Geschichte der Juden in Deutschland*, 7 (1937), pp. 197–198.

[23]*Sulamith*, I, 1, (1806), pp. 23–25.

[24]*Ibid.*, p. 30.

[25]*Ibid.*, p. 28.

[26]*Ibid.*, p. 28.

[27]Katz, *Tradition and Crisis*, *op. cit.*, pp. 172–174; Dan, *Sifrut ha-Musar veha-Drush*, Jerusalem 1975, pp. 31–45. For the inherited proem form still in use in the period see J. Heinemann, 'The Proem in the

The structure of the edification sermon, in contrast to the *derasha*, was rigorously analytical: it developed a single theme in a clearly demarcated three or four part structure. Benedictions both preceded and followed the sermon. The sermon attempted to be a model of decorum and reason, even when emotionally evocative. Its form was a re-working of a Protestant model, the "edification sermon" (*Erbauungspredigt*), that the *Aufklärung* had largely secularised. The ideologues of emancipation reshaped the edification sermon to fit their own needs by converting its highly secularised theological concept of edification into a religio-political category. *Erbauung* was a New Testament word meaning the "building up" of man with and through God. For the German Pietists of the late seventeenth and early eighteenth century this notion had a thoroughly Christian acceptation with an emotional cast: the sermon intended to create a community joined through its communion with God. Beginning in the 1760s, however, theologians sympathetic to the *Aufklärung* gradually secularised this form by emptying it of its Christian content. Johann Lorentz von Mosheim (1694–1755) reinterpreted it along rational lines: he thought the purpose of the sermon was to create a state of grace through knowledge. Subsequent clergymen like Johann Spalding (1714–1804) and Wilhelm Abraham Teller (1734–1804) defined *Erbauung* as the building up of a moral man without reference to Christian theological notions. The purpose of sermons was moralising and exhortation to improvement. The sermon for them was largely a pedagogical instrument aimed at individual perfection, and they adopted the concepts and language of the pedagogical revolution then underway in Germany.[28]

The ideologues could adopt the edification sermon without compunction about its Christian provenance: as a result of its gradual secularisation, the edification sermon seemed to belong as much to the general repository of German, and specifically *Aufklärung* culture, as to the Church.[29] It appeared to be part of the new public sphere (*Öffentlichkeit*) that the *Gebildeten* had created in the last decades of the eighteenth century. That public sphere had been a *sine qua non* for their emergence as a distinct social group.[30] Pastors had played a conspicuous role in shaping that public sphere by serving as writers of fiction and journalists. Yet they had also refashioned their own particular medium of the sermon into another element of it: the edification sermon propagated *Aufklärung* notions of individual perfection and eudæmonism.[31] In taking over

Aggadic Midrashim. A Form-Critical Study', in *Scripta Hierosolymitana*, 22, Jerusalem 1971, pp. 100–122.

[28]Alexander Altmann, 'The New Style of Preaching in Nineteenth-Century German Jewry', in *Studies in Nineteenth-Century Jewish Intellectual History*, *op. cit.*, pp. 87–97.

[29]*Ibid.*, pp. 75–77, 87–91; also Michael Meyer, 'Christian Influence on Early German Reform Judaism', in Charles Berlin (ed.), *Studies in Jewish Bibliography, History and Literature in Honor of I. Edward Kiev*, New York 1971, pp. 295–296.

[30]On the emergence of the public sphere see Jürgen Habermas, *Strukturwandel der Öffentlichkeit*, Darmstadt, 1962; Christa Bürger, Peter Bürger and Jochen Schulte-Sasse (eds.), *Aufklärung und literarische Öffentlichkeit*, Frankfurt a. Main 1980; and Ursula A. J. Becher, *Politische Gesellschaft. Studien zur Genese bürgerlicher Öffentlichkeit in Deutschland*, Göttingen 1978.

[31]On the role of pastors in the late *Aufklärung* see Alexandra Schlingensiepen-Pogge, *Das Sozialethos der lutherischen Aufklärungstheologie am Vorabend der Industriellen Revolution*, vol. 39, Göttinger Bausteine

this form, the ideologues inherited its emphasis on improvement yet gave it new meaning by turning it into an instrument of emancipation.

The edification sermon's intended audience differed as much from the *derasha*'s as its form. In the first volume of published sermons Joseph Wolf (1762–1826), one of the founders and co-editors of the *Sulamith*, stated that the blind adherents of the old and the undiscriminating admirers of the new would oppose his efforts.[32] The sermon was embroiled in a war on two fronts, then, against the traditionalists at one extreme and the secularists at the other.[33] It addressed a new sort of Jew, one whose Judaism could be expressed only through German forms.[34] According to David Fränkel, the sermon alone was able to address the middle classes.[35] By the 1830s, some ideologues were declaring it to be the most useful of the innovations introduced into the Jewish community in the nineteenth century.[36]

The institutions of the journal and the sermon represented a deliberate attempt to create a counterpart to the *Öffentlichkeit* of the German middle classes. The German-Jewish version took over from its model both the forms in which it reached its audience and the functions it attempted to fulfil for that projected audience. In its early stages (1720–1770) the German public sphere had supplied its audience with a form of secular identity, represented by the ideal of *Tugend*, through the discussion of religious, aesthetic and cultural issues.[37] In the 1770s the public sphere began to take a political turn.[38] This political turn resulted from a new stage of Germany's transformation: a further loosening of the estate structure with the emergence of a self-conscious, educated, bourgeoisie.[39] In this same decade that group began to adopt the ideal of *Bildung*, and thus their name, *Gebildete*. *Bildung* represented an ideal of integral self-development by which the whole man would fully develop his inherent form by transforming all of his faculties, mind and body, into a harmonious unity. This notion of form was borrowed from the recently redefined field of aesthetics in which a work of art was seen as an organic whole. The ideal of *Bildung* thus represented a doctrine of aesthetic individualism as opposed to the early *Aufklärung*'s doctrine of ethical

---

zur Geschichtswissenschaft, Göttingen 1967; and Hans Rosenberg, 'Theologischer Rationalismus und Vormärzlicher Vulgärliberalismus', in *idem.*, *Politische Denkströmungen im deutschen Vormärz*, Göttingen 1972, pp. 18–50.

[32]*Sechs Deutsche Reden*, Dessau 1812–1813, I, p. 2.

[33]Alexander Altmann, 'Zur Frühgeschichte der jüdischen Predigt in Deutschland. Leopold Zunz als Prediger', in *LBI Year Book VI* (1961), p. 15.

[34]Phöbus Philippson, *Biographische Skizzen*, 3 vols., Leipzig 1866, 3, pp. 119f.

[35]*Sulamith*, IV, 2 (1815), p. 248.

[36]See Ludwig Philippson in *Israelitisches Predigt- und Schul-Magazin*, 1 (1834) p. 288.

[37]For the early Enlightenment and its "cultural public" see Wolfgang Martens, *Die Botschaft der Tugend. Die Aufklärung im Spiegel der deutschen moralischen Wochenschriften*, Stuttgart 1971; Hans Wolff, *Die Weltanschauung der deutschen Aufklärung in geschichtlicher Entwicklung*, Berne 1949; and Eduard Winter, *Frühaufklärung*, Berlin 1966, pp. 47–106.

[38]On the politicisation of the public sphere see Falko Schneider, *Studien zur Politisierung der deutschen Spätaufklärung am Beispiel A. G. F. Rebman*, Wiesbaden 1978; and Jürgen Schlumbohm, *Freiheit. Die Anfänge der bürgerlichen Emanzipationsbewegung in Deutschland im Spiegel ihres Leitwortes, 1760–1800*, Düsseldorf 1975.

[39]Hans Gerth, *Bürgerliche Intelligenz um 1800*, 2nd edn., Göttingen 1976; and Ursula Becher, *Politische Gesellschaft*, *op. cit.*, pp. 12–15, 206–218.

individualism.[40] The increasingly self-conscious *Gebildete*, convinced of the powers of their legitimating ideal, now attempted to apply its rational criteria to politics, as they had previously applied them to literature, aesthetics and religion. In the burgeoning public sphere of journals, books and newspapers they thus took up the task of rationalising political authority.[41]

The German-Jewish public sphere attempted to accomplish all at once what the German public sphere had accomplished in successive historical stages: providing its audience with a form of identity as well as a new form of authority to legitimate it. But whereas in the majority culture the two functions of identity and authority had appeared in the course of the eighteenth century, in the Jews' media they appeared immediately. This accelerated development resulted from the politicisation of the Napoleonic era. It goes without saying that the journal and the sermon were not neutral instruments of expression, then. Rather were they integral to the radicalising of ideas from which the ideology emerged, and which brought the concept of *Bildung* to the fore.

The impact of the Napoleonic era can be seen in the relationship of the new media to the "Westphalian Consistory", the product of the French occupation. After his defeat of Prussia, Napoleon created a Kingdom of Westphalia in 1807 from territories confiscated from Prussia, Braunschweig and Hesse-Cassel, placing his brother Jerome on the throne. After emancipating the Jews of his newly-established Kingdom (15th November 1807), Jerome Bonaparte created a central organisation charged with reshaping and administering the Jews' lives, a Consistory, following Napoleon's example in France.[42] For after the successful conclusion of the Assembly of Notables and the "Grand Sanhedrin", which he had convened to give religious sanction to the Assembly's decisions, Napoleon created the Consistory as an institutional framework to sustain a now confessionalised Judaism. Modelled after the Gallican Church, the Consistory, among other things, made Judaism a rabbi-centred religion and required a sermon in the vernacular at regular intervals.[43] Jerome appointed Israel Jacobson, the Court Jew of Braunschweig and a tireless campaigner for Jewish rights, to head the Consistory. Jacobson co-opted David Fränkel, co-editor of the *Sulamith*, for the governing board. Fränkel, in turn, exerted a considerable radicalising influence over Jacobson, especially in regard to educational reform.[44]

[40]On the concept of *Bildung* see Rudolf Vierhaus, 'Bildung', in *Geschichtliche Grundbegriffe*, ed. by Otto Brunner, 4 vols., Stuttgart 1972, 1, pp. 508–551; Hans Weill, *Die Entstehung des deutschen Bildungsprinzips*, Bonn 1930; W. H. Bruford, *The German Tradition of Self-Cultivation*, Cambridge 1973. On the institutional history of the concept, especially in education, see Fritz Ringer, *The Decline of the German Mandarins*, Cambridge, Mass. 1969, pp. 14–61; and Charles McClelland, *State, Society and University in Germany*, Cambridge 1980.

[41]Habermas, *Strukturwandel der Öffentlichkeit*, *op. cit.*, pp. 69–75, 92–94; Schober, *Die deutsche Spätaufklärung*, Berne 1975, pp. 241–262; Becher, *Politische Gesellschaft*, *op. cit.*, *passim*.

[42]Jacob Rader Marcus, *Israel Jacobson. The Founder of the Reform Movement in Judaism*, Cincinnati 1972; Schwarzfuchs, *Napoleon, the Jews and the Sanhedrin*, *op. cit.*, pp. 147–156; Meyer, *Origins of the Modern Jew*, *op. cit.*, pp. 132–135.

[43]For Napoleon's consistory see the legislation contained in the *Transactions of the Paris Sanhedrin*, pp. 285–292. For a sustained study see Phyllis Cohen Albert, *The Modernization of French Jewry: Consistory and Community in the Nineteenth Century*, Hanover 1977.

[44]Marcus, *Israel Jacobson*, *op. cit.*, p. 143, note 33.

Jacobson instituted the first major reforms in Jewish ritual observance in the new Temple he had built at Cassel: a largely German liturgy, a choir, an organ and a German-language sermon. The sermon in particular was a legislated requirement.[45]

The Westphalian Consistory, however shortlived – it outlasted Jerome's Kingdom, which fell in December 1813, by a few months – enlisted the German-language media for a prominent role. During its heady five years the Consistory made the *Sulamith* its "veritable organ".[46] Fränkel interrupted the journal's normal format to provide extensive coverage of the Consistory's founding.[47] The journal subsequently carried copious news of the Consistory, publishing its legislation and its actual products, primarily sermons. The distribution of the first published sermons, Joseph Wolf's *Sechs Deutsche Reden*, issued in 1812–1813, also attests to this role. Wolf's sermons were pre-subscribed by patrons throughout the German states, with the exception of Bavaria. Orders came from the major cities of Berlin, Frankfurt and Hamburg; from as far north as Lübeck, as far south as Stuttgart, as far east as Lissa. Yet of 127 subscribers 76% were concentrated in the countries composing the *Rheinbund*, where the Consistory's legal requirement of sermons was strongly felt: the Kingdom of Westphalia itself (Cassel, Braunschweig, Magdeburg, Halberstadt, Hannover) accounted for 18%, while Saxony and Thuringia (Dessau, Dresden, Leipzig, Sondershausen, Weimar), where Wolf's reputation was probably best established, accounted for 58%.[48]

THE IDEOLOGY

To analyse the ideology which found expression in the German-language public sphere we will examine some of the earliest seminal formulations in the *Sulamith* along with later elaborations, particularly from sermons. We can proceed in this manner because the ideology underwent little change. The ideas of 1806–1808 were endlessly recapitulated without major revision down to the early 1840s. What the expectation of imminent emancipation begot, incomplete emancipation sustained. Three closely related ideas remained central to the ideology. First, the acceptance of the *quid pro quo* of regeneration for rights through the transformation of politics into pedagogy. Second, unquestioning faith in the tutelary State, which by definition required regeneration. Third, the lachrymose view of Jewish history, in which culture was the agent of historical change. The ideal of *Bildung* unified these ideas as well as the ideology's programme of regeneration – occupational restructuring, religious reform, and moral rehabilitation – by giving them internal coherence.

[45]*Ibid.*, p. 69.
[46]Simon Dubnow, *History of the Jews*, trs. by M. Spiegel, 4 vols., South Brunswick 1967–1971, 4, pp. 652–653. On Jacobson's use of the journal also Marcus, *Israel Jacobson, op. cit.*, pp. 90, 104.
[47]*Sulamith*, II, 1 (1808), p. 1.
[48]See the 'Verzeichnis der resp. Herren Subscribenten', *Sechs Deutsche Reden, op. cit.*, pp. iii–vi.

The expectation of imminent emancipation led the ideologues of emancipation to abandon whatever remained of the autonomous community's dualist political doctrine. They set the issue of regeneration in direct relationship to the problem of rights by transforming political ideas into pedagogical ones. They reduced Mendelssohn's argument from natural rights into a claim for a form of minimal autonomy that would allow the Jews to regenerate themselves.

In his introductory essay to the *Sulamith*, for example, Joseph Wolf reconstrued "natural rights" precisely as the inalienable right of every people to perfect itself according to its native traditions. While insisting on the central *Aufklärung* tenet of perfectibility, he refused to relinquish the particularity of different groups, the Jews among them. "Every people has its own characteristics and needs, its own concepts and abilities . . . Every people is therefore capable of formation (*Bildung*), the improvement of morals."[49] The worst injustice is therefore to impose a foreign culture in the name of perfection. That sort of imposition could only "destroy, or at the least suppress and deform", the group. Wolf accordingly declared the *Sulamith*'s purpose to be, "the development of the Jews' intensive educational ability".[50]

Wolf thus translated the political doctrine of natural rights into the pedagogical doctrine that the Jews have the right to improve. This transformation of politics into pedagogy provided the basis for the idea that emancipation rested on a *quid pro quo*. Whereas Wolf gave it explicit articulation when emancipation impended, later ideologues assumed it to be given. They limited themselves instead to tirelessly enjoining improvement, without having to specify what the reward would be. "Improvement", "perfection" and "ennoblement" thus became their code words for the regeneration they thought emancipation demanded. While these notions belonged to the lexicon of the "edification sermon", reflecting its *Aufklärung* origins, for the Jewish preachers they took on new meaning because of the "contract" of emancipation.

A few illustrations will suffice. We can begin with Wolf's own sermons. He incessantly calls for improvement and spiritual betterment. Yet he, of course, goes beyond mere injunctions. He defines life itself as a process of improvement; man's very vocation is an unflagging self-amelioration:

> "Living means being active, working usefully, creating good things, developing the spirit, guiding one's sentiments, improving oneself and everything around one. Any other life is empty for man, is merely animalistic, without consciousness or reflection, without spirit."[51]

While Wolf genuinely believed in these *Aufklärung* notions, there can also be no doubt that he understood that such improvement led to emancipation. Eduard Kley (1789–1867), who first preached in Berlin and later became one of two preachers at the new Temple in Hamburg, is another case in point. In the preface to his revised liturgy (1817) he wrote that the "divine gift of civic freedom" carried with it the new "duty of civic life". How better to demonstrate "worthiness (*Würdigkeit*)" – a code word to which we shall return – than to

[49] *Sulamith*, I, 1 (1806), pp. 1–2.
[50] *Ibid.*, p. 9.
[51] *Sechs Deutsche Reden*, 1, p. 117.

improve "our spiritual, our higher life?" Kley not only expressed his understanding of emancipation as a *quid pro quo*, but also conjured up the spectre of failure: "Woe betide us", Kley admonished, when we are scrutinised by the "sublime Monarch" and have not fully exploited our new opportunities.[52] In an 1823 sermon commemorating the destruction of the Jerusalem Temple Kley argued that the Jews' state had been destroyed because it lacked "justice, truth and peace". He declared those qualities to be the mainstays of all communities, and found the Jews of the present sorely lacking. The result is that, "we stand in opposition to the larger European, the smaller German community, that we remain the wreckage of that destruction 'of the Temple' . . . and can find no place in the structure of the state to which we belong". Kley's prescription for this diagnosis is self-improvement. A concerted effort must be made to overcome the barrier of "centuries of development" (*Bildung*) that separates Jew from Gentile.[53]

The same ideas expressed in the same language appear constantly in the 1820s and 1830s as well. Salomon Herxheimer (born 1801), for example, in a Passover sermon of 1838 in Anhalt-Bernburg, where emancipation remained typically incomplete, stressed the reciprocal dependence of freedom and improvement. A major impediment to freedom, is that too many Jews, "do not feel sufficiently acutely and inwardly the wretchedness of their civic position". They must instead exert themselves to attain the necessary improvement:

> "O if every one of us were to work in this spirit towards his own and his co-religionists' constant purification; if we were to free ourselves in this way from all sins and trespasses and to increase in all virtues; if we resolutely progress in useful industry and professional activities which were once at home in Israel; if we were to cease dividing ourselves through disunity, since we are already so fragmented and dispersed; if we were all to distinguish ourselves through honesty, since we are all often traduced because of one dishonest man; if we were ever more to acquire a modesty befitting the weak, ever more to awaken among us a spirit of sacrifice for the community, a thorough school education, a purer religious instruction, an enlightened pious religiosity . . ."[54]

The programme Herxheimer expounded is the ideology in miniature: individual and collective improvement through religious reform, occupational restructuring, and an improvement in manners and morals. The call for these reforms was made incessantly in the first four decades of the century.

David Fränkel had outlined this same programme of regeneration in the pages of the *Sulamith* in 1807. The Jews had to shift away from trade to the productive occupations of agriculture and artisanry. "Learn to value more highly the sciences and arts according to the example of numerous educated Jews (*gebildete Juden*) . . . Pursue agriculture with industry and effort; the cultivation of your own fields is a first-rate occupation . . . Remove your children, dear fellow believers, from miserable petty trade."[55] Such an occupational restructuring required a major overhaul of the educational system.

[52]E. Kley and C. S. Günsburg (eds.), *Die deutsche Synagoge oder Ordnung des Gottesdienstes für die Sabbath-und Festtage*, Berlin 1817, pp. vii–viii.
[53]*Die Feste des Herrn: israelitische Predigten für alle Festtage des Jahres*, Berlin 1824, pp. 344–357.
[54]*Sabbath-, Fest- und Gelegenheits-Predigten*, Bernburg 1838, pp. 197–213.
[55]*Sulamith*, I, 6 (1807), pp. 377–378.

The old text-based training of the *cheder* had to give way to a religious education that would teach morality and human dignity: "Try yourselves, or at least through judicious and good teachers, to excite the spirit of humanity in them so that they will feel their dignity as men even more and love morality above all."[56] Secular subjects and trades would also have to be taught. Beyond re-education, the Jews also had to acquire the civility – manners and morals – necessary to associate with their Christian neighbours:

> "The frightful oppression under which we groaned until now occasioned, to be sure, that many of our religious relatives became degenerate and therefore in their morals (*Sitten*) and total appearance conspicuously contrasted with the educated class of the Jewish confession (*gebildete Klasse jüdischer Konfession*) and especially their Christian brothers . . ."[57]

Finally, Judaism had to be turned into a decorous and morally pure religion:

> "As far as religious worship is concerned: there exists only one true Jewish religion. One should therefore take pains to fulfil all of that which best approaches this honourable original religion (*Urreligion*) and against that to dispense with all of that which, sanctioned by the former oppressive situation of the Jews, leads away from the true spirit of it."[58]

Israel Jacobson, President of the Westphalian Consistory, neatly captured the intent of this programme: "The purpose of all our institutions is to make those Israelites who are not yet what they ought to be, worthy respecters of their holy religion, true subjects of the government, and moral men."[59] With this programme of regeneration Fränkel had defined natural rights as the right to regeneration.

Because the ideology rested on a contract, showing proof of reciprocity became a chief preoccupation. "Show that you are worthy (*würdig*) of the name citizen and subject", Fränkel admonished his readers.[60] "Worthiness" became the ideology's code word designating the Jews' efforts to make themselves equal to their achieved or anticipated equality. It pointed to that regeneration which would infuse them with the very values which they held to be responsible for their attainment of rights.[61]

"Worthiness" also encompassed the values the *Aufklärung* propagated as appropriate to its ideal of the moral man, especially industry, family and the purposeful use of time. In 1822 Eduard Kley declared that "in work lies benediction".[62] In other sermons he asserted that work is a means to serve God, and that because God dictates that every man have a calling (*Beruf*), it is

[56]*Ibid.*, p. 378.
[57]*Ibid.*, p. 377.
[58]*Ibid.*, p. 378.
[59]Israel Jacobson in *Sulamith*, II, 2 (1809), p. 300. I have used Marcus's translation of the passage. See his, *Israel Jacobson*, p. 70.
[60]*Sulamith*, I, 6 (1807), p. 377.
[61]For two representative examples see H. J. Damier, 'Patriotische Gedanken und Wünsche', *ibid.*, II, 6, (1809), p. 414: "We must not surrender to an indolent joy, but must instead seriously strive to make ourselves worthy (*würdig*) of all forms of the government's benevolence." Levy Rubens, *ibid.*, II, 1, (1807), p. 107: "Then also he [Gregoire], our defender, our advocate before Kings, makes us realise through his hints, that we too must strive, that we too must make use of our full capabilities, to show that we are worthy (*würdig*) of all the advantages which his affable advocacy promises us, that we must work on ourselves . . ."
[62]The German reads: "in der Arbeit liegt der Segen". See *Die Feste des Herrn*, p. 248.

imperative that the individual choose his work judiciously.[63] Herxheimer asserted in the late 1830s that a well-chosen vocation is a "duty" and an "inner calling" (*innerer Beruf*). He also gave the concept of sanctification of God's name (*kiddush ha-shem*) new meaning. Rather than designating the choice of martyrdom over forcible conversion, as it had in the Middle Ages, it now meant choosing an occupation that brought honour to one's fellow Jews and to Judaism.[64]

The family became an independent value for the ideologues, and served as the topic of sermons, because it was seen as fundamental to the promotion of morality. Joseph Maier (Stuttgart 1840) declared that "family sense is what makes the holy day a holy day".[65] Clearly this understanding diverged from the notion that holy days were observed because God commanded it. The same J. Maier asserted that the family must be the location for education: in the long winter evenings they should pursue those occupations that contribute to their "spiritual development and education".[66] As Maier's sermon shows, time for the ideologues was a precious commodity to be exploited. But for them it is not that "time is money"; for them time is *Bildung*. Joseph Wolf included the irresponsible use of time in a catalogue of sins: "How gladly would I have back this precious time for development (*kostbare Zeit der Bildung*), in order to make scrupulous use of it, in order to apply it carefully."[67] S. L. Liepmannsohn (Rietberg 1829) asserted that time must be regarded "as a school in which I develop myself for my earthly and my eternal vocation and bliss".[68] J. Wolfsohn expressed this same concept of time: "Just as a happy consciousness follows a good deed, so satisfaction follows work, and only in the purposeful use of our time, in the free use of our powers, lies our true happiness."[69]

These values belonged to and reinforced the ideology's programme of regenerating the Jews: the sanctification of work went along with occupational restructuring, the family and the use of time with *Bildung*. And these were minority appropriations and re-workings of ideas found in the majority society: a heavy emphasis on work and moral development belonged to the "sacralisation of life" that characterised the Lutheran sermons of the immediately preceding period (1780–1810).[70]

The translation of natural rights into the right to regeneration depended upon the ideologue's idealisation of the tutelary State. The ideologues lacked a developed political understanding of the far-reaching transformation of State and society which made emancipation possible. The ideologues were a

[63]Kley (ed.), *Sammlung der neuesten Predigten*, 2, pp. 70–71; and E. Kley and G. Salomon (eds.), *Sammlung der neuesten Predigten*, Hamburg 1827, 3, p. 160.
[64]*Sabbath-, Fest- und Gelegenheits-Predigten*, pp. 231, 236.
[65]J. Maier, J. N. Mannheimer, G. Salomon (eds.), *Israelitische Festpredigten und Casualreden*, Stuttgart 1840, p. 105.
[66]The German is, "geistigen Entwicklung und Bildung". *Ibid.*, p. 107.
[67]*Predigt am Vorabend des Versöhnungstages*, Dessau 1823, p. 18.
[68]*Predigt am ersten Neujahrstage der Welt 5590*, Rietberg 1829, p. 5.
[69]*Predigten für wahre Religionsfreunde*, Dessau 1826, p. 35.
[70]Schlingensiepen-Pogge, *Das Sozialethos der lutherischen Aufklärungstheologie am Vorabend der Industriellen Revolution*, pp. 133–138.

generation of pedagogues who lacked both a philosophical grasp and the practical experience of politics. They avidly endorsed the *Aufklärung* notion that the State always acted on behalf of the best interests of its subjects, assuming that there could be no distinction between the subjects' and the sovereign's interests. They consequently viewed the State as the agent of emancipation, investing it with quasi-messianic status.

Joseph Wolf, in his introductory article to the *Sulamith*, argued that the "illustrious sovereigns" had brought forth the new age of humanity. They were the creators of the new dispensation, and as such deserved the Jews' total devotion: "Our hearts are dedicated to you, you who, animated with the spirit of humanity and liberality, have restored the lost rights of a humbled people".[71] The benevolent rulers had thereby successfully included the Jews in the family of humanity: "The times are past in which Jew and man were held to be heterogeneous concepts."[72] The Jews must reciprocate by making themselves suitable to the states that are now willing to accept them. To do this the Jews must not only accept the critical ideals of toleration and justice; they must also demonstrate that they can contribute to the commonweal. Being included in society requires that the Jews become "useful" members of it, "social beings".

Wolf thus accepted the *Aufklärung* notion of social utility that the *Maskilim* (Wessely, Mendelssohn, Friedländer) had espoused, but now related it directly to rights, because he thought a grant of rights was imminent. Regeneration was an act of reciprocity to the agent of emancipation, the tutelary State. Reforms were designed to make the Jews acceptable first and foremost to the tutelary State. As another contributor to the *Sulamith* put it: "Let them first be regenerated to be men, and then give them over to the State as useful members."[73]

This view of the State led to a doctrine of unrestrained etatism. David Fränkel thought that emancipation flowed solely from the beneficence of the individual sovereigns. He thought the "enlightened, noble-minded and philanthropic sovereigns",[74] by making "justice the sole norm"[75] of their actions had promised to confer rights on the Jews. In a discussion of the Jews' situation in France and Italy in 1807 he asserted that, "where you are treated in a humane fashion, where things go well for you, there is your Palestine, your fatherland, which you must love and defend according to its laws".[76] In another article of the same year he used a midrashic passage that described the slow progress of messianic redemption from country to country to explain the process of emancipation: "redemption (*geulah*)", he asserted, means "the elevation of the Jews to citizens and to men".[77]

[71] *Sulamith*, I, 1 (1806), p. 11.
[72] *Ibid.*, pp. 6–7.
[73] Maimon Fränkel, 'Über die Erziehung des Menschen zur Religion', III, 5, (1810), p. 349.
[74] *Sulamith*, I, 1 (1806), p. 23.
[75] *Ibid.*, p. 16.
[76] *Sulamith*, I, 2, (1807), p. 4. For one among numerous similar passages see Gotthold Salomon, *Auswahl mehrerer Predigten zunächst für Israeliten*, Dessau 1818, p. 92.
[77] *Sulamith* I, 6, (1807), p. 377. For an excellent analysis of the problem of messianism and religious reform see Barukh Mevorakh, 'Messianism as a Factor in the First Reform Controversies', *Zion*, 34 (1969), pp. 189–218.

Because Fränkel understood the Jews' emancipation to be entirely dependent upon the State, he cheerfully endorsed the augmentation of state power that occurred during the Napoleonic era. In those years the policies of enlightened despotism were realised to an unprecedented extent, the German states extending the scope and efficacy of their control, whether through imitation of the Napoleonic model or through indigenous alternatives to it. Fränkel thought, for example, that the State alone could dispel the age-old prejudices against the Jews, rehabilitating them in the eyes of the common man; that "only living examples from above are effective in enlightening and instructing the common man below".[78] Fränkel also thought that the State had ultimate responsibility for helping the Jews to become useful citizens: "No resident of a State can be regarded as un-useful and superfluous; a wise government can place each of them in the proper position so as to be of utility to the State."[79] He therefore proudly announced in his introductory article that the *Fürst* of Anhalt-Dessau along with one of his ministers had been among the first subscribers to the *Sulamith*, demonstrating their unequivocal support for the journal.[80] There was not a trace of embarrassment in this declaration.

Fränkel's response to the public debate (Rühs) following the Congress of Vienna utilised the same ideas. In response to this attack Fränkel first and foremost took recourse to the benign sovereigns. He saw them as a bulwark unmoved by the tirades of a few fanatics:

> "Fear not, brothers of the House of Jacob, the impotent rage of a few zealots of our age. Our truth-loving, good sovereigns will not allow themselves to be led away from the path of right and humanity by their sophisms and distorted facts."[81]

He also listed the names of the sovereigns who subscribed to the *Sulamith*. But he obviously felt that the turn of events was dangerous, calling the entire ideology into question. He speculated that "some weak ones" among the Jews might think that the efforts of the last decades were in vain. They might say:

> "To what end our efforts of many years for greater ennoblement and approximation [to Germans]? To what end our exertions to fulfil properly our duties as citizens? Does not all this go unnoticed by many of our Christian compatriots? . . . Would we not be happier if we had stayed in our earlier, isolated less cultivated situation . . . ?"[82]

Fränkel conceded that there might be some truth in this line of reasoning. He nevertheless admonished his fellow Jews to redouble their efforts at "inner ennoblement" in order to show their Christian neighbours that they were not "unworthy . . . of being their fellow citizens".

The sermons display the same ideas. Responding to the emancipation edict of 1812 and the patriotic enthusiasm aroused by the War of Liberation, Eduard Kley asserted that, "we belong to the State; the State, and what concerns it, concerns us as well; we must live and die for the State".[83] Leopold Zunz told his

[78] *Sulamith*, I, 4, (1806), p. 339.

[79] *Sulamith*, I, 6, (1807), pp. 363–364.

[80] *Ibid.*, 36. For other lists of "exalted subscribers" see V, 4 (1817–1818), pp. 209–210; and VI, 1 (1819–1821), pp. 3–4.

[81] *Sulamith*, V, 1 (1817–1818), p. 6.

[82] *Ibid.*, p. 7.

[83] *Erbauungen, eine Schrift für Israeliten zur Beförderung eines religiösen Sinnes*, Berlin 1813–1814, p. 8.

auditors in Berlin (*circa* 1820) that their "well-being is tied to the fatherland and its pious King", and that therefore "you must dedicate the highest which you have to the fatherland, the land to which you belong".[84] In Mainz (1831) Michael Creizenach asserted that citizens owe the sovereign the "trusting and cheerful respect of a child towards his father, of a mortal towards his maker". In the same sermon he said the Jews must be especially grateful to Hessen: "France has made us citizens; Hessen, however, has educated us to be citizens." Creizenach emphasised the fact that while the French had granted legal rights, the tutelary Hessen state gave the Jews the means for "moral, religious and civic development (*Ausbildung*)". He therefore asked in his closing benediction that the sovereign be granted the power to permit him "to raise his people to the highest level of well-being, morality and culture (*Bildung*) of which they are capable".[85]

In its idea of the right to regeneration and its faith in the tutelary state, the ideology accepted the liberal *Gebildete*'s and the reforming states' view that rights were contingent upon regeneration. With emancipation being realised during the Napoleonic era, the ideologues had no reason to doubt their own wisdom. When the reaction turned against them, they thought they needed only to bide their time to be vindicated. But in accepting the notion that rights required regeneration, the ideologues went farther than the Gentile proponents of emancipation: they relinquished the political framework of *raison d'état* and natural rights. They thereby retained only the most conservative elements of a liberal doctrine. The ideology's etatism and its view of *Bildung* as a form of politics were the most conservative aspects of the liberal politics in the still pre-parliamentary German states. These were the ideas which, in some ways, both impeded the growth of a potent liberal doctrine and hampered its political success.[86] In the political ideology of the minority group, then, the dilemmas of Liberalism were more acute, their dependence on the State even greater. The historical commonplace that the emancipation process led the Jews to Liberalism therefore has to be qualified in the case of the ideology of emancipation before 1830.[87] In its initial phase, emancipation at best disposed the Jews to the most conservative of Liberalism's ideas.

The ideology's fundamental notion that regeneration was an act of reciprocity to the tutelary State involved a distinct view of history, what Salo Baron has called the "lachrymose" view.[88] This posited that prior to emancipation, throughout 1,800 years of dispersion, the Jews had experienced unrelieved suffering and persecution which had deformed both them and Judaism. With the advent of the absolutist State, however, that deformity could be corrected, because the benevolent State transformed the *Aufklärung* ideal of

[84] *Predigten gehalten in der neuen Israelitischen Synagoge zu Berlin*, Berlin 1823, p. 182.
[85] *Predigt gehalten in der Synagoge zu Mainz*, Mainz 1832, pp. 17–23.
[86] On these issues see the recent perspicacious analysis in James J. Sheehan, *German Liberalism in the Nineteenth Century*, Chicago 1978, pp. 14–18, 35–48.
[87] See for example, Jacob Toury, *Die politischen Orientierungen der Juden in Deutschland. Von Jena bis Weimar*, Tübingen 1966 (Schriftenreihe wissenschaftlicher Abhandlungen des Leo Baeck Instituts 15), pp. 1–46. and Hans Liebeschütz, *Das Judentum im deutschen Geschichtsbild*, *op. cit.*, pp. 172–177.
[88] See his 'Ghetto and Emancipation', in *The Menorah Journal*, 14 (1928), pp. 515–526.

universal humanity into a political policy. In that view of history, then, culture is the motor of change. This idea of historical causality, while foreign to the predominantly "sensationalist" view of history among French and English *philosophes*, was typical of the *Aufklärung*, deriving from its "idealist" Leibnizian heritage and the need of German thinkers concerned with religious and ecclesiastical history to account for the developments of the Reformation and post-Reformation era.[89] This view of history explains the form which the ideologues thought the Jews' regeneration should take. Since the tutelary State presided over the realisation of the *Aufklärung*, the Jews' reciprocity was to elevate themselves to the same ideal that animates the State i.e., to make themselves exemplars of the ideal of *Bildung* that espouses toleration and the ideal of humanity. The Jews' natural right to regeneration under the aegis of the tutelary State is, then, the right to remake themselves and Judaism in the image of the *Aufklärung*.

Joseph Wolf, for example, argued that the Jews had lost their rights in the dark centuries during which they were the "victims of tyranny". In those centuries they had clung to their religion as a source of strength and consolation. But that religion was a pale shadow of its former self. Before the loss of independence Judaism, especially during the reign of Solomon, had achieved a "high degree of perfection". Not only did it create a healthy collective life by combining a "moral and political constitution" of enviable character; it transcended mere "national love", achieving "general love of mankind". Late biblical Judaism heightened appreciation for foreigners and their beliefs and thus spread "toleration, sympathy, satisfaction, peace and happiness" throughout the nation. For Wolf, then, Judaism was the source of those very virtues which were now making possible the emancipation of the Jews. He thought it was the "illustrious sovereigns'" acceptance of the ideal of justice that had engendered the concept of tolerance that allowed the Jews to be considered part of humanity. They had brought about the new age of humanity. Because prior to the centuries of persecution Judaism had been "entirely pure", the Jews could regenerate themselves by recovering their own heritage, their "primordial education" (*Urbildung*), which would restore their own notion of justice to them.[90] The Jews' reciprocity is to recover through their own heritage the very values which are responsible for their emancipation.

The process of the recovery of a lost heritage is the Jews' exercise of their natural right to regeneration, what Wolf meant when he asserted that the Jews had to perfect themselves according to their own traditions. With this idea Wolf echoes one of the axioms of the neo-humanist theory of education. Wolf manifestly adopted the concept of *Bildung* in the years in which, after having gained currency among the educated classes and the bureaucracy, it passed into the language of politics.[91] While he used the concept and the constellation of

[89]The *philosophes* tended to stress external factors: climate, geography and social and political structures. The *Aufklärung* also used these forms of causality, but introduced idealistic ones as well. On these differences see Reill, *The German Enlightenment and the Rise of Historicism*, pp. 161–189.

[90]*Sulamith*, I, 1, (1806), p. 9.

[91]See the emancipation edict of Baden (1809), quoted in the *Sulamith*, II, 3 (1809), p. 152. For the Reform Period in Prussia see Karl-Ernst Jeismann, *Das preussische Gymnasium in Staat und*

ideas associated with it, he did not subscribe to the vision of aesthetic individualism it entailed. He remained firmly attached instead to the *Aufklärung*'s notion of ethical individualism that was the *sine qua non* of emancipation since Dohm.

Bildung meant the development of that form which was an organic part of the individual. Wolf used this organic metaphor.[92] "Nothing foreign can be grafted onto man, neither the individual nor entire peoples"; rather, all "formation (*Bildung*) must come from within" as the development of innate characteristics. Wolf based his argument on the *Aufklärung* notion of eudæmonism. All human happiness rests on the concept of justice, and so the individual must place his relationship to society on that basis. In order to be capable of establishing such a relationship, the individual has to "develop and form" both his "reason and his will". Reason must be broadened by the acquisition of knowledge and sharpened through the appreciation of all that is good, beautiful and true, so that the individual can comprehend the meaning of justice; the will must be bridled by constant exercise so that he is capable of implementing what he understands. In other words, the whole man, the sensual as well as the cognitive, must be cultivated or formed, for the individual to achieve, "perfection in himself and connection with other individuals". The *Sulamith*'s purpose is thus to "enlighten the nation in its own self", to "improve it internally".[93] The means to achieve this are to be found in religion, in Judaism itself, and thus Wolf declared that, "religion is the essential intellectual and moral necessity of the cultivated man".[94] For the Jews this means a return to Judaism as it had been.

Wolf saw the "edification sermon" as a central instrument for the reconstruction of Judaism since he understood "edification" to represent all of the religious reforms necessary for moral regeneration. In the medium of the sermon, then, Wolf undertook the reform on native grounds necessary for emancipation. He put into effect the ideology's pedagogical understanding of natural right, realising the implications of the lachrymose view of Jewish history. The sermon's purpose, he stated, was the "ennoblement and completion of the human soul".[95] As Wolf had made clear in his introduction to the *Sulamith*, this process had two parts: the education of the head and the heart, both cognition and volition. Wolf consequently attempted to explain what morality was, but also to foster those emotions and dispositions necessary for its attainment. The preacher had to "promote an ever greater growth in the knowledge of morality, and thereby to try to win the hearts of his auditors for the good cause".[96] In the preface to his volume of sermons Wolf stressed this emotional aspect. He had been gratified with the response to his sermons over

---

Gesellschaft, Stuttgart 1974, pp. 223f; and *idem.*, *Staat und Erziehung in der preussischen Reform*, Göttingen 1969.

[92]*Ibid.*, p. 2, especially the references to "bildende Natur".

[93]*Ibid.*, p. 10.

[94]*Ibid.*, p. 9.

[95]*Sechs Deutsche Reden*, I, p. 30.

[96]*Ibid.*

the years because the congregants had obviously been moved by them: "During my sermons all had directed themselves towards me with devout decorum and each one was moved and edified."[97]

This emphasis on the emotional as well as the intellectual aspect of the religious service was integral to Wolf's attempted redefinition of Judaism. In his sermons Wolf undertook to separate the "kernel" from the "husk", excising the product of centuries of persecution in order to reveal the pristine Judaism conducive to morality. This meant the creation of a Judaism that spoke to both the head and the heart instead of one requiring mere ritual performance. In a sermon on Shavuot, the spring holiday commemorating God's giving of the Law at Mount Sinai, for example, he asserted that Judaism had been "externalised" during the centuries of persecution, becoming merely the outward bond that held the nation together. In serving as a form of national solidarity and a means of survival, Judaism had lost its *Bildung*, its primordial moral centre.[98] With the dispensation of the *Aufklärung* and the end of persecution, the Jews could now turn inward and recover true religious feeling. Wolf demonstrated what this meant in the first of his published sermons, also delivered on Shavuot. He thought that because Shavuot had no particular ritual or symbol attached to it, it was perfectly suited to the desired internalisation of Judaism. "To be sure no religious image points to the origins of today's festival, no ceremony makes the memory of it tangible for us; our divine service of today consists only in pure devotion, in the effusion of the heart and the elevation of the spirit", and thus "it is perfectly suited to lead us to reflections which are commensurate with the dignity of man".[99]

In understanding edification to encompass the cultivation of the head and the heart, Wolf made use of another Protestant understanding of the sermon. While he clearly took over the form of the *Aufklärung* edification sermon, he also utilised the romantic notions introduced by Friedrich Schleiermacher (1768–1834). In his *On Religion, Addressed to the Educated Among its Despisers* (1799), the young Berlin theologian had rebelled against the utilitarian view of religion that the *Aufklärung* had made predominant. He asserted that religion should not be the handmaiden of morality or philosophy, let alone culture, but should instead have its own sphere centred on the "intuition" and "feeling" arising from the individual's autonomous experience of the universe. Schleiermacher developed a distinct terminology of "spirit" (*Gemüt*) and "feeling" (*Gefühl*) to explore the interior of this experience.[100] Wolf took over this terminology in his sermons, and understood the entire religious service through it. He asserted that religious ceremony and especially prayer are without content if not performed with "true devotion, with innermost feeling and with warmest emotion".[101] While adopting Schleiermacher's vocabulary, Wolf

[97]*Ibid.*, I, p. viii.
[98]*Ibid.*, 2, pp. 74–75.
[99]*Ibid.*, I, p. 2.
[100]*Über die Religion. Reden an die Gebildeten unter ihren Verächtern*, Hamburg 1958, vol. 255, Meiners Philosophische Bibliothek, pp. 38–39.
[101]*Sechs Deutsche Reden*, I, pp. 41–66.

nevertheless maintained a utilitarian view of religion, regarding it as instrumental to morality. "Prayer is the most potent means to raise and ennoble our morality."[102]

Edification for Wolf thus represented the overall reform of Judaism, the internalisation necessary to transform it into a key means of regeneration. The role of edification in the sphere of religion, was comparable to that of artisanry and farming in the sphere of occupations: it made possible the morality that leads to *Bildung*. In creating this concept of edification Wolf did not limit himself to *Aufklärung* ideas. Just as Wolf assimilated the axioms of neo-humanist pedagogy in defining his pedagogical understanding of natural rights, so here he assimilated the romantic religious vocabulary of Schleiermacher to his essentially utilitarian, *Aufklärung* outlook. The sermon thus presents another example of the predominance of ethical individualism in the ideology of emancipation.

While the concept of "edification" appeared with striking frequency in the Jews' German-language sermons of the early nineteenth century, its romantic implications were always subordinated to the ideology's moral goals. Leopold Zunz, for example, took a markedly romantic theme, "enthusiasm" (*Begeisterung*) for the subject of his first published sermon. Using Schleiermacher's terminology Zunz argued that the emotion of enthusiasm, exemplified by the biblical prophets, was the seat of religion. It is the "high and divine . . . which inspires (*begeistert*) us"; only a truly "pious spirit (*Gemüt*) is capable of enthusiasm". Yet this enthusiasm was the instrument by which man comes to rule over his sensual nature and to establish the reign of morality. Zunz placed the religious emotion of enthusiasm within the *Aufklärung*'s framework of fundamental opposition between sensuality and ethics. The divine enabled man to recognise and follow his higher nature with unswerving constancy; true enthusiasm kept man on the strait path. It aided him in attaining "ethical magnitude", a love of duties and the ability to act for the commonweal. "Enthusiasm", Zunz concluded, "can only ennoble".[103]

A second example illustrates the assimilation of romantic notions to the ideology's *Aufklärung* framework. In the introduction to a sermon delivered in Mainz in 1831, the Chairman of the Community Board, Jacob Dernburg,[104] used Schleiermacher's terminology to describe the purpose of the sermon. The religious service is a means for man "to arouse his spirit" (*das Gemüt anzuregen*) and to "build up" religious feeling within himself (*anzubauen*). For this to succeed, the sermon must be delivered in German, because only in "the language of the fatherland" can it fortify the congregation's understanding with "clear concepts through . . . a clear presentation". Dernburg sensed no contradiction between awakening the spirit and clarifying concepts. Yet in the

[102] *Ibid.*, 1, p. 55.

[103] *Predigten gehalten in der neuen Israelitischen Synagoge zu Berlin*, Berlin 1823, pp. 3–14. Alexander Altmann has a very different analysis of this sermon. See his 'Zur Frühgeschichte der jüdischen Predigt in Deutschland', *loc. cit.*, pp. 41–42.

[104] Dernburg was an active "reformer". On his activity see J. M. Jost, *Neuere Geschichte der Israeliten*, in *Geschichte der Israeliten*, 10 vols., Berlin 1846, 10, Pt. 1, p. 151.

end he subordinated both of these themes to a preoccupation with moral improvement: the sermon fulfils the urgent need of "making us nobler and better".[105]

Central to the lachrymose view was the figure of Moses Mendelssohn. The ideologues saw Mendelssohn as the great progenitor of regeneration. Such a view of Mendelssohn was in keeping with the *Aufklärung* idea of the role of individual genius in history. The figure of Luther, for example, helped *Aufklärung* thinkers to account for the Reformation and post-Reformation era.[106] Mendelssohn, the ideologues maintained, had single-handedly introduced the Jews to that culture which was the motor of historical change. He had set in motion the Jews' necessary regeneration, introducing light where there had previously been darkness. Mendelssohn had been able to accomplish this because he was the prototypical self-made man of culture. Mendelssohn proved that "a son of Israel could also soar upwards to the height of pure morality and virtue, that he could reach this height even on his own, without direction or guidance".[107] "He was, as a man and as a writer, both teacher and model."[108] This image of Mendelssohn as a genius provided a form of legitimation for the ideology as well as a normative example for the Jew seeking to merit emancipation. But Mendelssohn's image served still another purpose. By making Mendelssohn the progenitor of regeneration, the ideologues also entered a plea that additional time was needed for regeneration to take place:

> "The period of illumination for the Jewish nation, in which Moses Mendelssohn first voiced his creative: Let there be light! is far too brief for one to perceive the manifold results of a different kind of thought in general."[109]

The originality of the ideology lay not so much in its component ideas as in the new combinations they gained within it. These ideas were already advocated by Dohm and the other liberal advocates of emancipation on the one side, or the *Haskalah* on the other. But the ideology transformed them into the articulate programme of a new public sphere. The ideologues intended their ideas to represent the interests of the Jews as a group; the institutions of the public sphere made that representation possible. The ideologues radicalised the *Haskalah*, turning a vision into a pragmatic programme, by setting its ideas in direct relationship to the emancipation process through the transformation of natural rights into the right to regeneration. They gave all of the *Haskalah*'s ideas for reform a new internal coherence through the unifying symbol of *Bildung*. *Bildung* was now the other term in the emancipation contract. It stood for both the goal of the ideology's programme of regeneration as well as being integral to its underlying ideas of the tutelary State and the lachrymose view of Jewish history.

[105]*Predigt gehalten in der Synagoge zu Mainz*, Mainz 1832, pp. 4–9.
[106]Reill, *The German Enlightenment*, pp. 172–180.
[107]Gotthold Salomon, *Licht und Segen oder auf welchem Wege können Völker wahrhaft erleuchtet und beglückt werden*, Hamburg 1829, p. 18.
[108]Leopold Zunz, *Rede gehalten bei der Feier von Moses Mendelssohns hundertjährigem Geburtstage*, Berlin 1829, p. 7.
[109]*Sulamith*, I, 1, (1806), p. 25.

We are now in a position to analyse the role the institutions of the public sphere played in radicalising the ideas of the *Haskalah*. Wolf's adoption of the long-standing Sephardi practice of translating sermons delivered in the vernacular back into Hebrew for publication provides a striking illustration.[110] Wolf stated that he translated his printed sermons into Hebrew for the benefit of his fellow Jews who had not yet learned German.[111] A comparison of the original with the renditions into a clear *maskilic* Hebrew (worthy of Wessely, his model of Hebrew style) reveal that the ideas central to the ideology of emancipation that are prominent in the German original are almost entirely effaced in the translation. Whereas Wolf translated some *Aufklärung* notions into Hebrew, he eliminated the code words and key concepts of the ideology because he thought the reception his *maskilic* or Orthodox Hebrew readers would give them did not merit the effort required to convey them in Hebrew. As Fränkel had argued in vindication of the *Sulamith*'s language, those who wanted *Bildung* would be able to read German. The result is that in the Hebrew Wolf ended up using words and images associated with traditional Judaism instead of the ideology of emancipation. The Hebrew sermons thus have a totally different import from the German originals.

Wolf concluded a New Year's sermon (delivered in German) which was devoted to the effect of the holy day on our moral lives with the following prayer: "Make our hearts ever purer and firmer, our spirits ever more enlightened and developed (*unsern Geist immer aufgeklärter und gebildeter*), our belief ever surer and innocent."[112] The prayer gives clear evidence of the assimilation of *Aufklärung* categories; Wolf sees the purpose of Judaism as being synonymous with education of the head and the heart, the bases of morality deemed necessary for regeneration. The Hebrew has an entirely different effect: to "strengthen our hearts in your precepts, enlighten our eyes in your Torah, and strengthen our belief in our midst".[113] The Hebrew retains the exclusivity of its language: its associations are entirely within the realm of historic Judaism. It contains nothing of the amalgam of secular culture and Judaism characteristic of the ideology.

Wolf's sermon on the last day of Passover provides a similar example. Wolf discussed the qualities of a pious man, emphasising the importance of religions. In the German he reiterated one of the key assertions of his introduction to the *Sulamith*: "Religion is an essential requirement of the educated man (*gebildeter Mensch*). It is the beloved daughter of heaven."[114] Wolf's Hebrew translation obliterated the over-arching category of *Bildung* and relocated "religion"

[110]See Leon de Modena's *Midbar Yehudah*, Venice 1602; the sermons were given in Italian but published in Hebrew. For this point see Penina Nave (ed.), *Yehuda Arye Modena. Leket Ketavim*, Jerusalem 1968, p. 113. For the sermons themselves see Ellis Rivkin, 'The Sermons of Leon de Modena', *Hebrew Union College Annual*, 23 (1950–1951) pp. 295–317. Wolf seems to have been alone in continuing this practice. I have not been able to find another preacher in the first decades of the century who translated a German sermon into Hebrew.

[111]*Sechs Deutsche Reden*, I, p. ix.

[112]*Ibid.*, I, p. 84.

[113]*Ibid.*, Hebrew section, p. 47.

[114]*Ibid.*, 2, pp. 56–57.

squarely in the realm of historic Judaism. The two clauses are rendered: "It is the source of living waters, from it flow faithful and strong ideas." In rabbinic Hebrew water serves as one of the many images associated with the Torah. In fact water can be used metonymically to represent the Torah.[115] Wolf plays off that usage here. In replacing the concept of *Bildung* with a felicitous image, Wolf returned to an entirely traditional range of associations.

An obscure critique of Wolf's sermons further highlights the radicalising effect of the German sermon. Meir Elkan Fürth was an admirer of Mendelssohn who was the author of a textbook on algebra and contributed mathematical puzzles and articles on mathematics to the *Sulamith*. He criticised Wolf on two counts. First, he attacked Wolf for "philosophising" in the synagogue. Fürth did not disapprove of "philosophising" in principle; he simply objected that the synagogue was not the place for it, nor the sermon the appropriate vehicle. Fürth understood the sermon's function in terms of the musar tradition: the sermon should show people the strait path of virtue (*derekh ha-yashar*) or coax them from sin with mellifluous words (*be-metek dvarav*). Wolf's sermons, Fürth asserted, only confused the masses, especially since they did not understand his German. If the masses no longer knew sufficient Hebrew to understand a *derasha*, then Wolf should make it his business to teach it to them. Second, Fürth took issue with Wolf's Hebrew renderings. Wolf had translated belief (*Glaube*) as "knowledge of the truth" (*hakarat emet*) in keeping with the *Aufklärung* notion that true religion consists of clear concepts. Fürth asserted that this translation was misleading because it did not specify the contents of belief. Fürth here invoked Mendelssohn. Assuming that Mendelssohn had thought in Hebrew even while writing German, Fürth argued that in his *Jerusalem* Mendelssohn had translated belief – the Hebrew equivalent being *emunah* – as trust, *Vertrauen*, and defined it as "knowledge of the duties that man has towards the creator". For Fürth belief meant nothing else than observance of the commandments. In support of this he strictly applied Wessely's distinction between the "teachings of man" and the "teachings of God": the *Aufklärung* applied only to the realm of "practical affairs", and could teach us nothing about belief.[116]

THE PROBLEM OF COMMUNITY

The theory of emancipation posited that through the removal of collective disabilities the Jews would be integrated into State and society. They would be transformed from an autonomous community – or, in the language of the day, a "colony" or a "nation" – into a confession distinguished from the rest of society by religion alone. The various theoreticians of emancipation understood the implications of this theory differently. Dohm, the practical bureaucrat, was unwilling to rush the transformation of society. He assumed that the Jews would retain some judicial autonomy, just as he thought the guilds should not

[115]R. Margaliyot, 'Endearments for the Torah' (Hebrew), *Sinai*, 17 (1953), pp. 150–151.
[116]*Mahshavot ha-Leiv*, n.d., n.p., pp. 19 & 22–23.

be abrogated even while economic freedom was being introduced.[117] Mendelssohn, in keeping with his natural rights theory, envisioned the Jews constituting themselves as a voluntary society without any vestiges of corporate autonomy, because bourgeois society as a whole would be structured in precisely that way.[118]

The ideologues fervidly advocated the dismantling of the autonomous community. Yet they did so without fully facing its consequences: the ideologues lacked the developed political philosophy or the practical political experience needed to come to grips with the implications of their ideas. They did not develop a coherent and fully articulated view of what the Jews' new status would be. They assumed that their programme of regeneration would also provide a basis for the cohesion of the new Jewish community. They thought their notions of religious reform, for example, would change Judaism from a religion dependent upon the authority of tradition to a religion that could command rational assent. They wanted the Jews to form a community on the foundation of rational rather than inherited authority by making the Jews and Judaism fully compatible with *Bildung*. They implicitly assumed that their notion of Judaism would provide the basis for a new form of religious community.

Because the ideology lacked a fully articulated view of the Jews' new status, a paradox was inherent in the very foundations of the ideology: the basis of separation and integration were identical. The same programme of regeneration based on *Bildung* which was to provide a new basis of internal cohesion was also designed to integrate them into society. The universal values necessary for integration were also to sustain particularism. This paradox went unattended for well over two decades.

The ideology's primary concern was to demonstrate conclusively that the Jews' collective existence did not militate against their integration into society – that they were not an unassimilable group, whether on religious, economic or social grounds, as the opponents of emancipation never tired of asserting.[119] The ideologues therefore devoted themselves to showing, in the first place, that Judaism taught toleration, love of fellow-man and a unitary ethic which did not permit different standards of treatment for Jews and non-Jews. They had to show, as we have seen, that Judaism was entirely compatible with the *Aufklärung* principles which they held responsible for their own emancipation. In Joseph Wolf's words, they demonstrated that Judaism in its reconstructed pristine form "is not in the least harmful to the individual or to bourgeois society".[120] They also tried to demonstrate, in the second place, that through their programme of regeneration – occupational restructuring and re-education, the acquisition of language, manners and morals – the Jews themselves

[117] *Über die bürgerliche Verbesserung der Juden*, 1, pp. 121–122; 2, p. 272.
[118] *JubA*, 8, pp. 145–204.
[119] For two representative examples see Johann David Michaelis's (1717–1791) rebuttal of Dohm in *Über die bürgerliche Verbesserung der Juden*, 2, pp. 31–71; and Friedrich Rühs's (1781–1820) *Über die Ansprüche der Juden an das deutsche Bürgerrecht*, Berlin 1816.
[120] *Sulamith*, I, 1, (1806) p. 8.

would be entirely acceptable to the larger society in that they would be as proper and educated, as *gebildet* as their Christian neighbours.

Alongside these professions, the ideologues also endeavoured to show that the Jews no longer saw themselves as a distinct political group. Fränkel declared in 1807: 'We no longer constitute a distinct entity (*wir machen kein Ganzes mehr aus*), but rather as citizens are merely individual members of the State; we belong to no guild and therefore must consider our brothers as neither Jew nor Christian, but merely as a fellow citizen."[121] Yet because he was so concerned to deny the Jews' former political status, he characteristically neglected to discuss what their new one would be. This overwhelming concern to establish that the Jews were no longer a political group can also be seen, for example, in the change made in the *Sulamith*'s subtitle in 1810. The journal's original subtitle read, 'A Journal for the Promotion of Culture and Humanity in the Jewish Nation' (*unter der jüdischen Nation*). At the beginning of its third year the title became 'among the Israelites' (*unter den Israeliten*). The adoption of the euphemism "Israelites" intended to signal an end to the Jews' former political status. (The euphemism had the additional purpose of avoiding the term "Jew," which was pejorative. In the first four decades of the century various German governments prohibited the use of the term, adopting one or another neutral euphemism. In so doing they were fulfilling Fränkel's and the other ideologues' hope: that the State, acting as the agent of emancipation, would attempt to remove the causes of prejudice.)[122]

Ceasing to regard themselves as a political group did not mean that the ideologues dissociated themselves from Jews in other countries. On the contrary: they were as well informed about the situation of Jews elsewhere as could be expected. During the Napoleonic era, for example, the *Sulamith* featured articles devoted to legislative changes throughout Europe.[123] In the *Vormärz* the ideologues monitored developments in education and religious reform abroad.[124] And the *Sulamith* reported on interesting events, such as Mordechai Noah's attempt to establish a utopian community in America.[125] In considering the Jews to be a confession the ideologues and their successors did not separate themselves, then, from the larger community of Israel. Instead, as with all groups, they paid attention to those aspects of their fellow Jews that interested them most. This meant that they saw Jews in other lands just as they saw themselves: through the sharply focused, if limited vision of their ideology.

When the ideologues did think about the problems of cohesion – what the basis of community would be – they obviously thought in terms of the perils their age presented. In particular, they feared that the pressure of emancipation would polarise the Jews into two irreconcilable camps: at one extreme

[121]'Die Lage der Juden alter und neurer Zeiten', I, 6, (1807), p. 382.

[122]For Baden's prohibition of the term "Jew" see Rürup, 'Die Emanzipation der Juden in Baden', in *Emanzipation und Antisemitismus*, *op. cit.*, p. 48.

[123]See, for example, 'Nachrichten und Berichtigungen, die bürgerliche Verbesserung der Israeliten in verschiedenen Ländern betreffend', II, 3 (1808), pp. 155–176; and 'Nachrichten aus verschiedenen Ländern', III, 4, (1811), pp. 274–280.

[124]'Nachrichten von den neuen Israelitischen Schulen', *Sulamith*, VI, 4, (1820), pp. 235–256.

[125]VI, 4, (1820), pp. 283–284.

undiscriminating advocates of integration, at the other, unyielding adherents of segregation and an unreconstructed Judaism. Such a polarisation, they thought, would end in the dissolution of Judaism. Their overriding concern was, therefore, to save Judaism by finding some common ground that could again unify the Jews.

This concern was prominent, for example, in the ideologues' notion of the sermon's audience (which we examined earlier): they thought that institution could perhaps mediate between the extremes. When Fränkel asserted that the sermon alone could address the new "middle class", he said that with the implicit wish that all of Germany's Jews, through regeneration, would become "middle class".[126] M. Neumann, director of the Breslau *Wilhelmschule*, made a similar point in reaction to the 1812 Prussian emancipation edict. Now that "all bonds of the Israelite nation are dissolved", he argued, the sole communal institution was the synagogue: "The synagogue is the only point where the Israelites' social interest is concentrated."[127] The synagogue therefore had to serve to unify the entire community, since no other institution could do so. Yet the basis of that unity, not surprisingly, lay in religious reform.

> "After the State has done so much for the improvement of our civic constitution (*bürgerliche Verfassung*), we for our part must do something for our moral, ecclesiastical (*kirchlich*) improvement. There is no doubt that the duration and strength of our civic constitution depends entirely upon our moral life. Only through the improvement of our ecclesiastical condition, the most infallible and often the only means to influence the moral character of a nation, will we make ourselves worthy (*würdig*) to enjoy fully our acquired rights . . . But if that alteration of the synagogue is to succeed, then the entire nation must willingly accept it, the entire nation must be taken into account, and no party can be granted anything at the expense of another."[128]

The obvious problem here is that the ideologues thought the means to the moral regeneration required by emancipation and the means to re-unite the community were one and the same. They wanted a reconstructed Judaism that would alienate none by commanding the assent of all. They sought to mediate between the extremes, and the key to mediation, they thought, – as with everything else – lay in *Bildung*. In his introduction to the *Sulamith* Joseph Wolf had asserted that "religion is the essential intellectual and moral necessity of the cultivated man".[129] For Wolf the recovery of Judaism's *Urbildung*, which was the very source of the *Aufklärung* values of toleration and humanity, would allow Judaism to regain the credence of all Jews. For Wolf this could be accomplished through a service and a German-language sermon that promoted "edification". For Wolf edification that led to *Bildung* was the answer. The author of the 1812 article similarly thought that a decorous service accompanied by a German sermon was the surest means to the "development (*Bildung*) of the Israelites".

[126]See note 23 above.

[127]Über die Verbesserung der kirchlichen Verfassung der Israeliten in den Königl. Preussischen Staaten', *Sulamith*, IV, 5 (1812), pp. 396–397. Although the journal had dropped the word "nation" from its subtitle, some contributors continued to use it. There was no terminological consistency.

[128]*Ibid.*, pp. 383 & 401.

[129]*Sulamith* I, 1 (1806), p. 9.

The ideology's fundamental paradox remained implicit during the years of its earliest formulation. In the *Vormärz* incomplete emancipation made the paradox explicit and acute. On the one side there were continuing demands for regeneration through religious reform from the states and the advocates of emancipation. The very process of emancipation continued to maintain the Jews' distinct status. On the other side the polarisation the ideologues had feared proceeded apace. The ideology's programme of regeneration through religious reforms became a divisive rather than a unifying factor, as the Jewish communities, especially in urban areas, were torn by controversy over religious and educational reform.[130] The ideology attempted to cope with this disappointing situation by extending its own immanent logic rather than by altering its ideas: it introduced the idea of the Jews' "mission". Rather than just improving themselves in order to gain emancipation, the Jews had a mission to improve non-Jews. Once their non-Jewish neighbours had been regenerated, emancipation would be realised, for society would then act on the high ideals it had attained. The ideology thus effected a theoretical reconciliation of its own inherent paradox: universal values could sustain the Jews' particularism, were indeed integral to it, since the Jews had a role to play on the stage of universal moral history.[131]

We can see these ideas in the sermons of Mendel Hess (1807–1871), for example. He subscribed fully to the ideology of emancipation. He believed that moral regeneration was the means to emancipation: "True education and inner worth are the foundations of civic freedom." He also understood religion's purpose to be the promotion of "moral purity and moral dignity"; he believed religion is what "makes men human". Finally, he advocated that the Jews adopt the "customs and genuinely human strivings of their neighbours". Yet the Jews must maintain one kind of distinctiveness: they must be moral exemplars. They must teach morality to the rest of the world. Hess articulated this idea by reinterpreting the concept of the Jews as the chosen people. In quoting from Deuteronomy (especially XIX:2) Hess shifted the emphasis of the concept from the Jews' relationship to God and His law to their relationship to the non-Jewish world. He argued that whereas in the past the Jews gave the world moral precepts (Wolf's argument), they must now give the world an unmistakable example: "As previously through its teaching, now through its

[130]There is an enormous literature on these controversies. Characteristic of the older scholarship is David Philipson, *The Reform Movement in Judaism*, 2nd edn., New York 1931. For the more recent scholarship see Michael Meyer, 'The Religious Reform Controversy in the Berlin Jewish Community, 1814–1823', in *LBI Year Book XXIV* (1979) pp. 139–156; and Stephen M. Poppel, 'The Politics of Religious Leadership. The Rabbinate in Nineteenth-Century Hamburg', in *LBI Year Book XXVIII* (1983), pp. 439–469.

[131]For a discussion of this contradiction between universal ideas and group particularism at the very end of the *Vormärz* era see Uriel Tal, 'German-Jewish Social Thought in the Mid-Nineteenth Century', in *Revolution and Evolution. 1848 in German-Jewish History*, edited by Werner E. Mosse, Arnold Paucker, Reinhard Rürup, Tübingen 1981 (Schriftenreihe wissenschaftlicher Abhandlungen des Leo Baeck Instituts 39) pp. 299–328, esp., pp. 306–309. For the problem in the thought of one prominent figure see Michael Meyer, 'Universalism and Jewish Unity in the Thought of Abraham Geiger', in Jacob Katz (ed.), *The Role of Religion in Modern Jewish History*, Cambridge, Mass. 1975, pp. 91–104.

example Israel must be exemplary for all peoples, must take the highest rung on the ladder of moral perfection."[132] In so doing they would also gain political emancipation.

The idea of mission justified the redefinition of Judaism according to the universal values which the ideology had promoted. It also provided grounds for continuing separation, thereby giving a new form to the ideology's fundamental paradox of the identity of universality and distinctness. The idea of mission was an attempt to achieve a theoretical resolution of the problem of the Jews' cohesion.

But was that theoretical resolution also the actual historical resolution? Did the idea of mission in fact provide a basis for cohesion? Or did the ideology of emancipation itself instead become the basis for a new sort of German-Jewish community? In radicalising the *Haskalah*, the ideology provided a coherent cultural system expressed in a new German-language public sphere. The ideology had its mythic hero in Moses Mendelssohn. It articulated a distinct political outlook (tutelary State); a view of history (lachrymose) and a notion of German Jewry, however ambiguous, as a community (confession). The symbol of *Bildung* unified and represented this cultural system through its ideal of man (ethical individualism) and the programme of regeneration (occupational restructuring; reform of religion, manners and morals) showed how that ideal could be attained. The system was sufficiently coherent to be able to assimilate new ideas by subordinating them to its own programme (e.g. Schleiermacher's religious romanticism). Moreover, it sufficiently resembled the majority culture to allow its adherents to see it as a means to integration.

Could it be the case that the ideology itself came to unite a community otherwise divided? Could it be that the ideal of *Bildung* became the new unifying factor for a community increasingly polarised over religious issues because it represented both the reciprocity which emancipation demanded and a means to integrate into the larger bourgeoisie of education? The answers to these questions might well suggest that the Jews' response to emancipation led to the creation of a new kind of identity which was primarily secular, but not for that reason any less Jewish or viable. They might suggest that emancipation did not lead to assimilation, but to an acculturation which had its own inherent legitimacy. Such a conclusion would indicate that a different approach to the study of Jewish identity in Germany is in order.

[132] *Predigten, Confirmations-, Trau- und Schuleinführungs-Reden*, Eisenach 1839, pp. 13, 55, 63–64, 90, 183. For other examples see Moses Dreifuss, *Israels Aufgabe* (n.p. 1840), *passim*; and Samuel Hirsch, *Friede, Freiheit und Einheit. Sechs Predigten gehalten in der Synagoge zu Dessau*, Dessau 1839, especially p. 52. On the idea of mission see Max Wiener, 'The Concept of Mission in Traditional and Modern Judaism', *YIVO Annual for Jewish Studies*, 2/3 (1948–1949), pp. 9–25.

Nineteenth-Century Antisemitism

Jews and Antisemites at Universities in Imperial Germany (II)

The Friedrich-Wilhelms-Universität of Berlin: A Case Study on the Students' "Jewish Question"

BY NORBERT KAMPE

The first part of this essay[1] concentrated on major structural developments in higher education, the university-trained professions and the place of Jews within that field. It described the situation during the last quarter of the nineteenth century, when an intensifying crisis in the academic labour market was nevertheless accompanied by growing enrolment figures. At this time, the German Jews acted as the vanguard of upward social mobility through education and became highly visible in some universities and professions. This gave antisemitic agitators the chance to blame Jewish students and graduates for the situation. Part I of this study foreshadowed the goals of the organised antisemitic student movement and some of its effects after 1880.[2] The following essay will study the development of the "studentische Judenfrage".

For various reasons the *Friedrich-Wilhelms-Universität zu Berlin* (F.W.U.) played a major role in the history of student antisemitism. Founded in 1810 according to the reforming ideas of the Prussian Education Minister Wilhelm von Humboldt, it had become the leading German university in many subjects because of its generous endowments and a skilful appointments policy.[3] Beyond that the F.W.U. enjoyed a considerable international reputation, resulting in a consistently large foreign student body, studying at their own expense. It had manifold connections with foreign universities, and in the USA for instance the German *Ordentlicher Professor* was held in the highest esteem.[4] In short, at the

[1]Norbert Kampe, 'Jewish Students: Social History and Social Conflict', in *LBI Year Book XXX* (1985), pp. 357–394 (hereafter, Kampe, 'Jewish Students'). For editorial help and translation of my two articles, I would like to thank Helga Braun, Cambridge, Janet Langmaid, Ottery St. Mary, Reinhild Weiss, Reading. These articles are English versions of sections of my *Bildungsbürgertum und Antisemitismus im Deutschen Kaiserreich. Der studentische Anteil an der Durchsetzung einer gesellschaftlichen Norm*, Phil. Diss., Technische Universität Berlin 1983 (unpubl.). The manuscript is available in the Leo Baeck Institutes, Germania Judaica, Cologne, and Zentrum für Antisemitismusforschung, TU Berlin.

[2]Kampe, 'Jewish Students', pp. 377–378.

[3]See especially Max Lenz (ed.), *Geschichte der königlichen Friedrich-Wilhelms-Universität zu Berlin*, 4 vols., Halle/Saale 1910–1918.

[4]See Charles F. Thwing, *The American and the German University. One Hundred Years of History*, New York 1928; Carnegie Foundation for the Advancement of Teaching (ed.), *The Financial Status of the Professor in America and Germany*, New York 1908. After Swiss, Austrians and Russians, students from the USA

foundation of the Empire in 1871, when the capital of Prussia was obliged rather hastily to expand into a European metropolis, the University of Berlin had already attained international status. Although the thinking of the average Berlin *Ordinarius* was undoubtedly "national", it remained in the tradition of the Liberal bourgeois unification movement; but this was at the very time that the reactionary forces associated with the anti-Liberal change of 1878–1879 were forging the weapon of demagogic and xenophobic nationalism to hamstring the "dangers" of equal manhood suffrage. Such a situation explains the angry reaction in Berlin academic circles when it appeared that the poisonous breath of antisemitism emanating from the anti-Liberal campaign might gain ground in their own ranks. Contrariwise, how enticing for the antisemitic "national" camp was the prospect of taking over the enemy bastion – "the specific Berliner progressive mentality",[5] defined as a particular intellectual alloy of "Liberal", "international" and "Jewish". Meanwhile, out of 53 *Ordinarien* in 1875, only one was a Jew;[6] however, there were many Jewish students – they outnumbered the Catholics, the second largest religious community in Prussia.[7] Moreover, although in the early 1880s most universities in Protestant Prussia and Saxony saw the new student generation reflected in nationalist and anti-Liberal voices, in Berlin significant numbers of students still opposed the contemporary trend. In the capital, therefore, there was enough backing on both sides to prevent a "lightning victory".

Another circumstance made the University of Berlin into a barometer for the political balance among students: only a few other German universities held regular elections for student committees.[8] These were closely observed – and not just by Berliners, a fact which further politicised the students. Such wide public interest has provided a research opportunity unique among German universities: by analysing the university press, it is possible to reconstruct the strength and composition of the different parties, as well as the level of student

---

numbering 173 in 1880 were the largest group, comprising 15·5% of all foreigners in German universities. Compare *Preussische Statistik* (hereafter PS), vol. 236 (1913), p. 67, tables pp. 39–69.

[5]Antisemitic students described their aims as "emancipation from the specific Berliner metropolitan spirit" (*Kyffhäuser-Zeitung*, No. 1, 6th August 1881) and in early 1882 complained to the Education Minister about the alleged preference for "specifically Berlin and Jewish" members of the *Akademische Lesehalle*; see below pp. 56ff. and note 72. An antisemitic and anti-modern book by August Julius Langbehn appeared anonymously as *Rembrandt als Erzieher. Von einem Deutschen*, Leipzig 1908 (48th edn.) pp. 117–121, which was enthusiastically received in the student fraternity press, contrasted expressly the perverted "Berliner spirit" and the original, unspoilt "pure German spirit".

[6]Jews seldom reached *Ordinarius* level; see Kampe, 'Jewish Students', note 19; Ismar Schorsch, 'The Religious Parameters of Wissenschaft. Jewish Academics at Prussian Universities', in *LBI Year Book XXV* (1980), pp. 3–19; Fritz K. Ringer, 'Inflation, Antisemitism and the German Academic Community of the Weimar Period', in *LBI Year Book XXVIII* (1983), pp. 3–9. For precise data see now Kampe, 'Jüdische Professoren im Deutschen Kaiserreich', in Rainer Erb and Michael Schmidt (eds.), *Antisemitismus und jüdische Geschichte. Studien zu Ehren von Herbert A. Strauss*, Berlin 1987, pp. 185–211.

[7]For the Jewish students at the F.W.U. Berlin see Figure II and Table III. See also Kampe, 'Jewish Students', Tables IVa (breakdown by religion) and IVc (indigent Jewish students in Berlin).

[8]Konrad H. Jarausch, *Students, Society, and Politics in Imperial Germany. The Rise of Academic Illiberalism*, Princeton 1982, pp. 382f. (Table 6–1).

politicisation, for almost every year between 1880 and 1914. By a fortunate chance, too, the relevant records of the rector's office have survived[9] and can be supplemented by certain other sources, so that the history of the struggle concerning the "studentische Judenfrage" in Berlin can be reconstructed with unusual completeness.

It may fairly be said that on this question the University of Berlin was both typical and unique. What was happening openly in Berlin was followed – often covertly – by other universities. This is shown by the tradition-conscious student *Verbindungen*, even though their strongholds were mainly in small-town universities in Southern Germany, rather than in the modern, large-scale University of Berlin, where *Nichtkorporierte* made up by far the majority. The traditional wing of the German student *Korporationen*, banded together in the big *Kartelle* of the colour-wearing and duelling *Verbindungen*, followed the example of their Berlin counterparts on the "Jewish Question": in the early 1890s they established a rigid anti-Jewish social norm.

Rather than depicting the amalgamation of traditional student attitudes with the antisemitic social norm,[10] this study concentrates on the politics of the student parties in Berlin. The formation of the first organised antisemitic student movement, the reaction of Liberal and academically educated Berlin and the student struggles regarding the "Jewish Question" will be considered in order to understand the reorientation among students in the 1880s and the early 1890s. The subsequent emancipation movement of the *Nichtkorporierten* and the Jewish students with their independent association will form a further point of analysis.

I. THE BEGINNINGS OF AN ORGANISED ANTISEMITIC STUDENTS' MOVEMENT

The antisemitic student movement, beginning in Protestant Germany in the early 1880s and concentrated in Berlin and Leipzig, was closely related to the first climax in the development of modern antisemitism which accompanied the severe crisis of political and philosophical Liberalism.[11] Parts of the student body – especially in the ideology-related faculties of philosophy, theology and law – no longer accepted the moral leadership, educationally so important, of

[9]Today held in the archive of the Humboldt Universität Berlin, under *Rektor und Senat* (hereafter cited HUA). I have to thank Dipl. Hist. Kossack and his staff for their most friendly help and also Mrs. Charlotte Gudereit for checking my transcriptions of the notoriously difficult professorial manuscripts.

[10]See Norbert Kampe, *Studenten und Antisemitismus im Deutschen Kaiserreich*, forthcoming (Kritische Studien zur Geschichtswissenschaft, Göttingen). Hereafter the term "antisemitism as social norm" is used, since student antisemitism was not just a "cultural code" of "little practical importance", "a sign of cultural identity, of one's belonging to a specific cultural camp", Shulamit Volkov, 'Antisemitism as a Cultural Code. Reflections on the History and Historiography of Antisemitism in Imperial Germany', in *LBI Year Book XXIII* (1978), pp. 34f. What is termed "social norm" in Klaus Felden, *Die Übernahme des antisemitischen Stereotyps als soziale Norm durch die bürgerliche Gesellschaft Deutschlands (1876–1900)*, Heidelberg, Diss. Phil. 1965, is really more a "cultural code".

[11]See, for the literature, Kampe, 'Jewish Students', notes 2–4.

their Liberal teachers. On top of that the ostentatiously antisemitic garb of the new student "illiberalism" had the "advantage" of giving provocation to Liberal professors.[12]

Among Berlin's peculiarities with the potential for sparking off a separate antisemitic student movement were Adolf Stoecker's *Berliner Bewegung*,[13] and the fierce public debate conducted between Professors Heinrich von Treitschke and Theodor Mommsen, both historians with a wide readership. Treitschke exemplified the changeover from (moderate) Liberalism to a Conservatism carrying a chauvinistic reinterpretation of traditional bourgeois nationalism; Mommsen was a symbol of (now "Left") Liberalism with republican tendencies. The "Christian Social Movement" of Court Chaplain Stoecker, as well as the debate between Treitschke, Mommsen and others which became known as the *Berliner Antisemitismusstreit*[14] have been extensively discussed in recent scholarly literature, and only the student aspect needs to be set out here.

Adolf Stoecker was a socially committed churchman who tried to make contact with the city proletariat. But he failed to alienate the workers from atheistic, revolutionary Social Democracy and to lead them into the Christian-Conservative camp. Not proletarians, who mocked his equation of "social question" and "Jewish Question",[15] but the lower bourgeoisie joined Stoecker's election campaign rallies, particularly when he indulged in antisemitic attacks against "Manchester Liberalism" and "big business". By such dubious successes Stoecker assumed the mantle of an influential antisemitic demagogue. Students sensitive to the "social question" saw in Stoecker a protagonist of non-revolutionary social reform within existing social relations. The position of a court chaplain close to the ruling circles of court and Conservative Party allowed students to believe that his antisemitism was more honourable than the *Radauantisemitismus* of failures like Wilhelm Marr or Hermann Ahlwardt.[16]

Heinrich von Treitschke set out to lend antisemitism academic respectability. In November 1879, as editor of the *Preußische Jahrbücher*, he published a political review, the whole second half of which was dedicated to the existing modern antisemitic movement. The article, showing the end of a ten-year process of

[12]Heinrich Claß, for example, later the leader of the *Alldeutscher-Verband*, when a student, because of the antisemitic attitudes he had absorbed at Treitschke's feet, characterised his parents' "old-fashioned" *Weltanschauung* indulgently: "three foreign words – patriotism, tolerance, humanity". (Claß, *Wider den Strom*, Leipzig 1932, pp. 14–17). See also *Akademische Blätter* (*Akad. Bll.*), 1 (1886/1887), p. 164.

[13]See Werner Jochmann, 'Stoecker als nationalkonservativer Politiker und antisemitischer Agitator', in Günter Brakelmann, Martin Greschat, Werner Jochmann, *Protestantismus und Politik. Werk und Wirkung Adolf Stoeckers*, Hamburg 1982, pp. 123–198. And Kampe, 'Jewish Students', note 54.

[14]Walter Boehlich (ed.), *Der Berliner Antisemitismusstreit*, Frankfurt a. Main 1962, and Michael Meyer, 'Great Debate on Antisemitism. Jewish Reactions to New Hostility in Germany 1879–1881', in *LBI Year Book XI* (1966), pp. 137–170. Michael Reuwen, 'Graetz contra Treitschke', in *Bulletin des Leo Baeck Instituts*, 4 (1961), pp. 301–335.

[15]Reinhard Rürup, 'Sozialismus und Antisemitismus in Deutschland vor 1914', in *Jahrbuch des Instituts für deutsche Geschichte*, Beiheft 2 (1977), Tel-Aviv, pp. 203–227. Rosemarie Leuschen-Seppel, *Sozialdemokratie und Antisemitismus im Kaiserreich. Die Auseinandersetzung der Partei mit den konservativen und völkischen Strömungen des Antisemitismus 1871–1914*, Bonn 1978.

[16]For Stoecker and the *Vereine Deutscher Studenten*, see Kampe, *Studenten und Antisemitismus*.

distancing himself from Liberalism,[17] is a masterpiece of political demagogy. Detailed analysis discloses in it the beginning of Treitschke's terrifyingly inhuman attitudes,[18] later to break through into his lectures on political science.[19] The author himself exposed as mere rhetoric his own claim to be keeping his distance from *Radauantisemitismus*, from the "filth" and "mob coarseness" for instance, when he uses "filth" in the context of baptised Jews. Similarly, his "decent" Jews serve a rhetorical purpose. In the end what was said and generally understood, was that this still vague antisemitic public feeling in truth derived from the "damage" done by the "Semites": these people now wielded too much power; they were largely answerable for the frivolity of non-Christian *littérateurs*, the "assiduity" of "third rate talents" and the "confidence tricks" and "wicked greed" of speculators and profiteers; and they were undermining the national consciousness of the German Empire, still tender after its recent revival.[20]

With great stubbornness Treitschke maintained his position unaltered throughout the year-long journalistic conflict of 1880, even though he became more and more isolated. The infamous statement, "The Jews are our misfortune!" – which he said was to be heard "up to and including the most highly educated levels" –[21] gained him new "friends", yet Treitschke later wished to dissociate himself from these people. Politically and personally isolated, at least he still received regular student ovations until his death in 1896.[22] Theodor Mommsen, in his pamphlet against Treitschke of November 1880, justifiably centres criticism on the damaging effect of Treitschke's effusions: the "immeasurable damage" and the "bombshell effect of those articles" was that they dragged the antisemitic movement out of the twilight of immorality.[23] As early as 18th March 1880 during a speech in the Friedrich-Wilhelms-University celebrating the Emperor's birthday, Mommsen exclaimed:

> "Is Kaiser Wilhelm's empire really still the country of Frederick the Great, the country of enlightenment and tolerance, the country where character and spirit are looked for rather than religious confession and nationality? . . . The battle of envy and ill-will has blazed up on all sides. The torch has already been thrown into our own ranks, and the chasm within the nation's aristocracy of scholarship already gapes wide."[24]

Meagre and biased as are the sources relating to the first attempts to organise the antisemitic trends among Berlin students,[25] the following reconstruction is still

[17]See Max Cornicelius (ed.), *Heinrich von Treitschke. Briefe*, vols. 1 and 2, Leipzig 1914–1918 (2nd edn.), vol. 3, Leipzig 1920.

[18]For example, improved education for the masses is alleged as the cause of their "increasing unruliness"; 'Unsere Aussichten', in *Preussische Jahrbücher*, November 1879; quoted in Boehlich, *op. cit.*, pp. 7–14, here p. 8.

[19]For example H. v. Treitschke, *Politik. Vorlesungen gehalten an der Universität zu Berlin*, ed. by Max Cornicelius, vol. 2, Leipzig 1922, p. 570.

[20]'Unsere Aussichten', *loc. cit.*

[21]*Ibid.*, p. 11.

[22]The only full critical biography is by Andreas Dorpalen, *Heinrich von Treitschke*, New Haven 1957. See also the biography by Georg Iggers, 'Heinrich von Treitschke', in Hans-Ulrich Wehler (ed.), *Deutsche Historiker*, vol. 2, Göttingen 1971, pp. 66–80.

[23]Theodor Mommsen, *Auch ein Wort über unser Judenthum*, (3rd edn.), Berlin 1880, p. 11.

[24]Theodor Mommsen, *Reden und Aufsätze*, Berlin 1905, pp. 89f.

[25]The most important source is Hermann von Petersdorff, *Die Vereine Deutscher Studenten*, Leipzig 1891 (^{2}1895 and ^{3}1900). For the later period Hans Weber, *Geschichte des Vereins Deutscher Studenten in*

possible. In the summer of 1880 some law students founded an *Akademisch Rechtswissenschaftlicher Verein* because the existing *Akademischer Juristischer Verein* was said to be full of Jews. Paul Dulon,[26] a Leipzig student spending the vacation in Charlottenburg managed to win over antisemitic law students to his plan of gaining considerable student support for the *Antisemiten-Petition*, in circulation since 1879. On 22nd October 1880, Dulon obtained Treitschke's full backing. He began covert agitation in Leipzig and aroused his Berlin student friends. It seems that one of the first major demonstrations by antisemitic students took place in Berlin at the beginning of November when Eugen Dühring lectured against the "over-estimation of Lessing". Apparently as a preventative, the Liberal *Berliner Börsen-Courier* commented that the student ovation for Dühring could not be regarded as evidence of sympathy for the currently circulating *Antisemiten-Petition*.[27]

The tide of antisemitism now appeared ready to flow beyond the student world. Perhaps in view of this threat, Mommsen and some of his colleagues, together with seventy-five others, all prominent in Berlin's political and social life, signed a declaration[28] which appeared in several Berlin daily papers on 12th November 1880. This celebrated *Notabelnerklärung* by representatives of the Liberal, educated Berlin bourgeoisie called for "the resistance of sensible men" to antisemitism, which was branded as "race hatred", "medieval fanaticism", "an infectious pestilence" and "artificially inflamed mob passion". Everyone well versed in politics could not but connect the following sentences of the declaration with Stoecker and Treitschke:

> "Although the leaders of this movement are now preaching envy and malice in the abstract, the masses will not hesitate to draw practical conclusions from such speeches. They try to overturn Lessing's legacy, these men who should be proclaiming from pulpit and rostrum

---

Berlin vom 2.-3. Kyffhäuserfest des Kyffhäuserverbandes (1891–1906), Graudenz 1912. The files of the *Kyffhäuserverband* (KV) in the *Preussisches Geheimes Staatsarchiv* disappeared after 1945; cf. the KV's *Praktisches Handbuch*, Tirschenreuth 1980 (4th edn. by Ludwig Biewer), pp. 212–214. And see now as the best survey on sources available today Hedwig Roos-Schumacher, *Der Kyffhäuserverband der Vereine Deutscher Studenten 1880–1914/18*, Gifhorn 1986. This author also touches on antisemitism in the KV, but tends to minimise its ideological and practical importance. Since the work confines itself to a history of ideas within the KV, the effect of the organisation's antisemitism and nationalism on the overall academic scene is out of its scope.

[26]Paul Dulon, later von Duelong (1858–1927), son of a Royal Prussian government surveyor, untypically neither became a senior member of the KV, nor ever again appeared in public in association with it. In Breslau, during the summer semester of 1881, Dulon created the best organised VDSt (112 members), soon followed by other associations (a more rigid hierarchy, obtained by changing from "faculty chairmanships" to only two chairmen – normally jurists – installation of a "reading room" and foundation of "departments" with special tasks). In the following winter semester, he gave up the chairmanship apparently "because of disagreements" and stayed away from all further development of the KV.

[27]In Dühring's most important writings on the *Judenfrage* (*Die Judenfrage als Rassen-, Sitten- und Kulturfrage. Mit einer weltgeschichtlichen Antwort*, Karlsruhe–Leipzig 1881 (2nd edn.). *Die Judenfrage als Frage der Rassenschädlichkeit*, Berlin 1888) he defined it as a purely "racial question" and thus became the spiritual leader of the most radical tendency within the antisemitic groups; von Petersdorff, *Die Vereine*, [3]1900, p. 12, where the *Börsen-Courier* quotation also appears.

[28]Reprinted in Boehlich, *op. cit.*, pp. 204–206. Signatories are given in Liebeschütz, *Das Judentum im deutschen Geschichtsbild von Hegel bis Max Weber*, Tübingen 1967 (Schriftenreihe wissenschaftlicher Abhandlungen des Leo Baeck Instituts 17), p. 341.

that our culture has overcome the isolation of that tribe which once gave to the world the worship of the One God. Already there is heard the call for emergency laws and the exclusion of Jews from this or that profession or employment, from distinctions and positions of trust. How long before the mob joins in?"[29]

On 17th November, the *Post* printed Treitschke's public rejection of the "defamation" of his lectures and "academic honour". He did not consider that his statements as a publicist on the German Jews had been refuted. Not all signatories of the *Notabelnerklärung* intended the relevant part of the text to refer to him.[30] Mommsen's prompt rejoinder was a personal declaration in the *Nationalzeitung* of 19th November: he had signed the declaration in the full knowledge "that this reproach primarily referred to Herrn von Treitschke". Treitschke was shifting the attack on him as a publicist on to the protected ground of the freedom of academic teaching. However, the signatories had assumed that Treitschke the academic teacher would not contradict Treitschke the publicist, who was still maintaining his "gospel of intolerance" published in the *Preußische Jahrbücher*.[31]

Meanwhile the core of antisemitic Berlin students had founded a *Comitee zur Verbreitung der Petition unter der Studentenschaft* (referring to the Antisemitic Petition). Law student Erich von Schramm[32] became prominent as its leader and the committee exploited the excitement caused among the students by the clear-cut embodiment of the opposed political positions in the persons of Professors Treitschke and Mommsen. On 19th November students attending Treitschke's lecture demonstratively applauded his entry. Von Schramm then proposed a cheer for the esteemed professor. The ensuing roar drowned out a few critical voices, followed by distribution of pamphlets held in readiness, together with the text of the students' petition and lists for signature.[33]

On 20th and 22nd November, amidst continued agitation in Berlin, Leipzig and other university towns for student participation in the petition, a debate on the *Antisemiten-Petition* was held in the Prussian Lower House.[34] This had been forced by Professor Albert Hänel, a member of the Left-Liberal *Fortschrittspartei*, as a means of making the Prussian government definitely withdraw from the promoters of the petition, who had up till then been able to assert without contradiction that Bismarck, Chancellor of the Empire and Prussian Prime Minister, looked favourably on the petition. The Prussian Ministry of State, however, took refuge in the evasive answer that there was no intention of changing the law giving equal rights to religious confessions.[35]

[29]Boehlich, *op. cit.*, pp. 204–206.

[30]*Ibid.*, pp. 206f.

[31]*Ibid.*, pp. 210f.

[32]Erich von Schramm, born into a Catholic noble Silesian family, son of a Prussian officer, himself a lieutenant in the 1870/1871 war and therefore afterwards a mature student, was the political leader of the *Kyffhäuser* movement, whose independence from the various antisemitic political groups he militantly enforced. The KV also has to thank von Schramm for finding a positive identity ("pure national", monarchistic, favouring authoritarian social reform) and restraining orthodox Protestant influence.

[33]See von Petersdorff, *Die Vereine*, ^{2}1895, p. 24.

[34]*Die Judenfrage im preußischen Abgeordnetenhause. Wörtlicher Abdruck der stenographischen Berichte vom 20. und 22. November 1880*, Breslau 1880.

[35]*Ibid.*, p. 4.

For its effect on public opinion, the parliamentary debate must also be considered a failure for Left Liberalism. The rejection of the motion condemning the *Antisemiten-Petition* agreed by the Conservative parties and the Catholic *Zentrum* gave support to antisemitism. The *Zentrum*, in particular, displayed blatant satisfaction at the opportunity of getting even with Liberalism. The party declared that the motion was biased in seeking equal rights for Jews, while Catholics were, as ever, still oppressed by Liberals. The Jews were not a weak minority in need of protection: in fact, "progressive Jewish terrorism" reigned in areas of particular antisemitic unrest.[36] Thus by the end of November 1880 the Prussian parliament had given clear and open confirmation that once again a "Jewish Question" existed.

The actual organisational head of the students' petition was still Dulon in Leipzig. On 15th November, he and 27 other students began the work of the Leipzig "Committee",[37] which sent other universities the texts of the general petition, the students' rider to it, the lists for signature and subsequently reports of an antisemitic students' meeting on 22nd November. The students' rider read:

> "German students believe that they must not lose the opportunity of adding their support to the feelings expressed in what has been said above, although their civic position and their point of view on social questions might not allow them to support every single demand. This is done in the full knowledge that the continuation of the struggle to maintain our nationality will to no small extent one day be put into their hands, and in the conviction, based on this fact, that the proclamation of their opinions in this place and at this time will help to strengthen the hope of an abiding success and increase the joy of creation among those circles of the people who are effective today."[38]

An accompanying letter was designed to win over the hesitant:

> "Whatever the difficulties, objections and doubts which might be raised against us from any side, we are secured by this slight amendment. This at least is the belief of one of our professors in Berlin who, by his status as academic teacher, statesman and representative of the people, certainly possesses an authority in this matter second to none. We, the students who first broached the matter in Berlin during the vacation, asked his advice in particular on whether such an amendment was opportune and also concerning our procedure in general; his very friendly and detailed reply to us ended with the words: 'Not only do I see no reason to dissuade you, rather do I wish you all possible success'."[39]

[36] *Zentrum* delegate Bachem, *ibid*, pp. 81f. For Virchow's contribution, see Kampe, 'Jewish Students', p. 375.

[37] See von Petersdorff, *Die Vereine*, [3]1900, p. 13.

[38] Three different editions were issued: *Die studentische Petition als Annex der allgemeinen Petition betreffend die Einschränkung der jüdischen Machtstellung. Bericht über die am 10. Dezember zur Besprechung der Frage privatim abgehaltenen zweiten Versammlung herausgegeben auf Grund des Protokolls*, Leipzig 1880, here pp. 4f; *Die studentische Petition als Annex der allgemeinen Petition betreffend die Einschränkung der jüdischen Machtstellung. Ein Beitrag zur Orientierung über Gründe und Zweck derselben*, Leipzig, [2]1881; *Die studentische Petition als Annex der allgemeinen Petition betreffend die Einschränkung der jüdischen Machtstellung. Reden gehalten am 22. November und 10. Dezember*, Leipzig 1881, pp. 30f. And see Ludwig Quidde, *Die Antisemitenagitation und die deutsche Studentenschaft*, Göttingen 1881, p. 13. Quidde had tried to fight student antisemitism in Göttingen. For his life as historian and later leading pacifist see Reinhard Rürup, 'Ludwig Quidde', in Hans-Ulrich Wehler (ed.), *Deutsche Historiker*, vol. 3, Göttingen 1972, pp. 124–147.

[39] From Mommsen, 'Auch ein Wort', in Boehlich, *op. cit.*, p. 225. On 15th December Mommsen had already added this quotation to the third edition of his pamphlet, issued because of heavy demand, and had called upon Treitschke to deny it. For Treitschke's evasive attitude, see the quotation from *Preussische Jahrbücher*, in Boehlich, *op. cit.*, pp. 232f.

By 25th December 1880 the agitation of the students' Leipzig "Committee" had resulted in 1,022 signatures for the petition. By mid-January 1881, about 1,700 students had signed in Berlin, some 41% of those enrolled. Other "Committees" reported on student signings: Göttingen some 400 (nearly 41%), Halle 350 (about 29% of the students), Kiel 80. There were said to be successes in Rostock, Tübingen and Erlangen. Despite strong agitation, failures were experienced by "Committees" in Jena – a stronghold of the *Burschenschaften* stemming from the Liberal and national unification *Vormärz* movement – and in Königsberg.[40] A direct link might be suspected between the number of Jewish students and a readiness to sign, but this is at once countered by a glance at the statistics. Königsberg, 8% of whose students were Jewish, came third among the Prussian universities. The highest proportion of Jews was found in Berlin and Breslau, each with 17% of their students being Jewish; however, in Breslau no student came forward to support the petition. In Göttingen, Halle and Kiel – universities with strong support for the petition – the proportion of Jewish students was minute (between 1 and 2 percent).[41]

On 13th April 1881 the petition demanding a derogation in the legal position of the Jews in Germany and bearing some 265,000 signatures of adult male citizens, including some 4,000 (or about 1·5% of all signatories) on the independent students' petition, was presented to Bismarck. While throughout the Empire only about 0·6% of the total population supported the petition, almost 19% of all German university students did so.[42] The successful "Committees" now decided to turn themselves into a permanent student organisation. The name chosen, *Verein Deutscher Studenten* (VDSt), was an indication of policy: the new foundation was to rank higher than the existing student corporations and should be open for non-corporation students as well. That was why *Verein*, the more open form, was chosen, and not the more traditional *Verbindung*. In the superior interest of "national" orientation, it was to maintain strict neutrality on the inner conflicts of the student factions – for example, on questions of duelling. The first *Vereine Deutscher Studenten* were founded in December 1880 in Berlin, in February 1881 in Halle-Wittenberg, Leipzig and Breslau, in March in Göttingen, in May in the *Technische Hochschule Charlottenburg*, in July in Kiel and Greifswald. Reaction of the various administrations ranged from the friendliest cooperation from the very outset (Leipzig), to the other extreme of constant suppression (Berlin), where – as the following section will show – the VDSt was permitted only in April 1882 following massive intervention by the Prussian Minister of Education.[43]

[40]*Die studentische Petition*, [2]1881, p. 31; von Petersdorff, *Die Vereine*, [3]1900, pp. 12–15.

[41]See Kampe, 'Jewish Students', Table IVa.

[42]Richard S. Levy, *The Downfall of the Anti-Semitic Political Parties in Imperial Germany*, New Haven – London 1975, pp. 21–23. No "official result" was ever announced by the promoters of the student petition. In sporadic later reports the number 4,000 was mentioned. See *Der Kyffhäuser 1* (1898), pp. 1f; Paul Blunk (ed.), *Praktisches Handbuch des Kyffhäuser-Verbandes der Vereine Deutscher Studenten*, Hamburg 1926, p. 18. Individual results mentioned in the KV literature amount to 3,552 signatures.

[43]See von Petersdorff, *Die Vereine*, [3]1900, pp. 69–73.

II. THE STRUGGLE FOR ACADEMIC ACKNOWLEDGEMENT OF AN ANTISEMITIC STUDENTS' ASSOCIATION

On New Year's Eve 1880, an inflamed mob marched through Berlin's inner city shouting "Juden raus", mistreated what they supposed to be Jewish customers in two cafés and smashed one café's windows. As some papers reported a large student participation, Rector von Hofmann made enquiries of the police president and was told that "there had indeed been many students amongst the thousands of rioters", "but they had not been observed to have originated or borne a conspicuous part in these excesses, nor on the whole to have attracted particular notice by unseemly behaviour".[44]

In the winter semester of 1880/1881, the crucial appointments of academic autonomy in the Friedrich-Wilhelms-University – the rectorate, the academic senate and the university judgeship – were held by distinctly Liberal professors and determined opponents of the antisemitic movement. Consequently the Rector, the chemist August von Hofmann, rejected the application for admission as a student association at the University of Berlin made by the supporters of the students' petition. Following that refusal, on 18th January a "VDSt Berlin" was registered with the police in accordance with the *Bürgerliches Gesetzbuch*.[45] (On that same day, Theodor Mommsen, speaking at an *Allgemeiner Studentenkommers* in celebration of the tenth anniversary of the Empire's foundation, was forced to break off because of heckling by antisemitic students.)[46] On the Day of Commemoration, 25th January, a telegram saluting Bismarck was sent by the VDSt and evoked a friendly answer.[47] The Chancellor's basic strategy at that time was to create a new Conservative majority in the *Reichstag* by supporting populist and even demagogic currents.[48] In their addition to the *Antisemiten-Petition* the antisemitic students already offered themselves as allies to the forces of change in home affairs. This line was from then on consistently followed.

[44]HUA, file 602, pp. 28f; von Petersdorff, *ibid.*, p. 32. Jews "were turned out of" the Café National and Café Bauer, and the Café Bauer had a brick thrown through the window.

[45]HUA, file 638, p. 7. At the request of the Rector, the Police President had the assembly watched: in January and February 1881, between 300 and 500 sympathisers took part. The "Student Jewish Question" predominated: the student Lohan defined the purpose of the VDSt according to §1 of the statutes: ". . . to confront Judaism". HUA, file 638, pp. 24f. The student von Schramm regarded the "Jewish Question" from the "positive-Christian" and "German-national" point of view and came to the conclusion that the Jews had "proved themselves unworthy" of God's revelation in Christ, that the German nation did not have to be grateful to the Jews. In view of the answer found by England, France and Spain [sic] even before the nineteenth century, only Germany was lagging. A solution was necessary because of Jewish criminal tendencies, but a mixing of the races was rejected as impossible. Instead the position of Jews in public life was to be limited and if necessary "emergency laws against them" brought in; Jews were to emigrate from Germany. *Ibid.*, pp. 26–28 (assembly on 13th January 1881), further minutes pp. 29–33.

[46]Michael Doeberl, Otto Scheel *et al.* (eds.), *Das Akademische Deutschland*, 4 vols., Berlin 1930/1931, here vol. 2, p. 542.

[47]Ernst Hunkel, *Der Verein Deutscher Studenten zu Berlin. Wesen, Ziele, Geschichte*, (H.1 der Deutsch-akademischen Schriften des VDSt), Berlin [2]1912, p. 13.

[48]For Bismarck's cynical exploitation of antisemitism, see Hans-Ulrich Wehler, *Bismarck und der Imperialismus*, Köln [3]1972, pp. 464–474.

It was in January 1881, too, that the first student counter-movement to antisemitism crystallised into a *Comitee zur Bekämpfung der antisemitischen Agitation unter den Studierenden* of some fifteen members, which launched a kind of counter-petition of its own with a pamphlet against "the destructive effect of antisemitism".[49] On 31st January the chairman, the law student Oskar Schubert, was summoned before the Rector and university judge and declared that he had collected 400 signatures for the counter-petition. Although they must have been more in sympathy with this action, the Rector and judge set their faces against "any political activity" by students. Under this pressure, Schubert put it on record that his "Comitee" was in the process of dissolving itself. Further activity was unnecessary, given "the small part played at the present time by the antisemitic movement in university circles proper".[50] This, however, was wishful thinking. In June 1881 the *Freie Wissenschaftliche Vereinigung* (FWV) emerged from the "Comitee", and for over thirty years worked continuously against student antisemitism in Berlin. Moreover, it was the first port of call for Jewish students politicised by their fellow-students' antisemitism.

The meeting of the academic senate on 9th February[51] showed that the lecturers agreed with the stringent measure of forbidding membership both of the VDSt and of the *Comitee zur Bekämpfung der antisemitischen Agitation unter den Studierenden*. The reason given was that such activities by associations infringed academic laws. The University vice-judge, Professor Hinschius, suggested the radical step of public prohibition. He was defeated by six votes to five and a less spectacular action was decided upon, the discreet summoning of the two chairmen. So on 11th February Schubert and Lohan (as a representative of the VDSt) were summoned before Hofmann and Hinschius, to be informed of the Senate's decision. Further activities of either association would lead to *Consilium abeundi* (recommendation to leave): furthermore the VDSt was not permitted to hold the assembly already convened. On the same day Lohan informed the Rector that a protest was being sent to the Minister of Education.[52] Matters thus escalated contrary to the hopes of the academic senate. In their protest, Lohan and other VDSt members told the Minister of their "truly patriotic aims" and asked for his protection against the senate's decision:

> "We further believe it necessary to inform Your Excellency that all students of Christian and true patriotic German mind in this university feel that from the beginning of the semester they have been slighted."[53]

The struggle which now began between the senate and the Ministry of Education on the question of the academic dignity of the VDSt was to last until

[49]HUA, file 638, pp. 4f.

[50]*Ibid.*, pp. 17–20, 37–39.

[51]*Ibid.*, pp. 53f. The names of the members of this militant senate should be noted: Rector Hofmann, Vice-Rector Beseler, Vice-University Judge Hinschius, Deans of the Faculty Dillmann (theol.), Dernburg (jur.), Schröder (med.) and Zupitza (phil.), and Senators Kummer, Bardeleben, Weierstraß, Tobler – all of them were, of course, professors.

[52]*Ibid.*, pp. 41–45.

[53]*Ibid.*, pp. 57f.

summer 1882. At the outset the senate stood firm on its maximum position of imposing a ban, though later could barely maintain its minimum requirement of not losing face. Five members of the academic senate worked out an unusually long and detailed answer to Lohan's protest.[54] They rejected the allegation of bias by a detailed documentation. After listing the formal legal offences which sanctioned dissolution of associations, they pointed out that in 1878 the university administration and the former Minister of Education had completely agreed on the banning of Social Democratic activities. No precedent should be created allowing other political parties to establish student associations. The police reports proved that the meetings of the VDSt were not meant to serve the cause of learning but chiefly

> "to develop political agitation, namely with regard to the so-called Jewish Question, which in our opinion is suitable neither to further the academic training of the participants, nor in the national interest. The complainant Lohan, the former chairman of the association, himself had to admit that antisemitic agitation is the primary purpose, when he put it on record that 'I have to acknowledge that it is also our purpose to fight Judaism as a hindrance to national development and as an internationally directed element'."[55]

More than once they expressed concern that if there were further agitation among the students the senate's disciplinary methods would no longer be effective. The students had impertinently conveyed to the press and so to the public the Rector's every step; they had even reported that he was about to resign over a ministerial intervention in favour of the VDSt. Minister of Education von Puttkamer himself confirmed that prohibition of the association was correct in law but his political interest led him to a completely different assessment:

> "Should the VDSt now restrict itself to students of this university it would have to be considered permissible, since there is insufficient reason to suppose that the existence of the association automatically endangers discipline as regards the relevant contents of the statutes, especially as there have been no excesses necessitating intervention."[56]

Only those parts of the Minister's decision confirming the academic senate's view were passed on by University Judge Schulz to the VDSt chairman, who at once applied for approval in a new form adapted to the legal situation.[57] Meanwhile, however, the spectacular Förster-von Schramm affair had brought about a split within the Berlin VDSt.[58] This incident showed that the attitude of the students towards the different antisemitic tendencies had not yet crystallised. Seizing his chance, the Rector offered a dissident group (21 members in the first instance) academic admission under a different name (*Vereinigung der Studenten an der Friedrich-Wilhelms-Universität zu Berlin zur Pflege des Deutschtums*).

[54] *Ibid.*, pp. 62–69.
[55] *Ibid.*, p. 66.
[56] *Ibid.*, pp. 77f.
[57] *Ibid.*, pp. 85–88. File 619, p. 2.
[58] Bernhard Förster hoped to acquire considerable influence over the antisemitic student movement, which had been brought together under "his" petition. But in this he met energetic resistance from von Schramm. On 31st March 1881 he was beaten up by von Schramm and another VDSt member. The incident disclosed hostilities between the somewhat paranoic antisemitic cliques in Berlin; conservative groups threatened to move away from the VDSt.

On 5th May 1881 the Rector announced to the former administrative board that he could not allow a second association with the same statutes.[59] This manoeuvre, however, had no lasting success. The two wings were reconciled on 6th August 1881 at the *Kyffhäuserfest*, which generally brought the whole movement (as a useful ally) closer to the men in power.[60] In September the new Minister of Education, von Goßler, at Lohan's request ordered the Rector to facilitate "the unification of both groups" under the desired name. "A full semester has gone by" since the VDSt ban, so that it was impossible to discern continuity between the two associations bearing the same name.[61]

On 16th November 1881 a delegation from the senate negotiated with von Goßler in order to prevent a complete defeat. He could not be induced to change his mind and agreed only to examine written objections in which the senate mainly argued against the idea of a break in continuity. The union of all *Vereine Deutscher Studenten* in German universities on the occasion of the *Kyffhäuserfest* had proved that the old VDSt Berlin had continued to exist despite the existing ban. The students would consider an amalgamation under the old name as "a triumph won through the ministry over their academic authorities". In any case, having accepted the *Vereinigung zur Pflege des Deutschtums* the senate was making consolidation possible. By insisting on the old name the students, however, aimed at damaging the "reputation of the academic authorities", "whose maintenance in the face of rising emotion was highly desirable".[62] Nonetheless, the Minister of Education did not compromise and now even threatened to investigate the doubtful legality of the existing prohibition of the VDSt. In order to maintain their authority he would in any event leave the rector and senate to negotiate directly with the students. The academic senate now decided to make the best of the situation, and to present a façade of apparent strength and support from the Minister. On 27th January 1882 Judge Schulz once again confronted Max Lohan with all his offences, threatened him with immediate expulsion from the university if there were any further transgressions and finally offered him a way out by applying to change the association's name.[63] Naturally neither Lohan nor the other leaders of the Berlin VDSt were impressed. Since March they had been receiving confidential hints that powerful influences were working for them and against the academic senate.[64] The defeat of the senate soon became even more obvious when the

[59]File 638, pp. 92–103. File 619, pp. 16–24.

[60]For controversy with the Rector, see the highly conservative *Kreuzzeitung* (*Neue Preussische Zeitung*), No. 239 (12th October 1881), 244 (18th October 1881).

[61]HUA, file 638, pp. 114f., 124f.

[62]*Ibid.*, pp. 116f., 120.

[63]*Ibid.*, pp. 126–131.

[64]Through the influential *Zentrum* politician Geh. R. Müller, von Schramm was in contact with Count Wilhelm von Bismarck, the Chancellor's second son, who with his father's approval was close to Stoecker's "Berlin movement". The VDSt learned from him (letter dated 21st October 1881) that the Minister of Education had given an order to the Rector which was generally favourable to Lohan's petition. *Akad. Bll.*, 42 (1927/1928), pp. 74f.; and see Jarausch, *Students, Society and Politics*, pp. 267–269.

Prussian Minister of Education cancelled disciplinary measures against some VDSt members.[65]

From March 1881 to January 1882 a secondary battleground of Liberal professors and students against organised student antisemitism was the *Akademische Lesehalle* (ALH) – a kind of club and library open to F.W.U. students paying fees for a semester. A *Kuratorium*, consisting of six lecturers, supervised the students' directorate of the *Lesehalle*.[66] On 2nd March 1881 in a surprise attack, led by VDSt member Johannes Meinhold, the antisemitic students "conquered" the *Lesehalle* by "deposing" the directorate.[67] They had called an extraordinary general assembly on some pretext, having mobilised about eighty sympathisers by postcard;[68] only twenty or so astonished ALH-members were present to face this onslaught. The statutes did not permit an extraordinary general assembly to elect a new directorate and accordingly the "deposed" directors asked for help from the *Kuratorium*, which included the declared enemies of student antisemitism – Hofmann, Aigidi, Virchow and Mommsen. Rector Hofmann and Judge Schulz began a disciplinary investigation of the VDSt chairman, the law student Theodor Greving, successor to von Schramm who had "emigrated" from Berlin. At this stage, the VDSt had only been registered with the police. Faced with the threat of mass expulsion, on 7th March the new directorate presented its resignation to Hofmann and Schulz and handed over the "conquered" club funds.[69]

Those Berlin students politicised by antisemitic agitation now gathered their forces to fight for the leadership of the *Lesehalle*. In the ordinary general

[65]In May 1881, theology student Johannes Meinhold, son of a Protestant superintendent from Kammin, received the *consilium abeundi* from the academic senate for publicly calling the Jews "the lice on the body of Germany". After he had complained to the Prussian Education Minister in November 1881, he was rehabilitated. Compare von Petersdorff, *Die Vereine*, [3]1900, pp. 43f., 83. Meinhold went to Greifswald, where he became co-founder of the local VDSt. Consequently Rector Landois wrote to Rector Kleinert of Berlin: "We fear that under cover [of cultivating German national thinking] are hidden antisemitic aims". He asked if Meinhold had been expelled for antisemitic speeches and whether the Berlin VDSt was still involved in "insidious antisemitic agitation". HUA, file 619, p. 10. Meinhold later became Theology Professor in Bonn, wrote a history of the Jews and tried to prove the "Aryan" origin of Jesus.

[66]For the *Akademische Lesehalle*, see HUA, files 553, 554 *passim*.

[67]The events of 2nd March 1881 are not isolated, but in the general student assembly, by points of order or manipulation of speakers' lists, the "nationals" also achieved appropriate decisions. Compare the protests from the student body in HUA, file 602, Bl. 52–85. Although Rector Hofmann and University Judge Schulz did not sympathise with antisemites, they rejected all petitions against irregularities. In August 1881, there were as many as 320 student signatories, about half of them perhaps of Jewish origin, to judge by their surnames. For manipulations see also *Deutsche Hochschule*, 4 (1885/1886), p. 3.

[68]Besides pamphlets, postal invitations to vote were a feature of the post-1880 election campaigns; the matter came to a head when in 1888 the Rector declared the election result invalid because of "vote-buying". VDSt members could present postcards entitling them to repayment of the 5 Mark entrance fee provided they voted for the FWV. Compare HUA, file 553, Bl. 314–324. For the postcard campaign of the FWV in 1885 on the occasion of the committee elections compare HUA, file 602, Bl. 195. In 1886 both sides further developed the "knocking-up" system: sympathisers or members who had not yet voted by the last possible day were collected from their homes. See *Allgemeine Deutsche Universitäts-Zeitung*, 1 (1887), pp. 31f., *Akad. Bll.*, 1 (1886/1887), pp. 158f.: ". . . all Sem was on its feet and collected everything that was in any way usable".

[69]HUA, file 553, pp. 87–103, 106.

assembly on 17th March 1881 the opponents of the VDSt in their turn resorted to a trick. When uproar broke out between the two hostile camps, the old directorate got itself "elected" on the spot by its own men, the actual voting going unnoticed by the other students. On 11th July, yielding to protest, Rector Hofmann declared the election invalid. Nevertheless, he ordered that the directorate should carry on for the time being. However, the eagerly awaited election of 30th November was cancelled by the directorate because of inadequate accommodation in the university. In the two days, 28th and 29th November, the number of members had risen considerably from 506 to 837 and on the proposed election date another 250 or so new members joined. Hofmann allowed the *Kuratorium* to postpone the election, but at the same time forbade it to use accommodation outside the university. He expressed his fears that "student party politics had an effect on the academic *Lesehalle* incompatible with an institution maintained principally by university funds". It was for those reasons that the *Kuratorium*, together with the new Rector Ernst Curtius and the Senate, wished to reform the statutes and therefore again asked the directorate to continue.[70]

With such support the directorate itself began to doubt Hofmann's interpretation of the statutes; however, in view of this "unusual state of affairs" it was prepared to carry on. A letter of thanks from Hofmann on 8th December 1881, sounding almost as if written to colleagues, makes it abundantly clear how important it was for him to secure the *Lesehalle* from the clutches of the antisemites. Up to January 1882 new statutes were being drafted containing most extensive provisions for intervention by the *Kuratorium*. University Judge Schulz pressed for a quick decision to enable acceptance of the new statutes by the current directorate. After agreeing to the name VDSt and its statutes, Rector Curtius hinted that now the organisation had been academically admitted, "justice" to it should also be done in the matter of the *Lesehalle*. Upon this, Mommsen, Virchow and Hofmann demonstratively left the *Lesehalle Kuratorium*. Schulz, an opponent of the changes initiated by Curtius, vainly tried to persuade the new Rector to begin disciplinary proceedings against Greving, the VDSt chairman: he stated that Greving had protested about the *Kuratorium* to the Minister of Education and had included false statements, particularly about Mommsen. The new "entente" between the VDSt, Curtius and von Goßler could now no longer be prevented. Greving withdrew his protest before it reached the Minister and expressed his "full confidence" to the new rector.[71]

At Schulz's earlier suggestion the provisional directorate of the *Lesehalle* had made a statement countering Greving's protest. This commented on the allegation that favour was shown to "spezifisch berlinisch und jüdisch" members. In fact such members were, according to the directorate, in a minority of 2 to 6 in the summer semester of 1881 and 4 to 6 in the winter semester of 1881/1882. Following up these statements, which appear to tally with the names in the membership lists, this would mean that during the mass

[70]*Ibid.*, pp. 108–123.
[71]*Ibid.*, pp. 134–167.

joinings of November 1881 Jewish students not merely maintained the existing ratio, but increased proportionally from one third to two thirds.[72] In the election, at last held in January 1882, the Liberals gained a small majority of 452 to 377. The "nationalists" therefore at first withdrew from the *Lesehalle* elections and concentrated their forces mainly on the *Ausschuß der Studierenden*. However, in 1886 the "national" coalition took over the chairmanship of the *Lesehalle* directorate, retaining it until 1895 without having to meet any threat.[73]

III. "MODERN NATIONALISM" AND STUDENTS' PARTIES IN THE ELECTION CAMPAIGNS OF THE 1880s

Contemporary observers had already coined the terms "student antisemitism" and "academic antisemitism". The *Alte Herren* of the old traditional corporations looked with displeasure at student politicisation by the "Jewish Question", and sought to differentiate the nationalism of their own student days by speaking of "modern nationalism".[74] By this they referred to a development by no means already destined to follow the lines laid down by the 4,000 student signatures to the *Antisemiten-Petition* of 1881. Figure I does after all clearly show a marked falling-off in membership of both opposing associations, the VDSt and the FWV, after the excitement of the first tidal wave of antisemitism gradually receded. It would be very unwise to assume that the signatories to the students' petition were already manifest antisemites.[75] Naturally the political climate in the universities could not remain completely uninfluenced by the general trend towards nationalism and imperialism. But what must attract scholarly interest is the fact that it was apparently among students that the terms "national" and "antisemitic" first became synonymous. Such a development could not originate from short-term activity, but only by persistent agitation as carried out in student meetings and election campaigns under the leadership of the VDSt.

Content analysis of the sources shows that "student antisemitism" after 1880 made no special contribution to the "general" antisemitic ideology – apart from certain idealistic phrases. Its particular "achievement" was an infection of the student environment. Thence the antisemitic views, now a respectable *Weltanschauung*, reached the educated German middle classes – although it was not only the student body which played a part.[76] "Student antisemitism"

[72] *Ibid.*, pp. 148f. Membership lists from pp. 70ff. Until 1879 the *Lesehalle* was a fairly conflict-free institution of some 50 students.

[73] For election results see Table II and for membership see Figure II.

[74] See for example *Nachrichtsblatt für den akademischen Turnbund* (*Nachr.-Bl. ATB*), 12 (1898/1899), pp. 121–124.

[75] Quidde, *op. cit.*, p. 14, for example reported that at Göttingen student signatures to antisemitic petitions were more often collected at the beer table than in action meetings.

[76] Literary, artistic or scholarly traditions of this kind run throughout the nineteenth century. But about 1900 they lead to what may be described as a "cultural code". The student antisemitic "social norm", however, has its real origin after 1880, whereas later both sources finally meet in the *Bildungsbürgertum*.

therefore grew into a unique historical phenomenon, less for its content than because of its aims, methods and consequences. From the very outset the fight against Jewish fellow-students was of course its chief aim. As its first discussion of "practical action within the student body", the 1891 *Taschenbuch für die Mitglieder der Vereine Deutscher Studenten* sets out:

> "Both in the election of student representatives and in the administration of their office, in the midst of vehement agitation and with total success, we have endeavoured to ensure that they should interpret their office in the spirit hitherto developed. Moreover, we have always regarded it as a matter of special importance that Jewish students should be barred from offices representative of academic youth."[77]

To achieve this first objective the catchphrase, that Jewish students lack "national mentality", was repeated with prayer-wheel monotony. Proof was neither possible nor necessary. The idea was overall discrimination so that it would seem impossible that Jews should belong in the same association, or speak for the student body. At first the ideologists of student antisemitism abstained from extreme radical prospects of a "solution of the Jewish Question", either to set themselves apart from *Radauantisemitismus*, or because of the untimeliness of such speculations in face of the definite "tasks" chosen. With growing awareness of the severe crisis in the academic labour market of the 1880s, the antisemitic aim of isolation was now also applied to Jewish professional men. The motif of "Jewish competition" was now thrust into the foreground with the underlying insinuation that Jews were lacking in professional academic ethics:

> "[The Jews inhabit] our universities in vast numbers and so Jewish doctors push out Christians, Jewish mouths disproportionately emit jurisdiction and law, that is why journalism and literature bear the stamp of Jewry to an almost terrifying extent . . . Furthermore, the debasement of the legal profession by Jews, the degradation of juridical practice to 'business', and the resultant diminution of the people's trust in judges and the law, these are highly dangerous."[78]

In each semester, the meetings of the various faculties and – as the climax of the election campaign – a general students' assembly by a simple majority vote elected sixteen representatives in all to the *Ausschuß der Studierenden*. This committee afforded the students only a modest participation in the university administration of student affairs. However, in view of the declared aim of the VDSt to create "national" majorities, it was given an importance far beyond its real position and the student body became polarised in the election campaigns. Several duels took place: two of them arising from the student "Jewish Question" ended fatally. Both cases will be analysed in section IV below as examples of the way in which student conflicts were resolved.

From the outset VDSt members realised that they could not "conquer" the F.W.U. student committee by themselves. For this reason the winning over of coalition partners played a prominent role, especially as traditional corporation

[77]'Die Bestrebungen der Vereine Deutscher Studenten', reprinted in *Akademisches Taschenbuch für Theologen. Sommersemester 1892*, Berlin 1892, pp. 17–36, here 26f.

[78]Matthias Meinhold, 'Über die Stellung des Kyffhäuser-Verbandes zur Judenfrage', in *Akad. Bll.*, 3 (1888/1889), pp. 12f., 20f.

egotism had wrecked the originally planned supra-corporation association and the VDSt was reduced to just one of many corporations. Skilled coalition politics, however, were only possible against the background of an unprecedented internal *Verein* structure. Although in social matters student tradition was followed and each VDSt member was bound by the traditional student code of honour – that insults must be avenged with weapons (the principle of "unconditional satisfaction") – the political aim clearly had priority within the VDSt. On controversial traditionalism[79] – for example, the constant problem of the protection of honour (*Ehrenschutz*) for non-duellists – it maintained a strictly neutral attitude. Nor did it include coloured ribbons or caps, sabres or duelling rooms, *Bestimmungsmensuren* or *Schmisse*, the scars borne like caste-marks on the faces of students belonging to elitist fraternities. The VDSt was thus open to lower middle-class students. Through the amalgamation of local VDSt branches into the *Kyffhäuserverband* (KV), the institution of annual meetings gave a means of disciplining associations which threatened to deviate from the "black principle" and the priority of the political over the social. The attitude of neutrality meant that political pacts rising above the organisational fragmentation of the student corporation system could be created between fraternities, associations, and even non-corporation students, and in these pacts the VDSt then assumed a key function. The KV, with its clear leadership structure, determined and long-standing pursuit of political aims, strict co-ordination of decision-making processes, establishment of offices for particular tasks, continuity ensured by close cooperation between *Alte Herren* and *Activitas*, and a brilliantly edited association organ (*Akademische Blätter*, beginning 1886), had an undoubted advantage over competitors and opponents.

The elections of January and March 1881 had shown that the VDSt could muster a majority.[80] The breakthrough was achieved by bringing together the first major coalition of "national" fraternities in May 1881, with a triumphant victory in all ballots; only once to be so clearly repeated, in December 1885. The general student meetings (permitted only up to December 1884) were judged by the members attending the largest student forum for political debate; and here the "nationals"/antisemites always got their candidates through. The theological was of all faculties their unchallenged stronghold. The majorities there were so obvious that the candidates were often simply confirmed by acclamation. The law faculty came next: here the Liberals, organised by the FWV, never reached more than half the number of their opponents' votes. On the other hand the medical faculty was a Liberal stronghold, probably due to the votes of the considerable Jewish student body, already to be seen there in the 1880s.[81] In medicine, moreover, the FWV had enjoyed a higher status than in any other faculty because of its honorary member, Professor Virchow.

[79]See Kampe, *Studenten und Antisemitismus*.

[80]See Table I.

[81]In the winter semester of 1886/1887, 481 Jews studied medicine, 38% of all medical students. For comparison 166 Jews (13%) studied law and 270 (13%) were in the philosophical faculty. See *PS*, 102 (1890), tables, p. 98.

The last faculty elections in December 1888 were generally looked upon as the first defeat for the "nationals", whose elected representatives were reduced to only three. Up to January 1885, they had usually numbered sixteen (once fifteen) and thereafter seven, with the prohibition of the general election meeting. One reason for this change was that the VDSt grew less able to integrate and its claim to leadership was increasingly rejected. In December 1883 for the first time a "national" splinter party, the *Mittelpartei*, managed to win over the large philosophy faculty; its 484 votes approached the 597 votes of the VDSt-coalition in the general election. The *Mittelpartei*, however, did not develop a programme of its own and immediately fell apart again.[82] In December 1887 even the traditionalist fraternity wing organised a *Couleurverband* and put up a list of its own. In July 1888, *Akademische Blätter* lamented:

> "In Breslau, in Leipzig, in Greifswald, in Berlin, in Halle, and so on, everyone joined us unreservedly. Shoulder to shoulder with the DC, the LC, the *Akademischer Turnverein Borussia* and other colour-wearing fraternities, as well as the majority of associations, we have fought the FWV and their adherents here in Berlin. . . . For others' benefit we have always fielded only a minute number of candidates, although we could have put up more . . . The FWV naturally fishes in troubled waters. It turns everything to its greatest advantage, laughing up its sleeve the while. What is lost to the national spirit in the student body is of course won by international Jewry . . . Our information is that in the latest *Lesehalle* election 90 out of 100 votes for the FWV were Jewish."[83]

Although the particularism of the traditional corporations led to a weakening of the VDSt coalition, this is not to say that "modern nationalism", that is, VDSt antisemitism, was rejected. On the contrary, simultaneously with antisemitism beginning to detach itself from the VDSt as the main representative, it was starting to spread. This is particularly well shown by the example of the large *Akademischer Turnverein* (ATV), which officially had taken part in the *Kyffhäuserfest* in 1881. In the 1870s, the "black" ATV Berlin had played a leading role as a strong opponent of student fraternities, attracting many non-corporation students. In June 1885 and December 1886 only by making concessions could it be kept in the VDSt coalition. In December 1888 the ATV managed to create a coalition of student associations under the title *Neue Mittelpartei*[84] to withstand leadership claims of the VDSt. The *Mittelpartei*, although its pamphlets stated that safeguarding student interests had nothing to do with party politics, nevertheless in practice maintained the policy of excluding the Jews, not considered as social equals.

The swing to antisemitism in the student *Activitas* of corporations with long-standing traditions rarely met with the approval of the *Alte Herren*. In the 1880s students silently arranged matters at local level on their own initiative simply by no longer admitting Jewish fellow-students, not seeking any formal decision

[82]E.v.F., 'Die deutschen Hochschulen und der deutsch-nationale Gedanke', *Neue deutsche Studentenzeitung* (*Neue Dt. Stud.-Ztg.*), 1 (1884), No. 8 (February). The author almost implores all corporations not completely allied with the VDSt to ensure for the *Mittelpartei* a strict organisation and discipline, comparable to that of the VDSt "which almost by itself dominates the whole student body".

[83]See von Petersdorff, 'Die Notwendigkeit der allgemeinen Studentenversammlungen in Berlin', in *Akad. Bll.*, 3 (1888/1889), pp. 65f.

[84]See Table I.

at *Kartell* level on the "Jewish Question". The *Alte Herren* themselves, hoping that the antisemitic wave would pass, on the whole tried to avoid this explosive topic. For this reason, it is particularly interesting that, ten years earlier than in other large student *Kartelle*, matters led to an outburst in the Berlin ATV, described in its fiftieth year *Festschrift* of 1910 as "the worst internal crisis that the ATV has ever undergone". The last straw was said to be the refusal to admit a student named Löwenthal, so that "the cup of displeasure, filled to the brim, overflowed".[85] Some (all Jewish?) *Alte Herren* tried to make the *Activitas* issue a clear statement against antisemitism.[86] However, students voted by 93 to 49 votes against taking any attitude, "as it is out of the question that Christians should dominate Jews or *vice versa*", and members had equal rights under the rules of the *Verein*. This was an attempt by the students against being forced to distance themselves from the antisemitic student movement – in other words, from the general trend.

In December 1881, some *Alte Herren* wanted final clarification of the matter, but obtained no more than the students' promise to remain "neutral" in the "Jewish Question". Thereupon the *Alter Herr* Siegfried Isaacsohn organised, by way of demonstration, a "mass withdrawal" of Jewish *Alte Herren*.[87] It appears from twelve letters to Isaacsohn that none of those approached doubted the reality of an antisemitic shift by the ATV students. Only two refused to sign the resignation list and these on tactical grounds, saying that such withdrawals for similar reasons had taken place in "medical circles", but had only done harm. The matter should perhaps "also be discussed with Christian *Alte Herren*, so far as they were not notorious antisemites". At an extraordinary general meeting, the students decided on the following statement:

> "The club regrets the withdrawal of Jewish members and declares that it was far from its intention to bring about this withdrawal by measures which the *Verein* has recently taken."[88]

This is where the painful process of splitting between the students, now nationalist-antisemitic, and the *Alte Herren* began as early as 1881; ten years later it would become the dominant theme in all the important student corporations of Germany.

[85]ATV-Berlin (ed.), *Festschrift zum 50jährigen Jubiläum des Akademischen Turnvereins zu Berlin (ATV)*, Berlin 1910, pp. 99f.

[86]On 6th March 1881 the *Berliner Börsen-Courier* had called the ATV-Berlin "an association of evil repute among the more enlightened students" because of its antisemitic tendencies. And see von Petersdorff, *Die Vereine*, [3]1900, pp. 46–48.

[87]I should like to thank Dr. Daniel Nadav, Ramat-Gan, Israel, for the reference to Isaacsohn's activities as well as for allowing me to see his great grandfather's correspondence. Dr. Nadav is working on a biography of Isaacsohn and will publish in full the letters quoted here. Isaacsohn, 1845–1882, a doctor of history and professor, worked as an *Oberlehrer* in Berlin. His main work (suggested by his "teacher" Droysen) was the *Geschichte des preussischen Beamtentums* (1874 and 1878), reprinted 1962. Compare Kurt Forstreuter and Fritz Gause (eds.), *Altpreussische Biographie*, vol. 3 (suppl. vol.), Marburg 1975, p. 962.

[88]Nadav Archive. See also the letter on the mass resignations by the *Referendar* Mankiewitz of Suhl, 16th December 1881: "It is a mark of the effrontery shown by the antisemitic movement that any organisation should force its honorary members and *Alte Herren* into resignation."

Lastly, it must be asked whether the elections for the student committee do indeed enable a representative quantitative statement to be made about the attitudes in the 1880s of the whole Berlin student body to the "Jewish Question". Participation in the election doubled from approximately 18·5% in May 1881 to 36·8% of the student body in December 1888;[89] but even then well over half the students did not vote. Their attitude towards the battle between the two main streams of opinion cannot be discovered by this means. In all the excitement of those years, the massive electoral campaigns, the pamphleteering and the rest, it really is highly improbable that this "silent majority" had heard nothing of the altercation. In comparison with the previous peaceful decade, however, it is possible to speak of an unusually intense politicisation resulting from the conflict on the "student Jewish Question" in the 1880s.

After forbidding the elections for the committee in 1888, Rector Hinschius wished to emasculate the corporations and put the "silent majority" on a par with them, in the hope that the committee's work would become more objective. In preparation for these reform plans, he caused the existing committee to compile an exact list of each corporation's numerical strength.[90] Comparison with the election result of December 1888 shows that there were 513 more votes than the total of corporation students. (Not all corporation students would have voted, so that out of 4,040 non-corporation students over 513 must have voted.) Of these 513 votes, closer social links meant that the great majority (481) went to *Vereine* candidates and only a few (32) to *Verbindungen* candidates. On the basis of these figures only about 12·7% of non-corporation students as against 36·7% of all students[91] took part in the election. Up to 1914 any further reform attempts had to confront this quantifiable apathy among the mass of Berlin students.

What was the particular stance of Jewish students in the committee elections? Although available figures permit only an approximate answer, this is nevertheless quite astonishing, especially in view of the presumption that a minority under heavy pressure will close its ranks. Firstly it must be remembered that in the 1880s there was as yet no consciously Jewish party. In practice, however, only the FWV was acceptable to Jewish students. The reasons for this were the FWV's aim, which adhered to the Liberal concept of legal and social Jewish integration; its tactics of support in principle for all likely-looking opponents of the VDSt coalitions while renouncing a clear-cut position of its own; and also its membership structure. By a scrutiny of members' names, it may be estimated that in the summer of 1881 over half the FWV members were "Jewish" in the widest sense. In the summer of 1882 under the skilful and energetic philosophy student Max Spangenberg, membership numbers reached their highest point of 179 and the proportion of non-Jews seems to have increased temporarily to over 50%.[92] In his speeches

[89]See Table I.

[90]HUA, file 602, pp. 55f.

[91]Franz Eulenburg, *Die Frequenz der deutschen Universitäten von ihrer Gründung bis zur Gegenwart*, Leipzig 1904, p. 306.

[92]HUA, file 623, pp. 4ff. Estimated on the basis of "typical Jewish names", though here there must be some uncertainty.

Spangenberg opposed what he considered the slur by the antisemitic press that the FWV was a "bulwark of Jewry reinforcing the national, confessional or social exclusiveness of the Semitic offspring from the Memel to the Rhine". The FWV, he said, did not defend Jews as "a chosen people", but out of basic Liberal convictions. Over-emphasis on the "counter-antisemitic tone" would be "harmful to our basic idea".[93] However, as the "Spangenberg generation" took their examinations, they dropped out of the daily battle. As it lost members,[94] the FWV also lost its state of parity between Gentile and Jewish members. From summer 1887 onwards, it seems that all members were Jewish. Were the succeeding generations even of potentially Liberal students no longer inclined to belong to a *Verein* which included Jews? Or does this mean that it was the "counter-antisemitic tone" that finally determined the character of the FWV and that it failed to build up a positive identity?

While membership dropped and none but Jewish students was recruited, the FWV paradoxically retained its significance as the sole ever-present opposition to the "national"/antisemitic party. It always obtained the relatively highest number of voters from outside its ranks. For example, in December 1888, of 155 votes in the medical faculty, 81% or more came from outside the FWV (given that it had only 30 members altogether in all faculties !). At the general elections of January 1882, the first ballot produced 340 votes for the candidate opposing the first major "national" coalition, although FWV registered members numbered only 134. In December 1884, it achieved votes in the faculties, although limited to 7 law students, 13 medical students and 11 philosophical faculty members. At the assembly for the general election, this handful of FWV members with the addition of one theology student obtained as many as 628 votes. In January 1885, at a by-election in the philosophical faculty following the arrest of the FWV member Oehlke for "manslaughter in a duel", his ten colleagues could nevertheless muster 168 votes against the "national" candidate.[95] Such numerical discrepancy between members and votes in favour allows only one conclusion to be drawn: that individualism and nonconformism were far more widespread among the Liberals than in the "national" camp. Despite incessant attacks on them, the Liberal and Jewish students were unable to make common cause in forming any long-term political defence founded on some such model as the *Vereine*.

Focusing only on the simple willingness of the Jewish students to take any part at all in elections, this characteristic seems to have been astonishingly small, often even less than the average among all students. Remember that in the winter semester of 1888/1889, 925 Jews were studying at the F.W.U. Had most (not even all) of the 816 German Jews voted[96] this would obviously have changed the election result of December 1888. If every single one of the 155

[93]Max Spangenberg, *Der Standpunkt der "Freien wissenschaftlichen Vereinigung an der Universität Berlin" zur Judenfrage und zur Wissenschaft. Zwei Reden, 4. Juli 1881 und 30. Oktober 1882,* herausgegeben im Auftrage des Vorstands der FWV, Berlin 1882, pp. 18–28.

[94]See Figure I.

[95]See Table I, and note 92.

[96]See Figure II; for the following numbers see sources to Figure II and Table I.

votes for the FWV in the medical faculty had been cast by a Jew, then even this best possible case would mean that of the 455 Jewish medical students only 34% had voted, as against 42% in the medical faculty overall. For comparison, take the faculty elections in December 1886 (omitted in Table I); there were 481 Jewish medical students, but only 248 votes for the Liberal candidate, who must of course have received some unascertainable number of votes from non-Jews; similarly, Jewish law students totalled 166, yet only 92 Liberal votes were obtained; and with 270 Jewish students in the philosophical faculty, there were only 82 Liberal votes. The assumption that the mass of Jewish students automatically became politicised and joined ranks against the antisemites (at least in the committee elections) is therefore illusory.[97] Indeed their predominantly petty bourgeois class structure now emerges as a probable factor; expressed in the typical student behaviour of social climbers (*Brotstudenten* who went to university as a means to a career): beyond their studies and concern about making ends meet they could not summon up the (psychological) resources to share in a *civitas academiae*, which for them ultimately remained alien.[98]

IV. THE STYLE OF STUDENT DEBATES AND THE DUELS OF 1885 AND 1888

Any synopsis of the student disputes about the "Jewish Question", each of them in principle following the same pattern, would necessarily lend them an appearance of being raised to a theoretical and intellectual level never reached in reality. Accordingly, it is better to illustrate the style and atmosphere of the disputes by the example of a student assembly, by setting out the proceedings at the general student meeting on 10th June 1884, which was one preliminary to the Holzapfel/Oehlke duel. Up to this meeting, the press had described the election campaign as comparatively mild. Victory was made easy for the "nationals "/ antisemites, since no candidates were put forward against them – except in the medical faculty – by their unorganised opponents. The final general assembly, after five hours of speeches, ended at midnight with a motion by the FWV proposing (with a realistic assessment of its weakness) that, in order to shorten the voting procedure, the "national" candidates should simply be confirmed by acclamation.[99] "The assembly was opened by the law student Wölbling, committee representative of the VDSt, and conducted in such a way as to give frequent rise to sharp disagreements on points of order."

Wölbling was attacked by the law student Morris with the argument "that this committee, which is surely 'German-national' in the VDSt sense, has done nothing at all in national affairs". For example, it had not arranged student

[97]For the political inactivity of the Jewish students in the *Akademische Lesehalle*, compare the membership numbers of the ALH and the number of Jewish students in Figure II.

[98]For the social structure compare Kampe, 'Jewish Students', sections II and III.

[99]*Deutsche Hochschule*, 3 (1884/1885), pp. 3–5. The other quotations also come from the report of the Berlin correspondent of this Liberal Prague newspaper. A similar description is found in *Neue Dt. Stud.-Ztg.*, 1, No. 25 (1884).

celebrations on such anniversaries as 18th January (Foundation of the Empire) or 22nd March (the Emperor's birthday). Defending the committee, the law student Freiherr von Zedlitz (VDSt) "touched off extremely brisk debates" by remarking that the celebration of the VDSt foundation which had taken place in January had rendered a further reunion for state celebration unnecessary. Various speakers rejected as "outrageous" the expectation "that all our fellow-students should have attended the festival of a specifically antisemitic association". *Cand. med.* Mantzel "stressed that the actual aims of the VDSt were not at all national; antisemitism as well as Christianity was international and Herr Stoecker, the honorary VDSt member, had allied himself totally with the Hungarian and Russian antisemites. Why didn't the VDSt more exactly and more openly call itself the *Verein deutscher Antisemiten*?"

Freiherr von Zedlitz retorted that the VDSt members were not Stoecker supporters.[100] Out of all the *Reichstag* political parties, only the *Konservative Partei* had responded to their invitation. "There must be a distinction between 'crass antisemitism' and 'decent antisemitism'; in the first semesters of its existence the VDSt had admittedly been strongly antisemitic; since then, however, such opinions had sorted themselves out, and this tendency had long been overcome; the VDSt was not against individual Jews but against what it saw as the disastrous influence of Jewry. How that was to be broken was immaterial; he would be quite happy if it came about simply through Jewish assimilation."[101] He also pointed out that Count Moltke and the poet Julius Wolff had attended the celebration of the VDSt's foundation, which contradicted references to the party-political nature of the occasion.

The VDSt's opponents tried to show that antisemitism was temporarily being played down for mere tactical reasons, in order for example not to frighten off men like Moltke. The law student Freudenberg (VDSt) dilated on "the evil effect of Jewry and later reproached Herr Oehlke for having unjustifiably depicted the VDSt as antisemitic to the poet Wolff. When, however, Herr Oehlke questioned him energetically and asked for a clear answer to the question whether the VDSt was or was not antisemitic, after several attempts at evasion he admitted that he could not give an answer as the VDSt was not united on this question".[102]

[100]Only a little later Stoecker was invited to the "Bismarck-Kommers" of the VDSt and received much applause after his speech; compare *Dt. Hochschule*, 4 (1885/1886), pp. 3f.

[101]In 1884 the law student Heinrich Freiherr von Zedlitz und Neukirch – later government assistant judge and then district president in Konitz – was chairman of the Berlin VDSt. He was regarded as "extraordinarily moderate on the Jewish Question" (von Petersdorff, *Die Vereine*, ^{3}1900, p. 90), and saw it as a political rather than a racial controversy. As some of the associations in the *Kyffhäuserverband* shared Zedlitz's point of view, a basic clarification of the role of antisemitism within the union became necessary. The question was debated early in 1888 between von Zedlitz and *cand. phil.* Matthias Meinhold, reorganiser of the VDSt Göttingen and brother of Johannes Meinhold (see footnote 65), *Akad. Bll.*, 2 (1887/1888), pp. 161f.; 3 (1888/1889), pp. 12f., 20f. See Paul Blunk, *Praktisches Handbuch des Kyffhäuser-Verbandes der Vereine Deutscher Studenten*, Hamburg 1926, p. 318; and *idem*, 'Kyffhäuser-Verband der Vereine Deutscher Studenten', in Doeberl and Scheel (eds.), *op. cit.*, vol. 2, pp. 409–422 on the victory of the radical racial tendency within the KV.

[102]See note 99.

Several Jewish students immediately repelled Freudenberg's antisemitic attacks in a way which shows how easily verbal assaults could turn to deadly earnest: *cand. med.* Oppenheimer (of the *Hellevia* fraternity who, with the support of the FWV, had been elected in the previous faculty elections as the medical students' second representative) demanded that Freudenberg "if he dared to doubt [Oppenheimer's] national convictions, might wait upon him". *Cand. med.* Ascher (FWV) was still more vehement: ". . . [Herr Freudenberg should prove to the speaker] in what way he was damaging the German people and [Ascher] would be happy to give him the opportunity to find out 'that we not only feel German, but can also cause German feeling'."

The climax of the five-hour battle was a dispute about the extent of the honorary guests' agreement with the VDSt aims. Here, von Zedlitz (VDSt) and *stud. jur. et phil.* Alfred Oehlke (FWV) especially rose to the heights of bitter mutual hostility. With supplementary evidence from later court statements, a reconstruction of the battle of words can be made as follows: despite the widespread notion – even appearing in the press – that Field Marshal Moltke and two celebrated authors of the day, Julius Wolff and Ernst von Wildenbruch, supported the VDSt, *stud. phil.* Franz Ganske declared that Wildenbruch had not even been present at the VDSt *Kommers* in January 1884. He had been told by the author "that after hearing what kind of association it was, he would not attend; and that furthermore the poet Julius Wolff had subsequently declared that he went there without having any idea of the association's tendencies."[103]

To the growing outrage of the "national" majority in the auditorium, Oehlke declared that he had approached Wolff after the *Kommers* and obtained authority to declare that Wolff would not have taken part had he known anything about the association's antisemitic tendencies. When von Zedlitz doubted the truth of this statement, Oehlke affirmed it on his word of honour. On the following day Wolff, questioned by the VDSt, denied giving Oehlke the authority he claimed.[104] On 9th December, at the first post-vacation meeting of the newly-elected committee, the 15 members present voted for von Zedlitz's motion, commenting on the committee member Oehlke "who, with at best inexcusable irresponsibility, had falsely given his word of honour".[105] Hard-pressed by Wolff's cowardice in not making public his private dislike of antisemitism, Oehlke saw nothing for it but to restore his impugned honour by challenging no less than five committee members. The first duel, on 15th December, ended with *cand. med.* Michaelis being shot in the knee. On 5th January 1885, there was an inconclusive exchange of shots with von Zedlitz; but in the third duel immediately afterwards, VDSt member Richard Holzapfel died after the first exchange.

[103]Hans Paalzow and Johannes Rindermann (eds.), *Das Duell Holzapfel-Oehlke vor dem Schwurgericht. Stenogr. Bericht der Verhandlungen vom 18. März 1885*, Berlin 1885, p. 37.

[104]Wolff deposed that he had refused Oehlke the desired declaration against antisemitism and the VDSt: he had said "You will have understood me even without a declaration, and you can also tell your friends some time that I do not harbour antisemitic tendencies." *Ibid.*, pp. 26f. See also *Dt. Hochschule*, 4 (1884/1885), 22nd January 1885, p. 4; 20th March 1885, pp. 4f.

[105]See von Petersdorff, *Die Vereine* ([3]1900), pp. 192–198.

This event excited the German public in Berlin and beyond. The Rector and senate saw as the main source of evil the polarisation occurring at general student meetings; these were at once prohibited. Every corporation in Berlin (apart from the Protestant *Wingolf*, which set its face against duelling) sent official representatives to Holzapfel's funeral. Oehlke having been arrested, his seat in the philosophical faculty became vacant. The result of the ensuing election is perhaps a measure of opinion: the "nationals" regained it by 235 to 168 votes.[106]

In March 1885, more headlines were made by the trial of the duellists – and especially by its remarkable outcome. All such trials saw a clash between bourgeois legal norms and the feudal code of honour. Often enough, juries, prosecutors and judges had accepted the code of honour as mitigating the offence, making it a case of necessity: light sentences had therefore been imposed. When Oehlke, von Zedlitz and Michaelis were tried, the prosecutor several times attacked the indulgent treatment of duellists in similar proceedings. The judge expressly instructed the twelve jurors – two *Rittergutsbesitzer*, one manorial bailiff, four (small?) businessmen, another aristocrat, the rest apparently being petty bourgeois – that their only duty was to decide on the fact of a criminal challenge to a duel, or participation or manslaughter in a duel; it was he who would pass the sentence. Nevertheless and despite the accuseds' own statements, the jurors found von Zedlitz and Michaelis not guilty of taking part in a duel. Oehlke, however, was found guilty on all counts, and was sentenced to four years' imprisonment in respect of the two duels – in which, the jurors had declared, von Zedlitz and Michaelis had taken no part. So the plea of necessity in a case of honour was accepted from only one side: this was sensational indeed. Was the verdict an expression of the jury's attitude on antisemitism? The question of antisemitism had several times been raised during the trial.

A second melodramatic duel, leading to the total abolition of an elected committee as a student body, was sparked off in the committee meeting of 1st December 1888 by Hugo Blum, a representative of the medical faculty. He declared it to be a disgrace that the VDSt could exist in the university when its only *raison d'être* was to follow the course of antisemitism. In reply to Eichler and Sänger, the two VDSt members present, Blum deliberately left open the question whether membership of the VDSt, too, was a disgrace. When he refused to retract, Eichler and Sänger challenged Blum "to a threefold exchange of shots with drawn pistols at ten paces". Nothing happened in the first exchange with Eichler and the arrival of a policeman put the parties to flight. The morning of 11th December in the Grunewald saw the third meeting: Blum was fatally wounded in the liver. It was said that he violently rejected attempts at reconciliation made by the seconds and neutrals.[107]

Publicity about this new case even exceeded that provoked by the Holzapfel-Oehlke duel. With an eye to defence, the *Akademische Blätter* portrayed Blum as a Jewish rowdy, a playboy who had fought over twenty duels, some with sabre and pistols. Blum's face, they said, was all distorted by duelling scars. He

[106]See Table I.

[107]*Akad. Bll.*, 3 (1888/1889), p. 157; von Petersdorff, *Die Vereine*, [2]1895, pp. 264–267.

had taken careful aim at the myopic Eichler. Following this, the public prosecutor extenuated Eichler's action under the notorious "necessity of honour" and the sentence handed down was two years' imprisonment. Moreover, all the jurors signed a petition for clemency, granted by the Emperor only six months later. For his challenge, Sänger was given seven days' imprisonment.[108]

However, the academic senate under Rector Paul Hinschius showed no mercy: Eichler and Sänger were immediately expelled from the university. A student member of the *Akademische Blätter* editorial staff was threatened with expulsion: but responsibility for the journal was immediately transferred to some VDSt *Alte Herren*, so taking it out of the Rector's control. Within days of the fatal duel all committee members were obliged to pledge their honour to University Judge Daude not to engage in any duel arising from discussions in the committee. From now on, the Rector decreed that the protection of committee members' honour (*Ehrenschutz*) should remain in his hands. Despite these precautions, Hinschius still regarded the situation as so tense that he eventually forbade the faculty elections due in Spring 1889.[109]

Rector Hinschius hoped to exploit the situation for a general reform of student representation: he also wished to democratise and depoliticise the committee. An active opponent of antisemites since the time of Rector Hofmann, he now embarked on a new strategy. As direct suppression of the "national" students was not politically possible in the face of the Ministry's opposition, it seems that he wished to activate counter-forces within what had so far been the "silent majority" of students. He tried to win over the academic senate by arguing that 740 corporation students were guaranteed seventeen representatives in the committee, while 5,000 non-corporation students had in recent days been able to vote only in the election of nine faculty representatives – and even these were mainly corporation students. He felt that elections, the cause of so much student excitement, were too frequent and simple majority decisions provoked many quarrels; pamphleteering should incur a special penalty. The main reason for Blum's attack on the VDSt had been its election pamphlet attacking Jewish students.[110]

In May 1889, academic senate representatives negotiated with Education Minister von Goßler, who ultimately agreed to "defeudalise" the committee. The corporations, however, refused to acquiesce in an abrogation of their power, and with rare unanimity fulminated against the "imposed statutes" and the downgrading of the committee to a "tool of the Rector". The committee chairman's duty to patch up affronts or report them to the Rector was rejected, it was "tale-telling". In the Rector's view, every challenge to a duel arising out

[108] *Akad. Bll.*, 3 (1888/1889), pp. 161f., 178f., 181; 4 (1889/1890), pp. 5, 51, 94; *Der Zweikampf Eichler-Blum. Stenographischer Bericht über die Verhandlungen des Schwurgerichts*, Berlin 1889. In the university year 1890/1891, Eichler achieved another "important national feat" in Leipzig by organising a collection to present an *Ehrenhumpen* (i.e. a beer mug) to Bismarck. Later he became editor of the *Deutsche Zeitung*. See von Petersdorff, *Die Vereine*, [3]1900, pp. 277f.

[109] HUA, file 602, pp. 295–297.

[110] HUA, file 604, pp. 1–32, 36–47.

of a committee meeting should entail immediate expulsion from the university. In reply, the corporations boycotted the elections at the end of 1889. The mass of non-corporation students could not yet use this chance of freeing themselves from tutelage. The question of reinstatement of the committee was now shelved.[111]

V. THE REACTION OF THE LIBERAL AND JEWISH BILDUNGSBÜRGERTUM IN THE CAPITAL

Under Rector Hofmann, the university administration in Berlin certainly fought a respectable fight against student antisemitism. It may, however, be doubted whether the highly political character of the whole procedure ever occurred to them. They saw their Liberalism to some extent as the politically neutral "normal position" and in other respects adhered to the traditional fiction of the university as an area of purely scholarly activity, an area free of politics. Rector and senate reacted, not politically, but on the level of order and disciplinary law, where, however, the Minister of Education had the last word as an immediate superior. The Prussian government, though, very clearly also wanted a move towards anti-Liberalism within the universities and saw the nationalistic-antisemitic student movement as a force for this end. Rather than using the initial vantage-point of university self-government and strengthening potential opposition within the student body, Rector, senate and university judge acted on the concept of "neutrality" and paralysed Liberal student activity. The "nationals" themselves, on the other hand, could be certain of sympathetic promotion from the "very highest" positions.

When Ernst Curtius (an internationally-acknowledged classical scholar) took over the rectorate, the politics of the old senate had reached an impasse. He believed the solution lay in upgrading the VDSt to a fraternity with equal rights. He may have hoped to depoliticise it by an incorporation into academic life. The VDSt reacted gratefully, even making Curtius an honorary member in the winter semester of 1882/1883.[112] It seemed that "domestication" had proved successful: but the "nationals" did not for one moment intend abandoning their primarily political character. Curtius was pained by hostility on the part of Liberal colleagues and their demonstrative resignation from the academic administration. In March 1882, however, he thought that he had managed to ease the tense situation at the F.W.U.:

> "In doing this I discovered that party differences among professors are far more bitter than among the young, whose representatives have proved to be much more sensible and conciliatory."[113]

[111] *Ibid.*, pp. 83–99. For press criticism of the "imposed" statutes see *Das Volk*, 14th November 1889 and *Vossische Zeitung*, 20th November 1889.

[112] With the other honorary members – Treitschke and Adolph Wagner (the political economist and Stoecker's ally in the Christian-Social Party) – Curtius was regarded as the truest and longest-standing friend of the Berlin VDSt; see Ernst Hunkel, *Der Verein Deutscher Studenten zu Berlin. Wesen, Ziele, Geschichte*, (vol. 1 of the Deutsch-akademische Schriften des VDSt), Berlin [2]1912, p. 10.

[113] Ernst Curtius, *Ein Lebensbild in Briefen. Neue Ausgabe von Friedrich Curtius*, vol. 2, Berlin 1913, pp. 166f.

The new course begun by Curtius was followed by his successors. It was of course much less trouble from the outset to avoid conflict with the Ministry and the side effects of subtle reduction in the authority of the academic administration. Of later rectors, only Paul Hinschius, Wilhelm Foerster and Rudolf Virchow did not follow this pattern and did not accept antisemitism as a political demand of "national"-minded youth. In addition, in 1885 the late University Judge Schulz was unfortunately succeeded in this important post by Paul Daude, who regarded himself as a long arm of the Education Minister and worked against the now rare Rectors of decidedly Liberal views. The *Kyffhäuser* movement was, as intended, successfully incorporated into academic life, but the VDSt, now upgraded, had a splendid position from which to carry on its incessant agitation against Jewish fellow-students – of course, completely according with the letter of "academic" forms. With minds fixed on conventional loyalty the ultimately disastrous effect of student antisemitism was lost sight of. An 1886 statement of Rector Kleinert on the Berlin VDSt is a key document for the attitudes of the various Rectors.[114] In this Kleinert frees the VDSt from its political and moral responsibility by explaining that polarisation (at that moment spectacularly obvious because of the fatal Holzapfel-Oehlke duel) arose from a more or less natural "difference of race and instinct" and from the effect of "extreme" party leaders. By this, however, he was not referring to Stoecker, Foerster, Henrici or to other leaders of antisemitic parties, but to Left-Liberalism ("a progressive body of opinion specific to Berlin against Conservative-patriotic movements in the student body"). How did the alleged "progressive Berlin" really react to student antisemitism?

The special situation of *Abwehr* against antisemitism in the academic world was derived from the "national" camp's strategy of punishing social communication with Jews by a reduction of prestige. All organisations of Christian-Jewish "parity" lived with this threat of sanctions. In 1882, the "Christian" FWV chairman, the student Max Spangenberg, described this recently encountered dynamic of "academic" antisemitism as a social norm:

> "It is precisely the diabolical effect of these brutal practices, not only to create a difference between Jews and Christians but likewise between Christian and Christian; and not least among students, for whom the question has often become one of social life. In obscure corners of the Wiener Café, on the open promenade of the Unter den Linden, wherever one goes, the first question on seeing an acquaintance is: Is he Christian? Is he Jewish? Is he pro-semitic? Is he antisemitic?"[115]

In November 1884 the educated Liberal middle classes of Berlin as a group reacted directly to the events at the F.W.U. by founding the *Akademisch Liberaler Verein* (ALV), intending to demonstrate solidarity between Christian and Jewish academics and the vitality of Liberalism as an intellectual attitude. The student founders of the ALV thought of themselves as the academic wing of the Left-Liberal party.[116] The ALV should therefore definitely not be reduced to the

[114]Staatsarchiv Marburg, Best. 305a Acc 1954/16 Nr. 70.

[115]Spangenberg, *op. cit.*, p. 31.

[116]At the beginning of 1884 the Left-Liberal *Deutsche Fortschrittspartei* (founded 1861) had just merged with a splinter group from the Right-Liberal *Nationalliberale Partei* to form the *Deutsche Freisinnige Partei*. See James J. Sheehan, *German Liberalism in the Nineteenth Century*, Chicago-London 1978;

character of a student corporation. The historical significance of the ALV in the record of organised *Abwehr* has not yet been recognised: it did in fact form a bridge of continuity between the November 1880 declaration against antisemitism and its promoters made by 75 prominent Berlin scholars, city administrators and businessmen, and the foundation of the *Verein zur Abwehr des Antisemitismus* in Berlin in 1893.[117] The ALV was in fact a direct predecessor of the *Abwehrverein* – although with limited aims: as an amalgamation of students and professional men, it defined its aim as averting the possibility that, because of indifference among a large part of the student body, "complete domination should be borne by one *Verein*" (meaning the VDSt)

> "which under the harmless flag 'German' and 'national' is sailing happily in reactionary waters. We are, however, convinced that there is still a considerable number of students of true liberal mind . . . Since a political association in the university would not obtain the acceptance of the academic administration, we have founded the *Akademisch Liberaler Verein* under the statutes governing clubs, which do not envisage a student form, but which only academically educated men may enter. Naturally any agitation by the club is out of the question."[118]

From 69 members in May 1885 (33 of them F.W.U. students), the association grew to 158 in February 1886 (65 of them students), and fell to 115 (48 students) in August 1886.[119] It became particularly effective in public through establishing academic assemblies, where well-known personalities were booked to lecture on political themes. Relatively high attendances were obtained, of 150 to 230 in 1885 and 1886.[120] The proud claim, based on these figures, to be "the largest academic corporation in Berlin" was rejected by the VDSt on the grounds that the ALV did not meet the definition of a "student corporation" and also because the Rector declined to give his recognition.[121] However it was described, by the late 1880s the ALV had become a factor in the capital's academic life, particularly from the point of view of quality: of the 158 members in 1886, 21 were *Reichstag* deputies; moreover, it included 35 doctors, 28 jurists, at least 21 in the mathematical, technical or scientific professions, but only 17 doctors of philosophy and students of the philosophical faculty and with only 3 theologians. Taking those members with more precisely-defined professions and noting which types appear most frequently (editors, merchants, writers, musicians), it is seen that the main

---

Gustav Seeber, *Zwischen Bebel und Bismarck. Zur Geschichte des Linksliberalismus in Deutschland 1871–1893*, Berlin 1965; Ludwig Elm, *Zwischen Fortschritt und Reaktion. Geschichte der Parteien der Liberalen Bourgeoisie in Deutschland 1893–1918*, Berlin 1968.

[117]The leading *freisinnig Reichstag* deputies and ALV members, Heinrich Rickert and Hugo Hermes, were among the 75 signatories. Rickert later became *de facto* and in 1895 also *de jure* leader of the *Abwehrverein* whose members also included National Liberals. The ALV on the contrary was clearly purely Left Liberal and in opposition to the Prussian-German government. As the ALV only accepted academics, only one leading politician, Ludwig Bamberger, can be mentioned. For further names see Liebeschütz, *op. cit.* (Notabeln). HUA, file 668, pp. 59–63, (members of ALV). Barbara Suchy, 'The Verein zur Abwehr des Antisemitismus (I). From its Beginnings to the First World War', in *LBI Year Book XXVIII* (1983), pp. 205–239, and see illus. between pp. 226–227 from the antisemitic *Politische Bilderbögen* in which the members of the Left-Liberal "*Judenschutztruppe*" are caricatured.

[118]From the pamphlet of about November 1884, distributed in the F.W.U., HUA, file 668, p. 2.

[119]*Ibid.*, pp. 45–73, *passim*.

[120]*Ibid.*, pp. 37, 82–91.

[121]*Akad. Bll.*, 1, No. 23 (1886/1887).

emphasis was on the self-employed and not on civil servants (probably fewer than 10 members were in the public services).[122] The high number of 21 *Reichstag* deputies was naturally a special case, explicable by the ALV's origins, but otherwise a comparison with the professional structure within the VDSt points up some revealing differences. In the latter theologians and civil servants, for example, clearly made up a higher proportion.[123] That the ALV did indeed maintain parity between members can be seen from the approximate proportion of 1:2 as between Jews and "non-Jews". Nevertheless it was of course dubbed the "Jüdisch-Deutschfreisinnige Partei", and the antisemitic *Staatsbürgerzeitung* talked of the "true Jewish endeavours which were to be found there".[124]

The foundation of the ALV immediately became a political stumbling-block as it threatened the Prussian government's long-term strategy of subduing the Liberal (*Bildungs-*)*Bürgertum* and its opposition to reactionary domestic politics, by means of its "sons", who had become nationalistic. The social and political elites of the capital really were split into two camps – roughly speaking, on the one side the *junkerlich* or re-feudalised government bureaucracy with allies from the *bourgeoisie*, and on the other the educated middle classes in the liberal professions and free-trade merchants, who maintained their position in the city council. While the conservative Prussian government flirted with antisemitism to test its populist possibilities, the Liberal Magistrature of the city of Berlin under Lord Mayor Max von Forckenbeck, who had initiated the *Notabelnerklärung* of 1880, removed the antisemitic agitators Dr. Jungfer, Dr. Bernhard Förster and Dr. Henrici from their posts as teachers in city *Gymnasien.*[125] How would the University rectorate, regarded as a bastion of the Liberal middle classes, behave in this field of tension between government and city? The ALV became a test case. Political activities of students to the left of *Nationalliberalismus*, which conformed to the regime, appeared intolerable to the Minister of Education. Social Democrat students were in any event subject to expulsion from the university and therefore had to disguise their opinions for fear of police and Right-wing student spies.

Rector Heinrich Dernburg and his successor Hugo Kleinert allowed themselves to be used by the Ministry without resistance. Dernburg argued that ALV registration with the police was inadequate, since after all its aim was to gain student members. Education Minister von Goßler called for information from the Rector and imposition of the strictest punishments. The Rector's ban on assemblies was enforced outside the university area with help from the Police

[122]HUA. file 668, pp. 59–63.

[123]In 1887, out of the 466 senior members of the *Kyffhäuserverband;* 162 were theologians; 44 of these held clerical appointments, the rest were awaiting ordination. 138 were jurists; only 8 of these were independent lawyers, 117 were assistant judges (therefore with careers still to be made). 13 were employed by the government or local authorities or were expecting to join the Civil Service. Of the rest, there were 72 philologists of whom 43 were in higher education or candidates for further degrees; 22 doctors (presumably independent). The remaining 72 worked mainly in public services, only 12 in trade or banking, 3 were factory owners and 12 farmers. *Akad. Bll.*, 2 (1887/1888), p. 182; 13 (1898/1899), p. 301.

[124]No. 176, A., 31st July 1886.

[125]Paul W. Massing, *Rehearsal for Destruction. A Study of Political Anti-Semitism in Imperial Germany*, New York 1967, p. 237.

President. On 16th December 1884, Dernburg announced that the ALV was illegal.[126] Now the outraged Left-Liberal *Bildungsbürgertum* of Berlin braced itself for an unexampled action; as a demonstration, large numbers from its ranks joined the ALV, averting the immediate threat to the student chairmen. In the same month of December 1884, the lawyer and *Reichstag* deputy Meibauer was elected as first chairman, the editor Dombrowsky as second. Another *Reichstag* deputy, Dr. Otto Hermes, the writer Franz Duncker and the lawyer Dr. Grelling became officers in the ALV.[127] Legal and parliamentary efforts meant that in March 1885 the decree of the Rector and *Polizeipräsident* was carried to an annulment by the *Oberpräsident* of the province of Brandenburg. Then Dernburg and von Goßler took the matter to the Ministry of the Interior: here, however, the conclusion was reached by the end of the year that it was not legally possible to reverse the *Oberpräsident*'s decision.[128] Though constitutional barriers and the massive efforts of the Left-Liberal Berlin *Citoyen* had prevented excessive spread of the Rector's disciplinary powers to persons and places outside the university, within the F.W.U. the new Rector nevertheless continued his predecessor's repressive course.

The Minister of Education for his part now hardly distinguished between Left-Liberal and Socialist students. Following the most insignificant press statements about ALV meetings, von Goßler demanded information from the Rectors Dernburg and Kleinert about "further excesses", as in his expectant enquiry in July 1886. As the Rectors could not show any "direct disturbances of university life" by the ALV, at least they had to provide addresses, nationalities and life stories of ALV students marked down as dangerous. The culmination of the witch-hunt was the persecution of Gustav Hoch, described as a student of "Mosaic religion". He had left the university, but spies said they had heard him making Social Democratic remarks in an ALV assembly. In Friedrich Althoff, an official adviser and future education minister, Goßler sent a key Ministry figure to University Judge Daude to take up Hoch's trail. University administrations throughout Germany became catspaws of the police and the Prussian education minister in order to watch the "dangerous Left-Liberal" Hoch. In March 1887 a namesake of his at Munich University temporarily fell victim to a macabre new version of *Demagogenverfolgung*. The motives of the Ministry did not really originate in antisemitism but they were anti-Liberal and anti-democratic within the general reactionary tendency.[129]

However, in its claim to establish a strong and lasting counterbalance to the "national" camp within the Berlin student body, the ALV did not succeed in the long run. The concerns of the party politicians rather seem to have been momentary image-creation and the demonstration of power. An important precondition of electoral successes in the university would have been to clarify its relationship with the FWV, since the ALV as a political club could not enter the university area. The FWV was after all the only student corporation which

[126]HUA, file 668, pp. 1–27.
[127]*Berliner Volkszeitung*, No. 300 (21st December 1884).
[128]HUA, file 668, pp. 30–56.
[129]HUA, file 668, pp. 64–69, 76–78, 95–136.

continuously represented the Liberal side. The representatives of political Liberalism, however, in effect ignored the FWV throughout the years. Rudolf Virchow and Theodor Mommsen did not represent their parties, but as lecturers had become honorary members of the FWV, that is, with "their" students. Of the two, incidentally, only Virchow supported the FWV continuously. Mommsen accepted only a few invitations to FWV events. He was on the whole a relic of the generation of Liberal *Honoratiorenpolitiker* – highly ethical in his thinking, quickly angered by "baseness", his reactions were ultimately unpolitical.[130]

With absolutely no justification, the "national" students had called the *Comitee zur Bekämpfung der antisemitischen Agitation unter den Studierenden* and its successor, the FWV, "a child of Eugen Richter" and of the *Fortschrittspartei*. A letter dated 18th January 1881 from Richter to Otto Hermes, his party colleague in the *Reichstag*, which by some means or other had found its way into the hands of the antisemites, was again and again referred to as proof of this.[131] Richter's letter surmised that the *Comitee* would be too clumsy to outdo the demonstrations of the antisemites. It suggested convening a general student meeting against the antisemitic student movement, at which various members of parliament might also appear as honorary guests. This letter alone speaks against the argument that the *Comitee* had a progressive origin. The FWV for its part always looked upon the ALV as a rather unfortunate competition, and had at most indirectly profited by votes from the ranks of the ALV students. It might also be suspected that the appearance of the ALV hastened the loss of the FWV's "parity" character, so that, in the eyes of the student body, it became no more than the party of "Jewish assimilants". Ironically, therefore, in the 1890s Liberalism within the student party spectrum was only kept alive by Jews and men of Jewish origin while by 1888 the ALV – the name which after all stood for the Christian and Jewish and educated Left-Liberal Berlin middle classes – had gone to sleep.[132]

VI. NEW STUDENT PARTIES AFTER 1892 AND THE WRECK OF THE "STUDENT PARLIAMENT" PROJECT ON THE "JEWISH QUESTION"

The colour-wearing student bodies in the post-1880 break-through phase of "modern nationalism" had been pushed to the edge of student political development. The call for a German *Weltpolitik*, first heard from certain areas of German public opinion in the 1890s, found a particular echo in the corporations. It was no accident that in 1893 the *Burschenschaftliche Blätter* began discussing the need for and path to an imperialistic modernisation of the political ideas in the student fraternities.[133] A continuity was inferred between the national ideals of

[130]For Mommsen's ambivalent attitude to the "Jewish Question" see Suchy, *loc. cit.*, pp. 225–227. See also Hermann Bahr, *Der Antisemitismus. Ein internationales Interview*, Berlin 1894, pp. 26–31.

[131]See von Petersdorff, *Die Vereine*, ³1900, pp. 32f. *Akad. Bll.*, 6 (1891/1892), p. 51.

[132]A last note about the chairmanship elections in the ALV appeared in May 1888 in *Akad. Bll.*, 3 (1888/1889), p. 42. The lawyer Dr. Grelling and *Privatdozent* Dr. von Kalckstein were elected chairmen; Franz Duncker, *Oberreg. Baumeister* Pinkenburg, *Sanitätsrat* Dr. Ehrenhaus and a lawyer named Jaffé became committee members.

[133]See *Bursch. Bll.*, 6 (1891/1892) ff.

the early *Burschenschaften* and the demand for imperialistic expansion and a claim was made for regaining the leadership of the student body. This discussion about the overdue modernisation of their own image took hold among all the traditional colour-wearing students and produced a race for the leadership. Whole fraternities entered the new imperialistic pressure groups (*Alldeutscher Verband, Kolonialverein, Ostmarkenverein, Flottenverein*, and others). In connection with this belated and therefore hasty determination of position, the debate about the *Kartell*'s official attitude towards the "student Jewish Question" was at last begun, having been delayed until now because of its threat to internal harmony. The result was an almost complete exclusion of Jewish students, even Jewish *Alte Herren*, from the German colour-wearing fraternities; the repercussions were felt in various *Vereine* – student, bourgeois- academic, and even petty bourgeois, completely outside the universities. Newly-founded students' *Verbindungen* and *Vereine*, for example the fraternities on the university model in the *Technische Hochschule*, at once adopted the antisemitic point of view to avoid the stigma of social inferiority and the risk of internal quarrels if Jewish students were admitted.[134] In this way, the antisemitic social norm, at least in fraternity circles, was already fully established before 1900. With the transition to imperialism, "modern nationalism" and with it antisemitism had been "raised" to a new, higher unity – in the Hegelian sense.

The *Kyffhäuserverband* of the *Vereine Deutscher Studenten* now suffered a severe crisis of identity, for its nationalism and antisemitism had largely been taken over. This could not be surmounted without curtailing its claims, the unique role of the KV in the transitional phase from *moderner Nationalismus* to *Weltpolitik* having been played out. As early as 1893, the *Akademische Blätter*, referring to the 11% loss of student members within a single year, declared:

> "Antisemitism was a strong magnet; since it is no longer the unique possession of the *Vereine*, the number of those attracted by it has diminished. The proportion between those drawn into the *Kyffhäuserverband* by chance and those drawn from genuine interest shifted towards the former. It is understandable that among them strongly-marked characters are generally rare. Thus our own interest urges us towards those further activities which our ideas already require from us. National thought does not stop at antisemitism."[135]

The student generation from the early days of the KV, now as *Alte Herren*, instructed their successors in the lasting significance of antisemitism, which as an immediate issue had retreated into the background, but only in that respect:

> "Because today the notion of *gesellschaftlicher Antisemitismus* has really more or less become a matter of course shared by all academic circles."[136]

[134]See details in Kampe, *Studenten und Antisemitismus*.

[135]Hans Wendland, 'Neue Aufgaben', in *Akad. Bll.*, 8 (1893/1894), pp. 25f.

[136]Karl Kormann, 'Wandlungen im Kyffhäuser-Verband?', *ibid.*, 5 (1910/1911), pp. 225f. For guidelines on antisemitism for their successors see for example, *ibid.*, 25 (1910/1911), p. 39. For the passages quoted, see Hans Wendland, 'Zur Ethik des Antisemitismus', *ibid.*, 11 (1896/1897), pp. 121f.; from 1892 to 1897 Dr. Wendland was editor of the *Akad. Bll.* and later of the *Kreuzzeitung*. As a racial antisemite, he enforced *völkisch* antisemitism within the VDSt and today may be regarded as the theoretician of a radical "academic" antisemitism. See also his articles 'Zur Abwehr', in *Akad. Bll.*, 11 (1896/1897), pp. 147–149; 'Zur Psychologie des Judentums', *ibid.*, pp. 161–163.

In contrast to "general" antisemitism as a "cultural code" without further intellectualisation, however, the authors of the KV, in adapting racism, claimed a particular scientific consciousness which could only "remain the exclusive property of the educated": although antisemitism had often been "characterised and treated as a catchword and attraction for the masses, they will never achieve a rational grasp of its true meaning . . .".

With the establishment of an antisemitic social norm in the fraternities, by about 1893 the first phase of "student antisemitism" had come to an end. All further developments took place in conscious awareness of widespread anti-Jewish attitudes. Two of these developments in the late *Kaiserreich* are especially important for the present topic: 1) from the ranks of hitherto passive non-corporation students, serving merely as a mass to be manipulated, emerged an anti-corporation movement: 2) a "Jewish party" came into existence as an express counter-foundation to the VDSt, based on positive identification with Judaism – this was the *Verein Jüdischer Studenten*, (V.J.St.). A third grouping, in which Jewish students cooperated in larger numbers, was the *Sozialwissenschaftliche Studentenvereinigung* (SStV), whose political classification lay between Social Democracy and *Kathedersozialismus* (represented by Professors Gustav Schmoller and Adolf Wagner). The SStV, like the ALV, was persecuted by the Minister of Education and the Rector, with the unsavoury assistance of VDSt members. The SStV entered election coalitions with the FWV against the "nationals "/ antisemites. However, after the turn of the century, politically active Jewish students increasingly joined the "Jewish party" and the movement of non-corporation students similar in structure to a trades union. The following brief synopsis down to 1914 restricts itself to these two new groups.

In the 1880s it had become clear to all students and professors with reasonably independent minds that, with the unceasing conflict about the "Jewish Question", a completely dysfunctional element had paralysed the politics relating to the interests of students. With his reform attempts in 1889, Rector Hinschius had hoped that those *Verbindungen* and *Vereine* almost totally identified with antisemitism would be deprived of power. He had, however, failed because of the political immaturity of the non-corporation students. What seemed a more favourable situation arose in 1892, when three older students thought that while the Rector, in the person of the astronomer Wilhelm Foerster, was a militant opponent of antisemitism, they could organise a movement among the "independent student body" on a basis of up to four thousand men.[137] Foerster supported the *Unabhängigen* to his utmost and in May 1892 decreed regulations giving complete equality for the election of a new

[137]Foerster was a signatory of the declaration of 1880 and became a longstanding member and vice-chairman of the *Abwehrverein*, as well as founder of the *Deutsche Gesellschaft für ethische Kultur*, 1892: see Suchy, *loc. cit.*, p. 223; Heinz Starkenburg, 'Die Bewegung der "Unabhängigen Studentenschaft" zu Berlin im Jahre 1892', in *Akad. Rundschau*, 1 (1896), pp. 32–36; Hans Weber, *op. cit.*, pp. 24–30; *Allgem. Dt. Univ. Ztg.*, 6 (1892), pp. 104–106, 124f., 135f., 155, 212–215, 222; *ibid.*, 7 (1893), p. 44; *Akad. Bll.*, 7 (1892/1893), pp. 175f., 192f., 207–209; *Nachr.-Bl. ATB*, 5 (1891/1892), pp. 132–137; 6 (1892/1893), pp. 8f., 57f.; Comite der Unabhängigen (ed.), *Die Bewegung der Unabhängigen Studentenschaft zu Berlin*, Berlin 1892.

student committee. A quorum of votes amounting to one-third of the student body should prevent the reconstituted *Ausschuß* from being dominated by small, determined groups. In June, Foerster permitted a general student meeting of the *Unabhängigen* within the university, the first general meeting since the prohibition in 1885. In consequence, it was thronged with representatives of the old parties as well, and the intended foundation meeting of the *Unabhängigen* was at once dominated by the VDSt and the FWV with the same old topics mooted since 1880 – the "Jewish Question" and "national thinking".

By the exclusion of corporation students from two more meetings, questions of organisation could be dealt with. But the call to the independent students of all German universities ("... who in contrast to old-fashioned traditions desired a vigorous reformation of all student life on a national and modern basis ...") to organise their interests had no sooner been formulated than the *stud. jur.* Sommerfeld attacked "the expression 'national' as characteristic of antisemitism, and found agreement among a large proportion of those colleagues who were still present".[138] The committee's proposal to replace the word "national" by *vaterländisch* was inadequate: on 23rd June, at the third meeting in the F.W.U. *auditorium maximum* controversies arose which simply could not be covered over by terminological cosmetics.

The Social Democratic wing rejected the word *vaterländisch* because science was international and, furthermore, demanded a vote on the declaration that the *Unabhängigen* stood for "a renewal of student life on the basis of the equality of all students without distinction of confession, nationality or race".[139] Loud applause greeted *stud. jur.* Philippsthal's protest at this: his reasons were that, precisely because he was himself a Jew, he must object to the attempt by the previous speaker and his "mostly Jewish supporters" to exploit the non-party movement of the *Unabhängigen* for the benefit of "philosemitic international Social Democracy". Antisemitism, the "old apple of discord", had nothing to do with the matter. The speech of the founder-member *cand. jur.* Hercher, representing himself as antisemitic, was very well received and probably marked the lowest common denominator of a purely pragmatic attitude towards the "Jewish Question":

> "If we let the Jews work with us, then they must also share in the harvest. Although no race distinctions should be made, of course we must hold fast by the fact that we stand on monarchist and patriotic ground. The committee should include no international elements, we want to be Germans. The Jews are monarchists like us and hold to the constitution. Should these gentlemen want to unite with us, they are welcome as collaborators; just as the fatherland stands for all of us, we are all united in this case."[140]

Soon, however, the meeting was anything but united. In the obviously tense and tumultuous situation, the chairman expressed indignation at the audacity

[138]Comite (ed.), *Die Bewegung* ..., p. 8. See also *Berliner Lokalanzeiger*, 21st June 1892, midday edition ("Herr stud. Sommerfeld wishes to see the word national eradicated, as either superfluous, being self-evident, or objectionable, if it is given a special meaning; this particular word, misused by a certain party, would be better avoided.")

[139]Also for the following Comite (ed.), *Die Bewegung* ..., pp. 10–13.

[140]*Berliner Börsen-Courier*, midday edition, 24th June 1892.

of gainsaying such terms as "German" and "patriotic" within a German university. For any "German-thinking" person, this was bound to create antisemitism. As he could not tolerate an assembly demonstrating against *Deutschtum* and monarchy, by means of a vote he enforced the division of those present into a *deutschvaterländisch* majority and an "international minority", and thereupon closed the meeting.[141]

Foerster's efforts towards a new student committee ended in failure. Despite several postponements of the closing dates only 1,212 students took part in the election, so that the one-third quorum (1,450 students) was not reached. With 512 votes for the non-corporation students there was no more talk of a "mobilisation of 4,000". Most corporation students showed their feelings by boycotting the election: and the antisemites ironically registered the rising total of nominees bearing Jewish-sounding names, to the amusement of those who were not involved.[142] In announcing the election results, the Rector expressed his personal regret about the failure of the committee project and his hopes for success in the following winter semester.[143]

The next Rector was Rudolf Virchow, a Left-Liberal member of Parliament and socially committed pathologist and physician. During his time of office, the independent student movement came to a sad end, and with it the attempt to reconstitute the *Ausschuß* in the winter semester of 1892/1893. The cause was entirely due to the continuing discord among non-corporation students on the "Jewish Question". Virchow was not afraid to use his official powers against the VDSt, and for his pains received a "correction" in favour of the VDSt from the Minister of Education.[144] In a speech at a commemoration of Friedrich Wilhelm III, Virchow declared with a pessimistic touch of resignation:

> "Our time, so self-confident and triumphant in its sense of science, readily ignores the mystical emotions which are being conveyed by venturesome individuals into the soul of the people. It still stands perplexed before the riddle of antisemitism; no-one knows the real desire of antisemitism; despite or perhaps because of this fact, it is fascinating even for educated young people. So far no-one has demanded a chair of antisemitism but, it is said, there are antisemitic professors."[145]

Virchow pointed out to newly-enrolled students "that in this university we know no difference between nations and confessions: they all have equal rights and duties".[146] However, because of perpetual dissent on the "Jewish Question", the *Unabhängigen*, after some more meetings, abandoned the committee elections project.[147]

[141]Comite (ed.), *Die Bewegung . . .*, pp. 10f.
[142]Weber, *op. cit.*, p. 26.
[143]HUA, file 603, p. 237. See also, for criticism of the *Nationalen*, Georg Siepmann, *Der Ausschuß und die Bewegung der "Unabhängigen" an der Berliner Universität*, Berlin 1892; *Univ.-Ztg.*, 6 (1892), pp. 212–214.
[144]*Wingolf Bll.*, 22 (1892/1893), pp. 177f., *Akad. Bll.*, 8 (1893/1894), pp. 101, 125f.; Arnold Bauer, *Rudolf Virchow. Der politische Arzt*, ed. by Heinz Ohff, Berlin 1981.
[145]*Allg. Dt. Univ. Ztg.*, 7 (1893), pp. 165f.
[146]*Wingolf Bll.*, 23 (1893/1894), p. 14.
[147]Weber, *op. cit.*, p. 27; *Akad. Bll.*, 7 (1892/1893), pp. 192f.; *Nachr.-Bl. ATB*, 6 (1892), pp. 57f.

In October 1892, some students had had several interviews with Rector Virchow, pretending to be canvassing for the committee project, and had persuaded him to allow a students' meeting to be convened in the *Auditorium maximum*. The invitation leaflet for this meeting was issued in the names of the VDSt and known antisemitic members of the earlier independent student committees; it revealed the real intentions of the organisers:

> "Fellow-students! All of you must know about the recent outrageous happenings. Opposing them will be a huge rally of the whole national student body of Berlin!"[148]

Virchow reacted at once. The students arriving at the *Auditorium maximum* found the doors locked, with a notice saying that Virchow had discovered he had been deceived and had therefore cancelled his permission: university rooms were not made available for the increase of internal discord. Signature sheets for a petition "against the suppression of academic freedom" were immediately spread out, but were confiscated by university beadles. On this, the "national" students returned to the *Akademische Bierhallen*, where they collected 360 protest signatures. *Alte Herren* of the VDSt called a meeting for 18th November in the *Tonhalle* to protest against "unequal treatment of national and international movements within the student body". Antisemitic and "philosemitic" ex-leaders of the independent student movement clashed before an attendance of 1,200.[149]

A second and finally successful attempt to initiate a supra-regional movement of non-corporation students began with students in Leipzig in 1896. Here too the "Jewish Question" became a question of survival for this "distinctively class movement"[150] of the mass of students. The first ten years of the *Freistudentenschaft/Finkenschaft* were marked outwardly by the struggle for recognition by the university administrations of their claim to represent all non-corporation students, and internally by constant debates about the position of Jews and foreigners in the *Finkenschaft*. The Leipzig *Urfinken*, for example, saw "the danger of *Verjudung*" of the whole movement when in the winter of 1898/1899 the *stud. jur.* Artur Blaustein and Georg Lewy founded a Berlin *Finkenschaft*.[151] Unlike its Leipzig model, this adopted a radical democratic constitution. Only after 1900 did the two *Finkenschaften* again draw closer to each other, after the opinion had gained ground in Leipzig that Jewish students should at least have equal rights, but that "these people are not regarded as altogether holding equal rank with others both in academic life and in society".[152] For this reason,

[148]*Allg. Dt. Univ.-Ztg.*, 6 (1892), pp. 222f.; HUA, file 603, p. 178.

[149]See the reproduction of longer passages in *Akad. Bll.*, 7 (1892/1893), pp. 207–209; and the report on German student life in the Belgian *Revue Universitaire*, transl. in *Bursch. Bl.*, 7 (1892/1893), p. 43. For a demonstration of 30–40 antisemitic students against Virchow in his lecture on 18th November 1892 see *Allg. Dt. Univ.-Ztg.*, 6 (1892), p. 234 and *Akad. Bll.*, 7 (1892/1893), p. 211.

[150]Friedrich Schulze and Paul Ssymank, *Das deutsche Studententum von den ältesten Zeiten bis zur Gegenwart*, München [4]1932, p. 375.

[151]Ssymank (who was a member and the first historian of the *Finkenschaft*) in *Deutsche Hochschul-Zeitung. Organ der Leipziger Finkenschaft*, cited from *Akad. Bll.*, 15 (1900/1901), p. 136. Blaustein and Lewy came from the "socialist" SStV.

[152]Arthur Heinzig, 'Über die Stellung der Juden in der Leipziger Finkenschaft', in *Dt. Hochschul-Ztg.*, November 1899, cited from *Akad. Bll.*, 14 (1899/1900), p. 241.

Jews should not hold representative offices, in order not to call in question the success of the movement. In the subsequent years, the delegates recognised the explosive potential of this ambivalent attitude and declared the "Jewish Question", like all the social norms of the corporations, was irrelevant. Later, however, there were considerable grass-roots tensions: for example, in 1905, at the great University of Munich, these led to a split in the *Finkenschaft.* The altogether positive development of the independent student body after 1900 however shows that antisemitism had long outgrown corporation circles and was not to be abolished by the single resolution of democratic deputies.[153]

The proportion of active Jews in the Berlin *Finkenschaft* was supposed to be quite high. But no precise numbers are available as the "corporation of non-corporation students" always declined to hand in a membership list and thereby give up its claim to general representation. In the case of Berlin too, student officials were elected by an elite drawn from the more consciously aware section of the student body. A precise quantitative expression of the ultimate spread of antisemitic attitudes among Berlin students must therefore remain speculative. There was, however, one test case: in 1910, the university administration needed at least a temporarily functioning *Ausschuß* in order to organise student contributions to the F.W.U. centenary celebrations. University Judge Paul Daude, known to oppose independent students, no doubt envisaged a colourful procession of uniformed corporations when he gave them privileges in the regulations for electing the *Ausschuß.* The consequent outrage moved an astonishing number of non-corporation students to join in the election. In order to split the non-corporation students, *nationale Finken* were quickly fielded, although they received only 560 votes against 2,071 for the democratic *Freisstudentische Partei.*[154] On this occasion the "Jewish Question" did not come to the fore, so that it is difficult to assume that the high voting percentage (about 30% of all Berlin students) represented an outright rejection of antisemitism. Yet at last there was a trend towards democratic potential: this, because of the overall political conditions, did not become effective until the early years of the Weimar Republic.

Until the war the student body did not manage to get any further with the *Ausschuß* question. About 2,000 students met on 23rd July 1914 to discuss the purpose of the newly founded *Ausschuß*, and it was decided that "questions of religion and politics should be withdrawn from it, but that German-national questions were not part of these". Jewish students regarded the term "German-national" as a possible cover for what were in fact antisemitic activities, and suggested instead the words *vaterländisch* or "patriotic". In turn, this provoked protests from *Korps* students for whom "German-national" was an indispensable term and did not, they said, include antisemitic activities. On this point the 1914 discussion was still at the same stage as in 1892. In this last attempt to reinstate a student committee, Rector Max Planck, the luminary of German natural science, accepted the "feudal" demand of the corporations for

[153]See Kampe, *Studenten und Antisemitismus.*

[154]Ernst Knoll, *Geschichte des Berliner Jubiläums-Ausschusses*, Guben 1910.

"equal representation" *vis-à-vis* the mass of students (16:16) and permitted something quite new – the culmination of unending years of xenophobic agitation: the abrogation of foreign students' suffrage.[155]

VII. THE "JEWISH PARTY" IN THE LESEHALLE AND THE INTERNAL JEWISH CONTROVERSIES

In the absence of a general student representation, the *Akademische Lesehalle* had functioned since 1888 as a substitute parliament. There was, however, no exact similarity here with the elections for the *Ausschuß*, for the *Akademische Lesehalle* comprised a student elite in both political and academic interests. Participation in the elections for the directorate of the *Akademische Lesehalle* was therefore always much larger than for the *Ausschuß* elections, varying between 55% and 85%.[156] A voting turnout of about 80% was reached whenever parties or coalitions campaigned to change the directorate majority. Low turnouts implied resignation to existing conditions.

Electoral enthusiasm within the hard core of the "national" camp was always quite high, as mastery of the student committees was transformed into a question of prestige, even a "national question". Furthermore the national coalition invariably put forward one list only, while their opponents – even when they intended to cooperate subsequently within the directorate – generally went into the campaign with three or more lists. Given the election rules, the coveted chairmanship of the directorate was generally safe for the "nationals". Moreover the VDSt was the backbone of the "nationals"/ antisemites, whilst the fluctuating allies varied according to chance and petty jealousy. The interest of the colour-wearing students in continued cooperation in the *Lesehalle* was somewhat limited. Nevertheless, in 1895 the *Burschenschaften* in the *Allgemeiner Deputierten Convent* (ADC) believed that here too they had to take over from the VDSt and assume leadership of the imperialistically modernised student body. But they were simply too weak for this; when it looked as if they would just fail to reach the magic threshold of 100 votes (to give one representative in the directorate), the SStV, disguised under the name "Committee of Non-Party Students", – it had been banned by Rector Pfleiderer as "Socialistic" – supplied the missing votes for the ADC. SStV support for the *Burschenschafter*, who latterly had also turned reactionary, was motivated by a shared opposition to the VDSt.

Berlin's press regarded the outcome as sensational: a united move by the opposition parties, who were far superior (460 to 272) in voting power, had snatched the chairmanship of the directorate from the VDSt, after nine years of the latter's unchallenged rule. Speculation was rife that the ADC would leave the "national" coalition. The VDSt raged that fraternity members had let their

[155]*K.C.-Blätter* (*K.C.-Bll.*), 4 (1913/1914), p. 256; *Akad. Turn-Ztg.*, 27 (1910/1911), p. 333; *ibid.*, 32 (1915/1916), pp. 61–63. For the failure of Rector Schmidt's reconstitution attempt in spring 1910 see *Akad. Bll.*, 24 (1909/1910), p. 383.

[156]HUA, file 553, *passim*. For election participation and strength of parties see Table II.

representative be served up to them by students "whose qualification is adequately explained by bearing such names as Löwenstein, Max Mosse, etc." Though the following heated excerpt in the *Akademische Blätter* need not be taken too seriously, it nevertheless gives a rough idea of the atmosphere and the extreme exaggeration of the significance attached to student elections:

> "Thus the inconceivable came about: the Berliner *Burschenschaften*, whose first generation had not feared persecution or imprisonment in their often over-passionate enthusiasm for the grandeur of the German nation . . . went hand in glove with international Jews and the friends of Jews . . . For ten years, we have made great sacrifices to hold on to the chairmanship of the directorate, in order not to let it fall into Jewish hands. Where were the other 'national' associations throughout those years . . . ? We are left with the irrefutable fact that the *Burschenschaften* have helped to raise the red-gold *Internationale* in the University of Berlin."[157]

The *Burschenschafter*, of course, saw the danger of being driven into a political corner on the Left, or being dubbed "philosemitic". A press statement by them confirmed that "they were not opposed to the political or national purposes of the VDSt", but only to its "uncomradely ways":

> "In no way, however, does the election ballot signify approval of, or a swerve towards, politically and socially suspect shades of opinion. For this the patriotic consciousness within the *Burschenschaften* is too deeply founded."[158]

After this neither the *Burschenschaften* nor other colour-wearing associations dared to keep a high profile at the expense of the "protectors of the Holy Grail of the national mind". In subsequent elections, the VDSt usually won the chairmanship. Either its opponents were disunited or the VDSt coalition on its own won an unchallengeable absolute majority.[159] The Catholics – in Berlin a minority like the Jews – pursued their 1880s line of support for the VDSt, with only one exception in 1899.[160]

The *Verein Jüdischer Studenten* (V.J.St.), ratified by the *Rektorat* in July 1895, was intended to be "the rallying point for all Jewish students who consciously feel as Jews and who want to take part in the development of a living Jewry".[161]

[157]Paul Becker, 'Die Lesehallenwahl und die Berliner Burschenschaften', in *Akad. Bll.*, 10 (1895/1896), pp. 77–79. The Protestant *Wingolf* as the most loyal appendage of the VDSt repeated this comment almost word for word, adding an alleged remark by "the Jewish students" [?]: "We are very content with the election" – "The DC should not let itself drift so far, although the behaviour of the VDSt, alleged to be the sole guardians of the national idea, has on several occasions already given offence in almost all student circles." *Wingolf Bll.*, 24 (1894/1895), p. 149. And see *Allg. Dt. Univ.-Ztg.*, 9 (1895), pp. 133f.

[158]Cited from Becker, *loc. cit.*.

[159]See Table II. On the occasion of the absolute majority of 8:6, reached in 1905, it was proudly announced (*Akad. Bll.*, 20 [1905], p. 308): "What the *Kyffhäuserverband* was attempting twenty-five years ago has to a large extent now come to pass . . . a clear break between *Deutschtum* and *Judentum* is becoming more and more obvious."

[160]*Allg. Dt. Univ.-Ztg.*, 14 (1900), p. 6. For VDSt relations with Catholics see *Akad. Bll.*, 19 (1904/1905), p. 317; and *ibid.*, 26 (1911/1912), p. 310.

[161]HUA, file 723. See also *Akad. Turn-Ztg.*, 25 (1908/1909), p. 292. Walter Gross, 'The Zionist Students' Movement', in *LBI Year Book IV* (1959), pp. 143–164, clearly shows the importance of the V.J.St. Berlin as a nursery of future leading Zionists; for example, Martin Buber, Erich Rosenkranz, Richard Lichtheim, Kurt Blumenfeld, Felix Rosenblüth and Siegfried Moses were active in the Berlin and supra-regional *Kartell* B.J.C. After the fusion of the B.J.C. and K.Z.V. in 1914, all member associations prefixed their own association's name by "V.J.St." – as a kind of

The founding members saw in the V.J.St. – the only Jewish association to take part as such in student election campaigns – the Jewish answer to the VDSt. (Its early history stretched back to 1892 and the unsuccessful attempt to reconstruct the student *Ausschuß*. At that time the Jewish students participated in the election under the neutral name *Kartell Akademischer Vereine*). Before the foundation of the sister association V.J.St. *Maccabaea* in December 1906, membership gradually increased from 11 to 50. Neither V.J.St. numbered more than barely 20 student members up to the war. About 180 further votes in the *Lesehalle* came from Jews outside the *Vereine Jüdischer Studenten* who did not want to support either the Liberals or the *Freistudenten.*[162] Notwithstanding imminent internal Jewish disputes, the V.J.St. continually maintained its function of integration. In this respect nothing changed, when, because of growing Zionist sympathies, the *Bund Jüdischer Corporationen* (B.J.C.) as the *Kartell* of those *Vereine Jüdischer Studenten* founded in other universities on the Berlin model merged with the *Kartell Zionistischer Verbindungen* (K.Z.V.), (emerging between 1902 and 1906). The fusion produced the new *Kartell Jüdischer Verbindungen* (K.J.V.).[163]

Pluralism within the Jewish student body meant that Berlin, with Breslau, became the birthplace of the various German-Jewish academic associations. Academically acknowledged at the beginning of 1883, the *Verein für jüdische Geschichte und Literatur*[164] existed till 1914, having up to 24 members and presenting itself as strictly scholarly; it did not engage in politics. In 1907 Heinrich Graetz became an honorary member. All further foundations were obviously reactions to the success of student antisemitism in excluding Jews from existing corporations. Explicitly *Abwehr* organisations were the Jewish associations in the *Kartell-Convent* (K.C.) starting in 1886 with *Viadrina* in Breslau. *Sprevia*[165] in Berlin was not founded until the end of 1894. The K.C. stressed its *deutsch-vaterländische Gesinnung* and its aim was "the fight against antisemitism and the education of its members as self-aware Jews". The idea was that special training in sword-fighting and a spirited retort to all insults (the principle of absolute satisfaction) would enforce social recognition. K.C. members were really dreaded as people for whom it was better to maintain a healthy respect. On the whole, however, this was a rather hopeless attempt to regain the ground of German student fraternity life which had already been lost to antisemitism.[166]

"trade mark". See also Jehuda Reinharz, *Dokumente zur Geschichte des deutschen Zionismus 1882–1933*, Tübingen 1981 (Schriftenreihe wissenschaftlicher Abhandlungen des Leo Baeck Instituts 37), pp. 34f., 66f.

[162]Compare the number of members in Jewish corporations with the votes for the "Jewish party". For the V.J.St. *Maccabea*, see HUA, file 801.

[163]See Doeberl and Scheel (eds.), *op. cit.*, *passim.* For the B.J.C. and K.Z.V. see Moshe Zimmermann, 'Jewish Nationalism and Zionism in German-Jewish Students' Organisations' in *LBI Year Book XXVII* (1982), pp. 129–153.

[164]HUA, file 649.

[165]HUA, file 721. See in general Adolph Asch, *Geschichte des K.C. im Lichte der deutschen kulturellen und politischen Entwicklung*, London 1964.

[166]Maintaining personal dignity, "the feeling of humiliation and the yearning for recognition of their honourableness" is a theme in all issues of the *K.C.-Blätter*. See, e.g., *K.C.-Bll.*, 1 (1910/1911), pp. 8–10. Not only was Judaism regarded as a value in itself and worthy of consideration, but baptism as a calculated step would always be a dishonourable stain and felt as such by "Germanic colleagues".

Nevertheless, the K.C. and Zionism each provided the way to a renaissance of Jewry in academic circles.

Jewish students without other backing now began to strengthen their self-awareness and preserve their dignity as Jews: this also signalled the end of the attraction of Liberalism for younger German-Jewish academic society. The old concept of emancipation – as antisemitic attacks only served to make especially clear – had reached a point where it cancelled itself out and triggered off a dialectical process, this time on the level of acculturation achieved. As a final visible proof of Liberal incapacity, faced with the antisemitic challenge, to develop an aggressive concept of minority protection, the *Reformburschenschaften* were active from 1883 onwards in the *Kartell* of the *Allgemeiner Deutscher Burschenbund* (ADB). Basically the ADB explicitly rejected the anti-Liberal and antisemitic development of the ADC, the largest *burschenschaftliches Kartell*. But its final aim was still the logical continuation of the Liberal emancipation concept, the "disappearance of Judaism by amalgamation with the German race".[167] For this same purpose social intercourse with Jews should continue, contrary to antisemitic views. Even while admitting the fact that Jewish students had been effectively excluded, Liberal bourgeois sharply objected to the same students' "voluntary separation". Even Mommsen, they said, had already recommended the Jews to give up their anachronistic existence, which had come about only by chance: there must be "a merging of the less in the greater, of the worse in the better". Thus Jews led "even today a pitiful separate existence and as a contribution to the perpetuation of the Jewish Question to all eternity, comes the very latest creation, the *Vereine Israelitischer [sic] Studenten*, which is gradually emerging at all the universities".[168]

[167]*ADB-Corresp.*, 1 (1890), pp. 142f. For the ambivalent attitude of the ADB see further: *Allg. Dt. Univ.-Ztg.*, 6 (1892), pp. 147f; 7 (1893), p. 162; 10 (1896), pp. 155f.; *Deutsche Academische Zeitung* (*Dt. Acad. Ztg.*), 3 (1886), No. 1 (Konrad Küster, *Unsere Zwecke und Ziele*); *Akad. Bll.*, 19 (1904/1905), pp. 145–147; Konrad Küster, 'Der ADB und das Judenproblem', in *Deutscher Burschenschafter*, 29 (1919), p. 57. Physician and *Alter Herr* Dr. Konrad Küster, together with the Jewish student (later Professor) E. Wolff, founded the *Reformburschenschaft* in 1883 in Berlin. Despite his narrow views, he is the outstanding figure in the traditionalist camp condemning antisemitism. For the conflict within the *Reformburschenschaft* concerning acceptance of Jewish fellow-students see Kampe, *Studenten und Antisemitismus*.

[168]The anonymous article 'Vereine israelitischer Studenten', in *Die Grenzboten*, 58, 1 (1899), pp. 117–170, was reprinted or discussed innumerable times throughout the corporation press. Although here there is room only for a few sentences, it can be regarded as the most representative statement about "Jewish exclusiveness" for the Right-Liberal *Bildungsbürgertum*. ". . . The members of the *Verein israelitischer Studenten* openly bear the mark of Cain inflicted on them in insult as a mark of exclusion by their Christian fellows; the *Verein* is living proof of those – from the standpoint of its members at least – regrettable relations . . . Under these circumstances it must appear somewhat inexpedient for Israelite students to keep themselves to themselves . . . The university years pass by, and one knows that in general they are much better used by Israelite students than by Christian ones . . . Even this anxiety [that Jews might be excluded from liberal professions through antisemitic agitation] does not disconcert the Philistine of the *Verein israelitischer Studenten*: the very accident of birth, which caused him to be born an Israelite, holds an irresistible power for him . . ." Despite the sympathies of older Jewish academics with the fight of the Jewish students against antisemitic attacks, they also display strong reservations about "voluntary" seclusion in an "academic ghetto"; see for example Dr. F. K., 'Jüdische Studenten-Verbindungen' in *Israelitisches Familienblatt*, 15th August 1901.

In Berlin internal Jewish differences also became apparent in student assemblies – to the great delight of the antisemites. Coupled with this, it emerged that Zionists and antisemites were fighting a common enemy – Liberalism, in both its Jewish and its general connotations. Despite a bitter mutual hostility, sometimes they paradoxically supported each other's anti-Liberal positions . In 1910 the K.C. conference even had to deal with a build-up of duels between members of strongly anti-Zionist views and others from the *Vereine Jüdischer Studenten* or the K.Z.V.[169] These Jewish student organisations, however, were united in the development of a phenomenon which might best be described as "defensive cultural nationalism", not always avoiding linguistic echoes of the racism in fashion at that time. This process, surprising at first glance, can only be properly evaluated in the light of the extreme pressure under which young Jews, and those the most sensitive, were living within a very largely antisemitic student subculture. The identity problem of this generation has often been discussed in terms of avoiding "Jewish self-hatred". Reappraisal and favourable estimation of the alleged racial characteristics attributed to Jews was for part of the Jewish students at least one way of preserving their identity.[170]

In Berlin, despite internal Jewish controversies, a *modus vivendi* between the FWV and the V.J.St. was reached during the *Lesehalle* elections. Previously the V.J.St. customarily abused the "Jewish FWV" as an association of characterless assimilants and deserters from Jewry.[171] During the elections there was cooperation: votes not yet cast were given to the side with the best chance of achieving the next full tally of one hundred votes. Notwithstanding all rhetorical and ideological differences, at least the Jewish members of the *Lesehalle* joined arms against the "national" coalition. However, a union of Jewish students and professional men in a wider framework – the aim of academic regional groups of the *Centralverein deutscher Staatsbürger jüdischen Glaubens* since 1902 – never succeeded.[172]

The majority of Jewish students in the University of Berlin stood outside corporations and *Lesehalle*: they saw no reason to organise as Jews, preferring rather to bear a part in the democratic movement of the *Finken/Freistudenten* –

[169]*K.C.-Bll.*, 1 (1910), pp. 14f. See also the article of Ludwig Holländer on B.J.C. hostility, *ibid.*, 3 (1912), p. 37. For an ironic report on differences among Jewish students in Berlin, see also *Akad. Bll.*, 7 (1892/1893), p. 148; *ibid.*, p. 209; 17 (1902/1903), p. 305.

[170]See Peter Loewenberg, 'Antisemitismus und jüdischer Selbsthaß. Eine sich wechselseitig verstärkende sozialpsychologische Doppelbeziehung', in *Geschichte und Gesellschaft*, 5 (1979), pp. 455–475.

[171]The V.J.St. pamphlet of December 1901 reproduced in *LBI Year Book XXX* (1985), opp. p. 373 is still relatively moderate. Under the influence of Siegfried Moses after 1904/1905 the Zionist wing gradually won ground. As editor of the union magazine *Der Jüdische Student*, in 1909–1911, Moses attacked FWV students of Jewish origin, who had come to a different conclusion on the meaning of their origin for them. See also Georg Herlitz, 'Siegfried Moses' Entwicklung und Stellung im KJV', in Hans Tramer (ed.), *In Zwei Welten. Siegfried Moses zum fünfundsiebzigsten Geburtstag*, Tel-Aviv 1962, pp. 17–26.

[172]See Ludwig Holländer, 'Akademische Ortsgruppen im Central-Verein deutscher Staatsbürger jüdischen Glaubens', in Doeberl and Scheel (eds.), *op. cit.*, vol. 2, p. 607; *idem*, *K.C.-Bll.*, 1 (1910), pp. 105–108. He was not the only person to combine the K.C. and C.V. in a quasi-personal union.

often in leading positions. Incessant verbal attacks and social humiliations were, it appears, largely neutralised by faith in continuing security under the law, by the manifold possibilities of social contacts within and outside the university and in the city of Berlin, or by the expectation of a professional career, realisable despite academic antisemitism. The Catholic student minority, in a somewhat similar situation, behaved completely otherwise. In answer to the "academic *Kulturkampf*" of 1904/1905, set on foot by "national" associations against the equality of Catholic corporations, Catholics achieved the highest degree of organisation: they had taken the path of internal unity and strengthened their numbers. This would be a worthwhile area for a comparative study of the causes of differing political and social behaviour between Catholics and Jews.

Towards the end of the Empire, the University of Berlin saw three more or less sharply drawn parts of the student body confronting each other: 1) A strong antisemitic nationalistic *völkisch* bloc, incorporating nearly all the fraternities and the biggest *Vereine*, because of its activism represented student politics to the outside world: 2) More or less equal in strength – under the most favourable circumstances – but disunited, the camp of Liberal or free students, advocates of student reform, Jewish and Socialist students saw itself as the opposition to the nationalist bloc: 3) At least half the Berlin students who were not interested in university politics. To take this as a rejection – unquantifiable – of antisemitism would certainly be a mistake. Often what was rejected was the so-called "everlasting quarrels between Jews and antisemites". Even for the *Freistudentische Bewegung*, because of the (very necessary!) rejection of further dealing with the "Jewish Question" it cannot be decided whether most members were really convinced opponents of antisemitism. The national bloc therefore was dominant not only by reason of the number of its supporters, their commitment to university politics or institutionalised corporation advantages, but most of all because of the lack of any comparably united opposition.

VIII. A SURVEY OF THE HISTORICAL RESULTS

For more than thirty years generations of Berlin students discussed the "Jewish Question" as a central topic, making their attitude on this one point a criterion for the formation of political and social groups. This discussion developed a dynamic of its own carrying just as much weight in explaining the spread of student antisemitism as the crisis in the academic labour market or the consensus of the elites to protect higher education against outsiders. In order to forestall exclusive concentration on the theory of competitiveness, this argument was raised in Part I of this essay, in the conclusion to the structural level investigation.

The student "Jewish Question" was, "Can a Jew be an equal member of academic society?" Members of most student fraternities and of many student associations in Berlin in the course of the 1880s gave the answer "No", and put it into practice, a decision which was not afterwards corrected. Rather, the antisemitic social norm of the corporation circles spread beyond Berlin; in the early 1890s it was officially confirmed by the supra-regional *Kartelle*, thereafter to be justified by pseudo-scientific racism. Social intercourse with Jews was penalised by the threat of loss of prestige or vilification for supposed sympathy with "Jewish-international" aspirations. Organisations with parity of membership between Jews and non-Jews came under heavy pressure: in consequence exclusive Jewish corporations arose, with members who no longer needed to hide their Jewish loyalty.

For most Jewish as well as non-Jewish students, a more realistic way out of social discrimination and tutelage became possible with the collective and radical rejection of the quasi-feudal and traditional student code of honour. It was not a path which could be followed with complete success because of the indifference shown by most non-corporation students in the *Kaiserreich*, but the corporations clearly recognised the threat to their anachronistic power position. On the failure of the independent student movement in 1892/1893, the corporations unexpectedly received help from the explosive force of antisemitism, already spread beyond their own circles. Making use of this experience, at and after the turn of the century so-called *nationale Finken* were deliberately played off against the democratically-inclined *Finkenschaftsbewegung*. Faced with the "free student" challenge, the corporations, originally divided by strong social, political or traditional differences, moved closer to one another on the new common basis of racist and imperialist ideology. This development continued after the war, when the (short) heyday of democratic student parliaments was answered by consolidation into the *Deutscher Hochschulring*. Even the Catholic fraternities, hitherto treated with hostility but now taken into the "national" consensus, were allowed to participate. In 1923 the *Hochschulring* included two-thirds of corporation students; the strongest student party, it was the hotbed of racist academic opposition to the Weimar Republic until the rise of the *NSD Studentenbund* from 1926 onwards. In the well-researched student history of the Weimar period,[173] the introduction of an "Aryan Paragraph" by the corporations in the early 1920s is seen as the beginning of a disastrous development – but in reality it is only the formal demonstration confirming a decision taken some thirty years earlier.[174]

[173]Two of the most important works are mentioned here: Michael H. Kater, *Studentenschaft und Rechtsradikalismus in Deutschland 1918–1933. Eine sozialgeschichtliche Studie zur Bildungskrise in der Weimarer Republik*, Hamburg 1975; Michael S. Steinberg, *Sabers and Brown Shirts. The German Students' Path to National Socialism 1918–1935*, Chicago 1977.

[174]For a modern critical history of students under the Empire see Jarausch, *Students, Society and Politics, op. cit.*, The work quoted on pp. 264, 267 by N. Schafferdt has reference to Kampe, *Bildungsbürgertum und Antisemitismus, op cit.* (see note 1). An evaluation of the importance of the *Kyffhäuserverband* can be found in: George L. Mosse, *The Crisis of German Ideology. Intellectual Origins of the Third Reich*, New York 1964, pp. 190–194; Hans-Jürgen Puhle, *Agrarische Interessenpolitik und preußischer Konservatismus im wilhelminischen Reich, 1893–1914. Ein Beitrag zur Analyse des Nationalismus in Deutschland am Beispiel des Bundes der Landwirte und der Deutsch-Konservativen Partei*, Hannover 1966. Puhle deals largely with Diederich Hahn, *Reichstag* deputy and the dynamic director of the landowners' lobby, *Bund der Landwirte*. See also Jürgen Schwarz, 'Deutsche Studenten und Politik im 19. Jahrhundert', in *Geschichte in Wissenschaft und Unterricht*, 20 (1969), pp. 72–94. I cannot agree with Detlef Grieswelle, 'Antisemitismus in deutschen Studentenverbindungen des 19. Jahrhunderts', in Christian Helfer and Mohammed Rassem (eds.), *Student und Hochschule im 19.*

In view of the significance of antisemitism that has been shown here – at least for the Berlin student body – it must be asked whether these students can more justifiably be described as a *Trägerschicht*, the foundation level, of modern antisemitism than can certain sections of the new and old middle classes. It was the *Kyffhäuserverband* in particular which brought forth a notable number of disseminators: *deutschnational* clergy and teachers, editors with key positions in the capital's Right-wing press, politicians who carried forward the students' organisational experience and strategies of the 1880s into the new generation of militant pressure groups during the 1890s.[175] Neither should the effect of less noisy followers of student antisemitism be forgotten: the feudal elite of corps students,[176] most favourably placed for a career in the ministerial bureaucracy, and their bourgeois or petty bourgeois imitators in the *Burschenschaften, Landmannschaften, Sängerschaften* and *Turnerschaften.* Student conflicts also threw into relief political and scholarly talents on the other side, Jews who would thereafter play leading roles in the *Abwehr* and, as conscious Jews, across the whole spectrum of Jewish organisations.[177]

Undoubtedly, with the transition to professional life, the student sub-culture lost its rigid function as an arbiter of conformity, and organised professional interests might have restored some balance. But no satisfactory declaration is possible here, until a fundamental examination becomes available concerning the role of "academic antisemitism" in the professional and social life of Berlin's academically educated classes and as to cooperation and antagonism between the Jewish and non-Jewish German *Bildungsbürgertum.*[178]

In its long term effects, too, the significance of bringing antisemitism into the social life of the academic generations before the First World War must

---

Jahrhundert, Göttingen 1975, pp. 366–379. Acceptable only as a first approach is Hans Winkel, 'Kyffhäuserverband der Vereine deutscher Studenten (KVDS) 1881–1919', in Dieter Fricke *et al.* (eds.) *Die bürgerlichen Parteien in Deutschland, 1830–1945*, vol. 2, Leipzig 1970, pp. 313–319. A social history covering the *Reich* and going beyond the attempt in Kampe, *Jewish Students*, does not yet exist and there is nothing at all on Jewish students in the Weimar Republic.

[175]For the professional structure of the *Alte Herren* see note 123. For politicians and lobbyists in the *Reichstag* see examples in Kampe, *Studenten und Antisemitismus.*

[176]Manfred Studier, *Der Corpsstudent als Idealbild der wilhelminischen Ära*, Phil. Diss., Erlangen-Nürnberg 1965.

[177]See Arnold Paucker, 'Die Abwehr des Antisemitismus in den Jahren 1893–1933', in Herbert A. Strauss and Norbert Kampe (eds.), *Antisemitismus. Von der Judenfeindschaft zum Holocaust*, Frankfurt a. Main–New York 1985, pp. 143–171, here 147; see also the fully annotated critical bibliography of literature on Jewish defence against antisemitism, pp. 164ff.*

*For further contributions to the growing literature on the Jewish Defence in Germany and the *Centralverein deutscher Staatsbürger jüdischen Glaubens* in particular see the essays by Evyatar Friesel, 'The Political and Ideological Development of the Centralverein before 1914', and David Engel, 'Patriotism as a Shield. The Liberal Jewish Defence against Antisemitism in Germany during the First World War', in *LBI Year Book XXXI* (1986) pp. 121–146 and pp. 147–171; and furthermore Arnold Paucker, 'Jewish Self-Defence', in *Die Juden im Nationalsozialistischen Deutschland/The Jews in Nazi Germany 1933–1943*, herausgegeben von Arnold Paucker mit Sylvia Gilchrist und Barbara Suchy, Tübingen 1986 (Schriftenreihe wissenschaftlicher Abhandlungen des Leo Baeck Instituts 45), pp. 55–65 – (Ed.).

[178]See Thomas Rainer Ehrke, *Antisemitismus in der Medizin im Spiegel der "Mitteilungen aus dem Verein zur Abwehr des Antisemitismus" (1893–1931)*, Diss. Med., Mainz 1978, though this does not cover everyday professional relationships.

probably be given a prominent place. In view of the losses in the two generations affected by the First and Second World Wars, reference has to be made to the phenomenon of a "long generation" in Germany,[179] meaning that those academics who finished their studies before 1900 held key positions in society and the state during the crisis years of the Republic they despised and during the Nazi period. Could they have been expected to interpret the new type of fierce antisemitism shown by the National Socialists as a warning sign? Did not the law of April 1933 "to reconstitute the professional civil service", the restrictions on admitting Jewish lawyers and doctors, the exclusion of Jewish students and scholars from the universities mean the fulfilment of dreams which were older than the Nazi movement?[180] Had not the *Deutscher Akademikertag* of 1925 already passed the following resolution?

> "A halt has to be called to infiltration (*Überfremdung*) of German universities by Jewish teachers and students. No more teachers of Jewish origin are to be appointed. A *numerus clausus* for students is to be introduced."[181]

Sources of the Weimar era can be used to show a qualitative leap from the thinking of *deutsch-national* and *völkisch* academics from the time of the Empire to the mentality of *NSD Studentenbund* members.[182] The question nonetheless remains: did the climate of imperial student life conduce to the achievement of a vantage-point from which this qualitative leap was all too easy? Admittedly such men as Dr. Stahlecker or Dr. Dr. Mengele were not representative of the mass of German academics, nor did Eugen Fischer and Otmar von Verschuer mirror the professors;[183] but where were the Western and Christian values, usually so prized in academics' words, when – after nearly a year of barbaric terror displayed before their eyes – some 700 professors sent their loyal address to Hitler in November 1933?[184] A legitimate and accepted counter to antisemitism on moral and intellectual grounds might have been possible to the educated German elite: yet it was destroyed. Can one strand of that destruction be traced back to the history of the Berlin students after 1880?

179 Henry C. Meyer (ed.), *The Long Generation. Germany from Empire to Ruin, 1913–1945*, New York 1973.

180 For the part played by civil servant elites in the preparation of the first anti-Jewish laws in 1933, Uwe Dietrich Adam, *Judenpolitik im Dritten Reich*, Königstein/Ts.-Düsseldorf ²1979, pp. 28–71; Max Weinreich, *Hitler's Professors. The Part of Scholarship in Germany's Crimes against the Jewish People*, New York 1946, at an early date showed that the professional apologists of Nazi ideology were by no means merely unimportant Nazi protégés but well-established scholars of high international repute (p. 7). See also Fritz K. Ringer, *The Decline of the German Mandarins. The Academic Community, 1890–1933*, Cambridge (Mass.) 1969; useful texts are also given in Gabrielle Michalski, *Der Antisemitismus im deutschen akademischen Leben in der Zeit nach dem Ersten Weltkrieg*, Frankfurt a. Main 1980, although the commentary is at best naive; Rainer C. Baum, *The Holocaust and the German Elite. Genocide and National Suicide in Germany, 1871–1945*, Totowa-London 1981, argues for the growing "moral indifference" among German elites.

181 Cited from Hans P. Bleuel, *Deutschlands Bekenner. Professoren zwischen Kaiserreich und Diktatur*, Bern 1968, p. 189.

182 See Anselm Faust, *Der Nationalsozialistische Deutsche Studentenbund. Studenten und Nationalsozialismus in der Weimarer Republik*, 2 vols., Düsseldorf 1973.

183 Benno Müller-Hill, *Tödliche Wissenschaft. Die Aussonderung von Juden, Zigeunern und Geisteskranken 1933–1945*, Reinbek 1984.

184 *Bekenntnis der Professoren an den deutschen Universitäten und Hochschulen zu Adolf Hitler und dem nationalsozialistischen Staat*, Dresden n.d. [November 1933].

APPENDIX

TABLE I

*Students' Committee (*Ausschuss*), Königliche Friedrich-Wilhelms-Universität Berlin: Selected Election Results 1881–1888*

Date	Faculties and General Assembly	Number of Representatives	Votes for FWV (support from anti-antisemites, Liberals, Jews)	Votes for VDSt coalition (antisemites, nationalists)	Other coalitions and individual corporations	Proportion of students taking part in election
			*Remarks and Voting Figures (based on first round of elections) – * indicates successful candidate(s) –*			
1881 January	Philosophy (by-election)	1		*VDSt candidate received 80% of votes		
March	Theology	2	?	?		
	Law	2		*		
	Medicine	2	*In these campaigns,			
	Philosophy	3	*non-organised Liberals were described as "philosemites" or "Jews"			
	General	9	Student election meetings forbidden by Rector			
May	All	9	*Comitee zur Bekämpfung der antisemit. Agit.* obtained only 102 votes in all	*Henceforward candidates put forward by a large coalition[1]		Approx. 685 out of 3709 students, or approx. 18·5%
	General	9	No candidate put forward	*Obtained between 550 and 583 votes in each election		
November	Theology	2		*Unanimous		
	Law	2		*"large majority"		
	Medicine	2	*non-organised Liberals			951 out of 4421 students: 21·51%
	Philosophy	3		*"large majority"		
1882 January	General	9	340	*570		

TABLE I (*continued*)

May			Henceforward FWV organises the anti-antisemitic party				
	Theology	2		*			
	Law	2		*			
	Medicine	1	* 86	23			
	Medicine	1	*FWV sympathiser				
	Philosophy	1	*				
	Philosophy	2	*FWV sympathisers				
	General	9		*"large majority"			
1884 December	Theology	2		*			
	Law	2	91	*200			
	Medicine	2	*143	48			
	Philosophy	1	* 84	80			
	Philosophy	2	166	*239			
	General	9	628	*710			Approx. 1500 out of 5006: approx. 30% (general election only)
1885 January	Philosophy (by-election)	1	168	*235			
			called after arrest of FWV rep. following death of VDSt member in duel				
June				Small coalition[2]			
	Theology	2		*108			
	Law	2	46	*143			
	Medicine	2	*174	98			
	Philosophy	3	155	*258			
	General	9	Because of duel mentioned above, Senate had forbidden meetings of whole student body				
1888 December					*Neue Mittelpartei*[4]	*Korporationsverband*[3]	
	Theology	2		*212	149	35	2049 out of 5576: 36.75%
	Law	1		*229	223	98	
	Law	1		218	*288	supported Mittelp.	
	Medicine	1	155	122	*201	103	
	Medicine	1	supported Mittelp.	supported Korporationsverb.	*280	210	
	Philosophy	3	supported Mittelp.	114	*327	81	

Numbers and percentages voting for each party – based on first round of voting in each faculty

The Academic Senate dissolved the *Ausschuss* and permitted no more election campaigns, in consequence of a second duel between a VDSt and a FWV member, in which the latter was killed.

Notes:

1: The large "national" coalition comprised: *Verein Deutscher Studenten, Akad. Turnverein, Akad. Gesangverein, Akad. Liedertafel, Kath. Leseverein, Wissensch. Vereine für Rechtswissenschaft, Mathematik, Erdkunde, Heilkunde, Küstriner Studentenverein* (the *Vereine*); *Sängerschaften* in CC, *Suevia* (Catholic), *Wingolf* (Protestant) (the *Verbindungen*).

2: The small VDSt coalition: VDSt, ATV, *Akad. Gesangverein, Akad. Theologischer Verein* (thc *Vereine*); the *Burschenschaften* in the DC, two out of six *Landsmannschaften* in the LC. From December 1885, there were in addition: *Akad. Liedertafel, Ascania* (Catholic student *Verein*), *Akad. Verein für Heilkunde, Gymnasialverband* (graduates from six Berlin *Gymnasien*) (the *Vereine*); *ATV Borussia* in the VC, *Suevia* (Catholic), *Wingolf (*Protestant*) (the Verbindungen)*.

3: *Korporationsverband* (*Couleurverband*) comprised: *Burschenschaften* in the DC, *Landsmannschaften* in the LC, *Sängerschaften* in the CC, *ATV Borussia* in the VC. With the sole exception of the corps in the KSC, all the colour-wearing and duelling *Verbindungen* formed part of the alliance.

4: *Neue Mittelpartei* comprised: ATV, *Akad. Liedertafel, Akad. Gesangverein, Akad. Wissensch. Verein* (only *Vereine* included)

Sources:

Akad. Bll., 2 (1887/88), p. 156; 3 (1888/89), pp. 65f.; 7 (1892/93), pp. 192f., 207–209; 24 (1909/10), p. 303.
Akad. Rundschau, 1 (1896), pp. 32–36.
Allg. Dt. Univ.-Ztg., 2 (1888/89), p. 286; 6 (1892/93), pp., 212f, 222f.
Bursch. Bll., 7 (1893), pp. 42f.
Dt. Hochschule, 3 (1884/85), p. 4.; 4 (1885/86), pp. 3f.
Der Kyffhäuser, 1 (1898), H. 7., p. 2.
Nachr.-Bl. ATB, 2 (1888), pp. 30–32, 40f., 89, 112; 5 (1892/93), pp. 132–138.

See in particular for the early 1880s, Hermann von Petersdorff, *Die Vereine Deutscher Studenten*, Leipzig 1900 (3rd edn.), pp. 58–262.

The Archive of the *Humboldt-Universität zu Berlin, Rektor und Senat*, (File 602, for December 1888 pp. 55f., 110ff., 196f.; File 603, *passim*) contains only the names of those elected with an occasional note of their affiliation, apart from the results of the December 1888 election.

The number of the Berlin student body is taken from Franz Eulenburg, *Die Frequenz der deutschen Universitäten von ihrer Gründung bis zur Gegenwart*, Leipzig 1904, p. 306.

And see unabridged version of above table in Kampe, *Bildungsbürgertum und Antisemitismus*, pp. 502–504 (referred to in footnote 1).

TABLE II

Akademische Lesehalle *of Berlin University: Election Results, 1882–1913*

Date	Voting Figures and *Korporationen* participating *Liberals*	*"Nationals" Antisemites*	*Others*	*Proportion of students voting*	*Remarks*
1882 January	477: FWV	452: VDSt			VDSt and FWV returned the same number of representatives: VDSt awarded chair by lot.
June	FWV chairman	VDSt declined to put up candidate			No change from this situation until 1886
1886 January	410: FWV	431: VDSt, ATV, Gymn. Verbd., Kath. Korpor., Wingolf		78%	Again equal representation: "nationals" obtained chair by lot.
June	349: FWV	261: with additional organisations AThV, AHV		75%	
December	503: FWV, ADB	529: with additional organisations AGV, ALT		77%	FWV in chair
1887 June	290: FWV	323: including all organisations shown above		68%	
December	—	—			Elections forbidden by Rector because of "vote-buying".

1888 June	129: FWV	282: without ATV, AGV, ALT		55%	
December	No candidate	Uncontested victor			No change until 1891
1891 June	151: FWV	236: VDSt, Gymn. Verbd., APhV, ARV, AHV, Akad. Wagner V., ThStV		72%	
1892 June	231: FWV	277: with same organisations		76%	
1893 June	217: FWV, Unabhängige	270: VDSt, ARV, AHV		66%	
1894 June	200: FWV 94: SStV	239: same organisations		77%	
1895 June	104: FWV	272: VDSt	256: Kom. d. Parteilosen 100: ADC	81%	ADC elected with assistance from Liberals
1896 June	207: Reform Committee (FWV, SStV)	345: VDSt, VC, Wingolf	136: Election Committee (Jewish: V.J.St., Sprevia)	80%	First test-case for a solely Jewish party
1897 June	259: Reform Committee	287: same organisations	Election Committee after Jewish-Liberal dispute gave only 65 votes to FWV	68%	
1898 December	447: Reform Committee	582: same organisations	100: Non-party Mittelpartei (AMV, AGV, ANV, APhV)	81%	
1899 December	100: FWV 200: SStV	631: additional organisations Nat. Vbd. wiss. V., Nat. Finken	300: Finken (non-corporation) 146: Kath. Korporationen	84%	

TABLE II (*continued*)

1900 December	108: FWV 214: SStV	625: additional organisation AR-V Teutonia; less VC, Wingolf	389: Finken 208: Kath. Korpor. 124: V.J.St.	85%	V.J.St. henceforward acts as the "Jewish party"
1901 December	100: FWV 103: SStV	709: same organisations	202: Finken 231: Kath. Korpor. 178: V.J.St.	85%	
1902 December	281: FWV	606: same organisations	213: Kath. Korpor. 201: V.J.St.	—	No Finken candidate, in protest against the continuing role played by the "Jewish Question"
1903 December	263: FWV	806: same organisations	244: Kath. Korpor. 221: V.J.St.	79%	
1904 December	207: FWV	837: additional organisations Akad. Ruderb., Ev. Bund	212: Kath. Korpor. 205: V.J.St.	73%	
1905 December	Supported Freie Verwaltungspartei	844: same organisations	256: Freie Verwaltungsp. 207: Kath. Korpor. 231: V.J.St..	78%	Freie Verwaltungsp. acts as surrogate after withdrawal of Finken representatives. No change between 1905 and 1908
1909 December	100: FWV Support also given to Freie V.	533: VDSt, Nat. Vbd. wiss. V., Nat. Finkenschaft	309: Freie V. (Freie Studentenschaft, Akad. Freibund) 201: Kath. Korpor. 100: V.J.St. (supports Freie V.)	73%	
1910 December	Over 100: FWV	Over 500: same organisations	Over 200: Freie V. Over 200: Kath. Korpor. Over 200:. V.J.St.	—	

1911 December	No candidate	Over 500: same organisations	Over 200: Freie V. Over 200: Kath. Korpor. Over 100: V.J.St.	—	No change in 1912
1913 December	No candidate	Over 600: same organisations	Over 100: Freie V.	Over 64%	Catholics and Jews describe elections as meaningless and resign

Note: Student parties were allocated one representative for each complete tally of 100 votes received. Accordingly, if it appeared that the final batch of votes would not reach this number, a group would often close its lists and direct remaining supporters to vote for another party with similar views. The FWV, in particular, lent backing to any non-antisemitic alternative to the VDSt coalition.

Chairmanship went to the party with most representatives: ties were determined by casting lots. The Rector did not accept post-election combination of lists.

Whatever the numbers voting, there were invariably 15 seats on the Directorate. Up to 1892, the chairman coopted the other members from his own party, thereby greatly magnifying his influence. After that date, Directorate members were coopted in proportion to the relative strengths of the parties.

List of Korporationen participating in election campaigns:

Opposed antisemites:	ADB[1]	Allgemeiner Deutscher Burschenbund (Reformburschenschaften; included Jews)
Joined antisemitic coalitions:	ADC[1]	Allgemeiner Deputierten Convent (Burschenschaften)
Joined antisemitic coalitions:	AGV[2]	Akademischer Gesang-Verein
Joined antisemitic coalitions:	AHV[3]	Akademisch Historischer Verein
Joined antisemitic coalitions:	ALT[2]	Akademische Lieder-Tafel
Joined antisemitic coalitions:	AMV[3]	Akademisch Mathematischer Verein
Joined antisemitic coalitions:	ANV[3]	Akademisch Naturwissenschaftlicher Verein
Joined antisemitic coalitions:	APhV[3]	Akademisch Pharmakognostischer Verein
Joined antisemitic coalitions:	ARV[3]	Akademisch Rechtswissenschaftlicher Verein
Joined antisemitic coalitions:	AR-V[2]	Akademischer Ruder-Verband
Joined antisemitic coalitions:	Akad. Ruderb.[2]	Akademischer Ruderbund
Joined antisemitic coalitions:	A Wagner V[4]	Akademischer Richard Wagner Verein
Joined antisemitic coalitions:	AThV[3]	Akademisch Theologischer Verein (Protestant)
Joined antisemitic coalitions:	ATV[2]	Akademischer Turn-Verein
Joined antisemitic coalitions:	Ev. Bund[3]	Evangelischer Bund (Protestant party, association of certain theological *Vereine* and non-affiliated Protestants

List of Korporationen participating in election campaigns (continued)

Opposed antisemites:	FWV[5]	Freie Wissenschaftliche Vereinigung (Liberals and Jews)
Joined antisemitic coalitions:	Gymn. Verbd.[2]	Gymnasial-Verband (graduates of certain Berliner *Gymnasien*)
Friendly to antisemites:	Kath. Korpor.	Katholische Korporationen ("Catholic party", association of various *Vereine* and *Verbindungen*)
Opposed antisemites:	Komitee d. Parteilosen[5]	(Cover name for SStV, temporarily forbidden by the Rector)
Joined antisemites:	Nationaler Verband wissenschaftlicher Vereine[3]	(Association of "nationals"/antisemitic *Vereine*)
Opposed antisemites:	Sprevia[1]	Jewish fraternity (Kartell K.C.)
Opposed antisemites:	SStV[5]	Sozialwissenschaftliche Studenten-Vereinigung ("Socialists", Jews)
Joined antisemitic coalitions:	ThStV[3]	Theologischer Studenten Verein (Protestant)
Joined antisemitic coalitions:	VC[1]	Vertreter-Convent (Turnerschaften)
Joined antisemitic coalitions:	VDSt[5]	Verein Deutscher Studenten (Kyffhäuser-Verband, leading antisemitic association)
Opposed antisemites:	V.J.St.[5]	Verein Jüdischer Studenten (Kartell B.J.C., the Jewish party, counter-foundation to VDSt)
Joined antisemitic coalitions:	Wing.[1]	Wingolf (Protestant fraternity, refusing to duel)

List of non-corporation bodies forming electoral parties

Opposed/ignored antisemites:	Finken(schaft)	Resemblance to trade union, "democratic" emancipation movement of non-corporation members, included Jews.
Opposed antisemites:	Freie Verwaltungspartei	*Finken* remaining after official withdrawal of the elected *Finkenschaft* representatives from "fruitless politics" in the *Lesehalle*.
Antisemites:	"Nationale Finkenschaft"	Cover organisation for non-corporation antisemites, connected with VDSt.
—	Unabhängige	Forerunner of the *Finkenschaft* movement: foundered on internal disputes on the "Jewish Question".

1. *Verbindung*: traditionalists, colour-wearing and voluntary duelling fraternities.
2. *Geselliger Verein*: social student association, not wearing colours, not armed, duelling only if insulted (theologians did not usually duel).
3. *Gesellig-fachwissenschaftlicher Verein*: social and scientific interests.
4. *Gesellig-politischer Verein*: social and political.
5. Primarily political.

Sources: Current reports in *Akad. Bll.*, 1 (1886/87)–28 (1913/14); *Akad. Turn-Ztg.*, 8 (1891/92)–32 (1915/16); *Allg. Dt. Univ.-Ztg.*, 1 (1887)–13 (1899); *Berliner Hochschulztg.*, 2 (1900); *Dt. Hochschule*, 1 (1882)–5 (1886); *Finkenbll.*, 4 (1901)–8 (1906); *KC-Bll.*, 4 (1914); *Der Kyffhäuser*, 3 (1900); *Wingolfsbll.*, 10 (1881)–26 (1896/97).
Number of *Akademische Lesehalle* members taken from the Archive of the *Humboldt-Universität zu Berlin, Rektor und Senat*, file 553, 554 *passim*.

TABLE III

Religion of Students at Berlin University, 1886–1925

	Winter Semester				
	1886/87	*1890/91*	*1902/03*	*1911/12*	*1924/25*
Protestant	3,644	3,695	4,319	5,510	4,689
Catholic	515	563	949	1,262	788
Jewish	917	896	1,223	1,390	1,021

Note: The above figures comprise German and foreign students. Women, however, are included only in the year 1924/25.

Source: *Preussische Statistik*, Part II (Tables) in the following vols.: 102 (1890), p. 98; 125 (1895), p. 161; 193 (1905), p. 185; 236 (1913), p. 185; 279 (1925), p. 10.

FIGURE I

Membership of Selected Student Korporationen in the Friedrich-Wilhelms-Universität Berlin, 1880–1914 (Student Members only)

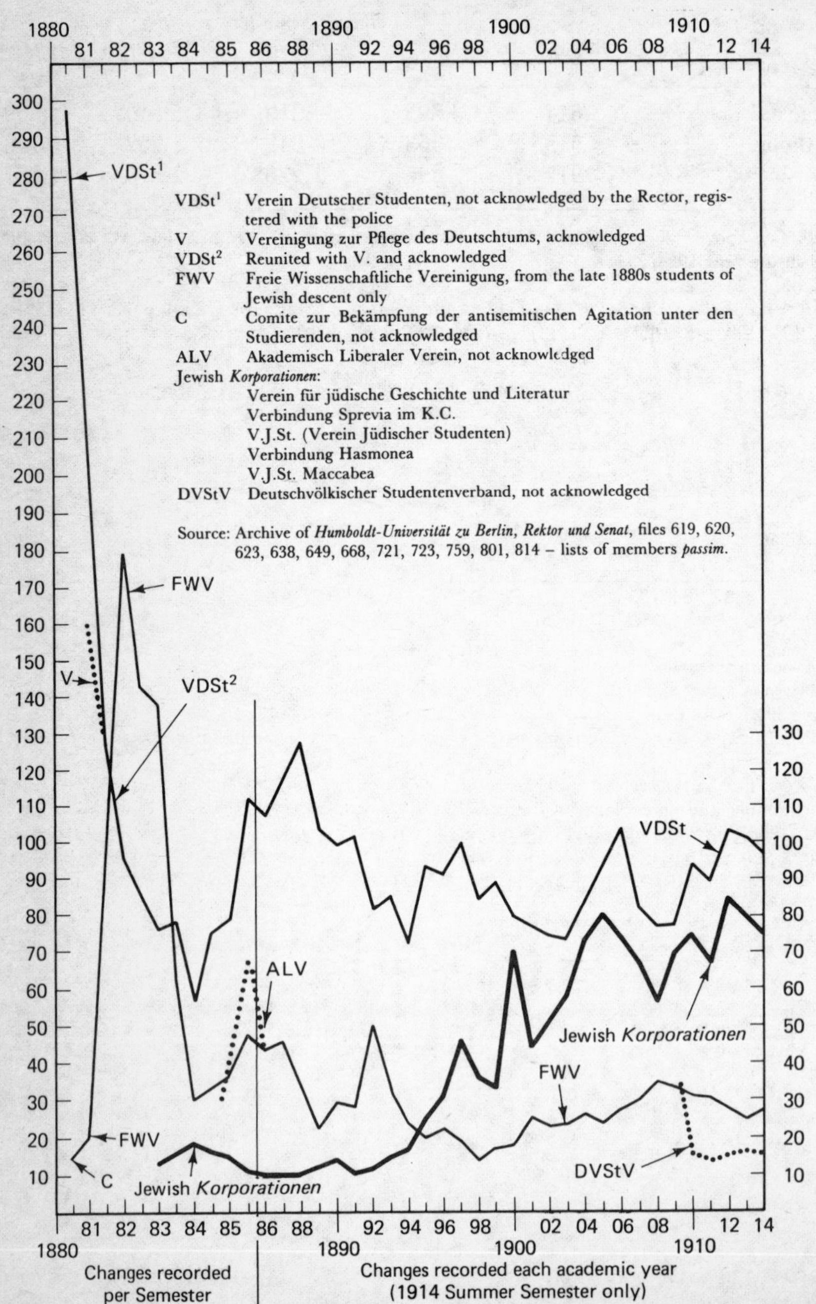

FIGURE II

Jewish Students at Friedrich-Wilhelms-Universität and all Members of Akademische Lesehalle (winter frequency, males only)

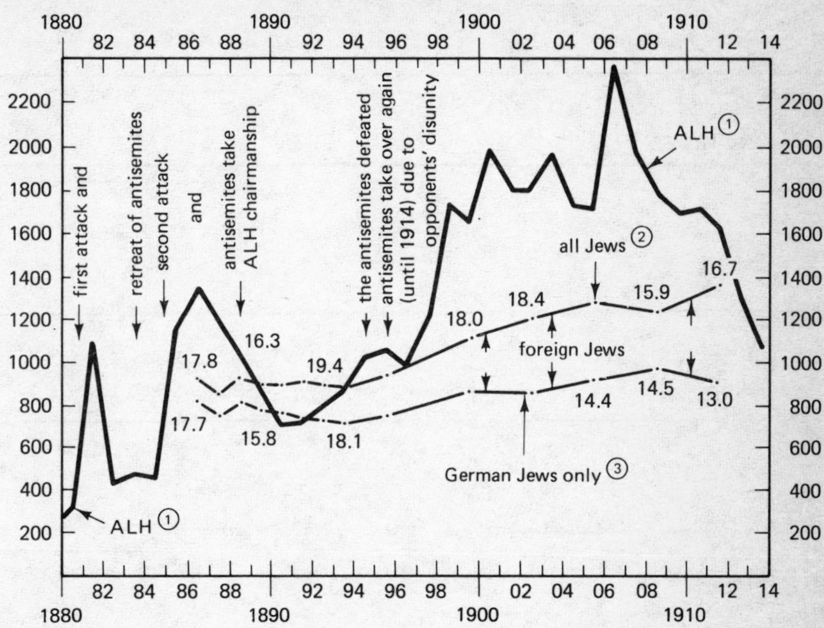

1 *Akademische Lesehalle*

2 Prussian, other German, and foreign (mainly Russian) nationality. The numbers (e.g. 16·7) are percentages of total Berlin student body (inflection points only).

3 Prussian and other German nationality. Percentages are related to all German students at F.W.U.

Sources: For ALH, Archive of the *Humboldt-Universität zu Berlin, Rektor und Senat*, file 553, 554, *passim*. For number and percentages of students *Preussische Statistik*, part II (tables) of the following vols.: 102 (1890), pp. 98f.; 106 (1892), pp. 67, 71; 112 (1892), pp. 155, 157; 116 (1892), pp. 161, 163; 125 (1895), pp. 161, 163, 373, 375; 136 (1896), pp. 177, 179, 387, 389; 150 (1899), pp. 183, 185; 167 (1901), pp. 183, 185; 193 (1905), pp. 183, 185; 204 (1908), pp. 183, 185; 223 (1910), pp. 189, 191; 236 (1913), pp. 183, 185.

Bavarians and Jews in Conflict in 1866: Neighbours and Enemies

BY JAMES F. HARRIS

This is a study of the relations between Christians and Jews in two Bavarian towns in 1866 almost on the eve of the war between Prussia and Austria.* Bavaria was already in the initial stages of military mobilisation in support of Austria when Christian excesses against Jews began to occur. It is the story of riots with roots both in Germany's antisemitic past and in the modern process of Jewish emancipation. As such it is a study in local history which must be viewed within the larger context of emancipation, Bavarian town life, and antisemitism. The local communal leadership used these excesses in a clever attempt to obtain Jewish renunciation of newly-acquired rights to communal goods in return for peace and quiet. On the other hand the Jews used the state and the military to bring pressure to bear on the community as a lever in bargaining for the defence of their rights. The relations of Jews and Christians to each other within the community and the relation of each to the state were the fundamental issues involved.

These at times sordid events took place in a picturesque rural area north-west of the older ecclesiastical city of Würzburg in an area enclosed by the Main river as it loops northward before continuing its way westward to Frankfurt and the juncture with the larger Rhine. Even today the communities seem amazingly similar in size, distinguished chiefly by location and relative prosperity. Karlstadt, on the Main about halfway north on the eastern side of the loop, was the seat of the local state office, the *Bezirksamt*. A few kilometres to the north-west, just over the line of hills that form the crest of the Main valley, lay the agricultural town of Wiesenfeld and its approximately eleven hundred inhabitants. To the south-west of Karlstadt, about as far as Wiesenfeld was to the north, the town of Laudenbach and its nine hundred residents perched on the shoulder of the hills forming a side valley of the Main. Where Wiesenfeld sprawled sleepily on very gently rolling land, Laudenbach's appearance was striking, the fine Catholic Church at its centre visible for miles. In Wiesenfeld the *Rathaus*, built in 1865, still stands on the major through road, but it can hardly be seen unless one is directly in front of it. Today there are no visible signs of the thriving Jewish communities of 1866.

Using the boundaries of 1871, Jews were never more than about one and a

*Research for this article was supported in part by the General Research Board of the University of Maryland.

quarter percent of the German population.[1] Bavarian Jewry was slightly larger in the early nineteenth century when 25% of all German Jews lived there. But the percentage fell rapidly as Bavarian Jews emigrated in larger numbers than Jews in the rest of Germany.[2] Nor were they evenly spread throughout the state geographically. The governmental district of Lower Franconia, where these towns were situated, one of eight such units, contained nearly 40% of all Bavarian Jews.[3] Moreover, these communities were rapidly changing demographically, socially, and economically: in 1840, 88% of all Jews lived in small towns and rural cities, whereas by 1910, 78% resided in very large cities such as Munich, Fürth, Nuremberg, and Würzburg.[4] Wiesenfeld and Laudenbach reflect the high concentration of Jews in Lower Franconia – Jews numbered about 11% of the population of Wiesenfeld and over 14% in Laudenbach.[5] They had lived there since at least the end of the Thirty Years War.[6]

Bavarian Jews received a substantial increase in legal rights as the result of the French Revolution and Napoleon, especially in the Edict of 10th June 1813. Although they fell far short of full emancipation, these gains, mostly economic, were very real. But there was a catch – Jews could not move freely within Bavaria. The 1813 law effectively froze the Jewish communities as they were, excluding Jews from moving into new areas or into areas where the number of Jews equalled or exceeded that of 1813.[7] The immediate consequences were twofold: Bavarian Jews remained rural longer than they might otherwise have done and many who did move left Bavaria entirely.[8] Subsequent attempts to further emancipate Jews met with vigorous, even violent, popular reaction. In 1819 (and in 1820 and 1821 as well) serious riots broke out in Würzburg, the capital of Lower Franconia, and in numerous other German cities, sparked in part by the introduction of legislation for emancipation.[9] During the Revolution of 1848 antisemitic riots and violence against Jews broke out again, chiefly in the rural areas of south-west Germany.[10]

[1]Avraham Barkai, 'The German Jews at the Start of Industrialisation. Structural Change and Mobility 1835–1860', in *Revolution and Evolution. 1848 in German-Jewish History*, edited by Werner E. Mosse, Arnold Paucker, Reinhard Rürup, Tübingen 1981 (Schriftenreihe wissenschaftlicher Abhandlungen des Leo Baeck Instituts 39), p. 124.

[2]Baruch Z. Ophir and Falk Wiesemann (eds.), *Die jüdischen Gemeinden in Bayern 1918–1945. Geschichte und Zerstörung*, Munich–Vienna 1979, p. 14.

[3]*Ibid.*, p. 13.

[4]*Ibid.*, p. 15.

[5]Baruch Z. Ophir, *et al.* (eds.), *Pinkas Hakehillot. Encyclopedia of Jewish Communities from their Foundation till after the Holocaust. Germany–Bavaria*, Jerusalem 1972, pp. 471, 504.

[6]Jonathan I. Israel, 'Central European Jewry during the Thirty Years' War', *Central European History* 16 (March 1983), pp. 5, 8.

[7]Stefan Schwarz, *Die Juden in Bayern im Wandel der Zeiten*, Munich–Vienna 1963, p. 182; Adolf Kober, 'Emancipation's Impact on the Education and Vocational Training of German Jewry', *Jewish Social Studies*, XVI (1954), pp. 3–32, 151–176.

[8]Kober, 'Emancipation's Impact', *loc. cit.*, p. 163.

[9]Eleonore Sterling, 'Anti-Jewish Riots in Germany in 1819. A Displacement of Social Protest', *Historia Judaica*, 12 (October, 1950), pp. 105–142; and Jacob Katz, *From Prejudice to Destruction. Anti-Semitism, 1700–1933*, Cambridge, Mass., 1980, pp. 92–104; and Schwarz, *Juden in Bayern, op. cit.*, p. 216.

[10]Reinhard Rürup, 'The European Revolutions of 1848 and Jewish Emancipation', in *Revolution and Evolution, op. cit.*, p. 35; and Monika Richarz, 'Emancipation and Continuity. German Jews in the Rural Economy', *ibid.*, pp. 100–102.

Failure of the Revolution in 1849 occurred before the Bavarian parliament could pass legislation for full emancipation. The government, however, fulfilling a royal promise of March 1848, introduced emancipatory legislation in 1849 which passed its first major hurdle in the lower house in December. A flood of petitions from all over Bavaria, 300 from Lower Franconia alone, opposed the bill and caused the administration to back away from it, finally withdrawing it entirely in 1850.[11] This time there were no riots, at least so far as the documents show. The story of the origin of this petition campaign, however, is muddled. Most historians describe the outpouring of sentiment as simultaneously democratic and antisemitic. Eleonore Sterling argued that the petitions did not represent public opinion, but only some activist, antisemitic elements, which were misinterpreted and used to sabotage the bill.[12] But documents uncovered in Würzburg and Munich suggest, if they do not prove, that Sterling was wrong – that these petitions were genuine and representative. Popular opinion in Unterfranken was antisemitic and the state cautiously supported emancipation.[13]

In any event the Jews in Bavaria gradually received more civil rights, especially in 1861 when the residence quotas were finally lifted. By 1866, although still lacking complete emancipation, Jews were legally on an equal footing with Gentiles. This progress, from 1813 to 1861, resulted largely from actions and initiatives by non-Jews, whether King or Parliament. Several historians have noted the passive and even fearful attitudes of many German Jews. Baron notes that Orthodox Bavarian rabbis in 1848 petitioned the government against Jewish equality.[14] Sterling notes the same in Baden where the Jews of Fechingen asked not to be emancipated because their lives had been threatened.[15] Jewish response to overt antisemitism seems to have been either to leave or to quietly seek state support against violence.

Conditions improved after the Revolution of 1848. Riots became a thing of the past, even if the very recent past. A modern German historian describes the 1848 riots against Jews as "old-fashioned" and writes that "by the end of the 1860s the progress of the Jews in German society and culture – despite wholly understandable friction – appeared well-established, or so the great majority of

[11]Schwarz, *Juden in Bayern*, *op. cit.*, pp. 274–304; Eleonore Sterling, *Er ist wie Du. Aus der Frühgeschichte des Antisemitismus in Deutschland (1815–1850)*, Munich 1956, pp. 176–179; Salo W. Baron, 'The Impact of the Revolution of 1848 on Jewish Emancipation', in *Jewish Social Studies*, XI (July 1949), p. 227.

[12]Sterling, *Er ist wie Du*, *op. cit.*, pp. 177–179.

[13]Bayerisches Hauptstaatsarchiv, Ministerium des Innern 44249; Bayerisches Staatsarchiv Würzburg, Regierung von Unterfranken, Präsidialakten Rep. 0.0. -3, 325. This will be developed further in a separate article. Also see R. Moldenauer, 'Jewish Petitions to the German National Assembly in Frankfurt 1848/49' in *LBI Year Book XVI* (1971), pp. 195–196 on a petition in 1848 from Karlstadt (in Unterfranken?), which, though undated, stemmed from spring 1848 and called for the Jews to be driven out of Germany.

[14]Kober, 'Emancipation's Impact' *loc. cit.*, p. 202.

[15]Eleonore Sterling, 'Jewish Reactions to Jew-Hatred in the First-Half of the Nineteenth Century', in *LBI Year Book III* (1958), pp. 105, 119–120; also Richarz, 'German Jews in the Rural Economy', *loc. cit.*, p. 103, and Michael A. Riff, 'The Anti-Jewish Aspect of the Revolutionary Unrest of 1848 in Baden and its Impact on Emancipation', in *LBI Year Book XXI* (1976), p. 29.

the bourgeois world as well as the Jews themselves saw it".[16] Monika Richarz also describes these years as, relatively, the most free period in German-Jewish history.[17] The fact is, as the documents show concerning the Jewish residents of Wiesenfeld and Laudenbach, that the Jews were neither aliens nor newly-arrived. Thus they could hardly be feared as Jews were feared contemporaneously in some of the bigger cities. The conflicts in 1866 provide a basis for evaluating the progress of emancipation in the countryside, for assessing the degree of acceptance there, and for questioning both the sources of rural antisemitism as well as the tactics of both sides in the struggle.

Students of Jewish communal life in nineteenth-century Germany will not find references to the riots of 1866. Only one source, a Hebrew language encyclopaedia, even mentions the upsets in the city of Würzburg. But there were two other types of related occurrences in Central Europe in 1866: pogroms in Bohemia and beer riots in Bavaria. The pogroms occurred in a series of smaller Bohemian cities in April and May 1866 and, while primitive, were neither new nor unusual.[18] The *Allgemeine Zeitung des Judenthums* provided news of the riots in Bohemia and repeated a comment from the *Münchener Neueste Nachrichten* that the shameful Bohemian pogroms had surfaced in the Bavarian towns of Laudenbach, Wiesenfeld, and Thüngen. The *Allgemeine Zeitung des Judenthums* itself commented that the pogroms in Bavaria were milder than in Bohemia, adding that these things occurred each year at bockbeer time, especially in the big cities. "From a general standpoint," they concluded, "these events have no significance, [although] locally they are very disturbing."[19] But Wiesenfeld and Laudenbach lie nearly one hundred miles from the Bohemian frontier and there was no report of similar outbreaks nearer than Würzburg. The Bohemian outbreaks were primitive expressions of prejudice while the Bavarian experiences, as will be shown below, were quite different. Nor is there any reason to believe that anyone in these areas knew of the Bohemian events – only a few Munich papers carried reports and then only in very limited fashion.

As noted by the *Allgemeine Zeitung des Judenthums*, beer did play a role in at least one antisemitic incident. Beer riots, "Krawalle", were a regular and frequent feature of Bavarian big city life in the nineteenth century, occurring almost every time the price of beer increased.[20] In May and June 1866 the brewers raised prices and riots promptly ensued. In Munich, Regensburg, Augsburg, and Würzburg the rioters included soldiers who had been mobilised as well as elements of the urban populations.[21] In one case what began as a beer

[16]Thomas Nipperdey, *Deutsche Geschichte 1800–1866. Bürgerwelt und starker Staat*, Munich 1983, p. 255.

[17]Monika Richarz (ed.), *Jüdisches Leben in Deutschland*, Bd. I, *Selbstzeugnisse zur Sozialgeschichte 1780–1871*, New York 1976, Veröffentlichung des Leo Baeck Instituts, p. 58.

[18]*Allgemeine Zeitung des Judenthums*, XXX, Nos. 17, 18, 19, 22, for (24th April, 1st, 9th, 19th May 1866), pp. 262, 282–283, 298, 346,. Also No. 32 (7th August 1866).

[19]*Allgemeine Zeitung des Judenthums*, XXX, No. 27 (3rd July 1866), p. 425 dated 'Aus Bayern im Juni (Privat)' and 'Von der bayerischen Grenze'.

[20]O. E. Breibeck, *Das fünfte Element der Bayern. Eine unterhaltsame Bierhistorie*, Regensburg 1978, pp. 125–126.

[21]See the description in the *Augsburger Allgemeine Zeitung* No. 125 (5th May 1866), Beilage, No. 150 (30th May 1866), Beilage, No. 153 (2nd June 1866), No. 154 (3rd June 1866), and (3rd, 5th,

riot became an antisemitic riot. A correspondent for the *Augsburger Allgemeine Zeitung* from Würzburg, wrote on 11th June that his city had the "honour" of combining beer riots and Jew riots. Antisemitic wall posters had preceded the actual event by several days and a rumour spread that on Sunday, 8th June, both brewers and Jews should be punished. As far as can be ascertained, Jews were not brewers. No preventive measures were taken, according to the report, and when a brewer refused a crowd demanding that he sell his beer at the old price, his inn was smashed up. The crowd grew larger and moved on undeterred by a weak police force. After dark the crowd moved again, this time to the area where several Jews owned homes and stoned them. One man was shot defending his house and another mishandled. The crowd made no distinction, the writer indignantly noted, between respected Jews and usurers. The *Landwehr* eventually dispersed the mob, jailing fifty and wounding several.[22]

As tempting as it is to link Bohemian pogroms and Bavarian beer riots to the antisemitic outbreaks in rural Lower Franconia, as the *Münchener Neueste Nachrichten* and the *Allgemeine Zeitung des Judenthums* did, there is no evidence that either played any role at all. Documentation on the events in Wiesenfeld and Laudenbach is surprisingly rich. It is located in the files containing nearly all of the correspondence relating to the cases from the state office in Karlstadt.[23] No file could be found for Thüngen, but there are several references to disturbances there in other files. The contents of these documents show that the incidents were not entirely the product of 1866 – in Wiesenfeld, at least, they began in the summer of 1865, breaking out again in the late spring of 1866 largely before the Würzburg riots. Hence, while possibly affected by outside occurrences these "excesses" should be treated as local affairs, stemming from local problems.

The first known report of an incident dates from 25th June 1865 when Jakob Steigerwald of Wiesenfeld appeared at the state office in Karlstadt to report that "recently" excesses against Jews had "come" to his town. Specifically, he stated that on the night of 17th to 18th June, a Saturday evening, stones were thrown at his shuttered windows breaking some of them. Unknown people used clubs to beat on his front door and stones were thrown into his living room. He did not know who was responsible, but he requested protection. The state lawyer, Weingärtner, immediately directed the communal Chairman (the Bavarian equivalent of mayor in small towns) of Wiesenfeld to use all means to prevent a recurrence, informing him that if he were not successful, the *Landwehr* and even the military would be called in as allowed for by law.[24]

12th–13th, and 17th June 1866); reports in the *Regensburger Anzeiger, Regensburger Morgenblatt, Neues Bayerisches Volksblatt*, and the *Amberger Tageblatt* say essentially the same.

22 *Augsburger Allgemeine Zeitung*, No. 164 (13th June 1866), Würzburg, 11th June (Wed.), p. 2712. On Jews as brewers see Moldenauer, 'Jewish Petitions', *loc. cit.*, p. 186, who states: "All trades, with the exception of brewing, the selling of spirits, and catering, were open to them [Jews]."

23 Landratsamt Karlstadt, Files 1459 (Wiesenfeld) and 1461 (Laudenbach) in the Bayerisches Staatsarchiv, Würzburg, [hereafter: LRA 1459 or 1461]. Was file No. 1460, missing, the file for documents relating to Thüngen? Karlstadt alternates with Carlstadt in the documents. We have standardised it as Karlstadt throughout.

24 LRA 1459, Karlstadt, 25th June 1865.

What followed in Wiesenfeld in 1865 and in both towns in 1866 fell quickly into a pattern. Groups of unknown assailants appeared at night under cover of darkness and threw stones at windows and roofs, as well as beating on the doors and ground-floor shuttered windows with clubs.[25] Some variations are reported. A sabre was used against one house leaving behind tell-tale slash marks.[26] A field of newly-sown grain belonging to a Jew was "disturbed" and thereby damaged.[27] On another occasion the door of the house of a Jew was smeared with excrement. This latter case was complicated by the presence in the house that night of the father of a bride promised to the son of the host – the next day the visitor cancelled the marriage contract, fearful for his daughter's future in Wiesenfeld.[28] In addition Jews overheard comments on the street and in the inns which were, to say the least, unsympathetic and often intimidating, hostile, and bitter.[29] Two people were injured, a child by flying glass from a broken window and a serving maid by a stone which struck her shoulder.[30] Life for Jews in Wiesenfeld and Laudenbach became tense and several families fled, not to Karlstadt (as reported in the newspapers) where only one Jew was living in 1871, but to Würzburg.[31]

No one seriously challenged the basic descriptions of what occurred. Jews and Gentiles agreed even if the former tended to exaggerate and the latter even more to minimise. Most of the events were destructive, but not usually directly life-threatening. Some of the stones used by the vandals, however, weighed as much as five pounds. From the very beginning, the most significant aspect was that Jews like Steigerwald did not expect genuine help from the local community. Hence their repeated appeals to the state officials in Karlstadt. This was traditional in Bavaria, as Jews found more support from the modern state than from the more traditional "hometowns".[32] What was new in these conflicts was that Jews not only requested protection, but accused the local officials and the Christian community in general of lack of interest in preventing excesses and even of support for them. When vandalism began again in Wiesenfeld in May 1866 a delegation of Jews, Moses and Jakob Steigerwald, Kalman Grünebaum and Baruch Schild, went to Karlstadt to complain. Baruch Schild reported having called to the neighbourhood for help during an attack, but had no response. The Wiesenfelders, the Jews affirmed, said openly that the time had come to take revenge on Jews and "kill us all". We can, they concluded, expect no protection since our neighbours themselves want to know nothing about it.[33]

[25]The descriptions and even the assessment of the amount of damage may be found in numerous reports by Jews and non-Jews, officials and townspeople in both files.

[26]LRA 1461, Karlstadt 24th July 1866, testimony of Lazarus Frank.

[27]LRA 1459, Karlstadt, 25th July 1865 statement of Moses Steigerwald.

[28]LRA 1459, Karlstadt, 12th September 1865, statement of Marcus Braunold.

[29]LRA 1459, Karlstadt, 22nd May 1866, testimony of Moses and Aaron Steigerwald; LRA 1461, Laudenbach, 7th June 1866, testimony of Hirsch Frank the younger.

[30]LRA 1461, Karlstadt, 1st June 1866 and Laudenbach 7th June 1866, testimony of Samuel Strauss.

[31]LRA 1461, Laudenbach, 7th June 1866.

[32]See Mack Walker, *German Home Towns, Community, State, and General Estate 1648–1871*, Ithaca – London 1971, *passim*.

[33]LRA 1459, Karlstadt, 17th May 1866.

On 22nd May, Moses and Aaron Steigerwald described additional events to another state official, Hoermann, concluding: "Last night's excesses place all of us again in fear of our lives and property, since we can expect no protection from our Christian neighbours; when the communal Chairman read the order of the Royal State Office . . . the other neighbours said they would not provide a night watch, [that] the Jews should do that themselves."[34] In Laudenbach, also, a delegation of Jews complaining of similar vandalism, stated: "If the residents were firm and united [vandalism] could not happen"; but all of the Jews agreed that they could trust neither the communal administration nor the watch. The most recent event, they noted, had actually been announced ahead of time and the participants, contrary to the Chairman's assertions, were all native Laudenbachers.[35] Weingärtner, one of the officials in Karlstadt, stated in his report to the provincial office in Würzburg that the military was needed because the local police and *Gendarmerie* could not maintain public order and because "the majority of the members of the Christian community, while not in agreement with the excesses, have neither the will nor the strength to stop them . . ."[36]

As in all such cases, it was important to determine whether the perpetrators were natives of the town or not and, if they were, to identify them. Although this was both difficult and, for the Jews, potentially dangerous, it did occur. In Wiesenfeld Moses Steigerwald identified a whiskey distiller named Joseph von Obeisenn as well as the son of a *Gemeinde* official. Steigerwald noted that Obeisenn had been investigated before for throwing a stone through his window, but not convicted. Both were local inhabitants.[37]

Far more incidents occurred in Laudenbach over a longer period of time and more participants were identified. At first, as in Wiesenfeld, no one, including the *Landwehr*, identified any of the vandals.[38] But in testimony given on 7th June, Mayer Bach stated that he had recognised a former railway guard from Karlstadt, Johann Raudenkolb, who had threatened him; later on the same day, 21st May, a crowd of young men attacked his house, but he recognised none of them.[39] Hahum Süsser, however, named this same man as the leader of groups of rioters on several occasions. After Süsser's testimony, which came sixteen days after the fact, Jews made more identifications. In all eight more perpetrators were named, always by Jews. All were Laudenbachers! The men named included two railway workers, a farmer, a shepherd, the rest sons of prominent families, including one of the innkeepers. Jews also reported hostile comments made in conversation more freely after 7th June – comments made by native Laudenbachers. The early claim that foreigners, which is to say members of other Bavarian communities, had committed the acts gradually disappeared.

34LRA 1459, Karlstadt, 22nd May 1866.
35LRA 1461, Karlstadt, 29th May 1866.
36LRA 1461, Karlstadt, 1st June 1866.
37LRA 1459, Karlstadt, 22nd May 1866, 9 a.m.
38LRA 1461, 28th May 1866, report of Schuhmann and Enders, the *Brigadier*.
39LRA 1461, Laudenbach, 7th June 1866.

Both in Wiesenfeld and in Laudenbach the communal leaders uniformly agreed that the incidents were blown out of proportion by overly fearful Jews;[40] that outside elements, literally "foreigners", were responsible;[41] that the great majority of the community deplored the events;[42] and, after each incident, they insisted that there would be no repetition of such actions.[43] Investigations of the complaints by the Jews took place on several occasions and the files include, in addition to the evidence given by the Jews, testimony from the leaders of the communities, especially the chairmen, from the watch, from the officers and soldiers in the military and police units, and from the personal visits and evaluations by the state officials from Karlstadt.[44] Although inclining to believe the soothing explanations of the Chairmen, Schäfer in Wiesenfeld and Schuhmann in Laudenbach, the Karlstadt office ordered in state forces. Because of greater tension, and for other reasons to be treated below, the state sent out a military force of fifty men to Laudenbach to prevent repetition of antisemitic incidents.[45]

At this point it is necessary to dwell briefly on the provisions of Bavarian law governing military intervention in communal affairs. After the Revolutions of 1848, and probably in direct response to them, the state issued laws which stated that any community requesting state aid in putting down civil disturbances must pay the costs of such aid.[46] Hence the request by the Jews for protection began a process to be paid for by the community as a whole which was, of course, predominantly Christian. In this light the communal attempts to excuse the actions of the vandals may be understood on financial as well as on emotional grounds. Likewise, the Jews knew that one result of asking for outside protection would be to irritate the community, both by increasing its costs and by questioning the ability and integrity of the communal administration in the eyes of the state. In addition the state could intervene in a milder way by ordering the community to double or triple its guard and to maintain it overnight, which it did. In a farming community this was burdensome and greatly aggravated the townspeople. Both Chairmen tried to reduce this burden and opposition to an expanded watch explains in part the reluctance of the people to mount any guard. Jews, on the other hand, complained that the watchmen were often nowhere to be seen, including on some of the nights on which excesses occurred.[47]

[40]LRA 1459, 3rd July 1865, where the Chairman, Schäfer, minimised the damage and 15th September 1865; LRA 1461, Karlstadt, 22nd May, 1866, where the Chairman, Schuhmann, stated that the Jews were very fearful and sought to magnify everything in order to incite the state officials against the community administration.

[41]LRA 1459, 3rd July 1865; LRA 1461, Karlstadt, 28th May 1866 report to the government office in Würzburg.

[42]LRA 1461, Laudenbach 7th June 1866, Oehninger testimony.

[43]This literally occurred after each incident!

[44]Numerous reports throughout the documents.

[45]LRA 1461, Telegram from Weingärtner, Assessor in Karlstadt, to the Royal Ministry of the Interior Office in Würzburg, 1st June 1866.

[46]LRA 1459, Karlstadt, 17th May 1866, Weingärtner's *Beschluss* referring to the laws of 12th March 1850 and 4th May 1851. Also LRA 1461, 28th May 1866, report of the public meeting; also 29th May, 7:30 p.m. at a second meeting in Laudenbach; and the report of 30th May, Karlstadt, by Wiedenmann.

[47]LRA 1459, Karlstadt, 17th May 1866, Weingärtner's *Beschluss*.

Motivation for both the overt antisemitic acts as well as for the apathy regarding them is easily found in the form of traditional antisemitism. The communal board (or town council) in Laudenbach noted the Jews' record, historically, as usurers.[48] After the state requested quiet in late May 1866, placards appeared reading 'Down with the Jews on 2nd June'.[49] The infamous and inflammatory *Hep!-Hep!* cry of German antisemitism was reported on several occasions.[50] But the most complete and telling expression of anti-Jewish feeling may be seen in the voluntary testimony of one Philipp Oehninger, forty-six years old, retired, and living in Laudenbach. He was introduced by a Royal state official, Wiedenmann, as being "knowledgeable about the relations in the community [of Laudenbach] and enjoying the general respect and love [of the people]". Oehninger began by citing the "notorious" fact of Jewish usurious practices, adding that "any official . . . knew that. It is", he went on, "a further fact that here especially very many families have been ruined through the cheating and usury of the Jews."[51]

But the immediate source of bitterness in feelings as well as the explanation of the actions of some of the community is to be found in the process of emancipation described earlier. "Emancipation", Jacob Katz reminds us, is the restoration of a human condition lost at some earlier stage of development.[52] In communities like Wiesenfeld and Laudenbach that meant restoration of the right to participate in the community, in the *Gemeinde*, as full citizens, as *Bürger*. Voting, especially for a minority of about 10 to 15% of the population, was far less significant than more material factors. Emancipation in towns such as these meant the right to share in the common rights and goods, *Gemeindenutzungen*, including normally the right to share in the use of common lands for pasturage and wood.[53] Conflict over such rights won through state emancipation was a major cause of the antisemitic riots of 1866.

In Wiesenfeld the first reference to communal rights occurred in the statement of Moses Steigerwald on 25th July 1865. He stated that a possible motive was the Jewish role in Wiesenfeld in the rights to communal lands.[54] Nothing more was said of it, however, in 1865. But the next May, five days after the initial outbreak, Moses and Aaron Steigerwald arrived in Karlstadt in the morning of 22nd May to report on the previous night's events. Following their report of the facts as they saw them, they added that they were convinced that "all this" was due to their recent participation in the *Gemeindenutzungen*. "We are not usurers and this does not, as it might in other areas", they stated, "cause the agitation in Wiesenfeld". They continued:

[48]LRA 1461, 28th May 1866, Declaration of the *Gemeindeverwaltung*.

[49]LRA 1461, 30th May 1866, Wiedenmann report.

[50]LRA 1461, Laudenbach, 7th June 1866, testimony of Hirsch Frank the younger.

[51]LRA 1461, Laudenbach, 7th June 1866.

[52]Jacob Katz, 'The Term "Jewish Emancipation". Its Origins and Historical Impact', in Alexander Altmann (ed.), *Studies in Nineteenth-Century Jewish Intellectual History*, Cambridge, Mass., 1964, pp. 1–25.

[53]See Otto Gierke, *Das deutsche Genossenschaftsrecht*, 3 vols., Berlin 1868–1881; and Karl Bücher, *Die Allmende in Ihrer wirtschaftlichen und sozialen Bedeutung*, Berlin 1902.

[54]LRA 1459, Karlstadt 25th July 1865.

> "We also see clearly that we can find no sufficient protection for our persons and property from the Royal District Office on a permanent basis and that, if we carry through the establishment of a Royal Special Police Office (*Gendarmeriestation*) or even a smaller *Exekutionsgruppe*, the hate and bitterness against us will be even worse and more dangerous for us. If we could be certain that we would be left in peace, we would gladly give up participation in the communal revenues."[55]

That afternoon the Chairman of Wiesenfeld, Schäfer, reported in person in Karlstadt. He described the recent events from his perspective as well as his official role in ending them, adding the following statement:

> "Since no other ground for hate against the Jews exists, as I know from the Neighbourhood Watch, I am of the opinion that the peace will no longer be disturbed if the Jews renounce their *Nachbarholz* (common wood rights)."[56]

A governmental decree (*Beschluss*) followed Schäfer's report. It called for the military to intervene, but made the Communal Government responsible until the troops arrived. It noted that the Jews had declared their readiness to resign [their rights] in favour of their neighbours and to use more influence on the further actions of the Royal District Office. The Decree authorised the Communal Government to meet with the Jews to arrange for the renunciation of their participation in the *Gemeindenutzungen*.[57] The documents in the Wiesenfeld file end here, but a final comment exists in the correspondence relating to Laudenbach about a week later – in a report on the affairs in Laudenbach, the state official Wiedenmann noted that "Wiesenfeld is quiet and will remain so since the Jews have resigned their interest in the *Gemeindenutzungen*".[58]

Disturbances began in Laudenbach the night before the Wiesenfelders reached agreement on the communal rights, that is on 21st May. About the only difference between the events in the two towns prior to 7th June was the difficulty of trying to apprehend vandals in the dark in a town built on the side of a very steep hill. But the excesses were very bitter, more so than in Wiesenfeld. In an attempt to end the incidents, probably in light of the experience in Wiesenfeld, the Royal District Office ordered a meeting of all Christian heads of household for the evening of 28th May. This was highly unusual and possibly unique. Nearly all were present in the Neuland Inn, some 135 men in all. Wiedenmann lectured them on law and order, specifically reading aloud verbatim from the laws of 12th March 1850, especially article 342, and 4th May 1851.[59] But the excesses continued and the military was called for. Still seeking a solution, Wiedenmann called a meeting of all "Israelites" for 7th June to try to come to an understanding both about the excesses as well as the outlook for the future in terms of security.[60]

Evidently every Jewish head of household who was then in Laudenbach, twenty-one in all, took part. Nine more were absent: four were away on business trips, four had fled the town, and one was too old. Of those who appeared, four were merchants, ten were engaged in some form of agricultural endeavour, three

[55]LRA 1459, Karlstadt, 22nd May 1866, Vormittag, 9 a.m.
[56]LRA 1459, Karlstadt, 22nd May 1866, Nachmittag.
[57]*Ibid.*
[58]LRA 1461, Karlstadt, 28th May 1866, Nachmittag.
[59]LRA 1461, Laudenbach, 28th May 1866, from Wiedenmann.
[60]LRA 1461, Laudenbach, 7th June 1866; until noted the following material is from this source.

were weavers, one was a shoemaker, one a second-hand dealer, and one was the teacher in the religious school. As a group these Jews were afraid, despite the presence of the military. Since most of the military had been quartered with the Jews, they claimed knowledge of Christian sentiments obtained from the soldiers. The gist of this was that when the military left, Jews would be at risk. Levi Worms then stated that the former communal Chairman, Franz Diels, in front of his wife and servant, had stated on the 31st that they, the Jews, should settle the communal rights issue or the community could not be restrained. Other testimony substantiated the feeling that, when the troops left, conditions would worsen.

The assembled Jews asked for the military not to be withdrawn until conditions improved and the old good relations between Christians and Jews returned. They stated that, for their part, their behaviour would not fail to be compliant. The next paragraph, recorded by the Royal District Office, is important and reads:

> "It is always stated by the Royal District Office that it is our free choice whether to renounce our right to wood from the common forest. We are also prepared of our own free will for our persons to declare such renunciation, but only under the condition that the Christian community give up its hostile attitude to us and allow us again to enjoy protection; at the most we wished to retain the right to wood for a few poor."

Before further testimony was taken, the state official inserted a paragraph stating that he would not act as mediator between Jews and Christians in pursuit of such a settlement.

The public emergence of the issue of the *Gemeindenutzungen* on 7th June in Laudenbach was new, but, as the testimony of the Jews shows, the question of the participation of the Jewish community was longstanding. Indeed, the Communal Board (similar to a city council) had itself declared, on 28th May, that the "agitation" against the Jews in Laudenbach stemmed in part from their usurious occupations and in part from their legal sharing in the Communal Rights.[61] Both Samson Adler and Levi Worms later testified that the excesses were an attempt to force Jews to renounce their right to wood from the commons. So, too, Philipp Oehninger pointed to the wood rights as the source of conflict in Laudenbach. He held that Jews should not have the right since they had not previously supported the community. (By which he seems to have meant that they had not been members of it until emancipation.) The people, he said, saw this as a moral injustice, if not as actually illegal, and he agreed with them. Since their emancipation, he gratuitously commented, Jews had become more impudent.

It is not entirely clear what happened in Laudenbach after the meeting of 7th June. There is no document stating, as in the case of Wiesenfeld, that the two sides reached agreement. But the next day, 8th June, Wiedenmann recommended withdrawal of the military.[62] Two days later the military commander ordered the removal of the detachment of fifty to take place on the 11th and to

[61]LRA 1461, Laudenbach, 28th May 1866, Declaration of the *Gemeindeverwaltung*.
[62]LRA 1461, Karlstadt, 8th June, Wiedenmann to the Royal Government Office in Würzburg.

go to Würzburg.[63] Each official justified the action on the grounds "that the community has taken steps to prevent further actions". This of course could have meant only a better local watch; but it might well also indicate a bargain between Christians and Jews. Unlike the Wiesenfeld case there were further incidents, though few and very mild. In a few weeks even these ceased.[64] The crisis was over. The state demanded payment for the costs of the military and Laudenbach protested, taking the issue to court where the town lost and had to pay.[65]

In conclusion several points need to be made. The anti-Jewish riots in Wiesenfeld and Laudenbach had nothing in common with the events in Bohemia or Würzburg. Emancipation put a strain on relations between Christians and Jews, because Christians refused to accept full equality of Jews in the community. The Bavarian state acted quickly to end the crisis and was reasonably even-handed in doing so. Throughout the crisis the state officials favoured the Christian Community, but not to the serious detriment of the Jews. Jews recognised the nature of the problem, firmly fought for protection and their rights, and did so locally in an innovative manner. They used the military and its cost as a lever against the Christians, yet in the end they traded some of their newly-won rights for peace.

Whether this bargain worked well is not clear. Both communities declined in size over the ensuing decades, but nearly all such communities in Bavaria and Germany did so also. The files contain no further references to similar incidents in these towns, though some may have occurred. The Jewish Communal records give no hint about these matters. But the use of popular antisemitism, at times violent antisemitism, as a tactic in dealing with communal rights makes it clear that legal emancipation was not always successful. It was often merely the prelude to a more difficult process of social acceptance and assimilation on the local level. Later failure on the national level does not mean that failure must also have occurred in the locality.

Were the events in Wiesenfeld and Laudenbach unique? Here we must distinguish between the specific actions in these two towns in Unterfranken and the process whereby the Christian community attempted, successfully it must be remembered, to modify the legal emancipatory changes required by the state. Hints from research on other areas mentioned earlier[66] indicate that other communities may have used a similar process though in different fashion. It is quite possible that Jewish communities in some areas gave up or bartered some

[63]LRA 1461, Würzburg, 10th June 1866, 2:30 p.m. Telegram form, from the Royal General-Kommando Würzburg to the Karlstadt Bezirksamt.

[64]LRA 1461, Laudenbach, 25th July 1866, the final report of the Chairman noting no more incidents.

[65]LRA 1461, Laudenbach, 16th June 1866, statement from Würzburg.

[66]See above note 15. Bayerisches Staatsarchiv Würzburg, Präsidial Akten 325, Report of the Royal *Landrichter*, Büttner, in Karlstadt, 20th January 1850, who, in response to inquiry from Munich into the state of opinion regarding Jewish emancipation, stated that the cause of anti-Jewish sentiment was the damage it would do to Christian *Gemeindenutzungen*; he added that emancipation would cause violence to Jews, but no political reaction. Among the communities which sent petitions against emancipation to the *Reichsräte* in 1849–1850 were both Laudenbach and Wiesenfeld.

of the unimportant new rights for acceptance without the upsets of 1866. The fact is that the situation in Wiesenfeld and Laudenbach was not unique either for Jews or their Bavarian neighbours; a similar development elsewhere would not be surprising.

Finally, Monika Richarz has argued persuasively that there was a causal connection between agrarian antisemitism and agrarian economic depression. Indeed she inclines to belief that economic depression was the only cause.[67] But the events in Laudenbach and Wiesenfeld did not occur during a period of economic recession. There was a crisis, but it was political. Elsewhere Richarz writes that the reality of antisemitism is more important than its theory. She is right and this essay is an attempt to add to our knowledge of the reality of antisemitism in small-town Germany.

[67]Richarz, 'German Jews in the Rural Economy', *loc. cit.*, p. 105.

APPENDIX

Laudenbach 7. Juni 1866

Praes.	Exzesse gegen die
kgl. Reg. Rath Wiedenmann	Juden in Laudenbach
Rechtspr. Uhl	betr.

Man hat für angemessen befunden, heute die sämmtlichen Israeliten von hier zusammenkommen zu lassen, um sie theils über die jüngsten Vorgänge und Exzesse, theils über die ihnen für die Zukunft in Aussicht stehende Sicherheit zu vernehmen.

Die nebengenannte Kommission begab sich zu diesem Ende heute hieher und es haben sich im Gemeindezimmer im Neuland'schen Gastwirthshause dahier folgende Israeliten eingefunden.

1. Wolf Süsser, Kaufmann;
2. Levi Worms, Kaufmann u. Kultusvorstand;
3. Aaron Bernai, Kaufmann;
4. Abraham Hall, Trödler;
5. Lazarus Frank jung, Oekonom;
6. Hirsch Frank jung, Oekonom;
7. Lazarus Frank alt, Oekonom;
8. Salomon Khan, Oekonom;
9. Aaron Adler, Oekonom;
10. Samson Adler, ledig, 35 Jahre alt für seine Mutter Hanne Adler;
11. Hirsch Frank alt, Oekonom;
12. Gabriel Worms, Weber;
13. Joseph Worms, Schuhmacher;
14. Isak Adler, Oekonom;
15. Michael Frank, Oekonom;
16. Mayer Rosendorf, Weber;
17. Mayer Bach, Weber;
18. ? Adler, Oekonom;
19. Samuel Strauss, Kaufmann;
20. Hahum (?) Süsser, Oekonom;
21. Samuel Danziger, Religionslehrer

Ausser diesen Erschienenen sind noch weiter dahier ansässig:

1. David Grünebaum, Garküchner (?) in Lohr wahrscheinlich in Gerichtsgeschäften heute abwesend;
2. Sophie Grünebaum, Kaufmannswittwe, seit vorgestern nach Geldersheim zu ihrem Tochtermanne abgezogen aus Furcht vor den hiesigen Unruhen;
3. Isaak Bach, Trödler, seit einigen Tagen auf einer Geschäftsreise abwesend;
4. Aaron Hecht, Oekonom, welcher heute beim kgl. Landgerichte Carlstadt Geschäfte hat.
5. Joseph Strauss, Oekonom, in Geschäften heute abwesend.
6. Aaron Frank, Privatier, kann wegen Altersschwäche nicht erscheinen;
7. Benjamin Süsser, Oekonom, seit ungefähr einer Woche aus Furcht vor künftigen Unruhen nach Würzburg abgezogen, und dort eine eigene Wohnung bezogen habend;
8. Aaron Siegel, Oekonom, vergangenen Dienstag aus gleichem Grunde nach Würzburg abgezogen, sammt Familie und allem beweglichen Vermögen;
9. Süssel Süsser, Oekonom, aus gleichem Grunde mit Familie nach Würzburg abgezogen.

Diese Angaben über die Abwesenden gründen sich auf die Aussagen der

Comparenten, welch' Letztere auf Befragen deponiren: I. Wir halten trotz der Anwesenheit des Militärs die Sicherheit und Ruhe noch keineswegs für so hergestellt, dass wir nach dem Abzuge desselben nicht abermals Gefährdungen unseres Eigenthums und vielleicht noch grössere als die bisherigen und etwa auch unserer Personen besorgen mussten. Viele von uns haben bisher mit christlichen Familien im besten befreundetsten Verhältnisse gelebt, gegenwärtig schauen uns dieselben nicht mehr an, geben viel mehr nur Hass und Erbitterung zu erkennen.

Wir haben fast grösstentheils Soldaten einquartirt und von diesen vernommen, wie die christlichen Einwohner dahier sagen, wie das Militär fort sey, hätten die Israeliten die grössten Gefahren zu besorgen; alle Rache, die schon früher hätte genommen werde sollen, werde dann zur Ausführung kommen.

[Testimony from five Jews follows]

Wir Alle bitten, dass vorerst das Militär nicht entlassen wird, und zwar in so lange nicht, bis sich eine bessere Gesinnung gegen uns zu erkennen gibt, und bis das frühere gute Einvernehmen zwischen Christen und Juden wieder zurückgekehrt seyn wird; wir unsererseits werden es an zuvorkommendem Benehmen nicht fehlen lassen.

Es wurde uns von Seiten der königl. Behörde immer als unser freier Wille erklärt, ob wir auf unsere Holzrechte aus dem Gemeindewalde verzichten wollen. Wir sind auch aus freiem Willen für unsere Personen bereit, einen solchen Verzicht auszusprechen, aber nur unter der Bedingung, dass die christliche Gemeinde ihre feindliche Gesinnung gegen uns aufgibt und uns wieder Schutz angedeihen lässt; höchstens für einige Arme wünschten wir das Holzrecht erhalten. Weiter müssten wir uns vorbehalten, von den Gemeindelasten befreit zu werden.

Den Comparenten wurde hierauf sofort bewirkt, dass wenn sie einen solchen Verzicht und bezügliches Übereinkommen mit den christlichen Gemeindegliedern aussprechen bezw. treffen wollen, dies ihr freier Wille und es ihre Sache sey, hierwegen der Gemeinde eine Eröffnung zu machen, das kgl. Bezirksamt fühle sich aber nicht veranlasst, irgend welche Vermittlung zu übernehmen. [A list of damage follows, as well as additional testimony on the events, in twenty pages of manuscript.]

The Government of Baden against Antisemitism

Political Expediency or Principle?

BY MICHAEL ANTHONY RIFF

Baden has been regarded by historians of both the *Kaiserreich* and the Weimar Republic as a bastion of Liberalism in which an adherence to democratic principles, a spirit of political compromise and constitutionality combined to make the Grand Duchy the representative of the "other Germany" par excellence. However self-congratulatory and exaggerated this claim may at times sound, there is a certain underlying truth to it. It was no wonder, especially after the creation of the *Gross-Block* coalition between the Liberals and the Social Democrats, that Baden became a great hope for democrats throughout Germany.

This does not mean that the Grand Duchy was not afflicted by most of the same problems which plagued the rest of the country. Social strife was endemic in the industrial towns, demands for protectionism were heard up and down the countryside and the call for electoral reform came from both the under-represented Catholic and working-class segments of the population. Neither was Baden immune from the scourge of antisemitism which afflicted Germany from the late 1870s onwards. Characteristically, however, the extent to which organised Jew-hatred entered the political fabric of the Grand Duchy was limited both in geographic and electoral terms. Why this was so had a good deal to do with the diverse territorial and confessional make-up of the state as well as the direction of economic change. Perhaps unique to Baden was the role of the Government and the ruling house in reducing this antisemitism. The reasons for the state intervention were necessarily complex and had much to do with the special political circumstances of the Grand Duchy. The question is inevitably begged whether the policy of combating antisemitism was motivated by a sincere opposition to Jew-hatred or political expediency. In the following pages, it is hoped, an answer will be provided.

Despite significant progress both before and after the Revolution of 1848, the completion of Jewish emancipation in Baden had to wait till 1862. Even then, the measure was by no means universally popular. In 1848, after all, the feeling that Jewish emancipation was imminent helped trigger-off some of the worst and most widespread antisemitic violence Germany had seen since the Middle Ages.[1] By 1860, the anomaly in law which kept the Jews second-class citizens

[1]See Michael Anthony Riff, 'The Anti-Jewish Aspect of the Revolutionary Unrest of 1848 in Baden and its Impact on Emancipation', in *LBI Year Book XXI* (1976), pp. 27–40.

was, for the new Liberal leadership under August Lamey and the Grand Duke, no longer tenable. The liberal principle of equality for all citizens under the law had finally triumphed.[2] The worry, nevertheless, persisted that the measure would lead to violence as well as continued popular resistance. Local officials were requested to take the Government's case to the people and in certain areas the Gendarmerie and army were put on alert.[3] No serious disturbances took place, and what had been becoming a fact of life in all the larger towns and many villages since 1848 was embedded in law.[4] The Jews of Baden were full and equal citizens under the law with all the accompanying rights, privileges and obligations. The Government, for its part, not only tried to sway public opinion in favour of the measure, but made every effort to see that it was fully and properly implemented.[5] With emancipation completed, for the Jews of Baden the next thirty years or so were essentially marked by material progress and outward tranquility. While antisemitism had already become a factor in the political life of other German states in the 1880s, it left Baden relatively untouched until the early part of 1890 when the avowedly antisemitic *Deutsch-Soziale Partei* of Max Hugo Liebermann von Sonnenberg started agitating in the Heidelberg area, Lörrach and Müllheim. From the start the authorities showed a keen interest in the group's meetings which attracted supporters as well as opponents and, as a consequence, showed every potential for violence.[6] There was a certain precedent as well, in the anti-Socialist and anti-Catholic campaigns of curbing "dissident" political agitation from whichever quarter it came.

If the local authorities were hardly enamoured with the antisemites, neither were they in love with Jews. This is especially noticeable in the reporting of an antisemitic meeting of 2nd May 1890 in Müllheim. The *Bezirksamt* accepted a claim that Jews had ordered and paid for the attendance of a group of ten Social Democratic activists from Freiburg.[7] In its opinion, moreover, this was a move which could hardly be expected to win support amongst their true allies in the population (presumably the bourgeoisie) who would never become the bed-fellows of the Socialists.[8]

Prejudice amongst the lower echelons of the bureaucracy against Jews was by no means a new phenomenon. They had traditionally been prone to take the part of the peasantry in their complaints of exploitation at the hands of Jewish middlemen and money-lenders. This could be seen most clearly in the *Enquêtes* of the 1880s relating to "Wucher auf dem Lande".[9] It was not, furthermore, a

[2]Reinhard Rürup, 'Die Judenemanzipation in Baden', in *Zeitschrift für die Geschichte des Oberrheins*, 75 (1966), pp. 241–300.
[3]'Die Verhütung unruhiger Auftritte gegen die Juden', Badisches General-Landes-Archiv, Karlsruhe (abbr. GLA) 339/928; GLA 236/14706.
[4]Rürup, *loc. cit.*
[5]'Die Überwachung von Vereinen und Versammlungen. Die Antisemitische Bewegung betreffend', GLA 236/17241.
[6]*Ibid.*
[7]Report of the Bezirksamt Müllheim to the Ministry of the Interior, 2nd May 1890, GLA 236/17241.
[8]*Ibid.*
[9]See *Wucher auf dem Lande*, Schriften des Vereins für Sozialpolitik, Bd. 35, Leipzig 1887.

phenomenon exclusively confined to Baden. An instance comes to mind of an official in the Württemberg *Oberamt* of Ulm who at about the same time did everything except express outright support for the antisemitic stance taken by the local conservative newspaper.[10] Similarly, officials looking into the hop trade in Franconia were quite open in their antipathy towards Jewish involvement.[11]

Whereas in official reports one often has to read between the lines to discern an anti-Jewish bias, in the press such feelings were sometimes openly displayed. There is no mistaking the position, for instance, of the author of the following, which appeared at the time of the anti-Jewish agitation in South Baden in the Liberal *Freiburger Zeitung*:

> "Wer mit bäuerlichen Kreisen bekannt und vertraut ist, der wird mir Recht geben, wenn ich behaupte, daß an dem Rückgang unserer Landwirtschaft ein gut Stück davon auf das Kerbholz der Juden geschrieben werden muß. Daß daher die Bewegung gegen die Juden in diesen Kreisen Fortschritte machen muß, das liegt auf der Hand. An den Juden selbst liegt es ganz allein, wenn der Antisemitismus dominieren soll."[12]

The *Synagogenrat* of Freiburg, in fact, was so incensed by the above remarks that it took the matter up with the *Bezirksamt* in Freiburg and the *Landeskommissariat* for South Baden. In its plea the Jewish body pointed to the special position of the *Freiburger Zeitung* as an *Amtsblatt*. Interestingly, for its part, the *Landeskommissariat* while regarding the above remarks as "not very tactful and regrettable", did not feel that any action beyond informing the paper's editor of its displeasure was in any way necessary. One has a sense that the *Landeskommissariat* simply hoped the matter would sort itself out with a minimum of intervention. On the other hand, in a report of 29th May 1890 to the Ministry of the Interior in Karlsruhe it went a long way towards actually agreeing with the argument of the newspaper:

> "Die antisemitische Bewegung in der Stadt Müllheim, die vornehmlich in den Gemeinden Fernbach, Beblingen und Rheinminster Boden finden dürfte, hat vorzugsweise in den ungünstigen Ernten der letzten Jahre und der damit in Zusammenhang stehenden da und dort vorgekommenen Ausbeutung minder gut situirter Landwirte durch einzelne Israeliten der Bewegung gut ihrem Begier Vorschub geleistet . . ."[13]

While the attitude of the lower-level bureaucracy in Baden towards the incursions of the antisemites can at best be described as equivocal, at ministerial level the situation gives every indication of having been decidedly different. Action was taken, as it were, to nip the antisemitic movement in the bud. In May of 1890, within weeks of the matter having been brought to its attention, the Ministry of Justice, Religious Affairs and Education (*Ministerium der Justiz, des Kultus und Unterrichts*) through their local school boards informed several teachers, known to be active in the movement, that their participation

[10]See Antisemitische Hetze, 1891–1922, Haupt-Staatsarchiv Stuttgart (abbr.: *HStASt*), E 130a/406.

[11]Information supplied by William Tannenbaum of Stanford University to M. A. Riff, September 1983.

[12]*Freiburger Zeitung*, 6th July 1890, cited in GLA 236, 17241.

[13]Report of the *Landeskommissar* for the districts of Freiburg, Lörrach and Offenburg to the Ministry of the Interior, 29th May 1890, GLA 236/17241.

was not commensurate with their positions as public servants. The wording of the memoranda is instructive:

> "Wir müssen ein solch' offenes Eintreten in eine Bewegung, die, wenn auch vielleicht nicht nach der Absicht der einzelnen dabei beteiligten Personen, so doch thatsächlich geeignet erscheint, den Frieden unter den einzelnen Klassen der Bevölkerung zu stören, für durchaus unvereinbar erklären mit den für Professor Schumacher aus seiner Stellung als öffentlicher Lehrer sich ergebenden Verpflichtungen."[14]

There is a clear sense in the above that an anti-Jewish stance is not in harmony with the terms of emancipation and religious equality. Later in the letter the fear is also expressed that Professor Schumacher's antisemitism would find its way into the classroom. Individual as well as general prejudice against Jews was seen as a distinct possibility.[15] This is not surprising, since the warning letters were, at least in part, occasioned by a complaint from the father of one of Schumacher's Jewish pupils in Müllheim. Just how clearly the Ministry spelt out the consequences of involvement in the antisemitic cause for the teachers concerned can be seen from the following paragraph in a letter to the School Board in Weinheim regarding a teacher at a local state-registered private school:

> "We cannot help but feel that it is up to the institute to see to it that the teacher Sturm in future refrains from participating in the above-mentioned movement. Otherwise, we shall feel ourselves forced to regard the said teacher's conditions of service as having been violated. Put another way, we shall be forced to consider whether we should not apply for his dismissal."[16]

Clearly, government policy in this regard made itself felt as directly as possible. It had, however, an indirect effect on subordinate authorities which may have, in the last analysis, been more significant. They were given the clear message that the antisemitic movement was not going to be encouraged nor even tolerated. We find, for example, the *Landeskommissariat* for South Baden reporting to the Ministry of the Interior of the reprimand it had given to the mayor of the town of Wollbach for letting the Town Hall for an antisemitic meeting. This was only a matter of weeks after the *Landeskommissariat* had issued a report, in some senses, sympathising with the anti-Jewish mood in its area.[17]

Similar attitudes made themselves felt when, in 1894, a petition from the *Deutsch-Sozialer Verein* of Mannheim (which existed prior to the *Deutsch-Soziale Partei* of the same name) calling for an investigation into the laws of the Jewish religion, came up for consideration before the Upper House of the *Landtag*. One of the members of the committee charged with reporting on the petition, Presiding Judge Kamm, while rejecting the demand of the antisemites, expressed the mood of his colleagues in seeing the growing hatred of the Jews

> ". . . in certain realities of economic life . . . Anyone who has lived in the countryside will know that in just about every village there is a Jewish dealer or agent who exploits the local

[14]Memorandum from the Ministry of the Interior to the *Oberschulamt* Weinheim, 13th May 1890, GLA 236/17241.

[15]*Ibid.*

[16]Letter from the Ministry of the Interior to the *Oberschulamt* Weinheim, 7th June 1890, *ibid.*

[17]Report of the *Landeskommissar* . . ., 29th May 1890, GLA 236/17241.

population. On the stock exchanges, as well, most dealings involve the participation of Jews. Antisemitism is, therefore, not an artificially created movement."[18]

While being equally hostile to the aims of the antisemites as well as mindful of their potential for political and social disruption, the report of the commission reiterated the views of Kamm in maintaining that

> "... popular resentment against Jewry has not merely been superimposed through agitation. Much more, we see it as a grass-roots phenomenon which has been brought to the surface, nurtured and made politically and socially useful through agitation."[19]

Even so, perhaps one should not regard an understanding for the anti-Jewish position of the rural population as incompatible with combating antisemitism as a political movement. To whatever extent a *Landeskommissar* or high-ranking judge might share some of the prejudices of the antisemites, he saw himself as being first and foremost dedicated to preserving the constitutional *status quo* in Baden, of which Jewish emancipation was an integral part.

This was essentially the policy as well of the National Liberal Party in Baden. As early as June 1890 the election committee of the Party in Mannheim issued a memorandum to its electors in the Mannheim/Schwetzingen area to be on their guard against the activities of the *Deutsch-Sozialen*:

> "This party under the banner of popular reform pursues a policy of inducing and encouraging antisemitic feeling ... we address to you, therefore, the urgent plea to use all your powers to prevent this party from making any headway, so that in our constituency confessional peace may be preserved."[20]

Some months later, in November, the annual convention of the party in Baden went so far as to declare that it was a matter of honour to oppose the antisemitic faction of the Conservative Party led by von Stockhorn. Franz Thorbecke of Mannheim declared that it was the duty of any Liberal party to struggle against antisemitism and implored all local branches of the National Liberal Party in Baden to prepare pamphlets and other measures to counter the activities of antisemitic agitators in rural areas.[21]

The National Liberals of Baden were not far from the mark in identifying the antisemitic threat as coming at that time chiefly from the ranks of the Conservatives. Otto Freiherr von Stockhorn, one of their leaders, was, indeed, in the vanguard of those Conservatives who espoused the antisemitic cause. He was held, for example, to be responsible for the increasingly anti-Jewish stance of the Conservative daily, the *Badische Landespost*. Another omen of the time, according to the *Allgemeine Zeitung des Judentums*,[22] was that the notorious antisemite, *Hofprediger* Adolf Stoecker, was scheduled to speak before the annual conference of the Conservatives on 17th October whereas previously his supporters had not even been able to rent a hall in which he could speak.[23]

The role of Stockhorn in these events becomes all the more significant when

[18]*Karlsruher Zeitung*, 6th February 1894, cited in GLA 236/17241.
[19]*Ibid.*
[20]*Allgemeine Zeitung des Judentums*, 54, 12 (6th June 1890).
[21]*Ibid.*, 54, 45 (20th November 1890).
[22]*Ibid.*, 54, 35 (12th September 1890).
[23]*Ibid.*, 54, 27 (18th June 1890).

we bear in mind his later activity as the prime mover amongst the Conservatives in Baden for an alliance with the antisemites. He played a key role, for example, in arranging the candidacy in 1893 of the notorious Max Liebermann von Sonnenberg for the *Reichstag* constituency of Freiburg-Emmendingen-Walkirch. On that occasion he made his first attempt to forge an alliance between Protestant and Catholic voters in part on the basis of a common approach *vis-à-vis* the Jews. He was, of course, convinced that antisemitism would be a main factor in bringing like-minded voters, irrespective of denomination, together to challenge the National Liberals. To this end, for instance, he arranged for the distribution in the constituency of an excerpt from the infamous pamphlet by Father Josef Deckert, *Kann ein Katholik Antisemit sein?*[24] Von Stockhorn's efforts, as it turned out, were not entirely without effect, for it seems, even after taking into account the reduced voter turn-out, in 1893, Liebermann made a modest gain over the Conservative candidate's showing in 1890 at the expense of the *Zentrum*.[25]

One might add that in all the constituencies where they ran in 1893 the Conservatives aligned themselves behind their party's Tivoli Programme of 1892 and injected a strong dose of antisemitism into their campaigns. It was, moreover, not the first time. As early as the election of 1881, in fact, von Stockhorn involved himself in the cause. The occasion was the candidacy in the 10th *Reichstag* constituency Mannheim of his fellow Conservative, Freiherr Adolf von Marschall. Stockhorn joined the campaign after the first round of voting in which Marschall lost a considerable number of votes to the National Liberal candidate who had the support of some Social Democrats and Left Liberals. Openly antisemitic hand-bills claiming that Jews and their allies were responsible for the impoverishment of peasants and artisans were distributed in country areas. One of these was even displayed outside the home of a local official.[26] The culprit, a lower-echelon court clerk, was dismissed immediately.

With the above activity taking place in Baden it was not surprising that by 1890 fears were expressed in Jewish circles about the potential of the antisemitic movement in the Grand Duchy. As the following remarks made by one commentator in the *Allgemeine Zeitung des Judentums* indicate, what Jews and others especially feared was a spread of the movement from neighbouring Hessen:

> "Of late, the antisemites have been showing a preference for taking their campaign into Baden. They hope to find fertile ground there because Baden, after Hessen, Alsace-Lorraine and several Prussian provinces, has the highest per capita Jewish population according to the census of 1885 – 169 per 1,000 as opposed to 273 for Alsace-Lorraine and 256 for Hessen. As in Hessen they have set their sights on the rural population."[27]

Some three years later, in commenting on the participation of the antisemites for the first time in elections to the *Reichstag*, another writer, also in the *Allgemeine Zeitung des Judentums*, took a much more sober view of the matter:

[24]*Hinterlassung v. Stockhorn*, GLA/N 69/135.
[25]F. L. Sepaintner, *Die Reichstagswahlen im Grossherzogtum Baden*, Bern 1982, p. 145.
[26]GLA 236/15221.
[27]*Allgemeine Zeitung des Judentums*, 54, 31 (15th August 1890).

"If we objectively investigate the causes of this movement in Baden, we find the explanation solely in the discontent of the agricultural population. The economic situation in our otherwise fertile land has, following several bad harvests and as a consequence, as well, of a short supply of feed stuffs, taken a turn for the worse. In order to vocalise their discontent, farmers have shown a preference for antisemitism as opposed to Socialism without in the process becoming committed enemies of the Jews . . ."[28]

The article went on to defend the Jews against the often-made charge of exploitation by Jewish cattle-dealers and other middlemen in the rural economy. In some areas, according to its author, it was Christians and not Jews who engaged in unfair business practices. Jews and Christians had, in fact, banded together to found the *Landesschutzverein gegen wucherische Ausbeutung des Volkes*. In some areas, moreover, official statistics showed that Jews were completely impoverished and largely dependent on charitable support. Additionally, the antisemites had failed to keep their long-standing promise of producing a list of farm properties that had been sub-divided and sold by Jews. While the author emphasised that the Jews of Baden still had to be thankful to the National Liberals as the party largely responsible for bringing about their emancipation, he was disappointed at what he saw as the "highly indecisive position" the party was currently taking towards the antisemitic movement.[29]

He felt, for example, that such newspapers as the formerly "echt und recht" Liberal *Badische Landeszeitung* had adopted the language and tactics of the antisemites in holding the Jews responsible for the politics of the *Frankfurter Zeitung*. The Liberals in Baden, in his view, showed no inclination, furthermore, to meet the challenge of the antisemites head on, but rather, like their colleagues in Prussia, chose to issue hollow but high-sounding declarations. He left his sternest warning for the leading Jews amongst the ranks of the Liberals:

"Especially the Jewish Liberal *Grandees* of Mannheim and Karlsruhe who notice nothing of the antisemitic campaign . . . should take heed. The Jews in the countryside, who in any case find it exceedingly difficult to support themselves, are neither personally nor financially in the position to contribute very much towards the struggle against it. Here our intelligentsia must take the lead."[30]

All in all, however, the article took an optimistic view of developments and saw the antisemites in Baden as being unable to achieve the successes they had in Hessen and Saxony. In this regard, the author also took solace in the fact that the Catholics of Baden, representing two-thirds of the total population, had shown themselves particularly resistant to incursions by the antisemites. He was especially positive on the role of the Catholic press and clergy:

"Their newspapers constantly warn against this dragon-seed and their clergy emphasise the un-Christian aspects of the movement."[31]

As we shall shortly see, his trust was somewhat misplaced.

[28]*Ibid.*
[29]*Ibid.*
[30]*Ibid.*
[31]*Ibid.*

In coming back to the role of the Government of Baden towards the antisemitic movement it has to be stressed that as long it was in its infancy the containment of its activities was viewed both as a matter of principle and as part of the authorities' general responsibility to preserve law and order. Once, however, the antisemitic *Deutsch-Sozialen* showed themselves to be an independent and seemingly threatening force in the electoral arena the situation naturally changed. From that moment onwards, the Government of Baden's policy towards Jew-hatred became inexorably tied to its own struggle for self-preservation. It was not as if the *Deutsch-Sozialen* ever threatened to become a major political force in Baden. Their potential lay in possibly being able to make electoral gains in Protestant rural areas at the expense of the National Liberals and in the possibility of their making common cause with the right-wing opponents of the National Liberals, the Conservatives and the Agrarian League.

This situation was a product of the unique political, confessional and social structure of Baden. Although dominated by a Protestant ruling house and a National Liberal diet and bureaucracy, about 61% of the population of the state was Catholic. Moreover, of the forty *Amtsbezirke* in Baden twenty-eight had overwhelming Catholic majorities; only twelve were clearly "Protestant". The latter were concentrated in the Northern part of the state between Karlsruhe and Weinheim and the rural districts of the North-east. But even there such districts as Wiesloch, Tauberbischofsheim and Buchen had Catholic majorities of over 90%.[32] With the dismantling of the *Kulturkampf* in the 1880s and growing popular awareness of its potential, the Catholic Centre Party became increasingly assertive as an oppositional force in politics.

Industrialisation did not only bring about changes to the social structure and landscape of Baden, but also to its political configuration. Even though many of the workers in the new factories which came into being after 1870, whether in the cities of Mannheim or Karlsruhe or in the less urbanised settings of Wiesloch, Weinheim, Offenburg or Säckingen, returned to their villages and tilled their family farms after the day's work, from the mid-1880s onwards the strength of the Social Democrats increased significantly. The challenge of the Social Democrats and the *Zentrum* was only deflected thanks to an outdated indirect electoral system and advantageously drawn constituency boundaries. Pressure at the ballot box continued and the control of the National Liberals over the *Landtag* became increasingly tenuous.[33]

Even though the antisemites had been perceived as a threat earlier, it was only with the 1895 election to the *Landtag* that they became serious contenders for seats. It is, nevertheless, important to note that the *Deutsch-Sozialen* had taken part in previous electoral campaigns, both those for the *Landtag* as well as the *Reichstag*. They did not necessarily put up their own candidates, but sometimes chose rather to support those of other parties. There was, however, even an instance of one of their number, Liebermann von Sonnenberg, having

[32] *Badische Geschichte. Vom Grossherzogtum bis zur Gegenwart.* Hrsg. von der Landeszentrale für politische Bildung Baden-Württemberg. Stuttgart 1979, p. 110; Johnpeter Horst Grill, *The Nazi Movement in Baden*, Chapel Hill 1983, pp. 3 ff.

[33] *Ibid.*, pp. 83–84.

been chosen as the candidate of the *Deutschkonservative Partei* of the *5. Badischer Reichstagwahlkreis* (Freiburg, Emmendingen, Waldkirch). This was apparently the "brain-child" of the Conservative politician Otto Freiherr von Stockhorn who envisaged a grand coalition of the Right to include not only the antisemites and Conservatives, but also elements normally loyal to the *Zentrum*. The bond that would unite them in a new bloc, in his view, would be antisemitism. In the end, however, the overwhelming majority ignored the propaganda of Stockhorn and his associates and continued to vote along confessional lines.[34]

This did not mean that Catholic farmers, artisans, shopkeepers and other members of the lower and lower-middle classes did not have views about Jews similar to those of their Protestant neighbours and fellow countrymen – they had. In their end effect, the resentment felt by the Protestant and Catholic peasant against the Jewish cattle-dealer or that of the Protestant and Catholic artisan against the Jewish entrepreneur and banker were indistinguishable. To invoke "Catholic backwardness"[35] as a special animus in the rise of popular antisemitism in Baden would simply mean, moreover, imposing a pattern that did not fit.

For one thing, those Protestant areas where antisemitism took the strongest hold were just as economically "backward" as many Catholic areas in Baden. The Protestant peasants of the Kraichgau and Odenwald hardly lived in conditions any more advantageous than their Catholic counterparts in the Black Forest and South Baden. For another, however much resentment against Jews may have been harboured by Catholics in Baden, it was never, during the *Kaiserreich*, anywhere near a major factor in their political mobilisation. Catholics in Baden, to put it simply, voted along sectarian lines. Whatever deviation from this pattern took place was only amongst a small segment of the urban working class.

This did not mean that electoral and parliamentary alliances between the Centre Party and the antisemites were out of the question in Baden. At least one attempt, however, to mould an electoral alliance between the Conservatives, the *Zentrum* and the antisemitic *Deutsch-Sozialen* on the basis of a common position on the Jewish Question failed, as we have seen.

The policy of the Centre Party was to put up, whenever possible, candidates on their own. There was, moreover, the problem that both the *Deutsch-Sozialen* and their erstwhile Conservative allies were political groupings decidedly Protestant in character. Especially in Baden many of the same resentments that existed between Catholics and Liberals were present between Catholics and the Protestant politicians on the Right.

What did develop in the 1890s, however, was a certain amount of electoral cooperation between the *Zentrum* and the antisemites at constituency level.[36] In the first two instances – Weinheim in 1895[37] and Heidelberg-Land in 1897[38] – the

[34]*Hinterlassung v. Stockhorn* (see note 24).

[35]For an elucidation of this notion, see David Blackbourn, 'Roman Catholics, the Centre Party and Anti-Semitism in Imperial Germany', in P. Kennedy and A. Nicholls (eds.), *Nationalist and Racialist Movements in Britain and Germany before 1914*, London 1981.

[36]GLA 236/15095.

[37]*Pfälzer Bote*, 30, 241 (19th October 1895).

[38]*Heidelberger Zeitung*, 252 (28th October 1897).

Centre Party in multiple-round voting eventually withdrew its own candidate and advised its electors to vote for the candidate of the *Deutsch-Sozialen*. In each case the end result was the defeat of the National Liberal incumbent and the victory of the antisemite. The constituencies were, of course, neighbours and had strong Protestant majorities in which the Centre Party could only hope to play a marginal role, that is, as a junior partner of one of the other parties.

The primary aim of the *Zentrum*, both in Weinheim and Heidelberg-Land, was the unseating of the National Liberal incumbent in order to weaken his party's hold over the elected Second Chamber of the *Landtag*. This was made clear in their electoral propaganda and is borne out by similar behaviour elsewhere. In Karlsruhe, where the constellation of political forces was much different and there were no antisemitic candidates on the ballot, in the later rounds of voting in 1897 they threw their support behind two Social Democrats and a Progressive.[39]

The Centre Party, furthermore, was apparently not alone in helping to pave the way for the antisemites' initial victory in Weinheim. The Social Democrats did their share, so to speak, by withdrawing their support in the third round of balloting from the candidate of the Left-Liberal Democratic Party. As they made perfectly clear at the time, their intention, like the *Zentrum*'s, was not to elect the antisemite but to unseat the National Liberal.[40] As the two main opposition parties, the *Zentrum* and the Social Democrats, hoped that they would thereby bring the day nearer when they could force a change in the election laws of Baden so as to facilitate direct polling for the *Landtag* and ultimately the demise of National Liberal rule in Baden. Although this finally happened in 1905, the consequence was not the coming to power of the Centre Party, but the creation of the so-called *Gross-Block* coalition of Liberals and Social Democrats which remained intact right up to the end of the Weimar Republic.

While their support of the antisemitic *Deutsch-Sozialen* in Weinheim and Heidelberg-Land has to be seen as primarily tactically motivated, the Centre Party in Baden undeniably had within its ranks a decidedly anti-Jewish element. This can be seen most clearly in reporting by the *Pfälzer Bote* of the Dreyfus Affair in France. Take, for example, the following from a front-page article of 11th September 1899:

> "A most disturbing occurrence in the Dreyfus Affair is the behaviour of the Christian press. It cuts one to the quick to see them in the company of the Socialist press dutifully attending to the business of the Jews and vying with the *Frankfurter Zeitung* (*die Frankfurterin*) in condemning everything in France that is not Jewish, Socialist or anarchist (*jüdisch, sozzisch oder anarchistisch* . . .)."[41]

Continuing its attack on the Jewish press, the same tone was evident in the Catholic paper's leading article of the following day:

> "It is furthermore disturbing that the most widely read and distributed papers bring their influence to bear according to the interests of Jewry. Just as today a whole forest of pulped

[39]*Ibid.*
[40]*Mannheimer Volksstimme*, 17th October 1897, cited in *Badischer Volksbote*, 18th October 1895.
[41]*Pfälzer Bote*, 34, 207 (11th September 1899).

trees are made to roar to proclaim the innocence of the Israelite Dreyfus, so will tomorrow or the day after a law be praised to heaven or damned to hell, all according to whether it pleases the Israelite in charge . . ."[42]

One might add that about a month later the *Pfälzer Bote* came out in favour of not only the re-election of the antisemitic incumbent in Weinheim, but the candidacy of the notorious Pastor Specht whose bid for the *Landtag* constituency of Eppingen nevertheless remained unsuccessful.[43] A year earlier the paper at first welcomed the candidacy of the *Deutsch-Sozial* Dr. Rudolf Vogel for the *Reichstag* seat of Heidelberg-Mosbach-Eberbach as a friend of the *Mittelstand* (farmers as well as shopkeepers and artisans).[44] The intention of the *Pfälzer Bote*, probably, was to help acquire the support of antisemitic voters for the Centre Party in the inevitable second round balloting.

The would-be plan, however, partially backfired with the appearance in the Heidelberg dailies of advertisements, ostensibly paid for by a faction of the *Deutsch-Sozialen*, recommending the party's supporters to vote in the run-off election not for the Centre Party candidate, Judge Armbruster of Freiburg, but the National Liberal, Beck of Eberbach. The argument used was that appealing to Jewish voters and their supporters helped ensure Vogel's elimination from the run-off.[45]

Continuing the controversy, a notice appeared the following day in the Liberal *Heidelberger Tageblatt* sponsored by another group of antisemites which appealed to their followers to support Armbruster and not desert the *Zentrum*. It claimed that it was not the Centre Party, but the Conservatives in the Heidelberg region who were responsible for the poor showing of Vogel in the first round of voting.[46] On Election Day, a day later, three separate advertisements directed towards supporters of the *Deutsch-Sozialen* appeared in the Heidelberg papers. One was from the Executive Committee of the party for Baden, the Rhineland Palatinate and Alsace-Lorraine which implored its supporters to vote for Armbruster,

> ". . . since the *Zentrum* is much closer to us in economic policy, and in their voting for the Navy Bill also showed that in matters of the utmost national importance they are willing to pursue the best interests of the Fatherland."[47]

It was mentioned, as well, that the National Liberals, according to a report in the *Frankfurter Zeitung*, had advised their supporters in the *Reichstag* constituency of Giessen to vote for the Social Democrat and against the candidate of the antisemites. Immediately below appeared the second advertisement, a "Declaration", signed by "Many Members of the *Deutsche Reformpartei*" (the antisemites, that is), which made its preference for the Liberal known in the most certain of terms:

[42]*Ibid.*, 34, 208 (12th September 1899).
[43]*Ibid.*, 34, 250 (30th October 1899).
[44]*Ibid.*, 33, 115 (23rd May 1898).
[45]*Heidelberger Tageblatt*, 16, 142 (22nd June 1898).
[46]*Ibid.*, 16, 143 (23rd June 1898).
[47]*Ibid.*, 16, 143 (24th June 1898).

> "So we see ourselves with the choice of voting for a National Liberal or a man of the *Zentrum* who is more Roman (i.e. Catholic) than German. We must, therefore, choose the lesser of two evils, and with all the means at our disposal give our support to the National Liberal."[48]

The third appeal, signed "A Protestant for Many", called on all Protestant voters to stay away from the polls altogether, since the candidates of both the *Zentrum* and the National Liberals were Catholics.[49]

It is difficult to tell exactly what effect these various advertisements had on voting behaviour. Suffice it to say that the National Liberal candidate won by a margin of almost two to one. Even in the first round of the ballot, moreover, many communities which returned impressive majorities for the antisemitic candidate in the *Landtag* elections, went heavily for the National Liberal. Even if we take into consideration the difference in methods for electing each body, there is good reason to believe that the people of the districts concerned were much more willing to have themselves represented by an avowed antisemite in the parliament of the Grand Duchy than in the Imperial *Reichstag*. Ultimately, they could also have felt that the National Liberal Party was more in tune with their interests at imperial than at state level. One has to remember in this connection that the Liberals had dominated the political life of Baden since before 1848. By the 1890s the feeling had grown – and not just amongst the supporters of the Social Democrats and the *Zentrum* – that the time had come for a change.

To a certain degree, all the parties of the *Kaiserreich* behaved differently at state than at national level. This was, as David Blackbourn has shown,[50] even more the case for the Centre Party than for any of the other political groupings in Wilhelminian Germany. To *Zentrum* voters in the Heidelberg area let alone the party leadership, helping to elect an antisemite to the *Reichstag* may have seemed as ill-advised as it did to their Protestant neighbours.

At this point, of course, the question is begged whether, at least in Baden, support for antisemitic candidates, at whatever electoral level, largely amounted to a form of protest from those sections of society which felt their vital interests (most often, those of a "bread and butter" nature) were being ignored or neglected by the major parties. This comes out quite clearly, for example, in the reports on the *Landtag* elections by the *Bezirksämter*. As the following comment from Weinheim at the time of their first electoral victory indicates, the farming population was also eager to be represented by one of their own number rather than by a member of the local establishment (*die Honoration*):

> "The success of the antisemites is in part explained by the prevailing mood of discord, but also by the fact that the candidacy of the incumbent (i.e. the National Liberal), the apothecary Klein, evokes little sympathy. The agricultural population demands a representative from its own ranks."[51]

In this light, then, antisemitism became an issue into which others, such as depressed agricultural prices, protection of artisans, small shopkeepers and

[48] *Ibid.*

[49] *Ibid.*

[50] See esp. David Blackbourn, *Class, Religion and Politics in Wilhelmine Germany. The Centre Party in Wuerttemberg*, New Haven–London. Mainz 1980.

[51] GLA 236/15085.

farmers from domestic and foreign competition, the introduction of adequate rural credit facilities, the preservation of traditional "Christian" values and, later, the demand for increased imperial expansion, coalesced. In other words, however prevalent the hatred and resentment of Jews may have been in the rural areas of North Baden, or elsewhere for that matter, it was not the chief impetus behind support for the *Deutsch-Sozialen*. To cite the Israeli historian Shulamit Volkov, antisemitism became a cultural code[52] through which a whole complex of issues, revolving around the dislocation suffered and fears aroused by socio-economic change and the discontinuity in Imperial Germany between economic and political development, were expressed.

This helps to explain why in Baden, as in other areas of the country, a separate antisemitic political party only achieved limited and short-lived success. Support was funnelled-off, as it were, once the Conservatives, the Agrarian League as well as the National Liberals took up most of the issues originally put forward by the antisemites without necessarily adopting their single-minded and racialist views on the "Jewish Question".

In this regard, it must be remembered, the antisemites in Baden, like their colleagues in the other German states, contributed to their own demise. A contemporary account of their activities, by its own admission hostile, pointed to the role of the professional agitator in this process:

> "Because the antisemitic agitator holds meetings in order primarily to earn a living, because in its newspapers and pamphlets only the Jews are abused, so that journalists can earn a livelihood when they do not possess the ability to work for decent papers, the Antisemitic Party will never become a broadly based and popular movement (eine Volkspartei). Even the most ignorant amongst us can discern their true aspirations."[53]

As a consequence, however, rather than losing its importance as an issue entirely, antisemitism became deeply embedded in the political fabric of Germany and not just in those sections of society or areas of the country where it took hold in the 1880s and 1890s.

Nevertheless, even at the height of their political success, the antisemites in Baden could not automatically count on the support of their erstwhile allies when it came to the introduction of hard-core antisemitic measures. Attempting to regulate the department stores and money-lending or protecting the peasant and artisan against unfair outside competition was one thing, but attempting to roll back emancipation or trying to regulate the Jewish religion was another. When, for instance, in 1898 the antisemites in the Lower House of the *Landtag* tried to get government support for the Jewish religion withdrawn on the grounds that the funds were being used in part to translate and disseminate the immoral and unethical teachings of the Talmud, their only ally was the Conservative von Stockhorn.

The *Zentrum*, along with the Social Democrats and National Liberals, voted to proceed with the business of the day.[54] There was at least one other occasion

[52]Shulamit Volkov, 'Antisemitism as a Cultural Code. Reflections on the History and Historiography of Antisemitism in Imperial Germany', in *LBI Year Book XXIII* (1978), pp. 25–46.
[53]Julius Jacoby, *Die Antisemitische Bewegung in Baden*, Karlsruhe 1897, p. 15.
[54]*Allgemeine Zeitung des Judentums*, 62, 7 (18th February 1898).

when the Centre Party behaved likewise. This was when, in December 1893, a petition from the *Deutsch-Sozialer Verein* of Karlsruhe was presented before the Lower House of the *Landtag* calling for an investigation of the ethical and moral teachings of Jews as embodied in the *Shulhan Aruch.* The leader of the *Zentrum*, Theodor Wacker, joined his Social Democratic and Liberal colleagues in speaking against it. Were the House to recommend the petition's acceptance, he argued, the way would be paved for the state to pronounce on Christian teachings as well.[55]

With all this activity on the part of the *Deutsch-Sozialen* and their sometime allies, it is hardly surprising that they were eventually singled out for the same sort of attention as Social Democrats and Catholic priests by the authorities at election time. This began in earnest with the victory of Pfisterer in Weinheim with the help of the *Zentrum* in 1895. The good showing of the *Deutsch-Sozialen* in several other constituencies, notably Heidelberg-Land, Bretten and Sinsheim,[56] gave the threat they represented added significance, even though it was not until the next *Landtag* election, in 1897, that the antisemites managed to capture another seat. Predictably it was Heidelberg-Land, to which the popular farmers' leader, Mampel, held on until he was ousted by the National Liberals after electoral reform and the conclusion of the *Gross-Block* in 1905.[57] Despite a significant amount of internal dissension and rivalry with other right-wing groups, the *Deutsch-Sozialen* were a force to be taken seriously at the ballot-box. Their agitation had, moreover, in part paved the way later on for victories by the Conservatives and the Agrarian League in the *Landtag* constituencies of Bretten and Eppingen-Sinsheim.[58]

What perhaps made the authorities view the *Deutsch-Sozialen* as a threat to the political *status quo* even more than their erstwhile electoral successes was their possession of a party newspaper. It was called the *Badischer Volksbote* and although for almost its entire existence it had its editorial offices in Heidelberg, the paper began publication at the end of June 1890 in the northern Black Forest town of Todtnau. Although founded by the brothers Otto and Rudolf Vogel and the Protestant Pastor Specht from Zell, the paper was officially published by a certain professional agitator by the name of Bösenberg who after moving to Heidelberg soon found himself replaced by the Hessian antisemitic activist and associate of Otto Böckel, Thomas Reuther. The head of the movement in Baden, a shoemaker from Karlsruhe by the name of Joseph Schmidt, believed that he had found in Reuther a person who would lend new vitality to the antisemitic cause in the Grand Duchy. A printer by trade, he was also a prodigious writer, fiery speaker and successful fund-raiser.[59]

[55] *Karlsruher Zeitung*, 17th December 1893, cited in GLA 236/17241.

[56] GLA 236/15085.

[57] For details, see Jürgen Thiel, *Die Grossblockpolitik der Nationalliberalen Partei Badens 1905–1914.* Veröffentlichung der Kommission für geschichtliche Landeskunde in Baden-Württemberg. Reihe B: Forschungen. Bd. 86. Stuttgart 1976.

[58] GLA 236/15085; *Heidelberger Zeitung*, 43, 235 (8th October 1901).

[59] Jacoby, *op. cit.*, pp. 5–6.

While the *Badischer Volksbote* inevitably came to the attention of the authorities as soon as it began publication,[60] it was only after it set up operations in Heidelberg (1893) as a bi-weekly that it came under special surveillance. As early as March 1894 the *Staatsanwaltschaft* Mannheim suggested that it have its permission to publish rescinded. Although the reasons it gave were essentially technical and had mainly to do with the fact that Reuther was not thought to be a particularly savoury character, it is quite apparent that the very *raison d'être* of the paper was being questioned. The State Attorney soon turned word into deed and on 28th March 1894 Reuther was charged with five counts of violating the press laws by publishing openly antisemitic and inflammatory articles. In April, he was convicted and sentenced to six weeks imprisonment. While another prosecution of this type did not occur again, it is quite clear that the authorities kept a close watch on the paper's activities. They were particularly concerned about the criminal record of each successive editor. In fact, it seems that they all left just in time before the *Staatsanwaltschaft* could institute proceedings leading towards their dismissal.[61] What makes this case all the more interesting is that the impetus for surveillance seems to have derived locally. Taken together with the detailed reports on antisemitic agitation submitted by the *Bezirksamt*, it is abundantly clear that the authorities on the spot had an adequate appreciation of its potential for harm, not only to the electoral chances of the National Liberal Party but to the political and social well-being of the state.

If the policy of the ministerial and local bureaucracy towards antisemitism only becomes entirely discernible through inference and an examination of nuance, the attitude of the ruling house is at the very least unequivocal. For a start, the *Grossherzog* was from the early 1890s kept informed of the movement's activities.[62] It is safe to assume that this fact alone is adequate testimony to his own personal concern. His advice was even sought in the matter of *Hauptlehrer* Sturm who, it will be remembered, had in the eyes of the authorities jeopardised his position as teacher in Weinheim through active participation in the antisemitic movement. Since by that time he had already left the *Bendersche Institut*, where he was employed, of his own accord, the *Grossherzog* suggested that the matter simply be dropped. His attitude, which gives every indication of being connected to his support of the Zionist movement, gave rise, in fact, to his receiving a fair number of anonymous letters accusing him of a philosemitism not in tune with true "German" interests.[63]

However noteworthy the efforts of the Government and ruling house of Baden to combat antisemitism may have been, they were by no means wholly unique. Similar policies to those in effect in Baden were pursued in the neighbouring Grand Duchy of Hessen as well as the Prussian province of Hesse to the north. Both governments tried, as in Baden, to curtail the participation of teachers and other public servants in the antisemitic parties, and local authorities in both areas kept a close watch on the activities of the antisemites,

[60]GLA/236, 17241.
[61]GLA 356/4484.
[62]GLA 60/681.
[63]*Ibid.*

often going so far as to disperse or discourage meetings.[64] It has even been argued that these efforts may have been counter-productive, especially in Prussian Hesse where the Böckel movement may have been the beneficiary of anti-Prussian sympathies amongst the peasantry.

All in all, one is, nevertheless, left with the impression that the Government of Baden took the threat of antisemitism most seriously. Ironically, however, because of its unique electoral/confessional configuration Baden was the least likely of the three states to have an antisemitic party with a mass following. As has already been pointed out, the Grand Duchy's Catholic majority consistently loyal to the Centre Party and a growing urbanised working class together with a certain amount of "electoral geometry" ensured that the antisemites would never be able to capture more than a few *Landtag* constituencies.

Still, we are left with the question of motivation: why did the Government of Baden pursue its efforts against the antisemites with such intensity? On the basis of the facts at our disposal we can only give a balanced answer. On the one hand, it saw the antisemites as not only a threat to public order but to the Liberal *status quo*, of which Jewish emancipation had become an integral part. On the other hand, it viewed the antisemites in terms of their potential for combining with the *Zentrum* and the other opposition parties of the Right to threaten the hegemony of the National Liberal Party in the lower chamber of the *Landtag*.

As we all know, after the turn of the century the antisemitic parties were in any case a spent force. Electoral reform and the creation in 1905 of the so-called *Gross-Block* coalition between Liberals and Social Democrats made their marginality in Baden all the more marked. What had nevertheless been shown was that, given the right circumstances, in certain areas of Baden Jew-hatred could be politically mobilised.

[64]Richard S. Levy, *The Downfall of the Anti-Semitic Political Parties in Imperial Germany*, New Haven-London 1975, pp. 137 ff.

Antisemitism by Other Means? The Rural Cooperative Movement in Late Nineteenth-Century Germany

BY DAVID PEAL

This essay examines the problem of political antisemitism and rural cooperation as alternative means of combatting usury as it was understood in the German countryside in the late nineteenth century. It focuses on Kurhessen because the political antisemites won their first victories there. This was also the one place where political antisemitism, and its aims, did not fail in Imperial Germany, although it underwent two distinct phases: the populistic Böckel movement, from 1887 until 1894; and the more conservative, less populist stage of the next two decades. In analysing Kurhessian history I apply many of the insights of Reinhard Rürup. For Rürup, Jewish emancipation in 1869 formed only a part of the economic, political, and social reform measures passed in Prussia and the North German Confederation in the 1860s. Antisemitism emerged in the 1870s and 1880s not as a narrow rejection of Jewish emancipation but as a general and uncomprehending attack on the secular culture and material insecurities produced by liberal capitalism.[1]

Rürup has provided a valuable conceptual framework for understanding antisemitic politics in the context of the social upheavals accompanying the industrial revolution, but his analysis begs the question of exactly how Jews came to serve as proxy for the evils of capitalism. I would like to argue, on the basis of my analysis of the heartland of political antisemitism, that the prejudice against the "Jew-usurer" provided a crucial link between antisemitism and anti-capitalism. The preoccupation with usury among antisemites as well as non-antisemites had two major consequences. First, in the Böckel movement, usury was the principal evil associated with Jews, and the antisemitic cooperatives were the prime means of combatting it. Second, the non-antisemitic cooperative movement, the Raiffeisen credit-cooperative movement, represented in part an alternative means of combatting usury, in part a continuation of the Böckel movement by non-political means.

I

Kurhessen was a medium-sized state stretching from Frankfurt to Kassel, just south of Hanover. Wedged between the eastern and western provinces of

[1]Reinhard Rürup, 'Jewish Emancipation and Bourgeois Society', in *LBI Year Book XIV* (1969), pp. 67–91; *idem.*, 'Emancipation and Crisis. The "Jewish Question" in Germany 1850–1890', in *LBI Year Book XX* (1975), pp. 13–25. On the "failure" of the antisemitic parties see Richard S. Levy, *The Downfall of the Anti-Semitic Political Parties in Imperial Germany*, New Haven – London 1975.

Prussia, Kurhessen was annexed in 1866. Agriculture dominated the local economy until well into this century. As farm country Kurhessen was hilly, raw in climate, and generally inhospitable. Smallholders dominated the social structure. True peasants – landholders owning at least five hectares, enough to support a family – formed a minority even in the rich farming basins. The Jewish population of Kurhessen numbered just over 13,000 or 2.3% of the overall population in 1816. Before 1866 Jews increased in number at a faster rate than the general population, reaching over 18,000 in 1858 or 2.5% of the overall population. Jews lived in almost 300 communities, forming *c.* one and a half times as many synagogue communities. Like German Jewry generally in the early nineteenth century, Jews in Kurhessen were very much involved in the cattle trade, peddling, and the small-scale credit business. Unlike other German Jews, Kurhessian Jews remained in the countryside up to this century. As traders they experienced upward mobility and specialisation within the commercial sector, and they increasingly lived in the larger rural towns and the towns with large Jewish communities.[2]

Usury in Kurhessen, as elsewhere, meant by tradition the taking of excessive interest. Legally fixed interest maxima had an ethical rationale: like the fixed price of bread, the fixed interest rate protected the poor consumer. The man who borrowed to meet expenses arising from daily needs or unforeseen occurences could not repay more than a modest interest rate along with the principal. The usurer, in the traditional view, profited without working by speculating on the distress of poor consumers. The stereotype of the Jewish usurer dates from the twelfth century, when usury was viewed as a Jewish business. The confusion of the epithets Jew and usurer remained current long after Jews ceased being money-lenders and became traders, a process completed in Kurhessen in the late seventeenth century. The epithet Jew-usurer persisted even into the nineteenth century, but its focus had shifted from money-lending to petty commerce.[3]

[2]Ludwig Horwitz, 'Die Entwicklung der jüdischen Bevölkerung in Kurhessen', in *Zeitschrift für Demographie und Statistik der Juden*, IX (1913), pp. 99–101. By 1925, the proportion of Jews to the total population of Kurhessen (*Regierungsbezirk Kassel*) had fallen to 1.4% (15,000 of 1,092,000 persons). While in Prussia as a whole an average of 0.3% of the population of *Landkreise*, and 2.1% of *Stadtkreise*, was Jewish, in Kurhessen the figures were 1.6% and 1.3% – evidence of the rural character of Kurhessen's Jewish population and the rural character of Kurhessen itself, even in the twentieth century. Heinrich Silbergleit, *Die Bevölkerungs- und Berufsverhältnisse der Juden im Deutschen Reich*, vol. 1 (*Freistaat Preussen*), Berlin 1930, p. 32*. I use "Kurhessen" to refer to the post-1866 period; this corresponds to contemporary usage and to the real continuity of rural society in Kurhessen before and after 1866.

[3]On the origins of the confusion of "Jew" and "usurer", Dagmar Berman, *Produktivierungsmythen und Antisemitismus. Assimilatorische und zionistische Berufsumschichtungsbestrebungen unter den Juden Deutschlands und Österreichs bis 1938*, Munich University diss. 1971, pp. 20–34; on the moral reprehensibility of usury, Georg Ratzinger, *Die Volkswirtschaft in ihren sittlichen Grundlagen*, Freiburg im Breisgau 1880, pp. 287ff.; for an historical overview of the concept of usury and legislation pertaining to it, "Wucher", in *Handwörterbuch der Staatswissenschaften*, 4th edn., VIII, Jena 1928, pp. 1086ff.; from the Jewish perspective, "Usury", in *Encyclopedia Judaica*, XVI, Jerusalem 1971, pp. 27–33; more apologetic is Meyer Kayserling, *Der Wucher und das Judentum*, Budapest 1882; from the perspective of intellectual history, an account that neglects the social-historical reality as well as the persistence – to the present day – of the anti-usury current in popular culture, Benjamin Nelson, *The Idea of Usury. From Tribal Brotherhood to Universal Otherhood*, 2nd edn., Chicago 1969.

Jewish emancipation in Kurhessen, as elsewhere, was accompanied by Dohmian expectations: the emancipation acts of 1816 and 1833 were intended to remove the legal barriers that relegated Jews to the periphery of Christian society, in particular to bring about their conversion from petty commerce and usury (*Nothandel*) to more honourable occupations. In other German states of the time, emancipation was introduced either slowly, in phase with other liberal reforms in state and society, or at once, together with those reforms (1848–1849). In Kurhessen, however, emancipation was an anomaly. The electors clung to a rigid guild ordinance until 1866, discouraged the formation of joint-stock companies, delayed the construction of railways, and refused to join the *Zollverein* as long as possible.

In the circumstances of institutionally reinforced rural poverty, emancipation as an educative policy could only, and did, fail. Discontent with emancipation found expression in the pogroms of 1830 and 1848 as well as through bills and popular petitions in the 1850s. Sharing Dohm's *Handelsfeindlichkeit*, Kurhessian antisemites were innocent of his assumption that circumstances make men what they are. For them, Jews had an inborn disposition to practise usury; pauperisation of rural society was for them a result of Jewish rapacity. In 1858 three edicts restricted Jewish civil rights by tying them not to religion but to occupation.[4]

II

Annexation by Prussia and incorporation into the North German Confederation immediately brought Kurhessen the framework of what Rürup calls "bourgeois emancipation": freedom of movement, industrial freedom, full commercialisation of landed property, abolition of interest maxima, and, as part of the larger programme of civil equality and separation of church and state, unconditional Jewish emancipation.

Emancipation was now virtually inviolable. It was imposed from without and could not be revised on merely Kurhessian initiative. Emancipation now formed only one link in the liberal reforms of the 1860s. As part of the constitutional *status quo*, emancipation was defended, albeit tepidly, by the Prussian government in 1880. And in the 1880s even the Conservative parties reconciled themselves to Jewish civil equality. In these circumstances, so-called *Wucherfreiheit* became a sort of surrogate for Jewish emancipation, and not only in Kurhessen. For a decade and a half after 1878 the usury issue preoccupied antisemites as well as non-antisemitic publicists, scholars, civil servants, Jewish community leaders, legislators, and concerned middle-class social reformers.

[4]Ludwig Horwitz, *Die Gesetze um die bürgerliche Gleichstellung der Israeliten im ehemaligen Kurhessen in 1816 und 1833*, Kassel 1927; Gerhard Hentsch, *Gewerbeordnung und Emanzipation der Juden im Kurfürstentum Hessen*, (*Schriften der Kommission für die Geschichte der Juden in Hessen* [SKGJH], IV), Wiesbaden 1979. The first chapter of my dissertation contains the first full discussion of antisemitism in early nineteenth-century Kurhessen. *Anti-Semitism and Rural Transformation in Kurhessen. The Rise and Fall of the Böckel Movement*, Columbia University diss. 1985.

The discussion became virulent in the peak years of antisemitic agitation in the *Kaiserreich*, between 1878 and 1880 and between 1887 and 1893.

This public preoccupation with usury should be seen in two sets of circumstances. The first was general in character; Kurhessen was now subject to developments issuing from outside its borders. In 1878–1879, Bismarck brushed aside the Liberal *Reichstag* coalition and put together a new coalition of Conservative, *Zentrum*, and right-wing deputies from the *Nationalliberale Partei*. The members of the new coalition tried to secure and extend their electoral bases by appealing to popular prejudices. Conservatives sponsored, directly or indirectly, the antisemitic activities of Adolf Stoecker and Franz Perrot. For the *Zentrum*, the usury issue was the focal point of Catholic hostility toward Jews, Manchesterite economics, and political Liberalism. *Zentrum* deputy Schorlemer-Alst was the first to raise the issue, in the Prussian *Landtag* in November 1878. For Schorlemer's *Zentrum* colleague Schröder, new usury legislation would fill the need for a Jewish ordinance in Germany.[5]

Usury bills were submitted to the *Reichstag* by Conservative and *Zentrum* deputies in 1879, and a law was passed in 1880. Since the reintroduction of interest maxima was now irreconcilable with the working of the free market, usury was redefined in 1880 as the exploitation of "need, inexperience, and frivolity" in monetary transactions. This new definition conformed to the old ethical rationale for usury legislation, and deputies ranging from the *Sozialdemokratische Partei Deutschlands* (SPD) rightward had appealed to the popular legal consciousness in defence of the new bill.[6]

The more specific circumstance of the pre-occupation with usury in the late 1870s and 1880s was the agricultural depression, which had its origins in heavy grain imports from North America; in Kurhessen its effects were felt primarily in the forms of structural under-employment and acute credit scarcity. In general the fortunes of peasants and Jews diverged in the *Kaiserreich*, as a result of differing abilities to take advantage of liberal legislation. This disparity was sharpened after the onset of the depression. Tax data from the Frankenberg

[5]On Catholic antisemitism, David Blackbourn, 'Roman Catholics, the Centre Party, and Anti-Semitism in Imperial Germany', in *Nationalist and Racialist Movements in Britain and Germany before 1914*, edited by Anthony Nicholls and Paul Kennedy, London–Basingstoke 1981, pp. 106–129; for a recent assessment of Stoecker, Werner Jochmann, 'Stoecker als nationalkonservativer Politiker und antisemitischer Agitator', in *Protestantismus und Politik. Werk und Wirkung Adolf Stoeckers*, edited by Jochmann *et al.*, Hamburg 1982, pp. 123–198, and the literature cited there; for the dramatic first *Landtag* debate on usury legislation (before the problem was transferred to the *Reichstag* in 1879–1880), *Stenographische Berichte* (SB), *Haus der Abgeordneten*, 1878, vol. 1., 26th November 1878, (5th session), pp. 31ff. (Schorlemer-Alst interpellation), 47 (Schröder). One Liberal considered S-A's interpellation "the most aggressive challenge to the [liberal] legislation of the last ten years". *Op. cit.*, p. 34 (Meyer).

[6]*Reichsgesetzblatt*, Berlin 1880, pp. 109–111; on the new law, Karl von Lilienthal, 'Die Wuchergesetzgebung in Deutschland unter besonderer Berücksichtigung derselben im preussischen Staate', two parts, in *Jahrbuch für Nationalökonomie und Statistik*, new series, I (1880), pp. 140–161 and esp. pp. 366–385. The new definition was codified by the social philosopher, Lorenz von Stein, in *Der Wucher und sein Recht. Ein Beitrag zum wirtschaftlichen und rechtlichen Leben unserer Zeit*, Vienna 1880; for a critical discussion of Stein's work, see K. Th. Eheberg, 'Die Wucherfrage in Theorie und Praxis seit 1880', in *Jahrbuch für Gesetzgebung, Verwaltung und Volkswirtschaft im Deutschen Reiche*, VIII (1884), pp. 823–871.

village of Grüssen indicate that within village society, groups directly dependent on agriculture (peasants and their servants) took losses in income between 1877 and 1887 and decreased in number but remained well-to-do by village standards. More flexible casual labourers and petty craftsmen increased in number and enjoyed small income gains but remained poor in relation to peasants; these were the people who suffered most from credit scarcity during the agricultural depression.

Jewish traders, however, began as relatively affluent and registered gains in the decade after 1877. As creditors at a time when credit was scarce, the Jewish traders' economic position was comparatively good, even though the security of their debtors declined. Traders had the option of trading outside the agricultural sector and outside Kurhessen. As mediators of the depression they may have distributed its effects unevenly, to their own relative advantage. To the rural poor, Jews appeared to gain most, or were the only gainers, from annexation, emancipation, and liberal economic legislation. The figure of the usurer personalised the processes threatening to engulf the rural population.[7]

It is important to stress that the public concern over usury was not occasioned by an increased incidence of either high interest rates or the aforesaid exploitation of "need, inexperience, and frivolity". A survey of *Reichsbank* branches used by the *Reichstag* committee in drafting usury legislation in 1879 shows that mortgage and bill rates did not rise after the 1867-abolition of maximum interest rates. After the redefinition of usury in 1880 from the taking of excessive interest to "exploitation" – the number of usury suits in Germany actually fell, from 261 in 1882 to 131 in 1885; of these, only 153 and 54 suits, respectively, led to convictions. In Kurhessen, which was notorious in Germany as a den of usury, four persons were tried for usury in three cases and all four were convicted in 1882; no one was tried in 1885. It should be noted that the 1880 law was almost unenforceable because of the difficulty in establishing criminal intention to exploit, and because usurers, it was said, devised new forms of transactions to get around the law. The revised law of 1893 extended the 1880 law by prohibiting exploitation of need in non-monetary transactions.[8]

The concern over usury reflected less its actual incidence than the profound clash of economic realities discerned by the *Frankfurter Zeitung* at the opening of the *Landtag* debates in 1878: legislators in the 1860s "did not take into consideration that while the upper echelons of our society move fully within the framework of the capitalist economy [*Kapital- und Kreditwirtschaft*], the lower classes are still stranded in the conceptions and forms of the natural economy". This insight applies to Kurhessen and much of rural Germany, where the new liberal order imposed from without seemed to favour the calculating Jewish

[7]On income data, see my *Anti-Semitism and Rural Transformation*, chapter 2; for a Zionist's view of social relations in the countryside prior to the Böckel movement, Isaac Rülf, *Entstehung und Bedeutung des Antisemitismus in Hessen*, Mainz 1890; cf. the breathless general account of peasant-Jewish relations in Hans Rosenberg, *Grosse Depression und Bismarckzeit. Wirtschaftsablauf, Gesellschaft, und Politik in Mitteleuropa*, Berlin 1967, pp. 98–99.

[8]SB, *Reichstag*, 1879, second session, *Drucksache* 265 (committee protocols, inc. *Reichsbank* survey); Karl von Lilienthal, 'Der Wucher auf dem Lande', in *Zeitschrift für gesamte Strafswissenschaft*, VIII (1888), pp. 158–160 (trial data).

trader while denying villagers the social protection traditionally accorded them.[9]

In Kurhessen *Landwucher* – land speculation – was the focal point of the whole usury issue. By contributing to a free market in land, Jewish real-estate traders and creditors seemed to threaten the very basis of familial and personal independence in the countryside. Disapproval of the trading in land was nothing new in Kurhessen. In the 1847–1848 *Landtag*, von Buttlar introduced legislation that would have curtailed Jewish emancipation by denying Jews the right to resell land that came into their possession. Buttlar feared that Jews, pursuing their inborn commercial instincts, would undermine rural society by speculating in land. In the late 1870s identical and equally ill-founded allegations were made against the Jewish *Güterschlächter*, the "land butchers" who bought up peasant holdings, parcelled them, and resold them at profit to the land-hungry. In his quarterly reports to Berlin the Kassel *Regierungspräsident* called attention to the usurious practices of heartless Jewish creditors, which resulted in alarming rates of foreclosure, involving ever larger farms.[10]

As with usury in general in the late 1870s and 1880s, actual exploitation was not the issue here. Surviving court documentation of foreclosure cases in the county of Marburg and other sources show that the rate of foreclosure did rise after 1878 and peaked in 1881 but fell thereafter. As in the farm states of America in the mid-1980s, a combination of low land values, weak rural purchasing power, and agreements among farmers made foreclosure an unsatisfactory way of recovering a loan. Eleven to twelve debtors pressed claims in each foreclosure case. Debt-load exceeded sale-price by between 2:1 and 3:1 in Marburg, so that many debtors – including the small Jewish ones – "gingen leer aus". Although foreclosure rates declined, indebtedness increased, as a result of irregular income during the depression and the decreasing possibilities of liquefying assets through foreclosure.[11]

More important than the actual usury rates was the pervasive belief that mounting debts led inevitably to foreclosure and that foreclosure itself constituted usury. This view was given definitive expression in the very influential collective volume, *Der Wucher auf dem Lande*, published in 1887 by the *Verein für Socialpolitik*. Every page of the short anonymous report on Kurhessian conditions bristles with Jewish usurers. In *Wucher* and the antisemitic writings,

[9]This cutting is in the volume, 'Äusserungen der Presse über den Wucher', *Geheimes Staatsarchiv*, Berlin-Dahlem 84a/5725. Werner Sombart considered the traditional aversion towards the calculating and rational trader a deeper source of the anti-trade prejudice than the condemnation of deceptive trading practices. *The Jews and Modern Capitalism*, translated by M. Epstein, orig. German 1911, trans. London 1913, repr. New York 1969.

[10]*Staatsarchiv Marburg* (StAM) 165/6828, vol. 1 (quarterly reports to Prussian *Staatsministerium*). Discussion of *Güterschlächterei* in the Prussian Upper House in 1882 impelled the Kassel *Regierungspräsident* to undertake a survey of the problem. SB, *Herrenhaus*, 6th May 1882 session, pp. 249–251 (Schlieben interpellation); StAM 150/1180 and 165/1599. Results of the survey were leaked, by way of a government official, to the antisemitic press, whence they made their way into the antisemitic pamphlet and propaganda literature. Otto Böckel, *Die Güterschlächterei in Hessen*, Leipzig 1886.

[11]Statistics based on the 27 existing foreclosure cases in StAM 275 Wetter/acc. 1900/27, Nos. 57–61, 63–80, 84–87. See my *Anti-Semitism and Rural Transformation* for fuller analysis.

scholarly studies, and government usury surveys inspired by it, it was assumed that if a landholder could not meet a term, the "Jew" wanted it that way; that foreclosure, too, was planned; and that profit through resale reflected Jewish rapacity.[12]

III

Two recent scholarly analyses of the Böckel movement invoke the study *Wucher auf dem Lande* to show that usurious exploitation incited the rural poor to revolt in the 1880s.[13] This view may be rejected, because in other regions characterised by ambiguous economic relations between Gentiles and Jews, political antisemitism was of no consequence. The identification of Jew and usurer characterises almost all of the contributions to the *Wucher* volume; the few pages on Kurhessen are not the grimmest in the book.[14]

Political antisemitism was primarily a political phenomenon, which should be seen in light of the weak standing of the other parties in the countryside and the deficient political education of the rural population. In the 1880s, after the failure of Stoecker's Berlin movement,* the antisemites, as Werner Jochmann has written, "very deliberately" sought out regions where the other parties were "hardly present". Rural Protestant Kurhessen was such a region. Because of the unpopularity of the previous rulers, the particularists never established themselves after 1866. With the exception of the two partially industrialised districts of Hanau and Kassel, the SPD was of little importance before 1890. The *Zentrumspartei* was of significance only in Fulda. Of the established national parties, the National Liberals controlled the five rural Protestant *Reichstag* districts of Kurhessen until 1878; the Conservatives controlled them in the

[12]*Der Wucher auf dem Lande. Berichte und Gutachten, (Schriften des Vereins für Socialpolitik,* XXXV), Leipzig 1887; cf. the excellent critique of *Wucher* by Gottlieb Schnapper-Arndt, *Zur Soziologie der sozialen Enqueten mit besonderem Hinblick auf "Wucher" auf dem Lande,* Frankfurt a. Main 1888. Sombart considered *Wucher* methodologically "grundschlecht", yet as a whole "unübertrefflich gut", since the authors of the 27 reports, independently of each other, called attention to a great social problem: the plundering of small property owners. *Die deutsche Volkswirtschaft im neunzehnten Jahrhundert und im Anfang des zwanzigsten. Jahrhunderts,* 5th edn., Berlin 1921, p. 337. What the authors shared, as Schnapper-Arndt makes clear, was antisemitism.

[13]Bernhard vom Brocke, 'Marburg im Kaiserreich, 1866–1918', in *Marburger Geschichte,* edited by Erhart Dettmering and Rudolf Grenz, Marburg 1980, pp. 476, 482ff.; Wilfried Schlau, *Politik und Bewusstsein. Voraussetzungen und Strukturen politischer Bildung in ländlichen Gemeinden.* Cologne 1971, pp. 402ff. More judicious is Rüdiger Mack, 'Otto Böckel und die antisemitische Bauernbewegung in Hessen, 1887–1894', in *Neunhundert Jahre Geschichte der Juden in Hessen,* edited by Christianne Heinemann (SKGJH, VI), Wiesbaden 1983, pp. 382–383 (orig. appeared in *Wetterauer Geschichtsblätter,* XVI [1967]).

[14]Twenty of the 27 reporters in *Wucher auf dem Lande* identified the religion of the usurers in their regions. The following synonyms for "Wucherer" were used: "Handelsjude", "Schacherjude", "Wucherjude", "Pferdejude", "Viehjude", and simply "Jude". *Op. cit.,* pp. 39, 77, 154, 194, 224, 234, 262, 285, etc. In his very sensitive study of the pervasiveness of social and cultural conflicts between Jews and Gentiles in rural Württemberg, Utz Jeggle does not adequately explain why political antisemitism was of negligible importance. *Judendörfer in Württemberg,* Tübingen 1969.

*Cf. the first essay in this section of the current Year Book by Norbert Kampe, 'Jews and Antisemites at Universities in Imperial Germany (II)' – (Ed.).

1880s. Despite the national-level events of 1878–1879, turnout remained at the 50–60% level throughout the 1870s and 1880s.[15]

Virtually without opposition, then, the antisemite Otto Böckel won the district of Marburg-Frankenberg-Kirchhain in 1887. He discovered not only a political vacuum but also a reservoir of aggrieved, unorganised rural voters. To these rural poor he had a message of compelling simplicity: they were poor because of Jewish usurers, and they had been badly served by their earlier representatives; Böckel went into politics attacking the Conservatives and Jews with equal hostility. Two more Kurhessian districts fell to antisemites in 1890, and another two in 1893.

Before going into politics Böckel's speeches in Kassel and Berlin and his articles in antisemitic newspapers held fast to the tenets of racial antisemitism. In a series in Ludwig Werner's antisemitic Kassel *Reichsgeldmonopol* on the "natural history of emancipation", he wrote of the lasting attributes of the Jewish race. Armed with modern proofs that the Jews are short, born to trade, and excessively fertile, Böckel conjured up an old image – the Jews breeding like weeds among field crops – and bestowed on it an aura of scientific validity. He wrote:

> "The Jew wants to live at any cost . . . the Jew must be socially isolated . . . It must be made clear to him that he is only tolerated in Germany . . . Away with Emancipation! We need social defence against the alien Jew, otherwise he will run us into the ground. . . ."[16]

His own newspaper, *Der Reichsherold*, reads at first like other antisemitic newspapers. But articles on race theory quickly dwindled in number; this makes *Der Reichsherold* the least boring of all antisemitic newspapers. The reasons for this shift are indicated in a speech Böckel gave in his antisemitic *Reformverein* in October 1887. In addition to purely antisemitic agitation, he called for non-political measures against usurious exploitation, in particular cooperative self-help. His political goals in advocating what he came to call practical antisemitism were, in his words, "on the one hand, so that antisemitism does not exhaust itself, and on the other hand, so that we can create something positive".[17]

Practical antisemitism served several purposes in the Böckel movement. The stress on creating something "positive" separated Böckel clearly from his Conservative enemies, whose antisemitism was a matter of rhetoric, not policy. His break with Theodor Fritsch in 1888 reduced his commitment to Fritsch's racism. In addition, his complete isolation in the *Reichstag* may have convinced him that anti-Jewish legislation had no chance of passage – as if the effective inviolability of emancipation were not enough. Non-legislative means of

[15]Werner Jochmann, 'Struktur und Funktion des deutschen Antisemitismus', in *Juden im Wilhelminischen Deutschland 1890–1914*. Ein Sammelband herausgegeben von Werner E. Mosse unter Mitwirkung von Arnold Paucker, Tübingen 1976 (Schriftenreihe wissenschaftlicher Abhandlungen des Leo Baeck Instituts 33), p. 426. On all aspects of Kurhessian particularism, Enno Knobel, *Die Hessische Rechtspartei. Konservative Opposition gegen das Bismarckreich*, Marburg 1975; on politics in Marburg, Brocke, *op. cit.*, pp. 476ff. Chapters 2–4, and 7 of my dissertation, *op. cit.*, analyse in depth party politics in Kurhessen after 1866.

[16]*Reichsgeldmonopol*, 30th January 1886, 6th February 1886.

[17]*Protokollbuch des Deutschen Reformvereins*, 10th October 1887, StAM 340/Böckel "Nachlass".

combatting Jewry would also have to be found if the voters were not to desert him. They wanted more from politics than racism, nostalgia for the *Volk*, and a city boy's *Deutschtümelei*. Finally, cooperative cells would provide Böckel with a power base and institutionalise his movement in the villages.[18]

In a series of leading articles in 1887–1888 *Der Reichsherold* endorsed the credit cooperative, pioneered by Friedrich Wilhelm Raiffeisen in the 1860s in the Rhineland, as the chief instrument of practical antisemitism. The principles of the self-help credit cooperative, as spelled out in *Der Reichsherold*, were simple. Based on unlimited liability, it would make the Jewish creditor superfluous by providing personal credit at low interest rates and long terms, and this credit would be uncallable. Because the cooperative's scope was defined by the boundaries of the parish, its members would know each other This would reduce the risks of unlimited liability and foster mutual trust. The cooperative principle, economic strength and moral improvement through the organisation of vulnerable small producers, was flexible. If small borrowers could meet their credit needs by cooperating, why could not cattle raisers and grain producers market their products cooperatively, without the intervention of traders? From these considerations emerged a vision of a society based on an autonomous peasantry, organised in community-like cooperatives, buying and selling in all markets without the intervention of intermediaries.[19]

This vision became the dominating motif of *Der Reichsherold* after 1890; a recent American historian identifies it as the constitutive element of American populism as well. It was at the core of a larger social reformism opposed, essentially, to the unrestrained individualism of the free market. Antisemitic demands, often ridiculed for their multiplicity and apparent inconsistency, must be seen in this light. Böckel's newspaper demanded revision of industrial freedom, nationalisation of the *Reichsbank*, inalienable homesteads, and the abandonment of the gold standard – desiderata remarkably similar to those of American populists of exactly the same time. The anti-capitalism of the Böckel movement rarely strayed from rejection of the liberal economic order to the more fundamental anti-capitalism of the SPD, as some political enemies alleged. After 1890, *Der Reichsherold* never relented in its opposition to the SPD, which was beginning to agitate in the countryside. The cooperative utopia promised a middle way between liberal capitalism and Socialism; the utopia would be Jew-free but that did not seem to be its chief attraction.[20]

More than an ideal, cooperation was also the basis of the antisemites'

[18]On the break with Fritsch, Kurt Wawrzinek, *Die Entstehung der deutschen Antisemitenparteien (1873–1890)*, (*Historische Studien*, CLXVIII), Berlin 1927, p. 68. Kurhessian Conservatives adopted an antisemitic plank in their platform in May 1887 – five and a half years before the national party took this step in December 1892. *Casseler Journal*, 13th May 1887; cf. *Der Reichsherold*, 4th October 1887.

[19]*Der Reichsherold*, 9th, 16th September, 1st, 11th November, 6th, 9th December, 1887; 3rd, 13th March, 20th, 27th April, 8th, 15th May 1888, etc.

[20]On the cooperative vision in American populism, Lawrence Goodwyn, *The Populist Moment. A Short History of the Populist Revolt*, New York 1978; on the reformism of the Böckel movement, *Der Reichsherold*, 3rd, 7th May 1889 (taxes), 27th September 1889 (*Reichsbank*), 3rd, 17th, 21st June 1892 (revision of industrial freedom, etc.), 27th February 1894 (inalienable homesteads), etc.

organisations. In November 1888 they set up their first such organisation, the *Kurhessischer Bauernverein* (KBV). Like most peasant associations of this time in Germany, the KBV was directly modelled after Schorlemer-Alst's *Westfälischer Bauernverein* (WBV), which strove to improve the peasantry through lectures, legal counsel, and agricultural cooperation. Since the WBV's leaders also wanted the peasantry to help itself by political means, the WBV acquired the dual character of economic organisation and pressure group. Böckel appointed Alfred Winkler, a Catholic from Westphalia, to head the newly founded KBV. Winkler drafted the KBV statutes on the model of those of the non-antisemitic WBV. Despite organisational constraints imposed by the Prussian Assembly Law of 1850, KBV cell members were able to cooperate on an *ad hoc* basis to purchase seed, fodder, and fertiliser, and formal cooperatives were sponsored in a few of the Catholic villages of Kirchhain.[21]

In response to the antisemites' continuing agitation in the political off-season, other parties and organisations turned their attention to the usury issue and to cooperation as a way of combatting it. The appearance of *Wucher auf dem Lande* in the summer of 1887 seemed to identify the cause of Böckel's triumph in the usury inflicted by Jewish traders on peasants. The major Jewish organisation, the *Deutsch-Israelitischer Gemeindebund* (DIGB), and the "Jewish" *Vossische Zeitung* accepted the *Wucher* study, with its indictment of Jews, as objective.[22] The usury theme dominated the March 1887 meeting of the Marburg *Bismarckverein*, where the Left Liberal law professor Franz von Liszt said that "the only value" of the recent election was to draw public attention to the ravages of usury in Marburg. Usury also dominated the proceedings of the Marburg Agricultural Association's spring 1887 meeting, of the periodic gatherings of the regional economic elite (the *Wirtschaftliche Conferenz*) in 1887–1888, and of the national conference of the Protestant Inner Mission, held in Kassel in the autumn of 1888.[23]

Then, ten days after the founding of the KBV in November 1888, the budding Raiffeisen organisation in Kurhessen founded its own *Verein gegen den Wucher* (VgW). This organisation would not only combat usury; it would combat political antisemitism by eliminating its understood cause – usurious exploitation. At the founding meeting F. W. Raiffeisen's son Rudolf said that he had just returned from Spain, where usury was pervasive. But its practitioners were not Jewish. In Germany, he said, the Raiffeisen organisation must not become an *Antisemitenverein*; the rural poor should help themselves instead of

[21]*Der Reichsherold*, 23rd November 1888 (KBV statutes); on the KBV, Siegmar Krey, 'Der Kurhessische Bauernverein', Marburg University *Staatsexamsarbeit* 1963; on the WBV, Robert G. Moeller, *German Peasants and Agrarian Politics, 1914–1924. The Rhineland and Westphalia*, Chapel Hill 1986; see the useful general account by Martin Fassbender, an acquaintance of Böckel's, *Die Bauernvereine und die Lage der Landwirtschaft*, Paderborn 1888.

[22]*Die Jüdische Presse*, 28th July 1887 (on *Vossische Zeitung* article); March 1887 correspondence between Rabbi Munk and DIGB, Central Archives for the History of the Jewish People (CAHJP), M1/14.

[23]*Oberhessische Zeitung*, 27th, 29th March 1887 (*Bismarckverein*); 14th May 1887 session of Agricultural Association, Justus Kaiser, *120 Jahre Landwirtschaftlicher Kreisverein Marburg/Lahn*, Marburg 1975, p. 64; 7th December 1887 meeting of semi-official *Wirtschaftliche Conferenz, Zentrales Staatsarchiv*, Merseburg, *Handelsministerium*, rep. 120 BB/VI°/12/vol. 1, bl. 212–216, etc.; *Verhandlungen des 25. Congresses für Innere Mission zu Cassel, 10.–13. September 1888*, Kassel 1888, pp. 134–153.

attacking Jewish usurers. In its campaign to combat usury and set up cooperatives, the VgW enlisted the aid of Conservative government officials, including a dozen *Landräte* and the *Regierungspräsident*, as well as local notables and a number of rabbis. Largely through its efforts the number of Raiffeisen cooperatives in Kurhessen increased in its first year from 58 to 96. With various forms of state aid to individual cooperatives and cooperative unions, the Raiffeisen network expanded to 240 in 1895, encompassing approximately one rural household in six.[24]

Meanwhile, within the antisemites' KBV, conflict quickly broke out over the relative importance of practical and political antisemitism. Böckel had gone the way of practical antisemitism for tactical reasons: not only to create something "positive" but to serve his vaulting political ambitions. As the Marburg *Landrat* put it in 1889, "the purpose of the creation of all these cells is without doubt the promotion of electoral agitation".[25] Winkler, however, adhered to practical antisemitism as an end in itself. He wanted to curtail usurious exploitation, but he was no principled enemy of the Jews. He believed that Roman law and the free circulation of landed property were the ultimate causes of indebtedness and foreclosure in the countryside. The conflict between Böckel and Winkler came to a head in March 1890, when Winkler declared at a KBV general assembly that the organisation must not become subordinated to politics.[26]

To avoid the spectacle of a divided leadership Böckel did not dissolve the KBV but set up alongside it a new cooperative organisation, *Der Mitteldeutsche Bauernverein* (MdBV), later *Hessischer Bauernbund.* Under his chairmanship the MdBV expanded very rapidly, encompassing by 1892–1893 as many as 15,000 members in 500 cells in Kurhessen, the Grand Duchy, and Nassau. At this time subscription to the *Reichsherold* reached about 11,000, five times the subscription of its hated Conservative competitor, the *Oberhessische Zeitung.*[27]

Like the KBV, the MdBV was an instrument of political as well as practical antisemitism. As a political organisation the MdBV served Böckel and the antisemites of the anti-capitalist "reform" wing as a means of mobilising voters, getting out signatures for *Reichstag* petitions, breaking up rallies of enemies, and most important, financing the antisemites' campaigns.

As an instrument of combatting "usurers" the MdBV was even more ambitious. It took the Raiffeisen cooperative as its model, but the antisemites strayed from Raiffeisen's principles. They concentrated their efforts on the wholesale purchasing side of the cooperative enterprise, which was easier to organise and more lucrative but also more capital-intensive than the credit side. Concretely, MdBV leaders mediated the wholesale purchase of artificial fertiliser and fodder; turnover in 1892 reached 2 m. Mk. or about 150–200 Mk. per member.[28]

[24]*Jahresbericht des Vereins gegen den Wucher im Regierungsbezirk Cassel für 1889*; on Jewish approval of the *Verein*'s activities, Adolf Gotthelft to DIGB, 12th January 1889, CAHJP, M1/14; *Allgemeine Zeitung des Judentums*, 21st February 1889.

[25]StAM 165/4642.

[26]Krey, *op. cit.*, p. 33, *passim.*

[27]On the MdBV, Gisela Kalbfleisch, *Der Mitteldeutsche Bauernverein in Hessen von 1890–1894*, Marburg University *Staatsexamsarbeit* 1962, pp. 59ff (statistics); see my *Anti-Semitism and Rural Transformation*, ch. 5.

[28]*Der Reichsherold*, 6th, 16th December, 1892.

The cooperative organisation of the commodity business struck directly at Jewish "usurers", that is traders. The best known – because least successful – of the MdBV's projects was the attempt to set up "Jew-free" cattle markets in Upper Hessen in the Grand Duchy. These markets failed as markets, since they could not displace the mobile and well-informed Jewish trader, who always had cash in hand. Only as *Volksfeste* did they succeed. It is too easy to discredit the MdBV and miss the point of practical antisemitism by focusing on the fiasco of these markets. The point is that, in general, Jews could be more successfully combatted as "usurers" than as Jewish traders. Practical antisemitism was also what Böckel's voters wanted.[29]

Like the KBV, the MdBV was riven by conflict over the proper balance between practical and political antisemitism – between combatting Jews as usurers and combatting them as an evil race. The conflict was more than a clash of personalities. Rather, the two worked at cross purposes. The full realisation of practical antisemitism would have rendered Böckel's style of political antisemitism superfluous by reducing the vulnerability felt by smallholders in the liberal economy. The antisemites' financial exploitation of the organisation, for political purposes, violated the interests of MdBV members in the concrete advantages of practical antisemitism: after 1891 Böckel began taking 2% cuts in the fertiliser and fodder business mediated by the MdBV.[30]

The MdBV was undermined not only by internal structural tensions. More seriously, the functions it performed were increasingly taken over by national organisations that pursued them separately and more efficiently – but not primarily in the service of antisemitic politics. As a political organisation the MdBV lacked the resources and agitational prowess of the *Bund der Landwirte*, the national Conservative agricultural organisation founded in February 1893 in Berlin; the Marburg cell of the *Bund der Landwirte*, founded in March, set out immediately to win back Marburg for the Conservatives.[31] As an instrument of practical antisemitism the MdBV was more and more eclipsed by the state-sponsored Raiffeisen cooperatives, which shared many of the goals of practical antisemitism without being burdened by ulterior political purposes.

The inefficiency of the MdBV was brought home in the summer and autumn of 1893, during one of the worst droughts of the nineteenth century. The Raiffeisen organisation was mobilised by the state to purchase and distribute huge quantities of fodder. Without a network of credit cooperatives, the MdBV lacked the resources to respond to the crisis. Its limited resources were further strained as a result of the three *Landtag* and *Reichstag* elections it financed in 1893. And the organisation was circumvented by the state during the drought.

[29]On the cattle markets, Eugen Schmahl, 'Die antisemitische Bauernbewegung von der Böckelzeit bis zum Nationalsozialismus', in *Entwicklung der völkischen Bewegung*, edited by Schmahl and W. Seipel, Giessen 1933, pp. 78–80.

[30]*Der Reichsherold*, 17th July 1891; 17th, 23rd June 1893.

[31]On all aspects of the *Bund der Landwirte*, Hans-Jürgen Puhle, *Agrarische Interessenpolitik und preussischer Konservatismus im wilhelminischen Reich (1893–1914). Ein Beitrag zur Analyse des Nationalismus in Deutschland am Beispiel des Bundes der Landwirte und der Deutsch-Konservativen Partei*, 2nd edn., Bonn–Bad Godesberg 1975; on the founding of the Marburg cell of the *Bund der Landwirte*, *Oberhessische Zeitung*, 14th–15th, 23rd–24th March 1893.

Even Jewish wholesalers were preferred by Prussia to the MdBV in the task of getting fodder to hard-pressed smallholders.[32]

With his organisation weakened and his political space narrowed by the *Bund der Landwirte*, Böckel was forced from the MdBV leadership in September 1894 for reasons that are still unclear. The *Bund der Landwirte* probably had a hand in his dismissal. Böckel was the last obstacle to the unification of the wings of political antisemitism in a national party with *Fraktion* strength (16 deputies), which could have provided the *Bund der Landwirte* with decisive help in the *Reichstag*. Within a month of Böckel's downfall, the united *Deutschsoziale Reformpartei* (DSRP) was created at the joint conference of "conservative" and "reform" antisemites in Eisenach.[33]

IV

After seven years of extraordinary expansion the Böckel movement came to an end in the space of a few months in 1894, with Böckel's dismissal from the MdBV, the failure of his newspaper, and his departure from Marburg. What happened next? A 1933 history of the movement, still the most informative in the literature by virtue of its use of sources that were subsequently destroyed, identified the *Bund der Landwirte* and the non-antisemitic cooperative system as the successors of the Böckel movement.[34] While the *Bund der Landwirte* and its antisemitic allies in the *Deutschsoziale Reformpartei* have been well covered in the scholarly literature on antisemitism, the Raiffeisen organisation and non-antisemitic cooperative system generally have been completely neglected. This is especially surprising because the cooperative network was simply the largest and most thorough organisation in the German countryside; in Kurhessen every other rural household belonged to one of nearly 400 Raiffeisen cooperatives in 1913. In that year the bi-weekly *Raiffeisenbote* reached three times as many subscribers as *Der Reichsherold* had at its height. Without this far-flung organisation the villagers of Kurhessen could probably not have participated in the general economic expansion of the two decades after 1895.[35]

[32]StAM 165/724, vol. 2; and as in note 10, 180 Kirchhain/499 (Jewish distributor Strauss); *Der Reichsherold*, 22nd August 1893, etc.

[33]On Böckel's downfall, Levy, *op. cit.*, pp. 103–110; Mack, *loc. cit.*, pp. 398–400.

[34]Schmahl, *op. cit.*, pp. 121–122.

[35]*Jahresbericht des Verbandes ländlicher Genossenschaften Raiffeisenscher Organisation für Hessen* (JBR), 1913 (stat., unnumbered appendices). Three useful introductions to agricultural cooperation in Germany: Joseph R. Cahill, *Agricultural Credit and Cooperation in Germany* . . . , Washington D.C. 1913; Erich Lothar Seelmann-Eggebert, *Friedrich Wilhelm Raiffeisen. Sein Lebensgang und genossenschaftliches Werk*, Stuttgart 1928; Helmut Faust, *Geschichte der Genossenschaftsbewegung*, 3rd edn., Frankfurt a. Main 1977. None of these works explores in depth the political aspects of cooperation; see my dissertation, *op. cit.*, chapters 6–7. In 1913 there were more than 26,000 registered rural cooperative societies in Germany. Of these more than 20,000 belonged to the Haas system, named after its founder Wilhelm Haas (1839–1913), a Hessian *Kreisrat*; more than 5,000 to the Raiffeisen system. Friedrich Wilhelm Raiffeisen (1818–1888) founded the first cooperative, in the Westerwald, in 1864; in 1879 Haas and associates of Raiffeisen's broke from the Neuwied-based Raiffeisen organisation and founded a new system based in Darmstadt. The Haas organisation was less centralised, less committed to Christian principles, more strongly orientated to profit-

In what sense did the non-antisemitic cooperative system carry on the Böckel movement? This problem can be approached by looking at three aspects of rural cooperation in Kurhessen: the Raiffeisen ideology, the political affiliation of the cooperatives, and their economic functioning. The following comments apply primarily to Kurhessen but provide perhaps the starting point for a systematic comparison between Kurhessen and regions where political antisemitism was of negligible importance.

Much of the ideological affinity between the Raiffeisen organisation and political antisemitism was unintentional, arising from a shared preoccupation with the evils of usury. F. W. Raiffeisen's preoccupation with usury parallels that of the Böckel movement. Beginning in the 1881 edition of his book, *Darlehnskassenvereine*, Raiffeisen described usury in terms rivalling the antisemites': "Like the greedy carnivore feeding on the agitated and exhausted beast, the heartless and selfish bloodsuckers fall upon needy and defenceless rural folk, exploit their inexperience, and take over their property." However, Raiffeisen criticised the antisemites for offering superficial measures against usury, like pogrom and revocation of emancipation: "No one considers murdering them all. Taking away their civil rights would be just as inappropriate." He found more merit in the proposal to expel the Jews to Palestine. Their expulsion, however, would not change the conditions that enabled "the small heap of Jews" to acquire great wealth and power. With the Jews gone, Christian usurers would take their place. Raiffeisen hated usurers regardless of their religion; he was an equal-opportunity antisemite. In his view, self-help – institutionalised neighbourly love – was the proper means of combatting usury.[36]

The antisemitism of the early Raiffeisen cooperatives derived not from any affiliation with political antisemitism but from more traditional Jew-hatred. The importance of pastors as local initiators and leaders lent the early coops a pronounced Christian as well as anti-Jewish character. Pastor Seelig founded the Ottrau cooperative in Ziegenhain, just east of Marburg, in 1881; as chairman, Seelig opened the general assemblies with prayers and conducted them like sermons. He warned members that they would be expelled if they took part in "dangerous transactions" with *Wucherjuden*. Jews were excluded from membership in many early cooperatives, although Raiffeisen never went that far in drafting model statutes. "How much do the Jews here want to take part in our cooperative", said Seelig. "I will never offer them my hand, for that would

---

making, and more sympathetic to the needs of independent farmers than the Raiffeisen system. After the turn of the century the systems converged, merged in 1905, but separated again in 1913; in 1929–1930 a more thorough-going merger was enacted, which remains, in effect.

[36]F. W. Raiffeisen, *Die Darlehnskassenvereine* . . . , 5th edn., Neuwied 1887, pp. 127, 140. These passages first appeared in the third edition (Neuwied 1881, pp. 8, 149–150) of Raiffeisen's book, which was originally published in 1866 and revised in 1872. Böckel's *Der Reichsherold* printed an obituary for Raiffeisen, written by Martin Fassbender, in which Raiffeisen was named an "enemy of the antisemitic movement" who believed that "everything that it strove after could be achieved through cooperation"! 27th March 1888.

violate the purpose of the cooperative." Cooperative leaders still exploit the usury issue by reminiscing on the evils of usury before the days of self-help.[37]

This antisemitic tone was pervasive at the local level but less intrusive higher up in the Raiffeisen organisation, where outright antisemitic utterances would have discredited the Raiffeisen system. Only at moments of crisis in the organisation – in the late 1870s, in the early 1890s, in 1898, and in 1905 – was an antisemitic tone struck, to rally the rank-and-file and discredit the organisation's enemies.[38]

More important in the Raiffeisen ideology after 1895 was its positive cast: institutionalised neighbourly love was the reverse side of institutionalised hostility to usury. Community-mindedness grew out of Raiffeisen's dream of reinvigorating the Christian *Gemeinde*. After 1895 the Christian element diminished in significance, and community-mindedness itself became the cardinal virtue; and was evoked primarily to affirm the cohesion of the organisation. Since the Raiffeisen cooperative was becoming a bank like all banks – average indebtedness per member increased from 150 Mk. in 1895 to 979 Mk. in 1913 – it was also good for business to bind members by non-economic means.[39] Like Christian faith, devotion to the cooperative community could not be questioned; for Raiffeisen leaders, this devotion became a sort of religious faith in the cooperative mission.

Turning to the area of the party-political affiliation of the Raiffeisen organisation in Kurhessen, it should first be observed that the 1889 imperial cooperative law prohibited cooperatives from affiliating with parties and cooperative members from using general assemblies as forums for political discussions. With this qualification, it can be argued that an ideological and direct as well as indirect political affinity existed between the Raiffeisen organisation and Böckel's enemies, then successors, on the Right: the *Bund der Landwirte*, the increasingly antisemitic Conservative parties, and the *Deutschsoziale Reformpartei*. The cooperative ideology of community-mindedness, anti-individualism, and, sporadically, antisemitism, bears family resemblance to the *völkisch* ideologies of these political groupings. Pastor Adam Meyenschein, the ideologue of the Kurhessian Raiffeisen organisation, deployed an outspoken *völkisch* nationalism in his speeches at village and district Raiffeisen functions. He saw Raiffeisen as a "Siegfried" striding the land, who rescued "Brunhilde"

[37]*Gründungsunterlagen*, Ottrau cooperative, including protocols of general assemblies of 1882ff, in possession of the present-day Raiffeisenbank e.G., Neukirchen; *Idee, Leistung, Erfolg. 100 Jahre Raiffeisenverband Kurhessen, e.G.*, Kassel 1982, pp. 37ff.

[38]In 1879, the Haas renegades from the Raiffeisen organisation accused Neuwied of allowing a Stoeckerite "Judenhetze" to infest the cooperative system. Seelmann-Eggebert, *op. cit.*, pp. 356ff. After Raiffeisen's death in 1888 Haas agitators in Kurhessen accused the Raiffeisen organisation of engaging in antisemitic politics; this was in part a way of discrediting the Raiffeisen organisation with its state sponsors. See Raiffeisen pamphlet denying antisemitism, "An die verehrlichen Vorstände, etc.", in StAM 180 Marburg/2715. In 1898 and 1905 intra-cooperative conflicts yielded to conflicts between cooperatives and private traders; each side accused the other of engaging in usurious or sharp commercial practices. See my dissertation, *op. cit.*, chapter 6, for discussion of cooperative-trade conflicts.

[39]*Raiffeisenbote-Cassel* 23rd October 1904; Adam Meyenschein, *Vierzig Jahre Raiffeisen in Hessen. Festgabe zum Verbandsjubiläum*, Kassel 1922, pp. 36, 49.

from her captors. For him the Raiffeisen cooperative was a modern form of the "urdeutsch" cooperative concept. Like the *Bund der Landwirte*, the Raiffeisen organisation brought unity to the defenceless countryside.[40]

A more direct but still informal political relationship between cooperatives and parties of the Right arose from relations between leaders and members of individual cooperatives. Because the local leadership was drawn from the conservative village elite of pastors, teachers, and mayors, lending practices had a political dimension. As the Left-Liberal Marburg press alleged in 1911: "Unfortunately, the local [cooperative] chairmen have been incapable of refraining from being guided by party-political considerations. Peasants who do not go along with the agrarian reaction have received no credit."[41]

Some cooperative leaders engaged directly in politics. Although they took part in politics as individuals and not in their capacity as cooperative leaders, it may be conjectured that they mobilised their organisations by evoking the Raiffeisen ideology and bringing economic pressures to bear on the rank-and-file. Meyenschein, just cited, was a leader of the *Bund der Landwirte* who served as a Conservative *Landtag* deputy (Gelnhausen-Schlüchtern) between 1903 and 1913 and opposed finance reform in 1909. Georg Rexerodt, Eschwege estate owner and leader of the Kurhessian Raiffeisen organisation, was a Free Conservative and member of the *Bund der Landwirte*; his cousin Max Klingenbiel, prominent lawyer and chief Raiffeisen organiser in the Marburg region, was a Conservative party activist. At the national level, Hermann Dietrich, the Raiffeisen *Generalanwalt*, was a Conservative *Landtag* deputy between 1898 and 1918 and a *Reichstag* deputy of the Conservatives, later of the *Deutschnationale Volkspartei*, between 1898 and 1928, serving in 1919 as a vice-president of the *Reichstag*.[42]

Antisemites of the *Deutschsoziale Reformpartei* did not possess the same systematic access to the village, regional, and national cooperative organisations enjoyed by the more traditional Right. Direct links between political antisemites and cooperatives were established only sporadically, in cases where cooperative leaders happened to be political antisemites. Antisemitic agitation among Raiffeisen members may, however, have been unnecessary. As Max Liebermann von Sonnenberg, the deputy of the *Deutschsoziale* groupings for Fritzlar between 1890 and 1911, commented during the 1903 election race, "as far as I know, all Raiffeisen men are antisemitic". It can be argued that this antisemitism was inculcated on a day-to-day basis by the ideology and workings of their cooperatives.[43]

[40]Many of Meyenschein's pre-war speeches were reprinted in his *Raiffeisen und das deutsche Dorf*, Berlin 1917, p. 35 ("Brunhilde"), etc.; on the ideology of the *Bund der Landwirte*, Puhle, *op. cit.*, esp. pp. 78–83 and 111–140 (antisemitism).

[41]*Hessische Landeszeitung*, 17th October 1911.

[42]On Meyenschein, *Oberhessische Zeitung*, 28th September 1909 and sources cited in chapters 6–7 of my dissertation, *op. cit.*; Georg Rexerodt, *Aus den Anfängen des kurhessischen Raiffeisentums*, Kassel 1943, pp. 98–99; on Klingenbiel, *Hessische Landeszeitung*, 6th February 1903 and sources in my *op. cit.*; on Dietrich, Faust, *op. cit.*, pp. 376ff.

[43]Liebermann von Sonnenberg, 'Offener Brief', in *Flugblättersammlung, Universitätsbibliothek* Marburg, 1903 *Reichstagswahl*.

The clearest bonds of continuity between the Böckel movement and the Raiffeisen organisation can be located in the economic functioning of the cooperatives, which seemed to realise many of the goals of practical antisemitism. Again the apparent continuity resulted from the anti-usury programme shared by antisemites and cooperators. But more than in the case of the cooperative ideology, the economic workings of the parish cooperatives were often downright anti-Jewish. Pastor Seelig of the Ottrau cooperative could announce at the March 1882 general assembly that in the first two months of the year local Jewish cattle traders had lost 4,200 Mk. because the cooperatives had deprived them of their credit business; the Niederklein cooperative, founded in 1895, extended credit *zur Befreiung aus Wucherhänden*; and the Kirchhain granary was set up in 1903 with the explicit purpose of circumventing Jewish grain traders.[44]

Despite these instances of anti-Jewish economic policy, the self-help ideology was less a rallying cry for institutionalised boycott than a sort of advertising device. Like the MdBV, the Raiffeisen organisation increasingly engaged in the commodity business after 1895; one tenth of the Kurhessian organisation's turnover in 1913 was accounted for by the commodity business – double the national level; in 1913 the Kassel cooperative central sold more than 35 m. kg. of fertilisers.[45] The anti-usury ideology was invoked primarily to discredit private traders in those fields where they competed with cooperative traders, especially in the fertiliser and fodder business. For instance, the Kassel Raiffeisen press repeatedly claimed that private traders had no concern for the welfare of their clients and sold them Thomas meal with a low percentage of soluble phosphoric acid. When the private traders – Jewish as well as Gentile – began to fight back and the conflict became very ugly, Raiffeisen leaders used antisemitic slogans to discredit traders. Otherwise they claimed their organisation only combatted dishonest – "unreelle" – traders.[46]

This rhetoric of practical antisemitism was even used to divert members from the commercial practices of the cooperatives themselves, which the private traders were very willing to disclose. F. W. Raiffeisen had realised that the cooperative commodity business required minimal acceptance of capitalist principles like hard bargaining with suppliers and minute attention to profit and loss. With the expansion of the cooperative trade in fertiliser and fodder, Raiffeisen leaders had to grapple with the problems never confronted by F. W. Raiffeisen. They had to compete with the trader – the usurer – on his own ground. In no area of cooperative economic activity was this clearer or the anti-usury ideology more disingenuous than in the property business.[47]

[44]Ottrau cooperative documentation, as note 37; *Protokollbuch für den Vorstand, Niederkleiner Darlehnskassenvereine*, in possession of present-day *Raiffeisenbank* e.G., Kirchhain; the bank's own historical sketch of the granary (established in 1903) refers to its goal of circumventing Jewish traders; cf. Paul Arnsberg, *Die jüdischen Gemeinden in Hessen*, vol. 1, Frankfurt a. Main 1971, pp. 444–447 (effects of *Kornhaus*).

[45]JBR, 1913, pp. 44–45; Meyenschein, *Vierzig Jahre Raiffeisen in Hessen, op. cit.*, p. 49.

[46]*Raiffeisenbote*, 1st April 1898; Adolf Scherer, *Raiffeisen in Hessen. Die Geschichte einer sozialen Bewegung*, vol. 1, Kassel 1951, pp. 121ff.

[47]Raiffeisen, *op. cit.*, 3rd edn., p. 108.

In 1905, the *Raiffeisenbote* instructed the rank-and-file to boycott auctions held by known full-time parcellers and to allow their cooperatives to conduct all land business formerly handled privately. The credit cooperative should assume the responsibility for purchasing and reselling the farms of members compelled to sell. The Niederklein (Kirchhain) cooperative protocols give evidence of how one cooperative went into the land-trading business. At the annual general assembly in 1909, members adopted a new paragraph in its statutes by which the cooperative committed itself to buy all land sold by members and, if necessary, to parcel it. Members were now prohibited from buying parcels from private traders. Violators would be fined and non-signatories expelled from the cooperative. At least three cases of cooperative *Güterschlächterei* were undertaken by the Niederklein cooperative between 1909 and 1914. It is not clear whether these cases resulted from indebtedness to the cooperative itself, but the *Vorstand* protocols for the years after 1909 are filled with decisions to take action against delinquent debtors, by securing debts against land or by taking debtors to court. To render the usurer superfluous the cooperatives had to adopt what Böckel's antisemites had considered "Jewish" business practices.[48]

Summarising, the Raiffeisen ideology contained antisemitic elements, but they developed outside the political arena and in spite of F. W. Raiffeisen's intentions. It may be hypothesised that through its general assemblies, publications, and press, the cooperative organisation provided the institutional underpinnings of *völkisch* antisemitism in regions otherwise unblemished by political antisemitism. In Kurhessen after Böckel the Raiffeisen ideology bore a strong affinity with the ideologies purveyed by Böckel's political successors on the Right. However, both the conservative antisemites and antisemitic Conservatives were repugnant to the populist Böckel. The Conservative politicians among cooperative leaders did not belong to the Böckel tradition. The Raiffeisen organisation got its start in Kurhessen as part of the government's programme to combat political antisemitism in the 1880s, and Raiffeisen leaders continued to invoke the Böckel movement as the "wrong" sort of self-help in the 1920s.[49]

It was in the realm of practical antisemitism that the Raiffeisen cooperatives most directly and successfully – if not always intentionally – carried on the tradition of the Böckel movement. Through new usury laws, economic prosperity, and the very working of the cooperatives, usury ceased to be a political issue, much less a threat to the rural population after 1895. In competing with traders, cooperatives themselves behaved like "usurers," belying in practice an ancient prejudice.

There was more to the Böckel movement than hostility to the Jewish usurer. Böckel brought the racist dogma to the countryside, but discovered that on its own it found little resonance there. In part because the Raiffeisen cooperatives

[48]*Raiffeisenbote*, 9th May, 23rd September 1907, etc.; *Niederkleiner Darlehnskassenverein*, *Vorstand* and *Generalversammlung* protocols, 1909–1914, as note 44. See my dissertation, *op. cit.*, for detailed discussion. Raiffeisen touched on the possibilities of using the cooperatives to alleviate *Güterschlächterei* in the second edition (1872) of *Darlehnskassenvereine*, pp. 62, 294–300.

[49]From Meyenschein's collected postwar speeches, *Raiffeisen und das deutsche Landvolk, 1918–1933*, Kassel 1938, pp. 112–113, 181.

made smallholders more independent, the antisemitic ideology lost its populist impulse after 1895. It was absorbed by the *Bund der Landwirte*, the *Deutschsoziale Reformpartei*, and by the traditional parties of the Right. Once "Jewish usury" ceased to tie together anti-capitalism and antisemitism, the content of political antisemitism became more racist and chauvinist and less reformist and populist than it had been in Böckel's day.

Jewry under Nazi Rule

The Jewish Youth Movement in Germany in the Holocaust Period (I)

Youth in Confrontation with a New Reality

BY CHAIM SCHATZKER

In 1933 the existing Jewish youth movement in Germany was as old as the Weimar Republic. The *Blau-Weiss*, which had been the first Jewish youth movement, was established as a nation-wide movement in 1912 as a result of the merging of several hiking groups, the principal one being the *Wanderbund 1907, Breslau*.

Three additional Jewish youth movements were founded during the First World War: the *Jung-Jüdischer Wanderbund* (JJWB), *Esra*, and the *Kameraden*. One of the factions of the last-named movement later became known as *Der Kreis* and subsequently, after the movement had split, as the *Werkleute*. The *Kadimah* movement was created out of the remnants of the dissolved *Blau-Weiss* in 1926; and *Habonim-Hanoar Hachaluzi* was established in 1933 as a consequence of the union of JJWB – *Brith Haolim* with *Kadimah*. A year later, in 1934, the *Jüdischer Pfadfinderbund-Makkabi Hazair* was founded by the merging of the *Jüdischer Pfadfinderbund in Deutschland* and *Makkabi Hazair*. At about the same time, branches of both *Hashomer Hazair* and *Betar* were set up as well in Germany.[1]

It is important to observe in regard to our concerns in this study that when the National Socialists came to power they found a Jewish youth movement with a well-defined ideology and fully developed institutions and procedures of operation. This circumstance more than any other accounts for the ability of the Jewish youth movement to hold its own and successfully cope with the flood of capricious and perverse regulations that National Socialist authorities devised in order to limit and constrain its actions.

Moreover, most of the institutions and activities common to the Jewish youth movement and *Hechaluz* – that is to say, shared patterns of operation such as *hachscharah*, *hachscharah* communes and centres, training and administration at the branch offices of *Hechaluz*, arrangements for emigration to Palestine, and liaison with the labour movement and the various factions of the Kibbutz movement in that country – had already been laid down before 1933. Indeed, the success with which the Jewish youth movement fulfilled these functions and was able to absorb great numbers of young people in 1933, train them and encourage them to immigrate to Palestine, cannot be properly understood

[1]On the Jewish youth movement in Germany, the analysis of its fundamental features, and the phases of its development, see Chaim Schatzker, 'Martin Buber's Influence on the Jewish Youth Movement in Germany', in *LBI Year Book XXIII* (1978), pp. 151–163.

unless we take into account the fact that the tools for this purpose had been prepared and perfected beforehand.

The *Reichsausschuss der Jüdischen Jugendverbände*, too, had been established as early as 1924, on the initiative of the *Zentralwohlfahrtsstelle der Juden in Deutschland*, with the purpose of encouraging Jewish youth movements to do social work within the Jewish community. In time, and following the same pattern as the *Reichsausschuss der deutschen Jugendverbände*, this committee became a loose umbrella organisation of all Jewish youth movements and organisations, and represented the common interests of young people in Germany in such matters as access to youth hostels and reduced fares on railways. In 1927, the first joint enterprise was established, a young people's rest-house and resort in Seesen in the Harz Mountains. The rest-house eventually became a meeting place at which study days, leadership courses and a variety of other activities were held which furnished a context for the formation of a degree of intellectual communion among the diverse Jewish youth movements and organisations.[2]

The principal reason for the influence and power of the *Reichsausschuss der Jüdischen Jugendverbände* was that it was recognised by the office of the *Reichsjugendführer* as a negotiation partner in the capacity of sole responsible representative of Jewish youth organisations. Henceforth, all questions pertaining to young Jews would be transmitted through the *Reichsausschuss der Jüdischen Jugendverbände*, which would be responsible for the division into districts, and would from this time forward issue the credentials accrediting the leaders and membership of Jewish youth associations in the eyes of the authorities.[3]

In their efforts at centralisation and in trying to impose responsibility on the principal Jewish representative bodies, the Germans made use for the first time of existing Jewish representation in order to implement their policies, just as they would later do with the *Reichsvertretung der deutschen Juden*.

According to the regulations, the *Reichsausschuss* would represent the Jewish youth organisations in respect not only to the *Reich* authorities and local authorities in Nazi Germany, but to the *Reichsvertretung der deutschen Juden* as well. Eventually a close partnership developed between the two organisations that also came into play on an organisational level. Thus the *Reichsausschuss*

[2]Concerning the establishment of the *Reichsausschuss der Jüdischen Jugendverbände*, see *Die deutschen Jugendverbände*, hrsg. von Hertha Siemering, Berlin 1931, VIII, 'Jüdische Jugendverbände', von Dr. Georg Lubinski (Giora Lotan), Berlin, p. 234; and the *Reichsausschuss* organ, *Mitteilungen des Reichsausschusses der Jüdischen Jugendverbände*.

[3]See Reichsführer SS, Chef des Sicherheitsamtes, Lagebericht Mai/Juni 1934, p. 49. About the circumstances in which the *Reichsausschuss* came into being, see *Jüdische Jugend im Übergang, Ludwig Tietz, 1897–1933. Sein Leben und seine Zeit*, hrsg. von Gustav Horn; see also the criticism of this book by Chaim Schatzker in *Yalkut Moreschet Periodical*, No. 39 (May 1985), p. 195 (in Hebrew). Notwithstanding Tietz's proud and impressive comportment during negotiations with German authorities concerning the issues of the recognition of the *Reichsausschuss* and its new functions, as attested to by Gustav Horn (and such things were still possible in 1933), we should remember that the policy of Nazi authorities towards German Jews was not formed at the negotiation table. It was National Socialist political orientation in regard to Jews, and not Jewish representatives – impressive as their manner may have been – which ultimately determined the place and functions of the *Reichsausschuss*. See also *Gemeinschaftsarbeit der Jüdischen Jugend*, Berlin 1937, Verlag, Zentralwohlfahrtsstelle der Juden in Deutschland, hrsg. von Dr. Friedrich Brodnitz, pp. 86–88.

representative was involved in all those areas in which the *Reichsvertretung* was active that had to do with young people, such as vocational training, hostels and the like. Close cooperation was also established with the *Mittelstelle für jüdische Erwachsenenbildung* in matters of education and culture.

This, then, is the background against which we have to examine National Socialist policy towards the Jewish youth movement, and the position of the latter in the period under review.

The *Reichsausschuss der Jüdischen Jugendverbände*[4] comprised, apart from youth movements, organisations which, although not youth movements themselves, were in large measure maintained by them. Among these were *Hechaluz, Brith Chaluzim Datiim* (*Bachad*), as well as sports organisations such as the Zionist-orientated *Makkabi*, and the *Schild*, which was affiliated with the strongly assimilationist *Sportbund des Reichsbundes jüdischer Frontsoldaten.*

Also represented were youth organisations that were primarily concerned with supplementary education for young Jews – as, for example, the *Bund Jüdischer Jugend*, which was founded by the younger members of the *Verband der jüdischen Jugendvereine Deutschlands* (VjJD).[5] This organisation was moderately Zionist in its outlook at the time, and, in contrast to other Zionist movements, included within its ranks both *chaluzim* and non-*chaluzim.*

A distinct category was formed by youth organisations which served principally as a reserve force and young guard of political parties, and which in varying degrees assumed the characteristic features of German youth movements. Among these groups were the *Brith Hanoar* of *Zeirei Misrachi*, *Betar*, *Jüdisch-Nationale-Jugend "Herzlia"*, the youth groups of *Agudas Jisrael* (*Agudas Jisrael Junggruppen der B.Z.V.*, *Jugendorganisationen*, *Esra-Pirche-Aguda-Jugend mit Noar Agudathi*), and finally *Hashomer Hazair.*[6]

As opposed to these, the *Reichsausschuss* also included youth movements modelled on the classic *Bund* type of the German youth movement. Belonging to

[4]On the activities of the *Reichsausschuss*, see *Gemeinschaftsarbeit der Jüdischen Jugend*, *op. cit.*

[5]About the history of *Bachad*, see Joseph Walk, 'The Torah va'Avodah Movement', in *LBI Year Book XIX* (1974), pp. 97–102. For the history of the *VjJD*, see Herbert [A.] Strauss, 'The Jugendverband. A Social and Intellectual History', in *LBI Year Book VI* (1961), pp. 206–235; and Chaim Schatzker, *Tnuat ha-noar ha-yehudit be-Germania ben ha-shanim 1900–1933*, (The Jewish Youth Movement in Germany between 1900 and 1933), Ph.D. dissertation, Hebrew University in Jerusalem, 1969 (in Hebrew). Concerning sports organisations, see Paul Yogi Mayer, 'Equality-Egality. Jews and Sports in Germany', in *LBI Year Book XXV* (1980), pp. 221–241.

[6]In its origins, *Hashomer Hazair* was a youth movement. But at the time of its establishment in Germany in 1931, its branches in that country should properly be included in the above category, although it did retain many of the features of a youth movement.* *Zeirei Misrachi*, too, had many of the essential characteristics of a youth movement; see for example *Chayeinu*, the *Bachad* newspaper, No. 23 (January 1938).

*On the *Hashomer Hazair* see Jehuda Reinharz, 'Hashomer Hazair in Germany (II). Under the Shadow of the Swastika, 1933–1938', which follows this essay in the current volume of the Year Book, and *idem*, 'Hashomer Hazair in Germany (I). 1928–1933', in *LBI Year Book XXXI* (1986), pp. 173–208. See further Reinharz's more concise version on this topic 'Hashomer Hazair in Nazi Germany', in *Juden im Nationalsozialistischen Deutschland/The Jews in Nazi Germany 1933–1943*, herausgegeben von Arnold Paucker mit Sylvia Gilchrist und Barbara Suchy, Tübingen 1986 (Schriftenreihe wissenschaftlicher Abhandlungen des Leo Baeck Instituts 45), pp. 317–350 – (Ed.).

this category were such organisations as the *Werkleute, Habonim-Noar Chaluzi* and *Makkabi Hazair*, whose stages of development towards Zionism and Socialism we described earlier.

In this category, too, were the *Ring, Bund Jüdischer Jugend.*[7] The *Ring* grew out of a dispersed collection of groups calling themselves *Deutsch-Jüdische Jugend* (the first of which was founded in Hamburg in 1925), as well as out of a variety of youth groups affiliated with synagogues and the *Centralverein deutscher Staatsbürger jüdischen Glaubens* (C.V.). These groups were not youth movements but rather clubs that provided a young guard that fitted in with the outlook of the C.V. They defined themselves as "associations of young people who are German by culture and birth, and Jews by faith and origin".[8]

These groups joined together in Lehnitz in 1933 to form the *Bund deutsch-jüdischer Jugend*, whose ideology corresponded to that of the C.V., which looked upon the Jewish community in the Diaspora as representing the legitimate mode of Jewish existence. When, finally, circumstances made it impossible to reject out of hand the idea of Jewish emigration from Germany, other countries were considered as alternate places of settlement, and these did not necessarily include Palestine. Such alternative places of settlement might be sought in the South American countries or were offered by the "Cyprus Plan". To this end a Jewish educational establishment was founded on property in Gross-Breesen the purpose of which was to prepare Jews for immigration.[9]

The *Ring*, too, following a pattern similar to that of the *Werkleute*, instituted vocational training and preparation for emigration while resisting any break with German culture and despite the circumstances of the times, it launched a highly ramified cultural and educational campaign to prevent the cultural level of its members from declining.

In 1935 this movement was joined by young people from the *Schild* sports group, who were no longer satisfied with being a mere athletic organisation but wished to become a youth movement (their reasons were similar to those that led *Makkabi Hazair* to break away from *Makkabi*). The *Ring* was also joined by sections of the *Schwarzes Fähnlein*, which had been the "German" faction of the *Kameraden* movement and was disbanded in 1934. Another group that joined was the *Vortrupp*, which was founded by Hans Joachim Schoeps, of whose ideology we shall have occasion to speak later.

These groups bestowed upon the *Ring* the spirit and character of a youth movement. Indeed it was these characteristic features of a youth movement that accounted for the organisation's insistence upon its independence, and its explicit assertion that it would no longer regard itself as a manpower pool for the C.V. The process is comparable to the one that took place when the *Kameraden*

[7]On the history of the *Ring*, see Heinz Kellermann, 'Der "Bund"', in *Deutschjüdischer Weg. Eine Schriftenreihe*, Nr. 2. Wille und Weg des deutschen Judentums, Vortrupp Verlag, Berlin 1935.
[8]*Denkschrift der Deutsch-jüdischen Jugend*, Hamburg 1930, p. 20.
[9]On Gross-Breesen see Werner T. Angress, 'Auswandererlehrgut Gross-Breesen', in *LBI Year Book X* (1965), pp. 168–187; and *idem, Generation zwischen Furcht und Hoffnung. Jüdische Jugend im Dritten Reich*, Hamburg 1985.

broke with the C.V. in 1921.[10] Had there been sufficient time, the *Ring* too might have undergone the sort of transformation that was in the nature of youth movements, and eventually have evolved towards Zionism and the *chaluz* spirit.[11] However in 1933, and in the years immediately preceding and following, the *Ring* took an anti-Zionist, or non-Zionist, line and developed an ideology peculiar to itself that we shall consider later in this study. It is not surprising that some of the members of the *Ring* who had retired from the movement should have found it more congenial to work with the *Werkleute* than with non-Zionist adult organisations.

Regarding the multiplicity and fragmentation of the corporate organisations in the *Reichsausschuss der Jüdischen Jugendverbände*, it is hardly surprising that the agencies of the *Reichsjugendführung*, the German youth administration, should have been hard put to sort out the Jewish youth groups and to classify them on the basis of cut and dried criteria. There was some logic in proposing that the system which had been in force during the Weimar Republic should be adopted; namely, a functional classification of Jewish youth organisations into four categories: (1) youth *Bünde*; (2) religious youth groups; (3) sports organisations; (4) organisations dedicated to supplementary education, character building, and vocational training.

Some Jewish organisations rejected these principles of classification and proposed a system of division based on Jewish- or German-orientated organisational philosophies (i.e., Zionist and non-Zionist). In the end a compromise proposal was accepted that was put forward by Ludwig Tietz, who was one of the principal figures in the *Reichsausschuss* (Tietz died soon afterwards). His proposal was that the classification proposed by the authorities should be accepted, but that there should also be a parallel division according to region which would include regional committees (*Landesausschüsse*) and local organisations (*Ortsringe*). Apparently these left sufficient latitude for ideological considerations.

The policy of Nationalist Socialist authorities towards the youth movements was not consistent, and was subject to repeated changes in direction, with prohibitions being imposed, withdrawn, and imposed again.[12] Nevertheless a number of periods and of goals may be discerned.

[10]Chaim Schatzker, 'Toldot ha-"Kameraden". Gilgulim shel tnuat noar yehudit be-Germania' ('The History of the Kameraden. Metamorphosis of a Jewish Youth Movement in Germany'), in World Congress of Jewish Studies, vol. 2, Jerusalem 1976, p. 283 (in Hebrew).

[11]"The *Ring* had responded to a specific situation, a response that was in part anticipated by Zionist youth *Bünde* in their ideology and organisation . . ." See *Gemeinschaftsarbeit der Jüdischen Jugend, op. cit.*, p. 70.

[12]The author would like to take this opportunity to express his gratitude to the archives that put the documents used in this study at his disposal: The National Library at the Hebrew University in Jerusalem; The Central Zionist Archives, Jerusalem; Bundesarchiv Koblenz; Politisches Archiv des Auswärtigen Amtes, Bonn; Geheimes Staatsarchiv Preussischer Kulturbesitz, Berlin-Dahlem. The author's thanks are owed as well to his friend Otto Dov Kulka of the Hebrew University for putting at his disposal the sources in the American Document Center, Berlin; the Bayerisches Hauptstaatsarchiv, München; the Institut für Marxismus und Leninismus/Zentrales Parteiarchiv, Berlin, D.D.R. These were published in part in his study, 'Daat ha-Kahal be-Germania ha-Natsional-Sotsialistit ve-ha-beaya ha-yehudit' ('Public Opinion in National Socialist Germany and the Jewish Problem'), *Zion*, 40 (1974), pp. 186–290 (in Hebrew); and in *Ha-megamot be-fitron ha-beaya ha-yehudit ba-Raikh ha-Shlishi. Mivhar mekorot* ('Trends in the Solution to the Jewish Problem in the Third Reich. Selected Sources), Jerusalem 1977 (in Hebrew).

The sources are dispersed among a large number of archives: a variety of regulations were passed in different places in Germany, some of which were valid only within a given region while others applied to the country as a whole. A close consideration of the spheres to which each of these regulations applied might be useful in analysing legal and administrative matters. However we shall confine ourselves here to the general aims that are revealed in the sources.

I. 1933–1936

In this period, official policy consisted in four principal aims:
1. The concentration of Jewish youth organisations and movements.
2. Their differentiation and segregation from German youth movements and the German population.
3. The supervision and monitoring of their activities.
4. Putting those organisations and movements at a disadvantage which pursued a policy of encouraging Jews to remain in Germany, and favouring the ones that instituted vocational training programmes for the purpose of emigration.

1. The goal of centralising Jewish youth organisations was pursued according to the principle of transforming the *Reichsausschuss der Jüdischen Jugendverbände* from a loose and voluntary federation into an obligatory central body, and the establishment of a State Committee of Jewish Physical Training and Sports Organisations.[13] Only one Jewish sports organisation would be officially permitted in each city.[14]

2. A great many regulations, prohibitions, and limitations were instituted with the purpose of segregating Jewish youth movements and distinguishing them from both the German population and comparable German organisations. This policy was justified on the grounds of having to prevent Jews from making themselves conspicuous, a situation that could no longer be tolerated by either the German public or the young people of Germany. Such conspicuousness had been the result of their wearing uniforms, displaying symbols and flags, and the like. Also prohibited were field games, drill of a military character, and marching in unison.[15]

Nor could Jews be allowed to organise along lines that were similar to those of the *Hitlerjugend* or to use symbols that resembled those of that organisation. The *Ring*, which had ignored this prohibition and thereby proclaimed its desire to be

[13]See Geheimes Staatspolizeiamt Berlin, den 21. Februar 1935, an alle Staatspolizeistellen. Concerning the *Reichsausschuss der jüdischen Sportsverbände*, which included the *Makkabi* and *Schild*, see Paul Yogi Mayer, *loc. cit.*

[14]See note 12, Staatsministerium des Innern.

[15]Der Inspektor der Geheimen Staatspolizeistellen Berlin, den 2. August 1934, coming under pressure from the Olympic Committee, and "in consideration of foreign policy questions", lifted the prohibition on the display of symbols, but not without calling attention to the dangers that awaited those who displayed them from the violent reaction of the German population. See Geheimes Staatspolizeiamt, note 13.

part of the German nation, was disbanded.[16] Jewish youth hostels were only to be permitted in areas remote from residential areas, so that the inhabitants "should not perceive themselves as being discriminated against, or be caused unpleasantness in any other way"; nor should these be called "Jewish youth hostels," but rather Jewish overnight residences (*Jüdische Übernachtungsheime*).[17] Jewish organisations were also to be denied the use of the term *Ortsgruppe*, commonly employed in the Nazi Party, and were to adopt the name *Ortsverband* instead.[18] And it was clearly considered to be out of the question for the *Werkleute* to use the terms *Gauleiter, Kreisleiter,* and *Ortsgruppenleiter*.[19] Moreover, the *Reichsbund jüdischer Frontsoldaten* was to be prohibited from using the initials RjF, since these were employed by the *Reichsjugendführung* and confusion might therefore arise.[20] Further, it was to be forbidden for Jews to receive sporting emblems,[21] and moreover it was declared to be unthinkable that German youths should compete with Jews in handball games. The permission that had been granted in principle to some sports authorities in regard to matches in which Aryan and non-Aryan associations were to take part would of necessity undermine the educational means through which the natural sense of race was cultivated, and be the cause of a weakening of revulsion respecting this essentially foreign race. "If German youths compete with Jews in a handball game, they will lose all feeling of distance . . ."[22]

3. Many regulations were intended to augment official control over Jewish organisations and movements. Thus, no printed matter was to be distributed or sold through these groups.[23] Jewish youth hostels had to be located so as to be accessible to total supervision by local police authorities.[24] An exact listing was to be maintained of all youth movements as well as their membership and leaders.[25] All youth leaders were to be required to carry a document of

[16]Geheimes Staatspolizeiamt 1937, die jüdischen Organisationen in Deutschland, p. 34, and Geheimes Staatspolizeiamt, II 1B2 – 1371/36 J. Berlin, den 30. Dezember 1936. In an effort to establish some coherence among the prohibitions and regulations in force in various localities, the Prussian Ministry of Education reissued instructions concerning these, and added further prohibitions such as the one against hiking by Jews in groups of over twenty persons. Der Reichs- und Preussische Minister für Wissenschaft, Erziehung und Volksbildung, K II 9520/4. Juni 35; cited in *Gemeinschaftsarbeit der Jüdischen Jugend, op. cit.* In a summary on p. 8 of the different regulations and prohibitions proclaimed at various times and places, we find: "A description of the legal situation of the state of the different spheres of the activities of Jewish youth organisations, as revealed in the official written and oral instructions of the *Reichsjugendführung*."

[17]See Bayerische Politische Polizei, München, den 10. Januar 1936, and Der Reichs- und Preussische Minister für Wissenschaft, Erziehung und Volksbildung, K II 9520/4. Juni 35 – cited in *Gemeinschaftsarbeit der Jüdischen Jugend, op. cit.*, p. 94; and Bayerische Politische Polizei, den 10. Januar 1936.

[18]Geheimes Staatspolizeiamt, II 1B – 1371/36J, Berlin, den 30. Dezember 1936.

[19]Stapo, Lagebericht für den Monat Juni 1935, Aachen, den 5. Juli 1935.

[20]Lagebericht des Geheimen Staatspolizeiamtes für die Zeit vom 1. Oktober 1936 bis 28. Februar 1937.

[21]Geheimes Staatspolizeiamt, 7. Juni 1935, p. 35.

[22]Stapo, Lagebericht, Dortmund, Oktober 1934.

[23]Der Inspektor der Geheimen Staatspolizei an alle Staatspolizeistellen, Berlin, den 2. August 1934, betreffend Jüdische Jugendverbände, unter Bezugnahme auf den Erlass II 1 1642 vom 29. Mai 1934.

[24]See note 17.

[25]See *Gemeinschaftsarbeit der Jüdischen Jugend, op. cit.*, pp. 92–93.

identification as such; all changes of registration were to be submitted quarterly to the *Gestapo*;[26] advance notice was to be submitted in writing of every gathering and the purpose of such meetings.[27] *Hachscharah* groups were required to submit a detailed plan both of their study activities and practical work.[28]

4. This was apparently an idea of Heydrich's which became official policy – namely that of putting obstacles in the way of those youth movements encouraging Jews to remain in Germany, and of favouring movements that were engaged in vocational training for the purpose of leaving Germany and settling elsewhere. Thus in January 1935 Heydrich declared that the activities of Jewish youth organisations involved in vocational training in agriculture for emigration were in keeping with state policy, so that these should not be treated with the same degree of severity as was required in the case of German-Jewish organisations that advocated remaining in Germany.[29] In line with this policy *Brith Haschomrim* and *Herzlia-Betar** were to be permitted to wear uniforms – albeit only in enclosed places – in order to increase the motivation among young Jews to join them.[30] On the other hand, Heydrich forbade gatherings at which Jews were encouraged to remain in Germany.

For this reason official policy was to tolerate *hachscharah* groups until a very late date.[31] The regulations stress repeatedly that this is merely a stratagem for encouraging Jewish emigration from Germany and not an endorsement of Zionism, the attitude of which, as expressed by the World Zionist Organisation, was unequivocally hostile to National Socialism. Zionism, like every Jewish organisation, was in essence and by definition hostile to Germany. A strong Jewish Palestine would most likely become a significant factor in strengthening international Jewry in its struggle against Germany.[32]

[26] *Ibid.*, p. 100.

[27] Concerning the manner in which this supervision was implemented and the means used by Jewish organisations to deceive the authorities, see Stapo, Lagebericht, Berlin, 1935. The author of the report complains that the Jewish organisations were not conforming at all to the subjects which they had submitted, that some of the lecturers were wholly ignorant of which subject they were supposed to be talking about, and that there existed a tacit understanding to change over to the official subject the moment the police appeared.

[28] See Jizchak Schwersenz, *Mahteret halutsim be-Germania ha-natsit* (*The Chaluz Underground in Nazi Germany*), Kibbutz Hameuhad 1969 (in Hebrew).

[29] Preussische Geheime Staatspolizei, Berlin, den 17. Januar 1935, II 1B – 69681/1976, Vertraulich an alle Staatspolizeistellen.

*On the *Betar* see further the essay by Francis R. Nicosia, 'Revisionist Zionism in Germany (II). Georg Kareski and the Staatszionistische Organisation, 1933–1938', pp. 261–267 *passim*, and also the essay by Jehuda Reinharz, already cited, pp. 192–193, in this volume of the Year Book. – (Ed.).

[30] See Staatspolizeistelle 113/35 Hannover, den 6. April 1935; and Bayerische Politische Polizei, München, den 13. April 1935, and Geheimes Staatspolizeiamt, 10. Februar 1935.

[31] Lagebericht, Mai-Juni 1941, Chef der Sicherheitspolizei und Chef des Sicherheitshauptamtes. "We have no objection to this sort of vocational retraining (*Umschulung*), on condition that it is undertaken in closed groups and for the purpose of emigration in the future."

[32] Lagebericht, Berlin, den 20. Oktober 1936 An Stbf. (Stapobefehlsstellen) mit der Bitte um Vorlage bei C Betr.: Leitschrift "Die Zionistische Weltorganisation", p. 2; and 1. Vierteljahreslagebericht 1939 des Sicherheitshauptamtes, Band 3 Bericht. Die Zionistische Weltorganisation, Berlin den 20. Oktober 1936, p. 19.

II. 1936–1938

This was a period marked by increasing severity, with some of the Jewish youth organisations and movements being banned and dissolved by the authorities. The first to be dissolved were organisations encouraging Jews to remain in Germany, such as the *Ring*,[33] which was disbanded on the grounds that its members wore uniforms and participated in military drill. In 1939 the *staatszionistisch* organisations were banned and dissolved: the "Jewish National Youth", *Herzlia-Betar*, and *Brith Haschomrim*.[34] Their members were advised to join *Hechaluz* or other Zionist groups.[35] With the *Anschluss*, Jewish organisations were initially prohibited from operating in Austria, after which permission was renewed only in the case of Zionist organisations.[36]

III. From 10th November 1938 to 1941

The youth movements which until then had been allowed to operate freely, although under *Gestapo* surveillance, were first banned and then allowed to function once more under an altered guise.[37] Their activities were chiefly orientated towards emigration; no permission could be obtained for gatherings of more than fifteen members; youth leaders were arrested and deported to the East; and the ban on indoctrination of any kind made things particularly difficult for youth movements in the cities, although they did manage to continue their activities in semi-clandestine conditions.[38] Only *hachscharah* groups were able to operate with a fair degree of freedom within the framework of either *Hechaluz* or *Bachad*.[39]

At intervals the authorities would impose a ban on meetings and gatherings. Jewish youngsters who had completed elementary school were ordered to leave the cities for the countryside where they would be concentrated for the purpose of working on the land and being trained for emigration to other countries, "so that they should not be the cause of racial defilement in the cities". *Hechaluz* representatives in the *Reichsvertretung* were compelled to leave their posts. And persons of foreign nationality, as well as those having no national status, had to

[33]See Geheime Staatspolizei, Staatspolizeistelle München, 15. Januar 1937, and note 16.

[34]Der Reichsführer SS und Chef der deutschen Polizei im Reichsministerium des Innern, Berlin, den 25. Juli 1935.

[35]Geheime Staatspolizei, Geheimes Staatspolizeiamt, Berlin, den 25. August 1938, 11 112 315 C 422.

[36]Jahreslagebericht 1938 des Sicherheitshauptamtes, Band 1, p. 36.

[37]Jahreslagebericht 1938 des Sicherheitshauptamtes.

[38]See 'Mi-tik mikhtavim' ('From the Letter File'), Session of the German Department at Ein-Harod of 25th April 1936, and report of Shura in the session of the German Department of 18th April 1939.

[39]*Ibid.*, and Schwersenz, *Mahteret halutsim be-Germania ha-natsit, op. cit.*; On the *hachscharah* groups of *Bachad* see, The Hebrew University in Jerusalem, Centre for Contemporary Jewry, Department of Oral Documentation, Testimonies of Joseph Walk, Ezra Bromberger, Rudi Herz, David Beth-Arieh, Eliezer Seligmann; also *Den Netzen entronnen. Die Aufzeichnungen des Joel König*, Göttingen 1967.

quit their positions in the Zionist organisation and the Berlin Jewish community, a circumstance which badly affected both of these bodies since many of their active members were East European Jews. Even so, the lack of consistency that had been characteristic all along of official regulations in regard to Jewish youth movements and organisations was still evident in this period. For example, to the astonishment of the members of the *Hechaluz*, German authorities agreed in June of 1938 to permit an additional five new emissaries from Palestine to enter the country.[40]

IV. From the Beginning of Deportations to 1943

In this period the fate of the Jewish youth movement merged with that of German Jews as a whole,[41] with some pragmatic consideration given to *hachscharah* and the usefulness of Jewish labour in *Arbeitseinsatz* in factories, on roads, and so on.

We shall now consider the attitudes and responses of the Jewish youth movements in this atmosphere of prohibitions and violence. It is not our intention, however, to offer still another account of the experience of the Jews of Germany in these years. Neither shall we tell the story of one or another of these movements or *hachscharah* groups, nor shall we evaluate and judge the actions and failures of either the leadership of these organisations or those into whose hands their fate had been placed.

An account of the features that characterised these youth movements and differentiated them from other social organisations may be found elsewhere. What follows is an attempt to set out the history of the Jewish youth movement in Germany during the Holocaust and its response to that event, a response that was connected in an essential way with the fact of the organisations in question being youth movements. This contrasts with the conception that had then taken root in the *Hechaluz* movement and among some of the settlement movements in Palestine. For them 1933 marks the end of the historical role of romantic youth movements of the classic type, the place of which was taken – in the framework of *Hechaluz* – by youth movements dedicated to the principles of immigration to Palestine, settlement of the land, and the fulfilment of Zionist goals, which alone were regarded as constituting the ultimate purpose that supplanted all goals that had existed earlier.

Elsewhere we have been concerned with the four stages in which this third or fourth generation of German Jews since emancipation (and the attendant efforts to integrate into German society) had made its way to Zionism, Socialism and the ideology of fulfilment through a *chaluz* mode of existence. The youth movement did not look upon these stages as mere historical facts, but as a

[40]See 'Mi-tik mikhtavim' of the State of our Movement in Germany, pp. 18–19 (Hebrew); also the letter of MZ to the Secretariat of Kibbutzim dated 10th February 1939.

[41]See the descriptions and testimonies concerning the period in Anneliese – Ora Borinski, *Erinnerung 1940–1943*, Germany 1970; and Schwersenz, *Mahteret halutzim be-Germania ha-natzit*, *op. cit.*

necessary development which came in response to a spiritual and existential crisis. And in its view, there was no way of emerging from that crisis, nor of acting to achieve some sort of fulfilment, without undertaking to influence mental attitudes. Moreover, the youth movement did not believe in action for its own sake, action which was not derived from mental attitudes. It was for this reason that from 1934 onward the youth movement derived no great satisfaction from the large numbers of new members joining its ranks and those of *Hechaluz* under the compulsion of the times and of political and economic circumstances. Even then, the youth movement saw its chief function as consisting in "spiritual *hachscharah*", which was conceived of as being no less important than "physical *hachscharah*", and indeed the necessary condition of the last.

Nor was it a characteristic of the youth movement to respond directly to the facts of reality, troubling and cruel as these facts were. Rather did the youth movement concern itself with the spiritual and existential implications of that reality, which were the particular objects that it was intent upon addressing in its own fashion.[42] From this point of view, the manner of response of ideologically opposed youth movements was not dissimilar. Indeed, in this regard, movements such as the *Werkleute* and *Makkabi Hazair* were closer to the *Ring* than they were to their ideologically affiliated political camps and parties – as for example the Zionist Organisation of Germany or *Hechaluz* on the one hand, and the C.V. on the other. Thus physical resistance of the kind found among the Baum group* and the Prezlauer Berg group, some of whose members had formerly belonged to the Jewish youth movement, was uncharacteristic of Jewish youth movements as such, and it may well be that these individuals had left for the very reason that they were out of sympathy with the inward-orientated activities of these movements.

In the written sources of all of these youth movements we find repeated references describing the low point reached in 1933 as a deep and nearly total spiritual cæsura – not a physical one – between Jewish young people and their German external environment as a result of its having rejected them.[43] This is what emerges from the testimonies, among them even of seven-year-old children who were rejected by their non-Jewish classmates and friends.[44] Such was the pattern in all the educational and social spheres – at school, in the streets, and in the professions. The situation of young people living in small towns was especially bad in this regard, and we find very urgent requests to get these children away from these areas.[45]

[42]In the words of a member of *Habonim*: "For this revolution among German Jewry is not one of merely an economic nature but, first and foremost, one of a psychological nature." Leo St. 'Vor grossen Aufgaben', in *Haboneh, Älterenblatt der jüdischen Jugendgemeinschaft Habonim Noar Chaluzi*, Juli 1933, p. 2.

*A further contribution on the history of the Baum group is made by Eric Brothers, in his essay 'On the Anti-Fascist Resistance of German Jews', in this section of the current volume of the Year Book – (Ed.).

[43]See Bruno Sommerfeld, 'Die Sondersituation der jüdischen Jugendbewegung', in *Gemeinschaftsarbeit der Jüdischen Jugend, op. cit.*, p. 13.

[44]See 'Vorschläge von Alex Jacobsohn zur Propagandaarbeit', in *Jüdische Jugendgemeinschaft, Habonim Noar Chaluzi, Rundschreiben*, Nr. 5, Berlin, 27. Juni 1933, Anlage, p. 1.

[45]*Habonim, Bundesschreiben*, Nr. 29, Berlin, Januar 1936, p. 30.

The upshot was that the ties of Jewish young people with their peer group were broken, as were their relations with role models and their bonds of identity, all of which play an essential part in the process of socialisation.[46] They also experienced a breakdown in the scale of stable values, which is of especial significance for an adolescent in need of ordering his or her personality.[47] In looking around Jewish youngsters could find no valid and binding values offered by the environment; all that could be seen was a world in which values were being degraded, an *Entwertung aller Werte*. Everything seemed relative, so that they did not even try to discover alternate values in either themselves or their relationship with their environment.[48] In a lecture entitled 'Educational Problems in Our Work', a teacher who was active in *Habonim* reviewed his experience of the change being manifested by Jewish youngsters as a result of the events in those years. He spoke of the threat of psychological crippling, of the prospect of a generation given to superficial actualisation and unable to form personal ties of any lasting value.[49] Others spoke of the possibility of the emergence of feelings of inferiority attended by aggressive and arrogant behaviour that might result from the loss of psychological equilibrium.[50] Still another potential danger was that Jewish youngsters might internalise antisemitic doctrines in the course of adapting themselves to the patterns of Nazi thought and argument, notwithstanding the fact that these were being directed against them.[51]

It would appear, therefore, that the intellectual and psychological support which was the sole means for personality to develop harmoniously – and which Jewish youngsters had been deprived of by the force of circumstance – could only be obtained by young Jews within the milieu of the youth movement. This was virtually the only ambience available at the time to young Jews in which they could live as Jews without risking depression, humiliation, disorientation, or damage to their personalities.[52] A *Habonim* manual compares the benefits of such an ambience with the advantages of a compass on a journey: it gave a fixed point needed for orientation. In contrast to the parental home, where a young person met with reproaches, irritation, and tensions, the youth movement offered security, warmth, courage, the spirit of action, the joy of youth, and existential values.[53] The memoirs of Ora Borinski, Jizchak Schwersenz[54] and

[46]See note 42, *Haboneh, Älterenblatt, op. cit.*, p. 3.

[47]See *Hasolel, Blatt der Mittleren der Jüdischen Jugendgemeinschaft Habonim Noar Chaluzi; Werkleute, Bund deutsch-jüdischer Jugend, Bundesblatt*, Juni 1933, p. 12, 'Neuorientierung von Leni', p. 5.

[48]See note 42, *Haboneh, Älterenblatt, op. cit.*, p. 2 and Günter Friedländer, *Jüdische Jugend zwischen Gestern und Morgen*, Vortrupp/Jüdischer Bücherverlag/Berlin SW 29, 1938, pp. 24–25.

[49]Hans Gärtner (Jochanan Ginat), 'Erziehungsfragen in unserer Arbeit', in *Habonim Noar Chaluzi, Bundesschreiben*, Berlin, Nr. 28, 20. September 1935.

[50]See note 43, p. 14.

[51]See 'Mi-tik mikhtavim', p. 6. Brief des Hechaluz Dänemark an die Maskiruth Hakibuz von Fragen und Aufgaben der Pimpfenerziehung; Ernst, *Werkleute, Bund jüdischer Jugend*, 4. Bundesblatt, Juli 1933.

[52]See note 48, Günter Friedländer; also note 43, Sommerfeld, 'Die Sondersituation der jüdischen Jugendbewegung, *loc. cit.*, p. 14.

[53]Pony, 'Ein offener Brief/Einiges zu unserem jüdischen Problem', in *Hasolel*, p. 6, see note 47.

[54]Schwersenz, *Mahteret halutsim be-Germania ha-natsit, op. cit.*, p. 129.

others repeatedly testify to the conception of a society of young people that took the place of the family in inspiring a feeling of belonging and security in a shattered and ruined world. And as conditions steadily grew worse, and even reached the unmitigated disaster of Auschwitz and Birkenau, the individual's sense of merging totally with the society of his fellows and with the movement would grow to an extent never dreamed of by the youth movement. "Perhaps man really needs something like a barbed-wire fence so that he should always feel conscious of the value of living day to day in the group (*Gemeinschaft*)",[55] "until every person, even if he should remain alone, will feel that he himself is a society in each of his decisions". And in the cruel and hard decision of whether to join one's parents or remain with the group, it is often the group which tips the scale: "If only we could stay together, that is the wish that motivates us most strongly these days."[56] At Auschwitz, one member of the movement gathered together others in order to "try through arguing, talking, parties, and inquiries into the issues that concern us, to take their minds off the terrible ordeal of day-to-day existence".[57] And in the shadow of the crematoria of Auschwitz, a seventeen-year-old girl who was a member of the movement wrote:

> ". . . In my thoughts I am always with you . . . We never despair of the hope of one day seeing you again. Often we sing and talk amongst ourselves. And we still try to study. I have only one request: always take us into your circle at the hour of parting and never forget us . . ."[58]

Ora Borinski and Jizchak Schwersenz tell of nearly identical symbolic rituals that were practised at parting, in which the pieces of a torn flag and broken chain were given for safe keeping to members as a symbol and token of the continuity of the fellowship and its activity.[59]

Deprivation of the elements and components of education to which German Jews had until then been given equal access, and which were now taken away from them, required that the intellectual vacuum should be filled by a greater awareness of the elements and components of Jewish education. This was the task that the Jewish youth movement took upon itself and carried out in its own distinct way. In doing so, it did not so much address itself to the intellect as to palpable collective experience, at a time when young Jews were being forcibly separated from collective experience within their environment. The very same continuous analysis and re-examination of the educational goals of the youth movement focused everyone's attention upon the fundamental questions of Jewish existence in times such as these. This was the third and fourth generation since emancipation, and it was unwilling, indeed unable, to cut itself off from either European or German culture. It therefore did not so much cross the line separating Zionists from non-Zionists as that between Eastern and

[55]See note 41, Anneliese – Ora Borinski, *op. cit.*, p. 34.
[56]*Ibid.*, p. 47.
[57]*Ibid.*, p. 57.
[58]Concerning the episode connected with this letter, which was smuggled out of Auschwitz, see Schwersenz, *Mahteret halutsim be-Germania ha-natsit*, *op. cit.*, p. 29.
[59]*Ibid.*, p. 51; and Anneliese – Ora Borinski, *op. cit.*, p. 27.

Western European Jewry. In this, the *Werkleute*, the *Ring* and, at least to some extent, *Makkabi Hazair* were in the same camp. The principle issue in the intellectual struggle of the Jewish youth movements in Germany consisted now more than ever in a quest for what Hermann Gerson called the "living centre" (*die lebende Mitte*) by which a movement is unified, and from which it receives its meaning and content. And it may well be that it was the Jewish youth movement which succeeded in the meaningful fulfilment of this need, and that it did so by a creation of spiritual bonds.

> "A place where one knew how to look back into Jewish history and to learn from it pride, virtue, and instruction – there one was no longer powerless in the face of this cataclysm; this was already on the way to being overcome through organising the events into highly comprehensive, and even more highly comprehensive frameworks."[60]

This was what the *Ring* called the transition from "existential Judaism" (*Existenzjudentum*) to "historical Judaism" (*Geschichtsjudentum*).[61]

We should recall, too, that this was the period in which most of the youth movements created a new organisational and educational milieu in order to compensate for the loss of regular schooling. This consisted in "intermediate *hachscharah* (*Mittleren Hachscharah*)", which served schoolchildren who had completed their basic education (eight years) and offered both schooling for the higher grades and vocational training, thereby providing a solution to one of the most serious problems of Jewish youngsters in Germany.[62]

The psychological effect of the expulsion of young Jews from their German peer group – into which they had been born, and within whose culture they had grown up and with whose values they had identified – may be described as a sharp cæsura between reality, on the one hand, and the consciousness of Jewish youngsters concerning their environment, themselves, and their scale of values. From 1933 on, this contradiction grew rapidly more acute.

Indeed, the youth movement had always maintained that the decisive thing for man is not reality but consciousness of inner truth and the mental attitudes that derive from it (i.e., *innere Wahrhaftigkeit, Gesinnung*, and *Haltung*); and that it is therefore in accordance with these last that human existence must be shaped. Nor did the movement believe actions to have value – even when these were emigration, settlement in Palestine, and the practical realisation of Zionism in living as a *chaluz* – unless these actions emerged out of a pre-existing attitude of mind. In this regard, as well, a greater similarity may be discerned between youth movements such as the non-Zionist *Ring* and the *Kameraden*, which the events of 1933 had converted to Zionism, than between the latter and *Hechaluz*, which was dedicated to the practical fulfilment of Zionism. "Until now we supported working inside Germany, unequivocally and decisively, and regarded Germany as our homeland . . . Now we have been taught from the outside that we were mistaken" – so wrote Hermann Gerson, the leader of the *Kreis*

[60]Erich Hirschberg, 'Die Kameraden', in *Der Morgen*, IX (1933–34), pp. 339–347.
[61]Kellermann, 'Der "Bund"', *loc. cit.*, p. 31.
[62]See Paul Eppstein, 'Die Bildungsarbeit der Jüdischen Jugendbünde', in *Gemeinschaftsarbeit der Jüdischen Jugend, op. cit.*, pp. 22–27; and Georg Josephthal, 'Die Berufsfrage der Jüdischen Jugend', *ibid.*, pp. 40–48.

within the *Kameraden* who was later involved in the formation of the *Werkleute*. A mental attitude had to be formed before emigrating to Palestine, for without it the act would have no value:

> "Henceforth, as well, our ambition will be that only such persons will prepare themselves for the act of immigration to Palestine who possess an inner connection with it."[63]

> "The emigration towards which we are being impelled must become for us an inner process, as well, bringing us to *aliya* and inspiring us with new hope."[64]

In an article entitled 'New Orientation', one of the leaders of the *Werkleute* at the time writes that not all of the members of this group were able or would want to go to Palestine, and that it should be clearly understood that such persons were not in the least inferior. It is hard to know which is more difficult – to remain behind or to emigrate. Nor is this of any consequence; what is important is that the decision should be the result of a real inner choice, and not a response to ideologies.

> "And Germany, too, as well as its existence, which until now permeated so great a part of us, will continue to have a role. We are not allowed, nor would we any longer wish, to participate in its formation; but nevertheless, even now, we would not wish for the connection of our members with its culture to be dissolved."[65]

> "It is with our understanding of social facts and necessities that our principal responsibility begins, again and again, regarding the life of the private individual. And if we merge with the *Hechaluz* movement, out of the consciousness that productive participation in the life and realm of Germany is not possible, we do so even now from our own point of view. In this, we are the heirs of the old youth movement, and will so remain; it is with the renewal of the whole person that we are concerned."[66]

In the non-Zionist camp we find the same spirit expressed in the account of the leader of the *Ring* concerning the change that the events of the time had brought about in the intellectual principles of the association, so that young Jews rather than being urged to remain in Germany were now being encouraged to leave – though not for Palestine:

> "Changing one's country does not mean a change of *Gesinnung*. We sincerely hope and believe that people in possession of an inner truth will deny it neither to themselves nor to the outside, even in an alien environment, but will cling to the world of their values and ideas, if indeed they ever really acquired them. Thus we regard emigration neither as a change of residence nor as a means of improving one's lot, but as human daring in the face of a test. This test will prove not only whether the basic practical and necessary conditions [here language and vocational training] have been fulfilled, but whether a person has a certain true intellectual outlook and a firm character."[67]

Both groups would have agreed at this time with Buber, when he observed:

> "What matters is not only whether you stay or whether you go, but how you stay and how you go."[68]

[63] *Werkleute, Bund deutsch-jüdischer Jugend*, Berlin, den 21. April 1933, pp. 1–2.
[64] *Werkleute, Bund deutsch-jüdischer Jugend*, *Bundesblatt*, Juni 1933, p. 14.
[65] *Ibid.*, p. 6.
[66] *Ibid.*
[67] *Gemeinschaftsarbeit der Jüdischen Jugend*, *op. cit.*, p. 20.
[68] *Ibid.*

In concentrating on mental attitudes and the shaping of a mode of existence in conformity with them, the Jewish youth movements were able to diminish the role of external reality and, so to speak, dismiss them from consciousness. Even during the time of the Weimar Republic, Jewish youth movements managed to contend successfully in this way with the gap between the effort to integrate into German society and the irresponsiveness of the latter. They believed that the determining factor was not external reality but attitude of mind and individual choice. Now, in response to what was happening in 1933, the youth movements worked towards a complete disassociation between the domain of mental attitudes and that of reality:

> "The Zionist movements directed the whole of their education away from the real world of the young people themselves. Physically they were in Germany, but in their hearts they were in *Eretz-Yisrael.* Certainly it was unavoidable that they should have ties with their physical environment, with their families and culture, with their studies and work; but it would appear that all these, though they may have occupied a significant part of their thoughts and actions, had not permeated to the deepest layers of their souls. That place was filled with the message coming from Palestine, which confronted them with a demand for the whole of their personalities, heart and soul. This profound experience of Zionist youth-movement trainees was to have an especial significance in the period of totalitarian Nazi rule; for it assisted them in finding their way in the new conditions rapidly being established in 1933. Objectively, of course, their sufferings were in no way less acute than those of any other Jew; subjectively however their total devotion and aspirations to Palestine served as a buttress and a screen against the calamities raging outside."[69]

The account of Jizchak Schwersenz and the testimony contained in other sources substantially support the preceding analysis.[70]

While Zionist movements sought to steer the mental attitudes of their membership in a practical and creative direction, non-Zionist youth movements were intent on ignoring a reality that they found unacceptable and beyond bearing. The latter chose to escape, as though to a remote island in a sea of reality, seeking their refuge in a state of intellectual narcosis that could offer no solution or way out – only surrender to despair. And in the tension between the reality of 1933–1934 and their inner "truth", they chose the latter and paid the price of abandoning the domain of reality.[71]

"The things of reality collapse in the end, whereas those of the spirit remain standing forever."[72] This view was first advanced by one of the factions of the *Kameraden* that supported the idea of a pure "domain of youth". This faction had no transformative goal beyond itself and rejected all of the Jewish and Socialist aims and purposes maintained by the *Kreis*, which had been formed around the figure of Hermann Gerson. Initially it had been organised within the

[69]Shaul Esh, 'Introduction' to Schwersenz, *Mahteret halutsim be-Germania ha-natsit, op. cit.*, p. 6.

[70]See for example, the official response of the *Hechaluz* organisation to the Nazi take-over in *Informationsblatt*, hrsg. vom Hechaluz, Deutscher Landesverband, 6, Nr. 15/52 (Januar/Februar 1933).

[71]This mechanism is set out in Kellermann, 'Der "Bund"', *loc. cit.*, p. 34; and we are witness to it as well in *Der Deutsche Vortrupp. Blätter einer Gefolgschaft deutscher Juden*, Heft 6 (Oktober/November 1934), Schriftleiter, Hans Joachim Schoeps, especially the article of Ernst Horwitz, 'Zwischen Wahrheit und Wirklichkeit. Ein Bericht über die Berliner Führertagung am 22. und 23. September', pp. 4–9.

[72]Kellermann, 'Der "Bund"', *loc. cit.*, p. 45.

Kameraden under the name of the *Ring*. Later it was called the *Weisses Fähnlein*, and following that, the *Jungvolk* or *Jungenschaft* when led by Ernst Wolff and Hanne Davidson. Finally, when the *Kameraden* split in 1932, the faction took the name of the *Schwarzes Fähnlein* under the leadership of Günther Ballin, Paul "Yogi" Mayer and Günter Holzmann. In this last guise it opposed the *Kreis* and supposedly sought to revive the *Kameraden*. Since this was one of the most anomalous, extreme and bizarre groups to have emerged in the German-Jewish community in the years 1933–1935, as regards both its ideology and its actions, it would be worthwhile perhaps to trace the history of its birth and development in the period preceding that time in order to gain an insight into its later actions.

The first group of the *Kameraden* movement[73] was founded in Breslau in 1916, and the movement was consolidated organisationally on a country-wide basis in 1919. It included among its ranks a larger proportion of assimilated young Jews from upper middle-class homes than did any other Jewish youth movement in Germany.[74] The *Kameraden* may have represented a spontaneous attempt by young Jews to organise in reaction to the insecurity and despair at the close of the First World War,[75] and in order to demonstrate their feelings of profound sympathy with their German homeland in troubled times.[76] Or it may simply have been founded by the C.V. as an opposition movement to the *Blau-Weiss* to be used in the struggle against the spread of Zionism among young Jews.[77] At all events, it was grounded in the C.V., from which it received both moral and material support.[78]

Originally the *Kameraden* consisted of a confederation of societies (*Vereine*) of sport and hiking groups. But in time it became a youth movement, adopting the characteristic features and mechanisms associated with organisations of this type. It was by means of these mechanisms that many young people experienced the sort of change of consciousness that resulted in their return to Judaism, Jewish nationalism and, ultimately, to practical Zionism. The process of this transformation has been described elsewhere,[79] and we shall confine ourselves here merely to the principal directions that it took.

The identification of consciousness with feeling, and the strivings for an "inner truth" which endowed its possessors with a feeling of superior certitude, would prepare movement members for sensing "the Jew within them" as

[73]Concerning the *Kameraden* movement, see Elijahu Maoz, 'The Werkleute', in *LBI Year Book IV* (1959), p. 165; *idem*, '50 Jahre "Kameraden" Bewegung', in *Wochenzeitung des Irgun Olej Merkaz Europa*, Tel-Aviv, 34, Nr. 21 (27. Mai 1966); Hermann Meier-Cronemeyer, 'Jüdische Jugendbewegung', in *Germania Judaica, VIII*, Nos. 1/2, 3/4 (1969), pp. 51–56, 78–86, 109–110; Schatzker, 'Toldot ha- "Kameraden"', *loc. cit.*, p. 283.

[74]On the beginnings of the *Kameraden*, see *Blau-Weiss-Blätter*, 5, Heft 6 (April 1918), pp. 234–235; *Kameraden, Bundeszeitschrift des Reichsverbandes der "Kameraden" Verband Jüdischer Wanderer-, Sport-und Turnvereine*, Nr. 1–3, (Januar-März 1920), p. 18, and *Kameraden*, Nr. 4 (April 1920), pp. 5–8.

[75]*Kameraden*, 1, Heft 1–3, p. 2.

[76]*Mitteilungen des Verbandes der Jüdischen Jugendvereine Deutschlands*, 10, Heft 3/5, (Juli-September 1919), p. 58.

[77]*Ibid.*, and note 74, *Blau-Weiss-Blätter*.

[78]*Kameraden*, 2, Nr. 4, (April 1920), pp. 8–9.

[79]Schatzker, *Tnuat ha-noar ha-yehudit be-Germania ben ha-shanim 1900–1933*, *op. cit.*

something that transcended all other considerations. This attitude developed under the influence of Martin Buber, whose writings had made an especially deep impression on the *Kameraden*.[80] It was not one's "understanding" and rational analysis of one's Jewishness, but the introspective recognition and sense of oneself as a Jew that furnished the principle of this process – a process in which greater weight and significance were attached to the feelings represented by such expressions as "being swept up emotionally" (*mitschwingen*) than to logical argument. Only a small step separates the inner consciousness of "the Jew within one" from the ideas of Jewish nationalism.

We find innumerable instances of the factor of the *chavrutha* ("community", "fellowship") exerting a major influence on this process of transformation. The question of one's Jewishness or Germanness might be argued over at length, and a great many solutions could be offered that pertain to the sphere of rational thought and voluntary choice. But to the question of one's affiliation with the *chavrutha*, as a fact connected with the domain of feeling and sensibility, there was only one answer. Whoever aspired to *chavrutha*, as embodied in the youth movement, would eventually arrive at a commitment to the very *chavrutha* with which he was affiliated by virtue of his birth and feeling. It was this desire to actualise the *chavrutha* of the youth movement in life that eventually brought the *Kameraden* to Zionism and, under its later guise as the *Werkleute*, to the idea of emigration to Palestine and the choice of a collective mode of life.[81]

Throughout the writings of the youth movement we discern the impress of Buber's ideas concerning the spiritual dualism and division in both the world at large and among Jews in particular, as well as his concept of achieving redemption through a comprehensive and holistic unity. Thus the youth movement regarded itself as an agency through which young Jews, whose inner selves were spiritually divided, could achieve the sought-after goal of total spiritual unity. While Jewish political parties and groupings were concerned with a synthetic merging of the opposing polarities of German-Jewishness and Jewish-humanism, the youth movement sought this integration on the level of the inner spirit so as to arrive at a consciousness that "our deepest humanity and our deepest Jewishness are one", as Martin Buber had taught.

This totality of commitment of the youth movement was responsible for creating a sympathy among its members, when they matured, for *völkisch*-nationalist, Zionist and Socialist movements, which seemed to them, rightly or wrongly, to be committed to the realisation of the integrative wholeness that attained its ideal condition in the life of the collective. By the mid-1920s, two opposing groups had formed within the *Kameraden* that had committed themselves to this gradual and inwardly orientated process of transformation. One of these regarded this process to be too slow and much too remote from real life, which was becoming increasingly difficult under the Weimar Republic. It would therefore be necessary to abandon the line being taken by the youth

[80]On Buber's influence, see Schatzker, 'Martin Buber's Influence on the Jewish Youth Movement in Germany', *loc. cit.*, pp. 151–157.

[81]See Hermann Gerson, *Vom Werden des Kreises*, April 1934, p. 102; and *idem*, 'Warum der Kreis nach *Palästina* geht?', in *Werkleute, Bund deutsch-jüdischer Jugend, Bundesblatt*, Juni 1933, pp. 12–13.

movement, and to turn to political activity instead. This group, which had organised within the *Kameraden* and called itself the *Schwarzer Haufen*, broke with that movement to join the Socialist Party youth movement.

On the other hand, once it became obvious that this process of transformation would lead to a commitment to Judaism and Jewish nationalism, it inevitably aroused the opposition of assimilationists, for whom such a prospect was unacceptable. Already in the early 1920s this had been the cause of the C.V.'s estrangement from the *Kameraden*. And towards the end of the same decade, opposition would gather around the person of Ernst Wolff, who was then the principal figure in the *Jungenschaft*, the group that was organised to oppose the *Kreis*, led by Hermann Gerson. Wolff rejected all of the principles upon which the *Kreis* had been founded, and the debate took place entirely within the milieu of the movement and was conducted in terms that were peculiar to it.

Ernst Wolff first of all rejected the possibility of achieving absolute certainty by pursuing the sense of inner truth through introspection. According to Wolff, this sense of inner truth need not be the same for every member, nor need it consist in "Jewish" certitude. Even the shared feeling of disgust towards "society" does not include in itself any certainty concerning the course to be followed; if anything, it was much more likely to inspire pessimism than hope. Furthermore, Wolff doubted that it was possible actually to realise the *chavrutha*, which, being in want of a supreme and ultimate value, could not and must not attempt to direct young men and women towards a final collective goal. As opposed to these, Wolff set out the case of the private person, the individual who was aware of his inability to attain certitude of a supreme value that would enable him to cope with the "human condition", and who had no illusions concerning his spiritual redemption by means of a central and unifying idea, be it Jewish or Socialist. The individual must arrive at a choice exclusively by way of his own will.

From the point of view of the youth movement, Wolff's position represented a radically individualistic interpretation of the "Meissner formula", which spoke of youth's right "to shape its life through inner truth and on its own responsibility", and it laid that "responsibility" upon every individual separately, while it also rejected the *bündisch* interpretation.[82]

This pessimism and subjectivism, which also contained within it the seeds of anarchism, was not unknown in the world of the German youth movement. Contrary to the impression created by its external features and its symbolic underpinnings of sports and games, these were not at all the mere reflections of youthful innocence, or of the untroubled "domain of youth", or of an exuberant joy of life in nature. Rather they were from the very outset a "profound expression of pessimism about the human condition; and the very fact of it being organised is the fruit of despair and of the daring, almost heroic, idea of the total transformation of man".[83]

[82]Ernst Wolff, 'Aus der Führeraussprache', in *Kameraden*, 9. *Bundesblatt*, Oktober 1929, pp. 15–19.
[83]Schatzker, *Tnuat ha-noar be-Germania . . .*, *op. cit.*, p. 52, see note 6.

Such was the attitude of one of the faction's leaders, Günther Ballin, who denied the significance of life altogether. Accordingly, it made no difference how a person chose to order his existence – or if he decided to end it, for that matter. All of life, all action, and all experience ended in only one conclusion – nothing. And as a consequence of there being no meaning to life, and the impossibility of making an objective choice, there can be no criteria outside the will of the individual. But if "one wants to live", individuals cannot become a law unto themselves so long as they continue to exist within a social framework. Otherwise we would end up with a situation of everyone killing and being killed. Society has therefore established supposedly moral criteria, which are no more than an expression of its fear of the last conclusion. Only under the conditions of a complete psychic and physical break, as is represented by life on a remote island, or by the isolation of God, can the will of the individual become a supreme value.[84] The year 1933, and the ejection of Ballin and his comrades from German society, fulfilled the conditions that called for the sort of response that this logic demanded.

Though this controversy over the meaning of life and consciousness and the "human condition" may seem remote from the issues that concern us, it represented a struggle over the choice by young German Jews between Judaism and Germanism. It had always been characteristic of the youth movement to come to grips with reality by means of a symbolic system consisting in a code that was accessible only to initiates.

However as the "year of decision" neared, and as the forces of reality made themselves increasingly felt, ideas were expressed in a more explicit fashion. Thus, another leader of the *Jungenschaft*, Paul "Yogi" Mayer, proclaimed in an article that he had made a final and decisive choice in favour of Germany. Furthermore, he argued that since Judaism was only a religion, it must remain a matter of personal choice by the individual. But why, then, should the members of the *Jungenschaft*, having committed themselves so unequivocally to a "German" position after having organised themselves within a Jewish movement, now fail to follow the logic of their decision and affiliate themselves organisationally with the entity to which they were attaching their loyalty? Mayer's answer was along the lines of the response of Jewish assimilationists in Germany since the nineteenth century: "Being a Jewish society, the *Jungenschaft* augmented its chances of explaining the German youth movement to young Jews and bringing them closer to it."[85] This concept of a Jewish context in the role of a socialising agency for entry into German society was a sort of "order of the day" that was supposed to remain in force until the German side showed itself fully prepared to accept the Jews. "The *Jungenschaft* is the last stone in the bridge between the Jewish and German youth movement." The fact that these words were being written at a time when the other end of the bridge appeared to be moving ever further away – a circumstance that even Ballin was forced to recognise – did not deter the author in the least:

[84]*Kameraden*, 20. *Bundesblatt*, Dezember 1930, p. 97.
[85]Paul Yogi Mayer, 'Deutschland', *Blatt der Jungenschaft Kameraden*, Runde 4, 1932, pp. 23–24.

> "There is no hope that this dream, to which we all cling, will be fulfilled in the foreseeable future. Until that day, we shall gather young Jews together and prepare them to find their place in Germany and to occupy it in an appropriate manner."[86]

And even in 1935, when it had become altogether clear that the other end of the bridge would be barred to them, they persisted in employing the same metaphor, which had by now assumed a surrealistic character:

> "We have been withdrawn from our nations's revival – but we stand upon the bridge and wait . . ."[87]

The forms of education and system of symbols of this faction had been borrowed from the intellectual world of various German youth movements, especially from that of the *Deutsche Jungenschaft Eins/Elf* (*D.J. 1.11*) and "White Fox" scout movement. Moreover, their retreat into this domain of ideas in the general atmosphere immediately preceding the Nazi rise to power, and in the context of the fierce debate among the *Kameraden* on the Jewish problem, Socialism and politics, had about it something of the perverse and obsessive which derived from the disparity between their desire to merge with the German essence and a reality that was incompatible with it.[88]

> "The symbol of the *Jungenschaft* is the point of a bayonet . . . Thus spake the point of the bayonet: We favour the struggle. To join in the midst of battle – that is the meaning of life. To be a living part of a great struggle – that is our fate. To transform the long chain of Germany's defeats into ultimate victory, that is our mission . . ."

It is unlikely that these slogans could have had any real significance at this time for the members of the *Jungenschaft*, but neither was it intended that they should: "Young men have the right to be what they would like to be in their dreams, without the need of purpose or aim . . ." Elsewhere, in connection with the precious sense of life that was being destroyed by the new Socialist movement, we read:

> "We have the right to this; for every choice on behalf of values is made personally and freely, and has a meaning even when the order in which we live is actually doomed to destruction. To come to its aid, despite everything, is certainly in keeping with the *Haltung* of our movement."[89]

It seemed as though 1933 would be the year in which this same faction, which had been formed under the name of the *Schwarzes Fähnlein*[90] with the dissolution of the *Kameraden* movement in 1932, was to witness the shattering of still another of its greatly cherished life perceptions – namely the feeling of being part of the German nation. The efforts of this group to integrate into the "new order" of the Third *Reich* took the form of a demonstrative break with the association of German-Jewish groups in the *Reichsvertretung der deutschen Juden*, and an affiliation instead with the *Aktions-Ausschuss jüdischer Deutscher*, which they joined in concert

[86]*Ibid.*, p. 26.

[87]Klaus J. Herrmann, *Das Dritte Reich und die deutsch-jüdischen Organisationen 1933–1934*, Köln 1969, p. 44.

[88]See for example, *Blatt der Jungenschaft Kameraden*, Jungenschaft, Runde 4, 1932, pp. 3–16.

[89]Lothar Hecht, 'Wir Bürger', in *Kameraden*, 23. *Bundesblatt*, Mai 1931, pp. 35–36.

[90]Carl J. Rheins, 'The Schwarzes Fähnlein, Jungenschaft 1932–1934', in *LBI Year Book XXIII* (1978), pp. 173–197.

with radical assimilationist German-Jewish organisations. Additionally, they persistently applied to German authorities, and even to Hitler, to be allowed to do "labour service" (*Arbeitseinsatz*), and made other equally grotesque requests in order to demonstrate their loyalty to Germany and its new regime. And when these attempts ended in failure,[91] even the members of the *Schwarzes Fähnlein* had to admit that their hopes of joining the *völkisch* German order in a National Socialist state as a vanguard Jewish youth movement were untenable. For all of that, "to support it despite everything" was in perfect keeping with the movement's *Haltung*, since it was "not external success but a person's inner choice which is decisive".

> "By the readiness to descend into the abyss, I mean the kind of conviction [*Gesinnung*] which remains true to itself to the very end, with no thought for what may happen . . . To stand up for my fate, though it may have been decided against me – that is greatness . . . We are not optimists. We have need of a conviction which, when the occasion demands, will not flinch even at this ultimate choice; of people who will know – at the hour of need – how to plunge audaciously into the abyss, with *Gesinnung, Gesinnung und noch einmal Gesinnung* . . ."[92]

So it was that the youth movement's method of thinking was carried to an extreme conclusion, albeit one that was entirely logical and consistent from its own point of view. The elimination of *Gesinnung* entirely from the domain of real events now took the form of surrender to a despair from which there was no more thought of escape, a despair that was like a "universal seal".[93]

In line with the principle laid down at the time of the *Jungenschaft* that collective choices could not be made where values were concerned, some members of the *Schwarzes Fähnlein* declared in the Breitenhees Proclamation that "a communal [collective] solution to the Jewish problem does not exist". There was only an individual approach, which, in the case of those for whom Germany is the basis of existence, means making a complete break with Judaism in any form. Quite apart from the question of whether this position also entailed conversion from Judaism,[94] such a statement is clearly the product of a conscious and total severance of one's ties with Jewishness. Ballin even went so far as to join Max Naumann's *Verband nationaldeutscher Juden*, whose hymn professed: "We remain unquestioningly German, only our hearts affirm . . ."[95]

An organisation of young German Jews, whose zeal for joining the *völkisch* order of the National Socialist state equalled that of the *Schwarzes Fähnlein*, was known as *Deutscher Vortrupp* and had formed around Hans Joachim Schoeps. This group retained its Jewish base. Nevertheless, although Schoeps was critical of the *Schwarzes Fähnlein* for its break with Judaism and the anarchistic principles in its ideology, he too followed a policy of refusing to work together with Jewish organisations at large, and considered his own movement to be a

[91]For a detailed account, although apologetic in its tendency, see *ibid.*

[92]Günter Holzmann, 'Gesinnung', Schwarzes Fähnlein (Breslau), *Zeitschrift des Verbandes nationaldeutscher Juden*, April 1934, p. 34.

[93]See for example, *Der Vortrupp*, Heft 6 (Oktober/November 1934), pp. 8–9.

[94]On this controversy, see *Der Deutsche Vortrupp, Blätter einer Gefolgschaft deutscher Juden*, Heft 5, August 1934; and Carl J. Rheins, 'The Schwarzes Fähnlein', *loc. cit.*, pp. 193–194.

[95]*Schriften des Verbandes nationaldeutscher Juden*, Berlin, September 1934; Carl J. Rheins, 'The Verband nationaldeutscher Juden 1921–1933', in *LBI Year Book XXV* (1980), pp. 243–267.

Jewish fighting vanguard that was worthy of taking its place in the new order. But when he approached Nazi *Reichsminister* Frick in order to offer the services of his movement to the National Socialist regime, he was turned away.[96] Hence this movement, too, had to come to terms with a reality that they were hard put to accept. Indeed the *Vortrupp* was very much what its leader described it as being: "... a fraternity of misery, consisting of the impoverished and forsaken who had huddled together to await their hour – whether that hour sealed their doom or offered the possibility for a truly new life".[97]

The structural conception maintained by the youth movement described in the preceding pages was primarily concerned with changing the state of consciousness of its own membership. However, only a relatively small number of young German Jews came within the direct scope and influence of the structured framework of the youth movements; the large majority did not, although their need for it was certainly great. A description of the situation of the majority who had not joined the youth movement may be found in such sources as Günter Friedländer's *Jüdische Jugend zwischen Gestern und Morgen*, and in Jizchak Schwersenz's account. Both tell of young men and women who were incapable of commitment, and whose existence centred on the streets and on ice-cream parlours, cinemas and dance-halls; young people who were cynical of values and without the least will to discover a value system for and within themselves. This was a generation caught up in the process of the "devaluation of all values", a generation without a past, without faith, and without a future.[98]

But the significance of the Jewish youth movement in Germany resided in more than the subtle process of inner transformation we have been describing above. A highly significant and even practical contribution to the lives of young German Jews resulted from the manifold undertakings that were organised within the various youth movements themselves, as well as outside them in collaboration with local and central Jewish institutions, with the political parties and, principally, with the *Hechaluz* movement.

The sources of the youth movement as well as the German *Lageberichte*, or "situation reports", reveal that Jewish youth movements in Germany augmented their activities in the years following 1933. These reports contain a minute account of events, at times to the point of describing the content of lectures and cell meetings. Sometimes we find parallel descriptions of a particular activity, lecture or discussion both in *Gestapo* reports and in the records of the youth movements.

The attitude of German authorities to this heightened activity, which seemed to them to resemble those of a "state within a state",[99] varied with the circumstances. So, on the one hand, they tended to welcome those activities that seemed to have the purpose of preparing Jews to emigrate from Germany, or at

[96]See note 93.

[97]*Ibid.*

[98]Günter Friedländer, *Jüdische Jugend zwischen Gestern und Morgen*, p. 193; and Schwersenz, *Mahteret halutsim be-Germania ha-natsit, op. cit.*, pp. 40, 42.

[99]Such is the case, for example, in Stapo, Lagebericht, Halle, am 5. November 1934, p. 17.

the very least to segregate them from the body of the German people. However, if an activity appeared to be a continuation of the traditions of the German youth movement by its connections with German culture and intellectual values, or by its use of German symbols and organisational forms, it was treated with suspicion and regarded as being the work of Jewish impudence and guile, whose purpose was to encourage Jews in general, or the members of the group, to remain in the country.

The great range of the activities of the youth movement fell into two major categories: "internal work", which followed the special pattern that had always been a traditional part of the youth movement; and "external work", which the circumstances of the times called for, and which consisted in work within the community, social work, education, work in behalf of political parties, propaganda, vocational retraining, and involvement in a variety of other activities of a similar type.

There are innumerable sources[100] that describe the *chavrutha* activities of the youth movements. Such group activities included hiking trips, camping, singing, parties, rituals and ceremonies, celebrations of holidays, performances, callisthenics, sports, games, entertainment, local and national councils, Hebrew language studies, lectures on Jewish subjects, seminars, and a variety of similar events. With the increase of regulations designed to keep Jewish youth movements out of the public eye, attention was shifted to study activities, lectures, discussions and conferences. Nevertheless, the youth movements persisted, clandestinely and at great risk, in organising its hikes and marches even during the war, indeed up until the very implementation of the Final Solution.[101] It is only when we keep in mind the youth movement's system of "comprehensive education", designed to act upon the mental attitudes of members by way of symbols and to call forth their most intense emotional responses, that we can understand this stubborn devotion to the forms of youth movement activity and the readiness of the movement's members to put themselves at risk in order to maintain them, at a time when an outsider might have thought that circumstances had made such "games" and childish pre-occupations utterly obsolete.

As troubles mounted in the Jewish communities in Germany, especially in the smaller ones,[102] the Jewish youth movements threw themselves into social work, cultural activities, work in behalf of the Jewish National Fund, Zionist

[100]The German sources consist of the *Lageberichte*, as mentioned above, as well as the various regulations and prohibitions, all of which furnish evidence of the situation upon which they bear. The major Jewish sources are the newspapers of the youth movements, the accounts of *Hechaluz* emissaries to Germany and of its members who worked in Germany, as for example found in the *Tik ha-mikhtavim*, and the published memoirs of individual members such as those of Jizchak Schwersenz and Ora Borinski. A comprehensive and exhaustive survey of the activities of young German Jews is furnished in *Gemeinschaftsarbeit der Jüdischen Jugend*, *op. cit.*

[101]On this subject, see the detailed account by Schwersenz, *Mahteret halutsim be-Germania ha-natsit*, *op. cit.*, pp. 50–60.

[102]We read, for example, about a Hanukkah party organised by *Makkabi Hazair* at the synagogue in Weilburg which was the first Jewish activity there in twenty-five years. See *Jüdischer Pfadfinderbund Makkabi Hazair*, Hanhala Arzith, *Mitteilungsblatt* Nr. 12 (Januar 1937), p. 19.

propaganda, Hebrew studies, exhibitions on the subject of "Jewish labour",[103] and so on. Education continued to be the field to which members of the youth movement were most attracted, and for which they were best qualified. Thus they contributed their efforts to the *Jugendalija* School established by the Jewish community in Berlin, where they taught courses in general education, as well as Hebrew, Jewish History, and Zionism.[104] They also taught at other Jewish schools, particularly in those dedicated to vocational training.[105] At a time when adolescents aged fourteen to eighteen were being treated as adults in the matter of number of hours on the job and work conditions,[106] a variety of labour-service and watchman duties were required, as well, of members of the youth movement.[107]

Unemployment and vocational training were among the most immediately pressing problems facing German Jews.[108] According to Georg Josephthal, there were about 85,000 young Jews between the ages of ten and fourteen living in Germany in 1937. Because Jews had been forced out of the economy and the professions, unemployment had struck about a quarter of the Jewish families in Germany, with persons over the age of 35 being the principal victims.

The problem of vocational training was of special urgency. Firstly, some 5,000–6,000 Jewish young people were leaving school annually, of whom those who would face the greatest difficulties in finding jobs were 3,000 girls, since their employment opportunities were greatly circumscribed and the parents of many of them were unwilling to allow them to leave home for the purpose of vocational training.

There were four major contexts within which vocational training was undertaken, in three of which the youth movements played a significant and possibly even a crucial role:

1. Youth *Alijah*;
2. Intermediate and *Hechaluz hachscharah*;
3. Vocational training for those going to other countries (apart from Palestine);
4. Individual and non-collective vocational training.

But of the widest scope and greatest importance were the activities that the youth movement carried out together with *Hechaluz*. This will be the subject of the second of these two essays.*

[103]See Anneliese – Ora Borinski, *op. cit.*, p. 18.

[104]See Mi-tik ha-mikhtavim, Brief des Palästina-Amts Berlin an die Maskiruth Hakibbuz von 11. Mai 1939; and *Der Makkabi. Jüdische Turn-u. Sportzeitung*, 39, Nr. 4, (24. Mai 1938), 'Die Jugend Alijah des Makkabi Hazair', p. 4.

[105]Concerning this subject, see Schwersenz, *Mahteret halutsit be-Germania ha-natsit*, *op. cit.*, pp. 41–42.

[106]According to the 'Instruction for the Implementation of the Instruction concerning the Employment of Jews', dated 31st October 1941; see Schwersenz, *Mahteret halutsit be-Germania ha-natsit, op. cit.*, note 51 of Introduction, p. 186.

[107]See *ibid.*, pp. 86–87. On the participation of the youth movements in the recruitment for forced labour in *Arbeitseinsatz*, see also Anneliese-Ora Borinski, *op. cit.*

[108]On this subject, see Georg Josephthal, 'Die Berufsfrage der jüdischen Jugend', in *Gemeinschaftsarbeit der Jüdischen Jugend*, *op. cit.*

*'The Jewish Youth Movement in Germany in the Holocaust Period (II). The Relations between the Youth Movement and Hechaluz', in *LBI Year Book XXXIII* (1988) – (Ed.).

Hashomer Hazair in Germany (II) *Under the Shadow of the Swastika, 1933–1938*

BY JEHUDA REINHARZ

German Jewry was well aware of the deep-seated antisemitism within large segments of the population.* If any of them were in doubt as to its potential danger, they were convinced by the spectacular electoral success of the National Socialists in September 1930. Yet, despite Hitler's frank pronouncements concerning his hatred for Jews and other symptoms of violence, German Jewry was unprepared for the shocking measures taken against them during the winter and spring of 1933; it all seemed like a prolonged nightmare: their dismissal from government posts, the wild anti-Jewish agitation in the press, the beating of passers-by and the concerted terrorist activities directed against them after the burning of the *Reichstag* on 27th February and the boycott of 1st April 1933. The world which they had known and loved crumbled before them. Their faith in the bonds tying them to German culture and civilisation was cruelly shaken. Many tried to find solace and help in Zionism, which hitherto had attracted a small percentage of the 500,000 German Jews.

The rise of the National Socialists to power in 1933 and the new political and economic reality created by this situation, had an immediate impact on the Jewish youth movement and *Hechaluz* which were faced with organisational, social and human problems they had not anticipated and for which they were not fully prepared.** Nevertheless, they rose to the new challenges facing them and, on the whole, acquitted themselves well. Perhaps the key to understanding

*In writing this essay on *Hashomer Hazair*, I was fortunate to have the unflinching and cheerful support of Dan Fraenkel and Abraham Schiff of Kibbutz Daliah. This essay has also benefited from comments by Joseph Waschitz, Seew Weiss, Kurt Salinger, Gustav Horn and Zvi Raanan, all of whom played an important role in the movement's history in the 1930s. I also wish to record my thanks to all those who answered the questionnaire concerning various statistical data. The following kibbutzim responded: Daliah, Hazorea, Hamaapil, Gan Shmuel, Hazor, Shoval, Kfar Menahem, Kfar Masaryk, Lahavot Habashan, Mizra, Mishmar Haemek, Evron, Ein Hahoresh, Ein Hashofet, Shaar Haamakim, Tel Amal. The following abbreviations have been designated for the archives used in this article: The Archives of Hakibbutz Haarzi Hashomer Hazair, Merhavyah – H. H. (this archive has now moved to Givat Havivah; Archive of Hakibbutz Hameuhad – Personal Archive of Eliezer Livneh [Liebenstein], Efal – Liebenstein Archive; Archive of Kibbutz Daliah – Daliah Archive; Schocken Archive, Jerusalem – Schocken Archive; Central Zionist Archives, Jerusalem – CZA; Beit Lohamei Hagetaot, Archive of the Pioneer Movement – Archive of Kibbutz Lohamei Hagetaot; Archives of the Jewish Labour Movement, Tel-Aviv – Archives of the Jewish Labour Movement; Archive of Kibbutz Givat Brenner; Archive of Kibbutz Hazorea; Archive of Givat Havivah; Archive of Aliyat Hanoar/The Jewish Agency, Jerusalem); Archive of the Leo Baeck Institute, Jerusalem.

**On the Jewish youth movement in Nazi Germany in general see the preceding essay by Chaim Schatzker, 'The Jewish Youth Movement in Germany in the Holocaust Period (I). Youth in Confrontation with a New Reality', in this volume of the Year Book – (Ed.).

how they coped with new tasks, dangers and opportunities, lies in the fact that the youth movements and *Hechaluz* had crystallised their ideology and organisational make-up prior to 1933. Though geared towards a small membership, they had established educational guidelines, channels of communication within Germany as well as with their respective Palestinian counterparts, set patterns for *hachscharah* and immigration and methods of recruitment. All these educational and institutional tools had been streamlined and refined during the latter years of the Weimar Republic.[1] Zionist youth movements and *Hechaluz* – like other non-Zionist youth movements – were to some extent also protected through their membership in the roof-organisation, *Reichsausschuss der Jüdischen Jugendverbände*, which was re-organised by the Nazi authorities as their sole partner in all matters dealing with Jewish youth movements.[2] Moreover, the policy of the regime until 1938 – and to a lesser extent until 1941 – was to tolerate organisations and movements concerned with emigration out of Germany, thus giving Zionist bodies the opportunity to expand their operations. This did not mean, of course, that Zionist bodies could operate in total freedom. *Hashomer Hazair* for example, often conducted its activities in secret and other meetings were attended by members of the *Gestapo*.[3] Discussions dealing with Socialist themes were often conducted out of doors, in the woods or during hiking trips.

The impact of the disastrous events following January 1933 was perhaps felt most keenly by those amongst German-Jewish youth who themselves had hitherto stayed uncommitted to any political ideology or had come from assimilating families.[4] Their identity as German Jews was now called into serious question. Some of them opted for Socialist or Communist solutions, many found psychological and emotional refuge under the Zionist banner.[5] After the 1st April boycott, hundreds of Jews turned to the *Palästina-Amt* in Berlin. The *Hechaluz*, which up to 1933 had been struggling to keep its members, became a mass movement early in that year.[6] Its membership

[1]Chaim Schatzker, 'Tnuat ha-Noar ha-Yehudit be-Germanyah bitkufat ha-Shoah', in *Prakim be-Toldot ha-Hevrah ha-Yehudit. Mukdashim le-Professor Jacob Katz*, edited by Emanuel Etkes and Yosef Salmon, Jerusalem 1980, pp. 449–450.

[2]Shaul Esh, 'Historische Einführung', in Jizchak Schwersenz and Edith Wolff, 'Jüdische Jugend im Untergrund. Eine zionistische Gruppe in Deutschland während des Zweiten Weltkrieges', in *Bulletin des Leo Baeck Instituts*, 12, Nr. 45 (1969), p. 15. For a more detailed description of the genesis of this organisation and its supervision by Baldur von Schirach, the *Reich* Youth Leader, see the book by Leni Yahil, *The Holocaust. The Fate of European Jewry, 1932–1945*, Tel-Aviv 1987.

[3]In contrast to the period prior to 1933, the archives contain only few personal letters written in Germany. The extant private correspondence was, on the whole, written from Denmark, or other countries outside Germany. Likewise, detailed and real assessments were sent from across the German border, always marked: "highly confidential, not for publication!"

[4]See Chanoch Rinott, 'Major Trends in Jewish Youth Movements in Germany', in *LBI Year Book XIX* (1974), p. 94. See also the perceptive analysis of Ernst Fraenkel, 'Die Aufgaben einer jüdischen Erziehung im Bunde', in *Rundschreiben*, February/March, 1937. Daliah Archive, 901/3, file 6.

[5]An example of such a youth is Reinhard Bendix, now professor of political science at Berkeley. I am grateful to him for sending me in March 1983 a copy of his unpublished memoirs of this period. Since writing this, Bendix has published his memoirs in *Von Berlin nach Berkeley. Deutsch-Jüdische Identitäten*, Frankfurt a Main 1985.

[6]See copy of letter from Fritz Lichtenstein [Perez Leshem], 28th April 1933. Archive of Kibbutz Hazorea.

exploded by the summer of 1934 from 500 to 14,000, the number of local *Hechaluz* branches (*snifim*) which previously could be counted on two hands, increased to 140. The few *hachscharah* groups in existence in 1933 expanded to accommodate 3,500 members by 1934[7] and by 1935 the *hachscharah* centres were training some 5,000 people yearly; by the beginning of 1938 the number of men and women who had undergone this training in Germany and neighbouring countries reached 23,230.[8] The need to create a special institutional setting for younger people (14–18) led in 1935 to the creation of the so-called *Mittleren Hachscharoth*. Immigration to Palestine picked up considerably among the pioneer groups. Thus, 2,200 members of *Hechaluz* immigrated to Palestine between May 1933 and October 1934; of these 60% to kibbutzim.[9] This number surpassed the total German-Jewish immigration to Palestine throughout the Weimar Republic.[10] The *halutzim* were trained in *hachscharah* centres in Germany, Yugoslavia, Czechoslovakia, Lithuania, France, Luxembourg, Latvia, Denmark, Sweden and Holland.[11]

Unlike the *Hechaluz* which had always accepted into its ranks the *stam-halutzim* (those pioneers who joined *Hechaluz* directly, without first "graduating" through the youth movements), the youth movements – due to their particular educational philosophy and methods of training – were not geared towards an absorption of hundreds of new members. This was particularly true of *Hashomer Hazair*, the youngest German youth movement in the Zionist constellation. *Hashomer Hazair* objected on principle to accepting *bogrim* – those who were eighteen years or older – who did not join out of ideological conviction, but rather because of the newly created circumstances. Thus, its membership increased at a much slower rate than that of *Habonim*, whose constituent movements had established many branches throughout Weimar Germany; after 1933 *Habonim* was naturally in a better position to enlist new members. In April 1934 *Hashomer Hazair* encompassed 530 members: 330 in Berlin, 90 in Köln, 60 in Mannheim and 50 in Hamburg.[12]

[7]Der deutsche Hechaluz. Eine Darstellung 1 1/2 jähriger Arbeit in Zahlen', in *Werk und Werden. Eine chaluzische Sammelschrift*, Berlin 1934, pp. 29–30. Clearly not all figures given in official publications are absolutely reliable. For obvious propaganda purposes, it is quite possible that some of the figures given – by any of the youth movements or *Hechaluz* – may have been exaggerated.

[8]Abraham Margaliot, 'Megamot u-Drakhim be-Maavakah ha-Kalkali shel Yahadut Germanyah bitkufat ha-Redifot ha-Giziyot', in *Umah ve-Toldoteha*, edited by Shmuel Ettinger, Jerusalem 1984, p. 344.

[9]*Ibid.*, p. 32.

[10]See Jehuda Reinharz, 'Zur Einführung', in *idem* (Hrsg.), *Dokumente zur Geschichte des deutschen Zionismus 1882–1933*, Tübingen 1981 (Schriftenreihe wissenschaftlicher Abhandlungen des Leo Baeck Instituts 37), p. XLI. Between January and April 1933, 4,000 Jews applied for immigration through the *Palästina-Amt* in Berlin. See letter from Eliezer Liebenstein to [Ein Harod?], 28th April 1933. Archive of Kibbutz Hazorea. See also Michael Traub, *Die jüdische Auswanderung aus Deutschland*, Berlin 1936.

[11]'Der deutsche Hechaluz', p. 31. Between 1934 and 1938 *Hechaluz* invested out of public Jewish funds some four million *Reichsmark* in *hachscharah* centres. Hermann Meier-Cronemeyer, 'Jüdische Jugendbewegung', Zweiter Teil, *Germania Judaica*, Neue Folge 29/30. VIII. Jg., Heft 3/4 (1969), p. 107. These sums contrast sharply with rejection in April 1932 by the *Preussischer Landesverband jüdischer Gemeinden* of a 2000 RM subvention for *Hechaluz* activities. See Joseph Walk, *Hinukho shel ha-Yeled ha-Yehudi be-Germanyah ha-Nazit*, Jerusalem 1975, pp. 15–16.

[12]Schreiben des Geheimen Staatspolizeiamts an das Bezirksamt Bretten vom 17. April 1934. Generallandesarchiv Karlsruhe: 343, Zugang 1956, No. 30/516.

Ironically, while Communism and left-wing parties were outlawed in Germany after 1933, *Hashomer Hazair* was the only group with leftist leanings allowed to exist,[13] despite the fact that the police were well aware of its ideological orientation. For its part, *Hashomer Hazair* was careful – as in the period prior to 1933 – not to engage in German politics. Members who did not observe this rule were removed from its ranks.[14]

Many young people preferred *Hashomer Hazair* over other youth movements because of its small and homogeneous composition, which afforded the opportunity to people with a shared ideology to engage in intensive discussions within the framework of small groups. Others, who left the ranks of the Communists or Socialists after 1933, were attracted by *Hashomer Hazair*'s stance towards the Arab Question, class struggle and the movement's sympathetic view of the Soviet Union. No less important was the high intellectual level of many of the members. In his memoirs Reinhard Bendix, whose family had been highly assimilated, explains his motivations for joining *Hashomer Hazair* in 1935 when he was nineteen years old.

> ". . . In the world of my father and hence my own, Judaism as religion or as a way of life hardly existed. Culturally my father was steeped in the German classics. I grew up hearing quotations from Goethe, Schiller and Heine . . . rather than quotations from the Bible or the Talmud. . . .
>
> Pretty soon after joining the Hashomer I found myself a group-leader, largely I suspect because I was slightly older. I had no Jewish background, knew none of the songs the group sang, knew no Hebrew or Yiddish and was not committed to emigration to Israel. My only reason for joining was a genuine interest in finding out about Zionism (about which I knew nothing at the time), a quite urgent need to be in contact with some kindred souls, and probably my inclination to favor a left-wing group with an interest in Marxism. I remember we read [Ber] Borochov at the time and I was attracted by the idea of downplaying the nationalist appeal of Zionism in favor of some, vaguely-conceived solidarity with Arab residents of 'similar' class background. I was most impressed by those Chawerim who were studying Arabic in addition to their work on Hebrew and their apprenticeship in some trade or craft. Still, my first impressions were hardly theoretical. I was just happy to meet a group of boys and girls who believed in what they were doing and were eager to learn about everything there was to know.
>
> That pleasure had two aspects. One was frankly the gratitude of an assimilated German Jew at being received with such warmth in a community of young Zionists. No doubt, the solidarity of Jews at a time of great danger helped to overcome our differences in background. The good sense of personal relations in a youth movement played its part as well. And then there was an intellectual component. The Chawerim seemed eager to discuss anything of interest . . . My own memory is of discussing works of literature in the spirit of Georg Lukács's *Theorie des Romans*. I also seem to recall that we explored psychological problems like relations with parents and the meaning of work and that we read an essay by Max Weber on the causes of the decline of the Roman Empire. I imagine we also read some of Marx's writings."[15]

A member of Reinhard Bendix's group in Berlin, Israel Getzler, also recalled later in life the rich intellectual content of the group. Depending on the presence of the *Gestapo* there were always two themes for each session – a Socialist and a

[13]According to the testimony of Seew Weiss, there were a number of *Habonim* groups who after 1933 had strong leftist leanings. See letter of Zvi Raanan to the author [June 1986].

[14]One example of such a member is Helmut Eschwege who was expelled from the *Hashomer Hazair hachscharah* kibbutz in Faske, Denmark, as well as from other kibbutzim. Letter from Helmut Eschwege to Abraham Schiff, 28th March 1978. Private collection of Abraham Schiff of Kibbutz Daliah.

[15]Memoirs of Reinhard Bendix.

Zionist. On the whole the group was pro-Soviet and had its own clandestine library. Its members read the works of Karl Radek, Nikolai Bukharin and Leon Trotsky. Moreover they spent much time reading Joseph Conrad – for whom Bendix had a particular fondness – as well as Jakob Wassermann.[16] Much time was spent in analysing novels along the analytic framework set by Georg Lukács.[17] In fact, there was probably a good deal of intellectual snobbery among the members of *Hashomer Hazair* (as well as among other youth movements, especially the *Werkleute*). As the case of Reinhard Bendix shows, a man was judged by his education and knowledge of, among other fields, music, literature, psychology and philosophy. Bendix was accepted because of his intellectual prowess, not for his knowledge of Judaism or the theories of Socialist Zionists. It seems that the increasing proletarisation of *Hashomer Hazair* did not necessarily detract from the high level of discussion within its ranks.[18]

Clearly, these weekly or bi-weekly discussions left their imprint on many of the participants for decades to come. At the time they took place, within the context of an increasingly hostile and anti-intellectual world, they had a powerful and immediate impact. The opportunity to teach and be taught on a voluntary basis, outside the formal confines of a school, the immediacy of response and the warm relations with one's peers were all very significant for the young men and women for whom the small *Hashomer Hazair* group, indeed, the movement as a whole, became a second home. Within it they could express themselves freely on personal and intellectual problems, a luxury that became a scarce commodity within the Third *Reich*.

Yet *Hashomer Hazair* was not only a debating club, not simply a movement with stern ideological demands on its disciples. Many of its members recall the sheer fun of young people who were constantly on the move. The various groups had very active social programmes. They went on weekend walks as well as long hikes, camping and biking trips. They organised communal singing in the woods and played games, and on occasion they also celebrated Jewish holidays together. All in all, *Hashomer Hazair*, like other youth movements, generated many activities which demanded a great investment of time and energy by the *shlihim* and movement's leadership as well as from the rank and file.[19]

By 1932–1933 the German *Hashomer Hazair* had crystallised its educational approach – organisationally and pedagogically – to follow more closely the guidelines of the World Movement.[20] In conformity with these guidelines, for educational purposes, it divided its membership into age groups (*shichvot*) as follows: *Bnei Midbar* who were nine to twelve years old; *Zofim*, who were sub-

[16]Interview of Israel Getzler by Abraham Schiff (Bedolf), n.d.

[17]*Ibid.* and Bendix memoirs.

[18]See first part of my essay in *LBI Year Book XXXI* (1986), pp. 173–208. The status of Bendix in the movement was debated at the time, because as a *boger* he had not made a commitment to personal fulfilment (*aliyah* and kibbutz). Letter from Zvi Raanan [June 1986]. Nevertheless, he clearly played a role during his brief affiliation with the movement, as the testimony of those in his group demonstrates.

[19]Taped conversations during an all-day reunion of *Hashomer Hazair* activists from Germany in Kibbutz Maabarot, 8th December 1979.

[20]See Hahanhagah Harashit, Choser No. 5, 12th December 1933. Daliah Archive, 901/3.

divided into *Zofim Zeirim* (12–13) and *Zofim* (14–15) and *Bogrim* who were also sub-divided into *Zofim Bogrim* (16–17) and *Bogrim* who were eighteen years and older. The sub-division of the *Zofim* and *Bogrim* developed in 1933–1934 in order to suit educational programmes better to the needs of the various age groups. The various educational units among the *Zofim* – unlike the practice in other youth movements in Germany at the time – were not co-educational. Nevertheless, boys and girls did participate from time to time in common projects or activities. In fact, a number of groups of boys and girls together composed a larger unit referred to as the *Gdud*. The summer camps were open to all age groups and combined scouting, singing and dancing with more formal instruction: classes in Hebrew, Jewish history, ideology, geography of Palestine, fauna and flora, etc.[21]

A member of the *Hashomer Hazair* leadership (*Hahanhagah Harashit*) developed for each of the age groups educational programmes and a newsletter, and sent out memoranda as needed. A special circular (*hozer*) for the *Bogrim* was sent out once a month. The leaders (*madrichim*) of *Bnei Midbar* and the *Zofim* met often and on a regular basis to discuss common problems and new educational approaches. In order to keep track of the educational progress of their charges, they often kept group diaries. In addition, there were various intensive seminars for all the *madrichim* of all age groups which were also open to the *Bogrim*.

All meetings of the *Hashomer Hazair* leadership were conducted in Hebrew. The acquisition of Hebrew received high priority after 1933 and a number of the *Bogrim* were able to read the Hebrew newspaper *Davar* as well as other publications of *Hakibbutz Haarzi* and the World Leadership of the movement (*Hahanhagah Haelyonah*). The life of the movement was permeated by Hebrew songs intermingled with German songs.

The activities of every small unit within the movement – the *kvutzah* – included a discussion (*sihat hakvutzah*) once a week as well as a sports activity. On Friday night each age group (*shichvah*) met for an *Oneg Shabbat* in its own quarters. In smaller cities all members of *Hashomer Hazair* (the *ken*) met together for that occasion. *Hashomer Hazair* adopted the custom of the German *Wandervogel* of going on hiking trips every Sunday, sometimes leaving Saturday evenings at the end of the Sabbath, which included an activity (*peulah*) around the camp fire and sleeping in tents. *Hashomer Hazair* also continued the practice of long – and often arduous – hikes during the long school vacations, but the summer and winter camps soon became more popular and more educationally rewarding.

Beginning in 1937 – after prolonged reflection and discussion – *Hashomer Hazair* adopted co-education for all age groups. At the same time, due to the changing political climate and the increasing harassment of the youth movements, *Hashomer Hazair* began to accept into its ranks children aged seven to nine for whom special games and sports activities were devised. These new young units were referred to as *mahanot*.

In general, one can state that the educational policy for the *Bnei Midbar* revolved around an emotional approach: customs, symbols and various

[21]See e.g. Misrad le-shichvah Alef, "Naturkunde für Jüngere". Daliah Archive, 901/3.

"commandments" of the movement.[22] The educational emphasis for the *Zofim* was on character-formation and providing the basis for a Zionist-Marxist *Weltanschauung* and political education.[23] Among the *Bogrim* the emphasis was on a deepening of the ideological and political foundations of *Hashomer Hazair* in light of the political situation in the world and, in particular, in Palestine.[24] These educational activities continued unabated – and with increasing risk – under the Nazi regime.[25] The foundations of this educational approach were pioneer Zionism, Socialist Marxism and Jewish culture. Some of the basic texts read by the *Zofim* groups included the Communist Manifesto, Kropotkin, Gustav Landauer and others. The *Bogrim* read the works of Marx, Lenin, Plekhanov, Victor Adler, Bauer and Weber and, in the area of psychology: Alfred Adler, Freud, Sperber, Bernfeld and Reich. Moreover, they also attended lectures by Martin Buber, Ernst Simon and other spiritual and political representatives of German Jewry. In sum, the German *Hashomer Hazair* provided its members with a very full educational programme combining physical activity with ideological indoctrination and more formal instruction. Each one of those activities was geared, as much as possible, to the small groups within the larger movement.

The insistence of *Hashomer Hazair* on the small homogeneous nature of its groups did not mean that it had given up recruitment of new members. On the contrary, the immediate aftermath of the Nazis' rise to power was seen as a new opportunity for the expansion of the membership of *Hashomer Hazair*. Following his tour of major German cities in January 1933, Arthur Israelowitz wrote a report which brimmed with confidence. It was his assessment that *Hashomer Hazair* could make inroads in many cities and gain new members. He did add one *caveat*: success or failure in the period ahead depended first and foremost on *Hashomer Hazair* leadership. Without the proper number of qualified *shlihim* in the various locales, it was unlikely that much ground would be gained.[26]

Israelowitz's assessment concerning opportunities for *Hashomer Hazair* was confirmed by an unfriendly source. In a letter to the leadership of *Hakibbutz Hameuhad*, written the same day that Israelowitz had filed his report, Fritz Lichtenstein wrote:

> ". . . *Hashomer Hazair*, which for over a year has been at a standstill, has now intensified its work among its members with great skill. It has not captured the masses, but it has good control over its own membership and has established contacts, particularly among the West-European circles and groups, which, given their particular social class, would incline towards a homogeneous social setting. [*Hashomer Hazair*] has proceeded skilfully and has worked only among a few, but influential people, whom, on the whole, it has managed to attract . . . It is easy for these ideologues to propagandise with their socialist, radical theories

[22]Führerschriften No. 1. Bnei Midbar, 'Zur Theorie und Praxis der Erziehung in der ersten Schichwah', 1934. Daliah Archive, Library No. 6989.

[23]See e.g. Hahanhagah Harashit: "An alle Teilnehmer der Lernwoche!", 7th January 1935. See also *Hamenahel*, February/March 1937. Daliah Archive, 901/3.

[24]See Haschomer Hazair – Der Bundesrat. *Choser. Bundestag Budau*. August 1932. Daliah Archive, 9013/5.

[25]See e.g. Hahanhagah Harashit, Choser No. 8. 10th April 1934; *Hamenahel*, February/March 1937; *Igeret IV* – "Bishvil Menahalei-Hazeirim", January 1937. All in Daliah Archive, 901/3.

[26]Arthur Israelowitz to Hahanhagah Haelyonah, 30th January 1933. H.H. 2.12(1).

> and in addition to tell the Western European youth of the more extensive cultural work and higher social level within *Hakibbutz Haarzi*. We must honestly admit that this situation has created difficulties within our own ranks. . . .
>
> The demands of *Hashomer Hazair* for autonomy in education and within the *hachscharah*, have won for it a number of people from other movements . . ."[27]

Lichtenstein appealed to his colleagues for propaganda material and *shlihim* who could stem the dangerous influence of *Hashomer Hazair*.[28] A few months later Lichtenstein also warned that unless steps were taken immediately, the *Werkleute* would be drawn irreversibly into the orbit of *Hakibbutz Haarzi*.[29] His fear was echoed by other leaders of *Hakibbutz Hameuhad*.[30]

The subject of the *Werkleute* – originally a non-Zionist group – and their ultimate affiliation also preoccupied the leaders of *Hashomer Hazair*,[31] especially after the *Werkleute* had decided in April 1933 to establish their own kibbutz.[32] Though comparatively small in numbers, the members of the *Werkleute* were generally regarded with esteem and even a measure of awe for their intellectual prowess. Both *Habonim* and *Hashomer Hazair* made valiant efforts to draw them to their respective ideological camp. The former had the advantage of controlling the organisational structure and resources of *Hechaluz* and could thus more easily influence the *Werkleute*. On the other hand, some members of *Hashomer Hazair*, especially Mordechai Schenhabi, Milek Goldschein and Arthur Israelowitz, had established excellent personal contacts with the leadership of the *Werkleute*.[33]

According to a member of the *Bundesleitung* of the *Werkleute* at that time, the influence of Schenhabi and Goldschein expressed itself more in the area of psychoanalysis than in a Zionist-Marxist *Weltanschauung*. At that time the *Werkleute* opposed doctrinaire Marxist analysis and fought Communism as such, as the split in the *Kameraden* and the founding of the *Werkleute* shows. The discussions around the issue of Zionism were carried by the *Werkleute* mostly with those movements that eventually founded *Habonim* in 1933. In fact, during the winter of 1932–1933 there were discussions about a merger with the *Kadimah*, which did not materialise, probably because of the connection of the *Kadimah* with the ideology of *Hakibbutz Hameuhad*. *The Werkleute* believed deeply

[27]Fritz Lichtenstein to executive of the Histadrut, Lishkat Hakesher shel Brith Haolim and to Chawerim in Naane (Naan), and Raananah, 30th January 1933. Archive of Hakibbutz Hameuhad, container No. VI.

[28]*Ibid.*

[29]Copy of a letter from Fritz Lichtenstein, 28th April 1933. Archive of Kibbutz Hazorea.

[30]See letter from Eliezer Liebenstein, 28th April [1933]. Archive of Kibbutz Hazorea. Also Enzo Sereni to Mazkirut Hakibbutz Hameuhad, 11th August 1934. Archive of Hakibbutz Hameuhad, container No. 6.

[31]See e.g. Arthur Israelowitz to Moazah Harashit, 6th April 1933, H.H. 2.3(1); Ernst Fraenkel and Adolf Schiff to Hahanhagah Haelyonah, 28th April 1933, H.H. 2.12; Adolf Schiff to Hahanhagah Haelyonah, 17th June 1933, H.H. 2.3(1). The first "official" meeting between the *Werkleute* and *Hashomer Hazair* took place at the home of Ludwig Tietz soon after the Nazis assumed power. The *Werkleute* were represented at that meeting by Gustav Horn, Ernst Stillmann and Friedrich Altmann. *Hashomer Hazair* was represented by Arthur Israelowitz, Ernst Fraenkel and Adolf Schiff. See observations made by Schiff, November 1985.

[32]See Mordechai Orenstein to Vaad Hapoel des Kibbutz Arzi, 30th May, 1934. H.H. 3.8(1a).

[33]See Ernst Fraenkel to Hahanhagah Haelyonah, 23rd September, 1933. H.H. 2.12(1).

in the concepts of the close-knit society. This was an ideological and experimental touchstone of the movement which predated any connection with *Hashomer Hazair*. What is clear though, is that this *Weltanschauung* stemmed from the same sociological, cultural, emotional and intellectual sources that motivated those belonging to *Hashomer Hazair*. It is for these reasons, that the *Werkleute* demanded homogeneity and their own kibbutz and these factors brought them closer to *Hakibbutz Haarzi*. It is precisely for these motivating forces within the *Werkleute* that *Hakibbutz Hameuhad* lost interest in the *Werkleute* soon after they arrived in Palestine.[34]

The *Werkleute* had not decided in Germany which movement they would join. In fact, their alliance with *Habonim* in Germany was much stronger than their relations with *Hashomer Hazair*; a fact that was demonstrated by the election of Gustav Horn of the *Werkleute* as secretary of the *Hechaluz*. Clearly the influence of Sereni and Liebenstein on the *Werkleute* was very strong. The decision of the *Werkleute* to turn to Zionism and to move to Palestine as soon as possible was taken in a meeting of the *Bundesleitung* which took place after the elections of March 1933. The members of the *Bundesleitung* were Hermann (Menahem) Gerson, Rudi Baer, Friedrich Altmann (Yosef Amir), Gustav Horn and Leni Westphal (Yahil). Thus, the initial decision of the *Werkleute* to turn to Zionism was not influenced by the ideology of *Hashomer Hazair*. Once the decision had been taken,[35] the issue arose among the *Werkleute* as to which Zionist orientation they would adopt.

Given their thoughtful and methodical approach, the *Werkleute* solved the issue in their own unique manner. During the early summer of 1933 large numbers of the *Werkleute* went on *hachscharah* and that same autumn the first members were sent to Palestine. Since they had not yet decided which movement to join, they divided themselves among a kibbutz of *Hakibbutz Hameuhad* (Givat Haim) and one of *Hakibbutz Haarzi* (Mishmar Haemek).[36] By April 1934, the 40 members from both kibbutzim founded near Hadera the core group (*plugah*) that was to become Kibbutz Hazorea. In December 1936 this kibbutz settled in the Jezreel Valley and in 1938 affiliated with *Hakibbutz Haarzi*. Within a brief period most of the *Werkleute* left Germany and joined the new kibbutz.[37] There is little doubt that the decision of the *Werkleute* to join *Hakibbutz Haarzi* was an important moment in the history of *Hashomer Hazair* during the

[34]Letter from Leni Yahil to the author on 14th November 1985.

[35]There is a difference of opinion as to the nature of the discussion at the *Bundesleitung* which led to the decision to turn to Zionism. See letters to the author, by Leni Yahil, 14th November 1985 and 19th April 1986. Also the comment by Gustav Horn in *Bashaar*, 14th March 1986, pp. 10–11, and letter from Gustav Horn to the author, 22nd May 1986. The fact of the matter is that following this decision, it was agreed to send Baer to Palestine as a representative of the *Werkleute*, while Horn, Eliezer Beeri and Yosef Shatil were to serve the movement in Germany for a few more years.

[36]See letter from Rudi Baer to Mazkirut Hakibbutz Hameuhad, 26th December 1933. Archive of Kibbutz Hazorea.

[37]Eliyahu Maoz, 'The Werkleute', in *LBI Year Book IV* (1959), p. 178. On the history of the *Werkleute* and Kibbutz Hazorea see also Jacob Michaeli, *Kibbutz Hazorea. Zur Geschichte einer von Juden aus Deutschland gegründeten Gemeinschaftssiedlung*. Unpublished typed manuscript. I am grateful to Mr. Michaeli of Kibbutz Hazorea for sending me his ms. See also Menahem Gerson, 'Darkah shel "Werkleute" la-Kibbutz Haarzi', in *Sefer Hashomer Hazair*, (Tel-Aviv 1956), pp. 417–425.

Third *Reich*, not least for its psychological boost to morale. Yet throughout 1933–1938 there were sharp ideological disputes between older groups (*Bogrim*) of both movements concerning questions of Marxism and religious versus secular *Weltanschauung*. Only in 1938–1939 did the organisational ties between these two movements crystallise in the face of common dangers and the pressing need to save lives.

Indeed, already during the final few months of 1933 there were grounds for optimism. The early decision of *Hashomer Hazair* in Germany not to be tied to political parties, now served the movement well. Nevertheless, it became clear from the outset that the movement would have to establish *hachscharah* centres outside Germany – since 1932 it had had such a centre in Erfurt – and that with time, all training of *halutzim* must be moved to friendlier shores, primarily Denmark.[38] By mid-May 1933 Arthur Israelowitz reported to the movement's leadership in Warsaw that after a sojourn of a few weeks in Denmark, he was able to secure training sites on farms for some forty individuals as well as establish a *Beth-Halutz* in Copenhagen which would accommodate another twenty members. Though he had travelled as a representative of *Hechaluz*, Israelowitz saw to it that the initial group of fifteen *Hashomer Hazair* pioneers would be concentrated within a radius of 15–20 kilometers so as to enable them to have weekly meetings.[39] After 1933, the German *Hashomer Hazair* had *hachscharah* centres in Denmark (Lilderød), Yugoslavia (Gollenice), and Vilkaviskis in Lithuania. As the political situation worsened, *Hashomer Hazair* sent the fourteen to eighteen-year-old members to *Mittleren Hachscharah* to Silingtal (Silesia) in 1937–1938, and in 1938–1939 to Salman Schocken's Gut Winkel and Schniebinchen. *Hashomer Hazair* also established twice *Batei-Halutz* in Berlin – during 1933–1935 on Rankestrasse and during 1937–1938 on Essenerstrasse.[40]

The first few months of 1933 were marked by feverish activity and tense foreboding which began to relax somewhat by the end of April, after the first spate of anti-Jewish decrees had been issued and absorbed by the Jewish community. Ironically, it was at that very moment that *Hashomer Hazair* was struck a violent blow, not by the Nazi authorities, but by a German-Jewish youth movement, the Revisionist *Brith Trumpeldor*.[41] Both the *Brith Trumpeldor* and *Hashomer Hazair* occupied rooms in a building in Central Berlin[42] which had been made available, free of charge, by Margot Klausner, daughter of the owner of the Leiser chain of shoe shops and herself close to *Hashomer Hazair* activities.[43] Due to the location of the building, it was deemed best not to use the

[38]Arthur Israelowitz to Moazah Harashit, 6th April 1933. H.H. 2.3(1).

[39]Arthur Israelowitz to Hahanhagah Haelyonah (Warsaw), 12 May 1933. H.H. 3.5(1a). The most detailed description of *hachscharah* centres in Denmark is to be found in Jørgen Haestrup, *Passage to Palestine. Young Jews in Denmark 1932–1945*, Odense 1983.

[40]Letter from Dan Fraenkel to author, 31st May 1985. See also Kibuz Hachscharah Jugoslawien [1935]. Daliah Archive, 901/3, file 6.

[41]On the ideology and activities of *Brith Trumpeldor* in Germany, see Reinharz, *Dokumente zur Geschichte des deutschen Zionismus, 1882–1933*, *op. cit.*, pp. 439–441.

[42]Brunnenstr. 101. See Adolf Schiff to Hahanhagah Haelyonah, 3rd June 1933. H.H. 2.3(1).

[43]On Margot Klausner see Naomi Shepherd, *A Refuge from Darkness. Wilfrid Israel and the Rescue of the Jews*, New York 1984, pp. 62–63.

rooms of *Hashomer Hazair* during the uncertain turmoil of January to April 1933. When the members of *Hashomer Hazair* returned to the building on 19th April they discovered that during the preceding Easter holiday their *ken* had been totally demolished. The suspicion fell on their neighbour, the *Brith Trumpeldor*, whose leaders freely admitted their deed. Clearly, the Revisionists were confident that under the prevailing political circumstances, *Hashomer Hazair* – a left-wing group – would not dare file a complaint with the authorities.[44] The calculations of *Brith Trumpeldor* were indeed astute. *Hashomer Hazair* did not complain to the police and Arthur Israelowitz had to express his anger and disgust in a memorandum written to his colleagues from Copenhagen.[45]

The relations of *Hashomer Hazair* with *Brith Trumpeldor* remained tense throughout the 1930s,* but the movement's quarters in Berlin were soon restored[46] and there are no similar violent incidents recorded.[47] The most pressing issue now was the continuity of work, the adjustment to new conditions and the maintenance of the high level of experienced leadership. This last goal seemed in jeopardy since Arthur Israelowitz – the last *shaliah* of the original Palestinian group of *shlihim* which founded the movement in Germany – was about to return to Palestine in mid-May 1933.[48] The question as to who would replace Israelowitz came up in almost every letter written by German *Hashomer Hazair* members to the leadership of the movement in Palestine and Warsaw[49] and was a topic of frequent internal discussions. But it took almost a year – until March 1934 – before Mordechai Orenstein (Oren) arrived in Germany as the replacement for Israelowitz. This prolonged and much bemoaned delay, stood in stark contrast to the initiative of *Hakibbutz Hameuhad*, which in April 1933 sent some of its most forceful and talented emissaries to Germany – Eliezer Liebenstein and Enzo Sereni.[50] Other important Palestinian emissaries of *Hakibbutz Hameuhad* followed throughout the 1930s.

In the face of so formidable a delegation, *Hashomer Hazair* seemed bereft of experienced leadership, especially after the departure of Arthur Israelowitz. Moreover, those in the German *Hashomer Hazair* movement who qualified to take over key positions also tended to be among the first to go to *hachscharah*

[44]Arthur Israelowitz, 'Eine Tat des Brith Trumpeldor', 25th April 1933. H.H. 2.3(1).
[45]*Ibid.*
*Further, on the *Betar* in Germany see also the contribution of Chaim Schatzker, already referred to, pp. 164–165, and the following essay by Francis R. Nicosia, 'Revisionist Zionism in Germany (II). Georg Kareski and the Staatszionistische Organisation, 1933–1938', pp. 261–267 *passim*. – (Ed.).
[46]Adolf Schiff to Hahanhagah Haelyonah, 3rd June 1933. H.H. 2.3(1).
[47]Milek Goldschein, Mordechai Schenhabi and Arthur Israelowitz; see the first part of my history of *Hashomer Hazair* in Germany, in *LBI Year Book XXXI* (1986).
[48]He returned to Kibbutz Beit Alfa.
[49]See e.g. Arthur Israelowitz to Moazah Harashit, 6th April 1933, H.H. 3.2(1); Ernst Fraenkel and Adolf Schiff to Hahanhagah Haelyonah [Warsaw], 28th April 1933, H.H. 2.12(1) and 3.5(1); Ernst Fraenkel and Adolf Schiff to Hahanhagah Haelyonah, 5th May 1933, H.H. 2.3(1); Adolf Schiff to Hahanhagah Haelyonah, 17th June 1933, H.H. 2.3(1); Adolf Schiff to Hahanhagah Haelyonah, 9th July 1933, H.H. 2.3(1), Ernst Fraenkel to Hahanhagah Haelyonah, 23rd September 1933, H.H. 2.2(1); Adolf Schiff to Waad Hapoel des Kibbutz Arzi [Mishmar Haemek], 7th December 1933, H.H. 3.5(1a).
[50]Ruth Bondy, *Hashaliah*, Tel-Aviv 1974, p. 185. See also Ernst Fraenkel and Adolf Schiff to Hahanhagah Haelyonah, 28th April 1933. H.H. 2.12(1).

centres. This created special problems in all cities other than Berlin. Thus, the entire local leadership left the Mannheim *ken* by the end of April 1933, bringing activities there to a temporary standstill.[51] Native German-Jewish youth tried to fend for itself as best it could, and, on the whole, acquitted itself well. The central leadership in Berlin (*Hahanhagah Harashit*) consisted initially of Ernst Fraenkel and Adolf Schiff, who were joined in the autumn of 1933 by Joseph Waschitz (Seppl).[52] These young men tried to establish a "kibbutz" in Berlin, to send the members to Palestine and to *hachscharah* in Denmark, to continue relations with the *Werkleute* while holding the *Habonim* at bay and to lay the plans for future organisational and cultural activities.[53] These tasks were not easy for young people without experience. Though *Hashomer Hazair* as an organisation was not initially threatened by the Nazis, some of its members were taken to concentration camps in the spring of 1933.[54] Moreover, *Hechaluz* and *Habonim* were far from friendly even after 1933, especially after Liebenstein and Sereni had arrived.[55] Nevertheless, the German-born *Hashomer Hazair* leadership did better than could have been expected: the first ten male and five female members were sent to *hachscharah* in Denmark,[56] and *Hechaluz* was forced to accede to the demand that *Hashomer Hazair* establish its own kibbutz.[57] Yet time was running out. A month prior to his departure from Germany, Arthur Israelowitz wrote from Copenhagen a pessimistic report to the world leadership:

> "The general situation in Germany continues to be terrible. Though we are not yet directly hampered in our work, it is clear that we cannot conduct ourselves in a manner most beneficial for our goals. Thus, we must fear every day danger for our future work . . .
>
> The situation of the Jews in Germany is terrible . . . In a few months . . . – with few exceptions – the fate of German Jewry will be horrible . . . All in all a tragic situation, a hopeless situation, which we could not have imagined in our most daring analyses."[58]

The day on which Israelowitz wrote his letter to the "supreme leadership" in Warsaw with copies to the Palestinian leadership, the latter wrote that not much could be expected from the movement in Palestine. The Palestinian leadership could not on its own send an emissary to Germany who would devote his time to cultural activities (a *Tarbutnik*). The oldest group of *shomrim* in Germany would have to carry this burden. Nor were they ready in Palestine for a large and immediate immigration from abroad and could certainly not guarantee that the German *shomrim* would all be concentrated in one kibbutz.[59] Clearly the Palestinians were not yet fully aware of the dangers facing German Jewry. The Warsaw leadership, on the other hand – due to its physical

[51]Ernst Fraenkel and Adolf Schiff to Hahanhagah Haelyonah, 29th April 1933. H.H. 2.12(1).
[52]See 'Choser No. 1', 7th October 1933. Daliah Archive, 9013/5.
[53]Ernst Fraenkel and Adolf Schiff to Hahanhagah Haelyonah, 29th April 1933. H.H. 2.12(1).
[54]Arthur Israelowitz to Hahanhagah Haelyonah, 12th May 1933. H.H. 3.5(1a).
[55]*Ibid.*
[56]Ernst Fraenkel and Adolf Schiff to Hahanhagah Haelyonah, 5th May 1933. H.H. 2.3(1).
[57]Arthur Israelowitz to Hahanhagah Haelyonah, 12th May 1933. H.H. 3.5(1).
[58]Arthur Israelowitz to Hahanhagah Haelyonah, 12th May 1933. H.H. 3.5(1a).
[59]Letter from Ein Shemer to Histadrut Hashomer Hazair be-Germanyah, 12th May 1933. H.H. 2.7(2).

proximity to Germany – was much more aware of both the dangers and opportunities which existed in Germany and chided the Palestinians for their lack of understanding.[60] The lack of a Palestinian *shaliah* meant that German-Jewish youth would turn to *Habonim* and *Hechaluz*.[61] But the Palestinians were not to be moved. Indeed, often they delayed their answer, exasperating the German *Hashomer Hazair* leadership.[62] Moreover, they made it clear that when and if an emissary would be sent from Palestine, his or her travel expenses as well as maintenance would have to be underwritten by the German *Hashomer Hazair*.[63]

While the Palestinian leadership dragged its feet and continued to maintain an inflexible stance, it became increasingly urgent to have experienced men and women in Germany to handle the mounting and ever more varied responsibilities of the movement. One of these new tasks concerned the *Youth Aliyah* movement[64] which had begun sending children to kibbutzim in Palestine in October 1932.[65] Yet the Palestinian *shomrim* were slow to respond to the myriad questions connected with this complicated and emotionally draining issue.[66] Indeed, the Palestinians were in general uncompromising on the kind of people who could join their kibbutzim, unless they were perfectly suited ideologically and socially to those kibbutzim. This meant that many of the children from Germany were forced to seek a home in alternative kibbutzim.[67] The total number of German children who came on *Youth Aliyah* between 19th February 1934 and 1st October 1939 was 3,437.[68] The total number of children who went to *Hashomer Hazair* kibbutzim and to its high school, the *Mossad Hinuhi* (Mishmar Haemek) was 690. The number is composed of 28 different groups (*hevrot noar*), who between February 1935 and August 1943 stayed in thirteen different kibbutzim; of these, 421 eventually remained as kibbutz members, i.e., 61%.[69]

[60]Jehuda Gothelf to Mahleket Hahanhagah Haelyonah be-Eretz Israel, 28th May 1933. H.H. 2.7(2).

[61]Jehuda Gothelf to Mahleket Hahanhagah Haelyonah be-Eretz Israel, 7th June 1933. H.H. 2.7(2).

[62]See e.g. Adolf Schiff to Hahanhagah Haelyonah, 3rd June 1933. H.H. 2.3(1).

[63]Zvi Luria and Asher Schoenfeld to Histadrut Hashomer Hazair be-Germanyah, 26th June 1933. H.H. 2.7(2).

[64]Adolf Schiff to Hahanhagah Haelyonah, 3rd June 1933. H.H. 2.3(1).

[65]The Society for *Youth Aliyah* was formally established on 30th January 1933. See Recha Freier, *Let the Children Come. The Early History of Youth Aliyah*, London 1961, pp. 17–21. See also Eva Michaelis-Stern, 'Erinnerungen an die Anfänge der Jugendalijah in Deutschland', in *Bulletin des Leo Baeck Instituts*, 70 (1985), pp. 55–66.

[66]Adolf Schiff to Hahanhagah Haelyonah, 3rd June 1933. H.H. 2.3(1).

[67]Zvi Luria and Asher Schoenfeld to Histadrut Hashomer Hazair be-Germanyah, 27th June 1933. H.H. 2.7(2).

[68]See table: 'Zahl der Kinder, die in den Jahren 1934–1982 bei der Jugend-Alijah Aufnahme gefunden haben', in *Israelitisches Wochenblatt* [1983]. Archive of Kibbutz Daliah, 901/3. On general immigration figures of Jews from Germany see *The Jewish Immigration and Population*, issued by the Dept. of Statistics of the Jewish Agency, LBI Archive, Jerusalem.

[69]Archive of Aliyat Hanoar/Jewish Agency, Jerusalem. By June 1944 the total number of children who came on *Youth Aliyah* was 11,270. Of those, 4,547 (40.3%) went to kibbutzim; 987 to kibbutzim of *Hashomer Hazair*. See Abraham Fuerst, *Lemaan Hayeled ve-Hanoar*, No. 22, December/ January – 1944/1945, p. 3. I am grateful to Haim Seeligmann of Yad Tabenkin for drawing my attention to this reference.

The first group of *Youth Aliyah* which included ten *Hashomer Hazair* youths arrived in Palestine in February 1934. Five were sent to Ein Harod, five to Tel Yosef. These were followed in 1935 by groups which arrived in this order at the following kibbutzim: Mishmar Haemek, Merhavyah, Sarid, Mizra, Gan Shmuel, Afikim, and later – in 1937 – to Ein Hashofet. At first, each group was accompanied from Germany by a *Hashomer Hazair* leader (*Madrich*), e.g., Abraham Schiff spent a few months with the group he brought to Merhavyah, Zeev Katz was in Mizra, etc. Later, it was realised that such an arrangement was not necessary and then a member of the kibbutz took charge of the new arrivals. Prior to their departure the young people spent time in a *Vorbereitungslager* so that they could get to know one another.[70] Of course, many *Hashomer Hazair* youngsters from Germany immigrated to Palestine with their families and some of these joined kibbutzim later on. There were also those who arrived in Palestine on their own and also joined kibbutzim of *Hakibbutz Haarzi*.

The issue of *Youth Aliyah* (*Jugendhilfe*) greatly concerned *Hashomer Hazair* in Germany. Adolf Schiff and his colleagues were anxious to receive their share of certificates – of which three hundred arrived at the *Jugendhilfe* headquarters in Berlin in February 1934 – which would enable groups of children between the ages of fourteen to seventeen to come to kibbutzim of *Hashomer Hazair*. This required a two-pronged action – the agreement of Henrietta Szold, director of the social department of the *Vaad Leumi* in Palestine, and the *Palästina-Amt* in Berlin where Eliezer Liebenstein was in charge of all matters dealing with youth.[71] Yaakov Hazan, on behalf of the Palestinian leadership, replied at once notifying *Hashomer Hazair* in Berlin that he had informed Henrietta Szold that *Hashomer Hazair* kibbutzim[72] were willing to absorb 110 children immediately. In addition, the newly-founded high school in Mishmar Haemek (*Hamossad Hahinuhi*) could absorb another 25 children.[73] Of course, matters were not so simple as to have them resolved between the *Hashomer Hazair* leaderships of Berlin and Palestine. *Hechaluz*, which had an increasingly large voice in determining how certificates would be distributed for *Youth Aliyah*, tried to steer the *stam-halutzim* to kibbutzim of *Hakibbutz Hameuhad*..[74] The distribution of certificates for *Youth Aliyah* and others remained a complicated and controversial issue throughout the 1930s.[75] United within the framework of the *Arbeitskreis der Zionistischen Jugendbünde*, which was founded in the winter of 1934, both *Hashomer Hazair* and *Habonim* tried to enlist as many new members as possible in cities where youth was not yet organised.[76] This

[70]Notes sent to author by Abraham Schiff (Bedolf) on 1st June 1985.

[71]Adolf Schiff to Mazkirut Hakibbutz Haarzi, c/o Schenhabi, 1st March 1934. H.H. 3.8(1a).

[72]Such as: Merhavyah, Mizra, Sarid, Mishmar Haemek, Ein Hahoresh, Ein Shemer.

[73]Yaakov Hazan to Adolf Schiff, 13th March 1934. H.H. 3.8(1a).

[74]See e.g. Adolf Schiff to Vaad Hapoel des Kibbutz Arzi, 13th March 1934. H.H. 3.8(1a).

[75]See e.g. Mordechai Orenstein to Vaad Hapoel des Kibbutz Arzi, 4th April 1934, H.H. 3.8(1a), in which he complains that a *Hashomer Hazair* kibbutz, Mishmar Haemek, was placed third – following two *Hakibbutz Hameuhad* kibbutzim – on the list of kibbutzim to receive children from *Youth Aliyah*.

[76]See e.g. Michtaf-Choser No. 23 (signed by Bedolf), 22nd March 1934. H.H. 2.3(1).

added membership would presumably enhance the power of the respective movement within *Hechaluz* and strengthen its demand for certificates to Palestine.

The German leadership also sought to create a commune in Berlin (*Beit Chaluz*) and to publish a periodical to disseminate its ideas. For lack of people who could travel around the country, this seemed the next best vehicle for its ideology.[77] Schiff, Fraenkel, Joseph Waschitz, Heinz Ascher, Shimon Pilz, Norman Kahana and other leaders on the *Hashomer Hazair* executive in Germany continued their concerted effort throughout 1933 and 1934 to keep in touch with the *Werkleute* and to draw to their ranks members from other youth movements, particularly *Makkabi Hazair*. In general, they focused their attention on Western European youth who seemed rudderless and confused, seeking meaning and comfort within a new Jewish framework. Moreover, daily administrative and programmatic activities required a great deal of time and effort. Thus, with only three full-time men in the Berlin office, the movement prepared a three-week long summer camp (*moshavah*) for its members to take place in Denmark[78] and to be followed by a national convention (*veidah artzit*). All this was accomplished mainly due to the skill and dedication of *Hashomer Hazair* leadership, no mean feat given the constant interference and obstructionism of the *Hechaluz* organisation.[79]

The *Hechaluz* leadership in Germany, particularly Sereni and Liebenstein, were relentless in their opposition to *Hashomer Hazair* even after 1933. Apart from their general opposition to its ideology and their fear that it would capture the masses, there were also immediate practical areas of conflict, in particular the attitude of *Hashomer Hazair* to *stam-halutzim* and the issue of *hachscharah*. *Hashomer Hazair* – unlike *Habonim* and other youth movements – continued to oppose what was called *gemischte* or *gemeinsame hachscharah* (*hachscharah meurevet*), i.e., common training of members of the youth movements with the *stam-halutzim*. The background to the conflict between *Hakibbutz Hameuhad* and *Hechaluz* on the one hand and *Hashomer Hazair* on the other, was their varied conception concerning the nature of the kibbutz and its ultimate role. *Hakibbutz Hameuhad* believed in the concept of a large and open kibbutz and wished to develop communities capable of absorbing men and women of different backgrounds and even different ideologies who, together, would develop a multi-faceted economy. *Hashomer Hazair*, on the other hand (and also *Hever Hakvutzot*), believed in the small kibbutz which fosters unity. This concept was supported by the principle of common ideological views or, as it was called, "collective ideology". This then was at the root of *Hashomer Hazair*'s opposition to acceptance of the *stam-halutzim*.

Even after 1933 *Hashomer Hazair* – as well as the *Werkleute* – continued to maintain an elitist approach and insisted on having its own independent (*autonome*) *hachscharah* centres within *Hechaluz*. The *Hechaluz* could not exercise full control over the *hachscharah* activities of *Hashomer Hazair* in Denmark, but

[77] *Ibid.*
[78] Adolf Schiff to Hahanhagah Haelyonah, 9th July 1933. H.H. 2.3(1).
[79] Adolf Schiff to Hahanhagah Haelyonah, 17th June 1933. H.H. 2.3(1).

Sereni vowed that he would not permit the constitution of separate units (*gushim*) within the *Hechaluz* in Germany. It left the parent organisation bereft of its political power or its ability to educate the pioneering element in Germany towards common tasks and goals. The *Hechaluz* leadership maintained – with some measure of justification – that such disparity of treatment of *halutzim* within the youth movements made it difficult to attract the *stam-halutzim* to its ranks.[80] However, in light of the great pressure to accept new members into the ranks of *Hechaluz*, even *Hashomer Hazair* realised the need to shoulder some of the burden and offered to supply instructors (*madrichim*) for the new recruits, thus still keeping them apart from its own *hachscharah* centres. The proposal was rejected by *Hechaluz*, which realised that in effect it would simply give *Hashomer Hazair* the opportunity to recruit new members into its ranks.[81]

For his part, Sereni worked hard to prevent the success of the *hachscharah* centres of *Hashomer Hazair* in Denmark. In a letter to Gershon Ostrowski of the *Hechaluz* centre in Warsaw, Sereni was straightforward about his intentions:

> ". . . I know that you too are experiencing hard times right now and that you lack experienced people, but the situation in Denmark is particularly pressing. As far as we know, *Hashomer Hazair*, which has in Denmark a group of some twenty-five out of eighty, has turned to its 'headquarters' in Warsaw requesting that they send a *Tarbutnik* to Denmark. Naturally we want to prevent this from happening . . ."[82]

The *Hashomer Hazair* leadership was obviously aware of the attitude towards them and at an executive meeting of *Hechaluz* even went so far as to accuse its leaders publicly of disloyal conduct (*illoyales Verhalten*) *vis à vis Hashomer Hazair*[83]. Mutual mistrust between the two movements was such that when Sereni urged *Hashomer Hazair* members to emigrate to Palestine, it was suspected that Sereni was scheming to weaken the *Hashomer Hazair* by urging its leaders and most valuable members to desert the movement.[84]

Nevertheless, there was a semblance of civility and correctness in the relations between *Hashomer Hazair* and *Hechaluz* – an improvement when compared to the period prior to 1933. Even Sereni maintained this public posture. In fact, there was such disparity in their respective positions that it made little sense for *Hechaluz* – now a mass movement – to engage in a continuous public debate that could only draw attention to *Hashomer Hazair*. Since Arthur Israelowitz had departed for Palestine, *Hashomer Hazair* did not have a representative within the central committees of the *Hechaluz*. The movement tried instead to gain a power-base through work in the Jewish National Fund and the *Schule der jüdischen Jugend*. Its main support within *Hechaluz* was through members of the *Werkleute* who intervened on its behalf. What emerges from the documents is that *Hashomer Hazair* could not make much headway in Berlin among those groups closely allied to *Hechaluz* and its

[80][Sereni] to Merkaz Olami des Hechaluz, 27th May 1933. Archive of Hakibbutz Hameuhad.
[81]Adolf Schiff to Hahanhagah Haelyonah, 9th July 1933. H.H. 2.3(1).
[82][Enzo Sereni] to Gershon Ostrowski, 1st July 1933. Archive of Hakibbutz Hameuhad.
[83]Nachtrag zum Protokoll der Sitzung des erweiterten Merkas am 13.7.33. gez. Adolf Schiff, 16th July 1933. Archive of Kibbutz Lohamei Hagetaot, 2501.
[84]Ernst Fraenkel to Hahanhagah Haelyonah, 23rd September 1933. H.H. 2.12(1).

leadership, but it did make progress among other groups (e.g. *Makkabi Hazair* and *Jüdischer Pfadfinderbund Deutschlands* [I.P.D.]), especially in cities outside Prussia. By the autumn of 1933, *Hashomer Hazair* was increasingly aware of the importance of work among the *stam-halutzim* and other youth movements.[85]

The first achievement in gaining new members took place in Köln during the summer of 1933 when the local *Makkabi Hazair* joined *Hashomer Hazair*.[86] The four groups (*kenim*) comprising the movement in the autumn of 1933 were composed of the following numbers: Berlin – 261; Köln – 55; Mannheim – 55 and Hamburg – 35, a total of 406 members, not including fifteen in *hachscharah* in Denmark and another fifteen who had already immigrated to Palestine and were then in Kibbutz Mishmar Haemek.[87] This was hardly an impressive membership in terms of numbers and in fact the total membership was lower than on the day Hitler assumed power.[88] Though in its first phase – before 1933 – some 60% of the movement were *Westjuden* and 40% *Ostjuden*[89] (i.e., those with foreign passports), the proportions seemed to have reversed themselves by the autumn of 1933.[90] The executive of the German *Hashomer Hazair* made strong efforts after 1933 to recruit the liberal and unaffiliated *Westjuden*.[91] Likewise, they tried to gain female members who composed only 35% of the total *Hashomer Hazair* membership, resulting in situations where male *madrichim* instructed girls' groups.[92] The various reports for autumn 1933 stress the need for more expert male and female leadership before new *kenim* could be founded, more stress on Hebrew education and on the quality of new recruits to the movement.[93]

The period prior to the arrival of the new *shaliah* in March 1934 was marked by moderate success on the part of *Hashomer Hazair* in its work in Germany and continued frustration and disappointment in its dealings with the Palestinian leadership. The major accomplishment for the period consisted of the founding of a new *ken* in Essen in November 1933. This was achieved after intensive lobbying and debate from both sides which involved leaders of the two movements from Berlin – Georg Pape of *Habonim* and Adolf Schiff of *Hashomer Hazair*.[94] The fifty youths who constituted the new group – all *Ostjuden* – were a

[85]Ernst Fraenkel to Hahanhagah Haelyonah, 23rd September 1933. H.H. 2.12(1).

[86]Seppl (Joseph Waschitz), 'Bericht über die deutsche Histadrut "Hashomer Hazair"', 27th August 1933. H.H. 2.3(1).

[87]H.H., Choser No. 1, 7th October 1933. Daliah Archive, 9013/5. The total figures given in a report composed by Seppl show only 370 members. See 'Bericht über die deutsche Histadrut "Hashomer Hazair"', 27th August 1933. H.H. 2.3(1).

[88]On 30th January the total figure was 450. See H.H./Deutschland to Hahanhagah Haelyonah, 30th January 1933. H.H. 3.2(1).

[89]See Social Profile of *Hashomer Hazair*, Daliah Archive, 9013/12.

[90]See Seppl, 'Bericht über die deutsche Histadrut . . .', 27th August 1933. H.H. 2.3(1).

[91]Concerning efforts to penetrate the ranks of the assimilated Jews in Hamburg see Choser No. 3 of *Hashomer Hazair* in Hamburg, mid-January, 1934. Daliah Archive, 9013/8.

[92]*Ibid.*

[93]See e.g. Ernst Fraenkel to Hahanhagah Haelyonah, 23rd September 1933. H.H. 2.12(1) and Choser No. 1, 7th October 1933. Daliah Archive 9013/5. See also H.H. in Germany to Garin Kibbutz Germani, 30th November 1933. H.H. 3.5(1a).

[94]Ken Essen to [Mishmar Haemek]. Daliah Archive, 9013/13.

significant addition to the movement and a new outpost in the Rhineland.[95] At the same time it exacerbated the conflicts with *Habonim* and *Hechaluz* on the one hand and the Jewish community in Essen also disapproved of this new group.[96] Nevertheless, there was a note of confidence in the Berlin headquarters of the movement, remarking that *Hashomer Hazair* was continuing to gain members – some from defections in *Habonim* – and even carving for itself a place within *Hechaluz*.[97] But at the same time there was a persistent perception among the German leadership that their colleagues in Palestine were not doing enough to help. The failure to send reinforcements from Palestine was only symptomatic of the failure on the part of the Palestinians to comprehend the radically new situation in Germany.[98]

When reading the daily reports and correspondence of the *Hashomer Hazair* leadership in Germany, with its concerns for administrative matters, organisation-building and ideological struggles with opponents, it is easy to lose sight of the fact that *Hashomer Hazair*, like all other Jewish groups and organisations in Germany was constantly under surveillance by the authorities and often in danger. A glimpse into the reality of their world is given by a report written by Joseph Waschitz from Czechoslovakia in December 1933. The letter begins with a warning not to publish its contents and in any case not to send any material to Germany which would give the police cause to harass the movement. The *Gestapo*, according to Waschitz, was well aware that *Hashomer Hazair* was an international movement and knew about its Socialist-revolutionary ideology, especially in Poland.

> "We have therefore agreed with Sereni on the following ruse: the basis for the international movement is Zionism and scouting; the rest depends on the particular country. For example: in Poland there is a tendency towards revolutionary Socialism, in Palestine towards nationalism, in Lithuania there is an affinity to religion, whereas we are simply Zionists with a tendency towards constructive-pioneer-Socialism. The international headquarters of the movement is in Palestine, whereas Warsaw is only an emigration centre. This constitutes the basis of our relations with the police. They [police] visited us a few times, but behaved well. In general, the behaviour of the party [N.S.D.A.P.] and SA is more favourable, the higher the rank of the officers involved . . ."[99]

On the whole, the ruse seemed to work, but it is also quite clear from the extant police records that the authorities were generally well informed about the activities of *Hashomer Hazair*.[100]

The *Gestapo* was not always so friendly. *Hashomer Hazair* was forced to cancel

[95]Testimony of Hermann (Zvi) Sprung, interviewed by Abraham Schiff [n.d.]. Kibbutz Maabarot, 8th December 1979.

[96]*Ibid.* See also Adolf Schiff to Vaad Hapoel des Kibbutz Arzi (Mishmar Haemek), 7th December 1933. H.H. 3.5(1a).

[97]Adolf Schiff to Hahanhagah Haelyonah, 16th February 1934. H.H. 2.3(1).

[98]Adolf Schiff to Vaad Hapoel des Kibbutz Arzi, 7th December 1933. H.H. 3.5(1a).

[99]Joseph Waschitz to Hahanhagah Haelyonah, 28th December 1933. H.H. 2.3(1).

[100]See e.g. Schreiben des Geheimen Staatspolizeiamts Karlsruhe an das Bezirksamt Bretten vom 17. April 1934, betre. den jüdischen Pfadfinderbund "Haschomer Hazair", zu deutsch "Der junge Wächter". Generallandesarchiv Karlsruhe: 343 Zugang 1956 Nr. 30/516. Vermerk des Bezirksamts Bretten vom 25. April 1934: "Die Angelegenheit wurde in der politischen Sitzung mit der Kreisleitung der NSDAP in Anwesenheit des Kreisleiters . . . und des kommunalpolitischen Referenten . . . erörtert . . ." This document can be found in the Archive of Givat Havivah.

Hashomer Hazair in Germany
Reveille (mifkad)
Summer camp of the Mannheim group, 1936

By courtesy of Kibbutz Daliah Archive, Israel

Hashomer Hazair in Germany
Above: Rega Orenstein (Oren) leading a discussion of the Berlin group, early 1936
Below: Summer camp, 1935

By courtesy of Abraham Schiff (Bedolf) and Kibbutz Daliah Archive, Israel

Hashomer Hazair in Germany
Above: members of the Mannheim group, 1934
Below: bicycle trip of Cologne members, 1936

By courtesy of Kibbutz Daliah Archive, Israel

Kibbutz Bamifneh, May 1935

By courtesy of Kibbutz Daliah Archive, Israel

winter camps near Frankfurt and in the Rhineland in 1934, because the police made it clear that they would not guarantee the safety of the campers. In addition the *Gestapo* harassed the leadership from time to time. Thus, on one occasion Adolf Schiff had to present himself at *Gestapo* headquarters for interrogation[101]; on another occasion the police arrested Ernst Fraenkel and kept him in detention for three days.[102] A number of *Hanukkah* festivities were cancelled by the police in December 1933 because the authorities did not have enough policemen specialising in Jewish affairs to keep watch over these events. Other plans were also cancelled at will, often at the last moment or even in the midst of the event itself.[103] All meaningful activities had to take place outside Germany, mostly in Denmark. For example, the annual convention of *Hashomer Hazair* took place from the 2nd to the 5th August 1933 in Nodebo, a village on Lake Esrum, some twenty-five kilometers north-west of Copenhagen. It was there that Heinz Ascher, Ernst Fraenkel, Adolf Schiff and Joseph Waschitz were elected to the executive of *Hashomer Hazair* (*Hahanhagah Harashit*). These activities, outside Germany, enabled the members to discuss freely their plans and goals for the future. The few days or weeks abroad made it easier to bear the oppressive conditions when they returned to their homes.[104]

Soon after the Nazis came to power, and in the wake of the boycott of 1st April, Ernst Fraenkel and Adolf Schiff wrote to the Polish and Palestinian leadership of *Hashomer Hazair*:

> "We will do our utmost here. It is the responsibility of all of us. It will depend whether you, like the Kibbutz Hameuhad will fully know how to evaluate the [new] situation and will do *your* utmost to seize at the last moment opportunities that will never return."[105]

A day earlier Eliezer Liebenstein of *Hakibbutz Hameuhad* wrote an almost identical letter to his colleagues in Palestine.[106] Clearly, by sending some of its best people to Germany in April 1933 – Liebenstein and Sereni – *Hakibbutz Hameuhad* seems to have grasped earlier than *Hakibbutz Haarzi* what was at stake in Germany. It seems that only at the end of 1933 did the *Hashomer Hazair* leadership conclude that they had missed the boat. On the occasion of the 20th anniversary of *Hashomer Hazair* one of its more prominent members, Moshe Zippor, who had been a *shaliah* in Germany for a brief period prior to 1933, wrote a reflective piece on 'Hashomer Hazair in Western Europe'. In it he devoted much space to a critical evaluation of the movement in Germany:

> "The truth must be told: *'Hashomer Hazair'* has not yet come of age in Western Europe. This assessment does not necessarily relate to the quantitative weight of the movement in the West . . . It is a fact that we have not yet found the key to the masses of Jewish youth that live

[101]Interview with Adolf Schiff (Bedolf) on 16th May 1980.

[102]Joseph Waschitz to Hahanhagah Haelyonah, 28th December 1933. H.H. 2.3(1). Fraenkel was arrested by the SA because he entered a polling station with a suitcase full of material in Hebrew. The SA men brought him to the central prison in Berlin where he was detained for three days in the company of Communists. He was released after intervention by a ZVfD representative.

[103]*Ibid.*

[104]*Ibid.*

[105]Ernst Fraenkel and Adolf Schiff to Hahanhagah Haelyonah; Mahlakah Eretz Israel, Ein Shemer: Vaad Hapoel, Mishmar Haemek, 29th April 1933. H.H. 2.12(1) and 3.5(1).

[106]See Eliezer Liebenstein to [Ein Harod], 28th April 1933. Archive of Kibbutz Hazorea.

in those countries and have not succeeded in transforming *'Hashomer Hazair'* into a decisive factor in their education. Our movements in Austria, Germany and Czechoslovakia have no impact, not only because they encompass so few, but also because they have no ideological and qualitative impact which will make them a factor in the Jewish community. In Germany – there are only few people [in the movement] which has been at a standstill for a number of years . . .

Hashomer Hazair has not struck roots in the West and the question is: who is responsible for this, the special conditions in the region or perhaps the education and ideology of Hashomer Hazair which might not be suitable for the young in the West? One cannot blame this development on the objective conditions. They exist and the basic difference between East and West is not that in the West there is no mass Jewish settlement, but the fact that assimilation is still a decisive cultural factor and the attitude towards Zionism and the Jewish question is purely ideological without a feeling for the pulse of Jewish existence. Every individual must pass two stages here on the way to pioneer life (*halutziut*) and a decision for collective life. First, he finds his way back to Judaism and Jews in general and only after this process of intellectual and practical transformation of values is he capable of seeking a collective and historical solution for his quest to be part of the Jewish reality which he has found through an intellectual process. No doubt, the Jewish catastrophe in our days accelerates this process and it is easier to achieve the internal revolution and arrive at a negation of assimilation in Hitler's time than during other periods. But even Hitler can only act as an external force in recognition of the Jewish fate; the internal condition remains in force for a long time. The upheaval in the life of every individual must first pass the stage of *Ja-sagen zum Judentum* and every Zionist movement must start in the West as an individualistic movement which leads towards a collective solution, joining historical processes. Its starting-point must be the individual and his condition. It must start within the framework of the common fate of individuals who together pave the way towards acceptance of their fate as Jews. Only after this necessary process can the group of individuals turn into a movement with its own education, organisation, its special character. Our misfortune in the West is that we have not started with the individual and his needs, but from above with an educational apparatus, with the organisation of youth, without it becoming an independent entity of a unique and revolutionary movement . . ."[107]

Zippor's conclusion was that in the interest of expanding the organisation in Germany, insufficient time was given to the unique conditions in the West. What was needed was slow, organic development, which would permit those who grew up in youth movements to strike deep ideological roots before expanding the overall organisational framework of *Hashomer Hazair* in Germany. Zippor was, of course, echoing ideas that were current in the movement. Yet, in his criticism of developments in Germany, he ignored the special conditions prevailing there after 1933. Unlike *Brith Haolim, Kadimah* and other youth movements, which began their development in the mid-1920s, *Hashomer Hazair*, the last youth movement to be founded in Weimar Germany – began its ideological development only in 1931. The time was not propitious for a slow, organic process. As Joseph Waschitz noted in the same publication, what *Hashomer Hazair* needed to do more than anything else, was to take advantage of the moment and conquer the masses. This could be done only with the help of an appropriate *shaliah* from Palestine.[108]

This much awaited *shaliah* – Mordechai Orenstein (Oren) of Kibbutz Mizra – finally arrived in Berlin on 14th March 1934,[109] almost a year after Arthur

[107]Moshe Zippor, '"Hashomer Hazair" be-Maarav Europa', in *Hashomer Hazair, 1913–1933*, February 1934, pp. 57–58.

[108]Joseph Waschitz, 'Ba Shomer le-Germanyah', in *Hashomer Hazair, 1913–1933*, p. 59.

[109]See postscript by Orenstein to a letter from Adolf Schiff to Vaad Hapoel des Kibbutz Arzi, 13th March 1934. H.H. 3.8(1a).

Israelowitz had departed for Palestine. His arrival in Germany was perceived as an important boost for *Hashomer Hazair*. Orenstein was known for his energy and intelligence and was a respected member in the front ranks of the international leadership of the movement. But if the executive of *Hashomer Hazair* expected that Orenstein would play a role similar to that of Schenhabi, Goldschein or Israelowitz who had preceded him, they were soon in for a big disappointment.

Orenstein's mission in Germany began, as it were, with the wrong foot. Unlike the other *shlihim* of *Hakibbutz Hameuhad*, who were also emissaries of the *Histadrut*, Orenstein was merely sent by *Hakibbutz Haarzi* and therefore did not command the same status within the ranks of *Hechaluz*.[110] Orenstein was well-known as an avowed Marxist-Socialist, on the very left fringes of *Hashomer Hazair* and – unlike Schenhabi, Goldschein or Israelowitz – not a man of compromise. Moreover, Orenstein was a man possessed of great ambition to succeed quickly. Within two weeks of his arrival in Germany he made strong and unequivocal demands within the council of the *Jüdische Jugendhilfe* for the rights of *Hashomer Hazair*.[111] Within weeks new members joined the movement.[112] A number of groups from other movements joined *Hashomer Hazair*,[113] a development which clearly distressed the *Hakibbutz Hameuhad* people. Thus, the other *shlihim* – who obviously feared him – used the fact that Orenstein had no formal authorisation from the *Histadrut*, to deny him as much as possible access to sources of power within *Hechaluz*; their hope was to frustrate him and weaken his resolve.

They soon received help from unexpected quarters. Less than a month after his arrival in Germany, on 12th April 1934, anonymous letters were received by various Zionist institutions in Berlin, including the ZVfD and *Hashomer Hazair* executive, denouncing Orenstein as a well-known Communist leader in Palestine who supported the class struggle.[114] This was a most dangerous denunciation during the Nazi regime and since copies of the letter were sent in the mail to a number of different addresses, it was more than likely that it had been read by the police as well. An emergency meeting took place in which Levi Shkolnik (Eshkol) of the *Histadrut* (who had just arrived in Germany for a brief sojourn), Eliezer Liebenstein, and Gustav Horn of the *Werkleute* representing *Hechaluz*, as well as Ernst Fraenkel and Orenstein of *Hashomer Hazair*, participated. The consensus at the meeting, based on the wording of the letter, was that it was sent by the Revisionists. The *Hashomer Hazair* representative demanded at the meeting that *Hechaluz*, the *Histadrut* and the ZVfD, officially repudiate the denunciations and stand behind Orenstein. Otherwise the entire

[110]Adolf Schiff to Vaad Hapoel des Kibbutz Arzi, 22nd March. H.H. 3.8(1a).

[111]Mordechai Orenstein to Vaad Hapoel des Kibbutz Arzi, 4th April 1934. H.H. 3.8(1a).

[112]Mordechai Orenstein to Mazkirut Havaad Hapoel shel Hakibbutz Haarzi, 14th April 1934. H.H. 3.8 (1a).

[113]Ernst Fraenkel to Fritz Kupfer (Leipzig), 15th May 1934. H.H. 3.8(1a).

[114]The content of the letter: "... kam dieser Tage zur Erziehung jüdischer Jugend der 'Chawer' Orenstein nach Deutschland, der aus seiner Tätigkeit aus Polen und Palästina als ausgesprochener Kommunistenführer bekannt ist ..." Letter to Mazkirut Havaad Hapoel des Kibbutz Arzi (Mishmar Haemek), 16th April 1934. H.H. 2.3(1).

future of *Hashomer Hazair* in Germany would be at stake, and might encourage denunciations of other groups, including *Habonim* and *Hechaluz*. This demand was not accepted by the *Hechaluz* and *Histadrut* representatives. On the contrary, they felt that Orenstein could not be successfully defended and that *Hakibbutz Haarzi* had made a mistake by sending him to begin with.[115]

Orenstein's charge that the attitude towards him was motivated more by internal political considerations within the pioneer movement, rather than by fear of reprisals and suppression from the authorities, seems to have been true.[116] Clearly, had Sereni or Liebenstein been accused of Communist activities, there would have been a concerted effort to protect them. In the case of Orenstein the discussion at the meeting was narrowed to tactical considerations: how to pretend that his (proposed) departure from Germany was not due to pressure from the Revisionists. In fact, Orenstein was forced to consider leaving Germany because, as he pointed out, unless he had access to activities of the *Hechaluz* in Germany, there would not be much for him to do. Orenstein recognised that under the special conditions prevailing in Germany after 1933, it was *Hechaluz* and the *Palästina-Amt* which carried the most weight within the Jewish community, or at least within the Zionist movement. Without their blessing, or at least assent, there was no chance of meaningful work. He therefore demanded that the *Hashomer Hazair* leadership in Palestine request the executive of the *Histadrut* to condemn the attitude of their emissaries in Germany and declare that even if he was not an official representative of the *Histadrut*, he was entitled to the same treatment as any other Palestinian emissary.[117] This is not how the representatives of *Hechaluz* saw the matter. At a subsequent meeting which also included Hermann Gerson of the *Werkleute*, Adolf Schiff and Marduk (Mordechai) Schattner – one of the founders of *Brith Haolim* – the latter went so far as to declare that should *Hashomer Hazair* decide to retain Orenstein in Germany, he would suggest that *Hechaluz* sever all contacts with *Hashomer Hazair* in order not to endanger the *Hechaluz*. Shkolnik too cast doubts on Orenstein's usefulness for *Hashomer Hazair* and even the *Werkleute* equivocated.[118] Thus, within a month after his arrival, Orenstein had become a major liability for *Hashomer Hazair* in Germany.

Hakibbutz Haarzi had little choice but to bring the matter up before the executive of the *Histadrut*. A stormy debate ensued during which the leaders of *Hakibbutz Haarzi* threatened to make the attitude of the *Hechaluz* towards Orenstein public and even leave the *Histadrut*.[119] During a second meeting, a compromise formulated by David Ben-Gurion was accepted. It demanded that the representatives of the *Histadrut* inform all Zionist bodies in Germany that

[115]Mordechai Orenstein to Mazkirut Havaad Hapoel shel Hakibbutz Haarzi, 14th April 1934. H.H. 3.8(1a).

[116]This charge was also made by the leadership of *Hashomer Hazair* in Palestine. See Y[aakov] Hazan and B[unim] Steinberger (Shamir) to Merkaz Hechaluz be-Germanyah, 23rd July 1934. Liebenstein Archive.

[117]*Ibid.*

[118]Mordechai Orenstein to Mazkirut Havaad Hapoel shel Hakibbutz Haarzi, 23rd April 1934. H.H. 3.8(1a).

[119]Mordechai Orenstein to Vaad Hapoel des Kibbutz Arzi, 18th May 1934. H.H. 3.8(1a).

Orenstein was a loyal member of the *Histadrut* and the World Zionist Organisation, thus, *ipso facto*, entitled to the protection of the *Histadrut*.[120]

No sooner was this issue resolved than a new storm erupted around a pamphlet published by Orenstein in June 1934.[121] Orenstein began writing this brochure as soon as he arrived in Berlin and though he consulted his colleagues in Palestine and Warsaw as to content and form, he was solely responsible for the final product which was not seen by the leadership of *Hashomer Hazair* prior to its publication.[122] Though there is no extant evidence to substantiate it, it is more than likely that the controversy in Germany over the anonymous letter of denunciation may have sharpened some of the language in the brochure. Given Orenstein's character, it is quite possible that the personal attacks against him were in part rebuffed through ideological arguments. In any case, it was clear that he had intended the seventy-five page brochure, titled *Zur Problematik der Kibuzbewegung in Erez Israel*,[123] as a wide-ranging polemical debate against *Hakibbutz Hameuhad*.[124] Well aware of Orenstein's angry frame of mind, Yaakov Hazan wrote from Mishmar Haemek in the name of *Hakibbutz Haarzi* leadership, some three weeks prior to the publication of the brochure, a note of warning:

> ". . . We simply want to add one strategic-methodological remark. From the table of contents [of the brochure], it seems that it will not be merely theoretical, but polemical in nature. In fact, it is clear to us that there is no way to describe our ideology without comparing it to other segments of the kibbutz movement and without drawing the necessary consequences. Nevertheless, one must be very careful. Every word that is not well-considered, will immediately be turned against us by our enemies . . . We must be careful not to hand them weighty ammunition. We write all this because it is clear to us that at the moment you are extremely bitter [towards members of *Hakibbutz Hameuhad*] . . . this requires, therefore, extreme self-control while you write.[125]"

Hazan's warning either came too late or was not heeded. When Orenstein published his polemical tract in June 1934 it immediately became the focus of a heated debate which raged for many months.

It is impossible to summarise Orenstein's brochure in a few paragraphs. The importance of the tract lies less in its specific content which generally reflected well-known arguments within *Hakibbutz Haarzi*. It is perhaps more important to examine what those involved with *Hakibbutz Hameuhad* found objectionable in Orenstein's brochure. In accordance with their perceptions they reacted in a lengthy fifteen-page letter which was signed by Eliezer Liebenstein, Marduk Schattner and Enzo Sereni.[126] Their reply was sent to all *Hechaluz* groups in

[120]Yaakov Hazan to Mordechai Orenstein, 23rd May 1934. H.H. 2.3(1). In his letter, Hazan denied the reports received by Orenstein via Menachem Bader, that the *Histadrut* had refused to protect Orenstein. Whichever version is correct, it is clear from the correspondence that it was necessary to discuss the "Orenstein Affair" during two meetings of the *Histadrut* executive.

[121]The brochure came off the press on 23rd June 1934. See Mordechai Orenstein to Redaktion des Hashomer Hazair, 25th June 1934. H.H. 3.8(1a).

[122]See Mordechai Orenstein to Vaad Hapoel des Kibbutz Arzi, 4th April 1934. H.H. 3.8(1a).

[123]Führerschriften No. 2, Jüd. Pfadfinderbund 'Haschomer Hazair' (June 1934).

[124]See Mordechai Orenstein to Vaad Hapoel des Kibbutz Arzi, 18th May 1934. H.H. 3.8(1a).

[125]Yaakov Hazan to Mordechai Orenstein, 23rd May 1934. H.H. 2.3(1).

[126]See 'Bemerkungen zur Broschüre: "Zur Problematik der Kibuzbewegung in Erez Israel", von M. Orenstein'. Archive of Givat Havivah.

Germany. It highlighted aspects of Orenstein's brochure and then tried to reply to his arguments.

Orenstein claimed that *Hechaluz* had been disseminating one-sided information on the kibbutz movement which was intended to influence young people to join *Hakibbutz Hameuhad*; that the individual living in the Kibbutz Hameuhad tended to get lost amongst the large number of people and simply turned into a number, a wheel within a larger machine; that *Hakibbutz Hameuhad* had accused *Hakibbutz Haarzi* of not rising to the demands of the hour and accepting the large *aliyah*; that *Hakibbutz Hameuhad* and *Mapai* were constantly debasing the achievements and ideology of *Hashomer Hazair*; that *Hakibbutz Hameuhad* had turned into a mass movement, thus lowering the intellectual and cultural level of the pioneers; that *Hakibbutz Hameuhad*, through its economic, social and political actions was pushing the Arab population of Palestine into the arms of reactionary elements; that *Hakibbutz Hameuhad* had neglected the settlement of thousands of immigrants in order to pursue other political goals and that *Hakibbutz Hameuhad* and *Mapai* were unwilling or unable to unite with the various pioneer elements for the sake of common goals.[127] The charges listed here are, of course, only a small sample of Orenstein's lengthy tract, but they suffice to indicate its general nature.

As indicated before, Orenstein was not the first member of *Hashomer Hazair* to attack the policies of *Hakibbutz Hameuhad* sharply. Four months prior to the publication of *Zur Problematik der Kibuzbewegung*, another prominent member of *Hashomer Hazair*, Moshe Zippor, published an article in Hebrew which contained the following passage:

> "*Hakibbutz Hameuhad* has destroyed the great potential talents of the Jewish youth in Germany. It has squandered [its] constructive forces, it has destroyed the German *aliyah*, it has brought this *aliyah* to a state of degeneration and inner destruction. What has nevertheless been achieved in Givat Brenner and other places, is nothing but a small remainder, leftovers of a great *aliyah*, which has succeeded just in time in escaping the official, destructive policy of the Kibbutz [Hameuhad] and which, despite its will, managed to unite."[128]

This article did not go unnoticed by the members of *Hakibbutz Hameuhad* in Germany, but resulted in a mere written protest "for the record".[129] There is no indication that it was discussed in any major forum. Indeed, since the article was written in Hebrew, it was accessible only to the emissaries from Palestine as well as a few other German-born youths. What was different about Orenstein's pamphlet was that it was published in German with a large initial printing of close to 2,500 copies,[130] and that it was composed by an emissary of a pioneer movement resident in Germany. Moreover, Orenstein's far-ranging and thorough denunciation of *Hakibbutz Hameuhad* ideology and policy shattered the unwritten norms within *Hechaluz* which called for internal and civilised debate on a high intellectual level. Indeed, despite disagreements between the various

[127]*Ibid.*

[128]Moshe Zippor, 'Hashomer Hazair be-Maarav Europa', in *Hashomer Hazair 1913–1933*, February 1933, p. 58.

[129]See Liebenstein, 'Notiz für den Umlauf', 16th March 1934. H.H. 3.8(1a).

[130]See Mordechai Orenstein to Redaktion des Hashomer Hazair, 25th June 1934. H.H. 3.8(1a).

youth movements it had been possible for *Hashomer Hazair* in Germany to cooperate on a certain level with *Habonim* and *Hechaluz*. After the publication of the brochure this was no longer possible.

Three days after it came out, Liebenstein, Sereni and Schattner addressed a letter to Orenstein denouncing the brochure as lacking the most elementary norms of civility. They challenged him to a court of the *Histadrut* and declared that all personal relations between them were henceforth broken.[131] Naturally, Orenstein replied, denying all wrongdoing except for engaging in heated intellectual debate.[132] But Orenstein's defence did not even convince his own colleagues in Palestine. After some rather perfunctory compliments, Yaakov Hazan wrote, in the name of the executive, that the tone of the brochure was unnecessarily harsh and insulting, and that this might in the last analysis, be counter-productive.[133] Orenstein then turned to the headquarters of *Hechaluz* in Warsaw, asking that it interfere, lest the work of *Hechaluz* suffer from the internal friction.[134] But the executive in Warsaw was in no mood for compromises; it demanded an immediate halt to further distribution of the brochure until the *Histadrut* court had passed its judgement.[135]

The matter dragged on for months. Orenstein seems to have realised the potential danger of a further struggle with so formidable an opponent as *Hakibbutz Hameuhad* which was backed by *Mapai* and ultimately the *Histadrut*, and he sought a "normalisation" of relations with *Hechaluz*.[136] He suggested a neutral commission of inquiry to look into the affair.[137] The members of *Hakibbutz Hameuhad*, however, were not inclined to compromise and acted at once to shut out Orenstein as much as possible from all work within *Hechaluz*.[138] Moreover, Sereni and his colleagues pressed for a decision on the case from the executive of the *Histadrut* as well as for publication in Palestine of their brief against Orenstein.[139]

Yet, after all concerned had a chance to vent their anger, tempers began to cool by the end of the summer.[140] At the beginning of August 1934 the *Hashomer Hazair* executive in Germany published a circular sent to all members of *Hechaluz*. It was conciliatory in tone and after explaining the reasons for the

[131] Liebenstein, Sereni and Schattner to Mordechai Orenstein, 26th June 1934. Archive of Kibbutz Lohamei Hagetaot, 2501.

[132] Orenstein to Liebenstein, Sereni and Schattner, 13th July 1934. H.H. 3.8(1a). See also the reply: Shkolnik, Schattner and Liebenstein to Mordechai Orenstein, 24th July 1934. Liebenstein Archive.

[133] Yaakov Hazan to Mordechai Orenstein, 17th July 1934. H.H. 3.8(1a).

[134] Orenstein to Merkaz Olami des Hechaluz, 24th July 1934. H.H. 3.8(1a).

[135] Merkaz Hechaluz an den Hashomer Hazair, Bundesleitung, 30th July 1934. Liebenstein Archive.

[136] Orenstein to Vaad Hapoel der Histadrut Haowdim, 29th July 1934. H.H. 3.8(1a).

[137] Orenstein to Vaad Hapoel des Kibbutz Arzi, 30th July 1934. H.H. 3.8(1a).

[138] Mordechai Orenstein to Vaad Hapoel des Kibbutz Arzi, 1st August 1934, H.H. 3.8(1a); and [Merkaz Hechaluz] to Vaad Hapoel shel ha-Histadrut, 8th August 1934, H.H. 2.3(1).

[139] Enzo Sereni to Hakibbutz Hameuhad (Ein Harod), [13th] August 1934. Archive of Hakibbutz Hameuhad, Container No. 6.

[140] It seems that the last communication on the subject is a letter from Orenstein denying all charges made by the *shlihim* of *Hakibbutz Hameuhad*. It was written after Sereni, Liebenstein and Shkolnik had already left Germany. See Mordechai Orenstein to Vaad Hapoel der Histadrut, 13th October 1934. H.H. 3.8(1a).

publication of Orenstein's brochure, it offered to cease its distribution until the ruling by the *Histadrut*.[141] For his part, Sereni too, was pleased to end the fight with *Hashomer Hazair*.[142] Even Orenstein wrote that he hoped for a resolution[143] and the leadership of *Hashomer Hazair* in Palestine wanted to suppress the whole affair as quickly as possible before it could be decided by the executive of the *Histadrut*.[144] Towards the end of September 1934 the executive of *Hashomer Hazair* addressed another letter to all members of *Hechaluz* offering to end all conflicts between these two bodies.[145] Enzo Sereni and Eliezer Liebenstein left Germany in September 1934, thus facilitating a peaceful resolution. The affair ended formally in October of that year with a proposal by *Hashomer Hazair* to normalise its relations with *Hechaluz*.[146]

In retrospect, it is clear that the "Orenstein Affair" reflected conditions in Palestine – i.e., the struggle between *Hakibbutz Haarzi* and *Mapai* – rather than the situation in Germany. Most of Orenstein's efforts were devoted to political-ideological battles within *Hechaluz*. The yield from these debates was quite meagre, primarily because the social, economic, organisational and educational concerns of German Jewry lay elsewhere at the time. Their unique situation required adjustment and new skills from the Palestinian *shlihim*. Since Orenstein was unwilling to adjust to the particular needs of the German youth movements, he could not win the minds of those he was most interested in drawing to the ranks of *Hashomer Hazair*.

Orenstein's offensive against *Hakibbutz Hameuhad* ended then ignominiously, in total failure.[147] The failure was, on the whole, a personal blow to Orenstein, and did not necessarily affect the entire *Hashomer Hazair* movement in Germany. It is true that Orenstein arrived in Germany under a cloud of suspicion and prejudice against him. But it is also true that his personality was such that it inflamed those suspicions. The relations between *Hechaluz* and *Hashomer Hazair* were never very good, but just prior to Orenstein's arrival in Germany, it was possible for Arthur Israelowitz and Ernst Fraenkel to work within the larger movement. Within three months of his arrival, Orenstein had become a pariah within the group of *shlihim* in Germany.[148] By his own admission, Orenstein had been shut out from all activities of *Hechaluz* and thus from the very centre of the pioneering enterprise.[149] Even the *Werkleute* in Germany, who were generally

[141]Hashomer Hazair Bundesleitung, 'An alle Chawerim des Hechaluz! An die Älteren der chaluzischen Jugendbünde!', 10th August 1934. Daliah Archive 9013/13.

[142]Sereni to Mazkirut Hakibbutz Hameuhad, 11th August 1934. Archive of Hakibbutz Hameuhad, Container No. 6.

[143]Mordechai Orenstein to Yaakov Hazan, 3rd September 1934. H.H. 3.8 (1a).

[144]Y. Hazan and B. Steinberger to Mordechai Orenstein, 25th September 1934. H.H. 3.8(1a).

[145]Bundesleitung des Hashomer Hazair, 'An alle Chawerim des deutschen Hechaluz', 22nd September 1934. Daliah Archive, 9013/6.

[146]Vorschlag des Hashomer Hazair zur Normalisierung der Beziehungen zwischen Hashomer Hazair und dem Merkas Hechaluz [October 1934]. H.H. 3.8(1a).

[147]See Eliezer Liebenstein to Mazkirut Hakibbutz Hameuhad [September 1934]. Liebenstein Archive.

[148]See letter from Eliezer Liebenstein to Mazkirut Hakibbutz Hameuhad, 7th September 1934. Liebenstein Archive.

[149]Mordechai Orenstein to Mahleket Hahanhagah Haelyonah, 17th September 1934. H.H. 2.12(1).

close to *Hashomer Hazair*, kept their distance from him.[150] Orenstein's personal standing did not improve much even after the storm around his brochure had dissipated.

It is against this background that one must evaluate Orenstein's first comprehensive assessment of conditions in Germany, written at the end of September 1934:

> "Prior to my departure for Germany, there was much talk as to whether we have missed 'the historical moment' in Germany. I must now state that, in my opinion we have missed it . . . there is little chance that in the near future (next few years) we will become a movement of real consequence within the Jewish youth . . .
>
> We missed the opportunity during the period of deep shock which affected German Jewry during the national revolution . . . *Hakibbutz Hameuhad* has conquered Zionist public opinion and it is [*Hakibbutz Hameuhad*] which determines policy at Meinekestrasse. . . .
>
> '*Habonim*' in Germany is what *Hashomer Hazair* is in other countries. It preceded us and took our place. It has struck deep roots amongst youth . . . it is they who founded the *Hechaluz* . . .
>
> In all the large cities within which we tried to establish ourselves (and which have groups of '*Habonim*') we were unable to take hold for a simple reason, all those people who are suitable, are already organised in other movements . . .
>
> Both you [the Palestinian leadership] and the *Hanhagah Haelyonah* [in Warsaw], do not understand that in order to make a last effort, after the 'historic opportunity' has been missed – the help of the entire movement is required – and it makes no sense to send one person who sits here without any possibility for action. One needs many *shlihim* and a *great deal of money* . . .
>
> The situation as to youth is quite stable at this point, not like it was two years ago. In addition, there will be no possibilities for written propaganda after the publication of the new laws . . . which forbid any literary output by the Jewish youth movements . . .
>
> Oral propaganda is also impossible, it requires that I work within *Hechaluz* and the ZVfD. But the people of *Hakibbutz Hameuhad* know how to close this avenue to me . . . they also make it impossible for me to appear for a lecture before any group. . . .
>
> As to my situation: I came here not in order to spend my time corresponding with a few of the older youths in 6–7 *kenim* . . . I came on the basis of assurances of our people that we have not yet missed 'the opportunity', that there is a wide field of activity here. I came here with the assumption that I could work within *Hechaluz*, within the youth movements . . . and [would be able] to enlighten them on *Hashomer Hazair* ideology. . . .
>
> I came to the realisation that the situation is quite different . . . I think that sending me here was a mistake. I cannot make use of my talents here. There is no field of activity here . . . Thus it makes no sense to keep me here under the illusion that something can be done. My conclusion: in light of the situation described in this letter it makes no sense for me to remain here . . ."[151]

But the situation of *Hashomer Hazair* in Germany was not quite as bleak as described by Orenstein. In fact, it is worth noting that his own personal situation did not necessarily reflect that of the movement in Germany. On the contrary, as a circular of *Hashomer Hazair* in June pointed out, there was progress to report in all areas of their activities.[152] Mordechai Orenstein and others in the *Hashomer Hazair* leadership in Germany bemoaned in many letters the lack of a second *shaliah* from Palestine without whom it was impossible to

[150]Mordechai Orenstein to Vaad Hapoel des Kibbutz Arzi, 17th September 1934. H.H. 3.8(1a).

[151]Mordechai Orenstein to Hazan, Abraham Ravitzky and Arthur Israelowitz, 24th September 1934. H.H. 3.8(1a). See also Mordechai Orenstein to Hahanhagah Haelyonah shel Hashomer Hazair (Warsaw), 4th October 1934. H.H. 2.3(1). The letter to Warsaw is almost identical to the one written to Palestine.

[152]Hashomer Hazair, Hahanhagah Harashit, Choser No. 9, 22nd June 1934. Daliah Archive, 9013/6.

oversee properly the various existing groups in Germany, but at the same time they did report that the *hachscharah* centres in Denmark were doing very well. A Danish group of Jews constituted a "*Halutz*-Committee" which regularly visited the sixty-odd pioneers and even gave them an allowance.[153] In Germany, too, the movement had grown to seven *kenim* with a total membership of 750 people.[154] In fact, the expansion of *Hashomer Hazair* – despite the isolation of Orenstein from *Hechaluz* activities – greatly worried Enzo Sereni.[155]

Curiously, in his letter of 24th September Orenstein did not even mention one of the most exciting – and eventually the most significant – accomplishments of the German *Hashomer Hazair* – the establishment of its first kibbutz in Palestine.[156] The first cell (*garin*) of the kibbutz grouped its members in Kibbutz Mishmar Haemek beginning in May 1933.[157] The *garin* numbered at first eighteen people – twelve men and six women; of these, fifteen came from the German *Hashomer Hazair*. During the year they spent at Mishmar Haemek, others joined the *garin*: a number of people who had come from *Habonim*; a group of ten students of the *Kartell Jüdischer Verbindungen*, who had undergone agricultural training on an estate near Riga – and hence, called the Riga-*hachscharah* – led by a *Hashomer Hazair* member; a group which had been sent by *Hechaluz* to *hachscharah* in Ahlem and a few other individuals from Germany who had developed an intellectual and social affinity for *Hakibbutz Haarzi*.[158] A year later, on the 27th of May 1934, the *garin* became independent, counting thirty-four members; approximately two-thirds were men.[159] The new kibbutz, now called "Kibbutz Bamifneh," was given space for tents near Kibbutz Ein Shemer, close to the colony of Karkur. During five years of independent existence (27th May 1934–April 1939), they were joined by small groups of people who arrived from the German *Hashomer Hazair* and individuals from other German pioneer youth movements, some of whom had previously been in kibbutzim of *Hakibbutz Hameuhad*. There was considerable fluctuation in the absorption and departure of members. One of the reasons for this was the great disproportion in numbers between men and women. (See Table I.) Four of the members came from Switzerland,[160] two from other countries and the rest from Germany. The average age of the members was 23 1/2 years.[161]

[153]Mordechai Orenstein, 'Situationsbericht über Dänemark' [August 1934]. H.H. 2.12(1). See also Haestrup, *Passage to Palestine*, pp. 27–31.

[154]Mordechai Orenstein to Mahleket Hahanhagah Haelyonah, 17th September 1934. H.H. 2.12(1).

[155]Enzo Sereni to Mazkirut Hakibbutz Hameuhad, 11th Agust 1934. Archive of Hakibbutz Hameuhad, Container No. 6.

[156]This is particularly strange since Orenstein's brochure *Zur Problematik der Kibuzbewegung* was dedicated: "Dem Kibuz 'Haschomer Hazair' aus Deutschland in Karkur, Erez Jisrael – zum Beginn seines eigenen Schaffens und seiner Arbeit in der Moschawa".

[157]On the early period of this *garin* see letter (unsigned) of 15th December 1934 published in the *Informationsblatt* of *Hechaluz* in Daliah Archive, 902. For his help in the reconstruction of the history of Kibbutz "Bamifneh", I am very grateful to Dan (Ernst) Fraenkel of Kibbutz Daliah.

[158]Mordechai Orenstein to Vaad Hapoel des Kibbutz Arzi, 30th May 1934. H.H. 3.8(1a).

[159]Letter from the kibbutz to Mahleket ha-Hityashvuat shel Hasochnut, 12th June 1937. Daliah Archive 902.

[160]See Schweizer Chaluzim in Palästina, 'Wir bauen einen Kibuz' [1936]. Daliah Archive, 902.

[161]Letter from the kibbutz to Mahleket ha-Hityashvut shel ha-Sochnut, 12th June 1937. Daliah Archive, 902.

TABLE I

Numbers of Members in Kibbutz Bamifneh

Year		Men	Women	Total
Spring	1933	14	6	20
May	1934			32
Early	1935	37	12	49[162]
Early	1936	38	20	58
Early	1937	44	28	72
Early	1938	39	25	64 + 1 child
End of	1938	44	29	73 + 4 children
	1939	(at time of merger with Kibbutz Bamaaleh)		70

TABLE II

Number of German Hashomer Hazair People in Kibbutz Bamifneh-Daliah

	1933	Beginning of the *garin*	13
December	1936		~36
	1936	Kibbutz Bamifneh	57
	1945	Kibbutz Daliah	29
	1985		22

[Note: Between 1945 and 1985 only three of the original German members of the kibbutz left it voluntarily. Four have died. Both tables are based on material contained in Daliah archive, 902.]

During the period of Kibbutz Bamifneh, most of the male members worked as hired labour, especially in citrus plantations, construction and for a neighbouring British army installation. The women did house work in a neighbouring settlement (Gan Shomron). During periods of unemployment – especially in the winter months – the members were sent to work in the port of Haifa and some were sent to Hanita where they helped build the fence on the northern border. The members of the kibbutz also established for their own needs, and as preparation for their permanent site, a vegetable garden and later added dairy farming, a bee-hive, a locksmith's shop, carpentry, electric workshop, etc.[163]

The members spent much time pursuing cultural activities.[164] The major problem was to try to introduce the Hebrew language into all aspects of life on the kibbutz[165]: in general kibbutz meetings, in committees and later in public presentations and ideological debates.[166] The kibbutz newspaper appeared at first in German, then in Hebrew and German, and only in 1937 was it wholly written in Hebrew. It took, of course, much longer to make the Hebrew language part of daily discourse among the members and within families. Politically, too, there was a great awareness among members concerning questions in Palestine and in the world. It was expressed in many internal debates and lectures, in activity among the Jewish and Arab workers in the

[162]See "Vom Kibuz", Karkur, 1st March 1935. Daliah Archive, 901/3.

[163]See e.g. Kibbutz Hashomer Hazair "Bamifneh", 25th [July] 1936. Daliah Archive 902/3.

[164]See e.g. Bamifneh bereitet seinen ersten Neschef vor. August 1935. Daliah Archive 901/3, file 13.

[165]On some other problems of adjustment to the kibbutz way of life see Shimon Pilz to Ulrich Müller, 30th November 1937. Daliah Archive, 9013/11.

[166]See e.g. 'Baalei Tafkidim' (in German) and 'Mishpat al Hakibbutz' (in Hebrew). Both are public presentations made in 1935. Daliah Archive, 902. See also 'Eine deutsche Theateraufführung im Kibbuz vor 20 Jahren', *Jedioth Chadashoth*, 8th July 1955.

settlement of Karkur, marches during the celebration of 1st May, establishment of a *Hashomer Hazair ken* in Karkur, etc.[167]

Kibbutz Bamifneh began to explore the possibility for a permanent site soon after it settled in its temporary quarters near Karkur. The members of the kibbutz as well as *Hakibbutz Haarzi* leadership came to the conclusion that a prerequisite to a permanent settlement was a membership of some 120 people. A merger with another group was therefore necessary. Some also held the view that such a merger with a Palestinian or Eastern European partner was culturally and socially desirable. Under conditions prevailing in Mandatory Palestine in the 1930s, there was a long waiting period before kibbutzim could be granted land for permanent settlement. But Kibbutz Bamifneh had the advantage of considerable financial resources which were allocated by the German Department of the Jewish Agency. Beginning in 1937 there were negotiations for appropriate solutions with the Jewish Agency[168] and various potential partners were suggested for a merger.[169] In April 1939 it was decided to merge with Kibbutz Bamaaleh whose members came from *Hashomer Hazair* groups in Romania-Transylvania. The total membership of Kibbutz Bamifneh was then 70 and that of Bamaaleh 90. The members of Bamaaleh transferred to the camp of Bamifneh and on 1st May 1939 the first group of the united kibbutz settled on its permanent site in the proximity of Kibbutz Ein Hashofet. On 20th January 1940 it was decided to call the new settlement Kibbutz Daliah. On that date it had a total membership of 160, 90 male and 70 female members.[170]

Kibbutz Daliah was, of course, not the only kibbutz where members of the German *Hashomer Hazair* settled. It was the place where the first "generation" of *shomrim* from Germany settled in large numbers. The so-called second and third generations of German *shomrim* settled in many other kibbutzim such as Kfar Nahum, Hamaapil, Hazorea, Mizra, Maabarot, Sarid, Ein Hamifratz and Shaar Haamakim. In those kibbutzim – and in others as well – where they had often arrived through *Youth Aliyah*, they made up a considerable percentage of the population and their total aggregate numbers far outweigh the numbers of those who settled in Kibbutz Daliah. Nevertheless, Kibbutz Daliah retained a symbolic importance which is due to its status as the first creation of the German *Hashomer Hazair*.

The founding of Kibbutz Daliah completed a process that had begun some seven years earlier. As the Kibbutz Bamifneh developed year by year, it was watched with pride and satisfaction by the movement as a whole, but particularly by the *shomrim* in Germany. Even while in Germany, under the oppressive regime of the Nazis, they could identify with the work of their friends in Palestine. While waiting for their own certificates – in Germany or in

[167]See Siat Hashomer Hazair ve-Haligah ha-Sozialistit be-Karkur. Internal Bulletin No. 3. Intended only for members of *Hashomer Hazair* kibbutzim in Karkur, July–August, 1940. Daliah Archive, 902.

[168]See e.g. Kibbutz Bamifneh to Mahleket ha-Hityashvut shel ha-Sochnut ha-Yehudit, 12th June 1937. Daliah Archive, 902/41.

[169]See e.g. Kibbutz Bamifneh an den Bund, 30th November 1937. Daliah Archive, 902.

[170]The above description is based on material in the archives of Kibbutz Daliah, including the minute-book of the kibbutz. See Daliah Archive, 901/3; 902; 902/2.

hachscharah in Denmark or Yugoslavia – they could live vicariously through the process of construction in Karkur. The letters and reports from Palestine, and the occasional personal visits of *shlihim* or tourists from Palestine, kept up their spirits and encouraged them to work hard in Germany for their common ideals. Indeed, as suggested before, Mordechai Orenstein's gloomy report on the state of the movement in Germany was not shared by many others. Even the executive of *Hashomer Hazair* in Palestine suggested that his assessment was much too pessimistic. They tried to cheer him up with compliments on his work, by insisting that he was absolutely essential for the success of the movement and promising to send a larger group of *shlihim* to Germany.[171]

It is quite possible that from the larger perspective of the movement, it was necessary to keep Orenstein in Germany for a while, lest his departure be seen as a triumph of *Hakibbutz Hameuhad* people over *Hashomer Hazair*.[172] Though Orenstein agreed to remain in Germany for a few more months, his presence added little to the work at hand. Once again, it was left to Ernst Fraenkel and the older group of German-born *shomrim* to carry the burden of leadership with almost no assistance. Their situation was alleviated somewhat in 1935 when Mordechai Orenstein's wife, Rega, came to join him. While in Germany, she took part in the activities of *Hashomer Hazair*.

What were conditions like for Jews in Germany at the end of 1934? In brief, during 1934 there were very few official measures taken against Jews. It seemed for a while that the Nazi regime would allow the Jews a continued, if circumscribed existence. There were, of course, continued acts of harassment and boycotting, but these were without the official sanction of the government. The purge of the SA in June 1934 brought even these "spontaneous" incidents to an end. Many Jews took these developments as hopeful signs for a better future. In the wake of Hitler's takeover, an estimated 37,000 had left Germany. In 1934 the number dropped to 23,000. In fact, during the latter months of 1934 and early months of 1935, some 10,000 German Jews who had left, began to return. It was not until May 1935 that the introduction of anti-Jewish legislation recommenced.[173]

These relatively calm conditions were reflected in the situation of German-Jewish youth. On the whole the youth movements were calm. There was a tendency to consolidate that which had been achieved and even the non-Zionist youth *Bund deutsch-jüdischer Jugend* (B.d.j.J.) seemed to gain some strength. Certain segments of the Zionist youth – those allied to general Zionism – also gained in strength, particularly the *Makkabi-Verband* and the I.P.D.-*Makkabi Hazair* whose numerical strength (5,000) was equal to that of *Habonim*. Within the pioneer segment of the youth, *Hechaluz* continued slowly to gain strength,

[171] Y. Hazan and B. Steinberger to Mordechai Orenstein, 11th October 1934. H.H. 3.8(1a).

[172] Ernst Fraenkel to Vaad Hapoel des Kibbutz Arzi, 29th November 1934. H.H. 2.12(1).

[173] Karl A. Schleunes, *The Twisted Road to Auschwitz. Nazi Policy Toward German Jews, 1933–1939*, Urbana 1970, p. 116. The numbers quoted by Schleunes are taken from the *Völkischer Beobachter*, 17th May 1935 – during the rise of anti-Jewish agitation – and are probably exaggerated. Beginning in January 1943, the authorities began reacting to this phenomenon by sending returnees to concentration camps.

but, on the whole, was understaffed. Gustav Horn of the *Werkleute* even became the secretary of *Hechaluz* in June 1933 and the *Werkleute* gained in prestige. *Habonim* seemed to have reached numerical saturation and concentrated on intensifying their educational and ideological work within their membership.[174]

Hashomer Hazair in Germany did not expand in 1934 beyond its 750 members and nine *kenim*. There was a certain sense of stagnation in the movement which stemmed less from the lack of expansion, but was rooted in the lack of *shlihim* and older members who could lead the younger age groups. Moreover, in Ernst Fraenkel's estimate the movement seemed to lack élan and social cohesion which could express themselves in meaningful activity and deepening of Socialist-Zionist values. The *Hanhagah Harashit* itself was depleted and only very few people worked in its central offices in Berlin; this led to overwork and consequently diminution of efficiency. But there were some bright sides as well. A number of publications were issued – e.g., 'Um die zionistische Verwirklichung' – which seemed to find resonance in larger circles. Several important personalities, e.g., Max Kreutzberger, also began to show some interest in the work of *Hashomer Hazair*.[175]

What were the prospects for the future? The *Hashomer Hazair* leadership felt it could maintain its aggressive stance – which began with the arrival of Orenstein – only if more *shlihim* could arrive from Palestine. Quick action could still help expand *Hashomer Hazair*, though any hope for a movement of thousands was nothing but an illusion. The historic moment had been missed. Fraenkel and his colleagues believed that the winter of 1934–1935 was the very last chance to reach the *stam-halutzim*, the assimilated youth and those who were vacillating between the various movements. If the moment were not seized, *Hashomer Hazair* would remain a small movement with a strong ideology. What it needed above all, were three *shlihim*: an organiser and good representative on the model of Mordechai Schenhabi; an educator who would deal with the vast educational and psychological problems confronting young people in Nazi Germany; and a woman who could lead the groups of girls who have had no role model. It was imperative to have this delegation (*mishlahat*) by the end of December 1934, or at the latest, early January.[176]

The *shlihim* from Palestine did not arrive and to the extent that there was another "historic moment" to be seized, it too, like in 1933, was missed. *Hechaluz* continued to exclude Orenstein from its work until the spring of 1935. When *Hechaluz* finally relented, it assigned Orenstein to a desk job and tried as much as possible to prevent him from contact with its people.[177] When Orenstein refused to conform, he was given an official reprimand by Yitzhak Ben Aharon, the *shaliah* of *Hakibbutz Hameuhad* in Berlin.[178] The only member of

[174]The above is based mostly on a wide-ranging report from Ernst Fraenkel to Vaad Hapoel des Kibbutz Arzi, 29th November 1934. H.H. 2.12(1).

[175]*Ibid.*

[176]*Ibid.*

[177]See [Zeev] Orbach to Eliezer Liebenstein, 3rd May 1935. Liebenstein Archive.

[178]See Yitzhak Ben Aharon to Mordechai Orenstein, 28th June 1935 and Ben Aharon to Vaad Hasnif Berlin, 3rd July 1935. Archive of Hakibbutz Hameuhad, no file indicated. For his part, Orenstein also continued to take issue with various actions of *Hakibbutz Hameuhad*. See e.g.

Hashomer Hazair leadership to take active part in *Hechaluz* activities was Ernst Fraenkel.[179] The total membership of the movement remained constant for a while and declined as members went to *hachscharah* or emigrated to Palestine.[180] In some cases there were even defections from *Hashomer Hazair* to *Habonim* which, with the full support of *Hechaluz*, continued to be a vibrant movement.[181] There was a certain stagnation of the movement and some *kenim*, e.g., Hanover, seemed to be in a state of disintegration.[182] Perhaps the one ray of light in this period was the fact that in May 1935 a new kibbutz-*aliyah* called "Mischmar" was founded from *stam-halutzim* and declared its affiliation to *Hashomer Hazair*. Mordechai Orenstein played an important role in founding this kibbutz of *stam-halutzim*; in fact this was probably Orenstein's most important concrete accomplishment as a *shaliah*. Ben Aharon's anger against Orenstein was, no doubt, fanned by the founding of this group.[183] Eventually this group of twenty-five members joined Kibbutz Mizra and Kibbutz Ein Hahoresh.

Relations between *Hakibbutz Hameuhad* people and *Hashomer Hazair* improved somewhat in the autumn of 1935, perhaps due to the fact that Mordechai Orenstein had ceased taking an active role in *Hashomer Hazair* activities until his departure for Palestine in April 1936.[184] Another factor in the new search for unity among the pioneer youth movements may very well have been the pressure of new political circumstances in Germany.[185] After a relative calm in 1934, the Nazi government began again to introduce legislative actions against the Jews.[186] These climaxed, of course, in September 1935 with the Nuremberg Laws which were amended and supplemented during the following years. They effectively ended the process of German-Jewish emancipation through a legal process. The harassments, boycotts and physical abuse that had been a by-

---

Mordechai Orenstein to Merkaz Olami des Hechaluz, 22nd July 1935. Archive of Hakibbutz Hameuhad, no file indicated. See also Mordechai Orenstein to S. Adler-Rudel, 26th June 1935. H.H. 2.31(1), concerning the composition of a delegation to the approaching Zionist congress.

[179]See Hashomer Hazair, *Hedim*, March 1935, p. 15, Daliah Archive, 9013/6.

[180]*Ibid.*, pp. 7–12.

[181]See e.g. letter from Yaakov Simon (Shimoni) to Menachem Dormann, 11th April 1935. Archive of Hakibbutz Hameuhad, no file indicated.

[182]See 'Bericht an die Weltkonferenz des Haschomer Hazair über Haschomer Hazair in Deutschland' [Summer 1935]. H.H. 2.3(1).

[183]*Ibid.*, and Protokoll der Gründungs-Sichah des Kibuz-Alija "Mischmar", Berlin, 30th May 1935. H.H. 2.12(1). See also the circular of Kibuz-Alija "Mischmar" of 12th January 1937. Archive of Kibbutz Lohamei Hagetaot, 2501: "Der Kibuz-Aliyaj 'Mischmar' will die Chawerim in der Hachscharah des deutschen Hechaluz erfassen, die sich für den ideologischen und kibuzisch-gesellschaftlichen Weg des Kibuz Arzi entscheiden wollen. Die Zusammenfassung dieser Chawerim im Kibuz-Alija 'Mischmar' soll ihre organische Eingliederung in den Kibuz Arzi ermöglichen . . ." Concerning reactions of *Habonim* to the founding of Kibbutz "Mischmar," see Zeev Orbach to Eliezer Liebenstein, 3rd May 1935, and to Menachem Dormann, 16th July 1935. Both in Archive of Kibbutz Lohamei Hagetaot, 2501.

[184]See Yaakov Simon to Mazkirut Hakibbutz Hameuhad [September 1935] , Archive of Hakibbutz Hameuhad, no file indicated. In Essen there were even attempts by *Habonim* to merge with *Hashomer Hazair*, but this failed at the last moment due to objections from the *Hashomer Hazair* leadership. See Yaakov Simon to Menachem Dormann, 11th April 1935. Archive of Hakibbutz Hameuhad, no file indicated.

[185]See reports of Moezat Hechaluz, October 1935. Archive of Kibbutz Lohamei Hagetaot, 2501.

[186]See Uwe D. Adam, *Judenpolitik im Dritten Reich*, Düsseldorf 1972, and Joseph Walk (Hrsg.), *Das Sonderrecht für die Juden im NS-Staat*, Heidelberg 1981.

product of the Nazi rise to power – and which had started anew early in 1935 – now received, as it were, added official sanction; those who were now mistreated, or whose property was "aryanised" were, after all, no longer equal citizens before the law. In the period between 1936 and 1938 a number of Jewish youth movements were disbanded – especially those advocating an existence in Germany. While *Hechaluz* and other Zionist youth movements were not outlawed, they existed in constant peril.[187]

After 1935 there was a perceptible drop in public and open Zionist activities as a letter from Georg Josephthal of the *Hechaluz* clearly shows; all discussions that dealt with Socialism had to cease immediately.[188] There was also a marked decrease in the volume of publications and of official correspondence by *Hashomer Hazair* members in Germany (as was the case generally for all German Jews). Official reports tended to be even more bland and vague than before. Personal correspondence was kept to a minimum and valuable information was either smuggled out through couriers or written from abroad. A case in point is an unsigned letter probably written by Rega Oren[stein] from Berlin:

> "I don't think I have exaggerated [in my letter sent to Palestine via a courier] . . . On the contrary, I tried to go over well-known ground. It seems to me that the most important thing in a case like ours, where there is no possibility of active defence, is to try not to panic. So far not much new has happened. Except for Ben Aharon and Adler-Rudel, no one else has been expelled . . . We are waiting to see what tomorrow will bring. Is it possible that things will calm down? I doubt it. The fact that [Georg] Kareski [President of the *Staatszionistische Organisation*] has granted an interview to *Der Angriff* [on 23rd December 1935, in which Kareski had stated his support for the Nuremberg Laws], speaks for itself . . . the internal impact has been that the ZVfD is now a bit closer to *Hechaluz*, out of the healthy instinct which says it is better to pool our resources together . . . today it is clear that there is a general ceasefire [among all Zionist groups], all along the front. We do very little, are very careful . . . We are preparing a seminar for leaders . . . we have chosen a place where we will not be disturbed [by the *Gestapo*] . . . *Davar* [the *Histadrut* newspaper] is forbidden here. It is impossible to be here without any news at all, and we must find a way to solve the problem . . . We have removed from our own publications the name *Hashomer Hazair* from the title page so it won't be too prominent . . .[189]"

Yet, this letter does not tell the entire story. The history of *Hashomer Hazair* in Germany after 1935 is not easy to reconstruct, because the volume of correspondence among members in Germany, as well as with the movement abroad, diminished greatly due to self-censorship and fear of the *Gestapo* intercepting letters and memoranda. But contrary to public appearance, the activities of *Hashomer Hazair* continued in a clandestine fashion and at great personal risk. Discussions about Socialism may no longer have been reported to the authorities, but continued nevertheless. The *ken* in Köln, e.g., conducted a seminar in 1937 on three subjects: Socialist *Weltanschauung* after the failure of Communism in Germany (discussant: Dada Pilz); Marxism as a social science

[187]See Chaim Schatzker, 'Tnuat ha-Noar ha-Yehudit be-Germanyah bitkufat ha-Shoah', *Prakim be-Toldot ha-Hevrah ha-Yehudit*, p. 455.

[188]Georg Josephthal [writing from Copenhagen] to Mazkirut Hakibbutz Hameuhad, 11th January 1936. Archive of Hakibbutz Hameuhad, container 10 file 47. "Zur Zeit hat jede sozialistische Schulungsarbeit aufgehört." As the following discussion shows, Josephthal was referring to public pronouncements on the subject.

[189][Rega Oren] to Mazkirut Havaad Hapoel [December 1935]. H.H. 3.12(1).

and a philosophic *Weltanschauung* (discussant: Georg Schuster); and *Hashomer Hazair*'s view of Zionism-Borochovism and the cultural dilemma of the modern Jew (discussant: Zvi Frisch-Raanan). At this particular seminar a man from the *Gestapo* listened to some of the proceedings, a fact that forced the participants to use pre-arranged pseudonyms.[190]

Thus, certain Zionist activities, such as large public meetings and lectures, fund-raising events, etc., greatly diminished in number, giving the impression that *Hashomer Hazair* was decreasing its level of involvement. But beneath the surface and far from the public eye, *Hashomer Hazair* became even more active in other areas such as legal immigration and aid for those wishing to depart illegally. *Hashomer Hazair* also took active part in the general German-Jewish adult education activities through the *Mittelstelle für Jüdische Erwachsenenbildung* founded by Martin Buber and Ernst Simon.[191] *Hashomer Hazair* members were just as involved in the work of the *Schule der Jüdischen Jugend* and other institutions which specifically aimed to train candidates for *Youth Aliyah* as well as illegal emigration.

There was a desperate need, perhaps more after 1935 than ever before, for *shlihim* from Palestine. In the midst of chaos and turbulence, their mere presence in *Hechaluz* and the youth movements was a stabilising and psychologically comforting factor. Yet, as the above-cited letter indicates, some foreign nationals – like Ben Aharon and Adler-Rudel – had already been expelled; the presence of others, such as Boris (Baruch) Eisenstadt (Azniah), was being scrutinised by the *Gestapo*,[192] and others were simply not allowed to enter Germany. It seemed, therefore, a stroke of good fortune that Hilde Feblowitz, formerly of the *Kadimah* and later a member of *Hashomer Hazair* in Germany and of Kibbutz Bamifneh, had arrived in Germany in the autumn of 1935 to raise money for her kibbutz.[193] At the request of the executive of *Hashomer Hazair* in Palestine she was asked to function, *a fortiori*, as the movement's emissary to Germany for one year.[194] On the whole, she had a limited impact on the German *Hashomer Hazair*, but her knowledge of the movement was important and her talents as a public speaker and organiser were highly valued. She remained in Germany until the arrival in the autumn of 1936 of the next *shaliah* in Germany – Moshe Zippor of Kibbutz Sarid.[195]

As pointed out before, the ability of the *shlihim* from Palestine to do meaningful educational work in Germany, became quite limited after 1935. Their role was to operate within the existing framework of *hachscharah*, to oversee immigration and

[190]Letter from Zvi Raanan to author [June 1986].

[191]See Ernst Simon, *Aufbau im Untergang. Jüdische Erwachsenenbildung im nationalsozialistischen Deutschland als geistiger Widerstand*, Tübingen 1959 (Schriftenreihe wissenschaftlicher Abhandlungen des Leo Baeck Instituts 2).

[192][Rega Oren] to Mazkirut Havaad Hapoel [December 1935]. H.H. 3.12(1). Eisenstadt had to leave Germany in the spring of 1937 when it became too dangerous for him to remain. See letter from Aryeh Liebman (Lavi) to Eliezer Liebenstein, 31st May 1937. Liebenstein Archive.

[193]*Ibid.*

[194]Meir Yaari to Hilde Feblowitz, 17th March 1936. H.H. 3.12(1).

[195]Abraham Tarshish to Mazkirut Hakibbutz Hameuhad, 10th October 1936. Archive of Hakibbutz Hameuhad, container 10, file 47. Upon her return to Palestine, Hilde Feblowitz left the kibbutz and moved to the city. At the time, this was seen by the members of *Hashomer Hazair* as an act of treason and even caused a degree of demoralisation.

to bolster morale. Every activity of *Hashomer Hazair* had to be reported ahead of time to the *Gestapo* with a detailed description of the agenda, number of people participating, the place and the hour on which it would take place. Often a member of the *Gestapo* would be present at the meetings. If he failed to come, those present would listen or discuss a subject close to the ideology of *Hashomer Hazair*. As soon as warning was given that the *Gestapo* was approaching, the conversation would revert to the pre-arranged subject of which the police had been notified in writing.[196] Under these circumstances, it was quite difficult to sustain an educational programme for the various age groups. Nevertheless, the extant publications show that *Hashomer Hazair* – like the other pioneer youth movements – made strong efforts to sustain it. Those *shlihim* that could still remain in Germany played a major role here. Another important contribution of the *shlihim* for the historian lies in the detailed reports they sent and diaries they kept. Over a year after the Nuremberg Laws, Abraham Tarshish (of Kibbutz Naan), one of the most respected members of *Hakibbutz Hameuhad* who was then his movement's emissary in Germany, entered a long report in his diary in October 1936 describing conditions in Germany. A number of observations of general interest, as well as relevant to the youth movements (including *Hashomer Hazair*), are reproduced here:

> "... One cannot compare [the terrible] conditions in Poland to the feelings of powerlessness and humiliation which oppress the Jew to the utmost [in Germany] ...
>
> A few remarks concerning the economic condition of the Jews in Germany: Since Hitler came to power, 95,000 Jews have emigrated from Germany (36,000 to Palestine, 20,000 to countries overseas and 38,000 to countries close to Germany – Poland, Czechoslovakia, France). There now remain less than 400,000 Jews in Germany. 83,000 of those have received financial support, i.e., almost one fourth of German Jewry ... (These 83,000 German Jews last year received aid totalling some 3,000,000 Palestinian pounds ... Imagine what we could have done with this amount of money in Palestine!) ... In addition, there is the problem of the young finishing their schooling. Every year 6,000 students finish school and more than half of them have no employment ...
>
> Within the Zionist movement there is relative peace. The Revisionists are isolated, their numbers are small (400 in *Betar* and 1,300 in the Revisionist party) ... the Right is concentrated in the *Makkabi* ... The common problems unite [the various parties] ...
>
> The conference of *Hechaluz* took place in Leipzig ... One hundred delegates from 55 localities participated. A representative of the police was there which made it difficult to carry on ... The major pioneer movements are: *Habonim* (1,000 in *hachscharah*, 5,000 in their youth movement); *Makkabi Hazair* (350 in *hachscharah*, 5,000 in their youth movement); *Werkleute* (300 in *hachscharah*, 1,000 in their youth movement); *Hashomer Hazair* (50 in *hachscharah*, 600 in their youth movement): and *stam-halutzim* (1,800 in *hachscharah*, 3,000 in other various local groups). All in all, some 20,000 people of whom 4,000 are on *hachscharah* ...
>
> The speakers for the left-wing opposition [within *Hechaluz*] were *Hashomer Hazair* and the *Werkleute*. They concentrated on the Arab Question. In Germany the ground is fertile for this issue. After the unsuccessful experience of Orenstein, the new *shaliah*, Zippor, was careful not to use strong language during the debate ... He repeated the well-known arguments about the lack of 'active' political action on the Arab Question ... Demanded that the *Histadrut* organise 3,000 Arab workers. For the sake of peace one needs to declare a bi-national state and to agree to compromises even in the area of immigration. ... Rudi Baer of the *Werkleute* also complained about neglect of the Arab Question by the *Histadrut* ...

[196]Interview by Bedolf of Oskar Mussinger (Manor), n.d. given. See also testimony of Rega Oren who arrived in Germany in 1935. Archive of Givat Havivah.

On *hachscharah* – the *Mittleren-hachscharah* encompasses only 300 out of the 4,000 ... Approximately 900 [of the older *halutzim*] are on *hachscharah* abroad (Denmark, Sweden, Holland, Italy, Czechoslovakia, Yugoslavia, Danzig), half on farms in kibbutzim and the others as individuals working for farmers (coming together for meetings every Saturday and Sunday). The entire German *hachscharah* abroad is in agriculture. In Germany there are on *hachscharah* some 3,000 pioneers, of whom 1,200 are in agriculture (of these 700 are kibbutzim on farms and the rest work alone [*bodedim*] in twenty-five central locations). In the various *Beit Hechaluz* houses in the cities there are 600; scattered individuals in the cities comprise another 700 members ...

The lack of women is noticeable in the *hachscharah*. Their numbers reach only 20% (as compared to 65% in Lithuania and 50% in Poland). There is little progress with the study of Hebrew ...

Despite various problems one must see in the *hachscharah the major accomplishment* of this generation in Germany. A project which showed the way and saved a portion of the Jewish youth in Germany. *Hechaluz* has succeeded in placing its work in the centre of German Jewry's concerns ... The fact that among the 35,000 Jews who immigrated from Germany to Palestine, there are 6,000 *halutzim*, has had an influence on public opinion.

Youth Aliyah (*Aliyat Hanoar*) – thus far, 1,400 have immigrated to Palestine, 700 of them in the last year. There are another 1,000 candidates who stand ready to immigrate. *Youth Aliyah* has raised the prestige of Zionism in Germany more than any other project ... It is necessary to bring every year 1,000 children to Palestine and to organise the rest within the *Mittleren-hachscharah*.

Expenditures of the *Reichsvertretung* for *hachscharah* and immigration during 1936: for *hachscharah* – 800,000 Mark (of these 750,000 for *hachscharah* for Palestine); for immigration 1,600,000 Mark (of these 400,000 for immigration to Palestine). In addition, the Palestinian *hachscharah* has received directly from the Jewish communities another 550,000 Mark and for immigration another 200,000 Mark ...[197]"

In his diary, Tarshish devoted space to the question of the *Werkleute*, 300 of whom (out of 1,000) were then in *hachscharah*. His analysis of their ideological path led him to conclude that, at least in Germany, they had not yet made up their mind as to whether they would join *Hakibbutz Hameuhad* or *Hakibbutz Haarzi*.[198] In fact, there were some differences among the *Werkleute* in Germany and in Palestine as to which of the two movements they would join. Those living in Germany supported *Hashomer Hazair* on the Arab Question, but felt comfortable within *Hechaluz* where they played a large role in its cultural activities. In Palestine, on the other hand, there was a much greater affinity between the *Werkleute*, who by 1936 had already settled Kibbutz Hazorea, and *Hakibbutz Haarzi*. It was clear to the leadership of *Hakibbutz Hameuhad* that although the opinion of the *Werkleute* in Germany could delay a final decision, the outcome would be determined by the members of *Hazorea*.[199] Until a final decision was made by *Hazorea* in the spring of 1938 to join *Hakibbutz Haarzi*,[200] no effort was spared by members of *Hakibbutz Hameuhad* in Germany and in Palestine to dissuade them from this step.[201]

[197][Abraham Tarshish], *Yoman Germanyah*, 18th October 1936. Archive of Hakibbutz Hameuhad, container no. 10, file 47.

[198]*Ibid.*

[199][Fritz Lichtenstein] to [Ein Harod?], July 1936. Archive of Hakibbutz Hameuhad, container 10, file 47.

[200]See letter to Shimon Pilz (member of Kibbutz Bamifneh), 2nd February 1938. Daliah Archive, 9013/11.

[201]See Abraham Tarshish to Mahlakah Hagermanit (Ein Harod), 8th December 1936. Archive of Hakibbutz Hameuhad, container 10, file 47; Beni Marshak to Mazkirut Hakibbutz Hameuhad, 7th March 1937. Archive of Hakibbutz Hameuhad, container 10, file 47; [Fritz Lichtenstein] to

While winning the battle for the bodies and souls of the *Werkleute*, *Hashomer Hazair* was less successful in attracting other people to its ranks. *Hakibbutz Hameuhad* had placed a great deal of pressure on the *stam-halutzim* to join its kibbutzim. Since *Hakibbutz Hameuhad* controlled the *Hechaluz* and therefore also the distribution of certificates for immigration to Palestine or places within the *hachscharah* groups abroad – *Hashomer Hazair* had only one *hachscharah* kibbutz in Germany, in Silingtal, which functioned until the autumn of 1937 – it had powerful persuasive tools at its disposal. Most of the rank and file *halutzim* were impressed when arguments against *Hakibbutz Haarzi* and for *Hakibbutz Hameuhad* were made by such strong personalities as Tarshish or Georg Josephthal.[202] The protests of men like Moshe Zippor (Kibbutz Sarid) or Menachem Bader (Kibbutz Mizra) who came to Berlin for a few months, were to no avail in view of the control of resources of the majority who had the power to place Zippor at the bottom of the German delegation to the twentieth Congress (August 1937), thus making his participation unlikely.[203] As the number of certificates allocated to Germany dwindled, the situation of *Hashomer Hazair* became more precarious, since only a small percentage was allocated to its members. The situation worsened in 1936/1937 when the Mandatory authorities became less generous with the special allocation of certificates for *Youth Aliyah*.[204] Ironically, the world movement of *Hashomer Hazair* with a powerful membership of 58,000[205] and thirty-three kibbutzim in Palestine,[206] was unable to help its weak branch in Germany overcome ideological and organisational obstacles and ensure their proper allocation of certificates. At most, the German *Hashomer Hazair* was allocated 5% of the total certificates.[207]

But by the end of 1937, the situation in Germany had also become very difficult for *Hechaluz*. One gets an inkling of the terrible dilemmas facing *Hechaluz* on questions of immigration and other matters from a letter written by Jocheved Bat-Rahel (Tarshish), a *Hakibbutz Hameuhad shlihah* in Germany during 1936–1938, whilst on a trip to Warsaw:

> "I must fulfil my duty from here and inform you of a few things, something I can't do from Germany . . .

A. Tarshish, 7th April 1937. Archive of Hakibbutz Hameuhad, container 10, file 47; Aryeh Liebman to Eliezer Liebenstein, 31st May 1937. Liebenstein Archive. See also the urgent plea of the *Hakibbutz Haarzi* representative in Germany to his colleagues in Palestine concerning Kibbutz Hazorea. Moshe Zippor to Mazkirut Havaad Hapoel, 30th March 1937. H.H. 3.16(1).

202 See Moshe Zippor to Mazkirut Hakibbutz Haarzi, 16th March 1937. H.H. 3.16(1).

203 Moshe Zippor to Maskirut Havaad Hapoel, 30th March 1937. H.H. 3.16(1). This had also been the case with the German delegation to the Nineteenth Congress (August/September 1935). See letter from Mordechai Orenstein to Adler-Rudel, 26th June 1935. H.H. 2.3(1).

204 Abraham Tarshish, *Yoman Germanyah*, 18th October 1936. Archive of Hakibbutz Hameuhad, container 10, file 47.

205 Havaad Hapoel (Merhavyah) to Hahanhalah Hazionit – Mahleket ha-Irgun, 9th April 1937. H.H. 3.16(1).

206 See Menachem Bader to Kibbutz Bamifneh, 12th September 1937. Daliah Archive 9013/4.

207 See diary entry of Jocheved Bat-Rahel (Tarshish) of 11th January 1937: ". . . We demanded the following distribution of certificates: the German Hechaluz 80%; Makkabi 10%; Werkleute 5%; and Hashomer Hazair 5%. Jocheved Bat-Rahel (Tarshish), *Banativ Shehalachti* (Tel-Aviv 1981), p. 169. Concerning *Hashomer Hazair*'s battle for certificates see [Tarshish] to Mahlakah Germanit, Kibbutz Ein Harod, 21st June 1937. Daliah Archive (no file number indicated). See *Banativ Shehalachti*, pp. 138 ff.

Immediately after our return from the [twentieth] Congress [August 1937], we were placed in a very difficult situation within German Jewry and because of the attitude of the authorities toward us, the Jews are in a state of deep depression. There is total resignation concerning the Zionist enterprise . . .

About a month ago the authorities began to shower us with terrible decrees, one worse than the next. The first was the announcement that they are about to liquidate a concentration camp and wish to get rid of all the Jewish prisoners. They offered to send them to Palestine, because they do not want them sent to other countries where they might lobby against Germany. They think Palestine is the most appropriate place for them. We were shocked by the offer. At issue are certificates for 190 people, a great number of whom are certainly not people we want. Some of them are imprisoned because of defilement of race; but the political prisoners may be dangerous for us in Palestine, undesirable. With the very small number of certificates at our disposal, we could not imagine how we could take this burden upon us. A few days later we were informed that the authorities have decided that they have other means at their disposal for the liquidation of the concentration camp. They sent some families their relatives' clothing, in other words, they used this terrible means to exert pressure, by killing a few people. Once again our representatives were summoned and were told that the government had appointed a liquidation committee from among the Jews . . . The situation is such that we will have to transfer to Palestine a third of these people . . . Is there any hope of persuading the government in Palestine to get a few more certificates?

Two days later we received a demand to take all youths who have completed elementary school, move them out of the cities and train them in agricultural *hachscharah* so that they will be ready to emigrate to other countries. The official reason given for this order is: so that Jewish youth will not loiter in the cities and defile the [Aryan] race. The ZVfD has prepared for the authorities a plan for removal of the youths to *hachscharah* . . .

One of the severest problems is the announcement by the authorities that within two months all foreign nationals, or those without a nationality must leave their positions within the Zionist Organisation . . . The Zionist Organisation in Berlin alone employs seventy foreign nationals. The issue for us . . . is the survival of the movement. It is not by accident that many Jews from Eastern Europe had been working for the Zionist movement. They were the directors of the most important departments and their places can't be filled by people from the rank and file . . .

As you know, Germany has been emptied of *shlihim*. The only two remaining representatives of the *Histadrut* are me and Aryeh Liebman. We are being torn to pieces, unable to do what is required of us during such a period of crisis. We ask for visas for *shlihim*. The answer has been negative . . .

In addition to this general picture, there is yet another factor. During the last few days the authorities have arrested many Communists and among them four members of *Hechaluz* . . . The *Gestapo* is very interested in finding out why we don't bring these people to Palestine . . .

The difficult situation in the movement caused by these pressures, has created a great deal of controversy among our members. There is a heated debate among us as to how to plan our daily strategies. . . .

I have painted for you a canvas full of oppressive decrees and problems. Only one thing can now encourage the movement, infuse it once again with courage – immigration. If we had hope for a larger immigration, things would look different. Despair and depression gnaw at the movement because we face a difficult reality . . .

Please pay attention to the things I have written, most of all to the practical questions, such as: the question of the people in the concentration camp, settling people in Palestine and getting the funds to do so and the question of *shlihim* . . . You can write to me in code and I will understand your hints. I am enclosing a list of code words . . ."[208]

This letter reflects, of course, not only conditions in *Hechaluz*, but in all the Zionist-Socialist youth movements. The *Gestapo* had begun to tighten its control over their activities, which had decreased drastically. Everything had to be

[208]Jocheved Bat-Rahel (Tarshish) to Vaad Hapoel shel Hahistadrut, to the attention of Remez and Rosenstein, 10th October 1937. Strictly Confidential! Archive of Hakibbutz Hameuhad, no file indicated.

planned carefully so as not to give the authorities an opportunity for arrests or expulsions. By the end of 1937 the membership of *Hashomer Hazair* declined to some 500.[209] Some of the German leaders – e.g., Adolf Schiff and Ernst Fraenkel – had already emigrated to Palestine; Schiff in 1935 and Fraenkel in 1936. Moshe Zippor also returned to Palestine in October 1937,[210] and no new reinforcement of *Hashomer Hazair shlihim* were forthcoming from Palestine – the exception being Menachem Bader who came for a brief period until the *Kristallnacht*. Nevertheless, *Hashomer Hazair* continued to plan, often in cooperation with other youth movements, seminars and winter camps,[211] though after the autumn of 1937, due to new travel regulations, it became very difficult to plan those retreats abroad.[212] Publication of educational materials also continued as long as this was possible legally and financially.[213] The new leadership of *Hashomer Hazair* (*Hahanhagah Harashit*) consisted of Georg Schuster, Ulrich Müller (Meron), Ruth Müller (Meron), Friedel Nussbaum (Manor), Seew Weiss, Dada (Shimon) Pilz, Kurt Salinger and Richard Grüneberg (Raphael Givon).[214] Despite their inexperience and meagre resources, they managed to organise activities in the various *kenim* and in Berlin even opened a new meeting place (*maon*) on Sophienstrasse.[215] The number of certificates for immigration to Palestine became ever smaller; in October 1937, only four certificates were allocated to *Hashomer Hazair* by *Hechaluz*.[216] In January 1938, only six members of *Hashomer Hazair* could receive certificates.[217] The situation was only slightly better for *Youth Aliyah* certificates.[218] Work in the various *kenim* became increasingly difficult as their leaders and members emigrated to Palestine or went to *hachscharah*.[219] In some cases, e.g., in Frankfurt, the *ken* was dissolved.[220] All along there were new orders from the authorities which made it almost impossible to carry on. Some decrees were simply of nuisance value, such as a ruling by the NSDAP in January 1938 that the word "*Ortsgruppe*" could not be employed by Jewish organisations.[221] In

[209]See Michtaw-Kescher No. 166, 7th December 1937. Daliah Archive, 9013/8. The membership cited here is taken from an official publication of *Hashomer Hazair*. Nevertheless, the leadership of *Hashomer Hazair* which now lives in Israel disputes this figure. They claim for 1936–1937 a membership of about 1,000 in the three *kenim* in Berlin and 200 throughout Germany. Letters from Dan Fraenkel to the author, 31st May 1985 and 5th July 1985.

[210]Michtaw-Kescher No. 155, 29th October 1937. Daliah Archive, 9013/8.

[211]See e.g. Michtaw-Kescher No. 153, 15th October 1937. Daliah Archive, 9013/9. One of the last *shlihim* of the *Werkleute*, David Freund of *Hazorea*, also helped with activities for *Hashomer Hazair*. Letter from Dan Fraenkel to author, 31st May 1985.

[212]See Michtaw-Kescher No. 155, 29th October 1937. Daliah Archive, 9013/8.

[213]See e.g. Hashomer Hazair, Misrad le-Schichva Alef, *Informationsblatt der Edah*, 16th March 1937. Daliah Archive, 9013/13.

[214]See Michtaw-Kescher No. 155, 29th October 1937. Daliah Archive., 9013/8.

[215]See Uli [Müller] to Shimon Pilz, 8th January 1938. Daliah Archive, 9013/11.

[216]Michtaw-Kescher No. 155, 19th October 1937. Daliah Archive, 9013/8.

[217]See letter from Uli [Müller] to Shimon Pilz, 8th January 1938. Daliah Archive, 9013/11.

[218]See Michtaw-Kescher No. 166, 7th December 1937. Daliah Archive, 9013/8.

[219]See letter from Heinz Schwarz to Ilse [Pilz], 14th February 1938. Daliah Archive, 9013/11. See also Michtaw-Kescher No. 174, 23rd January 1938. Daliah Archive, 9013/8.

[220]See Michtaw-Kescher No. 172, 17th January 1938. Daliah Archive, 9013/8.

[221]*Ibid.*

other instances the *Gestapo* arbitrarily cancelled scheduled meetings or retreats.[222]

Despite all these difficulties, it is clear that the "second generation" of leaders of *Hashomer Hazair* – those who took over in 1935 – rose to the challenge and showed exceptional ability to adjust to rapidly changing circumstances. They were able to continue the organisational and educational functions of the movement on a high level and to exercise increasing moral influence within the larger circles of German Jewry. Moreover, they did so with ever fewer resources and under greater emotional and physical strain.

By 1938 *Hashomer Hazair* continued to make extraordinary efforts to keep up its educational programme,[223] while attempting to send to Palestine as many of its members as possible, either on the regular "certificate schedule" or through *Youth Aliyah.*[224] By the spring of 1938 the leadership of the German *Hashomer Hazair* decided to send on *Youth Aliyah* any young people who wished to go, regardless of wider social or pedagogic considerations concerning the larger enterprise.[225] They also demanded that the children be brought to such institutions as the *Mossad Hinuhi* in Mishmar Haemek rather than "Ahawah" or Ben-Shemen which had no institutional or ideological connection with *Hakibbutz Haarzi.* In fact, they made it clear that if German children could be boarded together in Mishmar Haemek, it would be possible to raise funds for an expansion of the *Mossad Hinuhi* from German-Jewish sympathisers.[226]

Paradoxically, there was more need for *Hashomer Hazair*'s educational activities in 1938–1939 than ever before. But these were now conducted secretly, in the private homes of the *shomrim* and not in the local headquarters (*kenim*), a fact which also strengthened the bond of the movement with the parents. At this time *Hashomer Hazair* served as an anchor of hope in the lives of many Jewish families. For many adults who had no previous contact with the organised Jewish community, the tie to *Hashomer Hazair* through their children seemed to offer both physical and emotional relief. In fact, during these last years, *Hashomer Hazair* was one of the very few movements which dared to continue its educational activities and maintain ties with its members – as well as non-members – who wished to escape from Germany.

Following the annexation of Austria in March-April 1938, the *Hashomer Hazair* leadership in Germany also greatly helped its fellow members there. For the German leadership it seemed like an exact replay of their own situation in 1933 and once again they urgently called for help from Palestine so that the "historic moment" which had been missed in Germany, would not be allowed

[222]Uli [Müller] to Shimon Pilz, 8th January 1938. Daliah Archive, 9013/11.

[223]See Michtaw-Kescher No. 174, 23rd January 1938. Daliah Archive, 9013/8.

[224]See e.g. letter to Shimon Pilz, 2nd February 1938, Daliah Archive, 9013/11; Richard Grüneberg to Shimon Pilz, 24th February 1938, Daliah Archive, 9013/11; Ulrich Müller to [Kibbutz Bamifneh] [February/March 1938], Daliah Archive, 9013/11.

[225]Ulrich Müller to Shimon Pilz and Joseph Waschitz (Seppl), Kibbutz Bamifneh, 17th May 1938. Daliah Archive, 9013/11.

[226]H.H. Hahanhagah Harashit to Vaad Hapoel (Merhavyah), 17th May 1938. Daliah Archive, 9013/11.

to slip by in Austria.[227] The letters requesting a *shaliah* became ever more insistent. But the German *Hashomer Hazair* leadership did not simply wait for help from Palestine. Though entry to Austria was forbidden for a number of months after the *Anschluss*, five German *Hashomer Hazair shlihim* arrived in Vienna one after the other, risking their lives by crossing illegally. The Austrian *Hashomer Hazair* movement – like the rest of the Jewish community – was in a state of shock and disintegration and it is to a large extent to the credit of these German *shlihim* who arrived in 1938 and 1939 and used their own experience to teach their Austrian colleagues how to function under the Nazis, that morale was bolstered and clandestine methods for operating were devised. Clearly their efforts were responsible for saving hundreds of young men and women who managed to flee Austria illegally and eventually arrived in Palestine, where many of them still live in the kibbutzim of Nir David and Haogen.

Ironically, the authorities were willing to authorise the visas of five new *shlihim* to Germany provided they were Palestinian nationals.[228] But by then time had run out. For the first time in its history, *Hashomer Hazair* could not muster the human and financial resources for a summer camp,[229] and though valiant efforts continued in all the *kenim*, their objective difficulties were such that most activities had to cease. The exception was the *ken* in Berlin which, as late as September 1938, organised a sports festival in Grunewald.[230] In the autumn of 1938, Georg Josephthal, the secretary of *Hechaluz*, and the *shlihim* of the *Histadrut*, Schura Oschorowitsch, Jocheved Bat-Rahel (Tarshish) and Aryeh Liebman returned to Palestine,[231] further weakening the organisational structure of the pioneer movements.

In November 1938, following the *Kristallnacht*, most Zionist-organised activities ceased. The headquarters of the ZVfD at Meinekestrasse 10 – which in this period also housed the offices of *Hashomer Hazair* – had been vandalised and its furnishings destroyed. Kurt Salinger – one of the last remaining leaders of *Hashomer Hazair* in Germany – who arrived at Meinekestrasse on the morning of 10th November – recalls that when the few Zionists on the scene began to collect the papers strewn everywhere, they were told to leave because the *Gestapo* was about to return.[232] The most badly damaged offices were those of

[227] *Ibid.* See also Hahanhagah Harashit to Vaad Hapoel, 18th May 1938. Daliah Archive 9013/11: "... dass in den wichtigsten Fragen der Bewegung derartige Verzögerungen eintreten, dass wir als Bewegung historische Augenblicke versäumen und uns selbst Schaden zufügen, den wir nie werden gut machen können. Es ist doch nichts natürlicher, als die Arbeit in den Ländern zu verstärken, aus denen zur Zeit ein grosser Teil der Olim kommen". See also Joseph Waschitz, 'Hashomer Hazair be-Germanyah – Be-Zel Zlav ha-Keres', in *Sefer Hashomer Hazair*, vol. I, p. 417.

[228] Ulrich Müller (Meron) to Kibbutz Bamifneh, 23rd June 1938. Daliah Archive, 9013/11 and Ulrich Müller to Vaad Hapoel shel Hakibbutz Haarzi, 24th June 1938. Daliah Archive 9013/11.

[229] See [Ulrich Müller] to Vaad Hapoel shel Hakibbutz Haarzi, 24th June 1938. Daliah Archive, 9013/11.

[230] See Michtaw-Kescher no. 195, 10th August 1938. Daliah Archive, 9013/8.

[231] *Ibid.*, and Jocheved Bat-Rahel (Tarshish), *Banativ Shehalachti*, p. 233.

[232] Testimony of Kurt Salinger, Archive of Givat Havivah. See also interview of Menachem Bader by Bedolf, n.d. given. Bader had been at the Tempelhof airport on the morning of 10th November. When his plane was delayed, he took a taxi to Meinekestrasse, trying to help place the files in order.

Hechaluz, which were on the ground floor. The offices of *Hashomer Hazair*, which were on the top floor, had been left untouched.[233] After the *Kristallnacht* all youth movements had to cease their activities and *Hechaluz* became the only legally recognised representative *vis à vis* the *Gestapo*. Once again it resumed activities at Meinekestrasse, trying to cope with the thousands of Jews who were desperate to leave Germany. For a while, *hachscharah* centres were expanded and new ones were even founded. *Hashomer Hazair* leadership had decided to terminate its own organisation and all efforts were focused on immigration, both legal and illegal. Contacts between the leaders of *Hashomer Hazair* and the youngsters continued until the summer of 1939, even though almost all the former had already left Germany. Ironically, it was then – during the last phase of the movement – that *shlihim* from *Habonim* arrived as well as from *Hashomer Hazair* (Arthur Israelowitz), who helped transfer people to Holland and England, before they could emigrate to Palestine.[234] Soon after the beginning of the war the offices in Meinekestrasse were closed forever on 4th September 1939.[235]

CONCLUSION

In evaluating the history of *Hashomer Hazair* in Germany, it is easy to see in retrospect that one of its major weaknesses was its inability to establish a strong political power base within German Jewry in general and within *Hechaluz* in particular. This weakness was due first and foremost to its small size. At its very height, the movement did not encompass more than 750 members, possibly 1,000 according to contemporary testimony. But size was not the only factor in hindering *Hashomer Hazair* from gaining political power. After all, the *Werkleute* and the *Bachad* were more or less equal in size to *Hashomer Hazair*, yet had more influence within *Hechaluz*. Rather, it seems that the lack of political clout was

[233]Testimony of Kurt Salinger.

[234]Testimony of Kurt Salinger.

[235]Letter from Pino [Ginsburg] to Mahlakah Germanit, 4th September 1939. Archive of Hakibbutz Hameuhad, container 10, file 49. On the possible activities after 1939 of some members of *Hashomer Hazair* in the so-called "Baum Gruppe", see Jizchak Schwersenz and Edith Wolff, 'Jüdische Jugend im Untergrund', *loc. cit.*, pp. 13 ff.; Helmut Eschwege, 'Resistance of German Jews against the Nazi Regime', in *LBI Year Book XV* (1970), pp. 143–180; Konrad Kwiet and Helmut Eschwege, *Selbstbehauptung und Widerstand. Deutsche Juden im Kampf um Existenz und Menschenwürde, 1933–1945*, Hamburg 1984 (Hamburger Beiträge zur Sozial-und Zeitgeschichte Band XIX), pp. 114–139; Wolfgang Wippermann, 'Die Berliner Gruppe Baum und der Jüdische Widerstand', in *Beiträge zum Thema Widerstand* (19), Informationszentrum Berlin 1981; Bernard Mark, 'Die Gruppe Herbert Baum. Eine jüdische Widerstandsgruppe in den Jahren 1937–1942', in *Blätter für Geschichte* XIV, Warsaw 1961, pp. 32 ff; Lucien Steinberg, *Jews Against Hitler*, Glasgow 1978. Also letter to the author by Mrs. Hannah Opher (1st December 1985), concerning the activities of her sister, Hilde Levy, a member of *Hashomer Hazair* in the *Baum-Gruppe*. Those members of *Hashomer Hazair* who joined the *Baum-Gruppe* did so as individuals and on their own responsibility. See also letter from Zvi Raanan to author [June 1986]. Raanan confirms the fact that some *Hashomer Hazair* members joined the *Baum-Gruppe*.*

*See also the essay by Eric Brothers, 'On the Anti-Fascist Resistance of German Jews', in this volume of the Year Book – (Ed.).

due to the ideology of *Hashomer Hazair*, which was more leftist-radical, less compromising, and therefore more threatening to the rest of the youth movements and *Hechaluz*.

Perhaps another one of *Hashomer Hazair*'s failures was its inability – especially after 1933 – to adjust ideologically and organisationally to the new situation prevailing in Germany, e.g., in failing to open its ranks early on and with enthusiasm to the so-called *stam-halutzim*. This inflexibility deterred it from cooperating with other youth movements and *Hechaluz* until, literally, the last moment when such cooperation was practically forced upon it by new circumstances.

One can, of course, contend that *Hashomer Hazair*'s ideology was by its very nature elitist and therefore precluded the admission of large groups of *stam-halutzim*. Indeed, its absolute demand for immigration to Palestine and for kibbutz life excluded many young men and women whose commitment to Zionism was of a different (as the movement would hold – less committed) nature. One could also argue from hindsight that unlike *Habonim*, which did admit the *stam-halutzim*, *Hashomer Hazair* members – on the whole – remained loyal to kibbutz life even when their personal fortunes took them to Palestine via long detours in England or Latin America. In other words, the power of *Hashomer Hazair* ideology is visible even today, whereas many of the *stam-halutzim* left their kibbutzim soon after arrival in Palestine. But this admitted success of *Hashomer Hazair* does not detract from the perception of many in the 1930s that in light of the special dangers facing German Jewry, more flexibility was necessary in admitting to *Hashomer Hazair* ranks those who needed its spiritual and physical framework.

While fighting for their existence, German Jews were obviously not in the position to sit back dispassionately to examine why *Hashomer Hazair* was unable to adjust ideologically to new conditions in Germany. This is a much easier task for the historian looking at the facts some five decades later. The following explanations seem relevant as background for this inflexible posture: (a) *Hashomer Hazair* was a typically elitist youth movement by virtue of its uncompromising demands for personal fulfilment which included pioneer work and kibbutz life – so much so that *Hashomer Hazair* formed a sect-like or order-like organisation. The movement actually cut the ties of its members to their own families. Emotionally and socially it became an alternate home for them and developed for them a rich inner life. It lacked the kind of warm Jewishness which characterised some other movements and this was reflected in its attitude to the *stam-halutzim*; not because of a condescension of superior beings towards those held in low esteem, but due to demands which the average person simply could not, or would not, fulfil.

(b) This extreme, almost fanatical attitude, fitted in well with Socialist political-ideological extremism. Thus, *Hashomer Hazair* was the last link between Jewish nationalism and Jewish cosmopolitanism – in its Communist and Liberal variants. Such extreme positions do not attract many people, while at the same time they invite attack from many sides.

(c) Due to different circumstances, this ideological extremism could draw to its ranks some 50,000 members and more in Eastern Europe, out of a total Jewish population of six million. Why did it not – proportionately – draw similar numbers in Germany? Probably due to the special Jewish-cultural complexity of German Jewry, which lived in two distinct worlds: culturally, it belonged to Germany; socially it lived within Jewish society while at the same time – in varying degrees – cut off from Jewish culture and an historical Jewish awareness. The lack of an emotional-national-Jewish foundation created enormous difficulties after the rise of the Nazis to power. None of the Zionist groups in Germany was able to find a totally satisfying solution to this problem. In Eastern Europe it was possible for *Hashomer Hazair* to rely on the existence of a strong Jewish identity and on this basis to require personal commitment from its members, i.e., pioneer life on the kibbutz. This element of strong Jewish identity was almost totally lacking in Germany. Indeed, the tie to Judaism was based almost exclusively on Zionist ideology. Perhaps one can go even further and state that their positive emotional tie to the Jewish nation was almost solely through the youth movement, while requiring a total break with their parents against whom they rebelled and who were, in any case, in a state of confusion and disorientation after the Nazis' rise to power. The young Jewish men and women became Jewish due to external forces and their decision for Zionism evolved through pride, without a positive Jewish cultural and national foundation. Thus, when a movement like *Hashomer Hazair* came and demanded an extreme Jewish-national commitment under the dual flag of pioneer Zionism and Socialism within the framework of the kibbutz, it could hardly expect that the masses would swell its ranks.

But a critical evaluation of *Hashomer Hazair* in Germany must also take into account the stance of its world leadership, both in Warsaw and in Palestine. After all, *Hashomer Hazair* in Germany was not a spontaneous phenomenon, but was initiated from the outside, finding an echo among German-born Jews. The documentation at hand does not clarify why the world movement had decided so late to found a branch in Germany, but it is clear that it had missed its chance when it failed to fill a vacuum in the early 1920s, when a number of youth movements in Germany had either split or gone out of existence. It is just as clear that the world movement missed the historic moment for the second time when it lacked the vision to seize the opportunities for expansion in Germany after 1933. It is this total failure to realise the crisis at hand which may explain why for an entire year after the spring of 1933, *Hashomer Hazair* in Germany was left without a *shaliah* from Palestine. After 1933, with the increase in the ideological and psychological importance of *Hakibbutz Haarzi* and the corresponding low morale and lack of confidence and human resources in Germany, it was more important than ever to send emissaries from Palestine.[236] It is difficult to find an explanation for this lack of foresight. One is tempted to generalise by blaming an essentially Eastern European leadership with lack of understanding for the needs of Western European Jewry. This argument fails, however, in light of the reaction of *Hakibbutz Hameuhad* leadership, composed of

[236]See Henry Near, *Hakibbutz ve-ha-Hevra, 1923–1933*, Jerusalem 1984, p. 41.

men and women with backgrounds and experiences very similar to those of *Hakibbutz Haarzi*. Why did *Hakibbutz Hameuhad* realise the momentous impact of 1933 and send to Germany such outstanding men and women as Enzo Sereni, Eliezer Liebenstein, Yitzhak Ben Aharon, Abraham and Jocheved Tarshish, while *Hakibbutz Haarzi* sent Mordechai Orenstein after a one year hiatus? As was shown, when Orenstein left in the spring of 1936, there were again many long gaps between the *shlihim* who followed him. Was the lack of help due to the fact that the small *Hashomer Hazair* in Germany could not provide the human resources necessary for building up the Palestinian movement? Were there ideological considerations that were not articulated? Perhaps part of the answer lies in the scarcity of human and financial resources,[237] but this is, at best, a partial answer. Whatever the reasons, clearly *Hakibbutz Haarzi* did not consider the small movement of *Hashomer Hazair* in Germany among its foremost priorities.

Perhaps, given the ideological and cultural condition of German Jewry as described above – more *shlihim* in Germany would have made little difference. But once again, this is possible to assess and state only in hindsight. The fact remains that the leadership of *Hashomer Hazair* at the time – throughout the 1930s – felt that more *shlihim* were an absolute necessity. Though the German-born leadership of *Hashomer Hazair* rose to the challenge facing them, they also felt demoralised and abandoned, especially since the *Habonim* and *Hechaluz* did receive more *shlihim*. It is quite possible that more *shlihim* would not have strengthened or expanded the movement physically, but it is impossible to underrate the moral boost they would have provided during these critical times. This, in any case, was the perception of the *shomrim* in Germany.

If one then looks at the record of *Hashomer Hazair* in Germany from 1931 to 1939 in light of the lack of support it received from its parent-movement and in light of the strong opposition of the *shlihim* of *Hakibbutz Hameuhad*, one must arrive at the conclusion that its achievements far outweighed its failures and that the failures, such as they were, were in large measure due to circumstances beyond its control.

What were the German *Hashomer Hazair*'s achievements? During the entire period of its existence, the movement succeeded in establishing and maintaining a lifestyle unique to the ideology of *Hashomer Hazair*, to bequeath the values of its ideology and to shape the personal identity of its members. Moreover it gave those involved, a political education on the basis of Marxist Zionism, without accepting Marxism blindly and clearly making some major modifications so as to streamline it with Zionism. Within the German pioneer-Socialist camp too (youth movements and *Hechaluz*), it fought for its right to express its own ideas and keep an autonomous stance in all matters relating to practical work and ideology – often at a cost to its organisational and intra-Zionist power base. In fact, one of the remarkable aspects about *Hashomer Hazair* – as well as other Jewish youth movements – is that, despite the National Socialist regime and in

[237]The total membership of *Hakibbutz Haarzi* in 1933 was 2,009, as compared to 3,200 of *Hakibbutz Hameuhad*. *Ibid*., p. 264.

the face of the acute danger which lurked for all of them, they continued with their ideological battles without giving ground. It is testimony to their high moral and intellectual qualities and an indication of their dynamism and vitality.

There were no ideological changes in the German *Hashomer Hazair* from its first *Bundestag* in Budau (Czechoslovakia) in August 1932. The guidelines established at that conference remained in force until the very end of the movement. All educational activities remained within their framework. Nevertheless, the last few years in the movement's existence saw greater emphasis on the acquisition of Jewish values in addition to the study of Marxist sources. There was also a heightened awareness – stemming from both Marxist and Jewish studies – on the need for Arab-Jewish cooperation. Throughout the 1930s the ideological battle of *Hashomer Hazair* concentrated on two fronts: against the so-called "red assimilation" and, within the pioneer movement, against the ideological stance of *Habonim* and *Hakibbutz Hameuhad*. There is little doubt that after 1933 *Hashomer Hazair* gave a segment of German-Jewish youth an emotional and psychological boost that for many served as their lifeline in a sea of hatred and misery.*

Perhaps the greatest strength of the German *Hashomer Hazair* was its pedagogic approach, which required a high level of commitment to the ideology and lifestyle while providing an all-embracing social and organisational framework that went beyond classrooms, occasional seminars and summer camps.[238] This approach, which was taught by example, certainly had an impact on a certain segment of the German-Jewish youth. One can also make the case that German members of *Hashomer Hazair* who had been directed to England,[239] Holland and Argentina were responsible for establishing the first *Hashomer Hazair* groups in those countries. Moreover, they continued to maintain their group ties and their educational and ideological activities. The result was that almost all members of the German *Hashomer Hazair* who had fled to England and elsewhere, eventually emigrated to Palestine and joined kibbutzim. Another practical achievement has been, of course, the establishment of Kibbutz Daliah, which has succeeded in absorbing and putting into practice the best values some of its members had brought with them from the German *Hashomer Hazair*. Many other kibbutzim have also greatly benefited from the large numbers of German *Hashomer Hazair* members who arrived via *Youth Aliyah* or through other legal and illegal means.

*A more concise version of this essay, 'Hashomer Hazair in Nazi Germany', was published in *Die Juden im Nationalsozialistischen Deutschland/The Jews in Nazi Germany 1933–1943*, herausgegeben von Arnold Paucker mit Sylvia Gilchrist und Barbara Suchy, Tübingen 1986 (Schriftenreihe wissenschaftlicher Abhandlungen des Leo Baeck Instituts 45) – (Ed.).

238An outstanding sample of this approach is Ernst Fraenkel's speech given in 1936 and published a year later under the title: 'Die Aufgaben einer jüdischen Erziehung im Bunde', in *Rundschreiben*, February/March 1937. Daliah Archive, 901/3, file 6.

239Arthur and Naomi Israelowitz (Ben Israel) of Kibbutz Beit Alfa were the *Hashomer Hazair shlihim* in England at the beginning of 1939. Members of *Hashomer Hazair* in England helped run a coal mine near Manchester. The men worked in the mine and the women as hired domestics.

Revisionist Zionism in Germany (II) Georg Kareski and the Staatszionistische Organisation, 1933–1938

BY FRANCIS R. NICOSIA

When Hitler became Chancellor in Germany on 30th January 1933,* the fortunes of Revisionism within the German Zionist movement were at perhaps their lowest ebb since 1925.[1] At a time when National Socialism had finally achieved the power with which to destroy the Jewish community in Germany, the Revisionist movement found itself in a state of bitter division, demoralisation and uncertainty. This rendered Revisionism not only incapable of achieving the dominant voice within the German Zionist movement that it had long sought, but also was an impediment to its ability to deal with the cataclysmic events that would soon befall the Jews of Germany.

After 1933, Revisionist Zionism in Germany was characterised by its own virtual isolation. The independent *Staatszionistische Organisation*, established early in 1934, absorbed the several Revisionist fragments left from the disintegration of the old Revisionist *Landesverband* in 1932 and 1933. Excluded from the *Zionistische Vereinigung für Deutschland* (ZVfD) and the World Zionist Organisation (WZO), it was also forced to maintain its independence from Jabotinsky's *Welt-Union*, later his independent New Zionist Organisation and from the Jewish State Party.[2] Thus, the *Staatszionisten* were not only cut off from the main body of the Zionist movement in Germany and abroad, they were also separated from the international Revisionist movement itself. A reflection of this isolation was the new organisation's obvious lack of a recognised leader of international stature, with strong international ties and influence, something which Richard Lichtheim had provided for the Revisionist *Landesverband* from

*I wish to thank Dr. Ronald Provost, Academic Dean of Saint Michael's College, Vermont, for his encouragement and much of the financial support that made the research for this essay possible.

[1]For the only account of Revisionist Zionism in Germany before 1933 in English or German see Francis R. Nicosia, 'Revisionist Zionism in Germany (I). Richard Lichtheim and the Landesverband der Zionisten-Revisionisten in Deutschland, 1926–1933', in *LBI Year Book XXXI* (1986), pp. 209–240. Of course Revisionist failures before 1933 must be considered within the context of the overall failure of the Zionist movement in Germany to neutralise the strong liberal inclinations and German national identity of the vast majority of German Jews, and specifically the failure of the *Zionistische Vereinigung für Deutschland* to replace the *Centralverein deutscher Staatsbürger jüdischen Glaubens* as the dominant Jewish political organisation during the Weimar Republic. See Donald L. Niewyk, *The Jews in Weimar Germany*, Baton Rouge 1980, p. 156.

[2]Herbert S. Levine, 'A Jewish Collaborator in Nazi Germany. The Strange Career of Georg Kareski, 1933–1937', *Central European History*, 8 (1975), p. 260. See also Abraham Margaliot, 'The Dispute over the Leadership of German Jewry (1933–1938)', in *Yad Vashem Studies*, vol. X (1974), pp. 129–148.

1926 to 1933.[3] It was a significantly different and greatly weakened Revisionist movement in Germany that would attempt to meet the crisis as well as the opportunities created for German Zionism by the National Socialist *Machtübernahme* in 1933.

German Revisionists had already embarked on a path somewhat different and independent from the Revisionist movement abroad during the stormy debates among Revisionists immediately following the Zionist Congress at Basle in 1931. Those debates were the culmination of several years of frustration and futility which had characterised the Revisionist effort to secure control of the world Zionist movement, and reflected the realisation that the successful removal of Chaim Weizmann from the presidency of the WZO had changed very little, and had not brought Revisionism any closer to the dominant position it sought within the Zionist movement. They centred around the question of separation from the World Zionist Organisation and of the creation of an independent Revisionist-Zionist movement, something that Vladimir Jabotinsky had been advocating since 1930 if not before.[4] In September, 1931, the Revisionist World Executive decided at a meeting in Calais to withdraw the Revisionist *Welt-Union* from the WZO and although permitting individual Revisionists to remain affiliated with the WZO through their respective national Zionist organisations, nevertheless imposed upon them strict Revisionist party discipline.[5]

The German Revisionist *Landesverband*, on the other hand, reflecting both the convictions of Richard Lichtheim about keeping the world Revisionist movement within the WZO, and the nature and overwhelming dominance of the traditionally more liberal German Zionist leadership in the ZVfD, took a different approach at its meeting in Berlin in October, 1931.[6] For German Revisionists, the more immediate problem had been their utter failure to secure any changes in the solidly entrenched leadership and policies of the ZVfD, even after Weizmann's temporary eclipse at Basle in 1931. Thus, reflecting an open

[3]Among Lichtheim's considerable efforts in the German and international Revisionist movements from 1926 to 1933, none was more noteworthy than his determined effort to keep the German and world Revisionist organisations within the World Zionist Organisation. It was his conviction that Revisionist Zionism had no chance whatever of success outside the world movement, one that contributed to his growing aloofness from Revisionist affairs after the events of 1931–1933, and after his departure from Germany for Palestine in 1933. See Nicosia, 'Revisionist Zionism (I)', *loc. cit.*, pp. 229–238.

[4]The most comprehensive accounts of Jabotinsky and the history of the Revisionist movement are: Joseph Schechtman[n]. *Rebel and Statesman: The Vladimir Jabotinsky Story. The Early Years*, New York 1956, and *Fighter and Prophet. The Vladimir Jabotinsky Story. The Last Years*, New York 1961; Joseph Schechtmann and Yehuda Benari, *History of the Revisionist Movement*, vol. I, Tel-Aviv 1970. A much more objective, although much less comprehensive, picture than the above defences of Jabotinsky and Revisionism can be found in: Walter Laqueur, *A History of Zionism*, New York 1972. On the opposite side, and in a decidely anti-Revisionist, anti-Zionist vein, there is the recently-published work by Lenni Brenner, *The Iron Wall. Zionist Revisionism from Jabotinsky to Shamir*, London 1984. Brenner's history of Revisionism seeks primarily to discredit the governments and policies of the State of Israel since the election of Menachem Begin and the *Likud* to office in 1977 by tracing their roots in Revisionist history, rather than to provide a comprehensive history of Revisionism itself.

[5]See Nicosia, 'Revisionist Zionism (I)', *loc. cit.*, p. 233.

[6]*Ibid.*, pp. 233–234.

split between Lichtheim and Jabotinsky over post-Basle Revisionist tactics, particularly in the matter of secession from the WZO, the Revisionist *Landesverband* in Germany chose to withdraw from the ZVfD, but to remain as a separate German Zionist party within the WZO. The separation of the Revisionist *Landesverband* from the ZVfD, which Lichtheim himself would later characterise as contrary to the traditional unity of all competing factions and political currents within German Zionism, was initiated by the Revisionists themselves.[7] The separation was confirmed by the *Geschäftsführender Ausschuss* of the ZVfD on 14th October 1931, when in effect it made membership in the Revisionist *Landesverband* incompatible with continued membership in the ZVfD, a move that was supported by the Zionist Executive in London in December.[8] Thus, by 1932, German Revisionism was cut off from the larger German and world Zionist movements; moreover the Hitler regime's traumatic assault on the Jewish community in Germany after 1933, and the wrenching debates over the proper Jewish response to that assault, would force a greatly weakened and reorganised German Revisionist movement to further isolate itself by avoiding links with Revisionist organisations abroad.

I. THE SHATTERED UNITY, 1932–1933

Whatever unity did exist in the ranks of the Revisionist *Landesverband* at its meeting in Berlin in October 1931, quickly evaporated in 1932. The deepening rift, within the world Revisionist movement, over the question of independence from the WZO specifically between Jabotinsky on the one hand and Richard Lichtheim and Meier Grossmann on the other, was not bridged at the World Conference of Zionists-Revisionists in Vienna in August 1932, where the Calais compromise was retained against the strong objections of Lichtheim, Grossmann and their supporters.[9] An already divided and weakened Revisionist *Landesverband* in Germany formally divided into two rival factions during the autumn/winter of 1932–1933, a split which reflected the larger division in international Revisionist ranks between Jabotinsky and his critics.

Although there are no reliable figures available, it appears that most of the German Revisionist membership supported Lichtheim's position that the world Revisionist movement should remain in the WZO, although the *Landesvorstand* sympathised with Jabotinsky, at least to the extent that Revisionist discipline should supersede that of the WZO. As a result of the failure of the Revisionist conference in Vienna in August to repudiate the Calais resolutions and to reaffirm Revisionist ties to the WZO, Lichtheim resigned his position as chairman of the *Landesvorstand* on 13th September 1932, and was replaced by Hans Bloch.[10] At the 1st November 1932 meeting of the reconstituted

[7]See Richard Lichtheim, *Geschichte des deutschen Zionismus*, Jerusalem 1954, pp. 241–242. Adolf Böhm perhaps best describes this tradition in German Zionism in his *Die zionistische Bewegung 1918 bis 1925*, Bd. 2, Berlin 1937, pp. 497–498.

[8]See Nicosia, 'Revisionist Zionism (I)', *loc. cit.*, pp. 235–236.

[9]See Nicosia, 'Revisionist Zionism (I)', *loc. cit.*, pp. 237–238.

[10]*Jüdische Rundschau*, XXXVIII, No. 4 (13th January 1933).

Landesvorstand of the Revisionist *Landesverband*, under the chairmanship of Bloch, there was much criticism of the Executive of the Revisionist *Welt-Union* in London, which was dominated by Meier Grossmann and his supporters opposed to separation from the WZO and to the primacy of Revisionist discipline.[11] While the minutes reveal the generally sympathetic posture of the *Landesvorstand* towards Jabotinsky in his battle with Grossmann and the Revisionist Executive in London, they also acknowledge the strong support within the German Revisionist movement for Grossmann and the Revisionist Executive, particularly that of Richard Lichtheim.

By the end of 1932, Lichtheim and some of his supporters decided to break with the *Landesvorstand* of the Revisionist *Landesverband*, and to establish a separate faction with allegiance to Grossmann and the Revisionist Executive in London, and full participation in the WZO. As he had done one year earlier with the secession of the Revisionist *Landesverband* from the ZVfD, Lichtheim again initiated a process of separation, although on a more limited scale, from the larger organisation in the effort to preserve and promote his view of Revisionist interests in Germany. Calling itself the *Verband Deutscher Zionisten-Revisionisten*, the new organisation officially came into being early in January 1933, in time for the elections to the Revisionist *Delegiertentag* of 8th January in Berlin.[12] Its *Landesvorstand* included Richard Lichtheim (chairman), Justus Schloss and Ernst Hamburger. According to the *Jüdische Rundschau*, the new organisation was the result of the unresolved differences within the Revisionist *Welt-Union* which had inevitably led to a parting of the ways within the German movement.[13] It also renounced Jabotinsky's leadership, declared its loyalty to the existing Revisionist Executive in London and its role of representing all German Revisionists who chose to remain in the WZO. Its activities were reported from time to time in the *Jüdische Rundschau* during the first half of 1933, and included the organisation of group tours of Palestine, the offering of courses in modern Hebrew, the dissemination of Revisionist literature, especially the writings of Richard Lichtheim, and lectures by Revisionist officials.

The new organisation was also quick to present itself as the only legitimate representative of Revisionist Zionism in Germany. An undated '*Communiqué*', signed by Ernst Hamburger and circulated to members of the German Revisionist movement probably in early January 1933, asserted in the following manner that the *Verband Deutscher Zionisten-Revisionisten* alone possessed the authority to represent Revisionist interests in Germany: "Der Verband Deutscher Zionisten-Revisionisten teilt mit, dass er allein berechtigt ist, namens der legal gewählten Instanzen der Revisionisten zu handeln, und insbesondere auch den anerkannten Sonderverband der Zionisten-Revisionisten (mit dem er

[11]Jabotinsky Institute (hereafter cited as JI)/Tel-Aviv: 2/5/21. Protokoll der Sitzung des erweiterten Landesvorstandes vom 1. November 1932. In the minutes of this meeting, Lichtheim was listed as absent without excuse.

[12]JI/Tel-Aviv: 2/5/21. Landesverband der Zionisten-Revisionisten in Deutschland an die Union der Zionisten-Revisionisten/London, 27. Dezember 1932.

[13]*Jüdische Rundschau*, XXXVIII, No. 40 (19th May 1933).

praktisch identisch ist) zu vertreten."[14] The '*Communiqué*' further counselled all Revisionists in Germany to direct all future correspondence and financial contributions to the new organisation, and reaffirmed its commitment to struggle for the principles of Revisionism, albeit within the framework of the World Zionist Organisation.

The issues dividing German Revisionists were given greater urgency just two days before their *Delegiertentag* of 8th January 1933. On 6th January, the WZO suspended the *Sonderverband der Zionisten-Revisionisten* which had been operating as an independent Revisionist organisation within the WZO since 1931.[15] Reacting to the decision taken by the Revisionist *Welt-Union* in Vienna in August 1932, which had reaffirmed the Calais resolutions and the primacy of Revisionist discipline, the WZO resolved that a higher "Disziplinpflicht" as well as independent political action were incompatible with membership in the WZO. The report in the *Jüdische Rundschau* also noted that the Zionist Executive in London had tried in vain to get the *Sonderverband* to adopt a clear position on these questions, presumably one opposed to that adopted by the Revisionists in Vienna. In Germany, however, the Revisionist movement was virtually paralysed by its own internal conflicts between August 1932, and January 1933, and Lichtheim and his supporters had not yet been able to assert their control and thus to repudiate the Vienna decisions.[16]

According to the *Jüdische Rundschau*, the Revisionist *Delegiertentag* of 8th January 1933, was dominated by the recent suspension of the *Sonderverband* by the WZO.[17] Jabotinsky attended the meeting and spoke forcefully about the questions of Revisionist discipline and independent political action in light of the suspension of the Revisionist *Sonderverband*. He posed the question: "Kann die Union bei ihren politischen Aktionen, auch nach dem Urteil des Ehrengerichtes, auf die aktive Leistung aller ihrer Mitglieder rechnen?" He further outlined the two choices faced by the Revisionist *Welt-Union*, namely complete subordination to the WZO and its policies, or a role as the only bearer of "Judenstaats-Zionismus", with the right to independent activity in every facet of the building of the Jewish State. As he had done for a long time, Jabotinsky favoured the second option, arguing: "Jede sentimentale oder schwärmerische Beziehung zu 'Kongresseroberung' muss aufhören."

[14]JI/Tel-Aviv: 2/5/21. *Communiqué* von Ernst Hamburger, no date. The *Sonderverband der Zionisten-Revisionisten* to which the *Communiqué* refers was the name of the Revisionist party which continued to operate as an independent faction within the WZO after the Calais meeting and resolutions of 1931. It consisted of those Revisionists who chose to remain in the WZO. The statement that the new *Verband Deutscher Zionisten-Revisionisten* was practically identical to the Revisionist *Sonderverband* in the WZO reflected the strong allegiance of the new organisation to the WZO, and perhaps its success in maintaining the support of most German Revisionists. It went to great pains during the first seven months or so to demonstrate that it did have that kind of support. See for example: JI/Tel-Aviv: 2/5/21. Verband Deutscher Zionisten-Revisionisten (Hamburger) an die *Jüdische Rundschau*, 28th May 1933; and *Jüdische Rundschau* XXXVIII, No. 45/46 (9th June 1933).

[15]*Jüdische Rundschau*, XXXVIII, No. 3 (10th January 1933).

[16]Lichtheim was not able to attract enough votes in the 4th January 1933 elections to be elected as a voting representative to the 8th January Revisionist *Delegiertentag*. This was the first time he had experienced such an electoral failure, and it was indicative of the divisions which still prevailed in Revisionist ranks in Germany, particularly in Berlin, by the beginning of 1933.

[17]*Jüdische Rundschau*, XXXVIII No. 4 (13th January 1933).

Clearly Jabotinsky was addressing the critical decision that individual Revisionists in Germany, most of whom appear to have favoured continued membership in the WZO, would have to make. To what extent would the suspension of their *Sonderverband* by the WZO affect their attitudes and conduct within the Revisionist *Welt-Union* which, as an organisation, had not been a part of the WZO since 1931, and which was no longer recognised by the WZO as a Zionist body? The decisions reached by the *Delegiertentag* reflected the ongoing divisions within the German Revisionist movement; they indicated that a compromise between Jabotinsky's supporters and Lichtheim's *Verband Deutscher Zionisten-Revisionisten* in the form of some combination of their respective positions was necessary to avert a complete breakdown. The delegates decided both to continue independent Revisionist political activities and, with Jabotinsky's reluctant support, to conduct an all-out election campaign for the forthcoming Eighteenth Zionist Congress.[18]

However, the compromise reached at the Berlin *Delegiertentag* in January 1933 was an utterly unrealistic attempt to resolve the problems facing the German Revisionist movement. The independent political activity that they resolved to continue was certainly incompatible with any role in the WZO, such as they presumably hoped to achieve with a strong showing in the elections for the Eighteenth Zionist Congress. Moreover the continuous and ever deepening struggle on the international level between Jabotinsky and the Revisionist Executive in London, leading towards a permanent split in Revisionist ranks later that year, only added to the pressures which were pulling the Revisionist *Landesverband* in Germany apart. At the meeting of the *Parteirat* of the *Welt-Union* in Kattowitz in March 1933, the familiar battle between Jabotinsky and Grossmann was fought again.[19] Jabotinsky reviewed the two major currents in Revisionism since 1931, namely independent political activity and organisation for the creation of a Jewish State in Palestine, versus a policy of trying to conquer the WZO from within. Grossmann countered with the argument that some independent political action was compatible with strict adherence to Zionist discipline, and that the Revisionists could indeed conquer the WZO from within. Both referred repeatedly to the Calais resolutions of 1931, and their reaffirmation in Vienna a year later, as attempts to reconcile the two, attempts which Jabotinsky also labelled as failures. At Kattowitz, the two sides again tried to avoid the inevitable split, as they had so often done in the past, and the *Parteirat* meeting ended in utter confusion, with nothing resolved.[20]

Shortly after the Kattowitz disaster, Jabotinsky decided to make use of his continued popularity among the rank and file of the Revisionist movement in order to make a clean break with his critics, and to subordinate the movement to his authority. On 23rd March, he suspended the Revisionist Executive and all other elected bodies in the *Welt-Union*, which had been dominated by Grossmann and other critics, personally assumed the full leadership of the

[18]*Ibid.* See also: JI/Tel-Aviv: 2/5/21. Ernst Hamburger an das Zentralbüro des Sonderverbandes, 12th January 1933.

[19]See *Jüdische Rundschau*, XXXVIII, No. 24 (24th March 1933), and No. 25, (28th March 1933).

[20]See Laqueur, *A History of Zionism*, *op. cit.*, p. 358.

organisation and set out to create a new provisional Executive.[21] This marked the final, formal split in the Revisionist movement that had been in the making since the Seventeenth Zionist Congress in 1931, and which was the critical first step towards the formal establishment of the fully independent Revisionist Zionist organisation that Jabotinsky had desired since 1930.

It also had an immediate, and equally disintegrating effect on the weak, divided Revisionist *Landesverband* in Germany. Jabotinsky's main support could be found in the *Landesvorstand* of the *Landesverband*, under the chairmanship of Hans Bloch. At its meeting of 27th March, 1933, the majority endorsed Jabotinsky's actions, as was reported in an article entitled 'Die Spaltung der Revisionisten' in the *Jüdische Rundschau*:

> "Der Landesvorstand der Zionisten-Revisionisten in Deutschland teilt mit: 'Der Landesverband der Zionisten-Revisionisten in Deutschland stellt sich eindeutig hinter die Führung Jabotinskys und hat in seiner Sitzung vom 27. März 1933 mit überwiegender Mehrheit beschlossen, entsprechend dem Aufruf Jabotinskys vom 23. März 1933 die politische Arbeit aufzunehmen.' "[22]

Two days later, the *Landesvorstand* informed the Executive of the Revisionist *Welt-Union* in London, which Jabotinsky had just dissolved, that the *Landesverband* no longer recognised the authority of the Executive, and that it would henceforth accept only the authority of Jabotinsky.[23] In this letter of 29th March, the *Landesverband* concluded: "Wir beendigen mit diesem Briefe unsere Korrespondenz mit der bisherigen Londoner Exekutive und werden uns in allen zukünftigen Fragen und Entscheidungen an das von Herrn Jabotinsky eingesetzte Sekretariat wenden."[24] Just one month later, the Revisionist Executive in turn dissolved the *Landesvorstand* of the German *Landesverband* with the following words:

> "Wir bestätigen den Empfang Ihres Schreibens vom 29. März und teilen Ihnen mit, dass das Exekutiv-Komitee wegen Ihres Disziplinbruches, der in Ihrer Resolution vom 27. März zum Ausdruck gekommen ist, beschlossen hat, den Landesvorstand aufzulösen."[25]

The London Executive also informed the *Landesverband* that it was entrusting Richard Lichtheim with the establishment and leadership of a provisional *Landesvorstand*.

Lichtheim and the leadership of the *Verband Deutscher Zionisten-Revisionisten* lost little time in asserting their authority over the entire *Landesverband* following the events of late March 1933. An undated circular (probably early April) to all

[21]*Ibid.* Jabotinsky also sought to neutralise the opposition of his critics by calling on all Revisionists to participate in the elections for the Eighteenth Zionist Congress, and thus refraining for the time being from demanding the formal creation of a separate, independent Revisionist organisation.

[22]*Jüdische Rundschau*, XXXVIII No. 27 (4th April 1933).

[23]See JI/Tel-Aviv: 2/5/21. Yehuda Benari, *History of the Revisionist Movement*, vol. II, unpublished manuscript.

[24]JI/Tel-Aviv: 2/5/21. Der Landesverband der Zionisten-Revisionisten an die Union der Zionisten-Revisionisten/London, 29. März 1933. This letter no longer contains the exact text of its 27th March resolution dissociating itself from the Revisionist Executive in London, as it has been cut out of the middle of the letter.

[25]JI/Tel-Aviv: 2/5/21. Exekutive der Welt-Union an den Landesverband der Zionisten-Revisionisten in Deutschland, 25. April 1933.

Revisionist *Ortsgruppen*, members and sympathisers from the *Vorstand* of the *Verband Deutscher Zionisten-Revisionisten* (Richard Lichtheim, Justus Schloss and Ernst Hamburger) sought to explain the events and the issues since the Kattowitz conference, and to rally the Revisionist rank-and-file behind the new leadership.[26] The circular charged that the Kattowitz meeting had done nothing to resolve the problems plaguing the Revisionist organisation, and characterised Jabotinsky's demands in Kattowitz, and his actions thereafter, as an implicit declaration of independence of the Revisionist organisation from the WZO. It emphasised the strong opposition to Jabotinsky from within the Executive as well as from the great majority of Revisionists, and regretted that Jabotinsky's action against the Revisionist Executive had split the *Welt-Union*.

The circular then reviewed the situation within the *Landesverband* in Germany. The previous *Landesvorstand* was held at fault for supporting Jabotinsky's actions over the objections of the majority of Revisionists in Germany. After its dissolution by Grossmann and the Revisionist Executive, the circular revealed the discussions that took place between the leaders of the two factions, which produced an agreement to form a new *Landesvorstand* consisting of Lichtheim, Schloss and Hamburger, which alone would possess the authority to speak and to act in the name of the German Revisionist movement. That the old *Landesvorstand* agreed to this, as the circular strongly implies, could also be an indication of the comparative unpopularity of Jabotinsky's position within the *Landesverband*. The circular followed with a warning to all German Revisionists:

> "Diejenigen Mitglieder, welche sich den Anordnungen der legalen Instanzen der Union nicht fügen, sind als ausgeschlossen zu betrachten. Wir ersuchen Sie alle, in diesem Sinne zu verfahren und die Mitglieder des 'Verbandes Deutscher Zionisten-Revisionisten' überall vor die Frage zu stellen, ob sie sich dem genannten Vorstand unterstellen und die legal gewählten Instanzen des Sonderverbandes anerkennen, oder ob sie es vorziehen, sich als ausgeschlossen zu betrachten."

It concluded with an optimistic report on the course of the Revisionist split in Eastern Europe, North and South America, Palestine and South Africa. It claimed that the great majority of Revisionists everywhere had remained loyal to the duly elected Revisionist Executive in London and its policies, and had rejected Jabotinsky's actions.[27]

Another undated appeal to all German Revisionists at about that time further demonstrated the determination of the pro-Executive *Verband Deutscher Zionisten-Revisionisten* to re-unify the divided Revisionist movement in Germany, and to prevent any further divisions.[28] It underlined the dangers of further division, and the need for unity at a time when the situation for Jews in Germany was rapidly deteriorating. It emphatically stressed the loyalty of the *Verband* to the Executive of the Revisionist *Welt-Union* in London, the need for all true

[26]JI/Tel-Aviv: 2/5/21. Verband Deutscher Zionisten-Revisionisten, Rundschreiben I an unsere Ortsgruppen und Mitglieder und Vertrauensleute (no date).

[27]The circular pointed with particular enthusiasm to the *Brith Hakanaim*, the new youth movement established by the few thousand *Betarim* who chose to remain loyal to the Executive and to leave the *Betar* which was overwhelmingly supportive of Jabotinsky.

[28]JI/Tel-Aviv: 2/5/21. Verband Deutscher Zionisten-Revisionisten: Aufruf an alle Gesinnungsgenossen (no date).

"Staatszionisten" to stand behind the Executive, and the conviction that a unified, strengthened Revisionist movement would eventually inherit the leadership of the entire Zionist movement. It concluded: "Wir wollen und werden diesen Kongress und diese Zionistische Organisation, den 'Judenstaat unterwegs', erobern und mit Herzlischem Geist erfüllen!"

None of this, however, ended the divisions and the confusion within the German Revisionist movement, especially since the deep rifts persisted on the international level, and were bound to affect the movement in Germany. In May 1933, Jabotinsky issued an order dissolving the Revisionist *Landesverband* in Germany, including the *Betar*, ostensibly because of the dangers to all German Revisionists posed by the strong, active, public support and participation of the international Revisionist movement in the growing economic boycott and propaganda campaign against National Socialist Germany.[29] It is not clear, however, whether this was in fact Jabotinsky's main reason, or whether it was simply a face-saving device for writing off a lost cause in Germany, or a combination of both. It is certainly true that the anti-German boycott and propaganda campaign, in which Revisionists the world over played an important role, was detrimental to the ability of Revisionists in Germany to compete with the ZVfD under the altered conditions of the Nazi state after 1933, a matter which will be considered in detail below. Yet it also seems clear that by May, Jabotinsky's supporters in Germany were in disarray, with most of their leaders abroad, and with Lichtheim's *Verband* still on the offensive. This is particularly evident in a written statement in Paris by Hans Bloch, the *Vorsitzender* of the old *Landesvorstand*. The statement was made on 24th May 1933, shortly after Jabotinsky's dissolution of the entire German *Landesverband*.[30] In his statement, Bloch referred to himself as "der . . . rechtmässig gewählte Vorsitzende des Landesverbandes der Zionisten-Revisionisten in Deutschland", and as such made it his official responsibility to execute Jabotinsky's directive dissolving the *Landesverband* in Germany. Bloch further criticised Lichtheim for taking advantage of the absence from Germany of most of the "legal" members of the *Landesvorstand*, for breaking Revisionist discipline and for damaging Jewish interests. He warned: "Wenn Herr Lichtheim einen Verband der Zionisten-Revisionisten aufmacht, so ist das eine missbräuchliche Aneignung des revisionistischen Namens, und ich warne alle Revisionisten, sich an dieser Organisation zu beteiligen."

Jabotinsky's dissolution of the Revisionist *Landesverband* in Germany had little practical effect on the activities of the reconstituted *Landesvorstand* under Richard Lichtheim. Certainly the most important step it was to take immediately following the dissolution attempt was the decision to reverse the October 1931 secession from the ZVfD, and to re-enter the German Zionist organisation. What would appear to have been a reversal of principle was rationalised by the Revisionist leadership as a practical step towards remaining true to the long-standing principle of remaining within the WZO. In its letter of

[29]Central Archives for the History of the Jewish People (hereafter cited as CAHJP)/Jerusalem: P82–44. Manuscript of an article by Jabotinsky for *Moment*, 22nd November 1935.
[30]JI/Tel-Aviv: 2/5/21. Erklärung von Dr. Hans Bloch, Paris, 24. Mai 1933.

28th May, 1933, to the Executive of the WZO in London, the German *Landesverband* requested permission to rejoin the ZVfD.[31] The letter asserted that the *Verband Deutscher Zionisten-Revisionisten* was the organisation of all German Revisionists who supported the Revisionist Executive in London, and who were loyal members and supporters of the WZO. The letter also described Revisionist reasons for seeking to re-enter the ZVfD as a means of reversing the January 1933 suspension of the *Sonderverband* by the WZO. As a condition for rejoining the ZVfD, the letter stated: "Der Eintritt erfolgt unter der Voraussetzung, dass die Zionistische Exekutive in London die Suspension des Sonderverbandes aufhebt, nachdem innerhalb des Revisionismus eine Klärung eingetreten ist." The objective of the move was primarily the re-instatement of the *Sonderverband* within the WZO, rather than a revival of the old policy of the 1920s of seeking to gain control of the ZVfD. This was reiterated in the concluding sentence of the 28th May letter: "Um den Eintritt des Verbands Deutscher Zionisten-Revisionisten zu ermöglichen und zu legalisieren (als deutscher Landesverband des Sonderverbands), bitten wir um Mitteilung, dass Sie unserem Wunsche entsprochen haben."

By the middle of July 1933, the *Verband Deutscher Zionisten-Revisionisten* found itself in an increasingly isolated and impossible position. It had not been able to return the *Sonderverband* to the WZO, was still shunned by the ZVfD, and was tied to a Revisionist Executive which was losing its battle with Jabotinsky for the allegiance of Revisionists in many parts of the world outside Germany.[32] Yet it still tried to build an effective Revisionist organisation through the summer of 1933 in spite of these impediments and the very difficult circumstances for all Jewish organisations in the Third *Reich*. Its circular of 13th July 1933, reiterated the continued allegiance of the *Verband* to the WZO, and to the deposed Revisionist Executive of Grossmann, Selig Soskin, Machover and Robert Stricker. It also provided a new justification for its commitment to remain in the WZO as the only avenue for Revisionist success:

> "Die Durchsetzung des revisionistischen Zieles kann nur innerhalb der Z.O. erfolgen. Die Z.O. ist die Titelinhaberin des Mandats. Diesen Titel braucht man, um überhaupt Politik

[31] JI/Tel-Aviv: 2/5/21. Union der Zionisten-Revisionisten/Landesverband in Deutschland (Ernst Hamburger), an die Exekutive der Zionistischen Weltorganisation in London, Hbg./Zr., 28. Mai 1933.

[32] If Kurt Blumenfeld's is typical of the attitude of the ZVfD towards the Revisionists during those years, it seems that that attitude was characterised by the tendency to ignore the Revisionists and to simply lump their two factions together as a single object of derision. See Blumenfeld's *Im Kampf um den Zionismus. Briefe aus fünf Jahrzehnten.* Hrsg. von Miriam Sambursky und Jochanan Ginat, Stuttgart 1976, Veröffentlichung des Leo Baeck Instituts, p. 117, and *Erlebte Judenfrage. Ein Vierteljahrhundert deutscher Zionismus* Hrsg. von Hans Tramer, Stuttgart 1962, Veröffentlichung des Leo Baeck Instituts, p. 199. Nahum Goldmann of the Radical Zionists dismissed the Revisionists as "Tolle Derwische", "Wortmaximalisten" and "antizionistische Auswüchse", while Alfred Berger likened them to Nazis, and described the *Betarim* as "Jewish Brownshirts". See *Die Neue Welt*, 9th September 1932, as cited in JI/Tel-Aviv: Yehuda Benari, *History*, vol. II, unpublished manuscript. Moreover, in the elections for the Eighteenth Zionist Congress in Prague in 1933, Revisionists elected 45 delegates from Jabotinsky's *Welt-Union* as opposed to 7 members from Meier Grossmann's new Jewish State Party, or 14% and 2% of the vote respectively. See *Stenographisches Protokoll des XIX. Zionistenkongresses und der Vierten Tagung des Council der Jewish Agency für Palästina, Luzern, 20. August bis 6. September 1935*, Wien, 1937.

> und damit Judenstaatspolitik zu machen; diesen Titel kann man nur erhalten, wenn man in der Z.O. die Macht erhält, und diese Macht wollen wir erobern."[33]

The circular further asserted that in advocating continued affiliation with the WZO the *Verband* did not intend that the Revisionist movement should remain forever an opposition party within the larger organisation. It expressed instead the firm but naive conviction that the time was ripe for a Revisionist conquest of the WZO as elections drew near for the approaching Eighteenth Zionist Congress.

II. THE JEWISH STATE PARTY AND THE STAATSZIONISTEN, 1933–1934

Important events occurred in the international Revisionist movement in the late summer and autumn of 1933, events in which the *Verband Deutscher Zionisten-Revisionisten* played no role, and which clearly demonstrated its virtual isolation from the larger Revisionist and Zionist organisations. The old Revisionist Executive under Meier Grossmann, to which the *Verband* had repeatedly pledged its loyalty, left the Revisionist *Welt-Union* to Jabotinsky, probably early in the summer of 1933, and called themselves and their supporters "Demokratische Revisionisten". Along with their supporters from other countries, they called a meeting of the suspended *Sonderverband der Zionisten-Revisionisten* in Prague for 20th to 28th August, to coincide with the Eighteenth Zionist Congress in Prague from 21st August to 4th September.[34] It was decided to change the name of the *Sonderverband* and the *Demokratische Revisionisten* to the *Judenstaatspartei* (Jewish State Party), to drop the term "Revisionist", and formally make a clean break with Jabotinsky's *Union der Zionisten-Revisionisten.*[35]

The purpose of the Revisionist conference was declared to be ". . . vor allem die Klärung der im Revisionismus geschaffenen Lage, sowie die Stellungnahme zu den Problemen des 18. Kongresses".

The conference elected an Executive which included the old Revisionist Executive of Grossmann, Machover, Soskin, Stricker and the absent Richard Lichtheim, as well as the authority to add three more members in the future. It also appointed a *Sekretariat* in Tel-Aviv under M. Weinstein, and an *Organisationsdepartment* in London under Robert Stricker for European countries. Its decisions included a repudiation of the Calais resolutions, a re-affirmation of Revisionist allegiance to the WZO and Zionist discipline, and somewhat

[33]JI/Tel-Aviv: 2/5/21. Verband Deutscher Zionisten-Revisionisten, Rundschreiben II, an unsere Mitglieder, Ortsgruppen und Vertrauensleute, 13. Juli 1933.

[34]The *Verband Deutscher Zionisten-Revisionisten* did not attend the Prague meeting, just as the ZVfD was not represented at the Eighteenth Congress, since the Hitler regime did not permit German Zionists to attend these meetings.

[35]See Central Zionist Archives (hereafter cited as CZA)/ Jerusalem: Z4/3296. Auszug aus dem *Bulletin der Judenstaatspartei*, No. 1 (25th December 1933). See also: *Jüdische Rundschau*, XXXVIII, No. 68 (29th August 1933), and No. 69/70 (1st September 1933). The full name of the new organisation was "*Judenstaatspartei* (*Sonderverband der Zionisten-Revisionisten*)".

naively concluded that: "Hiermit ist die Krise im Revisionismus geklärt".[36] Such a statement reflected yet another incident in the two years between 1931 and 1933 in which a part of the Revisionist movement went its own way, and claimed to speak for all Revisionists and to have resolved the internal conflicts within the movement. The events between 1933 and 1935 would demonstrate just how inaccurate this assertion really was.

Of course the events in Prague had little if any effect on the divided Revisionist movement in Germany. The adherents of the Jewish State Party in Germany, Lichtheim's *Verband Deutscher Zionisten-Revisionisten*, appear to have kept their name and to have continued to operate at least into the autumn of 1933.[37] By the end of the summer of 1933, however, it was the pressures imposed by the Nazi regime on all Jewish organisations rather than the continuing conflicts among Revisionists, that would have the decisive impact on Revisionist fortunes in Germany. It appears that this reality forced yet another re-organisation and the re-unification of the German Revisionist movement late in 1933 and early in 1934. The impossibility of attending the Revisionist meeting of the new Jewish State Party, and the Zionist Congress in Prague in August/September, as well as Jabotinsky's dissolution of the Revisionist *Landesverband* the previous May, left both factions of the German Revisionist movement completely isolated. Therefore, to ensure the survival of their common Revisionist Zionism in Germany, the two sides decided to come together in a unified organisation by the beginning of 1934.

The *Organisationsdepartment* of the Jewish State Party was able to report on

[36]In an interview in Poland in October 1933, Grossmann reaffirmed the policy of the new Jewish State Party towards the WZO in the following manner: "Wir betrachten uns als einen integrierenden Bestandteil der Z.O., in welcher wir ohne Rücksicht auf irgendwelche Konjunkturen verbleiben werden . . . Wir anerkennen das Primat der Disziplin der Z.O. gegenüber jeder Fraktion oder Föderation. . . ." See CZA/Jerusalem: Z4/3296. Grossmann interview in *Nowy Dziennik*, Krakow, 31st October 1933. This did not, however, put the question of discipline to rest. In January 1934, the Zionist Executive in London informed Grossmann that his Jewish State Party ". . . nicht den rechtlichen Status eines Sonderverbandes besitzt und im Sinne der Verfassung der ZO nur als eine Parteirichtung angesehen werden kann, deren Mitglieder und Vereine nur innerhalb der zionistischen Landesverbände ihre Existenz und Tätigkeit legal fortsetzen können". See CZA/Jerusalem: Z4/3296. Zionist Executive/London an Grossmann, 25. Januar 1934. Moreover the opposing positions of the WZO and the Jewish State Party (JSP) towards Jabotinsky's petition campaign in 1934 demonstrated this fact all too clearly. While the former condemned the campaign and ordered its members not to participate in it, the JSP as an organisation neither denounced it nor supported it, advising its individual members instead to sign if they chose. The WZO demanded that the JSP maintain Zionist discipline, and direct its members not to sign. That the JSP refused to do this is indicated in a resolution adopted at a JSP meeting in Warsaw in April 1935, which read: "Die Judenstaatspartei unterwirft sich der Disziplin der zionistischen Leitung und behält sich freies Handeln nur für den Fall vor, dass das höchste zionistische Gewissen es erfordert." Thus, the JSP's adherence to Zionist discipline was not complete. For an account of the petition movement, see Laqueur, *A History of Zionism*, *op. cit.*, pp. 366ff. For more on the WZO–JSP conflict over the petition issue, see CZA/Jerusalem: Z4/3296. *Die Neue Welt*, 2nd February 1934; *Jüdische Telegraphen-Agentur*, No. 96 (29th April 1935); and Organisationsdepartment an die Zionistische Exekutive/London, 9. Mai 1935.

[37]See for example the notice placed by the *Verband Deutscher Zionisten-Revisionisten* in the *Jüdische Rundschau*, No. 86 (27th October 1933), regarding its continued allegiance to the WZO, and its assurances that membership in the *Verband* made belonging to the WZO automatic. Richard Lichtheim emigrated from Germany to Palestine in September of that year.

Revisionist activities in Germany in January 1934. In its *Bulletin der Judenstaatspartei* of 28th January, published in Vienna, it was reported that although information from Germany was naturally "sehr spärlich", and that contact with German Revisionist leaders was very limited, Revisionist sentiment in Germany was strong.[38] The report drew attention to the realities which the situation in Germany imposed on the Revisionist movement, particularly its complete isolation from the larger Revisionist and Zionist organisations, and the consequent authority granted by the *Exekutivkomitee* to organise and to operate as a completely independent *Landesorganisation*. With some satisfaction, the report pointed to the success of German Revisionists in coming together in the face of the common disaster. It mentioned Revisionist meetings taking place throughout Germany, speeches given at these meetings by Justus Schloss, Ernst Hamburger, Hubert Pollack and Boris Silber, and expressed the special satisfaction of the Jewish State Party over the role of Georg Kareski in the unified Revisionist front in Germany:

> "Als ganz besonderen Erfolg der Judenstaatspartei, der weit über die Grenzen Deutschlands Beachtung und freudigste Zustimmung fand, ist zu verzeichnen, dass sich Herr Dir. Georg Kareski uns angeschlossen hat und sich im Hinblick auf eine erhebliche Verbreiterung der staatszionistischen Front entschlossen hat, den Vorsitz unserer Partei zu übernehmen."

It was not until April 1934, that a new, united Revisionist organisation, encompassing the remnants of the old Revisionist *Landesverband* loyal to Jabotinsky and Lichtheim's *Verband Deutscher Zionisten-Revisionisten* who supported the new Jewish State Party, was formally proclaimed. Calling itself the "*Staatszionistische Organisation (Vereinigte Revisionisten Deutschlands*)", the new organisation emulated the Jewish State Party in de-emphasising the word "Revisionist" because of the role of Revisionists abroad in the anti-German economic boycott.[39] It presented itself to all German Revisionists in the following manner:

> "Sämtliche Staatszionisten Deutschlands haben sich in der Staatszionistischen Organisation (Vereinigte Revisionisten Deutschlands) zusammengeschlossen. Sie ist damit die Einheitsorganisation aller in Deutschland lebenden staatszionistisch eingestellten Juden geworden. Der Zusammenschluss erfolgt in einer Zeit, in der die inner-zionistische Auseinandersetzung einen Grad erreicht hat, der zu einer endgültigen Klärung der politischen Situation innerhalb der zionistischen Reihen zwingt."

The organisation was to be governed by a presidium consisting of Georg Kareski as President, Adolf Hirschfeldt as Vice President, Justus Schloss and Ernst Hamburger, formerly of Lichtheim's *Verband*, as second and third Vice Presidents respectively, Willi Cegla as head of the *Nationale Jugend-Herzlia*, the new name of the German *Betar*, N. Scheinesohn and Louis Fleiss. Its official newspaper was to be *Der Staatszionist*.[40]

[38]CZA/Jerusalem: Z4/3296. *Bulletin der Judenstaatspartei*. Hrsg. vom Exekutivkomitee der Judenstaatspartei, 28th January 1934.

[39]JI/Tel-Aviv: 1/21/5/2c. Aufruf der Staatszionistischen Organisation (Vereinigte Revisionisten Deutschlands), 15. April 1934.

[40]Beginning as a bi-weekly newspaper with the 10th January, 1934, edition, *Der Staatszionist* soon became a monthly, and was published by the *Staatszionistische Organisation* until December 1935. Edited by Max Schulmann, it became a stencilled information bulletin by the end of its two-year

The conditions of Jewish life under National Socialism imposed a unity on German Revisionists that enabled the *Staatszionistische Organisation* to revive the Revisionist struggle with the ZVfD which had not been waged since 1931. Revisionists of all political inclinations were at least officially cut off from the larger Revisionist organisations and movement, be it Jabotinsky's *Welt-Union* and later his New Zionist Organisation, or the Jewish State Party. Therefore, the internal conflict between Jabotinsky and his opponents that had generated civil war in the international and German Revisionist movements since 1931, and which continued to divide Revisionists outside Germany, no longer imposed the old divisions on German Revisionists. Those battles must have seemed exceedingly inappropriate and altogether remote given the steadily deteriorating situation of German Jews, as well as the isolation of the German Revisionist movement. The choice between Jabotinsky and Grossmann, and their respective positions on discipline and the proper Revisionist relationship to the WZO as well as on other issues, which in any case had been a choice between different means rather than ends, was no longer particularly relevant for German Revisionists.

It is not entirely clear if the isolation of the *Staatszionistische Organisation* from the two Revisionist groups outside Germany was complete, or, if it was not, whether there might have been a preference for the *Welt-Union* or the Jewish State Party. In a 13th July 1934 letter to the *Reichsvertretung der deutschen Juden* complaining of ZVfD control over the *Palästina-Amt* and the distribution of immigration certificates for Palestine, Georg Kareski rejected ZVfD assertions that the *Staatszionisten* were still tied to the *Welt-Union* and the Jewish State Party, both supporters of the anti-German economic boycott.[41] Kareski asserted:

> "Trotzdem allen amtlichen Stellen der ZVfD zur Genüge bekannt ist, dass die Staatszionistische Organisation sich ausschliesslich auf Deutschland beschränkt und mit den revisionistischen Organisationen ausserhalb Deutschlands, also der Weltunion der Zionisten-Revisionisten und der Judenstaatspartei, in keinerlei organisatorischem Zusammenhang steht, wird seit vielen Monaten immer wieder der Versuch gemacht, die Staatszionistische Organisation mit dem von den ausserdeutschen Revisionisten proklamierten und geforderten Wirtschaftsboykott in Zusammenhang zu bringen."

Jabotinsky also claimed in 1935 that there existed no contact whatever between his *Welt-Union* and any Zionist group in Germany after his dissolution of the old Revisionist *Landesverband* in May 1933.[42] Nevertheless Yehuda Benari asserts in the unpublished second volume of his *History of the Revisionist Movement* that the *Staatszionisten* maintained unofficial, private contacts with Jabotinsky's *Welt-Union*, and to all intents and purposes felt themselves to be an integral part of it. Moreover it has already been mentioned that the Jewish State Party did have some contact with the new *Staatszionistische Organisation*, at least during the early part of 1934. This kind of contact, however weak, sporadic and private, to both

run. In 1934, the new organisation also put out a few editions of the *Staatszionistische Informationsblätter*.

[41]CAHJP/Jerusalem: P82/17, Georg Kareski an die Reichsvertretung der deutschen Juden, 13. Juli 1934.

[42]CAHJP/Jerusalem: P82/44. Manuscript of an article by Jabotinsky for *Moment*, 22nd November, 1935.

Revisionist movements, seems likely, especially since the *Staatszionistische Organisation* was made up of sympathisers and former adherents of both. However, such contact, if it did exist, could not have had much affect on Revisionist politics in Germany under the circumstances.

The unity and the renewed struggle against the ZVfD were especially apparent at the new organisation's first *Reichskonferenz* in October 1934. The meeting established the main points of conflict with the ZVfD that would characterise its political position for the coming years. While some of those points were the same ones around which the old battles of the 1920s raged, there were significant new political themes upon which the *Staatszionisten* based their arguments in the struggle with the ZVfD for support from Jews and from Nazi authorities.[43]

Seventy delegates representing twenty-four *Ortsgruppen* attended the conference that took place in Berlin on 13th and 14th October. The speeches by Georg Kareski, Ernst Hamburger, Adolf Hirschfeldt, Ludwig Goldwasser and others attacked the ZVfD on three recurring albeit utterly preposterous charges, namely that it promoted Jewish assimilation, that it was opposed to the establishment of a Jewish state in Palestine, and that it was a thoroughly Marxist organisation. These were the recurring themes on the Revisionist side of the propaganda battle between the *Staatszionisten* and the ZVfD until the dissolution of the former in 1938. While these themes were not entirely new, and had some basis in the Revisionist arguments during the 1920s, they were significantly different in emphasis as well as in intensity and scope after 1934. More familiar Revisionist grievances that were raised again at the Berlin conference included the question of ZVfD control over the distribution of immigration certificates for Palestine,[44] the question of compromise with the Arabs, and the need to provide German Zionists with the means of removing the entrenched leadership "clique" of the ZVfD, and replacing it with a new one. This last point was for the *Staatszionisten* still the most important, as it was deemed the basic reason or explanation for the alleged Marxist/assimilationist/anti-Jewish state nature of the ZVfD. On a practical level, the conference re-elected the old presidium of Kareski (President), Hirschfeldt, Hamburger and Schloss.

[43]For a complete account of the proceedings, see CZA/Jerusalem: Z4/3296. Staatszionistische Organisation (Vereinigte Revisionisten Deutschlands), Reichskonferenz am 13. und 14. Oktober 1934, (no date). See also *Jüdische Rundschau*, XXXIX, No. 84 (19th October 1934). See also the following publications of the *Staatszionistische Organisation* which reiterated the standard Revisionist concerns and demands: Georg Kareski, *Stürme über Eretz Israel*, Berlin 1936; Justus Schloss, *Frieden im deutschen Zionismus*, Berlin 1934; and *Der Staatszionismus* (no author, no date). These can be found at the Germania Judaica/Köln.

[44]The question of control over immigration certificates for Palestine had already become a hotly contested one during the summer of 1934. As mentioned above, Kareski wrote to the *Reichsvertretung* to protest both ZVfD control over the *Palästina-Amt* which distributed the immigration certificates, and the use of the *Palästina-Amt* by the ZVfD as an instrument in its campaign to destroy Revisionism in Germany. Kareski complained that the *Staatszionisten* were denied a voice in the distribution of certificates. See: CAHJP/Jerusalem: P82/17. Kareski an die Reichsvertretung der deutschen Juden, 13. Juli 1934. Shortly thereafter, Kareski and the *Staatszionisten* tried unsuccessfully to take over the *Palästina-Amt*. See Levine, 'Jewish Collaborator', *loc. cit.*, p. 265.

III. KARESKI, STAATSZIONISTEN AND THE ZVfD TO 1934

If the reality of Jewish life under National Socialism left little alternative to unity for German Revisionists, it tended to have the opposite effect on the relationship between Revisionists and the ZVfD. Herbert Levine correctly observes that the Jewish policy of the Hitler regime in general, and in particular the aim of removing the Jewish community from Germany, generated both an official "favouritism" towards Zionism as well as a "new receptivity" among the traditionally liberal/assimilationist German-Jewish community towards Zionism after 1933.[45] He further argues that these new realities greatly increased the stakes in the already bitter competition between the Revisionists and the ZVfD for the support and allegiance of Zionists in particular, and Jews in general, in Germany after 1933. This is certainly evident in the bitterly hostile relationship between the two that continued from 1933 to 1938.

Some of the antagonism between the ZVfD and the *Staatszionisten* during the 1930s was generated by the activities of the very controversial leader of the latter, Georg Kareski. As the word "collaborator" in the title of Herbert Levine's essay suggests, Kareski's role in the Jewish community and in Zionist affairs during the 1930s was one that has stirred considerable controversy and emotion ever since. Originally from Poznań, where he had naturally come into contact with East European Jewish traditions, Kareski was attracted to the Revisionism that became an important force in the Zionist *Jüdische Volkspartei* which in turn achieved a leading role in the political life of the Jewish community in Berlin in the late 1920s.[46] Attracted perhaps to the anti-Socialism and political style of the Revisionists, Kareski quickly became the dominant voice in the *Jüdische Volkspartei*, was elected to the *Gemeindevorstand* by the representative assembly of the Berlin Jewish community and became the chairman of the *Vorstand* in 1929.

Kareski's difficulties with the leadership of the ZVfD began several years before 1933, and ultimately drew him formally into the ranks of the Revisionist movement in 1934.[47] Kurt Blumenfeld acknowledged Kareski's general disagreement with the policies of the ZVfD in a letter to him in November 1929.[48] Two years later, Kareski expressed his disagreement with the economic

[45]Levine, 'Jewish Collaborator', *loc. cit.*, p. 263. For a detailed account of the role of Zionism in the Jewish policy of the Hitler regime, see Francis R. Nicosia, *The Third Reich and the Palestine Question*, Austin–London 1985, chapts. 2, 3, 4, 7, 8.

[46]See: Levine, 'Jewish Collaborator', *loc. cit.*, pp. 256–257. The Jewish People's party was founded in 1920 to represent Zionist interests on communal bodies, and ultimately to win over the Jewish communities in Germany for Zionism. For more on the *Jüdische Volkspartei*, see Kurt Jacob Ball-Kaduri, *Das Leben der Juden in Deutschland im Jahre 1933*, Frankfurt a. Main 1963, pp. 33, 39, 42, 122; Jacob Marcus, *The Rise and Destiny of the German Jew*, Cincinnati 1934, pp. 196–200; Niewyk, *The Jews in Weimar Germany*, *op. cit.*, pp. 148–152.

[47]Kareski's own complete and very detailed account of his political career and of his differences with the ZVfD during the 1920s and 1930s was presented to the *Beth Din* in Jerusalem in 1937 during his court action against the *Hitachduth Olej Germania*. See CAHJP/Jerusalem: P82/24a. Materialien für die Verhandlungen vor dem Beth Din. Angaben über die öffentliche Tätigkeit, eingeteilt in 3 Abschnitte, pp. 1–25. The trial will be considered below.

[48]CAHJP/Jerusalem: P82/16, Kurt Blumenfeld an Georg Kareski, 30. November 1929. See also Blumenfeld, *Erlebte Judenfrage*, *op. cit.*, p. 188.

policies of the ZVfD, and was harshly critical of Alfred Berger, a leading moderate in the ZVfD and supporter of Robert Weltsch and of Blumenfeld himself.[49] Kareski's support for the Catholic *Zentrumspartei* aroused some criticism from the mainstream of the German Zionist movement which, in line with the majority of the German-Jewish community, was transferring its support from the declining *Deutsche Demokratische Partei* (DDP) to the *Sozialdemokratische Partei Deutschlands* (SPD). For Kareski, the Centre Party was the only realistic option for German Jews in the waning years of the Weimar Republic. In an article entitled 'Juden und Reichstagswahlen' written for the *Jüdische Zeitung* shortly after the *Reichstag* elections of July 1932, he argued that the Centre Party was the only realistic choice for the Jewish community as the SPD was part of a fading Marxism that was in any case of little value for an overwhelmingly non-Socialist Jewish community, and because the *Staatspartei* was virtually dead.[50] Besides favouring the Centre Party as a non-Marxist one, he seems to have believed that the *Zentrum* and Franz von Papen would ensure the rights and security of the Jewish community. Robert Weltsch of the *Jüdische Rundschau* criticised Kareski for suggesting in a public speech in Geneva that ". . . die Regierung Papen hat den Schutz der Juden auf ihre Fahne geschrieben", something that, according to Weltsch, the Nazis were using in their propaganda campaign against the government.[51] Kareski was even inclined to accept a *Zentrum*-Nazi coalition at the end of 1932; presumably under the impression that the *Zentrum* would dominate such a coalition, Kareski reasoned:

> "Als Demokrat müsse man Wahlentscheidungen berücksichtigen. Wenn daher das Zentrum versuche, durch ein Abkommen mit den Nationalsozialisten eine brauchbare Regierungsgrundlage zu schaffen, so mag der Erfolg zweifelhaft sein. Grundsätzlich könne ich aber eine solche Politik nur billigen, auch wenn sie für mich als Jude gefühlsmässig eine gewisse Belastung darstellt."[52]

Perhaps the most interesting disagreement between Kareski and the Zionist leadership before 1933, certainly one with immense symbolic significance for what was to occur after 1933, was the attempt by a leading official of the NSDAP to open contact with the ZVfD in 1932. In the autumn of 1932, Gregor Strasser approached both Georg Kareski and Kurt Blumenfeld with a request to discuss the Jewish Question without any preconditions or obligations. During his testimony against the *Hitachduth Olej Germania* before the *Beth Din* in

[49]CAHJP/Jerusalem: P82/17. Georg Kareski an Kurt Blumenfeld, 29. Mai 1931. Along with Robert Weltsch and other moderates in the ZVfD, Alfred Berger was one of the founding members of the *Arbeitsgemeinschaft für zionistische Realpolitik* in 1929. It was a strongly anti-Revisionist group that came together to resist Revisionist propaganda in the autumn of 1929, in preparation for the ZVfD *Delegiertentag* in December and the coming showdown between the moderate leadership and the Revisionists. See Nicosia, 'Revisionist Zionism in Germany (I)', *loc. cit.*, pp. 220–222. See also Niewyk, *The Jews in Weimar Germany*, *op. cit.*, pp. 135–136.

[50]CAHJP/Jerusalem: P82/38. 'Juden und Reichstagswahlen', manuscript for the *Jüdische Zeitung*, (no date). Kareski himself had been placed by the Centre Party on its list of candidates in Berlin for the *Reichstag* for the September 1930 elections. He had no chance of winning as he was placed tenth on the list. See Niewyk, *The Jews in Weimar Germany*, *op. cit.*, pp. 28–29.

[51]CAHJP/Jerusalem: P82/16. Robert Weltsch an Georg Kareski, 19. Oktober 1932.

[52]CAHJP/Jerusalem: P82/21. Aufzeichnung Kareskis, (no date).

Jerusalem in 1937, which will be considered below, Kareski told of Strasser's overtures to himself and to Kurt Blumenfeld, of the latter's rejection of the Strasser request, and of his disappointment over Blumenfeld's refusal to meet with Strasser:

> "Im Herbst 1932 hatte Gregor Strasser bei mir anfragen lassen, ob ich mit ihm eine für beide Teile zunächst einmal völlig unverbindliche Unterhaltung über die Judenfrage haben wollte. Ich habe damals Kurt Blumenfeld informiert und hörte von ihm zu meinem Entsetzen, dass Gregor Strasser sich mit dem gleichen Wunsche an ihn gewandt habe, und dass er abgelehnt habe."[53]

Kareski further testified that Blumenfeld tried to justify his otherwise "völlig unverständliche Ablehnung" with the argument that as useful as such a meeting would be, the Jewish community would never understand it, particularly since the Nazis did not yet possess power, and that he (Blumenfeld) would be condemned. Kareski noted too that he had warned Blumenfeld of the consequences of such shortsightedness, that he had accepted Strasser's offer to talk, but that the talks never materialised due to Strasser's political problems and loss of power within the NSDAP.

By the middle of 1932, Kareski was drawn still closer to the Revisionist movement. In June, he received a letter from Jabotinsky thanking him for taking over the directorship of the Tel Hai Fond, and praising his energy, ability and particularly his loyalty.[54] In December of that year, Kareski received an appeal from Dr. Siegfried Stern of the Revisionist *Landesverband* which was in the process of disintegration as it entered the new year on the defensive against Lichtheim's *Verband Deutscher Zionisten-Revisionisten.*[55] Stern expressed his disappointment that the Revisionist movement in Germany was ". . . so gut wie zerfallen", and informed Kareski that he and friends from the *Landesverband* were determined to save what was left of the disintegrating Revisionist movement. He further noted that he and his friends were convinced that Kareski was the best person to take up the leadership of the *Landesverband*, and invited him to come to Munich for discussions on the matter. Although it is not known whether Kareski went to Munich to meet Stern and his colleagues, it seems clear that next to Richard Lichtheim he had become the most important

[53]CAHJP/Jerusalem: P82/24a. Materialien für die Verhandlungen vor dem Beth Din. Angaben über die öffentliche Tätigkeit, eingeteilt in 3 Abschnitte, p. 7. In his 'Zwei Jahre Reichsvertretung in ihrem Verhältnis zur ZVfD: Rechenschaftsbericht des politischen Referenten der Reichsvertretung an die ZVfD' of February 1936, Dr. Leo Plaut referred to this early contact with Strasser in a section of his report entitled 'Zionistische Ideologie und nationalsozialistische Bereitschaft'. He wrote: "Die Bereitschaft der neuen Männer, die Träger des Zionismus als Gesprächspartner, und in der Folge als Kontrahenten, anzuerkennen, ergab sich aus persönlichen Verbindungen und Gesprächen bereits im Jahre 1932." See CZA/Jerusalem: A142/86–2. 'Zwei Jahre Reichsvertretung in ihrem Verhältnis zur ZVfD: Rechenschaftsbericht des politischen Referenten der Reichsvertretung an die ZVfD', von Dr. Leo Plaut, Februar 1936. It is rather piquant to note in this context that the *Centralverein*, on the other hand, had contacts with Gregor Strasser's brother Otto, by then a renegade Nazi (though an approach via Otto to Gregor – usually one of the main targets of C.V. court actions – is also recorded). On all this see Arnold Paucker, *Der jüdische Abwehrkampf gegen Antisemitismus und Nationalsozialismus in den letzten Jahren der Weimarer Republik*, 2nd edn., Hamburg 1969, pp. 81–82, 119, 125, 169.

[54]CAHJP/Jerusalem: P82/18. Jabotinsky an Kareski, 9. Juni 1932.

[55]CAHJP/Jerusalem: P82/16. Siegfried Stern an Kareski, 23. Dezember 1932.

German Revisionist by the beginning of 1933. It is also apparent that he had become the favoured leader of the pro-Jabotinsky *Landesvorstand* of the Revisionist *Landesverband* in Germany.

Kareski's rise and activities in the politics of the Berlin Jewish community in 1931 and 1932 were rapidly propelling him into a head-on clash with some of the other parties, including the ZVfD. He was the target of a bitter attack by the leader of the *Vereinigung für das religiös-liberale Judentum* in Berlin in 1932, the basis of which was the contention that Kareski had become a deliberate, bitterly divisive force in a community in which all the parties were carefully trying to cooperate with one another for the common Jewish good. In a letter to Alfred Klee, one of the founders of the *Jüdische Volkspartei* and a supporter of Kareski, in October 1932, Heinrich Stern of the *Vereinigung für das religiös-liberale Judentum* charged that Kareski's personality and tactics had become a point of conflict between the parties as well as within them.[56] Stern argued:

> "Er hat eine Tonart eingeführt, die im Berliner Gemeindevorstand bisher nicht üblich war. Der politische Kampf hat sich verschärft und es ist bedauerlich genug, dass er auch auf unsere Reihen übergegriffen hat."

Stern further criticised Kareski for mis-management and mis-appropriation of Berlin community funds and for undermining the tireless efforts of himself, Klee and others to eliminate the conflicts among the parties, particularly between Zionists and Liberals, for the common Jewish good. Stern concluded with a plea to have Kareski removed entirely from *Gemeindedienst* for the sake of the continued cooperation of the parties in the Berlin Jewish community.

By the beginning of 1933, the misgivings about Kareski among mainstream Zionists in the ZVfD were no less intense. Following its bitter and mutual break with the Revisionists late in 1931 and throughout 1932, the ZVfD's relationship with Kareski reached a breaking point by the spring of 1933. Although he had tried to avoid becoming involved in the fierce Revisionist-ZVfD conflicts in the past, Kareski had come to identify himself more openly with the departed Revisionists, badly divided as they were, outside the politics of the Berlin Jewish community.[57] Even within the *Jüdische Volkspartei* in the Berlin *Gemeinde*, the ZVfD and the Revisionists had come to a parting of the ways by the summer of 1933. Early in June, the non-Revisionist members of the ZVfD in the *Jüdische Volkspartei*, led by Siegfried Moses and Alfred Berger, separated from the old party and formed their own *Zionistische Fraktion*.[58] This move was prompted in part by Kareski's growing role and influence in the Berlin *Gemeinde*, particularly through his dominant position in the *Jüdische Volkspartei*, and by the increasing resentment of the ZVfD towards his position and activities.[59]

[56]CZA/Jerusalem: A142/90–2. Heinrich Stern an Alfred Klee, 28. Oktober 1932.

[57]Kareski stated in 1937 that while he deliberately tried to stay out of the conflict between Revisionists and the ZVfD before 1933, he did nevertheless perform services for the Revisionists and the *Betar*, which, he noted, generated much suspicion within the ZVfD. See: CAHJP/Jerusalem: P82/24a. Materialien für die Verhandlungen vor dem Beth Din. Angaben über die öffentliche Tätigkeit, eingeteilt in 3 Abschnitte, p. 6.

[58]See CAHJP/Jerusalem: P82/21. Georg Loewenberg an Dr. Sammy Gronemann, 23. Juni 1933.

[59]After the secession of the *Zionistische Fraktion* from the *Jüdische Volkspartei*, what was left of the party under Kareski reorganised itself into the *Jüdischer Volksbund* in 1934. See *Jüdische Rundschau*,

One activity in particular had become the pretext for the June 1933 separation of the "Zionistische Fraktion" from the *Jüdische Volkspartei*, and ultimately would be used for Kareski's dismissal from the ZVfD. In May, Kareski apparently tried unsuccessfully to occupy a Jewish welfare office in Berlin, at the head of a group of uniformed members of the *Betar*.[60] Early in 1933, the Berlin *Gemeinde* had established a welfare office after the initial shock of the Nazi *Machtübernahme*. Kareski claimed that the office was placed under the direction of "assimilationists" led by Herr Bruno Woyda, and that the sharp differences between Woyda and himself had led to a *Betar* demonstration in front of the welfare office rather than a takeover attempt.[61] Nevertheless it was an indication of more unconventional political activities and strategies which he would use to promote Revisionist interests in the radically altered circumstances of the Third *Reich*.

On 9th May 1933, the *Geschäftsführender Ausschuss* of the ZVfD decided to ask Kareski to resign from the *Vorstand* of the Berlin *Gemeinde*, ostensibly because of his role in the attempted takeover of the Berlin Jewish welfare office. In a letter to Kareski informing him of this decision and demanding his resignation from the *Gemeindevorstand*, Kurt Blumenfeld berated him for this as well as other activities and policies in the following manner:

> "Ihr eigenmächtiges – misslungenes – Vorgehen hat nicht nur Ihrer Wirkungsmöglichkeit den Boden entzogen, sondern vor allem auch die zionistische Position geschädigt. Die Tatsache, dass Sie bei Ihren Aktionen allzu oft Einzeldinge – zuletzt eine nebensächliche Personalfrage – in den Vordergrund stellten, verhindert jeden grundsätzlichen Erfolg der zionistischen Bewegung, erschwert es uns, neue Verhältnisse in der Gemeinde zu schaffen und den Zionismus mit politischer Wirkung zu vertreten."[62]

Kareski ignored this and other communications from the ZVfD, until August, when he informed the ZVfD that in effect he did not recognise the authority of the *Geschäftsführender Ausschuss* to simply remove him from the positions he held in the Berlin *Gemeinde*.[63] As a result, Georg Landauer informed Kareski on 30th August that the *Geschäftsführender Ausschuss* of the ZVfD, having been authorised by the *Landesvorstand* at its meeting of 2nd July, had decided to expel him from the ZVfD.[64]

After his August expulsion from the ZVfD, Kareski did not formally attach

---

XXXIX, No. 89 (6th November 1934). On 7th November 1934, the two *Gemeindefraktionen* met in Berlin in an attempt to reunite the two groups in the Berlin *Gemeindevertretung*. Representing the *Jüdischer Volksbund* (JVB) were Drs. Ellenbogen and Klee, and A. Koczower, while Drs. Hirsch, Meyer and Tuchler represented the *Zionistische Fraktion* (ZF). They failed to achieve any kind of unity, particularly since the ZF demanded the subordination of the "zionistische Gemeindepolitik" to the discipline of the ZVfD, ". . . mit letztinstanzlichem Entscheidungsrecht des Geschäftsführenden Ausschusses". This was rejected by the representatives of the JVB. See CZA/Jerusalem: A142/53–4. Niederschrift über die Sitzung der von den beiden Gemeindefraktionen eingesetzten Kommission am 7. November 1934, 8. November 1934.

[60]Levine, 'Jewish Collaborator', *loc. cit.*, pp. 259–260.

[61]See CAHJP/Jerusalem: P82/24a. Materialien über die Verhandlungen vor dem Beth Din. Angaben über die öffentliche Tätigkeit, eingeteilt in 3 Abschnitte.

[62]CAHJP/Jerusalem: P82/16. Blumenfeld an Kareski, Mai 1933.

[63]See CAHJP/Jerusalem: P82/17. Kareski an die ZVfD, 7. August 1933.

[64]CAHJP/Jerusalem: P82/16. ZVfD (Landauer) an Kareski, 30. August 1933.

himself to the Revisionist movement until early in 1934, when he emerged as leader of the new *Staatszionistische Organisation*. During the autumn and winter of 1933–1934, he claimed to have spent six weeks hiding in Berlin from the SA which had a warrant for his arrest, which would have precluded his taking part in the establishment of the *Reichsvertretung*.[65] He was in Palestine from December 1933, until the end of February 1934. He noted in his testimony in Jerusalem in 1937 that he had been asked by the Revisionists several months before April 1934, to lead a new organisation, and that he had put forward several conditions before accepting such a task, the most important being the final end of the divisions and conflicts that had shattered Revisionist unity since 1931. His conditions were apparently met, and Kareski became the president of the new *Staatszionistische Organisation* in April 1934.

IV. GEORG KARESKI, THE HITLER REGIME AND THE ZVfD, 1934–1937

This essay cannot consider in detail the policies of the Hitler regime towards the Zionist movement, and its role in National Socialist Jewish policy during the 1930s.[66] There can be little doubt that before the Second World War, the regime pursued a policy or set of policies, albeit in a rather haphazard fashion, designed to remove the entire Jewish community and presence from Germany. The Zionist premise that the Jews constituted a distinct *Volksgemeinschaft*, possessing their own separate culture, traditions, history, language and, ultimately, their own land, that they were not a part of the German nation, and as such were aliens in Germany living in exile from their own homeland in Palestine, naturally made Zionism a useful vehicle in the regime's pursuit of a *judenrein* Germany. Certainly the assessment of Zionism among Nazi officials was by no means uniform throughout the multitude of government and Party agencies that in one way or another were responsible for Jewish policy. The willingness of the regime to accommodate the Zionist movement in Germany as a means towards its obvious ends was motivated if not by the belief that there were both good Jews and bad, then most certainly by the conclusion that some could be useful even if all were bad.

[65]See CAHJP/Jerusalem: P82/24a. Materialien für die Verhandlungen vor dem Beth Din. Angaben über die öffentliche Tätigkeit, eingeteilt in 3 Abschnitte. The *Staatszionisten* never supported the *Reichsvertretung*, and often attacked it. Kareski resented the cooperation of the *Centralverein* and the ZVfD and their joint dominance over the *Reichsvertretung* and, by extension, over all of German Jewry. He admitted as much in the above document, arguing that this kind of national organisation tended to neutralise whatever power and influence the Revisionists could muster, which was almost exlusively on the local and perhaps *Länder* level. The obvious example, of course, was the power and influence of the *Jüdische Volkspartei* in the Berlin Jewish community, and in the *Preussischer Landesverband*. The *Reichsvertretung* was clearly a reflection of Revisionist weakness, and the *Staatszionisten* considered it an impediment to their ambitions. See also CAHJP/Jerusalem: P82/25b. Kareski statement of 20th December 1937: *Der Staatszionist*, March 1935; Levine, 'Jewish Collaborator', *loc. cit.*, p. 259. For an account of the establishment of the *Reichsvertretung der deutschen Juden* in 1933, see Max Gruenewald, 'The Beginning of the "Reichsvertretung"', in *LBI Year Book I* (1956), pp. 57–67.

[66]This has been done most recently in Nicosia, *The Third Reich*, *op. cit.*, chapts. 2, 3, 4, 7, 8.

This utility, and the consequent support and encouragement that the regime showed towards the German Zionist movement, created opportunities as well as dilemmas for German Zionism during the 1930s. The obvious opportunities, although by no means relished by Zionists under the conditions imposed by the Nazi state on the Jewish community, would nevertheless mean the sudden and rapid victory of Zionism over liberalism and assimilationism among German Jews, and the transfer of considerable numbers of German Jews to the National Home in Palestine. However, the dilemmas inherent in this situation were numerous, not the least of which was the absolute necessity of cooperating with the regime as the only way of ensuring the safe and orderly emigration of the Jewish community from Germany. It is within this context that Kareski, the *Staatszionistische Organisation*, their policies, activities and their continuing battle with the ZVfD for supremacy in German Zionism after 1933 must be considered.

That this battle was a savagely divisive one for German Zionism, characterised by a degree of hostility perhaps unmatched by any other intra-Zionist conflict anywhere in the world, was evident in the court case before the *Rabbinatsgericht* in Jerusalem in November 1937, brought by Georg Kareski against the *Hitachduth Olej Germania* (HOG).[67] Shortly after his emigration from Germany and arrival in Palestine in the early autumn of 1937, the HOG published serious charges in its *Nachrichtenblatt* in October against Kareski and his activities while president of the *Staatszionistische Organisation* from 1934 to 1937.[68] There were four charges against Kareski altogether: that he sought, with the help of Nazi authorities and against the will of all Jewish organisations, to impose himself on the entire Jewish community as its leader; that he tried to destroy the ZVfD, after it expelled him in 1933, by constantly attacking it publicly as a Marxist organisation actively promoting Jewish assimilation; that he had permitted a death threat against Siegfried Moses, then *Vorsitzender* of the ZVfD, to appear in his newspaper *Das jüdische Volk*;[69] and that, as Director of the *Ivria Bank* which collapsed in 1937, he was responsible for ruining many small Jewish *Handwerker* and *Gewerbetreibende* as a result of his and the bank's questionable business practices. All of the charges against Kareski were upheld by the *Rabbinatsgericht*, which ruled that Kareski, with the assistance of German authorities, did attempt to assume his own personal leadership over German Jewry against its will, that he did try to destroy the German Zionist movement with his public charges that the ZVfD was a Marxist organisation, that he had allowed his newspaper to print a death threat against Siegfried Moses of the ZVfD, and that he was responsible for the failure of the *Ivria Bank* in Berlin.[70]

[67]An incomplete transcript of the trial can be found in CAHJP/Jerusalem: P82/22. The *Hitachduth Olej Germania* included German Zionists of all political views, including Revisionists, who had immigrated to Palestine. It was not a political party, although it was dominated by former members of the ZVfD. The presidium of the HOG at the time included Kurt Blumenfeld, Ernst Levy, Fritz Loewenstein, Julius Rosenfeld, Kurt Ruppin, Meinhold Nussbaum and Max Kreutzberger.

[68]CZA/Jerusalem: A142/87–39.

[69]This newspaper became the official organ of the *Staatszionistische Organisation* after *Der Staatszionist* ceased publication late in 1935.

[70]CZA/Jerusalem: A142/87–39. 'Das Urteil des palästinensischen Rabbinatsgerichts gegen Georg Kareski' (no date).

Against the backdrop of these charges, particularly the first three, this section will consider the specific activities and policies of Georg Kareski and the *Staatszionistische Organisation* from 1934 to 1937, in its triangular relationship with the ZVfD and the National Socialist state. The fundamental issue in the first three charges remained Kareski's relationship with the National Socialist regime and its role in his activities and in the pursuit of the objectives of the *Staatszionistische Organisation*, particularly in the conflict with the ZVfD. Certainly no Zionist or other Jewish organisation in Germany after 1933 could afford to take a public position that contradicted the policies of the Hitler regime, particularly its Jewish policies.[71] It was inevitable, therefore, that the *Staatszionisten*, like their counterparts in the ZVfD, would have little alternative to accommodating themselves publicly to government policies they might otherwise oppose.

One such example is the position of Kareski and the *Staatszionisten* towards the *Haavara-Transfer* agreement of August, 1933. Beginning with the Eighteenth Zionist Congress in Prague in August, 1933, through the rest of the decade, the entire Revisionist movement, including Jabotinsky and his followers as well as Meier Grossmann's Jewish State Party, adamantly opposed the accord.[72] In Germany, however, Kareski and the *Staatszionisten* saw no other choice but to support *Haavara*, albeit in a very subdued manner. Choosing for the most part to simply ignore the accord, neither Kareski nor other members said or wrote much about it in an obvious effort to avoid anything that might jeopardise their relations with the authorities and the achievement of supremacy over the ZVfD. An article critical of Kareski and the Revisionists entitled 'Die Chance zur Lösung der Judenfrage', which appeared in the *Israelitisches Gemeindeblatt*, probably in 1935, nevertheless noted that Kareski had expressed his support for the *Haavara* agreement in a speech in Mannheim that year.[73] There was also support for the transfer approach, if not specific mention of the *Haavara*

[71]The sensitive and very emotional nature of this question has been made even more acute by the recent publication of Edwin Black's *The Transfer Agreement. The Untold Story of the Secret Pact Between the Third Reich and Jewish Palestine*, New York 1984. Besides the wholly inaccurate statement made in the subtitle of this very controversial work, as well as its other questionable attributes, the book is precisely about the problem of cooperating with the Nazi regime in Germany as it undertook the liquidation of the German-Jewish community. Focusing on the *Haavara* Transfer agreement between the German government and Zionist representatives in 1933, Black condemns the deal, and in much broader terms, the refusal of German-Jewish organisations, particularly the ZVfD which had been a party to the *Haavara* negotiations, for not actively endorsing the international economic boycott movement against Germany, and indeed for having sabotaged the movement by entering into the *Haavara* agreement with the Nazis. For more on the public positions Zionist and other Jewish organisations felt they had to take in the battle between Nazi Jewish policy and the anti-German world opinion it generated, see Werner Feilchenfeld, Dolf Michaelis, Ludwig Pinner, *Haavara-Transfer nach Palästina und Einwanderung deutscher Juden 1933–1939*, Tübingen 1972 (Schriftenreihe wissenschaftlicher Abhandlungen des Leo Baeck Instituts 26), pp. 10–11, 15–20; Martin Rosenbluth, *Go Forth and Serve. Early Years and Public Life*, New York 1961, pp. 250–254. See also Bundesarchiv (hereafter cited as BA)/Koblenz: R/43–II:600. Reichsvertretung der deutschen Juden an Lord Melchett/London, 12th July 1933: and *Jüdische Rundschau*, XXXVIII, No. 26 (31st March 1933).

[72]See Black, *The Transfer Agreement*, *op cit.*, pp. 312ff.

[73]CAHJP/Jerusalem: P82/38. 'Die Chance zur Lösung der Judenfrage', in *Israelitisches Gemeindeblatt* (no date).

agreement itself, in Kareski's comprehensive emigration plan of 1935, as well as a very strong rejection, in complete contrast to the policy of Revisionists outside Germany, of the international boycott movement against Germany, and a proposal for actually promoting German goods in connection with the emigration of Jews from Germany:

> "Dem Boycott deutscher Waren im Ausland muss mit aller Entschiedenheit unter Hinweis auf die entgegenstehenden Interessen der gesamten Judenheit entgegen gewirkt werden. Die Juden aller Länder sind aufzufordern, im Interesse einer beschleunigten Durchführung der jüdischen Auswanderung aus Deutschland so viel als möglich deutsche Waren zu kaufen . . ."[74]

Jabotinsky's final, formal break from the WZO with the formation of his independent New Zionist Organisation (NZO) in Vienna in the summer of 1935 presented the *Staatszionisten* in Germany with a potential problem as well as an opportunity to prove their worth to the German authorities.[75] The German embassy in Vienna sent an observer to the first meeting of the NZO, and sent back to Berlin a detailed report on its proceedings. Among other things, the report noted the new organisation's strong support for the international anti-German boycott movement, and its loud condemnation of the *Haavara* agreement.[76] The Revisionist newspaper *Der Staatszionist* carried at least one decidedly neutral report, devoid of any editorial opinion, of the Vienna meeting in its 25th August 1935 edition. Kareski appears to have been in touch with Jabotinsky and the leadership of the NZO, and tried in vain, with the encouragement of the German government, to convince them to abandon their

[74]CAHJP/Jerusalem: P82/31. 'Die Durchführung des nachstehenden Planes einer Aussiedlung der in Deutschland lebenden Juden . . .' (no date). See also the letter of Dr. Siegfried Stern of the *Staatszionisten* to the German Foreign Ministry expressing the opposition of the *Staatszionisten* to the boycott, in Politisches Archiv des Auswärtigen Amtes (hereafter cited as PA/Bonn): Inland II A/B. Siegfried Stern an das Auswärtige Amt, 23. Januar 1935. The international boycott movement against Germany would always remain a stumbling block in Kareski's efforts to curry favour with Nazi authorities, and to discredit the ZVfD in the eyes of the regime. The German records clearly reveal not only the efforts of the ZVfD to ensure the authorities of its firm opposition to the boycott, and its efforts to stop it, but also the confidence of the Foreign Ministry and the police authorities in those assurances. See PA/Bonn: Inland II A/B. 83/21, Bd. 1, Kurt Blumenfeld an das Auswärtige Amt, 11. Juni 1934, 'Äusserung der ZVfD zur Stellung der Juden im neuen deutschen Staat', 21. Juni 1933, and Auswärtiges Amt an das Landesfinanzamt-Devisenstelle/Berlin, zu 83/21, 27/7, 14. August 1934. Those records are also replete with reports from German diplomatic missions abroad and from the *Gestapo* of the central role played by the two Revisionist organisations, outside of Germany, in the boycott movement. See PA/Bonn: Inland II A/B. 83–63, Bd. 3, Geheimes Staatspolizeiamt an das Auswärtige Amt, II 1 B2–61426/J.162/35, 6. Februar 1935; and Inland II A/B. 83–20, Bd. 3, Deutsches Konsulat/Genf an das Auswärtige Amt, Po. 22, 20. September 1935.

[75]For a good account of the last-ditch efforts of Jabotinsky's *Welt-Union* and the WZO to patch up their differences and preserve some semblance of Zionist unity late in 1934 and in 1935, and of the confusion within Revisionist ranks generated by the attempt, see *Jüdische Rundschau*, XXXVIII (12th October 1933, 9th November 1933), XXXX (11th January 1935, 18th January 1935, 30th April 1935).

[76]PA/Bonn: Inland II A/B. 83–20, Das Judentum allg., Bd. 3/II, Deutsche Gesandtschaft/Wien an das Auswärtige Amt, B4441, 19. September 1933. A copy of this report was then forwarded by the German Foreign Ministry to all German diplomatic missions on 30th September.

active support for the anti-German boycott.[77] Again, the *Staatszionisten* appear to have simply ignored this potentially harmful reality, keeping their distance from Jabotinsky and the NZO as their only viable option. That it seems to have worked, at least for a time, is evident in a brief report of *Abteilung* II–112, the section in the *Sicherheitsdienst* of the SS responsible for Jewish affairs, on the NZO in December, 1936. There is not the slightest hint or suspicion that the *Staatszionisten* maintained any connection to the NZO.[78]

Another question with potentially harmful consequences for the *Staatszionisten* was the debate over the recommendations of the Royal Commission on Palestine headed by Earl Peel in July 1937. The Commission recommended the partition of the Palestine Mandate into nominally independent Arab and Jewish states, with small areas to be left under British administration. Hence, the Zionist movement was confronted for the first time in its brief history with the real possibility of an independent Jewish state in at least a part of Palestine, albeit one that in its projected size fell far short of Zionist dreams. Of course Revisionists in Germany and elsewhere had been demanding for years the immediate establishment of an independent Jewish state in all of Palestine, including Transjordan; therefore the Peel Commission recommendation for a Jewish state in a relatively small portion of Mandatory Palestine was greeted by Revisionists throughout the world including Jabotinsky's NZO and Grossmann's Jewish State Party, with outrage and rejection.[79]

In this question too, it was simply easier and safer for Kareski and the *Staatszionisten* to avoid the issue publicly. The Hitler regime adamantly and publicly opposed the Peel Partition Plan.[80] The ideological basis for this opposition was the old antisemitic notion of an international Jewish conspiracy, which envisioned a Jewish state as nothing more than an independent power base from which the Jewish conspiracy against Germany could be directed. The more practical, strategic basis of this opposition was the conviction that the new state would be a powerful addition to the coalition of states opposed to the new Germany. Yet to have joined in the chorus of Revisionist opposition to the plan might have drawn attention to the very obvious fact that Revisionists opposed the partition of Palestine, which the Peel Plan called for, not the creation of a Jewish state which the Hitler regime opposed in any form.

Jabotinsky corresponded several times with Kareski during the summer of 1937, seeking his advice, support and a meeting in order to somehow head off

[77]See Levine, 'Jewish Collaborator', *loc. cit.*, pp. 251–252. Levine's evidence for this is weak, citing only Benno Cohen's "suggestion" in K. J. Ball-Kaduri, 'Protokoll No. VI. Sitzung des Arbeitskreises von Zionisten aus Deutschland am 5. März 1959', at Yad Vashem/Jerusalem: 01/245. It is certainly plausible, indeed likely, that Kareski would sense the potentially negative impact on the *Staatszionisten* of the new organisation and its renewed enthusiasm for the boycott, and that he would try to neutralise that threat.

[78]See BA/Koblenz: R/58–544. II–112 an II–1, A.Z. 1956/36, Betr. 'Ausbau der Arbeit der Abt. II–112 im Jahre 1937', 18. Dezember 1936.

[79]For more on the position and activities of the Jewish State Party against the partition plan, see Leo Baeck Institute (hereafter cited as LBI)/N.Y.: Wiener Library Material, Reel 40. *Kongress-Tribüne der Judenstaatspartei*, 5th August 1937, and *Die Neue Welt*, 29th June 1937.

[80]See Nicosia, *The Third Reich*, *op. cit.*, chapts. 2, 7.

the implementation of the plan.[81] Evidence of any replies to Jabotinsky's initiatives has not been found. As early as February 1937, when there was already much speculation over what the eventual recommendations of the Peel Commission would be, Kareski was supposed to address the topic of the Royal Commission publicly. In a lengthy 10th February speech entitled 'Dennoch Judenstaat! Unsere Antwort an die Königliche Commission', Kareski devoted much of his time to the problems of Polish Jews, and then to the general shortcomings of the official Zionist testimony, particularly Weizmann's, before the Royal Commission in Jerusalem.[82] He complained that the Jewish State Party as well as Vladimir Jabotinsky and the NZO were not permitted to testify before the Commission. While he did mention Jewish rights in Palestine towards the end of his speech, it was only in the very last sentence that he called for a Jewish State. In an article entitled 'Das jüdische Volk vor der Entscheidung', which appeared in the Revisionist newspaper *Jüdische Zeitung* on 9th April 1937, Kareski again reportedly dismissed Chaim Weizmann's testimony before the Peel Commission as ". . . eine zwar wirksame aber stark feuilletonistisch gehaltene Schilderung der Lage des jüdischen Volkes".[83] Beyond recognising the question of "Grosszionismus" versus "Kleinzionismus", Kareski simply reiterated the fact that there was little likelihood of an understanding between Jabotinsky and the WZO on this and other issues, and avoided the question of a Jewish state altogether.[84]

However, much more than by this kind of passive accommodation to specific policies of the Hitler regime, the efforts of Kareski and the *Staatszionistische Organisation* were characterised by an activist approach to the basic thrust of Nazi Jewish policy, namely the dissimilation and emigration of the Jewish community. They were designed to win the confidence of the authorities and to achieve the removal of German Jews under the best possible circumstances. They were also undertaken with an eye towards ultimately replacing the ZVfD as the dominant force in German Zionism, and as the proper vehicle for the liquidation of the German-Jewish community and its removal to *Eretz Israel*. It was this activist approach towards the German authorities which ultimately would be at the heart of the controversy that has surrounded Kareski and the *Staatszionisten* ever since.

The basis of Kareski's policy was an active, collaborative approach to the fundamental aims of Nazi Jewish policy during the 1930s. This meant not merely a passive, reluctant cooperation in the liquidation of German Jewry, which the ZVfD had little choice but to accept, but rather the active promotion of those aims within the Jewish community. In several public speeches before

[81]CAHJP/Jerusalem: P82/18. Jabotinsky an Kareski, 28. Juli 1937, Jabotinsky to Kareski, 20th July, 1937, Jabotinsky an Kareski, 10. August, 1937, and Jabotinsky an Kareski (postcard), 3. September 1937.

[82]CAHJP/Jerusalem: P82/31. 'Dennoch Judenstaat! Unsere Antwort an die Königliche Commission', Referat von Herrn Dir. Kareski auf der Kundgebung am 10.II.37.

[83]CAHJP/Jerusalem: P82/38

[84]The WZO, while rejecting the boundaries for the proposed Jewish state recommended by the Royal Commission, nevertheless accepted the principle of partition, and came out in favour of a larger Jewish state.

Revisionist *Ortsgruppen* in 1934 and 1935, Kareski asserted that the liquidation of the Jewish community in Germany, the aim of the Hitler regime, was a positive rather than a negative reality which was an essential ingredient of Zionism and which should be greeted with the support and enthusiasm of the Jewish community. In a speech in Stuttgart entitled 'In zwölfter Stunde: Rettung oder Untergang des jüdischen Volkes?', Kareski argued that the forced removal of the Jewish community from German culture and the liquidation of the German-Jewish community were positive developments, particularly for Zionism in Germany.[85] The very different styles of Kareski and the ZVfD were reflected in the former's assertion that the latter was wasting this unprecedented opportunity, as well as with his ringing "Ein Volk! ein Land! ein Gott!" with which he closed the speech.

Kareski offered a more comprehensive airing of this theme in a speech entitled 'Liquidation des deutschen Judentums: Konkurs oder Zwangsvergleich?'[86] After denouncing the "ganze Ohnmacht und sterile Impotenz" of the *Reichsvertretung* and its supporters in the ZVfD and the *Centralverein*, he asserted that Jews had to recognise the benefits of the current situation both for themselves as well as for Germans. He called for Jewish energies to be directed towards an orderly liquidation, warned against the dangerous illusion that the regime might change its policies, asserted that the Jewish policy of the regime reflected the wishes of the German people, and that the Jewish position in Germany was finished. He observed that the Jewish community in Germany had already been in the process of disintegration before 1933, as its size had been shrinking steadily. He called on the German authorities to assist young Jews in preparing themselves professionally for life in a new country, and in particular, to ease the economic difficulties in the emigration process and to ease the burdens imposed on Jews in Germany as they prepared to leave. He reasoned:

> "Es lohnt sich, wie ich glaube, auch vom deutschen Standpunkt aus zu prüfen, ob nicht eine solche Loslösung ohne Groll und Verbitterung angestrebt werden soll."

He concluded that the situation in Germany had provided German Jews with an unprecedented opportunity,

> ". . . an Stelle der aufzugebenden Verwurzelung im deutschen Wirtschafts- und Kulturbereich, unserem Leben einen neuen Inhalt und seinen tiefsten Sinn zu geben durch schöpferische Mitarbeit am Aufbau des Judenstaates, der allein für die durch die Jahrtausende schleichende Krankheit der Judenfrage hier und anderwärts die endgültige Heilung bringen kann".

Kareski's active theme of an orderly liquidation of the Jewish community in Germany through the cooperative efforts of German Jews and Nazi authorities for their mutual benefit generated specific emigration proposals that the

[85]CAHJP/Jerusalem: P82/38, 'In zwölfter Stunde: Rettung oder Untergang des jüdischen Volkes' (no date).

[86]CAHJP/Jerusalem: P82/31. 'Liquidation des deutschen Judentums: Konkurs oder Zwangsvergleich?' (no date). Levine suggests that the document containing the speech was dated March 1935. It is likely that this is correct, although the document has no date on it. See Levine, 'Jewish Collaborator', *loc. cit.*, p. 270, note 50.

Staatszionisten made to the authorities in Berlin.[87] A leading article by the editor, Max Schulmann, calling for the appointment of an *Auswanderungskommissar*, appeared in *Der Staatszionist* in August 1935.[88] Schulmann wrote that there was no one in the *Gemeindevertretung* and its leadership capable of successfully undertaking such a task, and that it would require a very strong will, with a strong hand,

> ". . . einen Juden, der von der Regierung die Vollmacht erhält, alle Massnahmen zu treffen, die erforderlich sind, die Umsiedlung einer halben Million Menschen mit Umsicht und Ordnung einzuleiten und energisch durchzusetzen".

He argued that there were legitimate Jewish needs to be met, namely an orderly emigration, occupational retraining, consideration of Jewish assets and help for the poor, as well as legitimate German interests, namely the removal of all Jews in ten years, the avoidance of pressures on German finances and the avoidance of difficulties for the German economy. Several weeks later, Schulmann sent a letter to the German Foreign Ministry asserting that the only solution to the Jewish Question was the total emigration of Germany's Jews to *Eretz Israel*, and offered the full cooperation of the *Staatszionistische Organisation* as the ideal partner in the process:

> "Das Interesse der deutschen Regierung an dieser Lösung kann als bekannt vorausgesetzt werden. Der Staatszionismus ist, wie an anderer Stelle dargelegt wurde, in der gleichen Weise daran interessiert, wenn auch von einem anderen Standpunkt aus . . . Dieses gleichgerichtete Ziel führt beinahe zwangsläufig zu einer Kooperation, die von keiner aussenstehenden Seite den Vorwurf einer unkorrekten Handlungsweise nach sich ziehen kann, da den letzten Ausschlag die nationalen Belange geben."[89]

Again, Schulmann called for the appointment of an *Auswanderungskommissar*.

Sometime in 1935, Kareski prepared a comprehensive proposal, already cited above, for the removal of the Jewish community from Germany.[90] Arguing that it could only be successful if the German government and the authorities in the Nazi Party recognised it as in the German interest, and if it was implemented by an authority set up by German Jewry and responsible to the German government and the Jewish community, the plan contained twelve points which were, for the most part, a reiteration of previous statements and opinions. Among the provisions of this plan was the demand that Jews recognise and accept the right of the German people to re-order their society, to reject the permanent Jewish presence in Germany, and to redefine the position of Jews in German society as guests. Kareski argued that it was against the common German and Jewish interest to resist or in any way to work against this desire. The plan also pointed out the problems and difficulties in the emigration process, and asked for patience and tolerance from German authorities until it could be completed. Kareski also asserted that the German government should

[87] See Levine, 'Jewish Collaborator', *loc. cit.*, pp. 269–270.

[88] *Der Staatszionist*, 25th August 1935.

[89] PA/Bonn: Inland II A/B. 83–21, Bd. 3. Max Schulmann an das Auswärtige Amt, 11. September 1935. See also: *Der Staatszionist*, 20th June 1935, and 25th September 1935.

[90] CAHJP/Jerusalem: P83/31. 'Die Durchführung des nachstehenden Planes einer Aussiedlung der in Deutschland lebenden Juden . . .' (no date).

direct Jewish emigration to a destination where no new "Jewish Questions" could arise, namely to Palestine. To facilitate the smoothest and fastest emigration process possible, the plan urged the German government to do everything to ensure the economic freedom and livelihood of Jews while they still resided in Germany, as well as to allow emigrating Jews to take with them a part of their assets so that they might more easily gain admittance to Palestine. At the same time, Kareski urged emigrating Jews to understand and accept the difficulty of the German economic situation and the impossibility of taking all their assets with them. His plan also stipulated that Jews with skills needed in Palestine, and particularly younger Jews, should be given priority over others, with the provision that people over the age of sixty should never be forced to emigrate and should be allowed to finish their years undisturbed in Germany. It insisted that no Jew should be forced to leave until he or she had obtained permission to enter another country. The plan also called for continuing support for the retraining of young Jews for life in Palestine, for the right of the Jewish community to tax its own assets in order to pay the emigration costs of poorer Jews, and the continuation and improvement of the transfer process to Palestine. In this context, Kareski clearly urged all Jews in Germany to oppose the anti-German boycott, and instead to urge Jews the world over to buy German goods as a means of promoting the smooth, orderly and mutually-advantageous emigration of Jews from Germany.

The most important political point contained in Kareski's plan was his suggestion of a Jewish emigration authority, or *Auswanderungskommissar*, to be appointed by the government, with control over the entire process. Kareski left little doubt about whom he thought should be named for the post:

> "In Anbetracht dessen, dass die deutsche Judenheit einer einheitlichen Führung ermangelt, eine solche auch ohne eine im Augenblick unerwünschte innerjüdische Auseinandersetzung in absehbarer Zeit nicht zu erzielen ist, wird die deutsche Regierung die Ernennung der mit der Durchführung dieser Vereinbarungen und mit der Bildung der dazu erforderlichen jüdischen Auswanderungs- und Finanzorgane zu beauftragenden Personen nach den Vorschlägen der Initiatoren dieses Planes vornehmen unter der Voraussetzung, dass diese die aktive Mitarbeit aller die Auswanderungsbestrebungen der deutschen Juden unterstützenden Organisationen und Verbände innerhalb der deutschen Judenschaft sichern und unter der weiteren Voraussetzung, dass sie sich des Vertrauens dauernd würdig erweisen, dass die Judenheit Deutschlands ihnen im Interesse einer erfolgreichen Durchführung dieses Planes entgegen bringen muss. Ernennungen und Abberufungen von leitenden jüdischen Beamten des zu schaffenden jüdischen Auswanderungsorganes sollen daher in einer zwischen der deutschen Regierung und den Initiatoren dieses Planes näher zu vereinbarenden Weise erfolgen."

While the regime was certainly willing to use Zionism and the Zionist movement to facilitate the dissimilation and emigration of German Jews, it was naive and presumptuous to think that it might share some authority with any individual Jew or Jewish organisation in the formulation and execution of its Jewish policy.

The publication of the Nuremberg racial laws in September 1935 provided Kareski with an opportunity to carry forward his activist approach to the new realities of Jewish life in Germany. Following the rationale of his arguments on the liquidation of the Jewish community in Germany, and of his comprehensive plan for Jewish emigration, he attempted to derive something positive from the Nuremberg Laws by using them to demonstrate the validity and the usefulness of his ideas to the authorities. On 2nd October 1935, Kareski was interviewed by Dr. Oskar Liskowsky, a subordinate of Hans Hinkel in the Propaganda Ministry.[91] The interview, published in Goebbels's *Der Angriff* on 23rd December 1935, brought the outcry against Kareski's methods and activities from Zionists and non-Zionists alike to a fever pitch. The text appeared under the front-page headline 'Reinliche Scheidung sehr erwünscht. Die Nürnberger Gesetze erfüllen auch alte zionistische Forderungen'.[92] Kareski opened the interview by generally supporting the Laws in so far as they sought the complete separation of the Jewish community from the non-Jewish, or "Aryan", majority:

> "Ich habe seit vielen Jahren eine reinliche Abgrenzung der kulturellen Belange zweier miteinander lebender Völker als Voraussetzung für ein konfliktloses Zusammenleben angesehen und bin für eine solche Abgrenzung, die den Respekt vor dem Bereich eines fremden Volkstums zur Voraussetzung hat, seit langem eingetreten."

Kareski went on to identify race and the importance of the family in Jewish life as the two factors responsible for the preservation of the Jewish people two thousand years after the loss of its national independence, its dispersion and lack of linguistic unity. He asserted that these two values had been the cause of much concern among Jews in recent times, and that the Nuremberg Laws were from the Jewish perspective a very positive development:

> "Die Unterbrechung des Auflösungsprozesses in weiten jüdischen Kreisen, wie er durch die Mischehe gefördert wurde, ist daher vom jüdischen Standpunkt rückhaltlos zu begrüssen."

Kareski's one reservation about the Laws, which he only indirectly addressed in the interview, concerned those provisions which stripped the Jews of their German citizenship. Implicit in Kareski's previous plans for the gradual liquidation and emigration of the Jewish community was the assumption that Jews would be permitted a reasonably free economic existence and the full protection of the law for as long as they remained in Germany. Fearing the dangerous implications that the loss of citizenship would have on these necessities, he endorsed the Laws with the following qualification:

> "Die Nürnberger Gesetze vom 15. September 1935 scheinen mir, von ihren staatsrechtlichen Bestimmungen abgesehen, ganz in der Richtung auf diese Respektierung des beiderseitigen Eigenlebens zu liegen."

Kareski's activist approach to the new realities of Jewish life under National Socialism was, as we have noted, both presumptuous and naive. It is

[91] Hinkel, with the support of the *Gestapo*, had backed Kareski's candidacy to be the Director of the *Reichsverband jüdischer Kulturbünde* in 1935. However in the face of almost unanimous opposition to Kareski's candidacy, including that of the *Reichsvertretung* and the ZVfD, Kareski was dropped in favour of Benno Cohen of the ZVfD. See Levine, 'Jewish Collaborator', *loc. cit.*, pp. 266–268.

[92] Liskowsky's transcript of the interview, sent to Kareski for his approval, can be found in CAHJP/Jerusalem: P82/17, 'Unterredung eines deutschen Schriftleiters mit dem Präsidenten der Staatszionistischen Organisation, Georg Kareski, Berlin, zu veröffentlichen, die mit Genehmigung der für die Überwachung der kulturellen Betätigung der Juden in Deutschland zuständigen Reichsbehörde stattfand' (no date). Kareski's approval of the transcript was contained in a letter to Liskowsky, also in CAHJP/Jerusalem: P82/17. Kareski an Liskowsky (no date).

certainly true that his ends were much the same as those of his critics and opponents in the ZVfD, that much of the logic behind his proposals for the liquidation and emigration of German Jewry simply reflected fundamental Zionist philosophy, and that many of his specific proposals had already been implemented or attempted by the ZVfD. However his means to those ends, substantially different in style as well as in substance, seemed to be based on the notion that the working relationship between Zionism and National Socialism for their common objective of liquidating the Jewish community in Germany could be one of mutual respect, sympathy and support between equally valid and worthy national movements. Of course, nothing could have been farther from the truth. The relationship was clearly one between unequals; the one holding all the power coldly and callously using the other as an instrument of its policy rather than embracing it as a legitimate partner with common objectives. There was no room for "good Jews" in the National Socialist *Weltanschauung*, only useful ones.

Nothing demonstrates this fact more than the attitude and reaction of German authorities to Kareski's activities and initiatives. Kareski himself testified before the *Beth Din* in Jerusalem in 1937 that the *Staatszionisten* did not receive any special consideration from the authorities different from that received by other Jewish organisations, apart from the special permission granted by police authorities to the *Nationale Jugend Herzlia* (*Betar*)* to wear uniforms at closed meetings.[93] The German documents tend to support Kareski's contention; while this does not refute the accusations that he tried to use what he believed was his intimate relationship with the authorities to destroy the ZVfD, it nevertheless does indicate that such a relationship simply did not exist, and that he could not have caused much harm to the ZVfD, even had he wanted to do so.

The only really positive assessment in the German documents of the *Staatszionisten* from the perspective of Nazi Jewish policy was contained in the above-cited police report of April 1935, granting Revisionist youth permission to wear uniforms at closed meetings. Beyond that, the attitude of the authorities seemed to range from indifference to suspicion, and by no means favoured the

*On the *Betar* see also the two preceding essays in this volume of the Year Book, Chaim Schatzker, 'The Jewish Youth Movement in Germany in the Holocaust Period (I). Youth in Confrontation with a New Reality', pp. 164–165 and Jehuda Reinharz, 'Hashomer Hazair in Germany (II). Under the Shadow of the Swastika', pp. 192–193 (Ed.).

[93]CAHJP/Jerusalem: P82/24a. Materialien für die Verhandlungen vor dem Beth Din. Angaben über die öffentliche Tätigkeit, eingeteilt in 3 Abschnitte (no date). There were some 500 members of the *Nationale Jugend Herzlia*, the new name adopted by the German *Betar* in 1933 after all links with Jabotinsky's movement were severed. See CZA/Jerusalem: S5/549. ZVfD/Jerusalem an die Jewish Agency/Jerusalem, 24. Dezember 1937. The police authorities made an exception for the *Betar* to the ban on uniform-like clothing at Jewish youth organisation meetings ". . . weil die Staatszionisten sich als diejenige Organisation erwiesen haben, die auf jede auch illegale Weise versucht hat, ihre Mitglieder nach Palästina zu schaffen und die durch ihre ernstlich auf Abwanderung gerichtete Tätigkeit der Absicht der Reichsregierung, die Juden aus Deutschland zu entfernen, entgegenkommt". See BA/Koblenz: Schumacher File 240/I. Bayerische Politische Polizei, B. Nr. 17929/35 I1B, an Polizeidirektionen, Staatspolizeiämter, Bezirksämter, Bezirksamtsaussenstellen, Stadtkommissäre, Kreisregierungen, 13. April 1935.

Staatszionisten over the ZVfD. There is no indication that any agency in the government or Party considered them better allies or more useful instruments in the process of removing the Jewish community from Germany.

By 1935, the *Sicherheitsdienst* (SD) and the *Gestapo* in the SS were becoming increasingly active in the formulation and execution of Nazi Jewish policy. The government agencies involved in Jewish policy since 1933, including the Interior, Economics and Foreign Ministries, had always dealt with the ZVfD in Zionist matters, such as the *Haavara* agreement, and would continue to do so right up to 1938.[94] Nevertheless the SD and the *Gestapo* did take an interest in the *Staatszionisten* and Kareski by 1935.[95] In the SD, section II–112 was responsible for Jewish affairs, with II–112/3 in charge of Zionist groups. In the spring of 1936, II–112/3 prepared a report on the various Zionist groups, including the *Staatszionistische Organisation.*[96] The report distinguished between three tendencies in German Zionism, namely a small and rapidly disappearing group which had never really been interested in emigration, a large group which it labelled the "Konjunkturzionisten" who were interested in the idea of the Jewish people in the abstract but were not in their convictions and outlook "nationaljüdisch", were really indifferent about a Jewish Palestine and who themselves would never see Palestine, and a third group ". . . dessen Anhänger mit ausgeprägtem Fanatismus immer wieder agitieren und für eine Verteidigung Palästinas, erforderlichenfalls mit Waffengewalt, eintreten". This last group was said to be composed of some old guard Zionists and, in increasing numbers, the *Staatszionisten.* The report then gave a general but very objective description of the *Staatszionistische Organisation*, its general Revisionist principles, its organisation in Germany including some of its *Ortsgruppen* and its youth movement. However the report did not make any attempt to portray the *Staatszionisten* in a positive manner, as an organisation worthy of special treatment or as being of any special value to the policy objectives of the regime. Another report in II–112 in October, 1936, entitled 'Die zionistische Weltorganisation', contained some brief remarks outlining the differences between the *Jewish State Party* and Jabotinsky's *New Zionist Organisation*, and nothing on the *Staatszionisten* in Germany.[97]

There is some evidence, however, that the SD did try to use Kareski briefly in its attempts to promote its own intelligence gathering capabilities and activities in the Jewish Question.[98] These efforts were particularly evident in II–112/3,

[94]The *Reich* Ministry of the Interior was the agency primarily responsible for the emigration process up to 1938. In March 1936 it rejected the proposals and possible visit to Germany of Professor Abraham Bensew, a Czech Revisionist who had been in close contact with Kareski, and had suggested a special "Palästinasteuer" to be paid by Jews to finance Jewish emigration from Germany to Palestine. The Interior Ministry, in a letter to the Foreign Ministry, reasoned that the number of assimilationist Jews was rapidly declining, and that special measures such as this or others were unnecessary. See PA/Bonn: Inland II A/B. 83–20, Bd. 3/2. Reichsministerium des Innern an das Auswärtige Amt, IA 3282/5012, 28. März 1936.

[95]For more on the emergence of the entire SS apparatus in Jewish policy by 1935, see Nicosia, *Third Reich, op. cit.*, pp. 54ff.

[96]BA/Koblenz: R/58–991. Lagebericht der Abteilung II-112, April-Mai 1936.

[97]BA/Koblenz: R/58–955. II–112, Bericht: 'Die zionistische Weltorganisation', 20. Oktober 1936.

[98]For more on these efforts, see: Nicosia, *Third Reich, op. cit.*, pp. 61–62.

the section under Adolf Eichmann that was responsible for Zionism and Zionist activities. A 17th February 1937 report in II–112 stated that discussions had been held with Georg Kareski and Max Schulmann of the *Staatszionistische Organisation* on 24th November 1936, and that the results of these discussions "... für die Arbeit auf dem Sachgebiet von grossem Wert war".[99] The report did not indicate what was discussed, or in what ways the discussions were of value to the SD. Later in 1937, the SD considered using Kareski in what was perhaps the only important intelligence contact it had made. The SD had established contact in Palestine with Feivel Polkes, who had been a member of the underground *Haganah*. A meeting between Polkes and both SD and *Gestapo* officials was arranged to take place in Berlin between 26th February and 2nd March 1937.[100] Polkes was interested in further facilitating Jewish emigration from Germany to Palestine, while Eichmann of II–112/3, who was in charge of the discussions, wanted to cultivate the contact in order to gather intelligence on assassination threats and attempts against German officials, including Hitler. In any case, Polkes invited Eichmann to Palestine, and the latter was given permission to pursue and develop the contact. In June, the SD considered using Kareski to obtain two tickets for ship passage to Palestine at no cost to the SD for Eichmann and a companion, but realised that to do so would run the risk of the journey becoming public knowledge, and therefore decided to foot the bill.[101]

If Kareski's activist approach to the policies and aims of the Hitler regime, as well as the regime's general indifference to his approach were both clear and undeniable, his activities *vis-à-vis* the ZVfD, the most serious part of the HOG charges against him in Palestine in 1937, were not. Indeed, three of the four charges against Kareski contained allegations in one form or another of his determination, with the assistance of German authorities, to destroy the ZVfD and to have himself appointed leader of the Jewish community and of its liquidation.[102] Specifically, he was accused of denouncing Jewish leaders and trying to use his relationship with the *Gestapo* in his struggle against them, of trying, with the help of the *Gestapo*, to win for himself and his supporters positions in the Jewish community at the expense of other groups, of acting as an informer or spy for the *Gestapo* against other Jewish groups, and of publicly supporting the defamation of the Jewish people with his published interview in *Der Angriff*. These charges have been more or less accepted by Richard Lichtheim in his history of German Zionism, and were supported by important witnesses during the trial in Jerusalem in November 1937.[103]

[99]BA/Koblenz: R/58–991. Tätigkeitsbericht 1.10.36 – 15.2.37, II–112–8/81, 17. Februar 1937.

[100]The Polkes affair is considered in Nicosia, *Third Reich*, *op. cit.*, pp. 62–64.

[101]See BA/Koblenz: R/58–954. Bericht betr. Feivel Polkes, II–112 984, 17. Juni 1937. Adolf Eichmann and Herbert Hagen of the SD made the trip in November, 1937, getting only as far as Egypt. They had posed as journalists, but were denied entry to Palestine. Polkes had to meet them in Egypt.

[102]See CAHJP/Jerusalem: P82/25a. Statement of HOG to the Oberrabbinat, 24. November 1937.

[103]Lichtheim, *Geschichte*, *op. cit.*, p. 259. See for example the testimony of two former *Staatszionisten*, Landesgerichtsrat Heymann and Dr. Hubert Pollak, who left the *Staatszionistische Organisation* "... mit der Begründung, sie könnten es nicht billigen, dass Herr Kareski den jüdischen

Kareski readily admitted that he had relations with the police authorities, in answer to a charge in *Das Israelitische Wochenblatt für die Schweiz* that he had close relations with the *Gestapo*. In his letter to the newspaper of 28th September 1937, he wrote: "Beziehungen zur Gestapo hat in Deutschland jeder politisch Tätige und muss sie haben."[104] However, he denied unequivocally that he ever used those relations in a dishonourable way, and rejected as slander charges to that effect. He continued to deny any wrongdoing in his dealings with the German authorities in his testimony in Jerusalem in November, and, as mentioned above, even admitted indirectly that his relationship with the *Gestapo* in the end was not what he had previously believed it to be. He denied charges that he had used his alleged connections with the *Gestapo* to secure *Redeverbote* against, as well as arrests and expulsions of, his Zionist and non-Zionist opponents.[105] After describing in detail each individual case of which he was aware, he mentioned a few cases in which he was able to use his influence and have a *Gestapo* decision reversed. He was quick to point out that two *Betar* leaders had also been arrested for no apparent reason, and that he was able to secure their release after much difficulty.

This essay will not dwell on the validity of the charges made against Kareski by the HOG in 1937. It is sufficient to mention here that the court essentially upheld them.[106] It found that he did attempt to have the German authorities make him head of the *Kulturbund*, and thus of the entire Jewish community [sic], against its will; although it concluded that it was an exaggeration to charge that he sought to become "Führer über die Juden", it was true ". . . dass er nach einem Platz an der Spitze gestrebt hat". Moreover, the charge that Kareski tried to harm or destroy the ZVfD with public charges of Marxism was upheld, even if, as Kareski argued, it had not been his intention to destroy or otherwise harm the ZVfD. The court reasoned that Kareski, as an experienced politician, must have known that, in the prevailing atmosphere in Germany, even the slightest suggestion that any Jewish organisation was Marxist or promoted Jewish assimilation (thus the court expressed itself) would place it in great danger. Thirdly, the court ruled that Kareski, having admitted reading the article entitled 'Der grosse und der kleine Moses' containing the death threat

---

Bruderkampf gegen die Meinekestrasse mit Hilfe der Gestapo führe". They also testified that this was the reason for others leaving the organisation. See CAHJP/Jerusalem: P82/25a.

[104]CAHJP/Jerusalem: P82/12a. Kareski an *Das Israelitische Wochenblatt für die Schweiz*, 28. September 1937.

[105]As early as June, 1934, the ZVfD had complained to the Zionist Executive in London that the *Staatszionisten* were deliberately undermining the organisation by infiltrating and attempting to break up its meetings, and by publicly denouncing the ZVfD as a Marxist organisation. The ZVfD also complained that this tactic had resulted in a temporary suspension of all ZVfD meetings. See CZA/Jerusalem: Z4/3567–8. ZVfD to Zionist Executive/London, 24th June 1934. In his statement to the *Beth Din* in Jerusalem, as well as during his testimony, Kareski admitted to several public comments about Marxists in the ZVfD, as well as his general opposition to Marxism, but denied that he tried to undermine and destroy the ZVfD with charges that it was a Marxist Organisation. See CAHJP/Jerusalem: P82/24a. Materialien für die Verhandlungen vor dem Beth Din. Angaben über die öffentliche Tätigkeit, eingeteilt in 3 Abschnitte, (no date). See also CAHJP/Jerusalem: P82/22. Transcript of 7th November, 1937.

[106]See CZA/Jerusalem: A142/87–39, and Z4/10262–1. 'Aus dem Urteil im Kareski-Prozess', Juni 1938.

Betar's evening party in Berlin, 1936
Above: in the front row, leaders of the Jewish community in Berlin. First from the left, Heinrich Stahl, Chairman of the community

By courtesy of the Jabotinsky Institute, Tel-Aviv

German Betar members en route to summer camp, 1936

Betar's evening party in Berlin, 1936
(On the left, Stahl)

By courtesy of the Jabotinsky Institute, Tel-Aviv

Performance by Betar, Berlin 1936

Betar in Germany, 1934

By courtesy of the Jabotinsky Institute, Tel-Aviv

Cartoon on Kareski by Arie Navon in the labour daily 'Davar', 18th October 1937

Reproduced with the assistance of the artist

against Siegfried Moses, and not stopping its publication in his newspaper *Das jüdische Volk*, was thus responsible for its publication and the consequent danger to Siegfried Moses. Finally, the charge that Kareski was responsible for the *Ivria Bank* failure was also upheld.[107]

Kareski's unorthodox and controversial methods of promoting the interests and aims of his *Staatszionistische Organisation* in Germany under the extraordinary circumstances of the Third *Reich* proved no more successful than those of the old Revisionist *Landesverband* of the Weimar years. During its lifetime between 1934 and 1938, it was a much smaller and weaker organisation than its Weimar predecessor. The police authorities characterised the organisation in 1936 as "ziemlich zurückhaltend" in its activities, perhaps a reflection of its weakness, and noted the dissolution of its *Ortsgruppe* in Zwickau and of the *Brith Hechajal* because of the lack of members.[108] According to the ZVfD, the *Staatszionisten* themselves listed their membership in Germany at the end of 1937 as just 1,000 members, with about 500 members in their youth movement, the *Nationale Jugend Herzlia* (*Betar*).[109] While recognising that the *Staatszionisten* did have some influence in Berlin, the ZVfD also concluded that they had virtually no influence on Jewish life in Germany:

> "Dieser sehr geringen numerischen Stärke der Organisation entspricht ihr Einfluss im Judentum in Deutschland. Die Organisation spielt im allgemeinen jüdischen Leben Deutschlands, insbesondere in der jüngsten Zeit, keine Rolle."

V. CONCLUSIONS: THE DISSOLUTION OF THE STAATSZIONISTISCHE ORGANISATION

It has been observed above that Kareski laboured for a time under the ingenuous assumption that the Hitler regime could be made to accept the *Staatszionistische Organisation* as a group apart from the other Jewish organisations, including the ZVfD. He presented his organisation as the only one that viewed the Jewish Question in Germany from a perspective similar to that of the regime, with similar objectives in mind, and therefore as the only Jewish organisation with which the regime could enter into a cooperative relationship based on some degree of mutual respect and support. He did not appear to

[107]For a detailed account of the history of the *Ivria Bank*, Kareski's role and the circumstances surrounding its failure, see Kareski's above cited testimony and statement before the *Beth Din* in Jerusalem, as well as CZA/Jerusalem: A142/87–39. See also Levine, 'Jewish Collaborator', *loc. cit.*, pp. 277ff.

[108]BA/Koblenz: R/58–991. Lagebericht der Abteilung II–112, April-Mai 1936. The *Brith Hechajal* was the association of Revisionist war veterans.

[109]CZA/Jerusalem: S5/549. Benno Cohen/ZVfD an Organisationsdepartment der Jewish Agency for Palestine, 24. Dezember 1937. It appears that the German *Betar*, like the *Staatszionistische Organisation*, was "ziemlich zurückhaltend". At its first and only national conference during the Third *Reich* in Berlin in November 1936, Heinrich Stahl and other non-Revisionist leaders had no misgivings about attending, and about praising the *Betar* for its discipline and its efforts to forge Jewish unity. Although Kareski was the official head of the *Nationale Jugend Herzlia*, it was actually controlled by Josef Fried, Josef Löw, Manfred Fein and Hans Mielczynski. See CAHJP/Jerusalem: P82/41. *Gemeindeblatt der jüdischen Gemeinde zu Berlin*, 29th November 1936.

accept the fundamental reality of the National Socialist racial philosophy, that all Jews were evil, even if some, such as the Zionists, might be used for facilitating the removal of Jews from Germany. Even the ZVfD, which, unlike the *Staatszionisten*, did not have the disadvantage of being identified in the end with the intensely anti-German, pro-boycott position and activities of a larger, overseas parent organisation, was never more than a convenient tool in Nazi eyes, as the SD reiterated in a report in 1936:

> "Selbst die naturgemäss in Deutschland sehr zurückhaltende Einstellung der ZVfD gegenüber den Behörden ändert nichts an der scharfen Gegnerstellung der 'Zionistischen Weltorganisation' zum nationalsozialistischen Staat . . . Wenn sich die ZVfD – als innerhalb der Reichsgrenzen bestehende jüdische Organisation – eine Zurückhaltung auferlegt hat, so ist der Grund nicht etwa in einer freundlichen Haltung dem Staat gegenüber zu suchen, sondern in der Erkenntnis, dass jede jüdische Organisation, gleich welcher Art, ein 100%er Gegner des Nationalsozialismus sein muss."[110]

Thus, the typically absurd Revisionist charges that the ZVfD was a Marxist nest, and was motivated by essentially assimilationist convictions, in contrast to the more compatible philosophy and inclinations of the *Staatszionisten*, were utterly meaningless to the Hitler regime.

It was inevitable that the *Staatszionistische Organisation* would ultimately be an object of even greater suspicion because of the active participation of both Jabotinsky's organisation and of the Jewish State Party in the anti-German boycott and propaganda campaigns. In the end, Kareski and the *Staatszionisten* were simply unable to convince Nazi authorities that they were not in some way connected with the Revisionist organisations abroad and their anti-German activities. Indeed, the notion that a Jewish group was not part of a larger international organisation or movement, conspiring to destroy the new Germany, could not be reconciled with Nazi ideology. Throughout the 1930s, both the police authorities and the Foreign Ministry followed closely and with alarm the activities of Vladimir Jabotinsky and his New Zionist Organisation, as well as those of Meier Grossmann's Jewish State Party.[111] As if the anti-German boycott and propaganda activities of the Revisionists abroad were not enough, the long-standing Revisionist demand for an immediate Jewish state in all of Palestine and Transjordan, made even clearer in 1937 with the publication of the Peel Partition Plan, was also in direct contradiction to the policies of the Hitler regime.

German fears of Jewish anti-German activities abroad, particularly in the United States, seemed to reach breaking point in the spring of 1937. In response to these activities, the police authorities suspended, until 10th June, all Jewish

[110]BA/Koblenz: R/58–955. II-112 Bericht, 'Die Zionistische Weltorganisation', 20. Oktober 1936.

[111]See PA/Bonn: Inland II A/B, 83–20, Bd.3. Geheimes Staatspolizeiamt an das Auswärtige Amt, B.Nr.II 1 B2–60625/J. 2435, 29. Januar 1935, and Bd. 3/2, Geheimes Staatspolizeiamt an das Auswärtige Amt, Reichsministerium für Volksaufklärung und Propaganda, Reichswirtschaftsministerium und Stellvertreter des Führers, Nr.II 1 B2–J.1208/35, 27. September 1935; Inland II A/B, 83–63, Bd. 3, Geheimes Polizeiamt an das Auswärtige Amt, II 1 B2–J. 24/35, 15. Januar 1935, Auswärtiges Amt an Geheimes Staatspolizeiamt, zu 83–63 15/1, 18. Januar 1935, Reichsinnenministerium an Geheimes Staatspolizeiamt, Nr.IA 324/5012, 19. Januar 1935, Deutsches Generalkonsulat/New York an das Auswärtige Amt, Nr. J. Nr. Ha.916, 28. März 1935, and Deutsches Generalkonsulat/New York an das Auswärtige Amt, Nr. Ha.925, 10. April 1935.

political organisations, including the *Reichsbund jüdischer Frontsoldaten*, the *Centralverein*, and the Zionist organisations.[112] By the end of 1937, the SD had come to the conclusion that the *Staatszionisten* were actively linked to Jabotinsky's movement, and were thus engaged in activities hostile to the state.[113] Early in 1938, the police authorities were warning that although the Zionist-supported emigration process had to continue at all costs, the *Staatszionisten* and their leaders had to be carefully watched, particularly their connections overseas.[114] In April, the police authorities decided to begin the process of dissolving the *Staatszionistische Organisation*, and all of its member groups, because of alleged ties to Jabotinsky's New Zionist Organisation.[115] The formal dissolution occurred on 31st August 1938, apparently because of the open relations between the *Nationale Jugend Herzlia* (*Betar*), the German Revisionist youth organisation, and the New Zionist Organisation. In a published annual report for 1938, the SD observed:

> "Besonders zu erwähnen ist in diesem Rahmen lediglich die Auflösung der 'Staatszionistischen Vereinigung', die nach Feststellung der staatsfeindlichen Verbindung ihrer Berliner Gruppe, der jüdisch-nationalen Jugend 'Herzlia', zur 'Neuzionistischen Weltorganisation' (Jabotynski) [sic] am 31.8.1938 erfolgen musste."[116]

The report also alluded to the weakness of the organisation when it concluded: "Nennenswerte Vermögensbestände konnten infolge der geringen Verbreitung der Organisation (etwa 1000 Mitglieder) nicht sichergestellt werden."

Kareski's methods had clearly failed to achieve Revisionist control over German Zionism. The ZVfD continued to function throughout the rest of 1938 and 1939 with the toleration of the German police authorities, although it had become increasingly irrelevant as an instrument and facilitator of Jewish emigration by the end of 1938 as the SS, acting on the success of the Eichmann model in Austria, began to implement its new direct deportation measures throughout the *Reich*. Even in this aspect of Jewish policy, the Hitler regime in the end showed its preference for using and relying upon established agencies, much as it had done in opting for the established agencies of the state over those in the NSDAP. In the end, the *Staatszionistische Organisation* was unable to neutralise its identity with the Revisionist movements abroad, and thus make Revisionism appealing to the Nazis. It also failed completely to reap the opportunities afforded by the National Socialist *Machtübernahme* to make Revisionism more attractive to German Zionists than the old *Landesverband* had been able to do. In fact, it proved in the end to be much less attractive.

[112]PA/Bonn: Inland II A/B. 83–21, Bd.6, Auswärtiges Amt an alle Missionen und Berufskonsulate, 83–21 15/4, 24. April 1937.

[113]BA/Koblenz: R/58–991. II–112, Tätigkeitsbericht vom 1.7.–31.12.37, 'Aufdeckung der staatsfeindlichen Betätigung der Staatszionisten', 15. Januar 1938.

[114]BA/Koblenz: Schumacher File 240/II. Geheime Staatspolizei/Staatspolizeistelle Würzburg, B.Nr. 1130/38 II B, 28. Februar 1938.

[115]See: BA/Koblenz: R/58–544. II–112, Aktennotiz betr. Einzelfälle, 26. April 1938.

[116]BA/Koblenz: R/58–1094. Jahreslagebericht 1938 des Sicherheitshauptamtes, Bd. 1 (no date). See also BA/Koblenz: R/58–991. Tätigkeitsbericht der Abt. II–112 vom 1.7.–31.12.38.

The B'nai B'rith Order (U.O.B.B.) in the Third Reich (1933–1937)

BY KARIN VOELKER

> "That which was the pride of German Jewry has been reduced to dust and ashes. Their philanthropies have been shattered and scattered to the four winds."

These words were spoken in January 1938 by Alfred Morton Cohen, the American President of the Order in his memorial address on the demise of the German District of the Order, founded in 1885.* After more than fifty years, on 19th April 1937, the Grand Lodge in Berlin and all the still existing individual lodges were disbanded and their assets confiscated by the National Socialist state apparatus.**

In 1843, Jewish immigrants in New York founded a Jewish association which they called "Sons of the Covenant" or, in Hebrew, *B'nai B'rith.*[1] These people lived on the East Side, also known as "Little Germany" (*Kleindeutschland*), a New York district with a predominantly immigrant population. Typical members of the group had come to the New World about ten years before and had managed to work their way up as solid traders or artisans. What they had in mind was the creation of a new Jewish fraternal community transcending the scope of a *Kahal*, a synagogue congregation, in order to reconcile the ethnically heterogeneous Jewish groups. The outcome of their efforts was a "secular synagogue", striving to forge out of the old traditions of Judaism what was to become a modern, American Judaism.

It will naturally be asked what reasons prompted the transplantation of the Order into old Europe at that particular juncture, forty years after its foundation. Indeed, inquiries and appeals from Berlin were met in New York at first with extreme reserve and a dose of scepticism.

*This essay was edited and translated from the German by Dr. Lux Furtmüller, Reading, to whom the Editor of the Year Book wishes to express his appreciation and gratitude.

**The present study had to be completed without access to the archives of the German Democratic Republic, Poland or the USSR. Material from the following West German archives has been used: Bayerisches Hauptstaatsarchiv München; Bundesarchiv Koblenz; Deutsches Freimaurermuseum e.V. und Archiv Bayreuth; Hessisches Hauptstaatsarchiv Wiesbaden; Hessisches Staatsarchiv Darmstadt; Nordrhein-Westfälisches Hauptstaatsarchiv Düsseldorf; Nordrhein-Westfälisches Staatsarchiv Münster; Nordrhein-Westfälisches Staatsarchiv Detmold; Politisches Archiv des Auswärtigen Amtes Bonn; Staatsarchiv der Freien und Hansestadt Hamburg; Staatsarchiv München; Staatsarchiv Würzburg; Stadtarchiv der Stadt Kassel; Stadtarchiv der Stadt Nürnberg. Thanks are due to the staff of these archives who helped the author in her search for relevant material as well as to the staffs of the Leo Baeck Institute in New York, London and Jerusalem; of the International B'nai B'rith in Washington; of the Wiener Library, London–Tel-Aviv; of the Central Archives for the History of the Jewish People, the Central Zionist Archives and the State Archives, all in Jerusalem.

[1]Cf. Deborah Dash-Moore, *B'nai B'rith. The Challenge of Ethnic Leadership*, Princeton 1981.

The main reason was undoubtedly the fact that German Jewry had been caught unawares by a sudden anti-Jewish turn in the climate of opinion.[2] Most German Jews had subscribed to the notion of "German citizens of the Jewish faith". Following the granting of full equality of civic status by the North German Confederacy in 1869, many Jews had become involved in politics in the ranks of the National Liberal Party. But in 1879 Bismarck abandoned his policy of collaborating with the National Liberals, which led to a split in the Party. From that time on Jewish influence in the realm of politics began to wane, and "a sharp-sighted Jew could not fail to notice that the recrudescence of antisemitism and the rightward turn in Government policy were mutually reinforcing".[3]

Among the circles of the educated bourgeoisie antisemitism was given the stamp of acceptability by Heinrich von Treitschke, the highly reputed historian at the University of Berlin, while the petty bourgeoisie, bewildered by the economic crisis, listened to the Court Preacher Stoecker, who pilloried Jewry as the guilty party responsible for capitalism, stock jobbery and Socialism alike.

Anxious to be accepted by the middle and upper bourgeoisie – the social groups most closely related to themselves on the strength of their economic standing and way of life – growing numbers of Jews entered Masonic Lodges,[4] considered to be strongholds of middle-class self-confidence. In the 1860s and early seventies Masonic Lodges in Prussia were open to Jews, but here, too, circumstances changed with the changing climate of opinion, and anti-Jewish tendencies came to the fore.

The development was not uniform; marked differences in the degree of tolerance shown in various regions as well as in individual Lodges have been recorded. As far as Berlin is concerned, we know the names of three members of Berlin Lodges (*System Royal York* and *Odd Fellows*[5] who at the beginning of the 1880s resigned on account of antisemitic incidents and endeavoured to found a new Lodge: Julius Fenchel, David Wolff and Moritz Jablonski.

In 1882, after two years of negotiations between Berlin and New York, the first Lodge of the U.O.B.B. (*Unabhängiger Orden Bne Briss*), the *Deutsche Reichsloge*, was established in Berlin. By the time of the installation of District VIII of the Order in 1885, altogether twelve Lodges had been founded, nearly all of them in Prussia.

A rough idea of the social structure of the membership can be obtained by a comparison with the figures for the economically active Jewish population of Prussia as a whole. Adopting Silbergleit's classification[6] – industry and artisan

[2]Cf. Jacob Toury, *Die politischen Orientierungen der Juden in Deutschland. Von Jena bis Weimar*, Tübingen 1966 (Schriftenreihe wissenschaftlicher Abhandlungen des Leo Baeck Instituts 15), p. 176.

[3]Peter Pulzer, 'Die jüdische Beteiligung an der Politik', in *Juden im Wilhelminischen Deutschland 1890–1914.* Ein Sammelband herausgegeben von Werner E. Mosse unter Mitwirkung von Arnold Paucker, Tübingen 1976 (Schriftenreihe wissenschaftlicher Abhandlungen des Leo Baeck Instituts 25), pp. 143–239, specifically p. 154.

[4]See Jacob Katz, *Jews and Freemasons in Europe 1723–1939*, Cambridge, Mass. 1970, p. 212.

[5]*Ibid.*, p. 271, note 11.

[6]Heinrich Silbergleit, *Die Bevölkerungs- und Berufsverhältnisse der Juden im Deutschen Reich*, vol. I, *Freistaat Preußen*, Berlin 1930, pp. 85ff.

trades (Group B), commerce and transport (Group C), administration and the professions (D), health care (E) – it appears that among the members of the three oldest Berlin Lodges (*Deutsche Reichsloge, Berthold-Auerbach-Loge, Montefiori-Loge*) Groups B and C were substantially over-represented during the period 1891 to 1928. During that period Groups D and E came to play an increasing part in the social structure of the Jewish population. This trend was even more pronounced in the membership of the Lodges. It must be noted that in spite of the prominence of Group B, hardly any Lodge members were artisans. East European Jews, too, were conspicuous for their absence. Lodges founded after the turn of the century in places where old-established Lodges already existed – such as the *Spinoza-Loge* and the *Jehuda Ha-Levi-Loge* in Berlin, founded respectively in 1904 and 1924 – exhibited a marked academic bias in the occupational structure of their membership, at least in the early years.

The development of the Order presented a picture of steady growth until 1925, when it had 107 Lodges with 15,278 members. The decline in membership after that year – to some 13,000 in 1933[7] – reflected on the one hand the deteriorating economic position of the Jews in the aftermath of the First World War and, on the other hand, a more restrictive admission policy designed to strengthen the spiritual element in the character of the Order. Ever since 1918 attempts had been made to interest more women and young people in the Order. A small band of reformers within the Order was animated by a crusading spirit. Together with committed members of the women's sections of the Order they campaigned for an end to the "ballot days", an admission procedure allowing the blackballing of candidates; they wanted to reduce the display of badges and emblems; to foster the broadest possible participation of the individual members in the life of the Lodges; and to discourage the promotion of an elitist self-image of the Order. However, fresh initiatives put forward in the course of the debate on the role of women and the need to strengthen the representation of youth failed to get majority support. As a result the Order entered the year 1933 in a phase of stagnation, with an over-aged membership.

To say this can in no way detract from the services rendered by the Order through the extensive welfare schemes and social work of the Grand Lodge and numerous individual Lodges. What had begun as a dispensing of charity to the poor developed during the fifty odd years of the life of the Order into a model of modern social welfare work.[8] Even after 1933 social welfare work continued in a number of Jewish communities with the assistance of the Lodges, the amount of which was not always undisputed. In any case, the financial strength of the Grand Lodge and the individual Lodges declined from year to year.[9]

[7]See Leo Baeck Institute (LBI) archives, New York, AR-C 1631/4082.

[8]See Alfred Goldschmidt, *Zum 50jährigen Bestehen des Ordens Bne Briss in Deutschland. U.O.B.B.*, Frankfurt a. Main 1933.

[9]See Hessisches Staatsarchiv, Abt. 483, No. 11 38/40, Darmstadt, for the minutes of the Dahlberg Lodge at Worms, 1936. Rabbi Dr. Rosenberg criticised the Lodge for what he held to be its insufficient contribution to the community's social welfare fund. On the ebbing financial resources consult also LBI Archives, New York, AR-C 1631/4082.

THE DECLINE OF THE ORDER IN THE THIRD REICH

To portray the fate of the Lodges in the years 1933 to 1937 means to trace, and to interpret, vestigial data. As a general rule it can be said that information about U.O.B.B. Lodges surviving beyond 1933 is available only in places where the history of the Jewish community during the National Socialist era is documented. This is the case for a number of towns,[10] but the relevant information never goes beyond a few sentences reporting confiscation of assets and dissolution. In view of the overriding significance of the events of 9th November 1938, less attention has been accorded to the oppressive measures to which the Jewish communities and Jewish organisations were subjected prior to that date. Understandably, scholars have concentrated on clarifying the fate of the Jewish communities and Jewish citizens during the years from 1938 to the end of the war, while less research effort was devoted to the period from 1933 to November 1938 (though this is now gradually being remedied).[11]

The dissolution of the Grand Lodge of the U.O.B.B. in Berlin and of all the individual Lodges throughout the *Reich* – carried out by the *Gestapo* on 19th April 1937, a birthday present for the *Führer* as it were[12] – constituted the final measure taken by a state authority against the U.O.B.B., the death blow ending the history of the Order in Germany, spanning over half a century.

After 1933 the living conditions of the Jewish population, which had already suffered from the results of a succession of economic crises, took a dramatic turn for the worse as vindictive attacks and threats against Jews and Jewish institutions increased in virulence. Under attack, the Jewish population became a community linked by bonds of solidarity, developing over the years into a community of destiny, in the emergence of which the Lodges played an important part. In the years 1932/1933 the press of the Order was dominated by the endeavour to forge a Jewish "Front of Inner Peace" transcending the quarrels of the various Jewish bodies.[13] At the same time the effects of the precarious economic situation could no longer be overlooked. At the last conference of the Grand Lodge in February 1933 the Order had to face the fact that 60 per cent of the revenue of the Grand Lodge had already been spent on "fraternal aid", for widows and orphans. In the individual Lodges the economic plight of the members threatened to wipe out the entire resources of the Lodges. Even before 1937 the individual Lodges throughout the *Reich* – though, as will be seen, in a manner varying from region to region – were subjected to gradually tightening oppressive measures ranging from close surveillance to the

[10] E. G. Lowenthal, 'In the Shadow of Doom. Post-War Publications on Jewish Communal History in Germany (III)', in *LBI Year Book XXIII* (1978), pp. 283–308; and (IV), in *LBI Year Book XXIX* (1984), pp. 419–468.

[11] See most recently *Die Juden im Nationalsozialistischen Deutschland/The Jews in Nazi Germany 1933–1943*, herausgegeben von Arnold Paucker mit Sylvia Gilchrist und Barbara Suchy, Tübingen 1986 (Schriftenreihe wissenschaftlicher Abhandlungen des Leo Baeck Instituts 45).

[12] See Oral History Division, The Institute of Contemporary Jewry. The Hebrew University of Jerusalem, No. 2355.

[13] See *Der Orden Bne Briss. Mitteilungen der Großloge für Deutschland* VIII, U.O.B.B., February/March 1932 to year end 1933.

banning of functions and the confiscation of assets. Documentary evidence also shows how tenaciously members of the Order endeavoured to ensure the continued existence of their Lodges. From Fulda the *Sicherheitsdienst* (SD) reported in February 1935 "that the local population has made a clean sweep of the Jewish Lodge". Yet, a year later an SS sergeant deplored the fact that the members of the *H.M.R.H. Schiff-Loge* in Fulda, "despite repeated protests pressed home by the strong arms of the National Socialist population, are bent on continuing their obnoxious activities".[14]

In Bavaria the campaign against the Lodges was initiated immediately after 9th March 1933, when the Nazification of the state was completed with the appointment of General Ritter von Epp as *Reich* Governor and Adolf Wagner as State Commissioner of the Interior. Wagner lost no time in appointing Himmler Munich Police Chief on 9th March and Head of the Bavarian Political Police on the 15th. Barely two months later the so-called Himmler Operation was launched against all Jewish organisations in Munich.[15]

On the morning of 12th May 1933 simultaneous searches were carried out on the premises of 54 Jewish organisations in Munich, including welfare and charitable associations as well as the two U.O.B.B. Lodges, ostensibly for subversive material. Their assets were "put on record and secured". On 13th May the Executive of the Israelite Board of Deputies in Munich recorded the events as follows:

> "On the morning of 12th May 1933 officials of the Political and Criminal Police called at the Welfare Office of the Board of Deputies as well as at the offices and homes of the Chairmen of nearly all Jewish associations and at some welfare institutions. The officials searched the premises, in some cases for several hours, and confiscated official records, correspondence, secretarial minutes, cash, savings books and other items. They declared that the organisations had been dissolved and that the Chairmen of the respective organisations would have to apply to the competent court to have them removed from the register. The organisations and their officers had to refrain from any further activity. The Chairmen of the organisations were made to sign a printed form which stated that the assets of the organisation had been expropriated in accordance with the provisions of the Bavarian Law of 4th April 1933 on the expropriation of assets applied to anti-national purposes."[16]

On 13th May the Board of Deputies sent a sharply-worded protest telegram to the *Reich* Governor Ritter von Epp, and on 20th May a letter addressed to the Minister of State for the Interior and signed by the Chairman of the Board of Deputies, Dr. Alfred Neumeyer, a Judge at the Supreme Regional Court, requested the Minister to revoke the measures concerned. Dr. Neumeyer pointed out that he had been told by the Political Police that "I had acted maliciously in informing the highest authorities that the organisations had been dissolved, whereas in actual fact the measure concerned was of a purely preventive nature. I was said to have deliberately made false statements to that effect."[17]

[14]Hessisches Hauptstaatsarchiv, Wiesbaden, Abt. 483, 11308.
[15]Cf. Peter Hanke, *Zur Geschichte der Juden in München zwischen 1933 und 1945*, Munich 1967, p. 66.
[16]Bayerisches Hauptstaatsarchiv München (BHM), Reichsstatthalter 432–1–4.
[17]BHM, Staatsministerium des Inneren, Letter Dr. Neumeyer to the State Minister of the Interior of 12th May 1933.

On 30th May 1933 the Commander of the Bavarian Political Police reported to the Bavarian State Chancellery that the operation of 12th May had been a "preventive police measure" designed to uncover subversive material and to ascertain and secure the assets of the organisations.[18] The most important provisional result of the operation was said to be the securing of material belonging to the *Centralverein deutscher Staatsbürger jüdischen Glaubens* (C.V.), including documents marked out "to be destroyed immediately, preferably by burning" in the event of police intervention. The report outlined what it described as the background necessary for an understanding of the operation. It was "the fundamentally hostile attitude of Jewry towards the national rising and the liberation of the German people, pursued openly up till the seizure of power [in Bavaria] on 9th March, as well as covertly since the appointment of the national Government, manifested also in the atrocity propaganda carried on abroad against the national Government".

Having given a bare outline of the events, it is now proposed to sum up the main features of the Himmler Operation of 12th May 1933 in Munich and to evaluate their significance in the wider political and historical context.

1. The operation was directed equally against all Jewish organisations, ranging from the important supra-regional C.V. to small groups centred on synagogues. The two Munich U.O.B.B. Lodges – *München-Loge* and *Jesaia-Loge* – were included.
2. Retrospectively the Bavarian Political Police described the operation as "preventive", intended only to check on certain aspects that had aroused suspicion. The official report imputed to the victims the intention of "distorting" the true facts by wrongly asserting that the police officials acting on behalf of the state had forced the organisations into voluntary liquidation. However, the document made it clear that the operation was justified in the first place on the grounds of ideologically motivated allegations (hostility to the National Revolution, underhand subversive activities and support for the so-called atrocity propaganda directed from abroad).
3. Two months later, on 13th July 1933, the majority of the affected organisations – including all synagogue, prayer-room and school associations, welfare and charitable organisations as well as a Jewish students' corporation – were re-admitted. But the ban on the C.V. was upheld, as the Police considered the confiscated material relating to its activities to be sufficiently incriminating.[19]
4. The operation gave rise to a wave of Jewish protests which is likely to have had some effect. Dr. Neumeyer called personally at the Police Directorate and sent protest telegrams to several Bavarian and *Reich* authorities.[20]
5. None the less it was Himmler who was the victor. At a time of "revolutionary events" in Bavaria in March 1933, a time characterised by the progressive disintegration of orderly administration and an anarchical uncertainty of

[18] *Ibid.*, Akz. 695–33, VI–4.
[19] *Ibid.*, Der Politische Polizeikommandeur Bayerns vom 13.7.1933 (Akz. IV/4, signed by Heydrich).
[20] *Ibid.*

official competencies, Himmler pioneered a new style, his very own style. Without any attempt to clarify the legal situation, far-reaching confiscations were carried out, which were given no more than a semblance of legality by the retrospective label of "preventive" measures, and which were clearly designed as a psychological move to intimidate the victims. The move was successful in that it spread fear and alarm. Overnight all manifestations of the collective life of the Munich Jewish community had simultaneously become paralysed. It was a humiliating blow. Every "decent German" was expected to avoid any contact with such events. The so-called preventive measure was in effect a terror measure launched with the aim of dragooning Jewish Germans, solid middle-class citizens, into voluntarily renouncing their status and liquidating their organisations. Was this the reason why some *B'nai B'rith* Lodges wound themselves up as soon as they were subjected to such oppressive measures? These measures aroused feelings of shame. Many a Lodge member must have thought that it was better to give in and liquidate the Lodge rather than allow it to be dragged down into the mire. What they failed to consider was that "the response of the prey may whet the appetite of the predator".[21] Here we have the first approach to a method which, according to the historian Hans Mommsen, was subsequently developed and applied with consummate skill by Heydrich, the method of charging the Jewish organisations themselves directly and indirectly with the task of executing the measures of persecution.[22] In Munich, for the time being, the method was pursued no further than the first stage, intimidation through terror, guiding the victims in a certain direction, in this case the direction of self-abandonment, of voluntary dissolution.

6. The so-called Himmler Operation of 12th May 1933 was an episode in the power struggle contested in Bavaria after 9th March 1933 between the National Socialist Government of the *Reich* Governor Ritter von Epp and the Premier Siebert ranged against the Minister of the Interior, Wagner, and his allies Himmler and Röhm. The main points at issue were the competencies of the SA, the status of the Special Commissioners and *Gauleiter*, and above all the question of the so-called "protective arrest", a device used during the early months of 1933 in the first place against members of other parties. Such practices brought about chaotic conditions in which "the authority of the state is placed in jeopardy by widespread instances of political functionaries interfering with the orderly working of the administrative machinery".[23] Himmler's wilful disregard of the law in his capacity as Police Commander – manifested in actions such as the Munich operation of 12th May and the subsequent seizure of the *Maimonidas-Loge* in Nuremberg (to be discussed

[21]Cf. Shlomo Aronson, *Heydrich und die Anfänge des SD und der Gestapo 1931–1935*, Diss. phil., Freie Universität Berlin 1967, p. 159.

[22]Cf. Hans Mommsen, 'Der Nationalsozialistische Polizeistaat und die Judenverfolgung vor 1938', in *Vierteljahrshefte für Zeitgeschichte*, X, 1 (January 1962), pp. 68ff.

[23]Minister of Justice Frank on 27th June 1933 to the Minister of the Interior: see Peter Diehl-Thiele, *Partei und Staat im Dritten Reich. Untersuchungen zum Verhältnis von NSDAP und allgemeiner innerer Staatsverwaltung 1933–1945*, Munich 1969, p. 5.

later) – was covered by Wagner. It was Himmler, too, who inspired the ideological justification of the terror measures as serving the struggle against "the subversive activities of purely Jewish Lodges and organisations".[24]

In 1933, at a time when his official authority was confined to Bavaria, Himmler had already conceived plans envisaging "the liquidation in the foreseeable future of all Lodges and Orders throughout Germany".[25] He tried to extend the policy of closing down all Lodges, Jewish Lodges in the first place, to Berlin, that is to say to the jurisdiction of the *Gestapo* headed by Rudolf Diels. His efforts were frustrated at first by the attitude of Diels, who forbade the execution of such plans by the SD.[26] However, on 20th April 1934 Diels was replaced as Head of the Prussian *Gestapo* by Himmler, a change – as will be seen – of major significance for the Lodges in general and the Jewish organisations in particular.

THE EVENTS IN NUREMBERG

On 20th July 1933 – exactly one week after the readmission of a number of Jewish organisations in Munich – the Bavarian Political Police took renewed action against Jewish organisations, with the exception of synagogues, prayer-rooms, school and welfare associations. The way in which this operation was carried out in Nuremberg is illustrated by the following report:

> "On 20th July 1933 some 300 Jews, mostly members of the *B'nai B'rith* Lodge, were taken from their homes and arrested. They were led through the streets, beaten up and eventually taken to an SA sports ground in a Southern district of Nuremberg. Some of those people were in their seventies. They were forced to work under most humiliating conditions. In the end a number of them were made to pull up grass from a lawn with their teeth. The Jews were forbidden to talk about it. So I was told by several persons who had been involved in that incident. I was given in particular a most accurate and reliable account by the man who preceded me in the position of manager at my office, Herr Moses Rülf of Lenbachstraße 11, Nuremberg. I have known this man for thirty years, and I am absolutely certain that he told me nothing that was untrue or exaggerated. In spite of his age – he was 77 – the men who took him from his home pushed him down the stairs because he was not walking fast enough. Another man who had been involved in the events told me that the operation had been carried out under the command of Wurzenbacher, at the time an SS-Colonel, and that Wurzenbacher had stated the operation had been ordered by *Gauleiter* Streicher."[27]

The two Nuremberg Lodges – *Maimonidas-Loge* and *Jakob-Herz-Loge* of the U.O.B.B., both at Untere Pirkheimerstraße 22 – had their premises searched on 20th July 1933 by the Nuremberg Police, who seized documents and blocked the bank accounts of the two Lodges. Thereupon both Lodges suspended their activities; only a catering establishment continued to serve members by special permission of the Nuremberg Police Directorate.

Months later, on 15th November 1933, members of the *Kampfbund für Deutsche*

[24]BHM, Staatsministerium des Inneren, Der Politische Polizeikommandeur Bayerns vom 30.5.1933, Akz. 695/33 VI/4.

[25]Letter from Dr. Best to the author, dated 30th January 1984.

[26]Rudolf Diels, *Lucifer ante Portas. Zwischen Severing und Heydrich*, Zurich 1949, p. 236.

[27]Bernhard Kolb, 'Die Juden in Nürnberg', Staatsarchiv Nürnberg, F5 QNG 404.

Kultur turned up at the offices of the two Lodges and took possession of the premises and terminated the tenancy of the catering establishment. Representations made by members of the two Lodges to the Political Police in Munich elicited the information that the seizure had been ordered by the Nuremberg Police Chief von Obernitz.

In a letter to the Ministry of the Interior in Munich, dated 20th November 1933, *Justizrat* Bing, a member of the *Maimonidas-Loge*, pointed out that the action of the Nuremberg Police had been devoid of any basis in law, that "in actual fact no measure so far taken by the Police Directorate could be legally effective, since no notification in writing, as required under Section 6 of the *Reich* Act of 26th May 1933, has been delivered. The two organisations are left in complete ignorance about the scope of the order affecting them. They do not know whether it is the intention of the Police Directorate to deprive them of the ownership and right of disposal also in respect of the contents of the house, including the library."[28] On 27th November work was started on structural modifications of the building. This prompted a letter, dated 5th December 1933, in which Bing and Dr. Sinauer appealed on behalf of the two Lodges to *Reich* Governor von Epp "with the utmost urgency to intervene without delay".[29] On 20th December, in a letter to the representative of the two Lodges the Police Chief, SS General von Obernitz, retrospectively "confiscated" the property together with its contents "on the strength of Section 4 of the Announcement of 4th June 1933 outlining executory regulations concerning the Acts of 4th and 11th April 1933 on the expropriation of assets applied for anti-national purposes".[30] It will be remembered that the identical argument was used in justification of the "Himmler Operation" of 12th May.

On 8th January 1934 the representatives of the two Nuremberg Lodges wrote again to the *Reich* Governor in Munich. Referring to the executory regulation invoked by the Police Chief, the letter said:

> "Quite apart from the fact that the very wording of the said provision makes it inapplicable in the present case, since at the time, long after the occupation of the premises by the *Kampfbund*, the situation was clearly not one that 'brooks no delay', it appears to us – as we may venture to point out – that the Acts of 4th and 11th April, to which the said Announcement refers, can no longer be applied to such cases, having been superseded by the *Reich* Acts of 26th May and 14th July 1933, which finally settled the question of expropriation. This is manifestly the view also of the Bavarian Government Departments, who, with explicit reference to those *Reich* Acts, have issued new rules concerning the question of sequestration in the Announcement of 19th September 1933 (*Bayerischer Staatsanzeiger* No. 218 of 21st September 1933). This question is of overriding significance, because under the *Reich* Act of 14th July 1933, it is an essential requirement for the expropriation of assets, that such assets should be used to promote tendencies which the *Reich* Minister of the Interior has found to be inimical to the people and the state. Since such a finding is out of the question in respect of the organisations represented by us – indeed, no such finding has been handed down, nor has any allegation been made to this effect – it appears that on this ground, too, there is no basis in law for the measures concerned. The

[28]BHM, Staatsministerium des Inneren. See note 16.
[29]BHM, Reichsstatthalter, 432–1–4 (see note 16).
[30]BHM, Staatsministerium des Inneren, Letter from Police Directorate Nürnberg-Fürth to *Bankdirektor a.D.* Sturmband, Karolinenstraße 16/I, dated 20th December 1933 Akz. No. 12 125/II.

> reason why in our view such a finding could not possibly be relevant is that the activities of all these organisations have been confined from the outset to charitable and cultural objectives as well as the promotion of social intercourse, whereas any political activity was strictly excluded."[31]

The legal arguments put forward in justification of the Himmler Operation and the action of the Nuremberg Police Chief were not used again, but the *Reich* Act of 14th July 1933 with its stipulation of a ministerial finding in respect of tendencies inimical to the people and the state was invoked – by the Berlin *Gestapo* as well as by other bodies – for the enforcement of the confiscation of assets throughout the territory of the *Reich*, a notable example being the crucial Ordinance of 10th April 1937, which dissolved all U.O.B.B. Lodges as well as the Grand Lodge in Berlin.

The course of events showed clearly that the state authorities in Bavaria were powerless to stop irregular confiscations, at any rate in the case of Lodge assets. This was an aspect of the aforementioned power struggle between the *Reich* Governor von Epp and the Bavarian Premier Siebert on one side, and the Minister of the Interior Wagner and his ally, the Commander of the Political Police, Himmler, on the other.

On 30th January 1934 the Nuremberg Administrative and Registration Court appointed Town Councillor Rollwagen trustee for the sequestrated assets of the two Lodges, in accordance with the joint Announcement of the Bavarian Ministries of the Interior, Justice and Finance, dated 19th September 1933, on the "sequestration for the benefit of the Bavarian State of Communist and other assets used for purposes inimical to the people and the state".[32] This was the very same Announcement invoked by the representatives of the two Lodges in challenging the sequestration.

What happened next is summarised in the "final" report addressed by the Commander of the Bavarian Political Police on 9th October 1934 to the Bavarian Premier:

> "The provisional sequestration of the propery was annulled by the Nuremberg-Fürth Police Directorate on 27th April 1934 as there was a prospect of negotiations with the Nuremberg Municipality with a view to the purchase of the Lodge building. The purchase of the property by the Nuremberg Municipality from the owners, *Maimonidas- und Jakob-Herz-Loge*, was duly completed, and the contract was attested on 30th April 1934 at the Municipal Notary's Office Nuremberg-V. On 16th May 1934 the sequestration of the contents and on 2nd June 1934 the sequestration of the library of the two Lodges was annulled, with the exception, in the latter case, of some of the books, in respect of which the sequestration was upheld on the strength of Section 1 of the Decree of the *Reich* President for the Protection of the People and the State, dated 28th February 1933."[33]

The sale of the premises was forced on the two Lodges by their deteriorating economic situation, as they could no longer meet their mortgage commitments. Another case of a Bavarian Lodge having to be sold is documented; it concerns the *Philo-Loge* in Aschaffenburg.

The events described here reveal a grotesque situation: the arguments put

[31]See note 16.
[32]Staatsarchiv Nürnberg, Bestand Amtsgericht Nürnberg, Vereinsrg. Abg. 1975, No. VR XI 5V.
[33]BHM, Staatsministerium des Inneren, Akz. No. 37624/34 I 1B. (Also see note 16.)

forward by the representatives of the Lodges proved to be valid within the terms of National Socialist legislation, whereas the case argued by the Commander of the Bavarian Political Police and the Nuremberg Police Chief, Himmler and von Obernitz, was untenable. In the end, however, superior legal pleading was of no avail either to the Nuremberg Lodges or to any others. To go by the limited documentation that has so far been made available, seizures of Lodge assets are nowhere found to have been reversed. The "revolutionary" pressure from below was opposed by other interests of a higher order, though certainly not with the aim of bringing back the rule of law in which the victims continued to believe.

Perhaps it was that unshakable faith in law and justice that motivated the lawyers *Justizrat* Bing and Dr. Sinauer when they added the following passage to their letter of 5th December 1933:

> "As regards the essential character of the Jewish Lodges, we should like to add that we have been able through the mediation of the central organisation of our Lodges, which is located in Berlin, to ascertain that the *Gestapo* Office in Berlin is fully apprised of the activities of the Lodges, and that no action has been taken against any of the Lodges, the great majority of which are situated within the jurisdiction of the *Gestapo* Office. Moreover, in connection with the admission of non-Aryan doctors – some of whom had been denied admission in the first place on the grounds of their possible membership of Jewish Lodges – the activities of the Lodges have now been scrutinised by the *Reich* Ministry of Labour as well: all decisions refusing admission on the ground of Lodge membership have been quashed in the absence of incriminating evidence against the Lodges."[34]

A case of naiveté? Not necessarily, bearing in mind the character of the Berlin *Gestapo* Office prior to 20th April 1934, when Himmler was appointed its Head. In the following it will be seen how the fate of an individual U.O.B.B. Lodge in a different part of the *Reich* was linked with the development of the *Gestapo* Office in Berlin.

THE RATHENAU LODGE AT MÖNCHEN-GLADBACH

The *Walther-Rathenau-Loge* at Mönchen-Gladbach, alongside the Munich and Nuremberg Lodges, is one of the few about whose fate we have documentary evidence. But it is reasonable to assume that similar events were repeated throughout the *Reich*, even though no written evidence remains.

The Mönchen-Gladbach Lodge differs from the others so far discussed in that its very name indicated a programmatic mission. The Lodge was founded on 29th October 1922, the 96th Lodge in the German District of the Order, and it was established as a memorial to the assassinated Walther Rathenau both as a German and a Jew. Speaking at the inaugural function of the Lodge, the Grand President Timmendorfer said that Walther Rathenau's ideas "were inspired by a generous precept of tolerance, according to which the state cannot afford the exclusion of any of its potential moral and intellectual forces".[35] Twelve years after, in 1934, government authorities were to describe the choice of name as a "provocation of the National Socialist population".[36]

[34]See note 16.
[35]*Der Orden Bne Briss*, January/February 1923.
[36]Nordrhein-Westfälisches Hauptstaatsarchiv Düsseldorf (N–WHD), RW–58/45618.

What happened in Mönchen-Gladbach? Here, as distinct from Bavaria, the first police investigations were connected with the charge of holding a political meeting, an indictable offence under the Decree of the *Reich* President of 28th February 1933 concerning the Protection of the People and the State. On 6th February 1934 the lawyer Vohssen wrote to the Mönchen-Gladbach Police Directorate on behalf of the Lodge, of which he himself was a member, requesting permission for the holding of a closed family gathering of the members of the Lodge, stating the venue and the exact time of the function, mentioning also that Dr. Walter from Berlin had been invited as a guest, however without explaining that Walter was Vice President of the Grand Lodge in Berlin. In addition the letter announced that the Lodge intended to resume its activities.[37] At the Police Directorate the matter was taken more seriously than the Lodge members seem to have expected. The Directorate's reply, issued on the same day, said:

> "I have passed on your letter in which you announce that the '*Walther-Rathenau-Loge*' intends to resume its activities. When a decision has been handed down concerning your application I shall arrange for you to be notified. Pending that decision, I request you to avoid any activities on the part of the Lodge. I would, however, point out to you immediately that the name of '*Walther-Rathenau-Loge*' cannot be retained in the future, as this name is provocative and offensive to the National Socialist population."[38]

It emerges from the official records that the Mönchen-Gladbach Police Directorate reported the matter to the *Gestapo* Office attached to the Regional Governor in Düsseldorf.

On 9th February 1934 a charge was brought against Vohssen of Mönchen-Gladbach, and Lodge President Joseph of Rheydt, also a lawyer: "Offence: Holding of a prohibited political meeting. Time of offence: 8th February 1934. Place of offence: Mönchen-Gladbach. Injured party: Public interest."[39] The documents attached to the charge show clearly that there had been a verbal agreement to tolerate the function as a tea party attended by the ladies rather than a statutory Lodge meeting. The meeting was watched from an adjoining room through a large hole in the wall (which presumably could not be seen from the meeting room) by an official from the criminal police. It seems likely that this arrangement was made possible with the help or tacit approval of the landlord of the premises. The Lodge President said in his statement that the landlord of the meeting room had checked with the Police Directorate by telephone that permission had been granted for the function.

The report by the official from the criminal police on the meeting constitutes an interesting document of intellectual incapacity combined with typical police misconceptions and officious zeal.

> "At about 21.00 the persons present, among them many women, were warned to be silent by the Chairman's bell. Introductory words were then spoken presumably by the Chairman, who welcomed the speaker of the evening, Dr. Walter from Berlin, who – he said – had exerted himself in order to address the brothers and sisters of the Mönchen-Gladbach

[37] *Ibid.*, Akz. 21.
[38] *Ibid.*
[39] *Ibid.*, Akz. 24–32.

Cartoon from a folder issued by the Oklahoma B'nai B'rith Association to show how the Order protects Jewish rights. 'B'nai B'rith Magazine', November 1933

community. The Chairman spoke so softly that one could not understand what he said. Furthermore, the undersigned was disturbed by late-comers who left their coats in the hall. Then Dr. Walter addressed the meeting, and the gist of his remarks was as follows: A voluntary abandonment of the existing community would never, not ever, be contemplated. If the present Government caused difficulties, such difficulties were there to be overcome and cleared out of the way. They wished to respect the existing laws. But if attacked, they would defend themselves with everything they had. If they were voluntarily to give up only one of their positions, all would be lost, and the damage could never be mended. They were a community within the People's Community. To separate the Jewish community in Germany from Jewish communities in other countries of the world was out of the question. Whatever may befall, they belonged together. They were one people and were determined to remain so evermore. They could not all that easily be liquidated in Germany, because there were so many such communities in the world, and they would receive aid from other brothers and sisters. Not for nothing had God chosen the Jewish people and entrusted them with the task of making laws. God had known that the Jewish people was the most brilliantly gifted in the world. Intellectually and culturally it was superior to the other peoples on earth. That was why the Jewish people, with its history of thousands of years, had not perished. They did not wish to leave Germany and would hold out as long as at all possible. Both during the war and afterwards the Jewish community in Germany had passed through trying times, but now things were on the mend. Today they could do nothing, since the *Führer* (Hitler) had behind him a large, newly-won following. But once those waves had subsided things would improve. Therefore the community must be fostered more steadfastly than ever. Every one must contribute as best he can to the wellbeing of the Jewish people and support the brothers and sisters to the best of his ability. Since the Jewish community could no longer afford to extend material aid in the same way as in the past, its togetherness should be strengthened at least spiritually and intellectually. The Jewish people living in Germany could not be wiped out as easily as the German Government had thought, in order to take them to the graveyards that were ready to receive them. So long as the possibility of a livelihood existed, they would stay in Germany. In any case, it was difficult nowadays to build up a livelihood in other countries.

It was clear that the German Government should look upon the choice of name as a sign of an attitude hostile to the state. There was no reason why they should take exception to this. The speaker stated that this evening's gathering was not the last. Even if meetings were banned for their community, they would find ways and means of fostering [their unity] by clandestine methods in the intellectual, cultural and moral respect. The speaker emphasised repeatedly that on no account should there be a voluntary liquidation of the community. This they were vowing to their God, they owed it to their people and to the memory of the founder of their community. After the end of the address, at about 21.45, the members stayed on, engaging in informal conversation.

This is the case of a purely political meeting, in which it was stressed that if attacked they would defend themselves."[40]

The two lawyers commented on this report as follows:

1. "Most certainly, the speaker did not say that in the event of our meetings being banned there was an intention of arranging to meet by clandestine methods. In actual fact, he said the opposite: 'Even if, at various places, we can no longer pursue our Lodge activities as we used to, an informal and relaxed gathering like the present one is sufficient to bring home to us from time to time the links that bind us together and to give one another mutual comfort in mind and spirit'."[41]

2. "The speaker said an opinion had occasionally been ventilated of late to the effect that there was only one thing left for us Jews in Germany to do, and that was to look after our cemeteries, to make sure we could be buried there.

[40] *Ibid.*, Akz. 17–20.

[41] *Ibid.*, Letter from Lawyer Joseph or Josephs, dated 9th February 1934.

He emphatically opposed this view and pointed out that there was still enough living space in Germany for the living, and that there were many tasks yet ahead of us. This incidentally bears out the sentence in the official report on the meeting, which said that in Germany the possibility of a livelihood existed, whereas it would be difficult to find such a possibility quickly in other countries."[42]

3. "I should like to point out most forcefully that the speaker emphasised repeatedly that we absolutely must respect the existing laws and remain faithful to the fatherland. He also appealed to the audience in stirring words not to slumber but to tread their path proud and erect in the knowledge that we had always fulfilled our duty to our fatherland. At no point in the proceedings was anything said that was hostile to the state. In any case, the Chairman of the meeting would most certainly not have tolerated such a remark."[43]

On 10th February the *Walther-Rathenau-Loge* was dissolved by order of the Police on the strength of the report by their criminal department.[44] But for once the Police were overruled. On 8th June 1934 the Chief Public Prosecutor at the Mönchen-Gladbach District Court notified the Mönchen-Gladbach Police Chief of the decision and wrote:

> "I have stopped the proceedings also in view of the fact that there was no question of an offence against Section 16, Para. 1, Fig. 1 of the Decree of the *Reich* President of 28th February 1933 for the Protection of the German People.
>
> This Section refers back to Section 1 of the same Decree, which makes it clear that the Provision applies to public political meetings. However, a meeting can qualify as being public only if admission to it is not restricted to persons individually identified by name or otherwise, but if anybody is admitted, whether or not subject to the fulfilment of certain conditions. The defendants have pleaded that the meeting in question was attended only by the registered members of the *Walther-Rathenau-Loge* with their wives as guests. Investigations carried out to check the facts have yielded no evidence indicating that the defendants' plea is incorrect, that the meeting was not in actual fact restricted to an individually identified group of persons. Accordingly, it cannot be proved that the meeting in question was a public political meeting subject to the penalties set out in the Provision referred to. Nor has there been evidence of any other punishable offence having been committed.
>
> The Berlin *Gestapo* Office to whom I reported the events agrees that there is no possibility of prosecuting the incriminated persons."[45]

What one would normally expect to happen after the decision of the Chief Public Prosecutor would be the reversal of the dissolution and the return of the sequestrated assets. What happened in actual fact was very different. In the meantime – that is to say between the banning order of 9th February and the termination of the proceedings on 8th June 1934 – the Police Chief had arranged for a detailed inventory to be made of the Lodge assets (using the requisite Form A), which, according to a later document, totalled 26,549.44 Marks.[46] It must be borne in mind that the dissolution of the Lodge and the

[42] *Ibid.*, Letter from Lawyer Vohssen (also Voossen, Vooßen), dated 9th February 1934.

[43] *Ibid.*

[44] *Ibid.*, Akz. 33.

[45] *Ibid.*, Akz. 6 J 109/34.

[46] N–WHD, Nebenstelle Kalkum, Handakte des Vizeregierungspräsidenten Dr. Bachmann, BR 1021/451 I, Akz. Abt. II/3105/70.02.

sequestration of its assets was not made valid in law until the Ordinances of April 1937. None the less, on 15th September 1934 a message was received in Düsseldorf from the *Gestapo* Office in Berlin, ordering that the sequestration be upheld.[47] During a period of three years, from April 1934 to April 1937, the Düsseldorf Regional Governor addressed queries at irregular intervals to the Regional *Gestapo* Office in the same building, asking how soon the Berlin *Gestapo* Office would be likely to ban the Lodges. On 7th October 1935 the Regional *Gestapo* Office informed the Regional Governor as follows:

> "According to a verbal communication from the Berlin *Gestapo* Office a definite settlement of all questions relating to the *B'nai B'rith* Order can be expected in the near future. In all likelihood this will involve also a decision concerning the *Walther-Rathenau-Loge* in Mönchen-Gladbach".[48]

It was indeed the case that the Berlin *Gestapo* Office in October 1935 had prepared a draft providing for a ban on the U.O.B.B. for the approval of the *Führer*.[49] Yet, Hitler for the time being refused to take action against the Order. The reasons for his caution will be discussed in the following.

WHY AND WHEN: THE POLITICAL BACKGROUND

The development of the Lodges during the period 1933 to 1937 is not documented except in a very few cases. In Bavaria, Himmler – to whom both Jewish and Masonic Lodges were anathema on ideological grounds – made use of his power base as Commander of the Bavarian Political Police to launch operations against the Lodges, which often enough ended with voluntary liquidation. In Nuremberg it appears that "revolutionary pressure" exerted by the Party influenced the course of events to some extent,[50] but elsewhere in Bavaria the operations were carried out officially by executive authorities of the state without the assistance of *vox populi*. Outrages of the population against U.O.B.B. Lodges – on record in a few cases, notably in Fulda – resulted in a scaling down of Lodge activities, but never in dissolution. In Mönchen-Gladbach, as has been seen, the Senior Public Prosecutor refused, on legal grounds, to endorse the Police measures against the *Walther-Rathenau-Loge*, and the matter was left in abeyance for years pending a decision by the *Gestapo* Office in Berlin, which since the assumption of supreme authority over the Police by the *Reich* was the competent quarter to issue further instructions.[51]

In Prussia Göring issued on 26th April 1933 what has been called the "first" *Gestapo* Law which set up the *Geheimes Staatspolizeiamt* as the central authority of the Political Police, subordinated directly to the Minister of the Interior. In

[47]Bundesarchiv Koblenz, R 58/984.
[48]Handakte Dr. Bachmann (as note 46).
[49]Bundesarchiv Koblenz, NS 1 9–1763.
[50]See note 27.
[51]Cf. Hans-Joachim Neufeldt, 'Über Entstehung und Organisation des Hauptamtes Ordnungspolizei', in Neufeldt *et al.*, *Zur Geschichte der Ordnungspolizei 1936–1945*, Schriften des Bundesarchivs No. 3, Koblenz 1957, p. 7.

contrast to the Bavarian Political Police under Himmler, the *Gestapo* Office in Berlin under Diels did not have a Department for Jewish Affairs. The impression which Diels made at the time on members of the Jewish organisations can be gathered from the reminiscences of Dr. Fritz Goldschmidt, son of the former Secretary of the Grand Lodge of the Order, Alfred Goldschmidt, and himself until 1937 a member of the Executive Committee of the Grand Lodge:

> "At that time the *Gestapo* was not yet headed by Himmler but by *Oberregierungsrat* Diels, formerly a member of one of the constitutional parties. We thought that it was on his initiative that *Justizrat* Brodnitz, the Chairman of the *Centralverein*, was summoned to an interview with the [Prussian] Premier Göring. Brodnitz told us that Göring had declared that he was fully aware of the fact that, contrary to press reports, the C.V. was not Communist; but he also knew how vehemently the C.V. had fought against National Socialism. That must stop, as Party and state were now closely linked. But it would be all right for the C.V. to represent Jewish interests *vis-à-vis* the authorities . . . Before long I had occasion to meet the Police Chief Diels personally. One evening at the beginning of April 1933 I was in the chair at a committee meeting of the Charlottenburg C.V. branch at the *B'nai B'rith* Lodge premises, Kleiststraße 10 in Berlin. All of a sudden the porter's wife rushed into the room with the cry 'The SA are coming!' I asked everyone to stay in their seats, and said I was going to negotiate with the SA if possible. Luckily it was not SA men but officials of the criminal police in civilian clothes who came in, led by a man with numerous duelling scars* on his face. I introduced myself as Chairman of the meeting and was told in reply that all those present except myself could leave the house in small groups, while I would have to stay for the time being in a room to which I was directed. While I was waiting there, the Lodge premises were searched. After about twenty minutes, the official in command entered the room. He carefully closed the door, keeping his subordinates outside, and introduced himself with the following words: 'Diels! All this is stuff and nonsense. I have come here to prevent worse unpleasantness! The SA wanted to come.' I told Herr Diels that I was a member of the Executive Committees of both the C.V. and the *B'nai B'rith* Lodges, and I asked him whether it was intended to place difficulties in the way of the continued functioning of these organisations. He said he would help us to the best of his ability. It was my impression that he was doubtful about the chances of the Hitler regime consolidating itself, and wanted to show that he had nothing to do with the brutalities."[52]

Indeed, after the war Diels protested over and over again that, together with Göring, he had worked against the extension of Himmler's "network of SD and SS" already established in Prussia, and that he had resisted the activities of Himmler's vanguard in Berlin. "I forbade further 'operations' by the SD, which were directed almost exclusively against the Lodges, Jewish Lodges in particular, and against the Catholic Action."[53] To accept these statements as evidence that Diels really meant to protect the Lodges would be premature; he was generally described as "a character of many hues, slippery as an eel, shifty and opportunistic",[54] an assessment that tallies with the impression this man made on Goldschmidt. Moreover, Diels was a member of a working party which in March and April 1933 had drafted a Bill intended to regulate the

*"*Schmisse*", scars resulting from fencing bouts, proudly worn by members of nationalist student corporations.

52 Fritz Goldschmidt, *Mein Leben in Deutschland vor und nach dem 30. Januar 1933*, reminiscences written in London in 1939, Wiener Library, London and Tel-Aviv, P.II.e.No. 756, pp. 8–9.

53 Diels, *op. cit.*, p. 236.

54 Günter Plum, 'Staatspolizei und innere Verwaltung 1934–1936', in *Vierteljahrshefte für Zeitgeschichte* 1965, pp. 191–224.

status of the Jews. Article 18 said *inter alia*: "The *B'nai B'rith* Order will be banned. Its assets are to be forfeited to the State."[55] Clearly, then, the option of banning the U.O.B.B. was being seriously considered as early as the first few months of the National Socialist regime, though it is not certain which interests were behind this Draft Bill in general and its Article 18 in particular. The driving force behind the Bill is believed to have been the top-level departmental bureaucracy in the Ministry of the Interior,[56] and Article 18 has to be seen in the light of Article 8 on the dissolution of Jewish societies and associations. In May and June 1934 – shortly after Himmler had taken over from Diels – the Berlin *Gestapo* Office issued a topical report entitled 'The Jewish Question', in which a whole section dealt with the Jewish Lodges. About the U.O.B.B. it said:

> "Yet, the most effective instrument for the imposition of a joint Jewish policy is likely to be the '*Unabhängiger Orden B'nai B'rith*', With close to 20,000 members it unites nearly the entire Jewish intelligentsia. It is significant that the Grand President of the Order simultaneously is President both of the *Reichsvertretung der deutschen Juden* and of the [*Allgemeiner*] *Deutscher Rabbinerverband*. Thus the three clamps that secure the cohesion of German Jewry are held in one hand."[57]

This assessment of the U.O.B.B. has to be regarded in the context of the situation at that particular juncture. In the spring of 1934 the Jewish population, while compelled to suspend all political activity, had retained some measure of economic strength, and thus was in a position "betwixt and between", which the authorities were "reluctant to legalise", lest "we may have to go so far as to recognise the Jews as a minority, and then that millstone will be round our necks for ever",[58] since the neighbouring countries were already crowded with 50,000 émigrés and experimental settlement schemes so far had not been promising. The reference to a position "betwixt and between" suggests the picture of a halfway house on the road from the status of a citizen enjoying full civic rights – the result of emancipation – via a multitude of ordinances, decrees and other measures which affected the position of Jews in public life and in many occupations, in short the "progressive restriction of the social living space allotted to the Jews",[59] ending in what may be called "dissimilation", that is to say the reversal of Jewish emancipation.

The report clearly shows that considerable importance was attached to Jewish organisational activities, which under increasing external pressure had greatly expanded. Apart from Jewish sports organisations, the report distinguished three types of Jewish organisations: Zionist, intermediate and national German. As to the attitude to be adopted by the authorities towards the *Reichsvertretung der deutschen Juden*, the report did not come to any definite conclusion. On the one hand, dealing with a central organisation would offer

[55]Politisches Archiv des Auswärtigen Amtes, Inland, Ref. Dt., Po 5 N.E. adh. 6 No. 1, vol. 1.
[56]Cf. Uwe Dietrich Adam, *Judenpolitik im Dritten Reich*, Königstein/Ts. 1979, p. 34.
[57]Lagebericht: Judenfrage, May/June 1934, National Archives, Washington, Himmler File T 175 (408)–2932 496–503.
[58]*Ibid.*
[59]*Ibid.*

the advantage of a "simplified negotiation technique and more effective surveillance", while on the other hand the very existence of such an organisation could foster a will for unification among Jews, and a unified representative body might even try to secure minority rights for the Jews. It appears that at that juncture the *Gestapo* Office was considered a number of different strategies. As regards the U.O.B.B., too, no definite policy had yet emerged by the spring of 1934. There was, of course, the option of a ban as a further step towards the goal of "dissimilation", but it was not yet clear what conclusions would be drawn from the role played by the U.O.B.B. as a force for cohesion. What is clear is that in Bavaria a drive by state authorities against Jewish Lodges is well documented, and that it is reasonable to assume that Lodges were generally subjected to interference and closures, though we do not know to what extent.

During the following months, from the spring of 1934 to the end of 1935, anti-Jewish measures included notably the Nuremberg Laws and on 31st May 1935 the first ban extending over the whole of the *Reich* on any meetings by the so-called German-Jewish organisations,[60] now described – following SD usage – as "assimilationist organisations". This label covered all organisations that came out in favour of the Jews staying on in Germany. The ban did not apply to Zionist groups, nor to sports and cultural organisations, provided they did not engage in "assimilationist" propaganda. The two main organisations affected by the ban were the C.V. and the *Reichsbund jüdischer Frontsoldaten*. A third organisation, the *Verband nationaldeutscher Juden*, which in 1934 was the butt of much ridicule on account of its nationalism, was banned altogether in November 1935.[61] It appears, then, that in 1935, a year after Himmler's taking over in Berlin, the differential (rather than uniform) approach to Jewish organisations which he had adopted in Bavaria in 1933 and 1935, was being extended to the whole of the *Reich*.

For a number of reasons a ban on the U.O.B.B. seemed imminent in the autumn of 1935:

1. The *Gestapo* knew of course that the U.O.B.B. was more than a Jewish welfare institution. The Order's function as a "bonding agent" – clearly recognised in the topical report of 1934 – did not suit the *Gestapo* strategy of 1935, which was based on Himmler's approach of "*divide et impera*".
2. Himmler's deep-seated hostility to Lodges of every kind had prompted action taken by the Bavarian Police in the summer of 1934 against representatives of German Freemasonry, including the Symbolic Grand Lodge as well as the Lodges of Perfection (*Obedienzen*) of the Scottish Rite, which fostered an internationalist and pacifist outlook. Others were persuaded into voluntary liquidation.[62] In these circumstances it was only natural that a great deal of Himmler's attention should be focused on the U.O.B.B.

[60]Joseph Walk (ed.), *Das Sonderrecht für die Juden im NS-Staat. Eine Sammlung der gesetzlichen Maßnahmen und Richtlinien – Inhalt und Bedeutung*, Heidelberg-Karlsruhe 1981, p. 117. See also Staatsarchiv Münster, Akte des Oberpräsidenten, No. 5025.

[61]Walk, *op. cit.*, p. 141.

[62]Cf. Helmut Neuberger, *Freimaurerei und Nationalsozialismus*, vol. 2, Hamburg 1980, p. 44.

3. Up till the autumn of 1935 the *Gestapo* Office in Berlin received repeated requests for guidance in matters affecting the U.O.B.B. The instruction to Düsseldorf to uphold the sequestration of the assets of the *Walther-Rathenau-Loge* contrary to the decision of the judicial authority was given on 15th September 1934; yet, a full year afterwards the nagging question as to when a ban would be officially decreed was still unanswered. We do not know how many such queries were addressed to Berlin, and which Lodges were referred to, but there can be little doubt that there was some administrative pressure in favour of an official ban.[63] In the autumn of 1935 such a ban seemed to be overdue. Indeed, in October – as already mentioned – the Düsseldorf *Gestapo* Office was informed from Berlin that "a definite settlement of all questions relating to the U.O.B.B. can be expected in the near future".

On 1st November 1935 Himmler reported to Hitler on the question of a ban on the U.O.B.B. Hitler, however, decided not to take any action against the Order for the time being.

The decisive document was a memorandum over the signature of Dr. Best, drafted in Section II/1/B2 of the SD, and dated 21st October 1935. This memorandum was submitted to Himmler. It ran as follows:

> "After the voluntary liquidation of all Masonic Lodges in Germany, only the '*Unabhängiger Orden B'nai B'rith*' remains. No action has so far been taken against this organisation, following an instruction given by the *Führer* in the summer of 1935 on foreign political grounds.
>
> Although the U.O.B.B. Lodges do not adopt the Masonic rituals, this organisation acts nevertheless as the headquarters of Freemasonry world-wide. In a letter of 30th August 1935 to the Prussian and *Reich* Minister of the Interior – III B2 6833/L 909/35 – I have drawn attention to the anti-state attitude adopted by the U.O.B.B. against the National Socialist state, and I requested a ruling on the question as to whether the U.O.B.B. was to be regarded as an organisation of the Masonic type and accordingly due to be dissolved on the strength of the Ordinance of the Prussian and *Reich* Minister of the Interior – III P Log. 189 – dated 17th August 1935. In the event of the lodge-like character of the U.O.B.B. being denied, I requested that the organisation be declared inimical to the People and the State under the terms of the Act of 14th July 1933, and that its assets should be seized and expropriated.
>
> So far no decision relating to that report has been forthcoming from the Prussian and *Reich* Minister of the Interior. However, according to information received confidentially from *Ministerialrat* Eickhoff, it appears that it is intended at the Ministry of the Interior to allow the *Gestapo* Office in the future a completely free hand in dealing with the U.O.B.B. This is evidently meant to enable the Ministry of the Interior to disclaim responsibility in the event of action against the U.O.B.B. leading to foreign political setbacks.
>
> For these reasons I beg to request a ruling as to whether the U.O.B.B. is now to be induced to dissolve itself voluntarily by agreement with the *Gestapo* Office, thus following the example of other organisations, such as the Druids and the *Altpreußen*, while ensuring at the same time that the entire archival, library and other documentary material is placed at the disposal of the *Gestapo* Office.
>
> Yet, I feel I have to point out that in view of the obstinacy so far shown by the U.O.B.B. the chances of such an attempt succeeding are slim, especially as a large proportion of the documents is likely to have been stored in synagogues. This material could only be procured by means of compulsory action against the U.O.B.B.
>
> Should voluntary dissolution of the U.O.B.B. be considered inappropriate, I would beg, in view of the *Führer*'s earlier instruction, that the *Führer* be approached for a new ruling. (Signed:) Dr. Best."[64]

[63] Bundesarchiv Koblenz, R 58/984.
[64] *Ibid.*, NS 19/1763.

On 6th November 1935, after his interview with Hitler, Himmler informed Dr. Best's department that the *Führer* had again decided not to take any action against the U.O.B.B. for the time being.[65]

Why did Hitler hold back? Why was action against the U.O.B.B. postponed?

The foreign policy of the Third *Reich* was not at first as successful as the seizure and consolidation of power in the domestic field. Critical situations resulted from a series of policy measures:[66] relations with Poland were affected in the spring, with the League of Nations in the autumn of 1933. The following year has been described as the most perilous for the Third *Reich* during the period before the outbreak of the Second World War.[67] The effects of the massacre of 30th June 1934, followed in July by the abortive coup in Vienna impaired relations with Italy and prompted France to work for the establishment of a European alliance to prevent acts of aggression. As regards National Socialist policy towards the Jews, some allowance was made for public opinion abroad – as for instance in the execution of the anti-Jewish boycott of 1st April 1933 – but Foreign Office assessments were not always heeded.[68] 1935, in contrast to the preceding year, appeared to be successful for Hitler in foreign policy terms, having brought the incorporation of the Saarland, the introduction of conscription and the Naval Agreement with Britain. But there was one problem that had yet to be tackled, and that was the occupation by German troops of the demilitarised zone of the Rhineland. This having been achieved in 1936 without giving rise to military sanctions on the part of the Western Powers, 1937 promised to be a year of tranquillity. Hitler had won some elbow room. He was able to press on with the re-armament drive and watch European trouble spots: civil war in Spain, tensions between Italy and the Western Powers, domestic strife in France. So much for the historical background to the operation of 19th April 1937.

Was there a misjudgement of the likely reaction of US public opinion? Here, it must be borne in mind that protests by the American public against the National Socialist Government and its anti-Jewish measures had been dismissed from the outset as "atrocity propaganda" mounted by Jewish organisations abroad. Attempts had even been made to treat the Jewish organisations in Germany as hostages, so as to put circles abroad on their "best behaviour".[69] From the point of view of the *Gestapo*, the connections of the American *B'nai B'rith* Order with circles of the US Administration only seemed to underline the need for a ban on the U.O.B.B. Seen in this context, the spring

[65] *Ibid.*

[66] Cf. Hans-Adolf Jacobsen, 'Zur Struktur der NS-Außenpolitik 1933–1945', in Manfred Funke (ed.), *Hitler-Deutschland und die Mächte. Materialien zur Außenpolitik des Dritten Reiches*, Düsseldorf 1978, pp. 137–185; also Wolfgang Michalka (ed.), *Nationalsozialistische Außenpolitik*, Darmstadt 1978, 'Einleitung', pp. 1–30.

[67] Charles Bloch, 'Die Wechselwirkung der nationalsozialistischen Innen- und Außenpolitik', in Funke (ed.), *op. cit.*, pp. 205–222.

[68] Uwe Dietrich Adam, 'Der Aspekt der "Planung" in der NS-Judenpolitik', in Thomas Klein, Volker Losemann and Günther Mai (eds.), *Judentum und Antisemitismus von der Antike bis zur Gegenwart*, Düsseldorf 1984, pp. 161–178.

[69] Message to the Auswärtiges Amt from the German Embassy in London, dated 27th September 1934, Politisches Archiv des Auswärtigen Amtes, Bonn, K 330 171.

of 1937 appeared to be a propitious moment for action. It was left to the German Ambassador in Washington, Hans Luther, whose term of office was known to be nearing its end, to bear the brunt of the tidal wave of protests from the American public, while leaving a clear field for his successor. Luther said immediately after the war that the international reputation he had earned as a former Chancellor and *Reichsbank* President in the Weimar Republic and as a prominent supporter of the Locarno policy had been deliberately exploited by the National Socialists.[70]

When Himmler on 6th November 1935 informed the SD of the *Führer*'s decision not to take any action against the U.O.B.B. for the time being, he added the rider: "However, I would request monthly reports on the Lodges, and close observation of the Lodges, in case they are up to machinations dangerous to the State."[71]

There is no record of the monthly reports ordered by Himmler, but there are other relevant documents, notably a Topical Report covering the period April/May 1936, issued on 25th June 1936 by Department II/112 of the SD, which a year before, in June 1935, had been charged with responsibility for the Jewish question. The Report noted retrospectively that the Department had not got into its stride with its "political work proper" until the end of 1935.

> "Until then, the time available – and it was short enough – was used to create a basis for future activity. Nevertheless, at that point in time an understanding of the basic aspects of the enemy and his political tendencies had already been achieved."[72]

The Report had this to say about the U.O.B.B.:

> "The activities of the U.O.B.B. follow a very regular pattern everywhere. The members continue to gather for their Lodge meetings. Ritual functions are in general no longer carried out. The main feature of the Lodge meeting is usually a talk on political events, followed as a rule by a friendly social gathering.
>
> Out of some hundred Lodges existing in 1933, 34 have been suspended. In addition to the 66 Lodges that are still functioning, there are about 25 women's societies distributed over the entire territory of the *Reich*.
>
> The Grand Lodge of the U.O.B.B. proposed to send Jewish children with the co-operation of foreign Grand Lodges to Czechoslovakia and Holland. The *Gestapo* Office sanctioned this scheme for sending children abroad only for children between the ages of six and ten years."[73]

From a report entitled 'Working Programme of Department II/112 for the Year 1937', dated 18th December 1936,[74] it emerges that extensive information had been gathered about the internal affairs of Jewish organisation. An unexpected sidelight is thrown on the methods of surveillance practised at the time by a report of the Berlin Police Chief, dated 21st January 1938. It concerned an application made in the aftermath of the sequestration of the assets of the Grand Lodge by ex-employees and dependants of members of the Grand Lodge to the Police Chief in his capacity as the competent Claims

[70]Bundesarchiv Koblenz, Nachlaß Hans Luther.
[71]See note 64.
[72]Bundesarchiv Koblenz, R 58/991.
[73]*Ibid.*
[74]Bundesarchiv Koblenz, RW 58/544.

Adjudicator (*Feststellungsbehörde*) for the payment of pensions out of the Grand Lodge's pension fund. The application was rejected out of hand,[75] and so was the subsequent appeal to the *Reich* Adjudication Centre at the Ministry of the Interior in Berlin, on the grounds that the Grand Lodge had pursued "objectives inimical to the People and the State". However, it is the arguments put forward in support of the claim that are of interest in the present context:

> "The complainant pleaded that the organisation for which he had been working was subject to the supervision and superior authority of the *Gestapo*, and that in consequence he himself was equally subject to that supervision and authority. The committee meetings of the *Großloge für Deutschland* and the affiliated Lodges were subjected to constant surveillance by the *Gestapo*. All committee meetings were duly notified in advance, and nearly always attended by watchful *Gestapo* officials. The *Gestapo* demanded that lists giving information about the members should be handed in."[76]

Collaboration between Gestapo and SD played an important part in all activities affecting the U.O.B.B. A report on the activity of Department II/112 during the period 1st October 1936 to 15th February 1937 noted:

> "Results of SD investigations which required no follow-up by the intelligence service were always placed at the disposal of the *Gestapo*. As mentioned before, interrogations of Jewish personages were carried out in conjunction with the Berlin *Gestapo* Office. Similarly, the surveillance of Jewish meetings has proved an excellent source of information for the SD."[77]

The files of the same Department contain the following comment, dated 7th April 1937:

> "The task of the *Sicherheitsdienst* is not confined to registering and reporting the general situation, a composite picture derived from many individual observations. On top of this it is the task of the Service to supply the State and the Party with incontrovertible evidence as a basis for legislative and police measures."[78]

The principal future tasks of the SD – investigation of the role of Jews in German economic life, all questions of emigration and transfer of assets – are only adumbrated here, but the importance of intelligence as a basis for police measures is clearly stated. A fortnight later, on 21st April 1937 – two days after the decisive action against the U.O.B.B. – the Department issued, over the signature of the same official, 'Guidelines and Instruction for the Regional Centres', which under Point V include the following passage:

> "1. The collaboration between the *Gestapo* Office and II/112 has up to date been excellent. This is due in the first place to the person of the Head of II B, *Regierungsrat* Dr. Hasselbacher. The collaboration between *Gestapo* and SD territorial branches is above all a question of personnel. One effective way of solving the problem would be for one and the same person to head the local *Gestapo* and SD offices in each place.
> 2. As regards executive action, the *Gestapo* has up till now acted in good time to secure the participation of the SD. A good example for the possibility of collaboration of SD and *Gestapo* in preparing an executive measure was set through the preparation of the action against the U.O.B.B.
> 3. The evaluation of the material gathered by the *Gestapo* is carried out almost exclusively by the SD. This form of collaboration must be maintained in the future. It indicates that the

[75]Bundesarchiv Koblenz, R 18/ANH. Vorl. 244, ruling dated 21st January 1938.
[76]*Ibid.*
[77]See note 72.
[78]See note 74.

Gestapo accepts a measure of intellectual guidance by the SD. In any case, other considerations apart, the *Gestapo* is not in a position to carry out such an evaluation on account of its staffing levels."[79]

Some light is thrown on the extent of the participation of Department II/112 in the operation of 19th April 1937 by an extant expense account, dated 29th April. It names one senior and five other SS officers who were involved in the operations from 19th to 28th April. (They spent 33.20 Marks on 41 taxi rides, 10 telephone calls and six meals.)[80]

With the operation of 19th April 1937 the SD ceased to be purely an intelligence service. It now claimed intellectual leadership as well as a vital role in preparing and carrying out executive actions. The operation against the U.O.B.B. was a successful pilot experiment foreshadowing worse to come.

THE END: 19TH APRIL 1937 IN BERLIN AND IN THE REICH

At seven o'clock in the morning on 19th April 1937 the premises of the Grand Lodge in Berlin and all the individual Lodges in Berlin and throughout the *Reich* were occupied and their assets were seized. This was done in pursuance of an Ordinance issued by the *Gestapo* Head Office (*Gestapa*) on 10th April. The Ordinance dissolved with immediate effect the U.O.B.B. "as well as all affiliated branch or parallel organisations and any Jewish organisations similar in character to the U.O.B.B.". Attempts to re-establish the organisation or to found a camouflaged successor organisation would be liable to prosecution. In addition the Ordinance declared that "the assets of the U.O.B.B. have been used or were destined to be used for purposes inimical to the People and the State". All SD Area Offices were instructed to "take action on 19th April 1937 at seven o'clock in the morning and occupy at one fell swoop" buildings, other premises and all U.O.B.B. institutions (Grand Lodge, individual Lodges, women's associations, hostels, rest homes, etc.); to arrest leading Lodge members (President, Secretary, Treasurer), keeping them under detention until the end of the operation, and search their homes for Lodge documents. When there was a suspicion that specific assets had been removed, searches could be extended to business premises. A 21-page appendix listed 79 towns with a total of 81 premises as well as the private addresses of 347 office holders (including those of the women's associations).[81] The question as to how many persons were arrested on that day, and for how long, cannot easily be answered. Thus, the US Ambassador in Berlin, Dodd, reported to the State Department that on Monday, 19th April, all office holders and employees of the Lodges had been ordered to go to the office premises of the Grand Lodge in the Kleiststraße where they were interrogated and had their passports confiscated, but were allowed to disperse in small groups. The Ambassador added that, in contrast to the Provinces, the Police operation in Berlin had been carried out in an orderly

[79] *Ibid.*
[80] Bundesarchiv Koblenz, R 58/986.
[81] Staatsarchiv Münster, Akte des Oberpräsidenten, No. 5025.

and courteous fashion. The US Consul General in Berlin, on the other hand, reported to Washington that in Berlin about 80 and in the Provinces about 70 Lodge members had been arrested.[82]

Reports on the events of 19th April 1937 have also been made by surviving Lodge members. In his reminiscences Dr. Fritz Goldschmidt reported how the criminal police had wildly rung the doorbell of his home at 6.45 in the morning of 19th April and asked after his wife who was Chairman of the Berlin District of the sister organisation of the Order, with its 800 members. He did not know at the time whether the operation was directed only against the Lodges or against other Jewish organisations as well.

> "A short while before, Dr. Leo Baeck, the President of both the Grand Lodge and the *Reichsvertretung der Juden in Deutschland* had reported to us in the Executive Committee that he had had a talk at the Ministry of the Interior with the official who dealt with the affairs of the Lodges. That official had recommended the voluntary liquidation of the Lodges."[83]

After their flat had been searched, he and his wife were taken to the Lodge premises at Kleiststraße 10.

> "We were led upstairs to the large meeting hall of the Lodge. At the entrance door an official asked me whether I was a 'simple member of the Lodge'. I thought it inappropriate to introduce myself as a member of the Executive Committee, and so I merely replied: 'My wife is Chairman of the sister organisation'. I was then ordered to sit down in the last row of chairs at the back of the hall.
>
> Seated in front were Dr. Baeck and the members of the Executive Committee who had already been arrested. I saw that my wife, too, was sitting in the front row. Any conversation was strictly forbidden. The 'interrogations' were held in another room. Those to be interrogated were called up by name. Teenage SS men were standing guard by the people arrested and told them with much relish that they would afterwards be taken away in the lorries waiting outside. Several hundreds of leading Lodge members, women as well as men, had been taken from their beds in the early hours. But whereas outside Berlin many of them were kept under arrest for several days and left in complete uncertainty about what was in store for them, in Berlin all arrested persons were released in the course of the day. They were told that the Order *B'nai B'rith* had been dissolved as an organisation hostile to the State and its assets had been sequestrated. Around midday those who had already been interrogated were allowed to leave the hall in groups of ten and return to their homes . . . From Munich we received the news that arrests there had been carried out in much the same way as in Berlin. As one of the arrested women was led away, she gave the woman next to her an apple. Taking it, the woman said 'God bless you' whereupon a young SS man shouted at her: 'There is no God here!' She replied quietly: 'Young man, there is a God and there is judgment'."[84]*

[82]Foreign Relations of the United States, Diplomatic Papers, vol. 1937, pp. 321ff. See also Benjamin B. Ferencz, 'Memorandum zur Rückerstattung des entzogenen Vermögens des U.O.B.B.', in Files "In the Matter of the Claim of B'nai B'rith under Title II of the War Claims Act of 1948, amended by Public Law 87–846", New York n.d. International B'nai B'rith, Archives, Washington DC, 1640 Rhode Island Avenue.

[83]Fritz Goldschmidt, *op. cit.*, p. 22.

[84]*Ibid.*, pp. 24–26.

*Translator's Note: The stunning simplicity of the woman's retort defies translation. She said at first "Vergelt's Gott" (may God requite you), the common form of thanking used especially by recipients of charity, implying that they themselves cannot requite the gift. Replying to the SS man, the woman said: "Junger Mann, es gibt einen Gott und es gibt eine Vergeltung." While the verb "vergelten" means to requite good or evil alike, the noun "Vergeltung" is virtually confined to the sense of retribution, as in Hitler's "Vergeltungswaffen".

The interrogations of members of several Lodges on 19th April 1937 are documented by *Gestapo* records. The members of the *Glückauf-Loge* in Essen had to sign the following form:

> "I have been informed that the '*Unabhängiger Orden Bnai Briss*' as well as all affiliated branch or parallel organisations and any Jewish organisations similar in character to the U.O.B.B. have been dissolved with immediate effect by the Ordinance of the *Reichsführer* SS and Head of the German Police, dated 10th April 1937: S-PP (IIB) No. 351–36.
>
> Having been reminded that I am liable to Police measures, I declare that, apart from the material confiscated today in the course of the search of my home (business premises), I am not in control of any other assets of the . . . ______________________________ and that I do not know whether, and if so where, assets of this Lodge may be hidden."[85]

Moreover it emerges from the records relating to the *Glückauf-Loge* that the local *Gestapo* went beyond the instructions of the Ordinance of 10th April by arresting all Lodge members rather than only the office holders. According to the minutes of an internal meeting on 17th April 1937,[86] eighteen *Gestapo* officials were being mobilised for fourteen Lodge members in Essen for the operation on the 19th, one for each member and four for the Lodge premises. Many a Lodge member who received his first summons on 19th April 1937 was summoned again in November 1938, perhaps to be placed under protective arrest and land in a concentration camp. The *Gestapo* files – neatly arranged name by name – present a painstaking official record of the road of suffering of many Lodge members, along with other Jews, from that fateful 19th of April 1937 onward, concluding with a note on emigration and loss of citizenship, or else with a bald entry "gone away" to the East.[87]

The police measures taken against the *Philo-Loge* at Aschaffenburg are particularly revealing in this connection. This Lodge suspended its activities as early as February 1933, as Dr. Ernst-Julius Rosenthal, the last Lodge President, stated during his interrogation on 19th April 1937, since

> "in view of the political situation we were afraid of unpleasant incidents . . . In 1933, soon after the seizure of power, the Aschaffenburg criminal police searched my home and confiscated all records and papers in my possession. The Lodge premises were also searched in 1933 or 1934, and all written records of any significance, in particular the books containing the minutes of Lodge meetings, were seized . . . In 1934, by order of the Mayor Wolgemuth, the Lodge premises were made available to be used by the Aschaffenburg *Bund deutscher Mädchen*. In 1935 negotiations took place between Mayor W. and myself with a view to transferring the property *freihändig* to a Party organisation. Before these negotiations were concluded, on 23rd July 1935, four or five officials of the Würzburg or Munich *Gestapo* called. They searched my home, seized the objects specified in the attached list, and ordered that all items forming part of the inventory of the Lodge and housed for the time being with Lodge members should be taken by me to the haulage contractor Birkart in Aschaffenburg. This I arranged to be done . . . According to the enclosed document of the Aschaffenburg Notary's Office I, No. 1830, dated 23rd August 1935, the Lodge property at Lamprechtstraße 21 was sold to the *Gau* Treasurer Schneider, Würzburg, on the terms registered in that document. The property is now owned by the NSDAP Aschaffenburg and was renamed 'Bauriedlhaus' . . ."[88]

[85]Staatsarchiv Düsseldorf, RW 58/37467.
[86]*Ibid.*
[87]Staatsarchiv Würzburg, Gestapostelle Würzburg, No. 2953/10281.
[88]*Ibid.*, No. 11 132.

It is significant that the only available documentation concerning those earlier encroachments on the Aschaffenburg Lodge should be dated April 1937.

With remarkable thoroughness the Ordinance of 10th April 1937 stressed the need to get hold of all personal files and related documents[89] a clear sign of the keen interest shown by the SD in the slightest personal details of the Lodge members. The files of the Grand Lodge in Berlin in particular are likely to have contained copious information of that character (membership applications, reports of the Auditing Commissions, decisions in the case of disputes, etc.). From the reminiscences of some Lodge members we know that papers such as manuscripts or essays were also seized. In short, the searchers took everything they could lay their hands on. One entry in an official file, dated 26th May 1937, stated that voluminous material had been transferred from the Berlin *Gestapo* Office to the SD Headquarters, also in Berlin.[90] What became of the files held at the Emser Straße in Berlin is not certain.

A further important provision of the Ordinance of 10th April 1937 deals with the assets of the U.O.B.B. "Attention must be given to cases in which on formal legal grounds the sequestration of assets (bank accounts, real estate, etc.) must be effected in the proper form (e.g. entry of blocking clauses)."[91] Reporting to the US Secretary of State on 29th April, Ambassador Dodd estimated the total amount of the sequestrated assets of the U.O.B.B. at 1.5 million Marks in cash and movables, plus 2 million in real estate. Furthermore he recalled that the American branch of the Order had in 1920 assisted the German District by a gift of $20,000 plus $40,000 earmarked for social welfare work. According to the US Consul General in Berlin,[92] the German District of the Order had received 86,000 Marks during the last three years and recently monies were coming in at a rate of 12,000 Marks monthly. The Berlin *Gestapo* Office compiled a list of the assets of the Grand Lodge and the individual Lodges, dated 31st October 1937, but it did not quantify values, except for the liquid assets.[93] In accordance with the executory regulations previously referred to, the competent territorial Government offices (Regional and Provincial Governors and Police Chiefs) called in all outstanding debts and loans of the individual Lodges, ranging from substantial mortgages to minor arrears.

Thus the outstanding loans of the *Walther-Rathenau-Loge* included a credit advanced to the merchant Winter of Mönchen-Gladbach to cover a residual mortgage repayment. This loan figured in a statement submitted in May 1940 by the Mönchen-Gladbach-Rheydt Police Chief to the Düsseldorf Regional Governor. The repayment schedule for this residual debt of 165.00 Marks, provided for monthly instalments of 3.00 Marks payable from 1st June 1935 until 1st October 1946, with interest charged at a rate of 6 per cent. W. died in January 1942 and his widow continued the payments until 31st July 1942. With reference to the residual amount of 102.00 Marks still outstanding the Police

[89]See note 81, p. 3 of the Ordinance (Az II B4-V12 J), signed by Heydrich.
[90]Bundesarchiv Koblenz, R 58/544.
[91]P. 3 of the Ordinance; see note 81.
[92]See note 82.
[93]Bundesarchiv Koblenz, R 18/2644.

Chief informed the Regional Governor: "The widow of the late merchant Abraham Isidor Winter of M.-Gladbach, Gasthausstr. 8, was deported with a mass transport on 27th July 1942 . . ."[94]

In addition to the Ordinance of 10th April, the sequestration of U.O.B.B. assets was formally validated by a second Ordinance issued on 19th April 1937 by the *Gestapo* Office (Stapo D 1a 777–37) and notified immediately to "the Chairman or Deputy Chairman of the Grand Lodge for Germany VIII, U.O.B.B. e.V. [registered society], Dr. Leo Baeck, or his Deputy".

Ignored by the press and radio, the events of 19th April 1937 did not come to the notice of the German public at large. But in those places where Lodges had still been functioning and where Lodge premises had been available, the Jewish communities felt that a decisive blow had been struck at their very existence, and the anxious question was asked as to what the future held in store. Perhaps there is some symbolic significance in the fact that April 1937 lies precisely halfway between the promulgation of the Nuremberg Laws in the summer of 1935 and the November pogrom in 1938.

In America the *Gestapo* coup mounted in the early hours of 19th April 1937 caused widespread dismay. The eloquent words of the American *B'nai B'rith* President Alfred M. Cohen, quoted at the beginning of this study, were typical of the Jewish reaction. But Christian circles, too, were horrified, as contemporary press comment shows.[95] In the years 1933 to 1935 the American *B'nai B'rith*, together with the American Jewish Committee had bombarded the State Department with demands for diplomatic efforts to ameliorate the situation of Jews in Germany.[96] So confident of its role was the American *B'nai B'rith* Order that it saw itself as a defensive shield against the inhuman attacks of the National Socialists on the rights of the Jews in Germany.[97]

Even in January 1938, in delivering his memorial address, the *B'nai B'rith* President did not confine himself to remembering and mourning the past, but ended on a hopeful note, looking to a better future:

> "Like all else Jewish in Germany, *B'nai B'rith*'s noble undertakings have met frustration and desolation. Only when a better day dawns for Germany itself will *B'nai B'rith* return, even as *B'nai B'rith* now functions and flourishes in Egypt, the land of the Pharaohs, whence our forefathers emerged as slaves in that ancient day. That better day will surely come . . ."[98]

[94]Staatsarchiv Düsseldorf, Nebenstelle Kalkum BR 1021/451.

[95]*New York Times*, 25th April 1937.

[96]Sheldon Spear, 'The United States and the Persecution of the Jews in Germany 1933–1939', in *Jewish Social Studies*, vol. XXX, No. 4 (1968), pp. 215–242.

[97]See the cartoon reproduced opp. p. 280.

[98]Report of Alfred Cohen, President, to the Executive Committee at its Meeting held in New Orleans, La., January 23–24 1938. International B'nai B'rith Archives (see note 82).

From Weimar to Nazism: Abteilung III of the German Foreign Office and the Support of Antisemitism, 1931–1935

BY DONALD M. McKALE

Did the 30th January 1933 and Adolf Hitler's assumption of the chancellorship mark such a significant break in Germany's political history?* This question remains a controversial one among European historians,[1] especially when it comes to the role of racism and antisemitism in Germany.[2] Scholars have dated the collaboration of the German *Auswärtiges Amt* (AA) with Nazi antisemitism from the memo by the AA's *Staatssekretär* Bernhard von Bülow, to the Foreign Ministry on the day Hitler took office. It urged the diplomats, most of them old-guard careerists, Conservatives, and nationalists who had entered the ministry during the Imperial and Weimar eras, to remain at their posts to exercise a temperate influence on the radicals.[3] Hence the impression, first developed following the Second World War by German diplomats, that the ministry acted only after Hitler's rise to power and more from fear and opportunism than sympathy in supporting him, has not been challenged.

However, as this essay sets out to show, one of the components of the AA, the Anglo-American and Oriental division (*Abteilung III*), involved itself in defending Nazi antisemitism against foreign criticism at least a year and a half before Hitler's appointment. This fact and the zealous nature of the *Abteilung*'s support of Nazi attitudes after Hitler took office, not only permitted but

*I wish to thank the National Endowment for the Humanities, Washington, D.C., and the Faculty Research Committee of Clemson University, Clemson, South Carolina, for grants that contributed to the completion of this study.

[1]According to Pierre Aycoberry, *The Nazi Question. An Essay on the Interpretations of National Socialism (1922–1975)*, trans. by Robert Hurley, New York 1981, p. 225: "This doubt leads to another: one cannot say for certain whether the Third Reich was a radical departure from, or a continuation of the preceding regimes. The question remains open, like a gaping hole in the historical consciousness. We still have not settled with the past." See, moreover, Andreas Hillgruber, *Endlich genug über Nationalsozialismus und Zweiten Weltkrieg? Forschungsstand und Literatur*, Düsseldorf 1982, pp. 18–32; and Ian Kershaw, '1933: Continuity or Break in German History?", in *History Today*, 33 (1983), pp. 13–18.

[2]For example, note the criticism by Konrad H. Jarausch, 'From Second to Third Reich. The Problem of Continuity in German Foreign Policy', in *Central European History*, 12 (1979), p. 81, of the contention of Thomas Nipperdey, '1933 und die Kontinuität der deutschen Geschichte', in *Historische Zeitschrift*, 227 (1978), p. 98, that antisemitism was not one of the "dominant continuities of German history".

[3]Peter Krüger and Eric J. C. Hahn, 'Der Loyalitätskonflikt des Staatssekretärs Bernhard Wilhelm von Bülow im Frühjahr 1933', in *Vierteljahrshefte für Zeitgeschichte*, 20 (1972), pp. 376–410; and Günter Wollstein, *Vom Weimarer Revisionismus zu Hitler. Das Deutsche Reich und die Grossmächte in der Anfangsphase der nationalsozialistischen Herrschaft in Deutschland*, Bonn 1973, p. 29.

encouraged by Bülow and the German Foreign Minister, Constantin von Neurath, suggest that the conservative and elitist bureaucracy of the AA agreed more with Nazi policy towards the Jews than was previously thought.[4] The following pages will demonstrate further how the diplomats concerned themselves more with tempering foreign reaction to Nazism than with moderating the latter's influence on Germany and world affairs.

By 1930, *Abteilung III*, which handled day-to-day relations with England, America, Africa, and the Middle East, illustrated how Germany's professional diplomats had re-asserted their conservative influence in the AA, despite the efforts at the beginning of the Weimar Republic to infuse the ministry with new men of democratic views and political insight and initiative.[5] Two officials, who joined the foreign service before the First World War and held the authoritarian and nationalist values of Imperial Germany, headed the division from the autumn of 1930. Dr. Hans Heinrich Dieckhoff, the *Abteilung*'s new *Ministerialdirektor*, began his diplomatic career in 1912, fought as a cavalry officer in the War, and served in the 1920s at the German embassies in Washington and London. His deputy (*Dirigent*), Dr. Curt Prüfer, trained as a Middle Eastern specialist and entered the AA in 1907, worked as chief of German intelligence and propaganda in Syria and Palestine in the War, and later held diplomatic posts in Switzerland, Soviet Georgia (Tiflis), and Ethiopia.

Dieckhoff, because of his efforts to prevent war while Ambassador to the United States during 1937 and 1938 was accorded the reputation of being ideologically independent of, and even opposed to, the Nazis.[6] But neither he nor Prüfer displayed such traits. Although they did not join the Nazi Party until long after Hitler had become Chancellor, they shared many views with the Nazis; both detested Communism and had little respect for the democratic principles of the Weimar Republic.[7] Moreover, allegations by Prüfer that the

[4]Christopher R. Browning, *The Final Solution and the German Foreign Office. A Study of Referat D III of Abteilung Deutschland, 1940–1943*, New York 1978, pp. 11–14.

[5]On the efforts to reform the AA in 1919 and 1920 and replace its authoritarian and aristocratic officials with new talent, see Kurt Doss, *Das deutsche Auswärtige Amt im Übergang vom Kaiserreich zur Weimarer Republik. Die Schülersche Reform*, Düsseldorf 1977, pp. 147–286; and Paul Gordon Lauren, *Diplomats and Bureaucrats. The First Institutional Responses to Twentieth-Century Diplomacy in France and Germany*, Stanford 1976, pp. 121–150, pp. 168–169.

[6]Note the assessment of him in Sander A. Diamond, *The Nazi Movement in the United States, 1924–1941*, Ithaca 1974, pp. 284–285; Warren F. Kimball, 'Dieckhoff and America. A German's View of German-American Relations', in *The Historian*, 27 (1965), pp. 219, 242; and Manfred Jonas, 'Prophet without Honor. Hans Heinrich Dieckhoff's Reports from Washington', in *Mid-America*, 47 (1965), p. 232. A biographical sketch of Dieckhoff is in 'Personalbogen', 20th July 1944, National Archives and Records Service, Washington, D.C. (hereafter NARS)/microcopy T–120 (Records of the German Foreign Ministry Received by the Department of State)/roll 2537/frames E308745–750. For Prüfer's background, note the same collection, roll 2539/E309772–777; and Dokument Neurath–4, *Der Prozess gegen die Hauptkriegsverbrecher vor dem Internationalen Militärgerichtshof Nürnberg. 14. November 1945–1. Oktober 1946*, Nuremberg 1948, pp. XL: 453–454.

[7]See the file, for example, showing their efforts during 1931 and 1932 to improve Germany's relations with Persia by suppressing and violating the civil rights of Persian and German Communists in the *Reich*, who had agitated against the Shah, in *Politisches Archiv des Auswärtigen Amtes*, Bonn (hereafter PA)/*Abteilung III*/serial L88 (*Politische Beziehungen Persiens zu Deutschland*). Also regarding that episode, note Heinz Gläsner, *Das Dritte Reich und der Mittlere Osten. Politische und wirtschaftliche Beziehungen Deutschlands zur Türkei 1933–1939, zum Iran 1933–1941 und zu Afghanistan*

Jews and Zionism represented "international" threats to Germany can easily be traced back to the First World War.[8] Already in April 1931, seven months after the startling Nazi victory in the election to the *Reichstag*, *Abteilung III* had tried to blunt negative foreign reaction to Nazism by restricting the freedom of expression and of association in the case of leading Jewish officials and the publicity abroad surrounding the mounting attacks against the Jews.

The division responded to a question posed to the AA from Jewish leaders in the United States and the then German Ambassador in Washington, Friedrich Wilhelm von Prittwitz-Gaffron, about "whether a position could be taken in some form by a recognised German authority against the antisemitic propaganda of National Socialism", which, the Ambassador warned, threatened to become "very harmful to German interests in the United States".[9] Responding to the Ambassador's suggestion, Dieckhoff and Prüfer dispatched the AA's liaison "officer" with Zionist and other Jewish groups since 1918, the Jewish professor of Oriental studies, Moritz Sobernheim, with Gaffron's telegram to the *Reich* chancellery to discuss the possibility of the Chancellor, Heinrich Brüning, making a public declaration against Nazi agitation.

The AA files give no indication of why the leaders of the *Abteilung* sent Sobernheim to Brüning's office; given their anti-Jewish and other views sympathetic to Nazism, they apparently did not wish to intervene personally on behalf of the Jews and, possibily even to downgrade the importance of the subject, sent therefore a subordinate instead. Moreover, with Sobernheim being himself Jewish, even less significance was consequently likely to be attached to his visit to the chancellery. Whatever the *Abteilung*'s motives, it made certain that the chancellery would not agree to Brüning's taking up the cudgels for the Jewish community in public, but instigated an altogether different and far less impressive affair. Sobernheim, who possessed close ties to German-Jewish groups, arranged with the chancellery a private meeting of Brüning with representatives from the principal German-Jewish defence organisation, the *Centralverein deutscher Staatsbürger jüdischen Glaubens*, and arranged for the dispatch of a report of this meeting to Jewish leaders abroad.[10]

During the summer of 1932, the *Abteilung* organised a more significant effort to limit publicity abroad regarding the anti-Jewish Hitler movement. Verbal and physical attacks by the Nazis on Jews had intensified and Hitler's followers increased their number of seats in the *Reichstag* from 107 to 230 in the July

---

1933–1941. Unpublished Ph.D. Dissertation, Universität Würzburg 1976, pp. 188–190; and Ahmad Mahrad, *Die deutsch-persischen Beziehungen 1918–1933*. Unpublished Ph.D. Dissertation, Freie Universität Berlin 1973, pp. 74–187. Dieckhoff entered the Nazi Party in 1941; see his 'Personalbogen', 20th July 1944, NARS/T–120/2537/E308749. Prüfer joined the Party in 1937; note his membership card in Berlin Document Center/Master File/folder *Curt Prüfer*.

[8]Prüfer to Paul, Count von Wolff-Metternich (German Ambassador in Turkey), 10th December 1915, microfilm, 'German Foreign Ministry Archives, 1867–1920', University of Michigan/reel 31/frames 0152–0153.

[9]See document No. 51 in Arnold Paucker, *Der jüdische Abwehrkampf gegen Antisemitismus und Nationalsozialismus in den letzten Jahren der Weimarer Republik*, Hamburg 1968, p. 221.

[10]*Ibid*. On Sobernheim, note Egmont Zechlin, *Die deutsche Politik und die Juden im Ersten Weltkrieg*, Göttingen 1969, pp. 133, 432, 556.

election. Following Hitler's unsuccessful negotiations with the *Reich* President, Paul von Hindenburg, and his advisers – amongst them the new chancellor, Franz von Papen – about forming a government, diplomatic dispatches arriving at the Wilhelmstrasse reflected a steadily growing concern abroad about the likelihood of such an event.

For example, the German Consulate General in Jerusalem reported to *Abteilung III* that "the increase in the antisemitic movement in Germany has been followed closely by local Jewry". The Consulate General in Antwerp noted that "with the clashes on the Kurfürstendamm" in Berlin (when Nazi hooligans fell on Jewish passers-by), "a certain disquiet had come over the city's Jewish community", which numbered "about 40,000" (this must refer to the approximately 35,000 Jewish inhabitants of Antwerp, otherwise there would be a curious numerical error; as Berlin counted some 160,000 Jews amongst its population). Similar complaints arrived from the German mission in Egypt and the embassy in Paris; the latter mentioned "the call for a boycott of German goods by the Jewish population in North Africa". Moreover, the publisher of the *American Hebrew* and *Jewish Tribune* newspapers in the United States, David Brown, asked for permission to visit the *Reich* "with a view towards ascertaining the true state of Jewish affairs there".[11]

Abteilung III rigorously defended Germany's reputation and honour abroad by attempting to control public statements by German Jews about the true situation. It ignored the daily reports of Nazi outrages against Jews and agreed with the *Reich* Ministry of the Interior, which informed the AA that "peace and order govern throughout Germany".[12] In August 1932, Dieckhoff and Prüfer sent the AA's specialist for Jewish affairs, Sobernheim, to observe an international conference of Zionists in Geneva. The meeting featured reports on antisemitism by Jewish delegations from North America, Romania, Germany, Russia, and Palestine and arrived at the decision to form a World Jewish Congress by 1934.[13] The *Abteilung*'s heads, apparently because Sobernheim was Jewish and acquainted with the members of the German-Jewish delegation to Geneva, and in a position to observe them closely, directed him to accompany them to Geneva and submit "a thorough report" on their behaviour and the remarks they made there. Moreover, one member of the group was the Berlin banker and leader of a splinter organisation among German Zionists, Georg Kareski, noted for his contacts with the

[11]Louis Rittenberg to Paul Schwarz (German Consul General New York), 14th July 1932; German Consulate General Antwerp to AA, 20th July 1932; German Embassy Paris to AA, 4th August 1932; German mission Cairo to AA, 14th July 1932; and German Consulate General Jerusalem to AA, 25th June 1932, PA/*Abt. III*/L1279 (*Jüdisch-politische. Angelegenheiten – Allgemeines*). For examples of Nazi attacks in the autumn of 1932 against Jews, note Richard Bessel, *Political Violence and the Rise of Nazism. The Storm Troopers in Eastern Germany, 1925–1934*, New Haven 1984, p. 89; Martin Gilbert, *The Holocaust. A History of the Jews of Europe during the Second World War*, New York 1985, pp. 30–31; and on Nazi violence in general, Volker Hentschel, *Weimars letzte Monate. Hitler und der Untergang der Republik*, Düsseldorf 1978, *passim*.

[12]*Reich* Ministry of Interior to AA, 15th September 1932, PA/*Abt. III*/L1279.

[13]Sobernheim to Prüfer, 2nd August 1932; and Prüfer, Memo, 4th August 1932, *ibid*.

Catholic Centre Party and also for his demands for a vigorous Jewish policy against Nazi antisemitism at that time.[14]

The AA intended Sobernheim's presence to moderate or lessen what German-Jewish delegates said at this meeting about the mounting anti-Jewish attacks. These tactics apparently produced satisfaction in *Abteilung III*. Sobernheim reported about Kareski's remarks:

> "The third speaker, Kareski, agreed that the situation in Germany was serious, yet one should not overestimate it. The government was determined to protect the Jews; what the future would bring, no one could foresee."[15]

The German consulate in Geneva praised Sobernheim's influence on the German Jews:

> "The conference took a firm stand regarding the signs of the antisemitic movement in Germany and how one could counteract them. All Jews, especially those from America, were willing to support the German Jews in their struggle to defend themselves . . . Thanks to the activity of legation counsellor Professor Dr. Sobernheim, the speeches of the German Jews, but also particularly the press reports, insofar as they could have had a negative effect on Germany, were weakened."[16]

The AA's pressure, however, did not stop with Sobernheim's mission to Geneva. When Kareski allegedly wrote an anti-German and anti-Hitler article in an Antwerp newspaper, *Neptune*, Prüfer questioned him. He denied having written the essay. Moreover, as Prüfer recorded later, Kareski claimed that he made his "view on the situation of the Jews in Germany" clear at the Geneva conference, in which "he indeed did not deny the antisemitic movement in Germany, but had emphasised the trust of the German Jews in the present government".* Kareski also informed Sobernheim that he planned "to protest to *Neptune* in Antwerp against the misuse of his [Kareski's] name and also to enlighten the Jewish papers in Antwerp".[17]

It is difficult to judge whether the campaign to muzzle Jewish leaders in Germany affected foreign reaction to Nazism. During the autumn and winter of 1932, fewer dispatches noting criticism of the anti-Jewish movement arrived at the AA from its missions abroad. That probably resulted, however, from the

[14]This incident is not mentioned in Herbert S. Levine, 'A Jewish Collaborator in Nazi Germany. The Strange Career of Georg Kareski, 1933–1937', in *Central European History*, 8 (1975), pp. 256–257, 265, note 36. Note, moreover, Prüfer to Sobernheim, 9th August 1932, PA/*Abt. III*/L1287 (*Prof. Sobernheim: Verschiedenes, 1929–1932*).

[15]Sobernheim, 'Bericht über die jüdische Weltkonferenz vom 14.–16. August 1932 in Genf', [n.d.], PA/*Abt. III*/L1279.

[16]German Consulate Geneva to AA, 22nd August 1932, *ibid.* The press reports appeared to bear out the Consulate's assessment; note 'Say Palestine Jews have Best Conditions', in *The New York Times*, 16th August 1932; and 'The Jewish Conference', in *The Times* (London), 18th August 1932, which noted only that the Conference "strongly protests against the anti-Jewish measures some states are still practising, and against attacks on Jews in some countries".

*See in great detail the contribution by Francis R. Nicosia, 'Revisionist Zionism in Germany (II). Georg Kareski and the Staatszionistische Organisation, 1933–1938', in this section of the current volume of the Year Book – (Ed.).

[17]Such behaviour was apparently typical of Kareski's style as "a wheeler and dealer" in both business and politics and which contributed to his collaboration with the Nazis during the Third *Reich*; see Levine, *loc. cit.*, pp. 264–281. Further, note Prüfer to German Consulate General Antwerp, 23rd September 1932, *ibid.*

decline of the Nazi vote in the *Reichstag* election in November and the popular opinion that the Hitler movement had lost its political momentum. Nevertheless, defending Germany against attacks from abroad and violating the democratic rights of German-Jewish leaders by seeking to keep them from expressing their views freely on events in their country became even more pronounced in *Abteilung III* and other sections of the AA, particularly *Referat Deutschland*, a new division created in the AA during the early months of the Hitler regime in 1933, when the Nazis unleashed their official persecution of the Jews.[18]

Already on 3rd March 1933, little more than a month after Hitler's appointment, Foreign Minister Neurath, ignoring the spread of physical violence against Jews and the removal of Jewish judges and other professionals from their positions, assured Sir Horace Rumbold, the British Ambassador in Berlin, that the Jews had nothing to fear from the new regime.[19] Similarly, Hitler's Vice Chancellor, von Papen, emphasised to the press that Jews would be treated like all other German citizens.[20] As for the AA, Bülow not only showed no sympathy for the Jews, he even justified the radical measures against them prior to the anti-Jewish boycott and first racial legislation in April.

The *Staatssekretär* joined Neurath in forming in March the *Referat Deutschland*, the ministry's liaison office with the Nazi Party designed to protect Germany against its foreign critics. Neurath and Bülow quickly approved, moreover, the adoption by Vico von Bülow-Schwante (Bülow's cousin and the head of the new office), of the party's crude antisemitic propaganda to allay opposition abroad.[21] Bülow-Schwante sent propaganda material, which claimed that Jews dominated German life and that a Communist-Jewish world conspiracy existed to ruin the *Reich*, to Dieckhoff and other division leaders and to the foreign missions.

Dieckhoff and Prüfer, however, had accepted such views for some time; they intensified their efforts, begun in *Abteilung III* before the establishment of the new government, to blunt foreign criticism of Nazi antisemitism. During March 1933 the division received a flood of cables from Leopold Hoesch, the anti-Nazi German Ambassador in London, warning of the damage done to Germany's reputation in England by the persecution of the Jews. Dieckhoff, setting the future tone for the *Abteilung*'s response, angrily replied to Hoesch on 27th March that the claims of mistreatment of Jews in Germany were "outrageous atrocity reports". "It is in fact correct", he maintained, "that nearly all English correspondents have no understanding of the revolutionary movement of the last weeks and, with something akin to cold hostility, derisively criticise

[18]Browning, *op. cit.*, pp. 11–13, which deals solely with the *Referat.*

[19]Rumbold to Sir John Simon, 3rd March 1933, *Documents on British Foreign Policy, 1919–1939* (2nd series; London 1947–), vol. IV, doc. No. 254; and also on Neurath's role in defending the regime's antisemitism, Wollstein, *op. cit.*, p. 57. See, further, Uwe-Dietrich Adam, *Judenpolitik im Dritten Reich*, Königstein/Ts.-Düsseldorf 1979, pp. 46–48; and for the SA wave of terror in the spring of 1933 against Jews in Eastern Germany, note Bessel, *op. cit.*, pp. 105–109. The outcry abroad is detailed in Gerhard L. Weinberg, *The Foreign Policy of Hitler's Germany. Diplomatic Revolution in Europe, 1933–36*, Chicago 1970, pp. 38–40.

[20]Eliahu Ben-Elissar, *La Diplomatie du IIIe Reich et les Juifs (1933–1939)*, Paris 1969, p. 26.

[21]Browning, *op. cit.*, pp. 11–13.

everything that suits them." He demanded that the Ambassador inform British leaders of the "scandalous behaviour of the English correspondents".[22] Three days later, anti-German opinion in the United States prompted a meeting of Dieckhoff, Prüfer, other members of the division, and Bülow-Schwante.

Although the reaction of the outside world and the intervention of Hitler's only nominal superior, President Hindenburg, through Neurath, helped restrict the Nazi Party's nation-wide boycott of Jewish businesses to one day, 1st April 1933, numerous beatings of Jews by Nazi mobs and SA accompanied the event. *Abteilung III* nevertheless continued to ignore the violence; it collaborated with Hermann Göring, the new Prussian Minister of the Interior, who ordered German-Jewish groups to contact Jewish organisations abroad and deny the atrocity reports. The division, through its London embassy, ensured that leaders of the *Centralverein* and of the *Zionistische Vereinigung für Deutschland* delivered a letter to Jewish groups in Britain, cautioning the latter against "any exaggerated or false news spread about the happenings in Germany".[23]

Because of the key place of Britain in German foreign policy till mid-1935, improving the *Reich*'s image there preoccupied the *Abteilung*.[24] It arranged through Bülow and the *Reich* Chancellery for Hitler to receive a pro-German and Conservative member of parliament, Colonel Thomas Moore, during the latter's visit to Berlin. On the other hand, the division refused to forward to Hitler a letter of protest against the "systematic brutality practised in the concentration camps" from prominent English leaders, among them the Archbishop of York, the Bishop of Chichester, the economist John Maynard Keynes, and the historians George Trevelyan and G. P. Gooch. Dieckhoff sloughed off the affair by asserting "that such impertinent pieces of writing to the *Reich* Chancellor cannot be considered".[25]

[22]Dieckhoff to Hoesch, 27th March 1933; Hoesch's protests against the German behaviour mentioned in German Embassy London to AA, 21st, 22nd, 25th, 29th, 31st March 1933, PA/*Abt. III*/5740 (*Politische Beziehungen zwischen England und Deutschland*). For Bülow-Schwante's distribution of the propaganda to the AA see *ibid.*, p. 227 note 5. See, too, Wollstein, *op. cit.*, pp. 57, 80–81; Eugene R. McCane, *Anglo-German Diplomatic Relations, January 1933–March 1936*, Unpublished Ph.D. Dissertation, University of Kentucky, 1982, pp. 55–60; and Barbara Benge Kehoe, 'The British Press and Nazi Germany', University of Illinois (Chicago Circle), 1980, pp. 75–82, for the details on the British opposition to the persecution of the Jews.

[23]In light of later events, a further statement in this letter reads strangely (though we must allow for the fact that the Jewish representatives acted under pressure and that they also used other channels of communication with their co-religionists abroad – where they were more outspoken): "We have come across certain reports giving details about women being assaulted, even little children being burnt. These reports are absolutely untrue and may, if reprinted, do very much harm to our cause." Note of Ludwig Tietz and Richard Lichtheim to Board of Deputies of British Jews and Anglo-Jewish Association (London), 2nd April 1933; and German Embassy London to AA, 3rd April 1933 ('Inhalt: Jüdische Delegation in London.'), PA/*Abt. III*/ 5740. Regarding those present to discuss the protests in the United States, see 'Besprechung im Auswärtigen Amt am 30. März 1933', PA/*Abt. III*/5747 (*Politische Beziehungen der Vereinigten Staaten von Amerika zu Deutschland*). On the alleged complaint by Hindenburg and "non-Nazis in the Cabinet" about the boycott, see Adam, *op. cit.*, pp. 62–63; and Lucy S. Dawidowicz, *The War Against the Jews, 1933–1945*, New York 1975, p. 54.

[24]See esp. PA/*Abt. III*/5740, and other files of the *Abteilung* dealing with Britain.

[25]Dieckhoff, memo, 25th May 1934, mentioning Prüfer's agreement; and Prüfer, memo, 22nd September 1933, on Moore's visit to Hitler, PA/*Abt. III*/5740. Regarding the visit of Moore and

The protests against the Nazi regime, however, were not limited to the Western countries alone. While the AA's gestures revealed some concern on Hitler's part for opinion abroad, he changed nothing in his domestic policy, and hence critical reaction from the world at large continued during 1933 and 1934. The barrage of foreign disapproval and boycotts of German exports intensified the belief in *Abteilung III* that an anti-German plot existed among the world's Jews. Prüfer, for example, already expected that Hitler would drive the Jews from Germany. Explaining the Nazi policies towards them to an Arab friend in Switzerland, he prophesied that the "avowed attitude of the *Reich* government to the Jewish Question naturally makes it appear desirable to promote the emigration of the Jews from Germany".[26]

The stream of reports sent to the *Abteilung* from German mission leaders in the Middle East also heightened the division's paranoia. An air of hysteria and lack of sympathy for Jews dominated the cables. Information on the Zionists abroad also reached the division from the *Gestapo*.[27] A long and bitter protest against the anti-Jewish policies came from Egypt. The German Minister in Cairo, Eberhard von Stohrer, one of the few Nazi Party members in the AA at the beginning of Hitler's regime, and a virulant antisemite, repeatedly denounced the local Jewish community's attacks against Nazism and its efforts to organise a boycott of German exports. Admitting that the "Jewish agitation" was "not solely comprised of Jewish elements, but also embraces other confessions", Stohrer demanded that the Egyptian government suppress the "anti-German movement" and urged that the AA take measures to halt it.

In June 1933, *Abteilung III* arranged with the Egyptian Minister in Berlin, Hassan Nachat Pasha, for the *Reich* Propaganda Ministry to interview a prominent Egyptian journalist visiting Germany to counter, in the division's words: "the especially active and poisonous Jewish agitation propaganda in Egypt". Prüfer suggested that the interview be published in Egyptian newspapers and used to explain "the attitude of the German government in the Jewish Question" and how "the [German anti-Jewish] boycott was nothing other than a warning against the unscrupulous atrocity agitation".

During the autumn the *Abteilung* received crass propaganda material from the Nazi Party organisation in Berlin, emphasising a familiar theme: an "international Jewish conspiracy against Germany in Egypt".[28] Through Stohrer the *Abteilung* attempted to persuade the Egyptian government to stop Leon Castro, a popular Jewish lawyer and defender of Egyptian Jews in a libel trial against the

the array of other influential British officials to Hitler and the significance for German policy, note Josef Henke, *England in Hitlers politischem Kalkül 1935–1939*, Boppard/Rh. 1973, pp. 32–33.

[26]Prüfer to German Consulate Geneva, 26th October 1933, PA/*Abt. III*/L1279.

[27]Gestapo to AA, 19th September 1934 ('Geheim! Betrifft: Bericht über die III. Jüdische Weltkonferenz in Genf von 20. bis 23. August 1934.'); and many more examples, *ibid.* Other sources that have noted the division's anti-Jewish views are Gläsner, *op. cit.*, p. 190; and Heinz Tillmann, *Deutschlands Araberpolitik im Zweiten Weltkrieg*, [East] Berlin 1965, p. 68, note 264. On the acceptance of the AA of the premise that the world's Jews were Germany's enemies, note Ben-Elissar, *op. cit.*, pp. 135–141.

[28]Wolfgang Diewerge (Nazi Party official in Berlin) to Prüfer, 29th September 1933; Prüfer, memo, 15th June 1933; German legation Cairo (Stohrer) to AA, 31st March and 3rd, 12th, 19th, 21st April 1933, PA/*Abt. III*/L1043 (*Politische Beziehungen Ägyptens zu Deutschland*).

Deutscher Verein in Cairo, from speaking at public meetings. But the division, despite its energetic measures to combat anti-German opinion in Egypt, stopped short of agreeing to Stohrer's suggestion in September that Germany boycott Egyptian cotton. The mere threat of the boycott, however, Stohrer claimed three months later, "strongly disturbed Jewry" and persuaded the Egyptian government to silence the alleged enemies of Germany. The *Abteilung* quickly exploited the situation by arranging for a radio broadcast by Nachat Pasha from Berlin to Egypt, which praised the close ties of Berlin and Cairo, the music of Richard Wagner, and Hitler as "the hero of the new Germany and the pillar of its revolution".[29]

The *Abteilung*'s attempts to conceal Germany's anti-Jewish policy from foreign opinion stretched well into 1935. Thus much attention focused on preventing an American rabbi, Ferdinand Isserman, from visiting Germany. It instructed the German legations in Europe not to issue Isserman a permit to return to the *Reich* because the rabbi, after travelling through Germany during the autumn of 1934, had "delivered very hateful lectures" in America on "the German situation". Despite such efforts, a bureaucratic mistake enabled Isserman to procure a visa from the German embassy in Paris and travel again in Germany for six weeks during August and September 1935. On his return to the United States, the rabbi did what the *Abteilung* had tried to prevent; he reported to the press that Nazism "has destroyed the universities, has exiled the great scholars, Jew and Christian alike, and has eliminated academic freedom".[30]

One of the final actions of *Abteilung III* on the Jewish Question, before the reorganisation of the AA abolished the division and submerged it into a massive new political department, reflected the conflict that characterised Nazi policy by 1935 towards the Jews. In the spring, Nazi Party radicals unchained a new wave of anti-Jewish terror, boycotts, and discrimination, sanctioned by the previous legislation which had banished the Jews from government service and professional life.

Although the records are unclear, the Party soon called a halt to the outburst; apparently, some leaders considered the violence against Jewish businesses premature, and Hitler and other officials disliked spontaneous mob brutality that was unpredictable and ungovernable. The regime, however, quickly channelled the violence into new legislation, resulting in Hitler's decreeing of the Nuremberg Laws that banned marriage and sexual relations between Germans and Jews and stripped the latter of their German citizenship. With the Jews completely disenfranchised and defenceless before the law, influence in the Jewish Question passed increasingly to the SS, which governed the police and concentration camps and began urging the forced emigration of the Jews.[31]

[29]'Übersetzung. Eine Rundfunkrede des ägyptischen Gesandten in Berlin in arabischer Sprache', 29th January 1934; Prüfer to Nachat Pasha, 20th January 1934; German Legation Cairo (Stohrer) to AA, 4th December 1933; Prüfer, memo, 6th November 1933; and AA (Prüfer) to German Legation Cairo, 10th November 1933, *ibid.*

[30]'Rabbi Isserman Reports Mumbling in Ranks of Nazis', in *Globe-Democrat* (St. Louis), 26th September 1935; and Prüfer to German missions in Europe, 13th August 1935, PA/*Abt. III*/5747.

[31]This is surveyed in Karl A. Schleunes, *The Twisted Road to Auschwitz: Nazi Policy Towards German Jews, 1933–1939*, Urbana 1970, pp. 92–213; Dawidowicz, *op. cit.*, pp. 61–69, 82–87; Adam, *op. cit.*, esp. pp. 204–212; and Yehuda Bauer, *A History of the Holocaust*, New York 1982, pp. 101–106.

What was to be done with the Jews also concerned the AA and other government authorities. Beginning in 1933, in keeping with Hitler's often repeated desire to make Germany *judenrein*, the regime had introduced measures that rather favoured Zionist aims, fostering the emigration of German Jews to Palestine, and permitting them to take a portion of their property abroad. The *Haavara* scheme was initiated for this purpose, instituting a German monopoly on the shipping of goods to Palestine. The Nazis exploited Jewish migration to the British Mandate as a device to expand German foreign trade and also to counter the threat of a world-wide Jewish boycott of German goods.

Despite the *Haavara* agreement and other German-Jewish efforts to facilitate emigration, however, the prejudices and economic fears of foreign countries led them to restrict significantly the number of German refugees they would accept.[32] Moreover, not only did bitter divisions exist over *Haavara* among the Nazi Party or within the AA, especially during 1936 and 1937 when Britain began considering the partition of Palestine and formation of a Jewish state there, but differences also existed within *Abteilung III* regarding the AA's pro-Zionist policy.

Prüfer, fearing the impact of the policy on Germany's relations with the Arab world, differed from *Referat Deutschland*, which supported *Haavara* till 1936 in the belief that it would succeed in eliminating the Jews from Germany. The deputy director of the *Abteilung* remained an ardent opponent of Zionism, promised his Arab friends that Germany did not intend to send its Jews to Palestine, and watched carefully the statistics of German Jews migrating there (Palestine accepted over one-third of those who left Germany between 1933 and 1937). On the other hand, Prüfer favoured Jews leaving the *Reich* for other countries, excluding the Arab lands.[33]

Several of his colleagues, however, including Dieckhoff and Bülow, showed themselves less sympathetic to arrangements other than *Haavara* for Jewish emigration. On 18th April 1935, Max Warburg, the prominent Jewish banker from Hamburg and chairman of the *Hilfsverein der deutschen Juden*, which assisted Jewish migration both to Palestine and other countries, visited the AA and talked with Prüfer. Warburg requested help from the *Abteilung* in stopping the Berlin police from changing the group's name to *Hilfsverein der Juden in Deutschland*. According to the chairman, the *Hilfsverein* received "considerable amounts of foreign currency from abroad" for "easing the emigration of Jews

[32]Details are in Werner Feilchenfeld, Dolf Michaelis, and Ludwig Pinner, *Haavara Transfer nach Palästina und Einwanderung deutscher Juden 1933–1939*, Tübingen 1972; (Schriftenreihe wissenschaftlicher Abhandlungen des Leo Baeck Instituts 26); Herbert A. Strauss, 'Jewish Emigration from Germany. Nazi Policies and Jewish Responses (I)', in *LBI Year Book XXV* (1980), pp. 339,344, and (II) in *LBI Year Book XXVI* (1981), pp. 349–357. David Yisraeli, 'The Third Reich and Palestine', in *Middle Eastern Studies*, 7 (1971), pp. 334–355; and Edwin Black, *The Transfer Agreement. The Untold Story of the Secret Pact Between the Third Reich and Jewish Palestine*, New York 1984, which focuses mainly on the origins of the agreement in 1933. Not an "untold" story really! Instead of this polemical book see now rather Francis R. Nicosia, *The Third Reich and the Palestine Question*, Austin 1985, especially pp. 194–264.*

*See also the essay by Nicosia, referred to above, in this volume of the Year Book, pp. 253–262 *passim* – (Ed.).

[33]See his letter to the German Consulate Geneva, 26th October 1933, PA/*Abt. III*/L1279.

from Germany", but its members disapproved of the name change imposed by the Nazis and threatened to close the group. Since 1933, Warburg told Prüfer, the *Hilfsverein* had acted "thoroughly in the spirit of the new Germany" by assisting over 11,000 Jews to emigrate.

What upset Warburg and others in the *Hilfsverein* about the change of name was its symbolic meaning: on the one hand a further isolation of the Jews from the rest of German society and on the other potentially greater obstacles to emigration. By 1935, culminating with the Nuremberg Laws, the regime no longer allowed Jews to call themselves Germans. Hence, Jewish organisations had to alter their names so that they spoke for "Jews in Germany" rather than "German Jews". Prüfer, apparently believing that contributing to a "Jew-free" Germany took precedence over depriving the Jews of this cherished "German" nomenclature, suggested that Dieckhoff and Bülow consider the complaint and sought backing for the *Hilfsverein* from the *Referat Deutschland*. Bülow, however, replied with a curt, "No thank you", and the *Referat* refused help by offering the simple bureaucratic memo "that it deals with a question for the responsibility of which only the domestic authorities are competent".[34]

The policy of *Abteilung III* from 1931 to 1935 regarding the Jewish Question in Germany provides a limited but striking example of continuity between the latter years of the Weimar Republic and the beginning of the Nazi regime. The effort by old-line Conservatives such as Dieckhoff, Prüfer, Bülow and their superior, Neurath, to silence German Jews and foreign criticism regarding Nazi antisemitism even before Hitler seized power, strongly suggests that such officials did not act because of Nazi coercion. Moreover, the history of *Abteilung III* illustrates that the Foreign Office's involvement with Nazi discrimination comprised significantly more in the early days of the Third *Reich* than solely the activities of *Referat Deutschland*, the office established in the AA by the Nazis in 1933, which historians have traditionally emphasised.[35] In this respect, the division cloaked such policies with a veneer of Conservative and Nationalist "respectability", which doubtless contributed to the survival of Hitler's regime during its first critical phase. It need not surprise us! We know that when a conservative-nationalist resistance at a late hour – in 1944 – attempted to topple Hitler, most of its protagonists may have been disgusted by mass murder, but few were even then willing to contemplate the restoration of full citizenship to the surviving Jews.[36]

[34]Prüfer, memo, 18th April 1935, at the end of which Bülow scrawled, "Danke nein. B."; and Prüfer, "zu III.O.1788", 24th April 1935, *ibid.* For the background on the *Hilfsverein* see a.o. Dawidowicz, *op. cit.*, pp. 189–190, 193; Bauer, *op. cit.*, p. 122; and Max M. Warburg, *Aus meinen Aufzeichnungen*, New York 1952, pp. 151–155, discusses his prominent role by 1935 in encouraging Jewish emigration.

[35]The main source is Browning, *op. cit.*, pp. 1–14.

[36]Cf. Christof Dipper, 'Der deutsche Widerstand und die Juden', in *Geschichte und Gesellschaft, IX*, No. 3 (1983), *Juden in Deutschland zwischen Antisemitismus und Verfolgung* (an issue edited by Reinhard Rürup), pp. 349–380.

The Kristallnacht as a Public Degradation Ritual

BY PETER LOEWENBERG

The pogrom in Nazi Germany and Austria of 9th–10th November 1938, was the most violent public display of antisemitism in German history. As such, it provides a turning point in Nazi techniques of persecution of Jews and a number of problems to historians of the Third *Reich*.

The major historical problem is: why did it happen? The *Kristallnacht* violated all the major behavioural norms of the German people. The National Socialists came to power on 30th January 1933 after four years of public agitation, street fights, and selective violence – usually against Communist, Socialist, Liberal, Jewish, and Pacifist political opponents. One of the meanings of Hitler's seizure of power for the German public, and one of the explicit promises to them by the Nazis was: now there will be public order, peace, and law ("*Ordnung*," "*Ruhe*," "*Recht*") and things will again function normally as they should.

This was the way it appeared that things had worked out to the mass of Germans who were not Jewish nor of the political Left. During the 1936 Olympic Games in Berlin special efforts were made to tone down antisemitism and internal repression to deceive the eyes of foreign tourists and visitors.[1] It is significant, by contrast, that Wilhelm Gustloff, the leader of the Swiss Nazi Party, was murdered by a Jew, David Frankfurter, in 1936. At that time Hitler considered and rejected the idea of taking collective revenge and imposing a fine on the Jews of Germany.[2]

We may speak of German cultural traits and behavioural norms as a starkly contrasting backdrop to the events of the *Kristallnacht*. I refer to such widely shared values as:

1. Respect for the private property of others: *Eigentumsrecht* and *Privatbesitztum* are among the most highly valued norms inculcated in German children and shared by the German people as adults.
2. Thrift: *Sparsamkeit* is likewise a strongly held value and civic duty for all Germans. They are taught to save, not waste, to maximise the use of goods, energy, and services.
3. There is also a deeply ingrained respect for religion, for houses of worship of any religion, and especially in the Catholic areas, a concern about incursions of the state into religion stemming from their experience with Bismarck's *Kulturkampf*. The violence and persecutions of the Reformation and the Wars

[1]Richard D. Mandell, *The Nazi Olympics*, New York 1971, pp. 92–94, 143.
[2]Otto D. Kulka, 'Public Opinion in Nazi Germany and the "Jewish Question"', in *The Jerusalem Quarterly*, No. 25 (Fall 1982), p. 136.

of Religion compelled a gradually-won historical and attitudinal compromise by which other religions were respected and one lived side by side as Germans.

4. A further value in German social culture is decency to neighbours. At the most intimate level it means helpfulness to the family next door ("*die Familie nebenan*").[3]

German Jews, of course, also shared these norms and counted on them for their inner peace and security. These are the value systems that make continuity of life possible for people in a society. Given these widely generalised beliefs and values in the German people and a desire for a legal orderly *Rechtstaat*, for *Ordnung*, *Ruhe*, and *juristisches Recht*, the outbreak of violence, destruction, plunder, stealing, and personal assault in November 1938 appears difficult to explain and make sense of in historical terms.

Modern psychoanalysis has made us sensitive to ambivalence about achievements at mastery. The fact that order, structure, discipline, and the rule of law have been secured means that the contrary emotions of impulsiveness, violence, and destructiveness have been controlled. But the sanction to unleash these repressed forces is always tempting, particularly when it may be done under the cloak of official legitimacy as on the *Kristallnacht*.

We are also aware of the power of anniversary phenomena of repetition and unconscious "undoing" for past humiliations and the re-enactment of past moments of triumph and glory.[4] The "Ninth" of November had a double significance in German history and National Socialist Party hagiography. November "Ninth" is the date when the German Revolution triumphed in 1918. The Kaiser's abdication was announced in Berlin and a Social Democrat, Philipp Scheidemann, proclaimed a Republic. This day in Nazi political lore was interpreted as filled with shame and humiliation. The events of the German collapse of 1918 and the birth of the Weimar Republic were shrouded in slogans of "betrayal at home" and "stab-in-the-back" at the front.

The 9th of November was also a date of special significance in Nazi Party history. On that day in 1923 Hitler staged his unsuccessful "Beer Hall *Putsch*" in Munich. His attempt to overthrow the Bavarian government was easily put down. Hitler was arrested, tried, and sentenced to five years in prison and released after serving less than a year. The anniversary of the *Putsch* was celebrated by the Party every year and the fallen "martyrs" of the 9th

[3]I am influenced in this formulation by William S. Allen, 'Die deutsche Öffentlichkeit und die "Reichskristallnacht". Konflikte zwischen Werthierarchie und Propaganda im Dritten Reich', in Detlev Peukert and Jürgen Reulecke (eds.), *Die Reihen fast geschlossen. Beiträge zur Geschichte des Alltags unterm Nationalsozialismus*, Wuppertal 1981, pp. 401–403. For a psychodynamic analysis of German values and cultural traits, see Paul Kecskemeti and Nathan Leites, 'German Attitudes and Nazi Leadership', in Elizabeth W. Marvick (ed.), *Psychopolitical Analysis. Selected Writings of Nathan Leites*, New York 1977, pp. 271–294.

[4]George H. Pollock, 'Anniversary Reactions, Trauma, and Mourning', in *Psychoanalytic Quarterly*, 39, No. 3 (1970), pp. 347–371; and 'Temporal Anniversary Manifestations. Hour, Day, Holiday', in *Psychoanalytic Quarterly*, 40, No. 1 (1971), pp. 123–131; George L. Engel, 'The Death of a Twin. Mourning and Anniversary Reactions. Fragments of 10 Years of Self-Analysis', in *International Journal of Psycho-Analysis*, 56 (1975), pp. 23–40.

November held a special place in Party mythology.[5] Thus, the 9th of November 1938 marked the twentieth anniversary of the German Revolution and the fifteenth anniversary of Hitler's *Bierkeller-Putsch.*

The foreign policy context of the November pogrom is that it was preceded by the Munich Agreements of 29th September 1938, which dismembered Czechoslovakia, marking the high tide of Hitler's diplomatic success. The Nazis felt they could now ignore foreign opinion with impunity. The caution and circumspection which marked Nazi antisemitic policy during the 1936 Olympic Games was no longer necessary. The diplomatic events of the Munich crisis of September and October 1938 had caused widespread tension and fear of war in Germany and anti-Jewish reactions. The *Lagebericht* of the *Sicherheitsdienst* (SD) reports:

> "The populace was very dejected due to the fears that the situation could deteriorate into large-scale military actions . . . During this tense time, it was noted that the Jews revived and seemed happy. Individual Jews even gave vent to malicious gloating and expressed the hope that matters would now take a turn."[6]

The facts of the background and pretext for the *Kristallnacht*, if not the motives, are well known. We also know the events and their effects. The formal economic aim of Nazi policy in 1938 was the expropriation of the property of German Jewry. This was administered by Hermann Göring, the chief of the Four Year Plan. From April 1938 on there was a series of decrees designed to detect and register with the government all Jewish assets in the *Reich.* An issue between Göring and the Nazi Party came out into the open in a *Reich* Air Ministry Conference on 14th October 1938, less than a month before the *Kristallnacht.* After setting out production goals, such as a five-fold increase in the *Luftwaffe*, Göring stated: "The Jewish Question must now be grasped by every available means for they [the Jews] must be removed from the economy." However, the loot was to go to the State, administered by himself, not to the opportunistic Party faithful. He declared: "What must be prevented at all events is a wild commissar-economy of the type that has developed in Austria. These wild actions must stop and no one must look on the settlement of the Jewish Question as a charitable institution for incapable Party members."[7] Unquestionably the *Kristallnacht* accelerated the pace of the seizure of Jewish property. Yet this economic explanation does not suffice to give us a logic for the particular ferocity and the quality of personal humiliation that marked the November pogrom. Assets could have been seized without destroying every synagogue in Germany and enacting public rituals of degradation in each town.

There were premonitory signs of an impending public disaster for the German Jews in the weeks immediately previous to the *Kristallnacht.* Reacting to an incident in Antwerp, the *Völkischer Beobachter* on 26th October 1938 issued an undisguised threat:

[5]Harold J. Gordon, jr., *Hitler and the Beer Hall Putsch*, Princeton, N.J. 1972.
[6]This is a September report from Würzburg, dated 10th October 1938. Cited in Kulka, *loc. cit.*, p. 137.
[7]Lionel Kochan, *Pogrom. 10 November 1938*, London 1957, p. 32.

> "Wir warnen das Judentum mit allem Nachdruck vor der Wiederholung solcher Banditenstreiche, wie es sie in Antwerpen ausgeführt hat, da sie leicht Folgen ausserhalb seines Machtbereiches zeitigen könnten, die ihm und seinen Einzelgliedern höchst unerwünscht und unangenehm sein dürften."

> "We warn the Jews emphatically against the repetition of such acts of banditry as they carried out in Antwerp, since these could easily have consequences beyond their sphere of influence, which might be extremely undesirable and unpleasant for both individual Jews and Jewry as a whole."[8]

The murder of Ernst vom Rath, the Third Secretary of the German Embassy in Paris, by Herschel Grynszpan on 7th November 1938 was the excuse for the *Kristallnacht*. Grynszpan was a Polish Jew distraught over the treatment of his parents who had been abruptly deported from Germany to Poland on 27th October. This shooting provided the public "trigger" or pretext for the pogrom. The day after the shooting the *Völkischer Beobachter* carried a leading article heavy with menace and intimidation towards the Jews:

> "Es ist klar, dass das deutsche Volk aus dieser neuen Tat seine Folgerungen ziehen wird. Es ist ein unmöglicher Zustand, dass in unseren Grenzen Hunderttausende von Juden noch ganze Ladenstrassen beherrschen, Vergnügungsstätten bevölkern und als 'ausländische' Hausbesitzer das Geld deutscher Mieter einstecken, während ihre Rassengenossen draussen zum Krieg gegen Deutschland auffordern und deutsche Beamte niederschiessen."

> "It is clear that the German people will draw their own conclusions from this new deed. It is an intolerable state of affairs that within our borders hundreds of thousands of Jews still control whole streets of shops, populate our recreation spots and as 'foreign' apartment owners pocket the money of German tenants, while their racial comrades abroad agitate for war against Germany and gun down German officials."[9]

Vom Rath died in Paris on 9th November. The news reached Hitler as he was leading the Party faithful in a celebration of the 1923 *Putsch* in the Old *Rathaus* of Munich. The total Party leadership and that of every Nazi organisation was at this moment in one place. Hitler had what is described by an eyewitness as "a very serious discussion" with Goebbels. Hitler was heard to say: "The S.A. should be allowed to have a fling."[10] Hitler departed and Goebbels made a speech suggesting that there were to be "spontaneous" demonstrations against the Jews and the Party was told not to oppose them. The message was clear and it went out over the telephone and teleprinter to all parts of the *Reich*: Organise a "spontaneous pogrom", but the Party is not to appear responsible for it.

At 1:00 a.m. on 9th November Himmler gave Heydrich orders: "The *Gestapo* is to obey the orders of the Propaganda Ministry." This important sentence establishes Goebbels's full responsibility for the *Kristallnacht*. Himmler stressed that the *Gau* propaganda offices would lead the action. He informed the SS leaders of his orders to the *Gestapo* and told them to keep out of the activity. Then Himmler dictated a memorandum in which he stated these orders came from his discussion with Hitler and were a *Führerbefehl*.[11] The *Gestapo* was only to

[8] *Völkischer Beobachter*, 26th October 1938, p. 1, as cited in Hermann Graml, *Der 9. November 1938. "Reichskristallnacht"*, Bonn, Bundeszentrale für Heimatdienst, 1957, p. 12.
[9] *Völkischer Beobachter*, 8th November 1938, p. 2, as cited in Graml, *Der 9. November 1938, op. cit.*, p. 17.
[10] Kochan, *Pogrom. 10 November 1938, op. cit.*, p.51.
[11] Graml, *Der 9. November 1938, op. cit.*, p. 29.

have protective tasks and to keep the riots within limits. It was to ensure that when synagogues were burnt precautions were taken against the spread of fire to neighbouring buildings.[12] Various *Bürgermeister* and local Nazi Party leaders reported the appearance, during the early morning hours, of strangers who came to participate in measures against Jews in their towns. Some came in Party and SA uniforms, others in civilian dress. The uniformed were sent home to change into ordinary clothes.[13]

What happened on the 9th and 10th November 1938 in Germany is in the historical record. Every synagogue in Germany was burnt down or demolished. Those that were so close to neighbouring buildings that they could not be burned, such as the temple in Vienna's Seitenstettengasse, were desecrated and plundered.[14] In all 36 Jews were killed and 36 severely wounded, 267 synagogues were burned or razed and 7,500 Jewish businesses in Germany and Austria were destroyed. Over 30,000 Jewish men between the ages of sixteen and sixty were seized from their homes and sent to Dachau, Buchenwald, or Sachsenhausen concentration camps. The *Kristallnacht* was the first pogrom in Germany since the Middle Ages, and what the British historian Lionel Kochan called "the first distinctive modern pogrom" in that it was centralised, planned, and controlled through twentieth-century communication techniques.[15]

The most important feature of the pogrom of 1938, and this is the clue to its historical meaning, is the systematic public humiliation and abuse of Jews in every city and village in the Third *Reich*. This was an emotionally significant open ritual of degradation and dehumanisation.[16] A contemporaneous account by David H. Buffum, the American Consul in Leipzig, reports:

> "Having demolished dwellings and hurtled most of the moveable effects to the streets, the insatiably sadistic perpetrators threw many of the trembling inmates into a small stream that flows through the Zoological Park, commanding the horrified spectators to spit at them, defile them with mud and jeer at their plight . . . The slightest manifestation of sympathy evoked a positive fury on the part of the perpetrators, and the crowd was powerless to do anything but turn horror-stricken eyes from the scene of abuse, or leave the vicinity. These tactics were carried out the entire morning of November 10th without police intervention and they were applied to men, women and children."[17]

The particular quality of public personal insults to which the Jews were subjected indicates that the aim was to degrade and humiliate. In Baden-Baden the Jewish men were marched through the city, then made to walk over prayer shawls, singing the *Horst Wessel Lied* twice. Dr. Arthur Flehinger reports that he was forced to read *Mein Kampf* aloud while being struck on the back of his neck: "During the lull we all had to troop out into the courtyard to relieve ourselves.

[12]Kochan, *Pogrom. 10 November 1938*, *op. cit.*, p. 55.

[13]Graml, *Der 9. November 1938*, *op. cit.*, pp. 20–21.

[14]Hugo Gold, 'Die Kristallnacht in Wien', in *Geschichte der Juden in Wien*, Tel-Aviv 1966, pp. 89–95.

[15]Kochan, *Pogrom. 10 November 1938*, *op. cit.*, p. 15.

[16]For the ideal typology of a degradation ceremony, see Harold Garfinkel, 'Conditions of Successful Degradation Ceremonies', in *American Journal of Sociology*, 61 (1956), pp. 420–424.

[17]David H. Buffum, American Consul in Leipzig to Ralph C. Busser, American General in Berlin, 21st November 1938, Doc: L 202, in Office of United States Chief Counsel for Prosecution of Axis Criminality, *Nazi Conspiracy and Aggression*, Washington, D.C.: United States Government Printing Office, 1946, 8 vols., vol. 7, pp. 1040–1041.

We were not permitted to use the WC; we had to face the synagogue while being kicked from behind."[18] In Frankfurt a. Main young Jews were forced to cut up the Torah scrolls and to burn them.[19]

The sadism, of course, increased as the Jewish men were incarcerated in concentration camps. In a social culture, such as the German one, which prizes cleanliness and privacy regarding lavatorial functions and where children learn excremental shame, sadism takes the special viciousness of exposure and humiliation concerning excretion and bodily cleanliness. I quote Simon Levi's report of conditions in Buchenwald after the *Kristallnacht*:

> "There certainly was a shortage of water and anybody who wanted to keep clean had to use what was left of the so-called coffee to have some sort of a wash . . ."

He describes the "severe diarrhoea" of the inmates:

> ". . . and in this very cold November/December weather we were made to sit on the concrete floor with very severe consequences and one can imagine that in the hygenic conditions of the camp it was very difficult, if at all possible, to clean up and a lot of methods were invented that one didn't have to sit and to sleep in one's own dirt for the rest of one's time in Buchenwald . . . For human needs some latrines were provided which were absolutely horrible and quite a number of people drowned in the dirt of these latrines."[20]

This is corroborated in the account of Bruno Bettelheim who was also in Buchenwald and Dachau and who recalls that:

> "Even during the transportation the prisoners were tortured in the way in which a cruel and domineering father might torture a helpless child; here it should be added that the prisoners were also debased by techniques which went much further into childhood situations. They were forced to soil themselves. In the camp defecation was strictly regulated; it was one of the most important daily events, discussed in great detail. During the day, prisoners who wanted to defecate had to obtain the permission of a guard. It seemed as if education to cleanliness would be once more repeated. It also seemed to give pleasure to the guards to hold the power of granting or withholding the permission to visit the latrines. (Toilets were mostly not available.)"[21]

As we see, the emphasis both on the *Kristallnacht* and in these early camp experiences was on terror, cruel mockery, and vicious humiliation of Jews. This is an extreme form in action of the fantasies of adolescents towards their fathers – they wish to ridicule and mock them, to cut them down to size.[22]

Germany's ministers were convened by Field Marshal Göring at the *Reich* Air Ministry on 12th November to consider the psychological and economic consequences of the *Kristallnacht*.[23] Those present included Goebbels, the

[18]Wiener Library, London, Doc. P IId, No. 93, as cited in Rita Thalmann and Emmanuel Feinermann, *Crystal Night. 9–10 November 1938*, Trans. by Gilles Cremonesi, London 1974, p. 76.

[19]*Ibid.*, p. 77.

[20]Simon Levi, report of 8th October 1983, in the possession of the author.

[21]Bruno Bettelheim, 'Individual and Mass Behavior in Extreme Situations (1943)', in *Surviving and Other Essays*, New York 1980, p. 76.

[22]For suggestive historical treatments of this theme, see Norman Cohn, *Warrant for Genocide. The Myth of the Jewish World Conspiracy and the Protocols of the Elders of Zion*, New York–Evanston 1967, p. 261; and Erik H. Erikson, 'The Legend of Hitler's Childhood', in *Childhood and Society*, 2nd edn., New York 1963, pp. 326–358.

[23]A question frequently put to historical researchers is: How can you empathise with Nazi leaders sufficiently to accurately portray them? The answer lies in pursuing fantasies – as one would the dreams and fantasies of analysands, no matter how bizarre or sadistic. By listening for the

Propaganda Minister; Funk, Economics Minister; Frick, Interior Minister; Gürtner, Justice Minister; Heydrich, Chief of the *Sicherheitspolizei* and the *Sicherheitsdienst*; Woermann, representative of the Foreign Ministry; Blessing, Director of the *Reich*'s Railways; Kehrl, Stuckart, Pfundtner, State Secretaries in the Interior Ministry; Fischböck, representative of Austria; Daluege, Chief of the *Ordnungspolizei*; and Schmeer, an official of the Economics Ministry. The conference lasted from 11 in the morning to 2.40 in the afternoon. The ministers spent most of these three hours and forty minutes in fantasising how to humiliate Jews more completely, of when and where to allow Jews in theatres, cinemas, trains, parks and on benches. The emphasis was clearly on fantasies of debasing the Jews and of treating them as contaminants. In each case they postulated a new degradation and in fantasy placed themselves in the position of the Jew to experience how it felt. The ministers were attacking the worthless, depreciated parts of themselves by projecting this part onto Jews and then relishing the anguish and humiliation they were imposing.

The most active and creative fantasisers were Marshal Göring and the Propaganda Minister, Joseph Paul Goebbels. Goebbels proposed that the Jews must tear down their own synagogues which had been burnt. Parking lots or new buildings could be erected on the space:

> "Goebbels: ... die Juden selbst die beschädigten oder ausgebrannten Synagogen zu beseitigen haben und der deutschen Volksgemeinschaft fertige freie Plätze zur Verfügung zu stellen haben."

> "The Jews themselves ought to clear away the damaged or burnt synagogues and present the German people with cleared free spaces for their own use."

Goebbels quickly turned to other public areas, suggesting that Jews be banned from attendance at theatres, cinemas, and circuses:

> "Ich bin aber der Meinung, dass es nicht möglich ist, Juden neben Deutsche in Varietées, Kinos oder Theater hineinzusetzen."

> "It is my opinion that it is impossible to have Jews sitting next to Germans in variety shows, cinemas or theatres."[24]

Goebbels announced that he had already issued such an order on the basis of existing law. He rapidly moved to the consideration of more intimate areas of fantasy of Jewish contact. He points out that Jews still share sleeping compartments on trains with Germans.

---

emotions in the latent discourse, the associations and identifications of imagery, one hears much more than the speaker intended to say. Analysis of these emotional contents reveals what is being said unwittingly – the deep psychological structure of the fantasies.

The verbatim stenographic protocol of the *Reichsminister* exchanging conscious fantasies of their identification with Jews in Germany after the *Kristallnacht* for over three hours provides the "playful", spontaneous, free associative expression from which latent depreciated unconscious parts of themselves may be derived.

[24]Stenographische Niederschrift von einem Teil der Besprechung über die Judenfrage unter Vorsitz von Feldmarschall Göring, im RLM (Reichsluftfahrtministerium) am 12. November 1938, 11 Uhr., in *Trial of the Major War Criminals before the International Military Tribunal, Nuremberg, 14 November 1945–1 October 1946*, Nuremberg 1948, vol. 28, pp. 499–540 (hereafter cited as *Ministerbesprechung*, 12th November 1938). The quotations are from pp. 508–509.

"Weiterhin halte ich es für notwendig, dass die Juden überall da aus der Öffentlichkeit herausgezogen werden, wo sie provokativ wirken. Es ist z.B. heute noch möglich, dass ein Jude mit einem Deutschen ein gemeinsames Schlafwagenabteil benutzt. Es muss also ein Erlass des Reichsverkehrsministers herauskommen, dass für Juden besondere Abteile eingerichtet werden und dass, wenn dieses Abteil besetzt ist, die Juden keinen Anspruch auf Platz haben, dass die Juden aber nur dann, wenn alle Deutschen sitzen, ein besonderes Abteil bekommen, dass sie dagegen nicht unter die Deutschen gemischt werden und dass, wenn kein Platz ist, die Juden draussen im Flur zu stehen haben."

"Furthermore, I consider it essential that Jews be ejected from public life wherever they are provocative. For instance, it is still possible today for a Jew and a German to share a common sleeping compartment. Therefore, there must be a decree issued by the *Reich* Transport Minister that special compartments should be equipped for Jews and that when this compartment is occupied, the Jews have no right to seats, that the Jews only get their special compartment after all Germans are seated, that they must not be mixed with Germans and that, if there is no seat, the Jews must stand in the corridor."[25]

Goebbels and Göring then bounce their fantasies back and forth on how to humiliate Jews more completely in a spirit of "try to top this!"

"Göring: Da finde ich es viel vernünftiger, dass man ihnen eigene Abteile gibt.
Goebbels: Aber nicht, wenn der Zug überfüllt ist.
Göring: Einen Moment! Es gibt nur einen jüdischen Wagen. Ist er besetzt, müssen die übrigen zu Hause bleiben.
Goebbels: Aber nehmen wir an: es sind nicht so viele Juden da, die mit dem Fern-D-Zug nach München fahren, sagen wir: es sitzen zwei Juden im Zug, und die anderen Abteile sind überfüllt. Diese beiden Juden hätten nun ein Sonderabteil. Man muss deshalb sagen: die Juden haben erst dann Anspruch auf Platz, wenn alle Deutschen sitzen.
Göring: Das würde ich gar nicht extra einzeln fassen, sondern ich würde den Juden einen Wagen oder ein Abteil geben. Und wenn es wirklich jemals so wäre, wie Sie sagen, dass der Zug sonst überfüllt ist, glauben Sie: das machen wir so, da brauche ich kein Gesetz. Da wird er herausgeschmissen, und wenn er allein auf dem Lokus sitzt während der ganzen Fahrt."

"Göring: I think it more reasonable to give them their own compartments.
Goebbels: But not when the train is over-full.
Göring: Just a minute! There is only one Jewish carriage. If it's occupied, the others must stay at home.
Goebbels: But let's suppose there are not so many Jews travelling to Munich on this train. Let's say two Jews sit in the train and the other compartments are overflowing. These two Jews would have a special section for themselves. Therefore we must say: the Jews only have a right to a seat after all the Germans are seated.
Göring: I would not formulate it specially that way. Rather, I would give the Jews a coach or a compartment. And if it ever came to the situation you speak of, that the train is full, believe me, we will handle it as is. For this I need no law: The Jew is thrown out, even if he as to sit by himself in the loo for the whole trip."[26]

At this point the Nazi leadership was more interested in how to humiliate Jews than in other issues. Goebbels, Göring, Heydrich and the others spent a great deal of time fantasising on the situation of a Jew who wishes to take a train journey. Can he go? When will he know if he may travel? If he does get on board the train, where may he sit? May he sleep? Under what circumstances will he be thrown out? At no point will the Jewish traveller feel secure in his person or his place. He will always be in a state of tension, anxious about being abused and humiliated, at the mercy of any German Gentile. The Jew who wishes to travel

[25]*Ibid.*
[26]*Ibid.*

is to be made to feel on tenterhooks, with his self-esteem derogated and in constant distress. The Nazi leadership were putting themselves in this Jew's place emotionally. They were identifying with this demeaning position while actually structuring it. This is the psychodynamic situation of the sadist who needs his victim and identifies with him.

Goebbels goes on to issues of closing swimming pools, beaches, resorts, and forests to Jews. Göring responds with the idea of giving Jews certain sections of forests stocked with animals who look "damned similar" to Jews, such as elks, who have hooked noses. Goebbels protests that Jews should not be permitted to sit in public places.

> "Göring: Also wir werden den Juden einen gewissen Waldteil zur Verfügung stellen, und Alpers wird dafür sorgen, dass die verschiedenen Tiere, die den Juden verdammt ähnlich sehen – der Elch hat ja so eine gebogene Nase – dahin kommen und sich da einbürgern.
>
> Goebbels: Ich halte dieses Verhalten für provokativ. Dann weiter, dass die Juden nicht in deutschen Anlagen herumsitzen können. Ich knüpfe an an die Flüsterpropaganda durch Judenfrauen in den Anlagen am Fehrbelliner Platz. Es gibt Juden, die gar nicht so jüdisch aussehen. Die setzen sich zu deutschen Müttern mit Kindern und fangen an zu mosern und zu stänkern.
>
> Göring: Die sagen gar nicht, dass sie Juden sind.
>
> Goebbels: Ich sehe darin eine besonders grosse Gefahr. Ich halte es für notwendig, dass man den Juden bestimmte Anlagen zur Verfügung stellt – nicht die schönsten – und sagt: auf diesen Bänken dürfen die Juden sitzen. Die sind besonders gekennzeichnet. Es steht darauf: Nur für Juden! Im übrigen haben sie in deutschen Anlagen nichts zu suchen.
>
> Als letztes wäre noch folgendes vorzutragen. Es besteht tatsächlich heute noch der Zustand, dass jüdische Kinder in deutsche Schulen gehen. Das halte ich für unmöglich. Ich halte es für ausgeschlossen, dass mein Junge neben einem Juden im deutschen Gymnasium sitzt und deutschen Geschichtsunterricht erteilt bekommt. Ich halte as für notwendig, dass die Juden absolut aus den deutschen Schulen entfernt werden . . ."

> "Göring: We will place a certain part of the forest at the disposal of the Jews, and Alpers will see to it that various animals which look damned similar to the Jews – the elk has a hooked nose for instance – are placed and settled there.
>
> Goebbels: I consider that provocative. Further, the Jews mustn't sit around in German recreational areas. I'm referring to the whispering campaign of the Jewish women around the Fehrbelliner Platz. There are Jews who do not look very Jewish. They sit next to German mothers with children and start to carp and create a stink.
>
> Göring: They don't even say they're Jews.
>
> Goebbels: I see an especially great danger in this. I consider it necessary to put certain places – not the most beautiful – at the disposal of Jews – and we say: Jews may sit on these benches. They are especially designated. It says on them: For Jews only! Otherwise they have no business in German parks.
>
> And finally, I wish to take up the following issue. The fact is that Jewish children still attend German schools. I consider this to be intolerable. I consider it out of the question for my boy to sit next to a Jew in a German *Gymnasium* and learn German history. I consider it necessary that Jews be absolutely excluded from German schools . . ."[27]

A representative of the German insurance industry, Herr Hilgard, was invited to report on damage claims. He said this had been a "very great catastrophe" ["eine sehr grosse Katastrophe"] for the German insurance industry.[28] The glass damage alone had been six million marks. It would take the Belgian glass industry half a year to replace the breakage and it would, of

[27] *Ibid.*, pp. 510–511.
[28] *Ibid.*, p. 517.

course, require hard foreign currency.[29] A single jeweller on Berlin's Unter den Linden had a claim for 1.7 million marks because the store was totally plundered.[30] He stressed the importance of the international reputation of the German insurance industry. He was concerned that trust in the reliability of German insurance should not be shaken ("so wäre das ein schwarzer Fleck auf dem Ehrenschild der deutschen Versicherung"). "It would be a black spot on the shield of honour of German insurance."[31]

Later in the discussion, Göring calls for a number of concerted actions: police, propaganda, cultural, so that in this week the Jews should get one cuff on the ears after another ("das Judentum in dieser Woche zack-zack eins nach dem anderen um die Ohren bekommt.").[32]

Heydrich then proposes personal insignia that must be worn by Jews.

Göring asks: "A uniform?" Heydrich will settle for a badge or some sort of marking.[33] This leads to proposals by Heydrich to deprive Jews of their driver's licences, ownership of automobiles, freedom of movement by declaring public places, cultural sites, frontier areas, and fortifications off limits. He also would exclude them from sharing hospitals with Aryans and from public transportation.[34]

At this point Göring asked for reactions to the idea of a one billion Mark contribution "as a punishment –"

> "Göring: Noch eine Frage, meine Herren: Wie beurteilen Sie die Lage, wenn ich heute verkünde, dass dem Judentum als Strafe diese 1 Milliarde als Kontribution auferlegt wird?"

> "One more question, Gentlemen: What would you think of my announcing today that a contribution of one billion Marks is being imposed on the Jewish community as a punishment?"[35]

He develops the idea, relishing how it will hit the German Jews, and identifying with how it will feel to be a Jew in Germany:

> "Göring: Ich werde den Wortlaut wählen, dass die deutschen Juden in ihrer Gesamtheit als Strafe für die ruchlosen Verbrechen usw. usw. eine Kontribution von 1 Milliarde auferlegt bekommen. Das wird hinhauen. Die Schweine werden einen zweiten Mord so schnell nicht machen. Im übrigen muss ich noch einmal feststellen: Ich möchte kein Jude in Deutschland sein."

> "I will choose the wording – that German Jews as a whole, in punishment for their wicked crimes, etc., etc., are assessed at a contribution of one billion. That will hit them where it hurts. The pigs will not commit a second murder so soon. Moreover, I have to say once again that I would not wish to be a Jew in Germany."[36]

The decree announcing the one billion Mark fine was published in the official *Reichsgesetzblatt* as 'A Payment in Atonement by Jews of German Citizenship'

[29] *Ibid.*, p. 513.
[30] *Ibid.*, p. 514.
[31] *Ibid.*, p. 515.
[32] *Ibid.*, p. 532.
[33] *Ibid.*, p. 534.
[34] *Ibid.*, pp. 536–537.
[35] *Ibid.*, p. 537.
[36] *Ibid.*, p. 538.

['Eine Sühneleistung der Juden deutscher Staatsangehörigkeit']. The fine was exacted because:

> "Die feindliche Haltung des Judentums gegenüber dem deutschen Volk und Reich, die auch vor feigen Mordtaten nicht zurückschreckt, erfordert entschiedene Abwehr und harte Sühne."

> "The Jews' hostile behaviour towards the German people and *Reich*, which does not shrink even from cowardly acts of murder, demands decisive measures and harsh atonement."[37]

The ultimate degradation for a victim is to have to humbly pay and apologise for the damage inflicted on him. This dynamic of humiliation was well understood by the Nazi leaders. Thus German Jewry was not only cruelly victimised, but had to raise the money collectively to repair the damage wrought against them and their property by Nazi bullies.

Göring then expressly threatens a "final reckoning" with the Jews if Germany enters into a foreign conflict. He had in mind emigration to Madagascar and North America:

> "Göring: Wenn das Deutsche Reich in irgendeiner absehbaren Zeit in aussenpolitischen Konflikt kommt, so ist es selbstverständlich, dass auch wir in Deutschland in aller erster Linie daran denken werden, eine grosse Abrechnung an den Juden zu vollziehen."

> "If the German *Reich* comes into foreign political conflict in the foreseeable future, naturally we in Germany will first of all think of carrying out a final reckoning of our account with the Jews."[38]

A moment later Goebbels said:

> "Im Augenblick ist er [der Jude] klein und hässlich und bleibt zu Hause."

> "At the moment he [the Jew] is small and ugly and stays at home."[39]

Two important and related points need to be made about this meeting. First, to address the current historiographic controversy regarding centralised control of policy in the Third *Reich*, we may clearly see in this conference the full powerlessness of the state administrative authority and the high degree to which it was subordinate to the Nazi Party. Ministers and State Secretaries had been demoted to being functionaries carrying out the wishes of Nazi bigwigs. They did no more than to shape the suggestions of Goebbels, Göring, and Heydrich into correct bureaucratic form. In this case, the formula "the party controls the state" applies fully. Whatever fantasies the Nazi leaders had about what transpired in sleeping compartments on trains, what Jews did on park benches, or the stigma of an identification mark, these became suggestions to senior civil servants and were then immediately drafted and promulgated as laws and regulations of the *Reich* by their offices.

A mark of the warped nature of the Third *Reich* is that these men had the power to actualise their cruellest fantasies instantly like oriental potentates. There was virtually no distinction between the bizarre wish and its realisation among the

[37] *Reichs–Archiv: Sammlung der das Rechtswesen betreffenden Gesetze, Verordnungen und Verfügungen*, Hans Bergmann (ed.), 25 (1983), vol. 3, Karlsruhe 1939, p. 1771, 12th November 1938.

[38] *Ministerbesprechung*, 12th November 1938, pp. 538–539.

[39] *Ibid.*, p. 539.

Nazi high command. The most grotesque fantasies of single minds in high places were transmuted into historical fact.

It is centrally significant for an understanding of the *Kristallnacht* to note that the *Reich* Ministerial Meeting of 12th November at the Air Ministry spent a great deal of time discussing how to humiliate Jews prior to the consideration of insurance claims and costs. The Nazi leaders gave precedence to destroying Jewish self-esteem before they considered material losses. Even the large financial fine on the Jews was conceived so as to be an "atonement" and as humiliating as possible. What Göring and Goebbels cared about was robbing Jews of dignity and self-respect as human beings. This was a dialogue about the fine points of degradation. Considering the available economic interpretations, the ideological background, and the bureaucratic-structural explanations of Nazi antisemitism, it is evident that the most relevant and neglected element in German anti-Jewish policy in 1938 is the heightened emotional tone of depreciation, of narcissistic devaluation, and of personal humiliation of Jews under Nazi power.

What was the historical meaning of the *Kristallnacht* for Jews, Germans, and Nazis in 1938? The Jews of Germany and Austria were severely demoralised. Their very identity as self-respecting human beings was totally assaulted. The reaction of Jews was to preserve their self-esteem from further onslaughts by accelerating as much as possible their withdrawal from contact with the German world, a process that had been in effect since the Nuremberg Laws of 1935.

What the German historian Hermann Graml has termed "a real hail of discriminating and oppressive laws and regulations clattered down on the German Jews in the next days, weeks, and months". ("Ein wahrer Hagel von diskriminierenden und bedrückenden Gesetzen und Verordnungen prasselte in den nächsten Tagen, Wochen und Monaten auf die deutsche Judenheit nieder.")[40] Virtually everything which was fantasised at the *Reich* Ministers' Conference of 12th November was rapidly converted to the law of the *Reich*. The Jews were excluded from the cultural life of Germany. They were made to wear the yellow star. They were without rights, socially and morally isolated, and robbed. For Jews it meant that there was now absolutely no prospect of continued life in Germany. Any hopes of lasting out the Nazi era and waiting "for better times" were finally dashed. A fifteen-year-old Jewish girl from Nuremberg recalls: "The question was not whether we would emigrate to America, but when we could emigrate." A seventeen-year-old boy from Breslau reported: "After the *Kristallnacht* everything changed. My mother and my grandfather now realised that they must get out of Germany if at all possible, but that as a minimum they had to get us, my brother and me, out whatever happened."[41]

[40]Graml, *Der 9. November 1938, op. cit.*, p. 61.

[41]As quoted in Werner T. Angress, *Generation zwischen Furcht und Hoffnung. Jüdische Jugend im Dritten Reich*, Hamburg 1985, p. 42.

Life was now intolerable and insecure every minute and every hour. As Kochan wrote: "The pogrom and the ensuing measures made, as was their aim, any organized Jewish life impossible."[42] There was no place for Jews in Germany. To stay in the Third *Reich* was dangerous. All the assumed behavioural norms upon which people had relied for mental security and comfort had been trampled on and destroyed.

For the German government the *Kristallnacht* signified a test of how much and how far the German public would condone and support antisemitic violence. The general finding was that there was no spontaneous public participation in or enthusiasm for the attacks on Jews, the plundering of their property, and the destruction of their synagogues. Data on this are found in the official secret "opinion" reports of the German government. There are also the foreign consular reports from within Germany, especially from the American and British consuls. A further source is the Social Democratic Party reports compiled and smuggled out of Germany to the exile leadership, first in Prague and later in Paris and London. These are first-hand reports from all parts of Germany that were assembled and digested by the Social Democratic Executive Committee in exile and passed on to leaders of opinion. Even the *Gestapo* relied on these reports because they came from a non-Nazi source. Finally, there are the eye-witness accounts by the victims, those deposited in the Wiener Library, London, and the oral history sources now being collected in the places where survivors still live.

The aspiration of the Nazi regime was to create a "spontaneous" pogrom in Germany. In this they did not succeed. It was obvious to all that the November pogrom was a centralised, co-ordinated campaign. The conclusion drawn by the Nazi leadership was that any violence against Jews was acceptable to the German public if it was carried out secretly and in an orderly manner. Thus, three years later, when the "Final Solution" was ordered, it was under the condition that it be secret. The very secrecy of the "Final Solution" demonstrates that the Nazi leadership felt it could not rely on popular support for the extermination of the Jews.

For the German people, the *Kristallnacht* proved that this regime was willing and able to invoke any level of terror necessary to carry out its racial aims. Any opposition was pointless and would be ruthlessly crushed. As we read in the Social Democratic Party reports to the exiled party Executive Committee:

> "Man muss sich allerdings . . . darüber klar werden, dass die Brutalität der Pogromhorden die Einschüchterung gesteigert und in der Bevölkerung die Vorstellung gefestigt haben, jeder Widerstand gegen die uneingeschränkte nationalsozialistische Gewalt sei zwecklos."

> "One must, however, . . . be clear about it, that the brutality of the pogrom gangs has heightened the intimidation and has strengthened the idea in the population that any resistance against the unrestrained power of National Socialism is pointless.[43]"

As a social phenomenon the *Kristallnacht* was a nation-wide public degradation ritual aimed at totally altering the identity of German and Austrian Jews. The

[42]Kochan, *Pogrom. 10 November 1938*, *op. cit.*, p. 11.

[43]*Deutschlandberichte der Sozialdemokratischen Partei Deutschlands*, 5, p. 1204 F. as cited in William S. Allen, 'Die deutsche Öffentlichkeit und die "Reichkristallnacht" . . .', *loc. cit.*, pp. 399–400.

events entailed public denunciation and labelling of Jews before the German people to the effect of declaring them banned and cursed, so as to say: "All Germans must bear witness that Jews are not what they appear to be and claim to be – moral human beings; they are, in fact, of a lower species." The rituals of degradation of the *Kristallnacht*, the synagogue burnings, the public humiliation of individuals, the destruction of shop fronts which are part of the business-man's *persona*,[44] his presentation to the world – served to effect the symbolic destruction of the Jews as German people. What was aimed at, and achieved, was the transformation of identities – the literal destruction of a group of social beings and the constitution of another social identity with the intent of making the present retroactive. The Jews as Germans ("Deutsche Staatsbürger jüdischen Glaubens") were transformed into Jewish outcasts and their past as Germans was undone. It was declared that they always were sub-human pariahs and it was so from the first instance to the present. The new identity was the "basic reality" – Jews were now seen as what they "in reality" had been all along – degraded *poseurs*, not real men and women. The upright, active, German Jews who participated in the intellectual, economic and military life of Germany for the past sixty years were now transformed into essentially non-human parasites in the body of Germany. All their previous achievements were denounced as mere appearance and the way Jews were seen now was taken as the essence of what they were. All their performances, past, present, and future, were to be properly understood with reference to the new *schema*, as undesirable pollutants who were now, as always, deceiving us. The Jews became, in the eyes of the Nazis and of many Germans, different people, or non-people. Ian Kershaw assesses this as the greatest Nazi success of the *Kristallnacht*:

> "Where the Nazis were most successful was in the depersonalization of the Jew. The more the Jew was forced out of social life, the more he seemed to fit the stereotypes of a propaganda which intensified, paradoxically, its campaign against 'Jewry', the fewer actual Jews there were in Germany itself. Depersonalization increased the already existent widespread indifference of German popular opinion and formed a vital stage between the archaic violence of the pogrom and the rationalized 'assembly line' annihilation of the death camps."[45]

Jews as persons and as a social collectivity were made to stand as "out of the ordinary". The two conceptions, "Germanic" and "Jewish" were made to appear as opposites, as counterconceptions. All the character traits of idealised Germans: strength, cleanliness, purity, courage, upright morality, were clarified by references to their opposite: Jewish weakness, corruption, filth, sexuality, cowardice, and debauchery. The qualities of the sexual pervert are the reverse of the healthy decent person. The alternatives were presented so that the choice for obvious goodness and virtue was morally required. For the German citizen witnessing the *Kristallnacht*, not siding with the Germanic values could only

[44]Persona – the individual's presentation to the world as distinguished from his inner self. Cf. C. G. Jung, 'The Persona as a Segment of the Collective Psyche', in *Two Essays on Analytical Psychology*, New York 1956, pp. 166–172; Erving Goffman, *The Presentation of Self in Everyday Life*, New York 1959.

[45]Ian Kershaw, *Popular Opinion and Political Dissent in the Third Reich. Bavaria 1933–1945*, New York 1983, p. 275.

mean a preference for their opposite, and identification with the degraded Jews. The public ceremonies of humiliation placed great distance between the German public and the helpless outcasts. The witnesses were made to experience emotional distance from the ostracised Jews. The Jews were placed "beyond the law". They were made "strange". They were defined as opposed to Germany, as enemies and outsiders.

In view of this intense social and political pressure to redefine reality it is remarkable how many acts of private sympathy, decency, and support were manifested by Germans during and after the pogrom of November 1938.* These are the German people who managed to maintain an autonomous sense of reality, who refused to succumb to the communally validated revision of the present and past perception of their Jewish fellow citizens and neighbours.

Ian Kershaw summed up the crucial effect of the *Kristallnacht*[46] for the social alienation and depersonalisation of Jews from the German people.

> "The 'Final Solution' would not have been possible without the progressive steps excluding the Jews from German society which took place in full public view, in their legal form met with widespread approval, and resulted in the dehumanization of the figure of the Jew."[47]

An in-depth structural understanding of the terrible event we have recounted as a public degradation, as a preparation for dehumanisation and murder, may show us how to identify, contain, and prevent such processes. For, while each historical situation is unique, the forces we have considered are not. As Albert Camus concluded in his great allegory of the Holocaust:

> "Le bacille de la peste ne meurt ni ne disparait jamais, qu'il peut rester pendant des dizaines d'années endormi dans les meubles et le linge, qu'il attend patiemment dans les chambres, les caves, les malles, les mouchoirs et les paperasses, et que, peut-être, le jour viendrait où, pour le malheur et l'enseignement des hommes, la peste réveillerait ses rats et les enverrait mourir dans une cité heureuse."

> "The plague bacillus never dies or disappears for good; . . . it can lie dormant for years in furniture and linen chests; . . . it bides its time in bedrooms, cellars, trunks, and bookshelves; . . . perhaps the day would come when, for the bane and the enlightening of men, it would rouse up its rats again and send them forth to die in a happy city."[48]

*On the attitude of the German population see also the following essay by David Bankier, 'The German Communist Party and Nazi Antisemitism 1933–1938', in this volume of the Year Book, pp. 339–340 – (Ed.).

[46]It has been argued that the word *Kristallnacht* belittles the gruesome events of November 1938 which were, of course, not limited to shattering glass. In the past half-century the term has acquired specific historical and emotional connotation, symbolising the whole pogrom as considered in this article. To cite only one example, Günter Grass made the shattering of glass by his dwarf Oskar a major symbol of Nazism in *Die Blechtrommel*. Grass was unmistakably time specific by associating the 9th November with the death of Oskar's Jewish friend and benefactor: ". . . den Tag . . . der zum Geburtstag meines Komplexes wurde . . . den neunten November achtunddreissig, denn an jenem Tage verlor ich Sigismund Markus", Darmstadt 1984, p. 170 (". . . the exact date when my complex was born . . . November 9, 1938", *The Tin Drum*, transl. by Ralph Manheim, New York 1964, p. 210).

[47]Ian Kershaw, 'The Persecution of the Jews and German Popular Opinion in the Third Reich', in *LBI Year Book XXVI* (1981), p. 289.

[48]Albert Camus, *La Peste*, Paris 1947, Bibliothèque de la Pléiade, 1962, p. 1474; *The Plague* 1947, New York 1972, p. 287.

The German Communist Party and Nazi Antisemitism, 1933–1938

BY DAVID BANKIER

The reaction of the *Kommunistische Partei Deutschlands* (KPD) to antisemitism in the Third *Reich* has not yet been subjected to scholarly treatment. Obviously the studies and documents published on this topic in Eastern European historiography and in particular in East Germany, cannot be taken as an impartially true reflection of historical reality because, touching on the Jewish Question incidentally – while dealing with the Communist underground in Germany – they portray the fight against antisemitism as an invariably consistent KPD line. However, this type of historical writing undoubtedly reflects the dictates of the ruling Communist Party, rather than independent research devoid of official ideology.

Looking at this literature we shall, not surprisingly, find that the KPD struggle against antisemitism, under both the Weimar Republic and the Third *Reich*, has been idealised, whereas the suggestive picture conveyed by the variegated documentary material at our disposal is not so clear cut.[1] It would appear that the changes in the political orientation of the KPD since its inception left an indelible mark on the varying attitudes to antisemitism. Thus, for instance, we learn of the prevalence of antisemitic elements in the Communist Party in the Weimar period from the lively controversy which raged among its different factions. Clara Zetkin, one of the most eminent party leaders in the early twenties, hurled some caustic accusations against the party's left-wingers, emphasising significantly the reactionary elements at work in this faction which included, she claimed, "fascist antisemites".[2]

Moreover, apart from these murmuring antisemitic undercurrents, it is well

[1]See for example the "official history" of the German workers' movement edited by the East German Communist Party: Institut für Marxismus-Leninismus beim Zentralkomitee der SED, *Geschichte der deutschen Arbeiterbewegung*, Berlin 1969, vol. X, pp. 72–73, 88, 213. Cf. S. Khan, 'Dokumente des Kampfes der revolutionären deutschen Arbeiterbewegung', in *Beiträge zur Geschichte der deutschen Arbeiterbewegung*, 2 (1960), pp. 522–565; Klaus Mammach, *Die KPD und die deutsche antifaschistische Widerstandsbewegung 1933–1939*, Frankfurt a. Main 1974, pp. 139, 220–222, 240. For a review of this literature, Reinhard Rürup, 'Die kommunistische Wissenschaft und der Antisemitismus', in C. D. Hernig (ed.), *Sowjetsystem und demokratische Gesellschaft. Eine vergleichende Enzyklopädie*, Freiburg 1968, vol. III, col. 401–403; Konrad Kwiet, 'Historians of the German Democratic Republic on Antisemitism and Persecution', in *LBI Year Book XXI* (1976), pp. 173–198. On this topic the only study which partially relates to the Nazi era is Eduard Silberner, 'Die Kommunistische Partei Deutschlands zur Judenfrage', in *Jahrbuch des Instituts für deutsche Geschichte*, VIII, Tel-Aviv 1979, pp. 283–334. See as well his *Kommunisten zur Judenfrage. Zur Geschichte von Theorie und Praxis des Kommunismus*, Opladen 1983.

[2]Quoted in Hermann Weber, *Die Wandlung des deutschen Kommunismus*, Frankfurt a. Main 1969, vol. I, p. 327.

known that in the first half of the twenties, the KPD made deliberately cynical and opportunistic use of antisemitism for its own political purposes. This is particularly true during the period in which it gravitated towards Karl Radek's methods of National Bolshevism, especially during the adoption of what was known as the *Schlageter Kurs*, *i.e.*, taking advantage of the nationalist climate for tactical reasons.[3] In this context, the speech given by the Jewish Communist Ruth Fischer before a students' gathering on 25th July 1923, stands out clearly:

> "The German *Reich* will be saved only when you, together with the German nationalists, understand that you must fight hand in hand with the organised masses of the KPD; those who combat Jewish capital are already fighting in the class struggle, even if they are unaware of it. Stamp out Jewish capitalists! String them from the lamp posts."[4]

The KPD voiced similar views during the election campaign for the *Landtag* in Thuringia. Then too, in April 1924, it disseminated Communist propaganda peppered with antisemitic remarks. At the time, the political propaganda agitated openly for a war against what the KPD termed "Jewish contaminated government".[5] The KPD undoubtedly resorted to these means to demonstrate to the local population that it would serve their interests better than any right-wing political body. It is therefore hardly surprising to find antisemitic remarks also in Communist pamphlets distributed before the elections. The chief police station in Nürnberg-Fürth, for example, in its report for April 1924, mentions that 70 circulars had been confiscated from the regional Communist office, bearing the call "Down with the Jewish Republic".[6] This becomes clear in 1931 again, when the KPD returned to this line and allowed antisemitic views to be published in the party's central organ *Die Rote Fahne*.[7]

[3]The Schlageter line was adopted by the KPD during the months of June–September 1923, following the execution of the *Freikorps* man Leo Schlageter by the French occupation army. Since the KPD feared that the occupation of the Ruhr might lead thousands of German workers to the Nationalist camp, it decided to appear as a party that cared about German national interests and Germany's territorial integrity. Radek also believed that a cooperation between Communists and Nationalists would create tensions between Germany and France and the Soviet Union would profit from it. On this topic see Ossip K. Flechtheim, *Die KPD in der Weimarer Republik*, Offenbach 1948, p. 89; Werner T. Angress, *Stillborn Revolution. The Communist Bid for Power in Germany 1921–1923*, Princeton 1963, pp. 332–340; Weber, *op. cit.*, p. 289.

[4]Cf. the apologetics of Ruth Fischer in her book, *Stalin and German Communism*, Cambridge, Mass. 1948, pp. 267 ff, 283. On the rapprochement between the Communist party and right-wing antisemitic circles see the following conversation between a Communist and a right-winger: "If the Communists would detach themselves from the Jews and fight them I would be the first to join them", answered by the Communist: "Well, you hang the Jews and we'll hang the Capitalists", quoted in, Otto Ernst Schuddekopf, *Linke Leute von Rechts. Die nationalrevolutionären Minderheiten und der Kommunismus in der Weimarer Republik*, Stuttgart 1960, p. 199. On National Bolshevism see G. Lövy, 'National Bolshevism in Weimar Germany. Alliance of Political Extremes Against Democracy', in *Social Research*, 23 (1956), pp. 450–480; K. von Klemperer, *Germany's New Conservatism*, Princeton 1957, pp. 139–150; A. Spencer, 'National Bolshevism', in *Survey*, 44/45 (1962), pp. 133–152.

[5]Hans-Helmuth Knütter, 'Die Linksparteien', in *Entscheidungsjahr 1932. Zur Judenfrage in der Endphase der Weimarer Republik*. Ein Sammelband herausgegeben von Werner E. Mosse unter Mitwirkung von Arnold Paucker, Tübingen 1965 (Schriftenreihe wissenschaftlicher Abhandlungen des Leo Baeck Instituts 13), p. 330.

[6]*Idem, Die Juden und die deutsche Linke in der Weimarer Republik 1918–1933*, Düsseldorf 1971, p. 186.

[7]Silberner, 'Die Kommunistische Partei', *loc. cit.*, pp. 293 ff.

These incidents, however, should not be given undue importance and must be seen in their proper context. What we have here is the party's momentary political opportunism and its temporary adoption of the National-Bolshevist tactic, rather than a consistent dominant line.

THE REACTIONS TO THE ECONOMIC BOYCOTT

The KPD's first reaction to antisemitic policy in the Third *Reich* followed swiftly upon the boycott of 1st April 1933. The *Rundschau*, a KPD organ published in Basle at the time, printed an elaborate article explaining that the said boycott of Jewish shops was a necessary by-product of the prevailing intimate relationship between capitalism and Fascism.[8] In reading this article, one is immediately struck by the typical dogmatic schematisation of Communist exegetics; as such, it totally ignored the qualitative differences between Nazism and other fascist movements. Because the interpretation of Nazism's antisemitic policies were consistently nurtured on the Communist analytical method and categorical system – instead of an analysis of the causes underlying the boycott, within the wider context of the special role played by the Jewish Question in Nazi ideology – we find a mechanical and rigid reductionist assertion that antisemitism is merely a functional tool, serving the dictatorial pragmatic needs of the Nazi regime.[9] Thus, the author arbitrarily asserts that the only people harmed by the boycott were petty merchants and professionals. Large Jewish corporations, he affirms categorically, banks and stockbrokers were not affected.[10] This fallacious argument – already well known from Communist literature of the twenties – and as we shall clearly see it will crop up again and again in the thirties – is based not only on fundamental ideological conceptions, but also serves pragmatic political tactics. Ideologically, it is based on the analysis of Fascism as the ineluctable outcome of the crisis of modern capitalism, and Nazism is therefore the embodiment of a sinister form of struggle between expiring capital and the revolutionary movement. Because it admirably serves the interests of capital as a whole, Nazism is utterly indifferent to the distinction between Jewish and Aryan capital. This is why, the article categorically maintains, Jewish capitalists were not harmed by the boycott.

Tactically and politically, by deliberately putting forth this argument, the KPD tried to undermine Nazi "leftist" slogans, arguing that Nazism was actually perverted pseudo-socialism, and in fact relied materially on money from Jewish capitalists. So that its antisemitism was merely part of an

[8]'Die Judenverfolgungen des deutschen Faschismus', in *Rundschau über Politik, Wirtschaft und Arbeiterbewegung*, (hereafter *Rundschau*), 8 (7th April 1933) p. 197.

[9]On the beginnings of the application of Marxist interpretation to the understanding of Fascism, see 'Die Gegenrevolution. Der deutsche Faszismus', in *Kommunistische Partei Korrespondenz* (15th December 1922), p. 272.

[10]Among the large number of Communist writings mentioning the support given by Jewish capitalists to the Nazis see, for example, F. Schprach, *The fascist counter-revolution and the Jewish bourgeoisie*, Moscow 1939. (in Yiddish). This author affirms that in Austria, during the struggle between the *Heimwehr* and the Nazis, Jewish capitalists gave their support to the Nazis, *ibid.*, p. 45.

intentionally deceptive scheme, and the boycott a classic diversionary tactic on the part of the Nazi dictatorship. Through it, Hitler sought to camouflage the fact that Nazism actually protects and preserves the capitalist regime. Still, the fact that Jewish firms did not reap benefits on boycott day did not escape the author, and explaining this matter posed a theoretical challenge to him. For, if terror is simply capitalism's desperate attempt to divert opinion and halt the proletarian revolution, what is the role of terror against Jewish capitalists? In extricating himself from this difficulty, the author's argument clearly shows how the failure to understand the essence of Fascism led him to a mistaken interpretation of antisemitism in the Third *Reich*. To deal with a situation which clearly contradicts the overall Marxist theory, he ultimately resorts to the scapegoat argument: the fact that some Jewish capitalists were harmed also points to the instrumental use of antisemitism. Rich Jews become a substitute onto which the masses, bitterly disappointed at the failure of the regime, can deflect their rage. The article finally concludes by naming one of the concomitant uses of antisemitism for Hitler's regime: by focusing public opinion in Germany and abroad on Jewish problems, it delusively diverts attention from the fate of the persecuted oppositionist elements. While, he observes, the newspapers are busy describing every last detail of the maltreatment of Jews, the regime has a free hand to step up its repressive measures against Communist opposition in the *Reich*.

This interpretation should be seen as part of the general trend of accepted Marxist reading of the Jewish Question, which denies a unique place to antisemitism, religiously depicting it as a by-product of repression of the masses. It is also the main argument in the official declaration made public by the KPD regarding its position on the persecution of Jews in the Third *Reich*.[11] In this manifesto, issued several weeks after the boycott, it particularly pointed out that the party fought all forms of capitalism whether Aryan or Jewish. And in its own typical fashion it authoritatively noted that Jewish industrialists, stockbrokers and capitalists had not been harmed by the boycott.

This myopic political exegesis, tinged with antisemitism, appeared also in underground publications widely disseminated in Germany during these months by the illegal KPD. In Halle, for instance, a Communist broadsheet was circulated bearing the caption "Organise the mass struggle against the fascist dictatorship", and pointed scornfully to the hypocrisy of the Nazi regime:

> "The real face of the capitalist dictatorship has been unmasked. Contrary to past declarations on Jewish capital and department stores . . . it is now patently clear that the regime is actually protecting Jewish capital"[12].

Similarly we learn from a *Gestapo* report, apparently from the Hamburg area, for March 1934, that a favourite topic in Communist subversive propaganda is the Jewish Question. According to this report the KPD stresses the fact that Nazism did not succeed in removing the Jews and their financial activities.[13]

[11] 'Die Stellung der KPD zu den faschistischen Judenverfolgungen in Deutschland', in *Rundschau*, 9 (12th April 1933), p. 234.

[12] *Organisiert den Massenkampf gegen die faschistische Diktatur*, Halle (21st March 1933), *Kommunismus Sammelrundschreiben*, Institut für Zeitgeschichte-Munich, MA 423/867315–6.

[13] Gestapo [Hamburg?], Lagebericht, Bundesarchiv Koblenz (hereafter BA) R58/1561.

THE ATTITUDE TO ZIONISM

A special space in the KPD's discussion of the Jewish Question was devoted to fighting Zionism. The relative decline in antisemitic terror at the end of 1933 provided the KPD with a convenient pretext for reviving the controversy with Zionism without straying so much as an iota from the Communist line of the twenties. Zionism continued to be defined according to the formula presented at the Second Congress of the Comintern in 1920 as "an utopian and reformist vision leading to counter-revolutionary consequences". An article published in the Comintern's *Inprecor*, in September 1933, held up the "transfer agreement" as incontestable proof of the bond between Fascism and Zionism.[14] According to the writer the fact that the Nazi authorities permitted the *Jüdische Rundschau* to continue operating, and even more so, the fact that they allowed the Viennese Revisionist organ *Der Judenstaat*, to be sold in Germany, showed just how strong the bond between Zionism and Fascism was.[15] This deep attachment between Zionism and Nazism, according to the KPD, thus explains the government's playing down antisemitism in the second half of 1933. The need to still the passions of the inflamed masses who, contrary to plan, might transfer their attacks on Jewish craftsmen to Jewish capitalists, as well as the "*Haavara* agreement" with the Zionist Organisation explains the relative moderation in antisemitic activity.* Here too the KPD's form of debate shows little originality. The same claims were raised at mass rallies in 1930. Hermann Remmele, for instance, one of the leaders of the Communist Party, then pointed out that the Nazis had deleted the end of their slogan "Deutschland erwache – Juda verrecke" because the Jewish banker Jakob Goldschmidt had placed his monies at their disposal.[16] Thus we find the adaptation of former arguments which have been recalled to explain the situation in the Third *Reich*. However, it is now the Zionist movement, rather than Jewish bankers, which has become a partner to Nazism. It need hardly be demonstrated that in view of this dogmatic position, the KPD conspicuously disregarded the fact that other views on solving the Jewish problem persisted during the months in which the transfer agreement took effect and other proposals pertained which all rejected the Zionist solution. Alfred Rosenberg, for instance, cautioned against Jewish emigration to Palestine lest no Jewish hostages remained in Germany when it became subjected to a world boycott, but the KPD held the German press's attacks on the resolutions of the Zionist Congress in Prague to be mere demagogic trickery to cover up the true sharing of interests and divert public opinion. One of the most malevolent attacks on Zionism was printed in a special issue on the Jewish Question of Willi Münzenberg's *Unsere Zeit*. Apart from the rigid repetition of the known ideological *clichés* to explain antisemitism and the criticism of the

[14]'Letters from Berlin, The "incorporation" of the German Jews in the State', in *Inprecor*, vol. 13 (15th September 1933), p. 1241.
[15]*Ibid.*
*On the *Haavara* see in more detail the essay by Francis R. Nicosia, 'Revisionist Zionism in Germany (II)', in the current volume of the Year Book, pp. 253–262 *passim* – (Ed.).
[16]Knütter, *Die Juden und die deutsche Linke, op. cit.* p. 189.

attempts of the Jewish community to adapt to the new situation, this periodical positively vilifies Zionism. Trying to show that antisemitism is a class question and thus also spread by the Jewish bourgeoisie, Paul Held writes about how Zionism received Nazism with gratitude and appreciation. Furthermore, he affirms, obviously without stating his sources, that Zionist leaders praise Hitler, and that the Jewish national poet Bialik proclaimed Hitler as a new Cyrus. This line, now notorious, persists to this very day.[17]

THE REACTIONS TO ANTISEMITIC VIOLENCE AND LEGISLATION IN 1935

In the summer of 1935, when the anti-Jewish riots reached tidal proportions and swept over Germany, the new situation obliged the party to take a stand. Now it had to clarify its position to its sympathisers, for the issue had moved to the centre of public interest. It is, therefore, not unexpected to have August's reports from the Potsdam and Bielefeld *Gestapo* stations informing us that the KPD disseminated underground propaganda material sharply criticising the pogroms, which, according to the reports, are explained as just simple diversionary tactics.[18] Moreover, turning to other publications of the Communist underground which have been preserved we can complete the picture conveyed by these reports, adding details on the exact content of the clandestine material. The familiar functional role attributed to antisemitism was again used to explain the disturbances in an underground pamphlet, presumably printed in Germany, entitled *Wir kämpfen – Organ der KPD*, August 1935, which states: "[through the use of pogroms the Nazis sought] not only to satisfy SA activism but also to please those who have anti-capitalist instincts".[19] The Jewish Question is treated incidentally in another underground pamphlet also, one intended as a manual on how to counter Nazi propaganda slogans. In reading the chapter on racial theory, one is immediately struck by the bewildering internal contradictions of dogmatic Communist interpretations, leading to absurd conclusions. The "Leadership Principle", for instance, is explained as a strategy aimed at establishing a capitalist regime and Nazi doctrine, it affirms, permits Jewish capitalists also to integrate in the leadership echelons: "Selbst dann, wenn der Kapitalist Jude ist, hat er allein Anspruch auf die Führung".[20]

[17]Paul Held, 'Die jüdische Bourgeoisie und der Faschismus', in *Unsere Zeit. Monatsschrift für Politik, Literatur, Wirtschaft, Sozialpolitik und Arbeiterbewegung* (4th June 1934), p. 26.

[18]Among the reports alluding to the KPD's responses to the riots, see: Gestapo Potsdam, Lagebericht für August 1935, Berlin-GStA, REP/90P; Gestapo Bielefeld, Lagebericht für August 1935, BA R58/1587.

[19]*Wir Kämpfen, Organ der KPD*, August 1935, National Archives, T175/R280/F2774327. On the presumable circulation of the clandestine publications, see Wilhelm Pieck, *Wir kämpfen für ein Rätedeutschland*, [n.p.] [n.d.], p. 61.

[20]*Wie antworte ich auf Schlagworte der Nazis? Viertes Thema. Die Rassenfrage*, Wiener Library Archives (hereafter WL), P 24. The basis for this absurd argument is the paradoxical situation created with the promulgation of the law to organise German labour (*Gesetz zur Ordnung der nationalen Arbeit*) on 24th January 1934. Jews were then excluded from the *Deutsche Arbeitsfront* and other Nazi labour organisations. Jewish employers, however, became *Betriebsführer* and thus enjoyed legally even

The racial doctrine's functional nature is also explained in another context, as serving a dual purpose. In internal policy, it glorifies capitalist exploitation by asserting that the Nordic masters were born to rule capital, and in foreign policy, it performs the function of a first-class means of predisposing the population to war. Thus, under the mask of racial theory, lies hidden Germany's long-standing imperialistic aspiration to world-rule. In explaining the nature of antisemitism, the pamphlet falls back on well-known theses: hatred of the Jews as an effective means of blurring class consciousness and diverting public opinion from the class struggle. The boycott and summer riots, for example, are explained in the following fashion: Hitler could not satisfy the demands of the workers, and even failed in the elections to the workers' councils – he therefore needed to institute terror against the Jews.

The publication of the laws on race and citizenship, in September 1935, brought in its wake additional reactions from the KPD to the new antisemitic policy, adding nothing new, however, to conceptions we are already familiar with. The first to respond was the *Junge Garde*, the central organ of the Communist youth. In its issue of September it again pointed out that only poor Jews had been harmed while Jewish bankers were stronger than ever.[21] Also *Die Rote Fahne*, the party's central organ, dealt with the matter. In October it published an article the title and subtitle of which: 'The significance of Nuremberg. Provocation for war, agitation for pogroms, starvation salaries' aptly sums up its contents.[22]

Some *Gestapo* reports for these months supplement the information on the response of the Communist underground to the riots and antisemitic laws. The Dortmund *Gestapo* station, for instance, reports in October 1935, that Communist youth issued a circular in Bochum, in an ambitious attempt to gain the sympathy of the local Catholics and Protestants. Alongside the traditional call for the release of political prisoners, the Communists asked for a show of tolerance towards the Jews.[23] The sharpest reaction, however, seems to have come from a KPD cell in Berlin. The local *Gestapo*'s September report informs us, in the paragraph on "the dissemination of inflammatory material" that propaganda against antisemitism occupies a particularly important place in underground leaflets. Some of the slogans printed by the illegal KPD in its pamphlets and stickers are quoted in the report. Still on the same topic, the reporter reveals that a "*Kampfschrift* Against Antisemitism and Racial Hatred", the *Anti-Stürmer*, was issued at the end of August. Responding to Streicher's speech, the author called on the workers not to let themselves be deceived by diversionary activities such as the antisemitic campaign; not to stand docile on the sidelines, but to combine the war against antisemitism with the war against Fascism in general, and transform the antisemitic rallies into anti-fascist

---

more rights than during the Weimar period. This paradoxical situation ended in 1938. See Helmut Genschel, *Die Verdrängung der Juden aus der Wirtschaft im Dritten Reich*, Göttingen 1966, pp. 66–67.

[21]'Sind die Juden unser Unglück?', in *Die Junge Garde. Zentralorgan des KJVD*, Ende September 1935.

[22]'Was bedeutet Nürnberg?', in *Die Rote Fahne*, Mitte Oktober 1935.

[23]Gestapo Dortmund, Lagebericht für Oktober 1935, BA R58/1143.

demonstrations.[24] Nevertheless, even though the KPD reacted vigorously to the persecution inflicted on the Jews in these months, its basic conception remained definitely unchanged. The various underground publications unfailingly resort to the same dogmatic assertions: only poor workers are arrested for race defilement, and the ban on employing housemaids of under 45 years of age is simply legal legitimisation for firing thousands of women from their jobs. It is interesting to point out that although the Jewish Question was discussed in underground publications smuggled into Germany, in the Communist press outside the *Reich*, intended for a different public, it was pushed aside. The *Tribunal*, for instance, devoted almost an entire edition to the United Front, while the Nuremberg Laws received only casual mention in a side column, albeit with the accompanying remark that "the Middle Ages pale in comparison".[25]

At the KPD's "Brussels Conference", which for reasons of secrecy was actually held near Moscow, we find the same motifs monotonously repeated. The functional use of antisemitism and the claim that only poor Jews had been harmed, recur tediously throughout most of the discussions.[26] One of the resolutions adopted by the conference was to condemn publicly antisemitism and racial agitation, mainly because it was so widely used as a diversionary tactic. Wilhelm Pieck, the secretary of the Comintern's executive and one of the founders of the KPD, summed up, stating the urgency of fighting antisemitism and racial hatred.[27] It seems that this decision quite likely grew out of tactical considerations.[28] It was undoubtedly an ingenious attempt to break out of political isolation and put out feelers to other anti-Nazi circles in the hope of establishing a popular united front, composed of Catholics, non-party intellectuals, pro-Communist elements on the German Left and others.[29] The article in October's *Rundschau*, for instance, calling on all the persecuted to unite, is to be viewed against this background. According to this, stripping German Jews of their property was part of an essential process for concentrating capital, and the bourgeois class could expect their turn to come next. The above-mentioned resolution was thus followed diligently by articles on the Jewish Question, printed in the party's press at the end of 1935. November's

[24]Gestapo Berlin, Lagebericht für September 1935, *ibid.*, R58/1138. It seems to be more plausible that the *Anti-Stürmer* was published by a Left-wing Zionist youth movement, the *Borochow Jugend* attached to the left *Poalei Zion*, and not by the KPD. This information was given by Professor Israel Getzler, who knew the printer of the pamphlet, Isidor Hecht. On the *Gestapo* reports see, Otto D. Kulka, 'Public Opinion in Nazi Germany and the "Jewish Question", in *The Jerusalem Quarterly*, 25 (Fall 1982), pp. 126–127. These events are not mentioned in the latest work of A. Merson, *Communist Resistance in Nazi Germany*, London 1985.

[25]*Tribunal, Zentralorgan der Roten Hilfe*, Oktober 1935.

[26]Klaus Mammach (ed.), *Die Brüsseler Konferenz der KPD (3.–15. Oktober 1935)*, Frankfurt a. Main 1975, pp. 48–49, 124, 137, 159, 192–194, 578, 583.

[27]*Ibid.*, p. 194. However, at the end of his speech Florin returns to the familiar thesis that Hitler took money from Jewish bankers and therefore did not harm them. Only poor Jews and Jewish intellectuals are persecuted, *ibid.*, p. 578. Similar statements were uttered in his address to the seventh congress of the Comintern held in August 1935, See: *Inprecor* (30th October 1935).

[28]Mammach, *Die Brüsseler Konferenz, op. cit.*, p. 578.

[29]On this period of KPD history, see H. Duhnke, *Die KPD von 1939 bis 1945*, Köln 1972.

issue of *Tribunal*, for example, carries a concise account of the attacks on Jews which are explained as being a preparation for war against the Soviet Union.[30] The war against antisemitism, therefore, is a struggle to save the "progressive components of bourgeois democracy" which Hitler is attempting to destroy. Hence revoking Jewish emancipation is only the beginning of this process.[31]

THE REACTIONS TO ARYANISATION

In 1936–1937, we do not find the KPD concerned with the Jewish Question apart from running occasional reports in its press on the physical and economic harm done to the Jews. However, from the Spring of 1938 when antisemitic policy was abruptly stepped up,[32] this new reality confronted Communist interpretation with an annoying theoretical dilemma. Up to this point, it had almost totally ignored the attacks on Jewish capitalists and consistently claimed that Nazism persecuted poor Jews only. Now it had to deal with the reasons why wealthy Jews were also being hurt.

The paradigm used to explain the Aryanisation process was again the definition of Nazism as "an open terrorist dictatorship of the most reactionary and imperialist elements of financial capital".[33] Indeed, contemporary Communist literature claimed that the Nazi state accords an organisational-operational basis to monopolistic industry by legislating antisemitic laws in the fields of economics.[34] However, this rigid adherence to ideological stereotypes unquestionably prevented the KPD from seeing that Hitler in fact viewed economic measures in general, and Aryanisation in particular, as an instrumental means to convert into fact his theoretical principles and attain his political objectives. The financial monopolies in the Third *Reich* certainly had no significant influence in shaping policy. They simply adapted, cynically and opportunistically, to the framework determined by the Nazi regime. Thus, here too, antisemitic policy in the area of economics, clearly operated according to its own laws, determined by Hitler and not by German capitalists, though they adhered to it unscrupulously.[35] As in 1938 Jewish enterprises were sold under

[30] *Tribunal*, November 1935.

[31] 'Antisemitism leads to the Strengthening of the Regime of Trusts', in *Inprecor* (9th November 1935), p. 1458. In a clandestine publication of the Trotskyite underground from this period we also find reactions to Nazi antisemitism, however, not essentially different from the KPD's. See for example, *Unser Wort, Halbmonatszeitung der IKD (Internationalen Kommunisten Deutschlands), Organ der deutschen Trotzkisten (IV. Internationale)* Oktober 1935. Cf. also, L. Trotzki, 'Schriften über Deutschland', in E. Mandel, *Trotzkis Faschismustheorien*, Frankfurt a. Main 1971.

[32] See details in Genschel, *op. cit.*, pp. 139–248.

[33] This definition issued in 1933 carries the name of the Bulgarian Communist leader Dimitroff. See also, *VII Congress of the Communist International. Abridged Stenographic Report of Proceedings*, Moscow 1939, p. 126; *Der Faschismus in Deutschland*, Moscow/Leningrad 1934, p. 277.

[34] See also Ulbricht who devotes an entire page to Aryanisation from this perspective. Walter Ulbricht, *Kriegsschauplatz Innerdeutschland*, Strasbourg 1938, p. 20; as well as Frida Lang [Rubiner], *Wesen des deutschen Faschismus*, [n.p.] [n.d.].

[35] The role of high finance in shaping the policy of the Third *Reich* is a highly controversial issue dealt with in many works, most of them of a polemical character, see, for example, A. Schweitzer, *Big Business in the Third Reich*, Indiana 1964. In my opinion the views stressing the primacy of politics

coercion to Aryan hands, the KPD could not longer remain blind to the new circumstances and had to respond. Out of classical Marxism, whereby policy is part of the superstructure of the economic system, came the explanation for Aryanisation. In both the Communist press and the underground material, it claimed that stripping Jewish capitalists of their wealth was a constituent part of the bitter war waged by the big banks and heavy industry against their smaller competitors.[36] This, too, is certainly a typical example of stretching the facts to fit the theory, as the only way to get around the unwillingness to test its validity when empirical facts defy blind faith in an all-embracing doctrine. For: Communist theory holds that the inner contradictions within the ruling class appear when conflicts sharpen between large monopolistic capital and small capital. However, the theory continues, these conflicts appear during the first stage of what is termed the "fascistification process", when the concentration of capital is accelerated, and the price of raw materials is determined by the monopolies. Only then does intermediate capital wane, unable to hold its own in face of technological advances with production dictated by large concerns. But, on the basis of Communist interpretation itself, these conditions characterise Germany at the end of the twenties and the beginning of the thirties, rather than 1938. Placing the Aryanisation process in this category, is thus inevitably a gross anachronism.[37] Moreover, it is true that while during the early years of the Third *Reich* big business refrained from making considerable investments because of the uncertainty as to the trend of the new policies, by 1936 a change had occurred in its readiness to support Hitler's policies. The armament policy altered the position of heavy industry and German banks. Hence, from the end of 1936, they willingly gave support to antisemitic policies in the economic field. However, the initiative did not come from economic circles. It was the political echelon which zealously determined the implementation of antisemitic policy and principles. For this period, we have no written proof that the economic leaders participated in determining anti-Jewish policies, although they reaped its material benefits. Furthermore the KPD interpretation ignores the clear fact that German capitalists supported a different social system from that which Nazism wished to institute. The removal of Hjalmar Schacht, who represented these economic circles, and to a certain extent restrained attacks against the Jews, shows that other considerations,

---

should be accepted. See T. Mason, 'Der Primat der Politik. Politik und Wirtschaft im Nationalsozialismus und Primat der Industrie', *Das Argument*, 41 (1966) pp. 473–494; D. Petzina, *Autarkiepolitik im Dritten Reich*, Stuttgart 1968. On the different views and their evaluation see the valuable work of Ian Kershaw, *The Nazi Dictatorship*, London 1985, especially pp. 42–60.

[36] *Deutsche Informationen*, 22 (31st March 1938, 22nd April 1938); *Deutsche Scholle* [Walter Ulbricht, *Kriegsschauplatz Innerdeutschland*], Berlin 1938, WL P3; W. Perres, *Luftschutz, Gas und Bomben drohen!* [*Kommunistische Internationale*, 5 (1938)], 1938.

[37] On the Communist interpretation of fascism, see Historicus [A. Rosenberg], *Der Faschismus als Massenbewegung*, Karlsbad 1934; A. Thalheimer, 'Über den Faschismus', in *Gegen den Strom*, 2–4 (11th, 18th, 25th January 1930); R. De Felice, *Il Fascismo. Le Interpretazioni dei contemporanei e degli storici*, Bari 1970, p. 272 ff; J. Cammet, 'Communist Theories of Fascism (1920–1935)', in *Science and Society*, 2 (1967), pp. 149–163; E. Lewin, 'Zum Faschismus. Analyse durch die Kommunistische Internationale', in *Beiträge zur Geschichte der deutschen Arbeiterbewegung*, 1 (1970), pp. 44–59; See the recent book by L. Luks, *Entstehung der kommunistischen Faschismustheorie*, Stuttgart 1984.

non-economic ones, gained predominance in 1937–1938. Primarily the initiatives of the *Sicherheitsdienst* (SD) became the leading force in the antisemitic policy.[38] The same is true of the Aryanisation process with respect to department stores. In KPD literature, it is interpreted as a tactic to accelerate the process of concentration of capital in the hands of the monopolies. However, since the assumption of power there was constant pressure from antisemitic economic organisations affiliated to the *Nationalsozialistische Deutsche Arbeiterpartei* (NSDAP) to requisition and transfer the department stores to Ayran shopkeepers. This pressure was modified somewhat at various government levels due to Schacht's intercessions, but his dismissal spurred on the *NS-Hago* to take a more aggressive stand and demand that department stores be in fact expropriated from Jews. So that here too, the policy is not to be seen as the result of German capitalists gaining control over petty Jewish capital, but as the consistent and formal implementation of principles of the party programme. In addition to realising the ideology, implementing this policy could also satisfy the middle class, which had been somewhat deprived because of the preferential status given to industry when rearmament policy had stepped up.

THE REACTIONS TO THE ANTISEMITIC PERSECUTION OF 1938

In the summer of 1938, a new eruption of assaults and arrests broke out against the Jews, more severe than the one which preceded the adoption of the Nuremberg Laws. For some reason the historiography dealing with the history of the Jews in the Third *Reich* has not related to these events with a comprehensive in-depth study. It would appear that the international crisis surrounding the Sudeten issue, and the Evian Conference, because of the historic significance they acquired, diverted the attention of researchers and overshadowed what was happening in the *Reich*. Also the Jewish press outside Germany devoted no more than short laconic reports to the new situation. The *Jewish Chronicle* for instance, reported the arrests of hundreds of Jews in Berlin, simply explaining it as a political exercise in the wake of the Evian Conference.[39] It was the Communist press outside Germany which carried a good deal of varied information on the new antisemitic policy. The *Deutsche Informationen*, for example, tells us that the present anti-Jewish wave started on June 18th beginning with the SA agitating outside Jewish shops in the Kurfürstendamm in Berlin; the following day, shop windows had already been smeared with denigratory slogans; on the third day, verbal provocation turned into physical aggression, synagogues and Torah scrolls were destroyed.[40] Herein lies the reason for the KPD's renewed and unprecedented response to Nazi antisemitism, contrary to the generally accepted assumption that the KPD did not react to it until the *Kristallnacht*.

[38]See particularly Otto D. Kulka, *The Jewish Question in the Third Reich*, Ph.D.Diss., Hebrew University of Jerusalem 1975, vol. II, introduction to documents 18, 24, 26, 27, and Cf. Genschel, *op. cit.*, ch. 7, 8.

[39]*The Jewish Chronicle* (30th June 1938).

[40]*Deutsche Informationen*, 60 (2nd July 1938).

If up till now the KPD viewed persecution of Jews as part of the regime's policy against all opposing elements, and as such, relegated propaganda against antisemitism to the side-lines, now, in the summer of 1938, it started a more extensive campaign on the Jewish Question. In underground radio broadcasts, in the press outside Germany and underground pamphlets within the *Reich*, the issue was allotted considerable place. The first to react was *Die Rote Fahne*, in an article entitled 'The shameful pogroms against the Jews'.[41] Alongside a review of the injuries and arrests in Vienna and Berlin, the newspaper pointed out that the rioting was organised and executed by the SA and Hitler Youth. It added that several cases of suicide had occurred among the Jews, following the period of terror. The usual interpretation appeared as well: the riots were diversionary and a poignant expression of the frustration felt at Hitler's failure in foreign policy. But there was also an appeal to the readers to explain the events to the German public, showing the true reason for the pogroms.

In addition to written propaganda, the Communist underground radio station for the first time devoted a broadcast to the Jewish Question in Germany. The programme went on the air at the end of June 1938, and the announcer called on listeners to take no part in the assaults on the Jews, but to cement solidarity with the persecuted, as part of the anti-fascist struggle.[42] A similar call was issued again at the beginning of July.[43] These months of crisis were also exploited by the KPD for distributing dozens of underground papers and at least two of these which we have managed to locate, deal specifically with the Jewish Question. They deserve a more detailed analysis for they are ideological-theoretical discussions, rather than the purely political propaganda we have seen till now.

One underground pamphlet, misleadingly entitled *Das Sportphoto*, was actually a camouflaged issue of the KPD's central ideological organ, *Die Kommunistische Internationale*. Among the various subjects it dealt with, was a comprehensive article on the Jewish Question by the Austrian Communist Friedel Fürnberg.[44] As may be expected, the author essentially reiterated the accepted conception of antisemitism as an instrument to distract public opinion. However, as well as dealing with current events, he also set out a general review of Jewish history which to a large extent seems to have been taken from Otto Heller's famous book, *Der Untergang des Judentums*.[45]

Fürnberg, like Heller, draws on basic assumptions from Marxist historiography which sees Jews as a social group with a specific economic function. By using Marx's sociological model of the nomads as the first bearers of trade to society, Fürnberg attempts to show that the Israelites who came into Canaan,

[41] 'Die Schande der Judenpogrome', in *Die Rote Fahne*, 5 (1938).

[42] 'Der deutsche Freiheitssender im Kampf gegen die antisemitische Hetze. Ein Appell auf Welle 29, 8"', *Sonderdienst der Deutschen Informationen*, 360 (28th June 1938).

[43] 'Der deutsche Freiheitssender im Kampf gegen die Judenhetze', in *Beilage der Deutschen Informationen*, 365 (9th July 1938).

[44] Friedel Fürnberg, 'Die Judenfrage und der Antisemitismus', in G. Riebicke, *Das Sportphoto [Die Kommunistische Internationale, 9 (1938)]*, Halle 1938, pp. 23–27.

[45] Otto Heller, *Der Untergang des Judentums. Die Judenfrage, ihre Kritik, ihre Lösung durch den Sozialismus*, Wien-Berlin 1931.

like other nomadic peoples, dealt in barter. Relying exclusively on this Marxist thesis, he continues to argue that the special nature of the geographical conditions in the land of Israel determined the forces of production and moulded the local socio-economic relations. That is how the Jews became a distinct nation of traders. Like Heller, Fürnberg claims that the final character of the Jewish people was consolidated only in exile. However, we are not here concerned with how the author arrived at his conclusions. What interests us is the portrait of the Jewish people as it takes shape in the article, and the political purpose which this portrait serves. The first step, therefore, is to distinguish between the purpose of Heller's book and the purpose of Fürnberg's article: While Heller intended primarily to attack Zionism and praise the Soviet solution to the Jewish Question, Fürnberg's article was written for propaganda purposes and aimed at a public totally subjugated by antisemitic indoctrination. Thus, a tone of pro-Jewish apologetics pervades the whole article. For instance, the claim that the Jewish collective existence is politically reactionary, is deliberately obscured. In an attempt to take the antisemitic sting out of pro-Nazi propaganda, the author emphasises the positive contribution made by Jews to world history. He points out, for example, that at the fall of the Roman Empire the Jews served as a bridge for transmitting the culture and civilisation of the classical world to the barbarian tribes. In this manner, they made a distinguished contribution to the Nordic peoples.[46] Furthermore, in Heller's book it sounds as if the fact that Jews lived among themselves in isolationist communities only perpetuated their social function as a nation of traders, while Fürnberg's article arrives at a diametrically opposite conclusion. He finds positive elements in the existence of the Jewish community in the Middle Ages. Because of their community, he writes, Jews had a more elevated culture than all their neighbours. Economically, he continues, just as they played a progressive role during the transition to the Middle Ages, so they filled a positive and valuable function during the transition to modern times. Their progressive nature can be seen in the fact that the structure of the Jewish communities contributed to the process of concentrating commercial wealth in the early capitalist era, and to the destruction of the feudal regime.[47] Most of his apologetics is devoted to citing the important contribution made by Jews to German culture, science and art. Countering antisemitic claims, he points out that the number of criminals of Jewish origin is far smaller than their number among other peoples, while the number of Jews in revolutionary movements is far greater than the percentage of other peoples. This fact, he says, will never be forgotten by the Socialist movement.[48] More than that, dealing with a popular motif of Nazi propaganda: the connection between Judaism and capitalism, Fürnberg distinctly parts company with Marx's *Über die Judenfrage* by pointing out that the Jewish people is composed of masses of workers, and the Judaism-capitalism connection is an antisemitic invention. It must be noted that Fürnberg's perception, particularly as regards the nature of National Socialist

[46]Fürnberg, *op. cit.*, p. 26.
[47]*Ibid.*, p. 28.
[48]*Ibid.*, p. 30.

antisemitism, was unorthodox and far sharper than is generally found in KPD propaganda. In his view, Nazism was not simply the extension of the antisemitic reactionary movements which preceded it. It was a mixture and a combination of anti-Jewish trends in a new movement, a fact which imbued it with a special quality absent in classic antisemitism. Unlike others of his time, and certainly unlike official Communist interpretation, Fürnberg held that antisemitism and racial theory were one of the essential cornerstones of the Nazi doctrine.[49]

Another underground KPD pamphlet smuggled into Germany that year, dealt entirely with the Jewish Question.[50] At the start of the pamphlet the anonymous author gives a factual and detailed account of the attacks on Jews in Berlin and Frankfurt in June 1938. Like his predecessor, the author asks that the voice of conscience be heard and wisdom be listened to, and that humanists such as Lessing and Herder, who condemned antisemitism, be followed. He connects the common destiny of Jews and Socialists, and is very careful to mention that in Bismarck's day, Stoecker was the common enemy of Jews and Socialists. Like Fürnberg he reiterates familiar motifs from German apologetic literature: the stability of the Jewish family, the contributions of Heine, Mahler, Meyerbeer, and others, to German culture. And finally, like his predecessor, he denies all connection between Judaism and capitalism. Unlike the propaganda pamphlets which reiterate stereotyped slogans one after another, we find in these illegal writings from 1938 a totally unexpected approach: KPD interpretation characterised by apologetics typical of the *Centralverein deutscher Staatsbürger jüdischen Glaubens*, certainly not of Communist literature.

The wave of terror which swept over Germany, the destruction of synagogues and Jewish property on the *Kristallnacht*, was the focus of KPD propaganda in November 1938.* How did the KPD interpret the underlying causes? An underground publication (camouflaged as guidelines set down by the Ministry of Transport for cyclists) contains a comprehensive article on the violence unleashed against the Jews.[51] The article discusses the chief factors which led to the riots and the author's main contention is that German capitalists were required to pay a political tax to the Nazis with whom they were connected. The reasons were varied: the annexation of Austria swelled the population in need of support, the addition of the Sudetenland to German territory introduced an industrialised area into the *Reich* which could not compete with German industry and as a result, local industry foundered and many workers migrated to the *Reich* proper, again swelling the population in need of support. Moreover, the tremendous cost of mobilising the army and keeping it on the alert during the Munich crisis added an additional billion marks to the national budget. Continuing to print money for the armament industry, the reinforcement of the fortified line, and conscription, met opposition from stock-exchange circles who

[49]*Ibid.*, p. 31.

[50]W. Pötsch, *Die Grundlagen des jüdischen Volkes. Eine notwendige Abrechnung*, Breslau 1935, WL P 90.

*On the November pogrom see also the preceding essay by Peter Loewenberg, 'The Kristallnacht as a Public Degradation Ritual', in this volume of the Year Book – (Ed.).

[51]*Radfahrer – Dein Verhalten* [*Die Internationale*, 3/4 (1938)].

refused to supply the necessary financing. The antisemitic riots, therefore, were simply a prelude to the confiscation of property, and this together with the billion mark fine imposed on the Jews of Germany, was the only means of covering the war costs. This explanation is interesting because it again defies Communist principles with respect to the thesis of "economic primacy". For it seems to imply – as in the Bonapartist "heretical" interpretation of Leon Trotsky, August Thalheimer or Otto Bauer – that Hitler and his movement are neither enslaved by, nor totally dependent on, the will of German capitalism. On the contrary: there is a clash of interests between the economic factor and the political factor, and in the final analysis, it is the political element which dictates policy by subjugating capitalists to its will. In addition to this explanation, the article naturally mentions also diversionary tactics as a central motif behind the violence against the Jews. At the end of the article the author returns to the Communist conception of the nature of antisemitism, and though he regards the racial doctrine as the *Staatsraison* of Nazism, he does not regard antisemitism as specifically anti-Jewish. On the contrary, the meaning of antisemitism is universal because it is not directed only against Jews, but against all those identified as Judaised. For this reason, antisemitism must be fought, not for specifically Jewish reasons, but out of concern for universal interests affecting all mankind.

Regarding responses to the pogrom itself, the Berlin *Gestapo* report for that month tells us that together with propaganda for the united front, the Jewish Question was of central interest to Communist activity throughout the *Reich*.[52] The reporter adds that the KPD call for solidarity with the Jews fell on sympathetic ears among the upper class and the Church, and even among certain sectors of the public who supported antisemitic policies but rejected vandalism. According to this *Gestapo* reporter, public discussion on the Jewish Question was more intense than it had been in years. We find similar reports from other *Gestapo* stations, from Schwerin,[53] and Köln,[54] in which we learn of lively debates in factories which had previously been under Communist influence. However, as a recurrent theme we see in all these reports that even though the KPD underground spoke out strongly after the pogrom, its chief claim was against the destruction of public property – which was contrary to the objectives of the four-year plan. In this respect there was no essential difference between the reaction of the KPD and the responses of other groups in Germany.[55] Condemnation of material damage and regret at the destruction of property came first, before the censure of the immorality involved in perpetrating violence against defenceless civilians. This is particularly evident in one of the underground circulars issued at the time:

[52]Gestapo Berlin, Lagebericht für November 1938, Institut für Marxismus und Leninismus, Zentrales Parteiarchiv der DDR (hereafter IML/ZPA). Cf. O. D. Kulka, '"Public Opinion" in National Socialist Germany and the "Jewish Question"', in *Zion*, 40 (1975), p. 279. (in Hebrew). On this issue I agree with Kulka and not with Kershaw's criticism, see Ian Kershaw, *Popular Opinion and Political Dissent in the Third Reich. Bavaria 1933–1945*, Oxford 1983, p. 271, n. 76.

[53]Gestapo Schwerin, Kommunistische Bewegung, November 1938, IML/ZPA, St 3/4216.

[54]Gestapo Köln, *Kommunismus*, November 1938, BA R58/446.

[55]O. D. Kulka, '"Public Opinion"', *loc. cit.*, pp. 236–237.

"... No one in Germany believes that the burning of synagogues, and Jewish homes, the destruction, the plunder, the setting fire to Jewish shops, warehouses and factories, the bestial maltreatment, the murder, the mass concentration of Jews in camps, is due to the 'rage of the German people'. Workers are calculating the number of extra hours they will need to work to repair the damage done to German national property. Workers' wives, who manage to buy something for their homes only after much work and hardship, watched the destruction of so much property with bitterness, and numerous housing candidates watched Nazis burn houses, villas, and synagogues with repressed rage."[56]

It was not coincidental that the KPD directed its words at the Catholic population; the KPD knew very well that the Catholics were particularly sensitive about the renewed terror against the "foes of Nazism". The Catholics instinctively feared that once terror was unleashed, the churches and religious leaders would be harmed next. The KPD, therefore, tried to win over the Catholics by drawing parallels between the fate of the Jews and the fate of the churches. Again and again it said that the *Kristallnacht* was the beginning of a process which would eventually destroy Christianity. A Communist underground leaflet, disseminated in the Rhine region, stated: "The Catholics are horrified to see that the burning of synagogues is frighteningly similar to the outburst of the Hitler gangs against the bishops' castles in Rothenburg, Vienna, and recently, Munich."[57]

Other KPD reactions took various forms. A special edition of *Die Rote Fahne* was distributed in Germany, citing numerous examples of real help extended to Jews during the pogroms, and also carrying the condemnation issued by the Central Committee. The underground radio station broadcast on several occasions, with the KPD repeating its call to the Germans to help the persecuted Jews. It recalled August Bebel's definition of antisemitism as the Socialism of fools, as well as Marx's Jewish origins.[58] A month later, in its newspapers outside Germany and in its underground publications, the KPD was still reporting cases of solidarity with the Jews on the part of the German public.[59] Clearly, we have no direct proof whether the many incidents reported in detail in fact occurred, or whether they were invented for propaganda purposes.

Summing up, it can be said that the investigation of this topic shows that although the KPD devoted only marginal interest to antisemitism in its political literature, we found, surprisingly, that a relatively strong effort was made to deal with the Jewish Question in underground material intended for the German population under the Third *Reich*. This line was adopted because of the erosion of ideology in the working class, which was exposed to the flood of antisemitic propaganda and integrated into the ruling Nazi party.

[56]'Gegen die Judenpogrome! Für den Frieden! Für den Sturz Hitlers! An die Bevölkerung von Rheinland-Westfalen, Kommunistische Partei Deutschlands, Abschnittsleitung Rhein-Ruhr', in S. Kahn, *loc. cit.*, pp. 558–560.

[57]*Ibid.*

[58]*Die Rote Fahne, Sonderausgabe gegen Hitlers Judenpogrome*, November 1938.

[59]*Excentric Shampoo. Das Beste für die Haarpflege*, 1939, [Paper bag camouflaging pamphlet about the November 1938 pogrom], WL P 88; *Praktischer Leitfaden des Schachspiels [Die Kommunistische Internationale*, 1 (1939) disguised].

Otto Hirsch (1885–1941)
Director of the Reichsvertretung

BY PAUL SAUER

On the occasion of the dedication of the Stuttgart synagogue on 3rd May 1861, Rabbi Dr. Joseph Maier concluded his special sermon with this homage to his home town: "Yes, hail to thee, beloved Stuttgart, our Jerusalem!"[1] These words were more than an emphatic demonstration of close ties between a prominent Jewish citizen and the city where he lived, they were programmatic. For many centuries the Jews living in dispersion, mostly in a condition of poverty and deprived of civil rights, had directed their hopes for the future to returning to the land of their fathers, to Palestine. On Passover, during the festive Seder meal, they expressed their longing for Zion by exclaiming, "Next year in Jerusalem!"[2] Now Maier replaced Jerusalem with Stuttgart, which to Orthodox Jews was something unheard of, even blasphemous. He provoked vehement protest with his candid avowal. However, a large part of his co-religionists in Stuttgart sided with him. During the first half of the nineteenth century, the avenue to civic equality with the Christian population was opened to the Jews of South West Germany, who had been living there for many generations. In 1861, they lacked only a few rights for complete emancipation; and they attained these in the following years.

The price the Jews had to pay for this – and were willing to pay – was high, namely a far-reaching assimilation to the culture of their Christian compatriots and thus renunciation of Jewish national existence. As another religion alongside the Christian denominations, and like them subject to state supervision, the Jewish religion adjusted to Christian, mainly Protestant, forms of ritual and for the most part replaced the Hebrew of the religious services with the German language. Rabbi Maier was the head of the Reform Movement in Württemberg. He saw himself as a Württemberger and a German. German was his native tongue and he felt at home within German culture. Like most of his fellow Jews, he rejected Jewish nationhood. He aspired to the total integration of the Jews into the state of Württemberg. Within the framework of a pluralistic society, he saw the place of the Jewish religious community thus: German citizens of the Jewish faith were to be of equal standing with Protestant and Catholic Germans. He considered antisemitic prejudice outmoded. He was confident that it might be overcome before long, the Jews' comportment and attitude would largely contribute to that.[3]

[1]Maria Zelzer, *Weg und Schicksal der Stuttgarter Juden*, Stuttgart 1964, p. 46.
[2]Robert Raphael Geis, *Vom unbekannten Judentum*, Freiburg 1961, p. 74.
[3]Hermann Dicker, *Aus Württembergs jüdischer Vergangenheit und Gegenwart*, Gerlingen 1984, pp. 19ff.

The spirit of Reform prevailed in the Jewish community of Stuttgart which had been founded in 1832 and grew fast in the decades following. Its members were open to innovations in the religious service, supported the liberal aspirations of the theological leadership and tried – some only hesitantly – to assimilate into the non-Jewish environment. They remained rooted in the Jewish religion, however, were nourished by it and remained faithful to its great spiritual and ethical values. A small Orthodox group, which closely adhered to the traditional Jewish form of service and the ritual precepts split off from the community in 1880; it established its own congregation, the *Israelitische Religionsgesellschaft.*[4] In 1843, the capital of Württemberg had a Jewish population of 230; in 1854, 265; in 1869, 1,314; in 1886, 2,568; in 1900, 3,015; and in 1933 – including Stuttgart-Bad Cannstatt – 4,900. As early as the middle of the nineteenth century, the Jewish congregation of Stuttgart ranked first among the Jewish communities of the Kingdom of Württemberg, "both from an ethical-religious point of view as well as economically", according to Rabbi Maier. Around 1880, its members were active in banking, wholesale and other trades. There was no one making a living from peddling as had been widely customary among Jews in earlier times. A large proportion of the Jewish population had turned to academic professions, particularly to medicine and the law. Jews were held in great esteem in the public life of the city.[5]

Otto Hirsch himself was descended from a local family.[6] He was born on 9th January 1885. His father, Louis Hirsch (born in 1858), was the owner of a wholesale wine company and was a righteous, open-minded man without prejudice who epitomised the best of civic virtues. Throughout his life he maintained close ties to the Jewish religious community. He approved of emancipation and acculturation, because they promised a better life for the Jews in Germany. Otto's mother, Helene, née Reis (born in 1860), was an educated, warm-hearted woman who was also filled by a life-affirming religiosity and shared her husband's love of Stuttgart and of Württemberg. Helene and Louis Hirsch valued their social contacts and offered generous hospitality, their circle of acquaintances including both Christians and Jews.

Both their sons – in 1888, Otto was followed by Theodor – received the best possible education. Starting in 1892, when he was only seven, Otto attended the *Eberhard-Ludwigs-Gymnasium.* His friends describe him as a popular, helpful schoolmate who mastered the scholastic requirements with ease and maintained his position at the top of the class, unchallenged. Even during his school days, he was interested by intellectual and related political trends. Among the great figures of history and culture who fascinated him were Pericles, Socrates, Plato, and Seneca. Later on – in addition to Goethe – there were the philosophers Arthur Schopenhauer and Kuno Fischer, as well as the politician Friedrich Naumann. One of his most outstanding character traits, which

[4]Zelzer, *op. cit.*, pp. 63ff.

[5]Paul Sauer, *Die jüdischen Gemeinden in Württemberg und Hohenzollern* (Veröffentlichungen der Staatlichen Archivverwaltung Baden-Württemberg Bd. 18), Stuttgart 1966, pp. 168ff.

[6]When no other source indicated Robert Nebinger, *Otto Hirsch (1885–1941). Persönliche Erinnerungen eines Freundes*, manuscript in the New York Leo Baeck Institute.

became evident rather early, was a marked sense of righteousness and justice; another was modesty. Substance was more important to him than mere appearance. Outward religious forms meant little to him, although he maintained close ties with the religion of his fathers and was always aware of the spiritual and ethical strength that Judaism gave him. In 1902, at the age of seventeen, he completed his *Abitur*. As the topic of his valedictory address he chose 'Das Deutschtum im Ausland', thus expressing his patriotic attitude. Germany was as much his home and fatherland to him as it was to his Christian classmates.

He would have liked very much to study classical philology and to pursue a teaching career, in line with his pedagogical inclinations. A teacher, to whom he confided this wish dissuaded him, however. Professional advancement in teaching at the higher school level – commensurate with his talents – would require baptism. Hirsch was by no means prepared to convert. Therefore he decided to study law. In the autumn of 1902, he enrolled in the University of Heidelberg. Even during the first semester he undertook an impressive work schedule. In addition to thirteen law courses, he enrolled in the same number of courses in the faculty of philosophy. He did not join a fraternity but found pleasure in discussions and good conversation, as his friends remembered, and in Heidelberg he also learned to fence, ride and dance.

In the autumn of 1903, he interrupted his studies to do his military service in Stuttgart with the "Olgagrenadiers", (I. Grenadier-Regiment Königin Olga, Württemberg No. 119). He did not dislike being a soldier. Repeatedly, his superiors expressed their satisfaction with the performance of the one-year volunteer. After reserve manoeuvres in the spring of 1905, he was promoted to *Vizefeldwebel*. Promotion to the rank of reserve officer was denied him, because he did not have the required prerequisite, the certificate of baptism.

Two semesters of study in Leipzig, from 1904 to 1905, were a particularly fruitful time for Otto Hirsch's personal and professional development. He spent the time in close company with his friend and schoolmate Robert Nebinger, who later became a chief judge of the Administrative Court of Württemberg-Baden. (From 1945–1952, North Baden and North Württemberg, under U.S. occupation, formed the state, "Württemberg-Baden".) Leipzig was the seat of the Supreme Court of the *Reich*. The university's law faculty had an excellent reputation. In the autumn of 1905, Otto Hirsch transferred to the University of Berlin, for two semesters. In addition to intensive studies, he and some of his fellow students found the time to give a group of ten labourers lessons in German, namely in spelling, grammar and particularly in composition. He liked his "private social work"; this activity was not entirely devoid of egotism. As before in Leipzig, he eagerly went to the theatre in Berlin. His main interest was in modern naturalism, in playwrights such as Gerhart Hauptmann, Henrik Ibsen and Björnstjerne Björnson. He used two semester breaks to study in Grenoble and Oxford. They offered a welcome opportunity to improve his knowledge of French and English. The last stop for his studies was Tübingen. In the autumn of 1906 he enrolled in the Swabian University on the Neckar. There, too, he did not confine himself to the legal field. In Leipzig he had been an enthusiastic student of the historian of civilisation, Karl Lamprecht; in Tübingen he was fascinated by a course on the political parties.

In the autumn of 1907, he passed his first state law examination with the excellent mark of Ib. He did the subsequent probationary period in Stuttgart and then passed his second state law examination in the spring of 1911, again with outstanding results. Dr. Richard Reis, one of the most prominent lawyers in Stuttgart and his mother's cousin, accepted him as an associate in his law office. He had only a year, however, to gain experience as an attorney. On 1st March 1912, he entered the service of the city of Stuttgart as an assistant legal counsellor. Dr. Reis had recommended his young colleague "most warmly" for that position in a letter of 26th November 1911 addressed to municipal councilman Gottfried Klein who was in charge of city personnel matters. He wrote: "Hirsch is one of those young lawyers one does not encounter too often, who combine excellent theoretical knowledge with a specific disposition for being able to find practical and intelligent solutions to difficult problems. A brilliant education in economics and an extended stay abroad may have combined to let him successfully avoid from the start an emphasis on formality. This emphasis is a stumbling block for all lawyers . . ." Furthermore, Reis praised his lively interest in all questions relating to public law, his unusually quick comprehension, the eloquence and ease of his delivery and his amazing capacity for work. He was not affiliated with any political party. "His unusually quiet temperament and the unwavering objectivity of his intellectual orientation" almost predestined him for a position in municipal administration.[7] The validity of Reis's evaluation was proved in Hirsch's dissertation presented in 1912, on 'Obligations in Connection with Construction as Defined in Article 99, Paragraph 3 of the Württemberg Construction Code of July 28, 1910'. There he elaborated practical solutions of legal questions related to the new Württemberg construction regulations.[8]

His election as assistant legal counsellor met with resistance in the Stuttgart municipal committees. The majority of the responsible committee of the municipal council favoured Hirsch's opponent, Dr. Lindenmeyer. Before the plenary vote, the Social Democratic municipal councillor Fischer spoke, saying that in his view Hirsch, who belonged to the Jewish religious community, was the more qualified candidate, he postulated that the municipal council base its decision solely on aptitude for filling the vacancy and completely ignore the aspect of religious affiliation, so as not to be suspected of antisemitism. The Mayor Dr. Karl Lautenschlager and municipal councillor Hermann Reihlen – the latter a supporter of Lindenmeyer's – protested against the suspicion of antisemitism, at least as far as they were concerned, and also advocated a totally objective decision. In the course of the subsequent vote, Otto Hirsch was elected by a small majority (18 against 16 votes).[9]

[7]Stadtarchiv Stuttgart: Personalakten Otto Hirsch.

[8]Württembergische Landesbibliothek: Wirt. R. qt. K. 125; Ratsassessor Dr. Hirsch/Stuttgart, 'Über die Baulasten im Sinne des Artikels 99 Absatz 3 der württembergischen Bauordnung vom 28. Juli 1910', in *Württembergische Zeitschrift für Rechtspflege und Verwaltung*, V (1912), pp. 241–246, 265–271, 289–308.

[9]Stadtarchiv Stuttgart: Personalakten Otto Hirsch.

The young assistant legal counsellor soon gained the reputation of being an excellent co-worker in the municipal administration. Mayor Lautenschlager sought to demonstrate his high esteem for him. To do so, he called a special meeting of the Municipal Council, obtained its consent to Hirsch's appointment as legal counsellor of the city of Stuttgart and had the certificate of appointment delivered to Hirsch on the very morning of his wedding day, 14th May 1914.[10] One of the first projects that Otto Hirsch had to deal with was the suburban settlement of Luginsland. All six parties of the municipal council acknowledged his outstanding expertise and his unusual professional commitment. In a letter of June 1918 to the Lord Mayor of Berlin, Dr. Adolf Wermuth, Mayor Lautenschlager concluded that there was "no man similarly competent" in the Württemberg municipal administration. In view of anti-Jewish tendencies which could not be totally suppressed in public administration – and of which he himself was not completely free as his argumentation shows – Lautenschlager declared: the thought of disqualifying Hirsch, a man of "thoroughly Christian mind", because of his affiliation with the Jewish community and thus discriminating against him professionally would be intolerable. Indeed, Lautenschlager would have liked to obtain a leading position in the *Deutscher Städtetag* for Otto Hirsch at that time.[11]

Like innumerable other men of his age, Hirsch would have rushed to the colours at the outbreak of the First World War to be of service to his beloved German fatherland in its hour of peril. But the city of Stuttgart did not release him. He was indispensable to the city in time of war. His main field of activity was related to construction and water regulations as well as to matters concerning the electricity supply; he was also assigned to drafting ordinances and the regulation of rationing. In 1915, he published an annotated edition of the Law of War Services of 13th June 1873, under the authority of the city.[12]

Sympathising politically with the Democrats (*Fortschritt/Freisinn*), he disapproved of chauvinism, which was widespread during the first years of the war. He followed the development of war events soberly and became increasingly anxious. The German victory that he so much hoped for seemed to recede farther and farther into the distance, becoming almost unattainable. Therefore, he approved of the peace resolution of the German *Reichstag* in 1917. Like so many Jews he saw redemption from the misery of war in a negotiated peace without annexations. But the German peace initiative failed and the bloody struggle continued. In the autumn of 1918, the *Reich* was finished militarily. To his friend Nebinger, Hirsch wrote: "The future lies ahead of us darker than ever, we lack even the ability to evaluate, and our actions run the danger of becoming dull and – since they are futile – of becoming ineffective. The more appropriate are the good wishes which I am expressing with the usual cordiality for your well-being and that of your dear ones and for the future of our poor

[10] *Ibid.*; Leo Baeck Institute New York: Schriftliche Mitteilung von Theodor Hirsch. Anhang zu Robert Nebinger, *op. cit.*, p. 46.

[11] Zelzer, *op. cit.*, pp. 276f.

[12] Württ. Landesbibliothek: A 7/1289. *Das Gesetz über die Kriegsleistungen vom 13. Juni 1873 mit den Ausführungsbestimmungen nach dem Stand von Ende Juli 1915.*

nation."[13] He did not leave any doubt that the *salus publica*, the general welfare, was his supreme axiom and that he was firmly determined to do everything in his power to contribute to Germany's reconstruction. An opportunity to do so soon occurred.

The Württemberg State administration had been aware of the highly talented lawyer for a long time. In March 1919, the Ministry of the Interior appointed him counsellor for questions related to waterways, supply of electricity and the utilisation of hydro-electric power. The city of Stuttgart released him most reluctantly. In the beginning he was granted leave of absence to enable him to reassume his position. On 31st March 1921 the city terminated his employment at his request.[14] Hirsch did excellent work in the Ministry of the Interior. The thirty-four-year-old was entrusted with tasks that were as difficult as they were responsible. Thus, the ministry sent him to Weimar to participate in the framing of the new Constitution. He assisted in the formulation of articles 97–100 on the waterways. In 1920, he participated in the peace conference in Paris, where he represented Württemberg's concerns during the negotiations on the internationalisation of the Danube.[15] Interior Minister Graf was so impressed by Hirsch's outstanding performance that he suggested to the *Staatspräsident* in March 1921, that Hirsch be appointed Ministerial Counsellor with retroactive effect from 1st April 1920. Never before had there been a thirty-six-year-old Ministerial Counsellor in Württemberg. Hirsch had even been exempted from the intermediary rank of *Oberregierungsrat*.[16]

The Legislature and Administration of Württemberg gave high priority at that time to the construction of the Neckar Canal from Mannheim to Plochingen in their plans for transportation and economic development. The canal was to improve the transport facilities of the state considerably and compensate for the locational disadvantages of Württemberg's industry.

On 15th June 1921, the *Neckar–Aktiengesellschaft* was established and it was incorporated on 12th November of the same year. Its chief tasks were the construction of the Neckar Canal and the future construction of a connecting canal from Plochingen to the Danube near Ulm, the construction and operation of hydro-electric plants, and flood protection.[17]

Otto Hirsch had been dealing with the Neckar canalisation project since his appointment to the Ministry of the Interior. He contributed decisively to the creation of the legal stipulations for this large-scale project. He also drafted the contracts between the federal government and the riparian states. On 4th October 1920, the *Reich*'s Ministry of Transport appointed him to the Neckar Construction Advisory Board at the suggestion of the Württemberg Ministry of

[13]Nebinger, *op. cit.*, p. 26.
[14]Stadtarchiv Stuttgart: Personalakten Otto Hirsch.
[15]Zelzer, *op. cit.*, p. 277.
[16]Hauptstaatsarchiv Stuttgart (=HStAS): E 151 a Bü 141.
[17]*Die Neckarkanalisierung Abschnitt Marbach – Stuttgart 31. März 1958*, 1958, pp. 13ff. B. Rümelin, 'Der Neckarausbau in volkswirtschaftlicher Hinsicht', in *Baden-Württemberg*, 3 (Freiburg 1969), pp. 8ff.; Hans Otto Strohecker, 'Neckarkanal. Technisches Meisterwerk des Jahrhunderts', in *Mittlerer Neckar. Mitteilungen und Meinungen der Industrie- und Handelskammer*, 9 (1981), pp. 17f.

the Interior.[18] Since the establishment of the Neckar Corporation, he had acted as its executive. At the first general meeting of the corporation's shareholders on 2nd July 1921, he was unanimously authorised to continue in that capacity until the election of a directorate. The two directors of the Neckar Construction Agency in Heilbronn, Chief Engineer Otto Konz and Chief Counsellor Dr. Klotz, were to assist him in this task. The shareholders gave him far-reaching authority. He was empowered to represent the firm, to be a sole signatory and to make decisions regarding the use of the corporation's paid-in capital.[19] The Neckar Corporation's chairman of the board and representative of the *Reich* Ministry of Transport, Undersecretary Dr. Paul Kirschstein, would have liked to see Hirsch appointed as the chief executive officer of the corporation right from the start. But Hirsch declined. Baden vetoed the election of Württemberg's candidate, Stuttgart Deputy Mayor Daniel Sigloch, which Hirsch had repeatedly and emphatically supported. Only then, on the urging of Privy Counsellor Peter Bruckmann of Heilbronn, one of the initiators of the canalisation project, and especially of his Ministry, Hirsch declared himself available at long last. The task, he stated, attracted him and the construction of the Neckar Canal was a matter close to his heart, yet he was not willing to lay himself open to accusations of pursuing personal, selfish interests.

On 17th September 1921, the board of the Neckar Corporation unanimously elected him first, and Otto Konz second as members of the directorate. Hirsch's and Konz's election to the directorate was strongly criticised by certain circles of the Baden press. The *Heidelberger Tageblatt* for instance, regarded both men as candidates of the *Reich* and expressed the view that, due to Baden's "parochial politics" regarding all matters related to the waterways, the State had "surrendered to the *Reich*". In a project like this, which was to be of the first rank in South West Germany's economic policies, "during the next decades all independence and local initiative were thus eliminated". Besides, Baden and Württemberg, with all their differences of opinion had put themselves at the mercy of a few subordinate bureaucrats. Both elected executives lacked practical experience. The paper voiced doubts particularly as to whether the lawyer Hirsch, used to making decisions based on theoretical considerations, would be able to "identify" with such a gigantic project. The paper feared that, after having failed to entrust the "real experts" with the execution of this project, it might be delayed by the bureaucracy.[20] This opinion was wrong, however. The required expertise and the necessary ability to get things done were by no means to be found among politicians only. Hirsch, Konz and the Baden chief engineer Fritz Landwehr – who had been employed at the railway general directorate in Karlsruhe before his election as third member of the corporation executive – made an excellent team. Despite the more than difficult economic situation in the beginning due to the rapid decline of the German currency, they not only kept the project going, but made it grow step by step. It was mainly due to the merits of Otto Hirsch and his two colleagues that

[18]HStAS: E 152 f Bü 52.
[19]*Ibid.*, Bü 53.
[20]*Ibid.*

fourteen years later, in 1935, the first Neckar Canal section, 113 km. long, between Mannheim and Heilbronn was completed and could be opened.

Even though the Ministry of the Interior in Stuttgart had unconditionally supported Hirsch for a leading position in the Neckar Corporation directorate, it did not want to forego his services in the future. Interior Minister Graf, in particular, was interested in having the young ministerial counsellor continue to work on the internationalisation of the German river systems, the Danube conference, the Danube commission, and other related projects as an official of the ministry. Therefore, Hirsch was given leave of absence from the civil service for three years. Besides that, generous provisions were made for his salary and pension entitlements. A return to the state civil service was open to him at any time. In the spring of 1924, it was uncertain, due to the precarious economic situation, whether the Neckar Corporation would be able to continue the construction work of the Neckar Canal after the completion of the hydro-electric plants at Wiblingen and Neckarsulm. At the request of the Corporation's chairman of the board, the Württemberg government extended Hirsch's leave of absence, first, until the end of 1925, and then until 31st March 1926. Not before this date was the continuation of the construction work on the canal assured by the required appropriation of funds by the *Reichstag*. Hirsch immediately requested his release from the Württemberg civil service. This was granted on 22nd June 1926. He retained the title of Ministerial Counsellor because of the quasi-governmental character of the Neckar Corporation and because governments, particularly the Government of Württemberg, were the Corporation's shareholders.[21]

During the following years, Otto Hirsch devoted all his professional energy to his economically highly important assignment, which seemed tailor-made for him. It required imagination, organisational talent, definite power of judgment, negotiating skill, courage to make far-reaching decisions and effective, cooperative leadership, all abilities he possessed amply.[22] The world economic crisis which was sweeping Germany with elemental force at the beginning of the thirties put his tolerance for stress to the test, both professionally and personally.

In 1931, the *Staatspräsident* of Württemberg, Eugen Bolz, appointed Otto Hirsch Chairman of the Board of the *Kraftverkehr Württemberg Aktien-Gesellschaft*, a State-controlled corporation which operated a large garage in Stuttgart ("Schwabengarage") and promoted the interests of highway users. Bolz sought to re-activate Otto Hirsch, who seemed eager to shoulder this additional responsibility in the service of the State of Württemberg. Needless to say that the Nazis lost no time in removing Otto Hirsch from that assignment, as soon as they had taken over the State Government.[23]

The Nazi assumption of power in the *Reich* and in Württemberg, in 1933, tore Hirsch from successful public service. Being Jewish, he did not stand a chance of maintaining his position at the helm of the Neckar Corporation. He had to

[21]HStAS: E 151a Bü 141.
[22]Nebinger, *op. cit.*, pp. 28f.
[23]Information supplied by Hans George Hirsch.

relinquish it under humiliating circumstances. Venomous slander was disseminated, which, however, left his personal integrity completely untouched. One Stuttgarter, in a vicious letter, dated 4th April 1933, addressed to the Nazi Minister Christian Mergenthaler, spoke in terms of scandalous mismanagement at the "Judaised" Neckar Corporation and demanded the immediate removal of the "Grossjude Hirsch". He maintained that "this member of the rabbinical class, the Jewish World International in Paris and active 'Zionsweise' " was a multiple salary earner. It was alleged that he not only received a salary from the Neckar Corporation, but also from the State of Württemberg as a ministerial counsellor and from the Salamander Corporation in Kornwestheim as an executive of the company, and that he received an additional salary as the President of the *Israelitischer Oberrat* in Stuttgart. This idea of Hirsch accumulating salaries was as grotesque as it was malicious. Since 1926, Hirsch had received his salary exclusively from the Neckar Corporation; as the President of the *Israelitischer Oberrat* he was paid a modest expense allowance. He had absolutely nothing to do with the Salamander Corporation. It was his brother who served as a director there. Chief Engineer Konz was also abused because he was married to a so-called non-Aryan. However, his opponents did not succeed in bringing him down. He was able to defend himself successfully against the accusation of having derived personal advantage from awarding large contracts.[24]

Suddenly the German fatherland, to which he still felt closely attached, had no need of Otto Hirsch. He found himself entirely restricted to the Jewish community. Fortunately, despite the liberalism he professed in his view of life and the world, he had never detached himself from the roots of the Jewish religion. Now being Jewish was even more a source of spiritual and moral support to him than in the years of his youth and his studies. He had always been an optimist inspired by high ethical values. At the age of twenty-four he had written to a Christian friend that performing those duties which are imposed on the human being for the sake of their performance was certainly the highest and most logical aim in life. Nevertheless, this kind of Kantian, rigorous idea of duty, so he wrote, went against his grain. A cheerful heart should ensue also. "We must feel love", he wrote, "towards our life and towards its fulfilment. And therfore, the demand for the mere performance of duties is exceeded by the postulate to do what needs to be done with love and joy." He was aware of just how difficult that often was. In his optimistic way of looking at things, he considered it appropriate and right to loosen the reins imposed on one by duty and to remember joyful pursuits whenever it seemed impossible to perform duty cheerfully. He was convinced that, "everything happens for good. This is not just an aphorism, or even worldly wisdom, but ethics of the highest order. Once we accept life as given and necessary – and this we must do – we have to live with all that it brings, justly, courageously and joyfully. If I am stranded on an island, I strive to get away from it; but as long as that is not possible, I make myself at home on it and take pleasure in all the beautiful things that may be found on any island."[25]

[24]HSt AS: E130b Bü 1418.
[25]Leo Baeck Institute New York; Otto Hirsch Collection.

Throughout his life he kept a cheerful heart and a belief that ultimately everything he encountered was for good. From his ethos of duty arose his willingness to shoulder and to bear responsibility for his fellow man and for the community. He hated everything petty, small-minded and base. The educationalist Ernst Simon stressed his "unsurpassable capacity to understand people in their individuality and to treat them accordingly and activate them without ever manipulating them". Simon further noted that "his presence inspired immediate confidence, which was never misplaced. Nobody talked badly about Hirsch; it was next to impossible to do so. He did not build bridges, for he himself was a bridge, made of that particular kind of firm material of the body and soul that supports against all the blows of life and turns a person into the natural centre of any circle he appears in. The circle in turn becomes a community through him as its focal point."[26] Rabbi Leo Baeck, who after 1933 worked closely with Hirsch for years in the *Reichsvertretung der deutschen Juden*, wrote in retrospect: "He was a man at one with himself and who therefore stood firmly on the ground, a man whom one could build on. He was without guile or flaws. Even if one had to contradict him, which was rarely the case, one had to love him."[27] His friend from student days, Theodor Heuss, whose political convictions he also shared for a period, called him a noble man. Knowing that Heuss abhorred any verbal bombast, it may be appreciated what the future President of the German Federal Republic meant to express by "noble". Theodor Heuss, by the way, as much as Ernst Simon, was fascinated by the harmonious synthesis of Swabian and Jewish elements characterising Hirsch's personality. Not only his speech but "also his somewhat melancholy sense of humour, always ready for quiet cheerfulness", linked him – as Simon put it – to the best people of the Swabian tribe, in whose midst he lived. Even in Hirsch's liberal Jewish observance, "tending towards a thoroughly rooted, but by no means overdone piety", Ernst Simon saw a synthesis between Jewish and Swabian, even ancient Württemberg cultural heritage.[28]

Otto Hirsch felt as a German, but he did not want to be German by surrendering his Jewishness and his Jewish self-respect. He did not want to assimilate completely. The Jewish religion was the foundation of his existence. Its spiritual-ethical potential was to enable him to live as a conscious German, as a German citizen of Jewish faith. It became a central concern for him to regain for himself, his Jewish friends and other Jews the sources of the Jewish religion which were distant and therefore not well known to him. He wanted to be a student and teacher as well. He considered men like Franz Rosenzweig and Martin Buber his intellectual mentors and companions in his quest. In 1926, he founded the Stuttgart Jewish *Lehrhaus* after the Frankfurt model, together with his friend Leopold Marx, an industrialist from Cannstatt, and Marx's brother-

[26]Ernst Simon, *Aufbau im Untergang. Jüdische Erwachsenenbildung im nationalsozialistischen Deutschland als geistiger Widerstand*, Tübingen 1959 (Schriftenreihe wissenschaftlicher Abhandlungen des Leo Baeck Instituts 2) p. 39.

[27]Robert Weltsch (ed.), *Deutsches Judentum. Aufstieg und Krise. Gestalten, Ideen, Werke*, Stuttgart 1963, Veröffentlichung des Leo Baeck Instituts, p. 312.

[28]Theodor Heuss, *Staat und Volk im Werden*, München 1961, pp. 48, 60f.; Simon, *op. cit.*, pp. 38f.

in-law, Karl Adler, who had been the director of the Music Conservatory for many years. Through Adler, but also through Hirsch himself, the *Lehrhaus* closely cooperated with the *Verein zur Förderung der Volksbildung* led by Theodor Bäuerle. The *Lehrhaus* soon acquired a prominent place in the cultural life of Württemberg's capital.[29] Here, completely assimilated and partially estranged Jews studied with Orthodox fellow Jews. In addition, the *Lehrhaus* also became – for the first time since Jews had settled in Württemberg – a place of encounter, dialogue and of learning to understand each other for both Jews and Christians. Lectures given by Martin Buber, Leo Baeck and Ernst Simon were widely noticed. Several Jewish theologians from Württemberg also participated actively in the curriculum. Thus, on 19th January 1927, Rabbi Dr. Max Beermann of Heilbronn lectured on the cultural impact of the Talmud, and Rabbi Dr. Abraham Schlesinger of Buchau spoke about modern Hebrew poetry. The Rabbi of Stuttgart, Dr. Paul Rieger, the vice-president of the *Lehrhaus*, headed a study group on Franz Rosenzweig's *Stern der Erlösung* in 1931–1932.[30] Martin Buber also contributed to the dialogue between Jews and Christians. The discussions he engaged in with Theodor Bäuerle, the Catholic writer Hermann Hefele and the Protestant writer Wilhelm Michel in 1928–1929 made a great impression on the audience. The *Lehrhaus* curriculum put special emphasis on Hebrew classes. Already during the first year (1926–1927), 320 students had enrolled, as the president proudly observed.[31]

Despite his heavy professional work load during the 1920s Otto Hirsch never questioned that he would follow his father's footsteps in service to the Jewish community, if he were needed. His father served for many years on the *Israelitischer Oberkirchenrat (Oberrat)*. As we know, the Jewish religious community did not become completely independent of state supervision until 1924. Otto Hirsch played a leading role in drafting its constitution of 18th March of that year. According to it, the community organised itself independently as a *Körperschaft des öffentlichen Rechts*.

The *Israelitische Landesversammlung* was the legislative body, which elected the *Oberrat* as its Executive. In 1930, Hirsch was elected President of the *Oberrat*.[32]

Taking as his example his predecessor Dr. Carl Nördlinger and the latter's deputy, Louis Hirsch (Otto Hirsch's father) who was also vacating his position on the *Oberrat*, Otto Hirsch promised "to serve the cause of Württemberg Jewry and of Judaism at large",[33] to the best of his capabilities. In his new responsible position the coming difficult years were to prove how seriously he had taken this vow. Yet, at the beginning of the thirties, Württemberg Jewry, numbering about 11,000, still viewed its future chances favourably. This in spite of the world-wide economic crisis and the rapid growth of Hitler's radical right-wing party which had declared the fight against Jewry as the chief ideological issue in its programme.

[29] *Ibid.*; *Gemeinde-Zeitung für die israelitischen Gemeinden Württembergs*, 1931/1932, Anhang IV.
[30] *Ibid.*, 1926/1927, p. 492 and, 1931/1932, p. 135.
[31] Zelzer, *op. cit.*, pp. 118ff.; *Gemeinde-Zeitung*, 1926/1927, p. 492 and 1931/1932, p. 135.
[32] On the *Oberrat* and Hirsch's role in it see also Leo Adler, 'Israelitische Religionsgemeinschaft of Wurttemberg. Its Development and Changes', in *LBI Year Book V* (1960), pp. 287–298.
[33] *Gemeinde-Zeitung*, 1929/1930, p. 299.

In 1931, the Jewish orphanage *Wilhelmspflege* in Esslingen and the *Oberrat* both celebrated their 100th anniversaries. In his address, Otto Hirsch praised the truly Jewish and truly Swabian spirit that had guided the orphanage in its admirable work.[34] The public showed vivid interest in the jubilee of the *Oberrat*. The presence of *Staatspräsident* Bolz and Minister of Cultural Affairs Wilhelm Bazille at the celebration, as well as the attendance of many high-ranking representatives of the Christian churches and the authorities of the *Reich* and the state of Württemberg gave the impression that the Jewish religious community was firmly integrated into the State and society and that it was well respected everywhere. In his speech, *Staatspräsident* Bolz called it "the chief task of a neutral state to protect the values and traditions of its existing religious communities. The Württemberg government was prepared to cooperate with the *Oberrat* also in the future and to protect and to promote Judaism's cultural values." The vice-president of the State Legislature, Dr. Hans Göz regretted that, more than ever, religious beliefs were drawn into political controversies. He welcomed the united front of all denominations in defence against atheism. In his closing speech Otto Hirsch said that the *Oberrat* could only give thanks for the many expressions of trust and the obligations they implied by "unswervingly continuing to work for the future of Judaism".[35]

In little more than a year, the basis of trust between the Jewish religious community and the State, which had existed for many decades, collapsed in Württemberg with the establishment of the totalitarian Nazi regime. Otto Hirsch, deeply shaken, could not accept the new situation. He courageously raised his voice for law and justice. In a speech to the *Israelitische Landesversammlung*, on 19th February 1933, he declared that a religious renaissance for the German nation, and the urgently needed raising of public and private morale – as propagandised by the Nazi Party leadership – were irreconcilable with a struggle against those who had received God's word and the basis of all ethics at the foot of Mount Sinai. He asked the new rulers not to reject the insight "that any state, today and in all eternity, can only endure if it practises what has already been commanded to our patriarch Abraham, namely law and justice".[36] When, at the end of March 1933, SA-men from Heilbronn badly mistreated Jews in several communities in Hohenlohe (Northern Württemberg) and beat two men to death in Creglingen, Hirsch wrote a sharply-worded letter of protest to the Württemberg government, demanding on behalf of the *Oberrat* there be an inquiry into the incidents and merciless punishment of the culprits.[37] Of course, his protest was in vain. In April 1933, the *Oberrat* sent a letter to the *Staatspräsident* of Württemberg protesting against the defamation of the Jews as having harmed the German nation. The *Oberrat* demanded that those falsely pilloried should be left "with the right and the opportunity for livelihood in their own country".[38]

[34] *Ibid.*, 1931/1932, p. 141.
[35] *Schwäbischer Merkur*, 15th December 1931; and *Gemeinde-Zeitung*, 16th December 1931.
[36] *Ibid.*, 1932/1933, p. 253.
[37] HStAS: Q 1/21 (Nachlass Theodor Bäuerle).
[38] *Gemeinde-Zeitung*, 16th April 1933.

Otto Hirsch and many of his friends were still optimistic. They were hardly able to imagine a further escalation of hatred against Jews after the Nazis had taken over political responsibility for the *Reich* and its states; rather, they expected the contrary to happen: an increasing moderation. But one thing Otto Hirsch was clearly aware of: everything had to be done to strengthen the moral resistance of the Jewish congregations. Therefore, he issued an order as of 27th March 1933 immediately cancelling all vacations for rabbis and religious teachers who now were to be available to their congregations at all times.[39] Hirsch countered the challenge of an anti-Jewish regime with a declaration of loyalty to a Jewry which was conscious of its great spiritual heritage and also rooted in the community of the German people. A Jew was not to lose his self-respect. The sources of strength he needed would arise from his Judaism and make spiritual resistance possible. Rabbis and teachers of religion would have a decisive function in this. They did not have to master the problems and difficulties which arose before them alone. The *Oberrat* gave them firm support. It exercised its authority more than formerly. Its President Otto Hirsch gave unequivocal directives. For example, he directed rabbis and teachers of religion to give a sermon on the dignity and holiness of labour on the 1st of May which the Nazi regime had proclaimed as the holiday of national labour. This was to be done after the Torah reading within the framework of the customary morning service.[40] It was to demonstrate that Jews, too, supported the idea of national labour, that they felt solidarity with the Christian population and that they were part of the German people. In response to the dismissal of numerous Jews from public service (pursuant to the so-called law for the re-establishment of the Civil Service of 7th April 1933), boycott measures and economic discrimination against Jewish citizens, the *Oberrat* came to the aid of those who had lost their jobs or suffered severe economic loss. On 16th July 1933, Otto Hirsch convened all rabbis and teachers of religion in Stuttgart, in order to discuss the situation and to confer with them about ways to help. Participation in this meeting was compulsory.[41] In the autumn of 1933 the *Oberrat* organised a course in modern Hebrew for teachers from Stuttgart and vicinity.[42]

Looking back on the previous year at the meeting of the *Israelitische Landesversammlung*, on 7th January 1934, Otto Hirsch called the wounds which had been inflicted on the Jews of Württemberg in their professional and economic lives very painful, particularly inasmuch as the Jews had felt a close kinship with their Gentile fellow citizens. The defamation, however, "that has been inflicted on our community, our lineage and ancestry time and again" he characterised as "much more severe". He continued:

> "The building of a new German *Reich* on the basis of race and ethnicity may necessitate an emphasis on the differences between Jews and their Gentile environment; but no community with a sense of honour and self-esteem can accept being branded as inferior and even useless without raising its voice in protest. We trust that this new German state, which itself

[39]HStAS: J 355 Bü 269.
[40]*Ibid.*
[41]*Ibid.*
[42]*Ibid.*, Bü 270.

> professes such a marked sense of honour and dignity, will grant this elementary sense also to our small community and, from its position of unshakable security will no longer tolerate such defamation of a small minority like ours, rather that it may use the unlimited power, that it possesses so miraculously, against such slander from now on. As far as we are concerned, we will maintain our honour and dignity best by searching for the historical meaning of this time and finding it by realising the necessity for self-reflection and for remembering the values of our Jewish religion and developing inner strength to master this calamity. We may be just a handful of people, but let us not become despondent, no matter how small we are in number, and let us not abandon anything that has been created in our religious community in terms of organisation in the state and in the congregations during these past one hundred years. The *Oberrat* is willing . . . to do its share in maintaining Württemberg Jewry as a part of German Jewry."[43]

The day before, a joint demonstration with a similar motto "For a united Jewry on German soil" had taken place. It was organised by the *Oberrat*, the Board of the Jewish congregation in Stuttgart, the *Centralverein deutscher Staatsbürger jüdischen Glaubens* (C.V.), the *Reichsbund jüdischer Frontsoldaten* (RjF), and the *Zionistische Vereinigung für Deutschland* (ZVfD). In his welcoming address Otto Hirsch had appealed to German Jews to unite. Differences should no longer make for separation. The Jewish groups should be aware of their solidarity and not falter in their will for survival.[44]

For German Jews, a sense of unity and clear, spiritual, common goals were dictated by the hour. They all were in the same boat – were they Zionists or members of the *Centralverein*. Despite his active role in the *Centralverein*, Hirsch had been appreciative of the Zionist idea of a Jewish state for a long time. In 1929, he had participated in an appeal which solicited support for the development of Palestine within the framework of the Jewish Agency.[45]

It was to be expected that a builder of spiritual bridges of his stature was to be entrusted with a major assignment in the Jewish religious community not only in Württemberg, but in Germany at large at a time of most grievous oppression. On 17th September 1933, the *Reichsvertretung der deutschen Juden* had been founded. It comprised the diverse political groups or factions of Jewry, such as the *Centralverein*, the ZVfD and the RjF. This body, which combined a wide spectrum of political and religious organisations, was to represent the interests of the Jewish community to the German authorities, and needed, as Ernst Simon called it, a non-extreme leadership.[46] The highly respected liberal Berlin Rabbi Leo Baeck, who headed the *Reichsvertretung* was a personality above partisanship, embodying, as it were, the essence of Judaism. Otto Hirsch, however, was entrusted with the executive direction of this highest political representation of the German Jews. For the President of the *Oberrat* of the Württemberg Jewish religious community, the change from working for his co-religionists in his own home state to this position representing Jews on an overall national level was not an easy one. In Württemberg, the partisan differences among Jews were far less marked than in the *Reich* at large. The

[43] *Gemeinde-Zeitung*, 1933/1934, p. 181.

[44] *Ibid.*

[45] Alfred Marx, 'In memoriam Otto Hirsch', in *Feiertagszeitschrift der Israelitischen Religionsgemeinschaft Württembergs*, April 1965, p. 24.

[46] Simon, *op. cit.*, p. 25.

members of the *Oberrat*, members of the *Israelitische Landesversammlung* and the congregations spoke the same language. By contrast, chill winds blew in Berlin. The atmosphere there was alien to Hirsch. But he consciously accepted the personal risks and dangers involved with this new office. He hoped to be able to help his Jewish fellow-sufferers from a forward position. Ernst Herzfeld of the *Centralverein* has compared him to an officer going into a seemingly hopeless battle out of a sense of loyalty and duty. Leo Baeck said of him that he was both a realist and an idealist at the same time. Each and every idea had become a task for him and each and every task he looked at and tackled from the points of view of the idea and the ideal.[47]

In March 1934, the *Oberrat* and the Presidium of the *Israelitische Landesversammlung* approved his request for a temporary one-year leave of absence. As of 1st April 1935, he had to vacate his position as President of the *Oberrat* in order to be able to dedicate all his energies to the work of the *Reichsvertretung*.[48] The void he left was painfully felt in Stuttgart. During the meeting of the *Landesversammlung* on 3rd February 1935, President Dr. Simon Hayum, expressed appreciation for his meritorious service.[49]

To Otto Hirsch, the call to Berlin brought a temporary separation from his wife and children. Since May 1914, he had been married to Martha Loeb. His tall, blonde wife (whose appearance as much as his own gave lie to the Nazi babble about typical Jewish racial features) was an equal companion to him. She took great interest in his work and provided a friendly and harmonious home.[50] His son Hans Georg (born 1916) and his two daughters Grete (born 1921) and Ursula (born 1925) were genuine children of Swabia. By the end of 1935, Otto Hirsch was able to move his family to Berlin. Their Stuttgart home (Gähkopf 33) had to be let and the Hirsch family rented a Berlin apartment. At first, their daughter Ursula was the only child who could join them in the *Reich* capital. Their older daughter, Grete, finished school before joining them in 1937. Hans Georg had already completed his *Abitur* in 1934. But the special certificate needed for studying at the university in that year was denied to him as a Jew – which was a bitter disappointment both for the young man and his parents. In the following year, the Nazi regime abolished the special certificate, and yet Hans Georg was denied enrolment at the Stuttgart-Hohenheim College of Agriculture in 1935. He was not discouraged but worked as a trainee on various farms in Württemberg, Bavaria and Silesia.[51]

The Nazi assumption of power had created a situation for which the German Jews were totally unprepared. Overnight, they had become an outlawed minority in their own German homeland, in which they had always believed themselves to be strongly rooted. Already in the spring of 1933, the largest group of Jewish scientists, artists, teachers, judges and other Jews working in

[47]Leonard Baker, *Days of Sorrow and Pain. Leo Baeck and the Berlin Jews*, New York – London 1978, pp. 164 and 253.

[48]*Gemeinde-Zeitung*, 1933/1934 and 1934/1935.

[49]*Ibid.*, 1934/1935, p. 189.

[50]Marx, *loc. cit.*, pp. 21f.

[51]Nebinger, *op. cit.*, p. 46 (Anhang); HStAS: J 355 Bü 167.

the public sector lost their jobs. Owners of industrial and commercial enterprises and free-lance workers suffered economic distress as a result of the boycott measures. The Jewish community was particularly hard hit by their exclusion from Germany's intellectual and cultural life; they were forced to find ways which made possible their spiritual and moral self-assertion and a modest economic and social survival. With discrimination, oppression and ostracisation constantly increasing, a ghetto – as yet invisible – was being created, segregating Jews from the rest of the population.

The *Reichsvertretung* was confronted with a growing number of tasks. Together with the *Zentralausschuss für Hilfe und Aufbau* – which had been founded before the *Reichsvertretung* and was later incorporated into it as one of its departments[52] – it had to organise and maintain an extensive network of economic assistance and social welfare, procure new jobs for dismissed teachers, artists and scientists; build up an independent Jewish school and educational system; provide occupational re-training programmes, establish agricultural and craft-related educational facilities; and open and maintain emigration counselling centres. In his capacity as executive chairman of the *Reichsvertretung*, Otto Hirsch's organisational talents, his negotiating skills, his unusual working capacity and his talent for dealing with people served him very well. Even now, he did not lose his trust which was based on a high moral ethos. Even under difficult circumstances he maintained his calm and his sense of humour. As late as the spring of 1939, he would say to Hugo Rosenthal, head of the Jewish boarding school in Herrlingen, near Ulm: "We are not entitled to despair. We must continue our work as long as they let us."[53] On occasion, he received tempting offers of posts abroad, but turned them all down. His sense of duty kept him in Germany. The task set for him in the *Reichsvertretung* was twofold: securing and maintaining decent living conditions for German Jews in their homeland, and at the same time, creating the prerequisites for emigration for all those willing and able to leave. For this purpose, he went on numerous trips abroad to Paris, London and the United States.

It was only with great reluctance, that Otto Hirsch familiarised himself with the thought, which Leo Baeck had expressed as early as 1933, that the Nazi regime meant the end of German Jewry. When asked for advice, he told his friends and acquaintances to stay in Germany and not to be forcibly expelled from their ancient homeland. The escalation of persecution, however, compelled him, step by step, to see things differently.

This painful inner conflict burdened him profoundly and further aggravated the condition of his health, which had been impaired for many years.[54]

In November 1933, Otto Hirsch saw the main tasks of the newly-founded *Reichsvertretung* in resisting the degradation of German Jews, in paving the way

[52]Esriel Hildesheimer, 'Cora Berliner. Ihr Leben und Wirken', in *Bulletin des Leo Baeck Instituts*, 67 (1984), p. 49.

[53]HStAS/Bibliothek: Ba 427.

[54]Nebinger, *op. cit.*, p. 30; Marx, *loc. cit.*, p. 24; Annedore Leber, 'Otto Hirsch, 9. Januar 1885–Juni 1941', in *idem* (ed.), *Das Gewissen entscheidet. Berichte des deutschen Widerstandes*, Berlin–Frankfurt a. Main 1957, p. 14.

for their integration into the new state and in securing their religious, cultural and economic basis of existence. He thought that all this was only to be achieved with the good will and support of the *Reich* government. Whether the Nazi government was prepared to cooperate in such an undertaking remained to be seen.[55]

During the meeting of the *Reichsvertretung* advisory board in February 1934, Hirsch declared that the most important objective for the work of the *Reichsvertretung* would be the preservation of the position of the German Jews within the German economy. Special emphasis after that was on the increase of Jewish settlements in Palestine, and the activation of the Jewish educational system in Germany. He appealed to the various Jewish groups to act in solidarity and desist from partisan quarrels. The advisory board supported this appeal.[56] In the same month, at a meeting of the Jewish congregation in Frankfurt a. Main, Hirsch spoke out against hasty and unplanned emigration. The *Reichsvertretung*, he explained, held the view that anyone who was economically capable of staying and had the spiritual strength and will power to do so should not emigrate. It believed that the possibility still existed, and had to be realised in Germany, for living as upright German Jews. Wherever this was not feasible for an individual, emigration should be well prepared. The emigrant was to maintain contact with German culture, but particularly with Judaism.[57]

During the early years of the Nazi regime a large proportion of Otto Hirsch's co-religionists shared his view that the Jews should under no circumstances accept the denial of the right to their German homeland. Some Gentiles also shared this point of view. A leading official of the Foreign Office in Berlin implored Otto Hirsch and Friedrich Brodnitz, when they came to him on an official visit: "Gentlemen, do not throw away what you have gained in 150 years of emancipation", counselling them not to give up. The official had no doubt that the Nazi spectre would disappear before long.[58] On the other hand, mass emigration encountered difficulties that were almost insurmountable. The main countries of immigration, such as the U.S., were not willing to accept large numbers of emigrants from Germany. American Jews generously donated large funds for the support of their distressed German fellow Jews, but advised against emigrating. Robert Weltsch, editor of the *Jüdische Rundschau* was told by a prominent American Jew when they met, that the German Jews were by no means to give up their citizenship through emigration. Weltsch did not conceal his anger: "You don't understand what is happening in Germany", he replied. In the following year, Max Kreutzberger and Otto Hirsch had to hear a similarly negative comment by American Jews regarding emigration to the U.S.

[55]*Die jüdische Emigration aus Deutschland 1933–1941. Die Geschichte einer Austreibung.* Eine Ausstellung der Deutschen Bibliothek Frankfurt a. Main. Hrsg. von Brita Eckert unter Mitwirkung von Werner Berthold. Mitarb.: Mechthild Hahner, unter Mitwirkung des Leo Baeck Instituts, New York, Buchhändlervereinigung, Frankfurt a. Main 1985, pp. 59f.

[56]*Ibid.*, p. 62.

[57]*Ibid.*, p. 60.

[58]Friedrich S. Brodnitz, 'Memories of the Reichsvertretung. A Personal Report', in *LBI Year Book XXXI* (1986), p. 277; Baker, *op. cit.*, p. 196.

the people with whom they conferred feared that the Nazi acts of violence might generate similar anti-Jewish actions in Poland and Romania if the U.S. were to open its borders to Jewish emigrants.[59] In 1935, a *Reichsvertretung* delegation negotiated with representatives of the large Jewish welfare organisations in New York in a rather tense atmosphere. The request made by Otto Hirsch and Max Kreutzberger, to fund re-training and emigration without time limit, fell on deaf ears. In 1936, several hundred young German Jews were forced to discontinue their studies in England, because the funds that had previously been raised through donations were now lacking.[60] Notwithstanding such obstacles, the *Reichsvertretung* did everything to facilitate emigration for children and adolescents, who particularly suffered from discrimination and persecution, and for young farmers and craftsmen as well. For them, Palestine was of central importance in this respect. Thousands of young people found a new home there.[61]

The establishment of a Jewish school system was one of the main priorities in the *Reichsvertretung*. This task was particularly close to Otto Hirsch's heart. He strongly promoted all types of Jewish schools and educational institutions, such as elementary schools, higher education establishments like the Herrlingen boarding school near Ulm and the *Hochschule für die Wissenschaft des Judentums* in Berlin, to whose transformation into a kind of Jewish university he contributed greatly.[62] In his book, *Days of Sorrow and Pain*, Leonard Baker described education as the primary weapon used by the Jews in their spiritual struggle against the Nazi regime.[63] Otto Hirsch might have seen it in a similar light.

The guidelines, issued by the *Reichsvertretung* in 1935 said that "the school is to be permeated by a self-analytical Jewish spirit. The child growing up should be sure of his or her Judaism with a sense of healthy consciousness . . . Jewish issues are to be made a focal point in all appropriate subjects . . . The entire education ought to be aimed at educating Jewish personalities that are strong-willed and stable . . . The Jewish child must be enabled to take up the imminent, particularly difficult, struggle for survival and master it . . ."[64]

The Jewish school system ranks among the most brilliant achievements of the persecuted Jewish community. Amidst hatred, injustice and violence, to which children were even more brutally and helplessly exposed than adults, thanks to the imagination and commitment of its founders and supporters, a humane pedagogical haven was provided, which continued to serve as a constructive and creative force and remained effective mainly in Palestine/Israel and the U.S. even after its destruction.

One of the Nazi rulers' first actions, in 1933, was the expulsion of Jews from German cultural and intellectual life, where they had played a prominant role for decades. The Jewish community reacted in an admirable way. In May 1933 the

[59]*Ibid.*, pp. 220f.

[60]Naomi Shepherd, *Wilfrid Israel. German Jewry's Secret Ambassador*, London 1984, pp. 159f.

[61]Herbert A. Strauss, 'Jewish Emigration from Germany. Nazi Policies and Jewish Responses (I)', in *LBI Year Book XXV* (1980), pp. 319f.

[62]Richard Fuchs, 'The "Hochschule für die Wissenschaft des Judentums" in the Period of Nazi Rule. Personal Recollections', in *LBI Year Book XII* (1967), pp. 8ff.

[63]Baker, *op. cit.*, p. 174.

[64]*Die jüdische Emigration aus Deutschland, op. cit.*, pp. 96f.

Kulturbund was founded which was soon to become the largest organisation of German Jewry, numbering 80,000 members, and to be integrated into the *Reichsvertretung* as an autonomous department. About 2,500 artists and scientists were involved in its work. In its wide repertory it reflected the entire spectrum of European culture.[65] Despite being under the surveillance of the *Gestapo*, it retained a remarkable degree of intellectual freedom and though limited to Jewish audiences under a totalitarian regime, succeeded in offering a modest refuge to the rich intellectual life of the Weimar era. Remarkable were the achievements of Jewish publishing firms with their numerous and important publications on Jewish literature, history, philosophy and theology. Forgotten authors were rediscovered; new authors' works were introduced to an interested and grateful audience.[66] After 1933, the Jewish community published the only relatively free and independent newspapers in Germany.[67] Until the prohibition of the public sale of Jewish papers and magazines, in 1936, the number of their buyers kept increasing constantly.[68]

The success of Jews in securing for their community an intellectual and social life of its own during the first years of Nazi rule, and – unlike German society which had been *gleichgeschaltet* – in retaining their religious and ideological heterogeneity, was largely due to men like Otto Hirsch. They respected the peculiarities of the various Jewish groups and united them into a federated community, meeting the difficult challenges in the social and economic as well as the intellectual and cultural sectors. Despite discrimination, oppression and terror, the Jews in Germany maintained a pluralistic-democratic society in a totalitarian despotic state. Even after the *Kristallnacht* of November 1938 and during the following years of growing persecution, this paradoxical phenomenon persisted: a certain freedom of thought and action among the Jews exposed to the arbitrariness of the Nazi regime. This was the freedom of the outlawed, or more correctly, of those doomed to die.[69]

With the Nuremberg Laws, issued in September 1935, the Jews were excluded from the national life of the German people, deprived of their civil rights and barred from marrying Gentiles. The *Reichsvertretung* reacted to these despotic laws in a public declaration which expressed the hope that from now on, at least defamation and boycotting would come to an end, that Jews and the Jewish communities would be allowed to retain a moral and economic basis for existence and that the *Reichsvertretung* would be acknowledged as the autonomous leadership of the Jewish community by the state authorities.[70] A prayer by Leo Baeck, a remarkable document of the unbroken Jewish will to resist, aroused the indignation of the regime. In it we read:

[65]*Marbacher Magazin*, 25 (1983): *In den Katakomben. Jüdische Verlage in Deutschland 1933–1938*, bearbeitet von Ingrid Belke, pp. 5f.

[66]*Ibid.*, pp. 6ff.

[67]*Die jüdische Emigration aus Deutschland*, *op. cit.*, pp. 89ff.

[68]Peter M. Baldwin, 'Zionist and Non-Zionist Jews in the Last Years before the Nazi Regime', in *LBI Year Book XXVII* (1982), p. 105.

[69]Otto D. Kulka, 'Major Trends and Tendencies in German Historiography on National Socialism and the "Jewish Question" (1924–1984)', in *LBI Year Book XXX* (1985), pp. 238ff.

[70]HStAS: J 355 Bü 254.

"In this hour all Israel stands before God, the judge and the forgiver.
In His presence let us all examine our ways, our deeds, and what we have failed to do . . .
With the same fervor with which we confess our sins, the sins of the individual and the sins of the community, do we, in indignation and abhorrence, express our contempt for the lies concerning us and the defamation of our religion and its testimonies.
We have trust in our faith and in our future . . .
We stand before our God. On Him we rely. From Him issues the truth and the glory of our history, our fortitude amidst all change of fortune, our endurance in distress.
Our history is a history of nobility of soul, of human dignity. It is history we have recourse to when attack and grievous wrong are directed against us, when affliction and calamity befall us.
God has led our fathers from generation to generation. He will guide us and our children through these days . . ."[71]

The prayer was meant to be read during the Kol Nidre services in all synagogues throughout Germany. Its contents, however, became known to the *Gestapo* beforehand. Baeck was arrested and the *Reichsvertretung* was ordered to inform all congregations in the *Reich* by telegram that reading the prayer was prohibited. Leading officials of the *Reichsvertretung* explained to the *Gestapo* that Baeck's absence from his pulpit on Yom Kippur would result in great worry and anxiety abroad. Otto Hirsch assumed responsibility for dispatching the text of the prayer and directed that it be read publicly. Thereupon Baeck was released after 24 hours in prison and Hirsch was taken into custody. He was permitted, however, to proceed to his family in Stuttgart for Yom Kippur, after he had given assurances that he would immediately report to the *Gestapo* after returning to Berlin. As he was leaving home after Yom Kippur, he told his wife and son that he was not expecting to be detained again. Yet on his return to Berlin he was arrested anew and sent to the Columbiahaus concentration camp, where he was detained for a week before being released some time before the end of Sukkot. This was his first imprisonment.[72]

Immediately afterwards, in the new spirit of "a unity unprecedented in the history of the Jews in Germany",[73] the *Reichsvertretung* presented a new work programme to the community whose living conditions had become even more aggravated after the Nuremberg Laws. It clearly showed the hand of Otto Hirsch. It appealed for unity, the strictest self-discipline and the greatest willingness to make sacrifices. The areas of work were listed under five headings. The first priority was to be given to the extension of the Jewish educational system. It was "to serve the education of young people to become religiously strong, upright Jews, who draw their strength from a deeply felt tie to the Jewish community, from work in the Jewish present and from a belief in the future of Judaism in order to be able to meet the difficult demands made by life". Apart from imparting knowledge, the Jewish school was to provide the basis for a future occupation. The programme was to offer Jews engaged in artistic and cultural pursuits a field of activities and to guarantee an

[71]Simon, *op. cit.*, pp. 39ff., English translation by Nahum N. Glatzer (here quoted), in *The Dynamics of Emancipation. The Jew in the Modern Age*, Boston 1965.
[72]Information from Hans George Hirsch.
[73]Baldwin, 'Zionist and Non-Zionist Jews', *loc. cit.*, p. 105; *Arbeitsbericht des Zentralausschusses für Hilfe und Aufbau bei der Reichsvertretung der Juden in Deutschland für das Jahr 1935* (mimeographed), p. 7.

Otto and Martha Hirsch, Berlin 1938

autonomous cultural life to Jews in Germany. The total exclusion of Jews from the national life of the German people necessitated responsiveness to the increasing demand for opportunities to emigrate by large-scale planning, which included above all Palestine, but also all other possible countries and was especially directed at young people. The *Reichsvertretung* wanted to do everything to increase the possibilities for emigration by creating training facilities. Those in need, the sick and the old required the support of the Jewish community in addition to public aid. For that purpose as well as for the other above-mentioned tasks substantial financial resources were required. Therefore, the *Reichsvertretung* considered it indispensable to secure the economic viability of entrepreneurs and businessmen by appropriate means and to safeguard sources of income for Jewish employees.[74]

Otto Hirsch was active in all the fields of endeavour to which the *Reichsvertretung* had assigned priority. He continued to pay special attention to the school system. Hugo Rosenthal (who later changed his name to Joseph Yashuvi in Israel), reported that Hirsch kept visiting the Herrlingen Jewish boarding school, then one of the most important Jewish teaching and educational institutions in South Germany, in order to inquire about the school and its teaching methods and to find out how its material and spiritual needs could be most efficiently met.[75]

The *Reichsvertretung* now accorded high priority to settlement in Palestine. At the beginning of 1936, Otto Hirsch and his wife undertook a journey to the Holy Land, which they had been contemplating for a long time. Hirsch wanted to inform himself about immigration opportunities on the spot. In Haifa, he met Friedrich Sally Grosshut, who had studied law and came from Frankfurt a. Main. He urged him not to return to Germany. Hirsch replied that he knew exactly what was in store for him, that he was determined, however, to pursue the course of duty, come what may.[76] He returned to his homeland, which had become inhospitably alien to him, and resumed his selfless work.

The increasing difficulties in placing young Jews in apprenticeships with non-Jewish craftsmen and farmers prompted the *Reichsvertretung*, after the proclamation of the Nuremberg Laws, to promote plans for leasing an agricultural training farm. In addition to the Zionist training facilities which had existed in Germany and neighbouring countries for a long time, young men and women who did not want to emigrate to Palestine, but to another country were to be trained on that farm in agriculture, domestic science or crafts.

The reduction of immigration opportunities into Palestine by the British Mandatory authorities suggested that emigrants should increasingly look for other destinations. A Polish-Jewish family made its manor house, Gross-Breesen,

[74]HStAS: J 355 Bü 256; *Gemeinde-Zeitung*, 1935/1936, p. 105.

[75]Hugo Rosenthal, *Das Landschulheim Herrlingen*, MS, HStAS Bibliothek, pp. 18f. On Herrlingen see now Lucie Schachne, *Erziehung zum geistigen Widerstand. Das jüdische Landschulheim Herrlingen 1933 bis 1939*, Frankfurt a. Main 1986 (Pädagogische Beispiele. Institutionengeschichte in Einzeldarstellungen, Band 3). It contains a.o., Hugo Rosenthal, 'Otto Hirsch und die Anfänge des jüdischen Landschulheims in Herrlingen', pp. 40–49, excerpts from an uncompleted book (Rosenthal died in 1980), *Das Landschulheim Herrlingen. Die Geschichte einer jüdischen Landschaft im nationalsozialistischen Raum*, MS., Yad Vashem, Jerusalem, 0866, probably identical with the MS. in HStAS Bibliothek.

[76]Nebinger, *op. cit.*, p. 34.

30 kilometers north of Breslau, available to the *Reichsvertretung* free of charge. In May 1936, the training facility began operations with over one hundred students under the supervision of the noted psychologist and educator Curt Bondy. Otto Hirsch, as one of the project's initiators, belonged to the supervising curatorium. Bondy himself placed an educational emphasis on the character formation of those entrusted to his care. Two years after its creation, the training farm was already economically self-supporting. For outsiders it was a somewhat peculiar, protected island in the midst of hatred, persecution and terror. Despite many attempts made by Otto Hirsch, who felt particularly attached to Gross-Breesen, and his friends of the *Reichsvertretung*, an area for a larger settlement abroad – a Neu-Gross-Breesen where the farm's trainees might have settled together – could not be acquired. The few who were able to emigrate by the autumn of 1938 ended up in all four corners of the world. This also happened to the large proportion of the teachers and those trainees, who, shortly after, as a result of the November pogrom were forced to leave their native country. By the end of 1939, 118 students and six teachers found refuge abroad. The training farm was badly ravaged by the SS during the *Kristallnacht*. The training programme was resumed, however, under *Gestapo* surveillance and was continued under increasingly difficult circumstances. In 1942, the training farm closed and those of the teachers and students who had remained later met their deaths in the extermination camps.[77]

As the situation of the Jewish community deteriorated steadily, the *Reichsvertretung* was forced to broaden the basis of support for its work, that is, to look for increased backing from the voluntary Jewish organisations, namely from the Zionist movement and the *Landesverbände* and local congregations. In August 1936 Otto Hirsch took the chair at a meeting of the *Reichsvertretung* organisational committee which passed the requisite resolutions concerning (1) an expansion of the presidential committee of the *Reichsvertretung* by four Zionists and one Orthodox representative; (2) the addition of Dr. Franz Meyer, chairman of the ZVfD, to the executive of the *Reichsvertretung* and close cooperation between him and the executive director; (3) the formation of a council of the *Reichsvertretung*, consisting of 15 representatives of the *Landesverbände* and local congregations, three representatives of the voluntary organisations and five co-opted representatives. The council had to be consulted on all basic questions. Its approval was needed in matters pertaining to the autonomy of the congregations. The council was to supervise the financial management of the *Reichsvertretung* and – together with the presidential committee – it had to decide on constitutional matters. The council was to fill vacancies of the presidential committee by election and to adopt the *Reichsvertretung*'s budget. Most importantly, the council was to cooperate closely with the now firmly affiliated *Landesverbände* and local congregations.[78] Through the constitutional expansion of August 1936, the *Reichsvertretung* achieved what it had been hoping

[77]Werner T. Angress, 'Auswandererlehrgut Gross-Breesen', in *LBI Year Book X* (1965), pp. 168–187; and *idem*, *Generation zwischen Furcht und Hoffnung. Jüdische Jugend im Dritten Reich*, Hamburg 1985, pp. 82ff.

[78]*Die jüdische Emigration aus Deutschland*, *op. cit.*, p. 85.

to accomplish since its establishment in September 1933. It became the generally accepted voice and representative body of German Jewry. Its work was now also fully supported by the ZVfD, the *Landesverbände* and local congregations. This support had previously been lacking. Despite this internal strengthening of the *Reichsvertretung* there was a good measure of vainglorious obstructionism, which hurt Otto Hirsch severely. Georg Kareski, leader of the Revisionists and an influential politician in the Berlin Jewish community for many years, resumed his offensive against the *Reichsvertretung* at the beginning of 1937, with the support of Heinrich Stahl, chairman of the Berlin Jewish community, who was himself a member of the presidential committee of the *Reichsvertretung*. The *Gestapo* demanded the presidential committee's resignation in order to be able to manoeuvre Kareski into a leading position.* Baeck rejected this categorically. Stahl then withdrew his support from Kareski. The *Reichsvertretung* remained unchanged. Kareski, who became involved in financial entanglements, left Germany.[79]

During 1936, when the disturbances in Palestine reduced immigration there and administrative restrictions continued to keep immigration into the United States very significantly below the statutory immigration quota of approximately 25,000 natives of Germany, South Africa temporarily emerged as a possible haven for German Jews. However, in the summer of 1936 the Government of South Africa announced the imposition of new immigration restrictions to take effect on 1st November. Shortage of regularly scheduled shipping threatened the emigration of hundreds of Jews from Germany, who held immigration visas for South Africa, which would only be honoured before that date.

In this crisis, the *Reichsvertretung* and the *Hilfsverein der deutschen Juden* working together, with Otto Hirsch in charge chartered the S.S. Stuttgart for a special voyage from Germany to South Africa. On 27th October 1936, four days before the deadline, 540 Jewish refugees from Germany were admitted to South Africa. This limited success – against the background of ever-increasing immigration restrictions throughout the world – buoyed Otto Hirsch's spirit greatly during the autumn of 1936. It was a tangible success, no matter how small, when everything else seemed hopeless.[80]

Beginning early in 1938, with the progressive displacement of Jews, by the Nazi regime, from the positions in the economy that had been left open to them the German Jews placed high hopes on the refugee conference, which President Roosevelt had initiated and which took place in the French spa of Evian on Lake Geneva in July 1938. Representatives of 32 countries participated in the conference and (without having been invited, delegates from a large number of

*On Kareski see the essay by Francis R. Nicosia, 'Revisionist Zionism in Germany (II). Georg Kareski and the Staatszionistische Organisation, 1933–1938', in this volume of the Year Book – (Ed.).

[79]Herbert A. Strauss, 'Jewish Emigration from Germany (II)', in *LBI Year Book XXVI* (1981), p. 393; and Jacob Boas, 'German-Jewish Internal Politics under Hitler 1933–1938', in *LBI Year Book XXIX* (1984), pp. 12–19.

[80]Report of Hans George Hirsch; and *Die jüdische Emigration aus Deutschland*, *op. cit.*, pp. 182f.

Jewish refugee and relief organisations also attended). From Germany came an official *Reichsvertretung* delegation, headed by Otto Hirsch. It delivered a memorandum in which it made clear – by referring to the Jews who had left Germany since 1933 – that the emigration problem of the German Jews could be solved within a reasonable time-frame. Primary importance, however, was attributed to a solution of the financial problem involved.

The rapid pauperisation of German Jews, they pointed out, necessitated increased financial help from abroad. It did not seem impossible, however, that new ways for a transfer of assets could be negotiated with the German government – as had already been the case with respect to Palestine – to give less affluent families the opportunity to emigrate. The drafting of a comprehensive plan for emigration and accelerated execution of all separate measures to increase emigration were urgently called for. Of all the countries represented at the conference, the Dominican Republic was the only one that was prepared to open its gates to the persecuted Jews from Germany. The United States agreed to admit in the future as many refugees as were authorised by the statutory immigration quotas for Germany and Austria. Previously administrative cutbacks had severely reduced the number of immigrants below the level of the quotas. An inter-governmental committee dealing with the emigration problem from Germany was established. In the following years this committee negotiated with German government agencies. On the decisive question, concerning the transfer of assets, no agreement was achieved, however, before the outbreak of the war in September 1939.[81]

The pogrom of November 1938 came as a total shock to most of the leading men of the *Reichsvertretung*. These dreadful events were really beyond their imagination. Hardly any of them would have considered such an outbreak of barbarism possible in a civilised country.* In the early morning of 10th November 1938 Leo Baeck had been so shaken by the reports of burning synagogues, destroyed or plundered shops, mass arrests of Jewish men and murderous violence, which were coming in from all over Germany that he – and this his friends found hard to believe – lost control of himself for a short while. But then he and Otto Hirsch set out rushing from one ministry to the other, hoping to be able to request of one of the government officials to put an end to the riots at once. But in vain. Nobody received them. The *Reich* Chancellery, where they had hoped to be able to talk to State Secretary Otto Meissner, and also the *Reich* Ministry of the Interior remained closed to them. A large number of the board members of the *Reichsvertretung* disappeared into prisons and concentration camps. The *Reichsvertretung* office was closed. Leo Baeck maintained a relief and emergency service in his own flat.[82]

On the day after the *Kristallnacht*, Otto Hirsch was also arrested and

[81]S. Adler-Rudel, 'The Evian Conference on the Refugee Question', in *LBI Year Book XIII* (1968), pp. 235ff.; *Die jüdische Emigration aus Deutschland, op. cit.*, pp. 203ff.; Shepherd, *op. cit.*, pp. 201ff.; and information from Hans George Hirsch.

*On the November Pogrom see in particular the essay by Peter Loewenberg, 'The Kristallnacht as a Public Degradation Ritual', in this volume of the Year Book – (Ed.).

[82]Baker, *op. cit.*, pp. 234ff.; *Deutsches Judentum. Aufstieg und Krise, op. cit.*, pp. 312f.; Marx, *loc. cit.*, p. 24.

imprisoned in the Sachsenhausen concentration camp for several weeks. The enforced stay in the concentration camp was a severe setback for his delicate health. However, despite the marks of his imprisonment he expressed not a word of complaint. His first remarks after his return to the *Reichsvertretung* office (which had been reopened by *Gestapo* order on 29th November) were even playful. One might have formed the impression, Leo Baeck wrote admiringly, that he had just returned from a trip.[83]

Following the November pogrom, the Jews were deprived of their last means of subsistence. They were forced to sell the crafts or trade establishments still in their possession. At the beginning of 1938, there had still been 40,000 enterprises.[84] From then on unskilled labour was the only way of making a living. The Jewish press was suppressed. Only a *Jüdisches Nachrichtenblatt* was still permitted. At least the *Kulturbund* could continue its work, if under very burdensome conditions. The November pogroms must have destroyed Otto Hirsch's last illusions about maintaining the most modest means of subsistence of the Jewish community in Germany. Now the agenda demanded the concentration of all efforts on emigration. Yet this enforced emigration continued to be faced with enormous difficulties. Almost no potential country of refuge was prepared to receive the persecuted hospitably and without endless red tape. Nearly everywhere, there were rigorous quotas, numerical restrictions, often even bans on immigration. The Executive Director of the *Reichsvertretung* was again under great stress. With the complete elimination of Jews from the economy, the number of persons in need of aid increased rapidly. In addition, so-called non-Aryans were excluded from the public welfare assistance. The *Reichsvertretung* was now alone in charge of emigration, the school system – Jewish children were no longer admitted to German schools – and welfare. It had to be reorganised structurally. Authority over the Jewish congregation and the large organisations was tightened and intensified.[85] In July 1939, the Nazi rulers replaced the *Reichsvertretung* with the *Reichsvereinigung der Juden in Deutschland*. While the *Reichsvertretung* had been a voluntary coalition, the *Reichsvereinigung* was a compulsory organisation directly subordinate to the *Gestapo*. All so-called racial Jews had to belong to it. The leadership of the *Reichsvereinigung* was authoritatively appointed. There was little change of personnel. Leo Baeck remained the president, Otto Hirsch the executive director. Yet, the position of both men was incomparably more difficult than before. They were aware of how much they were in the hands of the *Gestapo*. However, only in this way could they continue their relief and rescue work on behalf of German Jewry. Leo Baeck gave out the watchword to stay at one's post, as long as there was a single Jew left on German soil.[86]

[83]*Ibid.*; *Deutsches Judentum. Aufstieg und Krise*, *op. cit.*, pp. 312f.; Hildesheimer, 'Cora Berliner', *loc. cit.*, p. 55.

[84]Boas, 'German-Jewish Internal Politics', *loc. cit.*, p. 4.

[85]HStAS: J 355 Bü 254.

[86]Paul Sauer, *Die Schicksale der jüdischen Bürger Baden-Württembergs während der nationalsozialistischen Verfolgungszeit 1933–1945* (Veröffentlichungen der Staatlichen Archivverwaltung Baden-Württemberg Bd. 20) Stuttgart 1968, pp. 107f.

Otto Hirsch and Leo Baeck had become close friends during their many years of joint service in charge of the *Reichsvertretung* and *Reichsvereinigung*. They helped each other carry the heavy burden of obligations imposed upon them in the service of German Jewry. They would often visit one another in their apartments and they met with third persons for confidential discussions concerning political questions. Thus it was through Otto Hirsch that Leo Baeck came into contact with Theodor Heuss and other opponents of Hitler, such as the Stuttgart industrialist Robert Bosch and his managing director, Hans Walz. Through Bosch and Walz both men also obtained contacts with German resistance circles: with the former Leipzig mayor Carl Goerdeler and with members of the military opposition. These contacts ended only with the arrest of Otto Hirsch in February 1941 and Leo Baeck's deportation at the beginning of 1943.[87] By maintaining relations with the German resistance movement, the president and the executive director of the *Reichsvereinigung* not only showed unusual courage, but also consciously assumed a high degree of personal risk. They did not abandon their faith in a democratic Germany true to its great humanitarian spiritual heritage, despite the intensified persecution of the Jews which the criminal Nazi regime had started with the pogroms of November 1938.

In August 1939, a few weeks before the outbreak of the war, Otto Hirsch visited Great Britain. Together with Leo Baeck he had escorted a transport of children there. Eva Reichmann tried to stop both men from returning to Germany but in vain.[88] After the November pogrom, Great Britain freely admitted Jewish refugees. Therefore, Hirsch was confident that he would find favourable consideration of his request that the admission of refugees should continue in a generous manner. This was the only reason why he and Leo Baeck had come to London. However, the outbreak of the Second World War in September 1939, closed this gate of rescue. During the tense days at the end of August, Otto Hirsch had still been able to participate in a conference of the American Jewish Joint Distribution Committee in Paris.[89]

With the war, emigration opportunities kept dwindling more and more. All the same, Otto Hirsch did not cease in his efforts to get as many Jews out of Germany as possible.[90] It was essentially because of his tireless efforts that – before the ultimate prohibition of emigration on 1st October 1941 – about two thirds of the German Jews had found refuge abroad. And it was essentially by his merits that many of these people had been provided with the needed training prerequisites and that some of them had been able to bring modest means of their own to rebuild their lives in an alien environment.

From the year 1940 we also possess documentary evidence of Hirsch's interventions with Eichmann to halt deportations to France; his dauntless endeavours to learn from the Nazi authorities the whereabouts and destination

[87]Hans Reichmann, 'Foreword: The Fate of a Manuscript' to 'Excerpts from Leo Baeck's Writings' in *LBI Year Book III* (1958), pp. 361f.; Baker, *op. cit.*, pp. 164 and 249f.
[88]*Ibid.*, pp. 246f.
[89]Shepherd, *op. cit.*, p. 248.
[90]Leber, *op. cit.*, p. 16.

of deportees; and of his desperate efforts on behalf of the *Reichsvereinigung* to submit alternative plans for resettlement within Greater Germany, as possibilities of emigration shrank more and more.[91]

When emigration was altogether prohibited in the autumn of 1941, Otto Hirsch was no longer amongst the living. On 26th February 1941 he was arrested without being informed of any charges of an alleged infraction against the regulations of the Nazi state and was initially held in the Berlin Alexanderplatz prison. Gentile friends tried in vain to obtain his release. Robert Nebinger, who had approached an official of the *Reichssicherheitshauptamt*, was told that the Hirsch case had already been decided by the highest authority. As long as her husband was still held in Berlin, Martha Hirsch was permitted to visit him. He was unchanged, radiated calm and confidence and could cheer up his worried wife and encourage her. On 23rd May 1941, he was taken to the Mauthausen concentration camp in Austria. Only four weeks later, he died, on 19th June 1941. "Colitis ulcerosa" was given as the cause in the concentration camp's register of deaths. This statement seems at least doubtful. Perhaps Otto Hirsch was murdered intentionally; perhaps the harsh life in the concentration camp with its physical and mental torture was responsible for his death. A policeman was sent to inform Mrs. Hirsch of her husband's death. He performed his duty coldly as ordered without showing any kind of human sympathy: "I have to inform you", he disclosed to Martha Hirsch at the apartment door, "that your husband has died. The urn cannot be delivered to you. Heil Hitler."[92]

Cora Berliner, until 1933 a *Regierungsrätin* in the *Reich* Ministry of Economics and then one of the executive director's closest co-workers in the *Reichsvertretung*, considered Otto Hirsch its leading figure. The death of this man, who was also a good friend of hers, moved her deeply. To her friend Hans Schäffer in Sweden she wrote, ". . . You know, what he meant to us and what he meant to me personally. It is an unspeakable grief." Also in some of her later letters she eloquently expressed her sorrow. She took care of Martha Hirsch, went to see her from time to time and tried to help her emigrate.[93]

Otto Hirsch's mother had died in Stuttgart in 1939. The outrages of the November pogrom, which were totally incomprehensible to the 78-year-old woman had finally broken her will to live. At the age of 83, Otto Hirsch's father left for America in the summer of 1941. He did not arrive at his destination but died at sea on 16th August 1941. His son Theodor, accompanying him, had succeeded in keeping the news of Otto's death from him. As early as 1939, Martha Hirsch had said to friends, who were about to emigrate to Palestine:

[91]Cf. Otto D. Kulka, 'The Reichsvereinigung and the Fate of the German Jews 1938/1939–1943. Continuity or Discontinuity in German-Jewish History in the Third Reich', in *Die Juden im Nationalsozialistischen Deutschland/The Jews in Nazi Germany 1933–1943*, herausgegeben von Arnold Paucker mit Sylvia Gilchrist und Barbara Suchy, Tübingen 1986 (Schriftenreihe wissenschaftlicher Abhandlungen des Leo Baeck Instituts 45), pp. 359–361. This essay is based on work on the *Reichsvertretung* and *Reichsvereinigung* by Esriel Hildesheimer and Otto D. Kulka in Hebrew which was not accessible to the author.

[92]Marx, *loc. cit.*, p. 25; Nebinger, *op. cit.*, pp. 39 and 46 (Anmerkung von Theodor Hirsch).

[93]Hildesheimer, 'Cora Berliner', *loc. cit.*, p. 58.

"we shall die here!" She knew that their three children were safe: the son had been in the U.S. since 1938, both of the daughters in England since early 1939. Christian friends like Theodor Heuss and Robert Nebinger maintained contact with this brave woman and tried to assist her after her husband's death. Temporarily, it seemed that the gates of rescue to the West would open for her after all. She received an American visa. The *Gestapo*, however, took her passport away. She wrote a last letter to Alfred Marx in Stuttgart complaining about great loneliness. On 26th October 1942, she was deported from Berlin to the East. "Destination unknown."[94] Like Otto and Martha Hirsch most of the leading men and women of the *Reichsvereinigung* who remained in Germany, paid for their noble work in the service of the Jewish community by death in concentration or extermination camps. In St. John's Gospel, the words of Jesus have been transmitted to us: "Greater love hath no man than this, that a man lay down his life for his friends." (Ch. XV: 13) I believe that Otto and Martha Hirsch's sacrificial deaths and that of the other Jewish leaders who stayed behind with their flock in Germany cannot be expressed in any better way.

[94]Marx, *loc. cit.*, p. 25; HStAS: J 355 Bü 167; Walter Strauss (ed.), *Signs of Life. Jews from Württemberg*, Reports for the period after 1933 in letters and descriptions, New York 1982. (German transl. *Lebenszeichen. Juden aus Württemberg*, Gerlingen 1982, p. 117ff.); *Deutsches Judentum. Aufstieg und Krise*, *op. cit.*, p. 313; Heuss, *op. cit.*, p. 62.

On the Anti-Fascist Resistance of German Jews

BY ERIC BROTHERS

Considering the interest in and the relative wealth of written work on the Herbert Baum resistance group of Berlin,* it is surprising that the group's specific activities between 1933 and 1941 have hitherto received next to no attention. On the other hand research covering the years 1941 to 1942 is quite extensive owing to the existence of surviving trial records, interrogation reports and the written testimony of one surviving member of the group, Charlotte Holzer, as well as other documents available to us.[1] The partial destruction of the anti-Russian *Soviet Paradise* exhibit in the Berlin Lustgarten was indeed one of the more dramatic acts performed by a resistance group in Europe, and it was certainly the first example of resistance within Germany to be reported in the American press.[2] This courageous act deserves all the attention it has been given, but the time has also come for the Baum group's resistance work from 1933 to 1941 to be disinterred, substantiated and analysed. In addition to this, the brave young Jewish people who risked their lives in the resistance to Nazism must be treated and portrayed in individual terms. To some extent Margot Pikarski of the German Democratic Republic has dug beneath the surface to

*Of those who assisted me in my work I would like to thank here Dr. Tom Grunfeld, my professor at Empire State College, New York; Hermann Pichler, Associate Editor of the *Aufbau* who has helped me to contact people who were involved in anti-Nazi resistance. It was the late Yuri Suhl who first excited my interest by his essay in the book of studies on the resistance which he edited and translated and who supported my work. My thanks too to Dr. Arnold Paucker for his advice when preparing this essay for publication.

[1]To give but the most important studies: Bernard Mark, 'Z dziejow walki antifaszystowskiej mlodziezy Zydowskiej w Niemczech w latach 1937–1942', in *Biuletyn Zydowskiego Instiytutu Historiczenego*, No. 33, Warsaw (January/March 1960), pp. 3–45, and in Yiddish in *Bleter fun Geschichte*, No. 14, Warsaw (1961), pp. 27–63; Eliyahu Maoz, 'A Jewish Underground in Germany' (translated from Hebrew). This article was released by the Organisation Department of the World Zionist Organisation in March 1965 and included in a 'Lecturer's Kit' for the Anniversary of the Ghetto Revolts; Yuri Suhl (transl.), 'The Herbert Baum Group. Jewish Resistance in Germany in the Years 1937–1942' (English version of Bernard Mark's Yiddish essay), in Yuri Suhl (ed.), *They Fought Back. The Story of the Jewish Resistance in Nazi Europe*, New York 1967, [2]1976, pp. 55–68; Helmut Eschwege, 'Resistance of German Jews against the Nazi Regime', in *LBI Year Book XV* (1970), pp. 143–180; Lucien Steinberg, 'The Herbert Baum Campaign', in *Not as a Lamb. The Jews Against Hitler*, London 1974 (in French, 1970), pp. 26–53; Wolfgang Wippermann, *Die Berliner Gruppe Baum und der jüdische Widerstand*, Berlin 1981; Esriel Hildesheimer, *The Central Organization of the German Jews in the Years 1933–1945* (in Hebrew, soon to appear in English), Jerusalem 1982, pp. 286–299; Konrad Kwiet and Helmut Eschwege, 'Die Herbert-Baum-Gruppe', in their book *Selbstbehauptung und Widerstand. Deutsche Juden im Kampf um Existenz und Menschenwürde 1933–1945*, Hamburg 1984, pp. 114–139; Wolfgang Scheffler, 'Der Brandanschlag im Berliner Lustgarten im Mai 1942 und seine Folgen', in *Jahrbuch des Landesarchivs Berlin*, Berlin 1984, pp. 91–118.

[2]George Axelsson, 'Opposition Seen Within Germany', *The New York Times*, 18th June 1942, p. 4; 'Der Amoklauf beginnt', *Aufbau*, 19th June 1942, p. 1.

present relevant facts concerning anti-fascism during the 1930s.[3] Her work places Herbert Baum and his comrades in the midst of the different groups and individuals, Jews and non-Jews, who engaged in active resistance in Berlin, mostly under the direction and supervision of the *Kommunistische Partei Deutschlands* (KPD). Margot Pikarski does not promote the Baum group as Jewish, but the persecution of Jews, membership in Jewish and Zionist youth groups, and aspects of Jewish descent and heritage are, however, covered in her work. There are many questions to be asked when researching German-Jewish resistance: When did a strong militant anti-fascist attitude develop in the minds of these young Jews? What was their social and economic background? Was their decision to become active anti-Nazis an individual, moral act, or was it politically or socially motivated? What was the extent of Jewish resistance activities as early as 1933, almost immediately after the *Machtübernahme*? There are many more questions and countless problems one encounters in this type of research. Konrad Kwiet, to whom, together with Helmut Eschwege, we owe one of two most recent detailed accounts of the Baum group,[4] wrote in 1979:

> "All resistance research faces the basic problem that, since resistance could only exist under conditions of illegality and in a conspiratorial way, any production and preservation of records of resistance activities which had been carried out was contrary to the interests of the safety of the resistance fighters."[5]

The members of the Baum group did not keep diaries, or send letters to each other, nor, of course, did they keep samples of the leaflets and posters they produced in the underground. Thus the materials needed in order to document and analyse effectively the events of 1933 to 1941 simply do not exist. In this case does the historian ignore the years which lack this type of primary source? He does not, and the events, when reconstructed, are based on the existing documents, which are in this case the extant records of the trials of the resisters. But perusal of this material must be tempered with the knowledge of who the authors of these documents were – Nazi civil servants and German bureaucrats. There must be a way of balancing the decidedly slanted view of the instruments of the Nazi rulers against the more complete story of people who for the most part were killed in 1942 and 1943. To some extent this information exists in the testimony of Charlotte Holzer, but as she joined Herbert Baum only in 1939 she cannot provide data on the first six years of the group's development.[6] However there is a way to get a more complete picture of the Baum group's actual situation and this is through the use of oral history and further written testimony.

Through the use of direct personal interviews and, if that is physically impossible, through written depositions, one can discover much previously unknown information on the Baum group and one can gain an insight into the

[3]Margot Pikarski, *Jugend im Berliner Widerstand. Herbert Baum und Kampfgefährten*, Berlin (East) 1978, [2]1984.

[4]Kwiet/Eschwege, *Selbstbehauptung und Widerstand, op. cit.*, pp. 114–139.

[5]Konrad Kwiet, 'Problems of Jewish Resistance Historiography', in *LBI Year Book XXIV* (1979), p. 51.

[6]Charlotte Holzer deposited her testimony at Yad Vashem in 1963. Another version, written by her *circa* 1946, is in the author's possession.

past which would otherwise remain hidden. But who can still be contacted? As we have said, most of the group members were killed by the Nazis in 1942 or 1943, and the only documented survivors – Charlotte and Richard Holzer and Rita Zocher (née Meyer) – have died in the last ten years.[7] Yet the assumption that these were the only survivors has proved not to be true. There are former members of the Baum group and relatives, friends and co-workers of these people alive today who are willing to tell their story to those willing to listen. But how reliable are such "witnesses"? Konrad Kwiet observes that "the declarations of the anti-fascists themselves are only fragmentary" and then claims that further "information was collected with the aid of correspondence and 'oral history'". Yet he states: "These revealed hardly any concrete certifiable dates or facts."[8] Now I feel that here Kwiet writes off potential sources of valuable data that could help fill the gaps of the Baum group story. I differ from Kwiet's evaluation of this "oral history". To me the survivors of the Baum group are living, breathing "documents", which the historian cannot ignore but must probe and question. An example of such a reliable source is Alfred Eisenstadter (formerly Eisenstädter), whose name appears in Charlotte Holzer's testimony.[9] His name also figures misspelled as "Eisenblätter" in a trial document dated 21st May 1943.[10] It is extremely likely that the name was misspelled on purpose during interrogation in an attempt to protect Eisenstadter's father, who was resettled to the East during the latter part of 1941.[11] Eisenstadter has been cooperating fully in my search for further information. Charlotte Holzer stated in her testimony that in 1936–1937 the KPD had resorted to the strategy of removing Jews from its general underground movement and had them operate in the legal Jewish youth movements[12] (which had been officially recognised by the Nazi authorities).* Eisenstadter corroborates Charlotte Holzer's testimony by describing his own activities. In the summer of 1936 he was planning a vacation in Prague; Herbert Baum asked him to get in touch with someone there to see "what direction to take".[13] Alfred met his contact, as arranged in a spot where they could be unobserved, who told him:

> "Baum must not do anything that is illegal. We have suffered too many losses. Many anti-fascists have been killed or put in concentration camps in the last three years. It has been

[7]Richard Holzer died in 1975 and Charlotte Holzer in 1980; see: Pikarski, *Jugend*, *op. cit.*, pp. 157, 159. Rita Zocher died in 1983; information obtained in signed letter (L.S.) from P. Kirchner, E. Berlin, dated 11th January 1985.

[8]Kwiet, 'Problems', *loc. cit.*, p. 51.

[9]Even though Alfred Eisenstadter's name appears in Charlotte Holzer's Yad Vashem testimony and Maoz's 'A Jewish Underground in Germany', *loc. cit.*, p. 12, he has been mentioned only once since then as a Baum group member in Kwiet/Eschwege, *Selbstbehauptung und Widerstand*, *op. cit.*, p. 117.

[10]Document No. 10 J 328/43 g (21st May 1943), p. 5, Berlin Document Center.

[11]Alfred Eisenstadter and his mother received their American visas in early 1941.

[12]Arnold Paucker and Lucien Steinberg, 'Some Notes on Resistance', in *LBI Year Book XVI* (1971), p. 240.

*On the Jewish youth organisations in general under Nazi rule see the essay by Chaim Schatzker 'The Jewish Youth Movement in Germany in the Holocaust Period (I). Youth in Confrontation with a New Reality', in this volume of the Year Book – (Ed.).

[13]All dialogue set in quotes has been remembered and reconstructed by Baum group survivors, not by the author.

> decided that Communists are to work through legal German organisations. All the Jews in Baum's circle must get into legitimate Jewish groups."

He also told Alfred that no overt act of any kind was to be performed and absolutely nothing was to be published. This directive seems to have come from the exiled KPD, which was based in Prague. Eisenstadter was never told by Baum that he was meeting representatives of the KPD, but he never asked Herbert about what actual connections he had with the Communists: it was however generally assumed by his adherents that Baum was a high ranking figure in the *Kommunistischer Jugendverband Deutschlands* (KJVD).[14] Baum followed every point of the directive, which suggests that his group was indeed under the umbrella of the exiled KPD. The statements made to Alfred in Prague imply that Baum was, indeed, extremely active in overt anti-fascist resistance, which would contradict the theory ". . . that this Jewish Communist group . . . did not take up the anti-fascist resistance struggle until after the attack on the Soviet Union . . ."[15]

A specific resistance act for instance in which Herbert Baum participated took place on the 11th of July 1934. Explosives with detonators were contrived by the anti-fascist underground and placed in eight cans. A metal plate covered the explosive material and on top of the plate leaflets were stuffed. These cans were placed on rooftops. An hour later they blew up and scattered the leaflets onto the streets; their slogan read: 'Today the Red Army marches in Red Square – Tomorrow the workers' battalions will march in Socialist Berlin!'[16] I would vouch for my source; this action can definitely be considered as proof that Herbert Baum was engaged in clandestine anti-fascist propaganda a good seven years before the German invasion of Russia.

Another action can further attest to the Baum group's activities well before the outbreak of the Second World War. Alfred Eisenstadter, in reaction to the Nazi rape of Czechoslovakia in March 1939, was concerned with disseminating information in Berlin about this criminal act on the part of the Germans. He wrote a rough draft of a leaflet on the invasion and brought it to a group meeting. He told Baum and the others that "waiting for directives was useless – the time to act is now". Herbert agreed, possibly because he realised that since Prague was under German occupation, the exiled KPD was no longer operational. Baum, Eisenstadter, Felix Heymann and a few others rewrote the original draft and the leaflet was prepared for printing. They managed to manufacture between 500–1,000 copies on a primitive machine which Herbert kept hidden in the basement of his block of flats. About ten people went on this action; among the pairs involved were Alfred and Felix, and Herbert and Marianne Baum. They constructed small catapults which worked on the flat. At one end there was a punctured tin can filled with water; the water would drip out slowly. The leaflets were to be placed on the other end. When the water level became lower, the weight of the paper would exert sufficient pressure on

[14]Information obtained in interviews with Alfred Eisenstadter, New York, on 28th January, 7th June, and 5th October 1985.

[15]Kwiet, 'Problems', *loc. cit.*, p. 53.

[16]Information obtained in L.S. from anonymous source dated 23rd November 1985.

the catapults to propel the leaflets and scatter them on the street. These devices were to be secured on window sills. Alfred, Felix and the others spent a long time searching for suitable buildings with staircase windows facing the street and found quite a few of them on the Alexanderplatz. Alfred mounted the catapults while Felix acted as the lookout. The action went smoothly – no one was caught – and hundreds of these leaflets littered the streets of Berlin giving the anti-fascist (i.e. the truthful) version of the Nazi occupation of Czechoslovakia.[17]

Without the use of such participant observers the details of how Herbert Baum received directives from the Prague-based KPD, which confirm and expand upon Charlotte Holzer's testimony, could not possibly be established. The factual details of resistance would never come to light without employing either this type of oral history or knowledge gained from written testimony. The new material obtained sheds further light on the Baum group's motives, dedication and political bent. German-Jewish resistance historiography should accept that oral history is a useful tool in the collection of new information and the confirmation of existing data. (And after all, Jewish historiography has fully accepted these methods when retracing the camouflaged anti-Nazi propaganda battle waged by the *Centralverein deutscher Staatsbürger jüdischen Glaubens* for several years in the last phase of the Weimar Republic.)[18]

Yet a further example of using oral history to dig beneath the surface of material in existing documentation may be noted here. In a document of the year 1943 there is mention that in September of 1939 Felix Heymann had attempted to cross the border into Denmark illegally.[19] He was caught and placed in "protective custody" until the end of the year. But why did Heymann wait until late in 1939 to try to escape from Nazi Germany? The reason is not given in the existing documents. Alfred Eisenstadter, who was arrested with Felix Heymann, provides the answer. There was an unwritten agreement among the older group members that no one was to leave the country. They honestly felt that it was their duty as anti-fascists to remain in Germany and that by continuing resistance they could help in putting an end to National Socialism.[20] But that was before the 1938 *Kristallnacht*. At the very next group meeting within days of the November pogrom, about the middle of the month, Herbert Baum reversed his decision about staying in Germany. "As Jews we are too exposed and limited in what we can do", he said, "you should all try to

[17]Information obtained in interviews with Alfred Eisenstadter on 28th January, 7th June, and 5th October 1985.

[18]See Arnold Paucker, 'Kampf gegen den Nationalsozialismus', in his book *Der jüdische Abwehrkampf gegen Antisemitismus und Nationalsozialismus in den letzten Jahren der Weimarer Republik*, Hamburg 1968, [2]1969, pp. 110–128.

[19]Document No. 10 J 328/43 g (no date), p. 7; No. 10 J 328/43 g (second set of documents in series dated 21st May 1943), p. 3. Berlin Document Center; No. 10 J 328/4 g (21st May 1943), p. 3, Yad Vashem.

[20]The fact that Herbert Baum's parents emigrated to South America (L.S. from E. Deutsch-Verlardo, London, dated 15th April 1986) and group member Heinz Birnbaum's mother and sister emigrated to London c. 1938 (information in statements to the author by Alfred Eisenstadter and in an interview with E. Lewinsky-Arndt, Rochester, N.Y., on 18th April 1985) should add credibility to this statement.

emigrate." As the situation became worse for the Jews, Alfred and Felix devised a plan. They decided to board a train taking them to a spot a few miles from the Danish border and try walking across to freedom. They hiked through a forest and mistakenly assumed they were in Denmark, but were arrested and placed in "protective custody" in Flensburg prison. In the spring of 1940 Alfred received an official communication which read: "You are hereby ordered to be transported to Buchenwald concentration camp." But a week or so later Alfred and Felix were released from prison. Herbert Baum had used some of his Zionist connections to help them on condition that they would board a ship in Romania bound for Palestine.[21] This event in the history of the Baum group would have remained unknown without Alfred Eisenstadter's testimony. It shows that Baum and the others were confident of an eventual victory over Nazism until the November pogroms. From then they shared the general view of the Jewish community that the time to leave had come. Baum is shown to have had compassion for his friends' plight and that he had apparently sufficient pull with certain Zionist functionaries to manage to get them out of prison, provided that their immediate emigration was assured; in Alfred's case he saved him from almost certain death in Buchenwald.

Another surviving Baum group member is Ellen Compart. Born in the Prenzlauer Berg district of Berlin in 1920, she joined the *Bund deutsch-jüdischer Jugend* (B.d.j.J. or *Ring*) in 1933 and remained a member of this youth movement until it was outlawed with the remaining Jewish youth organisations in 1938. Ellen Compart was involved in resistance work from 1933 until 1942, when she went underground shortly after her close friend, and another member of the group, Hella Hirsch, was arrested at the I. G. Farben plant where they were both slave labourers. Ellen's life was saved by Willi May, a non-Jewish resistance fighter who worked with an anti-fascist group which was connected with the Baum group. Ellen Compart lived with May and his family under the guise of being May's sister-in-law until shortly before Berlin was liberated by the Red Army.[22]

Alfred Eisenstadter maintains that the Baum group was a two-tiered organisation; the older group (the Baums, the Kochmanns, Eisenstadter, Heymann and others) met privately, and the younger group were members of the B.d.j.J. whose main contact was Walter Sack.[23] Ellen Compart was in the younger group.[24] She was fully aware of the clandestine work from early on in the Hitler regime, but had no knowledge of Baum's, Sack's and other people's Communist Party connections.

The first people in charge of these members of the *Bund deutsch-jüdischer Jugend* were Hans Cassel, Rudi Barta and Walter Fuchs. Meetings were held in

[21]Information obtained in interviews with Alfred Eisenstadter on 28th January, 7th June, and 5th October 1985.

[22]Information obtained in statements made to the author by Ellen Compart, Boca Raton, Florida.

[23]Information obtained in an interview with Alfred Eisenstadter on 28th January 1985.

[24]It should be noted that there was a wide gap in the group members' ages in 1933. At that time Herbert Baum was twenty-one and Ellen Compart only thirteen. The two-tiered system broke down after the *Kristallnacht*, when the *Ring* was banned. Also, as the younger members of the B.d.j.J. grew up, they assumed leadership roles in the resistance.

buildings owned by the Jewish community on Choriner Strasse, Oranienburger Strasse and Rykestrasse. A typical discussion at a group meeting led by Rudi Barta followed these lines:

> "If we want a better world we must never cease to search, never cease to learn, never be afraid to revise or moderate – and must be prepared to do so over and over again. We must learn to understand ourselves and others in order to reach the common goal – the end of Hitler's *Reich.*"

Ellen Compart and the others were made aware of the fact that there were many such small groups of anti-fascists in Berlin and throughout Germany. It was suggested that people should visit another group if invited, but they were told never to reveal any names or details about other groups. Anyone who said "no" to the regime was a potential friend. It did not matter much if their political philosophy differed, for only in unity could there be strength. Contact between groups was through a few individuals who used code names; this was for everyone's protection to lessen the risk of revealing information under pressure or torture.[25]

On the topic of oral history and written testimony, Konrad Kwiet found: "What the few survivors were still able to give in the way of evidence after three decades were memories and experiences of their own battle for survival, descriptions of their state of mind at that time and the motivation of their own anti-fascism."[26] In response to this observation I would offer what amounts to a reconstruction of a group meeting of the *Bund deutsch-jüdischer Jugend* from about 1936 led by Walter Sack[27] and Ari Steinbach based on testimony by Ellen Compart. This meeting shows how young anti-fascist Germans were reacting to and dealing with Nazism, how they could lose their grip on the reality of the situation – and it also displays much muddled thinking. One must furthermore keep in mind that such discussions and soul-searching were by no means uncommon in the Jewish youth movement in Germany.

Ellen Compart remembers that Sack was the practical organiser and that Steinbach was the creative, inspirational force. The theme of the meeting was how to convince, relate to, influence and prepare younger members for the years ahead. Initially they talked about the authoritarian educational system that prevailed in Germany at the time.

> "Ari told the group about an English boarding school where there were no grades and the students developed their own study programmes. Some spoke of the schools they were attending or had attended. A young woman named Thea Lindemann, who had been to the *Karl-Marx-Schule* until it was closed down by the Nazis in 1933, proposed the following: 'It is important to teach more than the basic academic subjects. We have to teach about living and about society, the social contract we all have with one another. But most of all we have to be taught how to create alternatives.' Harry Oschinski, a young man with a burning desire to study medicine, spoke next, 'We have all ingested a lot of rubbish and have to unlearn it – we must be de-schooled.' 'Give me specifics', demanded Walter Sack, 'what do we have to free ourselves from? If I put this waste paper basket in the centre here, what

[25]Information obtained in a testimony by Ellen Compart, dated 28th June 1985.
[26]Kwiet, 'Problems', *loc. cit.*, p. 51.
[27]Walter Sack was considered as important as Herbert Baum to the resistance movement in Berlin. Information obtained in statements made to the author by Alfred Eisenstadter.

"rubbish" would you want to throw into it?' The answers came, fast and furious, from around the room. 'Competitiveness', 'Tradition', 'Convention', 'Nationalism', 'Hypocrisy'. 'They are all holding us back – off with the straight jacket!', declared Harry. 'Very good', said Ari Steinbach, 'but do we have new values to replace them with so that the web will hold together? Do we have a premise to build on – is the foundation firm in our minds?' 'Why don't we empty the basket and see what we would throw in for a new way of looking at things', Walter suggested. Harry was the first to respond: 'Birth control for everyone who wants and needs it.' Ismar Zöllner[28] said: 'Equality regardless of achievement. Equal opportunity will raise the quality of life for everyone, which will even out the difference in the contributions one is able to make.' Eva Rumjanek, a young singer-guitarist, said: 'For happiness and fulfilment, stress the development of creativity in everyone.' A young artist named Thomas Landau added: 'Teach classes in creativity from kindergarten onwards so that students can improvise and solve problems on their own. They must not be afraid of the unknown and must make great strides instead of moving one little step at a time.' 'Yes', Ismar responded, 'we have to take risks in our thinking and in relationships with other people and also learn to trust and be trustworthy.' Etta, who worked with children, volunteered: 'From early on teach responsibility for actions and behaviour, and how to accept and deal with any consequences. Do not punish – give incentives for doing what is good for everyone. Reinforce this and no punishment will be necessary. In time we may no longer need prisons. Cooperation over competition, a winner to winner instead of winner over loser situation. We could be free and soar together, grow together.' Walter stopped everything right then and there: 'Utopian fantasies – the opium of the oppressed . . . !' He let this sink in before he began to speak again. 'We must learn and teach defiance. In spirit. In thought. In action. Today – not tomorrow. The time is now. If you have ideas for the future, implement them now wherever you can.' Ari had been quiet for a while and found this to be the right moment to make his point: 'But what about the other opium? The "opium of the masses", as Karl Marx called it. We forget about religion. But who can stand up without looking over his shoulder and proclaim: "I have no religion. I am a complete atheist. God has no meaning for me?"' The room grew silent as he spoke and no one ventured a response. Ari the philosopher said nothing else. He sat down at the piano and played with sadness and joy simultaneously, which fitted both his mood and personality."[29]

Through the use of such recollections, one can sense what it was like to be a young member of the Baum group in 1936. No group members wrote down what was said during these discussion groups. But we can recreate what these oppressed teenagers were thinking and how important their ideals and ideas were to them. In the Baum group their idealism was an integral aspect of their need and desire to be active in the resistance. We now know how people like Walter Sack and Ari Steinbach motivated their resistance activities and gave direction to their lives, as well as showing these young people that others actually did care about them. Sack and Steinbach helped them to have a life filled with culture. "Illegal" books retained from the Weimar Republic were read and discussed, abstract concepts were analysed, music was played, banned Socialist songs were sung. Many of these young Jews had been expelled from school by the National Socialists, but Sack and the others were giving them much more than they could get out of any Berlin classroom. The memories of the survivors help to show us the members of the Baum group as ordinary human beings, not just as mere names inscribed on a monument honouring the

[28]Ismar Zöllner and Walter Sack worked as apprentice blacksmiths in Sack's father's business, which was attached to his apartment on Skalitzer Strasse. It was there that Eisenstadter met them both c. 1935. Zöllner later led a group in the *Ring*. He emigrated to Chile in 1939. Information obtained in statements made to the author by Alfred Eisenstadter.

[29]The group meeting has been reconstructed in a testimony provided by Ellen Compart, dated 28th June 1985.

resistance or as figures in Nazi trial records. It can also give us some clues as to why they were willing to risk their lives in the hope that Germany would be freed from Hitler's stranglehold.

In addition to their weekly meetings, or *Heimabende*, which carry so many features that were typical to all Jewish youth movements, there were numerous resistance actions performed by the group which distinguished them. Let us single out here one example of their anti-Nazi propaganda: one- and two-sentence leaflets devised by the group, probably in 1936. Walter Sack, Ari Steinbach, Thomas Landau, Ellen Compart and others produced such leaflets in Walter's father's workshop late at night. Sack had procured the originals from a friend unknown to the others. The group duplicated the handbills on a type multiplier with a wax plate or on an old printing press. Sometimes Ari brought along political cartoons from pre-Hitler days to reproduce and distribute. Walter Sack saw to it that the leaflets were never stored – they were always dispersed immediately. Each action was thoroughly planned with precautionary briefings repeated many times. Various escape routes were prepared well in advance. People usually worked in pairs – one placed the leaflet while the other would be on the lookout. Everyone took turns at distributing the material; it was carefully placed in telephone booths, post boxes and underground stations. The handbills were also left on park benches and under church doors and windshield wipers. Here are some slogans of such 1936 leaflets:

Read and Pass On

1) Say NO every way you
can. Say NO to the
ruin of Germany.

2) Adolf,
Germany's gravedigger.

3) Be a good citizen –
Think for yourself.

4) Love your country,
think for yourself.
A good German
is not afraid
to say No. [30]

In order to show Herbert Baum's dedicated anti-fascism also from before 1933, during the last years of the Weimar Republic, we propose to pay some attention to the part he played in the *Deutsch-Jüdische Jugend-Gemeinschaft*

[30] Information obtained from Ellen Compart in the above testimony. The German slogans of 'Lesen und weitergeben' leaflets are rough translations into English. Dr. Arnold Paucker remembers vividly one such leaflet 'Hitler, Deutschlands Totengräber' from his last weeks in Germany, September/October 1936 (to the author, 8th September 1986).

(DJJG), which he joined in 1927. This youth movement was comprised of assimilated German-Jewish boys and girls, which like other youth groups engaged in hikes in the forest, Jewish cultural events and weekly discussions led by an assigned group leader. In 1929 Herbert was made a group leader of about 15–20 eleven year-old boys. Norbert Wollheim (later a functionary in the *Reichsvereinigung der Juden in Deutschland*) remembers that Baum analysed information differently from other group leaders by using Communist theory when addressing himself to the social, political and religious issues of the day.[31] But Baum had to be subtle about this because, after all, he was acting within a Jewish youth movement.

In 1931 Herbert Baum made his ideological, but not cultural, break with Judaism and joined the Communist youth organisation, the KJVD. Yet he continued to adhere to the DJJG for a time after joining the Communists. He led the weekly meetings in different buildings owned by the Berlin Jewish community until 1931, when the organisation was disbanded. However, after the dissolution of the DJJG he kept his own Jewish group together and continued the meetings in his apartment on Köpenikerstrasse. Herbert Ballhorn, one of Baum's young *Pimpfe* (scouts) at the time, writes: "My memory of Herbert Baum is that of a wonderfully warm and fair-minded teacher-leader who encouraged and nurtured young kids to become adults . . . he was a born leader." Baum's girlfriend and later wife, Marianne Cohn, together with him led the meetings and hiking trips. Once the group was freed from the somewhat restraining influences of the DJJG, Herbert accelerated the Communist education and indoctrination of those in his charge.

On Sunday afternoons Baum arranged for his group to meet members of the Communist youth organisation *Rote Falken*. In the beginning these gatherings were rather strained; the Jewish boys came from middle-class or lower middle-class families while the young Communists belonged to the Berlin proletariat. Ballhorn remembers that the Jews dressed better and employed a somewhat more polished and educated German than their left-wing comrades, which tended to magnify the differences between them. On the other hand, the rampant antisemitism of the time made these young Jews wary of this or any other Gentile group. There were many barriers which Baum needed to break down if he wanted to make these two groups cohesive. He achieved the first step by eliminating the Jewish aspects of his group, which put them on an equal ideological footing with the Communists. Ballhorn recalls: "It seemed to me that our handful of Jewish boys were better equipped and versed in Socialist theory than the *Rote Falken* themselves. Herbert had done a good job on us."

The initial problems faded away after a few meetings as individual friendships between Jews and Communists were formed and they found a

[31]Information obtained in statements made to the author by Norbert Wollheim. Wollheim is quoted in Leonard Baker, *Days of Sorrow and Pain. Leo Baeck and the Berlin Jews*, New York–London 1978, from an interview of 1975. Here Wollheim reflects the *Reichsvereinigung* leadership's concern about the repercussions of the Lustgarten action on the remnants of the Jewish community in Berlin. Wollheim had been asked to use his former contacts to dissuade the Baum group from resistance actions.

"common language"; their talks stressed the concepts of Solidarity, Brotherhood and Class Struggle. On a small scale Herbert Baum felt he had here reached his goal of ending antisemitism and antagonisms and brought about total equality by applying Socialism.

War games were a frequent pastime of the young in Weimar Germany and of course *de rigueur* in the Nazi and Communist movements. Baum used them to speed up interaction between the two groups. One game took place in late 1932 in the Grunewald forest outside Berlin; after a picnic and political talk the boys were divided into "Red" and "Brown" groups. Ballhorn recalls: "Darkness was falling and I was crawling towards the 'enemy' alone, undetected and from an unexpected angle. By doing that I earned some extra points. At the end of the game Herbert praised me for it. I felt very proud . . ."

At the next meeting after Hitler had become Chancellor, Baum selected a few boys, including Ballhorn, to either distribute or sell the Communist Party newspaper, *Die Rote Fahne*, which had immediately been banned by the Nazis.[32]

Herbert Baum's strong anti-fascist stance in the late 1920s has been demonstrated here clearly. He worked as hard as possible – and as a convinced Communist of course – to warn people of the dangers of German fascism and Nazism well before Hitler took power in 1933. Baum's preparation for resistance was developed over a number of years and his actual – and soon to become clandestine – anti-Nazi work began only a few days after the inception of the Third *Reich*.

There have been many attempts to categorise Baum and his comrades; historians have called them either a Jewish, Communist, or Jewish-Communist group. When I asked Alfred Eisenstadter to describe what kind of group it was, he said it was an anti-fascist group comprised of Communists and fellow-travellers.[33] Ellen Compart stated that the group felt equal solidarity with Jews and other persecuted Germans.[34]

The activities and political bent of the group against the background of the antisemitic laws of the Nazi regime help to give us a clear picture of the group's changing focus over the years. Herbert Baum was a dedicated Communist who, however, never lost sight of his own Jewish heritage or the plight of German Jewry, and used his radical politics to try to educate all Jews and non-Jews with whom he came into contact. His basic policy was an adherence to the concept of Jewish assimilation joined to a united resistance front composed of left-wing Jews and non-Jews. His leadership ability is confirmed by the fact that he was a district leader in the KJVD from about 1932 to 1936 and a group leader in the DJJG and later in the B.d.j.J. (*Ring*). Since Baum had joined the Communist youth movement in 1931, it is only natural that the anti-fascist group which he had formed earlier on, in the late 1920s, and which included Marianne Cohn, Martin Kochmann, Sala Rosenbaum (later Kochmann) and Rita Resnik (later

[32]Information obtained in L.S. from Herbert Ballhorn, Moranga, Calif., dated 23rd November and 11th December 1984, 22nd January, 5th February, April and 22nd June 1985.
[33]Information obtained in statements made to the author by Alfred Eisenstadter.
[34]Information obtained in statements made to the author by Ellen Compart.

Meyer),[35] was Jewish. They all followed Baum's political example and joined the KJVD. Baum regularly distributed the *Rote Fahne* and the KJVD's *Junge Garde* organ after the KPD was banned in 1933. The two-tiered organisational structure of the Baum group of about 1935 as described by Alfred Eisenstadter would appear to us as a Communist Party in microcosm with a "central committee" consisting of the Baums, Kochmanns, Eisenstadter, Heymann and others, with Walter Sack as liaison between the above group and the unwitting "party members" in the *Ring*. The act of resistance Baum organised in July 1934, which is mentioned earlier in this essay, was performed with both Jewish and non-Jewish KJVD members. The fact that Herbert Baum followed the directives of the Prague-based KPD in exile to the letter also displays his total commitment to Communism. Thus it can be claimed that the Baum group was a Communist body with strong ties to the KPD-inspired and -led resistance movement throughout Germany. However, since Baum and the others were Jewish, their activities take on a different hue. The view can be put forward that the group's activities do not fall under the category of "Jewish" resistance. Their work was not based on Jewish religious or national grounds, but on the political and moral basis of Communism and anti-fascism. The Baum group's activities in the early 1930s could be called, if we like, the Communist resistance of Germans of Jewish heritage. But since in its later years the group consisted of a mixture of Communists, Socialists, Zionists,[36] and some practising Jews as well, their overall activities can certainly be defined as the anti-fascist resistance of German Jews.

It is difficult to document the group's work after the outbreak of the Second World War. Dedicated Communist that he was, Herbert Baum was set adrift after losing his official contacts in Prague in 1939. The Nazi-Soviet non-aggression pact was also a blow to Baum and the others. Alfred Eisenstadter recalls that most of the older group members condemned the signing of the pact; Herbert Baum was the only one to justify it, and wholeheartedly at that. Eisenstadter, a Socialist and Communist sympathiser up until that time, made his ideological break from Communism there and then. Eisenstadter did not spend much time in Berlin after 1939. He was in prison with Felix Heymann for half a year, and worked on farms, in labour camps and as a slave labourer at Siemens for a short time before leaving for the United States in January of 1941.

[35]Rita Resnik-Meyer's testimony is deposited at Yad Vashem under the name Rita Zocher.

[36]They had, of course, belonged to the dissolved Zionist-Socialist youth movements such as the *Hashomer Hazair*,* which, during the period of legality, generally held the belief that, while one sympathised with the anti-fascist struggle of the German working class, the task of young Jews was not to participate in it but to go to Palestine and build Socialism in the Jewish homeland. Yet there were individual exceptions when some members did involve themselves in occasional resistance activities – and these young people were most unlikely to have been covert Communists. Dr. Paucker, formerly of the *Werkleute*, recollects sporadic distribution of anti-Nazi leaflets and even a case of sabotage in the aircraft industry at the outset of the Spanish Civil War with which some Jewish youth were linked (to the author, 8th September 1986). With the outbreak of the war, deportations and mass extermination, Jewish attitudes to resistance were, of course, changing.

* On the *Hashomer Hazair* and its attitude to resistance see the essay by Jehuda Reinharz, 'Hashomer Hazair in Germany (II); Under the Shadow of the Swastika, 1933–1938', in this volume of the Year Book, especially pp. 216–221 – (Ed.).

At a farewell gathering for Alfred at Sala Kochmann's home, Herbert Baum told him: "Good for you – you are getting out!" Sala asked Alfred to contact a relative of hers in America, but Herbert said: "Do not do anything for me." Eisenstadter remembers feeling that Baum would have remained in Berlin even if he had been offered an American visa.[37]

Ellen Compart, as we saw, remained in Berlin – underground from 1942 until 1945 – and is therefore in a position to provide some information about resistance shortly before the *Soviet Paradise* action, which is not presented in detail in this essay as it has been described more than once elsewhere. Based on her information it seems that the overall group fragmented into smaller groups after the *Kristallnacht*, and into even smaller cells once the remaining Berlin Jews were sent into forced labour for the munitions industry. The period from 1941 until the arrest and execution of the group has been well documented by Helmut Eschwege, Konrad Kwiet, Margot Pikarski, Wolfgang Scheffler, Ber Mark and others. However, it is the objective of the present author to add to this more data on actual resistance acts and the structure of the various groups operating in liaison with Herbert Baum.

One such action of which we have evidence and which took place in April 1942 should be mentioned here. The organisers of the act were "Ede" and "Unku",[38] young Jews who led a splinter group consisting of Baum group members. Helmut Neumann, Ellen Compart, Ursula Ehrlich, Lothar Salinger, Hella Hirsch, Felix Heymann, Siegbert Rotholz, Lotte Jastrow, Ede, and his girl friend met at Unku's apartment. The object was to cover all of Berlin with the slogan, "No to Hitler's Suicidal Politics! No! No! No!" Unku mentioned a part of town which he then pointed out on a map. He told the group: "If there is enough time to spell out the sentence, do so. If not, then write, 'No! No! No!' Paint on everything in reach. Use whatever paint, chalk, wax crayon you can get hold of. Anything that will make a line or form a letter. We want Berlin covered in one night!"

Ways to avoid capture were discussed. The group was told to wear dark clothing and to work in pairs – one to write or paint the slogans while the other was to act as lookout. The black-out in Berlin would help to cover the action. Helmut Neumann, always ready to laugh or joke in even the most dangerous situations, declared: "We *must* appear harmless. Go as a couple and if anyone walks by, take cover – or disappear into the nearest building – or just leave. Put your paint can under the girl's coat, then hug and kiss."

Altogether there were at least ten people involved – none of whom was caught. The next day the slogans were to be seen everywhere; householders, shopkeepers and street sweepers were busy cleaning up the mess. People either shook their heads or smiled when they saw the slogan. The group – young Jews in the Berlin of 1942! – was in an elated mood when they met Willi May, the non-Jewish resistance fighter who belonged to both a cell in a Siemens plant and the Ede and Unku group, who asked, "How much good did it do?" The

[37]Information obtained in statements made to the author by Alfred Eisenstadter.
[38]These names are nicknames.

young people spoke for a while and agreed that sowing discontent and protest was bound, eventually, to have an effect. "Its impact and value cannot be measured, but every show of defiance brings us a step closer", said Ellen Compart.[39]

The present essay represents only a small percentage of the data this author has been able to gather through the use of oral history and the collection of written testimony. Since the material these people have provided dates back to the 1930s and 1940s, the value of it will be realised when the survivors are no longer with us. Thus an important duty of resistance historians is to meet all the remaining Baum group members, their families and comrades, and record all their personal and resistance experiences for future generations of scholars and students. Using the methodology employed in this essay – and extending it to other Jewish resistance groups which existed –[40] documents which have been preserved can be analysed in greater depth and the complete story of Herbert Baum and his comrades, who deserve a place in German resistance history alongside the *Weisse Rose*, will one day be told in full – together with that of Jewish anti-Nazi activity in general, which has been greatly underestimated.[41]

Once these oral histories are stored in the archives of the Federal Republic of Germany, the German Democratic Republic, Israel, England and the United States, supplementary data will be available to stimulate much further research into the anti-fascist resistance of German Jews.

[39]Information obtained in a testimony by Ellen Compart, dated 28th June 1985.

[40]To give one example, our knowledge of a small Jewish non-Communist resistance group led by Eva Mamlok stems entirely from the testimony of the sole survivor, Inge Berner (Inge Gerson), New York. Cf. Paucker/ Steinberg, 'Some Notes on Resistance', *loc. cit.*, pp. 241–242.

[41]Cf. Arnold Paucker, 'Jewish Self-Defence', in *Die Juden im Nationalsozialistischen Deutschland/The Jews in Nazi Germany 1933–1943*, herausgegeben von Arnold Paucker mit Sylvia Gilchrist und Barbara Suchy, Tübingen 1986 (Schriftenreihe wissenschaftlicher Abhandlungen des Leo Baeck Instituts 45), p. 62.

Far West/Far East

Baron de Hirsch, The Jewish Colonization Association and Canada

BY KENNEE SWITZER-RAKOS

I

Towards the end of the nineteenth century, Jews from Russia and Eastern Europe flooded into the West in unprecedented numbers: between 1881 and the First World War, more than two million Jews were to settle in the United States, Canada, the Argentine, and in the towns and cities along their paths of migration.[1] These decades were ones of great suffering for the four million Jews confined within the Pale of Settlement.[2] The assassination of Tsar Alexander II, on 1st March, 1881, heralded an era of repressive autocracy throughout Russia, and it was during the reign of Tsar Alexander III that antisemitism was transformed into organised violence against Jews; two hundred and fifty pogroms erupted during 1881 and the first wave of pogroms to be directed against the Jews in the Ukraine, White Russia, Besserabia, and Poland during the years before the First World War. However, the pogroms were only one manifestation of renewed government persecution; in May 1881, a campaign of harassment was instituted against all Jews living outside the Pale of Settlement. They were required to present documentation proving their right of residence and only those with the most watertight permission were allowed to remain outside the Pale. The rest were rounded up and deported. The result was an influx of destitute Jews into the already overcrowded and violence-beset Jewish communities of the Pale of Settlement. In May 1882, more restrictive legislation, known as the 'Temporary Orders concerning the Jews', or the 'May Laws', were enacted which restricted the Jewish rights of residence even within the Pale, and had the effect of creating a Pale within the Pale of Settlement. They also limited economic opportunities: Jews could no longer engage in farming, or any secondary industry or trade that resulted from agriculture, they were prohibited from the keeping of inns or taverns, and they were barred from the professions and from academia. In 1891 all Jews living in the interior of the Russian Empire were expelled to the Pale. Consequently, thousands of Jews who had resided, for decades, throughout Russia were forced into the slums of Warsaw, Lodz, Minsk, Bialystock and the Jewish sections of the other towns and cities. This, of course, created all the problems of over-congestion and ghettoisation: disease, poverty and unemployment became common features of Jewish life in Russia at the turn of the century.[3] The economic infrastructure of

[1]Howard Morley Sachar, *The Course of Modern Jewish History*, London 1958, p. 309.
[2]David Vital, *The Origins of Zionism*, Oxford 1975, p. 30.
[3]On this see Salo Baron, *The Russian Jews under Tsar and Soviets*, New York–London 1969.

the Jewish ghettos and *shtetlach* of the Pale of Settlement could not cope with the increased demands placed on it by edict and pogrom, and the result was that most Jews lived on the fringes of the Russian economy. During the early twentieth century, the situation continued to deteriorate: in 1903, the Jews of Kishinev and Gomel were visited by pogroms, in the aftermath of the failed 1905 Revolution, and in 1906, the Jews of Bialystock were the victims of further violence.

Jewish life in the Russian ghettos and *shtetlach* represented almost every ideology and orientation: there were Zionists, Bundists, revolutionaries, religious revisionaries and more. Yet, whether Zionist or Bundist, national cultural autonomist or Social Democrat, one message echoed throughout the writings and the thoughts of the Jewish intellectuals and activists: life in Russia had become intolerable and Eastern Jewry could no longer afford to remain passive. Hence, while Jewish economic and social life was being strangulated by the long arm of the Tsarist regime, Jewish intellectual life was in a state of great fermentation and dynamic renascence, "of extreme restlessness, feverish collective dreaming, pretentious ideological effort"[4] and intense experimentation. Some joined the forces of revolution, others went to Palestine, but the vast majority of the Jews who took action did so by packing up their few belongings and by setting out for new and free lands. Neither the promises of Socialism nor the dreams of national revival could subdue their drive for new beginnings in the New World. They emigrated to America and Canada and the Argentine, not only because life beyond the Pale was difficult, but because they desired to take their destiny in their own hands.[5] The migration of Eastern Jewry represented more than a "flight ahead of catastrophe": it reflected a spontaneous yet collective reaction to repression and, perhaps, to the foreboding of destruction by a people in search of new modes of life.[6]

As the numbers of Jewish emigrants leaving the Pale of Settlement increased, Western Jewry was confronted with the question as to what were the best solutions to the dilemma of Jewish existence in the Russian Empire? Thus, the Russo-Jewish Question was addressed in the Jewish communities of the West, as well as in those of the East, during the years before the First World War. It is difficult to summarise the prevalent attitude of so diverse a group as Western Jewry to such a complex and multi-faceted issue as the Russo-Jewish Question: certainly the Jews of the West were always concerned about the persecution of their co-religionists, anywhere. They believed it was their role, as emancipated Jews, to intervene on behalf of oppressed Jewry and to do all that was possible to improve their condition. The foundation of the *Alliance Israélite Universelle* (1860), and its growth, both in influence and in strength, throughout the nineteenth century attests to the seriousness of Western Jewry's commitment to this principle. But when its members gathered to discuss the flight from Russia

[4]Irving Howe, *The World of Our Fathers. The Journey of the Eastern European Jews to America and the Life They Found and Made*, New York 1976, p. 16.

[5]On the intellectual Jewish renascence in Russia see Vital, *op. cit.*, p. 59.

[6]David Rome, 'On Anti-Semitism in Canada, 1929–1939', in *Clouds in the Thirties*, Montreal 1980, Section 8, p. 142.

and Eastern Europe at the turn of the century, they concluded that emigration was not the answer to the Russo-Jewish Question and therefore, it should be discouraged. Their decision was determined by the pressure of receiving, assisting, accommodating and settling the numerous impoverished refugees in the Jewish communities of the West. However, it was motivated by more than self-interest; it reflected the manner in which the leaders of Western Jewry understood the meaning of progress and historical evolution. The emancipation of the Jews throughout the Western world had broken down the barriers which had prevented them from participating in civil and secular society, but while they basked in the enlightened policies of their governments, their co-religionists in the East still lived in the Dark Ages. Hence, emancipation had also opened an almost unbridgeable schism in the way in which Eastern and Western Jewry viewed the world. The different social, political and economic realities in which these two Jewries resided produced divergent, and at times opposing dreams, aspirations and philosophies. For the assimilated, Western Jew, emancipation was historically determined – an inevitable by-product of industrial development – and would be bestowed upon the Jews of the East once their governments donned the cloak of modernity. However, Eastern Jewry must not sit back and passively await Russia's entry into the modern era; it must actively promote industrial and social progress because this would lead to emancipation. Therefore, the Western Jew's view of the world was premised on his own historical experience, and prevented him from understanding that the Jews of Russia lived in a hostile environment where emancipation might not be the inevitable outcome of modernisation.

II

There were Western Jews, both intellectuals and humanitarians, who could not abide the suffering of their co-religionists and who dissented from the mainstream of Western Jewish opinion. Theodor Herzl and the Zionists represented one such response – they advocated a return to statehood in Palestine – and Baron de Hirsch represented another. He was a proponent of the idea of agricultural auto-emancipation in lands where Jews could live free from oppression and discrimination. Maurice de Hirsch was born on 9th December, 1831,[7] the son of Joseph and Karoline von Hirsch auf Gereuth, banker to Kings Ludwig I, Maximilian II, and Ludwig II of Bavaria. The von Hirsches were a prosperous and cosmopolitan family who had, through their own efforts and accomplishments, attained a privileged position in society. Yet, they never forsook their Jewish origins, values or identity in order to rise in society. Thus, Maurice grew up in an atmosphere pervaded not only by a strong desire to succeed but by an equally fierce determination to acquire what was morally and socially just: recognition of Jews' rights and privileges as citizens

[7]All the material on Baron de Hirsch's family background has been taken from a private publication the Hirsch family commissioned, unless otherwise indicated. Josef Prys, *Die Familie von Hirsch auf Gereuth*, Munich 1931.

among compatriots. Perhaps their struggle for emancipation played as formative an influence on the young Maurice as did his birth into a wealthy family. Throughout his life, he upheld a sense of loyalty towards "being Jewish" despite his assimilated and non-religious life-style. At a time when many Jews renounced their origins to gain entrance into society, and at a time when this resulted in genuine acceptance, Maurice adhered to his Jewish roots with impunity. This should not be dismissed as mere lip-service by a man of wealth and status for it reflected a deep commitment to his Jewishness that would later express itself as a commitment to less fortunate Jewry. He believed he could rise to the very pinnacle of society and enjoy all its benefits without compromising his Jewish heritage, and he achieved this goal during his lifetime.

Maurice followed in his father's footsteps; he entered the banking world at seventeen years of age, an ambitious and enterprising young man eager to leave his mark. His accomplishments as a banker were many, but his greatest coup was the financing and the building of a railway from Vienna to Constantinople.[8] While supervising his project, he visited the Jewish communities along his railway lines, and was appalled at the poverty and backwardness of the Jews of the Ottoman Empire. They were not the victims of government repression, but of ignorance, and economic stagnation. From this time on, he donated considerable sums of money to the Jews of Turkey and in December 1873, he offered the *Alliance Israélite Universelle* one million francs to establish educational and vocational training programmes for them:[9] "Pouvoir à l'instruction et à l'éducation de la jeunesse, c'est le remède le plus efficace qu'on puisse apporter à ce mal."[10] Baron de Hirsch hoped that education would improve not only their standard of living, by opening up many more opportunities for economic advancement, but the quality of their lives as well. Thereafter, his ties with the *Alliance Israélite Universelle* grew steadily closer and in 1879, he was elected to its Central Committee.[11]

Baron de Hirsch disdained the traditional form of Jewish philanthropy, the giving of alms (*tsedakah*) which was practised by the prominent Jews of his day and which sustained the *Yishuv* in Palestine. He was especially wary of its effects on the recipient: it "only makes so many more beggars and I consider it the greatest problem in philanthropy to make human beings who are capable of work out of individuals who otherwise must become paupers, and in this way create useful members of society."[12] He believed it was necessary to eradicate the causes of poverty and not just to relieve their symptoms. He maintained that

[8]For a fuller discussion of Baron de Hirsch's financial accomplishments see Kurt Grunwald, *Türkenhirsch. A Study of Baron Maurice de Hirsch, Entrepreneur and Philanthropist*, Jerusalem 1966, and Kennee Switzer, *Baron de Hirsch, The Jewish Colonization Association and Canada, 1891–1914*, unpublished Ph.D. dissertation, University of London, 1982 pp. 34–41.

[9]Narcisse Leven, *Cinquante Ans d'Histoire, l'Alliance Israélite Universelle, 1860–1910*, vol. 2, Paris 1920, p. 24.

[10]*Ibid.*, p. 23, from a letter by Baron de Hirsch to the Central Committee of the Alliance Israélite Universelle.

[11]S. Adler-Rudel, 'Moritz Baron Hirsch. Profile of a Great Philanthropist', in *LBI Year Book VIII* (1963), p. 15.

[12]Baron Maurice de Hirsch, 'My Views on Philanthropy', in *North American Review*, No. 416 (July 1891), p. 1.

the most debilitating aspect of Jewish discrimination was the exclusion of the Jews from the economic infrastructure and as a believer in, and beneficiary of, the Industrial Revolution, he advocated the reintegration of "ghetto" Jewry into the economic order of the nineteenth century. The only remedy for Jewish poverty, and the only means of normalising the Jewish position in society was through productive labour: the Jewish masses must be given the opportunity to become useful and independent labourers, tradesmen, artisans and agriculturalists. The existence of a self-sufficient Jewish working force would improve their standard of living and it would also demonstrate to the rest of the world that despite prejudice and restriction Jews were capable of playing a "useful" role in society. It was in this spirit that he endowed the *Baron Hirsch Kaiser Jubiläums-Stiftung* in Austria with twelve million kronen in 1888, to celebrate the fortieth anniversary of Franz Joseph's ascension to the throne. The money financed the establishment of vocational and agricultural schools for young Jews of Galicia and Bukovina.

Baron de Hirsch was also actively involved in efforts to aid Russo-Jewish refugees: he contributed one million francs to the Emergency Fund for Refugees of the *Alliance Israélite Universelle*[13] and he sent his private almoner, Emmanuel Felix Veneziani, to the border town of Brody, where most of the refugees were fleeing, to supervise and fund relief operations.[14] From 1881 on, he turned his attention almost exclusively to the Jews of Russia and Eastern Europe whom he considered the most desperate and downtrodden of World Jewry. In 1886, he offered to organise a fund of fifty million francs to provide them with a network of educational and training programmes, along the lines of the *Baron Hirsch Kaiser Jubiläums-Stiftung*, but the Russian government would not cooperate and he abandoned this idea.[15] Nevertheless, the Jews continued to pour out of the Pale of Settlement and Baron de Hirsch concluded that the only effective means of assisting them would be to remove them from the clutches of the Tsar and to resettle them in countries whose governments were committed to freedom and equality:

> "What I (Baron de Hirsch) desire to accomplish, what . . . has come to be the object of my life and that for which I am willing to stake my wealth and my intellectual powers, is to give to a portion of my companions in faith the possibility of finding a new existence, primarily as farmers and also as handicraftsmen, in those lands where the law and religious tolerance permit them to carry on the struggle for existence as noble and responsible subjects of a humane government."[16]

Hence, he had understood that the Russian government was not just looking to bully its Jews into becoming assimilated members of society, but to eliminate them completely from Russia through expulsion, emigration, deprivation and pogroms.[17] Therefore, between 1886 and 1891, he arrived at a wholly new

[13]Hirsch read about the urgency of the situation from a pamphlet by Moriz Friedlaender, Secretary of the Hungarian *Israelitische Allianz zu Wien*. The pamphlet described the wretched conditions in the border towns.

[14]*Jewish Chronicle*, London, 24th April 1896.

[15]For a fuller discussion of the sequence of events surrounding his offer see Switzer, *op. cit.*, pp. 49–51.

[16]Hirsch, 'My Views on Philanthropy', *loc. cit.*, p. 2.

[17]Baron Maurice de Hirsch, 'Refuge for Russian Jews', in *Forum*, vol. 2, (August 1891), p. 627.

approach to the Russo-Jewish Question – one that differed radically from that adopted by most of the influential and prominent Jewish leaders of the day. The struggle had only begun for the man who was willing to "stake his wealth and intellectual powers"[18] on a cause that was not supported by the Jewish establishment: immigration, agricultural resettlement and auto-emancipation.

In 1887, Hirsch had sent Veneziani and a group of engineers on a tour of Palestine to investigate its potential for agricultural development and Jewish colonisation. Veneziani's report was hardly encouraging: he related the experiences of the Bilu settlers, who despite their idealism and their high degree of motivation were forced to abandon their dreams of farming in the Holy Land.[19] Veneziani concluded that the land had deteriorated beyond the point of redemption and that any agricultural effort, whether Jewish or non-Jewish, could never become successful. Consequently, Baron de Hirsch cast about for other lands in which to carry out his programme of Jewish regeneration.

What induced Baron de Hirsch to balk at the accepted and to advance a new and fundamentally different answer to the Russo-Jewish Question? Hirsch willingly accepted that the acquisition of great fortune carries with it the assumption of new responsibilities towards society and its downtrodden and he wholeheartedly embraced the duties incumbent upon his social position. One of his biographers suggests that his motivations for being generous may not have been altogether altruistic: "He felt the mere fact of being a millionaire was not sufficient to secure him the position in the world he aspired to . . . It was . . . a mixture of 'Gewissensbisse', of pangs of conscience, and social ambition which made Hirsch the outstanding philanthropist of his time."[20] This is a harsh judgement on a man who donated so much of his fortune to so many different causes. Some of his donations, such as the money he offered the London hospitals,[21] may have reflected his need to conform to the social and moral code of conduct of the upper class, but this does not explain why he focused so much attention, and so much energy, on resettling Russian Jews. To appreciate his motivations truly, one must remember the values that had been prevalent in his home: a commitment to "being Jewish", a desire to be treated equally, and a strong spirit of generosity and kindness towards the less fortunate citizens of this world. It was these influences which translated themselves into a loyalty towards disadvantaged and oppressed Jewry, be they in the Ottoman Empire or the Pale of Settlement. Furthermore, ever since the death of his only son, Lucien, in 1887,[22] he had been slowly extricating himself from the world of finance, and time may have weighed heavily on the bereaved father. He was a healthy and active man with both the time and the money to expend on "saving Russian Jews" and so he plunged into the project of removal and resettlement

[18] *Ibid.*

[19] Many of the early *Bilu* colonisers were forced to leave their colonies because of disease or lack of food.

[20] Kurt Grunwald made this accusation, in *Türkenhirsch*, *op. cit.*, p. 63.

[21] He donated all the money he earned from his race horses and when their winnings were scant, he made up the difference between what they won and what he had donated the year before from his pocket.

[22] Lucien de Hirsch died of pneumonia.

with gusto and fierce determination. Although he had lost his natural heir, he could still leave a legacy to his people.[23] For whatever reason, or combination of reasons, he spent vast amounts of time and money to found an organisation that would realise his goals. He employed the most experienced legal minds to draft the *Articles and Memorandum of Association of the Jewish Colonization Association* and the most qualified social service workers and administrators to supervise and to carry out its work. He submitted the *Articles and Memorandum of Association* to the Board of Trade in England on 24th August 1891 and the Jewish Colonization Association was registered as a limited liability company with two million pounds capital on 10th September 1891. The Association's capital was divided into twenty thousand shares (of one hundred pounds each): Hirsch owned 19,993 shares, and Nathaniel (First Lord) Rothschild, Sir Julian Goldsmid, Salomon H. Goldschmidt, Benjamin L. Cohen, Frederic David Mocatta, Edouard Kohn and Eugene Pereire were each given a share.[24] Each share carried the right to one vote and hence, Hirsch remained in complete control of the Association and its direction throughout his lifetime. He appointed as executive director his long time associate and trusted friend, Dr. Sigismund Sonnenfeld.[25]

The purpose and objectives of the Association were explicitly elaborated in the *Memorandum of Association of the Jewish Colonization Association*: it was

> "to assist and promote the emigration of Jews from any part of Europe or Asia, and principally from countries in which they may for the time being be subjected to any special taxes or political or other disabilities, to any other part of the world, and to form and establish colonies in various parts of North and South America and other countries for agricultural, cultural, commercial and other purposes".[26]

To realise these goals, the Jewish Colonization Association was empowered to purchase, or to acquire, any territory outside of Europe from governments, states, municipal or local authorities, corporations or persons.[27] It was also given the power

> "to establish emigration agencies in various parts of Europe, Asia and other parts of the world, [and] to construct, hire, charter and equip steamships and other vessels for the purpose of facilitating emigration".[28]

Therefore, Hirsch imbued his foundation with extensive powers to achieve his objectives: the removal of Jews from Russia and their resettlement.

[23]In response to a letter of condolence, Baron de Hirsch stated: "My son I have lost, but not my heirs. Humanity is my heir." ICA Archives, Haim Avni, *Argentina, the Promised Land. Baron de Hirsch's Colonization Project in Argentina*, unpublished Ph.D. thesis (trans. by Sydney Lightman), Jerusalem 1968[?]. For the book edn. see note 33.

[24]Switzer, *op. cit.*, p. 76.

[25]The Association underwent only one formal transformation during Hirsch's lifetime: on 26th August 1892, he donated an additional £7,000,000 specifically for Russian Jewry. This money was to remain separate from the initial £2,000,000 endowment and from then on the Jewish Colonization Association consisted of two entirely distinct funds: its original share capital which was to be expended according to the *Memorandum and Articles of Association* and the £7,000,000 trust fund which was to be spent only on Russian Jewish refugees. Switzer, *op. cit.*, p. 83.

[26]*Memorandum and Articles of Association of the Jewish Colonization Association*, London 1891, p. 1.

[27]*Ibid.*, Clause 3b, p. 1.

[28]*Ibid.*, Clause 3k, p. 3.

Once the Jewish Colonization Association had been certified by the British Board of Trade, Hirsch sent a representative to the Russian government to request official recognition and the right to organise the departure of Jews. On 11th June 1892, the Jewish Colonization Association received approval from the government and permission to operate, provided a one million rouble bond be deposited in the State Bank as a guarantee that the Association would remain a law-abiding philanthropic agency. Hirsch's representative immediately set about forming a working committee, but it took almost a year to assemble the right men. In February 1893, Hirsch was informed that the Central Committee of St. Petersburg had been formed and included such men as Baron Horace Günzburg, Baron David Günzburg, Jakob Lazar Poliakoff, Abraham Zak, Alexander Passower, Isaac Krasnoselky, I. A. Valvelburg, and Dr. Raffalovitch, some of Russia's most prominent Jewish leaders.[29] The principle function of the Central Committee of St. Petersburg was to select candidates for resettlement on the Association's farms overseas and to organise their departure from the Pale of Settlement.

The Jewish Colonization Association's primary sphere of operation, while Baron de Hirsch was alive, was Argentina, but it also became involved in Jewish agriculture at the settlement that bore his name, Hirsch, Canada, in 1892. Hirsch concentrated on Argentina because his advisers had informed him that politically, economically and geologically, its pampas were ideal for Jewish agricultural development. Furthermore, a group of Russian Jews were already settled on the land in Santa Fé province (this colony would later be named Moïseville) and therefore, there was already a Jewish presence in the farming sector of the Argentine economy. However, another factor may have induced him to consider settling Jews so far from the traditional paths of immigration: Jewish leaders in Europe and in the United States of America were becoming increasingly anxious about the Jewish flight from Russia. They were discouraging their co-religionists from packing up their household goods and moving to London, Berlin, Frankfurt or New York. Hence, when presented with the Argentine alternative, Hirsch was pleased because, apart from its other attractions, his project would not impose on the resources of the established Jewish communities nor would it depend on their hospitality in any way. Therefore, his choice was motivated by practical considerations and by the continuous crystallisation of events: he believed the pampas of Argentina would provide him with an ideal location, where he could assist oppressed Jewry without antagonising emancipated Jewry.[30]

Hirsch's choice of Argentina as the site of his colonisation project may have been inspired by one other factor: his ultimate goal, and his dream for the

[29]Jewish Colonization Association (ICA) Archives, Séance du conseil d'administration du 15 juillet, 1894.

[30]There appears to be no credence to the rumour that Baron de Hirsch was financially involved with the *Banque Murietta* which went bankrupt in the early 1890s, and was said to have left him with vast tracts of land in Argentina. See Mark Wischnitzer, *To Dwell in Safety. The Story of Jewish Migration since 1800*, Philadelphia 1948, pp. 90–91; or Benjamin G. Sack, 'A Historical Opportunity Forfeited', in *Canadian Jewish Yearbook*, vol. 3, (1941–1942), p. 98.

Jewish future. Soon after the foundation of the Jewish Colonization Association, he wrote to Dr. Loewenthal:

> "Il en existe peut-être et bien qu'il puisse paraître fantastique à la première vue, il ne rentre pas moins aujourd'hui dans le domaine de possible. Je [Baron de Hirsch] veux parler de l'achat d'un pays tout-entier réunissant toutes les conditions désirables et dont les colons deviendraient les (propriètaires) incontestés."[31]

Hirsch envisioned the eventual establishment of "une sorte d'état plus ou moins autonome" where the Jews from beyond the Pale could be settled, and where they could enjoy a productive and prosperous life.[32] He suggested to Loewenthal that all the Jewish colonies be concentrated in one province of the Argentine Republic because he believed its laws permitted every locality populated with one thousand inhabitants the right to elect a local council, and every territory with sixty thousand inhabitants the right to become an autonomous province.[33] He had misunderstood, or perhaps Loewenthal had misrepresented, the Argentine Constitution which did not provide for the eventual secession of any province. Furthermore, although the Argentine government pursued a rather open immigration policy, it anticipated the complete absorption and assimilation of the newcomers into its native society. The law-makers had no intention of encouraging the concentration of any ethnic or national group in one area of the country, or of affording any group special autonomous status. It is even doubtful whether they would have permitted the immigration of Jews into the Republic, had they believed they would cling to their cultural, and spiritual, identity by maintaining geographic exclusivity. Nevertheless, Hirsch, under the misapprehension that it would eventually be possible to achieve autonomous status, was disappointed that Loewenthal did not locate the Association's colonies within the same province.[34]

Unfortunately, Jewish agriculture in the Argentine was problematic. The first group of three thousand colonists arrived before their colony, then called Mauricio, was ready to receive them, and it took almost two years to complete their installation. Their premature arrival proved so demoralising, and created so many complications, that it left a bitter legacy which was never truly overcome. Furthermore, the Central Committee of St. Petersburg never instituted an appropriate method of selecting candidates and this too undermined progress. More often than not, the number of unfortunates clamouring for refuge in the New World overwhelmed the emigration agents in Russia, and if there was any selection at all, it was carried out in a haphazard fashion, usually at the ports or at the Western borders and often based on the testimony of the eager emigrant rather than on careful research by caseworkers. (The orderly and discriminating resettlement of refugees would have to wait for

[31]ICA Archives, letter, Baron de Hirsch to Dr. Loewenthal, 2nd October 1891.

[32]ICA Archives, letters, Baron de Hirsch to Lousada, 19th and 27th October 1891.

[33]Haim Avni, *Argentina Ha-aretz Ha-y'udah, Mifal Ha-hityash-vut Shel Ha Baron de Hirsch b'Argentina*, Jerusalem 1973, p. 123, from a letter Baron de Hirsch wrote to the ICA administration, Buenos Aires, 12th July 1893.

[34]ICA Archives, Baron de Hirsch to Loewenthal, 2nd and 16th October 1891. Loewenthal was opposed to the idea because he believed it would antagonise the Argentine government.

the more sophisticated social service personnel of the post-1945 era.) Consequently, many colonists were not commited to the agrarian way of life and were unwilling to leave Buenos Aires, once they had tasted the riches of city life in the democratic Republic. Others were unable to adapt to the rigours of life on the frontiers and, after untold difficulties, returned to the capital. Reports of deprivation, disease and disaffection were sent to the head office of the Association, and after many attempts to remedy the situation, Hirsch opted for drastic measures. He ordered his agents in Argentina to expropriate all disorderly and unproductive colonists and to resettle them in Buenos Aires or in the United States.[35] However, the selection committees in Russia and the colonists were not the only antagonists in this disappointing story: the Association's agents and managers in Argentina must also share the responsibility for the slow progress. Hirsch could not find effective yet empathetic administrators who were willing to exchange the luxuries of city life for the starkness of life on the pampas. His first two representatives proved incompetent, and when the situation had hardly improved by 1895, after a parade of four different managers, Hirsch decided to halt all emigration to his colonies.[36] He sent Sigismund Sonnenfeld and one of his Russian agents, David Feinberg, to the Republic to investigate the problems and the potential for further growth and development. Their assessments were positive, but unfortunately Hirsch died on the 20th April 1896 before they could report their findings:

> "I (Feinberg) regretted that Baron de Hirsch was unable to see this colony (Moïseville) and to behold the metamorphosis in the mode of life in the colonies. I could not imagine that in such a brief period people previously unaccustomed to agriculture could become excellent farmers and adjust . . . to life on the farms."[37]

Hirsch, like any astute and accomplished businessman, had provided for a time when he might no longer be in control of the Association and its direction: at his death, its administration was to be assumed by its shareholders. During the last five years of his life, he had negotiated for the transfer of four thousand five hundred and ninety-five shares to the Anglo-Jewish Association and the *Alliance Israélite Universelle* and three thousand six hundred shares to the Jewish communities of Frankfurt a. Main, Berlin and Brussels.[38] The shareholders elected a new Council of Administration to oversee the operations of the Jewish Colonization Association: it consisted of S. H. Goldschmidt, Narcisse Leven, Salomon Reinach, Alfred L. Cohen, Herbert Lousada, Chief Rabbi Zadoc

[35]ICA Archives, lettre, Paul Barrelet (Baron de Hirsch's personal secretary), par ordre de Baron de Hirsch to the direction, ICA, 26th July 1892; and letter, Baron de Hirsch to Director, ICA, 14th October 1893.

[36]Loewenthal was the first agent and colony manager. Adolphe Roth replaced him. Then A.E.W. Goldsmid took the position for one year, to try to remedy the situation. Conditions improved under his supervision, but his successors, David Cazès [Kazis], Samuel Hirsch (no relation to the Baron) and Maxim Kagan proved unable to sustain Goldsmid's legacy. For a fuller discussion see Switzer, *op. cit.*, pp. 99–100.

[37]David Feinberg, 'A Survey of the Colonization of Russian Jews in Argentina', in *American Jewish Historical Society*, vol. XLIII, (September 1953), p. 62.

[38]Switzer, *op. cit.*, p. 97.

Kahn, Claude J. G. Montefiore, Leopold Schloss, Julius Plotke, Dr. Edmund Lachmann and Franz Philippson.[39] The new administrators retained Sigismund Sonnenfeld as executive director and appointed Emile Meyerson to help him with his duties. Hirsch's desire that the Association's work be carried on without any serious interruption after his death became a reality.

In their first annual report (1896), the new administrators affirmed their commitment to Jewish agriculture in Argentina, but the problems and complications, which had so disheartened Hirsch, continued to impede their development. The colonists struggled from year to year; every time there was hope for an abundant yield, nature intervened. One year the crops were devastated by drought, the next by early frost, the year after by locusts and so on. And, finally when the farmers harvested bumper crops, the over-abundance of foodstuffs throughout the region drove the prices so low that the colonists were unable to recoup their costs (1899). The slow progress of the agricultural colonies discouraged the council members and periodically, they followed the Baron's example and suspended emigration all together. Yet, unlike their predecessor, they held few illusions about the ability of the colonies to absorb large numbers of Russian Jews, or about the possibility of Argentina ever becoming a centre of Jewish immigration. They believed the colonies suffered from chronic and incurable problems and had very little potential for growth: stability and self-sufficiency would be great enough achievements. Therefore, over the next decade, they sent fewer and fewer Jews to Argentina and by 1913, only those immigrants who could pay their way across the ocean, without the aid of the Jewish Colonization Association, or of any other agency, were invited to be apprenticed as colonists.

The new administrators did not turn their backs on the Jewish farmers of Argentina, or allow the colonies to be disolved, but they did very little to encourage or to stimulate Jewish agriculture on the pampas. This reflected more than their frustration with the slow and troubled progress of the colonies: it represented their fundamentally different approach to the Russo-Jewish Question. The men who assumed leadership of the Jewish Colonization Association were influential and prominent Jewish leaders, part of the group which had been opposed to emigration out of Russia in the first place.[40] Thus, they shifted the focus and orientation of the Association from migration and resettlement to reconstruction and *in situ* assistance, and eventually to immigrant aid in the countries of reception. During the pre-war era, the Jewish Colonization Association funded the establishment of many programmes designed to rebuild and revitalise the infrastructure of the Jewish communities in Russia and Eastern Europe. It opened up trade and agricultural schools, Talmud Torah schools and model farms, it offered subsidised apprenticeship and vocational retraining programmes and it founded "caisses de prêts et d'épagne" where Jewish businessmen could borrow money. It sponsored Jewish agricultural and industrial development throughout Russia and Eastern

[39] *Ibid.*, pp. 106–107.
[40] For a fuller discussion of Baron de Hirsch's motivations and objectives see *ibid.*, pp. 122–125.

Europe, in an effort to eradicate economic marginalism, and in an attempt to fashion from the Jewish masses a productive and self-sufficient work force that could contribute to their countries of residence. Nevertheless, Russian and Eastern Jewry continued to migrate westward, in numbers that grew steadily, year after year. Their journey across the European continent and their arrival at ports in the New World – New York City, Montreal and Buenos Aires – placed a heavy burden on the Jewish communities along their paths of migration. Hence, the administrators were forced to accept their responsibility as directors of one of the richest Jewish organisations, and to assist the immigrants, and their host communities, as each struggled to accommodate the other.

III

The story of Jewish settlement in Canada before the First World War is the saga of a country nearly new – Canada only gained independence from Britain in 1867 – a native Jewish population barely large enough to call itself a community – there were only 2,443 Jews in Canada in 1881 – and then came wave after wave of Jewish immigrants – 75,681 of them between 1881 and 1914.[41] It was the interplay between these elements that determined not only the nature of Canadian Jewry but the scope and context of the Jewish Colonization Association's role during these early years of Canadian development. It was to the 2,443 Jewish "Canadians" that the task of immigrant reception and assistance fell, and, while only too willing, for they too had only recently partaken in the immigrant experience, their financial situation proscribed them from all but the merest gesture. There were no local Barons de Hirsch, Moses Montefiores or Jacob Schiffs in Canada and therefore, while London and New York "contain(ed) a large number of the wealthy Jews – some of the wealthiest in the world"[42] – and still complained about receiving too many Jewish refugees, the Jews of Canada, the majority of whom lived in Montreal, could barely support their local poor, let alone absorb the newcomers. Consequently, they turned to their wealthier neighbours to the South and overseas for financial assistance.

In 1890, L. Aronson, a member of the Board of Directors of the Young Men's Hebrew Benevolent Society,[43] suggested that the Jews of Montreal request money for immigrant aid from the Baron de Hirsch Fund of New York.[44] Their

[41]L. Rosenberg, *Canada's Jews*, Montreal 1939, p. 10.

[42]ICA Archives, letter, D. A. Ansell to President of the ICA, 18th September 1890.

[43]The Young Men's Hebrew Benevolent Society was the central Jewish philanthropic organisation in Canada at the end of the nineteenth century. In March 1900, the Society was reincorporated under the name Baron de Hirsch Institute and Hebrew Benevolent Society of Montreal. The "Hebrew Benevolent Society of Montreal" was dropped and the Society has become known as the Baron de Hirsch Institute. For a fuller discussion of the foundation of this society see Switzer, *op. cit.*, pp. 133–138.

[44]The Baron de Hirsch Fund was founded in New York on 9th February 1891. The Baron endowed it with $2,400,000 to be used to help receive and resettle immigrants from Russia, Romania and Eastern Europe. It also offered them vocational retraining and agricultural training programmes.

request was refused because its charter prohibited it from sending money outside the United States of America and therefore, the directors of the Young Men's Hebrew Benevolent Society decided to appeal directly to its benefactor, Baron de Hirsch. On 20th May 1890, they sent a letter to Paris, explaining the purpose of their Society and its financial predicament. The Baron replied:

> ". . . as I appreciate the usefulness of your action and the object which you pursue, I am ready to contribute a sum of $20,000 which I enclose in a cheque. I shall be glad to hear from you, from time to time, about the progress of your work and may perhaps in a future time further assist you, but cannot in this respect undertake any engagements."[45]

The Young Men's Hebrew Benevolent Society received the twenty thousand dollars in August 1890. This was to be the first time Baron de Hirsch had any contact with the Jewish community of Canada and although the letter specified the opposite, his donation marked the beginning of what was to develop into a sustained and, from the Canadian perspective, a seminal relationship with the Jewish Colonization Association.

Twenty thousand dollars may not have been a substantial amount of money for the wealthy Baron, but for the members of the financially insolvent Young Men's Hebrew Benevolent Society, it was a windfall of good fortune, "a munificent donation",[46] and they elected him Honorary Life Member of their Society and inscribed him as their patron. Part of the donation was used to purchase a building at 7, St. Elizabeth Street (on 21st September 1891), which was converted into an immigrant shelter and school: they named it The Baron de Hirsch Institute and Free Day School. The shelter was to house all newcomers until they could establish themselves in their new community and the school was to be responsible for educating Jewish children.[47] (It was the first day school in Montreal to be free and open to students regardless of their ability to pay tuition.) The school offered courses which were designed to familiarise its students with their new homeland: its curriculum consisted of English, Canadian history, geography, customs and civics. "The (Young Men's Hebrew Benevolent) Society . . . consider(ed) that the best way of doing good was by helping the children help themselves and (by) making them understand the language, customs and institutions of their land of adoption."[48] Hence, the members of the Young Men's Hebrew Benevolent Society hoped to transform the children of the immigrants into loyal, industrious and economically successful "Canadians" by imbuing them with the proper values and education in much the same way as did the founders of the Educational Alliance in New York City. However, they realised that the Baron's donation would not last for ever, and that, if the school was to be maintained year after year, they must

---

For a fuller discussion of the Fund see Samuel Joseph, *History of the Baron de Hirsch Fund*, New York 1935.

[45]National Archives of the Canadian Jewish Congress (CJC), Simon Belkin, *Forty Years of ICA Work in Canada*, unpublished manuscript, 1931, p. 5.

[46]National Archives of CJC, *Minutes* of the 18th August 1890 meeting of the Young Men's Hebrew Benevolent Society.

[47]The Baron de Hirsch Institute and School were formally opened by the Mayor of Montreal on 17th June 1891.

[48]ICA Archives, letter, H. Vineberg and S. W. Jacobs to Baron de Hirsch, 23rd June 1891.

secure a more permanent source of income. In October 1891, they appealed to the *Alliance Israélite Universelle* and the newly founded Jewish Colonization Association for endowment: both organisations responded positively. The *Alliance* sent one thousand francs as a one time donation and the Jewish Colonization Association agreed to underwrite the cost of running the school.[49] (It continued to sponsor Jewish education in Montreal throughout the pre-war period.) Thus, the 20,000 dollar donation not only provided the Young Men's Hebrew Benevolent Society with a permanent home and a somewhat eased financial situation, but it created a link between the Jewish community of Canada and the Jewish Colonization Association, a link that was to prove indispensable to the Jews of Canada as they struggled to assume their responsibility towards their fellow Jews.

Throughout the pre-war era, the primary focus and concern of the Jewish agency in Montreal remained immigrant reception: its volunteers met the boats at the ports of entry – Montreal and Quebec City in the summer, and Halifax and St. Johns, New Brunswick when the St. Lawrence River was frozen over in the winter – guided them through the immigration process and escorted them to the immigrant shelter at the Baron de Hirsch Institute.

> "As soon as the immigrant family reaches Montreal, we [the volunteers of the Jewish agency] take a personal interest in them. We look after their immediate wants, we find employment for them. We watch their conduct. We try to let them feel our equals. We visit them in sorrow and poverty."[50]

Yet, while the leaders of the Jewish community of Montreal asserted that it was both their desire and their duty to receive their persecuted brethren, they feared the repercussions of large-scale immigration, just as the leaders of their sister communities in America and overseas did. Consequently, they sought to impress upon the Canadian government and the Canadian people the benefits these immigrants could bring to the young nation. They believed that the best way in which to keep the doors to Canada open and to avoid any anti-immigrant, and anti-Jewish, agitation, would be to integrate the newcomers into the Canadian economic order. Thus, their foremost goal became the dispersion of the Jewish immigrants throughout the nation: "It is absolutely necessary that congestion of immigrants in Montreal and other cities should be prevented."[51] The existence of Jewish ghettos would be interpreted by the Canadian population as a sign of the immigrants' inability, or perhaps even unwillingness, to adapt to their new conditions and to become productive citizens in their adopted homes. The directors of the successor to the Young Men's Hebrew Benevolent Society, the Baron de Hirsch Institute, established a Labour Bureau in Montreal to place Jews in productive employment throughout the Dominion, and during its first year (1905), it successfully found jobs for 3,665 immigrants.[52] They also sought to hide all signs of Jewish

[49]ICA Archives, Bigart (of the *Alliance Israélite Universelle*) to D. A. Ansell, 21st January 1891.
[50]*Canadian Jewish Times*, Montreal, 28th March 1902.
[51]*Ibid.*, 24th March 1905.
[52]National Archives of CJC, *Annual Report of the Baron de Hirsch Institute*, October 1906 and ICA Archives, *Rapport de l'administration centrale au conseil d'administration, 1907–1914*. In 1907, the Labour

destitution or dissatisfaction from the rest of Canadian society and therefore, they organised a comprehensive assistance and relief programme which provided all in need, whether "native" or "newcomer", with shelter, food, fuel, clothes, an education and a Jewish funeral and cemetery plot. In 1909, a *Gemilath Chassodim* (Hebrew Free Loan Association) was founded to aid those Jews of Montreal temporarily in debt and to relieve pressure on the relief and assistance programmes of the Baron de Hirsch Institute. The Jewish Colonization Association underwrote all of the Jewish community's attempts and efforts to facilitate Jewish accommodation and adaptation to Canadian society throughout the pre-war period.[53]

However, most innovative of all the Jewish Colonization Association's programmes in Canada were those designed to stimulate Jewish agriculture on the prairies. At the turn of the century, the Canadian interior was virtually uninhabited and the government, anxious to populate it, pursued a homesteading policy. Anyone could acquire the exclusive rights to 160 acres of land for a nominal entry fee of ten dollars, and if they could erect habitable lodgings, seed 25 acres and break another 30 acres by the end of three years, they would receive the patent, or clear title, to their land. (When the homesteader qualified for his title, he was offered an adjoining quarter section or 160 acres at a very reasonable rate.)[54] In 1891, the members of the Young Men's Hebrew Benevolent Society had suggested that Baron de Hirsch take advantage of this homesteading policy and establish a "regular and properly organised scheme of colonisation" in North-western Canada.[55] This would serve the interests of the Jewish Colonization Association, which intended to found Jewish agricultural colonies; of the Jewish community of Canada, which was anxious to ensure the hasty absorption of Jewish immigrants into the Canadian economy; and the

Bureau found employment for 2,250 Jews, in 1908 for 2,390, in 1909 for 1,396, in 1910 for 3,822, in 1911 for 1,896, in 1912 for 1,271 and in 1913 for 11,275 Jews throughout Canada.

53

	ICA Expenditures on Local Relief	*ICA Expenditures on the Baron de Hirsch Day School*
1900	$ 9,092.46	$ 2,804.07
1901	7,426.11	3,460.40
1902	5.496.35	4,771.91
1903	7,998.83	4,941.41
1904	13,082.63	5,186.58
1905	16,988.64	9,072.69
1906	no figure available	no figure available
1907	17,110.43	4,043.08
1908	45,998.60	5,548.85
1909	33,805.24	2,666.46
1910	no figure available	no figure available
1911	32,868.86	3,901.30
1912	no figure available	no figure available
1913	12,723.37	no figure available
1914	14,123.58	no figure available

Source: National Archives of the CJC, *Baron de Hirsch Institute Annual Reports, 1900–1914*.

54 Originally the government offered an adjoining quarter section at the price of $1.00 per acre.

55 National Archives of CJC, *Annual Report of the Young Men's Hebrew Benevolent Society*, 1st October 1891.

Canadian government, which wanted to turn the prairies into the nation's breadbasket.

In January 1892, Baron de Hirsch and the Jewish Colonization Association agreed to spend 30,000 dollars (500 dollars per settlement of 60 families) for the establishment of a Jewish agricultural colony in the Canadian interior.[56] The members of the Young Men's Hebrew Benevolent Society petitioned the Canadian government for all the even-numbered homesteads at Township 3, Range 5, west of the second milial meridian in the extreme south of Assiniboia (Saskatchewan), near the Estevan mines. The land was reported to be fertile and the proximity of the mines would ensure the homesteaders plenty of fuel in the winter months, as well as employment, should they require supplementary income during the first few years. Furthermore, a small Jewish community had sprung up along the newly built branch line of the Canadian Pacific Railway, at Oxbow:[57] some of its members were shopkeepers and tradesmen while others were trying their hand at farming. The men in Montreal believed the presence of other Jews nearby would facilitate the adaptation of their settlers. Hence on 28th April 1892, a group of 27 brave Jewish pioneers left Montreal to found an agricultural colony: they were joined by 20 other Jewish men at Winnipeg and Regina.[58] All had signed contracts accepting their indebtedness to the Jewish Colonization Association and promising to begin repayment of their loans by the end of the first year. They named their settlement Hirsch, in honour of the man who had made it possible to realise their "impossible dreams". Their wives and children remained in Montreal, Winnipeg and Regina until the autumn when their houses had been built and their pantries stocked. By the end of 1892, the Jewish Colonization Association had sponsored, and the Young Men's Hebrew Benevolent Society had supervised, the establishment of an agricultural settlement of 11,040 acres of land, 211 horses and 213 bulls and cows on the Canadian prairies.[59] It proved "impossible to procure a man of the Jewish persuasion who was both responsible and capable and who, combined with these two qualities, had a knowledge of agriculture sufficient to enable him to impart instruction to the colonists and (to) supervise them in their agricultural pursuits",[60] so the men in Montreal appointed as manager the man they had consulted about the location of Hirsch, Mr. McDiarmid, for a twelve-month-period.

The first years at Hirsch were not as trouble-free as the settlers, or their sponsors, had anticipated: in 1892, a drought parched the soil, in 1893 hail destroyed the crops and in 1894 grasshoppers ate their way through the Canadian Midwest. Furthermore, most of the homesteaders were inexperienced farmers who had no knowledge about the climate and conditions of the North American prairies, and their manager, McDiarmid, could not rise to the

[56]For a fuller discussion see Switzer, *op. cit.*, pp. 172–175.

[57]The branch line went from Brandon to Estevan and was built in 1888 to service the mines.

[58]ICA Archives, 'Report on the Establishment of a Jewish Colony in Northwestern Canada', H. Vineberg to Sonnenfeld, 5th May 1892.

[59]ICA Archives, Séance du Conseil d'administration du 22 février 1905, vol. 3, p. 188.

[60]ICA Archives, letter, L. A. Hart to the Chairman of the ICA, 15th January 1893.

difficult task of managing their colony while teaching them how to become accomplished farmers. However, the greatest problem which plagued the young colony and impeded its development was undercapitalisation: 500 dollars per family was an insufficient amount of money to install a homesteader on virgin prairie land and consequently, the pioneers were always short of working capital. During the first three years, McDiarmid was to be dismissed, many of the original homesteaders to abandon their farms and the Jewish Colonization Association to increase its investment to 222,500 francs. However, in 1895, the farmers reported a large harvest of high quality grain which they could sell at reasonable prices. "The colony was now an established success."[61] In 1897, the Association approved funds for the construction of a community centre and a schoolhouse and appointed a teacher for the children of the settlers and therefore, by the turn of the century Hirsch had established itself firmly as an agricultural settlement. Nevertheless, the homesteaders continued to rely on the Jewish Colonization Association to subsidise their needs and to underwrite their costs, and although the financial position of the colony continued to improve year after year, it never became self-sufficient and free of debt.

The Jewish Colonization Association was directly involved in only one other agricultural experiment on the Canadian prairies: the establishment of a Jewish colony at Qu'Appelle, Assiniboia (which was later renamed Lipton and Cupar). In 1899, Jews began to flood out of Romania, by boat, train and foot, taxing the reception committees, immigrant aid societies and shelters along their paths of migration. In an effort to regulate and organise this exodus, the *Alliance Israélite Universelle* convened a special conference in June 1900. Delegates from all the major Jewish communities in the West attended and agreed that the Jewish Colonization Association be placed in charge of controlling "l'émigration roumaine".[62] Quotas were placed on the numbers of Romanian Jews to be "let out" each month and the Jewish Colonization Association was to ensure that these were observed. Not surprisingly, it was unable to stem the tide: between 1900 and 1903 approximately 100,000 Jews left Romania each year and their numbers rose slightly thereafter.[63] In response to this tidal wave, the Jewish Colonization Association was forced to find new homes at least for some of the refugees. Its administrators approached the Canadian emigration agent in London, W.R.T. Preston, on 10th July 1900 to sound out his government's reaction to receiving Romanian Jews. Preston indicated that Canada would be

> "desirous of welcoming able bodied and physically and morally suitable immigrants into the Dominion whatever their creed. What he (and his government) wished to avoid was that the immigrants, as certain of them have done, should infiltrate into the towns and swell the already overgrown population of the Canadian cities. A suitable immigration would be welcomed, would be afforded help and would be aided by government agents."[64]

[61]National Archives of CJC, Report by the Young Men's Hebrew Benevolent Society, 19th October 1896.

[62]YIVO Archives, HKM 15 (15.166–15.169), letter, secrétaire de l'Alliance Israélite Universelle to Director, ICA, 27th November 1900.

[63]Wischnitzer, *op. cit.*, p. 99.

[64]ICA Archives, Précis of Consultation on the Influx of Roumanian Jews, 10th July 1900.

Consequently, a second Jewish colony was founded in the Canadian interior to be settled by Jews from Romania. The Jewish Colonization Association provided the funds for the transport and installation of the colonists and Thomas Smart, the Deputy Minister of the Interior for the Canadian government was supposed to organise the selection of suitable candidates and the administration of their colony. Smart appointed Wolfsberg, a Hamburg Jew, recruitment officer and D. H. MacDonald of Fort Qu'Appelle, Assiniboia, a local businessman and banker, administrator of the settlement. Unfortunately, MacDonald proved to be an incompetent, unscrupulous and dishonest man who chose a tract of land far from the nearest railway station (it was twenty-five miles away), and notoriously difficult to farm. Smart, perhaps out of ignorance, filed for the homesteads with the Land Commissioner of the Canadian government at what came to be known as Qu'Appelle. Thus, from early on, the Deputy Minister displayed only the most scant interest in the project and left MacDonald free to manage the colony as he saw fit.

The first group of forty-nine Romanian Jews arrived in Winnipeg in the spring of 1901. Preston was waiting to escort them to their settlement, but unfortunately several members had contracted diphtheria and their installation was delayed for several weeks. When they finally travelled up to Qu'Appelle, their enthusiasm turned to despair: all they saw was barren prairie. MacDonald had neglected to have shelters erected to receive the travel-weary pioneers. He had appointed two men, Barnes and Morrison, as managers of the settlement, but these men were suspicious of foreigners and resented their presence in the Canadian hinterland. They were also resentful of the special treatment and consideration Jews seemed to be receiving from the Canadian government. They regarded the project as a joke, doomed to failure, and instead of helping the newcomers and teaching them how to cultivate the prairies, they undermined all its chances for success. They made no effort to install the Romanian Jews: instead of buying implements and chattels for farming, they spent all the Jewish Colonization Association funds on food and clothing which they doled out only when the necessity arose. The settlers turned to the equally ill-treated Indians from the nearby reservation for guidance. Complaints began to filter back to Europe but the administrators of the Association received reassurances from Thomas Smart that all was well in the colony. A second group of Romanian Jews were sent to Qu'Appelle in August 1901 and a third group in the spring of 1902.

The colonists were unable to support themselves or provide for their families and by the winter of 1903, 193 of the original 365 homesteaders had abandoned their land. Those who remained were facing starvation and deprivation.[65] A few of the homesteaders found their way to Milwaukee where they related their tales of woe to its Jewish community leaders. These stories were reported to the administrators of the Jewish Colonization Association who immediately ordered their own inspection. Louis Kahn of the Jewish Agricultural and

[65]ICA Archives, *Rapport de l'administration centrale pour l'année 1903.*

Industrial Aid Society of New York[66] was sent to Qu'Appelle, and when he confirmed the stories of the Milwaukee settlers, he was asked to stay on and to reorganise the colony. By the end of 1904, he had resuscitated the settlement: eleven vacant plots had been occupied, 13,480 acres of field had been cultivated and a *schochet* and a teacher had come to live in the settlement.

Qu'Appelle was the second agricultural settlement in Canada to be founded directly by the Jewish Colonization Association; it was also the last. The early years at Qu'Appelle had been no less problematic or disappointing than the early years at Hirsch, despite the promise of help from the Canadian government. If the men in Paris had been doubtful about the potential for Jewish agricultural development after their experience at Hirsch, they held no illusions after the painful experience at Qu'Appelle. However, this did not spell the end of the Association's involvement in Jewish farming on the Canadian prairies, even if it did herald the end of direct sponsorship. Throughout the early years of the twentieth century, young, idealistic and enterprising Jewish pioneers, anxious to try their luck in agriculture, took advantage of the government's homesteading policy and travelled into the interior, usually in groups of twenty or so men. They would discover an uninhabited corner of land and file their claim with the Land Commissioner of the Canadian government thereby giving birth to their own settlement. In 1886, Hermann Landau, a British representative of the Canadian Pacific Railway and a Jewish philanthropist, deposited 12,000 dollars with the railway company to settle John Heppner and four of his companions on land near Wapella, Assiniboia. By 1892 twenty Jewish families were farming the land around Wapella, the oldest independent Jewish agricultural community in Western Canada. In 1888 a Jewish farming settlement was founded at Oxbow, Assiniboia, and in 1903 Jacob Bender organised Bender Hamlet, 72 miles north of Winnipeg, Manitoba (later renamed Narcisse in honour of Narcisse Leven), the only Jewish agricultural colony to be modelled after an Eastern European village. In 1906 Edenbridge and Sonnenfeld were pioneered in Saskatchewan as were Rumsey and Trochu Valley in Alberta. Between 1905 and the outbreak of the First World War, a number of smaller Jewish farming establishments sprang up throughout Eastern and Western Canada: Sainte Sophie, New Glasgow, La Macaza, Saint Lin and Saint Vincent de Paul in Quebec, Ezra (South Alsask), Camper (New Hirsch), Pineridge, Springfield, Bird's Hill, Lorette, Transcoma and Kildonan in Manitoba, Rosetown and South Morse in Saskatchewan and

[66]Towards the end of the nineteenth century, Jacob H. Schiff suggested the establishment of a credit institution which would sponsor the Jewish immigrant in agricultural and industrial homesteads. He approached the ICA and negotiated an agreement for its foundation. The ICA accepted an arrangement whereby it would contribute $80,000 annually and the Baron de Hirsch Fund would advance $30,000 annually over a ten-year-period. The new credit agency was founded in February 1900, under the name The Jewish Agricultural and Industrial Aid Society. In 1922 its name was changed to The Jewish Agricultural Society because its labour placement bureau was dissolved. The agency funded agricultural projects and development, lent money to Jewish tradesmen, encouraged and facilitated the relocation of Jewish industry to the countryside and generally offered incentives for Jews willing to experiment with a rural lifestyle. For a fuller discussion see Joseph, *op. cit.*, pp. 116–183.

Montefiore in Alberta. Jews also cultivated garden farms near the larger Canadian cities of Montreal in Quebec, Toronto, Hamilton, London, Ottawa and Krugerdorf in Ontario, Winnipeg in Manitoba and Regina and Saskatoon in Saskatchewan.[67]

These venturesome Jewish pioneers, who took up agriculture in the Canadian interior, soon discovered what the men in Paris and Montreal had found at Hirsch and Qu'Appelle: ploughing virgin prairie and planting the first crops was a backbreaking task which required an endless source of income, energy and commitment. In most cases, their funds were exhausted long before they had achieved self-sufficiency and in some cases, even before they had harvested their first crops. The administrators of the Jewish Colonization Association empowered its agents in Canada to travel throughout the provinces, seeking out the independent Jewish farmers and farming communities and offering those with potential for development financial assistance and technological advice. If these inspectors believed the pioneers showed promise, the Association would provide them with loans at advantageous rates (four percent instead of the Canadian rate which was eight percent and over a longer period of time than traditional lending institutions.)[68] In 1912 the Jewish Colonization Association subsidised the establishment of a permanent office in Winnipeg to oversee the disbursement and collection of loans and the advancement of Jewish agriculture in Western Canada. "The primary object in opening up this office was in order that those of our people who desire to take up land might be in a position to obtain reliable information about their future possessions."[69] H. Rosenblatt was appointed manager of the Winnipeg office and was also placed in charge of settling people he believed could become successful farmers on the vacant plots of Hirsch and Qu'Appelle.

During the years before the First World War, the Jewish Colonization Association also financed the construction of synagogues and community centres throughout the colonies and independent settlements, and underwrote the cost of educating the farmers' children, in an effort to render life on the frontiers as comfortable and familiar as possible. (When the provincial governments legislated universal free education, the Association continued to sponsor Hebrew and religious instruction.)[70]

Nevertheless, the Jewish settlers fell prey to the many hazards of pioneering the Canadian hinterland – the hard climate, an unsuitable location far from a railway, a water supply, or a supplemental source of income, and under-capitalisation – and most were forced to abandon their dreams. Even the few Jewish farmers who survived the difficult pre-war years and who prospered from the war-time demand for foodstuff, suffered serious setbacks during the

[67]For more on this see Switzer, *op. cit.*, pp. 218–222 and pp. 272–273.

[68]It should be noted that the mortgages did stipulate that the farmer pay 8% interest, but there was a clause in the agreement that reduced the interest rate to 4% if the farmer made regular repayments.

[69]National Archives of CJC, Report of the Canadian Committee for year ending 1912, p. 18.

[70]National Archives of CJC, Letterbook of the Canadian Committee, 1911–1914, vol. II, letter, M. B. Davis and L. Cohen to Director, ICA, 3rd August 1911.

agricultural slump of the early 1920s and the economic depression of the 1930s. During the inter-war years, Eyre, Montefiore, Narcisse and New Hirsch disappeared completely while the other settlements saw their populations greatly diminished, and by the end of the Second World War, almost all of the Jewish colonies on the Canadian prairies had been dissolved. Therefore, the colonisation policy pursued by the Jewish Colonization Association in Canada proved to be of little enduring consequence.

The failure of Jewish agriculture in Canada can be attributed in part to the Jewish Colonization Association, in part to its representatives in Canada (the Young Men's Hebrew Benevolent Society and later the Canadian Committee of the Jewish Colonization Association), and in part to the settlers and their expectations. However, it is important to remember that Jews were not the only ethnic group unable to transform themselves into prairie farmers: immigrants whose families had been farmers in Europe for generations were also unable to adapt and prosper in the untamed North American interior.[71] The pioneer's destiny was determined as much by the harsh weather – a spring that arrived too late, a summer that was too wet or too dry, an autumn that lingered too long, or departed too abruptly, forcing the farmer to leave his unharvested crop in the field, covered in snow – as by any other factor. The stark and isolated nature of life on the prairies at the turn of the century, without any of the amenities or conveniences of city life, undermined the courage and conviction of many homesteaders. Moreover, throughout most of the twentieth century, Canada was undergoing a period of industrialisation and accelerated urbanisation and consequently, the pioneers who ventured into agriculture were going against the trend of economic development. Therefore, the utopian notions about agriculture and its regenerative powers, harboured by Baron de Hirsch and by the many Russian and Eastern European Jews, were simply not applicable to the Canadian context: it would not be possible to normalise the position of Jews in Canada by having them take up agriculture on the prairies in the twentieth century. Three other factors served to tip the balance still further against the Jewish colonists and their chances of transforming themselves into self-sufficient agriculturalists: the Jewish Colonization Association never formulated a systematic and rational method of settling Jewish people on farms in Canada (it only instituted "direct colonisation" in 1925), its agents in Canada were never able to provide the fragile communities with effective management and guidance, and the rigours of life on the frontiers of civilisation did not fulfil even the most independent Jew's need for contact with his culture and community. However, if agricultural colonisation was not the channel through which Eastern and Russian Jewry became absorbed into Canadian society, it must not be written off as a complete and utter failure. Its real significance must not be measured by traditional standards of success – productivity and profit – but by the motivations, aspirations and goals of the idealistic pioneers. At a certain level, their ideals and objectives resembled those

[71] The Norwegian community in North Dakota is one example of an immigrant group, which was familiar with farming, struggling to adapt. The Ukrainian immigrants in Canada also had adjustment problems.

of the *halutzim* in Palestine during the closing decades of Ottoman rule, and testify to the strength, and energy, of the quest for normalisation and renascence that fired the imagination of more than a few of the Tsar's persecuted subjects. Therefore, the Jewish experience with pioneer farming in Canada must be considered part of one of the most significant dynamics of twentieth-century Jewish life: the active and energetic search for a new and "normalised" Jewish presence in the modern world.

Baron de Hirsch arrived at his own conclusions about the shape and form of the Jewish future and he founded the Jewish Colonization Association to oversee the realisation of his vision. When he died, the Association was handed over to the Jewish communities of Europe, and their leaders broadened its purpose and redefined its objectives and goals. By the time the First World War broke out, it had become a very different agency from the one founded by Baron de Hirsch: it was no longer dedicated solely to the removal of Jews from Russia and Eastern Europe and to their resettlement in agricultural colonies, primarily in the Argentine, where they would undergo a process of auto-emancipation. The new administrators sponsored programmes they believed would make Jewish life thrive in the East and in the New World. They may have been unable to transcend their own historical experience and world view, or to throw their support wholeheartedly behind Jewish emigration to the West, but they were able to ensure that the Jewish Colonization Association played an increasingly active and influential role in the Jewish world. It was under their leadership that the Association dispensed aid to those in need beyond the Pale of Settlement, and it was under their direction that it assisted the fledgling Jewish communities in the New World as they struggled with the pressures of receiving, accommodating and absorbing the thousands, and hundreds of thousands, of Jewish immigrants searching for new lives in new lands. Canada housed just such a Jewish community at the turn of the century, and it was due to the guidance and tutelage of the administrators and personnel of the Jewish Colonization Association that its members could accept their role, and the role Canada would play, in the story of Jewish survival and renascence.

"Waiting Room Shanghai": Australian Reactions to the Plight of the Jews in Shanghai after the Second World War

BY SUZANNE D. RUTLAND

> "I have to transmit to you some information which should by now not be shocking to any Jew, but which nevertheless still horrifies one . . . The new Australian Consul in Shanghai said:
> 'We have never wanted these people in Australia and we still don't want them. We will issue a few visas to those who have relations there as a gesture.'"
> Adolph C. Glassgold, American Joint Distribution Committee, Shanghai,
> 2nd December 1948.

The story of the Jews in Shanghai deals with a group of German and Austrian Jews who found sanctuary in the Far East immediately before the outbreak of the Second World War and then had to flee again after the war. After 1945 a new search was begun for countries outside Europe which would accept Central European Jewish refugees from Shanghai. Australia was seen as one possible destination. In the immediate post-war period the Australian government introduced a new immigration policy which sought to increase substantially Australia's population by tapping previously restricted migrant sources, especially among the non-British Europeans displaced by the war (DPs). In this way the Australian Labor government and the newly created Department of Immigration under its minister, Arthur A. Calwell, introduced a radically new migration policy. The aim was that increased population would strengthen Australia's defences, decrease the threat of an Asian invasion and provide a larger labour force. Given this new policy it appeared that at least some of the Central European Jewish DPs in Shanghai would be granted a chance to re-create a new life in Australia. After initial optimistic developments, the fears and prejudices which had prevented a humanitarian approach to Jewish migration in the free world before the Second World War reappeared. The Australian government decided to oppose any significant Jewish migration from Shanghai, which resulted in intense disappointment for all those involved in the programme.[1]

Hitler's antisemitic policies created a refugee problem of immense proportions. For Jews who wanted to flee Nazi Europe most doors were shut. The

[1]I wish to acknowledge the assistance of Professor Konrad Kwiet, University of New South Wales; Professor Alan Crown who established the Archive of Australian Judaica, University of Sydney and archivist Sister M. Dacy; S. Field, President, the Australian Jewish Welfare Society, Sydney; and R. Benjamin, President, the Australian Jewish Welfare and Relief Society, Melbourne, and of all those who willingly agreed to be interviewed, including Sydney D. Einfeld, and Walter Lippmann.

United States, which had offered refuge to millions of Jews fleeing from Tsarist Russia in the nineteenth century closed her ears to the cries for help. Emma Lazarus's famous words in the statue of Liberty: "Give me your tired, your poor, Your huddled masses yearning to breathe free", no longer applied for most Jewish refugees. The inadequacy of international responses to the refugee issue was seen in the failure of the Evian Conference in June 1938, a failure which only encouraged Hitler in his antisemitic policies. Australia was to make a token gesture to the refugee problem by offering to admit 15,000 over three years in December 1938, after the pogroms of November 1938, the *Kristallnacht*. In all about 7,000 Jewish refugees arrived in Australia before the outbreak of the Second World War.[2] There was, however, only one place in the world where Jewish refugees could go without a visa – that was the port of Shanghai in China. Shanghai was traditionally a free port and its large International Settlement had proved a place of refuge for a previous group of Europeans, the White Russians. The Japanese, who controlled Shanghai after 1937, kept Shanghai open for Jewish refugees because they believed that Jews had considerable influence on the international scene.

To the Jews of Europe Shanghai seemed like an almost impossible haven of rescue. Most preferred to wait until they received visas from the United States or other parts of the free world. After the *Kristallnacht*, however, the wholesale urge for exodus from Germany and Austria propelled many to accept the uncertainties of the Orient. As one Viennese Jew stated: "'. . . I'm going to Shanghai!' 'To Shanghai! But you've only three more months to wait before your visa from America comes through. Why go to the Orient?' '. . . I almost took my life last week. Only this news, that one can easily get to Shanghai, kept me from doing it'."[3]

David Kranzler has stated:

> "Shanghai! By the end of 1938, the name had become a talisman for thousands of German and Austrian Jews, a talisman with which they could transform the nightmare of their lives into a hope of salvation. It was the only place where one could hope to escape the Nazi terror without that magic formula, that open sesame, a visa. . . ."[4]

In all about 18,000 Jewish refugees from Germany and Austria settled in Shanghai before the gates to emigration were closed by the Japanese with the outbreak of war in September 1939, while in 1941 1,000 Polish Jewish refugees who had fled from Lithuania to Kobe, Japan, were resettled in Shanghai.

Most of the German and Austrian Jews who had fled to Shanghai chose it as their final destination because of their need to leave Europe in haste. After the *Kristallnacht* many Jewish men were imprisoned in Dachau and other concentration camps. Those who were released were often freed on condition

[2]See Michael Blakeney, 'Australia and the Jewish Refugees from Central Europe. Government Policy 1933–1939', in *LBI Year Book XXIX* (1984), pp. 103–133; Andrew Marcus, 'Jewish Migration to Australia 1938–1949', in *Journal of Australian Studies*, No. 13 (November 1983), pp. 16–31; and Suzanne D. Rutland, 'Australian Government Policies to Refugee Migration 1933–1939', in *Journal of the Royal Australian Historical Society*, vol. 69, Pt. 4 (March 1984), pp. 224–238.

[3]David Kranzler, *Japanese, Nazis and Jews. The Jewish Refugee Community, 1938–1945*, New York 1976, pp. 25–26.

[4]*Ibid.*, p. 26.

that they left Germany and Austria within two to three weeks. For these men and their families, Shanghai was usually the only option. As one Austrian refugee commented:

> "We faced similar conditions to most. We had to leave Austria after father was released from Dachau. He was released only on condition that we leave the country within a few weeks. We managed to get tickets to Shanghai. As the boat was not leaving for another six to eight weeks, we lived in Switzerland with a Quaker family. We had no money. We had to pray every evening but they did not try to convert us."[5]

In this way, escape to Shanghai became a life-line of survival for many Central Europeans after the November pogroms.

Kranzler posed the question:

> "What kind of place was Shanghai, which so suddenly beckoned to thousands of refugees from Hitler's persecution? Although hardly a household word in the average Jewish family of Germany or Austria, Shanghai was no primitive village in some distant place. It was, in fact, the world's seventh largest port, and contained a sizeable cosmopolitan population, which resided in two foreign concessions under Western control."[6]

Shanghai was, indeed a heterogeneous international city with a native population of about four million. At the time of the arrival of the German and Austrian refugees, it included not one, but two distinct Jewish communities. The older one consisted of a small Sephardi community of about 700 members, which originated largely from Baghdad. The Sephardim settled in Shanghai after the port had been opened by the British in 1841. Many members of the Sephardi community held British citizenship and were associated with the prosperous Sassoon family or other wealthy families such as the Kadoories.[7] The second, a much larger and more recent group, was composed of Ashkenazi Jews, most of whom had escaped from Russia after the October Revolution of 1917. The Ashkenazim never matched the commercial success of the Sephardim. By the late 1930s there were about 4,000 White Russian Jews in Shanghai, in addition to other White Russian Jewish communities in China, the most important being at Harbin.[8]

By the time the refugees from Nazism arrived in Shanghai the economic position of the city had deteriorated. In 1937 the Japanese occupied Shanghai and closed the door to its traditional trade links with the Chinese interior. The refugees were faced with an extremely difficult task of re-establishing themselves in an adverse economic climate. They arrived at the *Bund* where they were collected by open trucks on the wharves and taken to a disused school in Hongkew, a suburb of Shanghai, which had been almost totally destroyed by the Japanese invasion of 1937 and became the centre of initial Jewish refugee

[5]Interview with Lisl Gerber, Sydney 1985.

[6]Kranzler, *op. cit.*, p. 39.

[7]*Ibid.*, p. 41; and interview with Reuben Moalem, member of the Sephardi Jewish community in Shanghai whose father, a British citizen, came from Aden and whose mother was from Baghdad. Moalem was born in Shanghai in 1899 and was closely associated with the Shanghai Jewish community and migrated to Australia in 1950.

[8]Kranzler *op. cit.*, p. 41; Fritz Kauffmann, 'Die Juden in Shanghai im 2. Weltkrieg. Erinnerungen eines Vorstandsmitglieds der Jüdischen Gemeinde', in *Bulletin des Leo Baeck Instituts*, 73 (1986), pp. 13–14.

settlement after 1938. The reception of the refugees was organised by a committee formed from the local Jewish community and was later taken over by the American Jewish Joint Distribution Committee (JDC/Joint).

A few of the refugees managed to leave Shanghai for Australia in the period 1939 to 1941. One interesting case was that of Dr. Mark Siegelberg who had been a chief-editor of a leading Vienna daily. After fourteen months in Dachau and Buchenwald, he was released in 1938 and emigrated to Shanghai where he published the *Shanghai Jewish Chronicle* for two and a half years. In late 1941 he was evacuated with the help of the British embassy for services rendered on behalf of the Allied cause and he settled in Melbourne where he began publication of a German-language newspaper.[9]

Until Pearl Harbour, Shanghai Jewry was left alone by the Japanese. After the Pacific war began many of the Sephardi community who had British citizenship were interned by the Japanese[10], who gradually came more directly under Nazi influence resulting in a reversal of their previously pro-Jewish policy. In February 1943 the Japanese decided to relocate all stateless refugees in a "designated area" in Hongkew which was cordoned off as a ghetto. The Jewish refugees who had managed to establish themselves outside Hongkew and become self-sufficient again lost their homes and many saw their businesses destroyed. The Japanese called on the White Russian Jews, who had been excluded from the edict, to supervise the relocation, thus creating a wedge between the Russian and Central European sections of the Jewish community.[11]

After 1943 the situation greatly deteriorated. Many of the refugees lived in conditions of pitiful poverty, aggravated by the decreasing level of relief available. The terrible conditions were described in a letter in the following terms:

> "In May 1943 we were given two months to look for other accommodation, and all Jews had to leave their flats to go and live together in a small district, which affords only the most primitive dwellings. Practically all are small, dirty Chinese houses, mostly one story, to which lead up wooden ladders, stone floors, leaking roofs and without toilets, stoves etc. In Europe we would not even have used such places to house animals.
> We have fixed up our homes as much as possible, but some rooms were difficult to adapt. I, for instance, live in a small room over the entrance of a lane: there is a stone floor and no floor covering can keep the cold out. There is a tin roof which makes the room very hot in summer and unbearably cold in winter; besides it is quite rusty and when it rains there are 1–2 cm. of water on the floor of my room . . . Just imagine that in this room I have spent two winters and am now roasting for the third summer."[12]

The Central European refugees were able to survive largely as a result of the activities of the JDC, which re-established funding links between Shanghai and America in December 1943 following representations from Laura Margolis. These funds were sent through neutral Switzerland.[13] By the end of the war

[9]*Sydney Jewish News*, 9th June 1944.

[10]Reuben Moalem was himself interned by the Japanese.

[11]Kranzler, *op. cit.*, p. 521.

[12]Letter from Shanghai, 16th August 1945, in B40 and B42, Correspondence Files, New South Wales Jewish Board of Deputies, Archive of Australian Judaica.

[13]Laura L. Margolis, 'Race Against Time in Shanghai', reprinted from *Survey Graphic*, Magazine of Social Interpretation, March 1944, in B37, NSW Jewish Board of Deputies, Archive of Australian Judaica; and Kranzler, *op. cit.*, p. 99.

11,000 out of the 18,000 Jews in the ghetto were dependent on the relief allocated by the JDC.[14]

The ghetto was liberated in September 1945 but its inhabitants faced an insecure future. After 1945 China was torn by civil war between the Kuomintang led by Chiang Kai-shek and the Communists led by Mao Tse-tung. On 26th November 1945 the Chiang Kai-shek government announced the deportation of all Austrian and German-Jewish refugees in Shanghai.[15] The refugees were opposed to repatriation so the Joint negotiated with the Chinese government to permit the refugees to remain in Shanghai while they initiated an orderly emigration programme. In December 1945 the Joint director in Shanghai, Manuel Siegel, was replaced by Charles Jordan[16] whose task it was to relocate the refugees. Jordan later summed up the plight of the Central European Jews in Shanghai in the following terms:

> "They are middle-class people and workers. They owe their allegiance to no 'isms'. They cannot remain in Shanghai, which offers no possibility for them to settle down, take roots and form the semblance of a normal citizen's life, such as they knew before the Nazis took their homes away from them and exterminated their loved ones. They have kept up their morale. Yes, they haven't faltered . . . yet . . . They are perfectly good, useful people still, but the world, which has helped them to survive, must not fail them in providing ways and means for their real rehabilitation."[17]

The problem was where could they go? The doors of "the world" which had remained firmly shut in the 1930s were still firmly closed to Jewish refugees after 1945, while immigration to Palestine was curtailed under the British Mandate.

One possible place was Australia. In August 1945 Australia's first minister for immigration, Arthur Calwell, had announced a migration programme for survivors of the holocaust on the basis of family sponsorship for humanitarian reasons.[18] This announcement had emerged largely as a result of the close personal ties between Calwell and a number of prominent members of Melbourne Jewry. Paul Morawetz, himself a refugee from Nazi Europe who settled in Melbourne before the war, had worked as an interpreter during the war and had established a personal friendship with Calwell who was then

[14]At the end of 1943 only 6,000 were dependent on relief; April 1944 this had increased to 7,300 and June 1945 to 11,000, *ibid.*, p. 560; and Kauffmann, *loc. cit.*, p. 23.

[15]'Waiting Room Shanghai', by C. K. Bliss, *New Citizen*, vol. 6, 15th September 1946.

[16]In 1942 the director of the AJDC, Laura Margolis, and her assistant, Manuel Siegel, were interned. Laura Margolis was repatriated to the United States in 1943 but Siegel was not released until after the war when he took charge of the Joint Office in Shanghai, *Almanac, Shanghai 1946/1947*, published by *Shanghai Echo*, Shanghai 1947, p. 37. Charles Jordan was born in Philadelphia in 1908, attended Schools of Social Work in Philadelphia and New York, and studied at the University of Berlin. He joined the JDC in 1941 as director for the Caribbean area; enlisted in the navy (1943–1945) and after the war rejoined JDC, serving as director of Far Eastern activities (headquarters Shanghai) (1945–1948); director of Paris office (1948–1951); assistant director, Europe (1951–1955); director general from 1955; and later in New York as Vice-President; dying tragically while visiting Czechoslovakia in 1967.

[17]Statement No. 1, p. 3 by Charles Jordan to the AJWS, Sydney Branch, 20th August–20th September 1947, in the archives of the AJWS, Sydney.

[18]*Sydney Jewish News* (*SJN*), 31st August and 21st September 1945 and AJWS Minutes, Victorian Branch, 27th August and 27th October 1945, in the archives AJW&RS, Melbourne.

minister for information.[19] It appeared to the Jewish leaders of the newly-established Executive Council of Australian Jewry (ECAJ) that Australia might be able to offer assistance and the chance of a new life to some of the Jews of Shanghai.

Under the family reunion scheme introduced by Calwell in August 1945 a number of Jews in Shanghai were able to obtain landing permits and visas for Australia, after Calwell agreed to include this group following negotiations with the ECAJ in October 1945.[20] The problem was that Australia had no apparatus to facilitate migration from Shanghai and there were no direct shipping routes. An Australian legation office was established in Shanghai after the war and acted as the representative of the Australian Department of Immigration in China. From mid-1946 H. M. Loveday, the third secretary at the legation, was in charge of processing landing permits and visas.[21] He co-operated with Jordan as the JDC helped organise shipping and paid the fares for the Jewish refugees to UNRRA.

In April 1946 the first group of 37 Jewish refugees from Shanghai, sponsored by relatives in Australia, arrived on the *SS Javanese Prince* at Newcastle. General Secretary of the Australian Jewish Welfare Society (AJWS), Sydney branch, Walter Brand, travelled to Newcastle to facilitate their reception and absorption into Australia.[22] Of the 2,000 Jewish refugees who had migrated from Shanghai to different countries by March 1947, 776 were destined for Australia. This constituted 38 per cent of the migrants, and Australia was second only to the United States in the number of Jewish refugees received from Shanghai at that time.[23]

The migration of these refugees did not proceed smoothly because of a shortage of suitable means of transport. In July 1946 a group of 299 Jewish refugees sailed to Hong Kong with Australian landing permits and visas, booked to travel on the troopship, the *SS Duntroon* to Australia. The *Duntroon* was supposed to be diverted to Hong Kong after returning Asian evacuees from Australia to China, but government permission for this diversion was withdrawn at the last moment. It was announced publicly by the Australian Department for External Affairs that the *Duntroon* could not be used by civilians

[19] Interview with Walter Lippmann, Sydney 1984.

[20] 'Shanghai Unit', Corres. 30th April 1945–25th March 1946, New South Wales Jewish Board of Deputies, Archive of Australian Judaica, Box B40. In August 1945 a provisional committee for Shanghai Jewish Refugees was formed in New South Wales under the chairmanship of Dr J. M. Machover. This committee requested Masel to negotiate with Calwell on behalf of the Shanghai refugees. It also dealt with plans to send a Jewish Relief Team to Shanghai, partly financed by the United Jewish Relief Fund, Australia. These plans were cancelled when UNRRA did not agree to assist with transport costs, although a Relief Team was sent later to Europe. Boxes B34, B37, B40 and B42.

[21] Report by H. M. Loveday, 21st March 1947 in 'Reports from Shanghai on Alien Immigration', CA 51, Dept. of Imm. 1945–1974, Corres. Files, Australian Archives Office, CRS A434, item 47/3/21.

[22] *SJN*, 12th April 1946 and Minutes of the AJWS, Sydney, 17th December 1945 and 18th December 1946.

[23] H. M. Loveday's report, 21st March 1947, 'Reports from Shanghai on Alien Immigration' (note 21).

from either Shanghai or Hong Kong as it was required by the army.[24] In a confidential report, however, a different reason was given. It was feared that a large number of refugees arriving by ship in Australia would provoke adverse comment due to the housing shortage after the war. It was felt that the refugees from Shanghai might take over accommodation left empty by the evacuees to the detriment of ex-servicemen and that for this reason it was undesirable to permit refugees to enter Australia at that time.[25] This decision was made despite an effort by the Australian embassy in Washington to persuade the Department of Immigration to act favourably in regard to the refugees because "apart from any other considerations the Palestine situation has made the Jewish refugee question an inflammatory public issue here" in America.[26] Further negotiations in regard to another troopship, the *SS Reynella*, envisaged to replace the *Duntroon* resulted in the same negative decision.[27]

These decisions left the group of refugees stranded in Hong Kong where they were accommodated in two large ballrooms of the Peninsula Hotel, one being used for men and the other for women. The refugees, including many elderly people, had to go out and buy camp-beds on which they slept in the ballrooms. In some cases they lived under these difficult conditions for up to six months while Jordan organised alternative transport by chartering ships and planes. One of the first of the chartered ships was the *SS Yochow*. Only young and healthy passengers were accepted for this trip as conditions on board were shocking. Fifty refugees were accommodated and as there were no cabins they slept in the hold in hammocks or on the deck on the camp-beds they brought with them from the Peninsula Hotel. Soup was served in the same bucket which people used to wash their feet and many passengers were sea-sick for most of the journey.[28]

The largest group of Jewish refugees to sail from Shanghai in 1946 came on the *Hwa Lien*, which set sail on the 30th December 1946 with 52 merchant marines and 474 refugees on board, of whom 306 were Jewish. All passengers on this ship had their tickets organised by the Joint which paid U.S. $50,000 for the Jewish refugees, while the non-Jews travelling on the same boat paid their fares at a much cheaper rate subsidised by the JDC.[29] Conditions on the *Hwa Lien* were also frightful. The boat was built in 1908 as a ferry boat named the *Maori* for crossing between the North and South Islands of New Zealand and it only had facilities for a twelve-hour journey. The boat had been purchased by a Chinese shipping company after the war, renamed the *Hwa Lien* and modified for longer sea journeys. On the upper deck two large containers for oil and

[24] *Ibid.*, Appendix 'D' and 'Shipping Jewish Refugees en route to Australia', CA 18, Dept. of Ext. Affairs (II) 1921–1970, Corres. Files, Australian Archives Office, A1067, item IC46/25/16.

[25] 'Refugees in Shanghai: Question of Providing Shipping Accommodation on ss *Duntroon* (or by aircraft) or ss *Reynella*', CA 51, Dept. of Imm., Corres. Files, Australian Archives Office, CRS A434, item 46/3/6058.

[26] *Ibid.*, Cablegram dated 13th August 1946, received 14th August 1946, to the Dept. of Imm. from the Australian Legation, Washington.

[27] 'Shipping Jewish Refugees en route to Australia' (note 24).

[28] Interview (taped) with Gerty Mueller.

[29] *SJN*, 7th February 1947.

water had been added, making the ship top heavy so that it "rolled like a rolling pin".[30] According to a letter from the Australian legation, Nanking:

> "The ship was ill-staffed, dirty and, at least from a layman's point of view, semi-seaworthy. The UNRRA Travel Authorities had booked a number of people being repatriated to Australia but, after inspection, they also decided that it was most undesirable to send any of their personnel on the *Hwa Lien*, and cancelled all their passages. The sailing of the ship was marked by complete disorder – passengers embarked on Sunday 29 December, but sailing was held up owing to engine trouble; meanwhile, apparently no facilities were prepared for feeding the passengers who, up to the time of sailing, are reported not to have had any meals on board."[31]

The hardships on the *Hwa Lien* were outlined in newspaper articles which referred to poor food, inadequate water and high prices charged for amenities.[32] There were restrictions on drinking water and the toilets and bathrooms only had salt water while there was no refrigeration on board. As the kitchen did not have facilities for cooking meals for the large number of people on board, drums were installed and the food was cooked with steam from the engine. There were three separate sittings in the dining room and both the food and the drinking water had a slight taste of petrol. By the fourth day of the journey the bread was stale and mouldy. When they arrived in Cairns fresh bread was delivered and when the crew continued to serve mouldy bread, the passengers revolted.[33] Such was the desperation of the refugees in Shanghai that they were prepared to accept any conditions at any cost, provided that they could leave Shanghai.

The composition of the refugees on the *Hwa Lien* is of interest. There were a large number of Polish Bundists, many from Bialystok.[34] These Polish Jews had arrived in Shanghai in 1941, having travelled from Lithuania via Kobe, Japan, to Shanghai as a result of the humanitarian actions of Dutch and Japanese consulates in Kovno, Lithuania.[35] The sponsorship of most of the Polish Jews who wished to settle in Australia was organised by Jacob Waks, a Bundist from Bialystok, who had managed to escape from Vilna, Lithuania, circuitously to Australia during the war.[36] His landing permit for Australia was arranged through his niece, Mina Fink, whose husband Leo Fink was to become President of the Australian Jewish Welfare and Relief Society, 1947–1960. As a Bundist, Waks soon became a strong Labor supporter in Australia and a friend of Arthur Calwell. In order to expedite the issuing of permits for his confrères in Shanghai, Waks rose from his sick bed to meet Calwell to request that he be allowed to sign all the Form 40 applications in person.[37] When questioned later by officials of the Department of Immigration about the sponsorship of Jewish migrants from Shanghai, not only by Jacob Waks but also by Leo Fink and

[30]Interview (phone) F. Gunsberger, Sydney 1985, a Viennese passenger on the *Hwa Lien*.

[31]Letter from the Australian Legation Nanking to the Dept. of Ext. Affairs, 23rd January 1947, 'Shipping Jewish refugees en route to Australia' (note 24).

[32]*Daily Telegraph* (Sydney), 27th January 1947.

[33]Interview with F. Gunsberger.

[34]Written testimony, H. Bachrach, Melbourne, 1985.

[35]See Marvin Tokayer and Mary Schwartz, *The Fugu Plan: The Untold Story of the Japanese and the Jews During World War II*, New York 1979; and Kranzler, *op. cit.*

[36]Interview (taped) with Chaskal Davis, Sydney 1985.

[37]Interview with Mina Fink, Sydney 1985; and written testimony of H. Bachrach.

Abram Sokol (also a Bialystoker who arrived in Australia during the war via Japan), Waks stated that the family description was correct as "all Jews were 'cousins' or 'brothers' ".[38] The shared experiences of persecution and flight from Lithuania to the East made Waks and Sokol feel that "all Jews are a family" and use this concept in sponsoring Jews from Shanghai under the family migration scheme. The Australian Consul General in Shanghai was suspicious of a large group all being guaranteed by one man, but he did not make any difficulties in issuing the visas.[39] This was probably because the Australian consular official, H. M. Loveday, believed that some Jewish migrants from Shanghai could make a positive contribution to Australian development.

The use of the close relative scheme in Melbourne to promote the entry of people who were not relatives but people from the same home town such as Bialystok, Lodz or Warsaw, led to conflict with the Sydney Welfare Society. In Sydney there were no "Landsmannschaften" and all European DP Jews were brought to Sydney on the basis of guarantees provided by relatives or very close friends.[40] The Sydney Jewish community, under the leadership of Saul Symonds, did not approve of the Bialystoker support for the Polish Jews in Shanghai. The rivalry and tensions between Sydney and Melbourne, the two largest cities in Australia, is legendary and was also reflected within the Jewish community. Before 1945 there were more Jews living in Sydney but, because Melbourne followed a more aggressive policy through the "Landsmannschaften", it attracted more Jewish survivors after the war and became the larger community.

Calwell was concerned at the Australian reaction to the refugees on board the *Hwa Lien*. He requested that Walter Brand of the Welfare Society travel to Cairns and board the *Hwa Lien* there in order to instruct the refugees in regard to their behaviour on arrival in Sydney. The Department of Immigration made all the arrangements for Brand to fly to Cairns. On his arrival there he learnt that the *Hwa Lien* had docked first in Darwin due to a shortage of fuel and water.[41] The *Hwa Lien* then travelled to Cairns where Brand joined the ship to prepare the refugees for Australian conditions. On its final leg of the journey the boat encountered a cyclone off the North Queensland coast after which it stopped briefly in Brisbane and then arrived in Sydney, bringing to an end a difficult journey.

In spite of all Calwell's efforts to minimise the effects of the arrival of the refugees, they were met by a hostile reaction from the general Australian public. This took the form of negative and alarmist headlines in the press, critical questions in Parliament and accusations made by the leaders of the conservative, right-wing groups such as Ken Bolton, President of the New

[38]'A. Masel. A Report on Activities in Shanghai', CA 51, Dept. of Imm., Corres. Files, CRS A434 item 49/3/4673.

[39]Bachrach, written testimony.

[40]Charles Jordan's Report, 20th August 1947–20th September 1947, p. 9, AJWS Minutes, Sydney.

[41]Letter from Saul Symonds, President ECAJ, to Alec Masel, Immigration Liaison Officer, Melbourne, 23rd January 1947, in ECAJ Corres. Files, Archive of Australian Judaica, University of Sydney, Box E7.

South Wales branch of the Returned Services League (RSL). The refugees were accused of bringing in large sums of money and gold bars illegally, of being Communist spies who threatened Australia's security and of competing for shipping space and accommodation with Australian ex-servicemen.[42] Such criticism of the refugees was in keeping with the alarmist headlines and anti-refugee sentiments expressed in the Australian press and Parliament with the arrival of the pre-war Jewish refugees, the "reffos" as they were known, in 1938 and 1939.[43]

The main accusation against the Shanghai Jews was that they arrived with large sums of money and other dutiable items even though the amount of money they were permitted to take with them legally from Shanghai was very limited and that they were trying to avoid customs duty. Newspaper headlines such as 'Jewish Refugees Have Huge Rolls of Money'[44] highlighted the wealth of the refugees, while articles claimed that refugees arrived with up to £40,000. The *Hwa Lien* was searched for "counterfeit money and gold bullion" because the captain stated that when the refugees boarded the ship £100 worth of counterfeit money was found.[45] It was feared that Australia would be swamped with 2,000 refugees from Shanghai[46] and that refugees were able to obtain shipping while Australian and British soldiers were still stranded in Asia. Methods of obtaining landing permits and visas were also questioned.[47] In an article in the Sydney *Sun* headed 'Bribes offered for Jews' it was claimed that one federal parliamentarian was offered £1,600 to sponsor eight German Jews in Shanghai who wanted to circumvent the long wait after applying for a landing permit.[48] The accusation was made that "bribery and attempts at bribery" were common practices in Shanghai by refugees who wanted to get to Australia. Some were suspected of having peddled forged passports.[49] When Max Falstein, MHR, planned a business trip to Taiping, China, it was alleged that the real purpose of his visit was to bring refugees to Australia.[50] Although Falstein denied this claim, the matter was still raised in Parliament.[51]

As there were a number of White Russians in Shanghai, it was also claimed that there were two rival organisations, one "White Russian" and one "Red Russian" running "rackets" in refugees.[52] Although this accusation was denied by the Commonwealth Investigation Branch, an editorial in the *Sun* entitled 'Checking the Strangers at our Gates' stressed:

[42]'Protest re Jewish Immigration', 4th April 1946, CA 51, Dept. of Imm., Corres. File, Australian Archives Office, A445, item 235/5/6.

[43]See Suzanne D. Rutland, 'Australian Responses to Jewish Refugee Migration before and after World War II', in Konrad Kwiet/John A. Moses (eds.), *On Being a German-Jewish Refugee in Australia, The Australian Journal of Politics and History*, vol. 31, No. 1 (1985), pp. 29–48.

[44]*Canberra Times*, 29th January 1947.

[45]*Age*, 20th January 1947.

[46]*Daily Telegraph*, 22nd January 1947.

[47]*Courier Mail*, Brisbane, 16th January 1947.

[48]*Sun*, Sydney, 22nd November 1946.

[49]*Sydney Morning Herald (SMH)*, 22nd January 1947.

[50]*Daily Telegraph*, 2nd January 1947.

[51]*Ibid.*, 28th February 1947.

[52]*SMH*, 22nd January 1947.

> "The news that semi-secret organizations, with foreign political backgrounds, are busily shepherding refugees into Australia must cause apprehension to every inhabitant of this country. The danger of infiltration by professional troublemakers whether Jewish terrorists or Communist agents, will arouse the natural suspicion of all who wish to see Australia keep Australian . . . But when it is revealed that some of these 'refugees' were left uninterned by the Japanese, that 'any price will be paid for admission' and that many of them possess huge sums of money, most people will suspect that the Minister may have allowed his sympathy to override his judgement.
> Beside a most rigorous health examination, a complete check should be made on the antecedents of these people who look for 'refuge' with so much money."[53]

This editorial summed up the popular perception of the Jewish migration from Shanghai. Australians could not understand the desperate position in which the Central European Jews in Shanghai found themselves because of Chiang Kai-shek's deportation order and their need to leave at any cost.

Some of the Jews in Shanghai did come to Australia with considerable wealth which, in a few cases, was smuggled out of Shanghai. Although they had arrived in Shanghai from Germany and Austria almost destitute and they did not know the native language, those with a trade or business skills were able to do very well through hard work and perseverance. Even after all Jews were moved to the "designated area" of Hongkew there were a number who continued to thrive. Although foreign currency was illegal in Shanghai, those with comfortable businesses did possess foreign currency and were able to smuggle it out from Shanghai after the war. For example, one refugee had a piano accordion built with a special compartment where the family's money was hidden during the trip to Australia. It was felt by this group that they had already been dispossessed once when they left Nazi-dominated Europe. They were not prepared to be dispossessed for a second time.[54] The poverty which many other refugees experienced in Shanghai was highlighted by this story, published in the *YMHA News* by Ben Caplan in February 1947, after the arrival of the *Hwa Lien*. Ben Caplan wrote as follows:

> "An old man with lined careworn features and speaking only Yiddish, stood guard over his single piece of luggage, a huge wooden case. When a Customs inspector demanded that it be opened he demurred, but finally agreed. To the astonishment of the inspector and those assisting the old man, the case was almost full of empty bottles. Asked why he had brought so worthless a commodity to Australia the old man patiently explained that in Shanghai one empty bottle is worth two packets of cigarettes. These, which he had painstakingly collected and hoarded over the years he had been there, represented the capital he brought to his new country."[55]

This side of the story was not highlighted in the general newspapers. A few of those without money or family to help them secure landing permits tried more desperate methods. In 1947 two young Jewish refugees from Shanghai, Hans Cohn and Selig Schulman, arrived in Australia as stowaways. They were immediately imprisoned and despite efforts by the AJWS were deported after six months in Australia.[56]

[53]*Sun*, Sydney, 23rd January 1947.
[54]Interview (phone) with A. Kohn, Sydney 1985.
[55]*YMHA News*, Sydney, 13th February 1947.
[56]AJWS Minutes, 31st March and 20th October 1947. Eventually Hans Cohn went to the United States in August 1947 and Selig Schulman went to Palestine.

Before the federal elections of September 1946 Calwell responded to this anti-refugee outcry. He imposed a limit on the number of Jewish refugees permitted to travel on any one ship from either Europe or Shanghai to 25 per cent of the total number of passengers. This quota, called "numerus clausus" as it was reminiscent of restrictions on Jews in Europe, made transport from Shanghai to Australia extremely difficult. It prevented the Joint from chartering boats and, later, planes for the refugees. By late 1946 200 Jews, who had received valid landing permits, were waiting in Shanghai for visas which could not be issued until transport was organised. In October 1946 Jordan wrote in desperation to the AJWS, Sydney stressing that:

> "Your repeated hints on the undesirability of sending shiploads of refugees seemed to make sense before the election . . . But since the Labor government and Calwell have won the election we are at a loss to understand why people holding valid Landing Permits for Australia should be discouraged from making use of these permits, particularly if the Australian legation in Shanghai and the British consulate are most co-operative . . . we have been hearing over and over again when we were trying to book passages, that passages are not readily available for refugees, because the shipping companies are afraid to offend the Australian government by bringing refugees into Australia."[57]

Despite this plea the President of the Welfare Society, Saul Symonds, stressed that the 25 per cent quota must be strictly adhered to or the programme of Jewish migration from Shanghai would be suspended.[58] The *Hwa Lien* was the only exception to this rule as 50 per cent of the passengers on board were Jewish refugees, this concession being negotiated with the help of Donald S. Kilpatrick of the Australian Embassy in Nanking.[59]

In spite of the shipping restrictions introduced by Calwell, he continued to negotiate on a sympathetic basis with Jewish leaders in Australia, above all with Alec Masel, foundation president of the ECAJ in 1945 and Victorian liaison immigration officer with the Australian government in 1946. In late 1946 Gertrude van Tijn arrived in Australia from Shanghai representing the JDC to negotiate on behalf of the Jews in Shanghai. On 14th December 1946 Gertrude van Tijn[60] together with Alec Masel and Walter Brand met with Calwell to discuss the question of Jewish migration from Shanghai. At this meeting van Tijn outlined the hardships which the DPs in Shanghai had suffered, stressed the "agonizing uncertainty of their future"[61] and then outlined the numbers suitable for migration to Australia, presenting Calwell with statistics on their employability. This statistical list had been prepared with the assistance of

[57]Letter C. Jordan to W. Brand, 8th October 1947, ECAJ Corres. Files, Archive of Australian Judaica, Box E18.

[58]S. Symonds to C. Jordan, 31st October 1946, ECAJ Corres. Files, Archive of Australian Judaica, Box E18.

[59]C. Jordan to S. Symonds, 7th December 1946, ECAJ Corres. Files, Archive of Australian Judaica, Box E7.

[60]Gertrude van Tijn was a Dutch survivor who was freed from Bergen-Belsen in 1945 and was employed as a social worker by the JDC in Holland and other parts of the world. She visited Australia to negotiate on behalf of Shanghai Jewry and also to see her brother. See also her article 'Werkdorp Nieuwesluis', in *LBI Year Book XIV* (1969), pp. 182–199.

[61]Report from G. van Tijn to Charles Jordan, ECAJ Corres. Files, Archive of Australian Judaica, Box E18.

S. D. Einfeld, Honorary Secretary of the ECAJ, whom van Tijn described as "an expert on labour matters".[62]

As a result of this meeting Calwell agreed to renew old permits issued before the outbreak of war in 1939, but not used because of the fighting, to classify the Shanghai group of refugees on the same basis as the European Jewish refugees and to grant landing permits, irrespective of numbers, to Shanghai Jews, provided that the new immigrants had qualifications suitable for Australia and their selection was verified by Alec Masel during his stay in Shanghai. Calwell also promised that all permits would be organised before March 1947 when UNRRA was scheduled to withdraw from Shanghai. Gertrude van Tijn completed her report of this meeting by stressing that "the attitude of the Minister was, throughout, one of great cordiality, and I was deeply impressed by his humane approach and his sincere desire to alleviate the lot of the unfortunate refugees in Shanghai".[63]

Calwell put his words into action by verifying his request, first made in November 1946, that Alec Masel visit Shanghai "as a private citizen" and report personally to him[64] with a list of young and skilled workers suitable for migration to Australia. Masel arrived in Shanghai on 14th February 1947 and shortly after wrote to Saul Symonds stressing that there was "excellent human material here".[65] Masel held a series of conferences with Charles Jordan of the JDC, representatives of communal organisations such as the Hebrew Immigration Aid Society (HIAS), ORT (Organisation for Rehabilitation through Training), OSE (Jewish Health Society), *B'nai B'rith*, Federation of Polish Jews, Christian organisations, the White Russian Association and members of the British consulate.

These activities in Shanghai created great excitement even though Masel stressed that he could not write out permits. As one refugee stated:

> "Masel took my name amongst many thousands. He was in Shanghai to prepare a 'golden book' of names. People who were worthwhile for Australia. Everyone tried to get their names into that book. It was generally assumed that if one's name was in that book, one would receive a landing permit."[66]

Masel did stress that he was not "a kind of modern Messiah", but that he would try his best to secure permits from the government[67] and for this purpose he interviewed in person many of the prospective applicants.

As a result of the large number of people arriving each day at the Joint's office, Jordan had to look for alternative office accommodation. He approached Dorian Ritterman who agreed to lend part of his office rent free. On arrival from

62 *Ibid.*

63 *Ibid.*, p. 2.

64 'A. Masel. Report on Activities in Shanghai', Cable to Australian Legation, Shanghai, from T. H. E. Heyes, 7th February 1947 (note 38).

65 A. Masel to S. Symonds, 20th February 1947, ECAJ Corres. Files, Archives of Australian Judaica, Box E7.

66 Interview (taped) with Hans Mueller, Sydney 1985. Mueller was elected vice-president of B'nai Brith International, representing non-American districts, in 1986.

67 Reported in the German Language *Shanghai Echo*, p. 3, 9 March 1947 in 'A. Masel. A Report' (note 38).

Vienna, Ritterman had established his business in the International concession and although he had been forced to move to Hongkew in May 1943 he was able to return to his original office after the war. Here Masel interviewed people.[68] Those who wanted permits were told to write to the Welfare Society in Melbourne, with donations for the immigration fund. In this way Masel wanted the wealthier Shanghai Jews to build up a funding basis which could be used for Welfare Society guarantees for their less well-off co-religionists in Shanghai and Europe. This "so-called immigration fund" only existed in Melbourne and was "not directly under the jurisdiction of the AJWS".[69] It became another point of conflict between Melbourne and Sydney Welfare Societies, as the Sydney office was not officially informed of its existence[70] presumably because it was felt in Melbourne that Saul Symonds would disapprove of this system of raising money through landing permits, which were part of the government's jurisdiction and did not involve a charge.

On his return to Australia, Masel drew up a list with a total of 1,865 persons whom he recommended to Calwell for favourable consideration. His recommendations were made in a report submitted to Calwell on 1st May 1947.[71] In his selections Masel claimed that he paid no attention to religion, nationality or humanitarian considerations. He was concerned only with white Europeans of good character who had suitable occupations for Australia, were prepared to live in any area designated by the Department of Immigration and would not become a charge on the State. The list contained 1,445 Jewish DPs under the administration of the JDC, 62 DPs of the Association of Central European Protestants, 98 members of the old-established Shanghai Jewish community (nearly all of Russian nationality), and 260 people of the Russian Emigrants Association (nearly all Orthodox). Masel stressed that the various religious groups would be responsible for the maintenance and education of the migrants in Australia to ensure that they would not become a charge on the State.[72] Masel suggested that, in order to facilitate refugee migrants from Shanghai to Australia, a senior officer of the Department of Immigration should be sent to Shanghai to process the landing permits and disseminate publicity about Australia.[73]

At the time Masel was in Shanghai, the consular official H. M. Loveday sent a favourable report on Jewish migration from Shanghai to the Department of Immigration in Canberra. Loveday indicated that there were problems associated with processing landing permits, especially in regard to security checks, health problems and the high level of corruption in Shanghai. While bearing this in mind, he stressed that there were some valuable potential migrants from the younger people who had been trained by the Guild of

[68]Interview with Dorian Ritterman, Sydney 1985.

[69]Jordan's Report, p. 18, AJWS, Sydney.

[70]See correspondence between Masel and Symonds, ECAJ Corres. Files, Archive of Australian Judaica, Box E18.

[71]A. Masel's Report, 1st May 1947, in 'A. Masel. A Report' (note 38).

[72]*Ibid.*, pp. 7–8.

[73]*Ibid.*, p. 8.

Craftsmen, a vocational training college, and would be able to fit easily into the departmental categories as being an economic advantage to Australia. In his report, Loveday also commented that Masel had "co-operated most readily with our suggestions".[74]

Calwell accepted Masel's report, including his recommendations in regard to the 1,485 Jewish refugees and the need to appoint a senior migration official. The Commonwealth Immigration Advisory Council, with Leslie Haylen, MHR, in the chair, met in May 1947 to consider the report and "endorsed the principle of securing the greatest possible number of suitable migrants from all sources as soon as possible",[75] but at the same time suggested that all the applications submitted by Masel should be investigated by the Commonwealth Migration Officer to be sent to Shanghai. Following this recommendation, Calwell set in motion the appointment of a senior migration official and in August 1947 L. A. Taylor was chosen to fill this position in Shanghai.[76]

In view of these positive developments Charles Jordan decided to visit Australia so that he could become better acquainted with Australian conditions and could investigate the funding situation. Jordan's visit to Australia was first suggested by Masel during his visit to Shanghai and the idea was followed up by Walter Brand in two letters where he stressed that it would be "of great benefit to you and to those whom you wish to help".[77] Jordan acceded to this request, as in July 1947 he was optimistic that, even with the transport problems, large numbers of Jewish DPs from the Masel list would be granted Australian landing permits, following the arrival of the migration officer in Shanghai in September 1947.[78]

Charles Jordan was highly respected as a devoted worker, dedicated to the alleviation of human suffering among the DPs, both Jewish and non-Jewish, in Shanghai and later in Europe.[79] He arrived in Australia on 20th August for a month, during which time he visited the Welfare Societies in Sydney, Melbourne, Perth, Brisbane and Adelaide and communicated with lay and religious leaders of the Jewish community, people involved in the Australian IRO (International Refugee Organization) migration programme such as Caroline Kelly, T. H. E. (later Sir Tasman) Heyes, Secretary of the Department of Immigration, Arthur Calwell and social workers in the migration field. A Jewish immigration conference was held in Melbourne, where the Federation of the Australian Jewish Welfare Societies was created to allow for a more co-ordinated migration programme and the seeking of further financial support from American Jewry.[80]

[74]H. M. Loveday's Report, 21st March 1947, in 'Reports from Shanghai on Alien Immigration. H. M. Loveday, O. C. W. Fuhrman and L. A. Taylor' (note 21).

[75]Letter from Leslie Haylen to A. Calwell, 2nd June 1947, in 'A. Masel. A Report' (note 38).

[76]'CMO Shanghai – Procedures to be Followed in Connection with Administration of Aliens from Shanghai', CA 51, Dept. of Imm., Corres. Files, Australian Archive Office, CRS A434, item 47/3/19.

[77]Letter from W. Brand to C. Jordan, 8th July 1947, Corres. Files, AJWS, Sydney.

[78]Jordan's report, p. 19, AJWS Minutes, 20th August–20th September 1947.

[79]Written testimony, H. Bachrach, Melbourne, May 1985, and *Almanac, Shanghai 1946/1947*, *op. cit.*

[80]Report by C. Jordan, AJWS Minutes, 20th August–20th September 1947.

In a report prepared after his visit, Jordan outlined the need for professional social workers in the migration programme and ways and means of improving fund raising in Australian Jewry. He stressed that the fund-raising capacities of the Welfare Societies in the different states was limited because they had been inactive from 1939 to 1947 and had failed to keep the immigration issue alive in this period. Given the large influx expected from Shanghai and Europe, Jordan claimed that the financial obligations of reception and absorption were beyond the means of Australian Jewry. For this reason Australian Jewry was appealing for US $100,000 as capital investment from the JDC to enable them to establish housing facilities to receive the newcomers. Jordan suggested that such financial backing would have a positive impact on the Australian government and supported the request for American financial backing, as well as suggesting that the Joint do all in its power to support "Symonds and his associates".[81] American Jewry's financial support combined with Calwell's agreement to Masel's report was an auspicious beginning for the prognosis of a successful programme of Jewish migration from Shanghai to Australia.

In the midst of all these optimistic preparations for the reception of large numbers of Jewish refugees from Shanghai, moves were being made behind the scenes which were almost to invalidate these developments. On 22nd July 1947 the newly-arrived Australian Consul General in Shanghai, Major-General O. C. W. Fuhrman, sent a top secret report to the Department of External Affairs, Canberra, in which he stressed that migration from Shanghai was dangerous and not in Australia's best interests.[82] This report was to have serious repercussions for all the efforts to sponsor Jewish migration from Shanghai to Australia. It reflected a fairly common public service approach of many of the Commonwealth countries as well as the United States, where Jewish refugee migrants were viewed with suspicion and even considered undesirable by some public servants. This attitude was expressed in the comment of a Canadian civil servant who, when asked about Jewish DP migration to Canada in 1945, commented that "none is too many".[83] In addition Fuhrman was influenced by the British Foreign Office attitudes which were coloured by the events in Palestine in the immediate post-war years.

Fuhrman arrived in Shanghai on 4th July 1947 and immediately sought background information on the Jews in Shanghai. He spoke with the British Consul-General, A. G. H. Ogden, who had 35 years experience in China; with H. F. Gill, special security officer with the British Consulate who also had many

[81] *Ibid.*, p. 20.

[82] 'Legal and Consular Immigration. Migration from Shanghai', Memo for the Dept. of Immigration, 22nd July 1947, from Australian Legation Shanghai, 5 pages, CA 18, Dept. of Ext. Affairs, Corres. Files, A1068, item IC47/31/15. Major (General) O.C.W. Fuhrman was Australian Consul General in Shanghai, 1947–1949. He was then appointed as first Minister for Australia in Israel and held this post until his retirement in 1953. He was perceived as playing a positive role in Israel in regard to developing Israel/Australia trade but he continued to oppose Jewish migration from Israel to Australia, even in the case of close relatives. Since the Jewish Agency and the AJWS wished to discourage people emigrating from Israel, there was no conflict with Fuhrman's migration policies in Israel from the Jewish point of view.

[83] Irving Abella and Harold Troper, *None Is Too Many. Canada and the Jews of Europe, 1933–1948*, Toronto 1983, p. v.

years of experience in China; and with Drs. Marshall, Jackson and Partners, who carried out the medical examinations on all intending migrants to Australia.[84] In his report Fuhrman gave an historical outline of the city of Shanghai, stressing the high level of corruption and depravity which existed in the city. He claimed that as a result of the deplorable economic conditions the refugee population of Shanghai had become influenced by the immorality of the city so that "intrigue, sharp practice, crime, espionage and acting as agents provacateurs for foreign governments have been profitable fields for adventure and have . . . reduced the morale of the refugee population to the lowest levels of depravity and despair".[85] Fuhrman also referred to the "foreigners" in Shanghai collaborating with the Japanese. He stressed that the Russian Emigrants Association had "a most unsavoury reputation", was "hand-in-glove" with the Japanese during the war and that its honorary secretary Emanoff was "unscrupulous and cannot be trusted". He pointed out that "one Masel of Melbourne whose name will be familiar to your department" had consulted with Emanoff and included members of the Russian Emigrants Association on his list.[86] There were additional problems in regard to checking health, good character and security. In conclusion Fuhrman stated:

> "The stateless persons of European and Russian origin are enigmas – their past unknown and unspeakable, their intentions obscure. They are and must continue to remain suspect; as must also citizens of the USSR domiciled in Shanghai . . . The latter, in my opinion and from the angle of security in Australia, are potentially dangerous."[87]

Clearly on the basis of this report non-British Europeans in Shanghai from any of the different ethnic groups were not suitable as immigrants to Australia.

As soon as the Commonwealth Migration Officer, Taylor, arrived in Shanghai he came under Fuhrman's influence to the extent that S. D. Einfeld later referred to him as "the enemy".[88] He immediately cabled to Heyes, the Secretary of the Department of Immigration, that an associate of Masel's, the honorary secretary of the Russian Emigrants Association, Emanoff, had contacts with Soviet Intelligence[89] making him, and by implication Masel, suspect. At the same time Taylor wrote a detailed report criticising both the Russian and Jewish refugee elements in Shanghai. Taylor had also spoken with the long-time British residents of Shanghai who stressed that neither the White Russians nor the refugees had been interned during the war and so they must all "be regarded as Japanese collaborators" who are "without doubt a human flotsam and jetsam", compelled to resort to crime during the war to make a living. Their crimes included prostitution, especially among the Jews, "key-

[84]'Legal and Consular Immigration. Migration from Shanghai', Memo for the Dept. of Immigration, 22nd July 1947, A1068, item IC47/31/15 (note 82), p. 1.

[85]*Ibid.*, p. 2.

[86]*Ibid.*, p. 4.

[87]*Ibid.*, p. 5.

[88]Interview (taped) with S. D. Einfeld, Sydney 1985. Einfeld was on the Executive Council of the AJWS, Sydney, 1948–1952, and President, AJWS 1952–1977.

[89]Letter Taylor to Heyes, 16th September 1947, in 'Reports from Shanghai on Alien Immigration', (note 21).

money rackets" and all the other forms of corruption.[90] Taylor also alleged that among the refugees who had already arrived in Australia were criminal and unsavoury elements. For example, he described at least six firms, operating under Australian names and controlled by recently arrived Shanghai refugees, which had sent samples to Hong Kong and then, when orders had been placed, followed them up with goods of inferior quality, thus damaging Australian trade in the Hong Kong area.[91]

Taylor stated that he had been informed by a British security officer that the refugees were expelled from Austria and Germany not because they were Jewish but because of their Communist leanings which, presumably, had not changed. He ended his report by stating:

> "37. Under no circumstances do I consider that humanitarian grounds or outside pressure should be allowed to influence the granting of permits to these people and, in spite of what many of the guarantors in Australia may say, I hold the view that it is an absolute impossibility for any person in Australia who has not been in constant *personal* contact with his friends or relatives in this area, since their arrival to this date, to have the slightest knowledge of their integrity or character.
> 38. I would point out that all Latin American countries have imposed almost complete restrictions, France is almost the same, and they have their own Security Services and the United States works on a limited quota. I would stress that apart from the fact that it is almost impossible for these people to obtain permission to return to China, even the Soviet passports issued here are not valid for return to the USSR unless specially endorsed to that effect. Australia will therefore be unable to rid itself of undesirables.
> 39. After careful consideration of the facts presented to me I consider I have no alternative but to recommend complete cessation of migration from here to Australia, so far as the Russian and European refugee classes are concerned, and I do this most strongly. Any further concession granted to them will to my mind render a great dis-service to our country."[92]

Although there was no validity in the claims made in point 37, other countries had excluded migrants from Shanghai as outlined in point 38. When the Secretary of the Department of Immigration, Heyes, received this report he immediately telegraphed Taylor, instructing him to cease the issue of landing permits and visas, to remain in Shanghai until Jordan returned from Australia and then to proceed immediately to Canberra.

Charles Jordan returned to Shanghai at the beginning of October and met Taylor together with Fuhrman in the Joint offices. They discussed the allegations made against the White Russians and the refugees, even though the Joint was only involved with the latter. At this meeting Fuhrman claimed that when the British nationals were interned by the Japanese, the refugees took over their homes and businesses "at cut prices" thereby robbing them of their possessions. For this reason most British nationals considered the Jewish refugees to be undesirable, a point of view which Fuhrman personally

[90] *Ibid.*, Taylor's Report, 16th September 1947.
[91] *Ibid.*
[92] *Ibid.* The problem of the stateless refugees in China not being re-admitted to China once they had departed, even if only on a tourist visas, was highlighted in an article by Norman B. Hannah, American Consul General, Shanghai, 1947–1949, entitled 'What Happened to Lydia', in *Quadrant* (Australia), November 1975, pp. 42–46.

endorsed.[93] Taylor stated that he was more concerned with the impossibility of screening the refugees to ensure that they would not be security risks, especially in regard to Jewish terrorists who were opposed to the British Mandate in Palestine.[94] After this meeting Jordan cabled Calwell to reconsider his decision to recall Taylor to Canberra. In the telegram Jordan stated that Fuhrman's "completely and utterly unreasonable attitude discounting desirability of any and every immigrant aspirant from Shanghai has been well known to me before I came to Australia", but Jordan was under the impression that "it would not cut any ice".[95] He went on to stress that there were both useful and morally and politically reliable people among the refugees and ended that telegram with this plea to Calwell:

> "I implore you sir not to let my people down stop Repeated assurances of your friendly intentions have kept up their hope and Taylor's arrival here signified to them the beginning of the end of a long and heartbreaking wait for deliverance stop If Taylor were to leave now and under the circumstances which I must by necessity discuss with the people under my care it will be a mortal blow to their flickering faith."[96]

Jordan followed this cable with a four-page letter written on the same day when he again appealed to Calwell's "great understanding and appreciation of human values and human needs" and also referred to Calwell's "courageous stand in the face of many bitter attacks against you". Jordan felt that he and many others had been inspired by such courage.[97]

It was difficult for Calwell, even with his integrity and courage, his great friendship with many Australian Jews and his admiration of the Jewish people, to withstand the intensity of the attacks on the integrity of the refugee Jewish community in Shanghai as presented by both Fuhrman and Taylor. Jordan failed in his request to Calwell. Taylor was recalled to Canberra where he presented a further report, 22 pages in length, which reinforced his earlier arguments in regard to the undesirability of Australia admitting any immigrants from Shanghai. In this respect Taylor quoted from the British passport control officer, Clarke, who had been in Shanghai for some twenty years. Clarke claimed that the Jews in Shanghai were "unmoral or immoral", that some of them controlled Shanghai's underworld and that most had co-operated with the Japanese. Since "money appeared to be their principal aim in life" Jews were involved in smuggling and the drug trade. While prostitution was common in this group Clarke further claimed that corruption in Shanghai had been unknown before their arrival in 1938–1940. Taylor pointed out that this view was supported by other British people he had interviewed, such as the Roman Catholic priest Father Wilcock, Gill, Eric Davis, and Captain Atkinson. Taylor also replied to many of Jordan's comments and pointed out that there were on Masel's list many Polish Jews and Central Europeans of Polish origins

[93]'Reports from Shanghai on Alien Immigration', letter Jordan to Calwell, 2nd October 1947, p. 1 (note 21).

[94]*Ibid.*, p. 2.

[95]*Ibid.*, cable Jordan to Calwell, 2nd October 1947.

[96]*Ibid.*

[97]*Ibid.*, letter Jordan to Calwell, 2nd October 1947, p. 4.

whom, he claimed, were "the most anti-British people in Shanghai". Taylor concluded on the note that although there were clearly some desirables in Shanghai the problem was one of selection.[98]

Taylor's British sources in Shanghai were biased and unreliable but there was a kernel of truth in the allegations made in his report. The Japanese had followed a pro-Jewish policy in some areas before the outbreak of war, including the organisation of conferences for the Jews in the Far East, held in China in 1937, 1938 and 1939. Japan had hoped that British and American policy could be influenced by fair treatment of the Jewish population in the Far East.[99] Even during the war, at the height of Nazi influence when the extermination of Shanghai Jewry was proposed, perhaps through the use of gas ovens, the Japanese refused to implement such measures against a civilian population. In July 1942 plans to liquidate all Jews in Shanghai were discussed by young Japanese officers under *Gestapo* influence. The Jewish Affairs Bureau was notified of these plans by a sympathetic Japanese vice-consul, Shibata, and the Bureau's vice-president, Fritz Kauffmann, attempted to take action. Immediately members of the Jewish Affairs Bureau were incarcerated in the "Bridgehouse" prison. Before his release, Kauffmann was informed that he had spread malicious rumours. His Japanese interrogators explained to him that "the Japanese would never behave in such an abominable manner . . . because such a way of acting was against the Bushido philosophy".[100] Given these circumstances, it is understandable that the Jewish population was not vehemently anti-Japanese. The official reports, however, failed to point out that the Sephardi Jews with British passports were interned during the war while the stateless Jews who had arrived between 1938 and 1941 were confined to the designated area of Hongkew after May 1943.[101] Some Russian Jews did work for the Allied cause and, according to one of the leaders of the American OSS underground, such Jewish assistance played an important role in Allied success.[102]

In relation to the allegations of the "criminal nature" of Shanghai Jewry, such activities which did exist among a limited number of refugees were the consequences of the difficult economic and social situation. In the stressful years of 1944–1945 seven Jewish women were officially registered as prostitutes while several lived with men in order to improve their financial position. In some cases arrangements were made with the full knowledge of husbands who shared in the economic advantages.[103] Given the destitute position of most of the refugees in that period, the criminal elements constituted only a tiny minority of the 18,000 Jewish refugees. Taylor further charged that the calibre of migrants who had been allowed into Australia was very low. He cited as proof that the

[98]*Ibid.*, Draft Report from L. A. Taylor, 22 pages, n.d.

[99]Kranzler, *op. cit.*, p. 227 and Tokayer and Schwartz, *op. cit.*, pp. 9–10.

[100]Interview with D. Ritterman; Kauffmann, *loc. cit.*, p. 20.

[101]The White Russian Jews were not interned because Japan wanted to avoid unnecessary friction with the USSR. Kranzler, *op. cit.*, p. 518.

[102]*Ibid.*, p. 534.

[103]*Ibid.*, p. 545.

"United States authorities thought so little of the passengers on the *Haleakala* that they refused to allow any of them ashore at Manila when the vessel was in transit through the Philippines".[104] (This charge cannot be substantiated. One Jewish passenger who travelled on the *Haleakala* vividly recalled that they did get off the ship at Manila where everyone appeared to carry a pistol and that when they went to the cinema there was a sign asking patrons to leave their pistols at the ticket office.[105])

In regard to charges of black market activities and corruption, these must be understood in relation to the overall nature of society in Shanghai. Both corruption and the black market were "a way of life in Shanghai" from which it was impossible to refrain.[106] For example, one refugee remembered riding a bicycle and having a big load on the back. He was stopped by a policeman who practically asked him for money and clearly he had to pay up.[107] Within government agencies it was impossible to get anything done without corruption. All officials expected to be paid and in the end everyone living in Shanghai accepted it.[108]

Both contemporary evidence and oral history have attested to the inventiveness and determination of the Jewish refugees in Shanghai. They arrived in the devastated area of Hongkew with nothing and in a short period of time built up businesses, often out of nothing.[109] Many of the young people were taught a trade at the schools run by the Craftsmen's Guild and the ORT. Jordan spoke of the high moral fibre of the majority of refugees stating:

> "I think that this is a truly remarkable record. The refugees in Shanghai never for a moment expected to remain in Shanghai for any length of time. They have lived suspended in thin air for years. They have faced threats to their very existence, starvation and grave spells of insecurity and frustration since the end of the war. The great majority of these people are fine, upstanding and deeply religious people with a tremendous courage and faith without which they could not possibly have survived their bitter experiences."[110]

This view was reinforced by an Englishwoman, Edith Adlam of the Society of Friends, Shanghai. During a visit to Australia in 1947 she referred to the fact that among the Jews in Shanghai were many suitable immigrants as she believed that many of the Jewish refugees in Shanghai had much to contribute to the Australian community and potentially were even better than the European migrants.[111] In spite of this type of evidence, the Australian authorities believed the charges made against the Jewish refugees to be correct and acted accordingly.

In Australia the Jewish leadership through the ECAJ protested against Taylor's report and stressed the quality of Shanghai Jewry. Their efforts to rectify the situation were limited by the communication gap which existed

[104]'Reports from Shanghai on Alien Immigration' (note 21).
[105]Interview with Hans Mueller.
[106]Interview with Gerty and Hans Mueller, Paul Engel, and Lisl Gerber, Sydney 1985.
[107]*Ibid.*
[108]*Ibid.*
[109]Interview with A. Kohn, Sydney 1985.
[110]Jordan's Report, Statement No. 1, AJWS Minutes, 20th August–20th September 1947.
[111]*Melbourne Herald*, 31st January 1947.

between Sydney and Melbourne Jewry. In September 1947, before Jordan returned to Shanghai, Symonds, Brand and Jordan met Calwell after he had received Taylor's report. At this meeting Symonds stated that the ECAJ was not acting for White Russians in Shanghai, only to be informed that the AJWS had signed guarantees for 40 permits on behalf of White Russians. Following an approach from the President of the Shanghai Russian Jewish Community, Alec Masel had discussed with Calwell the sponsorship of a number of White Russians before his departure to Shanghai. Calwell agreed to this request, but Symonds was not informed, even though he was at the time President of the ECAJ then located in Sydney.[112] Symonds claimed that his ignorance in the matter "cut the ground from under our feet and at the same time made us look most ridiculous".[113] This failure to inform Symonds of the inclusion of White Russian Jews led to acrimonious correspondence between Sydney and Melbourne with Symonds claiming that "it was most humiliating as far as I am concerned".[114] Calwell found himself affected by a Sydney/Melbourne dispute over the issue of the White Russians, although in the long term it was the attitude of the Australian government officials which had the greatest impact on Calwell's decisions.

Efforts made by the Jewish leaders in Australia and by Jordan in Shanghai failed to militate against the full impact of the two negative reports. On 24th October 1947 Calwell agreed to the resumption of the issuing of landing permits in Shanghai but only 300 Jewish DPs were to be accepted over a period of 12 months, while no White Russians were to be admitted except in exceptional circumstances. A Commonwealth Migration Officer was not sent to Shanghai because of the small numbers to be selected. Security and health checks were to be carried out by the Consul General, Fuhrman, after the landing permit had been granted in Canberra.[115] Fuhrman followed the instructions but was obstructive in every way possible.[116] In January 1948 30 people received Australian landing permits and required the visa passport endorsement to be ready for departure. Fuhrman wrote to them that:

> "I am prepared to examine these cases and, for the purpose of such exam, I want to view the complete case histories of each person who it is suggested should go to Australia. These case histories should be complete in every detail and must embody unimpeachable evidence, which I can have checked by security services, as to character, political affiliations and the like."[117]

These instructions applied to refugees who already had landing permits and only required a visa for shipping purposes. On receipt of a copy of this letter, Walter Brand pointed out that "the tone and diction is not in keeping with the courteous manner in which the Department of Immigration handle migration matters".[118]

[112]Masel to Symonds, 10th October 1947, ECAJ Corres. Files, Archive of Australian Judaica, Box E5.

[113]*Ibid.*, Symonds to L. Fink, President of the AJW&RS, 8th October 1947.

[114]*Ibid.*, Symonds to Masel, 21st October 1947.

[115]'Reports from Shanghai on Alien Immigration', Memo, Immigration into Australia of Aliens Resident in China (note 21).

[116]*Ibid.*, p. 3.

[117]*Ibid.* Letter Fuhrman to Jordan, 5th January 1948.

[118]*Ibid.* Brand to Heyes, 14th January 1948.

In 1948 the situation in Shanghai further deteriorated and the need to escape became more pressing. Jordan became concerned because, as he wrote in January 1948, "I hate to see these people get hurt once again"[119] and he commented on Fuhrman's tendency to make "it as tough as one can possibly imagine".[120] Fuhrman continued to reject applications on different grounds, even claiming unjustifiably that eight out of ten of the refugees had TB.[121] In the light of this attitude, Leslie Haylen, Chairman of the Commonwealth Immigration Advisory Committee visited Shanghai in August 1948 to investigate the situation and report to Calwell. Haylen was a leading figure in the Labour movement for many years and a member of the federal parliament.

In Shanghai Haylen was very sympathetic in his approach to Adolph C. Glassgold, the JDC representative who had replaced Jordan following his transfer to Paris in April 1948. Haylen was accompanied by F. Penhalluriack, a Commonwealth Migration Officer, who had worked for some time with Jewish refugee migration and was considered to be very sympathetic.[122] Haylen was exposed to the same British advisers as Fuhrman and Taylor before him and his confidential report came to the same conclusions. During his visit Haylen cabled a brief summary of the situation to Calwell and again issue of Australian visas was halted.[123]

On his return to Australia Haylen submitted a nine-page confidential report condemning Jewish migration from Shanghai. He referred to allegations of a high proportion being involved in the "black market, money 'niggers', brothel owners and drug runners" and claimed he had seen evidence to substantiate this report.[124] Haylen described Masel's visit as having done "great mischief" and commented, in regard to press reports of Masel as the "New Messiah", that at best he could "only be the new 'John the Baptist' who came to tell of the 'New Messiah' who was *Calwell of Canberra*".[125] He also referred to Emanoff and stated that Masel had included names on his list irrespective of merit. In addition a number of the White Russians, who had already migrated to Australia, possessed Soviet passports and Haylen warned that if J. T. Lang discovered this fact he would use it effectively against Calwell.[126] In reference to the Joint representative, Glassgold, he commented that he "belonged to the same group as [Walter] Brand and Masel" and "impressed me more as an

[119]Jordan to Symonds, 30th January 1948. ECAJ Corres. Files, Archive of Australian Judaica, Box E12.

[120]*Ibid.*

[121]This claim was made in a Memo from Denzil H. Clarke, IRO Representative, to Jennings Wong, Acting Chief, dated 17th March 1948, following a conversation with Fuhrman. Sent by Jordan to Symonds, 22nd March 1948, EACJ Corres. Files, Archive of Australian Judaica, Box E12.

[122]Letter Symonds to Jordan, Paris, 1st September 1948, ECAJ Corres. Files, Archive of Australian Judaica, Box E12, and interview with D. Ritterman.

[123]*North China Daily News*, 26th August 1948, 'Reports from Shanghai on Alien Immigration', (note 21). Leslie Haylen, a strong Labour man, was deeply affected by the poverty and corruption he saw in Shanghai in 1948 and later expressed his distaste for the situation in Shanghai in his book, *Chinese Journey. The Republic Revisited*, Sydney 1959, pp. 56–64.

[124]'Reports from Shanghai on Alien Immigration', Haylen's Report, 1948, p. 1 (note 21).

[125]*Ibid.*, p. 6.

[126]*Ibid.*, p. 2.

undertaker of live bodies than a migration authority" and continued with the claim that:

> "I am convinced after weary years of contact with the Jew that what humanity you can extend him is not because he is a Jew but *despite* it. Glassgold's facts were good and in triplicate, but on the matter of health and security he refused to be drawn."[127]

On the basis of the information he had gathered, Haylen concluded that Australia "had little to gain from Shanghai migration", but that in order to counter publicity a quota of 300 should be introduced as "a necessary face saver".[128]

Haylen's concern to avoid open conflict with the Jewish leaders was supported by Calwell. When Symonds approached Calwell on the question of Haylen's visit to Shanghai and warned him that "it was the Taylor affair all over again", Calwell assured him that this was not the case.[129] Penhalluriack was posted to Shanghai to process visas for Australia. In the critical period in December 1948 and January/February 1949 Calwell agreed that small planes could be chartered to bring refugees to Australia, irrespective of the quota restrictions. Ashkanasy was with Calwell when he personally phoned Heyes in Canberra to issue this instruction.[130]

These concessions were of a limited nature and Haylen's report was the final condemnation of Jewish migration from Shanghai. After September 1948 the number of Shanghai Jews who were permitted to migrate to Australia was limited severely. On 30th November 1948 the Federation of the Australian Jewish Welfare Societies was informed that, in future, non-British European residents in China would not be eligible for admission to Australia unless they were "well known to their nominators" who had to have "a close personal interest in them".[131] On 2nd December 1948 Glassgold wrote to Brand:

> "I have to transmit to you some information which should by now not be shocking to any Jew, but which nevertheless still horrifies one. From a most unimpeachable source there comes to me a statement by the new Australian Consul [Penhalluriack] in Shanghai that casts a pall of futility over the prospect of Australian migration. The consul said to my informant substantially the following:
> 'We have never wanted these people in Australia and we still don't want them. We will issue a few visas to those who have relatives there as a gesture'.
> . . . This information must serve only as background to your redoubled efforts to break the Australian blockade."[132]

The Jewish leadership did not manage to "break the Australian blockade" and by mid 1949 Leo Fink, President of the Australian Jewish Welfare and Relief Society in Melbourne, advised Walter Brand that there was no point in further

[127] *Ibid.*, p. 6.
[128] *Ibid.*, p. 9.
[129] Letter Symonds to Jordan, 1st September 1948, ECAJ Corres. Files, Archive of Australian Judaica, Box E30.
[130] Letter W. Lippmann to W. Brand, 17th December 1948, *ibid.*, Box E12 and Heyes to Shanghai, 17th December 1948, 'Legal and Consular Immigration. Migration from Shanghai' (note 82).
[131] Heyes to Brand, 30th November 1948, ECAJ Corres. Files, Archive of Australian Judaica, Box E12.
[132] *Ibid.*, Glassgold to Brand, 2nd December 1948.

negotiations with the government as "Shanghai has always been a sore point".[133] Australia was closed as a significant place of migration for the stranded Jews of Shanghai.

At the end of 1948 there were still 16,000 Europeans in Shanghai, of whom about 10,000 were Jewish. With the approach of the successful Communist armies the desire to leave Shanghai became pressing, especially for the White Russians. If Australia was not prepared to accept large numbers from Shanghai on a permanent basis, it was felt that she could offer them a temporary refuge. In November 1948 the Australian government was requested by America to receive up to 15,000 stranded refugees in temporary holding camps. When considering this request, Calwell advised the Prime Minister, Ben Chifley, that:

> "In view of our existing commitments, in particular our agreement to receive 100,000 DPs from Europe within the next 18 months and the scarcity of accommodation, we are in the position to make only a small contribution to the solution of this problem and we will be unable to accept the vast majority of these people from China."[134]

Calwell suggested that Japan would be a suitable location for a temporary staging area and that General MacArthur should be approached on this issue. MacArthur refused to use Japan and referred the problem to his government, which involved the IRO.

In January 1949 the Philippines agreed to accept 6,000 White Russians on a temporary basis. Under the auspices of the IRO there was a mass evacuation of White Russians from Shanghai to Samar in the Philippines. The Australian government reacted positively to an appeal to select some of these White Russians for migration to Australia. In February 1949 B. K. Lawrey was chosen as selection officer in charge of the selection team in the Philippines. It was decided that "in view of the refuge provided by Israel for the Jewish people, no Jews are to be selected other than exceptional cases where they will contribute to Australia's economy".[135] Between February and July 1949 two selection teams under Lawrey chose 1,313 people suitable for Australia. They arrived in three separate ships in June, October and November 1949. By the end of 1949 there were still 3,500 White Russians stranded at the IRO camp in the Philippines, but of the 2,276 who had been resettled Australia had received 60 per cent.[136] The government decided that Australia could not accept any more White Russians and this group of refugees was not completely relocated until 1953.

Most of the Jewish refugees remained in Shanghai and further attempts were made in 1949 to resettle some in Australia. The government remained firm in its opposition to any migration of non-British Europeans from China and

[133] *Ibid.*, Fink to Brand, 23rd May 1949.

[134] 'Evacuation of White Russian Jews and other Refugees from China, Pt. 1', Calwell to Chifley, 12th November 1948, CA 51, Dept. of Imm., Corres. Files, Australian Archives Office, CRS A445, item 235/3/7.

[135] *Ibid.*, Memo, 'Admission to Australia for Permanent Residence of Refugees from Shanghai now at Samar (Philippines)', By A. L. Nutt, 8th February 1949.

[136] 'Refugees and DPs in Shanghai, 1948–1953', Memo, 6th March 1950, Dept of Ext. Affairs, Corres. Files, Australian Archives Office, A1838, item 861/5/7.

continued to stress that Shanghai was "not a suitable field for immigration".[137] Although refugees in the Philippines were being dealt with as a special group on an humanitarian basis, the Australian government would accept no responsibility for those who stayed in Shanghai. In response to an appeal from the World Jewish Congress in May 1949 for Australia to accept another 200 Jewish refugees Walter Brand wrote to the ECAJ in Melbourne:

> "On humanitarian grounds I feel that the Department must do something. They have done it for the White Russians, so why should they not do it for the Jewish people in Shanghai? I am given to understand that Mr Lawrey who is now in Manila is processing White Russians and issuing visas without first recommending to the Department for their approval."[138]

No action was taken, however, as it was clear to the Melbourne leadership that the Department would not change its attitude in regard to Shanghai. A further meeting was held in July 1950 with Heyes because, as part of the embargo on migrants coming from Iron Curtain countries, people repatriated from Shanghai to Europe were also not eligible for immigration to Australia. The Jewish leaders were again unsuccessful in persuading the Department to change its mind.[139]

In March 1951 Glassgold spent eight days in Australia, four in Sydney, three in Melbourne and one in Canberra. Although Glassgold did campaign for the entry of 50 Jewish people from Shanghai, the main reason for his visit was financial. Families who had sponsored migration from Shanghai were slow in repaying their remittance to the JDC for transport costs. Since 1946 only £2,233 had been remitted and large sums were still owed to the JDC.[140]

For the Jews remaining in Shanghai emigration to the newly-created state of Israel was the only solution. The main difficulty was in finding suitable transport to evacuate refugees bound for Israel. Calwell agreed that the *Wooster Victory* and the *Castelbianco*, which together could carry 1,772 passengers, could be diverted from the Europe/Australia IRO route and sent to Shanghai. The IRO then requested that transit facilities be made available in Australia as the boats could not use the Suez Canal and had to go round the Cape to the Mediterranean ports in Italy. In a telegram to the IRO this request was rejected because:

> "Apart from accommodation problems acceptance Jews from Shanghai would, in view strength and activities local co-religionists, lead to difficulties when time came for them to leave. This would involve political issues which would cause government considerable embarrassment."[141]

A further telegram stressed that the Australian government had done everything it could to assist the refugees in general and Jews in particular. It

[137] *Ibid.*, 17th March 1949.

[138] Brand to Lippmann (Hon. Sec. ECAJ), 18th May 1949, ECAJ Corres. Files, Archive of Australian Judaica, Box E12.

[139] AJWS Minutes, Sydney, Report of meeting of Symonds, Einfeld and Brand with Heyes in Sydney, 31st July 1950.

[140] *Ibid.*, 5th March 1951.

[141] 'Evacuation of White Russian Jews and other Refugees', cable Calwell to Tuck, IRO, transmitted by Sec. Dept. of Imm., Heyes, to Sec., Dept. Ext. Affairs, for transmission to Europe, 10th December 1948 (note 134).

had granted 15,000 landing permits to Jews in Europe, together with its programme for the resettlement of 100,000 DPs through the IRO between 1949–1951. Australia was unable to offer any more assistance, not even for trans-shipment of refugees en route from Shanghai to Israel.[142]

By December 1948 half of Shanghai's remaining Jewish population of 10,000 had registered for resettlement in Israel. Although Israel had no diplomatic relations with Maoist China, the Chinese were co-operative and visas for Israel were readily issued.[143] In six years, from 1949 to 1956, 9,700 of these 10,000 left Shanghai for Israel with the co-operation of the Maoist regime. By 1957 only 100 Jews remained in Shanghai.[144]

In all about 2,500 Jews from Shanghai settled in Australia, the largest proportion of these arriving in 1946. The adversity they had experienced in Shanghai on the whole gave them drive and determination to succeed in their new homeland and to contribute to Australia's development in all fields. In addition money collected in Shanghai was utilised for the reception and absorption of Jewish refugees from Europe. In 1946 Abram Sokol had visited Shanghai and collected £6,000 which went towards the purchase of the Bialystoker Centre in Melbourne,[145] while Masel collected money for the Melbourne "Immigration Fund" during his stay in Shanghai.

Without the negative reports of Fuhrman, Taylor and, subsequently, Haylen, it is possible that many more Jews from Shanghai could have contributed positively to Australia's development. Calwell's strong desire to assist these Jews was frustrated by the undercurrent of antisemitism in the public service departments of immigration and external affairs and the fear of repercussions from such Jewish migration. The negative reports frustrated the efforts and hard work not only of the Jewish leaders in Australia but also of the leadership of the JDC Shanghai office. Despite Charles Jordan's valiant efforts, not only in regard to Australia but with other countries, it was only the creation of the State of Israel in May 1948 which provided the means of rescue for the stateless Jews of Shanghai.

[142]'Refugees and DPs in Shanghai', Cable Dept. of Ext. Affairs to Australian Embassy, Washington, 23rd December 1948. AAO, CRS A445, item 235/3/5.

[143]*China Press*, 6th December 1948, in 'Evacuation of White Russian Jews and other Refugees' (note 134).

[144]Kranzler, *op. cit.*, p. 581.

[145]'A. Masel. A Report', Memo, 19th August 1947 (note 38).

Jews and the Camera

Jews in Photography

BY NACHUM T. GIDAL

The title of this study provokes at once the question of its validity. Does the fact of Jewish birth or descent from one or two Jewish parents justify an assemblage under one qualifying – positive or negative – common denominator except for an outworn and inconsequential apologetic or defensive purpose?

There is no such thing as Jewish Photography, just as there is no specific Jewish sport – or, for that matter, Jewish picture framing. This is in contrast to, for instance, Bible-inspired photography of the Holy Land. The finest representatives of this genre have been religious and non-religious people, from French Catholics (if in name only) and British High Church adherents in the nineteenth century to contemporary non-religious Jewish photographers and Orthodox Jews.[1]

In order to prove or disprove a hypothesis, that a specific trait characterises photographers of Jewish parentage, it is hoped that this study will serve a legitimate purpose. First of all it is necessary to clarify the basic attitude towards visual representation in the Jewish religion since earliest times, and the initial section of this study will discuss these aspects, while the second and major part will concern itself solely with means of visual representation through photography.

I

The Second Commandment, given, according to Jewish religious belief, like others by God himself on Mount Sinai, says: "Thou shalt have none other gods before me. Thou shalt not make thee any graven image or any likeness of any thing that is in heaven above, or that is in the earth beneath, or that is in the waters beneath the earth: Thou shalt not bow down thyself unto them, nor serve them . . ." (Exodus XX:3–5 and Deuteronomy V:7–9).

In Exodus as well as in Deuteronomy, the Second Commandment is preceded by the pronouncement from which it draws its irrefutable authority, namely by the accepted recognition of the absolute sovereignty of God: "I am the Lord your God . . ."

The Second Commandment forbids the making of graven images (made with a graving tool), *for the purpose of worship* (italics mine). The making of graven images in itself was not forbidden. It was clearly blasphemous when the brother of Moses, the High Priest Aaron, made the image of a calf, fashioning it with a

[1]See the author's *Land of Promise*, Munich–New York–Tel-Aviv 1985, pp. 79, 84–89.

graving tool, to be worshipped by the people who had given up all hope of Moses ever returning to them again from the Mountain (Exodus XXXII:4). Moses himself, ordered to do so by God, "made a serpent of brass" (Numbers XXI:8–9). Only when in later centuries this symbol of God's power to heal became an idol for worship before which the Hebrews burned incense, did King Hezekiah (c.715–687 B.C.E.) order it to be destroyed (II Kings XVIII:4).

Visual representations as such, contrary to a traditional animosity towards them at certain periods of Jewish history, obviously do not come under the ban of the Second Commandment as long as there is not the slightest temptation "to bow down to them". Even in the Holiest of Holies in the Temple of Solomon, the ark was watched over by two "Cherubim", which were life-like figures with wings.

Jewish (and Moslem) monotheism and the absolute exclusion of visual cultic imagery are projections of an absolute invisibility of God in any form or representation of a material kind whatsoever. It is in the light of this religious tenet as an unconditional one, that the philosopher Immanuel Kant's apodictic judgement can be perceived: "There is no sublimer passage in the Hebrew Scriptures than the Commandment: 'Thou shalt not make unto thee a graven image'."[2]

Martin Buber, the leading philosopher of modern Judaism writes:

> "Moses . . . sah sich gewiss einer Gegentendenz gegenüber, nämlich jener natürlichen, in allen Religionen, von den rohesten bis zu den sublimsten, mächtigen Tendenz, über die Gottheit sinnlich zu verfügen. Der Kampf gegen sie ist nicht ein Kampf gegen die Kunst . . . sondern er ist ein Kampf gegen die sich wider den Glauben auflehnende Phantasie . . . Moses musste . . . das bildlose Dasein des Unsichtbaren, der sich zu sehen gibt, zum Prinzip erheben."[3]

The cultic veneration of man or woman (in contrast to the supra-sexual unity of the Jewish God) is seen by Martin Buber as an additional inherent content of idol worship. It made for an unbridgeable wall between unconditional monotheism and the image-connected religions of ancient Egypt, Mesopotamia, Greece, Rome and, later, of Christianity.

The "fence around the law" was put higher or lower with this aspect in mind. An example for this attitude were the emperor's statues, which in Roman times were part of cultic veneration – the slightest possibility of such veneration within the Temple led to revolts against the display of these statues there.

The more these mythical or religious meanings of images in the neighbouring cultures transcended the purely naturalistic, the more stringent became the borderline or indeed the avoidance of the slightest possibility of approaching the borderline for the Hebrews. On the other hand the more self-evidently the absolute monotheistic idea pervaded all thinking, the more open to visual representation the Jewish religion showed itself.[4]

This clear-cut attitude makes understandable the fact of the existence of

[2]Quoted by Carmel Konikoff in *The Second Commandment and its Interpretation in the Art of Ancient Israel*, Geneva 1983, p. 9.
[3]Martin Buber, 'Moses', in *Schriften zur Bibel*, München-Heidelberg 1984, p. 146.
[4]See also Kurt Schubert, *Die Kultur der Juden*, Teil II, Wiesbaden 1979, p. 86.

visual images in Palestinian and other Near East synagogues of the second, third and fourth century C.E., in the form of mosaics as well as of mural frescos.

Monotheistic Judaism saw no sacrilege in the mosaics of the Hammat Lifat, Tiberias and Beth Alpha synagogues of that period. Obviously, it saw nothing blasphemous in the wall paintings in the synagogue of Dura Europos, which seemed such a puzzling enigma when they were discovered and excavated between 1932 and 1935 at a site on the right bank of the Euphrates river, between Damascus and Baghdad.

The murals, showing scenes from the Hebrew Bible, date from before 256 C.E., when the Sassanians laid siege to the town, which was at the time in the possession of the Romans.

There are depicted "Moses with the Torah", "Elijah feeding the ravens", "Ahasuerus and Esther", "David sparing King Saul", "Moses at the burning bush", and other scenes.

Midrash cites the Palestinian rabbi Joshua ben Levi, who said: "At the time of Rabbi Jochanan (3rd century C.E.) they began to have paintings on the walls, and the rabbis did not hinder them" (Jerusalem Talmud, Aboda Zarah III.3).[5]

In the seventh century a reaction set in, when the Moslems conquered the Near East. They were unconditionally hostile to representational art, and this attitude unquestionably influenced the suppression of other than decorative picture-making in Moslem-dominated territories, strictly excluding human beings and fauna.

It is only in the twelfth century that we find visual images by Jewish hands again. Whether any or many of the thousands of Hebrew manuscripts before that time were illustrated or not, we have no means of knowing. During the crusades tens of thousands of Hebrew manuscripts were destroyed. At the instigation of Pope Gregory II copies of the Talmud and other Hebrew books were sought out for destruction. In 1242, only fifty years after Jews were allowed to settle again in France, twenty-four cartloads of the Talmud and other Hebrew manuscripts were burned at the stake in Paris, later on in other cities. Manuscript books by Rashi, Maimonides and others were destroyed. From the few surviving illustrated Hebrew manuscripts, we can deduce that a great number of those destroyed had been illustrated. A number of magnificently illustrated manuscripts, especially Haggadoth, have survived to this day.

A great part of these Hebrew manuscripts, including the Hebrew Bible, Maimonides's *Mishne Torah*, Prayer books and especially Pessach Haggadoth have not only decorative ornamentation, but also show animals and human beings, men and women in serious and in humorous forms.[6]

[5]Quoted in Rachel Wischnitzer, *The Messianic Theme in the Paintings of the Dura Synagogue*, Chicago 1948, p. 10.

[6]See Bezalel Narkiss, *Hebrew Illuminated Manuscripts*, Jerusalem 1969. A greater selection in Therese and Mendel Metzger, *Jewish Life in the Middle Ages*, Office du Livre, Fribourg, Suisse and Fine Arts, New York 1982. The standard work on printed illustrations is *A Jewish Iconography* by Alfred Rubens, London 1981; supplementary volume, London 1982.

Whether the illustrators of these manuscripts were Jews or not, is of no concern in this context. However, in some of them, Jewish illustrators are named in the colophon, for instance in the magnificent *Mishne Torah* of 1296, today in the collections of the Academy of Sciences in Budapest. Here, the artist by the name of Nathan ben Simeon Halevi from Cologne gives thanks "that He made me worthy to write, to complete and to furnish with painted pictures the book of ibn Maimon" (i.e. Moses Maimonides). From the thirteenth to the sixteenth century, many illuminated manuscripts have survived.

We also know that at the end of the seventeenth century, many wooden synagogues in Poland were completely covered with wall paintings of subjects including fauna and flora. Eliezer Sussmann "from Pohlen" painted in the same way the walls of synagogues in Horb, Bechhofen, Kirchheim and other small places in Franconia and Bavaria. He included also the village houses of Horb and imaginary pictures of Jerusalem.

II

The possibility of the reflection of the outside world through a tiny hole projected onto the wall of a darkened room or a dark box has been known for many centuries. This physical process has been described by the Arabian scholar Alhazen in the tenth century and then again by the biblical commentator, philosopher and mathematician Levi ben Gershom, known by his acronym RaLBag (1288–1344), in 1321. He may have taken a cue from observations by Aristotle. The RaLBag lived in French Provence, in Orange and Avignon. What he described was a fleeting image only, a moving reflection.

The problem of fixing this fleeting image of the *camera obscura* was solved, after many attempts by other inventors, in the twenties and thirties of the nineteenth century by Joseph Nicéphore Nièpce and L. J. M. Daguerre in France and by W. H. Fox Talbot in England.

The daguerreotype was a one-off picture, a reversed mirror image on a metal plate. Talbot's invention proved to be the more practical, as it resulted in a paper negative, from which positive photographs could be made in any number.

The Daguerre process was bought and made public property by the French Government in 1839, and immediately spread world-wide. Talbot took out patents, which for many years obstructed the spreading of his invention to the same extent.

The most outstanding artistic personality amongst the first daguerreotypists was Hermann Biow (1804–1850), who opened a portrait atelier in Hamburg in 1841. He was born in Breslau, the son of a decorative painter, Raphael Biow, who adopted the name – after the Moravian town Biowa – when family names were made obligatory for Jewish people.

During his nine remaining years of intense activity in this new profession, Biow practised his craft in Dresden, Frankfurt a. Main and Berlin. In Berlin he was commissioned to take pictures of King Friedrich Wilhelm IV and members

Alexander von Humboldt, 1847
Daguerreotype by Hermann Biow

King Frederick William IV of Prussia, 1847
Daguerreotype by Hermann Biow

By courtesy of the Museum für Kunst und Gewerbe, Hamburg

Samson Raphael Hirsch
Daguerreotype by J. Böhm, Hamburg
Lithograph by Schier, Prague

From the Archives of the Leo Baeck Institute, New York

[130] Bei W. Pascheles in Prag ist erschienen, und durch C. L. Fritzsche in Leipzig zu erhalten:

Portrait

von

Samson Raphael Hirsch,

k. k. Mährischer und Schlesischer Landes-Oberrabbiner.

Daguerreotypirt von J. Böhm in Hamburg. Lithographie und Druck von Schier in Prag.

Hochquart. Preis 20 Ngr.

Verlag von C. L. Fritzsche. Redakteur: Dr.

Advertisement of Hirsch portrait in 'Der Orient', 1847

Collection Dr. Nachum T. Gidal, Jerusalem

'A Snapshot in Paris', 1911
By Alfred Stieglitz

From 'Camera', Lucerne 1971

John C. Warburg
By E. O. Hoppé

By courtesy of The Royal Photographic Society, Bath

Albert von Rothschild (1844–1911), in costume ball dress
Atelier Albert von Rothschild, Vienna

Collection of Dr. Nachum T. Gidal, Jerusa

'London Roses', ca 1908
Lumière autochrome transparency by John C. Warburg

From Margaret F. Harker, 'The Linked Ring', London 1971

Fürstin Sulkowska, 1916
By Madame d'Ora, Vienna

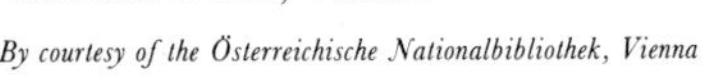

By courtesy of the Österreichische Nationalbibliothek, Vienna

'Paris, Slaughterhouse', ca 1955
By Dora Kallmus (previously Madame d'Ora)

By courtesy of the Museum für Kunst und Gewerbe, Hamburg
Collection Dr. Nachum T. Gidal, Jerusalem

Fürst Otto von Bismarck and the famous (Jewish) opera star Pauline Lucca
Photograph by Adele, Bad Ischl, in the 1880s

Yemenite scholars studying the Talmud, 1906
By Ephraim Moses Lilien, Jerusalem

Collection Dr. Nachum T. Gidal, Jerusal

'The White Fence', 1916
By Paul Strand

From 'Camera Work', New York 1917

'Awake and asleep', 1937
By Erwin Blumenfeld

'Woman', 1930
By Helmar Lerski

Collection Dr. Nachum T. Gidal, Jerusalem

The actor Paul Wegener
By Georg Gidal
'Münchner Illustrierte Presse', May 1930

By courtesy of the Folkwang Museum, Essen

'The face of fascism', 1928
Photomontage by John Heartfield

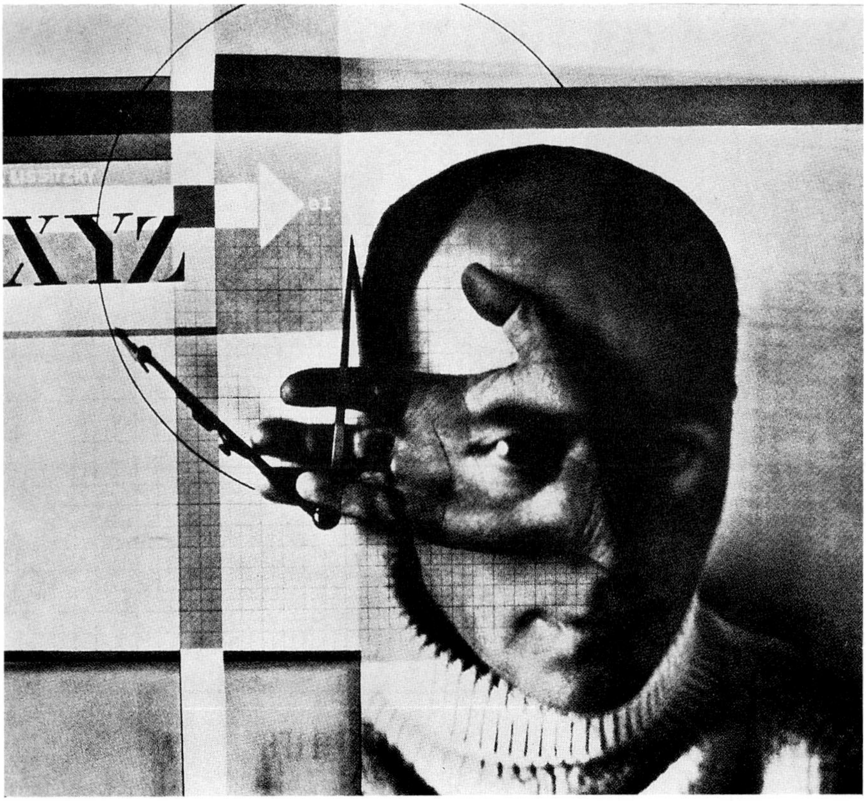

El Lissitzky
Selfportrait for the cover of 'Foto Auge', Stuttgart 1929

Collection Dr. Nachum T. Gidal, Jerusalem

)r. Erich Salomon shows his photographs of the League of Nations to Sir Austen Chamberlain in the Foreign Office, London April 1929

By courtesy of the Berlinische Galerie, Berlin

The British Prime Minister Ramsay McDonald at a reception in Berlin, August 1931
rom left to right: Prof. Max Planck, McDonald, Einstein, Minister of Finance Dr. Dietrich, Dr. Schmitz (I. G. Farben), Foreign Minister Dr. Curtius
By Dr. Erich Salomon

Collection Dr. Nachum T. Gidal, Jerusalem

'The Eye of Alfred Eisenstaedt'
Dust jacket, Thames and Hudson, London 1969
Left: African fishermen, 1936; right: Opera, New York, undated

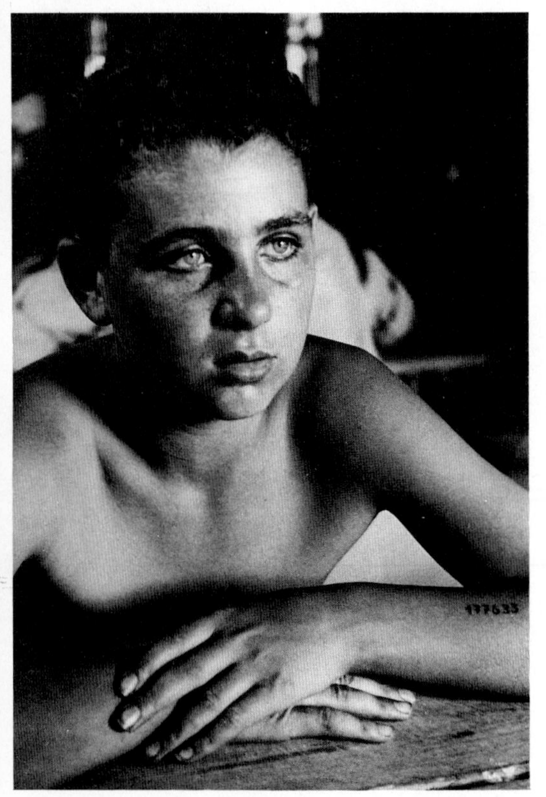

'No. 177633. Athlit Detention Camp 1945'
By N. T. Gidal

L'ag b'omer, Merom, Israel 1935
On the tomb of Rabbi Simon Bar Yochai
By N. T. Gidal

Collection Dr. Nachum T. Gidal, Jerusa

of the family in the Royal Palace. Amongst the daguerreotypes by Biow which are preserved today, are portraits of the philosopher Friedrich Wilhelm von Schelling, of the scientist Alexander von Humboldt, of the brothers Grimm, of the sculptor Christian Rauch and others. Lost is his photo-reportage of six daguerreotypes of the Great Fire in Hamburg in 1842. Biow planned a series of albums with portraits of famous contemporaries. For this project, he also took a number of pictures in 1848 of members of the *Deutsche Nationalversammlung*, the *Paulskirche* Parliament in Frankfurt a. Main.

The first of these albums was published in 1850: "*Deutsche Zeitgenossen*, herausgegeben nach H. Biows gesammelten Lichtbildern". As there was no practical photo-mechanical printing process known at the time, the daguerreotypes were transferred to copper engravings.

> "Hermann Biows Bildnisse sind von einer monumentalen Geschlossenheit, die den Blick des Beschauers in ein Auge-in-Auge mit dem Dargestellten zwingt. Er vermeidet das schmückende Beiwerk der gemalten Hintergründe, der altväterlichen Sessel, der Blumen und Pflanzen . . . Auf der spiegelnden Fläche der Daguerreotypie gelingt Biow echte Monumentalität wie sonst keinem."[7]

Biow also took the first known picture of Jewish people, the family Hahn (see the frontispiece of this Year Book).

The first known portrait of a rabbi is that of the Orthodox Samson Raphael Hirsch. As the only means of multiplication, daguerreotypes were copied by the graphic process of lithography. An advertisement was published in the weekly magazine *Der Orient*,[8] published by Dr. Julius Fürst in Leipzig. The advertisement said: "Portrait von Samson Raphael Hirsch, k.k. Mährischer und Schlesischer Landes-Oberrabbiner. Daguerreotypirt von J. Böhm in Hamburg. Lithographie und Druck von Schier in Prag."

The 1850s and 1860s were a good time for well-to-do travellers, some of whom were accomplished amateur photographers and achieved world fame with their photographs on the improved wax paper and, later, the glass plate negative. One of the foremost amongst these was A. F. Oppenheim from Dresden who had learned the process directly from its inventor Gustave Le Gray in Paris. His photographs of Spain (1852) and Greece (1853) were singled out at exhibitions with admiration: "Except Mr. Lorent (a rich amateur photographer in Mannheim, who also photographed in Palestine) I know nobody who manages this process better."[9]

It is wrong, and not in keeping with the facts, to assume, as many writers on sociological aspects of photography do, that the beginning of industrialisation in the 1850s meant the end of the "aura" period of photography. The chain of creative photographers, always limited to a few, certainly was never broken.

[7]Fritz Kempe, *Daguerreotypie in Deutschland*, Seebruck-München 1979, pp. 97ff. Kempe and other authors consider Hermann Biow the most important of all European daguerreotypists because his was a purely photographic vision (*Sehen*) quite uninfluenced by painting. In this, he had no precursor and no consequent successor in Europe for about twenty years, when Nadar in Paris and Julia M. Cameron in England created their powerful portrait studies.

[8]*Berichte, Studien und Kritiken für Jüdische Geschichte und Literatur*, Nr. 33, (13th August 1847), p. 527.

[9]E. Lacan quoted in Wolfgang Baier, *Geschichte der Fotografie*, Leipzig 1961 and Munich 1977, p. 454.

In the last quarter of the nineteenth century a number of photographers, who called themselves *Amateurs*, tried to elevate photography to the level of contemporary art, and to integrate their work within the mainstream of painting. Some of the leaders of these movements went from documentary realism to an *art nouveau* pictorialism and later back again to documentary purism.

The most powerful and influential proponent of these movements in America was, and in a way is to this day, Alfred Stieglitz. He has become for many the great myth and father figure of American photography, for others its destroyer. After the dismal failure of the German Revolution of 1848 and of the Frankfurt Parliament of that and the following years, many Jews, despairing of ever achieving human and legal rights in Germany, emigrated to America, "The Land of the Free". Amongst these early Jewish immigrants from Germany were the merchant-manufacturer Eduard Ephraim Stieglitz and his wife Hedwig. Like the majority of Jewish immigrants of the time, they were an assimilated family.

Alfred Stieglitz (1864–1946), the eldest son, was sent in 1881 to the *Realgymnasium* in Karlsruhe, which he left in 1882. In Berlin (Polytechnic and University), he studied mechanical engineering and photography with the famous Professor H. W. Vogel, a brilliant master of photographic chemistry and techniques, who had invented orthochromatic emulsions and had discovered the basic principles of colour photography. At the same time, Stieglitz won many prizes at photographic contests and exhibitions, often with photographically seen straight images. Some of these he gave, by using technical methods, painterly effects. In 1890 he returned to America where he became the founder and leader of the Photo-Secession group of pictorial photographers in New York in 1902. He also founded and edited the famed elitist magazine *Camera Work* (1903–1917), and other magazines.

In *Camera Work*, Stieglitz presented photographs side by side with reproductions of modern French and American paintings and sculptures.

Stieglitz wanted the American photographers to become equals of the then reigning pictorialists in England, in Austria and in Germany. With every means of salesmanship and photographic authority at his disposal, he was determined to win recognition for pictorial photography as a fine art, even if achieved not so much by the use of the camera alone, but by additional manipulations of a cosmetic kind of painterly "improvement". His fellow pictorialists sometimes went much farther in these manipulations than did Stieglitz himself, whose photographs were in content (i.e. before manipulation) often sensitive representations of a direct reportage nature.

In his later years it was again purist subject matter, printed in a direct way on normal photographic paper that he fought for and practised, now attacking pictorial photography as "trash".

> "Stieglitz was a non-stop garrulous bore, a cruel, domineering egomaniac and a vicious prima donna. His photographs are often dull, overrated and derivative . . . he was patient, generous, self-denying, a man of integrity. A saintly person. His photographs are strikingly original, full of depth and feeling, and have a rare beauty. They are among the finest ever made . . . There are excellent arguments for both versions . . . No matter what, he and his work matter."[10]

[10]David Vestal, *Contemporary Photographers*, London–New York 1982, p. 728.

Stieglitz's credo of photography as an independent creative medium has become the credo of American photography to this day.

The Pictorialist Movement in photography began in England, Germany and Austria. Two of the leading members of the Vienna Camera Club were the brothers Nathaniel and Albert von Rothschild. Nathaniel Rothschild (1836–1905) installed a private photo atelier in his castle at Enzesfeld in 1888. Baron Albert von Rothschild, the head of the Rothschild banking empire in Austria, learned photography with the well-known photographer H. Lenhard. In 1890 he installed an atelier in his town palace, with a technical manager and assistants. Visitors were sometimes startled by meeting people running along the corridors, clad in rather grubby white laboratory coats, reeking of chemicals.

Albert von Rothschild was an important representative of Austrian Pictorial Art Photography. His specialised work was in photographs of nature and astronomy. In these fields, he published theoretical papers and had photographs accepted at the great photographic exhibitions in Vienna (1901) and Dresden (1909).[11]

The original centre of Pictorial Photography as an art form was London. There, two of the most active theoreticians and practitioners were John Cimon (Simon) Warburg (1867–1931) and his sister Agnes (1872–1953).

Like the Hamburg Warburgs, they were descendants of Samuel Warburg (d. 1759). John C. Warburg, a private scholar of repute (in music, linguistics and entomology), took up photography in 1880. He was a member of the advisory committee for the famous Hamburg International Photographic Jubilee Exhibition of 1903. In 1916, he became a Fellow of the Royal Photographic Society in London. He worked in the pictorial style, using chiefly platinum and gum-bichromate processes and, after its invention by Lumière in 1907, he and his sister made many colour photographs by the autochrome transparency process. John C. Warburg also contributed many articles on Pictorial Photography to the Stieglitz publications and to German and Austrian magazines. Agnes Warburg's work was shown in many exhibitions too. She was also the founder member of a Women's Art and Crafts Association.

The centre of the Photo Pictorialists in Great Britain was the élitist club, The Linked Ring. In its photographic salon, the work of both Agnes and John Warburg was repeatedly shown.

> "Clive Holland, the art critic, said in 1905: 'Few English pictorial workers are better known, in this country, in the United States and also on the Continent than John C. Warburg!' It is a mystery why John Warburg and his sister Agnes, members of the wealthy and distinguished family of that name, were not elected to the Linked Ring Brotherhood . . . Many of the images have greater appeal than the work of several Links . . . The farmland, orchard, marsh and woodland scenes concentrate on features which the majority of photographers would ignore. John's ethereal portrait studies are reminiscent of the work of Symbolist painters."[12]

[11]I am indebted to Anna Auer, Director, Fotografis, Österreichische Länderbank, Vienna, for information on the photographic activities of the Rothschild brothers. See also *Geschichte der Photographie in Österreich*, Bd. II, Vienna 1983.

[12]Margaret Harker, *The Linked Ring*, London 1979, pp. 162–163.

The first entry in *The Journal of the Proceedings of the Linked Ring* records its first meeting on 9th May 1892:

> "After an excellent dinner, the menu of which is preserved amongst our archives, it was decided to form an Association having for its objects those which are now embodied in the Book of Our Constitution, and having regard to the mysticism and symbolism . . ."

In the same month the fifteen Founders met again, this time at the premises of the Camera Club, and "after a well-deserved dinner" finally adopted the title Linked Ring.[13]

There were "Purists" in the élitist photo club, The Linked Ring, as well as "The Impressionists", some famous to this day, but no Warburgs. As the criteria for acceptance into The Linked Ring were those of the highest quality of the photographic work of its members, it seems obvious that the blackballing of Agnes and John C. Warburg, "members of a distinguished and wealthy family" must have had reasons other than the quality of their outstanding work.

It is widely assumed that professional studio photography in the nineteenth century is characterised by the use of theatrical backdrops, of antique furniture and carpets, of flowerstands filled with artificial flowers, of stuffed birds and imitation-renaissance furniture. These were often the paraphernalia in photographic studios for the middle-class and lower middle-class clientele.

Hermann Biow, as we have seen, never used such theatrical paraphernalia. Many outstanding studio portrait photographers in the second half of the nineteenth century did not use them either, or only sparingly. One of these high-society photographers was Adèle Perlmutter-Heilpern, (1845–?) who was known by her professional trademark as "Atelier Adèle". The co-owners were her brothers Max and Wilhelm. In 1862, their father Joseph Perlmutter, a photographer from Zlocar and Tarnopol, founded the family enterprise "Adèle" in Vienna. Adèle Perlmutter, the outstanding photographer amongst the three, also established an atelier in Bad Ischl in 1874.

Her full-length portraits of Emperor Franz Joseph II and of many members of Court Society were (probably) the first studio photo portraits taken against a monochrome wall with only an armchair to lean on. This artistic approach was later taken up by other professional photographers who, however, added impressionistic effects by the use of artificial lighting devices.

The most competent, and most famous practitioner of these light arrangers was the Viennese society photographer Madame d'Ora. The studio-owner was Dora Kallmus (1881–1963), daughter of a lawyer, who had studied with the excellent pictorialist Nicola Perscheid in Berlin. Together with Benda, another student of Perscheid's, who had made gum prints in different colours in the Art Nouveau style, she opened the "Atelier d'Ora" in Vienna in 1907. While Dora Kallmus directed the arrangement and the lighting, Benda, a non-Jew, did the camera work. Splendid photographs of Arthur Schnitzler and his family, of Gustav Klimt, Karl Kraus, Felix Salten, Anna Pavlova, Duke Metternich, the world of art and high society, the world of the Viennese Decadence, of the Art

[13]*Ibid.*, pp. 83ff.

Deco period, of the imperial court, of the military and civilian aristocracy, the world of the decadent sensuality of Vienna's upper classes is mirrored in these atelier photographs. Beautiful as many of them still are, they also show that they have been posed, often *à la mode*, by an "arranger".

In 1925 a second atelier was opened in Paris.

Parallel to the beautiful, but also artificially beautifying, school of the Pictorialists there has always existed a "naturalistic" straight approach to photography. With the invention of the practical handcamera around 1896, which did not have to be supported by a tripod, the reportage approach of photographs taken unobserved with short exposure influenced photography everywhere.

In France, one of the first practitioners of reportage photos (which could by then be printed in newspapers), was the Alsatian Gerschel. His photographic reports of the Dreyfus Trial in Rennes in the year 1898 remain perhaps the most penetrating photo-reports of these decades.

In a similar unobserved reportage approach, Dr. Emil Mayer in Vienna captured scenes of everyday life. One of his finest achievements was a series of photos taken in Vienna's amusement and recreation park, *Der Prater.* He published a selection of these photographs, with the text by Felix Salten, in a book, *Der Wurstelprater.*[14]

But he also photographed, a precursor of modern Life-Photography, the people in the fashionable shopping centres and in the workers' quarters. He broke through the by then conventional pictorialist studio approach. People come to life in his photographs, as they do for instance in Molnar's *Liliom.*

Mayer, from 1907–1927 president of the prestigious *Wiener Amateurphotographen-Klub* also wrote a practical guide to photography and produced cityscapes using the brome-oil technique. (When the Germans occupied Austria in 1938, Dr. Mayer and his wife chose to commit suicide rather than fall into their hands.)

The first person in Europe to use photographs with the definite aim of bettering the living conditions of the working classes through social legislation was Albert Kohn (1857–1926) in Berlin.

A prominent member of the *Sozialdemokratische Partei Deutschlands* (SPD), he lived with his family in abject poverty during the time of the suppression of the SPD by Bismarck (1878–1890). Afterwards, he became a leading member of the party and the adviser of its parliamentary representatives in all their socio-political struggles and motions for improvement in the living conditions of the proletariat.

Kohn became the director of the Berlin Workers' Health Insurance with its 500,000 members and in consequence of Germany's *General-Krankenkassen.* He based his work on a combination of health insurance and sickness insurance with social sciences and social medicine – the basis for today's social medicine in many countries.

In order to convince the powers-that-be of his arguments, namely, of the appalling conditions of the workers' living quarters (only having eight or more persons in one room was at the time officially acknowledged as "unsanitary"),

[14]Emil Mayer/Felix Salten, *Wurstelprater*, Wien-Leipzig 1911. Neuauflage Wien 1973.

every year from 1900–1919 Albert Kohn published surveys of the living conditions of the working classes.

In a pioneering approach beginning in 1903, he sent out photographers to document these inquiries and had the photographs published in the yearly research reports of the workers' sanitary commission. These photographic illustrations carried immediate conviction and contributed directly to improvements in the living conditions and consequently in the health conditions of the working classes in particular and of the population as a whole.[15]

Ephraim Moses Lilien (1874–1925) was a successful illustrator and printmaker in Berlin. He is best remembered for his *art nouveau* illustrations to the Bible. He is also known for the famous photograph he took in the year 1902 of Theodor Herzl on the balcony of an hotel during the Zionist Congress. Lilien visited Palestine four times between 1906 and 1916, the last time as a soldier in the Austrian Army.

What is not well known is the fact that he took many photographs in Palestine, mainly of Sephardi Jews, which in their powerful feeling and honesty are reminiscent of the portraits by Hermann Biow, by the great English photographer Julia Margaret Cameron, and of some memorable contemporary portrait studies.

Even before the First World War, the *l'art pour l'art* approach of the main streams of photography had given way to attempts at letting the objects express themselves by way of the camera instead of the photographer expressing himself through the lens. Stieglitz recognised this new approach when he saw the photographs of his admirer, the young Paul Strand (1890–1976, the son of Jacob Stransky and the grandson of German-speaking immigrants from Bohemia, Stransky and Arnstein):

> ". . . the number of photographers (with the) competence to produce images that will bear comparison with the work of, say, a Matisse or a de Kooning, is extremely small. In this century, America has produced, by general agreement, only three photographic artists of this calibre: Alfred Stieglitz, Edward Weston and Paul Strand."[16]

Strand mastered the technique of the Pictorialists and soon rejected their soft focus approach. His basic concept he often explained as a respect for objective reality stemming from his conviction that the arts as well as the sciences had one ultimate goal: the understanding of truth.

Stieglitz exhibited Strand's photographs in 1916. He devoted the entire last volume of his *Camera Work* to Strand, who by then was the first to advocate the new realism in photography for its importance in social and economic forces in society. Objectivity in photography in its possible form of truth subjectively observed, became the touchstone of its validity.

The legitimate exceptions of course are Fashion Photography and Advertising Photography. They are both founded on flights of fantasy in a surrealistic or

[15]See Eduard Bernstein, *Die Geschichte der Berliner Arbeiterbewegung*, Bd. 3, Berlin 1910, pp. 382f.; Florian Tennstedt, 'Albert Kohn – ein Freund der Kranken', in *Die Ortskrankenkasse*, Bde. 23–24, Kassel 1977, p. 237.

[16]Harold Rosenberg, *Essays on Art*, New York 1975.

fairy-tale construction (an approach used occasionally also by the studio-portraitist d'Ora).

The danger of monumentalising the human face in the service of national propaganda was evidenced in some of the great Russian films in the first post-war years. This new visual culture, mistakenly aligned with German Expressionist Art, was in photography essentially a self-reflecting pre-occupation with the powerful possibilities of the camera. Its main representative was Helmar Lerski (1871 Strasbourg–1956 Zürich), who after an unsuccessful career as an actor in America, turned to portrait photography and film making. From 1915–1931 he lived in Berlin as a cameraman and portrait photographer, from 1931–1948 in Tel-Aviv. He prided himself on being able to transform in his photographs the face of one single person into twenty or more different characters by the use of make-up, mirrors, and light-reflecting face creams. His monumentalisation of faces ("anonymous portraits" of heroic expression) found a follower in the films and photobooks of Leni Riefenstahl, which the art critic Susan Sontag has called "Fascinating Fascism".

In direct, though unconscious, opposition to this monumentalising photography shown in Russian films and by Lerski, the post-war years, in the wake of other spiritual, intellectual and artistic movements, brought the liberation of the camera and of the photographer, in the service of a newly-found naturalness and simplicity, above all in the new field of Modern Photojournalism. Photojournalism, as the word implies, is a visual expansion of journalism. Modern Photojournalism is chiefly manifested in photo-reports, photo-stories and photo-essays. The text is essential, but subordinated to the photographs.

Modern Photojournalism can be said to have originated in Germany between 1928 and 1931. Three main factors caused its breakthrough: the emergence of a new generation of sensitive photo-reporters, who came mainly from an academic or intellectual background and who opened up new areas of photo reportage as witness of their own experiences in their own time. They became the creative realisers of Modern Photojournalism with the tools developed a few years before: the small cameras, above all the Leica and the Ermanox and the increasingly sensitive negative material available for the picture carrier, the film. Some editors of the illustrated magazines were immediately prepared to integrate these new photo reports in their publications. Last but not least, the owners of the magazines recognised Modern Photojournalism as a weapon in the competition for higher circulation for more advertisements and, in consequence, for higher financial returns.

Of far-reaching importance was the fact that the new kind of photo-reportage took its cues not from art or literature, but from the many and varied aspects of the *condition humaine* itself. The emphasis was placed almost exclusively on the human element. Modern Photojournalism became a medium of human communication directed primarily, in its essential examples, towards the individual in the mass rather than towards the mass instinct in the individual. Sensationalism and indiscretion had no place in true photojournalism. The corrupting method of programming of stories beforehand in the offices of magazines or picture agencies, as it was later arbitrarily practised in magazines like the New York magazine *Life*, was the rare exception.[17]

The greatest figure in this field of photo reportage was Dr. Erich Salomon, who at first, for four years beginning in 1928, worked exclusively with a plate camera 4 by 6 cm, the Ermanox. It was in fact the most powerful lens available in 1928, to which was attached the small body. With the Ermanox, Salomon remained the undisputed master of unobserved and candid photographs in his special fields of political meetings, sessions of artists, writers, court proceedings, concerts. Other Jews amongst the small number of eight or ten pioneers of Modern Photojournalism were Georg and Nachum (Tim) Gidal, Alfred Eisenstaedt, Kurt Hübschmann, Martin Munkasci, who had come from Hungary in 1927. Also working for German magazines was the Jewish Hungarian Andrée Kertesz in Paris.

Tim Gidal and Kurt Hübschmann (Hutton) later became two of the three chief photoreporters of the British weekly *Picture Post* which was founded in 1938. Gidal joined the British Eighth Army in 1942 and became chief photoreporter of the Weekly Illustrated Army Magazine *Parade* in the North African Campaign, in most countries of the Middle East, in India, on the Burma front 1944 and in China.

Alfred Eisenstaedt emigrated to New York and became one of *Life* magazine's most famous photoreporters. In another field, Fritz Gorodisky (Goro), assistant manager of the *Münchner Illustrierte Presse*, also joined *Life* magazine. He is considered a pioneer of nuclear science photography.

Foremost amongst the editors of illustrated magazines was Kurt Korff, who with unbounded imagination attracted new talent in photography and writing and made the *Berliner Illustrirte* the illustrated magazine with the highest circulation – close to two million copies per week in 1931.

The Berlin picture editor of the *Münchner Illustrierte Presse*, from 1932 till his arrest in March 1933, was Stefan Lorant, its picture editor in Munich, a Jewish Hungarian.

Kurt Korff and his right-hand man Kurt Szafransky designed in 1935/1936, after their flight from Germany, the visual presentation of *Life* magazine for the owner of *Time* magazine Henry Luce.

Stefan Lorant became editor-in-chief of the famed *Picture Post* in London, from 1938 to 1940. Assisted by a small group of young journalists, he made *Picture Post* into the most popular and successful illustrated weekly magazine through his outstanding selection of photographs and visual layouts over four, six, eight and more pages. He brought the visual experiences of the photoreporters to their highest fruition in the form of photo-essays, photo-stories and photo-reports.

Modern Photojournalism was also advanced by new photo-agencies in Berlin which concentrated on this new field: Rudolf Birnbach, the owner of the agency *Weltrundschau*, and Simon Guttmann, the head of the photo-agency *Dephot* (*Deutscher Photo Dienst*).

[17]See Tim N. Gidal, *Modern Photojournalism, Origin and Evolution*, New York 1973, p. 5.

Martin Munkasci left Berlin in 1934 and went to New York. He became for a number of years the foremost American fashion photographer working with *Vogue* and *Harpers Magazine.*

Also famous in this field was Erwin Blumenfeld (1897–1969), who, after his discharge from the German Army in 1918, opened a leather-goods shop in Amsterdam with a darkroom and studio in the back. In 1936 he had his first one-man exhibition in Paris. Imprisoned with his family in concentration camps in France and Algiers in 1941, they reached New York in the same year. "His talent was a combination of experimental and commercial approaches, often raising the latter to a level of art by his natural inventiveness." (Jacob Deschin). "He showed a powerful grasp of the psychological as well as artistic effects of photography . . . His quest is not reality but the mystery of reality." (Ebria Feinblatt).[18] Blumenfeld's quest for experimenting with never-before-used means of photographic expression stemmed from the time when he was, in Berlin in 1924, a member of the Dadaist group.

The photographer/painter Paul Citroen belonged to this same circle of friends. His *Metropolis* has become one of the most outstanding examples of non-political photo-collages. Hans Richter, another *avant garde* photographer/painter, became a theoretician and practitioner of the surrealistic film. John Heartfield (Helmut Herzfeld, 1891–1968), originally a member of the Dadaist group in Berlin too, became the powerful master of photomontage used as a political weapon. He worked mostly for the Communist weekly *Die Arbeiter-Illustrierte-Zeitung* and did most of the book jackets for the *Malik Verlag*. His collages show simultaneously foreground and background, the façade and the reactionary/military/fascist powers behind it. "To make the invisible visible" was the purpose of his biting satires of the politically anaemic Weimar Republic at a time when art, music, literature, theatre were flowering as never before or after.

Among avant-gardists during these culturally exciting times with its hope for a better future were also László and Lucia Moholy-Nagy, originally from Hungary and Czechoslovakia. Together they produced playful photo-collages and fotograms (a process in which more or less transparent objects are placed in the darkroom on photographic paper, which is then developed after exposure to a light source: they are cameraless photographs). These collages and fotograms are considered as an art by some people, arty by others. While photo-collages and fotograms had been made before, László Moholy-Nagy constructed a new photographic theory based on their experiments. László and Lucia Moholy-Nagy also made outstanding photographs of the "New Vision" kind of the other *avant garde* photographers. Lucia Moholy then went her own way with a new approach to architectural photography.

In strong contrast to the studio portraits of, for instance, Madame d'Ora, Lotte Jacobi in Berlin, born in 1896 in Thorn, a fourth-generation photographer, whose great-grandfather had bought his camera in Paris from

[18]Quoted from Lee D. Witkin and Barbara London, *The Photograph Collectors Guide*, Boston 1979, p. 87.

Daguerre himself, made portraits in a completely unposed reportage way: studies of the landscape of the human face as expressions of the inner life. She emigrated in 1935 to the United States. In 1983, together with the author she received the Dr. Erich Salomon Prize from the *Deutsche Photographische Gesellschaft*.

The modern cityscape was photographed by the architect Erich Mendelsohn (1887–1953) in the way inaugurated by the photoreporters, the way of the liberated camera, looking right and left, up and down like the human eye. His books, *Amerika* (Berlin 1925) and *Russland-Europa-Amerika* (Berlin 1928), with large-size architectural photographs and accompanying captions were meant as interpretations and explanations of three contemporary cultures.

A classic of another kind is the "all-round" photographer Gisèle Freund. In 1932, she was a student of Sociology in Frankfurt a. Main. She made a powerful photo-reportage with her Leica at a mass demonstration against the fascist-sympathising government. In 1933 she emigrated to Paris, where she finished her studies in 1935 with a thesis on photography in France in the nineteenth century. She then worked as a freelance photoreporter for *Paris Match*, for the London *Picture Post*, the New York *Life* magazine and others. At the same time she took portraits of famous people in the world of art and literature. Freund was the first photographer to use colour film for miniature cameras (which came on the market in 1937) for portraits of people. They have, in the course of years, become timeless witnesses to characteristic traits in writers such as Walter Benjamin, James Joyce, Paul Valéry, Romain Rolland, Hermann Hesse, Virginia Woolf, Colette, Sartre, Simone de Beauvoir, Peggy Guggenheim, General Peron and his wife Eva, and many others. But she also continued, in many countries, with her photo-reporting. "My camera led me to pay heed to that which I took most to heart: a gesture, a sign, an isolated expression. Gradually, I came to believe that everything was summed up in the human face."[19]

A new generation of photoreporters from Germany carried on the impulse given by the pioneers of Modern Photojournalism in France, Britain, America and Palestine.

Madame d'Ora's portrait studio in Paris was as successful as it had been in Vienna. Her well-posed and well-lit portraits showed, as before, society people in the way she thought they wanted to be seen. These posed photographs were often influenced by, and in turn influenced, fashion photography. Just as the world of Joseph Roth's *Radetzky Marsch* is visible in her Vienna portraits, so the world of post-Proustian Paris still flickers on in her Paris studio portraits.

However, one day, the Germans marched into Paris, many of them no doubt "beautiful-looking" would-be sitters ready for just such a photographer, except for the fact that Madame d'Ora, for years a Catholic, had on this day become again the Jewess Dora Kallmus. Dora Kallmus went into hiding and survived. During this time, she made autobiographical notes. In 1942 she wrote: "Seen through my eyes in 1942, almost all portraits of men are bad, mine included,

[19]Quoted in *Contemporary Photographers, op. cit.*, p. 254.

because they are copies of a copy, of which the true original has almost never been seen." But she continues, ". . . For the portrait of men there is only one kind of photography and this is the reportage photo, which I otherwise hate."[20]

She drew wrong conclusions of other people's work from her own approach of posing the people she photographed, and imposing therefore her effect-directed will on others.

In the post-war years, Madame d'Ora continued to do atelier portraits and to work for fashion magazines. But from now on, she took the photographs herself, and with the handy small reporter's camera Rolleiflex. Parallel to these portraits and ballet scenes she made reportage photos, beginning, in 1945/1946, with a photo-report of an Austrian refugee camp, perhaps in search of her sister and other relatives. She was to learn that they had all been killed in the Nazi death camps.

It was probably in around 1949 that Madame d'Ora, or rather Dora Kallmus, began to visit the abattoirs of Paris and from then on, again and again, she took photographs of the butchers at their work, severed animals' heads, "still lives" of their intestines in black and white and even more cruel naturalistic colour photographs. "Perhaps she rebelled, an old woman now, against the fashionable world of her life, perhaps, and this seems to be more likely, the horror to which she exposed herself again and again, was an equivalent for her survival, which was not granted to those whom she had loved and who had perished in Hitler's concentration camps."[21] Dora Kallmus herself refused to comment on these slaughterhouse photographs.

In the 1950s and 1960s, a few new photographers of German-Jewish and Austrian-Jewish descent made an impact on the photographic scene in the U.S.A., in France, and in Israel – all of them of the same post First World War generation.

Robert Frank was born in Zürich in 1924. He was influenced by the Swiss photographer Gotthard Schuh, who in turn was influenced by the reportage work of Georg Gidal for the *Züricher Illustrierte*.[22]

Robert Frank emigrated to the United States in 1947. In 1959, he shocked the American public with his photo-book, *The Americans*, which had first been published a year earlier in Paris. The photos debunked almost everything which seemed at the time to be the American dream achieved. "Affluent, free and deep in the middle of an American dream that blanketed the memories of Hiroshima and the Holocaust, Americans did not want to be caught dimeless in front of the jukebox, have their cocktail parties ruined by a funeral procession, or be reminded that blacks on a bus actually rode in the back. No one much appreciated seeing the stars and stripes so translucent, hanging across a

[20]Quoted in Monika Faber, *Madame d'Ora*, Vienna 1983, p. 195. On Madame d'Ora see also Arthur Benda and Nicole Perscheid, *Madame d'Ora*, Dokumente der Photographie, Band I, herausgegeben von Fritz Kempe, Katalog, Hamburg 1980 and *ibid*, Band II, herausgegeben von Fritz Kempe und Bodo von Dewitz, Katalog, Hamburg 1983.

[21]Fritz Kempe, quoted *ibid.*, p. 45.

[22]As told to the author by Arnold Kübler, editor of the *Züricher Illustrierte*, 1974.

Fourth of July picnic like prison bars, or church and state – St. Francis and City Hall – separated by a greasy garage."[23]

The impact of Robert Frank's harsh and often brutal treatment of actual facets of American life and society have had a lasting influence on American photographers for many years. Nonetheless, by concentrating on debunking and using at the same time aesthetic concepts of form, the reportage content seems to suffer from a preconditioned approach.

Of the same generation as Robert Frank, and standing or lying on the exactly opposite end of the spectrum of photography's possibilities, is Helmut Newton. Born in 1920 in Berlin, he emigrated in 1936 with his family to Australia and after the war to Paris. Newton began his career as an apprentice to a fashion photographer in Berlin. In Paris he became the photographer extraordinaire of all highbrow to lowbrow magazines the world over, from *Vogue* to *Playboy*. He specialises in a voyeurist approach. His scandalising photographs bordering on the pornographic and often more than hinting at sexual mores of the most varied kind, often reach out in the direction of a Marquis de Sade in modern dress. It is a world of fantasies and dreams of aggressive male sexual obsessions – always presented in a splendidly tasteful execution.

While Frank and Newton wander in opposite directions, the one to the social landscape, and the other into purely personal fantasies, straight photo-reportage as such has survived. It has given new impetus to the film, too. German, French, Italian, British film makers before and after the Second World War made films with a straight and realistic reportage approach.

In the face of growing sensationalism and voyeurism in the mass media and television, "honest" photo-reportage survived in some documentary television "shorts", made mostly by independent freelance photographers turned film makers. It also survived in a few strong personalities in the shrinking field of straight photo-reporting, who were able to withstand the pressures, financially and otherwise, of the mass media.

To this small group, now a pioneering group for the dignity of the individual, belongs David Rubinger. Born in Vienna in 1924, of the same generation as Frank and Newton, he escaped to Palestine in 1939. Rubinger works mainly in Israel, but also in other countries. His reportage photos are published in *Time* magazine (he is a member of its staff) and in other magazines world-wide. He has made many visual documents of lasting impact, fulfilling one of photography's basic tasks, which is to show the "condition humaine".

To select a few from amongst the essential photographers of time-proven impact only because of their Jewish background or their Jewish heritage must have a valid reason. The justification for our inquiry is the attempt either to prove or to disprove certain traits in these photographers which may contribute to a distinguishing common denominator.

[23]Arno Rafael Minkkinen in *Contemporary Photographers*, *op. cit.*, p. 249.

A negative result would show the redundancy of selecting this, or any, ethnic group in a given sociological situation for such an inquiry. If the result would show it to be of a purely apologetic nature, it would serve no legitimate purpose.

A common denominator however seems indeed to be discernible in the personal traits of most of the photographers dealt with in our study, all of them selected for their importance in the field of photography: by far the majority were, or are, explorers or revolutionaries in a new field, pioneers or outspoken proponents of new movements in photography.

There is discernible a quest to explore the unknown, to experiment, to take risks, to accept new ideas, to find and fight for new vistas as well as new visions. A similar phenomenon can be observed in art and music in modern times. Of decisive importance is the fact of this participation by Jews, far above their relative numbers, in *avant garde* and revolutionary movements.

Our survey, for obvious reasons, limits itself to photographers of German/Austrian Jewish parentage and to those born in other countries who were influential during their stay in Germany. If the results of this study lead to further and complementary research, its purpose has been served.

Post-War Publications on German Jewry

A Selected Bibliography of Books and Articles 1986

Compiled by
IRMGARD FOERG and ANNETTE PRINGLE

Leo Baeck Institute
4 Devonshire Street
London W.1.

CONTENTS

BIBLIOGRAPHY 1986

I. HISTORY

A. General

22898. *Ashkenaz – the German Jewish heritage.* Exhibition. New York: Yeshiva University, 1986–1987. More than 900 exhibits. [The most comprehensive exhibition ever shown in the USA on Jewish cultural life in Germany from the beginning to the 20th century. Cf.: Umfangreiche Dokumentation zur Kulturgeschichte der Aschkenasim (Monika Ziegler) [in]: Aufbau, No. 11–12, New York, March 14, 1986, p. 13, illus. Wiedergeburt und Ehrenrettung der 'Jekkes' (Hans Steinitz) [in]: Aufbau, No. 15–16, New York, Apr. 11, 1986, p. 9. Deutsch-jüdische Kultur in New York (Irène Speiser) [in]: NZZ, Nr. 125, Zürich, 3. Juni 1986, p. 39.]

22899. Barkai, Abraham: *Die Juden als sozio-ökonomische Minderheitsgruppe in der Weimarer Republik.* [In]: Juden in der Weimarer Republik [see No. 22915]. Pp. 330–346, tabs., notes.

22900. Beer, Udo: *Die Juden, das Recht und die Republik; Verbandswesen und Rechtsschutz 1919–1933.* Frankfurt am Main: Lang, 1986. 385 pp., bibl. (329–382). (Rechtshistorische Reihe, Bd. 50.) Zugl.: Kiel, Univ., Diss., 1986 u.d.T.: Die jüdischen Organisationen und der von ihnen betriebene Rechtsschutz in der Weimarer Republik. [Cont.: 1. Einleitung (17–34; incl. Antisemitismus in der Weimarer Republik; Perioden und Arten des Antisemitismus). 2. Das jüdische Lager (35–86; incl.: Organisationen der Juden). 3. Definition des Begriffes 'Rechtsschutz' (87–88). 4. Organisationen, die . . . Rechtsschutz geleistet haben (89–94). 5. Beziehungen zwischen den Vereinigungen (95–112). 6. Rechtsschutz von nichtjüdischen Organisationen und Einzelpersonen (117–120). 7. Anstrengungen des Deutschen Reiches und seiner Länder (121–128). 8. Arbeitsweise der jüdischen Organisationen (129–228). 9. Felder der Rechtsschutzarbeit (229–300). 10. Ergebnisse (301–306).]

22901. Breuer, Mordechai: *Jüdische Orthodoxie im Deutschen Reich 1871–1918; Sozialgeschichte einer religiösen Minderheit.* Eine Veröffentlichung des Leo Baeck Instituts. Frankfurt am Main: Jüdischer Verlag bei Athenäum, 1986. 525 pp., notes (364–496), list of names (518–525), bibl. (501–517). [Cont. the chaps.: 1. Der Umkreis der Orthodoxie (15–60). 2. Jüdische Orthodoxie und deutsche Kultur (61–90). 3. Erziehung und Ausbildung (91–139). 4. Literatur, Kunst und Wissenschaft (140–197; a.o., Presse; Jüd. Wissenschaft). 5. Wirtschaft und Gesellschaft (198–254; a.o., Stellung und Gestalt der Rabbiner; Religionsgesetz im Wandel der Zeit; Vereinsleben). 6. Im Deutschen Reich (255–316; a.o., Emanzipation; Flucht in die Konfession; Die Orthodoxie und der Antisemitismus). 7. Neuorientierung (317–350; a.o., Selbstkritik; Nationalbewegung; Studentenbund; Jugendbewegung; Im Weltkrieg). Epilog (351–360).]

—— Burgard, Friedhelm: *Bilder aus der deutsch-jüdischen Geschichte.* [See section B in No. 23084.]

—— Carsten, F. L.: *The Court Jews: a prelude to emancipation.* [See in No. 23684.]

22902. Cellarius, Helmut: *'Ons goed Moyses': Wilhelm von Oranien und die Juden – Vorkämpfer für Toleranz.* [In]: Tribüne, Jg. 25, H. 98, Frankfurt am Main, 1986. Pp. 155–164, footnotes. [William I of Nassau, Fürst of Oranien, 1533 Dillenburg— 1584 Delft; incl. William's connection with Jewish moneylenders of Frankfurt am Main.]

22903. Cohn, Emil Bernhard/Perelmuter, Hayim Goren: *Von Kanaan nach Israel: kleine Geschichte des jüdischen Volkes.* (Die Kapitel 25–33 wurden von John Kessel [et al.] aus dem Amerikan. übersetzt.) Deutsche Erstausg. München: Deutscher Taschenbuch-Verl., 1986. 148 pp. (dtv, 10685.) [E.B.C., pen-name also E. Bernhard-Cohn, data see No. 21817/YB XXXI.]

22904. *Danzig, between East and West: aspects of modern Jewish history.* Ed. by Isadore Twersky. Cambridge, Mass.; London: Harvard Univ. Press, 1985. XVIII, 172 pp., notes. (Harvard Judaic tests and studies, 4.) [Papers presented at a symposium held at Harvard Univ. March 24–26, 1982. Incl.: Introduction (Isadore Twersky, IX–XVIII). The image of Germany and German Jewry in East European Jewish society during the 19th century (Israel Bartal, 1–17). Problems of Western European Jews in the 20th century: a comparative study of Danzig and Paris (Yerachmiel Cohen, 19–35). From Ghetto to

Zionism: mutual influences of East and West (Jacob Katz, 37–48). The German model of religious reform and Russian Jewry (Michael A. Meyer, 65–91). The death of Sigismund Markus: the Jews in Danzig in the fiction of Günter Grass (Siegbert Prawer, 93–108). The rise of Jewish nationalism on the border of Eastern and Western Europe: Rabbi Z. H. Kalischer, David Gordon, Peretz Smolenskin (Joseph Salmon, 121–137). Art as social history: Moritz Oppenheim and the German vision of emancipation (Ismar Schorsch, 139–172, illus.).]

22905. *Das Deutsche Judentum und der Liberalismus.* Internationales Seminar des Leo Baeck Instituts London und der Friedrich-Naumann-Stiftung, 21-23. Mai 1986 in Königswinter. [The Conference volume will be published by the Friedrich-Naumann-Stiftung in 1987. For detailed report on the various lectures see]: Judentum und Liberalismus in Deutschland: Bilanz einer schwierigen Symbiose (Charles E. Ritterband) [in]: NZZ, Nr. 248, Zürich, 25/26. Okt. 1986, p. 37. [Further reports]: Juden und deutscher Liberalismus [in]: AHF Information, Nr. 31, München (Nussbaumstrasse 8), Arbeitsgemeinschaft ausseruniversitärer historischer Forschungseinrichtungen in der Bundesrepublik Deutschland, 23. Juni 1986, 2 pp. Die deutschen Juden und der Liberalismus (Barbara Suchy) [in]: 'Allgemeine', Nr. 41/24, Bonn, 13. Juni 1986, p. 5. Juden im deutschen Liberalismus (Werner Becker) [in]: Deutsche Universitätszeitung DUZ, Jg. 42, Nr. 15–16, Bonn, 1986, p. 26. Deutsche Juden und der Liberalismus (Peter Honigmann) [in]: Illustrierte Neue Welt, Wien, Juni/Juli 1986, p. 5.

22906. Doerry, Martin: *Judentum zwischen Anpassung und Selbstpreisgabe: 134 Briefe Moritz Ellstätters (1827–1905).* [In]: Zeitschrift für Geschichte des Oberrheins, 132, Stuttgart, 1984. Pp. 271–304. [Documentation.] [M. Ellstätter, Karlsruhe March 11, 1827–June 14, 1905, politician, the first Jew to become a minister in a German state: responsible for the ministry of finance in Baden 1868–1893.]

22907. Eban, Abba: *Das Erbe; die Geschichte des Judentums.* (Ins Deutsche übertragen von Peter Hahlbrock.) Frankfurt am Main: Ullstein, 1986. 399 pp., illus., ports., maps. [Transl. of No. 20807/YB XXX.]

22908. Erb, Rainer: *'Jüdische Güterschlächterei' im Vormärz.* Vom Nutzen des Stereotyps für wirtschaftliche Machtstrukturen, dargestellt an einem westfälischen Gesetz von 1836. [In]: Internat. Review of Social History, Vol. 30, Pt. 3, Assen, Netherlands, 1985. Pp. 312–341, facsim., footnotes.

22909. Gay, Peter: *Freud, Juden und andere Deutsche; Herren und Opfer in der modernen Kultur.* Aus dem Amerikan. von Karl Berisch. Hamburg: Hoffmann & Campe, 1986. 342 pp., illus., ports., notes (295–326). [Transl. of No. 14996/YB XXIV. Collection of essays, incl.: Sigmund Freud: ein Deutscher und sein Unbehagen (51–114). Begegnung mit der Moderne: die deutschen Juden in der Wilhelminischen Kultur (115–188; first publ. in: 'Juden im Wilhelminischen Deutschland 1890–1914', see No. 13387/YB XXII). Der berlinisch-jüdische Geist: Zweifel an einer Legende (189–206; first publ. in English as 'Leo Baeck Memorial Lecture', 15, New York, Leo Baeck Institute, 1972, see No. 10185/YB XVIII). Hermann Levi: eine Studie über Unterwerfung und Selbsthass (207–238). Eine Lanze für Beckmesser: Eduard Hanslick – Opfer und Prophet (263–284).] [Cf.: Besprechung (Sabine Richebächer) [in]: NZZ, Nr. 179, Zürich, 6. Aug. 1986, pp. 29–30. Liebesaffäre mit tödlichem Ausgang (Peter Reichel) [in]: Die Zeit, Nr. 46, Hamburg, 7. Nov. 1986, p. 17.]

22910. Heid, Ludger: *'Mehr Intelligenz als körperliche Kraft': zur Sozialgeschichte ostjüdischer Proletarier an Rhein und Ruhr 1913–1923.* (Mit Dokumentenanhang). [In]: Jahrbuch des Instituts für Deutsche Geschichte, Bd. 15, Univ. Tel-Aviv, 1986. Pp. 337–362, footnotes.

22911. Jersch-Wenzel, Stefi: *Der 'mindere Status' als historisches Problem; Überlegungen zur vergleichenden Minderheitenforschung.* Berlin, 1986. 20 pp. (Historische Kommission zu Berlin; Informationen, Beiheft 6.) [Also on the legal status of the Jews.]

22912. *Jettchen Geberts Kinder: der Beitrag des deutschen Judentums zur deutschen Kultur des 18. bis 20. Jahrhunderts am Beispiel einer Kunstsammlung [Leo Baeck Institut New York].* Berlin: Publica Verlagsgesellschaft, 1985. 184 pp., illus. [For detailed entry see No. 21830/YB XXXI]. *Reviews*, selection [continuation of No. 21831/YB XXXI]: Panorama eines furchtbaren Verlustes: Eröffnung der Ausstellung 'Jettchen Geberts Kinder' im Rheinischen Landesmuseum Bonn (Roland Gross) [in]: 'Allgemeine', Nr. 41/33, Bonn, 15. Aug. 1986, p. 6, port. Jettchen Geberts Kinder, oder: Verfall einer jüdischen Familie (Renate Heuer) [in]: Archiv Bibliographia Judaica, Jahrbuch 1, 1985, Bad Soden/Ts., 1986, pp. 185–204.

Ausstellung 'Jettchen Geberts Kinder' geht in zahlreiche deutsche Städte [in]: Aufbau, No. 23–24, New York, June 6, 1986, p. 31. Die Bildersammlung des Leo-Baeck-Instituts wurde in Frankfurt ausgestellt (Rolf Vogel) [in]: deutschland-berichte, Jg. 22, H. 3, pp. 26–35. Die Ausstellung des LBI New York wurde in Bonn eröffnet (Rolf Vogel) [in]: deutschland-berichte, Jg. 22, Nr. 9, Bonn, Sept. 1986, pp. 34–37. Jettchen Geberts Kinder (Hans Kricheldorff) [in]: Neue Deutsche Hefte, Jg. 33, H. 1 (189), Berlin, 1986, pp. 202–203.

22913. *Die Juden im Nationalsozialistischen Deutschland = The Jews in Nazi Germany 1933–1943.* Hrsg. von Arnold Paucker mit Sylvia Gilchrist und Barbara Suchy. Mit einem Geleitwort von Fred Grubel und einer Einleitung von Peter Pulzer. Tübingen: Mohr, 1986. XXIV, 426 pp., footnotes, index of names (411–420). (Schriftenreihe wissenschaftlicher Abhandlungen des Leo Baeck Instituts, 45.) [Papers presented at the International Historical Conference *Self-assertion in adversity: the Jews in National Socialist Germany, 1933–1939*, held by the Leo Baeck Institute in Berlin, Oct. 28–31, 1985 (see Nos. 21839–21840/YB XXXI). The sixth symposium volume on the history of the German Jews publ. by the LBI. Contributions are in German or English with summaries in the complementary language. Cont.: Geleitwort = Foreword (Fred Grubel, XIII–XVI; XVII–XX). Redaktionelle Vorbemerkung = Editorial note (Arnold Paucker, XXI–XXII; XXIII – XXIV). *Einleitung = Introduction.* Der Anfang vom Ende = The beginning of the end (Peter Pulzer, 3–15; 17–27). *Weimar.* In Deutschland zu Hause . . . : die Juden der Weimarer Zeit (Peter Gay, 31–43). German Jews: citizens of the Republic (Werner E. Mosse, 45–54). Jewish self-defence (Arnold Paucker, 55–65). German Judaism: from confession to culture (Ismar Schorsch, 67–73). Orthodox Jewry in Germany: the final stages (Julius Carlebach, 75–93). *Entrechtung = Emancipation revoked.* Das Ende der Emanzipation: die antijüdische Politik in Deutschland von der 'Machtergreifung' bis zum Zweiten Weltkrieg (Reinhard Rürup, 97–114). The struggle for survival of rural Jews in Germany 1933–1938: the case of Bezirksamt Weissenburg, Mittelfranken (Steven M. Lowenstein, 115–124). Jewish autonomy within the limits of National Socialist policy: the communities and the Reichsvertretung (Herbert A. Strauss, 125–152). Der wirtschaftliche Existenzkampf der Juden im Dritten Reich, 1933–1938 (Avraham Barkai, 153–166). A Jewish bank during the Schacht era: M. M. Warburg & Co., 1933–1938 (A. J. Sherman, 167–172). Jewish welfare work under the impact of pauperisation (David Kramer, 173–188, tabs.). Ausländische Juden in Deutschland, 1933–1939 (Trude Maurer, 189–210; incl. East European Jews). Jüdische Jugend zwischen nationalsozialistischer Verfolgung und jüdischer Wiedergeburt (Werner T. Angress, 211–221). Die jüdische Turn- und Sportbewegung als Ausdruck der Selbstfindung und Selbstbehauptung des deutschen Judentums (Hajo Bernett, 223–237; also on the Olympics in 1936). Jüdische Erziehung als geistiger Widerstand (Joseph Walk, 239–247; on the Jewish school system in Germany after 1933). Die Private Jüdische Waldschule Kaliski in Berlin, 1932–1939 (Michael Daxner, 249–257). Kultur 'nur für Juden': 'Kulturkampf' in der jüdischen Presse in Nazideutschland (Herbert Freeden, 259–271; on the Jüdischer Kulturbund). Jüdische Verleger, 1933–1938 (Volker Dahm, 273–282). Courage and choice among German-Jewish women and men (Claudia Koonz, 283–293). Jüdische Frauen nach dem Pogrom 1938 (Rita R. Thalmann, 295–302). Emigration – Planung und Wirklichkeit (Abraham Margaliot, 303–316). Hashomer Hazair in Nazi Germany (Jehuda Reinharz, 317–350; H.H., a Zionist Youth group). *Vernichtung = Destruction.* Die Reichsvereinigung and the fate of the German Jews, 1939/1939–1943: continuity or discontinuity in German-Jewish history in the Third Reich (Otto D. Kulka, 353–363). German popular opinion and the 'Jewish Question', 1939–1943: some further reflections (Ian Kershaw, 365–386). *Schlusswort und Diskussionen = Conclusion and debates.* Conclusion (Peter Gay, 389–392). Zusammenfassung der Diskussionsbeiträge (Werner T. Angress, 393–409).] [Cf.: Zum Buch über die Historikerkonferenz des Leo-Baeck-Instituts: Selbstbehauptung in der Not (E. G. Lowenthal) [in]: 'Allgemeine', Nr. 41/50, Bonn, 12. Dez. 1986, p. 4. Jüdisches Leben unter Hitler [in]: Husumer Nachrichten, Nr. 254, 31. Okt. 1986. Besprechung (E. Picard) [in]: Judaica, Jg. 43, H. 1, Basel, März 1987, pp. 62–63.]

22914. *Juden in der deutschen Wissenschaft.* Internationales Symposium (des Instituts für Deutsche Geschichte, Univ. Tel-Aviv), Apr. 1985. Leitung: Walter Grab. Tel-Aviv: Nateev-Printing, 1986. 348 pp., diagrs., footnotes, bibl. (Jahrbuch des Instituts für Deutsche Geschichte, Beiheft 10.) [Cont. the articles (each followed by report on the ensuing discussion): Der Aufbruch der Juden in die Wissenschaften (Jacob Toury, 13–51). Vom Elend der Aufklärung: jüdische Philosophiegeschichtsschreibung im 19. Jh. (Friedrich Niewöhner, 53–73). Deutsche Juden als Akademiker: das Beispiel Bonn (Otto Dann, 75–94). Juden in der deutschen Klassischen Philologie (John Glucker, 95–111, bibl.). Die Leistung der Juden für die Alte Geschichte im deutschen Sprachraum (Heinrich Chantraine, 113–145; incl. biogr. data, also on fate during the Nazi period and in exile). Deutsch-jüdische Neuhistoriker in der Weimarer Republik (Gottfried Niedhart, 147–177). The social origins of success in science: Jews in 19th century Germany; abstract (Shulamit Volkov, 179–185). Ernst Cassirer's interpretation of Judaism and its function in modern political culture (Joseph Mali, 187–215). Walther A. Berendsohn, 10. Sept. 1884–30. Jan. 1984 (Margarita Pazi, 217–247; on exile in Denmark and Sweden and B.'s studies on exile literature). Hedwig Hintze (1884–1942): die Herausforderung der traditionellen Geschichtsschreibung durch eine linksliberale jüdische Historikerin (Robert Jütte, 249–279). Integrationschancen jüdischer Wissenschaftler in Grundlagenforschungsinstitutionen im frühen 20. Jh. (Jörn Behrmann, 281–327, bibl. 314–326). Einstein and Germany (Gerald E. Tauber, 329–343, bibl.).]

22915. *Juden in der Weimarer Republik*. Hrsg. von Walter Grab, Julius H. Schoeps. (Internationales Symposium, veranstaltet vom Forschungsschwerpunkt 'Religion und Geschichte des Judentums' Univ. Duisburg und dem Institut für Deutsche Geschichte Univ. Tel-Aviv, Okt. 1984.) Stuttgart: Burg Verl., 1986. 386 pp., diagrs., index of names (381–386), notes. (Studien zur Geistesgeschichte, Bd. 6.) (Jahrbuch des Instituts für Deutsche Geschichte, Beiheft 9.) [Cont.: Vorwort (W. Grab/J. H. Schoeps, 7–8). Juden in der Kultur der Weimarer Republik (Jost Hermand, 9–37). Der S. Fischer Verlag als Wegbereiter der Weimarer Kultur (Jacob Toury, 38–60). Die Kraft des Intellekts – Jakob Wassermanns 'Der Fall Maurizius' (Margarita Pazi, 61–87). Linke Poot – Alfred Döblins satirische Kommentare zur Zeit, 1919–1922 (Ingrid Heinrich-Jost, 88–106). Rudolf Frank – Theatermann und Schriftsteller (Josef Heinzelmann, 107–126). Franz Rosenzweig und Gerhard Gershom Scholem (Michael Brocke, 127–152). Das Verhältnis von protestantischer Theologie und Wissenschaft des Judentums während der Weimarer Republik (Leonore Siegele-Wenschkewitz, 153–178). Jonas Cohn: Philosoph, Pädagoge und Jude; Gedanken zum Werdegang und Schicksal des Freiburger Neukantianers und seiner Philosophie (Margret Heitmann, 179–199). Der ungeliebte Aussenseiter: zum Leben und Werk des Philosophen und Schriftstellers Theodor Lessing (Julius H. Schoeps, 200–217). Egon Erwin Kisch und das Judentum (Walter Grab, 218–243). Paul Levi – ein Symbol der Tragödie des Linkssozialismus in der Weimarer Republik (Charles Bloch, 244–262). Leonard Nelson und die sozialistische Arbeiterbewegung (Susanne Miller, 263–275). Harry Epstein – ein Anwalt der Ostjuden in der Zeit der Weimarer Republik (Ludger Heid, 276–304). Von der Notwendigkeit politischer Beleidigungsprozesse – der Beginn der Auseinandersetzung zwischen Polizeivizepräsident Bernhard Weiss und der NSDAP (Dietz Bering, 305–329). Die Juden als sozio-ökonomische Minderheitsgruppe in der Weimarer Republik (Abraham Barkai, 330–346). Deutsche Juden oder jüdische Deutsche? Zur Identität der Juden in der Weimarer Republik (Alphons Silbermann, 347–355). Protokolle der Debatten (Doris Mendlewitsch, 356–372).] [Cf.: Am Vorabend der Katastrophe: erfreulicher Tagungsbericht (Yizhak Ahren) [in]: 'Allgemeine', Nr. 41/51–52, Bonn, 19./26. Dez. 1986, p. 16. Besprechung (Karlheinz Dederke) [in]: Das Historisch-Politische Buch, Jg. 34, H. 12, Göttingen, 1986, p. 385. Reiche Palette: ohne sie ist heute vieles farblos (Joachim H. Knoll) [in]: Die Zeit, Nr. 15, Hamburg, 3. Apr. 1987, pp. 21–22.]

22916. KAHN, LOTHAR: *Early German-Jewish writers and the image of America (1820–1840)*. [In]: LBI Year Book XXXI, London, 1986. Pp. 407–439, footnotes. [On Börne, Moritz Saphir, and especially Eduard Gans, Heine and other members of the Verein für Cultur und Wissenschaft der Juden who took up the idea of German-Jewish settlement in the USA.]

22917. KATZ, JACOB: *Aus dem Ghetto in die bürgerliche Gesellschaft: jüdische Emanzipation 1770–1870*. Aus dem Engl. von Wolfgang Lotz. Deutsche Erstausg. Frankfurt am Main: Jüdischer Verlag bei Athenäum, 1986. 291 pp. [For English orig. 'Out of the ghetto', 1973, see No. 11054/YB XIX; paperback edn. see No. 15001/YB XXIV.]

22918. KATZ, JACOB: *The Jewish response to modernity in Western Europe*. [In]: Jerusalem Quarterly, No. 38, Jerusalem, 1986. Pp. 5–13. [Particularly in 19th-century Germany.]

22919. KESTENBERG-GLADSTEIN, RUTH: *The Jewish 'Vormärz' in Germany and Bohemia*. [In Hebrew].

[In]: Proceedings of the 9th World Congress of Jewish Studies, Division B, Vol. 2: The history of the Jewish people. Jerusalem, 1986. Pp. 27–34.

22920. KLAUS, HARALD: *Deutsche Juden im Militärdienst.* Ein Beitrag zur Gleichberechtigung. – Zur Geschichte der Juden in Hessen. [In]: 'Allgemeine', Nr. 41/39, Bonn, 26. Sept. 1986. Pp. 19 & 21.

22921. KÜTHER, CARSTEN: *Räuber und Gauner in Deutschland; das organisierte Bandenwesen im 18. und frühen 19. Jahrhundert.* 2., durchgesehene Aufl. Göttingen: Vandenhoeck & Ruprecht, 1986. 197 pp., map, notes (151–175), bibl. (176–190). (Kritische Studien zur Geschichtswissenschaft, Bd. 20.) [Revised edn. of No. 13391/YB XXII. Incl. chap.: Zigeuner und Juden (24–27), and also refers generally to Jews.]

22922. LAPIDE, PINCHAS: *Der Undank des Vaterlandes; zur Geschichte der deutschen Juden im Ersten Weltkrieg.* [In]: Süddeutsche Zeitung, Nr. 90, München, 19./20. Apr. 1986. P. 170, ports.

22923. LIBERLES, ROBERT: *Emancipation and the structure of the Jewish community in the nineteenth century.* [In]: LBI Year Book XXXI, London, 1986. Pp. 51–67, footnotes. [Compares the situations in England, France, and Germany.]

22924. LIBERLES, ROBERT: *Was there a Jewish movement for emancipation in Germany?* [In]: LBI Year Book XXXI, London, 1986. Pp. 35–49, footnotes.

22925. LOWENSTEIN, STEVEN M.: *Governmental Jewish policies in early nineteenth century Germany and Russia: a comparison.* [In]: Jewish Social Studies, Vol. 46, No. 3–4, New York, Summer – Fall 1984. Pp. 303–320.

22926. LOWENTHAL, ERNST G.: *Subjekt – oder nur Objekt der Geschichte? Zur deutsch-jüdischen Geschichtsschreibung in unserer Zeit.* 1–2. [In]: 'Allgemeine', Nr. 41/24 (pp. 3–4) & Nr. 41/25 (pp. 3–4, illus.), Bonn, 13. & 20. Juni 1986. [Lecture by E.G.L., one of the recipients of the Dr.-Leopold-Lucas-Preis 1986, conferred by the Univ. Tübingen on him and Christoph Albrecht, Berlin/East.]

22927. MAURER, TRUDE: *Ostjuden in Deutschland 1918–1933.* Hamburg: Christians, 1986. 972 pp., notes (773–937), bibl. (938–956). (Hamburger Beiträge zur Geschichte der deutschen Juden, Bd. 12.) [Publication of the author's dissertation (see No. 21842/YB XXXI). Cont. the sections (titles condensed): Einleitung: Begriffsprobleme und Vorgeschichte (11 ff.). *Teil A*: Die ostjüdischen Wanderer in Deutschland: Versuch einer demographischen Skizze (46 ff.). *Teil B*: Das Porträt der Ostjuden im Spiegel der öffentlichen Meinung (104 ff.). *Teil C*: Die deutsche Politik gegenüber den Ostjuden (192 ff.). *Teil D*: Die deutschjüdische Gemeinschaft und die Ostjuden (508 ff.). Zusammenfassung: Ostjudeneinwanderung, deutsche Gesellschaft und deutsches Judentum (760–769).] [Cf.: Nur wenige fühlten sich ihnen verwandt: die erste wissenschaftliche Darstellung (Ludger Heid) [in]: Die Zeit, Nr. 15, Hamburg, 3. Apr. 1987, p. 21.]

22928. MEHNERT, ALMUT: *A selective discussion of historical and ideological aspects of German Jewish 'emancipation'.* A study. 1985. 29, 4, 14 (bibl.) pp. [At head of title: Arguments of German Jewish liberalism.] [Typescript, available in the LBI New York.]

22929. MENCKEN, FRANZ E., ed.: *Stachel in der Seele; jüdische Kindheit und Jugend.* Weinheim: Quadriga, 1986. 260, 26 pp., illus. [Collection of autobiographical texts, 1750–1942; incl. Kitty Hart, Ludwig Kalisch, Fritz Kortner, Fanny Lewald, Salomon Maimon, Moritz Oppenheim, Rahel Straus, Jakob Wassermann.]

22930. MONDOT, JEAN: *Der Aufklärer Wilhelm Ludwig Wekhrlin und die 'bürgerliche Verbesserung' der Delinquenten, der Juden und der Frauen.* [In]: Jahrbuch des Instituts für Deutsche Geschichte, Bd. 15, Univ. Tel-Aviv, 1986. Pp. 91–116, footnotes. [On W.'s attitude towards Jews, pp. 103–110.]

22931. NA'AMAN, SHLOMO: *Jüdische Aspekte des Deutschen Nationalvereins (1859–1867).* [In]: Jahrbuch des Instituts für Deutsche Geschichte, Bd. 15, Univ. Tel-Aviv, 1986. Pp. 285–307, footnotes.

22932. NICOSIA, FRANCIS R.: *Moritz Sobernheim and the Jewish Affairs section of the German Foreign Office, 1918–1933.* [In]: Proceedings of the eleventh European Studies Conference. Ed.: Karl Odwarka. Cedar Falls: Univ. of Northern Iowa, European Studies Journal, 1986. Pp. 185–193, notes (190–193). [A considerably expanded version of this paper will be publ. [in]: LBI Year Book XXXIII, 1988, under the title: 'Jewish affairs and German foreign policy during the Weimar Republic: Moritz Sobernheim and the Referat für jüdische Angelegenheiten'.]

22933. POMMERIN, REINER: *Die Ausweisung von 'Ostjuden' aus Bayern 1923: ein Beitrag zum Krisenjahr der Weimarer Republik.* [In]: Vierteljahrshefte für Zeitgeschichte, Jg. 34, H. 3, München, Juli 1986. Pp. 311–340, footnotes.

22934. *Revolution and evolution: 1848 in German-Jewish history.* Ed. by Werner E. Mosse, Arnold Paucker, Reinhard Rürup. [See No. 17885/YB XXVII.] *Reviews* [continuation of No. 21848/YB XXXI]: Review (Steven E. Aschheim) [in]: Studies in Contemporary Jewry, Vol. 2, Bloomington, Indiana Univ. Press, 1986, pp. 372–377.

22935. RICHARZ, MONIKA: *Landjuden und Wirtschaft: jüdische Schlachter und Viehhändler im deutschen und internationalen Viehhandel des 19. Jahrhunderts.* (Kurzfassung). [In]: Studia Rosenthaliana, Vol. 19, No. 2, Assen, The Netherlands, Oct. 1985. Pp. 357.

22936. ROSENSWEIG, BERNARD: *Taxation in the late Middle Ages in Germany and Austria.* [In]: Diné Israel; an annual of Jewish law, Vol. 12, Tel-Aviv, 1986. Pp. 49–93.

22937. RÜRUP, REINHARD: *The tortuous and thorny path to legal equality: 'Jew Laws' and emancipatory legislation in Germany from the late eighteenth century.* [In]: LBI Year Book XXXI, London, 1986, Pp. 3–33, footnotes.

22938. STEINHARDT, WOLFGANG O.: *Mein Vater – deutscher Bürger jüdischen Glaubens.* Berlin: Arcus, 1986. 271 pp., illus., ports. [Biography of Max Steinhardt, 1880 province of Poznań – 1932 Berlin, physician, married to a Gentile.]

22939. SUCHY, BARBARA: *Vom 'Güldenen Opferpfennig' bis zur 'Judenvermögensabgabe'; tausend Jahre Judensteuern.* [In]: Mit dem Zehnten fing es an; eine Kulturgeschichte der Steuer. Hrsg. von Uwe Schultz. München: Beck, 1986. Pp. 114–129, facsims., notes.

22940. SVETSINGER, ROBERT: *Was the pied piper of Hameln Jewish?* [In]: Midstream, Vol. 32, No. 8, New York, Oct. 1986. Pp. 32–34. [Also on the fact that many people in the 'pest-control profession' are of German-Jewish origin.]

22941. TOURY, JACOB: *Jewish textile merchants in south-west Germany before the age of industrialization.* [In Hebrew]. [In]: Zmanim, No. 21, Tel-Aviv, Spring 1986. Pp. 51–55 [See also the author's book: Jüdische Textilunternehmer in Baden-Württemberg 1683–1938 (Schriftenreihe wissenschaftlicher Abhandlungen des Leo Baeck Instituts, 42), No. 20839/YB XXX; and the author's essay, No. 20840/YB XXX.]

22942. TOURY, JACOB: *Self-improvement and self-defence in Central Europe 1890–1933.* [In Hebrew]. [In]: Yalkut Moreshet, No. 42, Tel-Aviv, Dec. 1986. Pp. 7–54. [On Austria and Germany.]

22943. VOGT, ARNOLD: *Volle Gleichstellung nie erreicht: Chancen und Grenzen jüdischer Religion im deutschen Militär bis zum Jahr 1918.* 1–2. [In]: Tribüne, Jg. 25, H. 99 (pp. 122–136) & Jg. 26, H. 101 (pp. 120–141), Frankfurt am Main, 1986–1987. Illus., footnotes. [For the author's book 'Religion im Militär' see No. 22400/YB XXXI.]

22944. VOLKOV, SHULAMIT: *Selbstgefälligkeit und Selbsthass: die deutschen Juden zu Beginn des 20. Jahrhunderts.* [In]: Geschichte in Wissenschaft und Unterricht, Jg. 37, H. 1, Seelze, Jan. 1986. Pp. 1–13.

22945. WAGENKNECHT, CHRISTIAN: *Isachar Falkensohn Behrs 'Gedichte von einem pohlnischen Juden': ein Kapitel aus der Literaturgeschichte der Judenemanzipation.* [In]: Juden in der deutschen Literatur [see No. 23676]. Pp. 77–87, notes.

22946. WASSERMANN, HENRY: *Jews in Jugendstil: the Simplicissimus, 1896–1914.* [In]: LBI Year Book XXXI, London, 1986. Pp. 71–104, facsims., footnotes.

22947. WASSERMANN, HENRY: *'Was ist des Juden Vaterland?' – Zum Selbstverständnis der deutschen Juden in der Zeit der Assimilation.* [In]: Geschichte in Wissenschaft und Unterricht, Jg. 37, H. 1, Seelze, Jan. 1986. Pp. 14–29, notes (27–29). [Revised version of a lecture printed in Hebrew under the title: 'The cultural identity of German Jewry', see No. 20842/YB XXX.]

22948. YUVAL, ISRAEL JACOB: *A German Jewish autobiography from the 14th century.* [In Hebrew, with English summary]. [In]: Tarbiz, Vol. 55, No. 4, Jerusalem, July-Sept. 1986. Pp. 541–566. [An anonymous autobiography by a Jew from Andernach, beginning in the year 1370 when he was 13 years old and went to study in Mainz. Ms. found in the Bodleian Library, Oxford, comprising 2 pp., in Hebrew, given here on pp. 564–566.]

Linguistics/Western Yiddish

22949. *Auseinandersetzungen um jiddische Sprache und Literatur.* Hrsg. von Walter Röll, Hans-Peter Bayerdörfer. [In]: Kontroversen, alte und neue, Bd. 5. Akten des 7. Internat. Germanisten-Kongresses, Göttingen 1985, hrsg. von Albrecht Schöne. Tübingen: Niemeyer, 1986. Pp. 3–103. [Incl.: Zum literarischen Charakter und der literarischen

Intention des altjiddischen Schmuelbuchs (Barbara Könnecker, 3–12). Frühneuzeitliche Fassungen des altjiddischen 'Artushofs' (Robert G. Warnock, 13–19). Der 'Knick' in der Entwicklung des Frühneuhochdeutschen aus jiddistischer Sicht (Erika Timm, 20–27). Das deutsch-jiddische Sprachkontinuum: neue Perspektiven (Ulrike Kiefer, 28–52). Bestandteile des deutschen Gegenwartwortschatzes jiddischer oder hebräischer Herkunft (Walter Röll, 54–62). Die Kontroverse um Sobols Musical 'Ghetto' (Thomas Freeman, 81–93). Die Beschäftigung mit dem Jiddischen und der Kanon der Wissenschaften (Klaus Cuno, 94–103).]

— BAUMGARTEN, JEAN: *Une traduction de la Bible en yiddish.* [See pp. 237–252 in No. 23460.]

22950. BIRNBAUM, SALOMO A.: *Das hebräische und aramäische Element in der jiddischen Sprache.* 2. Aufl., unveränderter Nachdr. der Dissertation Würzburg 1922. Mit einem Nachwort von Walter Röll. Hamburg: Buske, 1986. IV, 60 pp.

22951. — BIRNBAUM, SALOMO A.: *Die jiddische Sprache; ein kurzer Überlick und Texte aus 8 Jahrhunderten.* 2., erweiterte und überarb. Aufl. Hamburg: Buske, 1986. XII, 183 pp. [Augmented edn. of No. 12658/YB XXI.] [See also in No. 22967.]

22952. — DENMAN, HUGH: *Solomon Birnbaum's contribution to Yiddish linguistics.* [In Hebrew]. [In]: Ha-Sifrut, No. 35/36, Tel-Aviv, Summer 1986. Pp. 252–262. [Transl. from English.]

22953. BLUM, ANDRÉ/RAPHAËL, FREDDY: *Josouillet Rabat-Joie.* Epopée en judéo-alsacien d'André Blum. Présentation et commentaires de Freddy Raphaël. [In]: Revue des Sciences Sociales de la France de l'Est, No. 12, Strasbourg, 1983. Pp, 389–424, footnotes.

— FISHMAN, JOSHUA A.: *Nathan Birnbaum's 'second phase': the champion of Yiddish and Jewish cultural autonomy.* [See No. 23591.]

22954. FRAKES, JEROLD C.: *Accessibility, audience and ideology: on editing old Yiddish texts.* [In]: The German Quarterly, Vol. 59, No. 2, Cherry Hill, N.J., Spring 1986. Pp. 187–202, notes.

22955. FUKS, L. & R.: *Yiddish language and literature in the Dutch republic.* [In]: Studia Rosenthaliana, Vol. 20, No. 1, Assen, The Netherlands, July 1986. Pp. 34–57, footnotes.

22956. GELBER, MARK H.: *Das Judendeutsch in der deutschen Literatur; einige Beispiele von den frühesten Lexika bis Gustav Freytag und Thomas Mann.* [In]: Juden in der deutschen Literatur [see No. 23676]. Pp. 162–178, notes.

22957. *Die 'Historie von dem Kaiser Octaviano'.* Hrsg. von Theresia Friderichs-Müller. *Bd. 1*: Transkription der Fassung des Cod. hebr. monac. 100 mit 18 Federzeichnungen von Isaak bar Juda Reutlingen. *Bd. 2*: Faksimile des Drucks Augsburg, Matthäus Franck (ca. 1568). Hamburg: Buske, 1981. VIII, 176; XI, 274 pp. (jidische schtudies: Beiträge zur Geschichte der Sprache und Literatur der aschkenasischen Juden. Hrsg. von Walter Röll, Bd. 1–2.) [Vol. 1 incl.: Einleitung (1–32; a.o., Die Rezeption der deutschen Volksbücher bei den Juden; Die jiddische Bearbeitung des 'Kaiser Octavian'; Das Verhältnis des jiddischen 'Kaiser Octavian' zur deutschen Vorlage).]

22958. HOLZAPFEL, OTTO: *Yiddish folksong documents in the German Folksong Archives [at Freiburg i.Br.].* [In]: Proceedings of the 9th World Congress of Jewish Studies: Art, folklore, theatre, music. Jerusalem, 1986. Pp. 135–141.

22959. KATZ, DOVID: *Hebrew, Aramaic and the rise of Yiddish.* [In]: Readings in the sociology of Jewish languages. Ed. by Joshua A. Fishman. Vol. 1. Leiden, NL: Brill, 1985. Pp. 85–103.

— KATZ, DOVID: *Josef Herzens 'Esther': Zentral-Westjiddisch in Fürth.* [See pp. 24–27 in No. 23010.]

22960. KATZ, DOVID: *On Yiddish, in Yiddish, and for Yiddish: 500 years of Yiddish scholarship.* [In]: Identity and ethos [see No. 23677]. New York; Berne: Lang, 1986. Pp. 23–36, notes.

— MILFULL, HELEN: *'Weder Katze noch Lamm'? Franz Kafkas Kritik des 'Westjüdischen'.* [See pp. 178–192 in No. 23674.]

22961. PRAWER, SIEGBERT S.: *'Das verfluchte Gemauschel': jiddische Dichtung im Kampf der Sprachen.* [In]: Kontroversen, alte und neue. Bd. 1: Ansprachen – Plenarvorträge – Berichte. Hrsg. von Albrecht Schöne. Tübingen: Niemeyer, 1986. Pp. 97–110.

22962. RÖLL, WALTER: *Bemerkungen zur Sprache eines lateinschriftlichen Jiddisch-Glossars.* [In]: Proceedings of the 9th World Congress of Jewish Studies, Division C: Jewish thought and literature. Jerusalem, 1986. Pp. 133–140. [Describes Cod. hebr. 294 in the Hamburg Staats-und Univ. bibliothek.]

22963. SCHISCHA, ABRAHAM: *'The Prince and the Nazir' and its Yiddish translator; a translation and its fate.* [In Hebrew]. [In]: Alei Sefer, Vol. 12, Ramat-Gan, 1986. Pp. 111–123. [On the Frankfurt am Main 1769 edition, printed by Isaac Hamburg and transl. from Hebrew to Yiddish by Raphael Halevi.]

22964. STACKMANN, KARL: *'Dukus Horant' – der Erstling jüdisch-deutscher Literatursymbiose.* [In]: Juden in der deutschen Literatur [see No. 23676]. Pp. 64–76, notes.

22965. *Studies in Yiddish literature and folklore.* Jerusalem: Hebrew Univ., 1986. 235 pp. (Research projects of the Institute of Jewish Studies, monograph series, No. 7.) [An English translation of lectures delivered at the First International Conference on Research in Yiddish Language and Literature, Oxford, 1979. Incl. articles discussing old Yiddish in Germany: Can the Cambridge manuscript support the 'Spielmann' theory in Yiddish literature? (Chone Shmeruk, 1–36). Yiddish works on women's commandments in the 16th century (Agnes Romer Segal, 37–59). The evolution of the poetical contest in Ashkenaz (Chava Turniansky, 60–98).]

—— SÜSS, HERMANN: *'Esther' – die 'Fürther Megille' von Josef Herz.* [See pp. 16–24 in No. 23010.]

22966. TIMM, ERIKA: *Das Jiddische als Kontrastsprache bei der Erforschung des Frühneuhochdeutschen.* (Antrittsvorlesung Trier, Juli 1985.) [In]: Zeitschrift für Germanistische Linguistik (ZGL), 14,1, Berlin, 1986. Pp. 1–22, bibl. (19–22).

22967. TRIER, UNIVERSITÄT, Fachbereich Sprach- und Literaturwissenschaften, Abt. Jiddistik: *Von Raschi zu Moses Mendelssohn: Zeugnisse des Jiddischen.* Begleitheft [zur] Ausstellung im Gebäude A. (Ausstellung und Katalog: Erika Timm.) Trier, 1986. 24 pp., facsims. [Mimeog.] [See also: Rest von Mameloschn: als einzige Universität Europas bietet Trier das Fach Jiddistik an [in]: Der Spiegel, Nr. 41, Hamburg, 6. Okt. 1986, pp. 98 & 101. Eine Sprache, die man verleugnen muss: an der Universität Trier wird das Jiddische vor dem Vergessen bewahrt (Wolfgang Stauch-von Quitzow) [in]: Süddeutsche Zeitung, Nr. 203, München, 5. Sept. 1986, p. 47, port. (of Salomo A. Birnbaum; article on the occasion of the Univ. of Trier bestowing an honorary doctorate on Salomo A. Birnbaum; eulogy was delivered by Walter Röll).]

—— TURNIANSKY, CHAVA: *An unknown [Yiddish] song on the Frankfurt am Main events (1612–1616).* [In Yiddish]. [See No. 23008.]

22968. WOLF, SIEGMUND A.: *Jiddisches Wörterbuch mit Leseproben.* Wortschatz des deutschen Grundbestandes der jiddischen (jüdischdeutschen) Sprache. Korrigierter Nachdr. der Ausg. Mannheim 1962. 2., durchgesehene Aufl. Hamburg: Buske, 1986. 203 pp., facsims.

B. Communal and Regional History

1. Germany

22969. GENERAL. DIAMANT, ADOLF: *Vor hundert Jahren eingeweiht: zur Geschichte von neun deutschen Synagogen.* [In]: 'Allgemeine', Nr. 41/39, Bonn, 26. Sept. 1986. P. 25. [Refers to Kaiserslautern, Lechenich, Niedermendig, Nieder-Mockstadt, Nördlingen, Oberwesel, Papenburg, Reiskirchen, Usingen.

22970. ALPEN. SCHMITTER, PETER: *Geschichte der Alpener Juden.* Dokumente vom Alpener Beginn bis zum Leidensweg in der NS-Zeit. Alpen: Theuysen, 1986. 140 pp., illus., ports., maps.

22971. ALSFELD. DIETER, H.: *Aus der Geschichte der Alsfelder Juden.* [In]: Hessische Heimat, Jg. 35, Marburg/L., Hessischer Heimatbund, 1985. Pp. 77–82.

22972. ALTDORF. KUBY, ALFRED H.: *Die jüdische Gemeinde Altdorf, 1796 bis 1815, nach dem Zeugnis der Standesakten.* [In]: Pfälzisch-Rheinische Familienkunde, Jg. 35, Bd. 11, H. 1, Ludwigshafen, 1986. Pp. 8–10.

22973. ALTENKUNSTADT. MOTSCHMANN, JOSEF: *Altenkunstadt – Saaz – Berlin – Jerusalem: Stationen einer jüdischen Familie in drei Jahrhunderten.* [In]: Vom Main zum Jura (Postfach 41, D-8621 Weismain), H. 2, Lichtenfels, 1985. Pp. 45–56, illus., ports., notes (55–56). [On the family Grünfelder.]

22974. — MOTSCHMANN, JOSEF: *'Die Kultur im Dorfe': jüdisches Vereinsleben in Altenkunstadt zu Beginn des 19. Jahrhunderts.* [In]: Vom Main zum Jura, H. 2, Lichtenfels, 1985. Pp. 35–44, illus., port., notes (43–44).

22975. — MOTSCHMANN, JOSEF: *'Masel tow': zur Bedeutung des Hochzeitssteins an der Synagoge von Altenkunstadt.* [In]: Vom Main zum Jura, H. 3, Lichtenfels, 1986. Pp. 51–58.

22976. ALTONA. WINKLE, STEFAN: *Johann Friedrich Struensee und das Judentum.* [In]: Jahrbuch des Instituts für Deutsche Geschichte, Bd. 15, Univ. Tel-Aviv, 1986. Pp. 46–90, footnotes, facsims. [On Jewish life in Altona where Struensee (1737–1772) lived as a physician for 10 years, on his friendship with the Jewish physician Hartog Gerson (1730–1801), and his tolerant attitude towards Jews when he became minister of the Danish king Christian VII.]

22977. ASCHENHAUSEN. Köhler, Günter: *Aschenhausen – eine 'Insel' in der Geschichte deutscher jüdischer Gemeinden.* [In]: Nachrichtenblatt des Verbandes der Jüd. Gemeinden in der DDR, Dresden, Sept. 1986. Pp. 8–9, illus. (synagogue, cemetery).

22978. BAMBERG. Brachs, Meinrad: *Das bayerische Judenedikt vom 10. Juni 1813 und die Wiederverleihung erledigter Matrikelstellen an Bamberger Juden.* [In]: Bericht des Historischen Vereins Bamberg, 121, Bamberg, 1985. Pp. 153–185, tabs., footnotes.

22979. — Mistele, Karl H.: *Bamberg: verlorene Heimat der Juden.* Bamberg, 1986. 31 pp., illus. [Available in the LBI New York.] [Incl. the persecution during the Nazi period.]

—— BAVARIA. [See Nos. 22933, 22978, 23804.]

22980. BECHHOFEN. Lang, Adolf: *Bechhofen und seine zerstörte Synagoge.* [In]: Ansbach gestern + heute, H. 42. Ansbach (Postfach 1741): Städtisches Verkehrsamt, 1986. Pp. 990–1002, illus., notes. [Also on the Nazi period when the richly decorated and painted synagogue was burnt down.]

22981. BERGEDORF. Richert, Harald: *Juden in Bergedorf 1695–1945.* [In]: Zeitschrift des Vereins für Hamburgische Geschichte, Bd. 71, Hamburg, 1985. Pp. 145–160.

—— BERLIN. [See also Nos. 23503, 23520, 23617, 23630.]

22982. — Engelmann, Bernt: *Berlin – eine Stadt wie keine andere.* München: Bertelsmann, 1986. 320 pp., illus., map. [Covers also the participation of Jews in the history and cultural development of Berlin.]

—— — Fontane, Theodor: *Adel und Judenthum in der Berliner Gesellschaft.* [And]: *Die Juden in unsrer Gesellschaft.* [See in No. 23838.]

22983. — Friedrich, Otto: *Before the deluge: a portrait of Berlin in the 1920s.* With a new foreword by the author. New York: Fromm, 1986. 432 pp., illus. [Refers to many German-Jewish personalities. Paperback edn. of No. 9251/YB XVII.]

—— — Gay, Peter: *Der berlinisch-jüdische Geist: Zweifel an einer Legende.* [See pp. 189–206 in No. 22909.]

22984. — *Geschichtslandschaft Berlin: Orte und Ereignisse.* Hrsg. von Helmut Engel, Stefi Jersch-Wenzel, Wilhelm Treue. *Charlottenburg; Teil 1: Die historische Stadt.* Mit Beiträgen von Berthold Grzywatz [et al.]. Berlin: Nicolaische Verlagsbuchhandlung, 1986. 636 pp., 576 illus., ports., maps, index of names, bibl. references. (Publikation der Historischen Kommission zu Berlin aus Anlass der 750-Jahr-Feier der Stadt Berlin 1987.) [Refers passim to Jewish personalities, covers also the Nazi period, especially in an article by Marie-Luise Kreuter (pp. 178–199, bibl.) on the 'aryanisation' of the Aron Elektricitäts-zähler-Fabrik GmbH owned by Manfred Aron until 1936, from then on called Heliowatt Werke Elektrizitätsgesellschaft mbH.] [For 'Charlottenburg' pt. 2, see No. 21866/YB XXXI.]

22985. — Goldstein, Heinzwerner: *Auf der Suche nach der Vergangenheit: Fränkelufer – eine Berliner Synagoge besteht 70 Jahre* [In]: 'Allgemeine', Nr. 41/39, Bonn, 26. Sept. 1986. P. 28. [Also on Rabbi Isidor Bleichrode.]

22986. — Honigmann, Peter: *Die Austritte aus der Jüdischen Gemeinde Berlin 1873–1941.* Statistische Auswertung und historische Interpretation. [1986?]. 177 pp., notes (166–177). [Typescript, available in the LBI New York.]

22987. — Kagan, Zipora: *Writings on the wall.* [In]: The Jerusalem Quarterly, No. 36, Jerusalem, Summer 1985. Pp. 42–58. [On Jewish culture in post-World War I Berlin.]

22988. — Melcher, Peter: *Der Jüdische Friedhof in Weissensee; ein Denkmal der Assimilation und ihres Scheiterns.* [In]: Materialien des Pädagogischen Zentrums zur Lehrerfortbildungsveranstaltung 'Stätten des Judentums und der Judenverfolgung in Berlin', Berlin, 1985. [45] pp., illus., plan, bibl. [44].

22989. — Melcher, Peter: *Weissensee: ein Friedhof als Spiegelbild jüdischer Geschichte in Berlin.* Berlin: Haude & Spener, 1986. 131 pp., illus., notes (126–129).

22990. — Metzger, Karl-Heinz/Dunker, Ulrich: *Der Kurfürstendamm; Leben und Mythos des Boulevards in 100 Jahren deutscher Geschichte.* Berlin: Konopka, 1986. 285 pp., illus., ports., facsims., plans, bibl. [Refers to Jews and the part they played in intellectual and economic life around the Kurfürstendamm; incl. chap.: 'Arisierung': Enteignung, Entrechtung und Vertreibung der Juden (pp. 173 ff.).]

22991. — Offenberg, Mario, ed.: *Adass Jisroel, die jüdische Gemeinde in Berlin (1869–1942), vernichtet und vergessen.* Berlin (Hardenbergstr. 12): Museumspädagogischer Dienst, 1986. 332 pp., illus., ports., facsims., plans, tabs., bibl. references. [History of the Orthodox congregation 'Israelitische Synagogen-Gemeinde Adass Jisroel zu Berlin' from constitution in 1869 to destruction during the Nazi period, on its first rabbi, Esriel Hildesheimer, his founding of the Berlin Rabbiner-Seminar in 1873, on the school system of Adass Jisroel and its own social institutions, also on present-day condition of its cemetery. Publication on the occasion of the exhibition 'Adass Jisroel – vernichtet und vergessen' in the Landesarchiv Berlin, June 29 – Sept. 21, 1986.]

22992. — STÜRZBECHER, MANFRED: *Das Berliner Israelitische Krankenheim der Synagogengemeinde Adass Jisroel.* [In]: Die Berliner Ärztekammer, Jg. 29, H. 3, Berlin 1986. [4] pp., tabs.

—— — WESTPHAL, UWE: *Berliner Konfektion und Mode; die Zerstörung einer Tradition 1836–1939.* [See No. 23224.]

22993. BIELEFELD. MINNINGER, MONIKA: *Frau in einer bürgerlichen Minderheit – Bielefelder Jüdinnen, ca. 1850–1933.* [In]: Frauen-Alltag in Bielefeld, Hrsg.: Ilse Brehmer, Juliane Jacobi-Dittrich. Bielefeld (Heeper Str. 132): AJZ Verl., 1986. Pp. 145–200. [See also in same book]: Josepha Metz, 1871–1941: eine Bielefelder [jüdische] Schriftstellerin (Heidrun Macha-Krau, pp. 227–254).

22994. BIESENTHAL. KRATZSCH, GERHARD/MARKAU, WERNER: *Eine Entdeckung in Biesenthal.* [In]: Nachrichtenblatt des Verbandes der Jüd. Gemeinden in der DDR, Dresden, Juni 1986. P. 8. [On the Jewish cemetery.]

22995. BODERSWEIER. NUSSBAUM, HANS/BRITZ, KARL, eds.: *Das Schicksal der Juden von Bodersweier.* Erinnerung und Mahnung. Dokumentation nach dem Jubiläum '1100 Jahre Bodersweier'. Bodersweier: Stadtverwaltung, 1984. 48 pp., illus. [Covers also the Nazi period. Cf.: Erinnerungen von erstaunlicher Offenheit (Daniel Krochmalnik) [in]: 'Allgemeine', Nr. 42/11, Bonn, 13. März 1987, p. 6.]

22996. COLOGNE. FUSSBROICH, HELMUT: *Gedenktafeln in Köln – Spuren der Stadtgeschichte.* Köln: Bachem, 1985. 212 pp. [Refers in several chaps. to the history of Jews in Cologne.]

—— DANZIG. *Danzig, between East and West.* [See No. 22904.]

22997. — MEILI-DWORETZKI, GERTRUD: *Heimatort Freie Stadt Danzig.* [And]: OMANSEN, THOMAS: *Gdańsk-Danzig-Gdańsk; Rückblicke.* Düsseldorf: Droste, 1985. 260 pp., illus. [Reminiscences of G. Meili-Dworetzki, 1912–1977, psychologist: from childhood to expulsion by the Nazis. Book incl. also survey of the history of Gdańsk by Th. Omansen.]

22998. DEGGENDORF. WESTERHOLZ, S. MICHAEL: *Da wvrden die Ivden erslagen; zur Geschichte der Juden im Landkreis Deggendorf.* Straubling: Isr. Kultusgemeinde, [1986?]. 52 pp., illus., ports.

22999. DEUTZ. ROHRBACHER, STEFAN: *Ein 'Godesberger' Grabstein auf dem Deutzer Judenfriedhof.* [In]: Godesberger Heimatblätter, 22, Godesberg, Verlag für Heimatpflege und Heimatgeschichte, [1985?]. Pp. 158–159, 1 illus. [Refers to Schönchen Godesberg, 1610–1710.]

23000. DIERSBURG. BAR-GIORA BAMBERGER, NAFTALI: *Der jüdische Friedhof von Diersburg.* [In]: Die Ortenau, Bd. 65, Offenburg, 1985. Pp. 364–375.

23001. DRAMBURG. MANASSE, ERNST M.: *The Jewish graveyard.* Transl. by Judy Goldstein. [In]: The Southern Review, Baton Rouge, La., Spring 1986. Pp. 296–307. [On the history of the Jews in Dramburg, especially the Manasse family, also on antisemitism.]

23002. DROVE. BÖLL, HEINRICH: *Die Juden von Drove.* Hauzenberg: Edition Toni Pongratz, 1986. 1 vol. (unpaged). [Essay, previously publ. in: Köln und das rheinische Judentum, see No. 20870/YB XXX.]

23003. DUISBURG. KLEIN, BIRGIT/TEMMINGHOFF, SUSANNE/GRÜNER, ELVIRA: *Spuren der Vergangenheit: eine Friedhofsmauer mahnt.* Duisburg 17 (Marienstr. 21): Birgit Klein, [1984]. 5 pp., 2 facsim. documents (6 pp.), 4 photos, 1 sketch. [Available in the LBI New York.] [Documentation on Jewish epitaphs in Duisburg by students from the St. Hildegardis-Gymnasium in Duisburg under the guidance of Werner Goeke, which won a prize in 1984 from the Bundeszentrale für Politische Bildung, Bonn.]

23004. — RODEN, GÜNTER von: *Geschichte der Duisburger Juden.* In Zusammenarbeit mit Rita Vogedes. Mit Einzelbeiträgen von Yehoshua Amir [et al.]. Teil 1–2. Duisburg: Braun, 1986. XVI, 790; IX, 791–1535 pp., illus., ports., facsims., plans, bibl. (1397–1420). (Duisburger Forschungen, Bd. 34, T. 1–2.) [Covers also economic aspects. Incl.: Namensliste Duisburger Juden, ca. 1900–1945 (1013–1367; lists also professions). Cf.: Eine Würdigung mit Vorbehalten (Ernst L. Siebenborn) [in]: 'Allgemeine', Nr. 41/39, Bonn, 26. Sept. 1986, p. 23.]

23005. EMSLAND. *Jüdische Friedhöfe im Emsland.* Katalog zur Sonderausstellung des Landkreises Emsland vom 25. Okt. bis 12. Nov. 1985. Meppen: Landkreis Emsland, 1985. 88 pp., illus.

[Cf.: Relikte untergegangener jüdischer Gemeinden (Adolf Diamant) [in]: 'Allgemeine', Nr. 41/9, Bonn, 28. Feb. 1986, p. 14.]

23006. ESCHWEGE. ZIMMER, ANNA MARIA: *Zur Geschichte der jüdischen Gemeinde in Eschwege, unter besonderer Berücksichtigung der Zeit des Nationalsozialismus.* N.p., Schriftliche Hausarbeit für das Lehramt an Grund- und Hauptschulen, 1975. 110 pp., illus., plan, tabs., bibl. (107–110). [Typescript, available in the LBI New York.] [Incl.: Mitglieder der jüdischen Gemeinde Eschwege zwischen 1931 und 1942 (pp. 94–107).]

23007. FRANCONIA. GUTH, KLAUS/LAU, EVA: *Judendörfer in Oberfranken.* [In]: Bamberger Universitäts-Zeitung, Jg. 6, Nr. 4, Bamberg, 1985. Pp. 2–7, illus., port., facsims., plans.

—— FRANKFURT am Main. BÖRNE, LUDWIG: *Die Juden in Frankfurt am Main.* 1807. [And]: *Juden in der freien Stadt Frankfurt.* 1820. [See in No. 23681.] [See also pp. 239–253 in No. 23683.]

—— — MANN, VIVIAN B.: *The Golden Age of Jewish ceremonial art in Frankfurt.* [See No. 23634.]

23008. — TURNIANSKY, CHAVA: *An unknown [Yiddish] song on the Frankfurt am Main events (1612–1616).* [In Yiddish]. [In]: Proceedings of the 9th World Congress of Jewish Studies, Division C: Jewish thought and literature. Jerusalem, 1986. Pp. 423–428 [of Hebrew section].

23009. FRIEDBERG. HERRMANN, FRITZ H.: *Ein Gutachten des Wiener Reichshofsrats von 1659 und seine Bedeutung für die Friedberger Judenschaft.* [In]: Wetterauer Geschichtsblätter, 34, Friedberg, 1985. Pp. 77–79.

23010. FÜRTH/Bavaria. *Nachrichten für den jüdischen Bürger Fürths.* Fürth (Blumenstr. 31), Sept. 1986. 60 pp., illus., ports., facsims. [Incl.: 'Esther' – die 'Fürther Megille' von Josef Herz; Schluss (Hermann Süss, 16–24, illus., facsims., map, bibl.; for preceding pts. see Nos. 20882/YB XXX & 21888/YB XXXI). Josef Herzens 'Esther': Zentral-Westjiddisch in Fürth (Dovid Katz, aus dem Jidd. übers. von H. Süss, 24–27). Gedichte vermischten Inhalts (Josef Herz; Auszug aus der von J. Suhler bearb. Ausg., Fürth 1871, pp. 57–58). Juden und Freimaurerei in Fürth, I (Werner Heymann, 28–29, bibl.). Bibliographie der in Fürth gedruckten Siddurim (Mosche N. Rosenfeld, 35–45, facsims.). Fürth und Nürnberg vor 100 Jahren: im Spiegel der Zeitschrift Israelit (Günter Heinz Seidl, 46–51, facsims.). Hachawer Naftali Herz Rosenblatt – ein Sofer in Fürth (Max Rosenblatt, 52–53, illus., port.). Rede zur Einweihung des Denkmals für die Fürther Juden und Synagogen am 26. Juni 1986 (Ruben Rosenfeld, 54–56, illus., port.). Further contributions are listed according to subject.]

23011. GELNHAUSEN. DIAMANT, ADOLF: *Die Gelnhausener Synagoge.* [In]: Das Neue Israel, Jg. 38, H. 10, Zürich, Apr. 1986. Pp. 20–21, illus. [Title condensed.]

23012. GELSENKIRCHEN. DIAMANT, ADOLF: *Aufstieg und Untergang jüdischer Gemeinden: zum Beispiel Gelsenkirchen.* [In]: Aufbau, Nr. 3–4, New York, Jan. 17, 1986. P. 36, illus. [Short survey, also on the Nazi period.]

23013. GESCHER. ROTHSCHILD, HENRY: *Die jüdische Gemeinde in Gescher im 20. Jahrhundert.* [In]: Unsere Heimat; Jahrbuch des Kreises Borken, 1985. Pp. 108–110. [Incl. the Nazi period.]

23014. GÜTERSLOH. BARLEV, JEHUDA: *Die einstige jüdische Schule in Gütersloh.* [In]: Gütersloher Beiträge zur Heimat- und Landeskunde, N.F., H. 6/7, Gütersloh, Sept. 1985. Pp. 137–138.

23015. — BARLEV, JEHUDA: *Die Gütersloher Zeitung Anno 1891 über Juden und Judentum.* [In]: Gütersloher Beiträge zur Heimat- und Landeskunde, N.F., H. 8/9, Gütersloh, 1985. Pp. 174–177, bibl. (177). [Refers to antisemitism.]

23016. HAGEN. GASE, BARBARA: *Geschichte der Juden in Hagen.* Hrsg.: Stadtarchiv Hagen. Hagen: v.d. Linnepe, 1986. 78 pp., illus. (Hagener Hefte, H. 14.)

23017. HAMBURG. ASENDORF, MANFRED: *Der Hamburger Pädagoge und Politiker Anton Rée; ein Beitrag zum Verhältnis von Emanzipation und Bildung.* Hamburg: Landeszentrale für Politische Bildung, 1985. 31 pp., port. (Nachdrucke, 1985, 2.) [Reprinted from: Jahrbuch des Instituts für Deutsche Geschichte, Beiheft 6, see No. 20818/YB XXX.] [Anton Rée, Hamburg Nov. 9, 1815–Jan. 13, 1891, educationalist and politician, teacher and director of the Isr. Freischule in Hamburg.]

23018. — JOCHMANN, WERNER/LOOSE, HANNS-DIETER, eds.: *Hamburg: Geschichte der Stadt und ihrer Bewohner. Bd. 2: Vom Kaiserreich bis zur Gegenwart.* Hrsg.: Werner Jochmann. Hamburg: Hoffmann & Campe, 1986. 488 pp., illus., ports., facsims., tabs., notes, bibl. (469–472). [Cont.: *Handelsmetropole des Deutschen Reiches* (Werner Jochmann, 15–130; incl.: Die Juden, pp. 54–57; Die Antisemitenparteien, pp. 74–76.) *Der Stadtstaat als demokratische Republik* (Ursula Büttner, 131–264). *Im Dritten Reich 1933–1945* (Werner Johe, 265–376; incl.: Die

Verfolgung der Juden, pp. 332–338; Konzentrationslager Neuengamme, pp. 359–362; Die Ermordung der Hamburger Juden, pp. 363–364). *Hamburg seit 1945* (Arnold Sywottek, 377–468; incl.: Die Ära Weichmann, pp. 447–451). Vol. also refers passim to Jewish personalities. Volume 1, ed. by Hanns-Dieter Loose, with the subtitle: 'Von den Anfängen bis zur Reichsgründung', was publ. 1982, 560 pp.]

23019. — Klötzel, C. Z.: *Jugendjahre im jüdischen Waisenhaus am Papendamm.* [In]: Hamburgische Geschichts- und Heimatblätter, Bd. 11, Hamburg, 1984. Pp. 105–127. [C.Z.K., Feb. 8, 1891 Berlin – 1951 Israel, publicist.]

23020. — Oran-Pinkus, Ben Zion: *The Portuguese community of Hamburg in the 17th century.* [In Hebrew]. [In]: Mi-Mizrach u-mi-Ma'arav (East and Maghreb), Vol. 5, Ramat-Gan, 1986. Pp. 7–51.

23021. HECHINGEN. Werner, Manuel: *Die Juden in Hechingen als religiöse Gemeinde.* T. 1. [In]: Zeitschrift für Hohenzollerische Geschichte, 20, Sigmaringen, 1984. Pp. 103–213.

23022. — Werner, Otto: *Wie alt ist der Hechinger Judenfriedhof? Wo bestattete die Hechinger Judenschaft ihre Toten vor dessen Errichtung?* Hechingen: Glückler, 1984. 14 pp.

23023. HEIDELBERG. Heinemann, Günter: *Geschichte der Juden in Heidelberg bis zur Emanzipation im 19. Jahrhundert.* [In]: Ruperto Carola, 37, Heidelberg, Aug. 1985. Pp. 168–175.

23024. HEILBRONN. Angerbauer, Wolfram/Frank, Hans Georg: *Jüdische Gemeinden in Kreis und Stadt Heilbronn.* Geschichte, Schicksale, Dokumente. Heilbronn: Landkreis Heilbronn, 1986. 402 pp., illus., ports., facsims., 1 map, bibl. (384–396). (Schriftenreihe des Landkreises Heilbronn, Bd. 1.) [Incl. the Nazi period.]

—— HESSE. [See also Nos. 22930, 23631.]

23025. — Battenberg, Friedrich: *Gesetzgebung und Judenemanzipation im Ancien Régime; dargestellt am Beispiel Hessen-Darmstadt.* [In]: Zeitschrift für Historische Forschung, Bd. 13, H. 1, Berlin, 1986. Pp. 43–63, footnotes.

23026. — Peal, David: *Anti-Semitism and rural transformation in Kurhessen: the rise and fall of the Böckel movement.* Ann Arbor, Mich.: University Microfilms Internat., 1985. XII, 563, XLVIII pp., diagrs., maps, tabs., bibl. (516–563). [Photocopy of typescript.] New York, Columbia Univ., Thesis, 1985.

23027. — Sharman, Walter: *A Jewish master tailor: Jacob Schartenberg (1803–1880) from Zierenberg and the beginning of emancipation in Hesse-Kassel.* Newcastle upon Tyne, England (2 Carlton Close): W. Sharman, 1986. 22 pp., port., facsims., notes (15–16). [English version of Nor. 21954/YB XXXI.]

23028. HESSLOCH. *150 Jahre Synagoge Hessloch 1836–1986.* Hrsg.: Ortsgemeinde Dittelsheim-Hessloch, 1986. 1 booklet. [Obtainable from: Pfarrer Schaab, D-6521 Dittelsheim-Hessloch.]

23029. HIRSCHAID. Mistele, Karl H.: *Die Synagoge in Hirschaid.* [In]: Nachrichten für den jüdischen Bürger Fürths, Isr. Kultusgemeinde Fürth (Blumenstr. 31), Sept. 1986. Pp. 32–34, plans.

—— HOFGEISMAR. [See No. 23632.]

23030. HOHENLIMBURG. Böning, Adalbert: *Der jüdische Friedhof in Hohenlimburg.* Hagen: Presse- und Informationsamt, 1986. 1 vol.

23031. — *Jüdisches Erbe in Deutschland; Botschaft und Herausforderung.* Bericht der Bürgeraktion Synagoge Hohenlimburg. Hohenlimburg, 1984. 200 pp., illus., ports., facsims. [On the history of the Jews in Hohenlimburg.]

—— HORB. [See No. 23635.]

23032. JÜLICH. Bers, Günter: *Statut für die Synagogengemeinde Jülich.* Photomechanischer Nachdruck der Ausg. von 1926. Jülich: Stadtverwaltung, 1986. 59 pp.

23033. KASSEL. *Juden in Kassel, 1808–1933.* Eine Dokumentation anlässlich des 100. Geburtstages von Franz Rosenzweig. Ausstellung des Kulturamts der Stadt Kassel, 23. Nov. 1986–31. Jan. 1987. (Katalog: Ingrid Kräling, Konrad Scheurmann, Carsten Schwoon.) Kassel: Thiele & Schwarz, 1986. 288 pp., illus., ports., facsims., bibl.(284–287). [Title on cover: 'Ich bleibe also Jude': Franz Rosenzweig.] [Incl.: Der politische Antisemitismus vom ausgehenden 19. Jahrhundert bis zum Ende des Kaiserreichs unter besonderer Berücksichtigung des Nord- und Mittelhessischen Raumes (Erwin Knauss, 15–32). Streiflichter zur neueren Geschichte der Jüdischen Gemeinde Kassel (Dietfrid Krause-Vilmar, 33–42). Die religiösen und sozialen Verhältnisse in der jüdischen Gemeinde Kassels vor der Katastrophe (Max Spangenthal, 43–48). Bilder [des Malers Wilhelm Thielmann] aus der Synagoge: zur Selbstdarstellung des Kasseler Judentums im 19. Jahrhundert (Karl-

Hermann Wegner, 49–58). Rudolf Hallo und das jüdische Museum in Kassel (Ekkehard Schmidberger, 59–68). Der Weg der jüdischen Gemeinden in Hessen nach 1945 (Wolf-Arno Kropat, 69–74). Katalog (127–280). For articles on Franz Rosenzweig see No. 23538.]

23034. KAUFBEUREN. EGELHOFER, L.: *Die 'Judenhalde' in der Stadt Kaufbeuren: auch Flurnamen sind erhaltenswerte Denkmale der Heimat.* [In]: Kaufbeurer Geschichtsblätter, Bd. 10, Kaufbeuren, Heimatverein, 1984/85. Pp. 199–205.

— KOBLENZ. [See No. 23435.]

23035. KÖNIGSWINTER. REY, MANFRED van: *Leben und Sterben unserer jüdischen Mitbürger in Königswinter.* Ein Buch des Gedenkens. Königswinter: Stadtdirektor, 1985. 200 pp., illus., diagrs. (Königswinter in Geschichte und Gegenwart, H. 1.)

23036. KONSTANZ. WIEHN, ERHARD R.: *Schon im 13. Jahrhundert haben Juden in Konstanz gelebt.* [In]: Aufbau, Nr. 47–48, New York, Nov. 21, 1986. P. 27. [Incl. the Nazi period.]

23037. LAUPHEIM. BERGMANN, JOHN H./SCHÄLL, ERNST: *Der gute Ort: die Geschichte des Laupheimer jüdischen Friedhofs im Wandel der Zeit.* [In]: Ulmer Forum, Winter 1983/84. Pp. 37–47, illus., bibl. (47).

23038. LIPPSTADT. MÜHLE, EDUARD: *Jüdische Ansiedlungsversuche in Lippstadt während der ersten Hälfte des 19. Jahrhunderts (1808–1847).* [In]: Westfälische Forschungen, Bd. 34, Münster, 1984. Pp. 190–206.

23039. MACKENSEN. MITTENDORF, HANS NORBERT: *Die jüdische Gemeinde in Mackensen im 18. und 19. Jahrhundert.* [In]: Einbecker Jahrbuch 36 (1985). Pp. 93–103.

23040. MARBURG. ERDMANN, AXEL: *Der Friedhof der Marburger Juden.* [In]: Studier' mal Marburg, Nov. 1985. P. 4, 1 illus.

23041. MARKTBREIT. WENZEL, JOHANNES: *Die jüdische Gemeinde von Marktbreit im 19. Jahrhundert.* Marktbreit: Gress, 1985. 48 pp. (Beiträge zur Kultur, Geschichte und Wirtschaft der Stadt Marktbreit und ihrer Nachbarschaft, H. 12.)

23042. MEMEL. ROSS, ERHARD: *Moses Jacobson de Jonge: ein Jude aus Niederland und seine Familie in Memel (1664–1722).* [In]: Preussenland, Jg. 24, Nr. 2–3, Marburg, 1986. Pp. 33–45.

23043. MEPPEN. LEMMERMANN, HOLGER: *Geschichte der Juden im alten Amt Meppen bis zur Emanzipation (1848).* 2., erweiterte Aufl. Sögel: Emsländischer Heimatbund, 1985. V, 123 pp., illus., map. (Schriftenreihe des Emsländischen Heimatbundes, Bd. 2.)

23044. MOISLING. SCHLOMER, EISAK JACOB: *Liebes, altes, jüd'sches Moisling.* 2., durchgesehene Aufl. [Nachdr. der Ausg.] Lübeck, Werner & Hörnig, 1909. Erneut hrsg., mit Texterläuterungen, einem Nachwort, sowie einer Karte versehen von Peter Guttkuhn. Lübeck (Zweite Ochsenkoppel 18): P. Guttkuhn, 1985. 40, 24 pp., map. [Orig. title: Erinnerungen aus dem 'alten Moisling'. First edn. of this reprint see No. 21917/YB XXXI.]

23045. MONTABAUR. WILD, MARKUS: *Die Geschichte der jüdischen Gemeinde von Montabaur.* Eine Dokumentation. (Hrsg.: Rolf Homann.) 1. Aufl. Daubach bei Montabaur (Schulstr. 8): M. Wild, 1984. 124 pp., illus.

23046. MÜHLHAUSEN. BACKHAUSEN, MANFRED J.: *Jüdische Zeugnisse in Mühlhausen Thomas-Müntzer-Stadt.* [In]: Nachrichtenblatt des Verbandes der Jüd. Gemeinden in der DDR, Dresden, März 1986. Pp. 10–11, illus. (synagogue, cemetery).

23047. NAUHEIM. BRÜCHER, ERICH: *Einige Funde über Nauheimer Juden in der 2. Hälfte des 17. Jahrhunderts.* [In]: Wetterauer Geschichtsblätter, Bd. 33, Friedberg, 1984. Pp. 81–86.

23048. NEHEIM-HÜSTEN. SAURE, WERNER: *Juden in Neheim und Hüsten.* [In]: 625 Jahre Neheim und Hüsten. Arnsberg: Der Stadtdirektor, 1983. (Städtekundliche Schriftenreihe der Stadt Arnsberg.) Pp. 124–172, illus.

23049. NEUSS. ROHRBACHER, STEFAN: *Juden in Neuss.* Neuss: Verlag Galerie Küppers, 1986. 324 pp., illus., ports., facsims., maps, footnotes, list of places and persons (307–324). [Refers also to the economic situation; incl. the Nazi period, 'aryanisation' of shops, emigration, deportation, and 'Verzeichnis der nach dem 30. Jan. 1933 in Neuss wohnhaft gewesenen Juden' (260–276).]

23050. — ROHRBACHER, STEFAN: *Vergessene Namen aus vergangenen Zeiten; ein bebilderter Gang über den jüdischen Friedhof in Neuss.* [In]: Zeitgeist; die Neusser Stadtzeitung, Neuss, 1984. Pp. 17–20, illus., ports.

23051. NIENBORG. NACKE, ALOYS: *Ein Geleitbrief für Juden in Nienborg 1572.* [In]: Westfälische Forschungen, Bd. 34, Münster, 1984. Pp. 185–189. [Documentation.]

23052. ORTENAU. SCHNEIDER, HUGO: *Judengeleit und Judeneid in der Landvogtei Ortenau im 17. und 18. Jahrhundert.* [In]: Die Ortenau, Bd. 65, Offenburg, 1985. Pp. 356–359.

23053. PALATINATE. Kukatzki, Bernhard, comp.: *Dorfsynagogen in der Pfalz.* Eine Bestandsaufnahme erhaltener Synagogengebäude. 2., verbesserte und erweiterte Ausg. Schifferstadt: Die Grünen, Bezirksfraktion Pfalz; Schifferstadt (Robert-Schumann-Str. 43): B. Kukatzki, 1986. 52 pp., illus., facsims. [First edn. 1985.]

23054. POSEN. Jaworski, Rudolf: *Handel und Gewerbe im Nationalitätenkampf; Studien zur Wirtschaftsgesinnung der Polen in der Provinz Posen (1871–1914).* Göttingen: Vandenhoeck & Ruprecht, 1986. 205 pp. (Kritische Studien zur Geschichtswissenschaft, Bd. 70.) [Also on the activities of the Jewish population in trade and business. Cf.: Besprechung (Konrad Fuchs) [in]: Das Historisch-Politische Buch, Jg. 34, H. 12, Göttingen, 1986, pp. 381–382.]

23055. PRUSSIA. Braun, Johann: *Die 'Lex Gans' – ein Kapitel aus der Geschichte der Judenemanzipation in Preussen.* [In]: Zeitschrift der Savigny-Stiftung für Rechtsgeschichte, Bd. 102, Wien, 1985. Pp. 60–98, footnotes.

23056. — *Preussen: Gesetz-Sammlung für die Königlichen Preussischen Staaten.* 1806/10–1866. Reprint [der Ausg.] Berlin 1810–1866. Bad Feilnbach: Schmidt Periodicals, 1985. 42 vols. [Incl. the decrees and laws relating to Jews.]

23057. — Rohdich, Walther: *Friedrich-Faszination: 200 Tage aus seinem Leben.* Friedberg: Podzun-Pallas, 1986. 675 pp., 220 illus., bibl. (668–674). [On Friedrich II (the Great 1712–1786). Incl. chap.: Juden in Preussen.]

23058. RECKENDORF. Mistele, Karl H.: *Jüdische Sachkultur auf dem Lande: der Nachlass des Mosche Wolf aus Reckendorf.* [In]: Bericht des Historischen Vereins für die Pflege des ehemaligen Fürstbistums Bamberg, 120, Bamberg, 1984. Pp. 589–596.

23059. RECKLINGHAUSEN. Koppe, Werner: *Noch ein Nachtrag zur Geschichte der Juden im Vest Recklinghausen.* [In]: Vestische Zeitschrift, 82/83, Recklinghausen, 1983/84. Pp. 327–329.

23060. REXINGEN. Gekle, Gebhard: *Rexingen und seine jüdischen Mitbüger.* [In]: deutschland-berichte, Jg. 22, Nr. 7/8, Bonn, Juli/Aug. 1986. Pp. 13–21. [Also on the economic situation and professions of the Jewish population (15–17); incl. the Nazi period.]

23061. RHEINBISCHOFSHEIM. Honold, Nikolaus: *Der Rheinbischofsheimer Judenstein.* [In]: Die Ortenau, Bd. 65, Offenburg, 1985. Pp. 360–363.

23062. RUCHHEIM. Barth, Friedrich: *Die Geschichte der Juden in Ruchheim.* [In]: Ruchheim gestern und heute. Ludwigshafen, [1979?]. (Veröffentlichungen des Stadtarchivs Ludwigshafen, Bd 4.) [23 pp.], illus., ports. [Available in the LBI New York.]

23063. SAFFIG. Marbach, Wilfried: *Ein österreichischer Katholik rettet deutsche Synagoge [in Saffig bei Koblenz] aus der Vergessenheit.* [In]: Aufbau, Nr. 29–30, New York, July 18, 1986. Pp. 6–7, illus. [Abridged version of an article orig. publ. in: Heimat-Jahrbuch 1986 des Kreises Mayen-Koblenz. on the history of the Jews in Saffig from the 18th century to 1943, and on the restored synagogue.]

23064. SCHLESWIG-HOLSTEIN. Beer, Udo: *Juden in der Schleswig-Holsteinischen Armee.* [In]: Zeitschrift der Gesellschaft für Schleswig-Holsteinische Geschichte, Bd. 111, Neumünster, 1986. Pp. 215–219, footnotes.

23065. SCHMALLENBERG. Tröster, Helga: *Geschichte und Schicksal der Juden in Schmallenberg* [In]: Schmallenberger Heimatblätter, Ausg. 55, Jg. 1983–85, Schmallenberg; Schützengesellschaft, 1985. Pp. 51–104, illus., facsims., photo of synagogue on black cover. [Incl. the Nazi period. In same issue also: 'Jüdische Zeugen sagen aus' (pp. 105–106).]

23066. SCHWÄBISCH HALL. *Der Jüdische Friedhof in Schwäbisch Hall-Steinbach.* Eine Dokumentation . . . erstellt von Schülern der Realschule im Schulzentrum West. Schwäbisch Hall, 1985. [9] pp., [40] pp. of illus., 2 folding plans. [Available in the LBI New York.]

23067. — Wendnagel, Ilse: *Zur Geschichte der Juden in Schwäbisch Hall vom Mittelalter bis zur Gegenwart.* [Schwäbisch Hall, 1986?]. 100 pp., illus., tabs. Zulassungsarbeit zur II. Dienstprüfung für das Lehramt an Volksschulen. [Available in the LBI New York.] [Incl.: Liste über die in Schwäbisch Hall wohnhaft gewesenen Personen mosaischen (jüdischen) Glaubens (16 tabs.).]

23068. SELIGENSTADT. *Zur Geschichte der Seligenstädter Juden aus Dokumenten und Berichten.* Hrsg.: Der Magistrat der Stadt. (Bearb.: Marcellin P. Spahn.) Seligenstadt, Hessen, 1986. 199 pp., 64 illus., ports., facsims. [Incl. the Nazi period.]

23069. SILESIA. *Mitteilungen des Verbandes ehemaliger Breslauer und Schlesier in Israel.* Hrsg.: Erich Lewin. No. 51. Ramat-Gan (Mazadastr. 27), 1986. 52 pp., illus., ports., facsims. [Incl.: Die Schule Reimann in Berlin (Julius Sachs, 24 & 27). Erich Rosenblüth, Führer und Freund (Hans Chanoch Meyer, 37–38).] [See also]: Eine Zeitung besonderer Art – zum Tode von Erich Lewin (E. G. Lowenthal) [in]: 'Allgemeine', Nr. 42/10, Bonn, 6. März 1987, p. 22.

Zum Gedenken an Erich Lewin (A.F.) [in]: MB, Nr. 19, Tel-Aviv, Dez. 1986, p. 4. [E. Lewin, born in Rosenberg, Upper Silesia, died Dec. 1986 in his 85th year in Ramat-Gan, Israel, formerly cantor, from 1939 in Palestine.]

23070. — SCHWERIN, KURT: *Wie sich die Emanzipation auswirkte: die Juden Schlesiens und ihr überregionaler Einfluss.* [In]: Aufbau, Nr. 33–34, New York, Aug. 15, 1986. Pp.26–27 [&]: Leserbriefe [in]: Nr. 43–44, Oct. 24, 1986, p. 34 [& in]: Nr. 47–48, Nov. 21, 1986, p. 30. [Also on the participation in economic life.]

23071. SOEST. *Inventar des Stadtarchivs Soest.* Bestand A. Bearb. von Wilhelm Kohl. Münster: Aschendorff, 1983. XXX, 948 pp. (Inventar der nichtstaatlichen Archive Westfalens, N.F., Bd. 9.) [Incl.: Landesherrliche Verordnungen: Juden (p. 85). Judensachen (p. 293).]

23072. — KÖHN, GERHARD: *Fragen an unsere Soester Geschichte.* [In]: Mitteilungen; Verein für Geschichte und Heimatpflege Soest, 11. Okt. 1985. Pp. 5–12, facsims. [On the history of the Jews in Soest.]

23073. SOUTHERN GERMANY. MANDELBAUM, HUGO: *Jewish life in the village communities of Southern Germany.* New York: Feldheim, 1985. 94 pp., illus. [Personal recollections on Jewish life in Sommerhausen near Würzburg, Geroda in the Rhön, Braunsbach in Württemberg, and Buttenhausen.] [H. Mandelbaum, born 1901 in Sommerhausen, teacher at the Talmud-Tora-Schule in Hamburg, emigrated in 1939 to New York, professor of mathematics and geology, now living in Jerusalem.]

23074. SULZBÜRG. WAPPLER, KURT: *Die Geschichte der Sulzbürger Juden.* (2., verbesserte und erweiterte Aufl.) Sulzbürg, 1983. 36 pp., illus. (Sonderdruck Nr. 2 aus der kleinen Reihe 'Das Landlmuseum' der Arbeitsgemeinschaft Heimatmuseum Sulzbürg.)

23075. TRIER. HAVERKAMP, ALFRED: *Die Juden in der spätmittelalterlichen Stadt Trier.* [In]: Verführung zur Geschichte: Festschrift zum 500. Jahrestag der Eröffnung einer Universität in Trier. Trier, 1973. Pp. 90–103.

23076. ULM. ENGEL, ANDREA: *Juden in Ulm im 19. Jahrhundert; Anfänge und Entwicklung der jüdischen Gemeinde von 1803–1873.* Tübingen, Univ., Freie wissenschaftliche Arbeit für die Magisterprüfung, 1982. 72 pp., tabs., bibl. (65–71). [Typescript, available in the LBI New York.]

23077. WERNE. FERTIG-MÖLLER, HEIDELORE: *Juden in Werne.* Münster (Warendorfer Str. 24): Landschaftsverband Westfalen-Lippe, Landesbildstelle Westfalen, 1985. 37 pp., illus., 12 slides, bibl. (36–37). (Westfalen im Bild, H. 4.)

23078. WERRA. KOLLMANN, KARL/WIEGAND, THOMAS, eds.: *Spuren einer Minderheit; Judenfriedhöfe und Synagogen im Werra-Meissner-Kreis.* Mit Beiträgen von Herbert Reyer und Anna Maria Zimmer. Waldkappel-Wichmannshausen: Museumsverein Bischhausen-Wichmannshausen, 1986. 80 pp., illus., map, bibl. (79–80).

23079. WESTPHALIA. ASCHOFF, DIETHARD: *Ein Adelsstreit um Juden im südlichen Münsterland vor über 400 Jahren.* Mit Quellenanhang. [In]: Vestische Zeitschrift, 82/83, Recklinghausen, 1983/84. Pp. 165–176.

23080. — ASCHOFF, DIETHARD: *Juden in Westfalen.* Münster (Warendorfer Str. 24): Landschaftsverband Westfalen-Lippe, Landesbildstelle Westfalen, 1985. 45 pp., illus., facsims., map, ports., 12 slides, bibl. (44–45). [Incl. the Nazi period.]

23081. — ASCHOFF, DIETHARD: *Probst Hermann von Scheda, der erste jüdische Konvertit Westfalens.* [In]: Der Märker, Jg. 33, Altena, 1984. Pp. 204–209.

23082. — RIBBERT, UTA: *Juden in Westfalen.* [In]: Westfalenspiegel, 1–3, Dortmund, 1981. 12 pp., illus., facsims., map, bibl. (12). [Incl. the Nazi period.]

23083. WILHERMSDORF. MAHR, HELMUT: *Die Synagoge in Wilhermsdorf.* [In]: Nachrichten für den jüdischen Bürger Fürths, Isr. Kultusgemeinde Fürth (Blumenstr. 31), Sept. 1986. Pp. 30–31, illus., plans.

23084. WITTLICH. BURGARD, FRIEDHELM: *Bilder aus der deutsch-jüdischen Geschichte.* Katalog zur Ausstellung in der Kultur- und Tagungsstätte Synagoge Wittlich, vom 25. Nov.–31. Dez. 1985. Wittlich: Stadt Wittlich, 1985. 67 pp., illus., ports., facsims., maps, bibl. (66–67). [Cont. the sections: A. Die Juden in der Stadt Wittlich im Spätmittelalter bis zur Vertreibung aus dem Erzstift Trier 1418 (5–26). B. Bilder aus der deutsch-jüdischen Geschichte: Exponate aus dem Bestand des Jüd. Museums in Frankfurt am Main (27–45). C. Jüdisches Haus und Kult (47–62). D. Die Wittlicher Juden unter der nationalsozialistischen Gewaltherrschaft; eine Schülerarbeit der Klasse 9a der Staatl. Realschule Wittlich unter der Leitung von Irmgard Staab (63–65).]

23085. — FRECKMANN, KLAUS: *Die ehemalige Synagoge zu Wittlich* [In]: Jahrbuch 1978 für den Kreis Bernkastel-Wittlich. Pp. 57–62.

23086. WÖHRD. SEIDL, GÜNTER HEINZ: *Die Juden zu Wöhrd bei Nürnberg.* [In]: Mitteilungen des Vereins für Geschichte der Stadt Nürnberg, 72 (1985). Pp. 84–116.

23087. WÖRLITZ. ROSS, HARTMUT: *Aufklärung, Toleranz und Gartenkunst.* [In]: Nachrichtenblatt des Verbandes der Jüd. Gemeinden in der DDR, Dresden, Sept. 1986. Pp. 6–7. [On the synagogue in Wörlitz designed by Erdmannsdorff in 1788, one of the few synagogues not destroyed in 1938.]

23088. WORMS. SCHWERIN, KURT: *The synagogue at Worms: symbol of a thousand years.* A lecture in connection with the exhibit 'Jews in Germany under Prussian rule' at the Univ. of Illinois in Chicago, Jan. 2–31, 1985. Chicago, Bernard Horwich Jewish Community Center, 1985. 21 pp. [Typescript, available in the LBI New York.]

—— WÜRZBURG. GRIEB-LOHWASSER, BIRGITT: *Jüdische Studenten und Antisemitismus an der Universität Wüzburg in der Weimarer Republik.* [See No. 23815.]

1a. **Alsace**

—— BLUM, ANDRÉ/RAPHAËL, FREDDY: *Josouillet Rabat-Joie.* [See No. 22953.]

23089. CARON, VICKI: *Between France and Germany: Jews and national identity in Alsace-Lorraine, 1871–1918.* Ann Arbor, Mich.; Godstone, Surrey, England: University Microfilms Internat., 1985. 405 pp., New York, Columbia Univ., Phil. Diss., 1983.

23090. HERBERICH-MARX, G./RAPHAËL, FREDDY: *Transmettre autrement; recours à l'image et au rite dans la religion populaire des catholiques et des juifs en Alsace au XIXe et au XXe siècles.* [In]: Actes du 109e Congrès National des Sociétés Savantes, Dijon, 1984. Section d'histoire moderne et contemporaine, tome 1: Transmettre la foi. Paris: Ministère de l'Education Nationale, Comité des Travaux Historiques et Scientifiques, 1984. Pp. 337–359.

2. **Austria**

23091. FAERBER, MEIR: *Jakob Baschewy von Treuenburg: der erste Jude Österreichs, der geadelt wurde.* [In]: 'Allgemeine', Nr. 41/39, Bonn, 26. Sept. 1986. P. 37. [Jakob Bassevi von Treuenberg (Treuenburg), 1570 Prague – 1634 Jungbunzlau, court financier, favourite of Wallenstein.]

23092. KARNIEL, JOSEF: *David Michael Levy: ein jüdischer Agent der habsburgischen Gegenspionage zur Zeit Kaiser Josephs II.* [In]: Jahrbuch des Instituts für Deutsche Geschichte, Bd. 15, Univ. Tel-Aviv, 1986. Pp. 117–138, footnotes.

23093. KARNIEL, JOSEF: *Die Toleranzpolitik Kaiser Josephs II.* (Aus dem Hebr. von Leo Koppel.) Gerlingen: Bleicher, 1986. 616 pp., illus., footnotes, index of persons (609–616), bibl.(588–608). (Schriftenreihe des Instituts für Deutsche Geschichte, Universität Tel-Aviv, 9.) [Refers also to the Jewish population of the Habsburg Empire, incl., a.o., Bohemia and Moravia, the Bukovina, Galicia, Prague, Silesia, especially in the chaps.: *3: Die Judenpolitik zur Zeit der Mitregentschaft. Die Juden als Faktor im preussisch-österreichischen Konflikt* (243–310; incl.: Jüd. Beitrag zur Wirtschaft; Jüd. Handwerk; Ärzte). *5: Die neue Politik Joseph II. gegenüber den Juden (1780–1790). Dohms Schrift und ihre Wirkung* (378–474; incl.: Joseph von Sonnenfels' Beitrag).]

23094. LOHRMANN, KLAUS: *Zur mittelalterlichen Geschichte der Juden in Österreich.* Forschungslage und Literaturüberblick seit 1945. [In]: Mitteilungen des Instituts für Österr. Geschichtsforschung, 93, Wien, 1985. Pp. 115–134.

—— ROSENSWEIG, BERNARD: *Taxation in the late Middle Ages in Germany and Austria.* [See No. 22936.]

—— TOURY, JACOB: *Self-improvement and self-defence in Central Europe 1890–1933.* [In Hebrew]. [See No. 22942.]

23095. BUKOVINA. SCHAARY, DAVID: *The Jewish National Council in Bucovine in the transition period from Habsburg Monarchy to Rumanian rule.* [In Hebrew]. [In]: Proceedings of the 9th World Congress of Jewish Studies, Division B, Vol. 2: The history of the Jewish people. Jerusalem, 1986. Pp. 55–62.

23096. GALICIA. GOLCZEWSKI, FRANK: *Rural anti-Semitism in Galicia before World War I.* [In]: The Jews in Poland. Ed. by Chimen Abramsky [et al.]. Oxford: Blackwell, 1986. pp. 97–105.

23097. GÖRZ. COVA, UGO: *Un privilegio degli Ebrei delle contee di Gorizia et Gradisca: il godimento di diritti reali su beni immobili.* [In]: Mitteilungen des Österr. Staatsarchivs, 37, Horn, 1984. Pp. 120–148.

23098. GRAZ. BRÜHL, KURT D.: *Juden in Graz und in der Steiermark vom Mittelalter bis heute.* [In]: Das Jüdische Echo, Vol. 35, No. 1, Wien, Okt. 1986. Pp. 140–143, illus.

23099. — SEEWANN, HARALD: *Die Jüdisch-akademische Verbindung Charitas Graz, 1897–1938; ein Beitrag zur Geschichte des Zionismus auf Grazer akademischem Boden.* Mit einem personenkundlichen Teil von Theo Weichmann. Graz (Leonhardstr. 27): Steirischer Studentenhistoriker-Verein, 1986. 106 pp., facsims., notes & bibl. (39–70). (Schriftenreihe des Steirischen Studentenhistoriker-Vereines, Folge 12.) [Incl.: Mitgliederliste der 'Humanitas' (75–77), der 'Charitas' (86–93).]

23100. LINZ. MARCKHGOTT, GERHART: *Fremde Mitbürger: die Anfänge der israelitischen Kultusgemeinde Linz-Urfahr 1849–1877.* [In]: Historisches Jahrbuch der Stadt Linz, 1984. Pp 285–309.

23101. TIROL. *Die Geschichte der Juden in Tirol von den Anfängen im Mittelalter bis in die neueste Zeit.* Schriftleiter dieser Nummer: Günther Pallaver. [In]: Sturzflüge, Jg. 5, Nr. 15/16, Bozen, Mai-Aug. 1986. Pp. 1–164, illus. [Cont. 19 contributions covering especially antisemitism through the ages, incl.: 'Wir werden den Juden schon eintunken!' Geschichte der Juden in Innsbruck, Vorarlberg und Tirol (Maria-Luise Stainer, 17–32). Zwischen Duldung und Verfolgung: zur Geschichte der Juden in Vorarlberg (Harald Walser, 33–40). Studentischer Antisemitismus an der Univ. Innsbruck (Michael Gehler, 73–88). 'Ich bin mit Judenstein aufgewachsen!' Die Geschichte vom 'Anderl von Rinn' (Nadine Hauer, 109–126). Simonino da Trento: ein Ritualmordprozess und seine Folgen, 1475–1975 (Günther Pallaver, 127–136). Niemals vergessen! Die Jüdische Kultusgemeinde in Meran (Federico Steinhaus, 161–162). Die Jüdische Kultusgemeinde in Innsbruck (163–164).]

23102. VIENNA. ALEXANDER, GABRIEL: *Dr. Karl Lueger, the Christian Social Party, and the Jews of Vienna at the end of the Habsburg Empire.* [In Hebrew, title transl.]. Jerusalem, Hebrew Univ., Dept. of History, M.A. Thesis, Sept. 1984. [7], 126 pp. [Covers the period 1897–1910.]

23103. — BELLER, STEVEN: *Fin de siècle Vienna and the Jews: the dialectics of assimilation.* [In]: The Jewish Quarterly, Vol. 33, No. 3, London, 1986. Pp. 28–33, notes.

23104. — KOLLER-GLÜCK, ELISABETH: *Das Wunder von der Seegasse: von einem uralten Vertrag, vergrabenen Grabsteinen und einem sprechenden Fisch.* [In]: Das Jüdische Echo, Vol. 35, Nr. 1, Wien, Okt. 1986. Pp. 185–188, illus. [On the oldest Jewish cemetery in Vienna, restored in 1984.]

23105. — PALMON, ABRAHAM: *The community of Vienna and the Austrian Republic (1918–1938).* [In Hebrew, with English summary]. [In]: Jewish History, Vol. 1, No. 1, Haifa, Spring, 1986. Pp. 9–32. [On the struggle regarding government support in financing the communities.]

23106. — PULZER, PETER: *Liberalismus, Antisemitismus und Juden im Wien der Jahrhundertwende.* [In]: Wien um 1900; Aufbruch in die Moderne. Hrsg. von Peter Berner [et al.]. Wien: Verlag für Geschichte und Politik, 1986. Pp. 32–38, footnotes.

3. **Czechoslovakia**

23107. BÜCHLER, ROBERT J.: *Kurze Übersicht der jüdischen Geschichte in dem Gebiet der Slowakei.* (München: J. Herp, 1982.) 47 pp. (Schriftenreihe des Slowakischen Matúš-Černák-Instituts, Nr. 7.)

23108. IGGERS, WILMA, ed.: *Die Juden in Böhmen und Mähren.* Ein historisches Lesebuch. München: Beck, 1986. 391 pp. [Collection of historical, literary and autobiogr. texts covering Jewish life from 1744 to 1952.]

—— KESTENBERG-GLADSTEIN, RUTH: *The Jewish 'Vormärz' in Germany and Bohemia.* [In Hebrew]. [See No. 22919.]

23109. WLASCHEK, RUDOLF M.: *Die tödliche Gefahr nicht erkannt: zur Geschichte der Juden in Nordostböhmen.* [In]: Tribüne, Jg. 25, H. 99, Frankfurt am Main, 1986. Pp. 146–150. [Preview of a forthcoming book, ed. by Hans Lemberg.]

23110. PRAGUE. BARREY, KNUT: *Die Jüdische Gemeinde in Prag.* [In]: Frankfurter Allgemeine Zeitung, Nr. 215, 17. Sept. 1986. Pp. 9–10.

23111. — COHEN, GARY B.: *Jews in German liberal politics – Prague, 1880–1914.* [In]: Jewish History, Vol. 1, No. 1, Haifa, Spring 1986. Pp. 55–74.

—— — PETR, PAVEL: *Ghetto oder Integration? Zu den Identitätsproblemen der Prager jüdischen Schriftsteller.* [See pp. 176–181 in No. 23576; see also essay by Bak and Brolsma-Stancu in same No., pp. 182–186; 187–195.]

23112. — Rohan, Bedrich: *Kafka wohnte um die Ecke; ein neuer Blick aufs alte Prag*. Orig.-Ausg. Freiburg i.Br.: Herder, 1986. 123 pp. (Herderbücherei, 1337.) [Memoirs by the journalist B.R., who emigrated in 1938 to England; cover the Czech as well as German and Jewish components of Prague; on the 'Prager Tagblatt' circle, theatre, and German and Austrian emigrants after 1933.]

4. **Hungary**

23113. Gates, Rebecca: *Eighteenth-century Schutzherren: Esterházy patronage of the Jews*. [In]: Jewish Social Studies, Vol. 47, No. 3–4, New York, Summer–Fall 1985. Pp. 189–208.

23114. Schreiber, Hermann: *Im Getto gekaufter Protektion: die Judengemeinden im Burgenland*. [In]: Damals, Jg. 17, Giessen, 1985. Pp. 981–985.

23115. Silber, Michael K.: *Roots of the schism in Hungarian Jewry; cultural and social change from the reign of Joseph II until the eve of the 1848 revolution*. [In Hebrew, with English summary]. Jerusalem, Hebrew Univ., Diss., Feb. 1985. [10], 338, X pp.

23116. Yaron, Baruch: *Jewish assimilation and radicalism in Hungary*. [In Hebrew]. Jerusalem: Magnes Press, Hebrew Univ., 1985. 146 pp. [At the beginning of the 20th century.]

5. **Switzerland**

—— Guggenheim, Benny: *Die jüdische Sportbewegung in der Schweiz*. [See No. 23611.]

23117. Hausmann, Erich: *'. . . da also diese Religionsgebräuche mit allen Gesetzen des Staats sich vereinbaren können . . .': ein rabbinisches Gutachten aus der Zeit der Helvetik*. [In]: Isr. Wochenblatt, Nr. 39, Zürich, 26. Sept. 1986. Pp. 67–69 & 71, notes, port. (David Sintzheim), facsims.

23118. *Judaica. Jg. 42, H. 1* [with the issue title]: *Juden in der Schweiz – Geschichte und Gegenwart*. Basel: Stiftung für Kirche und Judentum, März 1986. 1 issue. [Cont.: Zur Geschichte des spätmittelalterlichen Judentums: die Juden im Gebiet der heutigen Schweiz und der europäische Kontext (Beat Meier, 2–6, notes, bibl.; incl.: Die wirtschaftliche Funktion der Juden, pp. 7–10; publ. also in: Isr. Wochenblatt, Nr. 9, Zürich, 28. Feb. 1986, pp. 20–26). Eine zu publizierende geschichtliche Quelle aus dem 18. Jahrhundert (Uri Robert Kaufmann, 17–21, facsim., notes). Die Ambivalenz des Schweizer Liberalismus gegenüber den Juden: Augustin Keller, 1862 (Uri Robert Kaufmann, 22–27, notes). Schweizerischer Protestantismus und jüdische Flüchtlingsnot nach 1933: Tradition und Neuaufbrüche (Hermann Kocher, 28–40, notes). Das Wohnverhalten der Basler Juden seit 1910 (Schimon Stern, 41–47, tabs., map). Wie lange noch Juden in der Schweiz (Ralph Weill, 49–57, diagrs.).]

23119. BASEL. Jenny, Kurt: *Basel und seine Israelitische Gemeinde in neuerer und neuester Zeit*. [In]: Schweizerisches Reformiertes Volksblatt, Jg. 120, Nr. 6, Basel, 25. Juni 1986. Pp. 9–12.

23120. WINTERTHUR. Herzka, Marc D.: *100 Jahre Israelitische Gemeinde Winterthur*. [In]: Isr. Wochenblatt, Nr. 18, Zürich, 2. Mai 1986. Pp. 35–45, illus., ports., facsims.

23121. ZÜRICH. Israelitische Cultusgemeinde, ed.: *Festschrift 100 Jahre Synagoge Löwenstrasse, 1884–1984*. Red.: Roger Cahn. Zürich: M & T Verlag, 1984. 28 pp., illus., ports., facsim.

C. **German Jews in Various Countries**

23122. Aronsfeld, C. C.: *Deutsche Juden in Irland*. [In]: 'Allgemeine', Nr. 41/9, Bonn, 28. Feb. 1986. P. 19. [On German immigration of the 19th century.]

23123. Berrol, Selma C.: *Julia Richman and the German Jewish establishment: passion, arrogance, and the Americanization of the 'Ostjuden'*. [In]: American Jewish Archives, Vol. 38, No. 2, Cincinnati, Nov. 1986. [Julia Richman, 1855–1912, American educator of German-Jewish background, played a prominent part in the Americanisation of East European Jews.]

23124. Böhm, Günter: *Judios en el Peru durante el siglo XIX*. Santiago: Universidad de Chile, 1985. 184 pp., illus., ports., facsims. tabs. [Incl. short biographies of Jews in Peru in the 19th century (115–173), many of them originating from Germany.]

23125. DAMROSCH Family. Martin, George: *The Damrosch dynasty; America's first family of music*. Boston: Houghton Mifflin, 1983. XIII, 526 pp., illus., ports. [Leopold Damrosch, 1832

Posen – 1885 New York, composer and conductor, emigrated to New York in 1871; his sons, Frank and Walter, both born in Breslau, were also leading figures in America's concert world.]

23126. EDGAR, IRVING I.: *Early sites and beginnings of congregation Beth El, Detroit, Michigan.* [In]: Michigan Jewish History, Vol. 26, No. 1, Bloomfield Hills, Mich., 1986. Pp. 13–21, ports., illus., notes (20–21). [Several rabbis from Germany served the Detroit congregation.]

23127. EHRLICH, EVELYN: *A history of the Hebrew Tabernacle Congregation of Washington Heights; a German-Jewish community in New York City.* With an introduction by Robert L. Lehman. New York, 1985. 59 pp., notes (55–59).

23128. EXILE. BANKIER, DAVID: *El movimiento Alemania Libre y la comunidad Judía de México.* [In]: Proceedings of the 9th World Congress of Jewish Studies, Division B, Vol. 3: The history of the Jewish people. Jerusalem, 1986. Pp. 329–336.

23129. — BAUM, PETER: *Hitlers wertvoller 'Export': deutsch-jüdische Emigranten in Grossbritannien.* [In]: 'Allgemeine', Nr. 41/20, Bonn, 16. Mai 1986. Pp. 19–20.

23130. — BETZ, ALBRECHT: *Exil und Engagement; deutsche Schriftsteller im Frankreich der dreissiger Jahre.* München: Edition Text u. Kritik, 1986. 338 pp., bibl. (205–280). [Incl. bibliography of books and articles publ. by German-speaking authors in France up to 1940.]

23131. — BOHM-DUCHEN, MONICA: *Fleeing Hitler: German émigré artists in England.* [In]: The Jewish Quarterly, Vol. 33, No. 3, London, 1986. Pp. 26–27, illus. [See also No. 23138.]

23132. — ENGELMANN, BERNT: *Die unfreiwilligen Reisen des Putti Eichelbaum.* München: Bertelsmann, 1986. 350 pp., illus. [Experiences in exile in several European countries and in the USA.] [Putti E., now Richard Essex, born 1921 in Berlin, son of a lawyer, now living in Munich.]

23133. — GROTH, MICHAEL: *Die bitteren Exiljahre deutscher Journalisten: Tschechoslowakei, Frankreich, Amerika.* [In]: Aufbau, Nr. 23–24, New York, June 6, 1986. Pp. 8–9, ports.

23134. — GRUNENBERG, ANTONIA: *'Ich wollte Montezumas Federhut nach Mexiko bringen'.* Ein Gespräch mit Bruno Frei über das kommunistische Westexil und die Nachkriegszeit in Österreich. [In]: Exilforschung, Bd. 4, München, 1986. Pp. 243–253. [B. Frei, data see No. 17176/YB XXVI.]

—— — HAFTMANN, WERNER: *Verfemte Kunst.* [See No. 23285.]

23135. — HARTWIG, THOMAS/ ROSCHER, HANS-JOACHIM, eds.: *Die verheissene Stadt: deutsch-jüdische Emigranten in New York.* Gespräche, Eindrücke und Bilder. Berlin: Das Arsenal, 1986. 175 pp., illus. [Incl.: Leo Baeck Institut: Gespräch mit Fred Grubel (pp. 109–119); also further interviews with, a.o., Ilse Blumenthal-Weiss, William G. Niederland, Hans Steinitz.]

23136. — HIPPEN, REINHARD, ed.: *Satire gegen Hitler; Kabarett im Exil.* Zürich: pendo-Verl., 1986. 178 pp., illus., ports., facsims., scores. (Kabarettgeschichte-n, 14.) [Incl. the German and Austrian Jewish cabaret artists in exile all over the world.]

23137. — KAUFFMANN, FRITZ: *Die Juden in Shanghai im 2. Weltkrieg: Erinnerungen eines Vorstandsmitglieds der Jüdischen Gemeinde.* [In]: Bulletin des LBI, 73, Frankfurt am Main, 1986. Pp. 13–23. [Incl. the attitude of the Japanese towards the Jewish refugees.]

23138. — *Kunst im Exil in Grossbritannien, 1933–1945.* (Eine Ausstellung der Neuen Gesellschaft für Bildende Kunst in den Räumen der Orangerie des Schlosses Charlottenburg vom 10. Jan.–23. Feb. 1986. Red.: Hartmut Krug, Michael Nungesser.) Berlin: Frölich & Kaufmann, 1986. 295 pp., illus., bibl. [Exhibition was also shown in London, Camden Arts Centre, until Oct. 5, 1986, under the title: *Art in exile in Britain 1933–1945*, organised by Zuleika Dobson [et al.], and with an illus. catalogue, introd. by Monica Bohm-Duchen.]

23139. — LUBLINER, MANFRED: *Nach der Rettung einen Altar errichtet: jüdische Emigration nach Südamerika am Beispiel Chile.* [In]: 'Allgemeine', Nr. 41/20, Bonn, 16. Mai 1986. P. 18.

23140. — MOCK, WOLFGANG: *Technische Intelligenz im Exil: Vertreibung und Emigration deutschsprachiger Ingenieure nach Grossbritannien 1933–1945.* Düsseldorf: VDI-Verl., 1986. 207 pp., bibl. (181–187).

23141. — OREN, DAN A.: *Joining the club: a history of Jews and Yale.* New Haven, Ct.; London: Yale Univ. Press, 1986. 448 pp. (The Yale scene university series, No. 4.) [Deals also with students of German-Jewish origin and refugee scholars from Nazism. Cf.: Cowardice versus democracy (A. J. Sherman) [in]: TLS, London, Aug. 8, 1986.]

23142. — *One-way ticket to Hollywood.* Exhibition at the Max Kade Institute for Austrian-German-Swiss Studies at the Univ. of Southern California. (Exhibition and catalogue by

Doris Angst.) Los Angeles, Calif., 1986. 100 pp., illus., ports., facsims., filmography. [On émigrés in the film industry. Catalogue incl. introductory essay and short biographies.]

23143. — Pearle, Kathleen M.: *Ärzteemigration nach 1933 in die USA: der Fall New York.* [In]: Medizinhistorisches Journal, Jg. 19, No. 1–2, Stuttgart, 1984. Pp. 112–137.

23144. — Pohle, Fritz: *Das mexikanische Exil; ein Beitrag zur Geschichte der politisch-kulturellen Emigration aus Deutschland (1937–1946).* Stuttgart: Metzler, 1986. XIII, 495 pp., illus. (Germanistische Abhandlungen, 60.) [See also the author's essay in No. 23664.]

23145. — Pütter, Conrad: *Rundfunk gegen das 'Dritte Reich': deutschsprachige Rundfunkaktivitäten im Exil 1933–1945.* Ein Handbuch. Unter Mitwirkung von Ernst Loewy und mit einem Beitrag von Elke Hilscher. Erarbeitet im Auftrag des Deutschen Rundfunkarchivs. München; New York: Saur, 1986. 388 pp., bibl. (353–372). (Rundfunkstudien, Bd. 3.) [Incl. German-Jewish refugees.]

23146. — Rutkoff, Peter M./Scott, Wiliam B.: *New School; a history of the New School for Social Research.* New York: The Free Press, 1986. XIV, 314 pp., illus., ports., notes (255–300). [Cf.: Ein Buch über die New School mit leider zu vielen Fehlern (Henry Marx) [in]: Aufbau, Nr. 23–24, New York, June 6, 1986, p. 10.] [A 'Postgraduate Faculty of Political and Social Science' which later became known as 'University in Exile' was founded in 1933 by the New School's president Alvin Johnson and Emil Lederer (1882 Pilsen–1939 New York); it provided teaching opportunities for many German- and Austrian-Jewish refugee academics.]

23147. — Schaper, Ralf: *Mathematiker im Exil; zur Rolle der Emigranten in der angewandten Mathematik.* Kassel: Gesamthochschule Kassel, 1983. 34 pp., bibl. (Mathematische Schriften Kassel; Preprint 1983, Nr. 7.)

23148. — Söllner, Alfons, ed.: *Zur Archäologie der Demokratie in Deutschland. Bd. 1: Analysen von politischen Emigranten im amerikanischen Geheimdienst 1943–1945. Bd. 2: Analysen von politischen Emigranten im amerikanischen Aussenministerium 1946–1949.* [Bd. 2]: Originalausg. Aus dem Amerikan. übers. von Sabine Gwinner [et al.]. Frankfurt am Main: Fischer, 1986. 312; 310 pp. (Fischer-Taschenbücher, Bd. 4360–4361.) [Vol. 1 is the paperback edn. of No. 19295/YB XXVIII and refers especially to Otto Kirchheimer, Herbert Marcuse, Franz Neumann. Vol. 2 contains documents by these and various other emigrants, publ. now for the first time.]

23149. —Strauss, Herbert A., ed.: *Jewish immigrants of the Nazi period in the USA.* Sponsored by the Research Foundation for Jewish Immigration, New York. New York [et al.]: Saur, 1979 ff. *Vol. 5: The individual and collective experience of German-Jewish immigrants 1933–1984; an oral history record.* Comp. by Dennis Rohrbaugh. 1986. 308 pp. [This work will comprise 6 vols.; for previously publ. vols. 1–3, pts. 1–2 see No. 18959/YB XXVIII.]

23150. — Strauss, Herbert A.: *Our people in the USA: American Federation of Jews from Central Europe.* [In]: AJR Information, No. 7, London, July 1986. P. 4.

23151. — Toliver, Suzanne Shipley: *The outsider as outsider? German intellectual exiles in America after 1930.* [In]: American Jewish Archives, Vol. 38, No. 1, Cincinnati, Apr. 1986. Pp. 85–91. [Review essay.]

23152. — Trommler, Frank/McVeigh, Joseph, eds.: *America and the Germans; an assessment of a three-hundred-year history.* Philadelphia: Univ. of Pennsylvania Press, 1985. 2 vols. (XXXII, 376; XVIII, 369 pp.), illus., ports., facsims., tabs., notes. [Revised versions of papers presented at a conference in Philadelphia 1983. Incl.: Transplanted and transformed: German-Jewish immigrants since 1933 (Herbert A. Strauss, Vol. 2, pp. 245–264). For German edn. and further contents see following entry.]

23153. — Trommler, Frank, ed.: *Amerika und die Deutschen; Bestandsaufnahme einer 300jährigen Geschichte.* Opladen: Westdeutscher Verl., 1986. IX, 698 pp., illus., ports., facsims., tabs., index of names, notes. [Incl. the sections: *X. Einwanderung nach 1933* (with the papers): Kontinuität im Wandel: der deutsch-jüdische Einwanderer seit 1933 (Herbert A. Strauss, 583–602). Kassandras mit deutschem Akzent (Anthony Heilbut, 603–610). Weder Staat noch Synagoge: der linke deutsch-jüdische emigrierte Intellektuelle als repräsentativer Jude (Paul Breines, 611–616). Die Kritische Theorie in den USA: Gedanken über vier Jahrzehnte ihrer Rezeption (Andrew Arato, 617–624). Die literarische und akademische Abwanderung aus dem Dritten Reich in die USA: ein Forschungsbericht (John M. Spalek, 625–638). *XI. Exkurs in die Psychoanalyse* (with the paper): Freuds Amerika (Peter Gay, 639–650).]

23154. — *Vor fünfzig Jahren: Emigration und Immigration von Wissenschaft* (21. Symposium der Gesellschaft für Wissenschaftsgeschichte, 12.–14. Mai 1983 in Wolfenbüttel.) [In]: Berichte zur Wissenschaftsgeschichte, Bd. 7, H. 3, Weinheim, Sept. 1984. Pp. 129–194, notes, bibl., summaries in English. [Cont.: The effect of the scientific environment in Britain on refugee scientists from Germany and their effects on science in Britain (Gustav V. R. Born, 129–143; see also No. 21993/YB XXXI). Technische Intelligenz im Exil: zum Einfluss emigrierter deutschsprachiger Ingenieure auf die Ingenieurwissenschaften in Grossbritannien 1933 bis 1945 (Wolfgang Mock, 145–159). Amtsenthebung und Emigration Klassischer Philologen (Walther Ludwig, 161–178). Die Emigration der Kulturwissenschaftlichen Bibliothek Warburg und die Anfänge des Universitätsfaches Kunstgeschichte in Grossbritannien (Dieter Wuttke, 179–194).]

23155. — *We were so beloved.* A 150–minute film. Director: Manfred Kirchheimer. [Interviews with about a dozen German-Jewish refugees who have settled in Washington Heights, New York: on their experiences in Nazi Germany and in exile, and what they think about present-day problems in their neighbourhood. Cf.: Porträt einer Generation (Henry Marx) [in]: Aufbau, Nr. 35–36, New York, Aug. 29, 1986, p. 15.] [M. Kirchheimer, born in Bremerhaven, went as a five-year-old to the USA.]

23156. — *Widerstand und Exil 1933–1945.* Frankfurt am Main; New York: Campus, 1986. 302 pp. [Appeared also]: Bonn, 1985: Schriftenreihe der Bundeszentrale für Politische Bildung, Bd. 223. [Incl.: Wissenschaftler im Exil: ein Versuch nach fünfzig Jahren (Richard Albrecht, 223–228). For further contents see explanatory note to No. 23417.]

23157. GUTTMANN, LUDWIG. Goodman, Susan: *Spirit of Stoke Mandeville: the story of Sir Ludwig Guttmann.* With a foreword by HRH the Prince of Wales. London: Collins, 1986. 191 pp., illus., ports. [Sir L.G., July 3, 1899 Tost – March 18, 1980 Aylesbury, Bucks., neurosurgeon, emigrated from Hamburg to England in 1939, founder director of the National Spinal Injuries Centre at Stoke Mandeville Hospital, founder of Stoke Mandeville Games, the 'Olympics of the Paralysed', knighted in 1966.]

23158. HAMLYN, PAUL. Till, Ernest Redmond: *Ein Komet namens 'Octopus'; das enfant terrible Paul Hamlyn gebietet jetzt auch über die Heinemann-Gruppe.* [In]: Börsenblatt für den Deutschen Buchhandel, Jg. 41, H. 75, Frankfurt am Main, 20. Sept. 1986. Pp. 2389–2391, port. [P.H., orig. Hamburger, brother of the poet and writer Michael Hamburger, born Feb. 12, 1926 in Berlin, emigrated with his family in 1933 to England, from 1949 active in publishing.]

—— Kahn, Lothar: *Early German-Jewish writers and the image of America.* [See No. 22916.]

23159. KELLER, HANS. Kenyon, Nicholas/Donat, Misha: *Hans Keller 1919–1985.* [In]: The Listener, Nov. 14, 1985. [Further obituary [in]: The Times, Dec. 7, 1985. See also: A personal memoir of Hans Keller (C. F. Flesch) [in]: AJR Information, No. 1, London, Jan. 1986, p. 4. The case for turning off the sound (Paul Driver) [in]: The Sunday Times, London, Feb. 23, 1986, p. 41.] [H.K., March 11, 1919 Vienna – Nov. 6, 1985 London, emigrated to England in 1938, musicologist, from 1959 BBC Music Division.]

23160. Kissinger, Henry A.: *Weltpolitik für morgen; Reden und Aufsätze 1982–1985.* (Aus dem Amerikan.) München: Bertelsmann, 1986. 319 pp. [Transl. of No. 22022/YB XXXI.]

23161. LEVY, OSCAR. Aronsfeld, C. C.: *Ein Jünger des Übermenschen: Nietzsches deutsch-jüdischer Apostel in England.* [In]: 'Allgemeine', Nr. 41/39, Bonn, 26. Sept. 1986. P. 40. [On Oscar Levy, born in Stargard, physician, settled in England in 1892 at the age of 25, translated Nietzsche's works in 18 vols., died 1946 in Oxford.]

23162. Petrie, Graham: *Hollywood destinies; European directors in America, 1922–1931.* London: Routledge & Kegan Paul, 1985. 257 pp., 58 illus. [Incl. Ernst Lubitsch and other German-Jewish film directors. Cf.: Continental legacies (S. S. Prawer) [in]: TLS, Feb. 21, 1986, p. 200.]

23163. Raphael, Chaim: *The Manchester connection.* [In]: Commentary, Vol. 82, No. 3, New York, Sept. 1986. Pp. 48–53. [On the Manchester Jewish community and its German-Jewish immigrants of the 19th century, some of whom rose to prominence in the cotton industry and merchant banking, a.o., the Bauers, Franklins, Sichels.]

23164. Sarna, Jonathan D., ed.: *The American Jewish experience.* New York: Holmes & Meier, 1986. 303 pp., bibl. references. [Collection of articles and book excerpts covering also the influence of German-Jewish immigration.]

23165. Tennenbaum, Shelley: *Immigrants and capital: Jewish loan societies in the United States, 1880–1945.* [In]: American Jewish History, Vol. 76, No. 1, Waltham, Mass., Sept. 1986. Pp.67–77, notes. [Refers to many German Jews, a.o., Edward Filine, Boston department-store owner.]

23166. WEIDENFELD, GEORGE. Arnim, Gabriele von: *George Weidenfeld.* Fotos: Hermann

Dornhege. [In]: Frankfurter Allgemeine Magazin, H. 304, Frankfurt am Main, 27. Dez. 1985. Pp. 8–14, illus. [Lord G.W., publisher, data see No. 18032/YB XXVII.]

23167. WEISSER, MICHAEL R.: *A brotherhood of memory: Jewish Landsmanshaften in the New World.* New York: Harper & Row, 1985. 303 pp., appendix. [Refers, a.o., to relief organised by Jews of German origin and also their effort to Americanise the new East-European immigrants. Cf.: Beyond the pale (Alan Brinkley) [in]: TLS, London, Aug. 8, 1986, p. 855.]

23168. WOLFF, ILSE R.: *Porträt: Ilse Wolff.* Interviews. Sendung des Deutschsprachigen Dienstes der BBC, Sonntag, 31. Aug. 1986, 20.10 Uhr, 33 Minuten. London (P.O.B. 76): Deutschsprachiger Dienst der BBC, 1986. [See also: Ilse Wolff's achievement: a literary contribution to Anglo-German friendship [in]: AJR Information, No. 7, London, July 1986, p. 4.] [I.R.W., librarian, publisher, data see No. 22031/YB XXXI.]

II. RESEARCH AND BIBLIOGRAPHY

A. Libraries and Institutes

23169. ARCHIV BIBLIOGRAPHIA JUDAICA, Frankfurt am Main. *Jahrbuch 1, 1985: Probleme deutsch-jüdischer Identität.* Hrsg. von Norbert Altenhofer und Renate Heuer. Bad Soden/Ts.: Woywod, 1986. 212 pp., notes, bibl. [Contributions are listed according to subject.]

23170. DEUTSCHES LITERATURARCHIV, Marbach am Neckar. *Jahrbuch der Deutschen Schillergesellschaft.* Jg. 30. Im Auftrag des Vorstands hrsg. von Fritz Martini [et al.]. Stuttgart: Kröner, 1986. VII, 717 pp., footnotes. [Incl.: Essays on Kafka's 'Der Verschollene' (Manfred Engel,533–570), and on Kafka's 'Das Schloss' (Ulrich Hohoff, 571–593). See also No. 23838.]

23171. DUISBURG, UNIVERSITÄT – GESAMTHOCHSCHULE, ed.: *Forschungsschwerpunkt 'Geschichte und Religion des Judentums'; Forschungsbericht 1982–1986.* (Red.: Birgit Ahlborn, Julius H. Schoeps.) Duisburg (Lotharstr. 65): Universität – Gesamthochschule, 1986. 62 pp.

23172. GERMANIA JUDAICA, Kölner Bibliothek zur Geschichte des deutschen Judentums, ed.: *Arbeitsinformationen über Studienprojekte auf dem Gebiet der Geschichte des deutschen Judentums und des Antisemitismus.* Ausgabe 13. (Bearb.: Monika Richarz, Christa Aretz.) Köln (Josef-Haubrich-Hof 1), 1986. 121 pp. [See also: Germania Judaica: Cologne's Institute of German-Jewish history (Monika Richarz) [in]: AJR Information, No. 9, London, Sept. 1986, p. 2.]

23173. — MÜLLER-JERINA, ALWIN: *Germania Judaica – Kölner Bibliothek zur Geschichte des deutschen Judentums; die Entwicklung und Bedeutung einer wissenschaftlichen Spezialbibliothek.* Köln: Greven, 1986. IV, 153 pp., bibl. (141–151). (Kölner Arbeiten zum Bibliotheks- und Dokumentationswesen, H. 8.) [Incl.: Ausländische Bibliotheken zur deutsch-jüdischen Geschichte: Wiener Libary (117–12); Yad Vashem (121–125); Leo Baeck Institute (126–133).]

23174. INSTITUT FÜR DEUTSCHE GESCHICHTE. *Jahrbuch des Instituts für Deutsche Geschichte, Universität Tel-Aviv.* Bd. 15, 1986. Hrsg. und eingeleitet von Walter Grab. Tel-Aviv: Nateev-Printing, 1986. 697, XIV (summaries in Hebrew) pp., footnotes. [Incl.: Register des Jahrbuchs von Bd. 11, 1982 bis Bd. 15, 1986 (pp. 661–689; sequel to the index for 1–10 in Jahrbuch 10, 1981). Contributions relevant to German Jewry are listed according to subject.] [For Jahrbuch, Beiheft 9, see No. 22915; Beiheft 10, see No. 22914.]

23175. JÜDISCHES LEHRHAUS, Frankfurt am Main. ARBEITSKREIS JÜDISCHES LEHRHAUS (Frankfurt am Main): *Diskussionsbeiträge aus dem Jüdischen Lehrhaus in Frankfurt am Main.* Eine Sammelschrift. (Hrsg. von Brigitte A. A. Kern.) Frankfurt am Main: Lehrhaus-Verl., 1986. 137 pp., illus., notes.

23176. LEO BAECK COLLEGE, London. NAVÈ LEVINSON, PNINA: *Gegründet von deutschen Juden: 30 Jahre Leo Baeck College.* [In]: 'Allgemeine', Nr. 41/44, Bonn, 31. Okt. 1986. P. 7.

23177. LEO BAECK INSTITUTE. *Bulletin des Leo Baeck Instituts.* Nr. 73–75. Hrsg. von Joseph Walk, Daniel Cil Brecher und Eve Strauss. Frankfurt am Main: Jüdischer Verlag bei Athenäum, 1986. 72; 78; 99 pp., notes. [3 issues]. [*Nr. 73* incl.: Namensregister 1985: Bulletin Nr. 70–72 (pp. 69–72). Individual contributions are listed according to subject.]

23178. — *Leo Baeck Institute Year Book XXXI.* From the Wilhelminian era to the Third Reich III. Ed.: Arnold Paucker. London: Secker & Warburg, 1986. X, 594 pp., illus., ports., facsims., footnotes, bibl. (465–572). [Cont.: Preface (Arnold Paucker, VII–X). Individual contributions are listed according to subject. For vols. I & II of 'From the Wilhelminian era to the Third Reich' see LBI Year Books XXV & XXVII.] [Cf.: Before emigration and after: bridge between the generations (Richard Grunberger) [in]: AJR Information, No. 3, London, March 1987, p. 2. Das neue Jahrbuch des LBI (Henry Marx) [in]: Aufbau, Nr. 49–50, New York, Dec. 5, 1986, p. 22. Revue (Paul Giniewski) [in]: Dialogues, No. 61, Paris, Déc. 1986. Les annales de l'Institut Léo Baeck, 1986 (Paul Giniewski) [in]: Jüdische Rundschau, Nr. 50, Basel, 11. Dez. 1986, p. 10.]

23179. — — *Selected reviews.* LBI Year Book XXIX [in]: Shofar, West Lafayette, Ind., Purdue Univ., Spring 1986, pp. 39–41. Year Book XXX (James Wilson) [in]: The Army Quarterly and Defence Journal, Tavistock, U.K., 1986, pp. 251–252. (Rolf Vogel) [in]: deutschland-berichte, Jg. 22, H. 10, Bonn, Okt. 1986, pp. 37–38. German-Jewish complexities (Vernon Bogdanor) [in]: Jewish Chronicle, London, Aug. 8, 1986, p. 21. Judentum in der Geschichte (Robert Jütte) [in]: Tribüne, Jg. 25, H. 97, Frankfurt am Main, 1986, pp. 193–194.

23180. — LBI New York. *Library and Archives News.* Ed.: Gabrielle Bamberger. Nos. 23–24. New York: Leo Baeck Institute, Winter & Summer 1986. 8; 8 pp. (2 issues.]

23181. — — *LBI News.* Ed.: Gabrielle Bamberger. Nos. 51–52. New York: Leo Baeck Institute, Winter & Summer 1986. 16; 16 pp., front illus., illus., ports., facsims. [2 issues.] [*No. 51* incl.: Self-assertion in adversity: the Jews in National Socialist Germany, 1933–1939: report on the LBI Internat. Historical Conference, Berlin, Oct. 28–31, 1985 (2–7). Vignettes from the past: a sampling from the LBI archives spanning five centuries of Jewish history in Germany (8–11). Reports on LBI New York events. Obituaries: Gustav Jacoby, 1904–1985 (attorney, member of the LBI New York board of directors). Axel Springer, 1912–1985. *No. 52*: The world of the theater (2–5). The Jews of Alsace and Lorraine: an exhibit at the LBI New York (6–7). Reports on LBI New York events.]

—— — *Das Deutsche Judentum und der Liberalismus.* Internationales Seminar des Leo Baeck Instituts London und der Friedrich-Naumann-Stiftung. [See No. 22905.]

23182. — Grubel, Fred: *'Jettchen Geberts Kinder': Geschichte und Geschichten der Kunstsammlung des New Yorker Leo Baeck Instituts.* [In]: MB, Nr. 11, Tel-Aviv, Apr. 1986. Pp. 10–11. [Excerpts from an essay orig. publ. in No. 21830/YB XXXI, pp. 7–18.] [See also No. 22912.]

—— — Grubel, Fred: *Leo Baeck Institut.* Gespräch. [See pp. 109–119 in No. 23135.]

23183. — Gruenewald, Max: *Bild und Text: Bemerkungen zu 'Jettchen Geberts Kinder'.* [In]: MB, Nr. 13, Tel-Aviv, Juni 1986. P. 4.

—— — Müller-Jerina, Alwin: *Germania Judaica.* [On the library of the LBI, pp. 126–133]. [See No. 23173.]

23184. — Pruschnowski, Itzchak/Ott, Rainer K. G.: *Das Leo Baeck Institut: eine Dokumentation.* [Textbuch zum 45 Minuten TV-Film am 10. Mai 1986, 3. Programm, 20.15 Uhr.] Red.: Jürgen Tomm. Berlin: Sender Freies Berlin, Abt. Literatur und Geschichte, 1986. 25 pp. [Mimeog.] [Covers the activities of the three LBI centres in Jerusalem, London, New York, also the Internat. Historical Conference of the LBI, Oct. 28–31, 1985 in Berlin, and the LBI art exhibition 'Jettchen Gebert's children' shown at the same time. Cf.: Das LBI im deutschen Fernsehen (E. G. Lowenthal) [in]: 'Allgemeine', Nr. 41/23, Bonn, 6. Juni 1986, p. 5 [& in]: Aufbau, Nr. 23–24, New York, June 6, 1986, p. 31 [& in]: MB, Nr. 13, Tel-Aviv, Juni 1986, p. 4. Wesen, Werden und Wirken des deutschen Judentums (ha) [in]: Hamburger Abendblatt, 10./11. Mai 1986, p. 16.]

23185. — *Selbstbehauptung in der Not: die Juden im nationalsozialistischen Deutschland 1933–1939.* Diskussionsrunde anlässlich der Internat. Historikertagung des LBI in Berlin. Leiter der Diskussion: Jürgen Schiller. Diskussionsteilnehmer: Abraham Barkai, Julius Carlebach, Stefi Jersch-Wenzel, Rita Thalmann, Radio-Sendung am 10. Nov. 1985, Berlin, RIAS I, 50 Min.

23186. — Stern, Stephanie M.: *Houses of the book: the Leo Baeck Institute: programs, collections, and organization of the library.* [In]: Judaica Librarianship, Vol. 2, No. 1–2, Spring 1985. Pp. 57–59.

23187. — Vogel, Rolf, ed.: *Bundeskanzler Dr. Helmut Kohl zur deutsch-jüdischen Frage in Verbindung mit der Rolle des Leo-Baeck-Instituts.* Eine Darstellung der deutschland-berichte. Bonn (Birkenweg 14): R. Vogel, [1986]. 35 pp., illus., ports. [Collection of addresses (a.o., by Carl Carstens, Max Gruenewald, Helmut Kohl, Axel Springer), and interviews by Rolf Vogel with Fred Grubel, Helmut Kohl, Arnold Paucker.]

23188. Martin Buber Institut, Köln. Maier, Johann: *Judaic studies in the Federal Republic of Germany: the case of the Martin Buber Institute.* [In]: Jewish Book Annual, Vol. 44, New York, 1986/87. Pp. 70–79, notes.

23189. Wiener Library, London. *The Wiener Library Newsletter.* Ed.: A. J. Wells. Vol. 1, Nos. 3 & 4 (Apr. & July 86) [&]: Vol. 2, Nos. 1–2 (Oct. 86–Jan. 87). 3 issues (4 pp. each), illus. [See also pp. 117–121 in No. 23173 and No. 23364.]

23190. Yad Vashem, Martyrs' and Heroes' Remembrance Authority. *Yad Vashem Studies.* 16. Ed. by Aharon Weiss. Jerusalem: Yad Vashem, 1984. XIV, 446 pp. [Publ. simultaneously in Hebrew and in English. Contributions relevant to German Jewry are listed according to subject.]

B. **Bibliographies and Catalogues**

—— *Arbeitsinformationen über Studienprojekte.* [See No. 23172.]

23191. Cargas, Harry James: *The Holocaust: an annotated bibliography.* 2nd edn. Chicago: American Library Association, 1985. VIII, 196 pp., index. [Bibl. of books from US publishers only; covers primary and secondary sources from the rise of Nazism to studies of survivors' offspring, incl. films, oral histories, photo collections.]

23192. Duisburg, Stadtbibliothek. *Judentum.* Literaturverzeichnis zur Woche der Brüderlichkeit: 'Bewährung liegt noch vor uns'. (Bearb. von Ulla Hoffmann [et al.].) Duisburg: Stadtbibliothek, 1986. 109 pp., illus.

23193. Edelheit, Abraham J./Edelheit, Hershel, eds.: *Bibliography on Holocaust literature.* Boulder, Co.: Westview Press, 1986. 842 pp., authors & periodicals indexes. [Lists more than 15,000 items starting with material written in the 1930s, incl. sections on Jewish life in pre-war Europe, antisemitism, and the aftermath of the Holocaust.]

23194. Eitinger, Leo/Krell, Robert/with Rieck, Miriam, eds.: *The psychological and medical effects of concentration camps and related persecutions on survivors of the Holocaust; a research bibliography.* Vancouver: Univ. of British Columbia Press, 1985. XII, 168 pp. [A bibl. of books, articles, and manuscripts, lists also many German titles.]

23195. *Encyclopedia of Jewish history; events and eras of the Jewish people.* Ed. by Joseph Alpher. General eds.: Ilana Shamir and Shlomo Shavit. New York; Oxford: Facts on File, 1986. 324 pp., illus., gloss., appendices. [Comprises 100 historical essays, incl. 'Jewish communities in Europe and the East' and 'The Holocaust of European Jewry'.]

—— *Das Grosse Lexikon des Dritten Reiches.* [See No. 23283.]

23196. *Hebräische Beiträge zur Wissenschaft des Judentums, deutsch angezeigt.* (Ein Referatenorgan.) Im Auftrag der Lessing-Akademie (Wolfenbüttel) hrsg. von Michael Graetz und Karlfried Gründer. Jg. 1/1985, H. 1/2. Heidelberg: Schneider, 1985. 176 pp. [Abstracts in German of books and articles publ. in Hebrew, covers the fields of history and archeology, linguistics and literature, biblical studies, the Talmud.]

23197. *Index of articles on Jewish studies.* No. 25: 1984 (with additions from previous years). Comp. and ed. by the editorial board of 'Kiryat Sefer'. (This vol. was ed. by Bitya Ben-Shammai, Susie Cohen [et al.].) Jerusalem: The Jewish National and University Library Press, 1986. XXXII, 389, [VI] pp. [A selective bibliography, incl. articles on German-speaking Jewry.]

23198. Kleeberger, Peter: *Eine Arche des deutschen Judentums: vom Entstehen eines einmaligen Werkes: die 'Encyclopaedia Judaica'.* [In]: Tribüne, Jg. 25, H. 100, Frankfurt am Main, 1986. Pp. 264–272, facsim. [The founding story of *Encyclopaedia Judaica; das Judentum in Geschichte und Gegenwart,* ed. by Jakob Klatzkin and Ismar Elbogen, publ. Berlin, Eschkol, 1928–1934; 10 vols., A–L, had appeared when the Nazis stopped the enterprise; also on the role which Nahum Goldmann played in this connection. See also No. 23644.]

—— Kulka, Otto D.: *Die deutsche Geschichtsschreibung über den Nationalsozialismus und die 'Endlösung'.* [See No. 23301.]

23199. Laska, Vera: *Nazism, resistance and Holocaust in World War II; a bibliography.* Metuchen, N.J.: Scarecrow Press, 1985. XXII, 182 pp.

23200. Merowitz, Morton J.: *'Once a Jew, always a German'; an annotated bibliography of English language materials on Polish-Jewish relations and history prior to 1939.* [In]: The Polish Review, Vol. 30, No. 2, New York, 1985. Pp. 185–202.

—— Personal Bibliographies. [See Nos. 23493 (Ernst Ludwig Ehrlich). 23510 (Walter Laqueur). 23556 (Salomon Ludwig Steinheim).]

23201. *Post-war publications on Germany Jewry; a selected bibliography of books and articles 1985.* Compiled by Irmgard Foerg and Annette Pringle. [In]: LBI Year Book XXXI, London, 1986. Pp. 465–572.

—— Rohrbaugh, Dennis, comp.: *The individual and collective experience of German-Jewish immigrants 1933–1984.* An oral history record. [See No. 23149.]

—— Rosenfeld, Mosche N.: *Bibliographie der in Fürth gedruckten Siddurim.* [See in No. 23010.]

23202. Schreckenberg, Wilhelm: *Literaturbericht: das Judentum in Geschichte und Gegenwart.* T. 1–2. [In]: Geschichte in Wissenschaft und Unterricht, Jg. 37, H. 8 & 9, Seelze, Aug. & Sept. 1986. Pp. 503–526; 570–592, notes. [Deals extensively with the pubications of the LBI.]

23203. Yassif, Eli: *Jewish folklore: an annotated bibliography.* New York: Garland, 1986. 500 pp., index. [Covers the entire field of Jewish folklore, excluding Yiddish, from the first scholarly contributions to the early 19th century; lists books and articles orig. written in English, French, German, Hebrew, and Spanish.]

III. THE NAZI PERIOD

A. General

23204. *L'Allemagne nazie et le génocide juif.* Colloque de l'Ecole des Hautes Etudes en Sciences Sociales. Paris: Gallimard, 1985. 600 pp. (Hautes études.)

—— ALPEN. [See No. 22970.]

—— ALTENKUNSTADT. [See No. 22973.]

23205. Angress, Werner T.: *Die 'Judenfrage' im Spiegel amtlicher Berichte 1935.* [In]: Büttner, Ursula, ed.: Das Unrechtsregime, Bd. 2. Hamburg: Christians, 1986. Pp. 19–44, notes.

23206. Angress, Werner T.: *Jüdische Jugend zwischen nationalsozialistischer Verfolgung und jüdischer Wiedergeburt.* [In]: Die Juden im Nationalsozialistischen Deutschland [see No. 22913]. Tübingen: Mohr, 1986. Pp. 211–221, summary in English, footnotes. [On the establishment of Jewish schools and training farms after 1933.]

23207. AUSCHWITZ. Breitman, Richard: *Auschwitz and the archives.* [In]: Central European History, Vol. 18, Atlanta, Ga., Sept.–Dec. 1985. Pp. 365–383. [Review article.]

23208. — Fürstenberg, Doris, ed.: *Jeden Moment war dieser Tod; Interviews mit jüdischen Frauen, die Auschwitz überlebten.* Eine Dokumentation. Düsseldorf: Schwann, 1986. 178 pp. (Geschichtsdidaktik: Studien, Materialien, Bd. 40.)

23209. — Kulka, Erich: *Escape from Auschwitz.* Foreword by Herman Wouk. Introd. by Yehuda Bauer. South Hadley, Mass.: Bergin & Garvey, 1986. XVII, 150 pp., illus., map. [Fictionalised account of true events.]

23210. — *The Liberation of Auschwitz.* The complete filmed record made by the Russians when they liberated Auschwitz in 1945. Directed by Irmgard von Zur Mühlen; produced by Bengt von Zur Mühlen. Federal German Republic: Chronos-Gesellschaft. A 60–minute film.

23211. AUSTRIA. Bukey, Evan Burr: *Hitler's hometown: Linz, Austria, 1908–1945.* Bloomington: Indiana Univ. Press, 1986. 288 pp. [Incl. the persecution of the Jews in Linz.]

—— — *Die Geschichte der Juden in Tirol.* [See No. 23101.]

23212. — Karner, Stefan: *Die Steiermark im Dritten Reich, 1938–1945.* Aspekte ihrer politischen, wirtschaftlich-sozialen und kulturellen Entwicklung. 2., ergänzte Aufl. Graz: Leykam, 1986. 636 pp., illus., bibl. (583–609). [Incl.: Die Juden (168–170). Die 'Reichskristallnacht' in Graz (171–172). Der Schluss des 'Holocaust' (173). Konzentrationslager in der Steiermark (184–188).]

23213. — Pauley, Bruce F.: *Hitler and the forgotten Nazis; a history of Austrian National Socialism.* Chapel Hill: Univ. of North Carolina Press, 1986. 292 pp. [Also on Austrian persecution of the Jews.]

23214. Bacharach, Walter Zwi: *Konsequenz und Manipulation der nationalsozialistischen Rassenideologie.* [In]: Büttner, Ursula, ed.: Das Unrechtsregime, Bd. 1. Hamburg: Christians, 1986. Pp. 49–58, notes.

23215. BADEN. Toury, Jacob: *Die Entstehungsgeschichte des Austreibungsbefehls gegen die Juden der Saarpfalz und Badens (22./23. Okt. 1940 – Camp de Gurs).* [In]: Jahrbuch des Instituts für Deutsche Geschichte, Bd. 15, Univ. Tel-Aviv, 1986. Pp. 431–464, footnotes.

—— BAMBERG. [See No. 22979.]

23216. Barkai, Avraham: *Deported German Jews in Eastern European Ghettos.* [In Hebrew]. [In]: Proceedings of the 9th World Congress of Jewish Studies, Division B, Vol. 2: The history of the Jewish people. Jerusalem, 1986. Pp. 197–204.

23217. Barkai, Avraham: *'Schicksalsjahr 1938': Kontinuität und Verschärfung der wirtschaftlichen*

Ausplünderung der deutschen Juden. [In]: Büttner, Ursula, ed.: Das Unrechtsregime, Bd. 2. Hamburg: Christians, 1986. Pp. 45–68, notes.

23218. BARKAI, AVRAHAM: *Der wirtschaftliche Existenzkampf der Juden im Dritten Reich.* [In]: Die Juden im Nationalsozialistischen Deutschland [see No. 22913]. Tübingen: Mohr, 1986. Pp. 153–166, summary in English, footnotes. [See also abridged version [in]: Aus Politik und Zeitgeschichte; Beilage zur Wochenzeitung Das Parlament, B 31, Bonn, 2. Aug. 1986, pp. 39–46, footnotes. Cf.: Auch ihre Deportation mussten sie bezahlen (W. Struminski) [in]: 'Allgemeine', Nr. 41/34, Bonn, 22. Aug. 1986, p. 5.]

—— BECHHOFEN. [See No. 22980.]

23219. BEN-AVNER, YEHUDA: *Trends of unification and division in Orthodox Jewry in Germany, 1934–1935.* [In Hebrew, with English summary]. [In]: Keshev, Vol. 1, Ramat-Gan, Dec. 1985. Pp. 5–14.

—— BERGEDORF. [See No. 22981.]

23220. BERING, DIETZ: *Von der Notwendigkeit politischer Beleidigungsprozesse – der Beginn der Auseinandersetzung zwischen Polizeivizepräsident Bernhard Weiss und der NSDAP.* [In]: Juden in der Weimarer Republik [See No. 22915]. Pp. 305–329, notes. [B. Weiss, data see No. 18075/YB XXVII.]

—— BERLIN. [See also Nos. 22984, 22986, 22990–22991.]

23221. — DAXNER, MICHAEL: *Der Erfolg der Überlebenden: die Private Jüdische Waldschule Kaliski in Berlin 1932–1939.* [In]: Neue Sammlung, Jg. 26, H. 1, Stuttgart, Jan.-März 1986. Pp. 68–78, facsims., footnotes. [Documentation.]

23222. — DAXNER, MICHAEL: *Die Private Jüdische Waldschule Kaliski in Berlin, 1932–1939.* [In]: Die Juden im Nationalsozialistischen Deutschland [see No. 22913]. Tübingen: Mohr, 1986. Pp. 249–257, summary in English, footnotes.

23223. — GEHRIG, BERIT: *'Bist 'ne Jüdische? Haste den Stern?'* Erzählt im Gespräch mit Bruno Schonig. Berlin-Kreuzberg: Nishen, c1985. 31 pp., illus. (Erzähltes Leben 6.) [Report on the difficult childhood of B.G. who stayed with her Gentile mother in Berlin while her Jewish father lived underground from 1943.]

23234. — WESTPHAL, UWE: *Berliner Konfektion und Mode; die Zerstörung einer Tradition, 1836–1939.* Berlin: Edition Hentrich, 1986. 203 pp., illus., ports., facsims., list of names (200–203), notes (195–197), bibl. (198–199). Stätten der Geschichte Berlins, Bd. 14.) [incl.: Wie jüdisch war die 'jüdische Konfektion': Legendenbildung und Wirklichkeit (85–86). Der Anteil der Juden in der Bekleidungsindustrie der zwanziger Jahre (87–96). Die NS-Gesetze zur Verdrängung der Juden aus der Wirtschaft in Deutschland zwischen 1933 und 1939 (102–105). Die Rolle der Industrie- und Handelskammer Berlin bei der 'Arisierung' jüdischer Konfektionsfirmen (117–119). Die publizistische Ebene im Dritten Reich zur Isolierung der jüdischen Geschäftsleute der Konfektion in Berlin (125–138). Beispiele der 'Arisierung' und Emigration aus der Berliner Konfektionsbranche (139–166). Firmen und Emigranten aus der Berliner Damenkonfektion (174–194).] [Cf. The Jewish share in Berlin's 'rag trade' (David Maier) [in]: AJR Information, No. 3, London, March 1987, p. 6.]

—— BIBLIOGRAPHY. [See Nos. 23191, 23193–23194, 23199.]

23225. BOAS, JACOB: *The shrinking world of German Jewry, 1933–1938.* [In]: LBI Year Book XXXI, London, 1986. Pp. 241–266, footnotes.

—— BODERSWEIER. [See No. 22995.]

23226. BÖCKENFÖRDE, ERNST-WOLFGANG, ed.: *Staatsrecht und Staatsrechtslehre im Dritten Reich.* Heidelberg: C. F. Müller, Juristischer Verl., 1985. 262 pp., bibl. (237–256). [Incl.: Personelle Veränderungen in der Staatsrechtslehre und ihre neue Situation nach der Machtergreifung (Bettina Limperg, 44–70; on the dismissal of Jewish university professors). Die Rechtsstellung der Juden (Kai Henning/Josef Kestler, 191–211).]

23227. BOEHM, ERIC H.: *We survived; the stories of fourteen of the hidden and the hunted of Nazi Germany.* As told to Eric H. Boehm. [3rd edn.] New York: ABC/Clio, 1986 (c1949). 337 pp. [Incl. reminiscences by Leo Baeck; Erich Hopp, journalist and playwright; Rolf Joseph, carpenter in Berlin; Heinrich Liebrecht, judge; Moritz Mandelkern, tailor born in Poland, from 1918 in Berlin; Alice Stein-Landesmann, novelist and playwright; Jeanette Wolff, socialist politician; Valerie Wolffenstein, artist.]

23228. BREMEN. MARSSOLEK, INGE/OTT, RENÉ: *Bremen im Dritten Reich; Anpassung – Widerstand – Verfolgung.* Unter Mitarbeit von Peter Brandt [et al.]. Bremen: Schünemann, 1986. 542 pp., illus., bibl. (519–525). [Covers also the persecution and deportation of the Bremen Jews.

Cf.: Eine genaue, beispielhafte Durchleuchtung (Volker Ullrich) [in]: Süddeutsche Zeitung, Nr. 51, München, 3. März 1987, p. 34.] [See also No. 23361.]

— Brent, Lucie: *The architects of Jewish self-assertion during the Nazi era.* [See No. 23457.]

— Brodnitz, Friedrich: *Memories of the Reichsvertretung.* [See No. 23621.]

23229. Browning, Christopher R.: *Nazi resettlement policy and search for a solution to the Jewish question, 1939–1941.* [In]: German Studies Review, Vol. 9, No. 3, Tempe, Ariz., Oct. 1986. Pp. 497–519, notes. [See also No. 23259.]

23230. Büchler, Yehoshua R.: *Kommandostab Reichsführer-SS: Himmler's personal murder brigades in 1941.* [In]: Holocaust and Genocide Studies, Vol. 1, No. 1, Oxford, 1986. Pp. 11–25, notes (21–25).

23231. Büttner, Ursula, ed.: *Das Unrechtsregime.* Internationale Forschung über den Nationalsozialismus. Bd. 1–2. Hrsg. unter Mitwirkung von Werner Johe und Angelika Voss. (Festschrift für Werner Jochmann zum 65. Geburtstag.) Hamburg: Christians, 1986. 2 vols. (XXXII, 560; 478 pp.), notes. (Hamburger Beiträge zur Sozial- und Zeitgeschichte, Bd. 21–22.) *Bd. 1: Ideologie – Herrschaftssystem – Wirkung in Europa. Bd. 2: Verfolgung – Exil – Belasteter Neubeginn.* [Contributions relevant to German-Jewish history are listed according to subject.] [See also: Verdiente Ehrung: zum 65. Geburtstag von Werner Jochmann (Ernst G. Lowenthal) [in]: 'Allgemeine', Nr. 41/30, Bonn, 25. Juli 1986, p. 4. Werner Jochmann – 65 (Karl-Heinz Janssen) [in]: Die Zeit, Nr. 33, Hamburg, 8. Aug. 1986, p. 42. . . . aber doch Wahrheit genug: Anmerkungen zu einer Festschrift für W. Jochmann (Jost Nolte) [in]: Die Zeit, Nr. 14, Hamburg, 27. März 1987, p. 20.]

23232. CHURCH. Bethge, Eberhard: *Christologisches Bekenntnis und Antijudaismus: zum Defizit von Barmen.* [In]: Barmer theologische Erklärung, 1934–1984; Geschichte – Wirkung – Defizite. Hrsg. von Wilhelm Hüffmeier und Martin Stöhr. Bielefeld: Luther-Verl., 1984. (Unio und confessio, Bd. 10.)

23233. — Conway, John S.: *The political theology of Martin Niemöller.* [In]: German Studies Review, Vol. 9, No. 3, Tempe, Ariz., Oct. 1986. Pp. 521–546, notes. [Also deals with Niemöller's attitude towards the Nazi persecution of the Jews.]

23234. — Ericksen, Robert P.: *The political theology of Paul Althaus: Nazi supporter.* [In]: German Studies Review, Vol. 9, No. 3, Tempe, Ariz., Oct. 1986. Pp. 547–567, notes.

23235. — Ericksen, Robert P.: *Theologen unter Hitler; das Bündnis zwischen evangelischer Dogmatik und Nationalsozialismus.* Aus dem Amerikan. von Annegrete Lösch. München: Hanser, 1986. 342 pp., bibl. (323–339). [On Paul Althaus, Emanuel Hirsch, Gerhard Kittel. Transl. of No. 22088/YB XXXI.]

23236. — Jonca, Karol: *Schlesiens Kirchen zur 'Lösung der Judenfrage'.* [In]: Büttner, Ursula, ed.: Das Unrechtsregime, Bd. 2, Hamburg: Christians, 1986. Pp. 123–148, notes.

23237. — Liebster, Wolfram: *Christlicher Glaube als 'unüberbrückbarer religiöser Gegensatz zum Judentum'? Neutestamentliche Wissenschaft im Dritten Reich.* Ein Tagungsbericht, Arnoldshain 17.–19. Jan. 1986. [In]: Judaica, Jg. 42, H. 4, Basel, Dez. 1986. Pp. 240–254, notes.

23238. — Meyer-Zollitsch, Almuth: *National-Sozialismus und Evangelische Kirche in Bremen.* Bremen: Staatsarchiv, 1985. 388 pp. (Veröffentlichung aus dem Staatsarchiv der Freien Hansestadt Bremen, No. 51.) [Deals, a.o., with Nazi antisemitism and the attitude of the Protestant Church towards the Jews.]

23239. — Norden, Günther van: *Die Barmer theologische Erklärung und die 'Judenfrage'.* [In]: Büttner, Ursula, ed.: Das Unrechtsregime, Bd. 1. Hamburg: Christians, 1986. Pp. 315–350, notes.

23240. — *Nürnberger Gesetze und Steglitzer Synode 1935.* Markustag vom 20.–22. Sept. 1985, Evang. Markuskirchengemeinde Steglitz. Berlin, 1986. 57 pp., illus. (Evangelisches Bildungswerk Berlin, Haus der Kirche, Dokumentation 51.)

23241. — Oesterreicher, Johannes: *Wider die Tyrannei des Rassenwahns.* Rundfunkansprachen aus dem ersten Jahr von Hitlers Krieg. Mit einem Nachwort von Robert A. Graham: Rundfunkprediger gegen Hitler. Wien: Geyer-Edition, 1986. 120 pp., port. (Publikationen des Instituts für Kirchliche Zeitgeschichte, 2,18.)

23242. — Reichrath, Hans: *Die Judenfrage – ein Defizit der Barmer theologischen Erklärung von 1934?* 1–2. [In]: Pfälzisches Pfarrerblatt, Jg. 75, Nr. 11 & 12, Homburg (Untere Allee 56), Nov. & Dez. 1985. Pp. 208–214; 243–244.

23243. — Schmidt, Johann Michael: *Martin Luther's attitude towards the Jews and its impact on the Evangelical Church in Germany in the beginning of the Third Reich.* [In]: Proceedings of the 9th World Congress of Jewish Studies, Division B, Vol. 3: The history of the Jewish people. Jerusalem, 1986. Pp. 157–164.

23244. — Scholder, Klaus: *Die Kirchen und das Dritte Reich.* Geringfügig ergänzte Ausg. *Bd. 1: Vorgeschichte und Zeit der Illusionen: 1918–1934.* Frankfurt am Main: Ullstein, 1986. 952 pp., illus. (Ullstein-Buch, Nr. 33073.) [Also on the attitude towards the German Jews after 1933. Vol. 2: *Das Jahr der Ernüchterung 1934* appeared in hardcover at Siedler, Berlin, 1985, 477 pp.]

23245. Cochavi, Yehoyakim: *Cultural and educational activities of the German Jews 1933–1941 as a response to the challenge of the Nazi regime.* By Yehoyakim Cohavi. [In Hebrew, with English abstract]. Jerusalem, Hebrew Univ., Phil. Diss., Jan. 1986. 396, XX (abstract) pp., notes (325–396). [Cont. the chaps. (in Hebrew): *1. Culture activities* (1–140; on the Jüdischer Kulturbund). *2. Jewish education for adults* (141–204; incl.: 'The Center for Jewish Adult Education'; The Lehrhäuser). *3. Periodicals* (205–265). *4. Books* (266–308; incl.: Publishing houses; Books and themes; Appendix: list of publishing houses).]

23246. Cochavi, Yehoyakim: *Kultur- und Bildungsarbeit der deutschen Juden 1933–1941: Antwort auf die Verfolgung durch das NS-Regime.* [In]: Neue Sammlung, Jg. 26, H. 3, Stuttgart, Juli-Sept. 1986. Pp. 396–407, footnotes. [Articles forms the final chapter of the author's dissertation, see preceding entry.]

23247. Cochavi, Yehoyakim: *Towards a 'Jewish school in its essence'.* By H. Kochavi. [In Hebrew]. [In]: Massuah; a yearbook on the Holocaust and heroism, Vol. 14, Tel-Aviv, Apr. 1986. Pp. 32–37. [On the Jewish educational system in the 1930s in Germany, the debates between the Zionists and the liberals.]

23248. CZECHOSLOVAKIA. Kárný, Miroslav: *Zur Statistik der jüdischen Bevölkerung im sogenannten Protektorat.* [In]: Judaica Bohemiae, Vol. 22, No. 1, Prague, 1986. Pp. 9–19, tabs., footnotes.

23249. *Dachauer Hefte.* Studien und Dokumente zur Geschichte der nationalsozialistischen Konzentrationslager. Red.: Wolfgang Benz und Barbara Distel. Dachau (Alte Römerstr. 75): Verlag Dachauer Hefte, 1985 ff. Jg. 1, H. 1: *Die Befreiung.* 1985. 231 pp. [Incl. reminiscences by the painter Max Mannheimer, who survived Theresienstadt, Auschwitz and Dachau.] Jg. 1, H. 2: *Die Sklavenarbeit im KZ.* 1986. 1 vol.

— DANZIG. [See. No. 22997.]

23250. Dürkefälden, Karl: *'Schreiben, wie es wirklich war . . .'; die Aufzeichnungen Karl Dürkefäldens aus der Zeit des Nationalsozialismus.* Bearb. und kommentiert von Herbert und Sybille Obenaus. Hannover: Niedersächsische Landeszentrale für Politische Bildung, 1985. 136 pp., map, bibl. (132–136). [Diary of the German engineer K.D. (1902–1976) who lived in Celle from 1934; also on antisemitism, persecution of the Jews, the November Pogrom.]

— DUISBURG. [See No. 23004.]

— EAST FRIESLAND. [See No. 23361, 23454.]

23251. Edvardson, Cordelia: *Gebranntes Kind sucht das Feuer.* Aus dem Schwedischen von Anna-Liese Kornitzky. München: Hanser, 1986. 133 pp. [The author, born 1929 in Munich and now living in Israel, daughter of the 'half-Jewish' writer Elisabeth Langgässer and a Jewish father, reports on her difficult childhood after 1933, her deportation to Theresienstadt and Auschwitz, the post-war years in Sweden and her settling is Israel. Cf.: Für immer ausgesondert und abseits (Boike Jacobs) [in]: 'Allgemeine', Nr. 41/23, Bonn, 6. Juni 1986, p. 7. Den Blick in die Vergangenheit wagen: C. Edvardson erhielt den Geschwister-Scholl-Preis 1986 (Ellen Presser) [in]: 'Allgemeine', Nr. 41/49, Bonn, 5. Dez. 1986, p. 7. Cordelias Geschichte (Horst Krüger) [in]: Neue Deutsche Hefte, Jg. 33, H. 4 (192), Berlin, 1986, pp. 719–750. Cordelias Opfergang durch die Hölle von Auschwitz (Horst Krüger) [in]: Die Zeit, Nr. 13, Hamburg, 21. März 1986, p. 15.]

23252. EMIGRATION. Freeden, Herbert: *'Bleiben oder gehen?': ein Kapitel aus der jüdischen Presse im nationalsozialistischen Deutschland.* [In]: Publizistik, Jg. 31, H. 1–2, Konstanz, 1986. Pp. 91–107, notes, summary in English. [First publ. in: Bulletin des LBI, 70 (1985).]

23253. — *Die Jüdische Emigration aus Deutschland 1933–1941: die Geschichte einer Austreibung.* Eine Ausstellung der Deutschen Bibliothek Frankfurt am Main unter Mitwirkung des Leo-Baeck-Instituts New York. Frankfurt am Main, 1985. [For detailed entry see No. 22103/YB XXXI.] *Reviews*, selection [continuation]: Besprechung (Bernt Ture von zur Mühlen) [in]: Aus dem Antiquariat, Nr. 1, [Beilage zum] Börsenblatt für den Deutschen Buchhandel, Nr. 9, Frankfurt am Main, 31. Jan. 1986, pp. A 13- A 16, facsims. Besprechung (Rolf Vogel) [in]: deutschland-berichte, Jg. 23, Nr. 1, Bonn, Jan. 1987, pp. 22–26. Besprechung (Margarita Pazi) [in]: Das Neue Israel, Jg. 38, H. 12, Zürich, Juni 1986, pp. 39–40. Die Vertreibung der deutschen Juden (Wilfried F. Schoeller) [in]:

Süddeutsche Zeitung, Nr. 49, München, 28. Feb. 1986, p. 49. Dokumente diabolischen Hasses (Edita Koch) [in]: Tribüne, Jg. 25, H. 97, Frankfurt am Main, 1986, pp. 52–56 [&]: Leserbrief (Esriel Hildesheimer) [in]: Tribüne, Jg. 26, H. 101 (1987), p. 200.

23254. — *Die Jüdische Emigration aus Deutschland 1933–1941: 60 exemplarische Biographien.* Ein zusätzliches Kapitel zur Ausstellung der Deutschen Bibliothek, Bonn, 7. Okt. 1986–4. Jan. 1987. Frankfurt am Main: Deutsche Bibliothek, 1986. 40 pp., ports.

23255. — MARGALIOT, ABRAHAM: *Emigration – Planung und Wirklichkeit.* [In]: Die Juden im Nationalsozialistischen Deutschland [see No. 22913]. Tübingen: Mohr, 1986. Pp. 303–316, summary in English, footnotes.

23256. — *Wohin und zurück.* [Set of three TV-films]: *An uns glaubt Gott nicht mehr* [&]: *Santa Fe* [&]: *Welcome to Vienna.* Directed by Axel Corti, script by Georg Stefan Troller. [On the forced emigration of Viennese Jews, their plight in various countries, settling in the USA, the young protagonist's return to Vienna and experience as a US Army officer. Cf.: 'Eine österreichische Emigranten-Trilogie im Fernsehen DRS (Walter Weiss) [in]: NZZ, Nr. 31, Zürich, 7. Feb. 1986, pp. 77–78.]

—— ESCHWEGE. [See No. 23006.]

23257. ESSEN. *Essen unter Bomben: Märztage 1943.* Mit Beiträgen von Franz Josef Gründges [et al.]. [Ausstellung in] Essen, Alte Synagoge. Essen: Klartext Verl., 1984. 100 pp., illus., ports., facsims., map, notes (95–96). [Also on the persecution of Jews in Essen. Incl.: Juden in Borbeck (70–72).]

23258. — HEID, LUDGER: *Lazar Finger [1887–1939]: Österreicher, Deutscher, Ostjude.* Für Ignaz Finger zum 70. Geburtstag am 25. Mai 1984. [In]: Beiträge zur Geschichte von Stadt und Stift Essen, H. 99, Essen, 1984. Pp. 215–238, illus., ports., facsims., footnotes. [On the persecution of Jews in Essen during the Nazi period.]

—— EXILE. [See Nos. 23128–23156, 23252–23256, 23366–23381, 23664–23670.]

23259. FINAL SOLUTION. BROWNING, CHRISTOPHER R.: *Fateful months; essays on the emergence of the Final Solution.* New York: Holmes & Meier, 1985. IX, 111 pp., illus., notes (88–107).

23260. — CARR, WILLIAM: *A final solution? Nazi policy towards the Jews.* [In]: History Today, Vol. 35, London, Nov. 1985. Pp. 30–36, illus. [See also ensuing Letter to the Editor]: With malice aforethought? (John P. Fox) [&]: Reply (William Carr) [in]: History Today, Vol. 36, Apr. 1986, p. 58.

23261. — GRAML, HERMANN: *Zur Genesis der 'Endlösung'.* [In]: Büttner, Ursula, ed.: Das Unrechtsregime, Bd. 2. Hamburg: Christians, 1986. Pp. 2–18, notes.

23262. — HIRSCHFELD, GERHARD, ed.: *The policies of genocide; Jews and Soviet prisoners of war in Nazi Germany.* With an introd. by Wolfgang J. Mommsen. London; Boston: Allen & Unwin [for] The German Historical Institute, 1986. XIII, 172 pp., maps, bibl. references. [Incl.: Hitler's Final Solution and its rationalization (Lothar Kettenacker, 73–92). The realization of the unthinkable: the 'Final Solution of the Jewish Question' in the Third Reich (Hans Mommsen, 93–144). Chronology of destruction (Gerhard Hirschfeld, 145–162.]

23263. — STEINBACH, PETER: *Die Planung des Unvorstellbaren: schon 1930 wurde die 'Endlösung der Judenfrage' konzipiert.* [In]: Tribüne, Jg. 25, H. 99, Frankfurt am Main, 1986. Pp. 84–94, footnotes.

23264. FRANK, ANNE: *De Dagboeken van Anne Frank.* Ed.: Harry Paape, Gerold van Stroom, David Barnouw. Amsterdam: Rijksinstituut voor Oorlogsdocumentatie, 1986. 714 pp. [New critical edn. of A.F.'s diaries, contains all three versions and proves that the Diary is not a fabrication. Cf.: The Diary of Anne Frank [in]: Patterns of Prejudice, Vol. 20, No. 3, London, July 1986, pp. 36–38.]

23265. — *Anne Frank in the world, 1929–1945 = Die Welt der Anne Frank.* Amsterdam: Anne Frank Stichting, 1985. 144 pp., chiefly illus., ports. [Textbook in English and German for an exhibition travelling to Berlin in April 1986, and London, then throughout the USA.]

23266. — — MULISCH, HARRY: *Death and the maiden.* [In]: The New York Review of Books, July 17, 1986. Pp. 7–8. [Also German version]: *Das Mädchen und der Tod: Anne Frank zum Gedenken.* (Aus dem Holländ. von Johannes Piron.) [In]: Die Zeit, Nr. 17, Hamburg, 18, Apr. 1986. P. 44. [Excerpts from the address delivered at the opening of the exhibition 'Anne Frank in the World' at the Berlin Academy of Fine Arts in Apr. 1986. H. Mulisch was the first young writer to receive the Anne Frank Prize in 1957.]

23267. — *'Früher wohnten wir in Frankfurt . . .'; Frankfurt am Main und Anne Frank.* Frankfurt am Main: Historisches Museum, 1985. 91 pp., illus., ports., facsims., bibl. (87–91). (Kleine Schriften des Historischen Museums, Bd. 24.)

23268. FRANKFURT am Main. DIAMANT, ADOLF: *Das zweite Buch Ruth: der Leidensweg einer Frankfurter jüdischen Familie bis in das Vernichtungslager.* Frankfurt am Main (Eysseneckstr. 56): A Diamant, 1986. XI, 110 pp., illus., ports., facsims. [On Ruth Wetterhahn, born Apr. 9, 1925 in Bockenheim, and her parents who perished in Auschwitz and Riga.]

23269. — *Spuren des Faschismus in Frankfurt: das Alltagsleben der Frankfurter Juden 1933–1945.* Eine kommentierte Materialsammlung. [Zusammengestellt von der] Arbeitsgruppe 'Spuren des Faschismus in Frankfurt' beim Hessischen Institut für Lehrerfortbildung. Kassel (Fuldatal 1): Hessisches Institut für Lehrerfortbildung, Hauptstelle Reinhardswaldschule, 1984. 150 pp., illus., ports., facsims., diagrs., map.

23270. — *Spuren jüdischer Geschichte in Frankfurt am Main 1933–1945.* (Text und Zusammenstellung: Angelika Rieber [et al.].) Frankfurt am Main: Staatliche Landesbildstelle Hessen, 1985. 72 pp., illus. (Beiheft zur Diareihe, Staatliche Landesbildstelle, Frankfurt am Main, 108111.)

23271. — WIPPERMANN, WOLFGANG: *Das Leben in Frankfurt zur NS-Zeit. Bd. 1: Die nationalsozialistische Judenverfolgung.* Darstellung, Dokumente, didaktische Hinweise. Frankfurt am Main: Kramer, 1986. 273 pp. [The following 3 vols. of this work cover other Jewish aspects of life in Frankfurt 1933–1945.]

23272. FREEDEN, HERBERT: *Sprachrohr der Opfer: die jüdische Presse in Nazideutschland.* [In]: Das Parlament, Nr. 42, Bonn, 18. Okt. 1986. P. 13, facsims. [Advance excerpt from H. Freeden's book 'Das Ende der jüdischen Presse in Nazideutschland', to be publ. 1987 by the Leo Baeck Institute.]

23273. FREIBURG i.Br. BRÄUNCHE, E. B.: *Die 'Reichskristallnacht' in Freiburg.* [In]: Schau-ins-Land, Bd. 103, Freiburg i.Br., Breisgau-Geschichtsverein, 1984. Pp. 149–160.

23274. *Gedenkbuch – Opfer der Verfolgung der Juden unter der nationalsozialistischen Gewaltherrschaft in Deutschland, 1933–1945.* (Bearb. vom Bundesarchiv, Koblenz und dem Internat. Suchdienst, Arolsen.) Bd. 1–2. Koblenz (Postfach 320): Bundesarchiv, 1986. 2 vols. (XVI, 950; VII, 951–1823 pp.).

—— GELSENKIRCHEN. [See No. 23012.]

23275. GERBER, DAVID A., ed.: *Anti-Semitism in America.* Champaign: Univ. of Illinois Press, 1986. 428 pp. [Incl. the State Department's response to Nazi antisemitism.]

—— GESCHER. [See No. 23013.]

23276. GIESSEN. *Dokumentation über die Gedenktage vom 26. bis 31. August 1982 für die jüdischen Mitbürger, die während der Zeit von 1933–1945 deportiert und ermordet wurden.* Giessen: Stadtverwaltung, 1982. 97, [63] pp., illus., ports., facsims., plans.

23277. — HEYNE, K. [et al.]: *Judenverfolgung in Giessen und Umgebung 1933–1945.* [In]: Mitteilungen des Oberhessischen Geschichtsvereins Giessen, N.F., Bd. 69, Giessen, 1984. Pp. 1–315.

23278. GINZEL, GÜNTHER B.: *Jüdischer Alltag in Deutschland 1933–1945.* Düsseldorf: Droste, 1984. 252 pp., illus., ports., facsims., notes (248–251). [A pictorial account of Jewish life in Nazi Germany; expanded entry of No. 21093/YB XXX. Incl.: Zeittafel (8–16). Alltag eines jüdischen Kindes (19–21). Bildteil (22–206). Zur Sozial- und Wirtschaftsstruktur der Juden in Deutschland (214–226). Jüdische Jugendbünde (227–232). Novemberpogrom 1939 (234). Menschen, die Juden halfen (239). Widerstand (240–283).]

23279. GÖTTINGEN. DAHMS, HANS-JOACHIM: *Verluste durch Emigration: die Auswirkungen der nationalsozialistischen 'Säuberungen' an der Universität Göttingen.* Eine Fallstudie. [In]: Exilforschung, Bd. 4, München, 1986. Pp. 160–185.

23280. GOSLAR. CRAMER, HANS DONALD, ed.: *Das Schicksal der Goslarer Juden 1933–1945.* Eine Dokumentation. Mit Beiträgen von Horst-Günther Lange, Friedrich Deiniger und Werner Hillebrand. Goslar: Geschichts- und Heimatschutzverein, 1986. 204 pp., illus., ports., facsims., bibl. (200–201). (Beiträge zur Geschichte der Stadt Goslar, 36.)

23281. GRENVILLE, JOHN A. S.: *Die 'Endlösung' und die 'Judenmischlinge' im Dritten Reich.* [In]: Büttner, Ursula, ed.: Das Unrechtsregime, Bd. 2. Hamburg: Christians, 1986. Pp. 91–122, notes.

23282. GROSS-GERAU. KAUFMAN, MENACHEM: *Kristallnacht in a small town: Gross-Gerau, November 1938.* [In]: The Jewish Quarterly, Vol. 33, No. 1, London, 1986. Pp. 47–53. [For Hebrew version see No. 22124/YB XXXI.]

23283. *Das Grosse Lexikon des Dritten Reiches.* Hrsg. von Christian Zentner und Friedemann Bedürftig. München: Südwest-Verl., 1985. 686 pp., illus., bibl. (671–682). [Refers in various entries to Jews and their treatment during the Nazi period. Cf.: Ersatz für eine ganze Bibliothek (Georg Schwinghammer] [in]: Tribüne, Jg. 25, H. 100, Frankfurt am Main, 1986, pp. 300 & 302.]

23284. GÜTERSLOH. LOHMEYER, LUDWIG: *'Die Synagoge brennt!' Der Bericht eines Augenzeugen.* [In]: Gütersloher Beiträge zur Heimat-und Landeskunde, N.F., H. 8/9, Gütersloh, 1985. Pp. 177–178.

23285. HAFTMANN, WERNER: *Verfemte Kunst; bildende Künstler der inneren und äusseren Emigration in der Zeit des Nationalsozialismus.* Hrsg. von Berthold Roland. Köln: DuMont, 1986. 420 pp., 336 illus., short biogr. of artists (388–410), bibl. [Incl.: Kunstdiktatur-Verfolgung-Gleichschaltung (19–46). Also chaps. on the various countries where exiles found refuge, a.o., Rudolf Levy in Italy (140–141).]

—— HAMBURG. [See also No. 23018.]

23286. — HUNGER, ROLAND [et al.], eds.: *Paul Dieroff, (1928–1944).* [Hrsg. im Auftrag der] Gesamtschule [Hamburg-]Niendorf. Hamburg: Zerr, 1986. 112 pp., illus. 1 map. [P. Dieroff, born 1928 in Badenstedt near Bremen, his Gentile father died when he was two, deported to Theresienstadt in 1943 where his Jewish mother survived while he was killed in Dachau on Dec. 15, 1944.]

—— HEILBRONN. [See No. 23024.]

23287. *Heimatgeschichtlicher Wegweiser zu Stätten des Widerstandes und der Verfolgung 1933–1945.* Hrsg. vom Studienkreis zur Erforschung und Vermittlung der Geschichte des Widerstandes 1933–1945 und dem Präsidium der Vereinigung der Verfolgten des Naziregimes – Bund der Antifaschisten. Red.: Ursula Krause-Schmitt [et al.]. Bd. 1 ff. Köln: Pahl-Rugenstein, 1984 ff. *Bd. 1: Hessen.* 1984. 136 pp., illus., maps. *Bd. 2: Niedersachsen. 1: Regierungsbezirke Braunschweig und Lüneburg.* 2. Aufl. 1985. 116 pp., illus. *Bd. 3: Niedersachsen. 2: Regierungsbezirke Hannover und Weser-Ems.* 1986. 206 pp., illus., diagrs., maps.

23288. HERRLINGEN. SCHACHNE, LUCIE: *Erziehung zum geistigen Widerstand: das jüdische Landschulheim Herrlingen 1933–1939.* Frankfurt am Main: dipa Verl., 1986. 266 pp., illus., ports., facsims., notes (235–241), bibl. (242–245). (Pädagogische Beispiele: Institutionengeschichte in Einzeldarstellungen, Bd. 3.) [Incl.: Otto Hirsch und die Anfänge des Jüdischen Landschulheims in Herrlingen (Hugo Rosenthal, 40–49). Wer waren die Lehrer und wer die Schüler (94–124; reminiscences by former teachers and pupils). Kurzbiographien ehemaliger Lehrer/innen und Schüler/innen (259–265).] [Hugo Rosenthal, founder of Herrlingen, educationalist, Dec. 13, 1887 Lippe–Dec. 6, 1980 Israel.]

—— HESSE. [See vol. 1 of No. 23287.]

23289. HILDESHEIMER, ESRIEL: *The fate of synagogues and Jewish cemeteries after the 'Crystal Night'.* [In Hebrew]. [In]: Proceedings of the 9th World Congress of Jewish Studies, Division B, Vol. 2: The history of the Jewish people. Jerusalem, 1986. Pp. 169–172.

23290. HILLGRUBER, ANDREAS: *Zweierlei Untergang: die Zerschlagung des Deutschen Reiches und das Ende des europäischen Judentums.* Berlin: Siedler, 1986. 110 pp., notes (100–108). [See also Nos. 23298–23299, 23303.]

23291. HISTORIOGRAPHY. BROSZAT, MARTIN: *Nach Hitler; der schwierige Umgang mit unserer Geschichte.* Beiträge von Martin Broszat, hrsg. von Hermann Graml und Klaus-Dietmar Henke. München: Oldenbourg, 1986. 326 pp. [Collection of essays publ. 1957–1986. Incl.: Hitler und die Genesis der 'Endlösung': aus Anlass der Thesen von David Irving; 1977 (187–229). Zur Kritik der Publizistik des antisemitischen Rechtsextremismus; 1979 (262–270). 'Holocaust' und die Geschichtswissenschaft; 1979 (271–286). Soll das Leugnen oder Verharmlosen nationalsozialistischer Judenmorde straffrei sein? 1982 (292–294). Die Ambivalenz der Forderung nach mehr Geschichtsbewusstsein; 1986 (310–323).]

23292. — BROSZAT, MARTIN: *Plädoyer für eine Historizierung des Nationalsozialismus.* [In]: Merkur, Jg. H. 5 (435), Stuttgart, Mai 1985. Pp. 373–385.

23293. — BRUMLIK, MICHA: *Neuer Staatsmythos Ostfront: die neueste Entwicklung der Geschichtswissenschaft der BRD.* [In]: Taz Magazin, Berlin, 12. Juli 1986. P. 14.

23294. — EUCHNER, WALTER: *Die Naziherrschaft – eine Normaltyrannei?* Über den Missbrauch geschichtsphilosophischer Deutungen. [In]: Die Neue Gesellschaft/Frankfurter Hefte, Jg. 33, Nr. 12, Bonn, Dez. 1986. Pp. 1116–1119.

23295. — FRIEDLÄNDER, SAUL: *From anti-Semitism to extermination: a historiographical study of Nazi policies toward the Jews and an essay in interpretation.* [In]: Yad Vashem Studies, 16, Jerusalem, 1984. Pp. 1–50. [See also: Saul Friedländer: Pavel, Paul, Shaul; Erfahrungen mit der deutschen Verdrängung: ein Historiker aus Tel Aviv in Berlin (Klaus Pokatzky) [in]: Die Zeit, Nr. 21, Hamburg, 16. Mai 1986, p. 77.]

23296. — GIORDANO, RALPH: *Ist Auschwitz vergleichbar? Gedanken zu einer aktuellen Diskussion.* [In]: 'Allgemeine', Nr. 41/45, Bonn, 7. Nov. 1986. Pp. 1–2. [See also: Vor Selbsttäuschung ist zu warnen: der Umgang der Deutschen mit ihrer Geschichte (n.) [in]: 'Allgemeine', Nr. 41/44, Bonn, 31. Okt. 1986, pp. 3–4.

23297. — GREBING, HELGA: *Deutscher Sonderweg oder zwei Linien historischer Kontinuität in Deutschland?* [In]: Büttner, Ursula, ed.: Das Unrechtsregime, Bd. 1. Hamburg: Christians, 1986. Pp. 2–23, notes.

23298. — HABERMAS, JÜRGEN: *Eine Art Schadensabwicklung: die apologetischen Tendenzen in der deutschen Zeitgeschichtsschreibung.* [In]: Die Zeit, Nr. 29, Hamburg, 11. Juli 1986. P. 40. [Review article of: Andreas Hillgruber: Zweierlei Untergang, see No. 23290. See also ensuing discussion [in]: *Die Zeit:* 'Geschichte ist auch eine Frage von Marktlücken': Streit um die Einmaligkeit der Hitlerschen Greuel (Leserbriefe, incl.: Ernst Nolte) [in]: Nr. 32, 1. Aug. 1986, p. 12. Die elende Praxis der Untersteller: das Einmalige der nationalsozialistischen Verbrechen lässt sich nicht leugnen (Eberhard Jäckel) [in]: Nr. 38, 12. Sept. 1986, p. 3. Wird die deutsche Geschichte umgeschrieben? Waren die NS-Verbrechen einmalig? (Hagen Schulze) [in]: Nr. 40, 26. Sept. 1986, p. 7. Wo sich die Geister scheiden (Martin Broszat) [in]: Nr. 41, 3. Okt. 1986, p. 12. Unter der Herrschaft des Verdachts (Thomas Nipperdey) [&]: Sinnstifter unter sich (Gerhard Spörl) [in]: Nr. 43, 17. Okt. 1986, p. 12. Die Sache auf den Kopf gestellt: gegen den negativen Nationalismus in der Geschichtsbetrachtung (Ernst Nolte) [in]: Nr. 45, 31. Okt. 1986, pp. 9–10. Vom öffentlichen Gebrauch der Historie (Jürgen Habermas) [in]: Nr. 46, 7. Nov. 1986, pp. 12–13. Leserbriefe [in]: Nr. 49, 28. Nov. 1986, pp. 38–39.]

23299. — HILLGRUBER, ANDREAS: *Jürgen Habermas, Karl Heinz Janssen und die Aufklärung Anno 1986.* [In]: Geschichte in Wissenschaft und Unterricht, Jg. 37, H. 12, Seelze, Dez. 1986. Pp. 725–738, notes. [Response to the article by J. Habermas, see preceding entry.]

23300. — HOFER, WALTHER: *Fifty years on: historians and the Third Reich.* [In]: Journal of Contemporary History, Vol. 21, No. 2, London, Apr. 1986. Pp. 225–251, notes.

23301. — KULKA, OTTO D.: *Die deutsche Geschichtsschreibung über den Nationalsozialismus und die 'Endlösung': Tendenzen und Entwicklungsphasen 1924–1984.* [In]: Historische Zeitschrift, Bd. 240, München, Juni 1985. Pp. 599–640. [Transl. of No. 22171/YB XXXI.]

23302. — LORECK, JOCHEN: *Kontroverse Darstellungen über das 'Wirken' Hitlers: die Entsorgung der Vergangenheit.* [In]: Vorwärts, Bonn, 9. Aug. 1986.

23303. — MALANOWSKI, WOLFGANG: *'Vergangenheit, die nicht vergehen will': über A. Hillgrubers Buch 'Zweierlei Untergang'.* [In]: Der Spiegel, Jg. 40, Nr. 36, Hamburg, 1. Sept. 1986. Pp. 66–67 & 70. [See also [in]: *Der Spiegel,* Jg. 40: Die neue Auschwitz-Lüge (Rudolf Augstein) [in]: Nr. 41, 6. Okt. 1986, pp. 62–63. Auschwitz, 'asiatische Tat' (Imanuel Geiss) [in]: Nr. 43, 20. Okt. 1986, p. 10.]

23304. — MEIER, REINHARD: *Deutsche 'Revisionismus'-Kontroverse: NS-Vergangenheit und nationales Selbstverständnis.* [And]: CATTANI, ALFRED: *Die Last des Bösen.* [In]: NZZ, Nr. 222, Zürich, 25. Sept. 1986, p. 5. [See also: Suchbild der Vergangenheit (Hanno Helbling) [in]: NZZ, Nr. 224, Zürich, 27./28. Sept. 1986, p. 65.]

23305. — MOMMSEN, HANS: *Suche nach der 'verlorenen Geschichte'? Bemerkungen zum historischen Selbstverständnis der Bundesrepublik.* [In]: Merkur, Jg. 40, H. 9/10 (451/452), Stuttgart, Sept./Okt. 1986. Pp. 864–874.

23306. — NOLTE, ERNST: *Between myth and revisionism: the Third Reich in the perspective of the 1980s.* [In]: Aspects of the Third Reich, ed. by Hans W. Koch. London: Macmillan, 1985. Pp. 17–38. [See also review of this book with special reference to Nolte's article (Klaus Hildebrand) [in]: Historische Zeitschrift, Bd. 242, München, 1986.]

23307. — NOLTE, ERNST: *Vergangenheit, die nicht vergehen will.* [In]: Frankfurter Allgemeine Zeitung, 6. Juni 1986. [See also [in]: *Frankfurter Allgemeine Zeitung*: Aufklärung? Habermas und die Geschichte (Frank Schirrmacher) [in]: 11. Juli 1986. Das Zeitalter der Tyrannen (Klaus Hildebrand) [in]: 31. Juli 1986. Erläuternder Leserbrief (Jürgen Habermas) [in]: 11. Aug. 1986. Leserbriefe (Michael Stürmer et al.) [in]: 16. Aug. 1986. Die geschuldete Erinnerung: zur Kontroverse über die Unvergleichlichkeit der nationalsozialistischen Massenverbrechen (Joachim Fest) [in]: Nr. 199, 29. Aug. 1986, pp. 23–24. Verschwiegene Zeitgeschichte; Leitartikel (Johann Georg Reissmüller) [in]: 14. Nov. 1986. Leserbriefe (Richard Löwenthal/Andreas Hillgruber) [in]: Nr. 277, 29. Nov. 1986, p. 11. Leserbriefe [in]: 24. Jan. 1987, p. 7.]

23308. — OPPENHEIMER, FRANZ: *Vorsicht vor falschen Schlüssen aus der deutschen Vergangenheit: die Verführung einer kollektiven Schuldbesessenheit.* [In]: Frankfurter Allgemeine Zeitung, Nr. 110,

Frankfurt am Main, 14. Mai 1986. Pp. 10–11. [F.O., a lawyer in Washington, publ. this article previously in English under the title 'Treacherous signposts' [in]: The American Spectator, Nov. 1985. See also: Leserbrief (Michael Stürmer) [in]: Süddeutsche Zeitung, München, 25. Juni 1986.]

23309. HITLER, ADOLF. JÄCKEL, EBERHARD: *Hitlers Herrschaft: Vollzug einer Weltanschauung.* Stuttgart: Deutsche Verlags-Anstalt, 1986. 183 pp. [Incl. chap.: Weg zum Mord an den Juden. For preceding vol. see following entry.]

23310. — JÄCKEL, EBERHARD: *Hitlers Weltanschauung: Entwurf einer Herrschaft.* Erweiterte und überarb. Neuausg., 3. Aufl. Stuttgart: Deutsche Verlags-Anstalt, 1986. 175 pp. [First ed. 1969, see No. 7731/YB XV. Incl. chap. referring to Jews.]

23311. — SPIELVOGEL, JACKSON/REDLES, DAVID: *Hitler's racial ideology: content and occult sources.* [In]: Simon Wiesenthal Center Annual, Vol. 3, White Plains, N.Y., 1986. Pp. 227–246.

23312. — WIPPERMANN, WOLFGANG, ed.: *Kontroversen um Hitler.* Frankfurt am Main: Suhrkamp, 1986. 305 pp., notes, bibl. (299–301). (Suhrkamp-Taschenbuch Wissenschaft, 639.) [Incl.: Forschungsgeschichte und Forschungsprobleme (W. Wippermann, 13–116). Die 'Endlösung' und das deutsche Ostimperium als Kernstück des rassenideologischen Programms des Nationalsozialismus (Andreas Hillgruber, 219–247). Die Realisierung des Utopischen: die 'Endlösung der Judenfrage' im 'Dritten Reich' (Hans Mommsen, 248–298).]

23313. — WISTRICH, ROBERT: *Genesis of Nazism? Hitler's Vienna years.* [In]: Religion, ideology and nationalism in Europe and America. Jerusalem: The Historical Society of Israel and The Zalman Shazar Center for Jewish History, 1986. Pp. 107–117, footnotes.

—— HOLOCAUST. [See also Nos. 23191, 23193–23195, 23199.]

23314. — LANZMANN, CLAUDE: *Shoa.* Mit einem Vorwort von Simone de Beauvoir. Deutsch von Nina Börnsen und Anna Kamp. (Enthält zusätzlich ein Interview mit Claude Lanzmann von Heike Hurst.) Düsseldorf: Claassen, 1986. 279 pp. [Transl. of No. 22148/YB XXXI.]

23315. — LIPSON, ALFRED: *The myth of Wehrmacht 'innocence' in the Holocaust.* [In]: Jewish Frontier, Vol. 53, No. 2, New York, Feb./March 1986. Pp. 12–15.

23316. — MILTON, SYBIL: *Images of the Holocaust.* Pt. 1. [In]: Holocaust and Genocide Studies, Vol. 1, No. 1, Oxford, 1986. Pp. 27–61, illus., notes (55–61). [On the historical evidence of photographs taken during the Nazi period; incl. illus. of Jews in Germany 1933–1939.]

23317. HOLOCAUST REACTION. COHEN, MICHAEL J.: *Churchill and the Jews: the Holocaust.* [In]: Modern Judaism, Vol. 6, No. 1, Baltimore, Febr. 1986. Pp. 27–49, postscript, notes.

23318. — LAQUEUR, WALTER/BREITMAN, RICHARD: *Breaking the silence.* New York: Simon & Schuster, 1986. 320 pp., notes. [Also German edn. under the title]: *Der Mann, der das Schweigen brach; wie die Welt vom Holocaust erfuhr.* (Ins Deutsche übertragen von Erwin Duncker.) Frankfurt am Main: Ullstein, 1986. 304 pp., illus. [Story of the German industrialist Eduard Schulte who was the first to inform the West about the 'Final Solution'.]

23319. — LIPSTADT, DEBORAH E.: *Beyond belief; the American press and the coming of the Holocaust, 1933–1945.* New York: The Free Press, 1986. 370 pp., notes. [Incl. press coverage of the Nazi seizure of power, passage of the Nuremberg Laws, Berlin Olympics, November Pogrom, Final Solution.]

23320. — PAUCKER, ARNOLD: *Die Haltung Englands und der USA zur Vernichtung der europäischen Juden im Zweiten Weltkrieg.* [In]: Büttner, Ursula, ed.: Das Unrechtsregime. Bd. 2. Hamburg: Christians, 1986. Pp. 149–162, notes.

23321. — WILHELM, HANS-HEINRICH: *The Holocaust in National-Socialist rhetoric and writings – some evidence against the thesis that before 1945 nothing was known about the 'Final Solution'.* [In]: Yad Vashem Studies, 16, Jerusalem, 1984. Pp. 95–127.

23322. HUNGARY. DON, YEHUDA: *The economic effect of antisemitic discrimination: Hungarian anti-Jewish legislation 1938–1944.* [In]: Jewish Social Studies, Vol. 48, No. 2, New York, Spring, 1986. Pp. 63–82, notes, tabs.

23323. — GROSSMAN, ALEXANDER: *Nur das Gewissen: Carl Lutz und seine Budapester Aktion.* Geschichte und Porträt. Wald (Zürich): Verlag Im Waldgut, 1986. 284 pp., illus., bibl. (231–237). [Carl Lutz, 1895–1975, Swiss Consul, from 1942 in Budapest, used his position in 1944–45 to prevent Jews from being deported, thus saving about 8,000 lives.]

23324. — KATZBURG, NATHANIEL: *Zionist reactions to Hungarian anti-Jewish legislation 1939–1942.* [And]: EREZ, ZVI: *The Jews of Budapest and the plans of Admiral Horthy, August–October 1944.* [In]: Yad Vashem Studies, 16, Jerusalem, 1984. Pp. 151–176; 177–203. [See also in same vol.: 'The politics of genocide: the Holocaust in Hungary' – notes on Randolph L. Braham's book, New York, 1981 (Bela Vago, pp. 437–443.]

23325. INTELLECTUALS. FUNKE, MANFRED: *Universität und Zeitgeist im Dritten Reich; eine Betrachtung zum politischen Verhalten von Gelehrten.* [And]: BRÄMER, RAINER: *Heimliche Komplizen? Zur Rolle der Naturwissenschaften im Dritten Reich.* [In]: Aus Politik und Zeitgeschichte; Beilage zur Wochenzeitung Das Parlament, B 12, Bonn, 22. März 1986. Pp. 3–14; 15–30, footnotes. [Both articles also cover antisemitism at German universities and the attitude of German professors towards their Jewish colleagues.]

23326. — HEIM, SUSANNE/ALY, GÖTZ: *Ein Berater der Macht: Helmut Meinhold; oder der Zusammenhang zwischen Sozialpolitik und Judenvernichtung.* Eine Arbeit aus dem Projekt 'Täterbiographien im Nationalsozialismus' des Hamburger Instituts für Sozialforschung. Hamburg (Laufgraben 37): Hamburger Institut für Sozialforschung, 1986. 72 pp., illus., ports., facsims., maps, notes. [Professor Dr. Helmut Meinhold, born 1914, involved in the persecution of the Jews in the 'Generalgouvernement', after 1945 Chief of the 'Sozialbeirat' of the Federal German Republic and member of the 'Institut für Weltwirtschaft' in Kiel.]

23327. — KLEE, ERNST: *Was sie taten – was sie wurden: Ärzte, Juristen und andere Beteiligte am Kranken- oder Judenmord.* Orig.-Ausg. Frankfurt am Main: Fischer, 1986. 355 pp., illus. (Fischer-Taschenbücher, 4364.)

23328. — KUDLIEN, FRIDOLF: *Werner Leibbrand als Zeitzeuge: ein ärztlicher Gegner des Nationalsozialismus im Dritten Reich.* [In]: Medizinhistorisches Journal, Bd. 21, H. 3/4, Stuttgart; New York, 1986. Pp. 332–352, footnotes. [W. Leibbrand, 1896–1974, psychiatrist in Berlin, married to a Jewess and friend of Jews: on life in Berlin during the Nazi period, persecution of the Jews, personal resistance.]

23329. — LIFTON, ROBERT JAY: *The Nazi doctors; a study of the psychology of evil.* London: Macmillan, 1986. 576 pp. [Also American edn. under the title]: *The Nazi doctors; medical killing and the psychology of genocide.* New York: Basic Books, 1986. 561 pp. [Cf.: Healers as killers (Daniel J. Goldhagen) [in]: Commentary, Vol. 82, No. 6, New York, Dec. 1986, pp. 77–80. The wound that will not heal (Alex Comfort) [in]: The Guardian, London, Nov. 14, 1986. The death doctors (Neal Ascherson) [in]: The New York Review of Books, May 28, 1987, pp. 29–34. Their speciality was murder (Bruno Bettelheim) [in]: New York Times Book Review, Oct. 5, 1986.]

23330. — RABOFSKY, EDUARD/OBERKOFLER, GERHARD: *Verborgene Wurzeln der NS-Justiz; strafrechtliche Rüstung für zwei Weltkriege.* Wien: Europa-Verl., 1985. 261 pp., illus. [On Wenzeslaus Graf Gleispach and the role he played in Nazi jurisdiction: born in Austria, from 1904 professor for criminal law, antisemite and anti-marxist, from Nov. 1933 professor in Berlin, died shortly before the end of the Second World War.]

23331. JOHE, WERNER: *Das deutsche Volk und das System der Konzentrationslager.* [In]: Büttner, Ursula, ed.: Das Unrechtsregime, Bd. 1. Hamburg: Christians, 1986. Pp. 331–346, notes.

—— *Die Juden im Nationalsozialistischen Deutschland = The Jews in Nazi Germany 1933–1943.* Hrsg. von Arnold Paucker mit Sylvia Gilchrist und Barbara Suchy. [See No. 22913.]

23332. KAPLAN, MARION: *Der Alltag jüdischer Frauen im NS-Deutschland.* (Übers. von Renate Steinchen.) [In]: Journal für Geschichte, Nr. 1, Weinheim, 1986. Pp. 50–58, illus., bibl. (58).

23333. KASSEL. KLEINERT, BEATE/PRINZ, WOLFGANG, eds.: *Namen und Schicksale der Juden Kassels, 1933–1945.* Ein Gedenkbuch. Mit einem Nachwort von Wolfgang Prinz. Kassel: Magistrat der Stadt – Stadtarchiv, 1986. 248 pp., ports., facsim.

23334. KATER, MICHAEL H.: *Everyday anti-Semitism in prewar Nazi Germany.* [In]: Yad Vashem Studies, 16, Jerusalem, 1984. Pp. 129–159.

23335. KATZ, STEVEN T.: *Hitler's 'Jew'; on microbes and Manichaeism.* [In]: Proceedings of the 9th World Congress of Jewish Studies, Division B, Vol. 3: The history of the Jewish people. Jerusalem, 1986. Pp. 165–172.

23336. KERSHAW, IAN: *German popular opinion and the 'Jewish Question', 1939–1943: some further reflections.* [In]: Die Juden im Nationalsozialistischen Deutschland [see No. 22913]. Tübingen: Mohr, 1986. Pp. 365–386, summary in German, footnotes.

23337. KOBLENZ. HILDA-SCHULE. *150 Jahre Hilda-Schule Koblenz, 1835–1985.* Bilder aus einer Schule in Erinnerungen und Berichten von Schülern und Lehrern des Hilda-Gymnasiums. Koblenz: Druck W. Perz, 1985. 166 pp., facsims. [Incl.: Jüdische Lehrer und Schüler der Hildaschule und ihre Schicksale im Dritten Reich (55–78).]

—— KÖNIGSWINTER. [See No. 23035.]

—— KONSTANZ. [See No. 23036.]

23338. Koonz, Claudia: *Courage and choice among German-Jewish women and men.* [In]: Die Juden im Nationalsozialistischen Deutschland [see No. 22913]. Tübingen: Mohr, 1986. Pp. 283–293, summary in German, footnotes.

23339. Koonz, Claudia: *Mothers in the fatherland: women, family life and Nazi ideology 1919–1945.* New York: St. Martin's Press, 1986. 640 pp. [Refers also to Jewish women under the Nazis and incl. material on Nazi antisemitism.]

23340. LEIPZIG. Lange, Bernd-Lutz: *Juden in Leipzig.* [In]: Leipziger Blätter, 9, Leipzig, Herbst 1986. Pp. 50–57, illus., ports. [Refers to the Nazi period.]

23341. LEMGO. Raveh, Karla, née Frenkel: *Überleben: der Leidensweg der jüdischen Familie Frenkel aus Lemgo.* Nebst Aufzeichnungen von Helene Rosenberg. Lembo: Archiv- und Museumsamt, 1986. VI, 119 pp., illus., ports., plan. (Forum Lemgo; Schriften zur Stadtgeschichte, H. 1.) [Incl.: Meine Erinnerungen an die letzten Tage in Deutschland 1942 und an die schrecklichen Jahre in Theresienstadt (Helene Rosenberg).]

23342. Lennert, Rudolf: *Zugehörigkeit, Selbstbewusstsein, Fremdheit: Erinnerung an eine dunkle Zeit.* [In]: Neue Sammlung, Jg. 26, H. 3, Stuttgart, Juli-Sept. 1986. Pp. 381–395. [Recollections of the Nazi period by a 'Mischling'.]

23343. LIECHTENSTEIN. Walk, Joseph: *Liechtenstein 1933–1945: Nationalsozialismus im Mikrokosmos.* [In]: Büttner, Ursula, ed.: Das Unrechtsregime, Bd. 1. Hamburg: Christians, 1986. Pp. 376–426, notes. [Also publ. in Hebrew in]: Proceedings of the 9th World Congress of Jewish Studies, Division B, Vol. 2: The history of the Jewish people. Jerusalem, 1986. Pp. 173–180.

23344. LINDAU. Schweizer, Karl: *Der NS-Faschismus in Lindau.* 2., überarb. und erweiterte Aufl. Lindau (Rickenbacherstr. 125): K. Schweizer, 1983. 30 pp., illus. [Also on the persecution of the Jews in Lindau.]

—— LOWER SAXONY. [See vols. 2 & 3 in No. 23287.]

23345. LÜBECK. *Nationalsozialismus in Lübeck 1933 bis 1945.* Eine Dokumentation zur Austellung im Lübecker St.-Annen-Museum vom 30. Jan. bis zum 4. Apr. 1983. Lübeck: Museum für Kunst und Kulturgeschichte, 1985. 132 pp., illus., diagrs. bibl. (Forschungen und Dokumentationen zur Stadtgeschichte, 1.) [Incl.: Die Zerschlagung der jüdischen Gemeinde (108–115).]

23346. Lühe, Barbara von der: *Aufbau im Untergang: das Leben der Juden in Deutschland nach 1933. [1–2].* [In]: Tribüne, Jg. 24, H. 95 (pp. 136–145, footnotes) [&]: Jg. 25, H. 97 (pp. 155–164, footnotes). Frankfurt am Main, 1985–1986.

23347. Malek-Kohler, Ingeborg: *Im Windschatten des Dritten Reiches; Begegnungen mit Filmkünstlern und Widerstandskämpfern.* Vorwort von Theodor Eschenburg. Orig.-Ausg. Freiburg i. Br.: Herder, 1986. 253 pp. (Herderbücherei, Bd. 1288.) [I.M.-K., born 1916 in Berlin, offspring of a mixed marriage, married to a German film-producer, reports on her experiences during the Nazi period in Berlin.]

23348. Maltzan, Maria, Gräfin von: *Schlage die Trommel und fürchte dich nicht.* Frankfurt am Main: Ullstein, 1986. 272 pp. [The author, veterinarian in Berlin, helped Jews during the Nazi period, saved the life of her Jewish friend by hiding him until the end of the war. See also: Prisoner of love: 'Forbidden', a film about a Prussian aristocrat who saved many Jews, opens in London on Feb. 28; a talk with the real countess in her Berlin flat (Janet Watts) [in]: The Observer, London, Feb. 16, 1986, pp. 51 & 48, ports.]

23349. Marchand, Carlotta: *Wie durch ein Nadelöhr; Erinnerungen einer jüdischen Frau.* (Aus dem Niederländ. von C. Marchand und Dorothea Ense.) Berlin: Sub-Rosa-Frauen-Verl., 1985. 150 pp., illus. [On antisemitism in the Netherlands after 1933 where the German-Jewish author grew up; her parents and her sister were deported while she, married to a Dutchman and living underground, survived.]

23350. Maurer, Trude: *Ausländische Juden in Deutschland, 1933–1939.* [In]: Die Juden im Nationalsozialistischen Deutschland [see No. 22913]. Tübingen: Mohr, 1986. Pp. 189–210, summary in English, footnotes. [Incl. East European Jews.]

23351. Milton, Sybil: *The observer: self-interest, voyeurism, and conformity, 1933–1945.* [In]: Dimensions; a journal of Holocaust studies, Vol. 2, No. 2, New York, Spring 1986. Pp. 4–9, illus., bibl. (8–9). [On Germans witnessing the persecution of the Jews.]

23352. MINDEN. Nordsiek, Marianne: *Fackelzüge überall . . . ; das Jahr 1933 in den Kreisen Minden und Lübbecke.* (Publiziert anlässlich der [gleichnamigen] Ausstellung des Kommunalarchivs Minden und des Mindener Museums.) Bielefeld: Westfalen-Verl., 1983. 128 pp., illus., map. [Incl.: Antijüdische Aktionen (pp. 83–85).]

23353. — Rüter, Karin Kristin/Hampel, Christian: *Die Judenpolitik in Deutschland 1933–1945 unter besonderer Berücksichtigung von Einzelschicksalen jüdischer Bürger der Gemeinden Minden, Petershagen und Lübbecke.* Minden: Gesellschaft für Christlich-Jüdische Zusammenarbeit, 1986. 223 pp., illus., bibl. (105–110). [Incl. hitherto unpubl. texts and illus.]

23354. MÜHLHEIM. Mirkes, Adolf/Schild, Karl/Schneider, Hans C.: *Mühlheim unter den Nazis, 1933–1945.* Ein Lesebuch. Frankfurt am Main: Röderberg, 1983. 160 pp., illus., bibl. (153–155). [Incl.: Die Juden (110–119).]

23355. NEUENGAMME. *Arbeit und Vernichtung: das Konzentrationslager Neuengamme 1938–1945.* Katalog zur ständigen Austellung im Dokumentenhaus der KZ-Gedenkstätte Neuengamme, Aussenstelle des Museums für Hamburgische Geschichte. (Hrsg. von Ulrich Bauche [et al.]. Hamburg: VSA-Verl., 1986. 259 pp., illus., bibl. (254–257). [Also on Jewish inmates and the murder of Jewish children at Bullenhuser Damm.]

23356. — Richter, Axel: *Das Unterkommando Vechelde des Konzentrationslagers Neuengamme; zum Einsatz von KZ-Häftlingen in der Rüstungsproduktion.* (Hrsg. von der Gemeinde Vechelde.) Vechelde: Druckerei Sander, Nov. 1985. 126 pp., illus., bibl. (71–78). [Incl.: Der Judentransport aus Auschwitz (p. 38); also refers to Jewish inmates of Neuengamme.]

—— NEUSS. [See No. 23049.]

23357. NIENBORG. Nacke, Aloys: *Nach 40 Jahren – Gedenken an jüdische Mitbürger [aus Nienborg].* [In]: Unsere Heimat; Jahrbuch des Kreises Borken, 1985. Pp. 110–112, illus., ports., facsim. [On the persecution during the Nazi period.]

23358. Noakes, Jeremy: *Wohin gehören die 'Judenmischlinge'? Die Entstehung der ersten Durchführungsverordnungen zu den Nürnberger Gesetzen.* [In]: Büttner, Ursula, ed.: Das Unrechtsregime, Bd. 2. Hamburg: Christians, 1986. Pp. 69–90, notes.

23359. NOVEMBER POGROM. Aronsfeld, C. C.: *The November 1938 pogrom: remarkable reactions inside Nazi Germany.* [In]: AJR Information, No. 11, London, Nov. 1986. P. 2 [&]: Letter to the Editor (Peter Prager) [in]: AJR Information, No. 1, London, Jan. 1987, p. 13. [See also Von 'Volkszorn' konnte damals keine Rede sein: Lehren des 9. Nov. 1938 (Niels Hansen) [in]: Frankfurter Allgemeine Zeitung, Nr. 279, 2. Dez. 1986, pp. 10–11.]

23360. — Schultheis, Herbert, ed.: *Die Reichskristallnacht in Deutschland nach Augenzeugenberichten.* Bad Neustadt a.d. Saale: Rötter, 1986. XXVIII, 405 pp., illus., notes (349–402). (Bad Neustädter Beiträge zue Geschichte und Heimatkunde Frankens, Bd. 3.)

23361. OLDENBURG. Heuzeroth, Günter/Wille, Sylvia: *Gelber Stern in brauner Zeit; Verfolgung und Vernichtung der jüdischen Mitbürger im Oldenburger Land, in Ostfriesland und der Stadt Bremen.* [In]: Unter der Gewaltherrschaft des Nationalsozialismus 1933–1945, dargestellt an den Ereignissen im Oldenburger Land. Bd. 2: Verfolgte aus rassischen Gründen. Oldenburg: Univ. Oldenburg, Zentrum für Pädagogische Berufspraxis, 1985. Pp. 17–226, illus., notes (213–217), bibl. (218–220). [Incl.: Ehemalige Synagogengemeinden im Weser-Ems-Gebiet: ein Überblick (120–183). Übersicht über die ungefähre Zahl der Opfer in den Synagogengemeinden im Weser-Ems-Gebiet (184–189).]

—— OLYMPICS. Bernett, Hajo: *Die jüdische Turn- und Sportbewegung.* [See No. 23610.]

23362. — Hart-Davis, Duff: *Hitler's games: the 1936 Olympics.* New York: Harper & Row, 1986. 256 pp., illus. [Deals, a.o., with the few Jewish or half-Jewish participants; also refers to anti-Jewish measures in sports by the Nazis.]

23363. — Ueberhorst, Horst: *Spiele unterm Hakenkreuz; die Olympischen Spiele von Garmisch-Partenkirchen und Berlin 1936 und ihre politischen Implikationen.* [In]: Aus Politik und Zeitgeschichte; Beilage zur Wochenzeitung Das Parlament, B 31, Bonn, 2. Aug. 1986. Pp. 3–15, footnotes. [Also on the question of the admission of German Jews to the Games.]

23364. — Wiener Library, London: *The 1936 Olympic Games in Hitler's Germany.* A Leonard Montefiore Memorial Exhibition, 10th June to 8th July 1986. Producer: P. Yogi Mayer. Ed.: Tony Wells. Assisted by Nana Wiessler. London: Wiener Library, 1986. 1 folded sheet, port., bibl. [Exhibition provides the background to the 1936 games and deals with the question of Jewish involvement. Cf.: Ausstellung und Buch [von Hart-Davis] zur Olympiade 1936 (William Stern) [in]: Aufbau, Nr. 33–34, New York, Aug. 15, 1986, pp. 24–25.]

23365. Rebentisch, Dieter/Teppe, Karl, eds.: *Verwaltung contra Menschenführung im Staat Hitler.* Studien zum politisch-administrativen System. Göttingen: Vandenhoeck & Ruprecht, 1986. 434 pp. [Incl. contribution by G. Kratzsch referring to 'Entjudung der Wirtschaft'.]

23366. REFUGEE POLICY. Boas, Jacob: *Boulevard des misères: the story of transit camp Westerbork.* Hamden, Conn.: Archon Books, 1985. XI, 169 pp., illus., bibl. (161–165).

23367. — *Deutschsprachiges Exil in Dänemark nach 1933.* Zu Methoden und Einzelergebnissen. Vorträge des Kolloquiums am 1. und 2. Okt. 1984. Hrsg. von Ruth Dinesen [et al.]. München: Fink, 1986. 215 pp., illus. (Kopenhagener Kolloquien zur Deutschen Literatur, Bd. 12.) (Text & Kontext: Sonderreihe, Bd. 21.) [Incl.: Auf dem Weg von Deutschland nach Palästina: jüdische Kinder und Jugendliche in Dänemark 1930–1945 (Jorgen Haestrup, 57–72; see also the author's book, No. 22192/YB XXXI). Die dänische Flüchtlingspolitik 1933–1941 (Hans Uwe Petersen, 73–94). Karin Michaelis – Porträt einer Helferin deutscher Emigranten (Birgit S. Nielsen, 153–177). See also No. 23670.]

—— — DÖBLIN, ALFRED: *Schicksalsreise.* [See No. 23685.]

23368. — *Exil in Schweden.* Ausstellung in der Akademie der Künste, Berlin, 9. Nov. 1986–4. Jan. 1987. (Gestaltung: Lorenz Dombois. Konzeption und Katalog: Lothar Schirmer.) Berlin: Akademie der Künste, 1986. 83 pp., illus. [Incl. introductory essay: Exil in Schweden (Helmut Müssener; covers Swedish refugee policy and reports on Jewish intellectuals who found refuge in Sweden).] [See also: Asyl in Schweden (Helmut Müssener) pp. 24–38 in No. 23831.]

23369. — FOSTER, JOHN, ed.: *Community of fate.* London; Winchester, Ma.: Allen & Unwin, 1986. 174 pp., illus., notes [Experiences of fourteen Jewish refugees from Nazi Germany who arrived in Melbourne, Australia, between 1938 and 1949.]

23370. — FRY, VARIAN: *Auslieferung auf Verlangen; die Rettung deutscher Emigranten in Marseille 1940/41.* Hrsg. und mit einem Anhang versehen von Wolfgang D. Elfe und Jan Hans. (Aus dem Amerikan. von Jan Hans und Anja Lazarowicz.) München: Hanser, 1986. 345 pp., [Orig. edn.: 'Surrender on demand', New York, 1945. The 'Emergency Rescue Committee', founded in New York in summer 1940, sent V. Fry to Marseilles where he established the 'Centre Américain de Secours' to help refugees to escape to freedom. Book refers, a.o., to Rudolf Breitscheid and Rudolf Hilferding and their refusal to leave France illegally.] [V. Fry, 1907–1967, worked in Marseilles from 1940 to 1942 when he was forced to leave Vichy-France.]

—— — KAUFFMANN, FRITZ: *Die Juden in Shanghai im 2. Weltkrieg.*[See No. 23137.]

23371. — KLARSFELD, SERGE: *Vichy – Auschwitz: le rôle de Vichy dans la solution finale de la question juive en France, 1943–1944.* Paris: Fayard, 1985. 409 pp., illus., appendices, bibl. [Refers also to the fate of German-Jewish refugees. For preceding vol. see No. 21150/YB XXX.]

23372. — KÖPKE, WULF: *Die Flucht durch Frankreich.* Die zweite Erfahrung der Heimatlosigkeit in Berichten der Emigranten aus dem Jahre 1940. [In]: Exilforschung, Bd. 4, München, 1986. Pp. 229–242.

23373. — KWIET, KONRAD: *Die Integration deutsch-jüdischer Emigranten in Australien.* [In]: Büttner, Ursula, ed.: Das Unrechtsregime, Bd. 2. Hamburg: Christians, 1986. Pp. 309–324, notes.

23374. — LEWIS, WARD B.: *Escape from the Third Reich: efforts of Kurt Pinthus to save Albert Ehrenstein and Alfred Wolfenstein.* [In]: German Life and Letters, New Ser., Vol. 39, No. 3, Oxford, Apr. 1986. Pp. 210–219, notes.

23375. — LOWENTHAL, ERNST G.: *Bloomsbury House: Flüchtlingshilfsarbeit in London 1939–1946.* Aus persönlichen Erinnerungen. [In]: Büttner, Ursula, ed.: Das Unrechtsregime, Bd. 2. Hamburg: Christians, 1986. Pp. 267–308, notes.

23376. — PFANNER, HELMUT F.: *Trapped in France: a case study of five German Jewish intellectuals* [In]: Simon Wiesenthal Center Annual, Vol. 3, White Plains, N.Y., 1986. Pp. 107–120.

23377. — POLLAK, ERNEST: *Departure to freedom curtailed; interned by the British.* From the original diary written on toilet paper during the internment in Canada in 1940. [N.p., n.d.]. 58 pp., illus., facsim. [Photoreproduction of typescript, available in the LBI New York.]

23378. — ROHWER, JÜRGEN: *Jüdische Flüchtlingsschiffe im Schwarzen Meer – 1934 bis 1944.* [In]: Büttner, Ursula, ed.: Das Unrechtsregime, Bd. 2. Hamburg: Christians, 1986. Pp. 197–248, notes.

23379. — SAHL, HANS: *Fluchtpunkt Marseille.* [In]: Die Zeit, Nr. 14, Hamburg, 28. März 1986. Pp. 61–64. [Incl. also: War ich je hier? Über Hans Sahl, einen deutschen Schriftsteller im Exil (Benedikt Erenz, p. 62).] [Reminiscences on Sahl's collaboration with Varian Fry (see No. 23370).]

—— — STRAUSS, HERBERT A.: *Asyl für Flüchtlinge der 30er Jahre.* [See pp. 11–21 in No. 23831.]

23380. — THALMANN, RITA R.: *Die Emigration aus Deutschland und die öffentliche Meinung Frankreichs 1933–1939.* [In]: Büttner, Ursula, ed.: Das Unrechtsregime, Bd. 2. Hamburg: Christians, 1986. Pp. 249–266, notes.

23381. — WYMAN, DAVID S.: *Das unerwünschte Volk; Amerika und die Vernichtung der europäischen Juden.*

Aus dem Amerikan. von Karl Heinz Siber. Ismaning bei München: Verlag Max Hueber, 1986. 586 pp. [Transl. of No. 21157/YB XXX; see also the companion volume 'Paper walls', No. 22204/YB XXXI. Cf.: Die USA und die NS-Vernichtungspolitik (Falk Piegel) [in]: Das Parlament, Nr. 12, Bonn, 21. März 1987, p. 14. Review (Patrick J. Heardon) [in]: Shofar, vol. 4, No. 1, West Lafayette, Ind., Purdue Univ., Fall 1985, pp. 63–65. Bitten um Hilfe überhört (Heiner Lichtenstein) [in]: Tribüne, Jg. 25, H. 99, Frankfurt am Main, 1986, pp. 205–208.]

—— RESISTANCE BY GERMANS. [See also Nos. 23199, 23414, 23417.]

23382. — DIPPER, CHRISTOF: *The German resistance and the Jews.* [In]: Yad Vashem Studies, 16, Jerusalem, 1984. Pp. 51–93. [For German orig. see No. 21159/YB XXX.]

23383. — MÜLLER, KLAUS-JÜRGEN, ed.: *Der deutsche Widerstand 1933–1945.* Paderborn: Schöningh, 1986. 267 pp. (UTB für Wissenschaft, 1398.) [Survey of German resistance from all angles, the various motives and aims.]

—— REXINGEN. [See No. 23060.]

23384. ROSENBERG, ALFRED. NOVA, FRITZ: *Alfred Rosenberg: Nazi theorist of the Holocaust.* New York: Hippocrene Books, 1986. XXI, 264 pp., bibl.

23385. RÜRUP, REINHARD: *Das Ende der Emanzipation: die antijüdische Politik in Deutschland von der 'Machtergreifung' bis zum Zweiten Weltkrieg.* [In]: Die Juden im Nationalsozialistischen Deutschland [see No. 22913]. Tübingen: Mohr, 1986. Pp. 97–114, summary in English, footnotes.

23386. RÜSTRINGEN. BÜSING, HARTMUT: *'. . . so viel' unnennbare Leiden erduldet' (Homer, Odyssee): zur Geschichte der Rüstringer und Wilhelmshavener Juden.* Wilhelmshaven: Historischer Arbeitskreis des DGB, 1986. 154 pp., illus. (Reihe: Arbeiter- und Gewerkschaftsbewegung in Rüstringen und Wilhelmshaven, Bd. 2.)

23387. SAARBRÜCKEN. PAUL, GERHARD: *Die jüdische Volksschule in Saarbrücken (1934–1939).* [In]: Zeitschrift für die Geschichte der Saargegend, 33, Saarbrücken, 1985. Pp. 157–184, facsims., tab., footnotes.

—— SAFFIG. [See No. 23063.]

23388. SALOMON, CHARLOTTE. *Charlotte Salomon – Leben oder Theater? Das 'Lebensbild' einer jüdischen Malerin aus Berlin, 1917–1943.* Bilder und Spuren, Notizen, Gespräche, Dokumente. (Zur 'Charlotte-Salomon'-Ausstellung der Akademie der Künste Berlin und der Hochschule der Künste Berlin. Hrsg. von Christine Fischer-Defoy.) Berlin: Arsenal, 1986. 163 pp., illus. (Schriftenreihe der Akademie der Künste, Bd. 18.) [Incl. contributions on and documents of the Jüdischer Kulturbund, also an interview with the singer Paula Lindberg, Charlotte's mother.] [Ch.S., data see No. 18690/YB XXVII.]

—— SCHMALLENBERG. [See No. 23065.]

—— SCHWÄBISCH HALL. [See No. 23067.]

23389. SCHWEINFURT. *Widerstand und Verfolgung in Schweinfurt 1933–1945.* Ausstellungskatalog, hrsg. und eingeleitet von Karl Werner Hoppe. Schweinfurt (Postfach 4440): Volkshochschule Schweinfurt, K. W. Hoppe, 1986. 56 pp., illus. [Also on persecution of Jews.]

—— SELIGENSTADT. [See No. 23068.]

23390. SHIRER, WILLIAM L.: *Das Jahrzehnt des Unheils; meine Erlebnisse und Erfahrungen in Deutschland und Europa 1930–1940.* Deutsch von Karl A. Klewer. Bern: Scherz, 1986. 479 pp. [Transl. of No. 22212/YB XXXI. Incl. reports on persecution and references to German and Austrian Jews.]

—— SILESIA. [See No. 23236.]

23391. SIMON, ERNST. BÜHLER, MICHAEL: *Erziehung zur Tradition – Erziehung zum Widerstand; Ernst Simon und die jüdische Erwachsenenbildung in Deutschland.* Berlin (Leuchtenburgstr. 39): Institut Kirche und Judentum, 1986. 201 pp. (Studien zu jüdischem Volk und christlicher Gemeinde, Bd. 8.) [See also E. Simon's book: Aufbau im Untergang: jüdische Erwachsenenbildung im nationalsozialistischen Deutschland als geistiger Widerstand. Tübingen: Mohr, 1959. 109 pp. (Schriftenreihe wissenschaftlicher Abhandlungen des Leo Baeck Instituts, 2.).]

23392. *Simon Wiesenthal Center Annual.* Vol. 3. Eds.: Henry Friedlander and Sybil Milton. White Plains, N.Y.: Kraus Internat. Publ., 1986. 386 pp. [Incl. *articles:* Writers in extremis (Guy Stern, 87–106; on, a.o., Gertrud Kolmar, Alfred Wolfenstein). *Review essays:* Lanzmann's 'Shoah' and its audience (Ruth K. Angress, 249–260). What should American Jews have done to rescue their European brethren (Leonard Dinnerstein, 277–288). Popular culture on Nazi Germany (Robert S. Wistrich, 331–336). How America abandoned the Jews in

World War II (Stephen E. Ambrose, 337–342). Further articles pertinent to German Jewry are listed according to subject.]

—— Suchy, Barbara: *Vom 'Güldenen Opferpfennig' bis zur 'Judenvermögensabgabe'*. [See No. 22939.]

23393. SWITZERLAND. Bleich, Hermann: *Die Schweiz hatte zwei Gesichter: Erinnerungen an den 8. Mai 1945 – so war die Flüchtlingszeit.* [In]: Isr. Wochenblatt, Nr. 19, Zürich, 9. Mai 1986. Pp. 29 & 31–35.

—— — Grossman, Alexander: *Nur das Gewissen: Carl Lutz und seine Budapester Aktion.* [See No. 23323.]

23394. — Karlen, Rudolf, ed.: *Fluchtpunkte: Menschen im Exil.* Basil: Lenos-Verl., 1986. 347 pp., illus. [On refugees in Switzerland 1940–1986. Incl.: Wir haben euch nicht gerufen: Erfahrungen eines jüdischen Flüchtlings (Hermann Bleich,, 15–34). Heimatlos in einer gnadenlosen Zeit: Flüchtlingsbriefe, zusammengestellt von Hermann Kocher (48–67). Dreimal zurückgestellt: die Schweiz als einziger Ausweg (Edwin Maria Landau, 68–78).]

—— — Kocher, Hermann: *Schweizerischer Protestantismus und jüdische Flüchtlingsnot nach 1933.* [See pp. 28–40 in No. 23118.]

23395. TELGTE. Rüter, Gregor/Westhoff, Rainer: *Geschichte und Schicksal der Telgter Juden 1933–1945.* Beitrag zum Schülerwettbewerb 'Deutsche Geschichte um den Preis des Bundespräsidenten'. Telgte: Stadt Telgte, 1985. 112 pp., illus., diagrs.

23396. Thalmann, Rita R.: *Jüdische Frauen nach dem Pogrom 1938.* [In]: Die Juden im Nationalsozialistischen Deutschland [see No. 22913]. Tübingen: Mohr, 1986. Pp. 295–302, summary in English, footnotes.

23397. THERESIENSTADT. Kryl, Miroslav: *A significant source of information about prisoners' recitation and theatrical activities in the Terezin concentration camp-ghetto.* Karel Heřman's collection dating from the years 1942–1945. [In]: Judaica Bohemiae, Vol. 22, No. 2, Prague, 1986. Pp. 74–86, footnotes. [See also in same issue a description of the 'Terezin Collection' in the State Jewish Museum, Prague (Markéta Petrášová, 87–95, footnotes, illus.).]

23398. — Marx, Henry, ed.: *Im Angesicht des Todes: Gedichte aus Theresienstadt – erstmals im Original veröffentlicht.* [In]: Aufbau, Nr. 9–10, New York, Feb. 28, 1986. Pp. 8–9, illus.

23399. — Midgal, Ulrike, ed.: *Und die Musik spielt dazu; Chansons und Satiren aus dem KZ Theresienstadt.* Orig.-Ausg. München: Piper, 1986. 183 pp., bibl. (182–193). (Serie Piper, Bd. 451.)

23400. — *Music written at Terezin.* Prague: Panton, [1986?]. 1 record. (Order No. 8111 0509 G.) [Cont. music by the composers Pavel Haas, Gideon Klein, Hans Krása, Viktor Ullmann, all of whom perished in concentration camps. Cf.: Besprechung (Walter Labhart) [in]: NZZ, Nr. 19. Zürich, 24./25. Jan. 1987, p. 113.]

23401. Toury, Jacob: *Ein Auftakt zur 'Endlösung': Judenaustreibungen über nichtslawische Reichsgrenzen 1933–1939.* [In]: Büttner, Ursula, ed.: Das Unrechtsregime, Bd. 2. Hamburg: Christians, 1986. Pp. 164–196, notes.

23402. UNNA. *Erinnerung und Mahnung; Gedenken an die jüdischen Opfer nationalsozialistischer Gewaltherrschaft in Unna.* Dokumentation zur Gedenkfeier am 1. Dez. 1985. Unna: Stadtdirektor, Referat für Öffentlichkeitsarbeit, 1986. 48 pp., illus.

23403. Weinstein, Lewis H.: *The liberation of the death camps.* [In]: Midstream, Vol. 32, No. 4, New York, Apr. 1986. Pp. 20–24. [Personal account by a US Army colonel.]

23404. WEISSENBURG. Lowenstein, Steven M.: *The struggle for survival of rural Jews in Germany 1933–1938: the case of Bezirksamt Weissenburg, Mittelfranken.* [In]: Die Juden im Nationalsozialistischen Deutschland [see No. 22913]. Tübingen: Mohr, 1986. Pp. 115–124, summary in German, footnotes. [The Bezirk Weissenburg comprised the Jewish communities of Ellingen, Pappenheim, Treuchtlingen.]

—— WESTPHALIA. [See Nos. 23080, 23082.]

—— WILHELMSHAVEN. [See No. 23386.]

23405. WITTLICH. Plohmann, Wilfried: *Die kulturelle und wirtschaftliche Bedeutung der Juden in Wittlich von 1933 ('Machtergreifung') bis 1938 ('Reichskristallnacht').* Wittlich, 1983, Facharbeit für Sozialkunde. 80 pp. [Typewritten manuscript, available in the Kultur- und Tagungsstätte Synagoge Wittlich, Himmeroder Str. 44, D–5560 Wittlich.] [See also section D in No. 23084.]

23406. WÜRZBURG. Steidle, Hans: *Diskriminierung und Emigration: das Schicksal der Würzburger jüdischen Apothekerfamilie Nussbaum vor und während des Dritten Reiches.* [In]: Berichte des Historischen Vereins Bamberg, Bd. 120, Bamberg, Selbstverlag, 1984. Pp. 299–311.

23407. WUPPERTAL. *Juden in Wuppertal – Verfolgung und Deportation.* Dokumentarischer Film, ergänzt durch Interviews mit Verfolgten und Überlebenden. Buch und Regie: Susanne Obermayer und Hans-Werner Robke, Kamera: Gerd Neumann. Videotechnik: Dietmar Kampmann. Wuppertal (Oberbrünewalder Str. 25): Medienzentrum Wuppertal, 1986. [Cf.: Vom Bahnhof Steinbeck in den Tod (Kurt Schöring) [in]: 'Allgemeine', Nr. 41/22, Bonn, 30. Mai 1986, p. 12.]

23408. ZIONISM. ALLAN, JIM: *Perdition.* London 1986/87. [In connection with this controversial play (withdrawn from the Royal Court Theatre) on the supposed collaboration of Hungarian Zionists with the Nazis in the destruction of Hungarian Jewry, the British press from January to March 1987 dealt on many occasions with allegations of collaboration by the German Zionists and the German-Jewish leadership with the Nazi regime; in the play itself and in correspondence defending the play, material quoted out of context or distorted is used. The reader is referred to this controversy [in]: The Daily Telegraph, The Guardian, The Independent, The Jewish Chronicle, The London Evening Standard, The Observer, The Stage und Television Today, The Sunday Times, The Sunday Telegraph, Time Out, The Times, Times Literary Supplement, and other British newspapers. Collection of press cuttings available in the Institute of Jewish Affairs, London, and The Wiener Library, London.]

—— — LEWIS, BERNARD: *Semites and anti-Semites; an inquiry into conflict and prejudice.* [Incl. chap.: The Nazis and the Palestine question.] [See No. 23820.]

23409. — NICOSIA, FRANCIS R.: *Fritz Grobba and the Middle East policy of the Third Reich.* [In]: National and international politics in the Middle East; essays in honour of Elie Kedourie. Ed.: Edward Ingram. London: Cass, 1986. Pp. 206–228, notes (224–228). [Refers also to the Nazi Palestine policy. Fritz Grobba, born in 1886, German ambassador in Iraq 1932–1939.]

23410. — NICOSIA, FRANCIS R.: *The Third Reich and the Palestine Question.* London: Tauris, [1986]. XIV, 319 pp., appendixes (203–221), notes (223–282), index (303–319), bibl. (283–302). [Edn. for England of No. 22240/YB XXXI; for cont. see same number.]

23411. — ORLAND, NACHUM: *Der Faschismus in zionistischer Sicht.* Frankfurt am Main: Lang, 1986. 77 pp. (Europäische Hochschulschriften: Reihe 31, Bd. 87.)

B. **Jewish Resistance**

23412. FRANKFURTER, DAVID: *The first fighter against the Nazis. (The case of the assassination of the Nazi Gustloff).* [In Hebrew]. Transl. from the German manuscript by A. Dash. Introd.: Joseph Nedava. Tel-Aviv: Reshafim, 1984. 188 pp. [Frankfurter's account of the assassination: expanded version of F.'s book 'Revenge', publ. in Israel in Hebrew in 1948; the introd. (pp. 9–37) has been added now.] [D.F., 1909 Yugoslavia – 1982 Tel-Aviv, studied medicine in Germany and Switzerland, shot the leader of the Swiss branch of the Nazi party, Wilhelm Gustloff, on Feb. 4, 1936 in Davos.]

23413. — LUDWIG, EMIL/CHOTJEWITZ, PETER O.: *Der Mord in Davos. Texte zum Attentatsfall David Frankfurter/Wilhelm Gustloff.* Hrsg. von Helmut Kreuzer. Herbstein: März, 1986. 223 pp., bibl. [Cont.: 1. E. Ludwig's book, first publ. Amsterdam, Querido, 1936, banned in Switzerland at that time. 2. Contemporary texts and documents, compiled and with comments by P. O. Chotjewitz.]

23414. JAHNKE, KARL-HEINZ: *Jugend im Widerstand 1933–1945.* Neu bearb. und erweiterte Aufl. Frankfurt am Main: Röderberg, 1985. 248 pp., illus. [Collection of short biographies, refers to Jews and also to the Herbert-Baum-group (83–85). First edn. 1970, publ. under the title 'Entscheidungen', see No. 8575/YB XVI.]

—— *Die Juden im Nationalsozialistischen Deutschland = The Jews in Nazi Germany 1933–1943.* Hrsg. von Arnold Paucker mit Sylvia Gilchrist und Barbara Suchy. [See No. 22913.]

23415. KWIET, KONRAD/ESCHWEGE, HELMUT: *Selbstbehauptung und Widerstand; deutsche Juden im Kampf um Existenz und Menschenwürde 1933–1945.* 2. Aufl. Hamburg: Christians, 1986. 384 pp., tabs., notes, list of names, bibl. (352–375). (Hamburger Beiträge zur Sozial- und Zeitgeschichte, Bd. 19.) [For detailed entry and cont., see No. 21207/YB XXX.] *Selected reviews* [continuation of No. 22259/YB XXXI]: Besprechung (Klaus Drobisch) [in]: Deutsche Literaturzeitung, Bd. 107, H. 4, Berlin/East, Apr. 1986, cols. 340–342. Besprechung (Haim Seeligman) [in]: Jahrbuch des Instituts für Deutsche Geschichte, Bd.

15, Univ. Tel-Aviv, 1986, pp. 654–657. Besprechung (Kurt Pätzold) [in]: Zeitschrift für Geschichtswissenschaft, Jg. 34, H. 5, Berlin/East, 1986, pp. 452–453.

—— LASKA, VERA: *Nazism, resistance & Holocaust in World War II; a bibliography.* [See No. 23199.]

23416. LÖWENTHAL, RICHARD: *Die Widerstandsgruppe 'Neu Beginnen'.* Berlin: Gedenkstätte Deutscher Widerstand, 1985. 36 pp. (Beiträge zum Widerstand 1933–1945, 20.) [See also Nos. 22260–22261/YB XXXI.]

23417. *Widerstand und Exil 1933–1945.* Frankfurt am Main; New York: Campus, 1986. 302 pp. [Appeared also]: Bonn, 1985. (Schriftenreihe der Bundeszentrale für Politische Bildung, Bd. 223.) [Collection of essays orig. publ. in 'Tribüne', 1984, and listed according to subject in the bibliography of YB XXX; covers 'Resistance' and 'Exile' from various angles, including the Jewish aspects.]

IV. POST WAR

A. General

—— AUSTRIA. [See also Nos. 23134, 23428, 23824.]

23418. — *Das Jüdische Echo.* Vol. 35, Nr. 1. Hrsg.: Vereinigung Jüdischer Hochschüler Österreichs und Jüdischer Akademiker Österreichs. Wien (Gonzagagasse 22), Okt. 1986. 224 pp., illus., ports., facsims. [Deals largely with present-day antisemitism in Austria. Incl.: Fünfzig Jahre danach (Heinz Kienzl, 27–33). Daran will ich mich nicht gewöhnen! (Helene Maimann, 37–39). Österreichertum und Judentum: über die Möglichkeit und Unmöglichkeit einer Koexistenz (Eduard März, 63–68). Kann man die Vergangenheit 'bewältigen'? (Erika Weinzierl, 75–79). Wiedergutmachung in Österreich: eine erste Bilanz (Brigitte Galanda, 85–86). Kurt Waldheim und die Zeitgeschichte (Herbert Steiner, 87–90). Vergangenheitsbewältigung (Peter Pulzer, 114–117). Historiker angesichts der Vergangenheit: hilflos? (Peter Malina, 127–134, bibl.). Further contributions are listed according to subject.]

23419. — LÖFFLER, SIGRID: *'Was habe ich gewusst? – Nichts'. Künstler im Dritten Reich: Fragen nach der verdrängten Vergangenheit.* [In]: Theater heute, H. 1, Zürich, Jan. 1986. Pp. 2–5, 9–11, illus. [See also]: Als Jude für die Hörbigers (Leon Askin) [in]: Morgen, Jg. 10, Nr. 47, Wien, Juni 1986, pp. 132–134 (title taken from cover). [On actors who soon after 1945 'forgot' that they had taken part in Nazi films with anti-Jewish tendencies.]

23420. — *Schalom für Österreich: christliche-jüdische Begegnungen in Wien.* (Hrsg.: Katholische Aktion Österreichs.) Wien: Herold, 1986. 96 pp., illus.

23421. — *Verdrängte Schuld, verfehlte Sühne; Entnazifizierung in Österreich 1945–1955.* Symposion des Instituts für Wissenschaft und Kunst, Wien, März 1985. Hrsg. von Sebastian Meissl [et al.]. München: Oldenbourg, 1986. 365 pp. [Covers denazification from all angles, a.o., in economy, of the press, in publishing and book trade, at universities. Incl. essay by Brigitte Galanda on restitution practice in Austria (pp. 137–140).]

23422. BÜTTNER, URSULA: *Not mach der Befreiung: die Situation der deutschen Juden in der britischen Besatzungszone 1945–1948.* Hamburg (Grosse Bleichen 23): Landeszentrale für Politische Bildung, 1986. 86 pp., facsims., notes (32–40). [Reprinted from: Büttner, Ursula, ed.: Das Unrechtsregime, Bd. 2 [see No. 23231], pp. 373–406, augmented by facsim. documentation (pp. 41–82).]

23423. FEDERAL GERMAN REPUBLIC. *Allgemeine Jüdische Wochenzeitung.* Jg. 41, Nr. 20: *Sonderausgabe 40 Jahre.* Bonn: Verlag Jüd. Presse Gesellschaft, 16. Mai 1986. 1 issue. [Incl.: Es fing bereits im Lager an: zum Neubeginn jüdischen Lebens in Deutschland (Alexander Ginsburg, 1 & 4). Vom 'Gemeindeblatt' zur 'Allgemeinen': persönliche Erinnerungen (E. G. Lowenthal, 3–4). Anfangszeiten der Wiedergutmachung (Otto Küster, 9 & 11). Erinnerungen und Gedanken: eine Jugend in Deutschland nach 1945 (Daniel Krochmalnik, 11–12).]

23424. — CRAMER, ERNST: *Juden in Deutschland – 40 Jahre nach dem Holocaust.* (Ansprache vor der Israelisch-Deutschen Gesellschaft in Tel-Aviv, 20. Mai 1986.) [In]: deutschland-berichte, Jg. 22, Nr. 7/8, Bonn, Juli/Aug. 1986. Pp. 7–11.

23425. — GAY, RUTH: *What I learned about Germany's Jews.* [In]: The American Scholar, Washington, D.C., Phi Beta Kappa, Autumn 1985. Pp. 467–484.

23426. — HOMANN, URSULA: *Jüdische Kultur in deutschen Städten: Pflege jüdischer Traditionen ohne Juden.* [In]: Tribüne, Jg. 25, H. 100, Frankfurt am Main, 1986. Pp. 273–284.

23427. — *Jüdisches Leben in Deutschland seit 1945.* Hrsg. von Micha Brumlik, Doron Kiesel, Cilly Kugelmann, Julius H. Schoeps. Frankfurt am Main: Jüdischer Verlag bei Athenäum, 1986. 278 pp., diagrs., bibl. [Papers of a symposium, Arnoldshain 1986. Cont. (titles condensed): *Historische Entwicklung der jüdischen Gemeinschaft in Nachkriegsdeutschland* (11–118; with the papers): Juden in der Bundesrepublik Deutschland und in der Deutschen Demokratischen Republik seit 1945 (Monika Richarz, 13–30). Die Lager der jüdischen Displaced Persons (Wolfgang Jacobmeyer, 31–48). Staat und Ethnizität: Der Aufbau der jüdischen Gemeinden im Kalten Krieg (Y. Michal Bodemann, 49–69). NS-Prozesse (Heiner Lichtenstein, 70–87). Die deutsch-israelischen Beziehungen (Michael Wolffsohn, 88–107). Jüdische Interessenvertretung in der Bundesrepublik (Hans Jakob Ginsburg, 108–118). *Jüdische Identität – sozialpsychologische Aspekte* (119–194; with the papers): Die Reparationsverträge und die Folgen der 'Wiedergutmachung' (Hans Keilson, 121–139). Religiöse Richtungen und Entwicklungen in den Gemeinden (Pnina Navè Levinson, 140–171). Zur Identität der zweiten Generation deutscher Juden nach der Shoah in der Bundesrepublik (Micha Brumlik, 172–176). Zur Identität osteuropäischer Juden in der Bundesrepublik (Cilly Kugelmann, 177–181). Von der Pubertät zum Erwachsenendasein: Bericht einer Bewusstwerdung (Sammy Speier, 182–194). *Die politische Kultur der Verdrängung* (195–274; with the papers): Die Anfänge des jüdisch-christlichen Dialogs (Martin Stöhr, 197–229). Die politische Linke und ihr Verhältnis zum Staat Israel (Detlev Claussen, 230–242). Negative Symbiose – Deutsche und Juden nach Auschwitz (Dan Diner, 243–257). Zu einigen jüdischen Figuren im deutschen Nachkriegsfilm (Gertrud Koch, 258–274).]

23428. — Sichrovsky, Peter: *Strangers in their own land: young Jews in Germany and Austria today.* Transl. from the German by Jean Steinberg. Foreword by Thomas Keneally. New York: Basic Books; London: Tauris, 1986. IX, 208 pp. [13 interviews with young Jews who now live in Germany and Austria: on their relationship with the past, treatment by non-Jews, and what they feel about being in Germany now. Transl. of No. 22271/YB XXXI. Cf.: In no man's land (Richard Grunberger) [in]: AJR Information, No. 1, London, Jan. 1987, p. 2. Reconciliation postponed (Robert S. Wistrich) [in]: TLS, London, Feb. 13, 1987, p. 153.]

23429. — Silbermann, Alphons: *Die Utopie vom jüdischen Bürger.* [In]: Der Spiegel, Nr. 18, Hamburg, [28. Apr.?] 1986. Pp. 52–54. [On the attitude towards Jews in present day Germany.]

23430. — Steinbach, Peter: *Mit der Vergangenheit konfrontiert: vom Erkennen der NS-Verbrechen zur 'Wiedergutmachung'.* [1–3]. [In]: Tribüne, Jg. 25, H. 97 (pp. 88–104, footnotes); H. 98 (pp. 137–154, footnotes); H. 99 (pp. 166–179, footnotes). Frankfurt am Main, 1986.

23431. — Berlin. Dawidowicz, Lucy S.: *In Berlin again.* [In]: Commentary, Vol. 82, No. 2, New York, Aug. 1986. Pp. 32–41, notes. [Author recalls her impressions of visits to Germany in 1939, 1947, and again in 1985 for the LBI conference.]

23432. — — Epstein, Edwin M.: *From Berkeley to Berlin: A Jewish journey to Germany.* [In]: The Northern California Jewish Bulletin, San Francisco, Calif., Jan. 23, 1987. Pp. 13 & 16.

23433. — — *Die Jüdische Gemeinde zu Berlin.* (Hrsg. vom Presse- und Informationsamt des Landes Berlin.) Berlin (Hardenbergstr. 20): Informationszentrum, 1985. 8 pp., illus. (Information Berlin, 85,2.) [See also: Das Leben der jüdischen Bevölkerung in Berlin [in]: NZZ, Nr. 188, Zürich, 16./17. Aug. 1986, p. 7. Wenn alte Vorurteile wieder aufleben: Moses Mendelssohn, Heinz Galinski und das Streben nach einer deutsch-jüdischen Symbiose: die Geschichte der Jüdischen Gemeinde zu Berlin (Volker Skierka) [in]: Süddeutsche Zeitung, Nr. 36, München, 13. Feb. 1986, p. 12. Der Schwierige: Heinz Galinski, Vorsitzender der Jüdischen Gemeinde Berlin (Gerda-Marie Schönfeld) [in]: Zeit-Magazin, Nr. 8, Hamburg, 14. Feb. 1986, pp. 42–45, ports.]

23434. — Düsseldorf. Suchy, Barbara: *Zwischen den Zeiten: die jüdische Gemeinde Düsseldorf von 1945–1948.* [In]: 1946 Neuanfang: Leben in Düsseldorf. Begleitbuch zur gleichnamigen Ausstellung im Stadtmuseum. Düsseldorf: Rheinische Post, 1986. Pp. 330–340, illus.

—— — Hesse. Kropat, Wolf-Arno: *Der Weg der jüdischen Gemeinden in Hessen nach 1945.* [See pp. 69–74 in No. 23033.]

23435. — Koblenz. *Zur Erinnerung an die Koblenzer Synagoge.* Zwei Beiträge, vorgelegt aus Anlass der Einweihung des Gedenkraumes im 'Bürresheimer Hof', der bis zum 9. Nov. 1938 die Koblenzer Synagoge war, am 18. Sept. 1986. Koblenz, 1986. 18 pp., illus., footnotes. (Veröffentlichungen der Stadtbibliothek Koblenz, H. 17.) [Cont.: Anmerkungen zur

Baugeschichte und Baugestalt der Koblenzer Synagoge (Udo Liessem). Lebensbilder jüdischer Koblenzer (Hildburg Thill).]

23436. — Nuremberg. PRESSE- und INFORMATIONSAMT: *Jüdische Mitbürger im Ausland: Adressenverzeichnis.* Nürnberg, 1985. 40 pp.

23437. — Schifferstadt. *Synagoge.* (Dokumentation über die Initiative des Kleinen Kulturvereins Schifferstadt für eine Synagogen-Gedenktafel.) Schifferstadt: Kleiner Kulturverein, 1983. 30 pp., illus.

23438. — Schwäbisch Hall. *Eine Reise in die Vergangenheit: Besuch ehemaliger jüdischer Bürger von Schwäbisch Hall, 28. Juni – 7. Juli 1985.* (Zusammengestellt von Michael S. Koziol.) Schwäbisch Hall: Verlag Haller Tagblatt, 1985. 63 pp., illus., ports.

—— GERMAN DEMOCRATIC REPUBLIC. [See also pp. 13–30 in No. 23427.]

23439. — *Nachrichtenblatt des Verbandes der Jüdischen Gemeinden in der Deutschen Demokratischen Republik.* Red.: Helmut Aris, Peter Kirchner. Dresden, März, Juni, Sept., Dez. 1986. 4 issues, illus. [Contributions are listed according to subject.]

—— HOLOCAUST TRAUMA. [See No. 23194.]

23440. PROSECUTION OF NAZI CRIMES. *Der Asche-Prozess.* Hrsg. vom Arbeitskreis Asche-Prozess. Kiel (Werftbahnstr. 8): Kieler Verlagsauslieferung, 1985. 135 pp. [Documentation on the trial of Kurt Asche, formerly SS-Obersturmführer and 'Judenreferent' in Belgium; also on the situation in Kiel during the Nazi period.]

23441. — GÖTZ, ALBRECHT: *Bilanz der Verfolgung von NS-Straftaten.* Köln: Bundesanzeiger, 1986. 165 pp., illus., bibl. (161). [Also on the prosecution of crimes against the Jews.]

23442. — GOLDSMITH, S. J.: *A memoir of Nuremberg.* [In]: Midstream, Vol. 32, No. 4, New York, Apr. 1986. Pp. 19–20. [American-Jewish reporter at the Nuremberg Trials.]

23443. — GRABITZ, HELGE: *NS-Prozesse – Psychogramme der Beteiligten.* 2., durchgesehene Aufl. Heidelberg: Müller, Juristischer Verl., 1986 (c1985). X, 171 pp., illus., bibl. (163–165). (Recht, Justiz, Zeitgeschehen, Bd. 39.) [About the persecutors of the Jews and the Jewish witnesses.]

B. **Restitution**

23444. JENA, KAI von: *Versöhnung mit Israel? Die deutsch-israelischen Verhandlungen bis zum Wiedergutmachungsabkommen von 1952.* [In]: Vierteljahrshefte für Zeitgeschichte, Jg. 34, H. 4, München, Okt. 1986. Pp. 457–480, footnotes.

—— KEILSON, HANS: *Die Reparationsverträge und die Folgen der 'Wiedergutmachung'.* [See pp. 121–139 in No. 23427. See also No. 23430.]

C. **Antisemitism, Judaism, Nazism in Education and Teaching**

23445. BEHLER, GABRIELE: *Aus der Geschichte lernen: Thesen zur schulischen Erziehung gegen den Faschismus.* [In]: Tribüne, Jg. 25, H. 100, Frankfurt am Main, 1986. Pp. 82–87, footnotes. [In same issue also]: Vorurteile und ihre Überwindung: eine Gedenkstätte und ihre Bedeutung für die Arbeit mit Jugendlichen (Angela Genger, 88–94, footnotes). Hoffnung auf ein Umdenken: Gespräch mit deutschen Gymnasiasten über die Judenfrage (Charlotte Petersen, 96–98).

23446. DÖRR, MARGARETE: *Warum sind so viele Menschen Hitler freiwillig gefolgt?* Ein Vorschlag, Autobiographien für den Geschichtsunterricht nutzbar zu machen. [In]: Geschichte in Wissenschaft und Unterricht, Jg. 37, H. 12, Seelze, Dez. 1986. Pp. 739–760, notes (755–760). [Refers also to the teaching on the persecution of the Jews.]

23447. DÜPPE, HARALD: *Das neue Gottesvolk; Konsequenzen für den Religionsunterricht.* Frankfurt am Main: Haag & Herchen, 1986. 155 pp., illus., diagrs., bibl. (142–155). [On Judaism and Christianity.]

—— Halbfas, Hubertus: *Das Judentum im Religionsbuch.* [See pp. 166–174 in No. 23803.]

23448. HOFFMANN, CHRISTHARD/PASSIER, BERND, eds.: *Die Juden; Vorurteil und Verfolgung im Spiegel literarischer Texte.* Für die Sekundarstufe. Stuttgart: Reclam, 1986. 155 pp., bibl. (152–155). (Universal-Bibliothek, Nr. 9596: Arbeitstexte für den Unterricht.)

23449. HOPF, CHRISTEL/NEVERMANN, KNUT: *Zum Geschichtsunterricht über die Voraussetzungen des Nationalsozialismus.* Eine empirische Studie. [In]: Aus Politik und Zeitgeschichte; Beilage zur Wochenzeitung Das Parlament, B 10, Bonn, 8. März 1986. Pp. 16–25, footnotes, bibl. [Incl.: Unterricht über die Traditionen des Antisemitismus (22–23).]

23450. INNOCENTI, ROBERTO/GALLAZ, CHRISTOPHE: *Rosa Weiss.* (Aus dem Engl. von A. Teuter.) Frankfurt am Main: Alibaba Verl., 1986. 32 pp., illus. [A picture-book for children: the story of Rosa, a German girl, who discovers a concentration camp near her hometown.]

23451. LICHARZ, WERNER/WILKE, BRUNO, eds.: *Juden und Christen; Informationen und Unterrichtsangebote für den Religionsunterricht.* Frankfurt am Main: Haag & Herchen, 1986. 193 pp., illus. (Arnoldshainer Texte, Bd. 41.)

23452. MARIENFELD, WOLFGANG: *Die deutsch-jüdische Beziehungsgeschichte von der Aufklärung bis zum Zweiten Weltkrieg in der Darstellung gegenwärtiger Schulgeschichtsbücher der Bundesrepublik Deutschland.* [In]: Internationale Schulbuchforschung, Jg. 7, Nr. 4, Braunschweig, 1985. Pp. 327–339.

23453. NIEDERLAND, DORON/FISCHER, LOUISE: *From segregation to integration; Jewish society in Central and Western Europe in the period of enlightenment and emancipation.* [In Hebrew, title transl.] Jerusalem: David Schoen Institute for Creative Jewish Education, 1986. 186 pp., illus., ports. [A history textbook for Israeli high schools. Deals with Germany (passim), Moses Mendelssohn (59–83), the Haskalah in Berlin (84–101).]

23454. *Ostfriesland im Nationalsozialismus.* Materialien und Hinweise für den Unterricht. Entwickelt vom Arbeitskreis 'Ostfriessland im Nationalsozialismus', Jobst Homeyer [et al.] Aurich (Georgswall 9): Ostfriessisches Kultur- und Bildungszentrum, 1985. 279 pp., bibl. (263–278). [Incl.: Judenverfolgung (219–245).]

23455. STEIN, GERD, ed.: *Begegnung und Auseinandersetzung; ermutigende Anstösse und wegweisende Beiträge zu deutsch-israelischer Schulbucharbeit.* Duisburg: Institut für Schulbuchforschung an der Univ. Duisburg/Gesamthochschule, 1986. 253 pp. (Impulse, Bd. 7.) [Publication on the occasion of the 60th birthday of Heinz Kremers.]

23456. TIMMERMANN, WALTRAUD: *Antisemitismus in spätmittelalterlichen und frühneuzeitlichen Medien.* Ein Unterrichtsvorschlag für den Deutschunterricht. [In]: Wirkendes Wort, Jg. 36, H. 5, Düsseldorf, Sept./Okt. 1986. Pp. 354–372, notes, facsims.

V. JUDAISM

A. Jewish Learning and Scholars

—— BAECK, LEO, BOEHM, ERIC H.: *We survived.* [See No. 23227.]

23457. — BRENT, LUCIE: *The architects of Jewish self-assertion during the Nazi era.* New York, Hunter College, M.A. Thesis, 1985. III, 131 pp., bibl. (128–131). [Typescript, available in the LBI New York.] [Cont. the chaps.: 1. Leo Baeck (12–34). 2. Martin Buber (35–60). 3. Robert Weltsch (61–86). 4. Jacob Rosenheim and Hans-Joachim Schoeps (87–116).]

23458. BARAS, ZVI, ed.: *The German Rabbinical Conferences 1844–1846.* [In Hebrew]. Introd. [in English]: M. Meyer. Transl.: Z. Jacobson. Jerusalem: Dinur Center, 1986. VII, 69 pp. ('Kuntresim' – texts and studies, 68.) [Consists of the protocols of the conferences in Brunswick, Frankfurt and Breslau.]

23459. BEER, PETER. MICHAEL, REUVEN: *Peter Beer (1758–1838) – author of the first monograph on Jewish sects.* [In Hebrew]. [In]: Proceedings of the 9th World Congress of Jewish Studies, Division B, Vol. 2: The history of the Jewish people. Jerusalem, 1986. Pp. 1–7. [P. B., teacher and writer in Prague.]

23460. BELAVAL, YVON/BOUREL, DOMINIQUE, eds.: *Le siècle des Lumières et la Bible.* Paris: Beauchesne, 1986. 872 pp., illus., bibl. (837–856). [Incl.: Une traduction de la Bible en yiddish (Jean Baumgarten, 237–252). La Bible et la musique synagogale en Europe (Frank Alvarez-Pereyre, 331–354). La Bible dans les attitudes juives face à la mort (Sylvie-Anne Goldberg, 397–414). La présence de la mystique dans les interprétations juives de la Bible (Roland Goetschel, 511–521). Les traductions et commentaires de Mendelssohn (Werner Weinberg, 599–621).]

23461. BEN-CHORIN, SCHALOM: *Als Gott schwieg; ein jüdisches Credo.* Mainz: Matthias-Grünewald-Verl., 1986. 95 pp.

23462. — BEN-CHORIN, SCHALOM: *Was ist der Mensch; Anthropologie des Judentums.* Tübingen: Mohr, 1986. 160 pp.

23463. BERNSTEIN, ARON. MEYER, MICHAEL A.: *Aron Bernstein: the enigma of a radical religious reformer*. [In]: Proceedings of the 9th World Congress of Jewish Studies, Division B, Vol. 3: The history of the Jewish people. Jerusalem, 1986. Pp. 9–16. [A.B., data see No. 18211/YB XXVII.]

—— BIRNBAUM, NATHAN. FISHMAN, JOSHUA A.: *Nathan Birnbaum's third phase: the activization of Jewish sanctity*. [See No. 23592.]

23464. BOAS, FRANZ. MESSER, ELLEN: *Franz Boas and Kaufmann Kohler: anthropology and Reform Judaism*. [In]: Jewish Social Studies, Vol. 48, No. 2, New York, Spring 1986. Pp. 127–140, notes. [F. Boas, July 9, 1858 Minden- Dec. 21, 1942 New York, from 1886 in the USA, father of American anthropology.] [K. Kohler, May 10, 1843 Fürth- Jan. 28, 1926 New York, from 1869 in the USA, Reform rabbi and president of the Hebrew Union College in Cincinnati 1903–1921.]

23465. BOUREL, DOMINIQUE: *Bulletin du Judaïsme moderne*. [In]: Recherches de Science Religieuse, Vol. 74, No. 4, Paris, Oct.–Déc. 1986. Pp. 559–574, footnotes. [Critical report on recent literature.]

23466. BREUER, ISAAC. HORWITZ, RIVKA: *Dispersion and redemption in the philosophy of Isaac Breuer*. [In Hebrew, title transl.]. [In]: Eshel Beer-Sheva; essays in Jewish studies, Vol. 3, Beer-Sheva, 1986. Pp. 281–301.

—— BREUER, MORDECHAI: *Jüdische Orthodoxie im Deutschen Reich 1871–1918*. [See No. 22901.]

—— BUBER, MARTIN. [See also Nos. 23247, 23457, 23543.]

23467. — BUBER, MARTIN: *Begegnung; autobiographische Fragmente*. Mit einem Nachwort von Albrecht Goes. 3., durchgesehene Aufl. Heidelberg: Schneider, 1986. 119 pp. [Also French transl. under the title]: *Fragments autobiographiques*. Récit. trad. de l'allemand par Robert Dumont. Introd. et notes de Dominique Bourel. Paris: Stock, 1985. 123 pp., notes, bibl.

23468. — BUBER, MARTIN: *The legend of the Baal-Shem*. Transl. by Maurice Friedman. Edinburgh: Clark, 1986. 224 pp.

23469. — BUBER, MARTIN: *On Zion*. Transl. by Stanley Godman. Edinburgh: Clark, 1986. 192 pp.

23470. — BECKER, DIETER: *Karl Barth und Martin Buber – Denker in dialogischer Nachbarschaft?* Zur Bedeutung Martin Bubers für die Anthropologie Karl Barths. Göttingen: Vandenhoeck & Ruprecht, 1986. 279 pp., bibl. (260–279).

23471. — BOUREL, DOMINIQUE: *De Bar-sur-Aube à Jerusalem: la correspondence entre Gaston Bachelard et Martin Buber*. [In]: Revue Internationale de Philosophie, Vol. 38, No. 3 (150), Bruxelles, 1984. Pp. 201–216, footnotes. [Incl. the hitherto unpubl. letters by Bachelard, 1931–1937.]

23472. — BOUREL, DOMINIQUE: *Six lettres [1951–1961] de Louis Massignon à Martin Buber*. [In]: Pardès, 2, 1985. Pp. 173–181, notes, footnotes. [L. Massignon, 1883–1962.]

23473. — DANNER, HELMUT: *Zum Menschen erziehen: Pestalozzi, Steiner, Buber*. Unter Mitarbeit von Otto Müller [et al.]. Frankfurt am Main: Diesterweg, 1985. III, 115 pp., bibl.

23474. — FRIEDMAN, MAURICE: *Martin Buber and the eternal*. New York: Human Science Press, 1986. 130 pp.

23475. — GROB, L. M.: *Non-violence: a Buberian perspective*. [In]: Journal of Jewish Studies, Vol. 37, No. 1, Oxford, Spring 1986. Pp. 76–87.

23476. — MENDES-FLOHR, PAUL: *Martin Buber's reception among Jews*. [In]: Modern Judaism, Vol. 6, No. 2, Baltimore, May 1986. Pp. 111–126.

23477. — OESTERREICHER, JOHN M.: *The unfinished dialogue; Martin Buber and the Christian way*. With introductions by Edward A. Synan and Michael Wyschogrod. New York: Philosophical Library, 1986. 133 pp., notes (113–126).

23478. — SCHWARZSCHILD, STEVEN S.: *A critique of Martin Buber's political philosophy: an affectionate reappraisal*. [In]: LBI Year Book XXXI, London, 1986. Pp. 355–388, footnotes.

23479. — STATMAN, DANIEL/SAGIE (SCHWEITZER), AVI: *A study of the relationship between religion and morality in Buber's thought*. [In Hebrew]. [In]: Daat, No. 17, Ramat-Gan, Summer 1986. Pp. 97–118.

23480. — SUTER, ALOIS: *Menschenbild und Erziehung bei Martin Buber und Carl Rogers; ein Vergleich*. Bern: Haupt, 1986. VI, 330 pp. (Studien zur Geschichte der Pädagogik und Philosophie der Erziehung, Bd. 6.)

23481. — VERMES, PAMELA: *The Buber–[Albert]Schweitzer correspondence*. [In]: Journal of Jewish Studies, Vol. 37, No. 2, Oxford, Autumn 1986. Pp. 228–245. [Incl. letters 1928–1955.]

23482. — WEINRICH, MICHAEL: *Der 'neue' Buber*. [In]: Kairos, N. F. 27, H. 1–2, Salzburg, 1985. Pp. 215–219. [Review essay.]

23483. — YASSOUR, AVRAHAM: *Martin Buber on Karl Marx*. [In Hebrew, title transl.]. [In]: Machbarot le-Machshava Sotzialistit, No. 9, Tel-Aviv, Apr. 1986. Pp. 161–172.

23484. CARLEBACH, JOSEPH. Gillis-Carlebach, Miriam: *The concept of 'mitzva' in Joseph Carlebach's thought.* [In Hebrew]. [And]: Rosenblüth, Pinchas: *R. Joseph Carlebach and his thought.* [In Hebrew]. [In]: Proceedings of the 9th World Congress of Jewish Studies, Division C: Jewish thought and literature. Jerusalem, 1986. Pp. 175–180; 181–186 [of Hebrew section].

23485. Carlebach, Julius: *Orthodox Jewry in Germany: the final stages.* [In]: Die Juden im Nationalsozialistischen Deutschland [see No. 22913]. Tübingen: Mohr, 1986. Pp. 75–93, summary in German, footnotes.

23486. COHEN, HERMANN. Dethloff, Klaus: *Hermann Cohen und die Frage nach dem Jüdischen.* [In]: Kairos, N.F. 27, H. 3–4, Salzburg, 1985. Pp. 241–256, notes (254–256).

23487. — Holzhey, Helmut: *Cohen und Natorp.* Bd. 1–2. Basel: Schwabe, 1986. 2 vols. *Bd. 1: Ursprung und Einheit; die Geschichte der 'Marburger Schule' als Auseinandersetzung um die Logik des Denkens.* XII, 419 pp., bibl. (387–407). *Bd. 2: Der Marburger Neukantianismus in Quellen.* Zeugnisse kritischer Lektüre; Briefe der Marburger; Dokumente zur Philosophiepolitik der Schule. 536 pp. [Vol. 2 incl. about 200 hitherto unpubl. letters and documents.]

—— — Horwitz, Rivkah: *Hermann Cohen und Franz Rosenzweig.* [In Hebrew]. [See No. 23537.]

23488. — Kluback, William: *Friendship without communication: Wilhelm Herrmann and Hermann Cohen.* [In]: LBI Year Book XXXI, London, 1986. Pp. 317–338, footnotes. [Wilhelm Herrmann, German philosopher, Protestant theologian.]

23489. — Kluback, William: *Hermann Cohen und Martin Heidegger: Meinungsverschiedenheiten oder Enstellung?* [In]: Zeitschrift für Philosophische Forschung, Bd. 40, H. 2, Meisenheim/Glan, Apr.-Juni 1986. Pp. 283–287.

23490. — Zac, Sylvain: *La philosophie religieuse de Hermann Cohen.* Avant-propos de Paul Ricoeur. Paris: J. Vrin, (c1984). 232 pp. (Bibliothèque d'histoire de la philosophie.)

23491. EGER, AKIVA, Bleich, Judith: *Rabbi Akiva Eger and the nascent reform movement.* [In]: Proceedings of the 9th World Congress of Jewish Studies, Division B, Vol. 3: The history of the Jewish people. Jerusalem, 1986. Pp. 1–8.

23492. EHRLICH, ARNOLD BOGUMIL. Kabakoff, Jacob: *Arnold B. Ehrlich – Bible scholar.* [In Hebrew]. [In]: Bitzaron, Vol. 8, No. 31/32, New York, Oct. 1986. Pp. 68–73. [A.B.E., data see No. 21260/YB XXX.]

23493. EHRLICH, ERNST LUDWIG. Stegemann, Ekkehard/Ehrensperger, Käthy, eds.: *Bibliographie Ernst Ludwig Ehrlich (1952–1985).* Zu seinem 65. Geburtstag zusammengestellt. [In]: Judaica, Jg. 42, H. 2, Basel, Juni 1986. Pp. 113–122. [See also: Am 9. Nov. wird Dr. E. L. Ehrlich die Ehrendoktorwürde durch die Theologische Fakultät der Univ. Basel verliehen (Alfred L. Rueff) [in]: Isr. Wochenblatt, Nr. 44, Zürich, 31. Okt. 1986, pp. 5 & 7–8 [&]: Bericht über die Feierlichkeit [in]: Nr. 46, 14. Nov. 1986, pp. 23 & 25, ports.]

23494. Fackenheim, Emil: *The Jewish thought of Emil Fackenheim.* A reader. Ed. and introd. by Michael Morgan. Selected in collaboration with Emil Fackenheim. Detroit: Wayne State Univ. Press, 1986. 560 pp. [See also No. 23543.]

23495. FRANK, JACOB. Werner, Klaus: *Versuch einer Quantifizierung des Frank'schen Gefolges in Offenbach am Main 1788–1818.* [In]: Frankfurter Judaistische Beiträge, H. 14, Frankfurt am Main, Mai 1986. Pp. 153–212, footnotes. [J.F., 1726 Korolowka, Podolia— Dec. 10, 1791 Offenbach, founder of the Frankists, a Jewish Sabbatian sect, set up his court in Offenbach where his daughter Eva resided after his death.]

23496. FRANKEL, ZACHARIAS. Schischa, Abraham: *On the controversy surrounding the book Darkei ha-Mishna.* [In Hebrew, title transl.]. [In]: Ha-Ma'yan, Vol. 26, No. 4, Jerusalem, Tammuz 5746 [= July 1986]. Pp. 41–46. [On the attack, started by Samson Raphael Hirsch, on Frankel's beliefs as expressed in the above book, publ. in Leipzig, 1859.] [Z.F., Sept. 30, 1801 Prague— Feb. 13, 1875 Breslau, rabbi and scholar, founding director of the Jüdisch-Theologisches Seminar in Breslau, editor of the Monatsschrift für Geschichte und Wissenschaft des Judentums.]

23497. GANS, DAVID. Neher, André: *Jewish thought and the scientific revolution of the 16th century: David Gans (1541–1613) and his times.* Oxford: Oxford Univ. Press, 1986. 240 pp. (Littman Library of Jewish civilization.) [D.G., born in Lippstadt, died in Prague, chronicler, astronomer, and mathematician. See also No. 21261/YB XXX.]

23498. GRAETZ, HEINRICH. Meyer, Michael A.: *Heinrich Graetz and Heinrich von Treitschke: a comparison of their historical images of the modern Jew.* [In]: Modern Judaism, Vol. 6, No. 1, Baltimore, Feb. 1986. Pp. 1–11, notes.

23499. GRAETZ, MICHAEL: *Anfänge der modernen jüdischen Geschichtsschreibung*. Wolfenbüttel: Lessing-Akademie, c1985. 20 pp., illus. (Lessing/Heft, H. 4.)

23500. GRAFF, GIL: *From 'Jerusalem' to Brunswick; the metamorphosis of 'Dina de-malkhuta dina'*. [In Hebrew]. [In]: Bitzaron, Vol. 8 (29/30), New York, Apr. 1986. Pp. 59–63. [On the issue of accommodation to state law as viewed by Moses Mendelssohn and religious reformers up to the Reform Rabbinical Conference at Brunswick, 1844.]

23501. GRUNWALD, MAX: *Spinoza in Deutschland*. Neudr. der Ausg. Berlin 1897. Aalen: Scientia, 1986. 380 pp., bibl. (361–370). [M.G., Oct. 10, 1871 Hindenburg, O/S.–Jan. 24, 1953 Jerusalem, rabbi, scholar, emigrated in 1938.]

23502. HERTZBERG, ARTHUR: *The return of Maimonides*. [In]: The New York Review of Books, Sept. 25, 1986. Pp. 58–61. [Report on the Maimonides Conference, Paris, Dec. 1985.]

23503. HILDESHEIMER, ESRIEL. AUERBACH, MOSHE: *The pathway of the Rabbinerseminar in Berlin*. [In Hebrew, title transl.]. [In]: Ha-Ma'yan, Vol. 27, No. 1, Jerusalem, Tishrei 5747 [= Oct. 1986]. Pp. 3–7. [Discusses the Rabbinerseminar and Rabbi Esriel Hildesheimer. See also No. 22991.]

23504. — ELLENSON, DAVID: *'Our brothers and our flesh': Rabbi Esriel Hildesheimer and the Jews of Ethiopia*. [In]: Judaism, Vol. 35, No. 1, New York, Winter 1986. Pp. 63–65. [Circular, publ. by E. Hildesheimer (1820–1899) in the Jewish press in 1864, concerning the status and plight of Ethiopian Jewry.]

23505. HIRSCH, SAMSON RAPHAEL. GRÜNEWALD, PINHAS PAUL: *Pédagogie, esthétique et Ticoun Olam – redressement du monde: Samson Raphaël Hirsch*. Berne: Lang, 1986. 230 pp. [See also No. 23509.]

23506. HIRSCH, SAMUEL: *Die Religionsphilosophie der Juden, oder Das Prinzip der jüdischen Religionsanschauung und sein Verhältnis zum Heidentum, Christentum und zur absoluten Philosophie*. Nachdr. der Ausg. Leipzig, Hunger, 1842. Hildesheim; New York: Olms, 1986. XXXII, 884 pp. [Orig. publ. as vol. 1 of the author's 'Das System der religiösen Anschauung der Juden'; no further vols. were published.] [S.H., philosopher, data see No. 19148/YB XXVIII.]

23507. HOFFMANN, DAVID. OPPENHEIMER, YAAKOV: *The attitude of Judaism toward the nations of the world; a selection of sources from the book of Rabbi David Zevi Hoffmann*. [In Hebrew, title transl.]. [In]: Shma'tin, No. 85/86, Bat-Yam, Nissan-Sivan 5746 [= Apr.–June 1986]. Pp. 87–94. [Discusses D. H.'s book of responsa 'Melamed le-ho'il', Berlin 1885.] [D.H., Nov. 30, 1843 Verbo, Slovakia–Nov. 20, 1921 Berlin, rabbi, biblical and talmudic scholar, from 1899 rector of the Rabbinerseminar in Berlin.]

23508. KATZ, JACOB: *Orthodoxy in historical perspective*. [In]: Studies in Contemporary Jewry, 2, Bloomington: Indiana Univ. Press, 1986. Pp. 3–17.

23509. KURZWEIL, ZVI E.: *The modern impulse of traditional Judaism*. Foreword by Norman Lamm. Hoboken: Ktav, 1985. XIV, 156 pp., notes (148–156). [Incl. chaps. on Isaac Breuer, Samson Raphael Hirsch, Moses Mendelssohn.]

23510. LAQUEUR, WALTER. *Walter Laqueur: a bibliography of his work [1947–1985]*. With an appreciation by Amos A. Jordan, and a response by Walter Laqueur. Washington, D.C.: Center for Strategic and International Studies, Georgetown Univ.; & Georgetown Univ. Press, 1986. 66 pp., port., biogr. data (p. 66).

23511. LEVISOHN, SOLOMON. COHEN, TOVA: *Shlomo Levisohn's system of exegesis in 'Melizat Yeshurun' [Vienna 1816]*. [In Hebrew]. [In]: Proceedings of the 9th World Congress of Jewish Studies, Division C: Jewish thought and literature. Jerusalem, 1986. Pp. 199–206. [S.L., Hebrew poet, scholar, precursor of the Wissenschaft des Judentums.]

23512. MACH, DAFNA: *Jüdische Bibelübersetzungen ins Deutsche*. [In]: Juden in der deutschen Literatur [see No. 23676]. Pp. 54–63, notes.

23513. MARCUS, LUDWIG. ESPAGNE, MICHEL: *Der König von Abyssinien: Leben und Werk des 'kleinen Marcus'*. [In]: Heine-Jahrbuch 1986, Jg. 25, Hamburg, 1986. Pp. 112–138, illus., notes (137–138). [L.M., Oct. 31, 1798 Dessau–July 15, 1843 Paris, polyhistor, member of the Verein für Cultur und Wissenschaft der Juden, friend of Heinrich Heine who wrote 'Ludwig Marcus, Denkworte', Paris, 1844. (See also: Eulogy of a lost cause: Heine's essay 'Ludwig Marcus' (Catherine Creecy) [in]: Heine-Jahrbuch 1983, pp. 83–95).]

—— MENDELSSOHN, MOSES. [See also No. 23509.]

23514. — ALBRECHT, MICHAEL: *Moses Mendelssohn, 1729–1786; das Lebenswerk eines jüdischen Denkers der deutschen Aufklärung*. (Ausstellung im Meissnerhaus der Herzog-August-Bibliothek Wolfenbüttel vom 4.–24. Sept. 1986.) Weinheim: Acta Humaniora, VCH Verlag, 1986. 195 pp., illus., ports., facsims. (Ausstellungskataloge der Herzog-August-Bibliothek, Nr.

51.) [See also: Erinnerung an Moses Mendelssohn: Vater der jüdischen Aufklärung (Cornelia Blasberg) [in]: Evangelische Kommentare, Jg. 19, Nr. 1, Stuttgart, Jan. 1986, pp. 45–46. Moses Mendelssohns 200. Todestag: zum 4. Jan. 1986 (Ernst Gottfried Lowenthal) [in]: Isr. Wochenblatt, Nr. 6, Zürich, 7. Feb. 1986. Pp. 19 & 21. Der deutsche Moses: aus der Chronik der Bürgerfamilie Mendelssohn (Edmund Wolf) [in]: Süddeutsche Zeitung, Nr. 117, München, 24./25. Mai 1986, p. 131.]

23515. — Bourel, Dominique: *Die Kontroverse zwischen Lessing und Mendelssohn um die Ewigkeit der Höllenstrafen bei Leibniz.* [In]: Lessing und der Kreis seiner Freunde. Hrsg. von Günter Schulz. Heidelberg: Schneider, 1985. (Wolfenbütteler Studien zur Aufklärung, Bd. 8.) Pp. 33–50.

23516. — *Deux-centième anniversaire de la disparition de Moïse Mendelssohn (1729–1786).* [In]: Communauté Nouvelle, No. 25, Paris, Juin-Juillet 1986. Pp. 114–139, illus., ports., facsims. [Cont.: Moïse Mendelssohn, le destin et la vocation d'un juif des Lumières (Maurice-Ruben Hayoun, 114–117). Moïse Mendelssohn: non à l'inquisition juive! (M.-R. Hayoun, 118–119). Introduction à la vindiciae Judeorum de Manasse Ben Israel; un plaidoyer en faveur de la tolérance des Juifs au XVIIIème siècle (Moïse Mendelssohn, présenté et traduit pour la première fois en français par M.-R. Hayoun, 124–127, 130–135, 138–139).]

23517. — Goldenbaum, U.: *Moses Mendelssohn – bedeutender Repräsentant der Berliner Aufklärung.* [In]: Deutsche Zeitschrift für Philosophie, H. 6, Berlin/East, 1986. Pp. 520–527.

23518. — Klein, Hans-Günter/Lowenthal-Hensel, Cécile: *Moses Mendelssohn; Leben – Werk – Aspekte seines Nachwirkens.* Ausstellung zum 200. Todestag am 4. Januar 1986. (Vom 7. Jan. 1986 – 4. Juni 1986 im Ausstellungsraum des Mendelssohn-Archivs der Staatsbibliothek Preussischer Kulturbesitz, Berlin.) Berlin: Mendelssohn-Archiv; Mendelssohn-Gesellschaft, 1986. 20 pp.

23519. — Kochan, Lionel: *Mendelssohn: true or false prophet.* [And]: Friedlander, Albert H.: *Mendelssohn and German Jewry.* [In]: European Judaism, Vol. 19, No. 2– Vol. 20, No. 1 (Issue No. 38), London, Winter 1985/Summer 1986. Pp. 41–45; 45–50.

23520. — Lowenthal-Hensel, Cécile: *Berlin 1786; der Philosoph und der König: Moses Mendelssohn und Friedrich der Grosse.* [In]: Der Tagesspiegel, Nr. 12245, Berlin, 4. Jan. 1986. P. 3.

23521. — *Mendelssohn Studien.* Bd. 6 [see No. 23690]. Berlin: Duncker & Humblot, 1986. [Incl.: Moses Mendelssohn: Philosoph und Menschenfreund (Klaus-Werner Segreff, 11–24). Friedrich Nicolai an Johann Peter Uz: ein frühes Zeugnis zu Moses Mendelssohns 'Lehrjahren' (Eva J. Engel, 25–40). Bendavids Trinkspruch auf M. Mendelssohn, Berlin 1829, übers. von Michael S. Cullen (Dominique Bourel, 41–47).]

23522. — Shmueli, Efraim: *Throes of culture – throes of language; Moses Mendelssohn and the problem of multiple languages in the literature of Israel.* [In Hebrew, title transl.]. [In]: Kivunim, No. 33, Jerusalem, Nov. 1986. Pp. 129–152. [On the struggle of the Emancipation movement with the problems of dual culture.]

23523. — Simon, Hermann: *Eine Episode aus dem Leben Moses Mendelssohns.* [In]: Nachrichtenblatt des Verbandes der Jüd. Gemeinden in der DDR, Dresden, März 1986. Pp. 9–10.

23524. — Tsamriyon, Tsemah: *Moses Mendelssohn and the ideology of the Haskalah.* [In Hebrew]. Tel-Aviv: Mif'alim Universita'iim, 1984. 212 pp. [Cf.: Review (Moshe Pelli) [in]: Hadoar, Vol. 65, No. 21, New York, March 21, 1986, pp. 16–18.]

—— — Weinberg, Werner: *Les traductions et commentaires de Mendelssohn.* [See pp. 599–621 in No. 23460.]

23525. — Yudkin, Leon I.: *The central seminal figure of modern Jewish history: on the 200th anniversary of the death of Moses Mendelssohn.* [In]: The Jewish Quarterly, Vol. 33, No. 4, London, 1986. Pp. 46–49, notes.

—— Meyer, Michael A.: *The German model of religious reform and Russian Jewry.* [See pp. 65–91 in No. 22904.]

23526. Mülhausen, Yom-Tov Lipmann: *Sefer Hanizzahon, the Hackspan edition, Altdorf-Nürnberg, 1644.* [In Hebrew]. Introd.: Frank Talmage. Jerusalem: Dinur Center, 1984. 54, 305 pp. ('Kuntresim' – texts and studies, 59/60.) [Y.-T.L.M., 14th–15th centuries, scholar, polemicist, philosopher, kabbalist, one of the great rabbis of Bohemia in his time.]

23527. Niewöhner, Friedrich: *Vom Elend der Aufklärung: jüdische Philosophiegeschichtsschreibung im 19. Jahrhundert.* [In]: Juden in der deutschen Wissenschaft [see No. 22914]. Pp. 53–73, footnotes.

23528. Pelli, Moshe: *Religious disputation in Hebrew Haskalah literature (Isaac Satanow's 'Divrei Rivot').*

[In Hebrew]. [In]: Proceedings of the 9th World Congress of Jewish Studies, Division C: Jewish thought and literature. Jerusalem, 1986. Pp. 193–198 [of Hebrew section].

23529. PREUSS, JULIUS. ROSNER, FRED: *Julius Preuss and his classic 'Biblisch-talmudische Medizin'.* [In]: Proceedings of the 2nd Internat. Symposium on Medicine in Bible and Talmud, Jerusalem, Dec. 18–20, 1984. (Koroth, Vol. 9, No. 1–2, Leiden, Fall 1985, Special Issue). Pp. 58–59. [See also: Julius Preuss: father of Hebrew medical research (Fred Rosner) [in]: LBI Year Book XXII, London, 1977, pp. 257– 269.] [J.P., 1861 Gross-Schönebeck, Uckermark–1913 Berlin, physician and medical historian.]

23530. PRIJS, LEO, ed.: *Lebensweisheit aus dem Judentum.* Gesammelt und eingeleitet. Orig.-Ausg. Freiburg i.Br.: Herder, 1986. 156 pp. (Herderbücherei, Bd. 1322.]

23531. ROSENZWEIG, FRANZ: *Comprendre ou se méprendre.* [Introd. et] traduit par Maurice-Ruben Hayoun. [In]: Communauté Nouvelle, No. 27, Paris, Nov. 1986. Pp. 180–189, ports.

23532. — ROSENZWEIG, FRANZ: *Théologie athée (1914).* Trad. et notes de Jean-Louis Schlegel. [And]: *Introduction* par Guy Petitdemange. [In]: Recherches de Science Religieuse, Vol. 74, No. 4, Paris, Oct.-Déc. 1986. Pp. 545–557; 537–544, notes.

—— — AMIR, YEHOSHUA: *Rosenzweigs Besuch bei Buber in Heppenheim am 3.12.1921.* [See pp. 107–118 in No. 23803.]

23533. — BROCKE, MICHAEL: *Franz Rosenzweig und Gerhard Gershom Scholem:* [In]: Juden in der Weimarer Republik [see No. 22915]. Pp. 127–152, notes.

23534. — BROCKE, MICHAEL: *The relationship between Franz Rosenzweig and Gershom Scholem.* [In Hebrew]. [In]: Proceedings of the 9th World Congress of Jewish Studies, Division C: Jewish thought and literature. Jerusalem, 1986. Pp. 187–192 [of Hebrew section].

23535. — CASPER, BERNHARD: *Von Einheit und Ewigkeit. Ein Gespräch zwischen Leib und Seele: ein unveröffentlichter Text Franz Rosenzweigs.* [In]: Bulletin des LBI, 74, Frankfurt am Main, 1986. Pp. 65–78, notes (68). [Incl. letters and texts by F. Rosenzweig (68–77).]

23536. — FRIEDMANN, FRIEDRICH G.: *Franz Rosenzweig, der Mensch und der Gelehrte, sein Martyrium und sein Werk.* Am 25. Dez. wäre er 100 Jahre alt geworden. [In]: Aufbau, Nr. 51–52, New York, Dec. 19, 1986. Pp. 6–8, ports. [&]: Leserbrief: Eduard Strauss vergessen (Elizabeth Strauss-Weiler) [in]: Aufbau, Nr. 3, Jan. 30, 1987, p. 4. [See also: Er suchte Wege, neu zu Gott zu finden (Wolfgang Madai) [in]: Neue Zeit, Berlin/East, 31. Dez. 1986. Stern der Erlösung: zum 100. Geburtstag von F.R. (Christoph von Wolzogen) [in]: NZZ, Nr. 299, Zürich, 24. Dez. 1986, p. 27.]

23537. — HORWITZ, RIVKAH: *Hermann Cohen and Franz Rosenzweig.* [In Hebrew, with English summary]. [In]: Mechkerai Yerushalayim be-Machshevet Yisrael (Jerusalem Studies in Jewish Thought), Vol. 4, No. 3/4, Jerusalem, 1985. Pp. 303–326.

23538. — *Juden in Kassel, 1808–1933.* Eine Dokumentation anlässlich des 100. Geburtstages von Franz Rosenzweig [see No. 23033]. Kassel: Thiele & Schwarz, 1986. 288 pp., illus. [Title on cover: 'Ich bleibe also Jude', Franz Rosenzweig.] [Incl.: Franz Rosenzweig, 1886–1929 (Erwin Seligmann, 75–86). Der Philosoph F. Rosenzweig: eine Vergegenwärtigung (Wolfdietrich Schmied-Kowarzik, 87–96). Jüdisches Denken und deutsche Sprache: zur Übersetzungstätigkeit F. Rosenzweigs (Esther Hass, 97–108). Der lernende Lehrer: Rosenzweigs Schulkritik und die Erneuerung jüdischer Erziehung und Bildung nach 1933 (Hildegard Feidel-Mertz, 109–118). Freies Jüdisches Lehrhaus 1920 – Jüdisches Lehrhaus 1986 (Brigitte A. A. Kern, 119–126).]

23539. — LAPIDE, PINCHAS: *Ich bleibe also Jude: Erinnerung an Franz Rosenzweig.* [In]: Evangelische Kommentare, Jg. 19, Nr. 12, Stuttgart, Dez. 1986. Pp. 719–722.

23540. — LICHARZ, WERNER/ KELLER, MANFRED, eds.: *Franz Rosenzweig und Hans Ehrenberg: Bericht einer Beziehung.* Frankfurt am Main: Haag & Herchen, 1986. 285 pp., illus., ports., bibl. (270–282). (Arnoldshainer Texte, Bd. 42.) [Hans Ehrenberg, cousin of F.R. See also No. 23797.]

23541. — MOSES, STÉPHANE: *Franz Rosenzweig in perspective: reflections on his last diaries.* [In]: Identity and ethos [see No. 23677]. New York; Berne: Lang, 1986. Pp. 193–210, notes.

23542. — NIEWÖHNER, FRIEDRICH: *Franz Rosenzweig in neuer Sicht: die Edition als Manipulation des Lesers.* [In]: Jahrbuch des Instituts für Deutsche Geschichte, Bd. 15, Univ. Tel-Aviv, 1986. Pp. 491–512, footnotes.

23543. — OPPENHEIM, MICHAEL D.: *What does revelation mean for the modern Jew? Rosenzweig, Buber, Fackenheim.* Lewiston, N.Y.: The Edwin Mellen Press, 1985. VIII, 151 pp., notes (129–149). (Symposium series, vol. 17.]

—— — SCHIVELBUSCH, WOLFGANG: *Auf der Suche nach dem verlorenen Judentum: das Freie Jüdische Lehrhaus.* [See chap. 2 in No. 23671.]

23544. SAALSCHÜTZ, JOSEPH L.: *Archäologie der Hebräer.* Für Freunde des Alterthums und zum Gebrauche bei akademischen Vorlesungen. Unveränd. Neudr. der Ausg. von 1855 und 1856. T. 1–2. Vaduz, Liechtenstein: Sändig-Reprints, 1986. 924 pp. in various pagings. [A pioneering work describing the dress, science, customs, and government of the Jews.] [J.L.S., Königsberg 1801–1863, rabbi, archaeologist, contributor to the early vols. of the 'Monatsschrift'.]

23545. SCHEIBER, ALEXANDER: *Essays on Jewish folklore and comparative literature.* Budapest: Akadémiai Kiadò, 1985. 396, 56 (Hebrew) pp. [Collection of more than 50 essays in several languages, selected by the author but publ. posthumously.] [A.Sch., data see No. 22370/YB XXXI.]

—— SCHOLEM, GERSHOM. [See also Nos. 23533–23534.]

23546. — BLOOM, HAROLD: *Scholem: unhistorischer oder jüdischer Gnostizismus.* [In]: Babylon, H. 1, Frankfurt am Main, Okt. 1986. Pp. 70–83.

23547. — HAYOUN, MAURICE-RUBEN: *Gershom Scholem: une vie entièrement consacrée à l'étude de la mystique juive.* [In]: Communauté Nouvelle, No. 25, Paris, Juin-Juillet 1986. Pp. 144–147, 150–151, ports.

23548. — MYERS, DAVID: *The Scholem-Kurzweil debate and modern Jewish historiography.* [In]: Modern Judaism, Vol. 6, No. 3, Baltimore, Oct. 1986. Pp. 261–286, notes.

23549. — SILBERMAN, LOU H.: *Scholem to Eisler on the publication of 'Das Buch Bahir'.* [In]: Studies in Bibliography and Booklore, Vol. 16, Cincinnati, 1986. Pp. 5–12, notes (7–8). [Incl. the letter by Scholem to Robert Eisler in the German original with English translation appended.]

23550. — WERBLOWSKY, R. J. ZWI: *Gershom Scholem – the man, the Jew, the scholar.* [In Hebrew, title transl.]. [In]: Molad, No. 42, Jerusalem, Winter 1985/86. Pp. 122–128.

23551. SCHORSCH, ISMAR: *German Judaism: from confession to culture.* [In]: Die Juden im Nationalsozialistischen Deutschland [see No. 22913]. Tübingen: Mohr, 1986. Pp. 67–73, summary in German, footnotes.

23552. — LANDAU, DAVID: *Holding the middle ground.* The head of Conservative Jewry, Ismar Schorsch, outlines his movement's position between Orthodox and Reform. [In]: The Jerusalem Post Internat. Edition, Week ending Dec. 27, 1986. [See also report in German]: Die Wahrheit in der Mitte: Ismar Schorsch über jüdische Fragen. [In]: Aufbau, Nr. 1, New York, Jan. 2, 1987. P. 17. [I.Sch., born 1935 in Hannover, from 1940 in the USA, professor of Jewish history, from 1986 Chancellor of the Jewish Theological Seminary of America in New York, Fellow, Executive Board Member, and until recently President of the Leo Baeck Institute New York.]

23553. SIEGELE-WENSCHKEWITZ, LEONORE: *Das Verhältnis von protestantischer Theologie und Wissenschaft des Judentums während der Weimarer Republik.* [In]: Juden in der Weimarer Republik [See No. 22915]. Pp. 153–178, notes.

23554. SIGAL, PHILLIP: *Judentum.* (Übers. aus dem Engl.: K. Hermans.) Stuttgart: Kohlhammer, 1986. 276 pp., bibl. (270–273). (Urban-Taschenbücher, Bd. 359.)

23555. STEINHEIM, SALOMON LUDWIG: *Die Offenbarung nach dem Lehrbegriffe der Synagoge.* Teil 1–4. Nachdr. der 1. Aufl. Frankfurt am Main 1835; Leipzig 1856 & 1863; Altona 1865. Hildesheim: Olms, 1986. 4 vols. (XXIV, 364; XVI, 468; XVI, 420; XI, 598 pp. [S.L.St., data see No. 21314/YB XXX.]

23556. — SHEAR-YASHUV, AHARON: *The theology of Salomon Ludwig Steinheim.* Leiden: Brill, 1986. VIII, 115 pp., illus., port., facsims., bibl. (111–112). (Studies in Judaism in modern times, vol. 7.) [Incl. complete bibliography of St.'s theological and philosophical writings and a list of the unpubl. manuscripts kept in the National and Univ. Library in Jerusalem; some of these ms. are publ. for the first time as appendixes.]

23557. TAL, URIEL. FRIEDLÄNDER, SAUL: *Uriel Tal – teacher and scholar.* [In Hebrew]. [In]: Yahadut Zemanenu (Contemporary Jewry), Vol. 3, Jerusalem, 1986. Pp. 13–18.

23558. — RASH, YEHOSHUA: *Uriel Tal's legacy.* [In Hebrew, with English summary]. [In]: Gesher, No. 114, Jerusalem, Summer 1986. Pp. 71–84. [See also]: In memoriam Uriel Tal (Yisrael Gutman) [in]: Yad Vashem Studies, 16, Jerusalem, 1984, pp. IX–XIV. [For further obituaries see No. 22378/YB XXXI.]

23559. TOURY, JACOB: *Der Aufbruch der Juden in die Wissenschaften.* [In]: Juden in der deutschen Wissenschaft [see No. 22914]. Pp. 13–51, footnotes.

23560. TSAMRIYON, TSEMAH: *The educational conception of 'ha-Me'assef'.* [In Hebrew]. [In]: Proceedings of the 9th World Congress of Jewish Studies, Division C: Jewish thought and literature. Jerusalem, 1986. Pp. 239–243 [of Hebrew section].

—— VEREIN FÜR CULTUR UND WISSENSCHAFT DER JUDEN. KAHN, LOTHAR: *Early Jewish writers and the image of America (1820–1840).* [See No. 22916.]

23561. VÖLKER, HEINZ-HERMANN: *Die Wissenschaft des Judentums: ihre Entwicklung in Deutschland von 1821 bis 1933.* [In]: Tribüne, Jg. 25, H. 100, Frankfurt am Main, 1986. Pp. 251–262, footnotes.

23562. WEINBERG, WILHELM: *Collected essays, lectures and sermons of Rabbi Dr. Wilhelm Weinberg.* Written between 1918 and 1951, covering events affecting the Jewish communities of Central Europe from the rise of Hitler to the reconstruction of Jewish communities in Austria and Germany. Compiled and organized by Norbert Weinberg. Whittier, Ca., 1986. 143 pp. [Typescript, text in German. Photoreproduction available in the LBI New York.] [W.W., 1901 Vienna–1976 USA, first Landesrabbiner of Hesse and Frankfurt am Main after the war, from 1951 in the USA.]

23563. WERSES, SAMUEL: *The relationship between belletristic literature and Jewish Wissenschaft in the Haskalah period.* [In Hebrew, with English summary]. [In]: Tarbiz, Vol. 55, No. 4, Jerusalem, July–Sept. 1986. Pp. 567–602. [On the Haskalah in Eastern Europe and in Germany.]

23564. WIENER, MAX. LUZ, EHUD: *Max Wiener as a historian of Jewish religion in the Emancipation period.* [In Hebrew, with English summary]. [In]: Hebrew Union College Annual, Vol. 56, Cincinnati, 1986. Pp. 29–46. [M.W., data see No. 19199/YB XXVIII.]

23565. WORMSER, SECKEL. HILDESHEIMER, MEIR: *Torah and wisdom; the historical image of Rabbi Seckel Leib Wormser ('Ba'al Shem of Michelstadt').* [In Hebrew, title transl.]. [In]: Proceedings of the American Academy for Jewish Research, Vol. 53, Jerusalem, 1986. Pp. 7–28.

23566. YUVAL, ISRAEL JACOB: *Rabbis and rabbinate in Germany 1350–1500.* [In Hebrew, with English summary]. Jerusalem, Hebrew Univ., Diss., Apr. 1985. 427, XXXI pp.

23567. ZUNZ, LEOPOLD. FELDMANN, RAINER: *Heinrich Heine und Leopold Zunz: Gespräche um den 'Rabbi von Bacherach'.* [In]: 'Allgemeine', Nr. 41/39, Bonn, 26. Sept. 1986. Pp. 39 & 41. [L. Zunz visited Heine in 1855 in Paris.]

23568. — RAHE, THOMAS: *Leopold Zunz und die Wissenschaft des Judentums.* Zum 100. Todestag von Leopold Zunz. [In]: Judaica, Jg. 42, H. 3, Basel, Sept. 1986. Pp. 188–199, notes.

23569. — SCHORSCH, ISMAR: *The production of a classic: Zunz as Krochmal's editor.* [In]: LBI Year Book XXXI, London, 1986. Pp. 281–315, footnotes. [Incl. 29 letters, 1840–1852, related to the preparation and printing of Krochmal's work.]

B. **The Jewish Problem**

23570. ALTENHOFER, NORBERT/HEUER, RENATE, eds.: *Probleme deutsch-jüdischer Identität.* Bad Soden: Woywod, 1986. 212 pp., notes, bibl. (Archiv Bibliographia Judaica, Jahrbuch 1, 1985.) [Incl.: Rabbi Faibisch Apollo: zum Spiel der Identitäten in Leben und Werk Heinrich Heines (Norbert Altenhofer, 7–27). Der Untergang der deutschen Juden: Felix A. Theilhabers Darstellung der jüdisch-deutschen Identitätsproblematik (Renate Heuer, 73–84). Treffpunkt Scheideweg (Elazar Benyoëtz, 95–145). Bücherschau zum Thema 'Probleme deutsch-jüdischer Identität', (R. Heuer, 175–212; Salomon Maimons Lebensgeschichte: die verlorene Identität. Jettchen Geberts Kinder, oder: Verfall einer jüdischen Familie. Gerty Spies: Drei Jahre Theresienstadt – die bewährte Identität).]

23571. COHEN, RICHARD: *'Return to the ghetto' as a motif in Central and West European Jewish society (1840–1881).* [In Hebrew]. [In]: Proceedings of the 9th World Congress of Jewish Studies, Division B, Vol. 2: The history of the Jewish people. Jerusalem, 1986. Pp. 21–26. [Discusses German-Jewish thinkers and artists as well.]

23572. COHN-BENDIT, DANIEL: *Ich lebe da, wo ich verliebt bin; Rede über das eigene Land.* [In]: Die Zeit, Nr. 50, Hamburg, 5. Dez. 1986. Pp. 52–53, port. [D.C.-B., born 1945 in France, of German-Jewish parentage, moved to Germany in 1958, leading figure of the 1968 youth revolution in Paris, after eviction from France finally settling in Germany.]

—— DINER, DAN: *Negative Symbiose – Deutsche und Juden nach Auschwitz.* [See pp. 243–257 in No. 23427.]

—— GAY, PETER: *Freud, Juden und andere Deutsche.* [See No. 22909.]

23573. Gay, Peter: *In Deutschland zu Hause . . . : die Juden der Weimarer Zeit.* [In]: Die Juden im Nationalsozialistischen Deutschland [see No. 22913]. Tübingen: Mohr, 1986. Pp. 31–43, summary in English, footnotes.

23574. Gilbert, Jane E.: *Ich musste mich vom Hass befreien.* Eine amerikanische Jüdin wird deutsche Staatsbürgerin. [In]: Die Zeit, Nr. 48, Hamburg, 21. Nov. 1986. P. 74, port. [A young woman of German-Jewish parentage in search of identity.]

23575. Gilman, Sander L.: *Jewish self-hatred; anti-Semitism and the hidden language of the Jews.* Baltimore, Md.: Johns Hopkins Univ. Press, 1986. XI, 461 pp., notes (393–445). [Cont. the chaps.: 1. What is self-hatred? 2. The drive for conversion (incl., a.o., The special language of the Jews; The Christian reaction; Luther's Judaeophobia and the Jewish convert). 3. The spirit of toleration. 4. The drive for assimilation (incl., a.o., Börne, Heine, Karl Marx). 6. The ashes of the Holocaust and the closure of self-hatred (incl., a.o., Anne Frank). Cf.: Judaeophobia (S. S. Prawer) [in]: Jewish Chronicle, London, March 21, 1986, p. 16.]

—— Grimm, Gunter/Bayerdörfer, Hans-Peter, eds.: *Im Zeichen Hiobs.* [See No. 23674.]

23576. *Jüdische Komponenten in der deutschen Literatur – die Assimilationskontroverse.* Hrsg. von Walter Röll, Hans-Peter Bayerdörfer. [In]: Kontroversen, alte und neue, Bd. 5. Akten des 7. Internat. Germanisten-Kongresses, Göttingen 1985, hrsg. von Albrecht Schöne. Tübingen: Niemeyer, 1986. Pp. 107–265. [Cont.: Jüdische Literaturdebatten im 19. Jahrhundert am Beispiel der 'Allgemeinen Zeitung des Judentums' (Hans Otto Horch, 107–112). Im Spannungsfeld Heine-Kafka: deutsch-jüdische Belletristik und Literaturdiskussion zwischen Emanzipation, Assimilation und Zionismus (Itta Shedletzky, 113–121). Das Opfer als Autor: poetische Assimilation in Michael Beers 'Der Paria', 1823 (Jürgen Stenzel, 122–128). Rezeption jüdischer Autoren durch deutsche Kritik und deutsches Publikum (Jakob Katz, 129–138). Assimilation in der Krise: die Thematisierung der 'Judenfrage' in Fritz Mauthners Roman 'Der neue Ahasver', 1882 (Jörg Thunecke, 139–149). Die Assimilationskontroverse im Spiegel der jüdischen Literaturdebatte am Anfang des 20. Jahrhunderts (Hanni Mittelmann, 150–161). Zwischen Identifikation und Distanz: zur Darstellung der jüdischen Charaktere in Arthur Schnitzlers 'Der Weg ins Freie' (Wolfgang Nehring, 162–170). Richard Beer-Hofmann: ein grosser Wiener jüdischer – und deutscher – Dichter: am Beispiel von 'Jaákobs Traum' (Kathleen Harris, 171–175). Ghetto oder Integration? Zu den Identitätsproblemen der Prager jüdischen Schriftsteller (Pavel Petr, 176–181). Hebräisch oder europäisch? Zur Denkweise in der Welt des Romans 'Der Prozess' (Huan-Dok Bak, 182–186). Der Prager Golem, ein Polygänger (Simona Brolsma-Stancu, 187–195). Ende der Hoffnung – Anfang der Illusionen? Der Erste Weltkrieg in den Schriften deutscher Juden (Bernd Hüppauf, 196–207). Thomas Mann und die Juden– eine Kontroverse? Thomas Manns Bild des Judentums bis zur Weimarer Republik (Jacques Darmaun, 208–214). Das Positive im Negativen: ein Problem der frühen Exilliteratur, erläutert am Beispiel von Ferdinand Bruckners 'Die Rassen' (Roy C. Cowen, 215–219). Stefan Heyms Ahasver: der ewige Jude als Sinnbild der Kontroverse (Rod Fisher, 220–224). Jurek Becker ringt mit seinem Judentum: 'Der Boxer' und Assimilation nach Auschwitz (Chaim Shoham, 225–236). Das sterbende Gedicht: deutsche Lyrik in Israel (Sigrid Bauschinger, 237–243). Deutschsprachige Schriftsteller in Palästina und Israel: ein Forschungsprojekt (Klaus Müller-Salget, 244–250). Deutschsprachige Literatur und Autoren in Israel (Margarita Pazi, 251–260). Im Nachhinein: anstelle eines Debattenprotokolls (261–265).]

23577. Koch, Rita: *Jüdische Identität und Holocaust.* [And]: Schubert, Kurt: *Das Problem der jüdischen Identität, von der Antike bis zur Gegenwart.* [In]: Das Jüdische Echo, Vol. 35, Nr. 1, Wien, Okt. 1986. Pp. 142–148, illus.; 151–154.

23578. Loewy, Ernst: *Jude, Israeli, Deutscher – mit dem Widerspruch leben.* [In]: Exilforschung, Bd.4, München, 1986. Pp. 13–42.

23559. Mittelmann, Hanni: *Das Problem der deutsch-jüdischen 'Symbiose' im zionistischen Roman.* [In]: Juden in der deutschen Literatur [see No. 23676]. Pp. 226–236, notes.

23580. Raphaël, Freddy: *L'étranger et le paria dans l'œuvre de Max Weber et de Georg Simmel.* [In]: Archives de Sciences Sociales des Religions, 61, No. 1, Paris, Jan.-mars 1986. Pp. 63–81, notes. [On the status of the Jew in Western history; incl. chap.: Les juifs, un peuple paria (66–74).]

23581. Robertson, Ritchie: *The problem of 'Jewish self-hatred' in Herzl, Kraus and Kafka.* [In]: Oxford German Studies, No. 16, Oxford, 1986. Pp. 81–108, footnotes.

23582. SCHUBERT, KURT: *Was ist jüdisch an der jüdischen Kultur?* [And]: MAIER, JOHANN: *Intellektualismus und Mystik als Faktoren jüdischer Selbstdefinition.* [In]: Kairos, N.F., Jg. 27, H. 3–4, Salzburg, 1985. Pp. 229; 230–240, notes.

23583. SCHULTZ, HANS JÜRGEN. ed.: *Mein Judentum.* München: Deutscher Taschenbuch-Verl., 1986. 244 pp. (dtv, 10632.) [For contributors see hardcover edn., No. 15328/YB XXIV.]

23584. SHAKED, GERSHON: *Die Macht der Identität; Essays über jüdische Schriftsteller.* Aus dem Engl. von Ulrike Berger, Matthias Morgenstern und Eve Strauss. Eine Veröffentlichung des Leo Baeck Instituts. Königstein/Ts.: Jüdischer Verlag bei Athenäum 1986. 232 pp., index of names (230–232). [Incl. the essays: Kafka: jüdisches Erbe und hebräische Literatur (14–36). Der ewige Jude in Kafkas 'Amerika' (37–58). Die Gnade der Vernunft und die des Unglücks: zum Briefwechsel zwischen Zweig und Roth (59–80). Wie jüdisch ist ein jüdisch-deutscher Roman? Über Joseph Roths 'Hiob' (81–94). Der Fall Wassermann (95–114). Kein anderer Ort: über Saul Friedländer (181–191). Die Macht der Identität: über deutsche und amerikanische Literatur von Juden (192–229).]

23585. SHEDLETZKY, ITTA: *Im Spannungsfeld Heine-Kafka: deutsch-jüdische Belletristik und Literaturdiskussion zwischen Emanzipation, Assimilation und Zionismus.* [In]: Bulletin des LBI, 75, Frankfurt am Main, 1986. Pp. 29–40, notes (39–40). [Orig. publ. [in]: Kontroversen, alte und neue, Bd. 5. See pp. 113–121 in No. 23576.]

23586. SHEDLETZKY, ITTA: *Ludwig Jacobowski (1868–1900) und Jakob Loewenberg (1856–1929): literarisches Leben und Schaffen 'aus deutscher und aus jüdischer Seele'.* [In]: Juden in der deutschen Literatur [see No. 23676]. Pp. 194–209, notes.

23587. SILBERMANN, ALPHONS: *Deutsche Juden oder jüdische Deutsche? Zur Identität der Juden in der Weimarer Republik.* [In]: Juden in der Weimarer Republik [see No. 22915]. Pp. 347–355, notes.

—— VOLKOV, SHULAMIT: *Selbstgefälligkeit und Selbsthass.* [See No. 22944.]

—— WASSERMANN, HENRY: *'Was ist des Juden Vaterland?'* [See No. 22947.]

C. **Jewish Life and Organisations**

23588. ALTMAN, ERWIN. MEIER, LEVI, ed.: *'Morenu': Our Revered Teacher, Guide and Counselor; a singular award-ceremony and tribute to an outstanding personality: Erwin Altman.* Los Angeles: Office of the Chaplaincy Cedars-Sinai Medical Center, 1986. 29 pp., ports., facsim. [Mimeog. record of the ceremony when the title 'Morenu' was bestowed on E.A., orig. Altmann, 1908 Salzburg–May 6, 1986 Los Angeles, jurist, emigrated via Holland to the USA in 1939, son of Adolf Altmann, Chief Rabbi of Trier.]

—— ANGRESS, WERNER T.: *Jüdische Jugend zwischen nationalsozialistischer Verfolgung und jüdischer Wiedergeburt.* [On the establishment of Jewish schools and training farms after 1933.] [See No. 23206.]

23589. BASNIZKI, LUDWIG: *Der jüdische Kalender; Entstehung und Aufbau.* Königstein/Ts.: Jüdischer Verlag bei Athenäum, 1986. 68 pp., illus. diagrs. [L.B., 1885–1957, from 1922 teacher in Heidelberg, emigrated in 1936 to Switzerland, in 1939 to Brazil.]

—— BEER, UDO: *Die Juden, das Recht und die Republik; Verbandswesen und Rechtsschutz 1919–1933.* [See No. 22900.]

23590. BIRNBAUM, NATHAN. FISHMAN, JOSHUA A.: *Nathan Birnbaum's first phase: from Zionism to Eastern European Jewry.* [In]: Shofar, Vol. 4, No. 1, West Lafayette, Ind., Purdue Univ., Fall 1985. Pp. 17–27, notes (24–27). [N.B., May 16, 1864 Vienna–Apr. 2, 1937 Scheveningen, Holland, political and philosophical writer.]

23591. — FISHMAN, JOSHUA A.: *Nathan Birnbaum's 'second phase': the champion of Yiddish and Jewish cultural autonomy.* [In]: Spracherwerb und Mehrsprachigkeit; Festschrift für Els Oksaar zum 60. Geburtstag. Hrsg. von Brigitte Narr und Hartwig Wittje. Tübingen: Narr, 1986. (Tübinger Beiträge zur Linguistik, Nr. 295.) Pp. 173–180, notes.

23592. — FISHMAN, JOSHUA A.: *Nathan Birnbaum's third phase: the activization of Jewish sanctity.* [In]: The Fergusonian impact; in honor of Charles A. Ferguson on the occasion of his 65th birthday, ed. by Joshua A. Fishman [et al.]. Berlin; New York: Mouton de Gruyter, 1986. (Contributions to the sociology of language, 42.) Vol. 2, pp. 325–336, notes.

23593. BORGES, SHMUEL: *The work and salary conditions of the teacher in Ashkenaz in the Middle Ages.* [In Hebrew, title transl.]. [In]: Bisdeh Hemed, Vol. 28, No. 3/4, Tel-Aviv, Shevat-Adar 5745 [= Feb.–March 1985]. Pp. 179–184. [Based on medieval rabbinical responsa.]

23594. CATANE, MOCHÈ: *L'élément français dans l'onomastique juive.* [In]: Revue des Etudes Juives, Vol. 144, Paris, Oct.-Dec. 1985. Pp. 333–342. [On the origins of Jewish names in France, incl. Alsace; traces Jewish names derived from German towns.]

—— CENTRALVEREIN (C.V.). [See also No. 23602.]

23595. — FRIESEL, EVYATAR: *The political and ideological development of the Centralverein before 1914.* [In]: LBI Year Book XXXI, London, 1986. Pp. 121–146, footnotes.

23596. — MATTHÄUS, JÜRGEN: *Das Verhältnis zwischen dem 'Centralverein deutscher Staatsbürger jüdischen Glaubens' (CV) und der 'Zionistischen Vereinigung für Deutschland' (ZVfD) im Ersten Weltkrieg.* Bochum, Univ., Schriftliche Hausarbeit zur Erlangung des Magistergrades, 1986. 147 pp., bibl. (139–147). [Mimeog.]

23597. — PAUCKER, ARNOLD: *Jewish self-defence.* [In]: Die Juden im Nationalsozialistischen Deutschland [see No. 22913]. Tübingen: Mohr, 1986. Pp. 55–65, summary in German, footnotes.

23598. — PFENNIG-ENGEL, SABINE: *Der Streit zwischen CV und ZVfD: die innerjüdische Diskussion am Ende der Weimarer Republik (1928–1933).* [In]: Tribüne, Jg. 25, H. 97, Frankfurt am Main, 1986. Pp. 143–154.

23599. — WIRTH, GÜNTER: *Erinnerungen an Otto Nuschke und seine Stellung zum Centralverein deutscher Staatsbürger jüdischen Glaubens.* [In]: Nachrichtenblatt des Verbandes der Jüd. Gemeinden in der DDR, Dresden, Dez. 1986. P. 6.

—— CHARITAS. Seewann, Harald: *Die Jüdische akademische Verbindung Charitas Graz.* [See No. 23099.]

—— COCHAVI, YEHOYAKIM: *Cultural and educational activities of the German Jews 1933–1941.* [In Hebrew]. [See No. 23245–No. 23246 (in German).]

23600. COHN, JOSEF. LOWENTHAL, E. G.: *Ein 'stiller Botschafter': zum Tod von Dr. Josef Cohn.* [In]: 'Allgemeine', Nr. 41/45, Bonn, 7. Nov. 1986. P. 12. [See also: Obituary [in]: AJR Information, No. 12, London, Dec. 1986, p. 11. Wir gedenken: Dr. Dr. h.c. Josef Cohn s.A. [in]: Isr. Wochenblatt, Nr. 44, Zürich, 31. Okt. 1986, p. 38. J. Cohn in memoriam (Walter Gross) [in]: MB, Nr. 19, Tel-Aviv, Dez. 1986, p. 4 (excerpts from obituary orig. publ. in 'Haarez', Jerusalem). Obituary (Veit Wyler) [in]: Das Neue Israel, Jg. 39, H. 5, Zürich, Nov. 1986, p. 24, port.] [J.C., Sept. 6, 1904 Berlin – Oct. 24, 1986 Zürich, emigrated via England to Palestine, 1935–1948 private secretary to Chaim Weizmann, from 1955 vice president of the European Committee of the Weizmann Insitute (Rehovot, Israel) in Zürich.]

23601. DAHM, VOLKER: *Jüdische Verleger, 1933–1938.* [In]: Die Juden im Nationalsozialistischen Deutschland [see No. 22913]. Tübingen: Mohr, 1986. Pp. 273–282, summary in English, footnotes.

23602. ENGEL, DAVID: *Patriotism as a shield: the liberal Jewish defence against antisemitism in Germany during the First World War.* [In]: LBI Year Book XXXI, London, 1986. Pp. 147–171, footnotes. [On, a.o., the Centralverein and the Zionistische Vereinigung für Deutschland.]

23603. EPSTEIN, HARRY. HEID, LUDGER: *Harry Epstein – ein Anwalt der Ostjuden in der Zeit der Weimarer Republik.* [In]: Juden in der Weimarer Republik [see No. 22915]. Pp. 276–304, notes. [H.E., Aug. 26, 1879 Duisburg–Aug. 25, 1973 Jerusalem, lawyer, emigrated to Palestine in 1934.]

23604. FEUCHTWANGER, NAOMI: *Interrelations between the Jewish and Christian wedding in medieval Ashkenaz.* [In]: Proceedings of the 9th World Congress of Jewish Studies: Art, folklore, theatre, music. Jerusalem, 1986. Pp. 31–36.

23605. GELBER, MARK H.: *The jungjüdische Bewegung: an unexplored chapter in German-Jewish literary and cultural history.* [In]: LBI Year Book XXXI, London, 1986. Pp. 105–119, facsims., footnotes. [On, a.o., Adolph Donath, Berthold Feiwel, Ephraim M. Lilien.]

—— GINZEL, GÜNTHER B.: *Jüdischer Alltag in Deutschland 1933–1945.* [Incl.: Jüdische Jugendbünde.] [See No. 23278.]

23606. HASHOMER HAZAIR. REINHARZ, JEHUDA: *Hashomer Hazair in Germany (I): 1928–1933.* [In]: LBI Year Book XXXI, London, 1986. Pp. 173–208, illus., ports., footnotes.

23607. — REINHARZ, JEHUDA: *Hashomer Hazair in Nazi Germany.* [In]: Die Juden im Nationalsozialistischen Deutschland [see No. 22913]. Tübingen: Mohr, 1986. Pp. 317–350, summary in German, footnotes.

23608. HILFSVEREIN DER DEUTSCHEN JUDEN. RINOTT, MOSHE: *Capitulations – the case of the German-Jewish Hilfsverein schools in Palestine, 1901–1914.* [In]: Palestine in the late

Ottoman period; political, social and economic transformation. Ed. by David Kushner. Jerusalem: Yad Itzhak Ben-Zvi; Leiden: Brill (Distributors), 1986. Pp. 294–301.

23609. HÜTTENMEISTER, GIL: *Pocket-calendars and wall-calendars from two genizot in Germany.* [In Hebrew]. [In]: Proceedings of the 9th World Congress of Jewish Studies, Division D, Vol. 1: Hebrew and Jewish Languages. Jerusalem, 1986. Pp. 183–189. [Found in the synagogues of Hechingen and Freudental.]

—— JEWISH NATIONAL FUND. HOFF, MASCHA: *Johann Kremenezky und die Gründung des KKL.* [See No. 23653.]

—— JEWISH SPORT. [See also Nos. 23362–23364.]

23610. — BERNETT, HAJO: *Die jüdische Turn- und Sportbewegung als Ausdruck der Selbstfindung und Selbstbehauptung des deutschen Judentums.* [In]: Die Juden im Nationalsozialistischen Deutschland [see No. 22913]. Tübingen: Mohr, 1986. Pp. 223–237, summary in English, footnotes. [Refers also to the Olympics in 1936.]

23611. — GUGGENHEIM, BENNY: *Die jüdische Sportbewegung in der Schweiz.* [In]: Sport und Kultur = Sports et civilisations. Freiburg/Fribourg 1984. Edité par Louis Burgener [et al.]. Berne: Lang, 1986. (Publications universitaires Européennes: ser. 35, vol. 10).

23612. — HANAK, ARTHUR: *Leibesübungen der Juden im Mittelalter und in der frühen Neuzeit.* Tel-Aviv: Eigenverlag der Maccabi Weltverbandbewegung, 1986. 44 pp., illus., notes (30–32), bibl. (33–37). [Largely on German and Austrian Jewry.]

23613. JÜDISCHER FRAUENBUND. *Das Heim des Jüdischen Frauenbundes in Neu-Isenburg, 1907–1942, gegründet von Bertha Pappenheim.* (Im Auftrag des Magistrats der Stadt Neu-Isenburg hrsg. von Helga Heubach.) Neu-Isenburg: Kulturamt, 1986. 103 pp., illus., ports., facsims., plan, tabs., bibl. (101–103). [Incl. an account by Helene Krämer of the home after B. Pappenheim's death. See also No. 23619.]

23614. JÜDISCHER KULTURBUND. FREEDEN, HERBERT: *Kultur 'nur für Juden': 'Kulturkampf' in der jüdischen Presse in Nazideutschland.* [In]: Die Juden im Nationalsozialistischen Deutschland [see No. 22913]. Tübingen: Mohr, 1986. Pp. 259–271, summary in English, footnotes. [See also No. 23245.]

23615. KRAMER, DAVID: *Jewish welfare work under the impact of pauperisation.* [In]: Die Juden im Nationalsozialistischen Deutschland [see No. 22913]. Tübingen: Mohr, 1986. Pp. 173–188, summary in German, tabs., footnotes.

23616. MARCUS, IVAN G.: *Hierarchies, religious boundaries and Jewish spirituality in medieval Germany.* [In]: Jewish History, Vol. 1, No. 2, Haifa, Fall 1986. Pp. 7–26.

23617. MORGENSTERN, LINA. FASSMANN, MAYA I.: *Die Mutter der Volksküchen: Lina Morgenstern und die jüdische Wohltätigkeit in Berlin.* [In]: Unter allen Umständen; Frauengeschichte(n) in Berlin. Hrsg. von Christiane Eifert und Susanne Rouette. Berlin: Rotation, 1986. Pp. 34–59, bibl. references. [L.M., née Bauer, Nov. 25, 1830 Breslau –Dec. 16, 1909 Berlin, educational theorist, philanthropist, writer.]

23618. PAPPENHEIM, BERTHA. FORRESTER, JOHN: *The true story of Anna O.* [In]: Social Research, Vol. 53, No. 2, New York, Summer 1986. Pp. 327–347, footnotes. [On Freud's interpretation of the case of Anna O., i.e. Bertha Pappenheim, and its importance for psychoanalysis.]

23619. — LOWENTHAL, E. G.: *Erinnerung an Bertha Pappenheim: zu ihrem 50. Todestag [am 28. Mai 1986].* [In]: 'Allgemeine', Nr. 41/19, Bonn, 9. Mai 1986. P. 11. [See also: Die Leiden und das Leben der Bertha Pappenheim: vor 50 Jahren starb die Frankfurter Sozialreformerin und Frauenrechtlerin (Arno Lustiger) [in]: 'Allgemeine', Nr. 41/39, Bonn, 26. Sept. 1986, pp. 38–39, port. See also No. 23613.]

23620. REICHSVEREINIGUNG DER JUDEN IN DEUTSCHLAND. KULKA, OTTO D.: *Die Reichsvereinigung and the fate of the German Jews, 1938/1939–1943: continuity or discontinuity in German-Jewish history in the Third Reich.* [In]: Die Juden im Nationalsozialistischen Deutschland [see No. 22913]. Tübingen: Mohr, 1986. Pp. 353–363, summary in German, footnotes.

23621. REICHSVERTRETUNG DER JUDEN IN DEUTSCHLAND. BRODNITZ, FRIEDRICH: *Memories of the Reichsvertretung: a personal report.* [In]: LBI Year Book XXXI, London, 1986. Pp. 267–277, footnotes.

23622. — STRAUSS, HERBERT A.: *Jewish autonomy within the limits of National Socialist policy: the communities and the Reichsvertretung.* [In]: Die Juden im Nationalsozialistischen Deutschland [see No. 22913]. Tübingen: Mohr, 1986. Pp. 125–152, summary in German, footnotes.

23623. ROUBICEK, FRITZ: *Von Basel bis Czernowitz; die jüdisch-akademischen Studentenverbindungen in*

Europa. Wien (Tuersgasse 21): Österr. Verein für Studentengeschichte, 1986. III, 90 pp., illus., bibl. (Beiträge zur österr. Studentengeschichte, 12.)

—— Schachne, Lucie: *Erziehung zum geistigen Widerstand: das jüdische Landschulheim Herrlingen 1933–1939*. [See No. 23288.]

23624. SCHATZKER, CHAIM: *Sozialisationsprozesse der jüdischen Jugend in Deutschland im 19. Jahrhundert*. [In]: Bildungsgeschichte als Sozialgeschichte; Festschrift zum 60. Geburtstag von Franz Pöggeler. Hrsg. von Heinrich Kanz. Frankfurt am Main: Lang, 1986. (Erziehungsphilosophie, Bd. 8.]

23625. SHAVIT, ZOHAR: *Der Anfang der hebräischen Kinderliteratur am Ende des 18. und zu Beginn des 19. Jahrhunderts in Deutschland*. [In]: Schiefertafel, Jg. 9, Nr. 1, Pinneberg, Apr. 1986.

23626. SHEDLETZKY, ITTA: *Literaturdiskussion und Belletristik in den jüdischen Zeitschriften in Deutschland 1837–1918*. [In German, with Hebrew summary]. Jerusalem, Hebrew Univ., Diss., 1986. V, 420, 33 pp.

23627. WALK, JOSEPH: *Jüdische Erziehung als geistiger Widerstand*. [In]: Die Juden im Nationalsozialistischen Deutschland [see No. 22913]. Tübingen: Mohr, 1986. Pp. 239–247, summary in English, footnotes. [On the Jewish school system in Germany after 1933. See also No. 23391.]

—— YASSIF, ELI: *Jewish folklore: an annotated bibliography*. [See No. 23203.]

—— ZIONISTISCHE VEREINIGUNG FÜR DEUTSCHLAND. [See Nos. 23596, 23598, 23602.]

D. Jewish Art and Music

23628. BAR-GIORA, NAFTALI: *Die bemalte Sukka aus Döttingen: ein Zeugnis aus dem 17. Jahrhundert*. [In]: Isr. Wochenblatt, Nr. 42, Zürich, 17. Okt. 1986. Pp. 15–16, illus.

23629. BENDT, VERONIKA: *Das Jüdische Museum Berlin; eine Abteilung des Berlin Museums*. Berlin (Hardenbergstr. 20): Informationszentrum, 1986. 76 pp., illus., ports., facsims., bibl. (72–73). (Berliner Forum, 5/86.) [Incl.: Die Geschichte des Jüdischen Museums in Berlin bis zur Zwangsschliessung 1938 (5–12).]

—— Burgard, Friedhelm: *Bilder aus der deutsch-jüdischen Geschiche*. [See section C in No. 23084.]

23630. GILAM, ABRAHAM: *Erich Goeritz and Jewish art patronage in Berlin during the 1920s*. [In]: Journal of Jewish Art, Vol. 11, Jerusalem, 1985. Pp. 60–72, illus., ports. [E. Goeritz, 1889 - 1955 London, industrialist, painter, art collector, especially of Liebermann and Corinth.]

23631. HALLO, RUDOLF: *Jewish folk art in Hesse:* Publ. 1928 for the 40th anniversary of the Sinai Lodge in Kassel. Transl. by Gertrude Hallo. 50 pp., 8 plates. [Transl. of: 'Jüdische Volkskunst in Hessen'. Typescript, available in the LBI New York.]

—— — SCHMIDBERGER, EKKEHARD: *Rudolf Hallo und das jüdische Museum in Kassel*. [See pp. 59–68 in No. 23033.]

23632. HOFGEISMAR. *Vertraut werden mit Fremden: Zeugnisse jüdischer Kultur im Stadtmuseum Hofgeismar*. (Redaktion: Helmut Burmeister und Michael Dorhs. Hrsg.: Verein für Hessische Geschichte und Landeskunde e.V. Kassel, Zweigverein Hofgeismar.) Hofgeismar, 1986. 16 pp., illus. (Führer durch das Stadtmuseum Hofgeismar, H. 2.)

23633. *Judaica Bohemiae*. Vol. 22, Nos. 1–2. Publication du Musée juif d'Etat, Prague. Rédacteur en chef: Otakar Petřík. Praha: Státní židovské muzeum v Praze, 1986. 60; 63–121 pp., illus., footnotes. (2 issues.] [*No. 1* incl.: Salomon Hugo Lieben – founder of the Prague Jewish Museum (Vladimír Sadek, 3–8). Morphologie der Schilde mährischer Provenienz aus den Sammlungen des Staatl. jüd. Museums (Jana Doleželová, 20–34). Acquisitions to the collections of the State Jewish Museum in Prague for the years 1981–1985 (Jana Doleželová/Arno Pařík, 35–46). Hebrew inscriptions in the old synagogue at Holešov=Holleschau (Vlastimila Hamácková/Jiřina Šedinová, 47–55). *No. 2*. Acquisitions to the collections of the State Jewish Museum for the years 1981–1985; II: Terezin Collection (Markéta Petrášová, 87–95). Der Hölle entronnen: Leo Haas – Zeitzeuge und Antifaschist (Wolf H. Wagner, 96–104; L.H., 1901 Troppau, Silesia–Aug. 13, 1983 Berlin-East, painter). Bolzanos Porträt von dem jüdischen Maler Aaron (Adolf) Pulzer (Lubomír Sršeň, 105–112. Further contributions are listed according to subject.]

—— KUKATZKI, BERNHARD, comp.: *Dorfsynagogen in der Pfalz*. [See No. 23053.]

—— LANG, ADOLF: *Bechhofen und seine zerstörte Synagoge*. [See No. 22980.]

23634. MANN, VIVIAN B.: *The Golden Age of Jewish ceremonial art in Frankfurt: metalwork of the eighteenth century*. [In]: LBI Year Book XXXI, London, 1986. Pp. 389–403, illus., footnotes.

23635. MOTSCHMANN, JOSEF: *250 Jahre Synagoge von Horb am Main.* Ein galizischer Künstler [Elieser Sussmann aus Brody] gestaltete 1735 eine fränkische Dorfsynagoge. [In]: Vom Main zum Jura (Postfach 41, D–8621 Weismain), H. 2, Lichtenfels, 1985. Pp. 7–33, illus., ports., notes (29–33). [See also No. 21353/YB XXX.]

—— OPPENHEIM, MORITZ. SCHORSCH, ISMAR: *Art as social history: Moritz Oppenheim and the German vision of emancipation.* [See pp. 139–172 in No. 22904.]

23636. PRAGUE, THE STATE JEWISH MUSEUM, ed.: *The Prague synagogues in paintings, engravings and old photographs.* (Written and designed by Arno Pařík. English version transl. by Slavoš Kadečka.) Prague: The State Jewish Museum, 1986. 72 pp., illus., plans, bibl.

23637. SCHUBERT, URSULA: *Was ist jüdisch an der jüdischen Bildkunst.* [And]: SCHUBERT, KURT: *Das jüdische Element in der Illustration der Pesach-Haggadot des 17. und 18. Jahrhunderts.* [In]: Kairos, N. F., Jg. 27, H. 3–4, Salzburg, 1985. Pp. 269–278, notes; 279–287, notes.

23638. SHMUELI, EPHRAIM: *Jewish music in Germany; Heine and the brothers Beer and Meyerbeer.* [in Hebrew, title transl.]. [In]: Hadoar, Vol. 66, No. 6, New York, Dec. 19, 1986. Pp. 14–16.

23639. SIMON, HERMANN: *Jüdische Exlibris.* [In]: Marginalien, H. 100, Berlin/East, 1986. Pp. 60–67, illus.

23640. *Synagogen und Tempel.* (Hrsg.: Informationszentrum Raum und Bau der Fraunhofer-Gesellschaft (IRB). Red. Bearb.: Ulrich Rombock.) Stuttgart: IRB-Verlag, 1986, 73 pp. (IRB-Literaturauslese, Nr. 837.)

—— WEGNER, KARL-HERMANN: *Bilder [des Malers Wilhelm Thielmann] aus der Synagoge: zur Selbstdarstellung des Kasseler Judentums im 19. Jahrhundert.* [See pp. 49–58 in No. 23033.]

VI. ZIONISM AND ISRAEL

—— BAUSCHINGER, SIGRID: *Das sterbende Gedicht: deutsche Lyrik in Israel.* [See pp. 237–243 in No. 23576.]

—— BIRNBAUM, NATHAN. FISHMAN, JOSHUA A.: *Nathan Birnbaum's first phase: from Zionism to Eastern European Jewry.* [See No. 23590.]

23641. BODENHEIMER, MAX: *So wurde Israel; aus der Geschichte der zionistischen Bewegung.* Hrsg. von Henriette Hannah Bodenheimer. 2., erweiterte Aufl. Köln: R. Biesenbach; Ijsselstein, Holland: Interpress Publications, 1985. 325 pp. [First edn. 1957; now augmented by some letters. Cf.: Der grosse Beitrag des deutschen Zionismus (Fritz Schatten) [in]: 'Allgemeine', Nr. 41/9, Bonn, 28. Feb. 1986, p. 7.] [M.B., March 21, 1865 Stuttgart–July 20, 1940 Jerusalem, lawyer, Zionist leader, emigrated to Palestine in 1935.]

23642. FISHMAN, ARYEI: *The Jewish ethic and the spirit of socialism: Karl Marx, Moses Hess, and the religious kibbutz.* [In Hebrew]. [In]: Proceedings of the 9th World Congress of Jewish Studies, Division B, Vol. 2: The history of the Jewish people. Jerusalem, 1986. Pp. 243–247.

—— GELBER, MARK H.: *The jungjüdische Bewegung.* [See No. 23605.]

23643. GOLDMANN, NAHUM. HERTZBERG, ARTHUR: *Nahum Goldmann; his political legacy.* [In Hebrew]. [In]: Gesher, No. 113, Jerusalem, Winter 1985/86. Pp. 16–23.

23644. — PATAI, RAPHAEL: *Nathum Goldmann: his missions to the Gentiles.* Tuscaloosa: The Univ. of Alabama Press, 1986. 320 pp. (Judaic studies series.) [Deals, a.o., with N.G.'s role as co-founder of the Eschkol Publ. House in Berlin and co-publ. of the Encyclopaedia Judaica (see also No. 23198), and G.'s postwar engagement for reparation payments of West Germany to Israel.]

23645. HERZL, THEODOR: *Zionistisches Tagebuch: 1895–1899 [&]: 1899–1904.* Bearb. von Johannes Wachten, Chaya Harel, in Zusammenarbeit mit Daisy Ticho, Sofia Gelman, Ines Rubin, Manfred Winkler. Berlin: Propyläen, 1984–1985. 2 vols. (999; 1151 pp.), indexes of persons and subjects (vol. 2, pp. 1019–1058; 1059–1145). (Theodor Herzl: Briefe und Tagebücher, Bd. 2–3. Hrsg. von Alex Bein, Hermann Greive, Moshe Schaerf, Julius H. Schoeps.) [First complete edn. of the Zionistisches Tagebuch in the original German language.] [Expanded entry of No. 21365/YB XXX.]

23646. — HERZL, THEODOR: *Theodor Herzl oder: Der Moses des Fin de siècle.* Hrsg. [und mit Einleitung] von Klaus Dethloff. Wien: Böhlau, 1986. 300 pp., bibl. (Monographien zur österr. Kultur-und Geistesgeschichte, 1.) [Collection of Herzl's writing.]

23647. — AVINERI, SHLOMO: *Herzl's Zionist utopia – dream and reality.* [In Hebrew]. [In]: Cathedra, No. 40, Jerusalem, July 1986. Pp. 189–200.

23648. — Be'eri, Eliezer: *The Herzl years.* [In]: The Jerusalem Quarterly, No. 41, Jerusalem, Winter 1986/1987. Pp. 3–18. [Deals with Herzl's attitude to and relations with the Arabs, based on the 'Altneuland' and on his correspondence with Yusuf al-Khalidi. Article is the English transl. of chapter 11 of the author's Hebrew book: 'The beginning of the Israeli-Arab conflict, 1882–1911', Tel-Aviv, Sifriat Poalim, 1985.]

23649. — Hadomi, Leah: *'Altneuland' – ein utopischer Roman.* [In]: Juden in der deutschen Literatur [see No. 23676]. Pp. 210–225, notes.

—— — Robertson, Ritchie: *The problem of 'Jewish self-hatred' in Herzl . . .* [See No. 23581.]

23650. — Wachten, Johannes: *Some unsigned articles of Herzl in 'Neue Freie Presse'.* [In Hebrew]. [In]: Proceedings of the 9th World Congress of Jewish Studies, Division B, Vol. 2: The history of the Jewish people. Jerusalem, 1986. Pp. 71–76.

23651. HESS, MOSES. Bar-Nir, Dov: *The modernism of Moses Hess.* [In Hebrew]. [In]: Me'asef, Vol. 16, Givat Haviva, 1986. Pp. 51–60. [See also No. 23642.]

23652. — Van der Ven, N.: *Moses Hess in Nederland.* Een onderzoek naar de ontvangst van 'Rom und Jerusalem' in de Nederlands-joodse pers. [In]: Studia Rosenthaliana, Vol. 20, No. 1, Assen, Holland, July 1986. Pp. 85–90, footnotes, summary in English (89–90).

23653. KREMENEZKY, JOHANN. Hoff, Mascha: *Johann Kremenezky und die Gründung des KKL.* Frankfurt am Main: Lang, 1986. 183 pp., bibl. (169–177). (Judentum und Umwelt, Bd. 14.) [J.K., 1850 Odessa–1934 Vienna, industrialist in Austria, Zionist, one of Herzl's close friends, one of the executors of his will, co-founder of the Herzl Archive, first head of the Keren Kayemeth Leisrael (Jewish National Fund).]

23654. Lavsky, Hagit: *The conflict with 'Binyan ha-Aretz' in Germany (1920–1921): was it analogous to the Brandeis-Weizmann controversy?* [In Hebrew]. [In]: Proceedings of the 9th World Congress of Jewish Studies, Division B, Vol. 2: The history of the Jewish people. Jerusalem, 1986. Pp. 101–108.

23655. Lavsky, Hagit: *The ideological and political role of German Zionism in the World Zionist Movement, 1918–1932.* [In Hebrew, with English summary]. Jerusalem, Hebrew Univ., Diss., March 1985. 2 vols. (285; 134, XVII pp.).

23656. LUFT, GERDA. Cattani, Alfred: *Gerda Luft gestorben.* [In]: NZZ, Nr. 114, Zürich, 21. Mai 1986. P. 2. [See also: Zum Tode von Gerda Luft (E. G. Lowenthal) [in]: 'Allgemeine', Nr. 41/22, Bonn, 30. Mai 1986, p. 7. G. Luft gestorben [in]: Isr. Wochenblatt, Nr. 20, Zürich, 16. Mai 1986, p. 72. Gerda Luft in memoriam (J. Lilienfeld) [in]: MB, Nr. 12, Tel-Aviv, Mai 1986, pp. 1–2, port.] [G.L., Apr. 20, 1898 Königsberg–May 12, 1986 Tel-Aviv, journalist, married to Chaim Arlosoroff, settled in Palestine in 1924. For G.L.'s memoirs see No. 20264/YB XXIX.]

—— Mittelmann, Hanni: *Das Problem der deutsch-jüdischen 'Symbiose' im zionistischen Roman.* [See pp. 226–236 in No. 23579.]

—— Müller-Salget, Klaus: *Deutschsprachige Schriftsteller in Palästina und Israel.* [See pp. 244–250 in No. 23576.]

—— Nazism and Zionism. [See Nos. 23324, 23408–23411, & in No. 23820.]

23657. Nicosia, Francis R.: *Revisionist Zionism in Germany (I): Richard Lichtheim and the Landesverband der Zionisten-Revisionisten in Deutchland, 1926–1933.* [In]: LBI Year Book XXXI, London, 1986. Pp. 209–240, ports., footnotes. [Also on Robert Weltsch and the views of the leadership of the Zionistische Vereinigung für Deutschland as expressed in the Jüdische Rundschau.]

—— Pazi, Margarita: *Deutschsprachige Literatur und Autoren in Israel.* [See pp. 251–260 in No. 23576.]

23658. Peles, Haim J.: *The training farms of the religious pioneers in Europe between the World Wars.* [In Hebrew]. [In]: Proceedings of the 9th World Congress of Jewish Studies, Division B, Vol. 2: The history of the Jewish people. Jerusalem, 1986. Pp. 109–114. [Deals also with training farms in Germany (111–113).]

—— Reinharz, Jehuda: *Hashomer Hazair.* [See Nos. 23606–23607.]

—— Rinnott, Moshe: *Capitulations – the case of the German-Jewish Hilfsverein schools in Palestine, 1901–1914.* [See No. 23608.]

23659. Rothschild, Eli: *Versöhnende Rufe.* Gesammelte Aufsätze. Hrsg. von Heinz Kremers und E. Horst Schallenberger. Zusammengestellt und bearb. von Alfred Tendick. Univ. Duisburg, Politische Wissenschaften. Köln: Brill, 1985. 176 pp., port., index of names. (Arbeitsmaterialien zur Geistesgeschichte, Bd. 3.) [Collection of essays, arranged in the sections: 1. Eli Rothschild – Autobiographisches (9–33). 2. Kraftquellen (34–41). 3. 2000 Jahre

Zionsliebe – Episoden (42–79). 4. Arabische Welt und Israel (80–94). 5. Mitstreiter (95–124; on Moritz Goldstein, Siegfried Lehmann, Max Marcus, Emanuel Roer, Pinchas Rosen, Hans Seelenfreund, Margarete Turnowsky-Pinner, Robert Weltsch). 6. Denkwürdigkeiten – Deutsches im Heiligen Land (125–139). 7. Deutschland von einem Freund aus Israel gesehen (140–159). 8. Epilog (160–164).] [E.R., born Dec. 7, 1909 in Lübeck, historian, emigrated to Palestine in 1933.]

23660. SALTEN, FELIX: *Neue Menschen auf alter Erde; eine Palästinafahrt [1924].* Mit einem Vorwort von Alex Carmel. Königstein/Ts.: Jüdischer Verlag bei Athenäum, 1986. IX, 189 pp. [First edn. 1925.] [F.S., orig. Siegmund Salzmann, Sept 6, 1869 Budapest–Oct. 8, 1945 Zürich, writer, emigrated from Vienna to Switzerland in 1938.

—— SEEWANN, HARALD: *Die Jüdisch-akademische Verbindung Charitas Graz.* [See No. 23099.]

23661. UNNA, MOSHE: *The training farms in Germany, cradle of the Religious Kibbutz Movement.* 1–4. [In Hebrew, title transl.]. [In]: Amudim, Vol. 35, No. 2 (pp. 56–58); No. 3 (pp. 97–101); No. 4 (pp. 143–148); No. 5 (pp. 193–194). Tel-Aviv, Cheshvan ff. 5747 [=Nov.–Dec. 1986; Jan.–Feb. 1987].

VII. PARTICIPATION IN CULTURAL AND PUBLIC LIFE

Section VII had to be drastically curtailed due to the excess of material stemming from the expansion of German-Jewish studies. Some of the entries now omitted will appear in next year's bibliography – (Ed.).

A. General

23662. AUSTRIA. ZOHN, HARRY: *'. . . ich bin ein Sohn der deutschen Sprache nur . . .'; jüdisches Erbe in der österreichischen Literatur.* Darstellungen und Dokumentation. Wien: Amalthea, 1986. 275 pp., ports., bibl. [Incl. essays on Beer-Hofmann, Brod, Alfred Farau, Herzl, Theodor Kramer, Karl Kraus, Ernst Lothar, Alfred Neumann, Robert Neumann, Schnitzler, Torberg, Ernst Waldinger, Stefan Zweig, and on writers in exile; in the bio-bibliographical appendix, 'Wiener Juden in der Literatur', 530 writers are listed (pp. 191–275).]

23663. BERLIN. HILDENBRANDT, FRED: *. . . ich soll dich grüssen von Berlin, 1922–1932.* Frankfurt am Main: Ullstein, 1986. 264 pp. (Ullstein-Buch, Nr. 20704.) [Reminiscences by the German editor of the Berliner Tageblatt feuilleton, appointed by Theodor Wolff; incl. chaps. on Paul Graetz, Kerr, Anton Kuh, Carola Neher, Max Reinhardt, Richard Tauber, and refers passim to many other German-Jewish writers.]

—— — WESTPHAL, UWE: *Berliner Konfektion und Mode.* [See No. 23224.]

—— EXILE LITERATURE. COWEN, ROY C.: *Das Positive im Negativen: ein Problem der frühen Exilliteratur.* [See pp. 215–219 in No. 23576] [See also M. Pazi: Walther A. Berendsohn, pp. 217–247 in No. 22914.]

23664. — *Exil.* Forschung, Erkenntnisse, Ergebnisse. Jg. 6, Nr. 1–2. Hrsg. von Edita Koch. Maintal (Goethestr. 122): E. Koch, 1986. 100; 99 pp., ports., notes, bibl. [*Nr. 1* incl.: Exil in Mexiko (Fritz Pohle, 5–18). Arthur Kronfeld zur Erinnerung: Schicksal und Werk eines jüdischen Psychiaters und Psychotherapeuten in drei deutschen Reichen (Ingo-Wolf Kittel, 58–65; A. K., 1886 Berlin–1941 Moscow). Aufzeichnungen eines Melancholikers: zu Walter Benjamins Fragmenten und autobiogr. Schriften (Josef Quack, 78–81). *Nr. 2*: Leo Perutz: eine biographische Skizze (Hans-Harald Müller, 5–17, notes). Jugend zweier Kriege: zur Weiterentwicklung der Zeitstückkonzeption in Ferdinand Bruckners Exildramatik (Johannes G. Pankau, 18–29). Die Autobiographie des Bankiers und Politikers Hugo Simon (Frithjof Trapp, 30–38; H. Simon data see in No. 20287/YB XXIX). Deutschsprachige Schriftsteller in Positano 1933–1945 (Heide-Marie Wollmann, 65–76).]

23665. — *Exilforschung.* Ein internationales Jahrbuch. *Bd. 4: Das jüdische Exil und andere Themen.* Hrsg. von Thomas Koebner [et al.]. München: Edition Text + Kritik, 1986. 310 pp. [Incl.: Der Jude als Paria:Hannah Arendt über die Unmündigkeit des Exils (Dagmar Barnouw, 43–61). Wer war Grete Bloch? (Wolfgang A. Schocken, 83–97). Further contributions are listed according to subject.]

23666. — FEILCHENFELDT, KONRAD: *Deutsche Exilliteratur 1933–1945; Kommentar zu einer Epoche.* München: Winkler, 1986. 255 pp., bibl. (233–243).

23667. — *Kulturelle Wechselbeziehungen im Exil = Exile across cultures.* Hrsg. von Helmut F. Pfanner. (Akten des vom 7.–10. März 1985 an der Staatsuniversität von New Hampshire, Durham, NH, USA, stattgefundenen Symposiums über deutsche und österreichische Exilliteratur.) Bonn: Bouvier, 1986. X, 394 pp. (Studien zur Literatur der Moderne, Bd. 14.) [Incl. essays, in German or English, on Vicki Baum, Broch, Ferdinand Bruckner, Freud, Else Lasker-Schüler, Robert Neumann, Max Ophüls, Hans Sahl-Walter Sorell-Otto Zoff, Ernst Waldinger; Film makers (Jan-Christopher Horak); Journalisten und Publizisten (Sigrid Schneider); Refugee photographers (Sybil Milton), Zürcher Schauspielhaus (Rolf Kieser).]

23668. — PATSCH, SYLVIA M., ed.: *Österreichische Schriftsteller im Exil: Texte.* Wien: Brandstätter, 1986. 309 pp., illus.

23669. — SOCIETY FOR EXILE STUDIES = GESELLSCHAFT FÜR EXILFORSCHUNG, ed.: *Nachrichtenbrief = Newsletter.* Nr. 5–6. Bearb. von Ernst Loewy unter Mitarbeit von Elsbeth Wolffheim. Frankfurt am Main 50 (Postfach 550207): Ernst Loewy, Dez. 1986. 147 pp. [Incl. bibl. of current books and articles referring to exile literature (60–129).]

23670. — WALTER, HANS-ALBERT: *Zeitgeschichte, Psychologie des Exils und Mythos in Anna Seghers' Roman 'Transit'.* Anmerkungen zu Interpretationsproblemen bei der deutschen Exilliteratur. [And]: KVAM, KELA: *Deutsches Exiltheater in Dänemark.* [In]: Deutschsprachiges Exil in Dänemark nach 1933 [see No. 23367]. München: Fink, 1986. Pp. 11–56; 178–198.

23671. FRANKFURT am Main. SCHIVELBUSCH, WOLFGANG: *Intellektuellendämmerung; zur Lage der Frankfurter Intelligenz in den zwanziger Jahren.* Frankfurt am Main: Suhrkamp, 1985. 176 pp., illus., notes (172–176). Suhrkamp-Taschenbuch, 1121.) [Refers in all chaps. to Jewish personalities. Cont.: 1. Soziologen, Georgianer, Stifter: die Universität. 2. Auf der Suchenach dem verlorenen Judentum: das Freie Jüdische Lehrhaus. 3. Die Frankfurter Zeitung. 4. Radio Frankfurt. 5. Der Goethe-Preis und Sigmund Freud. 6. Von der Verhinderung zur Liquidation: das Ende des Instituts für Sozialforschung.]

—— THE FRANKFURT SCHOOL. ARATO, ANDREW: *Die Kritische Theorie in den USA: Gedanken über vier Jahrzehnte ihrer Rezeption* [See pp. 617–624 in No. 23153.]

23672. — MARCUS, JUDITH/TAR, ZOLTAN: *The Judaic element in the teachings of the Frankfurt School.* [In]: LBI Year Book XXXI, London, 1986. Pp. 339–353, footnotes.

23673. — WIGGERSHAUS, ROLF: *Die Frankfurter Schule; Geschichte, theoretische Entwicklung, politische Bedeutung.* München: Hanser, 1986. 795 pp., bibl. (733–783). [See also chaps. 1 & 6 in No. 23671.]

23674. GRIMM, GUNTER E./BAYERDÖRFER, HANS-PETER, eds.: *Im Zeichen Hiobs; jüdische Schriftsteller und deutsche Literatur im 20. Jahrhundert.* 2., durchgesehene Aufl. Frankfurt am Main: Athenäum, 1986 (c1985). 372 pp., index of persons, notes. [Cont.: Einleitung (Konrad Kwiet/G. E. Grimm/H.-P. Bayerdörfer, 7–65). A.Schnitzler und das Judentum (Egon Schwarz, 67–83). 'Ich bin Jude, Gott sei Dank': E. Lasker-Schüler (Sigrid Bauschinger, 84–97). '-jüdisch, römisch, deutsch zugleich': K. Wolfskehl (Paul Hoffmann, 98–123). 'Verbrannt wird auf alle Fälle . . .': Juden und Judentum im Werk J. Wassermanns (Hans Otto Horch, 124–146). K. Kraus und das Judentum (Caroline Kohn, 147–160). "'Ghettokunst', meinetwegen, aber hundertprozentig echt": A. Döblins Begegnung mit dem Ostjudentum (H.-P. Bayerdörfer, 161–177). 'Weder Katze noch Lamm'? F. Kafkas Kritik des 'Westjüdischen' (Helen Milfull, 178–192). Max Brod – von 'Schloss Nornepygge' zu 'Galilei in Gefangenschaft' (Margarita Pazi, 193–212). Juden, Christen und andere Menschen: Sabbatianismus, Assimilation und jüdische Identität in L. Feuchtwangers Roman 'Jud Süss' (John Milfull, 213–222). '. . . mehr als die Juden weiss von Gott und der Welt doch niemand': zu Arnold Zweigs Roman 'Der Streit um den Sergeanten Grischa' (Jörg Schönert, 223–242). Die unkündbare Rolle: K. Tucholskys Verhältnis zum Judentum (Fritz Hackert, 243–257). Ein hartnäckiger Wanderer: zur Rolle des Judentums im Werk F. Werfels (G. E. Grimm, 258–279). 'Der begrabenen Blitze Wohnstatt': Trennung, Heimkehr und Sehnsucht in der Lyrik von N. Sachs (Russell A. Berman, 280–292). Die jüdische messianische Tradition und E. Tollers 'Wandlung' (Michael Ossar, 293–308). Joseph Roth: 'Hiob': der Mythos des Skeptikers (Bernd Hüppauf, 309–325). Vom Gewissen der Worte: E. Canetti und die Verantwortung des Dichters im Exil (Martin Bollacher, 326–337). 'Wachstum oder Wunde': zu Paul Celans Judentum (Theo Buck, 338–360).]

23675. HAMBURG. POHL, MANFRED: *Hamburger Bankengeschichte.* Mainz: v. Hase & Koehler, 1986. 264 pp., illus., index of banks and firms (259–264), bibl. (245–255). [Deals also with the Jewish merchant bankers and private banks in Hamburg, a.o., Salomon Heine, Mendelssohn & Co., M. M. Warburg.]

23676. *Juden in der deutschen Literatur.* Ein deutsch-israelisches Symposion [Jerusalem 1983]. Hrsg. von Stéphane Moses und Albrecht Schöne. Frankfurt am Main: Suhrkamp, 1986. 393 pp., notes. (Suhrkamp Taschenbuch Materialien, 2063.) [Incl.: Das Gedächtnis und die Geschichte: Gedanken beim Aufschreiben von Erinnerungen (Hans Mayer, 13–24). 'Ich bin der ich bin': über die Echos eines Namens – Ex.3,13–15 – (Hendrik Birus, 25–53). Zum Werk von Karl Emil Franzos (Martha Bickel, 152–161). Brecht und Benjamin als Kafka–Interpreten (Stéphane Moses, 237–256). Milena, Kafka und das Judentum: wie tief wirkt die intellektuelle Toleranz? (Hana Arie-Gaifman, 257–268). Der unbekannte Bote: zu einem neuentdeckten Widmungstext Kafkas (Jost Schillemeit, 269–280). Wie jüdisch ist ein jüdisch-deutscher Roman? Über Joseph Roths 'Hiob' (Gershon Shaked, 281–292). Das 'ungelebte Leben' Kurt Tucholskys (Margarita Pazi, 293–315). 'Grundriss einer besseren Welt': Messianismus und Geschichte der Utopie bei Ernst Bloch (Wilhelm Vosskamp, 316–329). Politische Theologie? Zur 'Intention auf die Sprache' bei Benjamin und Celan (Horst Turk, 330–349). 'Diese nach jüdischem Vorbild erbaute Arche' – Walter Benjamins *Deutsche Menschen* (Albrecht Schöne, 350–365). Letzte Morgenstunden der Aufklärung: oder Goethes ganz privater Ahasver (Elazar Benyoëtz, 387–394). Further contributions are listed according to subject.]

—— *Juden in der deutschen Wissenschaft.* [See No. 22914.]

—— *Juden in der Weimarer Republik.* [See No. 22915.]

—— *Jüdische Komponenten in der deutschen Literatur – die Assimilationskontroverse.* [See No. 23576.]

23677. LIPTZIN, SOL. *Identity and ethos; a Festschrift for Sol Liptzin on the occasion of his 85th birthday.* Ed. by Mark H. Gelber. New York; Berne: Lang, 1986. 412 pp., port., notes. [Incl.: Sol Liptzin-bibliography, selected, 1920–1986 (11–22). Sholem Asch, Joseph Leftwich, and Stefan Zweig's 'Der begrabene Leuchter' (Mark H. Gelber, 101–120). Adalbert Wogelein's justice, allegorical justice, and justice in Schnitzler's 'Die Frau des Richters' (Richard H. Lawson, 145–154). Neglected nineteenth-century German-Jewish historical fiction (Lothar Kahn, 155–168). The Austro-American Jewish poet Ernst Waldinger (Harry Zohn, 253–266). Further contributions are listed according to subject.] [S. Liptzin, born 1901 in Satanov, raised in the USA, professor of German.]

23678. PAPCKE, SVEN, ed.: *Ordnung und Theorie; Beiträge zur Geschichte der Soziologie in Deutschland.* Darmstadt: Wissenschaftliche Buchgesellschaft, 1986. VI, 458 pp., index of names. [Incl.: Diskurse im Institut für Sozialforschung um 1930: persönliche Erinnerungen (Willy Strzelewicz, 147–167). Siegfried Marck: Biographisches zur Wiederentdeckung des Philosophen, Soziologen und Sozialisten (Helmut Hirsch, 368–385; S. Marck, March 9, 1889 Breslau–Feb. 16, 1957 Chicago). Refers also passim to Jewish sociologists in Germany and in exile.]

23679. REINFRANK-CLARK, KARIN, ed.: *Ach, Sie schreiben deutsch? Biographien deutschsprachiger Schriftsteller des Auslands-PEN.* Gerlingen: Bleicher, 1986. 156 pp. [Collection of short autobiogr. accounts with selective bibliographies by 94 living PEN members, incl. German- and Austrian-Jewish émigrés.]

23680. REINICKE, PETER: *Die Berufsverbände der Sozialarbeit und ihre Geschichte von den Anfängen bis zum Ende des 2. Weltkrieges.* Frankfurt am Main (Am Steckborn 1–3): Deutscher Verein für Öffentliche und Private Fürsorge, 1985. 286 pp., bibl. [Cf.: Juden in der deutschen Sozialarbeit (E. G. Lowenthal) [in]: 'Allgemeine', Nr. 41/20, Bonn, 16. Mai 1986, p. 23.]

B. **Individual**

23681. BÖRNE, LUDWIG: *Ludwig Börne zum 200. Geburtstag. Für die Juden.* Hrsg. vom Archiv Bibliographia Judaica, Frankfurt am Main. (Auswahl und Nachwort [Ludwig Börne und die Juden] von Renate Heuer.) Bad Soden: Woywod, 1986. 79 pp. [Incl. a series of 4 articles which Börne publ. in Aug. and Sept. 1819 under the title 'Für die Juden' in 'Zeitschwingen', a periodical he edited at that time (8–19). Incl. also: Die Juden in Frankfurt am Main, 1807 [&]: Juden in der freien Stadt Frankfurt, 1820 (L. Börne, 5–7; 29–32).]

23682. — ENZENSBERGER, HANS MAGNUS, ed.: *Ludwig Börne und Heinrich Heine: ein deutsches Zerwürfnis.* Nördlingen: Greno, 1986. 378 pp., bibl. (366–368). [Collection of all texts, written by the two antagonists as well as by others in connection with the Börne-Heine controversy.]

23683. — Estermann, Alfred, ed.: *Ludwig Börne, 1786–1837*. (Ausstellungskatalog.] Bearb. im Auftrag des Dezernats für Kultur und Freizeit der Stadt Frankfurt am Main, hrsg. von der Stadt- und Universitätsbibliothek. Frankfurt am Main: Buchhändler-Vereinigung, 1986. 432 pp., illus., ports., facsims., notes, bibl. (359–424). [Incl.: Katalog der Austellung (A. Estermann/Walter Engel/Martin Herrchen, 19–154). Der grosse Judenschmerz: zu einigen Parallelen wie Differenzen bei Börne und Heine (Joseph A. Kruse, 189–197). Henriette Herz und Louis Baruch – Jeanette Wohl und Ludwig Börne (Norbert Altenhofer, 211–221). Die Frankfurter Juden zur Zeit Ludwig Börnes (Hans-Otto Schembs, 239–246). Ludwig Börne – Juif de Francfort (Georg Heuberger, 247–253).]

23684. CARSTEN, F. L.: *Essays in German history*. London: Hambledon, 1985; Ronceverte, W.Va.: Hambledon, 1986. 367 pp., bibl. F. L. Carsten. [Collection of essays from 1938 onward. Incl.: The Court Jews: a prelude to emancipation (orig. publ. [in]: LBI Year Book III, London, 1958, pp. 140–156).]

23685. DÖBLIN, ALFRED: *Schicksalsreise; Bericht und Bekenntnis: Flucht und Exil 1940–1948*. München: Piper, 1986. 326 pp. (Serie Piper, Bd. 549.) [First edn. 1949.]

23686. FRANZOS, KARL EMIL. Hubach, Sybille: *Galizische Träume; die jüdischen Erzählungen des Karl Emil Franzos*. Stuttgart: Heinz, 1986. 216 pp. (Stuttgarter Arbeiten zur Germanistik, Nr. 157.) [See also pp. 152–161 in No. 23676.]

23687. HEINE, HEINRICH. Prawer, S. S.: *Frankenstein's island; England and the English in the writings of Heinrich Heine*. Cambridge; New York: Cambridge Univ. Press, 1986. 357 pp., bibl. (340–348). (Cambridge Studies in German.) [Incl. Jews, antisemitism.]

23688. JACOB, PAUL WALTER. Naumann, Uwe: *Ein Theatermann im Exil: P. Walter Jacob; Hinweis auf einen Vergessenen*. [In]: Bulletin des LBI, 74, Frankfurt am Main, 1986. Pp. 3–15, notes. [P.W.J., data see No. 22603/YB XXXI.]

23689. KAUFMANN, JACOB. Pazi, Margarita: *Jacob Kaufmann: böhmischer Jude und deutscher Patriot*. 1–2. [In]: Bulletin des LBI, 73 (pp. 25–68, notes) [&]: 74 (pp. 17–49, notes), Frankfurt am Main, 1986. [Incl. texts by J.K. and letters to Gustav Freytag.] [J.K., Nov. 10, 1814 Nový Bydzov-Oct. 9, 1871 Wiesbaden, publicist.]

23690. MENDELSSOHN FAMILY. *Mendelssohn Studien*. Beiträge zur neueren deutschen Kultur-und Wirtschaftsgeschichte. Bd. 6. Hrsg. von Cécile Lowenthal-Hensel und Rudolf Elvers. Berlin: Duncker & Humblot, 1986. 288 pp., illus. [Incl. essays on Fanny Hensel née Mendelssohn Bartholdy, Felix Mendelssohn Bartholdy, Franz von Mendelssohn; and letters by Rebecka Dirichlet, Felix M.B., Philipp Veit. See also Nos. 23521 & 23692.]

23691. MENDELSSOHN & CO. Lemke, Heinz: *Finanztransaktionen und Aussenpolitik; deutsche Banken und Russland im Jahrzehnt vor dem Ersten Weltkrieg*. Berlin/East: Verlag der Akademie der Wissenschaften der DDR, 1985. 215 pp. (Studien zur Geschichte, 4.) [Refers, a.o., to the banking-house Mendelssohn & Co.] [See also No. 23675.]

23692. — Rasch, Manfred: *Die Bedeutung des Bankhauses Mendelssohn & Co. für die Industrialisierung Estlands*. Die Estnische Steinöl AG, Tallin, und der Heizöllieferveririag mit der deutschen Kriegsmarine von 1935. [In]: Mendelssohn Studien, Bd. 6, Berlin, 1986. Pp. 183–227.

23693. ROTH, JOSEPH. Johnston, Otto W.: *Jewish exile from Berlin to Paris: the geographical dialectics of Joseph Roth*. [In]: LBI Year Book XXXI, London, 1986. Pp. 441–454, footnotes.

23694. — Rosenfeld, Sidney: *Joseph Roth and Austria: a search for identity*. [In]: LBI Year Book XXXI, London, 1986. Pp. 455–464, footnotes.

23695. — Shaked, Gershon: *Wie jüdisch ist ein jüdisch-deutscher Roman? Über Joseph Roths 'Hiob, Roman eines einfachen Mannes'*. [In]: Bulletin des LBI, 73, Frankfurt am Main, 1986. Pp. 3–12, notes. [Also publ. in No. 23584 (pp. 81–94). and in No. 23676 (pp. 281–292).] [See also Hüppauf essay (pp. 309–325) in No. 23674.]

23696. ROTHSCHILD. Graetz, Michael: *Jewish entrepreneurship during the Second Industrial Revolution: the Rothschilds and the Russian oil industry 1886–1911*. [In Hebrew, with English summary]. [In]: Zion, Vol. 50, Jerusalem, 1985. Pp. 355–378.

23697. SCHEREK, JACOB. Toury, Jacob: *Wer war Jakob Scherek?* [In]: Bulletin des LBI, 75, Frankfurt am Main, 1986. Pp. 3–28, notes. [J.Sch., Dec. 31, 1870 Schrimm–July 26, 1927 Hango, Finland, writer, journalist in Berlin.]

23698. SCHNITZLER, ARTHUR. Allerhand, Jacob: *Jüdische Elemente in den Werken A. Schnitzlers, F. Kafkas, J. Roths und Paul Celans*. [In]: Kairos, N.F., Jg. 27, H. 3–4, Salzburg, 1985. Pp. 288–329, notes (324–329).

23699. THEILHABER, FELIX A. LEHFELDT, HANS: *Felix A. Theilhaber – Pionier-Sexologe.* [In]: Archiv Bibliographia Judaica, Jahrbuch 1, 1985, Bad Soden/Ts., 1986. Pp. 85–93. [See also pp. 73–84 in No. 23570.] [F.A.T., Sept. 5, 1884 Bamberg–Jan. 26, 1956 Tel-Aviv, physician, sociologist, Zionist writer.]

23700. WARBURG & CO., M. M. SHERMAN, A. J.: *A Jewish bank during the Schacht era: M. M. Warburg & Co., 1933–1938.* [In]: Die Juden im Nationalsozialistischen Deutschland [see No. 22913]. Tübingen: Mohr, 1986. Pp. 167–172, summary in German, footnotes. [See also No. 23675.]

23701. WERFEL, FRANZ. KÜHNER, HANS: *Zwischen Jahwe und Jesus: Franz Werfels Gedanken zur Synthese zwischen Juden-und Christentum.* [In]: Tribüne, Jg. 25, H. 99, Frankfurt am Main, 1986. Pp. 151–158.

VIII. AUTOBIOGRAPHY, MEMOIRS, LETTERS, GENEALOGY

23702. BEER-HOFMANN, RICHARD. BERLIN, JEFFREY B.: *The unpublished letters of Richard Beer-Hofmann to Hermann Bahr (with the unpublished letters between Beer-Hofmann and Theodor Herzl).* [In]: Identity and ethos [see No. 23677]. New York; Berne: Lang, 1986. Pp. 121–144, notes.

23703. BROCH, HERMANN: *Briefe über Deutschland 1945–1949; die Korrespondenz mit Volkmar von Zühlsdorff.* Hrsg. und eingeleitet von Paul Michael Lützeler. Frankfurt am Main: Suhrkamp 1986. 154 pp. (Suhrkamp-Taschenbuch, 1369.) [Cf.: Kontroversen über Deutschland (Heribert Seifert) [in]: NZZ, Nr. 112, Zürich, 16./17. Mai 1987, p. 111.]

23704. BRODY, BABETTE S.: *This was my grandfather Philip Stein, 1844–1922.* Assembled from recollections, old letters and historical facts. With research and editorial assistance by David Wolinsky. N.p., 1985. 175 pp., ports., geneal. tab. [Mimeog., available in the LBI New York.] [B.S. Brody, born 1907. Philip Stein, born in Stelle near Essen, judge.]

23705. DREIFUSS, ALFRED: *Ensemblespiel des Lebens; Erinnerungen eines Theatermannes.* Berlin/East: Buchverlag Der Morgen, 1985. 279, 32 pp., illus., ports. [A.D., born Sept 3, 1902 in Stuttgart, dramaturg, journalist, emigrated to Shanghai in 1939, from 1947 living in the GDR.]

23706. EISENBERG, LOTTE: *Pages from my life.* [In]: Hebrew, title transl.]. Jerusalem: Israel Economist, 1986. 92 pp., illus., ports. [For autobiography in German, see No. 16761/YB XXV.] [L.E., born in Königsberg, emigrated to Palestine in 1933, founder of the Galei Kinneret Hotel in Tiberias.]

23707. ELKAN FAMILY. HUSCHKE, WOLFGANG: *Genealogische Skizzen aus dem klassischen Weimar.* Genealogische Besonderheiten einer deutschen Residenzstadt an der Wende vom 18. zum 19. Jahrhundert. [In]: Genealogisches Jahrbuch, Bd. 19, T. 1, Neustadt/Aisch, 1979. Pp. 201–240. [Incl. chap.: Die Judenfamilien [Jacob] Elkan und [Gabriel] Ulmann (pp. 226–233, notes pp. 238–240). Discusses also the activities of both families as bankers.]

23708. FERENCZI, SÁNDOR/GRODDECK, GEORG: *Briefwechsel 1921–1933.* Deutsche Erstausg. Frankfurt am Main: Fischer, 1986. 110 pp., illus. (Fischer-Taschenbuch, 6786.) [S.F., psychoanalyst, data see No. 19378/YB XXVIII.]

23709. FEUCHTWANGER, LION/ZWEIG, ARNOLD: *Briefwechsel 1933–1958.* Bd. 1–2. Hrsg. von Harold von Hofe. Frankfurt am Main: Fischer, 1986. 2 vols. (599; 546 pp.), notes. (Fischer-Taschenbücher, 5783–5784.) [Paperback edn. for West Germany of No. 21701/YB XXX.]

23710. FREUD, SIGMUND: *Briefe an Wilhelm Fliess, 1887–1904.* Hrsg. von Jeffrey Moussaieff Masson. Bearb. der deutschen Fassung von Michael Schröter. Frankfurt am Main: S. Fischer, 1986. 613 pp., 19 illus., ports., facsims., bibl. (577–600). [For American edn. and reviews see No. 22778/YB XXXI.]

23711. FRIED, ERICH: *Mitunter sogar lachen; Zwischenfälle und Erinnerungen.* Berlin: Wagenbach, 1986. 149 pp., illus. (Quarthefte, 150.) [E.F., born May 6, 1921 in Vienna, poet, emigrated to London in 1938.]

23712. FYVEL, T. R.: *And there my trouble began.* Uncollected writings 1945–1985. London: Weidenfeld & Nicolson, 1986. XII, 240 pp. [Incl. reflections on German and Austrian Zionism, Nathan Birnbaum, Buber, the author's father Berthold Feiwel, the Jüdischer Verlag.] [T.R.F., 1907 Cologne – 1985 London.]

23713. GLÜCKEL VON HAMELN. WIEDEMANN, CONRAD: *Zwei jüdische Autobiographien im*

Deutschland des 18. Jahrhuderts: Glückel von Hameln und Salomon Maimon. [In]: Juden in der deutschen Literatur [see No. 23676]. Pp. 88–113, notes.

23714. GOLDNER, FRANZ: *Vorher und nachher; der Weg eines Österreichers.* Wien: Europa-Verl., 1985. 191 pp. [F.G., born Oct. 9, 1903 in Vienna, lawyer, publicist, emigrated to Paris in 1938, to New York in 1940, from 1946 living in New York.]

23715. GRÜNFELDER FAMILY. MOTSCHMANN, JOSEF: *Altenkunstadt – Saaz – Berlin – Jerusalem: Stationen einer jüdischen Familie in drei Jahrhunderten.* [See No. 22973.]

23716. GRUNBERGER, RICHARD: *Walking to school.* [In]: The Jewish Quarterly, Vol. 32, No. 4, London, 1985. Pp. 43–45. [About the author's childhood in Vienna and the Nazi takeover in 1938.]

23717. GURWITSCH, ARON: *Briefwechsel 1939–1959: Alfred Schütz – Aron Gurwitsch.* Mit einer Einleitung von Ludwig Landgrebe. Hrsg. von Richard Grathoff. München: Fink, 1985. XXXVIII, 543 pp., illus., bibl. (521–530). (Übergänge, Bd. 4.) [A. Gurwitsch, Jan. 17, 1901 Vilna–June 25, 1973 Zürich, philosopher, pupil of Husserl, assistant to Moritz Geiger, emigrated to France in 1933, to the USA in 1940, professor of philosophy at the New School for Social Research, New York.]

23718. HABE, HANS: *Ich stelle mich; meine Lebensgeschichte.* (Mit einem Nachwort von Licci Habe.) Erweiterte, neu durchgesehene Ausg. Berlin: Herbig, 1986. 558 pp. (Hans Habe: Gesammelte Werke in Einzelausgaben.) [Autobiography, first publ. 1954, see No. 750/YB I.] [H.H., orig. János Békessy, Feb. 12, 1911 Budapest–Sept. 29, 1977 Ascona, Switzerland, journalist, writer, emigrated in 1935 via Switzerland and France to the USA, chief of American Press in the US Occupied Zone of Germany 1945–1946, chief editor of 'Die Neue Zeitung', Munich.]

23719. HARTMANN, HEINZ: *Once a doctor, always a doctor; the memoirs of a German-Jewish immigrant physician.* Buffalo, N.Y.: Prometheus Books, 1986. 189 pp., ports. [H.H., born 1913 in Ostrow, Prussia, emigrated via Sweden in 1939 to the USA.]

23720. HELLER, HANS: *Zwischen zwei Welten.* Erinnerungen, Prosa, Bilder. Klagenfurt: Verlag Ovilava, 1985. 255 pp., illus., ports. [H.H., born 1896 in Vienna, writer, businessman, painter, emigrated via England in 1938 to the USA.]

—— HERZFELDE, WIELAND. [See No. 23744.]

—— HERZL, THEODOR: *Zionistisches Tagebuch.* [See No. 23645.]

—— — HERZL, THEODOR: *The unpublished letters between Beer-Hofmann and Th. Herzl.* [See No. 23702.]

23721. HODIN, JOSEF PAUL: *Dieses Mütterchen hat Krallen; die Geschichte einer Prager Jugend.* Hamburg: Christians, 1985. 414 pp. [Written in exile three decades ago, now publ. for the first time.] [J.P.H., born Aug. 17, 1905 in Prague, art historian, critic, librarian, emigrated from Berlin in 1933 to France, Sweden and England.]

23722. ISLER, EMMA: *Die Erinnerungen der Emma Isler.* [Hrsg. und eingeleitet von] Ursula Randt. [In]: Bulletin des LBI, 75, Frankfurt am Main, 1986. Pp. 55–99, notes (98), bibl. (99). [Hitherto unpubl. memoirs, written in 1874, cover the time of Jewish emancipation with personal recollections of life in Dessau, Leipzig, Berlin, Hamburg, and on Gabriel Riesser (pp. 96–98).] [E.I., née Meyer, Nov. 3, 1816 Dessau–June 22, 1886 Hamburg, married to Meyer Isler (1808–1888), librarian at the Hamburg Stadtbibliothek.]

23723. JACOB, ERNST M.: *Recollections of a metal merchant, 1922–1983.* [London?, 1985?]. 64 pp. [Typescript, available in the LBI New York.] [E.M.J., born in 1903.]

23724. KOHNER, HANNA & WALTER/KOHNER, FREDERICK: *Hanna und Walter: eine Liebesgeschichte.* Aus dem Amerikan. von Klaus Boer. München: Droemer Knaur, 1986. 190 pp. [For American edn. and data of Walter Kohner, film agent, see No. 21708/YB XXX. See also: Der Drehbuchautor Frederick Kohner gestorben [in]: NZZ, Nr. 170, Zürich, 25. Juli 1986, p. 45 (F.K., 1905 Teplitz-Schönau–July 6, 1986 Brentwood, Calif.]

23725. KRAUS, KARL: *Ein Brief von Karl Kraus an das 'Prager Tagblatt'.* Mitgeteilt und kommentiert von Georg Kranner. [In]: NZZ, Nr. 117, Zürich, 24/25. Mai 1986. P. 68. [Letter of Jan. 29, 1935, publ. for the first time.]

23726. KRAUSS, WALTER: *Austria to Australia; the autobiography of an Austrian Jew from birth to emigration 1904–1938.* [Melbourne, 198–?]. 125 pp. [Available in the Jewish National and Univ. Library, Jerusalem.]

23727. KREISKY, BRUNO: *Zwischen den Zeiten; Erinnerungen aus fünf Jahrzehnten.* Berlin: Siedler, 1986. 494 pp., illus., ports. [B.K., born Jan. 22, 1911 in Vienna, Socialist politician, postwar Austrian Bundeskanzler, emigrated in 1938 to Sweden.]

23728. KRONENBERGER, FRIEDRICH L.: *Erinnerungen und Betrachtungen*. Birkenfeld, 1986. 188 pp., illus., ports. (Schriftenreihe der Kreisvolkshochschule Birkenfeld, Bd. 18.) [F.L.K., born June 14, 1900 in Hoppstädten, physician, emigrated via various countries to Palestine, settled in England after the war.]

23729. LASKER-SCHÜLER, ELSE: *'Was soll ich hier?' Exilbriefe an Salman Schocken*. Dokumentarische Erstausgabe mit 4 Briefen Schockens im Anhang. Hrsg. und kommentiert von Sigrid Bauschinger und Helmut G. Hermann. Heidelberg: Schneider, 1986. 111 pp., illus., ports., list of names (99–101).

23730. — KLÜSENER, ERIKA: *Unveröffentlichte Briefe und Postkarten von Else Lasker-Schüler in der Stadt- und Landesbibliothek zu Dortmund*. [Hrsg. und eingeleitet.] [In]: Bulletin des LBI, 74, Frankfurt am Main, 1986. Pp. 51–63. [Incl. letters and postcards by E. L.-Sch. to the writer Adolf von Hatzfeld, Berlin, 1917–1930 (pp. 54–63).]

23731. LAZARUS, MORITZ: *Moritz Lazarus und Heymann Steinthal; die Begründer der Völkerpsychologie in ihren Briefen*. Bd. 2/2. Mit einer Einleitung hrsg. von Ingrid Belke. Tübingen: Mohr, 1986. VIII, 369–815 pp., illus., ports., index of persons (803–815), bibl. Lazarus & Steinthal (799–802). (Schriftenreihe wissenschaftlicher Abhandlungen des Leo Baeck Instituts, 44.) [Cont.: Letters by *Lazarus* (1824–1903) to university colleagues and contemporary writers, a.o., Paul Heyse; letters by Theodor Fontane and Wilhelm Dilthey to Lazarus. Letters by *Steinthal* (1823–1899) to his publisher and friend Julius Harrwitz, to his teacher Carl W. L. Heyse und the latter's son Paul Heyse, to colleagues and friends, to family members; incl. geneal. tab. of Steinthal. For preceding vols. see Nos. 10042/YB XVII & 20707/YB XXIX.] [Cf.: Lazarus-Steinthal komplett (E. G. Lowenthal) [in]: 'Allgemeine', Nr. 41/39, Bonn, 26. Sept. 1986, p. 41. Heymann Steinthal aus Gröbzig (E. G. Lowenthal) [in]: Das Neue Israel, Jg. 38, H. 8, Zürich, Feb. 1986, p. 41.]

23732. LOESER, FRANZ: *Sag nie, du gehst den letzten Weg; ein deutsches Leben*. Köln: Bund-Verl., 1986. 235 pp., illus., ports., bibl. (233–235). F. L., scholar and writer, now living in the USA, further data see No. 18677/YB XXVII.]

23733. LÖWITH, KARL: *Mein Leben in Deutschland vor und nach 1933*. Ein Bericht. Mit einem Vorwort von Reinhart Koselleck und einer Nachbemerkung von Ada Löwith. Stuttgart: Metzler, 1986. XVI, 160 pp., illus., ports. [Recollections, written 1940 in Japan for a competition by the Harvard University, covering the years from 1914: study at the universitities Freiburg and Marburg, connections with Heidegger and Husserl, life as a refugee in Rome and Japan. Cf.: 'Mit vielem ist es einfach vorbei' (Harry Pross) [in]: Merkur, Jg. 40, H. 11 (453), Stuttgart, Nov. 1986, pp. 963–967.] [K.L., Jan. 1, 1897 Munich–May 24, 1973 Heidelberg, philosopher, emigrated via Italy and Japan to the USA, returned to the Univ. Heidelberg in 1952.]

23734. LUKÁCS, GEORG: *Selected correspondence, 1902–1920; dialogues with Weber, Simmel, Buber, Mannheim, and others*. Selected, ed., transl. and annotated by Judith Marcus and Zoltán Tar. With an introd. by Z. Tar. New York: Columbia Univ. Press, 1986. 318 pp., ports.

23735. MARCUS, PAUL ERICH: *Heimweh nach dem Kurfürstendamm; aus Berlins glanzvollsten Tagen und Nächten*. Von PEM. Frankfurt am Main: Ullstein, 1986. 288 pp., illus., ports., facsims. (Ullstein-Buch, Nr. 34378.) [First edn. 1952.] [P.E.M., pen-name PEM, Jan. 18, 1901 Beeskow–Apr. 24, 1972 London, journalist, fled via Prague to Vienna in 1933, emigrated to London in 1935.]

23736. MARX, GUSTAV H.: *Von Germania zu Marianne*. Eine politische Biographie 1903–1944 mit Zeitbildern. Köln (Postfach 190452): G. H. Marx, 1984. 178 pp. [G.H.M., born 1903 in Düsseldorf, publicist, survived the Nazi period in France.]

23737. MEYER, HANS CHANOCH: *A short family story*. Haifa: The author, 1984. 81, 18 (Hebrew) pp., family ports., geneal. tab. (49–54). [H.C.M., born Oct. 3, 1909 in Krone, Poznań, rabbi, historian, emigrated from Berlin to Palestine in 1939, Landesrabbiner of Westphalia 1958–1963.]

23738. MÜHSAM, ERICH: *In meiner Posaune muss ein Sandkorn sein; Briefe 1900–1934*. Hrsg. von Gerd W. Jungblut. Bd. 1–2. Vaduz, Liechtenstein: Topos, [1986]. XXVI, 490; 491–927 pp., illus.

23739. REICH, WILHELM: *Zeugnisse einer Freundschaft; Briefwechsel zwischen Wilhelm Reich und A. S. Neill, 1936–1957*. Hrsg. und eingeleitet von Beverley R. Placzek. Aus dem Engl. von Bernd A. Laska. Köln: Kiepenheuer & Witsch, 1986. 599 pp. [Transl. of No. 19641/YB XXVIII.]

23740. SCHLEGEL, DOROTHEA: *Briefe von und an Friedrich und Dorothea Schlegel.* Die Periode des Athenäums: 25. Juli 1797– Ende Aug. 1799. Mit Einleitung und Kommentar hrsg. von Raymond Immerwahr. Paderborn: Schöningh, 1985. LIII, 494 pp., illus. (Friedrich Schlegel: Kritische Friedrich-Schlegel-Ausgabe, Bd. 24, Abt. 3.) [Friedrich Schlegel lived in Berlin from 1797–1799; his correspondence, reflecting this period of his life, refers a.o., to Rahel Varnhagen and the Berlin salons where he met Dorothea Veit, oldest daughter of Moses Mendelssohn, who went to live with him after her divorce in 1798. Cf.: '. . . erhabne Frechheit' (Martin Meyer) [in]: NZZ, Nr. 64, Zürich, 18. März 1986, p. 39.]

23741. SCHÖNBERG, ARNOLD: *The [Alban] Berg-Schoenberg correspondence.* Selected letters, ed. by Donald Harris [et al.]. New York: Norton, 1986. 225 pp., illus., ports., facsims. [A selection from more than 800 letters, publ. for the first time.]

23742. SCHOLEM, GERSHOM: *Briefe an Werner Kraft.* Hrsg. von Werner Kraft. Mit einem Nachwort von Jörg Drews. Frankfurt am Main: Suhrkamp, 1986. 165 pp. [Cf.: Der Freund als Mahner (Werner Fuld) [in]: Frankfurter Allg. Zeitung, Nr. 216, 18. Sept. 1986, p. 26. See also: In der Heimat der deutschen Sprache: Werner Kraft wird 90 Jahr [am 4. Mai] (Jörg Drews) [in]: Süddeutsche Zeitung, Nr. 101, München, 3./4. Mai 1986, p. 15.]

23743. SCHOTTLAENDER, RUDOLF: *Trotz allem ein Deutscher; mein Lebensweg seit Jahrhundertbeginn.* Orig.-Ausg. Freiburg i.Br.: Herder, 1986. 125 pp., (Herderbücherei, 1352.) [R.Sch., born Aug. 5, 1900 in Berlin, classical philologist, philosopher, survived the Nazi period in Germany, from 1961 living in East Berlin.]

23744. SEGHERS, ANNA/HERZFELDE, WIELAND: *Gewöhnliches und gefährliches Leben; ein Briefwechsel aus der Zeit des Exils 1939–1946.* Mit Faksimiles, Fotos und dem Aufsatz 'Frauen und Kinder in der Emigration' von Anna Seghers im Anhang. (Gesamtwerk hrsg. im Auftrag der Akademie der Künste der DDR von Ursula Emmerich und Erika Pick.) Darmstadt: Luchterhand, 1986. 204 pp., illus., ports., facsims. [Edn. for West Germany of No. 22811/YB XXXI. Also on the history of the exile publishing house 'Aurora', founded by Wieland Herzfelde in New York.]

23745. STARER, ROBERT: *Continuo.* [In]: The New Yorker, New York, Jan. 6, 1986. Pp. 23– 27. [Reminiscences on emigration to Palestine and on the author's teacher, the tenor Hermann Jadlowker.] [R.St., born Jan. 1924 in Vienna, composer, professor of music, emigrated to Palestine in 1938, living in the USA from 1947.]

—— STEINTHAL, HEYMANN: *Moritz Lazarus und Heymann Steinthal.* [See No. 23731.]

23746. TUCHOLSKY, KURT: *Farbige, weithin sichtbare Signalzeichen: der Briefwechsel zwischen Carl von Ossietzky und Kurt Tucholsky aus dem Jahr 1932.* Mit einem Nachwort hrsg. von Dietger Pforte. Berlin: Akademie der Künste, 1985. 63 pp., 2 ports. (Anmerkungen zur Zeit, 25.)

—— ULMANN FAMILY, Weimar. [See No. 23707.]

23747. VARNHAGEN, RAHEL: *Briefe und Aufzeichnungen.* (Hrsg. von Dieter Bähtz.) Frankfurt am Main: Insel, 1986; Leipzig: Kiepenheuer, 1985. 424 pp., illus.

23748. — VARNHAGEN, RAHEL: *Rahels erste Liebe; Rahel Levin und Karl Graf von Finckenstein in ihren Briefen.* Nach den Originalen hrsg. und erläutert von Günter de Bruyn. Frankfurt am Main: Fischer, 1986. 364 pp., bibl. (350–354). (Fischer-Taschenbücher, 5114.)

23749. WOLFF, CHARLOTTE: *Augenblicke verändern uns mehr als die Zeit.* Eine Autobiographie. Aus dem Engl. von Michaela Huber. Frankfurt am Main: Fischer, 1986. 318 pp. (Fischer-Taschenbücher, 3778.) [Transl. of No. 17777/YB XXVI.] [Ch.W., Sept. 30, 1904 Riesenburg, Eastern Prussia–autumn 1986 London, psychiatrist, feminist, emigrated from Berlin to France in 1933 and to England in 1936.]

—— ZWEIG, ARNOLD. [See No. 23709.]

23750. ZWEIG, STEFAN: *Stefan Zweig – Paul Zech: Briefe 1910–1942.* Hrsg. von Donald G. Daviau. Frankfurt am Main: Fischer, 1986. 248 pp., facsims., bibl. (Fischer-Taschenbücher, 5911.) [Edn. for West Germany of No. 22820/YB XXXI.] [See also pp. 59–80 in No. 23584.]

23751. — FLOR, CLAUDE: *Stefan Zweig und Meyer-Benfey.* Bisher unveröffentlichte Briefe, ein Psychogramm und die Erzählung 'Der Kampf um den Südpol'. Hamburg: Deutscher Literatur-Verl. Melchert, 1986. 128 pp. (DLV-Taschenbuch, Nr. 223.)

23752. — MYGDALIS, LAMPROS: *Unbekannte Briefe von Stefan Zweig.* [In]: Wirkendes Wort, Jg. 36, H. 4, Düsseldorf, Juli/Aug. 1986. Pp. 269–275, notes. [Incl. 3 letters by St. Zweig to Giorgos Anemojannis, 1939–1940, and a sketch written in German under the English title 'Autobiographic notes for an interview'.]

IX. GERMAN-JEWISH RELATIONS

A. General

23753. *Babylon.* Beiträge zur jüdischen Gegenwart. H. 1. Hrsg. Dan Diner [et al.]. Frankfurt am Main: Verlag Neue Kritik, Okt. 1986. 137 pp. [Incl.: Negative Symbiose: Deutsche und Juden nach Auschwitz (Dan Diner, 9–20). Die ästhetische Transformation der Vorstellung vom Unvorstellbaren: Anmerkungen zu Claude Lanzmanns Film Shoah (Gertrud Koch, 84–91). See also No. 23546.]

23754. FASSBINDER, RAINER WERNER. KAHN, LOTHAR: *The Fassbinder affair.* [In]: Midstream, Vol. 32, No. 2, New York, Feb. 1986. Pp. 50–52. [About the controversial attempt to stage Fassbinder's play, 'Garbage, the city and death', which has been charged with antisemitism.]

23755. — KIDERLEN, ELISABETH, ed.: *Fassbinders Sprengsätze; deutsch-jüdische Normalität.* Frankfurt am Main: Pflasterstrand, 1985. 96 pp. (Pflasterstrand-Flugschrift, 1.)

23756. — LICHTENSTEIN, HEINER, ed.: *Die Fassbinder-Kontroverse oder das Ende der Schonzeit.* Mit einem Nachwort von Julius H. Schoeps. Königstein/Ts.: Athenäum, 1986. 254 pp. [Cf.: Ende der 'Schonzeit' für Juden? (Ursula Homann) [In]: Tribüne, Jg. 25, H. 99, Frankfurt am Main, 1986, pp. 193–196.]

23757. — ZWERENZ, GERHARD: *Die Rückkehr des toten Juden nach Deutschland.* Ismaning bei München: Verlag Max Hueber, 1986. 254 pp. [On the author's novel 'Die Erde ist unbewohnbar wie der Mond' and its connection with Fassbinder's controversial theatre play, on antisemitism, old and new, in Germany.]

23758. FRIEDLANDER, ALBERT H.: *Begegnung nach 40 Jahren; Deutsche und Juden heute.* [In]: Der Monat, N.F. 297, Weinheim, 1985. Pp. 12–31.

23759. FRIEDMANN, FRIEDRICH GEORG, ed.: *Ja, es gab eine deutsch-jüdische Symbiose: Emigranten berichten über ihre ehemaligen Hausangestellten.* [In]: Aufbau, Nr. 15–16, New York, Apr. 11, 1986. Pp. 20–22 [&]: Leserbriefe [in]: Nr. 25–26, June 20, 1986, p. 34 [&]: Erinnerungen an frühere Hausangestellte [in]: Nr. 33–34, Aug. 15, 1986, p. 34.

23760. — LARSEN, EGON: *A tale of love, loyalty and courage: how Gentile maids stood by German Jewish families.* [In]: AJR Information, No. 8, London, Aug. 1986. P. 2. [Refers to the cóllection of letters publ. by F. G. Friedmann [in]: Die Zeit, see No. 22823/YB XXXI.]

23761. HARTMAN, GEOFFREY H., ed.: *Bitburg in moral and political perspective.* Bloomington: Indiana Univ. Press, 1986. XV, 284 pp., illus., bibl. (281–282). [Incl. contributions by Saul Friedländer, Jürgen Habermas, Raul Hilberg, Primo Levi.]

23762. KATZ, JACOB: *Rezeption jüdischer Autoren durch deutsche Kritik und deutsches Publikum.* [In]: Bulletin des LBI, 75, Frankfurt am Main, 1986. Pp. 29–53, notes (53). [Orig. publ. [in]: Kontroversen, alte und neue, Bd. 5. See pp. 129–138 in No. 23576.]

23763. KLAPPERT, BERTOLD: *Kollektivschuld und verweigerte Vergebung: 40 Jahre nach dem Ende des 2. Weltkrieges.* [In]: 'Allgemeine', Nr. 41/39, Bonn, 26. Sept. 1986. P. 20.

23764. KOEBNER, THOMAS: *'Feindliche Brüder': Stereotypen der Abgrenzung jüdischen und deutschen Wesens.* [In]: Archiv Bibliographia Judaica, Jahrbuch 1, 1985, Bad Soden/Ts., 1986. Pp. 29–55, notes, bibl.

23765. LEICHT, ROBERT: *Das Tabu zerbricht: Antisemitismus meldet sich wieder zu Wort.* [In]: Die Zeit, Nr. 8, Hamburg, 14. Feb. 1986. P. 1. [Refers to the Fassbinder controversy and to recent statements by German politicians. See also: Reiche Juden erschlagen: deutsche Kommunalpolitik 1986 (Heiner Lichtenstein) [in]: Die Neue Gesellschaft/Frankfurter Hefte, Jg. 33, Nr. 2, Bonn, Feb. 1986, pp. 101–102. '. . . endlich an der Zeit, nun Schluss zu machen . . .': anonymer Brief im August 1986 [an Peter Glotz]; Dokumentation [in]: Die Neue Gesellschaft/Frankfurter Hefte, Jg. 33, Nr. 10, Bonn, Okt. 1986, pp. 898 & 901. Welche Bedeutung hat Langemarck? Wie eine Stadt [Dormagen] mit der Geschichte umgeht (Roland Kirbach) [in]: Die Zeit, Nr. 15, Hamburg, 4. Apr. 1986, p. 20.]

23766. MAAS, HERMANN. *Redet mit Jerusalem freundlich: Zeugnisse von und über Hermann Maas.* Erarb. von Werner Keller [et al.]. Mit einem Vorwort von Klaus Engelhardt und Reinhold Zundel. Karlsruhe: Evangelischer Presseverband für Baden, 1986. 108 pp., illus. bibl. (107–108). [Incl. chap.: Der stadtbekannte Judenfreund (59–78).] [Prälat H.M., 1877–1970, clergyman, helped Jews during the Nazi period, banned from work and sentenced to slave labour in France, after the war instrumental in the re-establishment of German-Jewish relations.]

23767. RABINBACH, ANSON/ZIPES, JACK, eds.: *Germans and Jews since the Holocaust; the changing situation in West Germany*. New York: Holmes & Meier, 1986. VIII, 365 pp., bibl. (356–361). [Collection of articles, most of them previously publ. [in]: new german critique, No. 19 & 20 (1980), see No. 17780/YB XXVI.]

23768. STEINBACH, PETER: *Von der Revolution zum Völkermord: Entscheidungsjahre deutsch-jüdischer Beziehungen im 20. Jahrhundert*. 1–3. [In]: 'Allgemeine', Nr. 41/45 (pp. 3–4); Nr. 41/46 (pp. 3–4); Nr. 41/47 (pp. 3–4), Bonn, 7., 14. & 21. Nov. 1986.

23769. *Tribüne*. Zeitschrift zum Verständnis des Judentums. Jg. 25, H. 97–100. Hrsg. von Elisabeth Reisch. [And]: *Sach- und Autorenregister der Tribüne Jg. 1–25 (H. 1–100)*. Frankfurt am Main: Tribüne-Verl., 1986. 4 issues. [And index-vol.]: 196 pp. [*H.97* incl.: 'Gesagt, was sehr viele denken . . .': die Probleme der Deutschen mit ihrer NS-Vergangenheit (Georg Schwinghammer, 14–20). *H. 98*: Die Welt des Franz Goldstein (Klaus Täubert, 174–176; F.G., 1898 Kattowitz – 1982 Jerusalem, journalist). *H. 99*: Österreichs historische Last: Probleme nach der Wahl Kurt Waldheims zum neuen Bundespräsidenten (Georg Schwinghammer, 36–40). *H. 100*: 40 Jahre nach dem Holocaust: Umfrage über antisemitische Einstellungen bei deutschen Schülern (Rainer A. Roth, 59–72, diagrs.). Mitmenschlichkeit und Vertrauen: 'Wir Deutsche dürfen die NS-Verbrechen nie vergessen oder verdrängen' (Helmut Kohl, 112–119). 'Die Tabuschwelle hat sich gesenkt' (Tribüne-Gespräch mit Johannes Rau, 120–129). Gegen moralische Selbstlähmung: zum Verhältnis zwischen Deutschen und Juden (Franz Josef Strauss, 134–140). 'Nicht Auschwitz überlebt, um jetzt zu schweigen . . .' (Tribüne-Gespräch mit Heinz Galinski, 186–194). Begegnungen von Deutschen und Israelis (Herbert Rosenkranz, 223–230; Erich Rotter, 231–240). Im Zeichen der Ähnlichkeit: Antisemitismus – ein Element des deutschen Selbsthasses? (Herbert Freeden, 242–250). Further contributions are listed according to subject.]

—— VOGEL, ROLF, ed.: *Bundeskanzler Dr. Helmut Kohl zur deutsch-jüdischen Frage in Verbindung mit der Rolle des Leo-Baeck-Instituts*. [See No. 23187.]

23770. WEIGEL, HANS: *Man kann nicht ruhig darüber reden; Umkreisung eines fatalen Themas*. Graz: Styria, 1986. 141 pp.

23771. WEIZSÄCKER, RICHARD von. *Eine Rede und ihre Wirkung: die Rede des Bundespräsidenten Richard von Weizsäcker vom 8. Mai 1985 anlässlich des 40. Jahrestages der Beendigung des Zweiten Weltkrieges*. Betroffene nehmen Stellung. Hrsg. von Ulrich Gill und Winfried Steffani. Berlin: Röll, 1986. 191 pp. [Refers to No. 22253/YB XXXI.]

—— THE JEW IN LITERATURE. [See also Nos. 22946, 23754–23757, 23794, 23841–23844.]

23772. — ANGRESS, RUTH K.: *Gibt es eine 'Judenproblem' in der deutschen Nachkriegsliteratur?* [In]: Neue Sammlung, Jg. 26, H. 1, Stuttgart, Jan.–März 1986. Pp. 22–40, footnotes. [Slightly altered German version of No. 22829/YB XXXI.]

23773. — ANGRESS, RUTH K.: *Wunsch- und Angstbilder: jüdische Gestalten aus der deutschen Literatur des 19. Jahrhunderts*. [In]: Kontroversen, alte und neue. Bd. 1: Ansprachen – Plenarvorträge – Berichte. Hrsg. von Albrecht Schöne. Tübingen: Niemeyer, 1986. Pp. 84–96.

—— — Bremer, Natascha: *Das Bild der Juden in den Passionsspielen*. [See No. 23788.]

23774. — KAHN, LUDWIG W.: *The changing image of the Jew: Nathan the Wise and Shylock*. [In]: Identity and ethos [see No. 23677]. New York; Berne: Lang, 1986. Pp. 235–252, notes.

23775. — KARNICK, MANFRED: *Die grössere Hoffnung: über 'jüdisches Schicksal' in deutscher Nachkriegsliteratur*. [In]: Juden in der deutschen Literatur [see No. 23676]. Pp. 366–385, notes.

—— — KOCH, GERTRUD: *Zu einigen jüdischen Figuren im deutschen Nachkriegsfilm*. [See pp. 258–274 in No. 23427.]

23776. — KOCH, REINHARD: *Jud Süss: zur Darstellung von Juden in der deutschen Literatur*. Aachen: Bergmoser & Höller, 1986. 29 pp., illus. (Deutsch betrifft uns, 86,9.)

—— — PRAWER, SIEGBERT S.: *The death of Sigismund Markus: The Jews in Danzig in the fiction of Günter Grass*. [See pp. 93–108 in No. 22904.]

23777. — STEIN, ARJEH: *The image of the Jew in German society according to works of German non-Jewish authors, during the period of national unification until the Weimar era, as seen from a historical aspect*. [In Hebrew, with English summary]. Tel-Aviv, Univ., Diss., May 1985. 455, XX pp. in 2 vols.

23778. — STENZEL, JÜRGEN: *Idealisierung und Vorurteil: zur Figur des 'edlen Juden' in der deutschen Literatur des 18. Jahrhunderts*. [In]: Juden in der deutschen Literatur [see No. 23676]. Pp. 113–126, notes.

23779. — VOSS, JULIUS von: *Der travestirte Nathan der Weise*. Posse in 2 Akten mit Intermezzos, Chören, Tanz, gelehrtem Zweykampf, Mord und Todschlag. Faksimile-Druck nach der

Ausg. von 1804. Hrsg. und mit einer Einführung von Leif Ludwig Albertsen. Bern: Lang, 1975. 35, XXII, 192 pp. (Seltene Texte aus der deutschen Romantik.)

23780. — WODENEGG, ANDREA: *Das Bild der Juden Osteuropas.* Ein Beitrag zur komparatistischen Imagologie an Textbeispielen von Karl Emil Franzos und Leopold von Sacher-Masoch. Frankfurt am Main: Lang, 1986. 240 pp. (Europäische Hochschulschriften: Reihe 1, Bd. 927.)

B. **German-Israeli Relations**

23781. *deutschland-berichte.* Hrsg.: Rolf Vogel. Jg. 22, Nr. 1–12. Bonn, 1986. 11 issues & Themenregister (19 pp.). [*Nr. 12* incl.: Die 10. Deutsch-Israelische Konferenz: Ansprachen, Resolutionen (4–12). Further contributions are listed according to subject.]

23782. KÖGEL, HANS-WERNER: *Das Israel-Bild in Deutschland.* Dargestellt anhand von Presse- und Partei-Veröffentlichungen. Schmitten: Evang. Akademie Arnoldshain, 1985. 121 pp., illus., bibl. (Arnoldshainer Protokolle, 85,2.)

23783. MEROZ, YOHANAN: *In schwieriger Mission; als Botschafter Israels in Bonn.* Mit einem Geleitwort von Helmut Schmidt. Berlin: Ullstein, 1986. 253 pp. [Covers the years 1974–1981.] [Y.M., born 1920 in Berlin, emigrated in 1933 to Palestine.]

23784. SHAFIR, SHLOMO: *An outstretched hand; German Social Democrats, Jews, and Israel, 1945–1967.* [In Hebrew]. Tel-Aviv: Zmora, Bitan, 1986. 263 pp., ports.

23785. WIEHN, ERHARD R./WIEHN, HEIDE M.: *Dajenu: Tagebuch einer Israelreise.* Konstanz (Hegaublick 2): Verlagsbuchhandlung Hartung-Gorre, 1986. 305 pp., illus.

23786. WOLFFSOHN, MICHAEL: *Deutsch-israelische Beziehungen; Umfragen und Interpretationen 1952–1986.* München: Bayerische Landeszentrale für Politische Bildungsarbeit, 1986. 96 pp., illus., diagrs. (Zeitfragen, 27.) [See also essays by Wolffsohn (pp. 88–107) & Claussen (230–242) in No. 23427.]

C. **Church and Synagogue**

23787. BERGER, DAVID: *Mission to the Jews and Jewish-Christian contacts in the polemical literature of the High Middle Ages.* [In]: The American Historical Review, Vol. 91, No. 3, Washington, D.C., June 1986. Pp. 576–591, notes. [Refers also to Germany, especially the Rhineland, Cologne.]

23788. BREMER, NATASCHA: *Das Bild der Juden in den Passionsspielen und in der bildenden Kunst des deutschen Mittelalters.* Frankfurt am Main: Lang, 1986. 244, 44 pp., illus. (Europäische Hochschulschriften: Reihe 1, Bd. 892.) [Covers the 9th to the 16th centuries; incl. chaps.: Die Lage der Juden in der christlichen Gesellschaft; Synagoge und Ecclesia; Das Judasbild.]

23789. *Christian Jewish Relations.* Vol. 19, Nos. 1–4.Ed.: Norman Solomon. London: Institute of Jewish Affairs in association with the World Jewish Congress, 1986. 4 issues. [*No. 1* incl.: The Forgiveness debate, ed. and introd. by Norman Solomon (3–24, notes; cont.: Judaism and the concept of forgiving, by Albert H. Friedlander; Forgiveness reconsidered, by Anthony Phillips; Reconciliation in Germany, by Ursula Deist. For earlier material that prompted this debate, see No. 22251/YB XXXI). *No. 3*: The Forgiveness debate: letter to the editor (Eugene J. Fisher, 57–59). *No. 4*: Dr. Gertrud Luckner: on the occasion of her 86th birthday (Michael J. Pragai, 5–6).]

23790. COHEN, JEREMY: *Scholarship and intolerance in the medieval academy: the study and evaluation of Judaism in European Christendom.* [In]: American Historical Review, Vol. 91, No. 3, Washington, D.C., June 1986. Pp. 592–613, notes.

23791. EIDELBERG, SHLOMO: *On apostates and Christians in Ashkenaz in the late Middle Ages.* [In Hebrew]. [In]: Aharon Mirsky jubilee volume; essays on Jewish culture. [In Hebrew]. Ed.: Zvi Malachi. Lod: Habermann Institute for Literary Research, 1986. Pp. 25–30. [Discusses the case of Christoph David Bernard (27–29).]

23792. ERASMUS. GODIN, ANDRÉ: *L'antijudaïsme d'Erasme: équivoques d'un modèle théologique.* [In]: Bibliothèque d'Humanisme et Renaissance, Vol. 47, No. 3, Genf, 1985. Pp. 537–553.

23793. — MARKISH, SHIMON: *Erasmus and the Jews.* Transl. by Anthony Olcott. Afterword by Arthur A. Cohen. Chicago: Univ. of Chicago Press, 1986. 203 pp.

23794. HASAN-ROKEM, GALIT/DUNDES, ALAN, eds.: *The Wandering Jew: essays in the interpretation of a Christian legend.* Bloomington: Indiana Univ. Press, 1986. IX, 278 pp., illus., bibl. (272–278). [A survey of the most representative interpretations of the legend; incl.: The Wandering Jew: legend or myth? (Eduard König, 11–26, notes; a transl. of König's antisemitic book *Ahasver 'der ewige Jude'*, first publ. in 1907). The Ahasver-Volksbuch 1602 (Aaron Schaffer, 27–35; orig. publ. 1920 in German).]

23795. KOHN, JOHANNA: *Haschoah; christliche-jüdische Verständigung nach Auschwitz.* Mit einem Vorwort von Günther Bernd Ginzel. München: Kaiser; Mainz: Grünewald, 1986. 107 pp., bibl. (103–107). (Fundamentaltheologische Studien, Nr. 13.)

23796. KREMERS, HEINZ. *'Wer Tora vermehrt, mehrt Leben': Festgabe für Heinz Kremers zum 60. Geburtstag.* Hrsg. von Edna Brocke und Hans-Joachim Barkenings. Neukirchen-Vluyn: Neukirchener Verl., 1986. XIV, 250 pp. [See also: Laudatio auf den diesjährigen Preisträger der Buber-Rosenzweig-Medaille Professor Dr. Heinz Kremers (Johannes Rau) [&]: Dankwort (H. Kremers) [in]: deutschland-berichte, Jg. 22, Nr. 4, Bonn, Apr. 1986, pp. 28–31.]

23797. LIEBSTER, WOLFRAM: *Ein Judenchrist beginnt den Kirchenkampf: zum Gedächtnis von Hans Ehrenberg.* [In]: Jahrbuch für Westfälische Kirchengeschichte, Bd. 79, 1986. Pp. 265–286. [See also No. 23540.]

—— LUTHER, MARTIN. [See also Nos. 23243, 23575.]

23798. — AMARU, BETSY HALPERN: *Martin Luther and Jewish mirrors.* [In]: Jewish Social Studies, Vol. 46, New York, Spring 1984. Pp. 95–102.

23799. — DEGANI, BEN-ZION: *Layers of medieval Jew-hatred in Luther's writings and their influence on anti-Jewish writing in Germany.* [In Hebrew, title transl.]. [In]: Eshel Beer-Sheva; Essays in Jewish Studies, Vol. 3, Beer-Sheva, 1986. Pp. 179–227.

23800. — MICHAEL, ROBERT: *Luther, Luther scholars, and the Jews.* [In]: Encounter, Vol. 64, London, 1985. Pp. 339–353.

23801. — ROWAN, STEVEN: *Luther, Bucer and Eck, and the Jews.* [In]: Sixteenth Century Journal, 16, Northeast Missouri State Univ., Kirksville, Spring 1985. Pp. 79–90.

23802. — SÜSSMUTH, HANS, ed.: *Das Luther-Erbe in Deutschland.* Vermittlung zwischen Wissenschaft und Öffentlichkeit. Düsseldorf: Droste, 1985. 379 pp., bibl. [Incl.: Martin Luther und die Juden (Johann Michael Schmidt, 130–147). Ist Luthers Theologie in ihrem Wesen antijüdisch? (Johannes Brosseder, 148–154). Martin Luther und die Juden: eine Herausforderung für die Fernsehproduktion 1983 (Paul Karalus, 220–225).]

23803. MAYER, REINHOLD. *Wie gut sind deine Zelte, Jaakow . . .'; Festschrift zum 60. Geburtstag von Reinhold Mayer.* Hrsg. von Ernst Ludwig Ehrlich und Bertold Klappert in Zusammenarbeit mit Ursula Ast. Gerlingen: Bleicher, 1986. 278 pp., port., bibl. [Incl.: Der Reformprozess in der jüdischen Geschichte (Ernst Ludwig Ehrlich, 76–89). Rosa Luxemburg – eine Jüdin in Deutschland (Walter Jens, 96–106). Rosenzweigs Besuch bei Buber in Heppenheim am 3.12.1921 (Yehoshua Amir, 107–118). Das Judentum im Religionsbuch (Hubertus Halbfas, 166–174). Warum ich mich als Christ für die Juden interessiere (Franz Mussner, 191–195).]

23804. WOLF, GERHARD PHILIPP: *Zur Geschichte der evangelischen Judenmission im Bayern des 19. Jahrhunderts: zwischen Hoffnung und Enttäuschung.* [In]: Zeitschrift für Bayerische Kirchengeschichte, 54, Nürnberg, 1985. Pp. 127–152.

D. **Antisemitism**

23805. ARONSFELD, C. C.: *The first anti-Semitic International 1882–1883 [in Dresden].* [In]: Immigrants & Minorities, 4, London, March 1985. Pp. 64–75.

—— AUSTRIA. [See also Nos. 23101, 23106, 23418.]

23806. — BINDER, DIETER A.: *Der 'reiche Jude': zur sozialdemokratischen Kapitalismuskritik und zu deren antisemitischen Feindbildern in der Ersten Republik.* [In]: Geschichte und Gegenwart, 4, März 1985. Pp. 43–53.

23807. — WALLA, FRIEDRICH: *Johann Nestroy und der Antisemitismus.* [In]: Österreich in Geschichte und Literatur, Jg. 29, Nr. 1, Wien, 1985. Pp. 37–51.

23808. BEER, UDO: *Der falsche Priester; eine Borkumer Kampfschrift aus der Zeit der Weimarer Republik.* [In]: Jahrbuch der Gesellschaft für Bildende Kunst und Vaterländische Altertümer, Bd. 66, Emden, 1986. Pp. 152–163, footnotes. [Refers to Ludwig Münchmeyer, 1885–1947.]

23809. BERGMANN, WERNER/ERB, RAINER: *Kommunikationslatenz, Moral und öffentliche Meinung; theoretische Überlegungen zum Antisemitismus in der Bundesrepublik.* [In]: Kölner Zeitschrift für Soziologie und Sozialpsychologie, Jg. 38, Wiesbaden, 1986. Pp. 223–246, notes, bibl. [See also Nos. 23754–23757, 23765.]

23810. BLACKBOURN, DAVID: *The politics of demagogy in Imperial Germany.* [In]: Past & Present, No. 113, Oxford, Nov. 1986. Pp. 152–184. [Also on antisemitic movements.]

23811. BRODER, HENRYK M.: *Antisemitismus – ja bitte!* Ein Vorschlag für mehr Ehrlichkeit und weniger Heuchelei. [And]: *Ein falscher Fehler: ein Nachwort zu 'Antisemitismus – ja bitte!'.* [In]: Süddeutsche Zeitung, Nr. 14, München, 18./19. Jan. 1986. Pp. I–II [&]: Nr. 56, 8./9. März 1986, p. II.

23812. BRODER, HENRYK M.: *Der ewige Antisemit; über Sinn und Funktion eines beständigen Gefühls.* Orig.-Ausg. Frankfurt am Main: Fischer, 1986. 287 pp. (Fischer-Taschenbücher, 3806.) [See also: Vom pathologisch guten Gewissen: H. M. Broder gab einen Erfahrungsbericht über die Reaktionen auf sein Buch (Ellen Presser) [in]: 'Allgemeine', Nr. 41/50, Bonn, 12. Dez. 1986, p. 7.]

—— ENGEL, DAVID: *Patriotism as a shield: the liberal Jewish defence against antisemitism in Germany during the First World War.* [See No. 23602.]

23813. FLINT, VALERIE: *Anti-Jewish literature and attitudes in the twelfth century.* [In]: Journal of Jewish Studies, Vol. 37, No. 2, Oxford, Autumn, 1986. Pp. 183–205, notes. [Deals also with Germany, especially the Jewish community in Regensburg.]

23814. FREY, WINFRIED: *Die 'Epistolae obscurorum virorum' – ein antijüdisches Pamphlet?* [In]: Archiv Bibliographia Judaica, Jahrbuch 1, 1985, Bad Soden/Ts., 1986. Pp. 147–172, notes (164–172).

23815. GRIEB-LOHWASSER, BIRGITT: *Jüdische Studenten und Antisemitismus an der Universität Würzburg in der Weimarer Republik.* [In]: Ein Streifzug durch Frankens Vergangenheit. Hrsg. von Herbert Schultheis. Bad Neustadt a.d.S. (Postfach 1560): Rötter, 1982. (Bad Neustädter Beiträge zur Geschichte und Heimatkunde Frankens, Bd. 2.) Pp. 255–371, tab., bibl. (344–371).

23816. HURWITZ, EMANUEL: *Bocksfuss, Schwanz und Hörner; Vergangenes und Gegenwärtiges über Antisemiten und ihre Opfer.* Zürich: Nagel & Kimsche, 1986. 318 pp., bibl. (311–318).

23817. JATHO, JÖRG-PETER: *Dr. Ferdinand Werner; eine biographische Skizze zur Verstrickung eines völkischen Antisemiten in den Nationalsozialismus.* [In]: Wetterauer Geschichtsblätter, Bd. 34, Friedberg, 1985. Pp. 181–224, bibl. (220–224).

23818. KEILSON, HANS: *Zum Problem des linken Antisemitismus.* Vortrag zur 2. Jahreshauptversammlung der Gesellschaft für Exilforschung e.V. am 13. Feb. 1986. [Frankfurt am Main: Gesellschaft für Exilforschung, 1986.] 18 pp. bibl. (17–18).

—— KNAUSS, ERWIN: *Der politische Antisemitismus vom ausgehenden 19. Jahrhundert bis zum Ende des Kaiserreichs unter besonderer Berücksichtigung des nord- und mittelhessischen Raumes.* [See pp. 15–32 in No. 23033.]

23819. LÉMONON, MICHEL: *Die Verbreitung der Rassenlehre Gobineaus in Deutschland.* [In]: Büttner, Ursula, ed.: Das Unrechtsregime, Bd. 1. Hamburg: Christians, 1986. Pp. 39–48, notes.

23820. LEWIS, BERNARD: *Semites and anti-Semites; an inquiry into conflict and prejudice.* New York: Norton; London: Weidenfeld & Nicolson, 1986. 283 pp., notes. [Incl. chaps.: The Holocaust and after (25–41). The Nazis and the Palestine question (140–163). Cf.: Prejudicial encounters (Ernest Gellner) [in]: TLS, London, Aug. 22, 1986, p. 903.]

23821. MASSING, PAUL W.: *Vorgeschichte des politischen Antisemitismus.* Aus dem Amerikan. übers. und für die deutsche Ausg. bearb. von Felix J. Weil. Frankfurt am Main: Europäische Verlagsanstalt, 1986. VIII, 285 pp. (Taschenbücher Syndikat, EVA, Bd. 78.) [Paperback edn. of No. 1896/YB V; for American orig. 'Rehearsal for destruction; a study of political anti-Semitism in Imperial Germany', New York, 1949, see No. 824/YB I.]

23822. *Patterns of Prejudice.* Vol. 20, Nos. 1–4. Ed.: Antony Lerman. London: Institute of Jewish Affairs in association with the World Jewish Congress, 1986. 4 issues. [Contributions pertinent to German Jewry are listed according to subject.]

—— PAUCKER, ARNOLD: *Jewish self-defence.* [See No. 23597.]

—— PEAL, DAVID: *Anti-Semitism and rural transformation in Kurhessen.* [See No. 23026.]

23823. RYSZKA, FRANCISZEK: *Von der Idee zum Völkermord: Gedanken über den Antisemitismus.* [In]: Büttner, Ursula, ed.: Das Unrechtsregime, Bd. 1. Hamburg: Christians, 1986. Pp. 79–100, notes.

23824. SILBERMANN, ALPHONS/SCHOEPS, JULIUS H., eds.: *Antisemitismus nach dem Holocaust; Bestandsaufnahme und Erscheinungsformen in deutschsprachigen Ländern.* Köln: Verlag Wissenschaft und Politik, 1986. 194 pp., diagrs., bibl. (189–192). [Incl. (titles condensed):

Antisemitismus in Deutschland heute (Günther Bernd Ginzel, 19–32). Zerstörung und Schändung jüdischer Friedhöfe seit 1945 (J. H. Schoeps, 33–40). Bitburg: zu einem Lehrstück anti-jüdischen Ressentiments, 1985 (Hajo Funke, 41–52). Antisemitische Vorurteile in Österreich nach 1945 (Hilde Weiss, 53–70). Antisemitismus in der Schweiz nach dem 2. Weltkrieg (Willy Guggenheim, 71–90). Die Judendarstellungen in den deutschen Medien (Friedrich Knilli, 115–132). Judenfeindliche Tendenzen im Umkreis neuer sozialer Bewegungen (Micha Brumlik, 133–162).]

23825. SPIRO, E.: *Rembrandt and the Jews.* [In]: Jewish Affairs, Vol. 41, No. 6, Johannesburg, South Africa, June 1986. Pp. 25–30, illus., bibl. [Incl. chap.: Rembrandt – a symbol of a national rebirth of Germany through art (p. 29), referring to Julius Langbehn's book 'Rembrandt als Erzieher' and its antisemitic tendencies.]

23826. STERN, FRITZ: *Kulturpessimismus als politische Gefahr; eine Analyse nationaler Ideologie in Deutschland.* (Übers. aus dem Amerikan. von Alfred P. Zeller.) München: Deutscher Taschenbuch-Verl., 1986. 420 pp. (dtv, 4448.) [On Paul de Lagarde, Julius Langbehn, Arthur Moeller van den Bruck. For American orig. 'The politics of cultural despair', 1961, see No. 2994/YB VII.]

23887. STRAUSS, HERBERT A./KAMPE, NORBERT, eds.: *Antisemitismus; von der Judenfeindschaft zum Holocaust.* [2. Aufl.]. Bonn: Bundeszentrale für politische Bildung, 1985. 288 pp., footnotes, bibl. (Schriftenreihe der Bundeszentrale für politische Bildung, Bd. 213.) [For cont. and reviews see No. 22865–22866/YB XXXI. Cf.: Die Juden und die Vorurteile (Alphons Silbermann) [in]: Tribüne, Jg. 25, H. 98, Frankfurt am Main, 1986, pp. 188–190.]

23828. STRAUSS, HERBERT A.: *Antisemitism as a problem of periods in German history.* [In Hebrew, with English summary]. [In]: Gesher, No. 114, Jerusalem, Summer 1986. Pp. 21–34.

23829. STRAUSS, HERBERT A.: *Formen des modernen Antisemitismus und Probleme seiner Abwehr.* [In]: International Review of Social History, Vol. 30, Pt. 3, Assen, Holland, 1985. Pp.431–443, footnotes.

23830. VIRCHOW, RUDOLF: *Naturwissenschaftliches Zeitalter und das Rätsel des Antisemitismus.* [Auszug aus der Rede 'Die Gründung der Berliner Universität', gehalten am 3. Aug. 1893.] Mit einem Kommentar 'Die blinden Flecken des Rationalismus' von Lothar Baier. [In]: Freibeuter, 27, Berlin, 1986. Pp. 97–113, notes (106–113).

—— WASSERMANN, HENRY: *Jews in Jugendstil: the Simplicissimus 1896–1914.* [See No. 22946.]

23831. ZENTRUM FÜR ANTISEMITISMUSFORSCHUNG, Technische Universität Berlin. STRAUSS, HERBERT A./KAMPE, NORBERT, eds.: *Lerntag über Aysylrecht und Asylpraxis: 1933 vs. 1985* – gemeinsam mit der Research Foundation for Jewish Immigration, New York – am 24. Nov. 1985. Berlin: Univ.bibliothek der Technischen Univ., Abt. Publikationen, 1986. 85 pp. (Lerntage des Zentrums für Antisemitismusforschung, 3.) [Incl.: Asyl für Flüchtlinge der 30er Jahre (Herbert A. Strauss, 11–21). Asyl in Schweden (Helmut Müssener, 24–38).]

23832. — STRAUSS, HERBERT A.: *Vorurteilsforschung und Sozialstruktur.* Zu einem Forschungsprojekt des Berliner Zentrums für Antisemitismusforschung. [In]: International Review of Social History, Vol. 30, Pt. 3, Assen, Holland, 1985. Pp. 307–311, 1 illus.

23833. ZIMMERMANN, MOSCHE: *Aufkommen und Diskreditierung des Begriffs Antisemitismus.* [In]: Büttner, Ursula, ed.: Das Unrechtsregime, Bd. 1. Hamburg: Christians, 1986. Pp. 59–78, notes. [See also No. 23844.]

23834. ZIMMERMANN, MOSHE: *Wilhelm Marr; the patriarch of antisemitism.* Oxford; New York: Oxford Univ. Press, 1986. 192 pp. (Studies in Jewish history.) [For Hebrew orig. see No. 19714/YB XXVIII.] [W. Marr, 1819–1904.]

E. Noted Germans and Jews

23835. BENN, GOTTFRIED. GREVE, LUDWIG: *Gottfried Benn, 1886–1956.* Eine Ausstellung des Deutschen Literaturarchivs im Schiller-Nationalmuseum Marbach am Neckar. Marbach am Neckar: Deutsches Literaturarchiv, 1986. 398 pp., illus., index of names (381–389). (Marbacher Kataloge, 41.) [Also on Benn's connection with German-Jewish authors, a.o., Carl Einstein, Alfred Döblin (150–164), Else Lasker-Schüler, Carl Sternheim, and on his involvement with National Socialism.]

23836. FONTANE, THEODOR: *Die Briefe Theodor Fontanes on Fritz Mauthner.* Ein Beitrag zum literarischen Leben Berlins in den 80er und 90er Jahren des 19. Jahrhunderts. Teil 2.

Hrsg., eingeleitet und kommentiert von Frederick Betz und Jörg Thunecke. [In]: Fontane Blätter, Bd. 6, H. 1 (= 39), Potsdam, GDR, 1985. Pp. 7–53, port., notes (23–53). [Cont. letters 30–64 (Jan. 1890–Sept. 1898); for pt. 1 see No. 21789/YB XXX.]

23837. — FONTANE, THEODOR: *Drei Briefe an Otto Brahm [1894 und 1896]*. Hrsg. und kommentiert von Joachim Krueger. [In]: Fontane Blätter, Bd. 6, H. 2 (= 40), Potsdam, GDR, 1985. Pp. 127–130.

23838. — SCHILLEMEIT, JOST: *Berlin und die Berliner: neuaufgefundene Fontane-Manuskripte*. [In]: Jahrbuch der Deutschen Schillergesellschaft, Jg. 30, Stuttgart, 1986. Pp. 34–82, footnotes. [Incl. the hitherto unpubl. Fontane manuscripts: 'Adel und Judenthum in der Berliner Gesellschaft' and 'Die Juden in unsrer Gesellschaft' (pp. 37–38; 38–39 & notes: pp. 59–63; 63–66).]

23839. GOETHE, JOHANN WOLFGANG von. BARNER, WILFRIED: *Jüdische Goethe-Verehrung vor 1933*. [In]: Juden in der deutschen Literatur [see No. 23676]. Pp. 127–151, notes.

23840. JEAN PAUL. OCH, GUNNAR: *'. . . und beschenkten sogar Moses': Jean Paul und sein jüdischer Freund Emanuel Osmund*. [In]: Jahrbuch der Jean-Paul-Gesellschaft, 21, Bayreuth, 1986. Pp. 123–145. [E. Osmund, 1766–1842.]

—— LESSING, G. E. BOUREL, DOMINIQUE: *Die Kontroverse zwischen Lessing und Mendelssohn*. [See No. 23515.]

23841. — DESSAU, BETTINA: *Nathans Rückkehr; Studien zur Rezeptionsgeschichte seit 1945*. Frankfurt am Main: Lang, 1986. 279, 11 pp., illus. (Analysen und Dokumente, Bd. 22.)

23842. — FREIMARK, PETER [et al.], eds.: *Lessing und die Toleranz*. Detroit: Wayne State Univ. Press; München: Edition Text + Kritik, 1986. 374 pp. (Lessing Yearbook, Sonderband.) [Incl.: Erkenntliche Wahrheit: Anregungen Lessings zum Dialog zwischen Christen und Juden (Gerhard Freund, 131–145). Christian Wilhelm von Dohm und die Idee der Toleranz (Heinrich Detering, 174–185). 'Kein kleiner Raub, ein solch Geschöpf': Nathan der Weise und die Judenfrage (Alison Scott-Prelorentzos, 198–205).]

23843. — NEIS, EDGAR: *Gotthold Ephraim Lessing, Nathan der Weise; Paradigma eines religionsphilosophischen Dramas der Toleranz und Humanität*. Hollfeld, Obfr.: Bange, 1985. 160 pp., idagr. (Bausteine Deutsch.)

23844. — ZIMMERMANN, MOSHE: *'Lessing contra Sem': Literatur im Dienste des Antisemitismus*. [In]: Juden in der deutschen Literatur [see No. 23676]. Pp. 179–193, notes.

23845. MANN, THOMAS: *Pro and contra Wagner*. Transl. and ed. by Allan Blunden. Introd. by Erich Heller. London: Faber, 1985. 240 pp. [Deals also with Wagner's antisemitism. Cf.: Enthusiastic ambivalence (Norman Lebrecht) [in]: Jewish Chronicle, London, Jan. 31, 1986. Passion and suspicion (Michael Tanner) [in]: TLS, London, March 21, 1986.]

23846. — MANN, THOMAS: *Tagebücher 1944–1946*. Hrsg. von Inge Jens. Frankfurt am Main: S. Fischer, 1986. XVI, 913 pp. [For previously publ. 5 vols. see No. 19729/YB XXVIII.]

—— — DARMAUN, JAQUES: *Thomas Mann und die Juden – eine Kontroverse? Thomas Manns Bild des Judentums bis zur Weimarer Republik*. [See pp. 208–214 in No. 23576.]

23847. — SMALL, LAUREN COHEN: *The case of Thomas Mann's 'Joseph und seine Brüder'; an essay on German-Jewish cultural assimilation*. Ann Arbor, Mich.; Godstone, Surrey, England: University Microfilms Internat., 1986. 183 pp. Baltimore, Md., Johns Hopkins Univ., Ph.D., 1986.

23848. NIETZSCHE, FRIEDRICH. BROWN, MALCOLM BREWER: *Friedrich Nietzsche und sein Verleger Ernst Schmeitzner; eine Darstellung ihrer Beziehung*. Ann Arbor, Mich.; Godstone, Surrey, England: University Microfilms Internat., 1985. 149 pp. Standford, Ca., Stanford Univ., Ph.D., 1985. [Discusses also antisemitism.]

23849. — EISEN, ARNOLD M.: *Nietzsche and the Jews reconsidered*. [In]: Jewish Social Studies, Vol. 48, No. 1, New York, Winter 1986. Pp. 1–14, notes.

23850. — MATTENKLOTT, GERT: *Nietzscheanismus und Judentum*. [In]: Archiv Bibliographia Judaica, Jahrbuch 1, 1985, Bad Soden/Ts., 1986. Pp. 57–71, notes. [See also No. 23161.]

23851. PLANCK, MAX. HEILBRON, J. L.: *The dilemmas of an upright man: Max Planck as spokesman for German science*. New York; London: Univ. of California Press, 1986. 238 pp. [Also on Planck's attitude towards his Jewish pupils and colleagues, a.o., Max Born, James Franck, Lise Meitner. Cf.: Conservative revolutionary (Rudolf Peierls) [in]: The New York Review of Books, Nov. 20, 1986, pp. 56–57.] [M.P., 1858–1947, physicist, father of quantum theory.]

23852. RAABE, WILHELM. SAMMONS, JEFFREY L.: *Wilhelm Raabe and his reputation among Jews and anti-Semites*. [In]: Identity and ethos [see No. 23677]. New York; Berne: Lang, 1986. Pp. 169–192, notes.

23853. — THUNECKE, JÖRG: *Rezeption als Regression: Feuilletons zu Wilhelm Raabes 100. Geburtstag am 8. Sept. 1931*. [In]: Jahrbuch der Raabe-Gesellschaft, 1986. Pp. 129–149, footnotes, bibl. (141–149). [Refers also to Raabe and the Jewish question (136–139).]

23854. SHAW, GEORGE BERNARD: *Bernard Shaw's letters to Siegfried Trebitsch.* Ed. by Samuel A. Weiss. Stanford, Ca.: Stanford Univ. Press, 1986. XVI, 494 pp., illus., notes. [Cont. 531 letters 1902–1950, chiefly hitherto unpublished, reflecting, a.o., rise of Nazism, forced migration of German Jews.] [S. Trebitsch, Dec. 21, 1869 Vienna–June 3, 1956 Zürich, writer, translated most of Shaw's works into German, emigrated to France in 1938 and to Switzerland in 1940.]

23855. SOMBART, WERNER. HOROWITZ, IRVING LOUIS: *The Jews and modern communism: the Sombart thesis reconsidered.* [In]: Modern Judaism, Vol. 6, No. 1, Baltimore, Feb. 1986. Pp. 13–25, notes. [Refers to the reissue of S.'s 'The Jews and modern capitalism' in 1982.]

23856. STRAUSS, RICHARD. LIPMAN, SAMUEL: *The later and greater Strauss.* [In]: Commentary, Vol. 81, No. 5, New York, May 1986. Pp. 57–62. [Also on St.'s collaboration with Hofmannsthal and Stefan Zweig.]

23857. WAGNER, RICHARD. BUSI, FREDERICK: *The case of Richard Wagner: Wagner and the Jews.* [In]: Midstream, Vol. 32, No. 2, New York, Feb. 1986. Pp. 37–42, notes. [In same issue also: Wagner in the history of antisemitism (Morton Manilla, 43–46, notes). The Jewish Wagnerites (Elaine Brody, 46–50, notes).] [See also No. 23845.]

—— — GAY, PETER: *Hermann Levi.* [And]: *Eduard Hanslick.* [See pp. 207–238; 263–284 in No. 22909.]

23858. — KATZ, JACOB: *The darker side of genius: Richard Wagner's anti-Semitism.* Hanover, N.H.; London: Univ. Press of New England, publ. for Brandeis Univ. Press, 1986. XII, 158 pp., port., notes (135–152), bibl. (153–154). (The Tauber Institute for the Study of European Jewry series, 5.) [Also Hebrew edn.]: Jerusalem: Zalman Shazar Center, 1986. 131 pp. (Monographs in Jewish history.) [Transl. of: 'Richard Wagner; Vorbote des Antisemitismus. Eine Veröffentlichung des Leo Baeck Instituts', see No. 22878/YB XXXI. Cf.: Besprechung (Rolf Vogel) [in]: deutschland-berichte, Jg. 22, Nr. 12, Bonn, Dez. 1986, p. 44. Wagner's Jewish problem (Marc A. Weiner) [in]: Midstream, Vol. 32, No. 7, New York, Aug./Sept. 1986, pp. 62–63. Talk of destruction (John Deathridge) [in]: TLS, London, Nov. 14, 1986, p. 1270 [& ensuing]: Wagner's antisemitism (Jacob Katz) [in]: TLS, Jan. 9, 1987, p. 37.]

X. FICTION, POETRY AND HUMOUR

23859. APPELFELD, AHARON: *To the land of the cattails.* Transl. by Jeffrey M. Green. London; New York: Weidenfeld & Nicolson, 1986. 148 pp. [A Jewish mother and her son attempt in 1938 to return from Vienna to their native Bukovina.]

23860. BECKER, JUREK: *Bronsteins Kinder.* Roman. Frankfurt am Main: Suhrkamp, 1986. 302 pp. [On the conflicts of a Jewish family living in the GDR in the 1970s. See also: Wie ich ein Deutscher wurde: eine Begegnung mit Jurek Becker in Berlin und Anmerkungen zu seinem Roman 'Bronsteins Kinder' (Volker Hage) [in]: Die Zeit, Nr. 41, Hamburg, 3. Okt. 1986, pp. 1–2.] [See also pp. 225–236 in No. 23576.]

23861. FREUNDLICH, ELISABETH: *Finstere Zeiten.* Vier Erzählungen. Mit einem Nachwort von Werner Fuld. Mannheim: Persona-Verl., 1986. 203 pp. [Stories on the Nazi period and life in exile.] [E.F., born July 21, 1906 in Vienna, publicist, emigrated via France to the USA, lives in Austria.]

23862. HOFMANN, GERT: *Veilchenfeld.* Erzählung. Darmstadt: Luchterhand, 1986. 185 pp., [Life and death of a Jewish intellectual in a small German town around 1938 as seen through the eyes of a German boy.]

23863. HONIGMANN, BARBARA: *Roman von einem Kinde.* Sechs Erzählungen. Darmstadt: Luchterhand, 1986. 117 pp. [Autobiographical stories, also on Jewish identity in present day Europe; incl. 'Doppeltes Grab', a report on the author's meeting with Gershom Scholem in Berlin shortly before his death.] [B.H., born 1949 in East Berlin to where her Jewish parents had returned from exile, now living in Strasbourg.]

23864. MULISCH, HARRY: *Das Attentat.* Aus dem Niederländischen von Annelen Habers. München: Hanser, 1986. 242 pp. [On the traumatic effect of a boy's experience in the Netherlands during the years of German occupation.]

23865. WELT, ELLY: *Berlin wild.* New York: Viking, 1986. 368 pp. [On a partly Jewish 16-year-old who survives the Nazi period in hiding while his Jewish family is being killed.]

Index to Bibliography

List of Contributors

BANKIER, David, Ph.D., b. 1947 in Germany. Lecturer, Institute of Contemporary Jewry, Hebrew University, Jersualem. Author of *El Holocausto. Perpetrádores – Victimas – Testigos* (1986); 'Leftwing Opposition in Nazi Germany and the Jewish Question', in M. Zimmerman (ed.), *The German Opposition* (1986, in Hebrew).

BROTHERS, Eric, B.A., b. 1954 in New York City. Copy editor and freelance writer; has published plays and satirical pieces.

CRAIG, Gordon A., Ph.D., b. 1913 in Glasgow. Professor of History Emeritus. President of the American Historical Association. Author of *Politics of the Prussian Army 1640–1945* (1956); *Germany 1866–1945* (1978); *The Germans* (1982); *The End of Prussia* (1984); and of many other works on German and European history.

GIDAL, Nachum T., Dr.phil., b. 1909 in Munich. Formerly photo-reporter, university teacher, now writer and Visiting Associate Professor, Hebrew University Jerusalem. Author of i.a. *Jüdische Kinder in Eretz Israel* (1936); *Origin and Development of Modern Photojournalism* (1973); *Goldweights of the Ashanti – The Gidal Collection in the Israel Museum, Jerusalem* (1971); *The Land of Israel in Photographs, 1839–1973* (1978); *Eternal Jerusalem* (1980); *Jews in Germany. From Roman Times to the Weimar Republic. A Visual Documentation* (exhibition and catalogue, 1984); *Land of Promise* (1985); contributor to numerous newspapers and magazines including 'Jüdische Rundschau', 'Münchner Illustrierte', 'Picture Post', 'Life', and 'Parade'.

HARRIS, James F., Ph.D., b. 1940 in Cleveland, Ohio, U.S.A. Associate Professor in History. Author of *A Study in the Theory and Practice of German Liberalism. Eduard Lasker, 1829–1884* (1984). Editor of a volume of essays on German-American relations (forthcoming) and author of several articles on German history and the history of antisemitism. Currently working on the development of attitudes towards Jews in mid-nineteenth century Germany as part of a larger study of public opinion in Germany during the years 1848–1871. (Contributor to Year Book XX.)

KAMPE, Norbert, Dr. phil., b. 1948 in Berlin. Wissenschaftlicher Mitarbeiter am Zentrum für Antisemitismusforschung an der TU, Berlin. Author of *Studenten und Antisemitismus im Deutschen Kaiserreich* (1987); 'Co-editor, with Herbert A. Strauss, of *Antisemitismus. Von der Judenfeindschaft zum Holocaust* (1985). Compiler of volume 4, *The Expulsion and Migration of German Jews 1933– 1945: Annotated Sources of Jewish Immigrants of the Nazi Period in the USA* (1987). (Contributor to Year Book XXX.)

LOEWENBERG, Peter, Ph.D. (History), Ph.D. (Psychoanalysis), b. 1933 in Hamburg. Professor of History, University of California, Los Angeles. Author of i.a. *Decoding the Past: The Psychohistorical Approach* (1983); 'Die Psychodynamik des Antijudentums', in Walter Grab (ed.), *Jahrbuch des Instituts für Deutsche Geschichte*, vol. I (1972); 'Walther Rathenau and the Tensions of Wilhelmine Society', in David Bronsen (ed.), *Jews and Germans from 1860 to 1933: The Problematic Symbiosis* (1979); 'Antisemitismus und jüdischer Selbsthass: Eine sich wechselseitig verstärkende sozialpsychologische Doppelbeziehung', in *Geschichte und Gesellschaft. Zeitschrift für Historische Sozialwissenschaft*, 5:4 (1979); *Walther Rathenau and Henry Kissinger: The Jew as Modern Statesman in Two Political Cultures*, LBI Memorial Lecture 24 (1980); and of various articles on psychohistory.

MCKALE, Donald M., Ph.D., b. 1943 in Clay Center, Kansas, Professor of History, Clemson University, Clemson, South Carolina, U.S.A. Author of *The Nazi Party Courts: Hitler's Management of Conflict in His Movement, 1921–1945* (1974); *The Swastika Outside Germany* (1977); *Hitler: The Survival Myth* (1981); *Curt Prüfer: German Diplomat from the Kaiser to Hitler* (forthcoming); editor of *Curt Prüfer: The Original and Revised Diaries, 1942–43* (forthcoming); and of numerous articles on Nazi Germany.

MOSSE, George L., Ph.D., b. 1918 in Berlin. Bascom Professor of History, University of Wisconsin, Koebner Professor of History, Hebrew University, Jerusalem, co-editor, *Journal of Contemporary History*. Author of i.a. *The Struggle for Sovereignty in England* (1950); *The Culture of Western Europe. The Nineteenth and Twentieth Centuries* (1961); *The Crisis of German Ideology. Intellectual Origins of the Third Reich* (1964); *Nazi Culture. Intellectual, Cultural and Social Life in the Third Reich* (1966); *Germans and Jews. The Right, the Left, and the Search for a "Third Force" in Pre-Nazi Germany* (1971); *Towards the Final Solution. A History of European Racism* (1978); *German Jews Beyond Judaism* (1985); *Nationalism and Sexuality* (1986); 'Die deutsche Rechte und die Juden' in *Entscheidungsjahr 1932* (1965). Co-editor of *Europe in Review* (1964). Member of the Board of the New York LBI. (Contributor to Year Books II and XVI.)

NICOSIA, Francis R. J., Ph.D., b. 1944 in Philadelphia. Associate Professor of History, St. Michael's College, Vermont. Author of *The Third Reich and the Palestine Question* (1985); and of articles in scholarly journals and collections of essays on German Middle East policy during the inter-war period and on aspects of Zionism in Germany. Currently working on a biography of Fritz Grobba, German Ambassador in Iraq and Saudi Arabia during the 1930s. (Contributor to Year Books XXIV and XXXI).

PEAL, David, Ph.D., b. 1955 in Pennsylvania, U.S.A. Izaak Walton Killam Postdoctoral Fellow, Dalhousie University, Halifax, Canada. Author of *Anti-Semitism and Rural Transformation in Kurhessen: The Rise and Fall of the Böckel Movement* (Diss.); and of articles on German, Agrarian and Jewish History, incl. 'Purposeful Peasants?', in *Peasant Studies* (forthcoming) and

'Jewish Responses to German Antisemitism: The Case of the Böckel Movement, 1887–1894', in *Jewish Social Studies* (forthcoming).

Reinharz, Jehuda, Ph.D., b. 1944 in Haifa. Richard Koret Professor of Modern Jewish History and Director, The Tauber Institute for the Study of European Jewry, Brandeis University. Author of *Fatherland or Promised Land: The Dilemma of the German Jew, 1893–1914* (1975); *Chaim Weizmann, The Making of a Zionist Leader* (1975); and numerous essays; editor of volume IX of *The Letters and Papers of Chaim Weizmann* (1977); co-editor (with Paul R. Mendes-Flohr) of *The Jew in the Modern World: A Documentary History* (1980); editor of *Dokumente zur Geschichte des deutschen Zionismus, 1882–1933* (1981); co-editor of (and contributor to) *Mystics, Philosophers and Politicians. Essays in Jewish Intellectual History in Honor of Alexander Altmann* (1982); co-editor of (and contributor to) *The Jewish Response to German Culture From the Enlightenment to the Second World War* (1985); editor of *Living with Antisemitism. Modern Jewish Responses* (1987). (Contributor to Year Books XXII, XXIV, XXX and XXXI.)

Riff, Michael Anthony, Ph.D., b. 1944 in London. Formerly university lecturer, now Assistant Director of the Leo Baeck Institute, New York. Author of various essays on historical subjects; co-author with A. Polansky of 'Poles, Czechoslovaks and the Jewish Question', in *Germany in the Age of Total War.* Essays in honour of F. L. Carsten (1981). General editor of (and contributor to) the forthcoming *Encyclopedia of Modern Political Ideologies and Movements.* (Contributor to Year Books XXI and XXVI.)

Rutland, Suzanne D., M.A., b. 1946 in Sydney, Australia. Formerly teacher and lecturer in adult education. At present part-time lecturer, Judaic Studies, Sydney College of Advanced Education and research student. Author of *Seventy-Five Years: The History of a Jewish Newspaper* (1970); *Take Heart Again: The Story of a Fellowship of Jewish Doctors* (1983); 'Jewish Immigration to New South Wales, 1919–1939', in *Journal of the Australian Jewish Historical Society*, vol. VII, (November 1973); 'Australian Government Policies Towards European Refugee Immigration', in *Journal of the Royal Australian Historical Society* (March 1984); and of numerous articles on Jews in Australia. Currently preparing doctoral thesis on 'Impact of Post-War Jewish Immigration on the Evolution of Australian Jewry, 1945–1960'.

Sauer, Paul, Dr.phil., b. 1931 in Germany. Leiter des Archivs der Stadt Stuttgart. Author of i.a. *Die Schicksale der jüdischen Bürger Baden-Württembergs während der nationalsozialistischen Verfolgungszeit 1933 bis 1945* (1969); *Württemberg in der Zeit des Nationalsozialismus* (1975); *Demokratischer Neubeginn in Not und Elend. Das Land Württemberg-Baden 1945 bis 1952* (1978); and of numerous other publications.

Schatzker, Chaim, Ph.D., b. 1928 in Lwow. Professor of Jewish History (Strochlitz Professor of Holocaust Studies), Haifa University. Author of i.a. *Die jüdische Jugendbewegung in Deutschland* (1974); *Das Deutschlandbild in israelischen Geschichtslehrbüchern* (1979); *Die Juden in den deutschen Geschichtsbüchern* (1981); *Sozialisations- und Erziehungsprozesse der jüdischen Jugend in Deutschland, 1870–1917* (1986); and of various essays on historical and educational topics regarding the Holocaust. (Contributor to Year Book XXIII.)

Sorkin, David, Ph.D., b. 1953 in Chicago. Research Fellow, Oxford Centre for Postgraduate Hebrew Studies and St. Antony's College. Author of 'Wilhelm von Humboldt: The Theory and Practice of Self-Formation', in *Journal of the History of Ideas* 43 (1983); 'The Invisible Community: Emancipation, Secular Culture and Jewish Identity in the Writings of Berthold Auerbach', in *The Jewish Response to German Culture* (1985); *The Transformation of German Jewry, 1780–1840* (forthcoming). Currently working on a study of Gabriel Riesser. Member of the Board of the London LBI.

Switzer-Rakos, Kennee, Ph.D., b. 1953 in Montreal. Formerly lecturer in history, presently law student. Author of 'Albert Einstein's Concept of the Jewish State', in *Midstream* (November 1985).

Voelker, Karin, Dr.phil., b. 1941 in Gunzenhausen (Bavaria). Teacher and historian. Researcher on the history of B'nai B'rith in Germany, 1882–1937.

Abstracts of articles in this Year Book are included in *Historical Abstracts* and *America: History and Life*.

General Index to Year Book XXXII of the Leo Baeck Institute